# Civil Society and the Summit of the Americas:
# The 1998 Santiago Summit

Civil Society and the Summit of the Americas:
# The 1998 Santiago Summit

*Richard E. Feinberg and Robin L. Rosenberg, editors*

The publisher of this book is the North-South Center Press at the University of Miami.

The mission of the North-South Center is to promote better relations and serve as a catalyst for change among the United States, Canada, and the nations of Latin America and the Caribbean by advancing knowledge and understanding of the major political, social, economic, and cultural issues affecting the nations and peoples of the Western Hemisphere.

©1999 North-South Center Press at the University of Miami.

 Published by the North-South Center Press, University of Miami, and distributed by Lynne Rienner Publishers, Inc., 1800 30th Street, Suite 314, Boulder, CO 80301-1026. All rights reserved under International and Pan-American Conventions. No portion of the contents may be reproduced or transmitted in any form, or by any means, including photocopying, recording, or any information storage retrieval system, without prior permission in writing from the publisher. All copyright inquiries should be addressed to the North-South Center Press, University of Miami, P.O. Box 248205, Coral Gables, Florida 33124-3027, phone 305-284-8908, fax 305-284-5089, or email khamman@miami.edu.

To order or to return books, contact Lynne Rienner Publishers, Inc. at 1800 30th Street, Suite 314, Boulder,  CO 80301-1026, 303-444-6684, fax 303-444-0824.

Permissions to reprint the documents in this volume have been granted to the University of Miami North-South Center by each of the sponsoring agencies. Requests to reproduce, in whole or in part, any of the documents herein must be directed to the individual sponsoring agency.

The cover photograph is the official photograph of the Second Summit of the Americas, courtesy of the Department of Photography, Presidency of the Republic of Chile.

The North-South Center wishes to express its appreciation for the generous support of the Ford Foundation.

**Cataloging-in-Publication Data is on file at the Library of Congress.**

Civil Society and the Summit of the Americas: The 1998 Santiago Summit
    / Richard E. Feinberg and Robin L. Rosenberg, editors.
        p. cm.
    Includes index.
    ISBN 1-57454-074-2 (pbk. : alk. paper)

Printed in the United States of America
03 02 01 00 99  6 5 4 3 2 1

# CONTENTS

# Civil Society and the Summit of the Americas: The 1998 Santiago Summit

**I. Foreword/Acknowledgments**

**II. Prólogo/Preface**
    President Eduardo Frei Ruiz-Tagle ................................................. v

**III. Official Summit Documents and Speeches**
    Declaration of Santiago: Summit of the Americas ................................. 3
    Plan of Action of Santiago: Summit of the Americas ........................... 7
    Proposed Agenda for the Summit of the Americas ........................ 23
    *Speeches:*

        Remarks by the President of the Republic of Chile at the
        Inauguration of the Second Summit of the Americas .................... 25
            *Eduardo Frei Ruiz-Tagle*

        Remarks by the President of the United States at the
        Opening of the Summit of the Americas ...................................... 29
            *William Jefferson Clinton*

        Remarks by the President of the United States at the
        Closing of the Summit of the Americas ........................................ 33
            *William Jefferson Clinton*

        Palavras do Presidente da República Federativa do Brasil na
        Cerimônia de Encerramento da II Cúpula das Américas .............. 35
        *Fernando Henrique Cardoso*

        Presentation by the President of the World Bank at the Second
        Summit of the Americas ............................................................... 37
            *James D. Wolfensohn*

        Statement by the President of the Inter-American Development
        Bank on the Occasion of the Second Summit of the Americas ..... 39
            *Enrique V. Iglesias*

        "The Rights of Women" A Challenge for the Americas ............... 47
            *U.S. Secretary of State Madeleine K. Albright*

        Speech by the Secretary-General of the Organization
        of American States at the Second Summit of
        the Americas ................................................................................ 49
            *César Gaviria*

Palabras del Secretario-General de la OEA, en la X Reunión del Grupo
de Revisión e Implementación de la Cumbre de las Américas ............ 51
 *César Gaviria*

Statement by the Co-Chairs of the Meeting of Foreign Ministers of the
Nations of the Summit of the Americas ................................................ 57
 *U.S. Secretary of State Madeleine K. Albright and*
 *Chilean Foreign Minister José Miguel Insulza*

Remarks of the National Coordinator of Chile for the
Summit of the Americas ........................................................................ 61
 *Ambassador Juan Martabit, at the Inaugural Session of the*
 *Ninth Meeting of the Summit Implementation Review Group*

A Theme for the Santiago Summit ........................................................ 63
 *George A.O. Alleyne, Director,*
 *Pan American Health Organization*

## IV. Preparatory Work by Regional Organizations

The Hemispheric Summit Process and the Organization of American
States: The OAS and Its Contributions to the Santiago Summit .......... 69
 *The Organization of American States (OAS)*

Summit of the Americas Information Network, Responsible
Coordinators .......................................................................................... 75
 *The Organization of American States*

Report on Progress in Implementing the Health Initiative: Equitable
Access to Basic Health Services ............................................................ 77
 *The Pan American Health Organization*

Report of the Secretary-General on Bolivia Summit Implementation .. 97
 *General Secretariat, Organization of American States*

# PROPOSALS FROM NON-GOVERNMENTAL SECTORS

## V. Leadership Council for Inter-American Summitry

From Talk to Action: How Summits Can Help Forge a
Western Hemisphere Community of Prosperous Democracies .......... 131
 *The Leadership Council for Inter-American Summitry*

*Working Papers*

Democracy and Human Rights Since the 1994 Summit
of the Americas, and Postscript .......................................................... 155
 *Felipe Agüero*

Providing Equitable Access to Basic Health Services,
and Postscript ...................................................................................... 173
 *Cristina B. Cunico*

# Contents

Developing, Liberalizing, and Integrating Financial Markets,
and Postscript ............................................................................... 191
    *Manuel Lasaga*

Implementing the Education Recommendations of the 1994
Summit of the Americas, and Postscript ........................................... 219
    *Jeffrey M. Puryear, Ana Maria Andraca,
and Marcela Gajardo*

Monitoring Implementation of the Summit of the Americas:
Partnerships for Sustainable Development ....................................... 235
    *S. Jacob Scherr and Robert K. Watson*

Progress Toward Free Trade in the Western Hemisphere
Since 1994, and Postscript ................................................................. 249
    *Colleen S. Morton*

Combating Corruption, and Postscript ............................................. 313
    *Luigi Manzetti*

Combating Illegal Drugs and Related Crimes ................................... 329
    *Eduardo A. Gamarra*

## VI. Education: The Key to Progress

The Future at Stake: Report of the Task Force on Education,
Equity, and Economic Competitiveness in Latin America
and the Caribbean ............................................................................. 347
    *Partnership for Educational Revitalization in the Americas,
Inter-American Dialogue, Corporation for Development Research*

*Postscript:* Improving Education: A Comparison of Recommendations
on Education in the Plan of Action from the Santiago Summit and the
Report of the PREAL Task Force on Education, Equity, and
Economic Competitiveness in the Americas ..................................... 365
    *Partnership for Educational Revitalization
in the Americas (PREAL)*

Hemisphere at a Crossroads: Education and Human Capital for
the Information Age ........................................................................... 371
    *Caribbean/Latin American Action (C/LAA)*

## VII. Preserving and Strengthening Democracy and Human Rights

Establishing an Effective Government-Civil Society Dialogue ......... 385
    *Esquel Group Foundation (EGF)*

Civil Society Participation in the Summit of the Americas,
Santiago, Chile: A Report on the Peoples' Summit and
Various other Fora for Participation ................................................. 403
    *Nola-Kate Seymoar, International Institute for
Sustainable Development*

Social Capital and Civil Society ....................................................... 411
    *Damián J. Fernández, Florida International University*

The Indigenization of Latin America ................................................. 413
    *Kathleen R. Martín, Florida International University*

Signposts Toward Building a Hemispheric Community ..................... 415
    *Patricia L. Price, Florida International University*

Recommendations Concerning Corruption to the SIRG Ministers
for the Summit of the Americas, April 18, 1997 ................................. 419
    *Transparency International USA*

Workshop on the Role of Public Participation in Development
Actions and Eradication of Poverty Within the Framework of
the Summit of the Americas, November 4-7, 1997 ............................. 421
    *Transparency International USA*

## VIII. Economic Integration and Free Trade

Comercio y Desarrollo Sustentable: Recomendaciones de la
Sociedad Civil para la Integración Hemisférica .................................. 425
    *Red Nacional de Acción Ecológica (RENACE) and
National Wildlife Federation (NWF)*

Free Trade in the Americas: Fulfilling the Promise of Miami and
Santiago ................................................................................................ 451
    *Ambler Moss and Stephen Lande, North-South Center*

    Annex I: Executive Summary of Recommendations for
    the May 1997 Hemispheric Trade Ministerial in
    Belo Horizonte, Brazil ..................................................................... 472

    Annex II: FTAA Business Facilitation Proposals for
    Actions To Be Implemented before Year 2000 ............................... 475

    Annex III: NAM (National Association of Manufacturers) ......... 478

Santiago: Launching the FTAA: Report to the San José
Trade Ministerial .................................................................................. 483
    *Ambassador Julius L. Katz and Robert C. Fisher, Council of the
Americas; The U.S. Chamber of Commerce; and
The Association of American Chambers of Commerce
in Latin America*

Declaration by Non-Governmental Organizations of the
Hemisphere on the Occasion of the IV Ministerial of the
Free Trade Area of the Americas ......................................................... 493
    *NGOs at the IV Ministerial of the Free Trade Area
of the Americas on March 16-18, 1998*

Launching Negotiations for the Formation of a "Free Trade
Area of the Americas" .......................................................................... 497
    *Caribbean/Latin American Action*

# CONTENTS

Promoting Transparency Through the FTAA Process ........................ 509
    *Transparency International USA*

The Importance of Transparency in Government Procurement .......... 513
    *Transparency International USA*

Universal Elements of Sound Procurement Systems ........................ 515
    *Transparency International USA*

## IX. Eradication of Poverty and Discrimination

Propuesta de Afroamérica XXI ante el Taller de Participación
Pública en Acciones de Desarrollo de la Erradicación de la
Pobreza y la Discriminación en la Cumbre de las Américas .............. 519
    *Michael John Franklin, Presidente de la Organización
Pro-Avance de los Pueblos de Ascendencia Africana (OAA)*

Communiqué: To the Second Summit of the Americas
in Santiago, Chile ............................................................................ 521
    *The Inter-American Dialogue and The International
Center for Research on Women*

Women's Rights and Opportunities in Latin America:
Problems and Prospects ................................................................... 535
    *Mala N. Htun, The International Center for
Research on Women*

## X. General Proposals

Toward the Santiago Summit of the Americas: Policy
Options Resulting from Regional Civil Society Consultations .......... 555
    *Odette Langlais, Canadian Foundation for the Americas
(FOCAL)*

Partnership Between Government and Civil Society:
The Summit of the Americas ............................................................ 571
    *Corporación PARTICIPA*

Globalización y Orden Internacional ................................................ 581
    *Francisco Rojas Aravena, Director, Latin American
Faculty of Social Sciences (FLACSO)-Chile*

Final Declaration of the Summit: Peoples' Summit
of the Americas ................................................................................ 589
    *Western Hemisphere NGOs at the Peoples' Summit of the
Americas, Santiago, Chile, April 18-19, 1998*

Alternatives for the Americas: Building a Peoples'
Hemispheric Agreement .................................................................. 591
    *Alliance for Responsible Trade, Common Frontiers,
Red Chile por una Iniciativa de los Pueblos, Red
Mexicana de Acción Frente al Libre Comercio, and
Réseau Québécois sur l'Intégration Continentale*

## XI. Post-Santiago Evaluations

Mastering Summitry: An Evaluation of the Santiago Summit
of the Americas and Its Aftermath, Policy Report II, March 1999 ..... 625
> *The Leadership Council for Inter-American Summitry*

Report on Progress and Recommendations Toward Implementing the
1994 Summit Anticorruption Commitments, August 20, 1997 .......... 645
> *Transparency International USA*

The Importance of the OAS Convention Against Corruption,
October 1998 ............................................................................................... 649
> *Transparency International USA*

Recommendations of Transparency International on Combating
Corruption, November 16, 1998 ........................................................ 651
> *Transparency International USA*

Transparency International-Americas Informe de Avances Anti-
corrupción/Anticorruption Progress Report, November 2, 1998 ........ 653
> *Transparency International USA*

TI-Americas Anticorruption Progress Report, February 8, 1999 ....... 657
> *Transparency International USA*

The Civil Society Task Force Dialogue with the Responsible
Coordinators of the Civil Society Initiative of the Summit
of the Americas ...................................................................................... 659
> *Esquel Group Foundation*

## XII. Appendix: Summit Correspondence

October 27, 1997: Joint Letter to Mr. Carlos Murillo, President
of the Preparatory Committee, Free Trade Area of the Americas,
in Preparation for the Second Vice Ministerial Meeting, from
NWF and Western Hemisphere NGOs ............................................... 667

December 1, 1997: Organization of Africans in the Americas (OAA):
Correspondence from Director Michael J. Franklin to U.S.
Secretary of State Madeleine K. Albright ........................................... 669

December 18, 1997: Letter to Richard C. Brown, United States
Department of State, from OAA ......................................................... 671

February 8, 1998: Joint Letter to Vice-Ministers of Trade
Attending the Third FTAA Vice Ministerial Meeting
on Civil Society Participation from NWF and Western
Hemisphere NGOs ............................................................................ 673

March 10, 1998: Letter to Mr. Peter F. Allgeier, Associate
U.S. Trade Representative for the Western Hemisphere,
in Preparation for the Trade Negotiations Committee's (TNC)
Meeting in Suriname, from NWF ....................................................... 677

# Contents

June 19, 1998: Joint Letter to Ms. Kathryn McCallion, Chair of the Trade Negotiations Committee of the FTAA, in Preparation for the Trade Negotiations Committee's (TNC) Meeting in Argentina, from NWF and Western Hemisphere NGOs ..................... 681

October 16, 1998: Joint Letter to Ms. Kathryn McCallion, Chair of the Trade Negotiations Committee of the FTAA and Temporary Chair of the Committee of Government Representatives (CGR) for the Participation of Civil Society, in Preparation for the First Meeting of the CGR, from NWF and Western Hemisphere NGOs ...................................... 687

November 30, 1998: Letter to Mr. Peter F. Allgeier, Associate U.S. Trade Representative for the Western Hemisphere, in Preparation for the IV FTAA Ministerial of the Free Trade Area of the Americas ........................................................................ 691

Participating Organizations ................................................................ 695

Index ........................................................................................ 697

# I. FOREWORD AND ACKNOWLEDGMENTS

## Foreword

*"I am convinced that only insofar as civil society is directly and effectively involved in public life will democracy fully become a reality."*

Eduardo Frei Ruiz-Tagle
President of Chile

The Summit of the Americas "process," which began at the December 1994 Miami Summit, has opened up unprecedented opportunities for civil society actors to participate in the formulation and implementation of important initiatives in the economic, political, and social development of the Western Hemisphere. This "new diplomacy," which involves a wide array of organizations, from private sector business associations to academe, policy institutions, and non-governmental organizations, is oriented around the Summit's integrated hemispheric blueprint for the development of a community of prosperous democracies in the Americas. This volume documents the wide range of inputs from non-governmental sectors to the Summit of the Americas II in Santiago, Chile, in April 1998. It chronicles the contributions of civil society actors to the planning process for Santiago and evaluates progress in implementation of Summit of the Americas initiatives on priority issues such as trade, corruption, finance, and sustainable development.

Civil society involvement in summitry is part of a wider "power shift" in international relations, wherein the monitoring of international agreements has become a "growth industry" for non-governmental actors.[1] This involvement reaches into domestic affairs through inputs into national negotiating positions and through the participation of activist networks, think tanks, and academic organizations in the monitoring of international commitments in such areas as human rights, corruption, and the environment.[2] After the Miami Summit of the Americas in December 1994, the North-South Center published the first compendium of civil society inputs into the process of hemispheric summitry, *Advancing the Miami Process: Civil Society and the Summit of the Americas.* The present volume continues in this tradition, adding a major monitoring and evaluation component to the rich array of research and policy documents that were generated during the run up to the Santiago Summit of the Americas II.[3]

While the "new diplomacy" is by no means unique to the Western Hemisphere, it takes on special meaning in a region whose tortured history has been generally characterized by the primacy of government decisionmaking in the context of weak civil societies. In the Summit of the Americas, involvement of non-governmental actors in decisionmaking and implementation of public policy is expressed in terms of "partnerships" (*alianzas*) designed to lend stakeholder momentum to commitments made by heads of state and government. The acceptance by governments of the notion of partnerships, however, remains uneven across the region. Nor is there agreement on an operational definition for the term "civil society." Many Latin American officials and observers, for example, are reluctant to include private sector business organizations in the civil society mix. In contrast to the Anglo-Saxon perspective, which sees private business as an integral part of a vibrant civil society, many Latin Americans view society as composed of three separate entities: business, government, and civil society. There are also deep-rooted suspicions among Latin American officials of the political motivations of some civil society organizations. This manifests itself in the questioning of the "representativeness" (*representatividad*) of individual groups, which is often accompanied by allegations that such non-governmental organizations are not representative of national interests, but of powerful transnational interests or the interests of the developed countries of the hemisphere, particularly those of the United States. In negotiations for Summit texts, Latin officials focus equally on the notion of "responsible" participation, that is, what diplomats view as constructive, non-political, input. Thus, while civil society organizations emphasize rights and policies to facilitate the creation and participation of non-profit interest groups, governments put equal emphasis on the need to insure responsible behavior.

The Organization of American States (OAS), which has embraced Inter-American summitry as a vehicle for reform and renewal, is for the first time grappling with these questions. And, meanwhile, civil society continues to organize itself on the local, national, and regional levels, becoming an ever more powerful force in the constellation of institutions that compose the "Inter-American System."

This is not to say that governments are always listening. As this book chronicles, much of the activity by civil society actors around hemispheric summits is not "mainstreamed" into the governmental planning and negotiating processes. In some cases, significant activity transpires in parallel processes that implicitly protest the inadequacy of Summit of the Americas institutions to incorporate the contributions of the non-governmental sectors in meaningful ways. The 1994 Miami Summit set high standards for consultation with civil society actors during the planning process. The 1996 Summit of the Americas on Sustainable Development in Santa Cruz, Bolivia, included an elaborate, hemisphere-wide consultation mechanism for civil society. Although this mechanism ultimately failed to mainstream most Latin American and Caribbean civil society inputs into the negotiations process, the Bolivia Declaration and Plan of Action are replete with general references to civil society participation in decisionmaking and implementation of initiatives. The Bolivia Summit launched, at the OAS, the Inter-American Strategy for the Promotion of Public Participation in Decisionmaking for Sustainable Development (ISP), the only such initiative operative at the Inter-American level.

The Santiago Summit of the Americas II was characterized by an interesting mix of consultation, dialogue, and protest. While the Chilean hosts made some deliberate efforts to bring civil society expertise and perspectives into the planning and negotiation processes (see the contributions from Participa, the Facultad Latinoamericana de Ciencias Sociales (FLACSO), and Florida International University) and embraced inputs from such prominent groups as the Inter-American Dialogue (on education) and the Leadership Council for Inter-American Summitry (especially on process issues and Summit "institutionalization"), many non-governmental groups still chose to stage a parallel "Peoples Summit" at Santiago that, in turn, spawned a hemisphere-wide "alternatives" dialogue among a number of influential civil society organizations (see Section X). In its second policy report evaluating the Santiago Summit and its aftermath (see *Mastering Summitry*, Section XI), the Leadership Council for Inter-American Summitry concluded that "with regard to public access and influence over the summitry process, despite occasional references to civil society in the Plan of Action, Santiago stands as a setback against the gains of Miami, as foreign ministries reasserted their traditional prerogatives over foreign policy."

It is not surprising, then, that "civil society" should itself remain one of the major Summit of the Americas initiatives. Since the Miami Summit, the hemisphere recognized that "invigorating society" was a priority in democractic life. As President Eduardo Frei expresses so eloquently in his Preface to this book, "Those of us who believe in freedom and democracy, who share the basic principles that inspire the ideals, cannot fail to recognize that civil society's participation in the decision-making process is vital to the strengthening of democracy and the development of our peoples." Numerous non-governmental organizations continue to push this agenda for the Inter-American system with varying degrees of government support. Efforts range from ensuring local populations' involvement in development projects to a proposal to establish a fund at the Inter-American Development Bank to finance the participation of civil society in Latin American and Caribbean development. At its June 1999 General Assembly, the Organization of American States mandated the elaboration of guidelines to establish an accreditation program for civil society organizations by the end of 1999.

This volume is an attempt to capture the richness of the widening range of activities conducted by civil society actors around the process of hemispheric summitry. The scope of the documentation may be limited to regional

# I. Foreword and Acknowledgments

activities oriented around opportunities to contribute to Summit negotiations, but these contributions also reflect a perhaps greater ferment at the national level. At present, there is a tremendous gap in our knowledge of civil society activities at the national level in many countries, and even more limited knowledge of government efforts to implement Summit commitments at the national level. Monitoring mechanisms remain weak to non-existent.[4] As these contributions will show, civil society organizations can bring significant resources and expertise to bear in hemispheric efforts to monitor implementation.[5]

In designing this volume, we have been careful to follow the thematic orientation of the Santiago Summit Plan of Action, which also corresponds, in a general way, to the 23 Miami initiatives. After this Foreword and Chilean President Eduardo Frei's Preface, Section I and II, Section III presents official Summit documents and speeches, including the Santiago Summit *Declaration of Principles* and *Plan of Action*.[6] Regional inter-governmental organizations were very active in Summit preparation; Section IV includes the major contributions to the Santiago planning process. Most of the civil society inputs were directed to specific areas of the Summit agenda, reflecting the interests of the particular civil society groups: these contributions from non-governmental sectors are included in Sections V-IX. Those proposals that addressed more than one major initiative area are included in Section X, as "General Proposals." Section XI includes evaluations of the Santiago Summit and of the state of the art in hemispheric summitry.

In the spirit of "continuous summitry," these contributions are presented to the policy community as a solid, democratic basis for discussion and debate in advance of the Summit of the Americas III, scheduled for 2001 in Canada.

## Acknowledgments

The editors would like to express their gratitude to the many people and organizations that have made this book and the many activities that supported it possible.

First and foremost, we would like to thank Cristina Eguizábal of the Ford Foundation, who recognized the value of Summit monitoring and has provided ongoing support to the Leadership Council for Inter-American Summitry and the North-South Center's Summit-related activities.

The support and cooperation from the Chilean hosts of the Summit of the Americas II was instrumental. In his Preface to this book, President Eduardo Frei has shared his vision of the role of civil society in democratic development; Foreign Minister José Miguel Insulza consistently supported our efforts to bring non-governmental expertise into Summit planning; Ambassador Genaro Arriagada, formerly President Frei's Special Coordinator of Summit of the Americas II, and Ambassador Juan Martabit, former Senior Summit Coordinator, were particularly supportive during the preparations for the Santiago Summit; and Ambassador Carlos Portales, Permanent Representative of Chile and Chile's Senior Summit Coordinator at the OAS, gave us support and encouragement throughout.

We have also benefited from continuous engagement and assistance from within the U.S. government. Our gratitude goes to Thomas F. "Mack" McClarty, formerly President Clinton's Special Envoy to the Americas; Ambassador Richard Brown, former Senior Summit Coordinator; Mark Wells, formerly with the U.S. Department of State's Summit Coordinating Office; Zachary Teich, formerly with the U.S. Mission to the Organization of American States; and Ambassador Victor Marrero, Senior Summit Coordinator and Permanent Representative of the United States to the OAS for his unwavering advocacy of civil society involvement in hemispheric policy processes.

The government of Canada has been particularly supportive of this project. Ambassador Peter Boehm, Permanent Representative of Canada to the Organization of American States and Senior Summit Coordinator, has provided consistent support of civil society initiatives within the Summit process.

The editors must also acknowledge the many other government delegations that helped advance the civil society initiative throughout the negotiations for the Santa

Cruz and Santiago Summits, including, *inter alia,* Chile, the Dominican Republic, Costa Rica, Jamaica, Uruguay, and Venezuela.

At the OAS, we found great levels of engagement and interest from Secretary-General César Gaviria; Jaime Aparicio, Director of the Office of Summit Follow-Up; Christopher Hernández-Roy of the Office of Summit Follow-Up; Richard Meganck, Director of the Unit for Sustainable Development and the Environment; and Zoila Girón, Director of the Inter-American Strategy for the Promotion of Public Participation in Decisionmaking for Sustainable Development (ISP).

At the Dante B. Fascell North-South Center, many activities and publications have enriched this project. Thanks to Ambler H. Moss, Jr., Director, for his invaluable participation in this project and his steadfast support for our efforts to monitor the Summit of the Americas process; to Jeffrey Stark, Director of Research and Studies, for his good judgment and assistance with publications and research; and to Sherry Tross, Director of Programs, and Debbie Quinzi, Director of Finance and Administrative Services, for their ongoing support of the Center's programs on summitry.

To the professional staff of the North-South Center Press, we owe a particular debt of gratitude. Mary Mapes, Publications Director, lent her design talents to this and related publications and managed this book's production; Susan Holler gave painstaking attention to detail while putting together, formatting, and indexing the volume; Kathleen Hamman, Editorial Director, brought her high editorial standards to bear during the final stages; Jayne Weisblatt spent many hours copy editing and proofreading all documents and galleys; Michelle Perez meticulously typed several long documents for which disks were unavailable; and Mary D'León assisted in the translation of documents.

North-South Scholar and University of Miami doctoral student, Christie Kibort, provided indispensable research and organizational support for this book and the Center's Summit of the Americas activities. Special thanks to Lilly Iversen, Senior Staff Associate to the Deputy Director, who has been a pillar of support for all of the Center's Summit-related activities.

Finally, we would like to thank all of the participating organizations across the Western Hemisphere for generously providing their documents for publication in this volume.

*Richard E. Feinberg and Robin L. Rosenberg*

# Notes

1. See the seminal article on this challenge to traditional sovereignty, whose ramifications will be "seismic," in Jessica T. Mathews, 1997, "Power Shift," *Foreign Affairs,* January/February, 50-66.

2. An entire literature on the monitoring of international commitments has emerged in the second half of the 1990s. See, for example, Margaret E. Keck and Kathryn Sikkink, eds., 1998, *Activists Beyond Borders: Advocacy Networks in International Politics* (Ithaca, N.Y.: Cornell University Press). The monitoring of environmental regimes has been a subject of particular attention. See David Victor, Kal Raustiala, and Eugene B. Skolnikoff, 1998, *The Implementation and Effectiveness of International Environmental Commitments: Theory and Practice* (Cambridge, Mass.: MIT Press); and Lawrence E. Susskind, 1994, *Environmental Diplomacy: Negotiating More Effective Global Agreements* (Oxford, U.K.: Oxford University Press).

3. Robin L. Rosenberg and Steve Stein, eds., 1995, *Advancing the Miami Process: Civil Society and the Summit of the Americas* (Coral Gables, Fla.: North-South Center Press).

4. Among Summit of the Americas institutions, the foreign ministry-led Summit Implementation Review Group (SIRG) has assumed responsibility for monitoring Summit implementation. The Santiago Summit *Plan of Action* reaffirmed the primary role of the SIRG in organizing and monitoring Summits but also opened up the possibility of wider involvement by establishing the OAS as the "institutional memory" of the process. Addressing the need for a full-fledged secretariat, the Leadership Council for Inter-American Summitry recommended that the OAS Office of Summit Follow-Up, created in 1998 in response to the Santiago mandate, should take on greater responsibilities in the area of monitoring. See The Leadership Council for Inter-American Summitry, 1999, *Mastering Summitry: An Evaluation of the Santiago Summit of the Americas and Its Aftermath,* Policy Report II (Coral Gables, Fla.: Dante B. Fascell North-South Center). This document has been reproduced in section XI of this volume.

5. At the Santiago Summit in April 1998, the U.S. Department of State, whose Summit Coordinating Office was the de facto secretariat of the Summit of the Americas process from Miami to Santiago, released the only official report on Summit of the Americas implementation. Based on reports on Miami's 23 individual initiatives from 13 governments, the IDB, OAS, and the Pan American Health Organization, *Words Into Deeds: Progress Since the Miami Summit,* DOS Publication 10536, April 1998 (Washington, D.C.: U.S. Department of State, Bureau of Inter-American Affairs) is a major contribution and statement of the importance of follow-up and implementation of Summit commitments. Nevertheless, the document inevitably displays the methodological and resource problems plaguing current government efforts in Summit monitoring.

6. For a compendium of all the major official documents from the Summit of the Americas, from Miami to Santiago, and including the Santa Cruz, Bolivia, Summit of the Americas on Sustainable Development, see Organization of American States, Office of Summit Follow-Up, 1999, *Official Documents of the Summit Process from Miami to Santiago* (Washington, D.C.: OAS). See also the Office of Summit Follow-Up's excellent web site: http://www.summit-americas.org or http://www.cumbre-americas.org

# II. Prólogo

# Prólogo

Los días 18 y 19 de abril de 1998 Chile tuvo el honor de ser el país anfitrión de la II Cumbre de las Américas. Este acontecimiento, efectuado por decisión de todos los Jefes de Estado y de Gobierno de las naciones democráticas del hemisfero, vino a dar una solución de continuidad al diálogo que sostuvimos en Miami en diciembre de 1994 a instancias del Presidente de los Estados Unidos, señor William J. Clinton, con el decidido objetivo de avanzar en la solución de las distintas necesidades que afectan a nuestros países, sobre la base de una cooperación concreta y efectiva, como asimismo dar el impulso definitivo a la constitución de una sólida comunidad de naciones. Tengo la firme convicción que la cita hemisférica simbolizó el equilibro y madurez alcanzado en las relaciones hemisféricas, en el marco de un momento excepcional en la historia de las Américas. Agradezco pues las oportunidad de entregar algunas reflexiones sobre el particular.

En nuestra agenda de trabajo convergieron distintas inquietudes. Fue el resultado de un proceso de negociación en el que primó la transparencia, el consenso y la altura de miras. Los gobernantes le dimos forma concreta en la *Declaración de Santiago* y en el *Plan de Acción,* documentos que por una parte contienen nuestra apreciación sobre temas y problemas que, dadas las actuales circunstancias internacionales, requieren necesariamente de una conceptualización común y, por otra, compromisos concretos y efectivos en cuatro áreas fundamentales: como la educación — que fue el tema central de la cita hemisférica en cuanto áreas fundamentales para el desarrollo de las personas y para el desarrollo social; el desarrollo económico y comercial, la integración hemisférica, la democracia y los derechos humanos, la justicia, la erradicación de la pobreza y la discriminación, el medio ambiente, y otras de no menor importancia. Es preciso enfatizar que convencidos de la trascendencia de la integración y de la liberalización del comercio para las relaciones hemisféricas, y de la idoneidad del Area de Libre Comercio de las Américas (ALCA), para obtener esos objetivos, dispusimos el inicio de las negociaciones relativas a su establecimiento, reiterando nuestra decisión de alcanzar logros concretos para fines del presente siglo y de concluirlas a más tardar el año 2005.

La Sociedad Civil, tema que se ha escogido para esta publicación, está, en su más amplia acepción, tras los esfuerzos en pro del pleno desarrollo de nuestros pueblos, en que estamos involucrados los distintos gobiernos de las Américas. Los acuerdos y compromisos del *Plan de Acción* de la II Cumbre no son una entelequia sino una realidad concreta y tras la realidad concreta están los hombres, tanto como actores como destinatarios de los mismos. Los hombres, en definitiva, somos quienes conformamos y determinamos la Sociedad Civil. Quienes creemos en la libertad y la democracia, quienes compartimos los principios básicos que inspiran esos ideales, no podemos sino reconocer que la participación de la sociedad civil en el proceso de toma de decisiones es fundamental para el fortalecimiento de la democracia y para el desarrollo de nuestros pueblos. Ya al reunirnos en abril de 1998 se habían producido en el hemisferio importantes avances en este sentido. La Organización de Estados Americanos se encontraba formulando una Estrategia Interamericana de Participación Pública, y se organizaban los Consejos para el Desarrollo Sostenible a nivel nacional, de acuerdo a lo previsto en la Agenda 21 de la Cumbre de Río.

En la *Declaración de Santiago* nos comprometimos a impulsar la más activa participación de la misma. En el *Plan de Acción* dedicamos al tema un acápite específico del capítulo II dedicado a la "Preservación y Fortalecimiento de la Democracia, la Justicia y los Derechos Humanos", identificando acciones concretas, su ubicación ya por sí constituye un indicativo de la importancia atribuida a la materia. Ello sin perjuicio de que a todo lo largo del documento se contienen acciones en las cuales se vincula a la Sociedad Civil. Un análisis somero nos muestra que en la *Declaración de Santiago* existen al menos cinco párrafos vinculados de una forma u otra al tema, y en el *Plan de Acción* encontramos dieciocho párrafos de similar naturaleza. Ello responde al reconocimiento de inquietudes sociales cuya motivación proviene de demandas muy específicas, como, por ejemplo, lo que dice relación con el ejercicio de derechos y libertades, los derechos humanos y ciudadanos, el medio ambiente, cuestiones locales y regionales, demandas juveniles, reivindicaciones étnicas.

Se puede afirmar que en la medida que las decisiones adoptadas en Santiago se lleven a la práctica en la forma prevista, se cumple con la idea de que las respuestas a los desafíos que enfrentamos deben venir no sólo del aparato gubernamental sino también y en forma creciente de los protagonistas. He sostenido y sostengo que debemos empeñarnos en descubrir formas de hacer políticas y modalidades de renovación institucional que favorezcan el fortalecimiento de los distintos y muy variados componentes de la Sociedad Civil, y que el Estado, la actividad política y las instituciones establezcan un diálogo constructivo y una actitud de colaboración con la pluralidad de grupos que emergen de la sociedad.

En Chile estamos abocados a generar una política de Estado sobre la materia, entendiendo el fortalecimiento de la Sociedad Civil como un elemento clave para un desarrollo integral, eficiente y equitativo de nuestra comunidad. Creemos que esta política debe ser neutral, de manera que favorezca a todos los sectores de la sociedad civil; debe, al mismo tiempo, resguardar la autonomía — reconocida por lo demás constitucionalmente — de las instituciones sociales para cumplir sus fines específicos; contar con mecanismos de provisión adecuados que garanticen la equidad, la transparencia y calidad de los proyectos e iniciativas de la Sociedad Civil; garantizar la transparencia en todo el proceso de captación y movilización de recursos desde el Estado y sus agencias hacia los organismos ejecutores; coadyuvar a la mayor democratización del país en sus esferas políticas, económicas, sociales y culturales. Estoy convencido que sólo en la medida en que la sociedad civil se involucre efectivamente y directamente en el quehacer público, la democracia se hará plenamente realidad.

Eduardo Frei Ruiz-Tagle
Presidente de la República de Chile
Santiago, 23 de marzo de 1999

# II. Preface

# Preface

On April 18-19, 1998, Chile had the honor of hosting the II Summit of the Americas. This event, held by decision of all the heads of state and government of the democratic nations of the hemisphere, provided an opportunity for continuing the dialogue that took place in Miami in December 1994 at the invitation of U.S. President William J. Clinton. The Santiago Summit had as its purpose to continue searching for solutions to the different needs of our countries through concrete, effective cooperation and to give the final thrust to the establishment of a consolidated community of nations. I strongly believe that the hemispheric meeting symbolized the balance and maturity achieved in hemispheric relations within the framework of an extraordinary moment in the history of the Americas. I am, therefore, grateful for the opportunity to offer some reflections on this subject.

A variety of concerns converged in our work agenda. It was the culmination of a negotiation process in which transparency, consensus, and high expectations prevailed. We leaders gave it tangible form in the *Declaration of Santiago* and the *Plan of Action*, documents that include our assessment of issues and problems that, given the present international circumstances, inevitably require both a common conceptualization and effective and concrete commitments in four fundamental areas. (These areas include education, which constitutes the central theme of the hemispheric meeting in the important realm of the development of individuals as well as social development; economic and trade development and hemispheric integration; democracy, human rights, and justice; eradication of poverty and discrimination; the environment; and other issues of no less importance.) It should be emphasized that, convinced of the overarching importance of integration and trade liberalization for hemispheric relations and the unique capacity of the Free Trade Area of the Americas (FTAA) to accomplish the hemisphere's objectives, we launched the negotiations for the FTAA's establishment with renewed emphasis on the attainment of concrete progress by the end of this century and on concluding negotiations no later than the year 2005.

"Civil society," the focus of this publication, is, in its widest sense, behind those efforts promoting the full development of our peoples, efforts in which all the governments of the Americas are engaged. The agreements and commitments of the *Plan of Action* of the II Summit are not an abstraction, but a concrete reality, and behind this concrete reality are the people who are not only the protagonists, but the beneficiaries as well. We men and women, in the final analysis, are the ones who create and define civil society. Those of us who believe in freedom and democracy, who share the basic principles that inspire these ideals, cannot fail to recognize that civil society's participation in the decision-making process is vital to the strengthening of democracy and the development of our peoples. Significant progress had already been made in this regard by the time of our April 1998 meeting. The Organization of American States (OAS) was in the midst of formulating its Inter-American Strategy for

Public Participation, and Sustainable Development Councils were being organized at the national level as prescribed by Agenda 21 of the Rio Summit.

A commitment was made in the *Declaration of Santiago* to promote the greatest degree of civil society participation. In the *Plan of Action*, a specific section was dedicated to this topic in Chapter II on "Preservation and Strengthening of Democracy, Justice, and Human Rights," in which specific actions are identified. The very fact that it was included illustrates the importance that was given to this issue. And this is not to mention that throughout the entire document there are actions linked to civil society. A cursory examination reveals that there are at least five paragraphs in the *Declaration of Santiago* and 18 in the *Plan of Action* associated in some way with this topic. It is a reflection of the awareness of social concerns stemming from specific demands, such as those related to the exercise of rights and freedoms, human and civil rights, the environment, local and regional matters, youth demands, and ethnic claims.

It can be affirmed that, as long as the decisions adopted in Santiago are implemented in the manner foreseen, the idea that responses to the challenges that we confront must emerge not only from the governmental apparatus, but also — and increasingly — from the protagonists themselves, will be realized. I have said, and say again, that we must make an effort to find ways to create policies and mechanisms for institutional renewal that will invigorate the very diverse and complex components of civil society and that the state, political activity, and institutions must establish constructive dialogue and be willing to collaborate with a wide spectrum of groups that emanate from society.

In Chile, a state policy concerning civil society is under construction in the belief that a stronger civil society is a key element in the integral, effective, and equitable development of our community. We believe that this policy ought to be neutral so that all sectors of civil society will reap the benefits; it should simultaneously protect the autonomy — already recognized constitutionally — of social institutions in order to meet their specific goals; contain adequate mechanisms that guarantee fair, transparent, and quality projects and initiatives on the part of civil society; guarantee transparency in the overall process of mobilizing and capturing resources from the state and its agencies and transferring them to implementing organizations; and help advance the democratization of the country in the political, economic, social, and cultural spheres. I am convinced that only insofar as civil society is directly and effectively involved in public life will democracy fully become a reality.

Eduardo Frei Ruiz-Tagle
President of the Republic of Chile
Santiago, March 23, 1999

# III. OFFICIAL SUMMIT DOCUMENTS AND SPEECHES

# III. SUMMIT DOCUMENTS

# Declaration of Santiago:
## Summit of the Americas

### APRIL 18-19, 1998

We, the democratically-elected Heads of State and Government of the countries of the Americas, have met in Santiago, Chile, in order to continue the dialogue and strengthen the cooperation we began in Miami in December 1994. Since that time, significant progress has been made in the formulation and execution of joint plans and programs in order to take advantage of the great opportunities before us. We reaffirm our will to continue this most important undertaking, which requires sustained national efforts and dynamic international cooperation.

The strengthening of democracy, political dialogue, economic stability, progress towards social justice, the extent to which our trade liberalization policies coincide, and the will to expedite a process of ongoing Hemispheric integration have made our relations more mature. We will redouble our efforts to continue reforms designed to improve the living conditions of the peoples of the Americas and to achieve a mutually supportive community. For this reason, we have decided that education is a key theme and is of particular importance in our deliberations. We approve the attached Plan of Action and undertake to carry out its initiatives.

Since our meeting in Miami, we have seen real economic benefits in the Americas resulting from more open trade, transparency in economic regulations, sound, market-based economic policies, as well as efforts by the private sector to increase its competitiveness. Even as countries in our region have been tested by financial and other economic pressures, and as countries in other regions have experienced serious economic setbacks, the overall course in the Americas has been one of faster economic growth, lower inflation, expanded opportunities, and confidence in facing the global marketplace. A major reason for this positive record has been our countries' steadfast and cooperative efforts to promote prosperity through increased economic integration and more open economies. New partnerships have been formed and existing ones strengthened and expanded. A positive role is being played by sub-regional and bilateral integration and free trade agreements. We are confident that the Free Trade Area of the Americas (FTAA) will improve the well-being of all our people, including economically disadvantaged populations within our respective countries.

Hemispheric integration is a necessary complement to national policies aimed at overcoming lingering problems and obtaining a higher level of development. In its broadest sense, a process of integration based on respect for cultural identities will make it possible to shape a common, interwoven set of values and interests that helps us in these objectives.

Globalization offers great opportunities for progress to our countries and opens up new areas of cooperation for the hemispheric community. However, it can also heighten the differences among countries and within our societies. With steadfast determination to reap its benefits and to face its challenges, we will give special attention to the most vulnerable countries and social groups in the Hemisphere.

Education is the determining factor for the political, social, cultural, and economic development of our peoples. We undertake to facilitate access of all inhabitants of the Americas to preschool, primary, secondary, and higher education, and we will make learning a lifelong process. We will put science and technology at the service of education to assure growing levels of knowledge and so that educators may develop their skills to the highest level. The Plan of Action that accompanies this Declaration defines the objectives and goals we intend to achieve and the actions that will make them a reality. In order to meet our goals within the agreed timeframes, we reaffirm our commitment to invest greater resources in this important area, and to encourage civil society to participate in developing education.

The decisions adopted by our Ministers of Education at the Conference held in Mérida, Mexico, last February, reflect our desire to promote specific joint initiatives designed to improve access to education, with fairness, quality, relevancy, and effectiveness. In order to consolidate and lend continuity to our decisions, we have instructed that another Conference be held in Brasilia, Brazil, in July of this year.

Today, we direct our Ministers Responsible for Trade to begin negotiations for the FTAA, in accordance with the March 1998 Ministerial Declaration of San José. We reaffirm our determination to conclude the negotiation of the FTAA no later than 2005, and to make concrete progress by the end of the century. The FTAA agreement will be balanced, comprehensive, WTO-consistent and constitute a single undertaking.

We note with satisfaction the preparatory work by the Ministers Responsible for Trade over the past three years which has strengthened our trade policies, fostered understanding of our economic objectives and facilitated dialogue among all participating countries. We appreciate the significant contribution of the Inter-American Development Bank (IDB), the Organization of American States (OAS), and the United Nations Economic Commission for Latin America and the Caribbean (ECLAC), acting as the Tripartite Committee.

The FTAA negotiating process will be transparent, and take into account the differences in the levels of development and size of the economies in the Americas, in order to create opportunities for the full participation by all countries. We encourage all segments of civil society to participate in and contribute to the process in a constructive manner, through our respective mechanisms of dialogue and consultation and by presenting their views through the mechanism created in the FTAA negotiating process. We believe that economic integration, investment, and free trade are key factors for raising standards of living, improving the working conditions of the people of the Americas and better protecting the environment. These issues will be taken into account as we proceed with the economic integration process in the Americas.

The region has made significant advances in both monetary and fiscal policy as well as in price stability and liberalizing our economies. The volatility of capital markets vindicates our decision to strengthen banking supervision in the Hemisphere and to establish regulations relating to disclosure and reporting of banking information.

The strength and meaning of representative democracy lie in the active participation of individuals at all levels of civic life. The democratic culture must encompass our entire population. We will strengthen education for democracy and promote the necessary actions for government institutions to become more participatory structures. We undertake to strengthen the capabilities of regional and local governments, when appropriate, and to foster more active participation by civil society.

Respect for and promotion of human rights and the fundamental freedoms of all individuals is a primary concern of our governments. In commemorating the fiftieth anniversary of the American Declaration of the Rights and Duties of Man and the Universal Declaration of Human Rights, we agree on the need to promote the ratification and implementation of the international agreements aimed at preserving them and to continue strengthening the pertinent national and international institutions. We agree that a free press plays a fundamental role in this area and we reaffirm the importance of guaranteeing freedom of expression, information, and opinion. We commend the recent appointment of a Special Rapporteur for Freedom of Expression, within the framework of the Organization of American States.

Confident that an independent, efficient, and effective administration of justice plays an essential role in the process of consolidating democracy, strengthens its institutions, guarantees the equality of all its citizens, and contributes to economic development, we will enhance our policies relating to justice and encourage the reforms necessary to promote legal and judicial cooperation. To that end, we will strengthen national entities involved in the study of the administration of justice and expedite the establishment of a hemispheric center for studies on this subject.

We will combat all forms of discrimination in the Hemisphere. Equal rights and opportunities between men and women and the objective of ensuring active participation of women in all areas of national endeavor are priority tasks. We will continue to promote the full integration of indigenous populations and other vulnerable groups into political and economic life, with due respect for the characteristics and expressions that affirm their cultural identity. We will make a special effort to guarantee the human rights of all migrants, including migrant workers and their families.

Overcoming poverty continues to be the greatest challenge confronted by our Hemisphere. We are conscious that the positive growth shown in the Americas in past years has yet to resolve the problems of inequity and social exclusion. We are determined to remove the barriers that deny the poor access to proper nutrition, social services, a healthy environment, credit, and legal title to their property. We will provide greater support to micro and small enterprises, promote core labor standards recognized by the International Labor Organization (ILO), and use new technologies to improve the health conditions of every family in the Americas, with the technical support of the Pan-American Health Organization (PAHO), achieving greater levels of equity and sustainable development.

With deep satisfaction, we note that peace, an essential value for human coexistence, is a reality in the Hemisphere. We underscore that Central America has become a zone of peace, democracy, and development and we recognize efforts to eliminate antipersonnel mines and to rehabilitate their victims. We will continue to foster confidence and security among our countries through such measures as those mentioned in the Santiago and San Salvador Declarations on Confidence- and Security-Building Measures. We encourage the pacific settlement of disputes.

We will lend new impetus to the struggle against corruption, money laundering, terrorism, weapons trafficking, and the drug problem, including illicit use, and work together to ensure that criminals do not find safe haven anywhere in the Hemisphere. We are determined to persevere in this direction.

In forging an alliance against drugs and applying the Hemispheric Anti-Drug Strategy, we welcome the start of formal negotiations at the May 4 meeting of Inter-American Drug Abuse Control Commission (CICAD) to be held in Washington within the framework of the Organization of American States (OAS), to establish an objective procedure for the multilateral evaluation of actions and cooperation to prevent and combat all aspects of the drug problem and related crimes, based on the principles of sovereignty, territorial integrity of States, shared responsibility, and with a comprehensive and balanced approach.

We will strengthen national, hemispheric, and international efforts aimed at environmental protection as a basis for sustainable development that provides human beings a healthy and productive life in harmony with nature. The commitments undertaken at the Miami Summit and the Summit on Sustainable Development held in Santa Cruz de la Sierra, Bolivia, provide a solid basis for strengthening our actions. As parties to the United Nations Framework Convention on Climate Change, we underscore the importance of working together to further fulfillment of the agreement reached at the Conference in Kyoto, Japan, and to promote its ratification in our countries. Moreover, we will work closely to make preparations for a Conference of the Parties to be held in November of this year in Buenos Aires, Argentina.

We acknowledge that the development of energy links between our countries and the intensification of trade in the energy sector strengthen and foster the integration of the Americas. Energy integration, based on competitive and transparent activities, and in compliance with national conditions and objectives, contributes to the sustainable development of our nations and to the improvement of the quality of life of our people with minimum impact on the environment. Recognizing the importance of, and positive role played by hemispheric institutions, particularly the Organization of American States (OAS), we instruct our Ministers to examine the strengthening and modernizing of these institutions.

We reaffirm our will to continue strengthening intra-hemispheric dialogue and cooperation within the framework of friendship and solidarity that inspires our nations.

# III. Summit Documents

CUMBRE
DE LAS AMERICAS
CHILE 1998

# Plan of Action of Santiago:
## Summit of the Americas

We, the democratically elected Heads of State and Government of the Americas, recognizing the need to make a collective effort that complements the actions being developed and executed at the national level to improve the economic well-being and the quality of life of our peoples, mindful of our commitment to the continued implementation of the Miami *Plan of Action,* affirm our resolute determination to carry out this Plan of Action, which constitutes a body of concrete initiatives intended to promote the overall development of the countries of the Hemisphere and ensure access to and improve the quality of education, promote and strengthen democracy and the respect for human rights, deepen economic integration and free trade and eradicate poverty and discrimination. We have adopted this Plan of Action conscious that all the initiatives are inter-related and equally important to the attainment of our common endeavor.

## I. EDUCATION: THE KEY TO PROGRESS

The Hemisphere's commitment to education is reflected in the sweeping reform processes encompassing all levels of educational systems and is based on broad consensus with respect to the problems confronting education and the shared commitment and effort of societies as a whole to overcome them. These processes are based on the principles of equity, quality, relevance and efficiency. Equity is defined as the creation of conditions that ensure that all people have the opportunity to receive quality education services, thereby significantly reducing the effects of inequalities based on socio-economic status, disability and ethnic, cultural and gender discrimination. Quality implies the achievement of high levels of cognitive development, skills, capabilities and ethical attitudes. Relevance is defined as the ability of an educational system to meet the needs and aspirations of society as a whole, taking into account its social, cultural, ethnic and linguistic diversity. Lastly, efficiency is defined as the provision of adequate resources, used optimally, in order to enhance educational achievements.

Therefore, the Governments, fully recognizing and respecting national sovereignty and the responsibilities of the institutions of our respective countries with regard to education, reiterate the commitment of the Miami Summit to ensure, by the year 2010, universal access to and completion of quality primary education for 100 percent of children and access for at least 75 percent of young people to quality secondary education, with increasing percentages of young people who complete secondary education, and assume responsibility for providing the general population with opportunities for life-long learning. If these objectives are met, we are confident that we will provide our people with the tools, skills and knowledge necessary for and suited to the development of capabilities that ensure better conditions of competitiveness and productivity required by modern economies, thus allowing our people to contribute as worthy citizens to their respective societies.

*To achieve these objectives, Governments will:*

Implement targeted and inter-sectoral educational policies, as necessary, and develop programs that focus specifically on groups at a disadvantage in the areas of education, functional illiteracy and socio-economic conditions, with attention to women, minorities and vulnerable populations. Inter-sectoral programs in education, health and nutrition, as well as early childhood educational strategies, will be priorities, inasmuch as they contribute more directly to plans to combat poverty.

Establish or strengthen national or subnational and, where applicable, subregional systems to evaluate the quality of education, which permit assessment of the performance of various educational actors, innovations and factors associated with achievements in learning. To that end, information and national or subnational or, where applicable, subregional indicators will be made available that can be used to design, carry out and evaluate quality-improvement programs based on equity. Standards for reading and writing, mathematics and science shall receive special attention. Also, where appropriate, criteria and methodologies for collecting data that permit comparison of some educational indicators across countries in the Hemisphere shall be established.

Develop comprehensive programs to improve and increase the level of professionalism among teachers and school administrators that combine pre-service and in-service training, exploring incentive mechanisms tied to updating their skills and to meeting such standards as may have been agreed upon. Higher education must collaborate in this endeavor through research and pedagogy, both of which should be strengthened in order to meet this goal. Strengthen education management and institutional capacity at the national, regional, local and school levels, furthering, where appropriate, decentralization and the promotion of better forms of community and family involvement. Encourage the mass media to contribute to bolstering efforts being made by educational systems.

Strengthen preparation, education and training for the world of work so that an increasing number of workers can improve their standard of living and, together with employers, have the opportunity to benefit from hemispheric integration. In this regard, consideration will be given to the adoption of new technology based on different options and alternatives, ranging from specific occupational training to strengthening general employability competencies. Special attention will also be paid to the establishment or strengthening of mechanisms that permit workers to obtain certification of job-related competencies acquired through formal education and work experience. In order to confront changes in the labor market and to enhance employability prospects, actions that take into account the development of entrepreneurial skills will be included and will involve the different sectors and offer various options and alternatives.

Establish or improve, according to their internal legal framework, educational strategies relevant to multicultural societies, so as to be able to shape, with the participation of indigenous populations and migrants, models for bilingual and intercultural basic education. Similarly, the content of basic education will have to be enhanced, together with respect and appreciation for the cultural diversity of peoples, as well as to expand the knowledge of the different languages spoken in the countries of the Hemisphere, where resources and possibilities permit.

Develop, within and outside schools, with the assistance of families and other actors and social organizations, educational strategies that foster the development of values, with special attention to the inclusion of democratic principles, human rights, gender-related issues, peace, tolerance and respect for the environment and natural resources. Promote access to and use of the most effective information and communication technologies in education systems, with special emphasis on the use of computers, in combination with revised pedagogical methods and proper training for teachers in the use of these technologies. Special attention shall be paid to the ethical imperative of including the most vulnerable sectors. To that end, distance education programs shall be strengthened and information networks established.

Make efforts to increase the availability of teaching materials in collaboration with official institutions and, depending on the specific conditions in each country, with the private sector. Seek to use technology to link schools and communities as a way of establishing ties in the Hemisphere while encouraging the participation of higher education institutions that have advantages in this field.

Further scholarship and exchange programs for students, teachers, researchers and educational administrators using different strategies, including institution-to-institution ties, communications technology and internships which permit exposure to pedagogical and management innovations in the other countries of the Hemisphere. This will contribute to strengthening the institutional capacity of Ministries or Departments of Education, decentralized administrative entities and centers of higher learning.

## Funding, Horizontal Multilateral Cooperation Strategies and Follow-up

We, the Heads of State and Government, recognizing the cardinal importance of education as a foundation for development, agree, in accordance with our respective legislative processes, to promote allocation of the resources necessary for educational expenditure with a view to attaining greater levels of equity, quality, relevance and efficiency in the educational processes, emphasizing the optimal use of resources and a greater participation of other social actors.

We also reaffirm our commitment to promote horizontal and multilateral cooperation in the area of education. To that end, we:

Instruct the Organization of American States (OAS) and request the Inter-American Development Bank (IDB) and World Bank, together with the other national and multilateral technical and financial cooperation agencies operating in the Hemisphere, to provide, within their respective areas of action, support for programs and initiatives that are consistent with the goals, objectives, and actions proposed in this Chapter of the Plan of Action. To this end, the IDB is encouraged to work with member countries to substantially increase the share of new lending for primary and secondary education, by more than doubling the quantity over the next three years, compared to the previous three years. We also request that the IDB establish a special regional fund for education in the Hemisphere, utilizing the existing resources of this institution. This fund would support efforts to raise educational standards and performance throughout the Region.

Instruct the OAS and request the IDB, the World Bank, and United Nations Economic Commission on Latin America and the Caribbean (ECLAC), among other institutions, to use the mechanisms within their scope to develop and strengthen regional cooperation in areas such as distance education, using, among other means, satellite technology; internships and exchange programs; the development and use of information technology for education; the updating of education statistics; and quality assessment, while striving to ensure that this cooperation is in keeping with the specific needs of each country. We recognize the role and interest in these efforts of specialized international organizations, such as United Nations Education, Science and Cultural Organization (UNESCO). Likewise, we recognize the contributions of the private sector, philanthropic foundations, and pertinent non-governmental organizations.

Instruct the OAS to foster, articulate and facilitate, through ministerial meetings and other mechanisms being developed by member States in the framework of the Inter-American Council for Integral Development (CIDI), collaboration and joint effort in the Hemisphere and, to that end, to convene, in consultation with the coordinating countries, technical consultation forums of the countries in the Hemisphere in order to contribute to the implementation of the commitments included in this Chapter of the Plan of Action. Entrust the Meeting of Ministers of Education, to be convened by the OAS within the framework of CIDI's Strategic Plan for Partnership for Development, to be held in Brazil in July 1998, with the development of an implementation plan for this education initiative.

Instruct the OAS and request the IDB, World Bank, ECLAC, and other multilateral institutions to report on the execution of this Plan to the Government representatives responsible for review and follow-up of the commitments of the Summit of the Americas.

## II. PRESERVING AND STRENGTHENING DEMOCRACY, JUSTICE AND HUMAN RIGHTS

The strengthening of democracy, justice and human rights is a vital hemispheric priority. In this Plan of Action, we endorse new initiatives designed to deepen our commitment to these important principles. Specifically, we will intensify our efforts to promote democratic reforms at the regional and local level, protect the rights of migrant workers and their families, improve the capabilities of our justice systems and labor ministries to respond to the needs of our peoples, and encourage a strong and active civil society. We further resolve to defend democracy against the serious threats of corruption, terrorism, and illegal narcotics, and to promote peace and security among our nations. Taken together, these measures consolidate our democratic gains, reaffirm our commitment to democratic institutions, and commit us to building a Hemisphere of shared values.

## Democracy and Human Rights

### *Governments will:*

Define and develop, with the participation of civil society, comprehensive policies aimed at promoting and protecting human rights at a domestic level, in accordance with relevant international norms and principles, incorporating those policies, where appropriate, into national human rights plans and programs, as recommended by the World Conference of Vienna, 1993; and underscore as well the importance of promoting respect for the universally recognized principles of international humanitarian law.

Guarantee that all individuals have the right to due process of law, including the presumption of innocence and the right to trial within a reasonable period of time and the full respect for their constitutional and other legal rights. Governments will, in accordance with their legal framework, adopt measures intended to ensure that no person awaiting trial shall be detained for a period longer than permitted by law, taking fully into account the rights of the accused, the protection of society, crime prevention, the promotion of respect for the law, the rights of victims and other relevant considerations. Governments will continue their efforts to improve conditions of detention and enhance human rights education for the respective officials involved in the administration of justice.

Promote a review of their respective national legislation in order to eliminate or amend those provisions which may lead to any type of discrimination, for any reason, in contravention of their international commitments. In particular, they will seek to attain legal equality between men and women by the year 2002. In this context, priority should be given to the rights to equal treatment in the workplace, property, inheritance and child custody, as well as combating domestic violence.

Promote the adoption of legal, educational and social measures, as well as international cooperation, to combat the physical and sexual abuse of children, traffic in minors, child prostitution and child exploitation in all its forms, including pornography. At the same time, they will strengthen international cooperation through the implementation of a regional information system on affected children, based on national information systems, with the participation of and promotion by concerned international organizations, to analyze their condition and evaluate social policies to facilitate decision making in this sphere.

Promote the signature, ratification and accession to international human rights instruments to which they are not party, as well as observe the provisions contained in the instruments to which they are party.

Governments will also enhance cooperation with and support for the activities of the Organization of American States (OAS) in order to:

Strengthen the inter-American human rights system through concrete initiatives and measures which aim to reinforce its institutional structure and promote its links with national systems and regional entities that promote and protect human rights. In this context, Governments consider important the institutional strengthening of the Inter-American Human Rights Institute.

Support States that so request in the processes of promoting and consolidating democratic values, practices and institutions by strengthening the respective organs of the Organization, including the Unit for the Promotion of Democracy (UPD).

Strengthen the exercise of and respect for all human rights and the consolidation of democracy, including the fundamental right to freedom of expression and thought, through support for the activities of the Inter-American Commission on Human Rights in this field, in particular the recently created Special Rapporteur for Freedom of Expression.

Promote programs of cooperation, through the use of advanced information technology and with the support of the international institutions that deal with administration of justice, in areas identified by the OAS Working Group on Democracy and Human Rights, which include:

1. Training of police and correctional officers;
2. Necessary steps to remedy inhumane conditions in prisons and reduce drastically the number of pretrial detainees; and
3. Enhancing human rights education for judges, magistrates and other court officials.

## Education for Democracy

### Governments will:

Include in educational programs, within the legal framework of each country, objectives and contents that develop democratic culture at all levels, in order to teach individuals ethical values, a spirit of cooperation and integrity. To that end, the participation of teachers, families, students and outreach workers will be stepped up in their work related to conceptualizing and implementing the plans for shaping citizens imbued with democratic values.

## Civil Society

### Governments will:

Promote, with the participation of civil society, the development of principles and recommendations for institutional frameworks to stimulate the formation of responsible and transparent, non-profit and other civil society organizations, including, where appropriate, programs for volunteers, and encourage, in accordance with national priorities, public sector-civil society dialogue and partnerships in the areas that are considered pertinent in this Plan of Action. In this context the Organization of American States (OAS) may serve as a forum for the exchange of experiences and information.

In this process, draw upon existing initiatives that promote increased participation of civil society in public issues, such as relevant successful experiences from the National Councils for Sustainable Development and the Inter-American Strategy for Public Participation, among others. As soon as possible, Governments will adopt work plans to implement legal and institutional frameworks based on the principles and recommendations in their respective countries.

Entrust the OAS to encourage support among Governments and civil society organizations, and to promote appropriate programs to carry out this initiative, and request the Inter-American Development Bank (IDB) to develop and implement, along with interested States and other inter-American institutions, hemispheric financial mechanisms specially devoted to the implementation of programs oriented toward strengthening civil society and public participation mechanisms.

## Migrant Workers

*Governments will:*

Reaffirm that the promotion and protection of human rights and the fundamental freedoms for all, without distinction by reasons of race, gender, language, nationality, or religion, is a priority for the international community and is the responsibility of every state. Comply with the applicable international human rights instruments and, consistent with the legal framework of each country, guarantee the human rights of all migrants, including migrant workers and their families.

Seek full compliance with, and protection of, the human rights of all migrants, including migrant workers, and their families, and adopt effective measures, including the strengthening of public awareness, to prevent and eradicate violations of human rights and eliminate all forms of discrimination against them, particularly racial discrimination, xenophobia, and related intolerance.

Reaffirm the sovereign right of each State to formulate and apply its own legal framework and policies for migration, including the granting of permission to migrants to enter, stay, or exercise economic activity, in full conformity with applicable international instruments relating to human rights and in a spirit of cooperation.

Seek full respect for, and compliance with, the 1963 Vienna Convention on Consular Relations, especially as it relates to the right of nationals, regardless of their immigration status, to communicate with a consular officer of their own State in case of detention. Protect the rights of all migrant workers and their families, consistent with each country's internal legal framework, by taking steps, in case they do not exist, to: 1) provide, with respect to working conditions, the same legal protection as for national workers; 2) facilitate, as appropriate, the payment of full wages owed when the worker has returned to his/her country, and allow them to arrange the transfer of their personal effects; 3) recognize the rights of citizenship and nationality of the children of all migrant workers who may be entitled to such rights, and any other rights they may have in each country; 4) encourage the negotiation of bilateral or multilateral agreements, regarding the remission of social security benefits accrued by migrant workers; 5) protect all migrant workers and their families, through law enforcement and information campaigns, from becoming victims of exploitation and abuse from alien smuggling; 6) prevent abuse and mistreatment of all migrant workers by employers or any authorities entrusted with the enforcement of migration policies and border control; and 7) encourage and promote respect for the cultural identity of all migrants. Support the activities of the Inter-American Commission on Human Rights with regard to the protection of the rights of migrant workers and their families, particularly through the Special Rapporteur for Migrant Workers.

## Strengthening Municipal and Regional Administrations

*Governments will:*

- Within their legal framework and within a reasonable time, establish or strengthen mechanisms for the participation of groups of society in the process of local and other subnational decision-making, such as open public hearings and public budget reviews, and promote transparency in local and other subnational Government finance operations.

- In accordance with legislation at all levels, provide for financing options for local and other subnational Governments, including groups of local Governments, such as through transfers of national revenue, access to private capital markets, and authority for raising revenue locally, in order to expand the delivery of quality services as well as provide for training opportunities to strengthen local and other subnational administrative capabilities.

- In accordance with circumstances and the legal framework of each country, study the possible transfer of additional national governmental functions to local and other subnational levels as well as the possibility for enhancing such authorities.
- Share their experiences and information from existing and future programs supported by multilateral and bilateral cooperation institutions such as the Organization of American States (OAS), the Inter-American Development Bank (IDB) and the World Bank, to facilitate the implementation of this initiative.

## Corruption

### Governments will:

Resolutely support the "Inter-American Program to Combat Corruption" and implement the actions established therein, particularly the adoption of a strategy to achieve prompt ratification of the 1996 Inter-American Convention against Corruption, the drafting of codes of conduct for public officials, in accordance with respective legal frameworks, the study of the problem of laundering assets or proceeds derived from corruption, and the promotion of information campaigns on the ethical values that sustain the democratic system. Sponsor in Chile a Symposium on Enhancing Probity in the Hemisphere to be held no later than August 1998, in order to consider, among other topics, the scope of the Inter-American Convention against Corruption, and the implementation of the aforementioned program. They will also resolutely support the holding of workshops sponsored by the Organization of American States (OAS) to disseminate the provisions set forth in the Inter-American Convention against Corruption.

Foster within the OAS framework, and in accordance with the mandate set forth in the Inter-American Program to Combat Corruption, appropriate follow-up on the progress achieved under the Inter-American Convention against Corruption. Promote in their domestic legislation the obligation for senior public officials, and those at other levels when the law so establishes, to declare or disclose their personal assets and liabilities to the appropriate agency.

Encourage the approval of effective and specific measures to combat all forms of corruption, bribery, and related unlawful practices in commercial transactions, among others.

## Financing of Electoral Campaigns

### Governments will:

Propose the exchange of experiences that may be used as a support for each country so that, according to their own realities and legal systems, they adopt or develop internal rules that regulate contributions to electoral campaigns and independent internal control mechanisms. Consider the proposals resulting from the Meeting of Government Representatives on Contributions to Electoral Campaigns, held in Caracas in February 1998, under the auspices of the OAS.

Adopt or consider, as appropriate, measures to prevent financial contributions to electoral campaigns derived from organized crime and drug trafficking. Similarly, they will promote the adoption of measures designed to ensure transparency in the origin of all contributions.

## Prevention and Control of Illicit Consumption of and Traffic in Drugs and Psychotropic Substances and other Related Crimes

### Governments will:

Continue to develop their national and multilateral efforts in order to achieve full application of the Hemispheric Anti-Drug Strategy, and will strengthen this alliance based on the principles of respect for the sovereignty and territorial jurisdiction of the States, reciprocity, shared responsibility and an integrated, balanced approach in conformity with their domestic laws. With the intention of strengthening mutual confidence, dialogue and hemispheric cooperation and on the basis of the aforementioned principles, develop, within the framework of the Inter-American Drug Abuse Control Commission (CICAD-OAS), a singular and objective process of multilateral governmental evaluation in order to monitor the progress of their individual and collective efforts in the Hemisphere and of all the countries participating in the Summit, in dealing with the diverse manifestations of the problem. Strengthen national efforts and international cooperation in order to:

1. Enhance their national policies and plans with regard to the prevention of illicit drug consumption, and step up measures, particularly at the community level, in schools and those aimed at the most vulnerable groups, such as children and young people, in order to prevent the growth and spread of this consumption and to eliminate financial incentives to illicit trafficking;

2. Develop appropriate treatment, rehabilitation and reintegration programs with a view to alleviating the serious social effects, human suffering and other adverse effects associated with drug abuse;

3. Increase cooperation in areas such as the collection and analysis of data, standardization of systems that measure illicit consumption, scientific and technical training and exchange of experiences;

4. Develop or encourage the development of campaigns to foster greater social awareness of the dangers of drug abuse for individuals, the family and society as well as community participation plans;

5. Sensitize public opinion as to the serious effects of drug abuse and the activities of criminal organizations that deal with them, including at the wholesale and retail level;

6. Improve and update cooperative mechanisms to prosecute and extradite individuals charged with the traffic in narcotics and psychotropic substances and other related crimes, in accordance with international agreements, constitutional requirements, and national laws;

7. Establish or strengthen existing, duly trained and equipped specialized central units responsible for requesting, analyzing and exchanging among the competent State authorities information relating to the laundering of the proceeds, assets and instrumentalities used in criminal activities (also known as money laundering);

8. Reinforce international and national control mechanisms to impede the illicit traffic and diversion of chemical precursors;

9. Promote the rapid ratification and entry into force of the Inter-American Convention Against the Illicit Production and Trafficking of Firearms; promote the approval and prompt application of the Model Regulations on the Control of Arms and Explosives Connected with Drug Trafficking of CICAD; encourage States, that have not already done so, to adopt the necessary legislative or other measures to ensure effective international cooperation to prevent and combat illicit transnational traffic in firearms and ammunition, while establishing, or strengthening, systems to enhance the tracing of firearms used in criminal activity; and

10. Eliminate illicit crops through the increased support of national alternative development programs as well as eradication and interdiction.

Strengthen national drug control commissions, with a view to improving coordination in each country in the planning and implementation of their respective national plans and in streamlining international assistance in this area.

Underscore the valuable contribution of civil society, through its different organizations, in the areas of prevention of illicit consumption, treatment, rehabilitation, and social reintegration of drug addicts.

Encourage financial institutions to redouble their efforts to prevent money laundering and the appropriate business sectors to strengthen its controls to prevent the diversion of chemical precursors.

Give full support to the upcoming Special Session of the United Nations General Assembly which will be held in June 1998 for the purpose of promoting international cooperation with respect to illicit drugs and related crimes and encourage all States to participate actively, at the highest level, in that international meeting. They will make every effort to ensure effective implementation of international narcotics agreements to which they have subscribed, at regional and subregional levels, and for these to operate in consonance with the hemispheric effort and reaffirm their support for CICAD and its fundamental role in the implementation of these agreements.

## Terrorism

*Governments will:*

Take measures, as agreed in the Declaration and Plan of Action of Lima, in order to prevent, combat and eliminate terrorism, applying for that purpose the most decisive will to comply with the general objectives set forth therein.

Encourage States that have not yet done so to sign, ratify, or accede to, as appropriate, the international conventions related to terrorism, in accordance with their respective internal legislation.

Convene, under the auspices of the Organization of American States (OAS), the Second Specialized Inter-American Conference to evaluate the progress attained and to define future courses of action for the prevention, combat and elimination of terrorism.

## Building Confidence and Security Among States

*Governments will:*

Promote regional dialogue with a view to revitalizing and strengthening the institutions of the Inter-American system, taking into account the new political, economic, social and strategic-military factors in the Hemisphere and in its subregions. To that end, they will seek to expand further a climate of confidence and security among the States of the Hemisphere. Carry out, in the manner in which they are set forth, the measures and recommendations resulting from the Regional Conferences on Confidence and Security Building Measures, held in November 1995, in Santiago, Chile, and in February 1998, in San Salvador, El Salvador, under the auspices of the Organization of American States (OAS). Continue to support the efforts of small-island States to address their special security concerns, which are multidimensional in nature, and economic, financial, and environmental matters, taking into account the vulnerability and level of development of these States.

In furtherance of efforts to transform the Western Hemisphere into an antipersonnel mine-free zone, and in recognition of the contribution in this regard of the Convention on the Prohibition of the Use, Stockpiling, Production, and Transfer of Anti-Personnel Mines and on Their Destruction, including its early entry into force, they will encourage actions and support international humanitarian demining efforts in this area, with the goal of ensuring that priority is given to mines that threaten civilians and of ensuring that land can be restored for productive purpose. The latter will take place through effective regional and international cooperation and coordination, as requested by the affected States, to survey, mark, map, and remove mines; effective mine awareness for the civilian population and assistance to victims; and development and deployment of new mine detection and clearance technologies, as appropriate.

Continue promoting transparency in matters related to defense policy, among other aspects, with regard to modernizing the Armed Forces, comparing military expenditure in the Region, and strengthening the United Nations Register of Conventional Arms. Increase cooperation with United Nations peacekeeping efforts. Encourage the development of cooperative programs to deal with natural disasters and humanitarian search and rescue operations.

Pledge their efforts to ensure that the peaceful resolution of pending conflicts and disputes is achieved through existing mechanisms for the peaceful settlement of disputes within the Inter-American System and in keeping with international law and treaties in force, and express that said mechanisms and instruments should be strengthened. Acknowledge the value of ministerial or high-level meetings on the topics of international defense and security, such as the Defense Ministerials of Williamsburg and Bariloche, as an important contribution to regional dialogue on these matters, and, in this context, encourage interested countries to hold other meetings.

Entrust the OAS, through the Committee on the Hemispheric Security, to:

1. Follow up on and expand topics relating to confidence and security building measures;

2. Analyze the meaning, scope, and implications of international security concepts in the Hemisphere, with a view to developing the most appropriate common approaches by which to manage their various aspects, including disarmament and arms control; and

3. Pinpoint ways to revitalize and strengthen the institutions of the Inter-American System related to the various aspects of Hemispheric Security.

4. This process will culminate in a Special Conference on Security, within the framework of the OAS, to be held, at the latest, at the beginning of the next decade.

Support the convening of a follow-up Regional Conference to the Santiago and San Salvador Regional Conferences on Confidence and Security Building Measures, to further build mutual confidence in the Americas.

The progress achieved in these matters will be reported to States, thereby ensuring appropriate follow-up through the OAS, so that these topics may be discussed at the next Summit of the Americas.

## Strengthening of Justice Systems and Judiciaries

*Governments will:*

Develop mechanisms that permit easy and timely access to justice by all persons, with particular reference to persons with low income, by adopting measures to enhance the transparency, efficiency and effectiveness of the courts. In this context, they will promote, develop and integrate the use of alternative methods of conflict resolution in the justice system.

Strengthen, as appropriate, systems of criminal justice founded on the independence of the judiciary and the effectiveness of public prosecutors and defense counsels, recognizing the special importance of the introduction of oral proceedings in those countries that consider it necessary to implement this reform.

Step up efforts to combat organized crime, and transnational crime, and, if necessary, foster new laws and international conventions, as well as procedures and mechanisms for continuing to combat these scourges.

Adapt legislation and proceed, as soon as possible, with necessary institutional reforms and measures to guarantee the comprehensive protection of the rights of children and youths to meet the obligations established under the United Nations Convention on the Right of the Child and other international instruments.

Adopt as appropriate a clear distinction between procedures and consequences of violations of criminal law and measures established to protect children and youths whose rights are threatened or violated, and will promote social and educational measures to rehabilitate young offenders.

Foster the establishment and strengthening of specialized tribunals or courts for family matters, as appropriate, and in accordance with their respective legal systems. Expedite the establishment of a justice studies center of the Americas, which will facilitate training of justice sector personnel, the exchange of information and other forms of technical cooperation in the Hemisphere, in response to particular requirements of each country. To this end, they request the Ministers of Justice or other competent authorities to analyze and define the most suitable actions for the organization and establishment for such a center.

Promote, in accordance with the legislation of each country, mutual legal and judicial assistance that is effective and responsive, particularly with respect to extraditions, requests for the delivery of documents and other evidentiary materials, and other bilateral or multilateral exchanges in this field, such as witness protection arrangements. Support the convening of periodic meetings of Ministers of Justice and Attorneys General of the Hemisphere within the framework of the Organization of American States (OAS).

## Modernization of the State in Labor Matters

*Governments will:*

Promote measures by their Ministries of Labor to provide high quality programs and assistance for workers and employers, placing emphasis on greater decentralization of their functions, the incorporation of new technologies, active labor market policies, better and more timely information regarding the labor market, and improvement of safety and health conditions in the workplace.

Give special attention to the incorporation of socially disadvantaged groups into the workforce, including women, minorities, youth, the disabled and other vulnerable populations, and to the services offered by the Ministries of Labor that take into consideration their special needs. At the same time, Governments will further strengthen their overall efforts, and coordination among involved agencies, to address the issue of children at work. The Ministries of Labor will exchange experiences on best practices in these areas. Take actions towards assuring that the Ministries of Labor have the necessary means to carry out this Plan of Action in areas within their jurisdiction.

Request the participation of the International Labor Organization (ILO), the Inter-American Development Bank (IDB) and the Organization of American States (OAS) to assist Labor Ministries to support international activities and exchange information on modernization methods and strategies.

## III. ECONOMIC INTEGRATION AND FREE TRADE

### A. Free Trade Area of the Americas (FTAA)

*I. We instruct our Ministers Responsible for Trade to take the following actions:*

1. Initiate the negotiations for the Free Trade Area of the Americas (FTAA), in accordance with the principles, objectives, structure, modalities and all other decisions as set out in the San José Ministerial

Declaration, by convening the Trade Negotiations Committee no later than June 30, 1998, and the Negotiating Groups no later than September 30, 1998.

2. Exercise the ultimate oversight and management of the negotiations.

3. Achieve concrete progress in the negotiations by the year 2000 and agree on specific business facilitation measures to be adopted before the end of the century.

4. Ensure that the negotiating process is transparent and takes into account the differences in the levels of development and size of the economies in the Americas, in order to create opportunities for the full participation of all countries, including the smaller economies.

5. Conduct the negotiations in such a manner as to build broad public understanding of and support for the FTAA, and to consider views on trade matters from different sectors of our civil societies, such as business, labor, consumer, environmental and academic groups, presented to the committee of Government representatives established at the Fourth Meeting of Trade Ministers in Costa Rica.

*II. We instruct our Representatives in the institutions of the Tripartite Committee, in particular the Inter-American Development Bank (IDB), to allocate appropriate existing resources within those institutions to support the Administrative Secretariat for the FTAA negotiations.*

*III. We urge the Tripartite Committee to continue to respond positively to requests for technical support from FTAA entities. We ask the three institutions to consider requests for technical assistance related to FTAA issues from member countries —in particular from the smaller economies in order to facilitate their integration to the FTAA process — according to their respective procedures.*

## B. Further Actions

In addition to initiating the negotiations for the FTAA, we have defined a series of further actions which must be consistent with the FTAA negotiation, aimed at deepening the process of economic integration, as well as to create opportunities for the full participation of all countries, including the smaller economies. We have prepared a series of proposals to advance the modernization of financial markets, programs of science and technology, energy cooperation, and hemispheric infrastructure, in particular in the fields of transportation and telecommunications.

## Strengthening, Modernizing and Integrating Financial Markets

*Governments will:*

Strengthen banking supervision in the Hemisphere through: implementation of the Basle Core Principles for Effective Banking Supervision; training programs to strengthen supervisory capacity; and establishment of sound, high-quality reporting and disclosure standards for banks, and creation of a Working Group to assist countries in this process. Improve banking and securities market clearance and settlement systems in the Hemisphere, in order to facilitate the transparency, efficiency and security of internal and cross-border transactions.

## Science and Technology

*Governments will:*

Recognize that science and technology are related to various areas and objectives of this Plan of Action within and beyond economic integration, free trade and sustainable development. Continue implementing the Cartagena Plan of Action, agreed to in 1996, with emphasis on strengthening the capacity of the countries in the Hemisphere to participate and benefit from the knowledge-based global economy, promoting, among other actions, the growth of the communications and information industries as strategic components of national, subregional and regional integration processes. In the context of the Cartagena Declaration, recognize the important role that existing regional institutions play in implementing this Plan of Action.

Apply science and technology to mitigate the damages caused by the effects of "El Niño" and other natural hazards, such as volcanic eruptions, hurricanes, earthquakes, and floods, and their impact on the economy and ecosystems, based on improved forecasting, prevention and response capacity, improved research and training methods to deal with natural hazards, and the application of science and technology to address the effects of climate variability on health, agriculture and water. In this context, cooperative research and exchange of information about "El Niño" and other natural hazards will be emphasized. Support the development and use of science, technology and innovation indicators in fulfillment of the Cartagena Plan.

Promote actions to foster alliances among all sectors of society to advance cooperation and innovation in science and technology. It is recognized that university-industry relations, training in technology management and other human resource development programs, as well as participation of small and medium-sized companies, are important elements for utilizing science and technology to achieve hemispheric objectives.

## Regional Energy Cooperation

In accordance with the legal and constitutional rules of every State, as well as with the commitments that our Governments assume in the context of the negotiations of the Free Trade Area of the Americas (FTAA), in order to ensure sustainable energy development and further the energy integration of the Hemisphere,

*Governments will:*

Promote policies and processes that facilitate the trade of products, goods and services related to the energy sector. Give impetus to, in the shortest possible time, policies and processes that facilitate the development of infrastructure, including across international boundaries, to further the integration of energy markets.

Foster the creation and strengthening of transparent and predictable regulatory systems, which take into account the needs of the different parties involved. Promote legal, fiscal and regulatory systems in order to stimulate local and foreign private investment in the energy sector in those areas permitted by respective Constitutions. Increase access of rural inhabitants to energy services.

Support policies and programs that will stimulate the development of renewable energy and energy efficiency.

To support these actions, we will continue our cooperation efforts through the Hemispheric Energy Initiative.

## Climate Change

*Governments will:*

In light of their commitments in the United Nations Framework Convention on Climate Change and the decisions made at the Third Conference of Parties in Kyoto, Japan, and in view of the Fourth Conference of Parties to be held in Buenos Aires, Argentina, in November 1998:

Encourage the Parties to work toward achieving the objectives and goals of the United Nations Framework Convention on Climate Change.

Recognize the key role that technology plays in managing the environmental aspects related to energy, and encourage the exchange of technology, information and experiences, as well as share views on the Clean Development Mechanism.

## Hemispheric Infrastructure

### A. General Infrastructure

*Governments will:*

Charge the Inter-American Development Bank with the preparation of a draft set of voluntary principles to be adopted by each of the countries, to facilitate private sector participation in local and transnational infrastructure projects, that can serve as a basis for bilateral and multilateral agreements. This draft will be submitted to Governments not later than December 1998, to be further discussed during a meeting of ministers responsible for infrastructure to be held in 1999.

### B. Transportation

*Governments will:*

Undertake the necessary actions to implement, to the fullest extent possible, and taking into account subregional sectoral agreements, decisions, and projects, the Joint Ministerial Declaration of the Second Hemispheric Summit on Transportation, held in Santiago, Chile, in April 1996, aimed at: a) promoting market-oriented, integrated, financially viable, and environmentally sustainable transportation systems and services, and b) providing safe, efficient, and reliable passenger and cargo services that foster the economic growth and development of our countries.

Develop a plan aimed at ensuring the highest level of safety in air, sea and land transportation systems, improving infrastructure and increasing environmental protection by improving compliance with international standards and recommended practices established, such as those established by the International Civil Aviation Organization (ICAO) and the International Maritime Organization (IMO).

Engage in discussions to develop a cooperation program, taking into account the Santiago and San Salvador Declarations of the Regional Conferences on Confidence and Security Building Measures, which would address maritime and air transport of nuclear and other hazardous wastes and, where appropriate, work with the relevant international organizations to strengthen or develop standards governing the transport of such goods and its safety. Prepare a profile, with the cooperation of United Nations Economic Commission on Latin America and the Caribbean (ECLAC), of regional transportation systems and services taking into account agreements, decisions, projects and studies already prepared by regional and hemispheric organizations. Such a profile will identify the main problems and opportunities faced by the countries in the Hemisphere as a first step toward establishing regional transportation priorities and policies, with respect to, among other things, the harmonization of standards and the exchange of technology.

Seek, from international financial institutions, resources necessary to undertake, as soon as possible, transportation infrastructure projects in the Americas, including those which take into account the specific needs of the smallest economies.

## C. Telecommunications

*Governments will:*

Establish strategies to support the development and continuous updating of a regional telecommunications infrastructure plan, taking into account national plans, the need for universal access to basic telecommunications services throughout the Region and the evolution of Global Information Society.

Work together in close cooperation with the private sector to rapidly build out the telecommunications infrastructure in the Region, adopting strategies to make affordable access available to all for basic telephone service and the Internet, such as implementing the Inter-American Telecommunications Commission (CITEL) guidelines on value-added services and encouraging, the development of community information service centers that provide access to basic telephone and value-added services, computers, the Internet and multimedia services bearing in mind the diverse needs of the countries of the Region and divergent levels of development.

Promote, in cooperation with the private sector, the exchange and distribution of information concerning regulatory matters such as universal access/service, interconnection and the establishment of independent regulatory bodies, taking into account the commitments made in the World Trade Organization's Agreements on Trade in Basic Telecommunications Services (the GBT Agreement), developments in the Free Trade Area of the Americas process, and the Declaration and Plan of Action adopted by the 1996 Senior Telecommunications Officials Meeting held in Washington D.C. with a view to developing, wherever possible, and subject to national constraints, best practice guidelines and requesting when needed the assistance of CITEL, regional telecommunications organizations, the International Telecommunications Union (ITU), the Inter-American Development Bank (IDB) and others as appropriate. Foster, together with the private sector, the development of applications over electronic networks, such as the Internet, broadcast television and radio, that taking into account different socio-economic conditions and languages, will support education, health, agriculture and sustainable rural development, electronic commerce and other applications assisting small savers, Micro-enterprises and Small and Medium-size Enterprises (SMEs) and modernization of the State.

Encourage CITEL to address, with some urgency, studies of the standards coordination aspects of the telecommunications infrastructure, including the areas of Telecommunications Management Network (TMN) and Intelligent Networks (IN) so that the network can evolve to meet the interconnection requirements and to support the implementation of new applications in the regional context.

Continue to examine ways to develop consistent regulatory approaches among member countries leading to the promotion of greater commonality in the certification processes for telecommunications equipment and to the establishment of a framework and to move toward the negotiation and implementation of a Mutual Recognition Agreement (MRA) for telecommunications equipment encompassing all the countries of the Region.

## IV. ERADICATION OF POVERTY AND DISCRIMINATION

Extreme poverty and discrimination continue to afflict the lives of many of our families and impede their potential contribution to our nations' progress. To move toward a prosperous future for all, we will facilitate the provision of legal title to urban and rural properties and redouble our efforts to increase access to credit and to provide technical support for microenterprises, and protect the basic rights of workers. We will remove all forms of discrimination against women, indigenous communities, disadvantaged racial and ethnic minorities, and other vulnerable groups. We will seek to enhance the quality of life of all people of the Americas through efforts that ensure access to adequate health services, to improved health technologies, to clean water and proper nutrition. Taken together, these measures will facilitate the inclusion of all inhabitants, without exception, in the economic and democratic transformation of the Hemisphere.

## Fostering the Development of Micro, Small and Medium Size Enterprises

As a means to combat poverty and taking into account national differences, the Governments pledge to strengthen the development of micro, small and medium size enterprises by undertaking the following specific actions:

*Governments will:*

Ensure that a significant number of the 50 million micro, small and medium size enterprises in the Hemisphere, whose owners and workers are persons with low incomes, especially women from these enterprises, have access to financial services by the year 2000. Design and implement programs, with the support of the Inter-American Development Bank (IDB) and the United Nations Economic Commission on Latin America and the Caribbean (ECLAC) and in coordination with the World Bank and other development cooperation agencies, that promote appropriate financial policy reforms that accelerate the entry of formal-sector financial institutions into this market; support the development of institutions that work in the sector; and eliminate impediments that limit the access of micro, small and medium size enterprises to financial services.

Simplify and expedite the procedures for registration, obtaining licenses, complying with labor and tax regulations, and the formalization, where appropriate, of micro, small and medium size enterprises.

Support private-sector providers of non-financial services to enable them to expand access to new technologies and training for micro, small and medium size enterprises, which will permit them to enhance their competitiveness in national and global markets. Promote partnerships of micro, small, and medium size enterprises to allow them to take advantage of cooperative assistance in doing business and in modernizing business management.

Promote inter-institutional coordination by creating effective interchange mechanisms between national and local public institutions that support micro, small and medium size enterprises and facilitating their links with the private sector.

Design national plans for the achievement of the actions previously defined and convoke a regional meeting of ministers or senior officials responsible for public policies to support micro, small and medium size enterprises, for the purpose of exchanging information on those plans and thus improving the effectiveness of support policies. To this end, the IDB, in cooperation with ECLAC, will be asked to provide coordination for this meeting. Request that regional organizations and Government, multilateral, and bilateral development agencies involved in the Region assist in policy reform and invest between US$400-$500 million over the next three years in programs, including training and technical assistance, that support the actions identified in this Plan of Action.

## Property Registration

*Governments will:*

Streamline and decentralize, as necessary, property registration procedures by adopting transparent, simplified procedures for titling and registration; disseminating information regarding these procedures; utilizing, whenever feasible, state-of-the-art technologies for property georeferencing, computer-generated mapping and computerized records storage; incorporating alternative dispute resolution mechanisms; and avoiding overlapping administrative fees for titling and registration.

Recommend that multilateral and bilateral cooperation institutions, especially the Inter-American Development Bank (IDB) and the World Bank, strengthen their financial and technical assistance programs, including information exchange regarding experiences among countries, to support simplified property registration procedures and to assure access for the poor to those systems.

In accord with national legal frameworks, implement measures, where necessary, to protect rights accorded to indigenous populations, as well as information programs, if needed, to assure greater awareness of indigenous populations of their rights, in this respect.

## Health Technologies

*Governments will:*

Seek, through public and private efforts, or partnerships between them, to enhance the availability, access to, and quality of drugs and vaccines, especially for the most needy, by promoting efforts to safeguard the quality, rational selection and use, safety and efficacy of pharmaceutical products, with special emphasis on vital and essential drugs; and by supporting regional initiatives that by the year 2002 will facilitate research, development, production and utilization of vaccines, which will reduce the incidence of diseases, such as pneumonia, meningitis, measles, rubella and mumps.

Strengthen and improve existing national and regional networks of health information and surveillance systems, so that stakeholders have access to data to address critical health issues in the Region, in order to make appropriate clinical and managerial decisions. They will address the development, implementation and evaluation of needs-based health information systems and technology, including telecommunications, to support epidemiological surveillance, the operation and management of health services and programs, health education and promotion, telemedicine, computer networks and investment in new health technologies. Develop initiatives designed to reduce deficits in access to and quality of drinking water, basic sanitation and solid waste management, with special emphasis on rural and poor urban areas, by applying existing technologies or developing new, appropriate and effective low-cost technologies.

Make every effort to ensure that the necessary resources are allocated for the development of the lines of action of this Plan, with the technical support of the Pan American Health Organization (PAHO). They also will promote bilateral and multilateral collaboration, and will request the Inter-American Development Bank (IDB), the World Bank, and other financial and technical cooperation institutions to support the programs and activities included in this initiative, according to their own specific priorities and fields of action. Develop mechanisms for evaluating the relevance, cost and efficacy of the technologies introduced to deal with these and other priority health problems.

## Women

*Governments will:*

Strengthen and establish, where they do not exist, national mechanisms and governmental organs, as well as the respective regional and subregional networks in charge of promoting legal equality and equality of opportunities between women and men, focused on gender equity, and provide them with adequate and timely financial resources to enable these entities to promote, coordinate and carry out the commitments undertaken by the States at the World Conference on Human Rights, the International Conference on Population and Development, the World Summit on Social Development, the Summit of the Americas, the Fourth World Conference on Women, and the recent "Santiago Consensus" of the VII Regional Conference on Beijing Follow-up (ECLAC/UN).

Examine the existing laws and their implementation in order to identify obstacles limiting the full participation of women in the political, economic, social and cultural life of our countries. Whenever necessary, promote reforms or create new laws to eliminate all forms of discrimination and violence against women and to guarantee the protection of children's rights.

Implement and follow up on the commitments regarding the status of women as agreed to at the Summit of the Americas, with the support of the Inter-American Commission on Women (ICW), in collaboration with civil society, with the Inter-American Development Bank (IDB), the World Bank, United Nations Economic Commission on Latin America and the Caribbean (ECLAC), and other entities of international cooperation, using when appropriate the System of Indicators adopted by the countries of the Americas at Montelimar, Nicaragua. Promote policies designed to improve women's health conditions and the quality of health services at every stage of their lives.

## Basic Rights of Workers

*Governments will:*

Exchange informational materials regarding their labor legislation, with the objective of contributing to better mutual knowledge of such legislation as well as to promote core labor standards recognized by the International Labor Organization (ILO) -freedom of association; the right to organize and bargain collectively; the prohibition of forced labor; the elimination of all exploitative forms of child labor; and non-discrimination in employment. Such information will also include references to the mechanisms and/or legal authorities of Ministries of Labor to implement core labor standards as a fundamental component of productive workplaces and positive labor-management relations.

For these purposes carry out the exchanges by, among other means, furnishing informational materials on relevant changes to their labor legislation, mechanisms and/or legal authorities for implementation of core labor standards, and progress in the area of labor-management relations, to be provided at a meeting of the Inter-American Conference of Ministers of Labor, to be held in 1998 and their other meetings, as appropriate, including with the assistance of the Organization of American States (OAS), International Labor Organization (ILO) and Inter-American Development Bank (IDB).

Further secure their observance and promotion of internationally recognized core labor standards. In this context, they recognize the ILO as the competent body to set and deal with these standards and support the ongoing work of the ILO with regard to exchanges of information and the negotiation of a new Declaration of Principles on Fundamental Rights of Workers and appropriate follow-up; believe that economic growth and development fostered by increased trade and further trade liberalization contribute to the promotion of these standards and should lead to higher levels of employment; similarly reject the use of labor standards for protectionist purposes, and, in this regard, note that the World Trade Organization (WTO) and ILO Secretariats shall continue their collaboration.

## Indigenous Populations

To promote greater participation of indigenous populations in society through adequate access to education, health care, and occupational training, with the aim of improving their standard of living,

*Governments will:*

Support activities in the field of education aimed at improving the participation of indigenous populations and communities in society. Such activities would seek to strengthen the identity of indigenous populations and promote respectful coexistence among different social groups in communities and States.

Promote the widening of basic and secondary education services with training orientation, mainly in Regions with high percentages of indigenous populations, through greater support from Governments and international cooperation, at the request of interested Governments, so that indigenous and non-indigenous populations have the opportunity to receive technical training and contribute to the development of their countries. To the extent possible, the training areas which are implemented parallel to educational processes should respond to the needs of the Region and to productive strategies.

In cooperation with regional organizations, development institutions and NGOs, actively support and promote capacity building activities and productive projects, including agriculture, handicrafts, small trade and industry and marketing. To the extent possible, these should be guided and administered by indigenous populations.

Facilitate the organization of round-tables at the national and hemispheric level, in partnership with indigenous populations, with a view to promoting greater understanding of and cooperation in the areas of education and health, with a particular emphasis on women and children. Governments will also promote research initiatives on the relationship between indigenous populations, poverty and development.

Proceed with inter-governmental examination within the Organization of American States (OAS) framework of the "Proposed American Declaration on the Rights of Indigenous Peoples" prepared by the Inter-American Commission on Human Rights, with a view toward the possible adoption of a Declaration.

## Hunger and Malnutrition

*Governments will:*

Give the highest priority to reducing infant malnutrition, concentrating efforts on health, nutrition and education programs for the nutrition of infants, particularly those less than three, as those are the years of greatest vulnerability. To that end, emphasis shall be given to adequate nutrition and the correction of specific nutritional deficiencies, specifically with vitamin and mineral supplements combined with greater use of vaccinations and immunizations and monitoring during the growth of the child.

Give high priority to the nutritional and caloric needs of women before and during pregnancy and while they are breast-feeding. Governments therefore will promote breast-feeding as an important source of nutrition for babies. The nutritional needs of other high risk groups such as the elderly and the disabled will also be addressed.

Continue, as far as possible, with the dialogue begun at the Inter-American Conference on Hunger, held in Buenos Aires in October 1996, and they will explore the application, in their respective jurisdictions of the measures suggested there, in particular the creation of alliances with the private sector to fight hunger and malnutrition, the creation of food bank networks with volunteer participation and the creation of an Honorary Council dedicated to fostering activities to reach Summit objectives in this area.

## Sustainable Development

We recognize the effort made by the Organization of American States (OAS) in terms of follow-up of the Sustainable Development Summit, and instruct it, through the Inter-American Commission on Sustainable Development, to continue coordination related to fulfillment of its mandates. We ask the entities of the Inter-American System and the United Nations to strengthen cooperation related to implementation of the Santa Cruz Plan of Action.

## Cooperation

With the intention of achieving a greater impact in our national and collective efforts, we charge national agencies and organizations responsible for international cooperation with supporting the preparation and implementation of programs and projects which flow from the Plan of Action. Moreover, we request the participation of the multilateral cooperation institutions with the same objective.

## SUMMITS OF THE AMERICAS FOLLOW-UP

The Heads of State and Government will continue to meet periodically to deepen cooperation and understanding among the countries of the Americas, and, to that end, will strengthen the hemispheric institutional framework.

The Governments will bear primary responsibility for implementation of the mandates of the Summit. The mechanism established by their Foreign Ministers, called the "Summit Implementation Review Group" (SIRG), will continue functioning under their immediate authority. The National Summit Coordinators of the Foreign Ministries will guarantee rapid contact, through the appropriate channels, with all Government agencies involved in carrying out the mandates resulting from the Summit meetings.

The SIRG will meet on a periodic basis (two or three times a year) to monitor the follow-up process and assess the degree to which the Summit mandates have been fulfilled. It will be chaired by the country holding the Summit and co-chaired by both the country that has most recently served as host and the country that will serve as the next host ("troika"). Decisions will be adopted by consensus.

Senior representatives of the Organization of American States (OAS), the Inter-American Development Bank (IDB), the Pan American Health Organization (PAHO), and the United Nations Economic Commission on Latin America and the Caribbean (ECLAC), will be invited to support the Governments participating in the SIRG in order to follow up on the commitments of the Summit and to achieve greater coordination and effectiveness of these institutions in performing this task. To that same end, a representative of the World Bank will be invited. The OAS Secretariat will be assigned responsibility for operating as a record-keeping mechanism (the institutional memory of the process) and for providing technical support to the SIRG.

In accordance with Summit decisions, international organizations will have responsibilities in implementing this process and, as appropriate, according to Summit mandates, support will be provided by private sector organizations and civil society. In the case of specific mandates that require the convening of sectoral ministerials, these meetings, when appropriate, will take place under the aegis of the OAS Inter-American Council for Integral Development. Moreover, the OAS, IDB, PAHO, and ECLAC, as appropriate, will lend technical support to the meetings, the results of which will be reported to the States through the OAS Secretariat.

The SIRG will annually report on the progress achieved in the fulfillment of the Plan of Action to the Foreign Ministers, who will review this information on the occasion of the Regular Session of the OAS General Assembly.

Under the guidance of the Foreign Ministers, the SIRG will make preparations for the next Summit, bearing in mind the contributions of the pertinent organs of the OAS and other international organizations involved.

# III. Summit Documents

# Proposed Agenda for the Summit of the Americas
## Santiago - Chile

### I. EDUCATION

- Formulating actions in accordance with the proposals of the Responsible Coordinators in the Plan of Action they have prepared on the subject.

- Additional actions such as student and teacher exchange programs, distance education programs and incorporation of new technologies.

- Actions to develop training and skills improvement programs for workers with the aim of confronting under favorable circumstances changes resulting from the application and development of new technologies. Special attention should be given to programs for adult training.

### II. PRESERVING AND STRENGTHENING DEMOCRACY AND HUMAN RIGHTS

- Formulate actions based on the work that the Responsible Coordinators of this theme are carrying out.

- Actions in the area of education for democracy and full respect for human rights.

- Actions aimed at enhancing the participation of civil society.

- Actions aimed at strengthening municipal and regional administrations.

- Actions that guarantee the protection of the human rights of all migrant workers and their families.

- Actions aimed at reinforcing Hemispheric proceedings to confront corruption, narco-trafficking, and terrorism.

- Actions in the area of confidence and security building measures between states.

- Actions in the area of strengthening judicial systems.

- Actions aimed at cooperating on projects for modernization of the state that the countries of the Hemisphere may undertake in the administration of labor matters in accordance with the regulations and the legislation in force in each country.

### III. ECONOMIC INTEGRATION AND FREE TRADE

- Actions related to the negotiation of the Free Trade Area of the Americas (FTAA) in accordance with the progress achieved by the Ministers in charge of the subject.

- Actions on capital markets to be determined after the meeting of Ministers of Finance this December.
- Actions for the development of cooperation in science and technology.
- Actions related to regional energy cooperation.
- Actions for the establishment of an adequate hemispheric infrastructure, especially in matters of transportation and telecommunications.

    \* In accordance with the agreement of the Hemispheric Ministers of Transportation to the effect that the Western Hemisphere Transportation Initiative (HTI) be included in the agenda of the Summit of the Americas.

## IV. ERADICATION OF POVERTY AND DISCRIMINATION

- Actions in support of micro-enterprises and small and medium-sized businesses as a way of promoting the creation of new jobs through access to sources of credit, the development of vocational training, programs designed to obtain an increase in productivity, and the introduction and application of new and more advanced technologies.

    \* The education theme may be considered in any of these action initiatives.

- Actions for the implementation or modernization of effective systems of property registration for those countries that require it.
- Actions in the area of health based on the proposal of the Pan-American Health Organization (PAHO).
- Actions in accordance with the agreements adopted at the Conference on Women held in Managua, including a specific program related to education.
- Actions at the national level leading to the goal of ensuring quality jobs, and of safeguarding the basic rights and interests of workers and to this end, freely promote respect for relevant ILO conventions.
- Actions aimed at promoting greater participation of indigenous populations through adequate access to education, health and work training.
- Actions to combat hunger and malnutrition.

## SUSTAINABLE DEVELOPMENT

Considering the breadth of the Santa Cruz de la Sierra Plan of Action on the occasion of the Summit Conference to that effect, it is suggested that this theme be included in the Political Declaration that the Heads of State and Government will sign, recognizing in said Declaration the progress that the Secretary-General of the OAS will present in his report, and that reference be made to such agreements in the corresponding specific actions.

# III. SUMMIT DOCUMENTS

*Eduardo Frei Ruiz-Tagle is the President of the Republic of Chile. These remarks were delivered on April 18, 1998, in Santiago, Chile.*

# Remarks by the President of the Republic of Chile at the Inauguration of the Second Summit of the Americas

## Eduardo Frei Ruiz-Tagle

It is a great pleasure for the people and government of Chile to receive in our country the Heads of State and Government of the Americas. In the name of the women and men of Chile, I thank you for the honor which you have granted us in choosing our homeland as the location of the Second Hemispheric Summit, and I would like to express our very cordial welcome to our country.

We gather together today with joy and with hope. With joy, because the countries we represent share common principles and values, because they are expanding the scope of liberty and democracy, because they are rebuilding their economic potential, and because they are making a constructive contribution to peace in a world which still remains torn by conflict. And we gather with hope, because with the spirit of brotherhood and the desire for greater liberty and justice, we are setting out to construct a more equitable and mature hemispheric community.

The country that welcomes you today is a youthful and vital one. A country which is proud of having recovered its democratic tradition, but one which is still in the process of renewing its institutions. A country which during this decade has achieved economic growth at a rate unknown in its recent history, but which still confronts the challenges of defeating poverty and reducing the inequities suffered by broad sectors of our society. A country which is taking part actively, through its association with Mercosur, in the process of Latin American integration, but which is attempting to make this commitment compatible with increasingly close ties to other countries and regions of the world.

We are, simply, opening our doors. In doing so, we in no way intend to hold up our democratic reconstruction or our economic development process as ideal models. We are convinced that Chile is in need of further reconciliation and that our institutions must come to express their democratic character more clearly. We recognize that each country advances and develops in accordance with its own unique characteristics. This is a process in which there are no foolproof recipes or universal models to follow.

## A CONVERGENCE IN PRINCIPLES AND ASPIRATIONS

Our domestic priorities coincide with the priorities of our sister nations present here today. Never in the long history of inter-American relations has there been such a strong convergence of principles and aspirations among the countries of our hemisphere—a convergence of their dreams and concerns, of their goals and policies.

It was this convergence which made it possible for us to meet in the historic First Summit of the Americas, held in Miami in December 1994, in response to the visionary invitation extended to us by the President of the United States, William Clinton. On this occasion, 34 Heads of State and Government set forth the powerful vision of a community of nations united by the objectives of democracy, economic integration and social equity. The vision set forth in Miami retains all of its validity today. In Santiago, we hope to provide the definitive impulse toward the formation of a hemispheric community.

Individual nations can no longer formulate their policies without taking into account their place in a regional and global framework. The era of autarkies has ended. Our economic, political, social and environmental interests must increasingly be viewed from an international perspective. Standing alone, we cannot hope to grapple with challenges such as drug trafficking, organized crime or the spread of infectious diseases. Even issues which have traditionally been considered domestic in scope, such as social injustice, education, the modernization of the State and the fight against corruption, have taken on international dimensions. Global problems cannot be solved with unilateral policies.

## THE AGENDA OF THE SECOND SUMMIT OF THE AMERICAS

This summit will cover a broad and varied agenda. Identifying this agenda was no simple task; a spirit of great cooperation was necessary for it. Chile is profoundly grateful for the climate of consensus and generosity which surrounded the preparatory work for this Summit. We have always affirmed that an event of this magnitude must represent a collective effort, in which leadership is not only exercised by the host country and that which preceded it as the seat of the previous Summit, but is shared by a large number of nations.

We will discuss first of all the topic of education. We cannot hope to break down the barriers that divide social groups nor achieve sustainable economic growth as a region without effectively educating our people. We cannot participate in a competitive and globalized world if our people are not capable of applying the spectacular scientific and technical advances of our era. Education, in farms and factories as well as in schools and universities, is the best means of providing all of our citizens with the chance to improve their own lives. In a world that places increasing emphasis on knowledge, we must also develop active science and technology policies which will permit us to modernize our productive systems and make our economies more competitive.

The preservation and strengthening of democracy remain priority issues in the Americas. Beyond congratulating ourselves for successes already achieved, we must continue our vigilance against any attack against democracy in our region. In the past, our region's cycles of democratization were repeatedly interrupted by authoritarian interventions, in the face of passive regional and multilateral institutions. Today we resolve not to repeat this cycle. The great current of democratization which is carrying our peoples forward must continue its strong and unwavering advance toward a community of nations that is increasingly just, respectful of each other's liberties and more tolerant of each other's differences. This Summit must open new opportunities for cooperation in the consolidation and advancement of democracy in our countries.

As we seek to reinforce democratic values, the defense of human rights will always remain an essential task. Regional institutional mechanisms are already in place for the protection of these rights, and it is our duty to support initiatives to strengthen them.

We also recognize that all democracies require adequate legal systems to function. We share the necessity of creating judicial systems that are autonomous, effective and accessible to all sectors of society —systems that guarantee equality before the law and include safeguards against abuses of power in relations between the citizenry and the State. We have a great opportunity to identify concrete forms of cooperation for the interchange of experiences and technical assistance in this area.

The countries of our region also share a common concern about the destructive practice of drug trafficking in our hemisphere. Through the combined efforts of the producing, transit and consuming countries, supported with adequate national and multinational resources, the Anti-Drug Strategy which we have adopted can achieve real success.

In our efforts to build strong and healthy social institutions, the fight against corruption stands out as a further topic of great interest for hemispheric relations. We must work unceasingly to eradicate this evil. Its presence in the public or private spheres threatens democratic institutions and, at times abetted by interested groups, damages the public perception of politics and democracy.

## THE FREE TRADE AREA AND THE INTEGRATION OF THE AMERICAS

Integration and the liberalization of trade and investment are crucial focal points for the strengthening of our mutual relations.

It is undeniable that, whatever indicator one may choose: trade in goods and services, capital flows, migration, transportation and energy links, or political cooperation, the levels of integration achieved in Latin America so far are frankly spectacular. Mercosur, the Andean Community, the Central American Integration System, CARICOM and the North American Free Trade Agreement have modified the economic geography of our region, and in many cases also the political geography as well.

The Hemispheric Summit of 1994 raised the prospect of advancing toward free trade. Since then, preparations for the Free Trade Area of the Americas (FTAA) have been in motion and are scheduled to be finalized by the year 2005. This plan remains in full force. Our countries arrived at a highly significant agreement at the meeting of Ministers responsible for trade, held in March in San José. We must embark upon these negotiations with energy and enthusiasm. We are not starting from zero; in recent years, a truly impressive number of free trade accords have been signed in our region, providing a very solid base from which to continue our advance on the path toward liberalization of our commerce.

## THE SOCIAL DEVELOPMENT OF OUR PEOPLES

The economic transformation which is now taking place in our countries will only be sustainable over time if we succeed in improving the cohesion of our societies, and if we are able to provide greater equity to our people. The construction of a more peaceful, stable, prosperous and just order in the Americas will only be possible if a new ethical consensus is formulated among our nations, a consensus which firmly places a common ideal of social development at the foundation of our community of nations.

Equality of opportunity must also be extended to all women in our societies. Today, women are still denied opportunities that are routinely granted to men. Women make up an unacceptably high percentage of the poor in all nations of our hemisphere, including the more developed countries. This is a situation of injustice and inequity. At the same time, the exclusion of women also deprives our countries of great human potential and talent.

Great social and organizational challenges lie ahead, as well as challenges of national integration. We have the political and moral obligation to recognize that our histories show more than a few episodes of abuse and inequality with regard to our indigenous populations and communities. With this firmly in mind, the Second Summit of the Americas must spur new efforts to promote the effective integration of indigenous peoples, while respecting their cultural identities and their specific rights. We must continue to combat racial discrimination in our countries.

Finally, we would like to stress that the concept of sustainable development places great emphasis on the protection of the environment. After many years of neglect, the countries of our region have now begun to take environmental issues very seriously.

The Hemispheric Summit for Sustainable Development, held in 1996 in Santa Cruz de la Sierra, Bolivia, resulted in a plan for joint action in this field. The agreements we adopt during this Summit will take into consideration our determination to preserve our natural resources and our environment, but also the need to keep open effective opportunities for the countries of Latin America to continue in their development. Today we must reaffirm our will to adhere to these agreements and also to address new issues arising in this area.

## FINAL WORDS

We cannot construct a true inter-American community without solidarity. The diversity which characterizes our region, and the great differences which still persist in our relative levels of development, call for increased cooperation. We must mobilize the greatest of our national resources to support the smallest and most vulnerable economies of the hemisphere.

Our agenda is timely and relevant. We will not limit ourselves to issuing abstract, rhetorical declarations. We must approve a Plan of Action covering topics of direct concern for our people, who placed their faith and confidence in us as they cast their votes. Here there cannot be merely a declaration of intentions. We must have the will and determination to fulfill our agreements.

We are preparing to culminate a process of cooperative work which has lasted lengthy months, through the efforts and the generosity of many people, in Chile and throughout the region. We have a great responsibility to the men and women of all corners of our hemisphere.

But, above all, we have an enormous responsibility for the future of the Americas. We long for a continent united in its diversity, with freedom of expression for its peoples and just treatment of its children.

Visionary men, with Simón Bolívar leading the way, dreamed before us, as we dream with them now, of that free future for our people. Like that great Latin-American said in his inaugural address for the Angostura Congress, almost 180 years ago, "The rule of law is more powerful than that of tyrants ... ; good manners, not force, are the backbone of the law; ... the exercise of justice is the exercise of freedom."

We yearn to enter the 21st century as a continent that from the far north to its southern horn, and from one ocean to the other, speaks to the world in the common language of its united nations. A continent with a vigorous people prepared to assume the labors of development, each of the parts stamped with its unique story, but all converging in a common destiny.

The political democracy, economic growth, social justice and education of our societies are the objectives of this dialogue of the Americas that we take up again today in Santiago, Chile. But a loftier goal is sustaining our right to dream.

As we approach this historic crossroads, the culture of our emerging world makes us want to go exploring, with our reason, hearts and will. We are a continent of varied traditions and values; we have known pain and suffering; we have our shared hopes. As another of those visionaries from last century said, "America owes the earth a word." This is the time to speak it. Now that we are on the threshold of an epoch that will speak in many voices and tongues; of a humanity globalized by communications; of a culture that is open, diverse, inclined to discover in difference the deepest spiritual richness.

It is the deep voice that originates in the depth of our roots and our identity. It is the peaceful, solid voice for what we have achieved and what we have done. It is the voice of men and women and young people of our America who want to build and who want to live in a society with opportunities. It is the voice of the rulers who today have in our hands the decision to build the future together. It is, in the end, the word of many in our America who do not have a voice and who today want to break the chains of misery and poverty to build a future with dignity. That is why we have met. That is why we are here. To build together the future of the 21st century. To build the America that others dreamed of. And now that we are on the doorstep of the 21st century, we have this dream in our hands – a dream that we can turn into reality.

Thank you very much.

# III. SUMMIT DOCUMENTS

*William Jefferson Clinton is the President of the United States.*

*These remarks were delivered on April 18, 1998, in Santiago, Chile, at the Sheraton Hotel.*

# Remarks by the President of the United States at the Opening of the Summit of the Americas

## William Jefferson Clinton

President Frei, distinguished heads of state, leaders of the Chilean Congress, Supreme Court, members of the diplomatic corps, President Wolfensohn, President Iglesias, Secretary-General Gaviria, Secretary-General Ruggiero, Director General Alleyne: Four years ago in Miami, we, the democratic nations of this hemisphere, met in the historic Summit of the Americas and pledged ourselves to a common future rooted in shared values, shared burdens, shared progress, and embodied in our call for a free trade area of the Americas by 2005.

I thank all my fellow leaders and their governments for their faithfulness to the summit process. I thank especially those who helped us to begin the Summit of the Americas in 1994.

Now we come together in Santiago. What shall we do? First, we should celebrate a new reality in the Americas — the march of freedom, prosperity, peace, and partnership among our nations. Second, we should recognize that in all our nations too many people have not felt this new reality, and we should resolve to continue to work together until they do.

As we look back on the three and a half years since the Miami Summit, there is much to be proud of, as our report, "From Words to Deeds," documents. The economy of the region has grown 15 percent. Last year, average growth was five percent, and inflation was the lowest in 50 years. Chile and Uruguay have set the standard for poverty reduction and fiscal responsibility. Brazil and Argentina have slowed inflation to a crawl. Mexico has overcome adversity, transformed its economy, broadened its democracy. Bolivia has attracted new foreign investments and given its citizens a greater stake in their future. Venezuela's Apertura program is drawing investment to develop its energy resources. Peru and Ecuador, with a little help from their friends, are working towards a peaceful end to their decades-long border dispute. Central America, after years of strife, is well on the way to achieving its long-held vision of democracy and integration and growth. Caribbean nations are joining forces to expand their economies and to defend their shores against drugs and crime.

Together we have begun to create the Free Trade Area of the Americas, a thriving market of 800 million people invested in each other's future, enriching each other's lives, weaving a tapestry of interdependence that strengthens every nation. The Americas have set a new standard for the world in the defense of liberty and justice through our collective commitment to defend democracy wherever it is at risk in our hemisphere. Concerted action by neighbors and friends already has helped to restore or preserve democracy and human rights in Haiti, Guatemala and Paraguay.

29

Our cooperation in the fight against drugs has intensified, based on an understanding that drugs are a problem for all of us and all of us must work together to attack both demand and supply. We've adopted tough new measures against money laundering, forged the first multilateral treaty in the world to fight corruption, so that our societies will be governed by the rule of law.

We have signed an historic convention to stop the illegal trade in guns in our hemisphere. We're working to advance the environment and public health. Our people are healthier, our water safer, our air cleaner than four years ago. We are wiping measles off our hemisphere's map, dropping from more than 23,000 cases in 1994 to less than 500 so far this year. We're phasing out lead from gasoline. In 1996, 12 nations achieved this goal; by 2001, there will 20. We're working together to promote a clean energy future and to meet the challenge of climate change.

I thank the efforts of many people in this regard — the Vice President in our government, and many in other governments throughout this hemisphere.

The Miami Summit was a watershed in the history of our hemisphere as the leaders of free people embraced a common vision of the future and a common strategy for achieving it. The journey from Miami to Santiago has been filled with progress toward our goals. Now, here, and on the road forward from here, we must do more to ensure that the path of reform and democracy and integration actually lifts the lives of ordinary people in all our nations.

Poverty throughout the hemisphere is still too high, income disparity is too great, civil society too fragile, justice systems too weak, too many people still lack the education and skills necessary to succeed in the new economy. In short, too few feel change working for them. Therefore, with democracy and free markets now in place, we must vigorously launch a second generation of reforms for the next generation of Americans. No priority is more important than giving our children an excellent education.

The fate of nations in the 21st century turns on what all citizens know and whether all citizens can quickly learn. Too often, resources are spent primarily on higher education for the few. We must all redirect our focus toward higher quality education for all. I especially thank Presidents Frei, Cardoso, Menem, and Zedillo for their leadership to give all our children a good education, with well-equipped classrooms, well-trained teachers, high standards, and accountability. This is a goal we must vigorously embrace and work hard to realize.

We will also work here to deepen democracy and respect for human rights. We know free elections are democracy's first step, not the last. We'll support the Organization of American States' special rapporteur for freedom of expression; launch a regional justice center to train judges and prosecutors; strengthen local government institutions to bring power closer to people; and in its 50th year of the Universal Declaration of Human Rights, we will redouble our efforts to protect the human rights of all people.

We will also do more to defend democracy against its enemies — corruption, terrorism, and drugs. The new hemispheric alliance against drugs we will launch here will encourage, support, and improve all our nations' efforts to fight this common threat as partners. We'll continue to promote our common prosperity, by launching negotiations for a free trade area of the Americas.

I want to underscore the importance we attach to a special civil society committee that will allow a broad array of stakeholders within all our societies the opportunity to make their voices heard. If economic integration in a global economy is to work for all people, we must demonstrate that we can have economic growth and lift labor standards for all our workers. We must demonstrate that we can grow the economy and preserve, indeed, even improve the environment. This civil society committee will give the peoples of our nations the chance to make that argument, and we must prove that we can make the argument work.

Let me reaffirm to all my colleagues, the United States may not yet have fast track legislation, but we will. And I assure you that our commitment to the free trade area of the Americas will be in the fast lane of our concerns.

We must do that. After all, more than one third of the United States' growth in the last few years has come from expanded trade. More than 40 percent of our exports go to our neighbors seated on this platform. We can only continue to grow and create jobs in the United States if we continue to reach out to our neighbors for more open markets and freer trade. That is the fundamental observation that all of us share. Your prosperity lifts ours; our prosperity lifts yours. As more good jobs are created in any nation, as economies grow and people thrive, they become better partners for each other and for others around the world.

# III. Summit Documents

Finally, we must take further steps to lift people from poverty and spread the benefit of progress to every member of society, from supporting women's full participation in the lives of our countries to providing loans to microentrepreneurs, to broadening property ownership.

Now, this Santiago agenda is ambitious, but it is imperative. Again, let me applaud President Frei for his leadership, for bringing us all here together, and for supporting such a broad and deep agenda. If we are to seize the opportunities and meet the challenges of our time, we must pursue this agenda, and we must do it together.

The first broad meeting of representatives from our hemisphere took place in 1889 in Washington, D.C. Times were different and slower then. The delegates met for more than six months and toured around our nation by train. The only bad thing was they had to listen to even more speeches. But in that meeting our predecessors, drawing on Bolívar's vision of hemispheric unity, set a precedent for cooperation that grew over 50 years later from that seed into the OAS.

Four years ago at Miami, we planted the seed of a new partnership for a new century. Now we can and must do what is necessary for that seed to grow — to grow in freedom and opportunity and cooperation. The Americas can be a model for all the world in the 21st century. That is, after all, the spirit of the Summit of the Americas and the promise of Santiago.

Thank you very much.

# III. Summit Documents

*William Jefferson Clinton is the President of the United States.*

*These remarks were delivered on April 19, 1998, in Santiago, Chile, at the Sheraton Hotel.*

# Remarks by the President of the United States at the Closing of the Summit of the Americas

*William Jefferson Clinton*

President Frei, fellow of the Americas, First Ladies, distinguished Presidents of Senate, Chamber of Deputies, Supreme Court, members of the diplomatic corps, ladies and gentlemen of the Americas: Let me say first to you, Mr. President and I know I speak for all of us here we thank you and Mrs. Frei and your entire team for the warmth of your welcome, the wonder of your country, and the genuine leadership you have brought to this Summit of the Americas. Thank you very much.

At our first summit in 1994, we agreed on a common vision of a democratic, prosperous, peaceful, united hemisphere by the 21st century. We also formulated a comprehensive agenda to help us to realize that vision, an agenda to strengthen our democracies, tear down trade barriers, improve our people's quality of life.

Our journey from Miami to Santiago, as we have often said, was from words to deeds. Still, for all our progress, we all admit that too many of our citizens have not yet seen their own lives improved as a result of our participation as free nations in the global economy. Therefore, we have committed ourselves here to a second stage of reforms designed to bring the benefits of freedom and free enterprise to ordinary citizens throughout the Americas.

As we saw the truth in Miami, it is so here today — the real work of Santiago begins as we leave. And until we meet again in Canada, we must work every day to keep the commitments we have made to each other and to our people.

First, we must continue to stand fast for democracy for our entire hemisphere, with no hold-outs and no backsliders. We must support the integrity of the electoral process. We welcomed and participated in the restoration of democracy in Haiti. We supported its preservation in Paraguay. We now must support the OAS and Caricom as they support the people of Guyana in the integrity of their electoral process.

We must support our new special rapporteur on freedom of expression and work to prevent violence against journalists; get our new hemispheric justice system up and running; implement the OAS Illegal Firearms Convention to help to stop firearms from falling into the wrong hands; adopt the laws necessary to make our unprecedented anticorruption convention a reality. And most important, we must move aggressively to establish our alliance against drugs, so that we will have a more genuinely collective effort to protect our people against narco-trafficking and drug abuse, violence and organized crime.

Second, we must continue to bring the free economies of the Americas together. Today we launched comprehensive negotiations for a free trade area of the Americas and vowed to make concrete progress toward that goal by the year 2000, including greater transparency in government procurement and banking operations, a commitment to free trade in cyberspace, and steps to facilitate business, such as customs coordination.

And as we improve the climate for business contracts, we know we must also strengthen the social contract. The civil society committee we have established is designed to give all the voices of society the opportunity to be heard in shaping the new free trade area of the Americas. We want more trade and better working conditions, more growth and a cleaner environment.

The entrepreneurs of the Information Age can prosper in a way that increases opportunities for all who are willing to work hard. And we can reap the benefits of economic change and meet the challenge of climate change.

Finally, we have made it our mission to give our people the tools they must have to succeed in the new economy opening the doors of learning to all our children; doing more to lift our people out of poverty, supported by billions of dollars in new lending commitments for microenterprise and health care from the Inter-American Development Bank and World Bank.

By the time we meet again we should resolve that all our small entrepreneurs, especially our women, should have access to the loans they need to get their business off the ground; that poor urban and rural citizens should be able to gain titles to their property; that we should eradicate measles from this hemisphere; and, most important, that millions more of our children will be in school, not on the streets. We should achieve an 80 percent completion rate in primary school as work toward our goal of 100 percent by the year 2010. Our children, after all, will have more to say about the future we are trying to create than any of the rest of us.

The people of the Americas, as the President of Uruguay pointed out to us yesterday, have launched a profound revolution in the last few years, a revolution of peace and freedom and prosperity. Here in Santiago we embrace our responsibility to make these historic forces lift the lives of all our people. That is the future we can forge together. It is a future worthy of the new Americas in a new millennium.

Thank you very much.

# III. Summit Documents

*Fernando Henrique Cardoso is the President of Brazil.*

*This speech was delivered at the closing ceremony of the Second Summit of the Americas, in Santiago, Chile, on April 19, 1998.*

# Palavras do Presidente da República Federativa do Brasil na Cerimônia de Encerramento da II Cúpula das Américas

### Fernando Henrique Cardoso

Há momentos em que talvez fosse melhor calar. Depois do que ouvimos nas palavras inspiradas e inflamadas do Presidente Frei, confirmadas pelo Presidente Clinton, talvez devêssemos apenas aplaudí-los e pensar, no recôndito de nós próprios, sobre o significado do que foi dito e o significado do que estamos fazendo. Se ouso somar-me à voz daqueles que me antecederam, e de quem vai me suceder, é porque eu gostaria que nesse salão ecoasse também a língua do meu país: o português. E hoje, na verdade, nós dizemos em quatro línguas, as nossas quatro línguas — em espanhol, francês, inglês e português — a mesma coisa. Estamos unidos no sentimento, e este sentimento talvez pudesse ser comparado àquele dos pais fundadores, que formaram as bases éticas da democracia. Desde aqueles que, da Revolução Francesa, usavam palavras que todos nós repetimos desde estudantes, e sobre cujo significado profundo talvez não tivéssemos meditado — de igualdade, de solidariedade e de liberdade — às teses que foram proferidas em Filadélfia, que se repetiram nas constituições de todos os nossos países.

De alguma maneira, o espírito que nos traz aqui é o espírito de criação de uma nova comunidade, é constitucional. E o que temos reafirmado é que esse novo espírito, que une as nossas nações no hemisfério, se nasceu talvez de um impulso, ou de um sonho, que era econômico, que era de integração — e me apraz dizer isso aqui no Chile, na terra onde trabalhei com tantos chilenos e sob a inspiração de Prebisch, que lutava pela integração latino-americana — se o impulso foi econômico inicialmente dizia, pouco a pouco, sem abandonar a preocupação com a economia, que é fundamental, deixamos de falar apenas em taxas aduaneiras — em "aranceles", "tariffs" — e passamos a falar uma linguagem que toca mais ao coração dos nossos povos: pobreza, justiça, luta contra a impunidade, luta contra a droga, decência na administração pública, coisas concretas que realizam na prática, com um século de atraso, o que foi o sonho daqueles que fundaram, constitucionalmente, as idéias fundamentais da democracia, que são a expressão mesma, moderna, do mundo ocidental. Foi disso que se tratou.

De Miami a Santiago, se houve uma transformação, se houve uma evolução, foi nessa direção e foi no conhecimento recíproco. Se antes havia, talvez, alguma desconfiança de que a zona de livre comércio nas Américas talvez dificultasse o Mercosul ou, quem sabe, o Nafta fosse o caminho mais adequado — e que nós nos somássemos ao Nafta — ou quem sabe o Caricom um pouco à margem, ou o Acordo Centro-Americano de Livre Comércio, cada um olhando para o outro para medir suas vantagens e desvantagens. De repente percebeu-se que não, que o que nós fizemos, no Mercosul e em todos os outros blocos regionais, são passos constitutivos para ver este grande espírito americano, que é a zona de livre comércio, compreendida como nós a compreendemos hoje, como uma zona de liberdade, de paz e, sobretudo, de igualdade concreta na educação, no atendimento aos mais carentes, na luta contínua contra a pobreza.

Pobreza que, se no século XVIII não entrava sequer no horizonte dos que formulavam as grandes idéias da democracia, hoje não pode ser apenas uma declaração. Se no passado nossos países não tinham como combatê-la, porque não tinham sequer o desenvolvimento necessário, hoje, embora não tenhamos completado o ciclo do nosso desenvolvimento, combatê-la é um imperativo ético. Há pobres porque nós não estamos ainda moralmente comprometidos com a luta contra a pobreza. Já dispomos de recursos suficientes para, se estivermos juntos, lutarmos efetivamente contra a pobreza e nada... nem a história nos perdoará se das nossas palavras não resultar um progresso efetivo das condições sociais de vida do nosso povo. E, por isso, são tão bem-vindas as palavras, como as que aqui foram proferidas pelo Presidente Frei, de que não queremos armamentos, não queremos competições. Queremos, sim, solidariedade, novas formas de solidariedade para que nós possamos usar os instrumentos racionais de que dispomos, e os recursos materiais de que começamos a dispor, para mudar, efetivamente, não o mundo em termos de idéias, mas a vida concreta da população mais pobre, nas áreas rurais, nas favelas, nos bairros mais desamparados, que ainda existem perdidos em toda esta nossa América; e esta nossa América, aqui, é, com a palavra dita da maneira mais forte: vai, realmente, da Patagônia às áreas mais geladas lá no norte do Canadá e do Alasca. Porque também na América do Norte existem áreas de pobreza, áreas de carência e, portanto, também lá essa motivação, essa inspiração ética, há de movimentar as populações locais para que, em uma nova visão do que seja a vida em comum nesse hemisfério, nós possamos efetivamente transformá-lo num lugar onde todos sejam bem-vindos, onde todos se sintam em família, em casa, com tranqüilidade.

Mas me apraz dizer, Senhores Presidentes, Senhores e Senhoras, que os progressos foram muitos. Não gostaria de alongar-me — já fui além do que era necessário —, mas gostaria de dizer, como um dos países garantes do Protocolo do Rio de Janeiro, que nada nos satisfará mais no nosso continente do que a finalização desse processo de tranqüilização entre o Peru e o Equador — e os presidentes do Peru e do Equador são merecedores dos nossos agradecimentos pela maneira corajosa como têm desenvolvido os trabalhos que vão nos levar a que possamos dizer, com toda tranqüilidade: este é um hemisfério onde não há questões de fronteira. Este é um hemisfério onde a paz não é uma palavra, a paz é um modo de viver.

E também não gostaria de deixar de dizer uma palavra, uma que seja, sobre as muitas dúvidas e indagações que ouvi pelos corredores. Por que não todos? Falta talvez ainda um país. E esse país que falta firmou aqui, em Valparaíso, um compromisso com a democracia. Esse país que falta tem um contrato social, preocupa-se profundamente com a educação e com a saúde. Por que não dar os passos da democracia, que são tão bem-vindos por todos, para que amanhã nós todos possamos dizer: "nuestra América es una sola, democrática y hecha de hermanos".

Obrigado.

# III. SUMMIT DOCUMENTS

*James D. Wolfensohn is the President of the World Bank.*

*This presentation was delivered on April 19, 1998, in Santiago, Chile.*

# Presentation by the President of the World Bank at the Second Summit of the Americas

*James D. Wolfensohn*

## THE SANTIAGO CONSENSUS AND THE WORLD BANK

Your Excellency President Frei, Your Excellencies Presidents and Prime Ministers, Fellow Heads of International Institutions, Distinguished Ministers.

Let me first thank you all, and especially our host, for the opportunity you have given me, on behalf of the World Bank, to participate in this truly historic event.

Over the course of the many months of intensive preparation and discussions that led up to this Summit, a new consensus on economic and social policy in this hemisphere has been taking shape. And with your own here, you have placed the capstone in the arch. This new consensus is one based on recognition of the paramount importance of what I called a few months ago in Hong Kong "The Challenge of Inclusion," the challenge of ensuring that economic progress can become a reality in the lives of all the people of this region, especially the tens of millions who until now have been very largely left behind.

You have made a number of crucial commitments on the economic and financial side. One stands out: your agreements to translate the visionary promise made at Miami, to build a new model of Open Regionalism, into a concrete and detailed blueprint for attaining that goal.

But your new consensus goes beyond economics and finance. It recognizes that persistence with economic reforms, though essential, is not in itself enough. You are contributing today a new vision of the need to make the social dimension of development integral in your map for the years ahead. Not just for the next three years but for a decade and more, you are embracing the centrality of decent, modern and relevant education for all; good health care; the rights of women and indigenous groups; the right to justice and the right to live in safe societies ruled by democratically determined laws.

Today, surely, it is time to retire once and for all that tired old phrase of the so-called Washington Consensus. Today, you are giving your people a new vision — the Santiago Consensus.

Let me now speak very specifically about the commitment of the World Bank to support you and your efforts to make the Santiago Consensus a reality.

I will talk about financial resources in a moment. But first I want to talk about something more powerful still — the resource of global knowledge. The Bank's worldwide operations have long given us a unique opportunity to draw the lessons of development experience around the globe — what works, what doesn't work. But for years, this knowledge was largely concentrated in the memories of our staff and a small community of development practitioners. Now we are determined to harness the incredible power of new information technologies, and a new spirit of openness and partnership, to make knowledge of global best-practice in development accessible to all. We are already engaged in building the internal architecture of a "Knowledge Bank." We are starting to open-up access, and by the year 2000 we intend the clearing house of knowledge to have achieved comprehensive coverage and to be fully open to the world outside the Bank. This has already started, but we plan to make it into your first port of call when you want information on development experience.

I am not speaking of a one-way flow of knowledge, in which gurus in Washington presume to lecture the rest of the world. The "Knowledge Bank" will be a learning Bank, which forms partnerships with other agencies and groups, both official and nongovernmental and private, so that all can learn from each others' areas of strength. We are already forming these partnerships, and I look forward to many of them being in this hemisphere, both at the national level, and with our friends in the hemispheric multilaterals including IDB, OAS, CEPAL, and PAHO.

Returning more directly to the theme of the Santiago Consensus, the Bank of the future will be committed to pulling its weight in translating this consensus into reality at both the national and the regional level. Let me speak about the regional dimension. Already, since Miami and Santa Cruz, we have been working with you and the hemispheric multilaterals to help you develop regional strategies in a number of fields: work with ministers of finance on financial integration; work stemming from Santa Cruz on sustainable cities, which was submitted to you here through the OAS; work with IDB and other partners to support the Ministers of Education in preparing the central component of the draft Plan of Action.

We are ready to do a lot more in this area. From July, we are tripling our budget for regional policy studies and conferences. Specifically in the area of education, I am inviting your Ministers of Education and Finance to come together with experts on educational reform, business leaders and others to discuss, on June 5, what will be needed to bring your very bold targets for educational progress to fruition. We are also ready, again in partnership with our hemispheric colleagues, to offer support from our staff resources and experience to the work of your Summit Implementation Review Group, the SIRG, in monitoring and reporting to you the progress achieved in meeting the goals you set here in Santiago.

At the same time, a very large part of what needs to be done will take place primarily at national level. In each of your own societies, you will be called upon to build and sustain a social consensus that is both broad and deep, and also long-term in nature, to nurture the growth of the seeds of change you are sowing here today. At the national level, too, we are ready to do more. Over the past three years, a little over $10 billion of our lending in the Region of Latin America and the Caribbean —lending which in total amounted to $15 billion— has been directed to the broad areas of concern you have defined in your Plan of Action: education, governance, regional integration and infrastructure development, and the assault upon poverty and discrimination.

Today, I am challenging my colleagues, and proposing to you, a goal of raising this support for your own chosen priorities, as set out in the Plan of Action, to $20 billion over the three years until this group meets again. We will set out to increase our lending for education from $2 billion to at least $3 billion. We will plan to increase our lending for the attack upon poverty and discrimination from $3.5 billion to $5.5 billion or more. In the areas of governance and institution building, which in some cases are relatively new areas of engagement for the Bank, as for many of your countries, we will increase lending from $700 million to more than $2.0 billion. Finally, we expect to increase our lending for economic integration and free trade, including infrastructure, from $4.5 billion to around $9.0 billion.

We will expect to be held accountable not only for the quantitative aspects of our work, but also for quality and results, just as you have said that you will hold yourselves accountable for the commitments you are making here today.

Transforming the Americas, in the way you are setting out to do, is a very great challenge. It will call on each of us to give of his or her very best.

But nothing less would be worthy of those we are all, in the end, here to serve.

# III. Summit Documents

*Enrique V. Iglesias is the President of the Inter-American Development Bank and Chairman of the Board of Executive Directors of the Inter-American Investment Corporation.*

*This statement was delivered on April 19, 1998, in Santiago, Chile.*

# Statement by the President of the Inter-American Development Bank on the Occasion of the Second Summit of the Americas

*Enrique V. Iglesias*

## INTRODUCTION

The idea of a regional development bank for Latin America and the Caribbean had always been conceived, from the first suggestions aired at the Pan American Conference more than one hundred years ago, as an instrument for the promotion of closer integration among the nations of the region. This ideal found expression in the Agreement Establishing the Inter-American Development Bank in 1959, which charged the new institution, among other things, to "contribute to the acceleration of the process of economic and social development of the regional developing member countries, individually and collectively." Unstinting support for regional integration is, therefore, a value at the very core of the IDB's institutional culture. Accordingly, the renewed interest in economic integration and the success of the Summit of the Americas in focusing attention on the many dimensions of hemispheric cooperation have revitalized the Bank's commitment to this mission as we stand on the threshold of the new millenium, joining our efforts to improve the quality of life for all the people of our hemisphere.

In recent years, the Bank became the premier development institution for the countries of Latin America and the Caribbean, particularly the smaller ones where it now lends twice as much as any similar entity. Over the period 1994-1997, new lending by the Bank totaled around US$25 billion of which almost 40 percent was directed to projects designed with the objective of poverty reduction and social equity. As we look ahead to the next five years, the Bank would be capable of lending over US$40 billion to the region. We expect that one-half of this amount will continue to support the objective of poverty reduction and social equity and that at least US$4 billion will directly finance private investments in projects valued at US$20 billion for improving infrastructure in the region.

In many respects, the Bank's mandates coincide with the priorities adopted by Heads of State and Government at the Miami Summit of the Americas and those which will be endorsed at this Santiago Summit. Let me illustrate some of the initiatives that the Bank is taking to bolster the efforts of its member countries in the hemisphere to raise standards of living everywhere, not just in a material sense, but also in the many intangible ways that derive from the better functioning of civil institutions in a participatory democracy.

## THE PATH OUT OF POVERTY

The fundamental mandate of the IDB is to join efforts with its member countries to reduce poverty and income inequality by fostering sustainable development in the broadest sense throughout Latin America and the Caribbean. Among the many deeply rooted historical problems that remain to be resolved, perhaps the most compelling task is to face up to the unacceptably high levels of poverty founded, in large measure, on an unequal distribution of land and human capital. Income inequality is the worst of any developing region: the lowest one-fifth of the population receives barely 4.5 percent of national income, while the share of the highest fifth is 55 percent. Still, there is also genuine progress. In recent years, the share of the population living in poverty has been falling in a number of countries, even as the region has been buffeted by a major structural transformation. This progress, however, is fragile since some of the biggest gains have come from reduction in inflation and it would be difficult to sustain that pace of improvement. Most of the governments in the region perceive the urgency of implementing poverty-reduction policies.

We know that those born into poverty are likely to remain poor. There is a life cycle of social problems, beginning with inadequate prenatal care, followed by a disadvantaged childhood and troubled youth and evolving into a constellation of dysfunctional behaviors, including adolescent motherhood and single parenthood, alcoholism and substance abuse, and violence. Such social problems are costly — in the case of urban violence, doubling from 0.8 percent of GDP in the early 1980s to 1.6 percent in the mid-1990s — tear the social fabric, and slow down economic growth. At the same time, these characteristics point to the types of programs that are needed to break the transmission of poverty from one generation to the next. Accordingly, the Bank has launched a pioneering program to deal with urban violence. Two initial operations totaling US$73 million were signed recently in Cartagena. In addition, we are in the process of organizing a conference on poverty in Central America.

The Bank's experience shows that in addition to sustained economic growth, other complementary efforts are needed to help the poor earn their way out of poverty and improve their quality of life. These include investments in education, health, and other social areas; opening access to assets, such as land; supporting micro-enterprises that provide jobs for one-third of the region's workers and an outlet for the entrepreneurial energies of the poor; strengthening social networks; and targeting assistance to especially disadvantaged groups, such as indigenous populations and ethnic minorities. Taken together, these efforts are the foundation for a successful poverty-reduction strategy.

Developing programs geared to poverty reduction is an on-going test of the Bank's capacity for innovation and incorporating new themes in the regional development policy agenda. Among four projects dealing with domestic violence, one is geared to sensitizing judges and other judiciary personnel about women's issues, and another creates service networks in six countries to prevent domestic violence and provide treatment to victims of abuse. The Bank is funding a regional program to strengthen training for low-income women in many skill areas traditionally dominated by men. Increasingly, the Bank is financing free-standing programs, incorporating prenatal care, nutrition, health and school readiness activities, targeted to poor children. Particularly noteworthy is the work done with street children and related projects, carried out with the cooperation of civil-society organizations and involving grant funds of approximately US$70 million. In the case of indigenous communities that account for 10 percent of the region's population but constitute 25 percent of its poor, their interests have been explicitly addressed in several projects in the social sectors and environmental management as well as in a project for leadership training of indigenous women. Finally, the Bank played a decisive role in the creation of a regional Indigenous Peoples Fund that serves as an international forum for the exchange of information, negotiation, and conflict resolution and provides technical expertise to identify and develop projects that serve indigenous communities. The Fund has been ratified by 19 countries and has commitments of US$38.5 million available to it.

Support for micro-enterprises is an important vehicle for expanding income earning opportunities for the poor. While such entities account for 80 percent of all businesses in the region, less than 5 percent of them have access to formal financial services. This has led the Bank to take a pioneering role in micro-enterprise and small business financing for the past 20 years. In the course of that time, US$262 million has been provided in direct micro-enterprise financing, US$265 million in lines of credit for financial intermediaries in support of micro-enterprise and small businesses, and US$87 million in additional micro-enterprise and small business financing under the Multilateral Investment Fund (MIF). More than half of these micro-projects have been addressed to women, and an estimated one million micro-producers have benefited. In order to tackle this and other constraints to raising productivity and income levels in the micro-enterprise sector, the Bank has launched an ambitious program — MICRO 2001 — to invest US$500 million over a period of five years for micro-enterprise development. The program will fund institutions such as credit unions that make loans to micro-entrepreneurs; provide equity from resources of the MIF — a trust fund which it manages — to help transform experienced non-governmental organizations into formal financial institutions specialized in working with micro-enterprises; and provide enhanced support services through specialized business development and other institutions.

The Bank has substantially increased its lending in the social sectors since 1990. In 1997, such loans accounted for close to 40 percent of all lending, more than ever before in the Bank's history and one of the highest proportions posted by a multilateral organization. Today, the Bank's disbursements to the social sectors are the highest in its history, and it has a portfolio of social sector loans estimated at US$10 billion lined up through the end of the decade. These loans are reform-oriented, with the emphasis on improving the quality and coverage of primary education and basic health services within a framework that aims to change the structural conditions that perpetuate poverty and addressing issues of regional, linguistic, and socio-cultural discrimination. The objective is to provide a bundle of minimum services — quality education, basic health care, and adequate nutrition — that will enable the children of the poor to acquire the skills they need to earn a good wage and break the vicious cycle of poverty for themselves and their children.

## EDUCATION: A CATALYST FOR PROGRESS

This is education's moment in Latin America and the Caribbean. Today's consensus on the urgent need for educational reform responds as much to concern for social equity as to the imperative of becoming competitive in the global economy. Despite substantial gains in reducing illiteracy, improving gender equality, and providing access to primary education, much remains to be done to reduce the disparities in social and economic opportunities among citizens that undermine the region's development potential. The percentage of children who fail to complete the primary cycle is almost twice what would be expected given the region's level of income, and young workers enter the labor force increasingly ill-prepared to meet the demands of the modern workplace. Marked inequality in the distribution of income translates into disparities in educational opportunities, thus reinforcing social inequity. Learning in schools remains strikingly deficient both in the usual school subjects and in respect of inculcating citizenship, social responsibility, and the skills to participate in a democratic society.

The Bank has a strong commitment to promoting quality education for all by means of activities at the country and regional level and through innovation in its approaches to financing initiatives in this field. It is constantly seeking ways of responding to the growing demands of broad constituencies that include parents, students, teachers, businesses, civil society organizations, and governments themselves that are asking for more resources, new policies, and better decisions for the education sector. Several countries are pursuing the organizational and financial challenges of systemic reform, beginning to address problems of secondary education now that student flows are better established at the primary level, and are turning attention to training and vocational education in response to the economic restructuring taking place in the region.

Teachers occupy the center stage in any reform since, in the end, they will be the agents of change operating in the classrooms. They must be empowered to be effective in this role through training, incentives, school environment, pedagogic support, and facility with new techniques such as distance education. Substantial resources will be needed for this: not simply additional resources, but in the first instance through decisive improvements in using the resources already available.

The Bank has provided financial support for education in Latin America virtually since its inception and has pioneered the efforts of international financial institutions on this front. The first Bank loan for education was approved in March 1962; in the following months, the Bank extended four additional loans for education projects or programs, for a total of just over US$12 million in funding in the course of that year. Since then, the Bank has been affording steady support for initiatives to improve Latin American and Caribbean education systems. In recent years, the Bank has shifted its focus toward an explicit concern for such aspects of educational policy as managerial and pedagogic issues, support for quality improvement, and school-centered or community-based management. In accordance with the existing mandates approved by our Governors and our traditional support for regional initiatives, the Bank stands ready to complement actions in individual countries and to support a number of lines of activities that encompass more than one country and respond to priorities and preferences articulated by member countries in the Hemispheric Action Plan for

Education. These may include areas under study for submission in the near future to our Board of Executive Directors, such as

**Regional Program of Internships:** This program will allow practitioners who are working in new, experimental areas in education to interchange ideas with their colleagues abroad. It would also create a clearinghouse to facilitate internships for young professionals in enterprises located in other countries. The regional internship program will allow a more rapid diffusion of information about what works and help to promote experimental projects.

**The Virtual School:** There has already been much effort to improve the quality of teaching materials and methods for science and mathematics, two subjects of critical concern to educators in our region. The Bank would support the diffusion of these ideas on a regional level by selecting the best methods and bringing them to a number of average schools in participating countries using state-of-the-art concepts of distance learning and deploying technologies such as radio- and television-supported learning processes, or the still uncharted potential of inter-connectivity and computers.

**Distance Education:** Latin America is already a leader in the use of distance education, with programs such as Telesecundaria, Telecurso 2000, Tele-Escola, and Virtual University (Monterey), which are state-of-the-art by any standard. The IDB is prepared to provide technical and financial support to initiatives in distance education, including teacher training, the development of teaching materials, and, of course, ensuring accessibility across the region to the best practices that have been tried and tested in individual countries. In the past two years alone, the Bank has approved US$188 million in proposals in this area.

**Information for Education:** Until recently, official statistics remained in the straightjacket of a set of old practices that did not foster better management, improved quality, accessibility to the stakeholders, and comparability across countries, regions, and even schools. The systematic use of standardized tests to measure the quality of the output of the education system is particularly important. There is now the beginning of a small revolution in educational statistics and an emerging consensus in the region that are opening space for the IDB to support the countries in updating their information systems.

The successful implementation of regional programs of the kind described above on a sufficiently large scale will require the Bank to identify novel sources of financing. Fortunately, the shareholders are currently engaged in a fundamental reassessment of the sources and uses of concessional resources available to the Bank. The request of the Heads of State and Government in the Plan of Action of the II Summit of the Americas will be submitted to the Governors of the Bank for consideration in the context of the on-going review of concessional resources.

In recent years, the Bank has approved some US$300 million in educational loans annually. Considering potential demand from member country governments for projects in preschool, primary, secondary, and higher education, that figure could double by the end of the decade.

## STRENGTHENING JUDICIAL SYSTEMS

There is a broad consensus within the region about the importance of an independent, well-respected judiciary as a critical underpinning for the efficient functioning of a market-based economy. Confidence in the functioning of the judiciary assures all citizens of prompt and equal treatment before the law, protects property rights, provides validity to contracts, stymies corruption, and reduces risk for investors. The Bank took first steps to place this issue on the regional development agenda with a path-breaking Conference on Justice and Development held in Costa Rica in 1993, which was followed by a strong mandate from shareholders in 1994. Since that time, the Bank has financed operations in 13 countries, in addition to four regional operations, all with the primary objective of supporting the development of an independent judiciary, but incorporating characteristics that range from technical assistance for better administration to improving provision of justice in poor communities. The Bank has strengthened its operating capacity in this area and has projects in the pipeline that should lead to loans for a further six countries, as well as five regional operations, for an estimated US$76 million. In addition, to expedite rulings on commercial disputes, seven private arbitration tribunals have been sponsored and funded.

## CIVIL SOCIETY

In several countries in the region, civil society organizations are playing an increasingly vital role in partnership with governments and private businesses, in promoting civic responsibility and enhancing social and economic opportunities for all citizens. The Bank, in keeping with the mandate given by its shareholders in 1994, has been very supportive of this development, including innovative projects approved during the last year. We believe that our work in this area would be complemented and enhanced by efforts of another smaller entity dedicated to supporting partnerships and sustained dialogue among governments, civil society, and the private sector. The Bank will continue exploring options for creating complementary financing mechanisms for this purpose, consistent with its own mandate and in recognition of the request made in the Action Plan endorsed by this Santiago Summit.

## INFRASTRUCTURE

The accumulated effect of past neglect and the demands arising as the regional economies continue to consolidate their growth performance and integrate into the global economy, underline the grave deficiencies in physical infrastructure of all kinds: roads, ports, airports, telecommunications, water and sewerage, energy supply systems. The annual investment requirements far exceed the capacity of the public sector that traditionally undertook much of this type of activity and that continues to be challenged with the pressing demands for financing poverty-reduction initiatives. Against this background, the Bank has adopted a policy for provision of public services that aims at ensuring the long-term sustainability of the services; achieving economic efficiency in their provision; safeguarding their quality; promoting accessibility of the services to all citizens; and meeting wider national objectives, in particular, protection of the environment. While acknowledging that in many cases the private sector may be the best provider, the Bank recognizes that the public sector or public/private partnerships may offer a better fit in some countries or sectors or at different times in a given country or sector.

The Bank has several instruments that are well-suited to the implementation of its strategy in support of the efforts of countries in the region. These instruments include its traditional policy dialogue and lending to governments, its demonstrated capacity to attract private capital to projects that it finances or guarantees without sovereign recourse, and its ability to underwrite institutional reforms with MIF grants. The MIF has already supported governments in 22 countries in their role of policy making, regulating, and monitoring public services. In recent years, the Bank has been lending between US$1.5 billion and about US$2 billion annually for infrastructure projects, including a rising amount through its private sector window. Direct lending and guarantees to the private sector, which started in 1995, have reached a cumulative total of US$665 million for 19 projects in nine countries. This was complemented by an amount of US$866 million in B-loans and altogether helped to finance projects to a value of US$4.2 billion or 6.3 times the Bank's direct lending.

The Bank aims at fostering an increasing flow of resources to infrastructure in the years ahead. Accordingly, it will promote private sector investment, strengthen the role of the state as regulator, and support the most efficient use of scarce public resources. To implement this strategy, the Bank Group will seek to attract more resources for private infrastructure, design more attractive financial products, and support the development of local capital markets so that they can provide long-term financing for private infrastructure projects. Furthermore, the Bank will prepare a set of principles that countries may use to guide private participation in local and cross-border physical integration projects and that may also serve as the basis for bilateral and multilateral agreements.

## INFORMATION TECHNOLOGY

Information technology is revolutionizing the market for goods and services and the provision of public services. The countries of the region cannot afford to lag behind these important changes and must, therefore, take all necessary steps to facilitate broad access to communications technology, information, and knowledge. This will require major investments in the satellites, microwave stations, fiber optic cable, and computer workstations that are the essential infrastructure for the future.

The Bank would continue to work closely with the public sector to support efforts to use information technology to improve the delivery of public services. This will encompass areas such as social security, health and education systems, tax and customs administrations, land title registration, and case management in the judicial system. This field also offers great opportunities for building partnerships between the public and private sectors to create as rapidly as possible the basic components of the information infrastructure of the future. The Bank's Informatics 2000 Initiative, co-sponsored by many of the world's leading information technology companies, has already been identifying opportunities for partnerships in a range of substantive areas, and the Bank will join with both the public and private sectors in financing many of the resulting initiatives.

## CLIMATE AND ENERGY

We live in a world where the impact of energy use on climate is of increasing concern, given its regional and global dimension. The harmful effects of flood, drought, and pollution in one country may easily have their origin in a neighboring country.

Phenomena such as El Niño bring forcefully to our attention the dramatic impact that changes in climate can have in areas such as agriculture, fisheries, hydro-energy generation, human health, transportation, and the overall well-being of the economies of many countries. In recognition of the regional impact of weather and the need for adequate, reliable, and comparable measurements and forecasting tools, the Bank has started regional program efforts to improve the forecasting of weather with the objective of enabling countries to prepare themselves with timely managerial and mitigation measures to cope with the adverse effects of weather phenomena. An interesting example is the Ibero-American climate feasibility and design study, co-financed by Canada, Spain, and the United States, which involves the meteorological services of 13 regional countries with technical support from the World Meteorological Organization (WMO), among others. This experience is being used by WMO as a model for the design of a similar program in Southeast Asia.

The Bank has been very active in developing new instruments that are consistent with priorities in the energy sector, as endorsed at the Summit on Sustainable Development held in Santa Cruz de la Sierra, Bolivia. Sustainable Markets for Sustainable Energy (SMSE), an innovative pilot program that seeks to assist in the development of new markets for end-use energy efficiency and clean energy, has been chosen by the Hemispheric Energy Steering Committee as an example of the kind of action sought from multilateral institutions in support of the Summit's goals. The IDB, in partnership with the U.S. Department of Energy, USAID, and the European Union in the US$2 million pilot phase, hopes to demonstrate to the private sector the commercial feasibility of energy efficiency through the installation of clean energy sources (for example, renewable energy or hybrid systems in rural electrification activities); infrastructure development; and clean urban transportation systems.

Looking to the near-term future, the IDB — in cooperation with other international institutions — would also offer technical support to assist the countries of the region to analyze and develop operational approaches to the implementation of the Clean Development Mechanism in the Americas. This effort will be a part of IDB's continued support for enhancing the scientific, economic, and regulatory capacity on environmental issues in each country.

## BUILDING MODERN FINANCIAL SYSTEMS

Many countries in our hemisphere have confronted the problem of imminent systemic failure in financial markets and have had to shoulder costs that typically have been considerably higher than in the case of industrialized countries. The Miami Summit recognized the importance of establishing a sound regulatory framework for banking and for securities markets throughout the region and the Bank has been actively involved with hemispheric securities regulators and the Hemispheric Committee of Ministers of Finance in moving the agenda forward.

Clearly, governments are key to the proper functioning of the financial markets, but it must be recognized that no amount of regulation and supervision will smooth the functioning of these markets if the private sector is not a willing partner. Actually, over-regulation can be as bad as lax regulation. In this spirit, we encourage more self-regulation as a supplement to the role of the government as rector of the system.

The task ahead is difficult because the environment of financial markets is very dynamic, given the trend toward integrated services, the liberalization of markets, and the strength of cross-border capital flows, particularly of short-term funds. As in the case of infrastructure development, the Bank has a comparative advantage for working with partners in both the public and private sectors in light of the resources available through the IMF whose raison d'être is the promotion of private sector economic activity. The Bank has launched a Financial Markets Development Initiative, a comprehensive and systematic program to support the development of financial markets, working with both the public and private sectors.

On the private sector side, the program will include direct support to small and medium-sized banks for enhancing corporate management. A particular focus of this program will be the development and implementation, including training, of risk management and internal control systems, along the lines of proposals by the Basle Committee outlined in the "Core Principles for Effective Banking Supervision" and those contained in the draft on the "Framework for the Evaluation of Internal Control Systems."

The public sector's capacity for effective banking supervision needs to be significantly strengthened, even in those countries that have made a great deal of progress in the functioning of their regulatory agencies. In this regard, we will expand our current program of training and support for the implementation in each country of the Core Principles for Effective Banking Supervision. Similarly, in terms of securities markets and as requested in the Plan of Action adopted at the II Summit of the Americas in Santiago, the Bank will support the efforts of securities regulators and the private sector in bringing the Clearance and Settlements Systems to the framework outlined by the International Association of Securities Commissions (IOSCO) in the document entitled "Clearance and Settlements in Emerging Markets: A Blueprint."

## LABOR ISSUES

In recent years, the Bank has engaged in dialogue with representative labor organizations at the regional level, directed research efforts toward a better understanding of labor market issues, and used MIF grants to support novel programs sponsored by trade unions in some countries. Such consensus building and piloting activities have been the basis for moving issues firmly onto the regional development agenda in the past and may well have similar results in the case of labor issues. Accordingly, the Bank will keenly continue its efforts in this field in coordination with other international organizations as requested in the Action Plan of this Santiago Summit.

## ECONOMIC INTEGRATION AND FREE TRADE

The historic Free Trade of the Americas (FTAA) process launched at the Miami Summit is already bearing fruit, despite the skepticism often expressed about the chances of success of such an ambitious endeavor. This Santiago Summit will mark the start of formal negotiations as the assembled Heads of State and Government endorse the negotiating structure and framework for logistical and technical support adopted by the Trade Ministers at San Jose with the objective of achieving formal agreement of the FTAA by 2005. There is no room for complacency, however, since we are entering a phase of complex negotiation of many delicate issues. For example, it will be important to ensure the full and effective participation of all governments in the negotiations and to provide fora for expression of the concerns of labor, business, and civil society organizations in order to safeguard the acceptability of the terms of a final agreement. Another challenging area would be to coordinate the ongoing process of widening and deepening of subregional integration with the FTAA process.

The Tripartite Committee comprising the OAS, ECLAC, and IDB delivered, virtually against all odds, quality products that contributed to making the FTAA process one of the most advanced components of the Miami Plan of Action. The three institutions will have to redouble their collective effort in the years ahead to meet the demands of technical support to the negotiating tables and of placing the new temporary administrative secretariat on a firm footing. Beyond this, the Bank on its own is gearing up to intensify its technical assistance to individual countries in the area of trade. We are preparing a Regional Facility for Trade Development that will fund technical cooperation loans for countries interested in broad-based institutional strengthening in trade-related areas, including preparation and training in the new and somewhat unfamiliar areas of the international trade agenda and strengthening of technical negotiating capacity in the region's countries. In this spirit, we are proposing that the Board of Executive Directors approve a line of credit for up to US$100 million to finance technical-cooperation funding under a rapid approval approach to strengthen technical negotiating capabilities in the region's countries.

The FTAA is more than just another trade agreement. It is an important component of the hemispheric commitment to bring our people closer together. The FTAA is creating positive externalities such as incentives to accelerate deepening of subregional trade arrangements as well as to focus more intensely on multilateral issues and the broader challenges of globalization. All of this makes the launch of the FTAA in Santiago a very satisfying achievement and one in which the IDB is very proud to be an active participant and partner of the countries and other multilateral agencies.

# III. SUMMIT DOCUMENTS

*Madeleine K. Albright is the Secretary of State of the United States.*

*This statement was delivered at the colloquium hosted by the National Women's Service of Chile on April 18, 1998, in Santiago, Chile, as released by the Office of the Spokesman of the U.S. Department of State.*

# "The Rights of Women" A Challenge for the Americas

*Madeleine K. Albright*

### DEAR COLLEAGUES:

I send you greetings and good wishes for a successful colloquy today. I congratulate Minister Josefina Bilbao and the National Women's Service for organizing this important event and regret that I cannot join you in person.

As we will discuss and affirm during this Second Summit of the Americas, the march of democracy across the Americas in the last two decades means that all citizens of this hemisphere, with the exception of Cuba, live in vibrant, open societies, free from dictatorship or repression by unelected, military authorities. Peace has been consolidated throughout the Americas, with the end of civil strife in Central America. We now must turn our attention and our collective efforts to the next generation of reforms in Education, Deepening Democracy, Economic Integration, and Eliminating Poverty and Discrimination.

Make no mistake: defending and strengthening the status of women and girls in the Americas is essential to ensuring that the democracy and growing prosperity that we celebrate here in Santiago is equitable and durable. Women are more than fifty percent of the voters, the consumers, the heads of household, and the educators of our children, from the first moments of a child's life throughout the many phases of life. Women have roles and responsibilities that form the very fabric of society. We shape lives and are determinants of history, the history of our families, our communities, and our countries. However, many of our contributions are frequently undervalued or taken for granted.

In the Americas today, the reality is that women are not able to fully participate in the political, economic, and social lives of our countries because legal, economic, and societal barriers prevent us from doing so. There is a great disparity between the representation of women in our legislatures and the make-up of the electorate. Today, only eleven percent of elected legislators in this hemisphere are women. Great strides have been made in countries like Argentina, Costa Rica, and Mexico, that have changed their electoral codes to ensure greater participation of women as candidates and office holders. Admirable changes have begun, and you will no doubt discuss the impact of those changes here today.

Actions necessary to eliminate the formal barriers that are enshrined in law, as well as the informal barriers that are imbued in attitudes and in customs, limiting women's full contribution to political and economic life are addressed in the language of the Plan of Action our leaders will sign tomorrow. The goal of legal equality between women and men, with focus on gender equity, by the year 2002 lays a challenge before us that we can and must meet. In order to put our political commitments into action, government and civil society must work with our partners in the Inter-American system — the Inter-American Development Bank, the Organization of American States, and the Pan American Health Organization — to make serious, measurable progress.

Financial resources are already identified and posed for delivery to make implementation of these goals possible. The Inter-American Development Bank and its progressive president Enrique Iglesias have established programs in women's leadership, judicial reform, education and training for the needs of the twenty-first century, and to combat violence against women, an underestimated deterrent to development.

The substance of your discussions today, as well as the linkages and working relationships that will be fortified among each of the ministers taking part in this forum, can serve as the call to action for each one of us, whether elected official, educator, civil society leader, or journalist. The Plan of Action that is launched at this Summit gives us the tool to demand action and results, from our governments, law-makers, judicial authorities, schools and universities, and from the private sector.

I urge us all to waste no time in advancing the important work of turning the promise of the Summit into concrete achievements for women and men, girls and boys, for all the voices and beneficiaries of the more prosperous and democratic community of nations of the Americas that we celebrate and reaffirm our commitment to defend and advance as we prepare to cross the threshold of the next century.

Thank you, and warmest wishes for your colloquy.

*César Gaviria is Secretary-General of the Organization of American States.*

*These remarks were delivered at the Second Summit of the Americas in Santiago, Chile, on April 18, 1998.*

# III. Summit Documents

# Speech by the Secretary-General of the Organization of American States at the Second Summit of the Americas

## *César Gaviria*

I'd like to thank the American Presidents and Heads of State for the invitation made to the Organization of American States to accompany them in this new hemispheric meeting. My thanks to the Chilean people, to the city of Santiago, and to President Frei's government for their extraordinarily warm reception.

Forty months ago in Miami, we ended decades of isolationism, confrontation, and distrust. We abandoned the hostile language and a certain atavistic pessimism that characterized our political and economic manner of speaking. Since then, in the OAS, we have carried out instructions received at the First Summit of the Americas. With the IDB and CEPAL, we have sent technical support to the FTAA negotiations; we organized the Summit of Sustainable Growth with the government of Bolivia — I have brought an advance report from this event for your review; in the important areas of struggle against corruption, drug trafficking, terrorism or weapons control, the American nations here today have signed agreements or declarations which link them politically and legally.

With the mandate given us by our governments, we have created an American doctrine of solidarity with democracy in the OAS, which acts against any attempt of public powers to revoke the authority of others or against any military threat that tries to disrupt the democratic process in any country.

However, during these years, the OAS has also developed its own capacity to protect human rights and maintain public liberty; by assuring clean, just, and transparent elections through observation of the process; with the carrying out of post-conflict work in countries which have suffered internal confrontations; with removal of land mines; with the creation of measures to increase confidence and security.

With these projects, we have broken the chains that bound the OAS. However, we know that we still have a long way to go to make our institution a useful and efficient instrument to carry out the new tasks that you have assigned us. But the Santiago Summit sets forth a new and consistent political reality for us.

To this end, we are thinking of the Organization of tomorrow. We are undergoing a process of reform and of the creation of a new inter-American architecture at the Organization of American States as a result of this Summit.

And we have a vision of the Organization carrying out its theatrical role in the creation of inter-American law and as a trustee of treaties and agreements; as a prime forum of hemispheric political dialogue; as a center for exchanging experiences and of designing communal or collective policies; as responsible for building and maintaining hemispheric information systems; as a tool of continental solidarity through its cooperative projects. And, at the same time, we take on with satisfaction the task of being an institutional memory for the summit process and of giving technical support to the meetings of ministers and experts that will follow up in the Action Plan after this Summit meeting.

We know that the work that we have ahead of us is formidable and that it is necessary to find answers to the multitude of challenges that we face.

The questions are many and varied. How do we make integration not only a commercial process, but one of vast social and political consequence? How are we going to preserve political freedom of the governments, the legislatures, and public opinion in the entire hemisphere? How do we make all this effort benefit the smallest economies and the lowest wage earners? What is it that the OAS and the rest of the institutions are going to do so that our education systems prepare autonomous, informed, responsible, tolerant and information critical citizens; and to support the countries that need to attend to the immense demands that globalization and the information revolution places on their economies and culture? And we must also respond to other equally urgent fronts. We have to strengthen our institutions of human rights, to study deeply their financial, budgeted and operational autonomy in order to cover most events; to advertise more; to strengthen the mechanisms of investigation; to give more support and more self-support to national systems; to increase the atmosphere of protection of rights; to universally ratify the American Convention and the acceptance of the jurisdiction of the Court. And it is equally necessary to strengthen the right of free expression; to protect the rights of women, of ethnic minorities, of migrant peoples and their families; and to advance the elimination of all forms of discrimination. And, overall, we have to take strong and concrete steps so that America stops being the region of the greatest inequalities in the world.

We also have the enormous challenge of establishing mechanisms and procedures for evaluating the anti-drug policies of the countries in the heart of the CICAD, respecting the principles of the Letter of the OAS and accepting the principles of shared responsibility. In addition, we must contribute to strengthening judicial power, its independence, and the inter-American mechanisms for judicial cooperation, including subjects such as the struggle against money laundering.

All of these projects, all of them, demand that the OAS strengthen its mechanisms for citizen participation and permit a bigger presence of the civil society in the hemispheric dialogue and in the work of facing our collective problems.

Honorable Presidents and Prime Ministers

This conference has special importance for the OAS which will celebrate our 50th anniversary in a few days. Behind us lies a history of light and shadows, of rivalries and mistrust, of common enterprises and not a few misadventures, of great utopias but, also, of frustrations and disenchantment.

Today, we have an Organization more balanced and universal in its political objectives. An Organization that is preparing to become the enormous umbrella under which will cover the infinite actions to be put in motion by this Summit. With optimism and faith in the future of our America, we will be meeting in the following weeks first in Bogotá and then in Caracas, in order to pick up the legacy of collective action, integration, cooperation, coordination, and reform. It is this strong legacy from Santiago, Chile, which will be extended throughout the whole hemisphere for the benefit of our peoples.

Thank you very much.


Translation: Courtesy of Instituto Chileno-Norteamericano

# III. SUMMIT DOCUMENTS

*These remarks were delivered at the Tenth Meeting of the Summit Implementation Review Group on October 1, 1997, in Washington, D.C.*

# Palabras del Secretario-General de la OEA, en la X Reunión del Grupo de Revisión e Implementación de la Cumbre de las Américas

*César Gaviria*

Washington, D.C., 1 de octubre de 1997

Deseo comenzar expresando mis agradecimientos a los copresidentes del Grupo de Seguimiento y en particular al Embajador Juan Martabit por la amable invitación que se me ha hecho para dirigirme a ustedes en el día de hoy. En la medida en que pasan las semanas y se acerca la cita que nuestras naciones tienen en Santiago en abril próximo, crece también la atención sobre el desarrollo de los trabajos que aquí se adelantan con el decidido apoyo de los países del hemisferio.

La razón de que eso sea así recae en el hecho de que los temas que analizarán los presidentes y jefes de gobierno están estrechamente relacionados con la propia calidad de vida en las Américas. Este no es un ejercicio diplomático, ni una abstracción de las relaciones internacionales. Este es un proceso que responde directamente a las necesidades cotidianas de nuestros pueblos. Es con esa vara que seremos evaluados.

## SEÑORES COORDINADORES:

En la OEA vemos con entusiasmo los caminos y las oportunidades que se le abren a las naciones del hemisferio. Es por ello que la Organización está dispuesta y se prepara para poner lo mejor de sí en esta tarea histórica. Ello fue expresado de manera vehemente por nuestra Asamblea General a comienzos de junio en Lima, en donde los países aquí congregados demandaron mayor trabajo y le dieron más instrumentos a la Secretaría General para laborar conjuntamente con los grupos coordinadores en la preparación y seguimiento de aquellos temas en los que la Organización tiene conocimientos o experiencia.

A ese espíritu responden los documentos que hoy ponemos a su disposición. Frente a ustedes encontrarán dos trabajos de índole general. En el primero titulado "La OEA y la Cumbre de Miami" presentamos un panorama de lo que ha realizado la Organización en seguimiento de los mandatos que los Jefes de Estado y de Gobierno de las Américas le encomendaron en el Plan de Acción aprobado por la Cumbre. Se ofrece a ustedes este documento no sólo para rendir a este grupo cuenta de nuestras actividades, sino además como fundamento de las propuestas que la Secretaría de la OEA trae a su consideración sobre el rol de nuestra Organización, tanto en la preparación como en el seguimiento.

Como es por todos conocido, en el tema de la corrupción se dio origen a una convención que todos esperamos enriquezca pronto el derecho Interamericano. Otros encargos en temas tan complejos y esenciales como el combate al narcotráfico, la lucha contra el terrorismo o el desarrollo sostenible se han cumplido con el diseño común de estrategias y la suscripción de trascendentales pronunciamientos en materia de los principios o valores que guían las acciones de nuestras naciones y de planes de acción para darles eficacia. La OEA ha demostrado, en ese sentido, ser un espacio multilateral propicio para disipar suspicacias, profundizar consensos y entablar negociaciones equilibradas y sustantivas.

También se han logrado avances importantes en el campo de la defensa de la democracia y la protección de los derechos humanos; en integración comercial; en la identificación de nuestro papel en el campo del intercambio de experiencias en materia de política social; y en la reforma de las instituciones y el diseño de políticas para la lucha contra pobreza. Hemos avanzado, igualmente, en el diseño de instrumentos jurídicos que consagran derechos para enfrentar la discriminación de que son objeto las mujeres, los pueblos indígenas y los discapacitados.

El segundo documento, "La OEA y su contribución a la Cumbre de Santiago", adelanta algunas propuestas en relación con las futuras labores de seguimiento, como ya lo mencionamos, derivadas de la experiencia que hemos logrado del seguimiento de Miami. Como lo hemos dicho anteriormente, en la medida en que el proceso de diálogo hemisférico se transforma en una constante del nuevo multilateralismo de las Américas, creemos apropiado pensar en establecer mecanismos más adecuados para institucionalizarlo. El trabajo que presentamos hoy contiene algunas propuestas en cuanto a criterios ordenadores, y otras que hacen relación con los instrumentos y estructuras específicos para lograr ese propósito.

De manera paralela, pondremos a disposición de los países algunos documentos sustantivos sobre temas específicos que son parte del trabajo que este grupo tiene en los próximos siete meses. Estas iniciativas las hemos tomado de común acuerdo con la cancillería Chilena.

Queremos contribuir a la discusión sobre el tema de la Educación. Hemos asistido, gracias a la generosa invitación de las autoridades mexicanas, a algunas de las reuniones preparatorias en esta área. Creemos que el documento que los Estados han recibido de México contiene un enfoque programático que es fundamental para responder con eficacia a problemas concretos y urgentes que enfrenta la educación en nuestro hemisferio, y para que los compromisos adquiridos puedan evaluarse en su ejecución en el período que corre entre la celebración de las cumbres. Apoyamos plenamente ese planteamiento y pueden contar con la OEA para avanzar en su implementación.

Simultáneamente, creemos que dada la envergadura y complejidad del tema de la educación en las Américas, es también conveniente completar la primera discusión con una reflexión más analítica, quizás más crítica, de su realidad en nuestro hemisferio. En ese sentido pondremos a su disposición un documento de trabajo que se concentra en aquellos aspectos que tienen que ver con un diagnóstico de las políticas educativas y las instituciones que las ponen en práctica. Más que respuestas aspiramos a alimentar un diálogo sustantivo que nos permita identificar los problemas de que adolecen los sistemas educativos en el Hemisferio.

Un enfoque de esa naturaleza nos ayudará en la identificación de los programas más acordes con la índole de los males que aquejan a la educación en las Américas. Tal vez su utilidad haga más relación con sus aspectos de calidad que de cobertura, más con la educación primaria y secundaria que con la universitaria, más con los aspectos formativos que con la educación que demanda la formación de capacidades para enfrentar los retos de la globalización. Con este propósito también presentamos a ustedes un documento ejecutivo que analiza algunos aspectos generales de las políticas educativas y sus aspectos institucionales.

En el plano de la democracia entregamos a ustedes una versión revisada de un texto que recientemente fue circulado a los países miembros de la OEA. El documento identifica algunos de los principales problemas y desafíos que enfrentan nuestras democracias, y lo que de una manera ordenada, y a través fundamentalmente del intercambio de experiencias, podría hacer el sistema multilateral para apoyar a los países a enfrentarlos.

Sobre la base de ello proponemos algunas iniciativas que estimamos necesarias para que la OEA, aprovechando todas las posibilidades que la acción colectiva ofrece, pueda apoyar a los países de una manera más eficaz. Como por ejemplo, consolidar y fortalecer algunas instituciones de gobierno, avanzar en la modernización del Estado y promover espacios que permitan una mayor participación de la ciudadanía en la vida pública, mejorar las instituciones y políticas sociales, y enfrentar los problemas de la inseguridad ciudadana. Todos ellos son aspectos que demandan nuestra acción.

Con ese objetivo la OEA ha desarrollado dos iniciativas específicas sobre las cuales también les proporcionamos información. En primer lugar, la Organización está poniendo en marcha un Programa de Estudios sobre la Democracia que, con el apoyo del Banco Interamericano de Desarrollo, estará dirigido a promover la investigación y la capacitación sobre aspectos relacionados con el desarrollo democrático, dos áreas que a juicio de las dos instituciones presentan hoy graves deficiencias en lo que hace relación con organismos multilaterales.

Este programa también proveerá un espacio de más alto nivel político sobre el intercambio de experiencias, que también está haciendo falta, para que pueda ir más allá del que se realiza entre funcionarios de gobierno en temas atinentes a la gobernabilidad, el fortalecimiento de la democracia y la preservación de los derechos ciudadanos.

En segundo término, en colaboración con el BID y el Banco Mundial, con cuyos presidentes he examinado personalmente estas ideas, deseamos poner en marcha un Programas dirigido a apoyar a los gobiernos recién electos. Estos podrían así aprovechar mejor y más prontamente los recursos políticos con los que cuenta toda administración en sus primeros meses para promover los cambios necesarios de marco institucional y de políticas que se requieran para poner en ejecución sus programas. Creemos que ello puede constituir una contribución puntual y directa al proceso de darle credibilidad a nuestras democracias.

Este enfoque de mayor coordinación entre instituciones multilaterales también ha sido utilizado en torno a otro tema de creciente interés y preocupación para los Estados del hemisferio como es el de la seguridad ciudadana, en particular en las grandes ciudades. La Secretaría General ha elaborado algunas ideas y propuestas que hoy ofrecemos como insumos para la discusión general del tema y la posible colaboración multilateral. Simultáneamente estamos en condiciones de avanzar en la implementación de actividades específicas, junto con los Bancos, en la medida que los Estados así lo juzguen pertinente.

En el tema de Derechos Humanos también estamos trabajando. En torno de un seminario realizado por la Comisión Interamericana y de una reunión de expertos convocada por la el Consejo Permanente, hemos iniciado un proceso de reflexión y análisis tendiente a lograr el perfeccionamiento del sistema interamericano de protección de los derechos humanos.

A manera de resumen, he expresado que como parte del diagnóstico se ha avanzado en tres elementos. En primer lugar, a pesar de que la lucha contra el abuso de los derechos humanos siempre es un tema que tiene prioridad absoluta en nuestra agenda hemisférica, los procedimientos vigentes no aseguran siempre su eficacia. Además el sistema está afectado de una crónica deficiencia de recursos financieros y administrativos. En segundo lugar, las líneas de defensa de los derechos humanos están penetrando cada vez más el escenario doméstico. Los sistemas nacionales pesan cada vez más en la tarea de protección, y necesitamos modificar nuestro instrumento regional para poder estimular y fortalecer esa tendencia. En tercer lugar, no todos los Estados miembros son parte del sistema. Tenemos que encontrar los motivos por los cuales aún no hemos logrado una adhesión universal a éste y buscar una serie de soluciones eficaces para lograrlo.

Esto sólo para mostrar que sería útil que los Presidentes y Jefes de Gobierno se pronunciaran sobre la conveniencia de continuar ese proceso de reflexión y de invitar a los organismos nacionales de justicia, de policía y a todos los miembros de la sociedad civil a participar en este proceso. También podrían los Jefes de Estado y de Gobierno enunciar unos parámetros u orientaciones para avanzar en la reforma y perfeccionamiento del sistema. La Secretaría se propone, antes de la próxima reunión de este grupo de seguimiento, circular una propuesta en este sentido que contenga además algunos de los parámetros u orientaciones a los que me he referido.

Con nuestra Subsecretaría de Asuntos Jurídicos hemos iniciado un trabajo dirigido a identificar en qué medida es necesario impulsar la adhesión y ratificación de instrumentos existentes o el diseño de nuevos que nos permitan facilitar una amplia cooperación judicial para enfrentar los diversos problemas de criminalidad internacional en los cuales la OEA ha venido concentrando su trabajo después de la Cumbre de Miami. Esta ha sido ofrecida por los países en la Estrategia contra las drogas, en plan anticorrupción, en el plan de lucha contra el terrorismo, en el grupo de trabajo sobre la lucha contra el lavado de dinero y en la negociación de la convención sobre trafico ilegal de armas.

Entregaremos a ustedes un documento de trabajo, que está aún en una fase muy preliminar, sobre posibles áreas de cooperación judicial para hacer frente a realidades como el avance y la internacionalización del crimen organizado, fenómenos como el terrorismo, el narcotráfico, el lavado de dinero, la corrupción, el tráfico de armas y la explotación ilícita de recursos naturales.

No puedo terminar sin referirme brevemente a algunos elementos del documento sobre el papel de la Secretaria de la OEA en el proceso de preparación de la Cumbre y en las tareas de seguimiento. Entendemos este documento como una propuesta, como un insumo para iniciar un proceso de diálogo con los países que culminaría con la reunión de este grupo en enero próximo.

La propuesta que estamos presentando contiene, como ya lo hemos dicho, algunas propuestas de la Secretaría, no de los países, a ser usadas, si así se considera, en la etapa de preparación. Las propuestas para identificar un rol para la OEA en la etapa de seguimiento también son de la Secretaría pero le traerían responsabilidades a toda la Organización.

Consideramos fundamental para el proceso de seguimiento de la Cumbre de Santiago que se mantenga este grupo como la instancia superior de coordinación general del proceso. La eficacia de sus sistemas de coordinación sobrepasa en eficiencia los métodos parlamentarios que usa a veces nuestra organización en las negociaciones políticas o en las de creación de nuevos instrumentos jurídicos. Podría pensarse, después de la celebración de la Cumbre, que los propios jefes de Estado o la Asamblea de la OEA crearan en su seno un mecanismo nuevo, con la misma composición que éste, con viceministros o funcionarios investidos de amplias facultades, que utilizara los mismos métodos de coordinación a efectos de articular mejor todo el funcionamiento de sistema interamericano.

En la medida en que el proceso de Cumbres marche hacia su institucionalización, resulta conveniente establecer en la OEA un espacio claramente definido que lleve la memoria institucional del proceso, en el cual los Estados miembros, los gobiernos nuevos y la comunidad en general, puedan encontrar una relación clara de lo acordado, puedan acceder a los documentos entregados por las secretarías y los países, las constancias o elementos que los países hayan querido aportar y en general a cada uno de los hilos del rico tejido del proceso que se originó en Miami.

También puede ser conveniente, dada la multitud de reuniones ministeriales y de otras autoridades que se dan en el marco de la OEA, que ellas se amolden a la nueva arquitectura hemisférica, que formalmente empiecen a tomar sus mandatos de las Cumbres presidenciales y sirvan así al proceso de seguimiento. También podrían la OEA y el BID y las otras instituciones del sistema interamericano preparar documentos técnicos de trabajo para las reuniones ministeriales o de expertos, de lo cual el mejor ejemplo a seguir es el del trabajo que, BID, CEPAL y OEA realizan para los Ministros de Comercio. También pueden las instituciones internacionales y los organismos, de acuerdo con sus áreas de competencia, prestar el apoyo administrativo y técnico a esas reuniones.

Finalmente, cuando se examine el documento que sometemos hoy a su consideración sobre las tareas que ha realizado la OEA, se podrá identificar cómo son de útiles las Conferencias especializada y las reuniones de expertos, bajo los métodos de trabajo que utiliza la Organización, para el logro de algunos de los objetivos de acción colectiva interamericana. Creemos que cuando se tomen las decisiones de seguimiento de la próxima Cumbre se debe tener presente esta experiencia.

Dentro de esa lógica, deseo destacar las posibilidades que ofrece el Consejo Interamericano para el Desarrollo Integral, el cual cuenta con un marco jurídico aprobado por los Congresos del Hemisferio y maneja un importante volumen de recursos de cooperación internacional aportados por los países.

En el plano Financiero de la OEA, me gustaría hacer algunos comentarios. Es necesario continuar el proceso de redimensionamiento, de reasignación de recursos a las nuevas prioridades, y de sistematización con miras a adaptar mejor la estructura de la Secretaría y la asignación de recursos presupuestales a lo que constituye la voluntad d los Estados al más alto nivel político.

Es muy probable que la OEA, después de un período que ya alcanza más de cuatro años de congelación de recursos en términos nominales, pueda en un futuro próximo reexaminar con los países nuevas posibilidades de financiamientos.

De cara a la próxima vigencia fiscal, estoy convencido que la OEA puede asumir las tareas que he enunciado con una sola condición: que los países miembros y en especial los que llamamos grandes contribuyentes, nos paguen sus cuotas anuales completas. También nos haría bien que nos paguen las cuotas que están en mora. Si es así, creemos que va a ser muy difícil que este enorme ejercicio de identificar áreas de acción colectiva que estamos realizando aquí, encuentre tropiezos insalvables.

Hemos aprendido a enfrentar los grandes desafíos en términos más realistas. Hoy somos más capaces de mirar nuestros problemas sin voluntarismo, ni tozudez ideológica. Ello implica estar conscientes de nuestras limitaciones tanto como de nuestros entusiasmos, significa medir con detenimiento las expectativas que generamos, y significa asumir estas tareas como procesos graduales y acumulativos.

Palabras del Secretario-General de la OEA, en la X Reunión del Grupo de Revisión e Implementación de la Cumbre de las Américas

# III. Summit Documents

## SEÑORES COORDINADORES:

Debo ser claro en un punto: entregamos estos documentos como un ingrediente más de este rico y múltiple tejido. Las páginas que leerán contienen algunas ideas que no pretenden ser finales ni aspiran a ser enfoques cerrados. Tenemos muy claro que en última instancia la OEA es la Organización de los Estados Americanos y, en ese sentido, sólo interpretamos la partitura que los países y sus gobiernos nos asignen. Estamos seguros de que con la conducción de la Cancillería Chilena y el Departamento de Estado se va a decidir lo mejor para los pueblos de las Américas.

La OEA de hoy está mucho mejor preparada para desarrollar una función eficaz en el cumplimiento de los mandatos que los Jefes de Estado y de Gobierno emitirán en Santiago. Tenemos en marcha un plan de modernización administrativa y de reasignación de nuestros recursos a las nuevas realidades hemisféricas. Estoy seguro de que con las orientaciones que nos darán en la Cumbre quedará definida una arquitectura de instituciones que han de servir de marco a nuestras acciones para lograr una América más próspera, libre, justa y democrática.

Muchas gracias.

# III. Summit Documents

*Madeleine K. Albright is the Secretary of State of the United States.*

*José Miguel Insulza is the Foreign Minister of the Republic of Chile.*

*This statement was delivered on June 1, 1997, in Lima, Peru.*

# Statement by the Co-Chairs of the Meeting of Foreign Ministers of the Nations of the Summit of the Americas

*Secretary of State Madeleine K. Albright and Foreign Minister José Miguel Insulza*

The Summit of the Americas held in Miami in 1994, in which the 34 democratically elected leaders of the Western Hemisphere participated, permitted the building of a new framework of cooperation and hemispheric partnership. The Heads of State and Government agreed to develop a collective effort of cooperation intended to deepen the hemispheric dialogue, consolidate democracy, promote regional integration, improve the level and quality of life of the people, reduce poverty, and eliminate all forms of discrimination, while preserving the environment for future generations.

We, the Ministers of Foreign Relations of the Summit nations, met in Montrouis, Haiti in June 1995, and Panama City, Panama in June 1996, to review implementation of the commitments undertaken in Miami. At Panama, we reviewed ongoing activities and called for greater attention in those areas that until then were less developed.

The growing interest of the governments of the Hemisphere in continuing a balanced dialogue and taking additional actions towards realizing the objectives that inspired the leaders in Miami led us to decide on a new hemispheric summit and to accept the offer of Chile to hold such an event in Santiago. The date for such a meeting was fixed for March 1998.

In this context, we directed the Summit Implementation Review Group (SIRG) to initiate a process of consultations to develop the themes that might form part of the agenda for such a Summit. Since then our governments have taken concrete steps in this respect.

Now, as we convene in Lima, Peru, we note with satisfaction the progress attained in implementing the Miami *Plan of Action,* and we, the co-Chairs, present this report on the status of the Summit, the results of which have been attained thanks to the collective efforts of the governments and other entities party to the process.

## PROGRESS SINCE PANAMA

We made several important advances in our common agenda during the last twelve months. While not exhaustive, the following list includes several significant steps taken in the implementation of the Miami *Plan of Action:*

At the invitation of the Government of Bolivia, hemispheric leaders gathered for the Summit of the Americas on Sustainable Development held in Santa Cruz, at which time they adopted a bold, new plan to give even greater impetus to the theme of sustainable development in the hemispheric agenda. At the Organization of American States, the implementation of the Santa Cruz Plan of Action has begun in the areas of health and education, sustainable agriculture and forestry, sustainable cities and communities, water resources and coastal areas, and energy and minerals. We are pleased to note that such efforts are well underway in that forum, specifically in the newly formed Inter-American Commission on Sustainable Development. The Secretary-General of the OAS will present a written report on the subject at the Santiago Summit. In support of the Santa Cruz Plan of Action, the Inter-American Development Bank has designated $10 billion for ongoing and future projects and the World Bank, $11 billion in projected lending for sustainable development.

The Ministers of Trade met in Belo Horizonte, Brazil, and recommended to the Heads of State and Government that the negotiations for the Free Trade Area of the Americas should begin in Santiago, Chile in March 1998; twelve working groups on technical trade issues will continue to meet in order to prepare the next ministerial meeting in San Jose, Costa Rica in February 1998.

The Inter-American Convention Against Corruption has entered into force, with 23 signatories and two countries having deposited instruments of ratification. The Convention, the first of its type in the world, demonstrates the hemisphere's commitment to fight the scourge of corruption. We approved in December 1996 the Anti-Drug Strategy in the Hemisphere, which was finalized at the OAS Inter-American Commission for Drug Abuse Control, and thereby agreed to work together to counteract all aspects of the cycle of illicit drug production, trafficking, and abuse.

Law enforcement experts from countries of the hemisphere met in May 1997 at OAS headquarters to discuss ways to improve the exchange of information and other measures of cooperation among member states to prevent and combat terrorism.

The Working Group on Human Rights and Democracy, chaired by Brazil and Canada, met at the OAS in December 1996 and approved administration of justice as a main priority, specifically the areas of police training; minimizing the number of pre-trial detainees and remedying inhumane prison conditions; as well as human rights education for judges, magistrates and other court officers.

The Committee on Hemispheric Financial Issues established a Technical Working Group to assist in completion of the Survey of Financial Systems; developed initial plans for training banking and securities regulators and for technical assistance in combating financial crimes; and established a Working Group on Small Economies. The second meeting of Western Hemisphere Finance Ministers is scheduled to be held in Santiago, Chile in December 1997.

At the Senior Telecommunications Officials meeting in September 1996, Summit governments approved a hemispheric plan of action on telecommunications infrastructure and agreed to a comprehensive set of guidelines on value-added services and equipment certification. Implementation is being carried out in several fora, particularly in the Inter-American Telecommunications Commission (OAS/CITEL). Energy ministers agreed in Santa Cruz, Bolivia, in July 1996 on priority areas for cooperation, and as a result, projects are being developed in areas such as rural electrification and renewable energy resources.

The Government of Argentina convened an Inter-American Hunger Conference to discuss hemispheric strategies in this field, mainly with regard to the problem of nutrition. One of the results of the meeting was to establish an Honorary Inter-American Council charged with promoting the substantive agreements reached on this occasion. The governments of Jamaica and Uruguay, as Responsible Coordinators of the Miami initiative on invigorating society, made a progress report on the status of civil society in the hemisphere, which has served as a foundation for the beginning of a new hemispheric program on public participation via the OAS.

As Responsible Coordinator of Initiative 16 of the Plan of Action, Mexico, with the support of Argentina and Chile, has developed a proposal for a Plan of Action to Achieve Universal Access to Education that was presented for consideration to the VIII SIRG Meeting that took place in Washington, D.C. March 5-6, 1997. At the suggestion of Mexico, the SIRG agreed that this proposal be forwarded to the OAS Committee on Inter-American Summits Management with the request that a group of government experts be established to review said proposal and that it be presented for consideration by the OAS Inter-American Council on Integral Development (CIDI).

On the health initiative, the First Ladies of the Americas, with the technical support of the Pan-American Health Organization (PAHO), pursued an important hemispheric campaign against measles. This has allowed a reduction of reported cases from 23,583 in 1994 to 1,464 in 1996. Government experts on women's issues adopted on April 24-26, 1997 in Montelimar, Nicaragua, a System of Indicators to monitor progress in strengthening the role of women in society. PAHO has developed and is currently implementing a plan of action to improve sanitation conditions and safe water supplies throughout the hemisphere.

The Partnership for Pollution Prevention has continued its work to eliminate lead from gasoline in the hemisphere. PAHO, the World Bank, and several U.S. technical agencies organized workshops and training courses to assist countries in developing national action plans for lead phase out.

In addition, the SIRG has met on three occasions since our last meeting to conduct a policy-level review of activities in the initiatives on cultural values, democracy and human rights, counternarcotics, building mutual confidence, hemispheric infrastructure, tourism, and education. We are grateful to those responsible coordinating countries and organizations that have taken the lead in Summit implementation, whose work has been significant in carrying out the Miami *Plan of Action*.

## THE SANTIAGO SUMMIT OF THE AMERICAS

The Santiago Summit presents the opportunity to carry out a broad evaluation of the process initiated in Miami and to make decisions necessary to carry it out. To this end, we ask the Responsible Coordinators of the Miami initiatives to present, on that occasion, written progress reports to the leaders.

The Santiago Summit will also constitute an opportunity of special significance to continue advancing the political dialogue and collective actions based on our common interests. Its results should translate into concrete agreements intended to solve the urgent needs of our peoples and to design a framework that will permit us to effectively face the challenges that the next millennium will present. To this end, it is necessary to deepen and improve the hemispheric framework of coordination and consultation and to prioritize the initiatives intended to solve the serious social problems that still affect our countries.

With this spirit, and after several rounds of negotiations and consultations among the governments of the Hemisphere, we recommend that the agenda for the Santiago Summit should grant particular importance to the theme of education, an essential element to make significant progress in the objectives that we have laid out. To this end, we suggest that this referred agenda consist of the following initiatives:

1. Education, to include action items on: exchange programs, distance education, new technologies, adult education, and worker training and skills improvement.

2. Preserving and Strengthening Democracy and Human Rights, to include action items on: education for democracy and human rights, protecting the rights of migrant workers, public participation, municipal and regional governments, anticorruption, counternarcotics, anti-terrorism, confidence and security building measures, judicial systems, and modernization of the state in relation to labor matters.

3. Economic Integration and Free Trade, to include action items on: advancing the Free Trade Area of the Americas, which is a keystone for regional integration and economic liberalization, capital markets development, science and technology, regional energy cooperation, and hemispheric infrastructure in transportation and telecommunications.

4. Eradication of Poverty and Discrimination, to include action items on: microenterprises and small- and medium-sized businesses, health, hunger, women, indigenous people, effective systems of property registration, and promotion of internationally accepted labor norms.

We will continue to conduct Summit preparations guided by the principles of transparency, openness, and consensus, and we welcome the input of our respective publics in constructing an agenda that interprets the interests and realities of our nations. We are motivated by the will to increase our mutual cooperation, and to strengthen our hemispheric community, and as neighbors, partners, and friends, make a real and lasting difference in the lives of all our people.

# III. Summit Documents

*Ambassador Juan Martabit was the National Summit Coordinator for the Republic of Chile.*

*These remarks were delivered at the Inaugural Session of the Ninth Meeting of the Summit Implementation Review Group on May 20, 1997, at Punte Del Este, Uruguay.*

## Remarks of the National Coordinator of Chile for the Summit of the Americas

*Juan Martabit*

His Excellency Mr. Carlos Perez del Castillo, Acting Minister of Foreign Affairs of the Republic of Uruguay, Mr. Counselor Thomas MacLarty, Special Envoy of President Clinton for the Americas, Ambassador Jeffrey Davidow, Fellow National Coordinators, Representatives of Regional Organizations:

In response to the kind invitation of the government of Uruguay, we are meeting today in this hospitable city.

Calling a meeting of this nature at Punta del Este makes it an event filled with symbolism: shared aspirations and goals, willpower for a collective effort, the generation of great expectations. In sum, experiences from which we must profit.

Thirty years ago, nineteen hemisphere leaders met in this same place "for the purpose of giving a more efficient political thrust to the objectives of the alliance for progress and to agree on the most appropriate methods to accelerate its implementation."

That is, to decide upon actions designed to achieve agreements to make the economic and social development of their peoples possible through the implementation of a common market.

The results of that historic meeting, the positive aspects of the process, its failures, and its reformulations, are widely known.

Thirty years later, a similar objective has called us here, to the same place.

The international and regional contexts are different, of course, as are the nations. The current process of cooperation and integration is more broadly representative, the means chosen are not comparable and the scheme itself, initiated in Miami, has its own characteristics.

Nevertheless, the spirit that moved our leaders in 1994 to structure a pact for the development and prosperity of the Americas responds to the same interests of those who met in Punta del Este 30 years ago: to design a joint project to attain a quantum leap forward in the quality of life and the opportunities of our peoples.

The mere mention of earlier attempts to develop collective efforts to enable the Americas to confront the problems afflicting them and make adequate use of the hemisphere's resources imposes an additional responsibility on us here.

We must be capable of serving the real and urgent necessities of our peoples, through concerted, clear and precise actions so that tangible results can be seen within a specific time.

The Miami Summit was an important step in that direction, in that it established an appropriate framework for the development of a hemisphere cooperation scheme and brought together a relatively balanced plan of action, with concrete actions to transform the region into an area in which its inhabitants can finally enjoy their rights, profit from and develop their capabilities, satisfy their aspirations, and participate more fully in government decisions.

The governments of the hemisphere have advanced toward this goal during the past two years and five months, implementing initiatives in a series of areas.

Nevertheless, we must recognize that additional efforts are still required to fully meet such objectives and offer our peoples an integral response to their requirements.

The Santiago Summit will serve such goals by deciding upon actions that can deepen the advances thus far attained. That is why it is necessary to formulate programs closely related to the social agenda, particularly to those aspects related to human resources.

If we can contribute to the strengthening of human rights, improve education and broaden the people's rights we will have met that challenge appropriately.

"The time and the occasion." as President Eduardo Frei Montalva said thirty years ago at Punta del Este, "require grandeur in our vision and in the decisions we make. These times and this occasion are no less than those faced by the men who fought for our independence."

Our peoples know that they live poor in a rich continent. Not only is misery present among them but so is the awareness and meaning of that misery as well as the possibility of overcoming it in the near future, as other countries have already done.

Developing this shared process we can achieve the bases to reach our goals in the upcoming years. If we do so, we will fulfill the purpose to which our hemispheric effort is directed.

# III. Summit Documents

*George A.O. Alleyne is the Director of the Pan American Health Organization, Pan American Sanitary Bureau, Regional Office for the Americas of the World Health Organization.*

*This speech was delivered on March 6, 1997, at the Eighth Summit Implementation Review Group, Summit of the Americas, Washington, D.C.*

# A Theme for the Santiago Summit

## George A.O. Alleyne

Let me repeat the welcome I gave yesterday and say how pleased I am to have Mr. Iglesias, Mr. Gaviria and Mr. Rosenthal with us today. It is always gratifying to see the institutions of the Inter-American system working in concert. Like my colleagues, I wish to give some of our ideas of what the agenda for the Santiago Summit might be and what might be the focus of attention of the Heads of State and Government when they meet next year. It is a tribute to the SIRG process that we are able to have these discussions and hopefully this Process will allow us to participate in refining the agenda and program as we go along.

We have to consider the thematic possibilities in the light of the degree of completion of the Plan of Action, and we, like others, will be helping our Member Governments to report on their progress in the specific areas. But I believe that the main areas of emphasis will develop in very much the same open and transparent way as occurred in 1994. The agenda will deal with some major areas of concern for all the countries — some real and burning problems of our societies. The issues that flow from this concern must be politically viable and give the possibility of genuine intersectoral action, and this does not only refer to the public sector; we refer to many of those actors of civil society that are increasingly vocal in the governance of our countries. The final criterion I see as important is that the theme should have operational principles and plans of action should favor a Pan American approach. There should be some specific attention given to the possibility, nay, the necessity of the countries of the Americas working together.

But even as we look at these criteria for establishing some kind of agenda, we will have to indicate what level of progress, if any, there has been. I was pleased to hear yesterday of the significant advances and accomplishments in the various areas. I believe that the considerations of the Heads of State should not have a backdrop of negatives, because, at least in the field of which we have some knowledge, the countries of the Americas can show progress.

Let me refer to some of the standard indicators of health and the way they have changed for the better. All of our countries show a steady reduction of their infant mortality rates, and life expectancy of their citizens is increasing. The maintenance of our Hemisphere free of poliomyelitis has to be one of the triumphs of public health of this century. To have rid our children of the scourge of paralysis from polio through eradicating the virus from our Hemisphere is a monument to the commitment of our governments and the dedication of numerous health workers. I am pleased to be able to acknowledge the support of the IDB and President Iglesias' personal interest in this effort, as well as from USAID. However, until the rest of the world has caught up with the Americas, we must maintain our vigilance and continue to insist on vaccination of our children.

On the occasion of the Miami Summit, I was privileged to address the First Ladies and could persuade them to focus their attention on another major enterprise the elimination of measles from our Hemisphere. The First Ladies responded magnificently and as a result of concerted effort at the country level, the results have been impressive indeed. In 1994, there were 23,583 cases of measles reported and confirmed in the Region; in 1996, this figure had fallen to 1,464 and for the last 12 months, as far as we know, there has been not a single case of measles imported into the United States of America from Latin America and the Caribbean. This has been another fine example of the Pan American approach to problems.

Almost every one of our countries is involved in the reform of their health services and I believe that the process will accelerate during the coming years. I believe that there is a growing confluence of concepts and practices between ourselves, ECLAC and the Inter-American Development Bank in this area.

The situation for some other specific diseases is also heartening. The countries of the Southern Cone have made tremendous stride in eliminating Chagas' Disease that had plagued them for decades if not centuries. I would also point to advances in such areas as oral health and the public health approach to violence, particularly the domestic violence that is almost always directed against women. The improvement in environmental health has been slow but I believe that the Santa Cruz Declaration has given us more assurance of what is the proper course. What has been done and the progress made is a stimulus for doing even more.

But the truth is that there are still major problems in health that cry out for attention. There are too many unacceptable differences in health status between and within countries. Too many children still never live to see their first birthday and will never be able to profit from the proposed educational reforms. Women still die needlessly in childbirth and the health differentials between the rich and the poor, the urban and rural communities are unacceptable. Cholera is still with us as an indication of our environmental deficiencies. We estimate that about 300 million people of the countries of Latin America and the Caribbean are threatened by diseases transmitted through drinking water. These are diseases such as typhoid fever, and a myriad of gastrointestinal infections. We can find many specific aetiological agents for these problems but for us, the overarching concerns that impede progress in improving the public's health are poverty and its sister inequity. These will be as dominant in 1998 as they were in 1994.

To address the health consequences of poverty and the inequities in health. we will have to continue to work to secure equitable access to services as the 1994 Summit Plan instructed us to do, but in addition there has to be an appreciation at the highest level as to what are the true determinants of health. All must appreciate that it is the social and physical environment, the behavior patterns of groups and individuals as well as health services that impact on health. That appreciation is as critical as the understanding that concern for health is not only a moral imperative, but it is absolutely necessary if the investments made to increase economic growth are going to bear fruit. In this forum I need not explain the relationship between health and a country's economic development, or between health and the possibility of domestic stability and even democracy. I need not strengthen the arguments made yesterday for an emphasis on education by emphasizing how intimately health and education are linked and mutually supportive.

But it is not enough to suggest that we continue more of the same. There have been advances in the last few years that lead us to propose a major health theme for the Santiago Summit that builds on the agreements reached in Miami. It is a theme of the future that has the seeds of success in achievements of the past. I wish to see us explore the theme of "Health Technology Linking the Americas."

Why am I certain of success? It is because the history of health conditions of the Americas has shown the impact of health technologies in reducing the burden of disease, increasing life expectancy and decreasing the number of children and mothers who die. In addition, we now have the possibility of making even more health technology available to our countries and shortening the interval between generation of knowledge and development of the appropriate technology. I wish to cite a few examples of specific initiatives that could be developed under this rubric.

We would propose a Regional initiative for vaccines that will address research, development, production and utilization of vaccines. This initiative builds on the success of national immunization programs in the Region such as polio eradication and elimination of measles and neonatal tetanus. This initiative would incorporate the thrust in our Region for increased application of biotechnology. It could stimulate even more collaboration among some of the larger developing countries and would provide a concrete area of common interest to agencies like ours and the multilateral lending institutions. It is 100 years since the first vaccine was given, but the speed of development in the last few years and the real possibilities of the wide application of these agents make it clear to us that this is the technology of the future. If there is one thing on which all health workers agree, it is that vaccines represent the most cost-effective health technology yet devised.

We could have, in a relatively short time, millions of children and adults in the Americas protected against vaccine preventable diseases through the wide availability of quality vaccines. We could have a critical mass of scientists trained to participate in the new advances in biotechnology and we could envisage a genuine public-private partnership in which there is benefit to all. There are already some countries in Latin America that have made significant investment in constructing or modernizing their facilities. Such an initiative would strengthen them and make it possible to widen the net of those involved.

Health technology would embrace communications, because there is no doubt that the rapid development of information technology will revolutionize our approach to health. But the information to be managed by the new technology is in many ways restricted by the reliability of the basic data. Thus, we envisage a major effort to improve the capacity of all our countries of the Americas to capture health information, and perhaps restore some prestige and emphasis to the critical area of vital statistics. We will never be able to measure need and speak intelligently of inequities in health unless we have basic data on health.

The information technology will see other uses. The Region is moving towards the use of telemedicine as a mechanism for increasing access to some services. There are discussions on the development of simple devices that can capture data at the point of collection, thus facilitating analysis and use. The world of information technology also envisages the democratization of health information such that more persons have access to the data, information and knowledge to make decisions. There could be strengthening of existing regional networks of health science information through use of better technology such that all health care workers have access to material to help them make correct decisions.

We would envisage better communication to support the harmonization efforts in the area of essential drugs. There is much to be done in order to standardize and define better the common regulations and requirements to register and produce essential drugs in the countries of the Americas. PAHO has some experience in this area through its joint work with some of the subregional commissions on drugs.

A focus on health technology linking the Americas would include our capacity to monitor the emergence of new diseases and the resurgence or reemergence of old ones that we had ignored. AIDS will not be the last epidemic. The Ebola epidemic of Zaire frightened the world with the realization that diseases can be rapidly transmitted through our modern means of communication. We are now appreciating the magnitude of the problem of tuberculosis- an estimated 60,000 to 75,000 of our citizens in the Americas died from this disease in 1995 and over 400,000 new cases occurred. We cannot allow this to continue.

The foundation for any logical approach to these diseases is a good surveillance system, good research and laboratory infrastructure and perhaps strengthening of the International Sanitary Regulations. The possibility of a good surveillance system will depend in large measure on the use of suitable information technology.

We must not forget the possibility of new technologies improving our environmental health. We know that the water can be protected at various places - we can ensure the safety of the water sources, we can apply physichochemical means and try to make safe water available in conventional distribution systems. In some countries the systems that are proposed are no doubt efficient, but they are costly. Capital investment for piped water systems reach over $100 per person served. We can demonstrate technologies for use at the household level that cost no more than $1.00 to $4.00 per family per year. Once the water is available, there is no excuse for a family not to have it as a benefit rather than a risk to health. There are similar newer developments in the field of solid waste disposal and promising ideas for returning waste to agricultural areas, thereby in the medium term, enhancing food production. I believe that these approaches will allow us to give form and substance to some of the items of the Plan of Action for the Sustainable Development of the Americas that accompanied the Declaration of Santa Cruz de la Sierra.

An initiative for Health Technology Linking the Americas will have enormous potential for public-private partnerships in areas beside vaccine development. Telecommunications is one example that comes to mind immediately.

I said initially that any sectoral issues put before the Santiago Summit should be within the context of the overriding theme of reducing poverty and inequity, be politically viable, give possibility of intersectoral and interagency collaboration and foster the Pan American approach. I believe that the initiative of Health Technology Linking the Americas could fulfill these criteria. The basic thesis is that this would enhance health and reduce inequities. The wide application of the health technologies I have mentioned will improve health and thereby reduce poverty and particularly the health information technologies will help to define the inequities more clearly as well as giving the possibilities of reducing them.

I could show the political viability of this approach in a more detailed proposal pointing out the advantage of Presidents and Heads of State being able to inform their people of specific actions that affect their daily life and their living. And there is no doubt that all I have mentioned would facilitate collaborative work among the American countries.

Mr. Chairman, the Pan American Health Organization, by its very name, speaks to its purpose of improving the health of the Americas. We hope that the mandates of the Santiago Summit will, as did the Miami Summit, provide space for those actions that have health as a major concern.

We in PAHO will be ready to support a process of consultation with governments and civil society that will lead to a Pan American agreement in Santiago on improving Health for All in the Americas. Our mission is... to cooperate technically with the Member Countries and to stimulate cooperation among them in order that, while maintaining a healthy environment and charting a course to sustainable human development, the peoples of the Americas may achieve Health for All and by All.

We will continue to work, as President Clinton proclaimed in his closing speech at the Plenary Session of the I Summit, to ensure that dichos become hechos, that "words are turned into deeds."

# IV. Preparatory Work by Regional Organizations

# IV. PREPARATORY WORK BY REGIONAL ORGANIZATIONS

# The Hemispheric Summit Process and the Organization of American States:
## The OAS and Its Contribution to the Santiago Summit

*The **Organization of American States (OAS)** is the world's oldest regional organization, dating back to the First International Conference of American States, held in Washington, D.C., from October 1889 to April 1890. The OAS currently has 35 Member States. In addition, the Organization has granted Permanent Observer status to 37 States, as well as to the European Union.*

*The basic purposes of the OAS are as follows: to strengthen the peace and security of the continent; to promote and consolidate representative democracy, with due respect for the principle of nonintervention; to prevent possible causes of difficulties and to ensure the pacific settlement of disputes that may arise among the Member States; to provide for common action on the part of those States in the event of aggression; to seek the solution of political, juridical and economic problems that may arise among them; to promote, by cooperative action, their economic, social and cultural development and to achieve an effective limitation of conventional weapons that will make it possible to devote the largest amount of resources to the economic and social development of the Member States.*

© 1998 Organization of American States, Office of Summit Follow-Up

## 1. INTRODUCTION

In compliance with the mandate of the twenty-seventh regular session of the General Assembly, the General Secretariat is presenting a proposed Work Plan outlining the steps that need to be taken to effectively support the commitments made during the hemispheric process. These suggestions are put forth particularly in light of the upcoming Summit, which is scheduled to take place in Santiago, Chile, in 1998.

It has been noted on recent occasions that as the process of dialogue and hemispheric agreements begins to consolidate, it would be convenient that it be established on a solid institutional basis in order to ensure a gradual and cumulative process. In this sense, this proposal advances suggestions regarding the support that the Organization will be able to provide to the process of institutionalization and follow-up of the agreements of the hemispheric summits.

This proposal did not come in from the cold. Over the past three years, the OAS has gained invaluable experience by supporting the member states, through different mechanisms, in the execution of the initiatives adopted in the 1994 Summit *Plan of Action*. Specifically, the OAS has supported the work of 14 of the 23 initiatives approved in Miami. This has enabled the OAS to acquire valuable first-hand knowledge about the preparation of meetings of high-level government officials and experts; the elaboration of documents and technical support materials necessary for the discussions of the countries' delegates; and the compilation and distribution of documents in order to guarantee the successful outcome of the meetings. At the same time, the Organization has become a forum where the member states can easily access information and other support mechanisms.

In order to further this experience and better serve the member states, the Office of the Secretary-General has prepared this proposal. In accordance with the General Assembly mandate, this proposal focuses primarily on the tasks that will be required to undertake the activities that will ensure the follow-up of the initiatives adopted in Santiago, Chile, by the Heads of State and Government.

Furthermore, this proposal includes some ideas regarding the possible contributions of the OAS during the pre-Summit period. These suggestions address specific requirements expressed by some of the member states who play a coordinating role, in accordance with the agreements reached by the member states in the Summit Implementation Review Group (SIRG) meetings.

Finally, the proposed Work Plan addresses the financial implications of each task identified in this document. In this sense, we are only putting forth the general criteria which we consider essential to bear in mind during the discussions regarding the identification of responsibilities and assignment of tasks during the follow-up process. Ultimately, a detailed proposal will depend on the specific mandates that the Organization receives at the Santiago Summit.

## 2. THE OAS DURING THE PRE-SUMMIT PROCESS

The OAS, in coordination with the various institutions of the inter-American system, is prepared to provide support and contribute effectively to the work of SIRG and of the coordinating countries at the upcoming Summit of the Americas. The contribution of the OAS could be in terms of preparing the documents requested both by SIRG and by the countries coordinating the issues, as well as in terms of organizing and supporting the preparatory meetings according to specific issues.

With that perspective, the OAS is supporting the requests of some of the coordinating countries to prepare initiatives by subject matter. To date, the OAS is supporting activities in the following areas:

### a. Education

The OAS has participated in the preparatory meetings and is collaborating closely with the coordinating countries in the preparation of the document which is being submitted to the member states at this SIRG meeting. The OAS has also prepared a working document aimed at contributing to the global discussion on education policies.

### b. Preservation and Strengthening of Democracy and Human Rights

The General Secretariat has submitted to the member states two proposals which are in the process of being implemented with the participation of the multilateral banks. These are:

- The *Program for Studies on Democracy*; and
- *The Support Program for Newly Elected Governments.*

We have also distributed a revised version of the working document entitled "Representative Democracy in the Americas," which is a proposed framework for action for the inter-American system. This document, submitted to the member states by the Secretary-General in April 1997, contains some reflections as a contribution to the general discussion on this issue.

Regarding human rights, a proposal is being submitted on how to continue the process of strengthening the system to promote and protect human rights, an initiative of the OAS member states recently approved at the last General Assembly.

Finally, regarding both democracy and human rights, we are making available to the member states documents that include contributions on judicial cooperation, public safety and security, and corruption.

### c. Economic Integration and Free Trade

In addition to the work pertaining to Free Trade Area of the Americas (FTAA) being carried out by the OAS through its Tripartite Committee, the Organization has been asked to provide support to the Labor initiative as well. This undertaking will be carried out within the framework of the next meeting of the Inter-American Conference of Ministers of Labor to which the OAS already provides technical support.

The OAS will also support preparatory meetings in the areas of science and technology, as well as in telecommunications.

### d. Eradication of Poverty and Discrimination

The OAS is supporting two specific sub-issues.

- *Public participation:* We are cooperating with the coordinating countries in the identification of initiatives derived from the Inter-American Strategy for Public Participation.
- *Women:* The Inter-American Commission of Women (CIM), a specialized organization of the OAS, is helping with the organization of the second preparatory meeting scheduled to take place in October. At that time, the coordinators will assign specific tasks to CIM.

### e. Social Development

Finally, the OAS General Secretariat will submit, at the Santiago Summit, a progress report regarding the execution of the Santa Cruz Summit *Plan of Action*. This will include information on the progress made at the national level and on the advances made by the international organizations committed to the process.

## 3. FOLLOW-UP PROCESS OF THE SANTIAGO SUMMIT: THE OAS IS READY FOR THE NEW CHALLENGES.

Aware that the future of the OAS depends to a great extent on its ability to respond efficiently and in a timely manner to the needs and challenges of its member states, the Organization is prepared to play a useful and supplementary role in the fulfillment of the commitments undertaken by the Heads of State and Government at the next Summit. In this context, the General Secretariat recommends the establishment of a mechanism to institutionalize and follow up the process of hemispheric summits. It would be based on two main principles:

### a. Global Coordination of the Process under the Responsibility of the Foreign Ministries

The foreign ministries are responsible for the political negotiations and general coordination of the summits. One of the keys to the success of the summit process has been making the foreign ministries responsible for the negotiation of the agendas and for the fulfillment of the mandates of these meetings. The continuing participation of the Vice Ministers and other high-level officials, as forums for negotiations and general coordination, will guarantee a successful follow-up of the meetings of the Santiago Summit. This structure has been one of the main reasons why the follow-up process of the Miami Summit was so successful. Two factors in particular contributed to this success: first, the Vice Ministers participated in the meetings with full authority to adopt decisions and agreements quickly. Second, the work method proved to be responsive and enforceable, which enabled fluid and effective negotiations.

It is for these reasons that the General Secretariat has decided to introduce the possibility of adopting a similar mechanism to follow up on the Santiago meetings. Bearing in mind the objective to advance the process of institutionalization without altering the above-mentioned characteristics, the OAS could host the execution of these meetings at its headquarters and maintain a coordination mechanism at the Vice Ministerial level by providing the process with administrative and technical support, institutional memory, and at the same time maintaining the flexibility and efficiency of the process.

### b. Follow-up According to Specific Issues

Following up on the specific issues of the Miami Summit at regular meetings has also provided a global vision of the execution of the Miami *Plan of Action*. However, once this stage has been completed, we believe that in the future it would be more efficient to avoid using a uniform and homogeneous mechanism.

As the agreements of the *Plan of Action* of the Santiago Summit become more and more technical, the follow-up process must *be adapted to the characteristics and specificities of each issue in particular*. This would mean that, when appropriate, follow-up tasks would be assigned to the pertinent experts in each country as well as to the coordinators of the foreign ministries.

### c. OAS Contribution to the Hemispheric Summit Process

Based on those principles, the OAS is prepared to create a mechanism to support the follow-up of the hemispheric summits in order to carry out the general coordination of the work of the Organization in the following aspects:

- organize and support the regular meetings of the national coordinators of the foreign ministries and sectoral authorities;
- prepare the technical documents to support the work of those meetings;
- serve as administrative or technical secretariat, as required; and
- maintain the institutional memory of the process.

This coordinating mechanism could be implemented at no additional cost to the Organization within the framework of a timely fulfillment of the contributions of the member states. The individual responsible for coordination would work with the staff of the OAS. S/he would be located in the Office of the Secretary-General and be directly responsible to him. S/he would work in close coordination with the specific areas of the Organization which are already involved in support tasks. The coordinating mechanism could provide support to the OAS Special Committee on Inter-American Summits Management and will ensure a constant flow of information to the Permanent Council of the Organization. Finally, it will serve as a focal contact point to channel the requests that both members states and non-governmental organizations submit to the OAS. All this will ensure a centralized, organized, and efficient coordination under the political responsibility of the foreign ministries with responsive and effective OAS support.

Apart from the institutional arrangements that the General Secretariat of the OAS may adopt in the fulfillment of its responsibilities, the OAS has the capability to provide the following support:

- Serve as a multilateral political forum to create consensus in an institutionalized framework so that the processes become cumulative projects and the region's asymmetries are balanced.
- Support activities requested by the member states for the implementation of the activities defined in Santiago.
- Use of existing institutional mechanisms to facilitate summit follow-up, such as meetings and conferences of ministers and sectoral authorities of the member states. This is already taking place in the areas of education, labor, social development, environment, social investment funds, telecommunications, science and technology, drug abuse and drug trafficking, and women. This year the ministers of justice will be included. In all these meetings, the OAS has served as Technical and Administrative Secretariat. The use of these modalities will allow for a greater coordination between the execution of the agreements reached in the meetings and summits and the specific sectoral policies of each country. The Executive Secretariat of CIDI is preparing a study on the ministerial meetings that are taking place within the OAS framework. The study also describes the type of support that it is providing and suggests how to take on the follow-up of sectoral issues. This document will be submitted to the SIRG at its next preparatory meeting.
- Coordination among regional institutions. As has already been indicated, as long as the mandates that arise from the summits have an inter-sectoral nature, follow-up and support activities must be the responsibility of those institutions that have a comparative advantage in each area. This involves mobilizing resources and activities of organizations such as the Inter-American Development Bank (IDB), the Economic Commission for Latin America and the Caribbean, the Andean Development Corporation, among others. Effective follow-up of the process requires a specific mandate by the countries in order to establish a lasting system of coordination between the organizations providing support to the follow-up of the Santiago Summit.
- Survey of the region's various efforts on each subject, exchanging information with the international agencies in order to avoid a duplication of efforts among the countries, international organizations and cooperation agencies.
- Institutional memory, documentation center, and Website of the Summit Process. As the summit process and hemispheric dialogue consolidate as a mechanism of consultation and periodic deliberation, it is necessary to define where the institutional memory of the process will reside. At the same time, it's important to centralize this information to facilitate and guarantee easy access to it by the member states and governments. For this reason, the OAS would create a Website on the Internet which would include all information pertinent to the summit process beginning in Miami in 1994 and continuing with the work undertaken by SIRG.
- Coordinate all efforts by the member states and international agencies to create a technological Network of the Americas to exchange information in all areas regarding the follow-up of the Summit.
- Administrative Secretariat of the various follow-up meetings. The OAS has the necessary administrative structure to support the execution of these meetings. This includes, among other things, appropriate facilities, secretariat staff, and translation and interpretation services when the meetings take place at OAS headquarters.
- Technical Secretariat. Because of the high technical level and specificity of hemispheric dialogue, an in-depth analytical study in the various areas is required in order to nurture and focus it. The OAS, together with other institutions, can prepare documents for discussion, comparative studies, and other analytical instruments which will enrich the discussions of the regional authorities on sectoral policies.
- Forum for the exchange of experiences. Here, the OAS has ample experience which will enable the expansion of horizontal cooperation in the region in the areas defined in Santiago.

## 4. FINANCING AND INSTITUTIONAL ARRANGEMENTS AT THE OAS

The General Secretariat believes that the pre-Santiago Summit activities will not raise additional costs to the Organization. Each area's budget has resources which, although somewhat limited, are sufficient to finance the activities in this stage. On the other hand, the budget approved in Lima has a specific amount allotted for meetings and specialized conferences. All of this is obviously subject to the punctual fulfillment of the financial obligations of the member states to the Organization.

With regard to the following stage, and independently from the agreements and mandates which arise in Santiago, the consolidation of the summit process as an opportunity for hemispheric dialogue will require substantive decisions so as to optimize existing follow-up mechanisms, including:

Incorporating the Summit mandates through General Assembly Resolutions. The source of funding for the activities must be clearly defined. In this sense, the Special Committee on Inter-American Summits Management can make a significant contribution to the process.

The Committee on Administrative and Budgetary Affairs must be given the authority to expeditiously adjust the budget according to the mandates of the General Assembly.

Clear mandates by the Heads of State and Government to initiate an institutionalized process of coordination between the institutions of the inter-American system to optimize the implementation and the use of resources, as well as to better serve the countries of the region.

The member states must also study supplementary mechanisms to ensure the appropriate financing of the Summit agreements when they go beyond the capabilities of regional organizations. This is true for both specific follow-up tasks as well as for the meetings in general.

# IV. Preparatory Work by Regional Organizations

# Summit of the Americas Information Network, Responsible Coordinators

| Mandate | Responsible Coordinator | Co-Coordinator | Responsible Unit/Office in the OAS | Other Responsible International Organizations |
|---|---|---|---|---|
| 1. Education | Mexico | Argentina, Chile, United States | UDSE, CIDI | PAHO, IDB, World Bank, ECLAC, UNESCO |
| 2. Democracy and Human Rights | Brazil | Canada, Peru | UPD, IACHR | |
| 3. Education for Democracy | Paraguay | | UDSE, UPD | |
| 4. Civil Society | Dominican Republic, Jamaica | | UPD, UDSMA, OSFU, all areas of the General Secretariat | IDB |
| 5. Migrant Workers | United States | El Salvador, Mexico | IACHR, UDSE | |
| 6. Strengthening Municipal and Regional Administrations | United States | Chile, Honduras | UPD | World Bank, IDB |
| 7. Corruption | Venezuela | | Legal Affairs | |
| 8. Prevention and Control of Illicit Consumption of and Traffic in Drugs and Psychotropic Substances and other Related Crimes | United States | Argentina, Bolivia Colombia, Jamaica, Mexico | CICAD | |
| 9. Terrorism | Argentina | | Legal Affairs | |
| 10. Building Confidence and Security Among States | Chile | Argentina, Peru | Hemispheric Security Coordinator of the General Secretariat | UN |
| 11. Strengthening of Justice Systems and Judiciaries | Argentina, Uruguay | United States | Legal Affairs | |
| 12. Modernization of the State in Labor Matters | United States | Bolivia | UDSE | ILO, BID |
| 13. FTAA | Canada (rotating basis) | Argentina | Trade Unit | IDB, ECLAC |
| 14. Strengthening, Modernizing and Integrating Financial Markets | Mexico | | (Trade Unit) | IDB |

Continued on next page

| Mandate | Responsible Coordinator | Co-Coordinator | Responsibzle Unit/Office in the OAS | Other Responsible International Organizations |
|---|---|---|---|---|
| 15. Science and Technology | Colombia | Bolivia, Uruguay | Office of Science and Technology | |
| 16. Regional Energy Cooperation | Argentina, United States, Venezuela | | (Trade Unit, CIDI) | IDB, ECLAC |
| 17. Hemispheric Infrastructure: A. General Infrastructure B. Transportation C. Telecommunications | Chile, IDB Chile | Argentina Ecuador | (OSFU, Trade Unit) CITEL | IDB, ECLAC, ICAO, IMO ECLAC, ITU, IDB |
| 18. Fostering the Development of Micro, Small and Medium Size Enterprises | IDB | Argentina, Chile | (UDSE) | ECLAC, IDB |
| 19. Property Registration | United States | El Salvador | | World Bank, IDB |
| 20. Health Technology | PAHO | Argentina, Chile | | PAHO, World Bank, IDB |
| 21. Women | Nicaragua | Argentina, Chile | CIM | ECLAC, IDB, World Bank, PAHO |
| 22. Basic Rights of Workers | | Brazil | Legal Affairs | ILO, IDB, WTO |
| 23. Indigenous Populations | Canada | | UPD, Legal Affairs, UDSE | |
| 24. Hunger and Malnutrition | Argentina | | | (PAHO) |
| 25. Sustainable Development | OAS | Bolivia | UDSMA | UN |
| 26. Cooperation | Chile | Argentina, Brazil, Colombia, Mexico, United States, Venezuela | (CIDI, all areas, generally) | PAHO, ECLAC, World Bank, IDB, UNESCO) |
| 27. Summit of the Americas Follow-Up | All signatory governments, through the SIRG | — | Secretary-General of the OAS, through OSFU | PAHO, ECLAC, World Bank, IDB |

Entire contents © 1998 Organization of American States, Office of Summit Follow-Up

# IV. PREPARATORY WORK BY REGIONAL ORGANIZATIONS

*Pan American Health Organization, Regional Office of the World Health Organization*

*The **Pan American Health Organization (PAHO)** is an international agency specializing in health. Its mission is to cooperate technically with the Member Countries and to stimulate cooperation among them in order that, while maintaining a healthy environment and charting a course to sustainable human development, the peoples of the Americas may achieve Health for All and by All.*

# Report on Progress in Implementing the Health Initiative: Equitable Access to Basic Health Services

In accordance with the 1994 Miami Plan of Action, the Pan American Health Organization/World Health Organization (PAHO/WHO), in its capacity as regional coordinator, presents herewith a summary of progress achieved in regional work towards the goals of Initiative 17: Equitable Access to Basic Health Services. Progress in other initiatives also related to PAHO's work in the Hemisphere is also reported. In addition, in parallel with the SOA a Symposium on Health of the Children of the Americas was held by the Wives of Heads of States and of Governments of the Americas. Several actions have resulted from this symposium that also have an impact on Initiative 17 and related ones. These are also covered in this report.

## INITIATIVE 17: EQUITABLE ACCESS TO BASIC HEALTH SERVICES

Despite impressive gains in the Hemisphere, limitations on health services access and quality have resulted in persistently high child and maternal mortality among the rural poor and indigenous groups.

*Governments will:*

I. Endorse the maternal and child health objectives of the 1990 World Summit for Children, the 1994 Nariño Accord and the 1994 International Conference on Population and Development, and reaffirm their commitment to reduce child mortality by one-third and maternal mortality by one-half from 1990 levels by the year 2000.

### Actions taken since December 1994

2000 goal: Reduction of infant and under-five child mortality rates by one-third, between 1990 and the year 2000, or to 50 to 70 per 1,000 live births, respectively, whichever is less.

Infant Mortality Rate (IMR) ranges from 7 to 98 per 1,000 live births in Canada and Haiti respectively. Aruba, Cuba, the United States, and the Cayman Islands also show rates below 10 per 1,000. All other Caribbean countries, Argentina, Chile, Costa Rica, French Guyana, Panamá, Puerto Rico, Uruguay and Venezuela have rates higher than 10 but below 30 per 1,000 live births. Under-five mortality rates are at least 10 to 15% higher than the IMR values; the countries' classification remains the same.

The Americas have developed in these years stronger national surveillance systems for vaccine-preventable diseases, which are also being used to monitor other emerging and re-emerging diseases. Immunization coverage for children under 1 year of age for diphtheria, tetanus, pertussis, polio, measles and tuberculosis has reached, in average, levels above 80%. This figure confirms that the vast majority of children in the Region are protected against these diseases. There have also been important advances to improve the capacity of countries to assure that the vaccines children receive are safe.

**2000 goal:** Reduction of the maternal mortality rate by half from 1990 to the year 2000

Although there is a great discrepancy in regard to the reliability of maternal mortality data due to recognized sub-registration, efforts have been made to improve surveillance systems in order to permit more evidence based planning.

In only two countries, Canada and the United States, rates are below 20 maternal deaths per 100,000 live births. One-fourth of the countries, namely Argentina, Costa Rica, Cuba, Chile, Mexico and Uruguay, have levels ranging from 20 to 49 maternal deaths per 100,000 live births. Bolivia, Guatemala, Haiti, Honduras and Peru registered mortality levels above 150 maternal deaths per 100,000 live births, and the rest of the countries displayed values in the 50 to 149 range. Analysis of the information shows that most of these deaths were due to hemorrhage, abortion, and hypertension.

*Highlights of regional activities are the following:*

During the period, the majority of the countries of the Region have updated and revised their National Plans for the Reduction of Maternal Mortality.

PAHO actions in this area have been directed by the Regional Plan for the Reduction of Maternal Mortality in the Region of the Americas whose goals relating the reduction of maternal mortality, improvements in coverage and quality of care are similar to the Summit's. In addition, an agreement was signed between USAID and PAHO for a new regional project in which the Mother Care and Quality Assurance Project of University Research Corporation will participate. Its goal is to improve emergency obstetric care in eleven countries (Bolivia, Brazil, Dominican Republic, El Salvador, Ecuador, Guatemala, Haiti, Honduras, Nicaragua, Paraguay and Peru).

PAHO has initiated a new regional project for Adolescent Reproductive Health in 14 countries supported with UNFPA funds. It is expected that this will contribute to adolescent pregnancy prevention.

A recent increase in investment from several development banks (IDB, World Bank) and other donors in maternal health components and specific maternal mortality activities has been observed in their projects in Peru, Haiti, Ecuador, Colombia, Mexico, Caribbean Islands, Bolivia, Dominican Republic, El Salvador, Guatemala, Honduras, Paraguay, Venezuela and Nicaragua. These institutions have agreed to take the issue into consideration in the development of new projects.

The adoption of the maternal mortality issue as one of the priorities in the Wives of Heads of States and Governments of the Americas Meeting of La Paz, Bolivia 1996 has given strength and focus in many countries to actions to reduce this problem. A follow-up report was presented to their Seventh Conference, which took place in Panamá in October 1997.

## Future steps

### 1. Reduction of Child Mortality

The struggle over child and infant mortality has been more successful among the under-one than in the one-to-five age group. Nevertheless, it is believed that the pace of decline is sufficient to reach the goals in the Region, with the exception of the six countries — Bolivia, Brazil, Guatemala, Haiti, Nicaragua and Peru — which exhibit the highest values in both rates (their IMR rate is higher than 50 per 1,000 live births). Special programs are needed to double or triple the tempo of decline in these countries.

### 2. Reduction of Maternal Mortality

Most pregnancy-related deaths can be prevented by a combination of reproductive health services, proper management of labor and delivery, and access to life-saving essential obstetric care when unexpected complications arise. The Regional Plan contemplates a regional version of the "Mother-Baby-Package" recommended in the Safe Motherhood Initiative, training courses for birth attendants and decentralized application of integrated approaches to reproductive health — maternal care, family planning, prevention and treatment of reproductive tract infections — within the primary health care system.

Recognition of the maternal mortality tragedy as a social imperative for action is essential for achieving results. Keeping the problem in the public agenda and involving the community responsibilities for maternal care are strategies which will support change. Improvement and analysis in the surveillance systems, investigation of each maternal death, and policy and legislation changes to support safe motherhood will provide reliable information for planning.

II. Endorse a basic package of clinical, preventive and public health services consistent with World Health Organization, Pan American Health Organization (PAHO) and World Bank recommendations and with the Program of Action agreed to at the 1994 International Conference on Population and Development. The package will address child, maternal and reproductive health interventions, including prenatal, delivery and postnatal care, family planning information and services, and HIV/AIDS prevention, as well as immunizations and programs combating the other major causes of infant mortality. The plans and programs will be developed according to a mechanism to be decided upon by each country.

## Actions taken since December 1994

For a number of years, PAHO has worked with member countries to develop a package of basic services. While each country has a different pattern of health delivery services, and different mixes of private and public systems, there is general support for the concept of clinical, preventive and public health services packages. Such packages of health services are part of the general debate about sector reform being conducted in almost every country of the Region.

However, during the period, PAHO and UNICEF, in collaboration with the countries of the Hemisphere, have been working together to develop a strategy to combat in an integrated way the leading diseases that affect children younger than 5 years. The strategy for Integrated Management of Childhood Illness (IMCI) has proved an effective instrument for the early detection and appropriate treatment of the main health problems affecting children, as well as for the integrated education of parents and other caregivers regarding disease prevention and the provision of proper care in the home. The health problems selected and included under the IMCI strategy were found to be the reason for most consultations at the health services and most hospitalizations and deaths in infants after the first week of life, namely: pneumonia and influenza, intestinal infectious diseases, nutritional deficiencies, meningitis, septicemia, vaccine-preventable diseases (diphtheria, whooping cough, tetanus, and measles), and malaria. The importance of this group of illnesses in terms of infant mortality is that they account for 5 out of every 10 deaths both in infants 1 week to 11 months and in children 1 to 4 years of age.

With the cooperation of the Spanish Cooperation Agency, between 1996 and 1997, nine of the 12 countries (Bolivia, Brazil, the Dominican Republic, Ecuador, El Salvador, Haiti, Honduras, Nicaragua and Peru) with an estimated Infant Mortality Rate (IMR) over 40 per 1,000 live births (table 1) adopted the IMCI strategy and initiated its implementation at the level of the local health services. In addition, Argentina, with an IMR of fewer than 40 per 1,000 live births, also adopted the strategy and was the venue for subregional activities presenting the IMCI strategy (table 2). Paraguay also joins the countries adopting the initiative. In nine of these, Operational Plans were prepared for the national level and in five for the local level. Two more countries are in the process of finalizing Operational Plans.

IMCI Clinical Courses and training of health personnel were initiated in nine countries. Up to December 1997, 1,378 workers at different levels of the health systems have been trained, of which 1,105 correspond to the countries with the higher indexes.

USAID, the Pan American Health Organization (PAHO), and the Basic Support for Institutionalizing Child Survival Project (BASICS) collaborated also on the design of a five year LAC Regional IMCI results package for which USAID provided a 5 million dollar grant for the period 1997 to 2001. The activities have mainly targeted strengthening country-level IMCI capacity. PAHO and BASICS have been working in a unique partnership since the inception of the IMCI strategy and have been able to synthesize the evolving state-of-the-art in child health care and IMCI worldwide for adaptation and introduction of the strategy into the LAC regional context.

As regards to other diseases, activities conducted in several countries like Peru and Mexico were designed to raise the population's awareness about respiratory infections (also known as ARI's). The standardized protocol for the elimination of intestinal parasites in children (PEPIN) was used as part of the strategy in order to reduce morbidity from geohelminths through health education and social communication activities.

Finally, a number of countries are developing a "basic package" of health care to be guaranteed to all citizens, including access to family planning. The countries of the Region are moving towards the 70% mark of prevalence of contraceptive usage for women in union who are utilizing some method of family planning. Quality of care is an essential element of the delivery of reproductive health services, and several different initiatives are promoting this in the areas of family planning, Safe Motherhood, prevention of HIV/AIDS and cancer of the cervix. Close coordination among donors and other international agencies, like USAID, CIDA, SIDA, and GTZ, has resulted in increased activity of an efficient manner within the countries and better attention to priorities within the country plan of action.

## Future steps

In the coming years the regional and country level activities will focus on strengthening the application of the IMCI strategy in the health services and extending coverage. To achieve this there are two lines of action planned: One is to apply the appropriate organizational changes to the health systems to adapt them to the needs of the application of the IMCI strategy. The other is to incorporate Community Health Workers (CHW) into the application of the strategy while strengthening the social communication and educational component with the goal of improving the community practices with respect to care of children in the home.

In addition, the incorporation of mechanisms and instruments for monitoring and evaluation should continue to be emphasized. This follow-up on the results of the application of the IMCI strategy in terms of reductions in morbidity and mortality in children, as well as in the characteristics of their care both in the health services and in the home, is invaluable for future improvements to care.

Finally, the incorporation of the IMCI strategy in the rest of the countries of the Region, as in certain areas of the countries with higher IMRs, will require expansion plans to incorporate other illnesses and prevalent health problems, such as perinatal afflictions, accidents, developmental difficulties, etc.

III. Develop or update country action plans or programs for reforms to achieve child, maternal and reproductive health goals and ensure universal, non-discriminatory access to basic services, including health education and preventive health care programs. The plans and programs will be developed according to a mechanism to be decided upon by each country. Reform would encompass essential community-based services for the poor, the disabled, and indigenous groups; stronger public health infrastructure; alternative means of financing, managing and providing services; quality assurance; and greater use of non-governmental actors and organizations.

## Actions taken since December 1994

Health sector reform has been defined as a process directed at introducing substantial changes into the various functions of the sector, with the purpose of increasing equity in the provision of health services, efficacy in its management and efficiency in the satisfaction of the health needs of the population. In compliance with the mandate of the Summit of the Americas and the PAHO Special Meeting on Reform (subject to be addressed later on in this report), PAHO was the agency chosen to establish national evaluation mechanisms for monitoring the process of health reform, its results and effects, based on a conceptual framework encompassing elements like equity, quality, efficiency, sustainability, and social participation.

Currently, PAHO is developing a network for the exchange of experiences and a monitoring mechanism for sectoral reform in the Region, including national authorities, cooperation agencies, universities, NGOs, and health care providers and users. In this sense, subregional seminars were held in order to promote consensus building and negotiation in: San José, Costa Rica (with the collaboration of the IDB and the World Bank); Jamaica (with the Caribbean Community, CARICOM); and Guatemala (co-sponsored by the Central American Council of Social Security Institutions). Other events at the national level took place in Uruguay, Chile and Peru.

Several research projects and studies on reform processes have been conducted, as well — for instance, "Regional Study on the Health Sector of the Caribbean," conducted by IDB and PAHO, with support from the authorities of the countries involved, the Caribbean Development Bank, and the World Bank. Also, in 1996, a research competition on Financial and Organizational aspects of Health Sector Reform was organized by PAHO and 5 projects (Brazil, Uruguay, Peru, Colombia and Costa Rica) were selected from more than 90 proposals. In addition, major efforts have been devoted to Sector Reform Processes. Eight countries have been supported by PAHO in order to elaborate national plans (Barbados, Bolivia, Chile, Dominican Republic, Ecuador, Guatemala, Paraguay and Peru) and have established national commissions for health sector reform as consensus building mechanisms on reform among the various interest

# IV. Preparatory Work by Regional Organizations

groups, facilitating the preparation of proposals and the formulation of legislation to be submitted to the respective legislatures.

Special importance has been given to the management of human resources in the health sector. Several documents and workshops have been held in different countries of the Region in the fields of integral management, personnel administration, performance evaluation, and training.

## Future steps

As a consequence of the mandate of interagency collaboration in support to Health Sector Reform efforts in the countries of the Americas, PAHO and USAID are working on the identification of areas of regional cooperation to carry out the reform processes in the Region, and the evaluation of their impact. The purpose of the five-year project "Equitable Access to Basic Health Services" is to provide regional support to national processes of health sector reform, aimed at providing more equitable access to basic health services for their populations, developing tools and methodologies, monitoring of processes, gathering and dissemination of information, and networking and exchange of experiences which will support activities of the country programs.

IV. To strengthen the existing Inter-American Network on Health Economics and Financing, which serves as an international forum for sharing technical expertise, information and experience, to focus on health reform efforts. The network gathers government officials, representatives of the private sector, non-governmental institutions and actors, donors and scholars for policy discussions, analysis, training and other activities to advance reform; strengthens national capabilities in this critical area; fosters Hemisphere-wide cooperation.

## Actions taken since December 1994

The Inter-American Network on Health Economics and Financing (REDEFS) was established in 1994 by the Economic Development Institute of the World Bank, PAHO, and the Inter-American Center for Social Security Studies to promote training, research and information activities in health economics and finance. All three organizations have pooled their resources to develop a program to strengthen national capabilities in health economics and finance, and help countries apply economic instruments in allocating resources. In only a few years, the network has facilitated significant exchanges of knowledge and experience through technical seminars for high-level officials, training for trainers, policy-oriented research, and development and dissemination of policy papers, case studies, and training materials. A broad consensus exists on the need to ensure more equitable access to health care and allocate resources for it more efficiently. REDEFS directly responds to the need for health sector reform by providing the skills and tools policy-makers and high-level technical professionals need to develop sustainable health sector policies.

### Highlights of REDEFS activities during the period include:

In 1995, Seminar-workshop on "Modalities of Health Provider Contracting" in Argentina; Seminars on health economics in Peru and Uruguay; Seminar on "Health Services Financing" in Paraguay, and Seminar on "Financial Data and Hospital Costs for the Caribbean" in Trinidad and Tobago.

In 1996, International Seminar on "Methodological And Conceptual Topics in Health Economics" in Brazil; Course on "Health Systems Research Methodology, Focus on Health Economics" in Mexico; high-level technical seminars involving seven countries and 1,000 participants; support for the Fourth International Conference on Health Economics, entitled "Equity, Efficiency, and Quality: The Challenge of Health Models" in Argentina; organization of regional seminars on research in health economics in Chile; and the creation of a REDEFS home page on the Internet.

In 1997, Seminar on health economics in Ecuador and Paraguay; subregional meetings for preparing work programs and implementation strategy in Central America (Honduras), and the Southern Cone (Uruguay); seminar on "Critical Aspects of the Health Reform Process: Are Integrated Health Services Possible for All?" in Chile; and support for the Fifth International Conference on Health Economics, entitled "The Future of Health Reform" in Argentina.

## Future steps

Shift greater responsibility for program development and financing to national programs.

Strengthen in-service training and university programs through scholarships, fellowships, grants, and funds to support health economic associations.

Have a greater presence at international events and specialized conferences.

Formulate and test a basic curriculum for mid-level professionals in health economics.

V. Convene a special meeting of hemispheric governments with interested donors and international technical agencies to be hosted by the IDB, the World Bank and PAHO to establish the framework for health reform mechanisms, to define PAHO's role in monitoring the regional implementation of country plans and programs, and to plan strengthening of the network, including the co-sponsors' contributions to it.

## Actions taken since December 1994

The meeting was held as a special session of the XXXVIII Meeting of the Directing Council of PAHO at Washington, D.C., in September 1995, with the participation of multi-institutional government delegations, representatives of donor agencies and non-governmental organizations.

An interagency committee comprised of PAHO, the World Bank, IDB, OAS, ECLAC, UNICEF, UNFPA, USAID, CIDA, the Canadian International Development Research Center, and government officials from the Western Hemisphere was responsible for the preparations of the Special Meeting of Ministries of Health on Health Sector Reform in the Americas. The Directing Council of PAHO, based on the deliberations of the Special Meeting, adopted a resolution requesting the Member States to give priority to Health Sector Reform as a mechanism for guaranteeing equitable access to basic health services and achieving greater efficiency and effectiveness in health sector activities. It also requested the cooperation agencies to improve coordination and to increase their support for the Health Sector Reform processes. In addition, it requested PAHO, together with the countries and cooperation agencies, to develop a monitoring mechanism and an Inter-American network to support the reform.

## Future steps

An important challenge in the management of the reform processes is maintaining coherence and harmony among the different reform processes that take place in other sectors and government levels, but have an affect on the health sector. Some experiences seem to suggest that the reform processes require a combination of progressive changes at medium and long-term periods, with other more rapid changes of immediate impact, through an efficient strategic agenda that must have full support at the national level.

VI. Take the opportunity of the annual PAHO Directing Council of Western Hemisphere Ministers of Health, with participation of the IDB and donors, to develop a program to combat endemic and communicable diseases as well as a program to prevent the spread of HIV/AIDS, and to identify sources of funding.

## Actions taken since December 1994

At the meeting of PAHO's Governing Council in September 1995, a new Regional Plan was adopted for countering the threat of new, emerging and re-emerging diseases. This Plan was based on extensive consultations with technical experts from the Region at PAHO, who identified a number of actions needed to assure appropriate ability to identify and respond to outbreaks of new diseases as well as to monitor the re-emergence of older diseases and to monitor problems of drug resistance. This section will refer to four major problems of the Region: measles, dengue, malaria, and HIV/AIDS.

In September of 1994, in Washington, D.C., the Ministers of Health of the Americas adopted a resolution calling for the elimination of measles transmission from the Americas by the year 2000. During 1996 there were only 2,109 confirmed cases of measles, compared to 6,489 cases in 1995 and 23,583 confirmed cases in 1994. As of November 1, 1997, of the 18,132 confirmed cases of measles in the Region, 17,216 (95%) occurred in Brazil, primarily from an outbreak in the city of São Paulo. Twenty-five measles-related deaths have been reported; 12 occurred in infants less than 1 year of age. Conversely, in 1996, there were no measles-related deaths in the entire Region.

The epidemic in Brazil emphasizes the importance that countries fully utilize the vaccination strategy recommended by PAHO. In addition, it is necessary that the goal of measles elimination be recognized as a hemispheric effort. In this regard, collaboration among countries of the Region, as well as among governments, non-governmental organizations, the private sector, and society in general is critical and will have to be strengthened.

A follow-up report on the Measles Elimination Plan (attached) was presented at the Seventh Conference of Wives of Heads of States and of Governments of the Americas that took place in Panamá in October 1997.

# IV. PREPARATORY WORK BY REGIONAL ORGANIZATIONS

The 1995 meeting of PAHO's Governing Council was also the site of calls for intensified attention to the problem of dengue. Indeed, in 1996, a total of 276,758 cases of dengue and dengue hemorrhagic fever, and 47 deaths were reported. The XXXIX Meeting of the Directing Council of PAHO approved in September of 1996 a resolution urging countries to cooperate in the preparation of a Hemispheric-wide plan for the eradication of dengue, based on the conclusions of the Southern Cone and Brazil workshops held in 1996, and the Central American seminar held in 1995.

In addition, in 1995 a total of 1.3 million cases of malaria were reported, representing an increase of 14.6% over 1994 levels. PAHO has taken direct action to consolidate the global malaria control strategy by coordinating and mobilizing resources to foster sector decentralization processes under way in Brazil, Ecuador, Guyana, Mexico, Peru, and Venezuela; the development and dissemination of epidemiological criteria and guidelines that can be adapted to national policies; preparation of manuals for the clinical treatment of cases of malaria (Brazil, Colombia, Guyana, and Haiti); and organization of specialized and master's-level courses aimed at strengthening local health systems (Brazil, Colombia, Peru, and Venezuela).

HIV/AIDS continues to be a major health problem throughout the Region. At the XI International Conference on AIDS, held in Vancouver, Canada, in July 1996, the countries of the Region, in conjunction with PAHO, AIDS Prevention and Control Project and Family Health International, sketched a preliminary analysis of the epidemic in the Hemisphere. Available results show that during 1993-1995, cases increased dramatically compared to 1992, rising 66.87% in the Region as a whole, especially among young adults in urban areas. 1.8 million cases of AIDS were reported worldwide until September 30, 1997. Of these, about 50% were in the Americas. Underreporting is estimated at 50%. As far as HIV is concerned, of the 2.5 million regional cases, about one million are in Canada and the U.S.A. and the balance in Latin America and the Caribbean.

During the period, the countries of the Americas and several international agencies like PAHO, USAID and CIDA devoted much of their work and resources to establishing and consolidating interinstitutional and intersectoral mechanisms for cooperation in the operation of national AIDS prevention and control programs. In connection with the establishment of the new Joint United Nations Program on AIDS (UNAIDS), PAHO has prepared a regional plan for HIV/AIDS control. This plan was discussed and is being implemented in coordination with the countries of the Region. Countries had documented evidence of multisectoral and interagency participation in the planning, execution, and/or evaluation of their plan for the prevention and control of AIDS.

*For example:*
- In 1997, in collaboration with UNAIDS, PAHO developed comprehensive surveillance reports (EpiFact sheets) from 40 countries and territories in the Region of the Americas.
- Comprehensive information on prevention and management of opportunistic and on antiretroviral treatments was made available to all the countries.
- [a] In 1996, the seven countries of the Central American Isthmus (Belize included) conducted reviews of their achievements, lessons learned, and obstacles still to be cleared.
- The Directors of four National AIDS Programs (Mexico, Chile, Venezuela, and Paraguay) gathered to analyze the strengths and gaps of their programs, in 1996.
- In-country training in planning and program management was conducted in Peru, Colombia, Dominican Republic, Honduras, Panamá, Guatemala, Argentina, Cuba, Ecuador, Grenada, and Eastern Caribbean.
- All countries had achieved 100% screening of donated blood in urban areas.
- Workshops on comprehensive HIV/AIDS care were conducted for Argentina, Chile, Uruguay, Peru, Ecuador, and Paraguay.
- Data from eleven countries showed coordination of comprehensive care activities (Brazil, Colombia, Costa Rica, Argentina, Ecuador, Chile, Bahamas, Trinidad and Tobago, and Mexico).
- In 1995, projects were initiated in Costa Rica, Mexico, Nicaragua, and Brazil aimed at incorporating HIV/AIDS prevention into programs directed to improving women's health (e.g. prenatal care, cancer detection, family planning, etc.).

## Future steps

An important component for maintaining the interruption of measles virus circulation in the Americas is assuring high population immunity in infants. Efforts are needed to achieve at least 90% coverage for every cohort of newborns. Infants should receive measles-containing vaccine as soon as possible after their first birthday. In order to maintain high immunity levels in preschool-aged children, and to reduce the possibility of a measles outbreak, follow-up vaccination campaigns should be carried out when the estimated number of susceptible preschool children approaches the number of children in one birth cohort of the same year. Furthermore, measles surveillance needs to be strengthened throughout the Region. Reliable surveillance data can provide important information to improve the measles elimination strategy and orient it toward groups that run the highest risk of contracting the disease. Laboratory testing of suspected measles cases are also fundamental to confirm the circulation of the virus of measles. Finally, to achieve the target of measles elimination in the Americas, increased efforts are needed to eliminate the disease in other regions of the world. The only way of guaranteeing long-term regional interruption will be through the global eradication of measles.

> VII. Urge the March 1995 World Summit for Social Development and the September 1995 Fourth World Conference on Women to address the issue of access to health services.

## Actions taken since December 1994

PAHO was privileged to participate in both summit meetings, the UN World Conference on Populations and Development (Cairo, Egypt, 1994) and the UN World Conference on Women (Beijing, China, 1995), and is pleased both to report on the active participation of governments of the Region and to note the active role of many governments in raising the issue of access to health services at both meetings. The United States, Canada, Chile and many other member states played active and important roles in the successful outcome of both meetings. These summits highlighted violence against women as an obstacle to gender equality and a threat of great magnitude to the social and economic development of nations (the subject is addressed in the next section of this report).

## INITIATIVE 18: STRENGTHENING THE ROLE OF WOMEN IN SOCIETY

### Actions taken by PAHO since December 1994

As part of the commitment to achieve equity in health, in 1996 PAHO launched a series of local-level projects that directly benefited women, especially those living in poverty. One of the most significant was the regional project to prevent domestic violence and help abused women. PAHO mobilized financial resources from the governments of the Netherlands, Norway, and Sweden, and from the IDB in support of country efforts to address domestic violence. The cornerstone of this initiative was the creation of community-based networks that link health, education, and legal sectors, as well as representatives of religious and grassroots groups and women's organizations. These networks were formed in 18 communities in 10 countries of the Region (Belize, Bolivia, Costa Rica, Ecuador, El Salvador, Guatemala, Honduras, Nicaragua, Panamá, and Peru).

On the other hand, during 1996, PAHO, UNFPA, and The Netherlands joined forces to compile the experiences of 20 NGOs working in 12 countries in the areas of health and sexual and reproductive rights of adolescent and adult men and women.

A follow-up report on Progress in the Eradication of Violence against Women (attached) was presented at the Seventh Conference of Wives of Heads of States and of Governments of the Americas that took place in Panamá in October 1997.

These efforts will generate knowledge that will help to improve public health services in the area of reproductive health, and ensure broad access to high-quality services for both men and women.

### Future steps

While violence against women is a learned behavior, there are also structural obstacles to overcome for its reduction, such as the need for a certificate from the medical or forensic examiner to gain access to the courts. The medical examiner is responsible under the law for examining the victim and issuing an opinion about the case. Although some countries have changed this requirement (permitting the director of a clinic or a health post, for example, to perform the examination), the custom persists, and the reports issued by health professionals are not valid in a court of law.

# IV. PREPARATORY WORK BY REGIONAL ORGANIZATIONS

PAHO is preparing a research, training and lobbying project to show, document and correct gender access inequities in public health policies. It will cover both access to basic services (which fall under Initiative 17) as well as the responsibility and decision-making processes in health development, which fall under Initiative 18.

## INITIATIVE 23: PARTNERSHIP FOR POLLUTION PREVENTION

### Actions taken by PAHO since December 1994

PAHO convened the Pan American Conference on Health and the Environment in Sustainable Human Development in 1995, honoring the commitment assumed by the countries in the Summit of Miami, related to the fact that conservation and protection of health and the environment are a central concern in the new model of sustainable development being pursued by the countries of the Hemisphere. Technical cooperation from the Organization in this area focused on monitoring the action plan that emerged from the Conference, as well as building capacity to influence the sector and ensure that national decision-making processes involving development plans and projects give due consideration to public health issues.

Among the results obtained from this effort, governments of 10 countries have adopted formal political commitments, reflecting the recommendations made at the Conference, and seven have formulated action plans in the areas of health, environment, and human development.

In 1996, technical cooperation in the area of water supply and sanitation was targeted at expanding service coverage, improving the bacteriological quality of water intended for human consumption, and extending water supply and sewerage services to marginal urban areas and rural areas and indigenous communities. A major promotion effort was launched to promote investment in the sector through the Plan for Investment in Environment and Health (PIAS), including the preparation of sectoral studies, and reform and modernization of the sector and its institutions. Emphasis was placed on regulatory, technical, and technological activity to improve water disinfection in supply systems and in homes. PAHO, together with the Inter-American Association of Sanitary Engineering and the Caribbean Water and Waste Water Association, have established the Inter-American Water Day, which provides an important opportunity for national policy makers and communities to discuss their water problems and to educate the population about the issues of water supply and quality, and to increase their involvement in these matters.

With regard to urban solid waste, the sector received support for institutional strengthening and for building its organizational and regulatory capacity as part of the stepped up process of decentralization and privatization under way in the countries. Attention focused on waste management and promoting appropriate technologies for waste disposal, including hospital waste. One of the activities carried out under PIAS in this regard consisted of conducting sector studies in various countries to identify investment needs and formulate the respective projects to aid in the search in funding.

The OAS, PAHO, IDB, the World Bank, and USAID have worked together in several projects aimed at collaborating with the efforts carried out by the countries of the Region, in order to develop and implement national action plans to phase out lead in gasoline. In addition, PAHO, with the financial support of GTZ, continues to implement projects oriented to increase the epidemiological surveillance of the health effects of pesticides in Central America, as well as in Brazil, Chile, and Mexico. One example is the project known as PLAGSALUD, launched under the Environment and Health in the Central American Isthmus program, with strong support of DANIDA. The project aims to reduce the occurrence of pesticide-related diseases by one half, while promoting sustainable farming practices within the framework of the Alliance for Sustainable Development. During the project's initial phase between 1994 and 1996, work was completed on all activities in Costa Rica and Nicaragua, and demonstration projects were developed for the other five Central American countries.

### Future steps

The commitments assumed by the countries at the Summit of the Americas point to the fact that conservation and protection of health and the environment are a central concern in the new model of sustainable human development being pursued by the countries of the Hemisphere. PAHO's work in this area will focus on generating the necessary knowledge in the countries to ensure the sustainability of their actions and raise health levels, as well as facilitate intercountry cooperation and exchanges among agencies, institutions, and groups.

### Table 1. Mortality by Preventable Childhood Illness in Some Countries of the Americas (Latest Available Data)

| Country | Estimated Infant Mortality Rate Per 1000 Live Births* | Year | Less Than One Year Old – Total Recorded Deaths N* | Prevalent Childhood Illnesses N* | % | One To Four Years Old – Total Recorded Deaths N* | Prevalent Childhood Illnesses N* | % |
|---|---|---|---|---|---|---|---|---|
| *Countries with IMR above 40 per 1000 live births* | | | | | | | | |
| Peru | 55 | 1989 | 9391 | 4714 | 50.20 | 4147 | 2766 | 66.70 |
| Nicaragua | 52 | 1994 | 2592 | 932 | 35.96 | 615 | 372 | 60.49 |
| Guatemala | 48 | 1984 | 19196 | 7520 | 39.17 | 10616 | 8632 | 81.31 |
| Brazil | 47 | 1992 | 70695 | 22432 | 31.73 | 11096 | 5049 | 45.50 |
| Ecuador | 44 | 1995 | 4990 | 1510 | 30.26 | 2274 | 1118 | 49.16 |
| El Salvador | 44 | 1990 | 3623 | 1105 | 30.50 | 927 | 502 | 54.15 |
| Honduras | 43 | 1980 | 2437 | 1424 | 58.43 | 1460 | 993 | 68.01 |
| Paraguay | 43 | 1994 | 1604 | 676 | 42.14 | 522 | 361 | 69.16 |
| Dominican Republic | 42 | 1985 | 6032 | 2176 | 36.07 | 1760 | 1169 | 66.42 |
| **Sub-total** | | | **120560** | **42489** | **35.24** | **33417** | **20962** | **62.73** |
| *Countries with IMR between 20 and 40 per 1000 live births* | | | | | | | | |
| Mexico | 34 | 1994 | 48113 | 14125 | 29.36 | 10326 | 4092 | 39.63 |
| Suriname | 31 | 1992 | 102 | 29 | 28.43 | 35 | 14 | 40.00 |
| Colombia | 28 | 1994 | 10501 | 2622 | 24.97 | 3060 | 1005 | 32.84 |
| Panamá | 25 | 1989 | 981 | 174 | 17.74 | 266 | 118 | 44.36 |
| Argentina | 24 | 1993 | 14472 | 2084 | 14.40 | 2250 | 610 | 27.11 |
| Venezuela | 23 | 1994 | 13418 | 4371 | 32.58 | 632 | 1365 | 215.98 |
| Uruguay | 20 | 1990 | 1079 | 171 | 15.85 | 151 | 24 | 15.89 |
| **Sub-total** | | | **88666** | **23576** | **26.59** | **16720** | **7228** | **43.23** |
| *Countries with IMR between 10 and 20 per 1000 live births* | | | | | | | | |
| Trinidad and Tobago | 17 | 1994 | 266 | 23 | 8.65 | 60 | 12 | 20.00 |
| Chile | 14 | 1994 | 3362 | 544 | 16.18 | 646 | 111 | 17.18 |
| Costa Rica | 14 | 1995 | 1040 | 125 | 12.02 | 183 | 32 | 17.49 |
| Puerto Rico | 12 | 1992 | 808 | 35 | 4.33 | 114 | 11 | 9.65 |
| Cuba | 10 | 1995 | 1375 | 308 | 22.40 | 455 | 104 | 22.86 |
| **Sub-total** | | | **6851** | **1035** | **15.11** | **1458** | **270** | **18.52** |
| *Countries with IMR below 10 per 1000 live births* | | | | | | | | |
| United States | 8 | 1994 | 26278 | 1276 | 4.77 | 6532 | 434 | 6.64 |
| Canada | 7 | 1994 | 2088 | 49 | 2.35 | 487 | 30 | 6.16 |
| **Sub-total** | | | **28856** | **1325** | **4.59** | **7019** | **464** | **6.61** |
| **Regional Total** | | | **244933** | **68425** | **27.94** | **58614** | **28924** | **49.35** |

(*) For the period 1990-1994
Source: Health Statistics for the Americas, 1997 edition PAHO/WHO (in press).

# IV. PREPARATORY WORK BY REGIONAL ORGANIZATIONS

Table 2. Advances in the Implementation of the IMCI Strategy in the Region of the Americas, December 1997

| Country | Adoption of the IMCI Strategy By the MOH | Adaptation of the Strategy | Operational Plan National | Operational Plan Local | National Clinical Course | Trained Personnel |
|---|---|---|---|---|---|---|
| Argentina | ✓ | ✓ | X | X | ✓ | 89 |
| Bolivia | ✓ | ✓ | ✓ | ✓ | ✓ | 132 |
| Brazil | ✓ | ✓ | ✓ | ✓ | ✓ | 180 |
| Colombia | X | X | X | X | X | 22 |
| Ecuador | ✓ | ✓ | ✓ | ✓ | ✓ | 165 |
| El Salvador | ✓ | ✓ | ✓ | X | ✓ | 108 |
| Haiti | ✓ | ✓ | X | X | X | |
| Honduras | ✓ | ✓ | ✓ | X | ✓ | 34 |
| Nicaragua | ✓ | ✓ | ✓ | X | ✓ | 30 |
| Peru | ✓ | ✓ | ✓ | ✓ | ✓ | 528 |
| Dominican Republic | ✓ | ✓ | ✓ | ✓ | ✓ | 90 |
| Venezuela | ✓ | In Process | X | X | X | |
| Total | 11 | 10 | 8 | 5 | 9 | 1378 |

## PROGRESS IN THE ERADICATION OF VIOLENCE AGAINST WOMEN

### I. Program Objectives

The last two Conferences of Wives of Heads of State and of Government of the Americas, held in 1995 and 1996, respectively, have issued declarations in support of "the formulation and implementation of legal policies and norms, as well as regional educational campaigns designed to prevent and eliminate all forms of family violence." (Declaration of La Paz, VI Conference of Wives of Heads of State and Government of the Americas).

### II. Progress to Date

**i. Regional Review:** The countries of the Americas have made great efforts to prevent violence against women and assist women living in situations of domestic violence. Important among the regional activities in this area is the work of the Pan American Health Organization (PAHO) in 18 communities in 10 countries of the Region (Belize, Bolivia, Costa Rica, Ecuador, El Salvador, Guatemala, Honduras, Nicaragua, Panamá, and Peru) to improve the health sector's capacity to identify and refer women living in situations of domestic violence. At the end of 1996, the Board of Directors of the Inter-American Development Bank (IDB) approved this same project in six additional countries (Argentina, Brazil, Dominican Republic, Mexico, Paraguay, and Venezuela). That institution, with the cooperation of PAHO, produced a videotape depicting domestic violence against women as a social and economic development problem in the countries. This videotape has been distributed to the countries of the Region for airing on national television.

The regional vision of what is occurring in each Latin American and Caribbean country is particularly important in learning how to address domestic violence. Countries worldwide are still finding out how to best approach this social and political problem. Having an overview of what is working or not working in each country can be invaluable in advancing the global thinking on policies and programs that must be in place to protect women. Moreover, elevating the process underway at the community and/or national level to the regional and global level encourages experiences to be shared, improves knowledge and targeted activities, encourages countries that have taken no action, and contributes to the creation of a critical mass of professionals who are developing initiatives to prevent and combat violence.

**ii. Country Review:** All the countries have taken some action to put initiatives in place to reduce violence against women and punish offenders. Some of these are presented below.

**Costa Rica** has conducted three national campaigns "For a Life Without Violence" — the first in October 1995, the second in June 1996, and the third in August 1997. All this is part of its National Plan to Combat Violence. The regulatory agency spearheading this effort is the Center for the Development of Women and the Family, and various institutions actively participate in the implementation of the Plan by sector. This Plan is of a constitutional nature as the Law Against Violence holds the State accountable for developing social responses to the problem. On the other hand, very important steps have been taken in terms of training staff in the various institutions to address the problem of gender-based violence.

In **Paraguay**, the effort to tackle the problem of violence against women is led by the Ministry of Women, which has created an interinstitutional group with the participation of representatives from different public sectors and a number of women's NGOs. This group coordinates training activities and the dissemination of technical materials to operationalize the National Plan for Equal Opportunities for Women 1997-2001.

In **Bolivia**, the Vice Ministry of Gender and Generational Affairs has headed the effort to eliminate violence against women. However, regulations for the Domestic Violence Law, enacted in December 1995, have yet to be drawn up. To this end, national discussions to move forward with these regulations were supported, and their dissemination and promulgation at the national level is pending. Bolivia has also created the Family Assistance Policy Stations institutions for maintaining public order, which have used the law as an important instrument in cases of violence against women. In addition, pilot reforms in education are under way in selected sites, the objectives of which include incorporation of the gender perspective into school textbooks.

In **Chile**, the application of the 1994 Law Against Domestic Violence (No. 19,325) has helped to place the issue on the public agenda and launch activities between the government's interministerial commission and civil society to eliminate this scourge. As a result of regulations drafted under the law and their implementation, the number of complaints soared, reaching 57,939 in 1996. Some 73% of women that filed complaints stated that their situation at home had improved after the complaint had been filed. Of them, 39% estimate that their relationship with their partners improved.

**Belize** is making efforts to develop a National Plan to Combat Violence, involving different government agencies and the country's First Lady. **Guatemala** has approved the Domestic Violence Law. In **Honduras**, the Law Against Domestic Violence was approved on September 9th of this year, with immediate enforceability. In addition, efforts have been continued to strengthen the Family Bureaus, and today there are 12 such Bureaus in different parts of the country. In **El Salvador**, the recently formed Women's Institute has a National Plan to Combat Violence backed by the Anti-Violence Law. **Nicaragua** has continued to strengthen its Women's Commissariats, developing an integrated model to address the problem of violence.

In **Argentina**, the Executive Authority approved Decree 2385/93 in recognition of WORLD FOR NON-VIOLENCE AGAINST WOMEN DAY and to address Sexual Harassment in Public Administration. In addition, Law No. 24,417, "Protection against Domestic Violence," was approved in December 1994. However, since the 80s, and particularly in Buenos Aires, advocacy efforts ensured that the issue of domestic violence against women was at the forefront of public awareness as a social and political problem. Starting in the current decade, this work has been strengthened and extended to other jurisdictions. The Department of Community Care, through the pilot Project supported by IDB and PAHO, hopes to develop strategic guidelines for the development of a model of comprehensive care and of prevention duly coordinated with the different institutions committed to address this problem.

In **Peru**, progress is being made in the formation of self-help groups where women living in violent situations can meet. These opportunities are critical to ensure that women break their sense of isolation and guilt that afflicts them, provide them with a space where they realize they are not the only ones, that they are not crazy and that there are other women living in similar situations who are willing to listen to them and who can understand them.

In **Panamá**, there exists the Law Against Violence and the Sectoral Plan against Violence, which is framed at the community level within the initiative of "Municipios Century XXI." In the educational field, a graduate level is proposed for the education of professionals in the area of domestic violence in the National University.

## III. Successful Experiences

Most countries recognize that efforts to prevent the violence against women and assist those living in violent situations imply complex processes that require the commitment and the involvement of multiple actors of the public and civil sectors. In general, countries are using a two-pronged approach to respond to the situation: at the local level, coordinated community networks have been created where all actors, among them, the local health system, the legal system including the police and judges, churches, women's groups, other community-based groups and NGOs, meet on a regular basis to devise and implement a coordinated response to prevent violence and assist persons living in violent situations; and, at the national level, countries are promoting the adoption of legal norms and policies designed to strengthen the institutional capacity to effectively respond to violence against women. Additionally, many countries foster links with the media in an effort to modify social norms that posit the basic superiority of men and to communicate that violence against women is unacceptable.

Changing attitudes is one of the most complex challenges facing the efforts to put a halt to gender violence. There have been successes, however. In one community, for example, it was well known that the Deputy Prefect of the municipio was a batterer. Before the public was sensitized to this issue, the community turned a blind eye to the situation, considering it just one case among many. By opening a dialogue and raising consciousness about gender, violence, and human rights, the members of the network in that community succeeded in having this administrator removed from office, asserting that it was inappropriate to have an abuser of women as a community leader. In a very short time it was possible to lower the community's threshold of tolerance toward violence against women, a practice once regarded as part of daily life and now considered unacceptable behavior.

The countries are also increasing their efforts to train human resource so that women who seek help and guidance from public institutions are treated humanely. However, countries are aware that it is not enough to focus on women only. It is also necessary to work with men. Increasingly, at the country level, groups of men are being formed to work with aggressive men.

## IV. Obstacles Encountered

Violence against women is not the result of unfathomable cases of deviant or pathological behavior. On the contrary, it is a learned behavior, a conscious and directed practice that is the product of a social system based on inequality. In this regard, gender violence is the result of unequal power between men and women and is committed by those who feel they have the right to intimidate and control others. Inequalities stemming from gender and age are the main determinants of violent intrafamily relations.

Modifying these behavior patterns is the biggest obstacle facing the countries. However, there are also structural obstacles, such as the need for a certificate from the medical examiner or forensic to gain access to the courts. The medical examiner is responsible under the law for examining the victim and issuing an opinion about the case. Although some countries have changed this requirement—permitting the director of a clinic or a health post, for example, to perform the examination—the custom persists, and the reports issued by health professionals are not valid in a court of law. Furthermore, the work-up by the medical examiner entails a fee that many women cannot pay.

## V. Plans and Monitoring

Efforts at the national and regional levels are expected to help reduce and prevent the incidence of violence against women by changing the attitudes and beliefs that legitimize and justify it. The joint efforts of all social and institutional actors, public and private, in the participating countries are expected to yield a better response to the problem of gender violence. This and other regional forums are intended as a platform for learning about the problem and for political mobilization around this violation of human rights—a violation that, at the most intimate level of the relationship between men and women, has a clear directionality, for 92% of the cases of domestic violence are committed by men against women.

## MATERNAL MORTALITY REDUCTION PROGRAM: PROGRESS REPORT

## I. Background

The history of the commitment of the First Ladies with the important task of reducing maternal mortality in the countries of the American continent started in Costa

Rica, at the third conference of the First Ladies in 1993. A recommendation was made regarding the necessity to support actions in favor of the health of women, children and adolescents. Prevention of Maternal Mortality was identified as a priority action.

It is estimated that 35,000 maternal deaths occur each year in the Americas. The great majority of these deaths could be prevented by simple, well-known and inexpensive interventions. The death of a woman related to pregnancy or delivery is always a tragedy, but even more so if that death could have been avoided; the repercussions for the affected families are severe.

The magnitude of this problem varies from country to country, and within the countries significant differences exist between urban and rural areas, different regions and social groups. The significance of this situation for women in general, and specifically for women's health issues, is a challenge for sustainable human development and, therefore, deserves to be considered within the sociopolitical context of the countries.

At the fifth Conference of First Ladies of the Americas in Paraguay in 1995, the First Ladies, conscious of these issues, decided to actively and dynamically promote all actions that can contribute to the accelerated reduction of maternal mortality in the Americas. The Proposal: "Regional Initiative of the First Ladies to support the plans of maternal mortality reduction" is presented.

At the sixth Conference of First Ladies in Bolivia in December 1996, in the Declaration of La Paz, Bolivia, 1996, the First Ladies declared: "We reiterate our support for the implementation of programs to reduce maternal mortality, including access to prenatal care and delivery by trained personnel, the development of services able to solve obstetric emergencies, sexual education and reproductive health, and development of voluntary, accessible and high quality family planning services available to couples. Furthermore, we reaffirm our commitment to improve the quality of women's health care at all levels of the health system and in all stages of women's lives."

In The Action Plan of the sixth conference, the First Ladies state two major strategies to support the maternal and perinatal mortality programs:

a) promotion, revision, strengthening and follow-up of national policies, and

b) foster mobilization of institutions and different sectors of society.

## II. Objectives of the Program of the Regional Initiative of the First Ladies for Support of the Plans for the Reduction of Maternal Mortality

### General Objective

Contribute with decisive support to the specific regional and national plans to the accelerated decrease of maternal mortality in the Americas.

### Specific Objectives

- Promote the formulation or strengthening of specific national policies, plans and programs for the accelerated reduction of maternal mortality. Promote national campaigns of information, communication and education to increase sensitivity towards the importance and consequences of maternal mortality and promote major actions to prevent it.

- Foster the mobilization of public and private institutions, non-governmental organizations, grassroots organizations and others, so that they can contribute, from their areas of competence, to the development of national and local plans for the carrying out of measures with the greatest impact aimed at the accelerated reduction of maternal mortality.

- Facilitate the exchange of operations research and successful experiences between the countries that will allow them to identify and overcome the causes that impede appropriate access and utilization of the health services or that impede major impacts of the women health programs.

- Foster programs to improve information systems to facilitate follow up and monitoring of the maternal mortality epidemiological surveillance indicators at the country and regional levels, and to maintain a dynamic system of epidemiological vigilance at the community and institutional levels.

## III. Progress

The activities described here are the ones considered the most transcendental for the region, which occurred since the last meeting of the First Ladies in December 1996 through September 1997. These activities have already contributed to the maternal mortality reduction plan of the region.

# IV. PREPARATORY WORK BY REGIONAL ORGANIZATIONS

*Particularly notable are the following:*

- Six new governments of the Americas have explicitly confirmed their commitment to the national plans of maternal reduction, thereby stressing the importance of this issue for the development of their nations.

- Seven countries have recently updated and revised (between 1996 and 1997) their national plans for the reduction of maternal mortality.

- New regional projects: At the last meeting of the First Ladies an agreement for a new regional project was signed between US AID, PAHO MotherCare and Quality Assurance for the implementation of emergency obstetric management in eleven countries. The project includes political advocacy and lobbying, improvement of quality services and community mobilization. The countries involved in this initiative are: Bolivia, Brazil, Dominican Republic, El Salvador, Ecuador, Guatemala, Haiti, Honduras, Nicaragua, Paraguay and Peru.

- To contribute to the very important issue of continuation and growth of projects for the prevention of adolescent pregnancies, a series of projects are being carried out by different donor agencies and technical assistance entities—one of them is a regional project for adolescent reproductive health in 14 countries, carried out by PAHO with UNFPA financing.

- It has been observed that an increase of financial investment from several development banks (BID, World Bank), in maternal health and specifically maternal mortality, has occurred in several countries.

- By First Ladies or governmental initiatives, Mass Media Social Communication campaigns have been developed to contribute to the maternal mortality reduction programs. Within this context, resources have been mobilized with the active participation of different sectors of the society.

- Increased pro-active participation to improve the health of women, women's organizations, the civil society sector and other groups in the countries: The active and organized participation of these groups in the countries has increased the level of awareness regarding the maternal mortality problem. There are now many organized groups that are very active in political advocacy and lobbying for women's health issues. This has generated political pressure to accelerate legislative procedures for women's rights and assignment of resources for women's health issues. These groups also constitute a force that demands, facilitates and participates in the implementation of health programs for women, specifically in actions to decrease maternal mortality.

- Approximately twenty relevant documents have been distributed to the countries.

- Baseline data on the situation in the countries is being collected and verified.

- Evaluation of the Maternal Mortality surveillance systems has been completed in two countries.

- Preparations are under way in all countries to celebrate the year of Safe Motherhood, and kits have been distributed.

- Research is being conducted in 3 countries to develop policy and legislative guidelines.

## IV. Successful Experiences

Although the time period covered by this report is very short, some successful and interesting new experiences should be mentioned. One example of these interesting and successful experiences is Ecuador's First Lady's summons of different sectors of the society to ask for increased support and commitment for the maternal mortality reduction program. As a consequence of that meeting, the maternal mortality reduction program was reaffirmed as a priority objective by the government, donor agencies and technical cooperation agencies. This reaffirmation brought as a consequence reallocation of resources from the different sectors to increase the financial support for the program.

The First Lady of Bolivia, President of the National Comity for Safe Motherhood, promoted and fostered the implementation of a national Information, Education and Communication strategy for Safe Motherhood, directed to rural and marginal-urban areas of the highlands and valleys of Bolivia. The "Seguro de Maternidad y Niñez" (Maternal and Child Insurance) established in July 1996 has reached a coverage of 675.420 cases attended (from July 96 to June 97) in all Bolivia and is growing strongly.

In the Dominican Republic, a Plan of National mobilization for the reduction of maternal and infant mortality has been developed. This is a multisectional and multi-institutional effort that operationalizes the strategy of social development, showing the political goodwill of the current government.

In some countries, governments, donor agencies, technical cooperation agencies and development banks have reassigned and procured more funds and technical assistance for the maternal mortality reduction programs.

## V. Obstacles Encountered

The current tendencies of the countries to reduce government spending, especially in investments of the social sector like health and education, has weakened the physical, material and human infrastructure of the services for the most needy sectors of the society. The process of structural adjustment and the consequent reform of the health sector present the challenge of a rapidly changing context. This context determines the ability of the countries to mobilize for a rapid response of the system towards concrete and accelerated plans, like the accelerated plan to decrease maternal mortality, requiring the search for new implementation strategies and alliances.

Another notable obstacle specifically in this field is the appropriate planning, evaluation and follow-up. A feedback process to communities and health services is equally important. Many of the aforementioned problems are due to weakness in the collection and process of information, which results in a lack of confidence in the basic data.

## VI. Plans for the Future

Important progress has been obtained in the accelerated plan to reduce maternal mortality in the Americas. However, to further pursue and to obtain the objectives and goals proposed in the Initiative of the First Ladies, long-term support and personal commitment of the First Ladies and other participating sectors is indispensable.

Continuous monitoring of resources available for the plan is necessary to permit the implementation and operationalization of the objectives to obtain the desired goals. Advocacy and lobbying of the First Ladies with the different public forums are critical elements in this effort.

The high visibility of the public persona of the First Ladies in the countries of the Americas and their actions in favor of the well-being of women and their families represent an important model for all women in those nations. The actions of the First Ladies constitute an example that influences, stimulates and motivates many sectors of a society, which, in the context of the current democratic environment, work to improve the quality of life of all the elements of the society, specially for the most vulnerable and unprotected. Thus, the public attention will maintain focus on this unnecessary tragedy and provide the necessary recognition of the importance of this issue for the progress of the nations.

The roll of the First Ladies in fostering and supporting legislation in favor of women's rights is an action that has tangible, unmovable and irreversible short- and long-term benefits for the women of today and all future generations of women and their families.

Following the Regional Plan of the Reduction of Maternal Mortality, the AID/PAHO project previously mentioned is supporting the countries in various activities:

- Stimulation of the revision of the Regional Plan for Maternal Mortality Reduction as a basis for development of rational plans, emphasizing the obstetric emergency aspects in all countries.

- Creation of an interagency committee to coordinate and concentrate efforts, avoid duplications and provide attention to the priorities in a way that emphasizes the potential impact of activities.

- Regional and subregional meetings to share experiences, difficulties and successes.

- Improvements in basic information, the system of epidemiological surveillance and the use of information to improve the quality of services.

- The development of instruments to analyze legislation and policy aspects such as a matrix scheme, which explains the aspects needed to be addressed in the different sectors in order to contribute towards maternal mortality reduction and the development of a checklist for countries to examine their situation.

- The theme for World Health Day 1998 is Safe Motherhood (April 7, 1998). Efforts are being encouraged in all countries for the policy leaders and public figures such as the First Ladies to become involved in making Safe Motherhood and the reduction of Maternal Mortality a public agenda item. A workshop to bring other sectors into the efforts is being planned, and the information with technical support will be available later this year.

# IV. PREPARATORY WORK BY REGIONAL ORGANIZATIONS

## PROGRESS REPORT: MEASLES ERADICATION IN THE AMERICAS

### I. Background

Immunization is widely recognized to be one of the most cost-effective preventive health measures. Three million lives of children under 5 years of age are saved annually by vaccination. Measles continues to be the leading killer among childhood vaccine-preventable diseases, affecting mainly malnourished children and those who live in crowded urban conditions. Each year, approximately 1 million measles-related deaths are reported worldwide.

The Region of the Americas, with technical cooperation from the Pan American Health Organization, was the first in eradicating poliomyelitis in 1991 and in achieving the elimination of neonatal tetanus as a public health problem, a goal set by the World Summit for Children. The successes obtained have prompted countries to promote activities geared toward the control of vaccine-preventable diseases and to launch a new challenge of measles eradication from the Americas. In September of 1995, in Washington, D.C., the Ministers of Health of the Region of the Americas unanimously approved the Measles Eradication Plan of Action in the Americas by the year 2000.

The maintenance of these achievements and the fulfillment of new challenges require continuous political and financial commitment. The active participation of beneficiaries and other sectors has made immunization one of the most successful primary health care interventions. By building a broad base of support at the local levels, national immunization programs in the Americas have rapidly adapted to today's changing environment, which places a high priority on national self-sufficiency. However, it is necessary to recognize the leadership role of governments in assuring that immunization program goals are met in all areas of the country. The First Ladies of the Americas have also played a key role in emphasizing the importance of immunization, and during the Fifth Conference of Wives of Heads of State and of Government of the Americas held in Paraguay in 1995, the First Ladies prepared a Plan of Action that complements current efforts towards measles eradication.

Countries are also demonstrating an overwhelming commitment to the sustainability of national immunization programs. A key indicator for this is the increased allocation of national resources for regular program costs. Another excellent example of the priority accorded to this preventive health measure is the commitment by countries to establish a budget line for vaccination activities within the national budget. Venezuela approved the Immunization Law in March of 1996, and Ecuador's Congress passed a Law of Vaccines this past August.

### II. Progress Toward Measles Eradication

Considerable progress has been made toward the goal of measles eradication in the Americas. Transmission has been interrupted in many countries of the Region. While in 1990 there were more than 240,000 confirmed cases reported, the number of confirmed cases in 1995 had declined to 6,489 and to 2,109 in 1996. This general reduction of measles cases is a direct result of the vaccination strategy recommended by PAHO, which includes a one-time catch-up vaccination campaign of children 1-14 years of age, regardless of vaccination or disease history; maintenance of high coverage through routine vaccination of children 1 year of age (keep-up); and periodic follow-up campaigns to reduce the accumulation of susceptibles 1-4 years of age. In 1997, however, confirmed measles cases increased to 27,635, due in large part to a large outbreak in the State of São Paulo, Brazil (Figure 1).

A critical factor for documenting progress toward achieving the measles eradication goal will be the implementation of a sensitive and intensive surveillance system for suspected measles cases. This component is of utmost importance for the detection of remaining chains of transmission that could trigger an outbreak, and for dealing with imported cases. Given the difficulties of the current information systems in the Region to generate quality data in a timely fashion, PAHO is strengthening them through the implementation of a standardized Regional Surveillance System for Measles Eradication.

The timely investigation of suspected cases and outbreaks will also play a critical role in the successful conclusion of the measles initiative, since it allows determination with certainty whether or not a suspected case is due to measles. In this regard, the Regional Measles Diagnostic Laboratory Network supported by PAHO is collaborating with national reference laboratories to ensure the prompt confirmation of suspected measles cases.

During 1996 and 1997, evaluations of national measles surveillance systems were carried out in Brazil, El Salvador, Mexico, Nicaragua, Panamá, and Venezuela. These evaluations seek to identify obstacles that are impeding progress in the implementation of the measles eradication strategy.

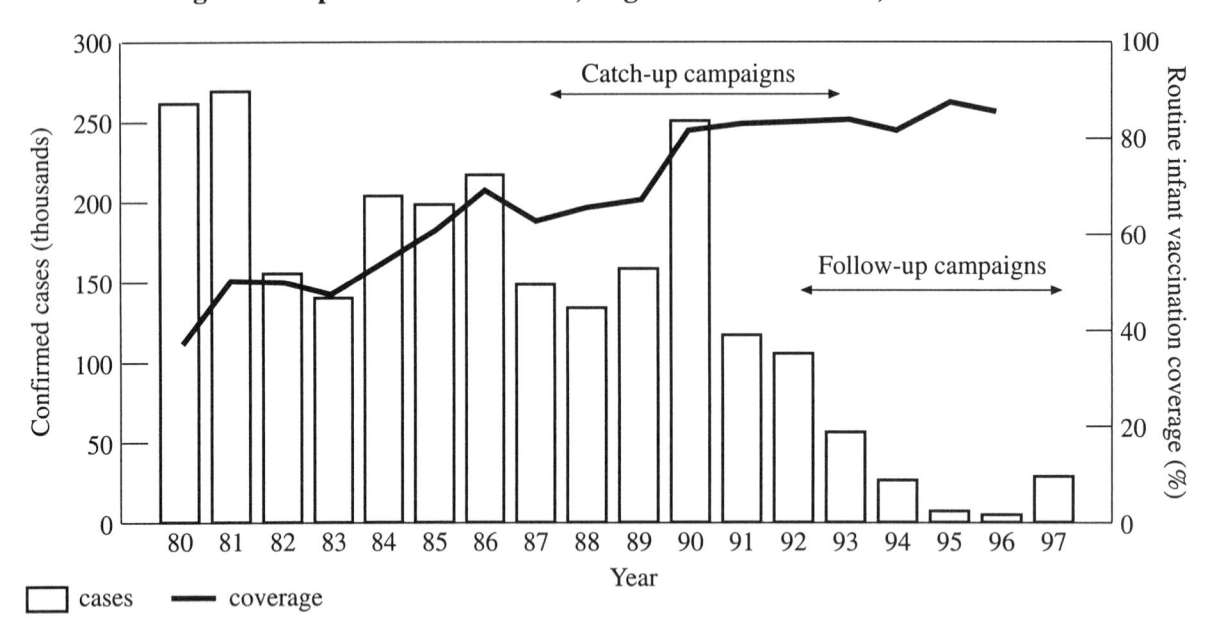

**Figure 1. Reported Measles Cases, Region of the Americas, 1960-1997*#**

Source: PAHO/WHO
* Coverage of children at one year of age.
# Data as of 21 February 1998.

## III. Obstacles

Despite the progress achieved in the Americas toward the goal of measles eradication, the virus continues to circulate in some countries of the Region. The low number of cases in 1996 produced a false sense of security. This is a particularly dangerous situation since many children remain susceptible in all countries of the Americas, due to low vaccination coverage in high-risk areas, and because vaccination schedules do not protect 5 to 10% of those who were vaccinated. Moreover, the recent outbreak in Brazil suggests there may be a large number of adolescents and young adults who remain susceptible to measles. These persons were often born too early for routine measles vaccinations, yet too late to have been exposed to the circulating measles virus.

In 1997, there were 27,635 confirmed measles cases in the Region, of which 26,348 (95%) were from Brazil, primarily from the State of São Paulo. The São Paulo measles epidemic has spread to other states in the country and to at least four more countries of the Region, and it has been responsible for twenty measles-related deaths. In addition, there have been five confirmed importations from Brazil into the United States. These are the first importations of measles into the United States from Latin America since 1994. Approximately half of the cases in Brazil correspond to persons 20 to 29 years of age. Other countries have reported similar but smaller outbreaks, with transmission occurring among young adults.

The latest measles outbreaks are a reminder of the ability of the measles virus to seek out susceptible individuals in areas that have achieved and maintained high levels of measles vaccination coverage. Even in a country with a strong routine immunization program, there will be many children who are vaccinated and yet do not become immune to measles. These children, in addition to those who escape vaccination, will combine to create a large pool of susceptible children. Over time, the size of this unprotected population will grow, and the risk of a measles outbreak will increase. It is always preferable to prevent measles outbreaks, because it is very difficult to control them, especially when the virus is circulating widely. Measles virus spreads faster than the activities conducted to contain outbreaks.

*Major Obstacles:*

- Insufficient resources to achieve the measles eradication goal.
- Routine vaccination coverage < 90%.
- Accumulation of susceptible children over time.

- Inadequate logistical support for investigating all suspected measles cases.
- Limited participation of the private sector and non-governmental organizations in reporting suspected measles cases.
- Insufficient dissemination and promotion of the Plan of Action for Measles Eradication at the national level.

The measles experience of 1997 clearly demonstrates that there are two major challenges to the Region's measles eradication goal by the year 2000. First, the countries of the Americas need to keep up their guard by maintaining the highest population immunity possible in infants and children, and targeting vaccination to adolescents and young adults who are at highest risk for exposure to the measles virus. Second, increased efforts are needed in other regions of the world to improve measles control and to decrease the number of exported measles cases to the Americas. As long as the measles virus circulates anywhere in the world, the Americas will remain at risk.

## IV. Follow-up

A critical component for maintaining the interruption of measles virus circulation in the Americas is assuring high population immunity in infants. Efforts are needed to achieve at least 90% coverage for every cohort of newborns in each municipality. Infants should receive measles-containing vaccine as soon as possible after their first birthday. Also, in light of data gathered from the recent outbreaks, specific risk groups among adolescents and young adults need to be identified and targeted for vaccination.

In order to maintain high immunity levels in pre-school-aged children, and to reduce the possibility of a measles outbreak, follow-up vaccination campaigns should be carried out when the estimated number of susceptible preschool children approaches the number of children in one birth cohort of the same year.

Measles surveillance needs to be strengthened throughout the Region. Information obtained through the surveillance systems is essential for monitoring the progress toward the goal of measles eradication. Reliable surveillance data can provide important information to improve the measles eradication strategy and to orient it toward groups that run the highest risk of contracting the disease. In addition, the laboratory testing of suspected cases is fundamental to determine areas where the measles virus is circulating.

All sectors of society should be mobilized to raise awareness and generate support for the measles eradication initiative. This includes government institutions at both the central and local levels, non-governmental organizations, the private sector and community leaders.

The successful completion of the measles eradication goal will require full implementation of PAHO's recommended vaccination strategy in all countries of the Region and improved measles control/elimination in other parts of the world. The only way for the Americas to assure regional measles eradication will be through the ultimate global eradication of measles virus.

### Areas for Immediate Action:

- Guarantee the availability of resources for vaccine procurement, as well as for follow-up measles vaccination campaigns and surveillance systems (vaccines, syringes, cold chain, per diem, transportation and staff);
- Support greater dissemination and support for the Measles Eradication Plan of Action at the national and regional level, through intersectoral contributions to mass-media campaigns, activities with well-known personalities in every country and distribution of promotional material;
- Support training activities;
- Guarantee the active involvement of society;
- Promote the involvement of the private sector and non-governmental organizations in vaccination activities and in the notification of suspected cases.

## Confirmed Measles Cases, 1995-1997*

| Region | Country | 1995 | 1996 | 1997 |
|---|---|---|---|---|
| Andean Region | Bolivia | 76 | 7 | 8 |
| | Colombia | 410 | 160 | 43 |
| | Ecuador | 919 | 42 | 0 |
| | Peru | 353 | 105 | 1 |
| | Venezuela | 172 | 89 | 27 |
| Brazil | Brazil | 793 | 580 | 26,348 |
| Central America | Belize | 4 | 0 | 0 |
| | Costa Rica | 35 | 24 | 15 |
| | El Salvador | 0 | 1 | 0 |
| | Guatemala | 23 | 1 | 8 |
| | Honduras | 0 | 4 | 6 |
| | Nicaragua | 5 | 0 | 0 |
| | Panamá | 19 | 0 | 0 |
| English-speaking Caribbean | Anguilla | 0 | 0 | 0 |
| | Antigua & Barbuda | 0 | 0 | 0 |
| | Bahamas | 0 | 0 | 1 |
| | Barbados | 0 | 0 | 0 |
| | Cayman Islands | 0 | 0 | 0 |
| | Dominica | 0 | 0 | 0 |
| | Grenada | 3 | 0 | 0 |
| | Guyana | 0 | 0 | 0 |
| | Jamaica | 15 | 4 | 0 |
| | Monserrat | 0 | 0 | 0 |
| | Netherlands Antilles | — | 0 | — |
| | St. Kitts & Nevis | 1 | 0 | 0 |
| | St. Lucia | 2 | 0 | 0 |
| | St. Vincent & Grenadines | 0 | 0 | 0 |
| | Suriname | 0 | 0 | 0 |
| | Trinidad & Tobago | 0 | 0 | 1 |
| | Turks & Caicos | 4 | 0 | 0 |
| | British Virgin Islands | 0 | 0 | 0 |
| | U.S. Virgin Islands | 0 | 0 | 0 |
| Latin Caribbean | Cuba | 1 | 0 | 0 |
| | Dominican Republic | 0 | 0 | 1 |
| | French Guiana | — | 0 | 0 |
| | Guadeloupe | 0 | 13 | 116 |
| | Haiti | — | 1 | 0 |
| | Martinique | — | 0 | 0 |
| | Puerto Rico | 11 | 8 | 0 |
| Mexico | Mexico | 244 | 180 | 0 |
| North America | Bermuda | 0 | 0 | 0 |
| | Canada | 2,357 | 327 | 570 |
| | United States | 309 | 489 | 135 |
| Southern Cone | Argentina | 655 | 59 | 96 |
| | Chile | 0 | 0 | 59 |
| | Paraguay | 73 | 13 | 198 |
| | Uruguay | 5 | 2 | 2 |
| **Total** | | **6,489** | **2,109** | **27,635** |

*Data as of 31 December 1997.

# IV. PREPARATORY WORK BY REGIONAL ORGANIZATIONS

*General-Secretariat, Organization of American States (OAS)*

The **Organization of American States (OAS)** *is the world's oldest regional organization, dating back to the First International Conference of American States, held in Washington, D.C., from October 1889 to April 1890. The OAS currently has 35 Member States. In addition, the Organization has granted Permanent Observer status to 37 States, as well as to the European Union.*

*The basic purposes of the OAS are as follows: to strengthen the peace and security of the continent; to promote and consolidate representative democracy, with due respect for the principle of nonintervention; to prevent possible causes of difficulties and to ensure the pacific settlement of disputes that may arise among the Member States; to provide for common action on the part of those States in the event of aggression; to seek the solution of political, juridical and economic problems that may arise among them; to promote, by cooperative action, their economic, social and cultural development, and to achieve an effective limitation of conventional weapons that will make it possible to devote the largest amount of resources to the economic and social development of the Member States.*

# Report of the Secretary-General on Bolivia Summit Implementation

## I. INTRODUCTION

In the context of the institutional arrangements set up in Santa Cruz de la Sierra, Bolivia, the Secretary-General of the Organization American States was given the mandate to submit a report on progress attained in the implementation of the initiatives of the Plan of Action on Sustainable Development. The report, to be made available prior to the 1998 Summit of the Americas, was intended as a follow-up on the commitments entered into in Bolivia. This paper is in compliance with the coordinating and follow-up roles entrusted to the Organization of American States (OAS).

### Background

The Summit of the Americas on Sustainable Development held in Santa Cruz in December of 1996 will perhaps be cited by historians as an effort which put the Western Hemisphere ahead of the rest of the world as the first region to prepare a blueprint on sustainable development within the framework of the global agreements reached at the United Nations Conference on Environment and Development in Rio in 1992. The Declaration of Santa Cruz built on the Rio Declaration and consolidated at the political level an understanding of the concept of sustainable development that reflects specific conditions in the Americas. The Bolivia Plan of Action also had the effect of setting priorities for the Western Hemisphere within the broad range of issues addressed in Agenda 21.

At the Summit of the Americas in Miami in 1994, the countries of the hemisphere reiterated their commitment to sustainable development and agreed on a series of actions to protect and ensure the efficient use of renewable natural resources and to combat pollution. At the Global Conference on Sustainable Development of Small Island Developing States held in Barbados in 1994, these governments further defined their priorities for action. Taken together with Agenda 21, the agreements reached in Miami and Barbados were the pillars on which the Bolivia Plan of Action was built.

In addition to mandating the holding of the Bolivia Summit in 1996, the Miami *Plan of Action* had called for "subsequent annual sustainable development ministerials," thereby setting in motion a significant process of inter-American dialogue on this issue. The Bolivia Summit gave additional impetus to this process.

The Bolivia Plan of Action is ambitious and includes initiatives in the areas of health, education, agriculture, forests, biodiversity, water resources and coastal areas, cities, energy and mining. Although the Declaration and Plan of Action are not comprehensive from the standpoint of sustainable development, they provide a foundation on which the countries of the hemisphere can gradually build new agreements on policies covering other elements critical to an environmentally sustainable approach to economic, social, and cultural development.

## Scope of This Report

One year is perhaps a very short period of time to evaluate the achievements of the Declaration and Plan of Action which the countries of the Western Hemisphere adopted at the Bolivia Summit. The mandate which the Secretary-General of the Organization of American States received to present this report was based on the desire of governments to assess promptly the progress being achieved on the 65 initiatives comprising the Plan of Action, which ultimately amounts to a strategy for seeking compliance with these initiatives.

The purpose of this report is to identify the major advances made in the region in implementing the Santa Cruz agreements and to make a series of recommendations designed to promote further implementation of the approved initiatives. It is important to stress that most of the activities linked to the initiatives were begun prior to the Summit, so it is not easy to determine to what extent they have been furthered as a result of the commitments made in Bolivia. In the main, these previously initiated activities were launched as a result of the commitments made in Rio de Janeiro, as expressed in the Declaration on the Environment and Development, and Agenda 21, as well as the Climate Change and Biodiversity Conventions, the Declaration on Forests, and other multilateral agreements or national initiatives of various origins. Quite frequently, the Santa Cruz initiatives were designed to strengthen activities that were already under way.

We are therefore looking at a very wide range of programs, many of which cannot be easily linked to the Bolivia Summit, either in terms of their origin or their achievements. This report makes an evaluation of the progress noted in the fields covered by each of the Santa Cruz initiatives, but it does not pretend to be comprehensive. It attempts to highlight successful strategies of implementation, identify obstacles encountered, and suggest new policies which may help to overcome difficulties.

The report singles out those activities that have been developed as a specific response to the mandates emanating from the Summit. While the number of such activities is relatively modest, they have a great deal of support, are very dynamic, and the outlook for them is promising.

## Principal Obstacles to Implementation of the Summit Initiatives

The modest progress made on actions undertaken as a direct result of the Summit can be attributed in part to the limitations inherent in the initiatives themselves, some of which go back to the preparatory process for the Summit.

Because of major disagreements that occurred in the course of the negotiations with regard to the scope of the Plan of Action and the responsibility that the different countries of the region should assume to implement the Plan, there was a great disparity in the support for the initiatives included in it. Furthermore, while many initiatives were the result of careful processes of technical preparation that included early political consultations, others were added during the very last part of the negotiations leading up to the Summit. Background studies were not conducted in issue areas such as sustainable cities, for example, and specific lines of action and implementation methods were not spelled out. The need to include such details was understood, but the time needed to further define the initiatives and make them operational was lacking. There was also a tendency in the final negotiating process to eliminate detail from some initiatives which had been more extensively crafted, in order to obtain a degree of homogeneity in the final document. Much useful detail about responsibilities for implementation was thereby deleted, most notably in the case of the chapter on water resources and coastal areas.

The shortage of financial resources to implement the initiatives has been another limiting factor. During the Bolivia Summit, there were major disagreements on this subject, similar to the differences of opinion encountered in other negotiating forums that took place after the Rio Conference. These differences have not been resolved and have ultimately made it impossible, so far, to implement some initiatives.

The fact of the matter is that there are too many initiatives in the Plan of Action and there has been too little money available in the short term to expect major advances. A major task for governments is to prioritize the initiatives and focus limited resources wisely. This is especially true at the inter-American level, where funds to support collective actions of the member states are extremely limited.

Many of the obstacles encountered in efforts to develop the agreements of the Rio Summit were repeated in the efforts to implement the Bolivia agreements. During the Special United Nations Assembly (Rio +5), the limited success achieved since Rio was acknowledged, but different interpretations of some of the fundamental agreements made at the Earth Summit made it impossible to develop strategies to overcome implementation problems. This situation, while worrisome in and of itself, should encourage the countries of the hemisphere to rise to the challenge and find ways to resolve this situation at a regional level.

Another obstacle to implementing the Bolivia Plan of Action is found at the national level. During the process of negotiating the initiatives, the institutions which had jurisdiction over the relevant areas in many cases did not participate adequately in the process, with the result that they were not fully committed to implementing the initiatives in question. This is a situation that can be resolved, but to do so will require decisive action at high levels of government. In the case of hemispheric actions mandated by the Summit, one proven strategy is to create focal points in countries and make sure that there is a clear assignment of responsibilities. Further substantive dialogue that fully involves all of the relevant institutions is clearly needed.

## A Forum of the Americas on Sustainable Development

### Background

The most meaningful follow-up to the consensus achieved at the Summit is not a report, on developments relating to those initiatives, or a series of such reports, but rather a continuing and constructive dialogue that will intensify efforts to fulfill the commitments that have been made.

The Plan of Action of the Summit on Sustainable Development is in many ways a piece of unfinished business. An organized forum process is greatly needed to further define priorities and to design practical, implementable actions. New initiatives may also be identified and new topics, not contemplated in the original Plan, may be incorporated. There needs to be a space in which the highest authorities of the hemisphere governments can exchange experiences on making the critical economic and social sectors environmentally sustainable. Such dialogue can serve as a basis for defining public policies at the national level and putting the concept of sustainable development into operation. To properly meet those needs, it is proposed that a ministerial-level forum on sustainable development be established within the framework of Inter-American Council for Integral Development (CIDI), as part of the agenda of its annual meetings.

### Functions

The Forum of the Americas on Sustainable Development would perform the following functions:

a) Work towards ensuring that the contents of the Declaration of Santa Cruz de la Sierra are reflected in regional, subregional, and national policies on sustainable development;

b) Promote implementation of the initiatives contained in the Plan of Action by defining goals, means of achieving them, and the agencies responsible for execution, and identifying new initiatives when necessary;

c) Promote a structured regional dialogue on experiences with solving problems of environment and sustainable development shared by the countries, as a strategy for increasing governments' capacity to define and implement relevant policies;

d) Adopt hemispheric positions for the negotiations taking place at the international level on environment and sustainable development issues.

### The Agenda for the Next Three Years

In view of the breadth of these functions, it is proposed that the Forum of the Americas on Sustainable Development concentrate each year on just two of the topics in the Bolivia Plan of Action. In particular, the following agenda is recommended for the next few years:

1999: Health and water

2000: Cities and energy

2001: Agriculture and biodiversity

One of the basic criteria for the selection of the two topics to be addressed simultaneously in any given year is that they should be closely interrelated and that the dialogue between the two sectors or issue areas could lead to the formulation of intersectoral policies. The two topics proposed for the first year, health and water, are good illustrations of the process. Many of the health problems in the region are associated with the lack of potable water and the unsatisfactory disposal of domestic and industrial wastewater. Such situations call for designing and putting into effect comprehensive policies and for coordinating the various sectors involved.

An agenda so conceived reduces the scope of debate to something manageable, while maintaining an integrated focus. The ministers of the relevant sectors would be asked to address the agenda along with the ministers of environment, economy, or planning, as appropriate. The focus should be on intersectoral issues in particular and the conclusions of the meeting could focus on actions to promote more effective coordination between sectors in order to help achieve sustainable development.

Furthermore, concentrating dialogue on issues at the interface between two sectors would have the effect of engaging higher authorities of government, which are needed to address problems or conflicts that cannot be resolved within the individual sectors. Such meetings are likely to promote the kind of high-level CIDI meetings which governments mandated in the OAS Charter. Through this mechanism, complex issues of sustainability could be addressed in a practical framework which does not attempt to treat the whole massive subject of sustainable development at one time.

Besides dealing with intersectoral topics, the agendas should also focus on specific issues that will advance the process of impelenting initiatives agreed at the Bolivia Summit, particularly ones requiring collective actions by governments.

Broad policy issues related to the Santa Cruz de la Sierra Declaration could also be included, with a view to furthering dialogue and action on a regional level and building hemispheric positions that could be advanced in global negotiations.

Ultimately, the ministerial meetings should be responsible for determining specific lines of action and should specify the relevant objectives, activities, expected results, financial resources, and the national and international institutions responsible for implementation.

It should be stressed that not all the possible elements of the topics to be considered in any given year would be included—only those in which there is a clear possibility of establishing a fruitful exchange of experiences aimed at policy recommendations or of deciding to implement specific proposals for action or of arriving at hemisphere-wide positions for use in negotiations at the world level. In each case, one of the priority criteria for the inclusion of a topic would be that its environmental and development dimensions could be treated in an integrated manner.

## Composition of the Forum, Convening Entities and Methods of Work

The Forum of the Americas on Sustainable Development, which would function within CIDI, could work as follows:

- It would operate through annual ministerial meetings, that would deal with an agenda set by CIDI at its regular meetings.

- Its participants would be ministers or leading officials of the sectors defined in the Bolivia Plan of Action along with the ministers of economy, national planning, and environment, or their national equivalents. Given the cross-sectoral nature of the Forum, the OAS would invite other organizations concerned with the topics, such as the Pan American Health Organization (PAHO), the Inter-American Institute for Cooperation on Agriculture (IICA), the Inter-American Development Bank (IDB), or the Latin American Energy Organization (OLADE), to participate in the meetings and assist in their planning and follow-up.

- During the twelve months prior to the annual ministerial meetings of CIDI on sustainable development, preparatory activities would be carried out at an adequate political and technical level to obtain needed consensus and to ensure that the lines of action submitted to the ministers for consideration would be viable if adopted. These preparatory activities would be undertaken in accordance with the nature of the topics to be discussed. They would include the preparation of studies and reports and the organization of workshops, seminars, or negotiating forums, among other things. The end product of these activities would be political and technical documents, which would contain specific recommendations for consideration and possible adoption by the ministerial meeting held under the auspices of CIDI.

- Efforts would be made to assure that the Forum of the Americas on Sustainable Development would be fully coordinated with the Forum of Latin American Ministers of Environment, so that their activities would be mutually complementary and not duplicative. As is well known, this strong forum has a remarkable history of achievement and concentrates primarily on topics that are the concern of the ministers of environment.

- The CIDI Forum, as mandated, should concentrate on intersectoral aspects of sustainable development. Efforts should also be made to coordinate the activities of the Forum on Sustainable Development with those of the FAO Forestry Commission for Latin America and the Caribbean and with the Central American Commission on Sustainable Development.

- The OAS Secretariat should also seek to utilize the inter-American technical dialogues operating under its auspices, such as the Inter-American Dialogue on Water Management and the one that is being created in the field of biodiversity, to support to the Forum of the Americas on Sustainable Development.

*Technical Secretariat*

The technical secretariat for the ministerial meetings and other technical dialogues would be under the responsibility of the OAS, in collaboration with other international and regional organizations as mentioned previously. Within the OAS, the Unit on Sustainable Development and Environment would function as the technical secretariat for the meetings, in association with other units as needed, under the overall coordination of the Executive Secretariat for Integral Development. Specialized Organizations of the inter-American system, such as PAHO and IICA, would be called upon to provide support to relevant sectoral dialogues.

## II. PROGRESS ON BOLIVIA SUMMIT INITIATIVE AREAS

This chapter summarizes progress made since the Santa Cruz meeting to implement the 65 initiatives adopted in Chapter II of the Plan of Action. The information for this report was provided by some countries and by several international organizations that have also made valuable inputs to the follow-up task. The agencies' contribution is an expression of the active role they have played and in some cases reflects their efforts within the Interagency Task Force to Support the Bolivia Summit Follow-Up, which is coordinated by the OAS Secretariat. The scope of this group, made up of a number of institutions in the United Nations and inter-American systems, has been expanded to include supporting the implementation of the relevant sections of the Miami Summit Action Plan.

## 1. Health and Education

There are still serious health problems in the Americas. Infant-mortality rates average 43 per thousand in Latin America and the Caribbean and reach as high as 70 per thousand in the poorest countries. Communicable diseases are still the main cause of morbidity and mortality in the region. Last year witnessed the first large outbreak of measles in a decade. The Americas must face additional challenges resulting from new and resurgent infectious diseases such as AIDS and cholera, increasing violence, and environmental hazards. Latin America and the Caribbean also face significant challenges in the area of education, which must play a key role in creating the social awareness needed for making commitments to sustainable development. The Bolivia Summit initiatives on health and education refer to environmental health (initiatives 1, 3, and 4), emerging and infectious/contagious diseases (initiatives 2 and 6), and education for sustainable development (initiative 5).

*a. Environmental Health*

Several actions have taken place that should increase access to safe drinking water:

- Baseline data on access to water disinfection levels and water quality have been established as part of PAHO's mid-decade evaluation. A regional meeting on drinking water quality was held in Peru in 1996.

- Projects on cholera prevention are under way in several countries in Latin America, which promote social mobilization of communities and development of basic technologies and small enterprises for the improvement of sanitation. A project for the improvement of basic sanitation in indigenous populations has been developed to address the problems of water supply.

- An Inter-American Water Day has been established by PAHO, the Inter-American Association of Sanitary Engineering (AIDIS), and the Caribbean Water and Wastewater Association (CWWA). Water Day provides an opportunity for policy makers and communities to discuss their problems, educate the population about issues of water supply and water quality, and strengthen their involvement in these matters.

- A working group on coordination of technical cooperation for improving access to and the quality of potable water has recently been formed under the Inter-Agency Task Force for Bolivia Summit Follow-Up. The group consists of PAHO, the United Nations Children's Fund (UNICEF), the World Bank, the U.S. Agency for International Development (USAID), the Canadian International Development Agency (CIDA), the OAS, the IDB, the National Sanitation Foundation, and the U.S. Environmental Protection Agency (USEPA). The purpose of the group is to prepare a plan of action for addressing crucial water quality issues and to design a conference.

- The Ministry of Public Health of El Salvador is preparing new rules and regulations on industrial and solid waste and on water and air quality. In coordination with several universities and with the support of PAHO a research project covering the whole country has been undertaken to determine levels of water, air, and soil contamination.

Efforts are underway to improve child health that will contribute in reducing the effects of environmental problems on the health of children:

- The countries of the region and PAHO have advanced during 1997 in developing a common framework, the Care of the Sick Child Strategy. This strategy would support the integral development of the child, with a focus on health promotion and prevention of illness in the growth and development process.

- Regional model standards on child health are being established and will be tested in Brazil to ascertain their applicability and the difficulties of implementing them before they are extended to other countries.

- In several countries laws are being revised on infants, and children's rights, the extension of access to and coverage of health and nutrition services, and educational opportunities.

[a] Immunization rates have risen as a consequence of policy decisions regarding extension of coverage. Children have been protected from environmentally borne diseases, including neonatal tetanus.

- Regional meetings to encourage the sharing of strategies on health promotion have been held. This practice will be brought into schools through the initiative "Health-Promoting Schools." Several countries are undertaking mass-media campaigns for health promotion and protection, including education on the abuse of alcohol, drugs and tobacco. All the countries of the region have developed programs for the integral development of adolescents.

The governments are also seeking to improve the coverage and quality of the available health services. They are giving priority to preventive and educational aspects and offering access to family planning information and services. The following actions have taken place in pursuit of these objectives:

- Many countries are using the themes of healthy cities, municipalities, islands, etc., to improve health promotion. Several countries are developing a basic package of health care that is to be guaranteed to all citizens. The Government of Venezuela has assigned priority to a program, based on equity and universal participation, to provide medications to outpatients. Special attention is given to vulnerable groups and especially to children, the elderly, and pregnant women. Nicaragua has also devised a package of basic services to the more vulnerable groups focused on preventive health to reduce infant mortality. Women and children are the priority targets of public health programs in the country. USAID supports programs in eight "child survival emphasis" countries in Latin America and the Caribbean: Bolivia, Ecuador, Peru, El Salvador, Guatemala, Honduras, Nicaragua and Haiti.

- Both non-governmental organizations (NGOs) and women's groups have been active in the implementation of national policies, especially in the delivery of reproductive health services and pre- and post-natal care.

- Close coordination among donors and other international agencies has resulted in greater and more efficient activities within the countries and closer attention to priorities of each country's plans of action.

- Efforts are under way to make a reality of the delivery of integrated reproductive health services. These include, at a minimum, family planning, safe motherhood, and prevention of HIV/AIDS and cancer of the cervix, as well as sexual education and the prevention of violence.

- PAHO is supporting the countries in building their capabilities to analyze and formulate health policies and plans, strengthening cooperation between them, and promoting exchanges among institutions and groups. PAHO has issued a document that sets out the parameters for reforming the health sector, in which emphasis is placed on the attainment of universal coverage with equity.

## b. Emerging and Infectious/Contagious Diseases

Key elements in addressing this topic have been as follows:

- The current PAHO Regional Plan of Action is an important instrument that provides guidance to countries in the prevention and control of emerging and reemerging diseases. A task force, convened in

# IV. Preparatory Work by Regional Organizations

1996, issued guidelines for its implementation and detailed recommendations on actions to be taken by countries and by PAHO. Implementation of it is in its early stages. A surveillance system for a limited number of diseases and syndromes was implemented on a pilot basis in 1997.

- A survey of national capabilities for the surveillance of emerging and reemerging infectious diseases in Latin America and the Caribbean was carried out. The results will serve as the basis for setting priorities for technical cooperation.

- A hemispheric plan to combat dengue was prepared by a task-force that met in Caracas in April 1997. However, its high cost makes its implementation difficult.

- Regarding response to disease outbreaks and disaster planning, preparedness, and mitigation, all the countries have continued to review their national and health sector plans in these areas

- In the Caribbean, response mechanisms have been strengthened by means of improved coordination between the United Nations Development Program (UNDP), the Caribbean Disaster Emergency Response Agency, the International Federation of Red Cross and Red Crescent Societies, and PAHO. The regional Safety System of the Caribbean and CARICOM collaborate in training programs for health administration in case of disaster. The multidisciplinary yearly exercise "Trade Winds in the Caribbean" provides each host country with an opportunity to test its plan for disaster preparedness.

- A symposium on emergency preparedness in the event of chemical disasters was held in Mexico in 1996. In September 1997, Peru organized a training course for the management of epidemic emergencies caused by "El Niño." All the Andean countries, several specialized agencies of the United Nations, and the Hipólito Unanue Accord participated in this course. A similar course is being organized for Central America, with PAHO support. These efforts are complemented by OAS, IDB, and World Bank support to member states to assess the vulnerability of economic and social infrastructure and define mitigation strategies. Several regional, sub-regional, and national organizations have joined in a partnership to develop a documentation center on disasters. The objective is to reduce vulnerability by facilitating access to and the dissemination of technical and scientific information.

- The International Committee of Experts in Hospital Mitigation, established as a follow-up to the International Conference on Mitigation of Disasters, is advising on the definition of technical policies for the implementation of mitigation programs. The European Union has supported studies in this field in several countries. Also, a series of technical training modules directed to professionals in structural engineering and design of hospitals have been prepared jointly with the UN Commission on Latin America and the Caribbean (ECLAC) and the International Decade for Natural Disaster Reduction.

- Also in relation to disasters, PAHO has prepared a guide on the vulnerability of water systems. In addition, technical documents were prepared based on case studies of damage caused by earthquakes in the urban water-supply systems in Costa Rica and Ecuador, by the volcanic eruption in Montserrat, and by landslides and floods in Brazil, among others.

## c. Education for Sustainable Development

Changes in educational and communications policy include instruction in sustainable development tailored to the different needs and realities of the hemisphere. Progress in this endeavor has been as follows:

- Several countries have developed multi-sectoral action plans for health promotion efforts. As a follow-up to international accords such as the World Summit for Children, the International Conference on Population and Development, the Fourth International Conference on Women, and the World Summit for Social Development, the involvement of different groups of civil society has also been promoted.

- In Peru, innovative initiatives in education are being promoted. The government's goal is to further diversify educational options and to raise its quality in public schools. A project on Andean ecological and environmental education is being developed at several teacher-training establishments.

- Initiatives for improving living conditions of indigenous people have stimulated studies and training within the health sector in many countries. There is increased awareness of the need to develop alternative models of communication and service delivery to reach diverse communities. The media are being more widely used for effective transmission of information in response to the identified needs of the population.

- Training models have been developed for quality of care, preparation of human resources, adolescent health, and other matters, which are based on an initial assessment and knowledge of what target populations see as their needs.
- The search for sustainable development in most countries has led to partnerships with NGOs and the private sector and to a redefinition of the role of ministries of health. These new partnerships have often resulted in greater efficiency and increased awareness of accountability.
- In Nicaragua, for instance, a National Committee for Environmental Education was established in 1994 with the participation of the ministries of education and health, other government agencies, and representatives of civil society. The Committee is an interdisciplinary institution that analyzes, prepares, proposes, and implements national policies in the areas of environmental protection and health. Several activities are currently under way on the matter of environmental education.
- The Ministry of Education in El Salvador is promoting policies directed toward transforming education at all levels of schooling. One subject in the curriculum deals with science, health, and the environment. Special attention has been given to groups such as women, youth, and children, with the objective of ensuring adequate training in sustainable development. An effort has been made to achieve equitable access to education, and support has been given to other innovative ways to improve the quality of education.
- USAID and PAHO resources will support a project on "Equitable Access to Basic Health Services." This five-year project (1997-2002) will foster regional or inter-country activities aimed at developing tools, providing support, and to designing, implementing and monitoring reform processes. The Central American Institute for Administration and Supervision of Education (ICASE) will develop a master's degree program in environmental education, under a project on Environmental Education for Latin America and the Caribbean, recently approved by OAS. The United Nations Educational, Scientific, and Cultural Organization (UNESCO) and the OAS will assist in the training of teachers on the topic of sustainable development. An international register of innovative practices to promote education, public awareness, and information on sustainable development will also be developed through the Internet.

*d. Obstacles*

Many countries share the difficulties encountered by Nicaragua in assessing its health sector: the need to clarify the functions of different actors involved in regulation, financing, and the provision of services. There are challenges posed by a lack of medical and non-medical supplies, inadequate infrastructure, and insufficient and poorly kept equipment. There is unmet demand in some services and the capacity for providing hospital care is saturated. Furthermore, in most countries access to services by underprivileged groups, such as indigenous and rural populations, is very limited.

The outbreak of measles in São Paulo, Brazil, in 1997 is threatening the successful eradication of the disease, after remarkable progress had been made. Recent evaluations have identified the major weaknesses of measles surveillance systems in the region. Some of these, which need to be overcome, are common to several places.

Education is inadequately funded, particularly during the first years, in public schools serving low-income groups. Improved access to quality education should contribute to strengthening the commitment to sustainable development. Awareness of the harm being done by polluting habits is not widespread and educational efforts to develop alternative behavior are inadequate.

*e. Recommendations*

Additional human and financial resources should be channeled to some key sectors that need to be strengthened, such as public education for low-income groups, and to improvements in the measles and other surveillance systems. A commitment should be made to bring health and educational services to the underprivileged.

The working group of the Interagency Task Force to support the Bolivia Summit Follow-Up in charge of preparing an action plan that will address major issues of water quality deserves full support. This initiative will bring together governments and relevant agencies in 1998 to adopt an action plan, that will integrate various health-related program components and develop specific projects.

A major problem for the hemisphere is the reduction of exposure to environmental pollution from hazardous wastes and the increased use of toxic chemicals. The decision to establish regional and subregional centers for training and technology transfer on the management of hazardous wastes should contribute to progress in this matter.

## 2. Sustainable Agriculture and Forests

The rural sector, traditionally the largest employer in Latin America and the Caribbean, suffers from widespread poverty. A lack of adequate techniques and know-how among farmers and their need to capture short-term economic benefits induce practices that cause soil erosion, desertification, and other harmful effects to the environment. As is currently practiced in many parts of the hemisphere, agriculture is not sustainable. Santa Cruz addressed this as one of the most serious problems of the region.

The Western Hemisphere has the largest forest cover on the planet, comprising boreal, temperate, and tropical forests. They contain the major share of the world's biodiversity, which is primarily concentrated in the tropical regions of the Americas. This great wealth, however, is threatened by acute deforestation, mainly in the tropicals, and forest degradation, which is occurring in many parts of the hemisphere. The Bolivia Plan of Action mandated a series of activities to move toward the sustainable use and management of biodiversity. The initiatives constitute a regional effort aimed at achieving the objectives established in the Convention on Biological Diversity signed in Rio de Janeiro. The Bolivia agreements were also directed at strengthening the measures adopted at the Second Conference of the Parties, which was held in Buenos Aires in late 1996. The Plan of Action includes initiatives on sustainable agriculture (7 to 16), sustainable forestry (17 to 22), and biodiversity conservation (23 to 31).

### a. Sustainable Agriculture

Progress in the area of sustainable agriculture has been as follows:

- Three principal land-management issues addressed at the Summit were the use of agricultural chemicals, soil conservation and desertification, and the preservation of traditional practices. Improved management of agricultural chemicals at the global, regional, national, and local levels was a goal. Globally, an International Instrument for Dangerous Substances and Pesticides in International Commerce is nearing agreement. Subregional groupings that include North America, Central America, MERCOSUR, and the Organization of Eastern Caribbean States (OECS) are also close to agreements on farm chemicals. Uruguay, Costa Rica, and Ecuador made striking advances in reducing the intensity of use of agricultural chemicals, while other countries conducted campaigns against specific troublesome pests and diseases. To reduce the need for farm chemicals, the Caribbean and Central American countries introduced integrated pest control and biological substitutes for pesticides, or instituted organic farming.

- Programs to achieve soil conservation and restoration and reduce desertification involve 20 governments, often cooperating closely with NGOs. Fourteen countries participate in the Network of International Cooperation on Arid and Semiarid Zones. Argentina, Bolivia, Chile, Ecuador, and Peru participate in the Action Program for the Sustainable Development of the American Puna. These programs also have important implications for agrarian reform and social welfare. Other countries have established specialized agencies such as Drought Commissions or National Commissions for Arid Lands. Argentina instituted a national diagnosis of soil degradation and operates several projects of soil and desertification management to achieve sustainable use of soils in arid, semiarid, and subhumid zones. Venezuela has instituted a program to stabilize river banks with bamboo plantations.

- Traditional practices that can have a beneficial impact on biodiversity include the use of organic fertilizers, mulch, and animal traction. Other practices include no-plow farming, integrated control of pests and diseases, the cultivation of native foods that favor conservation of biodiversity, and the application of sustainable management methods by small-holder producers of flora and fauna that have commercial potential.

- In keeping with the Summit directive to strengthen the efforts at the conservation of genetic resources and to generate appropriate research to support "whole system" (i.e., ecosystem, whole farm, or watershed) approaches, Mexico instituted a program of Productive Diversification and Wildlife in the Rural Sector offering new opportunities for economic development through diversification of crop and animal production with a base in the conservation of germ plasm. The program uses wild flora and fauna for the national chemical-pharmaceutical-cosmetic industry. Argentina,

Chile, Costa Rica, Dominican Republic, Paraguay, Peru, and Venezuela are stimulating research on national genetic resources. The English-speaking Caribbean is working on genetic improvement of table grapes, citrus, and native palm. At the hemispheric and subregional levels, IICA, the UN Food and Agriculture Organization (FAO), the Tropical Agronomic Research and Teaching Center (CATIE), and other international organizations are supporting research on genetic resources of native plants and animals.

- Significant steps have been taken to connect agricultural research more closely with ecosystem conservation. Canada is investigating new strains of crops and trees that promote biodiversity and yet bring benefits such as disease resistance, more efficient use of nutrients, and sequestration of $CO_2$. In keeping with the call to develop "whole system" approaches, there is increasing research on timing and methods of planting, fertilizing, rotations, green manure, and organic correctives in crops, pastures, and trees. Seed banks of forest species have been established as a source of quality seeds to preserve forest masses. A hemispheric research network for coconut production was established in which 12 countries participate.

- One approach to expanding agricultural exports is support for production by crop and by region. There is support for the commercialization of Andean products and for increasing the area planted to them; increasing Caribbean agricultural exports; improving the production and productivity of traditional crops, and capitalizing on comparative advantage, and for individual products such as fruits, peppers, tubers, sea-isle cotton, and small ruminants.

- Improved technologies and services such as information systems, quarantine periods for plants and animals, techniques that guarantee sustainable use of agricultural resources, and pre- and post-harvest improvements are being applied to enhance the quality of delivered products. Central America, with the technical support of IICA, has established agricultural exchange centers with electronic information systems that bring training, extension, and support for commercialization closer to the farmer. The new technologies demonstrate a consciousness of environmental issues: Argentina has promoted crops having environmental benefits, and the Caribbean has supported cleaner agroindustrial processes.

- Some countries have helped rural communities and indigenous people by promoting foreign markets for their crops, setting up export mechanisms, sheltering them from unfair competition, instituting land reform, and establishing incentives and subsidies. IICA, FAO, the United States, China, Germany, and the European Union have supported these efforts.

- An innovative approach to increasing agricultural exports was the development of ecotourism on individual farms and ranches. Paraguay has become a leader in this approach.

- In response to the need to overcome poverty in the agricultural sector, several countries have increased credit and technical support to small farmers, improved peasants' access to factors of production and packages of technology, and promoted organic farming. Some have created agricultural centers that showed small farmers how to increase long-term profits by incorporating environmental protection into their production systems. A number of governments helped their farmers with fish farming and forest crop production. Others devoted up to one percent of their GNP to agricultural research. A new concept called "activity chains" helped small farmers coordinate the steps in the agricultural process from the acquisition of inputs through land preparation, production, and transport to the marketing of selected crops.

- Meetings and training programs for indigenous people, peasants, and small businessmen on subjects like "Use of Tools Required to Operate Farm Enterprises" and "Augmenting Income and Competitiveness" are being widely offered by governments of the region. Attempts are being made to decentralize and privatize training activities. Training often focuses on business management for rural women and young entrepreneurs. Comprehensive exercises use integrated farms for training small operators. Emphasis is placed on transfer of technology with the goal of increasing productivity and competitiveness. Canada has supported programs of interchange of farmers from Latin America and the Caribbean. Twenty-four international meetings and conferences were convened on subjects related to the Santa Cruz initiatives on agriculture in 1997.

- Several countries strengthened local communities and rural organizations to promote conservation and sustainable agriculture. Bolivia established programs on equal opportunity for women and rural community development that help women assume a more active role in decision-making. To increase financial and technical assistance at the family level, Argentina is promoting the consolidation of associative groups of producers. Colombia's Rural Home Program supports low-income families in rural communities. Paraguay offers local leaders training in soil management. Peru helps small producers with fertilizer and certified seed for principal crops. Uruguay provides support for integrated pest control and crop diversification. The English-speaking Caribbean offers a similar array of support for small farmers.

- The most important feature of land reform is the distribution of land with certainty of title, but various national land-reform programs feature many other characteristics such as recognizing rights of indigenous populations, modernizing production, helping with credit, conducting rural cadastres, and inscribing rural properties in the public registry. Many countries strengthened their agrarian legal systems, passing in some cases titling or agrarian enterprise laws and enacting provisions to favor women with land rights.

- Some countries have improved the efficiency and quality of projects in their land-reform programs through decentralization. Bolivia, Brazil, Colombia, Chile, the Dominican Republic, and Saint Lucia incorporated agrarian reform into comprehensive programs of regional or rural development, poverty alleviation, or agroindustrial reform such as the replacement of sugar with other crops.

*b. Sustainable Forestry*

The following developments indicate progress in this subject:

- In accordance with the recommendation of the Bolivia Summit, governments in the region participated actively in the deliberations and between-meeting activities organized by the Intergovernmental Panel on Forests (IPF), which was co-chaired by a hemispheric country, Colombia. The parties were not able to arrive at a common position on the controversial issue of a convention on forests.

- The various activities organized between meetings included the following: the Study of International Organizations, Instruments, and Institutions in the Forestry Field, sponsored by Switzerland and Peru; the International Workshop on the Integral Application of Practices for the Sustainable Management of Forests, sponsored by Mexico, Canada, and Japan; and the Global Forum of Peoples Native to the Forests and Other Peoples Dependent on the Forests Regarding Preservation and Sustainable Management of Forests, organized by the Alliance of Peoples Native to Tropical Forests, in cooperation with the Indigenous Council of the Amazon Basin, with the sponsorship of the governments of Colombia and Denmark.

- After the Rio Conference, all the countries in the region strengthened their national forestry programs. This work gained momentum as a result of recommendations on the subject made by the Intergovernmental Panel on Forests. National programs were formulated and related activities were developed on the basis of co-financing arrangements involving World Bank and IDB credits in some countries. Resources obtained on favorable terms from bilateral and multilateral development assistance sources were also used. The activities included a Pilot Program on the Brazilian Amazon, financed through a special fund set up by the G-7. FAO also played an important role in supporting these efforts; it organized various workshops involving subregional or national experts in Brazil, Ecuador, and the Caribbean under the Regional Forum on National Forestry Programs for Latin America and the Caribbean.

- Some progress was also achieved in improving citizen participation in activities related to the sustainable management of forests. Several countries have adopted new policies and laws, and action has been taken to protect the cultural diversity of indigenous communities and their traditional know-how and skills. The Central American Council on Forests and Protected Areas has introduced various arrangements to guarantee that all relevant parties participate in decisions affecting forests. Numerous participatory projects for the sustainable management of forests have also been identified. These are promoted by national governments, by international agencies, such as the FAO Program on Forests and Local People, and by non-governmental organizations. Some countries have granted indigenous communities property rights to land that has been traditionally inhabited by their ancestors, or have adopted measures to organize the opening up of agricultural frontiers and clarify property titles for the new tracts of land. Under either plan, strategies have been designed to create conditions favoring sustainable management of wooded areas by rural property owners. The underlying assumption is that land holding and land rights play a vital role in the sustainable management of wooded areas, and that the process of regulating and legalizing these rights must be accompanied by technical assistance and credit programs. Moreover, while protected areas have increased in number and size, there is also growing recognition of the fact that to manage them adequately, the communities living there or in neighboring areas must participate in that management effort. Various participatory plans have been developed to that end.

- A number of programs involving bilateral and multilateral cooperation in the sustainable management of forests have emerged in the region. The International Program of Model Forests, the strengthening of which was recommended by the Santa Cruz Summit, is designed to promote the sharing of local experiences, know-how, and technology, with a view to achieving sustainable development. Representatives from Argentina, Canada, Chile, Costa Rica, the United States, and various regions of the host country attended the First International Forum of the Network of Model Forests, held in Mexico in 1997.

- In Central America and in the Amazon Basin, numerous cooperation programs are being developed under the auspices of the Central American Commission on Environment and Development and the Amazon Cooperation Treaty, respectively.

- Countries in the region are participating actively in international efforts to define and implement criteria and indicators for the sustainable management of forests. January 1997 saw the start of the process to define criteria and indicators for the seven countries belonging to the Central American Commission on Environment and Development.

- In mid-1997, the ninth meeting of the Montreal Initiative was held. Forty-five countries, including the six in the Americas that are part of that process—Argentina, Canada, Chile, Mexico, the United States, and Uruguay—attended the meeting.

- The Tarapoto Initiative, involving the eight countries belonging to the Amazon Cooperation Treaty, recommended to the member governments that a Proposal on Criteria and Indicators for the Sustainability of the Amazon Forest be adopted. The Tarapoto Proposal involves a comprehensive and multidisciplinary approach, which could give a considerable boost to national and regional efforts to develop an adequate tool for planning the sustainable development of forests.

*c. Biodiversity Conservation*

The following achievements can be underlined in this key area:

- Even before the Convention of Biological Diversity was signed in Rio de Janeiro, other multilateral agreements played an important role in furthering work on this matter in the hemisphere, such as: the International Convention on Trade in Endangered Species (CITES); the Convention on Wetlands of International Importance (RAMSAR); the Convention on the Protection of the World's Cultural and Natural Heritage; the Convention on the Law of the Seas; the International Treaty on Trade in Tropical Woods (ITTA); the Program for Regional Seas of UNEP; the UNESCO Program on Man and the Biosphere; and the Amazon Treaty. More recently, the Central American Alliance for Sustainable Development has also launched a number of initiatives directed towards the preservation of biodiversity.

- Implementation of the Convention on Biodiversity has not been satisfactory, although progress has been made in some specific areas. The United Nations "UNGASS" Program for the implementation of Agenda 21 stressed the fact that "there is an urgent need to ensure the preservation and sustainable development of biological diversity and the fair and equitable distribution of the benefits derived from using the components of genetic resources." UNGASS highlighted certain specific threats, including the destruction of habitat, overexploitation of both marine and land environments, pollution, and the inappropriate introduction of exotic plants and animals. Various ways to combat these threats were also the subject of agreements at Santa Cruz.

- Negotiations are currently under way to approve a Protocol on Biosecurity pertaining to the cross-border movement of live organisms which have been modified using modern biotechnology and could adversely affect the preservation and sustainable use of biological diversity, and even human

# IV. PREPARATORY WORK BY REGIONAL ORGANIZATIONS

health. At the same time, progress is being made on negotiations to bring the International Initiative on Genetic Plant Resources into line with the Convention on Biological Diversity. In an effort to protect genetic resources of plants at the national, regional, and global levels, this review includes access to genetic resources and the rights of farmers. Latin American and Caribbean countries are taking an active part in both negotiations.

- Many countries in the hemisphere have adopted national biodiversity strategies, strengthened their research and development capacity in the area of biological resources, and introduced legislation on access to genetic resources. The Andean countries have enacted regional laws and are developing national legislation. Argentina, Brazil, Costa Rica, and Mexico are also planning to either introduce or amend legislation on this subject.

- In early 1997, UNEP began a review of existing legislation in the region, as an essential component for an exchange of information to serve as a basis for further developing the body of law on the subject, so that the many complex provisions of the Convention can be applied. There are also various studies in progress on enhancing the economic value of biodiversity, and research project on the industrial demand for genetic resources and an analysis of the European market.

- In accordance with the Biodiversity Convention, specific strategies on a global or regional level aimed at furthering scientific knowledge of the biological diversity of forests, agriculture, and seas and coastal areas either have been defined or are in the process of being worked out. The Conference of the Parties endorsed the Global Initiative on Taxonomy, and the upcoming conference is expected to adopt the measures required to put it into effect. In addition, at the third meeting of the scientific group of the Conference of the Parties, the adoption of a preliminary series of indicators for biological diversity was recommended. This is a field in which work is being done by a number of countries in the hemisphere.

- An important achievement in the Americas in recent decades has been the creation of systems of protected areas, which reflects a key strategy for ensuring the long-range preservation of biodiversity. Its significance is reflected in the fact that the diversity of ecosystems can only be guaranteed *in situ*. A more recent development has been the identification and establishment of protected cross-border areas. In recognizing the importance of the network of protected areas, the Convention on Biodiversity indicated its intention that this would be one of the mayor areas for project financing by the Global Environmental Facility (GEF). The following projects are mentioned among those financed in the region: the regional Meso-American system of protected areas, buffer zones, and biological corridors; the establishment of a global representative system of protected marine areas; action for a sustainable Amazon region; regional strategies for the preservation and sustainable use of natural resources in the Amazon; and national projects to support the establishment and development of systems of protected areas, such as Brazil's Fund for Biodiversity, conservation of biodiversity and sustainable development in the conservation areas of La Amistad and La Osa in Costa Rica, and the programs of protected areas in Mexico and Guyana.

- In addition to projects for protected areas, the GEF has also financed various national projects for the protection of biodiversity, such as the following: consolidation and implementation of the program for management of the coastal area of Patagonia to preserve its biodiversity; protection and sustainable use of the biological diversity of the biogeographical Chocó in Colombia; preservation of biodiversity in the Lake Titicaca watershed; the integrated project for the protection of biodiversity in the Sartsún-Montagua region of Guatemala. Finally, the World Bank and the IDB have co-financed various projects in Latin America and the Caribbean related to preservation of biodiversity.

- The First Latin American Congress on National Parks and Other Protected Areas, which took place in Santa Marta, Colombia, in 1997, stressed the importance of the initiatives agreed to at the Bolivia Summit and the close relationship between preservation of biodiversity and management of national parks. It also highlighted the role that the OAS should play as a forum for moving forward the various recommendations emanating from the Congress, and especially those related to biodiversity.

- Effective protection and use of the traditional know-how, innovations, and practices of indigenous peoples and other local communities, and the equitable distribution of the benefits so derived, as agreed under the Convention on Biodiversity, have been identified as priority goals for the Americas. This topic was discussed at length in the Global Workshop on Indigenous Peoples and Forests, which took place in Leticia, Colombia, in December 1996. Ways to achieve this objective have been discussed in various forums and workshops sponsored for the most part by local non-governmental organizations. Also, a Workshop on Traditional Know-How and Biological Diversity was held in Madrid last November. However, five years after the Convention was concluded, little progress has been made in this area, which is of particular relevance to the Americas, a habitat with a great diversity of indigenous peoples.

- The Inter-American Biodiversity Information Network (IABIN) will be launched in September 1998 in an international conference to be hosted by the Government of Brazil. To support multilateral cooperation in the development of this initiative, the OAS convened a Meeting of Experts in October 1997 and a second one in early 1998. These have been successful in bringing about a common understanding and acceptance of IABIN and in helping Brazil to plan for the 1998 meeting. At the first meeting, experts from seven countries made some recommendations to the OAS, one of which resulted in a call for IABIN focal points from all OAS members. The second meeting was expanded to include additional countries and non-governmental organizations working in Latin American and Caribbean biodiversity. It also considered how to develop better coordination with the clearinghouse mechanism of the Convention on Biodiversity. During this period of implementation at least eight countries have committed resources and intellectual capital to IABIN as part of this organizing process.

## d. Obstacles

In the field of sustainable agriculture, as in the broader subject of sustainable development, insufficient domestic and international funding, human resources, and infrastructure for research and technology transfer are a paramount problem. Changing legislation to rationalize the use of farm chemicals is a slow process. The practice of exporting to developing countries chemicals that are banned in developed countries further hinders this effort. There is not enough coordination between governments and businesses to find suitable alternatives for unwanted pesticides. Constraints on resources for facing issues related to soil conservation, desertification, and traditional practices, combined with weaknesses in national information systems and lack of attention to indicators in areas where transformation processes lead to desertification, hamper progress in these matters.

Serious weaknesses in the institutional and policy framework must be overcome to strengthen genetic resource measures for valuing the rich heritage of the Americas. Agricultural exports from Latin America and the Caribbean continue to face significant obstacles. Trade liberalization is still a work in process. Technologies that simultaneously increase profits and protect the environment are difficult to find, which makes poverty eradication an even more elusive goal. In some cases, ambiguity of legal provisions has had negative effects on land-reform programs.

The main obstacles to curbing deforestation and degradation of forests have to do with a lack of firm commitment at the appropriate political level to combat their primary national and international causes. Political determination will develop as communities are able to participate in the decision-making processes affecting the environment, an approach that has been gaining substantial ground in the Americas.

Differences between developed and developing countries in the interpretation of certain agreements contained in the Convention on Biodiversity have hindered its implementation. The fact that the United States, the primary user of biodiversity in the world, has not ratified the Convention reduces the chances that it will succeed in achieving its main objective. International financing is also far from sufficient to meet all the objectives and commitments under the Convention. The GEF and individual donor countries have provided grant resources to developing countries to implement projects involving the protection and sustainable use of biodiversity, but international financing is far from adequate to meet all the objectives and commitments under the Convention. Very little is being done to combat the underlying national and international causes of the decline in biodiversity, and this has become one of the most formidable obstacles to halting that decline.

## e. Recommendations

Adoption of the FAO code on pesticides at the national and regional levels should help to improve the management of agricultural chemicals and reduce their harmful effects on the environment. With IICA support, governments should intensify their efforts to promote integrated pest-control practices and other programs that instruct farmers, producer associations, and unions in the safe use of pesticides. To increase needed research on agricultural chemicals and plant and animal health, associations between state and private organizations should be encouraged.

While national agencies in charge of research, technology transfer, and extension should be more responsive to producers and market indicators, greater participation by the private sector in extension and technical assistance activities should also be promoted. Measures should be taken to ensure that local communities have greater participation in resource conservation decisions, including the design of initiatives to control desertification and the adoption of sustainable development practices.

Changes to existing legislation could be considered to make the land market more open. In this respect, measures should be taken to ensure clean title to small parcels.

Because of the importance of agricultural exports for many countries in the Americas and the rapid changes in world trade, the farm sector needs to be more involved in multinational trade negotiations and be better trained in negotiating skills.

The countries should be encouraged to implement the IPF proposals for action. In order to achieve this objective the Regional Forestry Commission for Latin America and the Caribbean coordinated by FAO should be strengthened. All countries of the Americas should participate actively in the Intergovernmental Forum on Forests, which will be co-chaired by Colombia and Peru. The possibility of organizing a continental dialogue should be explored, with the goal of exchanging information on critical items of the agenda and identifying those on which a common position could be reached. Since the Intergovernmental Forum on Forests is expected to formulate its recommendations at the eighth meeting of the Inter-American Commission on Sustainable Development (CIDS), it is advisable that an item on forests be included on the agenda for the Forum of the Americas on Sustainable Development for 1999, as a strategy in preparation for the Intergovernmental Forum, and that ways of implementing the initiatives approved in Bolivia in the context of global agreements be identified.

The OAS should be requested to coordinate regional activities in order to further the process of exchanging experience and information on the identification and creation of cross-border protected areas in the hemisphere. The OAS should also look into the possibility of including in the Inter-American Strategy on Public Participation a pilot project in the field of sustainable management of forests, which would link the agreements under the Biodiversity Convention with those adopted by the Intergovernmental Forum on Forests.

The OAS could also be requested to carry out the steps needed to initiate talks on biodiversity at the inter-American level, which are specified in initiative 29. This would constitute supportive action to initiative 31 and the creation of IABIN. The GEF should provide support to IABIN, which is a priority for the hemisphere. In addition, the efforts of the IDB to explore new alternatives for financing protection and sustainable use of biodiversity should be reinforced.

## 3. Sustainable Cities and Communities

The cities of the region are experiencing dramatic and accelerating changes. Governments are channeling more resources and increased responsibilities to sub-national jurisdictions. In turn, many regional and local governments are facilitating business and community initiatives to expand and improve services in terms of coverage, quality and efficiency. International technical assistance and lending programs are supporting these changes. The Plan of Action refers to four areas under this subject: economic development (initiatives 32 to 35), housing (initiatives 36 to 40), pollution prevention and environmental protection (initiatives 38 to 45), and sustainable transport (initiatives 43 and 46).

### a. Economic Development

Cities have looked for greater coordination with national and regional governments, the private sector, and international cooperation, to face the challenges of urban unemployment:

- Some progress has been made in implementing new approaches to urban management or in applying them in an experimental way. USAID, for instance, has sponsored a number of programs and projects to foster the transition to democratic decentralization. Programs on strengthening municipal governments in Honduras and Nicaragua continued in 1997, and a new one on local communities' participation in development was launched in Guatemala. A conference on democratic decentralization was held in Guatemala City in September

1997, under the auspices of USAID and the Federation of Municipalities of the Central American Isthmus (FEMICA).

- The mayors of the Americas have met on several occasions in the last few years. These meetings have looked at issues of urban development in an integrated manner. Multilateral (OAS, IDB, World Bank) and bilateral (USAID) agencies have supported the mayors' meetings, most recently in Miami in October 1997.
- Decentralization has opened the way to multidisciplinary approaches to face the challenges of sustainable urbanization. Local authorities in Latin America and the Caribbean strive to create balanced, sustainable cities, enjoying some comparative advantages, in an environment where individual interests and collective services become compatible. Mendoza, Argentina; Curitiba and Porto Alegre, Brazil; Manizales, Colombia; and Quito, Ecuador, have been pioneers in their multidisciplinary and integrated approach to city management.
- Some progress has been made in decentralizing education and work training programs. In Argentina, Bolivia, Brazil, Colombia, Chile, and Peru, education programs have been successfully combined with on-the-job training. This is an area where city mayors could contribute because they are in a position to bring together knowledge of the local labor force and production potential as an input to shape educational and training programs.
- In Venezuela, support to decentralization has been given as called for in the IX National Plan and the Agenda Venezuela. A number of activities and services, such as health, education, sports, youth, and nutrition, have been transferred to state and municipal governments. The Intergovernmental Fund for Decentralization provides financial support to decentralize public administration, through the evaluation and financing of projects submitted by state and local governments.
- Lima, Mexico City, Rio de Janeiro, Chinandega and León (Nicaragua), and Medellin (Colombia) have undertaken programs aimed at facilitating municipal access to capital markets. They have also implemented programs to improve the capacity of low-income groups to obtain credit for financing productive activities, through the regularization of property titles, and the improvement of urban infrastructure and housing. Both Mexico City and Medellin prepared comprehensive strategic plans in 1997, including the strengthening of their competitive position and Bogota is completing a similar plan.
- In Bolivia, Honduras, and Nicaragua, incentives have been set in place to promote the involvement of local communities and governments in the joint planning of projects of construction and maintenance of urban infrastructure. Porto Alegre, Brazil, has broken ground in achieving the participation of different sectors of society in the preparation of the capital budget for the city. Other cities following this practice are Mendoza, Argentina; La Florida, Chile; Cali, Colombia; Tijuana, Mexico; and Ciudad Guayana, Venezuela.
- Under the sponsorship of USAID a new three-year, $3 million initiative was launched in 1997 to support job creation, labor productivity, microenterprise, and investment for the smaller economies of the Eastern Caribbean. USAID assistance, provided through the Caribbean Economic Diversification Program, in partnership with CARICOM, includes support for, among other things, microenterprises, short-term technical training for college students preparing to enter the labor force, and community-based projects for self employment opportunities.

## b. Housing

Some innovative approaches have been taken to face the unsatisfied demand for housing in the hemisphere:

- Several countries and many cities have diversified the instruments and mechanisms applicable to urban land acquisition, zoning, development, and regulation. Colombia, for instance, has enacted a law authorizing cities to appropriate, as resources of the local government, part of the increases in land values caused by administrative decisions. In Mexico, plans have been adopted to redistribute profits flowing from incorporation of suburban land or adjoining rural areas into the cities among previous owners, infrastructure financing, and environmental protection areas.
- Some Central American countries have undertaken programs to facilitate access to real-estate and capital markets and housing to low-income groups. Urban development is no longer a state monopoly

in Latin America and the Caribbean, as there is increased awareness and use of instruments to promote private-sector involvement. Metropolitan areas are conscious of the need for greater coordination between local and national governments in matters of planning, urban development, and environmental protection.

## c. Pollution Prevention and Environmental Protection

Progress has been made in incorporating all potential actors in policies, activities, and financing of environmental protection:

- Peru is one of several countries that have enacted laws to offer economic and fiscal incentives, as well as extended terms to comply with new standards, to those who abide by existing environmental regulations. Brazil, Colombia and Mexico are in the process of establishing some incentives to induce communities, the media, and financial markets to combat industrial pollution.

- Bilateral and multilateral development agencies have recently developed new principles and operative models to control industrial pollution. These models are based on interaction between governments, producers, and consumers; between business and communities; and between the public sector and the markets. International organizations are bringing forth new ideas regulating industrial pollution and new information on ways to reduce it.

- A substantial portion of IDB lending has been directed at urban environment and pollution control projects. In 1996, for instance, large-scale metropolitan sanitation projects in Mexico, Uruguay, Bolivia, and Guatemala made up the lion's share of the environmental portfolio of the bank. Major projects have also been financed for clean-up programs in Guanabara Bay, Bahia Todos os Santos, and Lake Managua and the Bank has supported innovative work upgrading low-income settlements in Brazil.

## d. Sustainable Transport

New policies have been put into effect in this context:

- Some cities, especially in Brazil, have adopted integrated policies on land use and urban transportation aimed at reducing the high expropriation costs associated with land acquisition for building urban transportation infrastructure. Cali, Colombia, will follow a similar approach to the construction of its city metro.

## e. Obstacles

Rapid urbanization poses serious challenges in terms of infrastructure and housing, common spaces and sustainable transportation, the prevention and correction of pollution, the disposal of industrial waste, the promotion of pollution free consumption habits, and the management of sustainable technologies. The accelerated pace of urbanization is creating new forms of social and economic marginality that nurture crime and violence at epidemic levels. The largest urban centers are just beginning to keep track of city crime and are learning the particular forms of metropolitan violence. They are beginning to experiment with new measures capable of effectively curtailing violence.

Decentralization is a means towards an end, not an aim in itself. Most national governments still maintain the structures that were established when the state was the party responsible for urban development. Cities are not yet fully recognized as valid counterparts in national or international discussions about urban development. Many restrictive regulations and long-held traditions of centralized administration deny them the management of some issues, like school programs and professional training, which they are in a position to undertake. There are also some unwarranted limitations on the management of local finances or on association between local government and the private sector.

Municipal governments suffer from weak structural and operational frameworks. Thus, local authorities are forced to spend an inordinate amount of time and resources to establish the organizational basis needed for planning, financing, implementing, and controlling social infrastructure projects and credit programs for income-generating activities.

Access to capital markets for infrastructure and urban development is still unduly restricted, and sufficient new forms of financing for this purpose have not yet been devised. External financial resources should be used to promote domestic savings and to finance low-cost housing programs in conjunction with domestic resources. Excessive red tape and lack of popular participation in the design and implementation of housing developments hamper their success.

Cities often expand beyond their planned limits, and official and informal systems to provide water, sewerage, waste disposal, and other common services to these areas tend to be insufficient and inefficient.

The existing fiscal and land-use policies are not conducive to facilitating adequate systems of urban transportation, nor is there a favorable environment for private participation in the transportation system. Different interest groups apply pressure to avoid updating and modernizing of urban traffic regulations.

## f. Recommendations

The most promising approaches to urban environmental management are to provide financial incentives and involve communities, business, and governments in consensus building on shared goals and actions. Legislation should be reviewed to allow private-sector participation in urban investment and also to promote joint financing of municipal programs by the national government, the private sector, and local communities. Tax laws should be enacted that take into account local participation in public revenues. Institutional arrangements should also be revised to reflect increasing decentralization. Efforts should continue to include issues relating to urban areas on the agenda of international organizations and national governments.

The OAS should continue to support the efforts of the Interagency Task Force to support Bolivia Summit Follow-Up and its working groups on sustainable cities and cleaner production which aim to integrate the efforts of international agencies in addressing complex urban environmental problems. An Interagency Seminar on Sustainable Cities which took place in February 1998 under the sponsorship of the World Bank helped to identify priority areas for action.

A combination of coercive measures and incentives should be applied to reduce pollution. Emphasis should be placed on those policies and actions that are beneficial to all parties involved, and that stimulate each potential polluting agent to comply with its commitments to environmental protection.

Regarding the transportation sector, cities should involve the private sector in the construction and operation of transit systems. The issues of low-income housing and regularization of land ownership must be faced head-on by the countries with the direct and active involvement of financing institutions.

## 4. Water Resources and Coastal Areas

Water resources management is at the very heart of the economic future of the hemisphere. Three of the largest river basins in the world (Amazon, Mississippi, and Plata) drain most of the land area of the Americas. South America has the largest volume of freshwater flow of any continent, and the freshwater produced in the hemisphere amounts to nearly twice the runoff of all the other continents combined. Common interest in the issues of management of the vast resources of the Caribbean Sea offers an opportunity for constructive interchange between the insular and continental states. Actions related to water resources and coastal areas are incorporated into the Plan of Action as initiatives on potable water (initiatives 1 and 47), integrated water resources management (initiatives 48 to 54), and coastal and marine resources (initiatives 55 to 58).

## a. Potable Water

There has been a significant shift from past trends, with their traditional projects on sewerage, wastewater collection and disposal, and solid-waste management. Nowadays, the water projects provide for comprehensive approaches to river-basin management and to integrated, multi-institutional environmental protection efforts. The Clean Water Program in Mexico and the Safe Water Project in Brazil, to ensure water fit for human consumption, are good examples of these new approaches. The programs include the protection of water sources, the installation and rehabilitation of equipment, and monitoring. In the Caribbean, Barbados, Belize, Jamaica, and Trinidad and Tobago are making impressive efforts in the areas of pollution control and coastal areas. Some examples of activities being implemented in the hemisphere are:

- Colombia is structuring a Clean Water Information System as a planning instrument for investment priorities. The system will facilitate coordination of actions to make water supply agencies more responsible for the conservation of watersheds.

- On the basis of a 1994 agreement, USEPA and the Central American Alliance for Sustainable Development (ALIDES) are working with seven Central American countries to develop compatible systems of environmental legislation, regulations, and standards.

- Most Latin American and Caribbean countries either have upgraded or are in the process of formulating their new water laws, incorporating concepts originated in Dublin (1991) and Rio (1992) and even going beyond Agenda 21 in the identification of mechanisms for implementation.

## b. Integrated Water Resources Management

Latin American and Caribbean countries are adopting integrated and comprehensive approaches to water management in river basins and coastal waters. The changes introduced in the legal framework have incorporated new concepts such as the principle that water-resources management should be decentralized, involve the participation of governments, users, and communities, and consider water as an economic asset. These trends favor the development of water markets, encourage water conservation, and promote private-sector participation. In Peru, five autonomous river basin authorities are being established in the Pacific Coast Watersheds. In Brazil, the Water Resources Management System will foster decentralization of governmental actions through the creation of river-basin committees and water agencies. The formulation of policies and legislation on integrated water-resources management and conservation has been given priority in the framework of the Central American Alliance for Sustainable Development. As a follow-up to the Bolivia Summit, several meetings were held in 1997 in the framework of the Inter-American Water Resources Network (IWRN). These included a Seminar on Water Resources Management for the Caribbean, including coastal-zone management, held in Port of Spain (Trinidad and Tobago), a Workshop on Integrated Management of Water Resources in Meso-America, held in Panama City, and an Inter-American Meeting on Water Resources, held in Fortaleza, Brazil. A workshop was held in Panama on October 1997, to review progress on implementation of initiatives 47 to 58 of the Action Plan. A regional forum on management of water resources in the context of MERCOSUR is planned for Montevideo in 1998. IWRN, established in 1994, is an important regional effort that joins governmental, non-governmental, academic, and international organizations with research groups, industry, and the private sector to transmit and exchange information and experiences related to water resources.

- Jamaica has approved legislation to strengthen water-resources management. Since January 1, 1997, an environmental permit and licensing system has been developed to monitor and minimize the negative impact of development on the environment through an effective process based on environmental audits and impact assessments.

- Peru is adopting innovative water legislation that supports both the private sector and decentralization. Under the new legal framework, the action of the state will be redirected from complete responsibility for water allocation and the construction and operation of water development projects to a role of mainly support and control, entrusting private users with the responsibility for managing water use.

As to public and stakeholder participation, greater access to information on projects and activities has enhanced the participation of communities in the making of decisions on water-resources management. Communities and interested groups directly affected by specific water projects have the opportunity to express their concerns, to propose alternatives, and to provide solutions for better management of water resources. Many countries have developed extensive education programs that cover a large spectrum of activities linked to the environment, not only through government institutions but also through academia, the private sector, professional societies, community associations, and NGOs. A few examples of ongoing projects in the hemisphere:

- In Brazil, the Secretariat of Water Resources is emphasizing the involvement of the communities in water resources development through a Citizens for Water Movement and the preparation and dissemination of informative publications and booklets for school children.

- Argentina is implementing a countrywide plan for educational activities for schools and user communities to make students and users aware of the importance of rationalizing water use. Peru is developing and implementing training programs for water users. A cycle of workshops on "Environment: Institutional Participation and Citizenship" is an annual event in different parts of the country.

In relation to transboundary water issues, Canada and the United States have long cooperated on such issues. Currently the protection of the Great Lakes has developed enough information to warrant a Great Lakes Information Network conference held in October 1997. Cooperation between Mexico and the United States has focused on shared water resources and the water quality in arid watersheds. Ground, and surface-water conservation and management are being discussed binationally for several shared watersheds along the border, including, for example, the Upper San Pedro river basin, the Santa Cruz

River, and the Rio Grande. Furthermore, through NAFTA side agreements on the environment, the United States and Mexico are working together to certify and leverage funds for a wastewater treatment facility. The 1992 Integrated Border Environment Plan is entering a second phase aimed at reducing pollution and improving understanding. Belize and Mexico are negotiating an agreement for joint monitoring of the Hondo River. The Dominican Republic and Haiti have reactivated the technical Joint Commission in charge of the development of the frontier zone, which involves the Artibonite River Basin. Colombia and Venezuela are implementing joint activities along border areas, especially in the Orinoco River. The same approach is envisaged for the Catatumbo, Carraipía-Paraguachón, Táchira, Arauca, and Meta River Basins. In the Amazon River basin, joint undertakings in the border areas are being implemented with the assistance of the OAS General Secretariat. They include the Integrated Development Program for the Peruvian-Brazilian Border Communities (Iñapari and Assis), and Land-Use Planning and Ecological-Economic Zoning between Santa Elena de Uairén-Pacaraima Border Area (Brazil-Venezuela), and the Plan for the Integrated Development of the Putumayo River Basin (Colombia-Peru). Other recent transboundary initiatives in Latin America are the following:

- A GEF-funded project for the formulation of the Strategic Action Plan of the Bermejo River Basin between Argentina and Bolivia. The OAS is the executing agency jointly with United Nations of Environmental Programs (UNEP).

- A joint project between Brazil and Uruguay for the integrated management of the Cuaréim River Basin.

- Twelve projects for coordinated management and border integration in Meso-America.

- The GEF-funded Caribbean Project for Planning for Adaptation to Climate Change, executed by the OAS, which is assisting eleven Caribbean countries to cope with the adverse effects of global climate change, particularly sea-level rise in coastal areas, through vulnerability assessment, adaptation planning, and capacity building. Incentives are being developed for more efficient use of water in these areas.

Several countries, including Argentina, Brazil and Mexico have adopted the "user/polluter pays" principle to improve the allocation of water resources and the effectiveness of pollution control. A number of water supply and sanitation projects in Latin America and the Caribbean promote water conservation through tariff rationalization and the reduction of unaccounted-for water. Peru is introducing economic principles in the allocation of water resources, through a system of tradable water property rights. Two ongoing projects, the Land and Water Resource Management Project and the Water Management and Coastal Pollution Control Project, will assist in establishing water markets. Mexico has implemented an effluent-fee system taking into account the quality of the body of water as a mechanism for pollution control. The system is being tested in the Lerma-Chapala Basin.

### c. Coastal and marine resources

- Despite the efforts of the last few years, the Caribbean countries face many challenges for managing their water resources in a socially acceptable, environmentally sustainable, and economically efficient manner. Environmental degradation is a serious threat, caused by oil activities and by the release of urban wastewater and industrial waste. There has been a great effort in recent years to overcome these conditions, and environmental institutions are generally adequate. However, they face constrains in terms of finance, management, and enforcement capability. A good example of cooperation is the current Planning for Adaptation for Climate Change project mentioned above. The recommendations of the joint IBRD/ECLAC/OAS Seminar on Integrated Water Resources Management: Institutional and Policy Reform, held from June 24 to 27 1997, in Port of Spain, Trinidad, focused on the urgency of managing water resources in an integrated manner: the need to take strategic rather than reactive action, to address freshwater, marine, and coastal resources as a management continuum, and to develop strategic partnerships and networks for fostering information sharing and exchange.

- In the Caribbean, increasing emphasis has been placed on coastal-zone management by exploring the options for strengthening existing agencies and collaborating mechanisms among relevant agencies, or establishing specialized units with responsibility for coordinating coastal zone management. Donor support has been secured from the GEF, the IDB, the Caribbean Development Bank, FAO, and CIDA and from the governments of France, the Republic of China, Japan, and the United States for projects that address selected aspects of coastal-resource management.

- Jamaica has been participating in the negotiation of the Protocol on Land-Based Sources and Activities that Pollute the Marine Environment, being developed in relation to the Convention on the Protection of the Marine Environment of the Wider Caribbean Region (the Cartagena Convention).
- The Government of Saint Lucia signed a letter of agreement with the UNEP for an integrated coastal-zone management project for the southeast coast of the island in March 1995. The general objective of this project is to prepare an integrated management plan for the sustainable use of the resources of the southeast coast. The results of this study should allow replication in other parts of the island. The government has also recently embarked on the second phase of a coastal conservation project aimed at the development of a coastal-zone management plan for the northwest coastline of the island.

## d. Obstacles

Chronic problems of water quality and quantity, human health, natural disasters, and degradation of ecosystems will persist in the future. Most of them can be alleviated through integrated water-resources management that includes integration of water sources and demands, coordination of water resources planning, decentralization of government services, stakeholder participation, and consideration of the needs of aquatic ecosystems. To cover increasing costs for the operation and maintenance of water systems, market pricing of water is a necessary but not sufficient mechanism to ensure the efficient allocation of water and improve water delivery services.

There is a need for an assessment of transboundary water resources issues in the Americas, identifying the main challenges and opportunities to improve the management of shared resources. Maximum use should be made of management mechanisms, such as international treaties, water resources authorities, commissions, or other institutional arrangements. The first stage of these assessments could be implemented in South America. In this region, just three of the international river basins (Plata, Amazon, and Orinoco) cover more than 73% of the entire area. The treaties for Amazonian Cooperation and for the Development of the Plata River Basin join 11 of the 12 South American countries and provide an adequate institutional framework.

In relation to coastal and marine resources, the Caribbean countries have identified four key areas for action: institutional coordination, water resources policies, public awareness and education, and innovative financing.

## e. Recommendations

Achieving integrated water resources management calls for some general guidelines for action. It is necessary to coordinate water-resources and user-sectors planning and to integrate those resources with development planning at the regional, state and national levels. Other goals are the coordination of water resources management with environmental and land-use management, and the integration of the management of river basins with the management of estuary systems and coastal areas.

Coordination between states and countries should be promoted to formulate water-resource strategies and action programs and to consider their harmonization when appropriate for transboundary areas and regional seas.

An assessment of transboundary water resources issues in the Americas is needed. To complete the assessment maximum use should be made of mechanisms such as the IWRN, which operates under the auspices of the OAS, and the newly created Global Program of Action for Land-Based Sources of Marine Pollution, under the auspices of UNEP. Once the first phase is finished, a series of international meetings should be held to share experiences and derive lessons learned in the Americas and elsewhere. The OAS Secretariat could be the catalyst to implement these activities, with the active participation of interested countries and other international agencies.

As for coastal and marine resources, the guidelines for action should include the identification and establishment of appropriate coordination units for promoting cooperation at regional and national levels. The primary goals for regional collaboration would be to foster the development of professional networks to address the various components of water-resources management, such as watershed management and pollution control, and to share and exchange information through electronic networks.

In the Caribbean, integrated water resources management policies and strategies are needed for each island based on the principle that water-resources activities need to be self-financed and that demand management is a cost-effective policy option.

Programs to develop appropriate public awareness and education strategies on this matter should be devised and implemented. Specific actions may include pilot projects for managing watersheds, strategies for sensitizing policy makers and for promoting changes in public attitude and behavior, and the development of primary- and secondary-school curricula especially aimed at sensitizing school children.

The following seems advisable in relation to the economic valuation of water: improve the efficiency of irrigated agriculture and drinking water systems as a priority concern, improve legislation and effective regulatory systems, and develop the institutional capacity for better local response to demand.

To strengthen stakeholder involvement courses, seminars, workshops and publications must be designed and implemented to engage the active participation of the many communities living in river basins or particular ecosystems, in order to increase their awareness of environmental concerns, avoid the disruption of the ecological balance, and promote the protection of their habitats.

The importance of the IWRN should be recognized and its role as a water forum in the Americas strengthened.

The public information efforts of the World Bank, the IDB, CAF, and other international organizations should be directed towards letting the general public know, on a timely basis, about plans for projects, their social and environmental impacts, and their costs.

Internet sites should be established in the major national water management agencies and information centers to publish electronically policies, legislation, environmental impact statements, plans, project descriptions, and other information of interest to the public and the water-resource community.

## 5. Energy and Minerals

The Western Hemisphere is the world's foremost energy consumer, owing mainly to the high per capita use in the US and Canada. Likewise the emissions of greenhouse gases from this region are the world's largest. It is expected that the rate of energy use in Latin America and the Caribbean will grow at a rate among the highest in the world over the next 15 years. Energy production and management will be major factors in the ability of the region to attract investment and expand production, as they have been in the past. During the past decade, the electricity sector of many countries has been characterized by institutional reform that has resulted in a shift toward increased private-sector participation. During the same period the region has expanded its output of raw energy resources, as it continues to be a key supplier of fossil fuels to the world. Five Summit initiatives were directed at energy. These address the major challenges facing this sector throughout the region: recognition and support of the Hemispheric Energy Steering Committee of the Summit of the Americas, with emphasis on encouraging hemispheric, regional, and cross-border energy cooperation (initiatives 59 and 63); promotion of regulatory and institutional frameworks and technology exchange initiatives to facilitate investments in clean energy projects, such as energy efficiency and renewable energy (initiatives 60 and 62); and, increasing access to energy services for underserved areas, especially rural and indigenous communities (initiative 61).

Mineral resources—metallic, non-metallic, and coal—continue to be very important to the economic stability of several nations in the hemisphere. Mining is a source of employment and income contributing to alleviate poverty and promote regional development. At the same time, mining creates social and environmental problems. The Santa Cruz Summit addressed these issues (initiatives 63-65).

### a. Regional and Cross-Border Energy Cooperation

Key advancements in the promotion of regional and cross-border energy cooperation have been as follows:

- The opportunities for energy cooperation mentioned in Santa Cruz recognize the importance of integration and cooperation if the hemisphere is to succeed in attracting energy-sector investment and expand its capacity. Cooperation among senior energy officials has improved dramatically as a result of the Miami and Santa Cruz Summits. Energy ministers from the hemisphere have gathered three times over the past three years (Washington, Santa Cruz, and Venezuela) to further the goals of the Summits and explore possible areas of cooperation. Additionally, the hemisphere's ministers of energy have authorized the establishment of the Hemispheric Energy Steering Committee and, most recently, the creation of a Energy Coordination Secretariat to facilitate improved communications among the various countries of the hemisphere.

- Electricity infrastructure integration is being assessed in several regions of the hemisphere. In South America, serious discussion and study has begun regarding the feasibility of an interconnected continent. Already, commercial and industrial demand has led to interconnections between Chile and Argentina and between Venezuela and Colombia. Planned expansion of the Guri hydroelectric facility in Southern Venezuela will permit the sale of electricity to the northern states of Brazil by means of a 1500-km interconnection. Further expansion in this regional interconnection is expected via transmission lines between Ecuador and Colombia.

- In Central America, discussion of its regional interconnection was initiated in 1976, but recent progress on this subject makes the System of Electric Interconnection of Central America (SIEPAC) feasible by 2002. This may open opportunities for a connection that extends from Mexico to South America. A first link of the SIEPAC line will interconnect Mexico and Guatemala by 1999.

- Natural gas interconnections are proceeding and include the Bolivia-Brazil Gas Pipeline and two planned gas pipelines from Argentina to Chile. The Bolivia-Brazil line will run from Santa Cruz to São Paulo, Curitiba, and Porto Alegre. The total investment is estimated at US$2 billion.

- The lines from Argentina to Santiago, Chile, are under construction. One is from Mendoza, at an estimated cost of US$600 million, and the other is from Lomo La Lata, with an estimated cost of US$1.7 billion. Santiago is also expanding its distribution network. Additionally, three proposals, ranging in cost from US$600 million to US$790 million are competing to provide the copper industry in northern Chile with thermoelectricity generated from Argentine natural gas.

- The World Bank has completed studies concerning two additional natural gas lines linking various countries of the region. The first would connect reserves in Trinidad and the Eastern Caribbean islands to Florida. The second would connect Eastern Venezuela and Colombia to Central America, Mexico, and ultimately Texas.

- Increased concerns regarding global climate change have led to more hemispheric cooperation and cross-border investments in clean energy projects. Many such project have risen out of the Joint Implementation Initiative (JI), a program inspired by the 1992 UN Rio Accord. JI encourages investments in energy and land-use projects that avoid or sequester greenhouse-gas emissions. Investors from developed nations are encouraged to participate in such projects in developing countries. Of the 28 projects approved by the U.S. JI Initiative worldwide, 21 have been in Latin America and the Caribbean. Projects have been approved in Belize, Bolivia, Costa Rica, Ecuador, Honduras, Mexico, Nicaragua, and Panama. This includes 10 renewable energy projects totaling approximately 180 MW, which could avoid up to 20 million tons of carbon-dioxide emissions over the life of these projects.

- OLADE has contributed to the process of regional energy integration through support of the projects described above, and to others including an electricity interconnection between Latin America and the Caribbean, gas interconnections between Mexico and Central America, alternatives for expanding the refineries in Latin America and the Caribbean, and a study on the elimination of lead in gasoline.

### b. Regulatory, Institutional, and Cooperative Initiatives for Clean Energy Projects

The following actions have been taken on regulatory and institutional reform and on technology exchange to facilitate investments in clean energy projects such as energy efficiency and renewable energy:

- Improved policy and regulatory frameworks for the development of renewable energy have been put in place in several countries, including Costa Rica, Bolivia, Peru, Guatemala, Nicaragua, St. Vincent and the Grenadines, and the United States. Numerous grid-tied alternative renewable energy projects have been launched in the past three years. For example wind energy projects have been completed in Costa Rica (20 MW), Argentina (6.5 MW), the United States (61 MW), Brazil (2 MW), and Mexico (1.6 MW). Additional projects are planned in Mexico (54 MW), Honduras (60 MW), Brazil (up to 320 MW), Ecuador (30 MW), Peru (10 MW), Costa Rica (47 MW), and the United States (800 MW). Geothermal power development has grown as well, with major projects under way in Mexico (adding 100 MW to the existing 800 MW), Nicaragua (70 MW), St. Vincent and the Grenadines (20 MW), Costa Rica (24 MW), and El Salvador (upgrading 105 MW).

- Multilateral development bank financing alternatives for sustainable energy projects have expanded with the creation of the IDB's Sustainable Markets for Sustainable Energy Program (SMSE) and the

World Bank's Solar Initiative (SI). The SMSE was established in 1996 to support the creation of sustainable markets for "sustainable energy" (energy-efficient systems, technologies, and practices and clean energy sources) by creating an environment in which there is sufficient full-scale financing for large numbers of energy-efficiency and clean-energy-source projects.

- The SI was established at the World Bank in 1994 to play a coordinating, strategic, and catalytic role in removing barriers that impede the introduction of renewable and other environmentally sustainable technologies in developing countries. At present it has US$163 million in renewable energy projects in the funding pipeline for Latin America.

- Currently 17 countries in the hemisphere have active programs to promote energy conservation and the use of energy-efficient technologies. These countries are Argentina, Brazil, Bolivia, Canada, Colombia, Chile, Costa Rica, Cuba, El Salvador, Guatemala, Guyana, Mexico, Nicaragua, Paraguay, Peru, the United States, and Venezuela.

- OLADE is playing an important role in supporting the creation of positive regulatory and institutional settings to reduce barriers to investments in energy efficiency and to promote projects of renewable energy and other clean-energy technologies that are economically feasible and socially desirable. It has worked on this with a number of countries, among them, Argentina, Brazil, Costa Rica, Chile Ecuador, Guatemala, Honduras, and Peru.

## c. Rural Electrification

The following advances resulting in increased access to energy services by underserved areas, especially rural and indigenous communities have occurred:

- Providing increased access to electricity services to the rural population of Latin America and the Caribbean is one of the greatest challenges facing the energy sector in this hemisphere. More than 50 million people, or 10 million households, remain without basic electric service. Significant steps have been taken over the past four years to address this challenge. Approximately half of the countries in the hemisphere have active programs of rural electrification. For example, Argentina has launched a US$300 million program to provide universal electric coverage over the next decade. This effort relies on the active cooperation of the public and private sectors with support from the World Bank. Brazil's rural electrification initiative, PRODEAM, will invest over $50 million to electrify community services with renewable-energy technologies in 5,000 communities by 1999. The Mexican Government has electrified approximately 34,000 rural households with solar energy over the past 6 years.

## d. Mining

Some positive steps have been taken in the mining sector:

- Given the non-renewable nature of the mining sector and increasing pressures on the industry to become more environmentally friendly, the ministers of mining have initiated discussions on a number of issues which will help quicken needed reform in this sector.

- At the Meeting of the Ministers of Mining of the Americas, held in mid-1997 in Santiago, an expert group examined the Bolivia initiatives related to the mining sector. Six working groups were subsequently appointed and they reported their findings at the September 1997 meeting of ministers in Arequipa, Peru. Regional collaboration on a wide range of issues affecting the industry continues to be active, including regular exchanges on clean technology strategies, ground-water controls through better management of tailings, environmental-hazard assessment, and developing markets for by-products.

- Common environmental standards, including incentives for restoration of mining sites and groundwater recharge zones and control of the contamination of adjacent soils and aquatic environments, is a very high priority for consideration by the ministers at their next meeting.

## e. Obstacles

Latin America and the Caribbean are blessed with an abundance of natural energy resources. Petroleum, natural gas, hydro reserves, solar radiation, and other resources offer the region tremendous opportunities for generating electricity, powering vehicles, and fueling other energy services. However, the region continues to face severe energy challenges, such as urban electricity brownouts and blackouts, inadequate electricity service for the rural poor and significant environmental concerns. Addressing these and other challenges through increased hemispheric integration and cooperation, policy and regulatory reform, and the expanded use of sustainable energy technologies is part of the solution, as laid out by the Summit. Such solutions, however, face major obstacles.

Energy integration and cooperation has increased significantly since the Summit of the Americas and the Summit on Sustainable Development. However, more substantial integration is faced with the problem that the countries of the hemisphere are very unequal in per capita income and lifestyle. This means that the nature of the problem for each country varies tremendously, as does the contribution of each country to global and local environment problems. Also, there remain specific trade barriers and uneven product standards for fuels and electricity supplies that impede integration.

While there has been a trend toward increased privatization of the energy sector over the past decade, energy policy and regulations continue to vary substantially by country. In many cases, neighboring countries have opposite approaches to the sector: while one continues to operate a public monopoly over energy production and delivery, another has completely privatized the sector and open competition is the rule. Given such differences at every level of policy and regulation, integration across national borders and throughout the region is extremely difficult.

Utilization of clean and efficient energy sources is a potential solution for many problems, such as environmental degradation, long-term energy security, and stemming the tide of urbanization by improving the conditions of the rural poor. Increased use of renewable energy technologies, clean advanced fossil-fuel technologies, and energy-efficient technologies and services requires changes in policy and regulations in a way that makes such options more attractive in competition with conventional energy supplies. While these reforms are not necessarily very costly, they do require a serious commitment from senior policy-makers and face major opposition from much of the existing conventional energy industry.

The mining industry faces broad constraints in achieving sustainable development. There is a great variation in mining regulations covering claims, titling, and ownership rights and responsibilities from country to country. Salaries are low in the mining sector, and professional personnel are scarce. There are few schools offering any specialized training programs in Latin America and the Caribbean. The sector has often faced protracted court proceedings as untouched mineral deposits sometimes occur in national parks or highly productive agricultural lands, creating conflicts of interest.

Small-scale mining often occurs in communities confronting serious difficulties when they do not enjoy the economies of scale that would enable them to compete with large-scale operations of a multi-national nature.

## f. Recommendations

Increasing hemispheric energy integration and enhancing the sector's sustainability are the central themes of the energy chapters of the Summit of the Americas and the Summit on Sustainable Development. Cooperation among the hemisphere's energy actors to achieve the goals of the Summit should be strengthened through the Hemispheric Energy Symposium Steering Committee and its Coordination Secretariat and OLADE.

The countries of the hemisphere should assess the potential applications of sustainable energy technologies and energy-efficiency measures in their efforts to further develop this sector while managing its impacts on environmental, social, and economic conditions. This might include policy reviews, local and global environmental impact training and assessments, and information exchange to permit greater use of these alternatives. International organizations such as OLADE, the OAS, the World Bank, and the IDB should contribute to the success of this process.

Competition for investment capital for the energy sector is now global. The regions and countries that succeed in attracting investment will be those with the most transparent, stable, and equitable market conditions. The OAS can play a role in assisting countries to reform policy by facilitating a dialogue between the investment community, policy-makers, and other experts. It is also in a position to work with the multilateral banking institutions to target financing to areas with the greatest need, as well as encouraging them to support projects that improve the sustainability of this sector.

The mining industry, governments, and the academic sector should cooperate to improve legislation, human resources, and research on innovative technology and to establish policy instruments that mitigate negative effects of emissions, effluents, solid waste, and land use derived from the production, transformation, transport, and use of metals and minerals, giving particular attention to tailing piles, acid runoff, ground-water controls, and the marketing of by-products.

The OAS could assist governments in holding a meeting to help design guidelines and policies for conflict resolution. The governments should attempt to coordinate their efforts to design and implement a series of training courses with support from an appropriate source, such as the Andean Development Corporation.

## III. PROGRESS IN INSTITUTIONAL, FINANCING, TECHNOLOGY AND COOPERATION ASPECTS

Besides the 65 initiatives to be carried out by the governments in several sectors, the Bolivia Plan of Action also calls for some actions to be taken on institutional, financial and technological aspects, and on the matter of public participation, in order to create a framework that will facilitate the implementation of those initiatives.

### 1. Institutional Arrangements

The OAS was entrusted in Santa Cruz with the responsibility of coordinating follow-up on the different initiatives of the Summit of the Americas on Sustainable Development. Several agencies of the United Nations and of the inter-American system were requested to collaborate in this endeavor.

#### a. Interagency Coordination and Collaboration

The Summit Plan of Action calls on the organs, agencies, and entities of both the United Nations system and the inter-American system "to develop adequate mechanisms to collaborate and coordinate with the OAS within their respective areas of action and mandates to support national regional, and hemispheric efforts towards sustainable development." In response to those instructions, a group of agencies of the UN system and the inter-American system, including all major development banks in the region, came together in February 1997 under the coordination of the OAS Secretariat to form an Interagency Task Force to Support Bolivia Summit Follow-Up.

The initial members of the Task Force were the OAS General Secretariat, the World Bank, the IDB, UNDP, UNEP, ECLAC, PAHO, IICA, CAF, USAID, and CIDA.

The objectives of the Task Force were defined as an interagency effort to:

- Provide a forum to discuss implementation of goals of the Summit especially where coordinated action of international agencies and financing institutions will facilitate government initiatives.

- Promote the financing of high-priority actions identified by hemispheric leaders at the Summit on Sustainable Development.

- Organize working groups to address specific initiatives contained in the Summit Plan of Action, particularly those requiring collective action by member states which can benefit from the coordinated support of international agencies and financing institutions.

- Serve as a clearinghouse to facilitate the collection and assembly of information from agencies regarding actions taken to assist governments in the implementation of the Plan of Action.

The group selected a few priorities from the large array of Summit initiatives and created a series of practical working groups to design joint projects, produce specific joint studies, or collaborate in holding technical conferences to facilitate Summit follow-up efforts of governments and agencies alike. The principal criterion for the establishment of interagency working groups on specific subjects is that they must produce "value-added" cooperation. The product of these joint efforts has already demonstrated that it can save money and improve the quality of agency efforts to assist governments in the implementation of Summit initiatives. The work of the task force has recently been expanded to include supporting the implementation of initiatives from the relevant section of the Miami Summit Plan of Action as well as the Bolivia Summit. The present report on Summit implementation has been made possible in large part by the contribution of the agencies that make up the task force.

#### b. Environmental Law Network

The Plan of Action calls for the creation of a hemispheric network of officials and experts in environmental law, enforcement, and compliance to facilitate the sharing of knowledge and experiences. The network is also to be a focal point for carrying out efforts to strengthen laws, regulations, and their implementation and also to provide training in these areas. In calling for the establishment of the network, the countries said that the effort would be made in coordination with the OAS.

- The OAS has taken a leadership role in this initiative. In the Interagency Task Force on Bolivia

# IV. PREPARATORY WORK BY REGIONAL ORGANIZATIONS

Summit Follow-Up it chairs a working group on environmental law that includes the UNDP, UNEP, USAID, and the USEPA. Funding has been included in the OAS budget to prepare an initial technical meeting to launch the network. It has also participated in informal meetings with agencies based in Washington, D.C., to explore possible contributions of various organizations to the development of the network.

- The OAS-funded activities constitute a crucial minimum effort to establish this initiative but are not sufficient to guarantee its success. Other supporters of the initiative should be encouraged to finance additional activities during 1998, including meetings of network participants to share knowledge and experiences, and for training purposes.

## 2. Financing

The Plan of Action calls for the mobilization of financial resources in keeping with the commitments made at the Rio Summit. It also states that those resources should be complemented with innovative financing mechanisms and highlights the importance of international organizations and financial institutions in supporting the efforts of the hemisphere.

- The OAS was called upon at Santa Cruz to assist in the identification of avenues and means of strengthening public and private finance for sustainable development in the hemisphere. The IDB, UNDP, the World Bank and ECLAC were among the hemispheric and international institutions asked to help with this. A working group has been established to this effect, with the participation of OAS, the IDB, UNDP, the World Bank, ECLAC and CAF. A technical meeting on financing sustainable development will take place later in 1998.

- Efforts have been made to attract private capital to programs and projects sponsored by international organizations. The OAS Secretariat has established the Trust for the Americas, a foundation which will seek to mobilize resources from the private sector for actions related to mandates from Summit meetings. It will also work closely with foundations in the hemisphere to facilitate work that complements follow-up activities to the Summits, as outlined in CIDI's "Strategic Plan for Partnership for Development 1997-2001." The Trust will place emphasis on human resources development, information sharing, and interdisciplinary research with an inter-American focus to enhance the quality of technical cooperation.

- The IDB and 15 Latin American and Caribbean countries, led by Colombia, have joined forces to create the Regional Fund for Agriculture, which is an endowment fund for financing high-priority strategic agricultural research. The Bank is also considering the possibility of establishing a Foundation of the Americas to provide financial support to civil-society initiatives in Latin America and the Caribbean.

- In the 1990s, several major trends in finance for sustainable development can be identified in Latin America and the Caribbean. Greater interest and activity in developing innovative domestic and international financial mechanisms have led to reductions in environmentally damaging and economically distorting subsidies and the increased use of environmental charges, user fees, and, in a few cases, emissions-trading programs.

- Private flows of financial resources from abroad have expanded. Foreign private funds have become the dominant source of capital for many countries in the region. However, the net impacts of foreign private capital upon sustainable development are difficult to determine.

- Heavy debt burdens have been a major hindrance to sustainable development. Although the debt situation of middle-income countries has, on the whole, improved significantly, and many have reentered international capital markets, heavily indebted poor countries continue to face burdensome external debt service, despite a decade of international efforts. The problem has been addressed by a World Bank/IMF initiative aimed at reducing their debt burden to sustainable levels and to complete a rescheduling process within six years.

As private flows of financial resources have become the dominant source of capital for many countries in the region, policies that result in stable macroeconomic conditions, transparent and fair laws and public administration, open trade and clear investment rules, and adequate infrastructure and human resources become more relevant since these are key determinants of foreign private capital flows. Countries should channel financial flows to promote sustainable development through sound social and environmental policies and not simply short-term, unsustainable economic growth. International financial assistance directed to sustainable development should be increased and, to be fully effective, should be used wherever appropriate, to leverage greater foreign and domestic private investment consistent with sustainable development, especially in poverty reduction.

## 3. Science and Technology

The principal regional mechanism to address science and technology issues is the Meeting of the Ministers of Science and Technology. This forum, which last met in Cartagena in 1996, issued a Plan of Action for addressing priorities and coordinating activities and investments in science and technology cooperation. The decision to charge the Common Market of Scientific and Technological Knowledge (MERCOCYT) with the responsibility of monitoring the implementation of the Cartagena Plan of Action was acknowledged in the Bolivia Plan of Action. The OAS was given a specific mandate to collaborate with MERCOCYT in designing a science and technology program.

- The OAS Secretariat designed a program to address some priority issues defined in the Science Plan of Action, which includes projects in science and technology innovation indicators, food enterprise technologies in the Caribbean, the use of biotechnology in vegetable production, institution building in Central America, and technology transfer in key industry sectors.

- The first of the key-industry-sector meetings which focused on the agri-food sector, was held in Costa Rica in mid-1997 with the participation of 76 industry associations from 21 countries and representatives from four financial institutions. The OAS joined forces with GTZ, the German technical cooperation agency, to offer workshops in five countries on ISO 9000 and ISO 14000, focusing on chemical-discharge management in industrial effluents. USAID has also sponsored seminars on ISO 14000 and clean technology for the industrial-export sector in South America and for the Caribbean tourist hotel sector. In addition, the Specialized Information System on Biotechnology (SIMBIOSIS) project which received special attention in Cartagena, is providing training on biotechnology applications in seven countries to treat industrial pollutants such as those from mining.

- In October 1997 the UNDP started a preparatory assistance project for the establishment of the Network for Sustainable Development of the Americas, which will provide information and means of communication for analysis and decision-making on sustainable development issues. The preparatory project will formulate the program document supporting the establishment of the Network and create a pilot version of its design and a critical mass of core modules to test how it provides basic information and services to users. In April 1998 a program document supporting the establishment of the hemispheric network will be submitted to the Summit of the Americas in Santiago, Chile, in compliance with the mandate given UNDP in Santa Cruz.

Most of the difficulties encountered in transferring scientific and technological information relate to an increasing gap between countries which invest in innovative technologies and those which cannot adequately support research and development. Fast-paced advances in technologies such as informatics, microelectronics, biotechnology, new materials, and digital communications equipment require substantial investments in training and institutions. This technological gap has significant impacts on the well-being of the nations concerned since, in large part, it determines the differences in productivity, which, in turn, affect income levels and distribution within and between countries.

Strong support should continue to be given to the work of MERCOCYT as a means of responding to both the Cartagena and the Bolivia Action Plans. Developing a regional innovation system to raise the level of cooperation on science and technology, establish common policies on generating, transferring, and accessing new technologies, and support subregional efforts such as the Scientific and Technological Commission for Central America and Panama (CTAP) deserves priority.

## 4. Public Participation

Governments of the hemisphere, through recent global and regional summits, have recognized that strong civil-society engagement in decision-making is fundamental for enhancing democracy, promoting sustainable development, achieving economic integration and free trade, improving the lives of all people, and conserving the natural environment for future generations. In the area of sustainable development, the Declaration of Santa Cruz de la Sierra specifically endorses this principle, committing its signatories to supporting and encouraging, as a basic requisite for sustainable development, broad participation by civil society in the making of decisions on policies and programs and their design, implementation, and evaluation.

# IV. Preparatory Work by Regional Organizations

- Important progress has been made since the Miami Summit of the Americas and the Bolivia Summit on Sustainable Development in addressing the need for public participation in decision-making and in identifying and developing the means to strengthen civil society.

- The Organization of American States, in compliance with the Bolivia Summit mandate, is currently formulating the Inter-American Strategy for Public Participation (ISP) to identify concrete mechanisms for securing transparent, accountable, and effective participation by individuals, civil society, and governments and to promote participatory decision-making in environment and sustainable development issues. This strategy is being formulated by conducting demonstration studies, analyzing relevant legal and institutional frameworks and mechanisms, sharing information and experiences, and establishing a basis for long-term financial support for public-private alliances. The ISP is a significant effort to support collective actions by OAS member states to strengthen partnerships between the public sector and civil society. The Global Environment Facility, the OAS, USAID, UNESCO, and other donors are financially supporting this effort. Several consultations and meetings have been held and technical studies are being conducted to identify lessons learned and best practices for public participation mechanisms to be recommended as the final Strategy.

In most countries of the hemisphere, civil-society participation still needs to be fully integrated into sustainable development decision-making processes, enabling citizens to participate responsibly in decisions regarding their country's and community's development path. Even where mechanisms do exist to facilitate and enable effective participation, many remain unaware of their scope and application, or lack the tools to take advantage of available processes. The failure to fully integrate stakeholder participation into environment and sustainable development policies continually deprives governments of the unique contribution and perspective of civil society and limits the full participation of citizens in determining their future. Up to now, the main obstacle to the implementation of the ISP has been maintaining coordination and information flow between governments and civil-society organizations. The experiences of OAS implementing the ISP, could lead to broader support for civil-society participation in public issues in areas considered pertinent by the Santiago Summit.

## IV. CONCLUSIONS

The short time since the Bolivian Summit is enough to take meaningful account of some progress made in implementing the 65 initiatives of the Plan of Action. At the same time, some obstacles have been identified that are common to most of those initiatives, and some institutional arrangements that could facilitate progress have been devised. Previous sections of this report have summarized specific accomplishments, obstacles, and proposals for action in the five areas of the Plan of Action. A brief review has also been made of progress achieved on the recommended institutional, financial and technological actions, which were mandated to establish a favorable framework for implementation of the Plan. This chapter brings together some of the more general conclusions, which have been suggested in this report.

### 1. Rationale for a Forum of the Americas on Sustainable Development

The significant accomplishment of the Americas in being the first region of the world to agree on a regional agenda for sustainable development should be followed up by concrete measures designed to expedite the implementation of the initiatives and actions approved in Santa Cruz de la Sierra.

Serious differences between developed and developing countries on issues related to the concept of and the means to achieve sustainable development have not been resolved. The mutually agreed upon initiatives for action also in many cases need to be more precisely defined. They require additional refinement, including practical ways to put them into effect, before they can be implemented. Both bridging the gap and fine-tuning the initiatives can be attained through further constructive structured dialogue at the technical and political levels. Many of the initiatives involve the coordination and cooperation of two or more sectors. Cross-sectoral dialogue is greatly needed to resolve issues at the interface between sectors, with the involvement of the relevant government agencies of planning and finance.

A ministerial-level forum should be established for continuing governmental contacts towards finding common grounds for policy and for action, and also for undertaking the necessary additional analysis and improvement of the initiatives and goals of the Plan of Action. A Forum of the Americas on Sustainable Development should be established at the ministerial level and be open to government representation in specific sectors to be considered at its meetings.

## 2. Institutional Framework for the Forum

The appropriate institutional place for a Forum of the Americas on Sustainable Development is the Organization of American States, the political forum of the countries of the hemisphere. The OAS was entrusted in Santa Cruz with the role of coordinating the follow-up of the various decisions of the Summit of the Americas on Sustainable Development. Within the OAS, the Forum should be established in the context of the Inter-American Council for Integral Development (CIDI) and could take place at its annual ministerial meeting. The guidelines for its functioning are presented in the Introduction to this report. As explained there, it is necessary that the proposed hemispheric forum work in close coordination with other international organizations and fora dealing with the environment and sustainable development issues at regional and subregional levels.

The Santa Cruz Plan of Action instructed the Inter-American Commission on Sustainable Development (CIDS) to review the progress of the Plan as part of its agenda. The OAS General Secretariat has been providing technical secretariat services to this Committee. The OAS should continue to support CIDS and also function as the source of technical and logistic support to the proposed Forum within CIDI.

## 3. Coordination of Support from International Organizations

The Interagency Task Force to Support Bolivia Summit Follow-up has made a valuable contribution to a process of selecting activities within the Plan of Action and identifying means for implementation which can attract the support of financing and technical cooperation agencies.

While governments, together with their civil societies, are primarily responsible for implementing the Plan of Action for the Sustainable Development of the Americas, the active participation of agencies of the United Nations and inter-American systems can offer substantial support to the technical, operational, and financial aspects of the Plan of Action. The work of the Interagency Task Force in this regard, with its coordinated action by specialized international and inter-American institutions, should be stimulated and maintained.

A number of bilateral and multilateral agencies have presented detailed statements of their policies and inventories of their projects in the area of sustainable development, which accompany this report. Some of those organizations, such as the IDB, USAID, and the World Bank have channeled substantial technical and financial resources to support the implementation of Summit initiatives. The appended compilation of their policies and projects will be useful to the countries as indicators of possible sources of future support. The priority assigned by the agencies to different aspects of sustainable development shows the extent to which the international community is backing the initiatives of the Santa Cruz Plan of Action.

## 4. Financial Resources for Sustainable Development

A lack of sufficient financial and technological resources has been identified as one of the main constraints in implementing many of the initiatives launched in Santa Cruz. Constructive dialogue is needed to explore innovative financial mechanisms that can be accepted by all parties concerned to supplement the funding available for sustainable development. Dialogue can also contribute to overcoming difficulties in transferring scientific and technological information.

The OAS has responded to the mandate received at Santa Cruz to look for new instruments and sources of financing for sustainable development, with the support of other international institutions. The working group of the Interagency Task Force established for this purpose is collaborating on plans for a technical meeting on financing sustainable development, which is expected to take place later in 1998.

The OAS has opened its doors to private capital through the establishment of a foundation that will try to mobilize resources from the private sector for financing development programs and projects. The IDB has strengthened its financial support to Latin America and the Caribbean by establishing new instruments in the fields of agriculture and energy. The Bank is also considering the creation of a foundation to support civil-society initiatives.

There is a fortunate trend in Latin America and the Caribbean towards reducing environmentally harmful subsidies and increasing the use of environmental charges and user fees. As private flows of financial resources have become the dominant source of capital for many countries of the region, policies that are key for private investment are gaining in importance.

# IV. Preparatory Work by Regional Organizations

## 5. Environmental Law

The efforts made by the OAS to begin establishing the basis on which a network of hemispheric experts and officials on environmental law can be created should be encouraged. Institutional arrangements in the region, among them the legal framework, are critical to the success of the common effort to promote sustainable development. The environmental law network should contribute to modernize laws and regulations and to improve their enforcement.

The initial OAS technical meeting to launch the network should serve as the occasion for other international institutions to initiate their support to the development of the network.

## 6. Public Participation

The OAS has responded promptly to the mandate it received to assist in the formulation of an inter-American strategy for the promotion of public participation in decision-making for sustainable development. Following the guidelines embodied in the Plan of Action, the strategy will promote the exchange of experiences and information among representatives of government and civil society on policies, programs, and legal and institutional mechanisms.

Civil society involvement is an essential component of sustainable development, since it amounts to recognition that development is a task of and for the citizens. Interaction between the government and groups such as non-governmental organizations, civic associations, labor unions, and civil society in general provides a broad basis upon which sustainable development efforts can be founded. The relative scarcity of human resources can be overcome through attracting the whole community to share in the drive for development. The effort the OAS is undertaking in this context deserves full support. The cooperation that the GEF, USAID, and UNESCO are providing in this effort is to be commended.

# Proposals from Non-Governmental Sectors

# V. LEADERSHIP COUNCIL FOR INTER-AMERICAN SUMMITRY

# V. LEADERSHIP COUNCIL FOR INTER-AMERICAN SUMMITRY

*The **Leadership Council for Inter-American Summitry**, established in 1997, is an independent, non-partisan initiative composed of citizens from throughout the Americas working in private business, legislatures, academia, public policy institutes, the scientific community, and other civic organizations.*

*Project Directors:*
*Richard E. Feinberg, Professor of International Political Economy and Director, APEC Study Center, University of California, San Diego*

*Robin L. Rosenberg, Deputy Director, North-South Center, University of Miami*

© *1998 University of Miami. Published by the University of Miami North-South Center Press.*

## From Talk to Action:
### How Summits Can Help Forge a Western Hemisphere Community of Prosperous Democracies

*A Policy Report: March 1998, by the Leadership Council for Inter-American Summitry*

### PREFACE AND ACKNOWLEDGMENTS

The Leadership Council for Inter-American Summitry, established in 1997, is an independent, non-partisan initiative composed of citizens from throughout the Americas working in private business, legislatures, academia, public policy institutes, the scientific community, and other civic organizations. While many members have held high public office, none is currently employed in the executive branch of government. The Leadership Council is united in its aim to strengthen the forces fighting for effective democratic governance, market-oriented economic reforms, and social justice. These same goals are embedded in the declarations issued at the 1994 Summit of the Americas in Miami. The Leadership Council believes that periodic summits that gather the Western Hemisphere's heads of state and government can make a significant contribution toward achieving these goals but that significant reforms are required in the summitry process if its promise is to be fully realized. It is in that hopeful spirit that the Leadership Council issues this report.

The Leadership Council seeks to serve as a bridge between experts outside the executive branch of governments and the officials who organize the summits, between organized civil society and the public sector, and, in the spirit of inter-American summitry, between the northern industrialized nations and the southern developing nations of the region. The Council's membership includes individuals active in the civil society of their nations, as well as individuals with extensive experience at senior levels of government and in summit meetings in the Americas, the Asia Pacific region, and the industrialized world.

---

The project directors wish to express their appreciation for the generous support of the Ford Foundation.

Special thanks to Sherry Tross, Program Coordinator, North-South Center; Lilly Iversen, Staff Associate to the Deputy Director, North-South Center; Christie Kibort, North-South Scholar, North-South Center; Mamie Barrett, Program Coordinator, APEC Study Center, University of California, San Diego; Jeffrey Stark, Director of Research and Studies, North-South Center; Jeffrey Schott, Senior Fellow, Institute for International Economics; Kathy Hamman, Editorial Director, and Mary Mapes, Publications Director, of the North-South Center Press.

Council members have had many conversations with officials responsible for the preparation of the second Summit of the Americas, scheduled for April 1998, in Santiago, Chile. We especially wish to express our gratitude to Thomas "Mack" McLarty III, Counselor to the President of the United States and Special Envoy to the Americas; Richard Brown, Senior Summit Coordinator, U.S. Department of State; Genaro Arriagada, Advisor to the President of Chile for the Summit of the Americas; and Juan Martabit, General Coordinator of the Summit of the Americas in Chile.

The work of the Leadership Council has been informed by two series of detailed working papers that surveyed implementation of the key initiatives of the Miami *Plan of Action* — the only such independent survey. We wish to thank those authors for their pioneering work in monitoring summit follow-up. This project, directed by Richard E. Feinberg and Robin L. Rosenberg, was made possible through the encouragement and support of the Ford Foundation.

The members of the Leadership Council wholeheartedly endorse this report's overall content and tone and support its principal recommendations, even as each member may not agree fully with every phrase. Members subscribe as individuals; institutional affiliations are for purposes of identification only.

## EXECUTIVE SUMMARY

The first Summit of the Americas provided us with a cogent vision of a community of democracies united by the dream of economic integration with social justice. The Leadership Council for Inter-American Summitry affirms that the Miami vision remains valid today. The challenge is to fulfill its promise by correcting the shortcomings of the Miami process.

The Leadership Council for Inter-American Summitry strongly believes that summits can make a difference in the lives of the peoples of the Americas. As the Summit of the Americas in Miami in December 1994 demonstrated, summits can create a political process whereby the hemisphere can agree upon shared values and a common agenda; summits can codify norms and rules to guide the behavior of governments and civil society; and summits can place new issues on the international agenda and catalyze collective action behind consensus goals.

## Evaluation of the Miami Process

Based upon its own independent survey in late 1997, the Leadership Council found that progress on key initiatives agreed upon in Miami was on average modest. More has been accomplished than the public is aware of, but progress has fallen short of the promise of Miami.

The Leadership Council found a number of flaws in the Miami process. There were far too many initiatives and action items. Some initiatives lacked the essential elements of good public policy — measurable goals, timetables, priorities, and accountability. Leaders failed to allocate sufficient technical and financial resources for some initiatives. Many governments did not have the requisite institutional and financial capacities to carry out some of the action items. The regional organizations, notably the Organization of American States (OAS) and the Inter-American Development Bank (IDB), sought to implement some initiatives but allowed other mandates to slip. Monitoring mechanisms were weak to nonexistent.

## The Substantive Agenda

The Leadership Council underscored seven challenges facing the region that summitry, to be credible and effective, must confront:

- the shallowness of democratic institutions (notably in the areas of corruption and narcotics trafficking),
- the weaknesses of civil society,
- persistent poverty and worsening inequality,
- failing schools,
- environmental degradation,
- sluggish export performance and low savings rates, and
- the insufficiency of inter-American institutions.

## Recommendations for the April 1998 Santiago Summit of the Americas

The Council offers recommendations for inclusion in the Santiago Summit *Plan of Action*, as worthy responses to each of these seven challenges. These recommendations are intended to underscore the importance of taming the summit process, that is, regarding realism, focus, selectivity, timetables, tangible targets, and accountability.

## *Democracy, Education, Environment, and Poverty*

To strengthen democratic institutions, the Leadership Council finds that the Inter-American Convention Against Corruption represents a major accomplishment of hemispheric diplomacy. The Santiago Summit should transform the Convention into a realistic work plan and mandate the OAS to establish an independent, expert Inter-American Commission on Corruption to promote implementation of priority goals.

The Leadership Council recommends that the Santiago Summit regularize the participation of non-governmental expertise and the private sector throughout the summitry process. The proposed summit secretariat should issue an annual report tracking transparency-related initiatives.

To yield a more equitable distribution of the fruits of government, the Santiago Summit should accelerate educational reform, seek reduction in diseases that disproportionately attack the poor and weak, strengthen labor ministries to enhance their capacity to enforce code labor standards, and seek to assure an enabling environment that provides equal opportunity for entrepreneurial talent. Priorities for educational reform include reaffirming the Miami commitment to ensure universal completion of quality primary education by the year 2010, establishing standards and quantifiable indicators for basic skills, and promoting early access to new technologies, such as the worldwide web and distance learning through such media as television.

To address environmental degradation, leaders should select a manageable number of items from the Miami and Santa Cruz, Bolivia, Summits for priority attention. Good candidates include sustainable water management, especially in urban areas; sustainable forest management; and the reduction of air pollution.

## *Trade Integration and Financial Stability*

The Leadership Council is concerned that the Miami Summit's 2005 date for completion of negotiations for the Free Trade Area of the Americas (FTAA), rather than serving to spur negotiations, has become an excuse for delay. To reignite the sense of urgency, the Council proposes that the Santiago Summit accelerate the target date for completion of negotiations to 2002. As the leaders agreed in Miami, trade negotiators should still seek concrete progress by the end of the century.

Since Miami, some governmental and private-sector leaders have failed to build public support for free trade and the FTAA. We urge leaders, particularly in the big markets of the United States and Brazil, to engage in concerted efforts to build the public case for the FTAA. Specifically, the U.S. administration must mobilize sufficient political support to gain fast track authority that encompasses regional trade agreements. The government of Brazil should explain to its citizens that the FTAA is in the national interest and is compatible with MERCOSUR's basic objectives.

In the Miami Summit, free trade was implicitly linked with democratic freedoms. At Santiago, the Leadership Council believes that the time has come for the Western Hemisphere to announce clearly that only democratic nations will be welcome to participate in the formation of the Free Trade Area of the Americas.

The recent turmoil in Asian financial markets has illuminated the importance of financial market reform in developing countries. The Leadership Council urges finance ministers to meet at least annually to exercise self-surveillance of national macroeconomic policies and of international economic trends as they affect the region. This new regional forum — which might be labeled the Inter-American Financial Council — could assess steps being taken at the national and international levels to build market confidence and to avoid contagion from the current financial volatility in East Asia.

## Seven Steps Toward More Effective Summitry

At this stage in the development of inter-American relations, priority must be given to institutional mechanisms that can insure compliance with Summit accords. The Leadership Council proposes seven steps to improve the process of summitry in the Americas.

- Initiatives should be responsibly crafted to contain practical goals, quantifiable targets, and realistic timetables.

- Initiatives should be assigned to mechanisms with adequate technical and financial resources, and leaders should mandate that existing regional institutions, notably the OAS and IDB, be fully integrated into the summitry process.

- Governments should appoint a senior official to coordinate summit planning and implementation.

- Networks of functional ministries should be solidified.

- The participation of the private sector and other non-governmental organizations should be regularized.
- Monitoring responsibilities should be assigned for each initiative to an official regional mechanism with adequate capacity.
- Most important, Summits should be institutionalized. Inter-American Summits should be held every two years. In interim years, ministers of foreign and economic affairs should meet to monitor the transformation of talk into action. Leaders in Santiago should establish a small, permanent Summit Secretariat to better coordinate, monitor, and assess the implementation of summit agreements.

## Centerpieces for Santiago

The Leadership Council proposes that at Santiago the heads of state and government focus on four of the initiatives we have proposed as summit centerpieces whose implementation would improve the well-being of millions of our citizens:

- acceleration to 2002 for completion of negotiations for the Free Trade Area of the Americas — with participation open to democratic nations only;
- formation of an Inter-American Financial Council to improve regional economic cooperation and enhance market confidence;
- creation of an Inter-American Commission on Corruption to spur implementation of the Convention Against Corruption; and
- institutionalization of summitry through biannual summits and a summit secretariat. Together, these centerpiece initiatives would assure the success of the Santiago Summit and revitalize summitry in the Western Hemisphere.

## POLICY REPORT

## I. The Mission of the Leadership Council on Inter-American Summitry

Never before in the history of the Western Hemisphere have its peoples enjoyed better opportunities to realize the cherished ideals of democratic values, market-driven economic prosperity, environmentally sustainable development, and social justice; and to work together toward these common goals. Never before have these values been so widely shared, nor have conflicting perspectives been so diminished. Never before have the institutions and processes that could cement hemispheric cooperation shown so much promise. Rarely has the global environment been more conducive to the fulfillment of these hemispheric ideals.

The Western Hemisphere has drawn the correct lessons from its tortured history. Our peoples have learned that military authoritarianism does not guarantee good government and that fiscal profligacy will not lead to sustainable prosperity. Leaders in the United States have recognized publicly that the Cold War sometimes blinded their government to the worthy aspirations of oppressed or exploited peoples. Throughout the hemisphere, there is a growing appreciation for the democratic virtues of tolerance, diversity, pragmatism, and compromise and for the economic virtues of sound fiscal and monetary policies and market-driven, open economies. In inter-American affairs, leaders are replacing suspicion and distrust with realism and cooperation.

Recent financial crises in Asia highlight the progress made in Latin America and the Caribbean, both in macro-economic stabilization and political democratization. Latin America has also made progress in building institutional infrastructures for sustainable development; for budget controls, regulatory regimes, and open financial systems; for parliaments, political parties, and labor unions; and for independent media — even if much remains to be done in these and other areas. The Western Hemisphere can take pride in the accomplishments of the last decade.

Indeed, the turbulence in the economies of East Asia underscores the logic behind cooperation in the Western Hemisphere. Today, both the United States and Latin America are enjoying sustained economic expansion with price stability, and their interdependent markets offer bright prospects for growing exchange. In the political realm, the entire Western Hemisphere (save Cuba) shares the common denominator of democratic values.

Yet, in the Western Hemisphere there is a real danger of backsliding and missed opportunities. In too many countries, the people feel betrayed by elected governments that fail to reform corrupt institutions. In too many cities, prosperity is not shared, and the gap between rich and poor, already glaring, has widened further. Inter-American cooperation has too often been stymied by demagogues or narrow interests that appeal to old prejudices, and official inter-American institutions are not yet strong enough to capitalize on the new dynamism and expertise that characterize the private sector and a diverse civil society.

# V. Leadership Council for Inter-American Summitry

At the 1994 Summit of the Americas, the leaders declared:

> The elected Heads of State and Government of the Americas are committed to advance the prosperity, democratic values and institutions, and security of our Hemisphere. For the first time in history, the Americas are a community of democratic societies. Although faced with differing development challenges, the Americas are united in pursuing prosperity through open markets, hemispheric integration, and sustainable development. We are determined to consolidate and advance closer bonds of cooperation and to transform our aspirations into concrete realities.

The Leadership Council for Inter-American Summitry shares these hopes and objectives. In this Policy Report, we seek to explain the potential contributions of summits for inter-American relations, to analyze the strengths and weaknesses of the Miami Summit and its aftermath, and to propose recommendations for the 1998 Santiago Summit of the Americas and for the process of summitry in general. Based upon the most extensive research undertaken by any non-official group, we evaluate follow-up to the Miami *Plan of Action* and make the case for a more serious, realistic, and transparent approach to summitry in the Americas.

First, we wish to situate these policy discussions in the context of the opportunities and obstacles facing the men and women of the Americas, within which summits will convene.

## II. Opportunities and Challenges

### *The Foundations for Success*

The physicist Marie Curie once said, "One seldom notices what has been done, one can only see what remains to be done." Before we discuss our agenda for future action, we want to review the accomplishments of the last decade or so — critical transition years for most nations of the hemisphere and for inter-American relations.

Politically, the swing begun in the mid-1970s away from authoritarian rule toward democracy and free elections has by now encompassed all but one country in the hemisphere. Over the past dozen years, every country except Cuba has had at least two consecutive elections to select a head of government, and most have had three or more. Since 1980, only one elected president has been ousted by military force—Haitian President Jean-Bertrand Aristide, who eventually completed his term in office. The media has become more open and vigorous throughout the region. Civil society is better organized and more effective, ethnic and racial minorities are playing more active roles, and women are more visible in political life in some countries. Public opinion polls indicate that the majority of citizens — the large majority in many countries — prefer democracy to any other type of government.

Economically, the robust U.S. economy has become the world's growth dynamo, and the Latin American economies, after a decade of tough structural reforms, have attained growth rates in the 3 percent to 4 percent range with dramatically lower inflation. Whereas the average annual GDP growth rate during the 1980s among Latin American and Caribbean economies stagnated at a little over 1 percent, from 1991 through 1996, output expanded at a respectable 3.2 percent rate. In 1997, the region's economies grew by an estimated average of 5.3 percent, one of the highest growth rates for the region in the last 25 years. Governments have slashed fiscal deficits, disciplined monetary policy, sharply reduced barriers to international trade and investment, and, to varying degrees, have privatized parastatals and taken the state out of counter-productive regulatory activities.

Exports have become an engine of expansion for important economic sectors. After stagnating for much of the 1980s, total Latin American goods exports soared from $137 billion in 1991 to over $250 billion in 1996. Particularly robust has been the growth of intraregional trade. Latin American exports to the United States more than doubled from $60 billion in 1988 to $130 billion in 1996, and U.S. exports to Latin America grew almost as fast. U.S. exports to Latin America as a percentage of total U.S. exports jumped from 14 percent in 1988 to 18 percent in 1996. Including Canada, the Western Hemisphere accounted for 39 percent of U.S. exports. Even more impressive, Latin American intra-regional trade is exploding, up 113 percent from 1990 to 1995. Booming intra-MERCOSUR trade as a proportion of members' total trade rose from 14 percent in 1992 to 21 percent in 1996.

Contrary to popular perceptions, social conditions for many citizens in Latin America and the Caribbean have gradually improved over the last generation. Primary school enrollment rates progressed markedly, and adult literacy rates rose from 73 percent to over 84 percent between 1970 and 1990. Girls now outnumber boys at both secondary and tertiary levels of education. As an indicator of the availability of health services, under-five-years-of-age mortality rates dropped by two-thirds from

1960 to 1994. Fertility has declined significantly — dropping 40 percent or more over the past two decades in many countries, and the total fertility rate has fallen from 4.8 to 3.2 percent. In contrast to the 1980s, when fiscally strapped governments cut social expenditures, during the 1990s, the level of public spending allocated to social sectors has risen in most countries in the region.

These trends — particularly the swings toward democracy, more open markets, and regional integration — converged with new directions in U.S. foreign policy to create conditions for a renaissance in hemispheric relations in the 1990s. At the Summit of the Americas in Miami in 1994, hemispheric leaders seized this favorable moment to forge a new agenda of cooperation for the Americas.

## Seven Critical Challenges

At the Miami Summit, the leaders recognized that there was no shortage of problems remaining before the region. We wish to underscore seven challenges that summitry, to be credible and effective, must confront in the years ahead. Summits cannot and should not pretend to resolve these complex problems in their entirety, but they should tackle issues — pragmatically and selectively — that address each challenge.

*1. Shallowness of Democratic Institutions.* Dissatisfaction with democratic institutions is a worldwide phenomenon. In Latin America in a recent survey of 9 countries, only 25 percent of the people expressed satisfaction with the way that democracy was working in their countries. Overextended and crusty central bureaucracies, inept parliaments, unfair and inaccessible judicial systems, and inefficient regulatory bodies are among the major problems that confront democratic states throughout the region.

Law enforcement and personal security have also emerged as central concerns. The return of democratic rule has been accompanied by a destructive upsurge in criminal violence. In the aggregate of 11 countries, the murder rate per 100,000 population has jumped from 8 in the late 1970s to over 17 today. In one poll, 75 percent of those surveyed expressed dissatisfaction with their judiciaries, and only one quarter expressed strong confidence in their police. In Rio de Janeiro, nearly 88 percent of residents believe that the police have links to organized crime. Corruption, often linked to drug trafficking, is perceived to be widespread in many countries, undermining faith in democracy and efficiency in economic policy. In one extensive poll, business executives listed corruption as the number-one obstacle to doing business in Latin America — ahead of tax policy or government regulation.

*2. Weaknesses of Civil Society.* Beginning in Miami, the process of summitry has opened up unprecedented opportunities for the participation of civil society — non-governmental organizations (NGOs), private-sector associations, the scientific community, political parties, labor unions — in hemispheric policy initiatives. The 1996 Santa Cruz, Bolivia, Summit on Sustainable Development opened the Organization of American States (OAS) to civil society input for the first time. Nevertheless, in many countries, civil society organizations face the formidable challenges of weak institutional and legal frameworks for effective and responsible participation. Many governments remain reluctant to provide opportunities for meaningful participation. Official suspicion of the increasingly dynamic civil society organizations is impeding the creation of the public-private partnerships necessary to make the promise of inter-American summitry a reality.

*3. Persistent Poverty and Worsening Inequality.* During the debt-ridden 1980s, the percentage of Latin Americans living in poverty rose from an average of 35 percent to 41 percent. In the first half of the 1990s, the incidence of poverty declined to 39 percent of households (as growth resumed and inflation fell). In absolute terms, the number of Latin Americans and Caribbeans living in poverty — 210 million — is higher now than ever before. The percentage of indigent households — those unable to meet basic food needs — stood at 17 percent in 1994, a slight improvement over 1990 but up from 15 percent in 1980.

Latin America has the most unequal distribution of income in the world. The richest 20 percent of households appropriate 60 percent of the income, whereas the bottom 40 percent receive only 10 percent. Income distribution worsened in the 1980s, although it appears to have stabilized during the 1990s. The mean national level of unemployment stood at just under 10 percent in 1996. Some 55 million Latin Americans still lack access to health services, and 110 million lack access to safe drinking water. Modest GDP growth, persistent high unemployment in some countries, and inadequate social services all contribute to the perpetuation of widespread poverty.

In the United States, the gap between the rich and the rest of the population has also widened since the 1970s. By 1994-1996, the gap between families with the highest income (the top 20 percent) and those with the lowest income (the bottom 20 percent) reached nearly 13:1. In New York state, the gap has expanded to nearly 20:1.

In Latin America and the Caribbean, if the deteriorating trends in poverty and income distribution of the 1980s have been halted, the 1990s have not brought about significant improvements. Not surprisingly, many citizens complain that democracy is not delivering the goods and that they are not benefiting from the fruits of the economic recovery.

*4. Failing Schools.* Increasingly, quality education is recognized as a key ingredient to greater social equality, democratic participation, and international economic competitiveness. Yet, in Latin America the average citizen receives just five years of formal education. Quality is also generally poor, as a result of outmoded curricula, anachronistic teaching methods, and insufficient instructional materials. Many public universities, once the crown jewels of national culture, have deteriorated under the weight of budget constraints and burgeoning enrollments. Latin America and the Caribbean spend about 8 percent of per capita GNP on pre-primary and primary education, as compared to 13 percent for developing countries in general and nearly 18 percent for developed countries.

*5. Environmental Degradation.* Air quality in many Latin American cities has become a serious health hazard, causing an estimated 2.3 million cases of chronic respiratory illness every year among children and over 100,000 cases of chronic bronchitis among the elderly. Increasingly, the region's carbon emissions are contributing to global climate change. Deteriorating water quality threatens the well-being of burgeoning urban populations. Due to the expansion of the agricultural frontier, deforestation is stripping some 6 million hectares of dense forests per year. Tropical deforestation accelerated from 5.6 percent in the 1960s to a stunning 7.4 percent in the 1980s. The region's vital biodiversity reserve is threatened in many globally outstanding ecoregions, as is the natural resource base upon which future development depends.

*6. Sluggish Export Performance and Low Savings Rates.* Latin American merchandise exports grew only 3.4 percent from 1980 to 1993, compared to well over 10 percent for many East Asian nations. Latin America lost significant market shares — its percentage of world exports fell from about 12.5 percent in the 1950s to about 3.5 percent in 1990, the lowest point in a century. Smaller economies, such as those in the Caribbean, are struggling to diversify their export base in the face of stagnant markets for their traditional crops.

Loss of competitiveness and slow labor productivity growth are associated with low savings and investment rates. At about 18 percent of GDP, savings rates in many countries are below the levels attained in the 1970s and far short of those reached by East Asian nations.

*7. Insufficiency of Inter-American Institutions.* The Inter-American Development Bank (IDB), the OAS, and other regional institutions are struggling to take advantage of new opportunities in the post-Cold War world. They are just beginning to explore how to build coalitions with dynamic forces in inter-American relations, such as corporate and financial private sectors, non-governmental organizations, and decentralized intra-ministerial working groups. Despite the election in 1994 of a dynamic new Secretary-General, the OAS has not gained significantly in stature or credibility, according to The Inter-American Dialogue.[1] After many years of remaining marginal to the region's needs, the IDB has just begun to grapple with critical development issues and has become a serious player in inter-American affairs. After years of mutual suspicion, the OAS and IDB are starting to cooperate in such areas as trade integration and democracy promotion. Still, these institutions are not yet providing the inter-American system and summitry with adequate administrative structures and resources.

### III. The Role of Summitry

There have been remarkably few Western Hemisphere summits. Since World War II, the hemisphere's leaders of state and government have convened only three times — in Panama in 1956, in Punta del Este in 1967, and in Miami in 1994. In other years, policy conflicts, cultural distrust, or simply lack of interest kept leaders apart. The collective decision to convene another full Summit of the Americas in Santiago, Chile, this year — only three years and four months after Miami — reflects a widespread political will to benefit from our shared geography and to work together on common problems.

The Leadership Council strongly believes that summits can make a difference in the lives of the peoples of the Americas. Summits can:

- Create a political process whereby the hemisphere can agree upon shared values and a common agenda.

---

1. Inter-American Dialogue, *The Americas in 1997: Making Cooperation Work* (Washington, D.C., 1997) 4. However, the OAS made an important contribution to the collective defense of democracy with its 1991 "Declaration of Santiago," requiring the OAS to take emergency action in the event of a challenge to democratic rule.

For example, the Miami-Santiago process has placed freer trade and quality education at the center of a regional agenda for action.

- Codify consensus norms and rules to guide the behavior of governments and civil society. Miami reinforced the unique legitimacy of democratic norms.

- Catalyze collective action behind consensus goals. Miami fostered action to eliminate lead in gasoline and to eradicate measles. Santiago may mobilize financial resources to help the region's smaller economies implement the leaders' decisions.

- Place new issues on the international agenda. Before Miami, official corruption was rarely discussed in diplomatic fora. Today, many international bodies are working to halt bribery and other illicit commercial practices.

- Build personal relationships between leaders and networks among national bureaucracies, motivate cross-border ties among civil societies, and foster public-private sector partnerships. The Miami-Santiago process scheduled periodic ministerials and brought together private sector groupings with senior government officials to discuss such issues as trade, finance, and energy.

The Western Hemisphere is only at the early stages of learning what summitry can contribute to regional progress, but Miami gave us a sense of the potential for summitry to accelerate the forward march of history.

Summits cannot tackle all of our problems successfully. Some issues are better left in the hands of existing institutions specifically designed to handle them; for example, the Bretton Woods institutions bring massive expertise and resources to correcting imbalances in countries' external finances.

Nor can summits manufacture national political will where none exists. Summits can lead but cannot get too far out in front of public opinion. Summits can, however, bolster already committed national leaders and strong social reform movements. Summits can make a difference but only where summit accords add their impetus to local forces already in motion.

## *The New Inter-American System*

Summits are part of the larger inter-American system emerging in the post-Cold War era. Summits stand at the zenith of a rich and growing array of hemispheric institutions and agreements that rest on three legs. The first leg consists of the regional institutions — especially the Organization of American States, the Inter-American Development Bank, and the UN Economic Commission on Latin America and the Caribbean (UNECLAC). The second leg is the series of ministerial meetings and working groups set in motion by the Miami Summit. The third leg is the growing array of partnerships between public-sector agencies and civil society organizations, forged in some instances in order to implement the Miami *Plan of Action*.

Summitry gives leaders opportunities to provide guidance to the various components of these three legs and to forge more coherence among them. Summitry also offers opportunities to explain this new inter-American system to the broader public. Too many people still associate the inter-American system solely with the OAS. Today, the inter-American system is much broader and richer and more directly relevant to the lives of millions of our peoples.

Outside the Western Hemisphere, summits can enable the formation of a regional "caucus" to express common positions in global fora, such as those dealing with women's rights, financial market liberalization, and climate change. In this way, in December 1996, at the Santa Cruz, Bolivia, Summit, the Americas became the first region of the world to establish a common definition and agenda for action on sustainable development. The forging of a common cause on global issues is one of the great promises of regional summitry.

## IV. Evaluation of the Miami Process

Lack of adequate information makes it very difficult to evaluate progress toward realizing the goals of the *Plan of Action* adopted in Miami. Predictably, governments will claim considerable success. However, lack of hard data and the near total lack of public dissemination of information on Summit-related activities has created the impression — not fully accurate in our opinion — that governments departed Miami and promptly forgot their pledges.

To begin to fill this information void, the North-South Center at the University of Miami and the Institute for International Economics commissioned independent experts to assess progress on many of the more important Miami initiatives (hereafter referred to as the "independent survey"). Undertaken with very limited resources and completed during the second half of 1997, these surveys can only be an incipient effort at assessing summit implementation.[2] The official "responsible coordinators" — governments and international organizations that play leading roles in coordinating implementation of individual Summit initiatives — will release their own surveys at the Santiago Summit. While these official reports will be welcome contributions, we fear they may suffer from unclear methodology, incomplete data bases, and insufficient resources.

Table 1 displays the Leadership Council's assessment of progress on key Miami initiatives, informed by the independent surveys as well as by Council members' own judgments. Ratings from one to five (five being the best) judge progress made toward the goals announced in Miami. The average rating is 2.44, or somewhere between "modest" to "good" progress. While other observers might award somewhat different ratings to individual initiatives, we are confident that our overall rating represents a reasonable and fair assessment. It suggests that more has been accomplished than public opinion is aware of but that progress has fallen short of the promise of Miami.

**Table 1. Assessment of Progress on Key Miami Initiatives**

| Initiative | Rating |
|---|---|
| Democracy/Human Rights | 2 |
| Civil Society | 3 |
| Corruption | 2 |
| Narcotics and Money Laundering Trade | 2 |
| Capital Market Liberalization | 3 |
| Education | 2 |
| Health | 4 |
| Sustainable Development | 2 |

Source: Leadership Council Independent Survey, 1997.
Note: Ratings of Progress toward implementation of the Miami *Plan of Action*:
5 = very strong, 4 = very good, 3 = good, 2 = modest, 1 = minor to none.

The independent surveys point to a number of summit successes. For example, in the area of democracy and human rights, enough countries ratified the Washington Protocol, which provides for the expulsion of a state from the OAS if democracy is interrupted, for this historic commitment to come into force. By 1997, at least six countries had established human rights ombudsmen. The collective defense of democracy in Paraguay in April 1996 may be attributed, in part, to the summit's negation of the authoritarian option. In early 1996, the hemisphere successfully concluded negotiations on the world's first regional anticorruption convention, and nations began to develop technically sophisticated centers to combat money laundering. To foster capital market liberalization, the IDB undertook to catalogue member countries' capital market regulations and to increase the transparency of financial transactions. Several countries carried out sweeping educational reforms and formed a network of educational policy reform partnerships. In the health area, the hemisphere began a new regional initiative to eradicate measles and continued efforts to lower maternal and child mortality rates. Many countries made progress on health reforms pursuing increased equity, quality, and efficiency of services. This is by no means an exhaustive list of Summit-related accomplishments.

Progress toward the centerpiece goal of negotiating a Free Trade Area of the Americas (FTAA) by 2005 was slowed by domestic political pressures in some key countries, but the foundations for future negotiations were put in place. A series of ministerials and a dozen working groups developed a detailed agenda for future negotiations and began to establish a hemispheric community of trade officials. The new OAS Trade Unit earned a reputation for quality work by compiling in-depth comparative studies of subregional free trade arrangements. The private sector coalesced into an Americas Business Forum with the potential capacity to advise governments and influence public opinion.

In their review of the sustainable development partnerships, experts from the Natural Resources Defense Council (NRDC) explained the reasons for the dramatic success of the initiative to eliminate lead — a clear health danger — in gasoline by the year 2000. The initiative was sharply focused, easily understood, and politically attractive. The initiative went beyond general regional discussions to include targeted assistance at the national level. Each government identified a focal point responsible for information and data collection. The World Bank provided technical expertise, and governments, particularly Canada's, provided financial support. The Bank and other agencies carried out case studies on leaded gasoline phaseout in a number of countries, assisted in developing national phaseout plans, and convened a workshop to review success stories. The overall effort was steered by an ad hoc committee, chaired by the World Bank, that

---

2. These surveys are available through the North-South Center's Worldwide Web page at <www.miami.edu/nsc/>.

included the OAS, IDB, Pan-American Health Organization (PAHO), U.S. Environmental Protection Agency (EPA), U.S. Department of Energy, U.S. Agency for International Development (USAID), and the NRDC.

At the same time, the independent surveys and the personal observations of Leadership Council members suggest a number of flaws in the Miami process:

- There were far too many initiatives and action items. The hemisphere simply lacked the institutional capacity and political will to implement the more than 150 action items.

- Some initiatives lacked the essential elements of good public policy — measurable goals, timetables, priorities, and accountability.

- Leaders failed to allocate sufficient technical and financial resources for some initiatives, particularly in the social and environmental areas, that required significant investments.

- Many governments, especially the smaller, poorer states in Central America and the Caribbean, did not have the requisite institutional and financial capacities to carry out some of the action items, and the Summit did not offer compensatory resources.

- The regional organizations, notably the OAS and the IDB, sought to implement some initiatives but allowed other mandates to slip.

- Monitoring mechanisms were weak to nonexistent. There was no strong central coordinating mechanism responsible for overseeing and monitoring implementation.

A preliminary assessment by the OAS of the 1996 Summit of the Americas on Sustainable Development in Santa Cruz reached remarkably similar conclusions regarding that effort at regional summitry. The draft report found "modest" progress on most of the 65 initiatives approved at the Bolivian conference. Initiatives, the report concluded, often lacked specific lines of action, implementation methods were not spelled out, and priorities were not established. Another limiting factor has been the shortage of financial resources. The OAS report also found that at the national level, where relevant agencies did not participate adequately in the preparatory process, they were not fully committed to implementing the initiatives in question, and national-level responsibilities were not clearly designated.

## V. Recommendations for the Santiago Summit

The Leadership Council has laid out seven critical challenges facing the Western Hemisphere on the eve of the second Summit of the Americas (see section II). Furthermore, our independent surveys of the Miami process have provided important lessons for policymakers. We have also indicated the various ways that summitry can contribute to the betterment of the Americas. Based on these findings, we now offer recommendations for the Santiago Summit, first with regard to substance, and second with regard to process.

### *The Substantive Agenda*

Each summit should not try to cover the whole gamut of issues in inter-American relations. If summits are overly ambitious in scope, they will inevitably fall far short in implementation. The Leadership Council believes that the following policy proposals for the Santiago Summit are worthy of the attention of heads of government and that the inter-American system has or could have the capacity to implement them. Significant progress is attainable on each of the proposals prior to a third Summit of the Americas.

These recommendations seek to build upon the lessons of the Miami Summit, the Santa Cruz Summit on Sustainable Development, and other inter-American events since 1994. They are intended to be illustrative rather than exhaustive and to underscore the importance of "taming" the summit process, that is, regarding realism, focus, selectivity, timetables, tangible targets, and accountability.

The Leadership Council offers the following substantive recommendations for inclusion in the Santiago *Plan of Action*, as worthy responses to the seven challenges outlined earlier:

**Challenge 1:** Shallowness of Democratic Institutions — Corruption and Narcotics Trafficking

*Summit Response A:* The Inter-American Convention Against Corruption represents a major accomplishment of hemispheric diplomacy. The Santiago Summit should transform the Convention into a realistic work plan and select a few priority goals for national implementation prior to the next Summit.

Candidates for priority attention include the following goals:

- Creating standards of conduct for public officials, including clarification of conflict of interest codes and creation of national mechanisms to enforce these standards of conduct;
- Establishing systems for publicly registering the income and assets of persons who perform senior-level public functions; and
- Outlawing bribery in international commercial transactions.

To spur compliance with the Santiago Summit work plan, we recommend that the leaders mandate the OAS to establish an independent, expert Inter-American Commission on Corruption to monitor implementation of priority goals, circulate model legislation and examples of best practices, and help to coordinate technical assistance. Inspired by the success of the OAS's Inter-American Commission on Human Rights, a commission on corruption would use the power of objective, non-partisan information to enhance compliance with international norms. Periodic reports on country performance, made available to the public, would provide governments and civil society with the information required for an informed public debate. In light of the OAS's very tight budget, we urge governments to make special financial contributions to support the work of the recommended Inter-American Commission on Corruption.

*Summit Response B:* As a follow-up to Miami, the OAS Inter-American Drug Abuse Control Commission (OAS/CICAD) reached agreement on "An Anti-Drug Strategy in the Hemisphere." Again, the Santiago Summit should transform this 40-plus-point agreement into a realistic work plan and select a few priority, quantifiable goals that address supply and demand for prompt national implementation.

In addition, a multilateral mechanism, probably within OAS/CICAD, should periodically measure and assess tangible progress toward key consensus goals, not to issue report cards but instead to alert countries regarding shortcomings and to direct technical assistance and resources toward trouble spots. Such a transparent, candid regional self-evaluation would be preferable to unilateral judgments and one-sided sanctions. The proposed civilian-led Multinational Counternarcotics Center in Panama would complement this cooperative, balanced approach.

**Challenge 2:** Weaknesses of Civil Society

*Summit Response:* An excellent way for summitry to encourage civil society participation in hemispheric decisionmaking is by setting an example. In principle and initiative by initiative, we recommend that the Santiago Summit regularize the participation of non-governmental expertise and the private sector throughout the summitry process, stretching from the design to the assessment of progress phases of work. The summit secretariat proposed below should issue an annual report on civil society participation in Summit implementation.

We urge government leaders to direct their ministries to create mechanisms to facilitate civil society participation in the national implementation of Summit initiatives.

We applaud the initiative of the IDB to establish a Foundation of the Americas to enhance the competence and contributions of civil society organizations and to engage them in productive partnerships with governments and private business. We propose that this new Foundation give priority to projects that advance initiatives mandated by the Summits of the Americas.

An ample supply of information is a precondition for an efficient and fair democracy. Throughout this report we underscore the importance of greater transparency in public-sector operations. We suggest that the summit secretariat proposed below also issue an annual report tracking transparency initiatives in such areas as anticorruption measures, financial market trends, tax policy and collection, indicators of social progress, and military purchases.

**Challenge 3:** Persistent Poverty and Worsening Inequality

*Summit Response:* Sustained private-sector-led economic growth with price stability provide the best context for poverty alleviation. In particular, open trading markets create good jobs and reduce unemployment. However, more specific interventions are urgently needed to yield a more equitable distribution of the fruits of growth.

Possible priority initiatives in the key areas of education, health, labor rights, and entrepreneurship include the following:

- Accelerating educational reform (outlined below);
- Building on PAHO's successful measles vaccination campaign to seek reduction in other diseases that disproportionately attack the poor and weak, such as influenza, pneumonia, mumps, and rubella;

establishing indicators to monitor and evaluate the impact of health reforms; and setting specific targets that help to define reform output;

- Strengthening labor ministries to enhance their capacity to enforce code labor standards, particularly the right of free association, and requesting that ministers of labor at their 1998 meeting agree to establish means to report on and assess national labor code reviews; and

- Assuring an enabling environment that provides equal opportunity for entrepreneurial talent. Governments should review financial market practices, accounting standards, legal and tax systems, and management training programs to ascertain whether unfair disincentives are squashing individuals, especially women and minorities, with ideas and drive but without large initial endowments. In coordinating this initiative, the microenterprise office of the IDB should work closely with expert NGOs and established private-sector firms.

**Challenge 4:** Failing Schools

*Summit Response:* Practical priorities for educational reform throughout the hemisphere include the following:

- Reaffirming the Miami commitment to ensure, by the year 2010, universal access to and completion of quality primary education for 100 percent of children and access for at least 75 percent of young people to secondary education;

- Establishing standards (that allow for differences among countries), quantifiable indicators for basic skills, and methods for the accreditation of institutions of higher education, to be compiled and published by mechanisms chosen at the time of the educational ministerial scheduled for August 1998; and

- Promoting early access to new technologies, including the worldwide web and distance learning through media such as television. Leaders should mandate a survey of existing programs and urge partnerships with the private sector.

We propose the establishment of an educational reform steering committee, consisting of the IDB, World Bank, relevant bilateral donors, responsible coordinator governments, and expert NGOs, to coordinate implementation, monitor progress, and direct additional assistance to countries that are lagging behind. The education ministerial should consider establishing an expert-level working group to focus on goals for elementary and secondary education.

**Challenge 5:** Environmental Degradation

*Summit Response:* Sustainable development initiatives are presently spread out among the three sustainable development partnerships from Miami (energy, biodiversity, and pollution prevention) and the 65 initiatives in the *Plan of Action* from the Santa Cruz, Bolivia, Summit of the Americas on Sustainable Development. At this time, the organizers of the Santiago Summit agenda plan to address sustainable development and environmental issues only through 1) the respective reports by the OAS Secretary-General on Santa Cruz implementation and the Miami responsible coordinators for the implementation of the Sustainable Development Partnerships, 2) a brief reference to sustainable development in the Santiago Summit Declaration, and 3) a short discussion of the reports among the Summit leaders.

The Leadership Council believes that, given the importance of the sustainable development agenda and the backlog of over 100 sustainable development commitments by governments, the Santa Cruz and Miami "processes" should not be forced artificially onto separate tracks. Future summits should integrate the processes of sustainable development and summitry, and their implementation provisions should be consolidated within the single institutional framework proposed below. At Santiago, leaders should select a manageable number of items from the Miami and Santa Cruz Summits for priority attention. Good candidates include sustainable water management, especially in urban areas; sustainable forest management; and the reduction of air pollution, including the completion of the successful initiative to eliminate lead from gasoline.

In particular, we note with approval that the joint U.S.-Venezuelan proposal to the Summit Implementation Review Group (SIRG) calls for establishing an organizational body to give institutional structure to the energy initiative, to include a permanent secretariat.

**Challenge 6:** Sluggish Export Performance and Low Savings Rates

*Summit Response A:* Intraregional trade has become an engine of growth, and as long as it remains consistent with "open regionalism" and WTO standards, regional economic integration will enhance each nation's international competitiveness. The Leadership Council is concerned that the Miami Summit's 2005 date for completion of negotiations for the FTAA, rather than serving to spur negotiations, has become an excuse for delay. To reignite the sense of urgency, we propose that the Santiago Summit accelerate the target date for completion of negotiations to 2002. This deadline would still provide plenty of time to overcome any technical obstacles, and those who worry about political adjustments should remember that actual implementation of trade liberalizing measures would be phased in gradually over 10 to 15 years or more. As the leaders agreed in Miami, trade negotiators should still seek "concrete progress" by the end of the twentieth century. Candidates for such an "early harvest" include business facilitation measures (customs harmonization, standards, and testing) of the sort currently under discussion in APEC and between the United States and the European Union, as well as possibly dispute settlement mechanisms.

This timely affirmation of faith in hemispheric economic prospects and the commitment to close cooperation would reassure international investors made wary by the Asian financial crisis. It would also draw the attention of the U.S. Congress to tangible market prospects contingent upon the granting of fast-track authority for trade legislation.

The Santiago Summit should designate the OAS Trade Unit as the temporary secretariat for the FTAA. The Trade Unit should focus on providing the necessary infrastructure for the all-parties negotiations and for fostering convergence among the various subregional trading arrangements, especially MERCOSUR and NAFTA.

Since Miami, some governmental and private-sector leaders have failed to build public support for free trade and the FTAA. We urge leaders, particularly in the big markets of the United States and Brazil, to engage in concerted efforts to build the public case for the FTAA. We also believe that the broader Summit agenda outlined here — with its emphasis on more honest and open government, a better distribution of the fruits of growth, more equal opportunity through access to education and the protection of labor rights, as well as the protection of the environment — if properly explained and implemented, would alleviate many of the fears that are driving citizens toward trade protectionism. Conversely, any real or perceived lack of progress toward the FTAA should not be used to block progress on the rest of the Santiago agenda.

Specifically, the U.S. administration must mobilize sufficient political support to gain fast-track authority that encompasses regional trade agreements. The government of Brazil should explain to its citizens that the FTAA is in the national interest and is compatible with MERCOSUR's basic objectives.

In the Miami Summit, free trade was implicitly linked with democratic freedoms. Only democracies were invited to a Summit whose centerpiece was regional integration. Since Miami, MERCOSUR demonstrated clearly the value of an explicit free trade-democracy linkage in its valiant defense of democracy in one of its member states (Paraguay). The pursuit of free trade by Latin American nations with the European Union — with its explicit defense of democracy and human rights — is another example of the linkage between economic and political systems.

At the Santiago Summit, the Leadership Council believes that the time will have come for the Western Hemisphere to announce clearly that only democratic nations will be welcome to participate in the formation of the Free Trade Area of the Americas.

*Summit Response B:* The recent turmoil in Asian financial markets has illuminated the importance of financial market reform in developing countries. Therefore, we propose that the Western Hemisphere maintain its leadership in this sector with its pivotal role in stimulating savings and allocating investment:

- At Santiago, based on the IDB's comprehensive survey of national capital market regulations, leaders should determine priority areas for market liberalization and progressive integration of financial systems at the subregional and hemispheric levels. The results of the IDB survey should be made public to increase transparency as a step toward liberalization and integration.

- We urge that the Deputies-level Committee on Hemispheric Financial Issues (CHFI) intensify its work, particularly with regard to strengthening the regulatory regimes that supervise banking and capital markets, implementing IMF disclosure standards, and reviewing ratification and implementation of the recent WTO accord on financial services. In advancing financial market liberalization, the CHFI should pay more attention to the sequencing of financial reforms, taking into account national differences and progress made by the sub-regional groups.

- We also urge finance ministers to meet at least annually to review the work of the CHFI as well as to exercise self-surveillance of national macroeconomic policies and of international economic trends as they affect the region. In its recent Manila Framework Declaration, APEC leap-frogged the Western Hemisphere by establishing such a regional forum, which is long overdue in the Americas. This new regional forum, which might be labeled the Inter-

American Financial Council — could assess steps being taken at the national and international levels to build market confidence and to avoid contagion from the current financial volatility in East Asia. The ministers of finance could also review measures taken by the Bretton Woods institutions to cope with new market realities and to ratify that the rapid dispersal of enhanced resources made available to Asian nations is also available to the Western Hemisphere. Private-sector financial market associations should be involved more routinely in the work of the CHFI and the proposed Financial Council.

**Challenge 7:** Insufficiency of Inter-American Institutions

*Summit Response:* The Leadership Council's recommendations for reform of the inter-American system are outlined in the section that follows. We believe that at this stage in the development of inter-American relations, priority must be given to institutional mechanisms that can insure compliance with Summit accords.

The Leadership Council considers that, taken as a whole, this pared-down, seven-point agenda maintains ambitious objectives yet sets limited goals that we believe are achievable within the recommended time frames. Properly explained and complied with, this agenda would enhance the credibility of summitry and make a difference in the lives of our citizens.

## Improving the Process of Summitry in the Americas

The Leadership Council is concerned that the process responsible for drafting the declarations for the Santiago Summit, under the guidance of the SIRG, rather than building on the successes of Miami and correcting its flaws, appears bogged down in drawing up yet another very lengthy composite of action items. This bureaucratized ritual of drafting "laundry lists" of proposals — however well intended and full of good ideas — threatens to burden the hemisphere with another overly ambitious agenda that it lacks the capacity to implement. Yet, if summitry fails to raise its implementation grades, it will lose credibility.

As the first Summit in a generation, it made sense for the Miami Summit to establish a comprehensive agenda for the region, giving voice to a long backlog of initiatives that had accumulated during the Cold War. However, future summits should take the Miami texts as antecedents and build on them rather than reinvent them. APEC follows this cumulative process to good advantage.

We recommend that future Summit declarations, beginning with Santiago, contain these elements:

- A reaffirmation of the basic principles agreed upon in Miami, amended as necessary to take into account the passage of events;

- Succinct guidelines for ministers and other implementation mechanisms to continue their work on the Miami agenda, while noting where enhanced efforts or somewhat new directions are called for, based upon an assessment of accomplishments to date. To underscore the need for progress in key areas, the leaders should 1) provide specific goals and deadlines, 2) assign responsibilities, and 3) allocate requisite resources; and

- A few detailed "centerpiece" initiatives, which build on previous work and, on occasion, respond to current crises. To enhance the coherency and continuity of the summit process, leaders should also propose key issues for priority attention at the subsequent summit.

Summits should deal with presidential matters. Leaders can generally leave it to their ministers and experts to design, evaluate, and refashion their assigned work plans. Ministerials and other implementation mechanisms (including the responsible coordinators) should submit more detailed reports to the leaders through the SIRG that the leaders' declarations can simply take note of and perhaps comment upon.

## Seven Steps Toward More Effective Summitry

Based upon our assessment of the accomplishments and shortcomings of the Miami Summit and its aftermath, we offer these specific recommendations for improving the process of summitry in the Americas:

*1. Initiatives should be responsibly crafted to contain practical goals, quantifiable targets, and realistic timetables.* Hemispheric Summits should be characterized by responsible public policy practices that are effective in their results and that enhance, not diminish, public respect for hemispheric diplomacy.

*2. Initiatives should be assigned to mechanisms with adequate technical and financial resources or the authority to mobilize them.* These mechanisms can be one or a combination of the three legs of the inter-American system — the international institutions, ministerials and working groups, and public-private sector partnerships.

# V. Leadership Council for Inter-American Summitry

Together, the IDB and World Bank lend over $10 billion per year to the region. Their support for certain of the Miami initiatives has been critical to their successes. Yet, neither institution has placed its full weight behind the Miami-Santiago process. *Leaders should mandate that existing regional institutions, notably the OAS and IDB, be fully integrated into the summitry process.* In response to mandates issued by the summit process, the IDB and World Bank should explicitly assign staff and financial resources to each initiative.

*We welcome the proposal floated by the Chilean government to establish a "virtual" regional fund to assist the poorer countries of Central America and the Caribbean to implement Summit initiatives and urge all governments to contribute.* Recipient governments should co-finance external donations with counterpart funds. The Chilean concept is for governments to manage their own contributions, so as to avoid creating a new bureaucracy. We suggest that governments consider asking the Inter-American Development Bank to help coordinate these bilateral funds and to provide technical assistance where necessary.

*3. Governments should appoint a senior official to coordinate summit planning and implementation.* Drawing on the experience of the Group of Seven industrialized nations and of APEC, a powerful, knowledgeable "sherpa," who reports to the president or prime minister, can impose "double discipline" to curb the inherent bureaucratic tendency toward a proliferation of diluted initiatives. Combining authority and expertise, such senior officials can bring discipline to their own internal political process as well as discipline to the diplomatic negotiations on the summit agenda. They can also mobilize resources to assure summit follow-up.

*4. Networks of functional ministries should be solidified.* A major contribution of the Miami process was the building of linkages among counterpart agencies in such areas as trade, finance, energy, law enforcement, and the environment. Such decentralized cooperation among ministries that house expertise and resources is one promising response to the dilemma created by international agreements that require domestic-level implementation. These networks can be solidified by the creation of coordinating offices in select ministries, use of e-mail and teleconferences, and collaboration with an international organization. Each national ministry should name offices or individuals that serve as focal points or points of contact to facilitate communication with counterpart agencies throughout the region.

*5. The participation of the private sector and other non-governmental organizations should be regularized.* Governments should routinize the participation of representatives of non-governmental organizations in the formulation and implementation of Summit initiatives. NGO involvement provides expertise, impetus, and political depth to the summitry process. The participation of private-sector firms in the Americas Business Forum at the time of the trade ministerials suggests a precedent applicable to other issues. The Natural Resources Defense Council has played a valuable role on the steering committee implementing the non-leaded gasoline project. Governments might follow the U.S. and Chilean examples of including NGO representatives in their SIRG delegations.

*6. To assure accountability, transparency, and adequate information feedback, monitoring responsibilities should be assigned for each initiative to an official regional mechanism with adequate capacity.* National governments should assist by gathering statistics. In addition, governments and regional mechanisms should cooperate with responsible non-governmental efforts to undertake parallel independent surveys of summit implementation. The purposes of monitoring are to assist countries in realizing their aspirations and to indicate to governments and the international community where additional efforts may be necessary — not to pass judgment.

*7. Most important, Summits should be institutionalized.* Inter-American Summits should be held every two years. This schedule would maintain momentum for implementation and innovation but not overburden leaders' calendars. In interim years, ministers of foreign and economic affairs should meet to monitor the transformation of "talk into action."

If the Leadership Council's recommendations on acceleration of FTAA negotiations are successfully pursued, the summit in 2000 would bless the "early harvest" progress, and the following summit in 2002 would celebrate the completion of FTAA negotiations. The Leadership Council believes that Brazil, as the leader of the region's most dynamic integration movement, would be a fitting site for the Summit of the Americas in 2000.

We urge that the leaders in Santiago establish a small, permanent Summit Secretariat to better coordinate, monitor, and assess the implementation of Summit agreements. It could also prepare special reports requested by Summit leaders. A partial precedent is the modest APEC Secretariat, located in Singapore, that helps to schedule ministerials and working group sessions, circulate and store documents, maintain a web page, and prepare reports. A Western Hemisphere Secretariat could build upon the existing Tripartite Committee, which coordinates some activities among the OAS, IDB, and UNECLAC. Officials could be seconded primarily from these organizations and bilateral governments. Such a regional secretariat could also provide services and continuity to the Summit Implementation Review Group, for which the United States, as host of the Miami process, has to date served as a de facto secretariat.

A Western Hemisphere Secretariat would provide the Summit process with a much-needed institutional memory. In negotiating the Santiago texts, the SIRG has too often reinvented initiatives de novo, with little to no reference to the Miami texts and their implementation or lack thereof. A secretariat would also facilitate the review of working-level issues, clearing the Summit agendas for focus on presidential matters.

In some cases, individual initiatives would also benefit from their own secretariats. The OAS Trade Unit is evolving into a secretariat for the FTAA process. The Hemispheric Energy Symposium is serving as an incipient secretariat for the energy initiatives. Such secretariats can be embedded within an international organization or a national agency, or can be a "virtual" secretariat uniting several ministries.

These recommended process reforms would give summitry the infrastructure it needs to succeed and would demonstrate to the peoples of the Americas that their leaders are genuinely committed to the goals of summitry, to the realization of their pledges, and to the participation of civil society throughout the Summit process.

## Centerpieces for Santiago

The Leadership Council proposes that at Santiago the heads of state and government focus on four of the initiatives we have proposed as summit centerpieces whose implementation would improve the well-being of millions of our citizens: acceleration to 2002 for completion of negotiations for the Free Trade Area of the Americas — with participation open to democratic nations only; formation of an Inter-American Financial Council to improve regional economic cooperation and enhance market confidence; creation of an Inter-American Commission on Corruption to spur implementation of the Convention Against Corruption; and institutionalization of summitry through biannual summits and a summit secretariat. Together, these centerpiece initiatives would assure the success of the Santiago Summit and revitalize summitry in the Western Hemisphere.

## Conclusion

The first Summit of the Americas provided us with a cogent vision of a community of democracies united by the dream of economic integration with social justice. We affirm that the Miami vision remains valid today. The challenge is to fulfill its promise by correcting the shortcomings of the Miami process.

Our futures are not predetermined. The Western Hemisphere is poised at a moment of great opportunity, but there are counter-currents that threaten progress toward deeper democracies, more prosperous economies, and more equitable societies. Summitry can make a significant contribution to a more optimistic vision for the Americas — if we are wise enough to build on its successes and courageous enough to correct its early errors. We present this Policy Report to the leaders and peoples of the Americas in the fervent hope that it helps to mold inter-American summitry into a powerful instrument for the construction of a hemispheric community of prosperous democracies.

## VI. Supplemental Comments

### Supplemental Comment of Dr. Winston Dookeran

I am pleased to associate myself with this timely report. However, I would like to add the following points regarding the role of subregional institutions and smaller economies.

We in the smaller economies of the Caribbean region recognize that the Summit process is a unique opportunity to bring to the attention of the larger regional economies the special position and problems of the Caribbean countries. As we approach the twenty-first century, many Caribbean countries face a future filled with challenges and uncertainties. The demise of traditional preferential arrangements for Caribbean exports will have differential impacts on each of the affected economies. At the same time, the establishment of the FTAA also implies that new economic relationships will now be possible; however, these new arrangements will also be devoid of any special trade and tariff advantages unless we use the Summit process to bring our unique characteristics to the fore. The Caribbean must be fully engaged in the Summitry process as the region attempts to become more competitive and to compete against many larger economies that are well endowed with natural resources and greater economic and financial capacities.

Much of the work of the hemispheric Summitry process can be accomplished through the participation of existing institutions and groupings at the subregional level. As the first strategic and comprehensive effort to formalize a pan-Caribbean movement aimed at strengthening regional integration and promoting sustainable development among the nations and peoples of the Americas, the Association of Caribbean States (ACS) is well placed as a regional mechanism for information feedback and monitoring responsibilities. The developmental diversity of its current membership may also provide substantive and practical ideas for identifying concrete ways to bring smaller economies into the developmental mainstream, especially within the framework of the Free Trade Area of the Americas.

*Dr. Winston Dookeran*

### Supplemental Comment of President Gonzalo Sánchez de Lozada

I am very pleased to endorse this excellent and important report. I do, however, have two comments. First, I believe that it would be more realistic to schedule hemispheric summits every four years rather than every two years as the report proposes, and in interim years the leaders could convene conferences on specific issues, as we did in holding the 1996 Santa Cruz Summit on Sustainable Development. Second, I agree with the report's proposal that a summit secretariat should be established, but in the long run those functions should be fully absorbed by the OAS. In the post-Cold War world, Summits will be at the forefront of the inter-American system, and the OAS should therefore play a central role in summitry. If the OAS is not yet equipped to perform those functions, the Santiago Summit should establish a task force to examine the OAS' roles and capacities.

*President Gonzalo Sánchez de Lozada*

### Supplemental Comment of Dr. Luis Moreno Ocampo

I am pleased to endorse the excellent Policy Report of the Leadership Council for Inter-American Summitry. I respectfully wish to emphasize the importance of those aspects of the report that deal with the issue of transparency and the fight to eliminate corruption in government.

• Corruption and the lack of transparency threaten the consolidation and functioning of key institutions; distort procurement, privatization, and other economic programs; and exacerbate the effects of poverty by diverting funds from social programs for the poor, sidetracking income to a small elite and discouraging foreign investment and aid. Thus, corruption must be seen as a core issue of the "Shallowness of Democratic Institutions" and not be confined specifically to law enforcement issues and solutions.

• Opportunities for meaningful participation by civil society in public policy formulation and implementation are still elusive; yet it is critical that governments be accountable to civil society. To achieve this requires fulfilling the 1994 Summit commitment to guarantee the right of access to and the regular publication of governmental information and to permit meaningful public review in all aspects of government function.

• Governments should agree to participate in a free-standing commission at the OAS with adequate funding and political authority to encourage implementation of anticorruption legislation and the establishment and dissemination of the best practices, as provided in the OAS Inter-American Convention Against Corruption, with periodic progress reports to the OAS General Assembly. The commission should permit and encourage input from the private sector and civil society. National leaders might also consider creating individual standing for communications to the commission.

• We note that the current Asian "turmoil" resulted, in some measure, from a failure of transparency and from outright corruption. Specific steps to be considered at the Summit should include the intensification of work to insure transparency in procurement and privatization.

• Finally, the private sector and NGOs should be called upon to aid in the formulation and implementation of current and future Summit initiatives. The Summit implementation process itself should serve as a model: national governments and regional mechanisms established for the purpose should act to insure accountability and transparency in the process, cooperating with and making information accessible to non-governmental monitoring and feed-back efforts.

*Dr. Luis Moreno Ocampo*

## Supplemental Comment of Senator José Serra

I am pleased to associate myself with this report. However, I would like to add some remarks regarding the FTAA and related issues:

My main comment refers to the "Summit Response" to "Challenge" number 6, which proposes that the Santiago Summit "accelerate the target date for completion of negotiations to the year 2002," on the basis that (i) the commitment on the year 2005 has operated as a pretext for delays, and (ii) the effective implementation of measures for trade liberalization would take from 10 to 15 years, or even longer. In my understanding, however, for Brazil in particular, and Mercosul in general, revising the 2005 goal is not executable.

On the other hand, it is reasonable that measures aimed at facilitating trading and mechanisms for the settlement of disputes may be natural issues for an "early harvest," i.e., agreements that may be hammered out before the negotiations' deadline.

It may appear odd in the current situation that Brazilian leaders, as suggested in this section of the Policy Report, would endeavor to make a public case in defense of the FTAA. In any case, since in Santiago not much can be expected on matters related to decisions on the actual parameters for negotiations, it makes sense that "any real or perceived lack of progress toward FTAA should not be used to block progress on the rest of the Santiago agenda." I think Brazil and other countries of the region are interested in stressing social and educational issues, since, with respect to trade issues, the U.S. administration will scarcely be able to count on "fast track" negotiating authority before April 1998, in the event that it is even requested from and granted by the Congress.

In the same section, the "Summit Response" to "Challenge" number six, as a sort of corollary, it is especially odd to indicate that the Brazilian Government should explain to its citizens that the FTAA represents a national interest and is compatible with the basic aims of Mercosul. And it is unrealistic to suppose, as stated in item number 7 in the section, "Seven Steps Toward More Effective Summitry," that Brazil, as the leader of the most dynamic integration movement in the region, would be an appropriate place to host the 2000 Summit of Americas, if only because such a meeting on such a date had never been mentioned before.

The report mentions, on page 6, that Latin-American exports to the United States had more than doubled between 1988 and 1996, from US$60 billion to US$130 billion, adding that U.S. exports to Latin America increased at almost the same rate. It is worth remembering, however, that in recent years Latin American countries are accumulating widening trade deficits with the U.S. and that Brazil's trade deficit with the U.S. in 1997 reached almost US $5 billion, virtually half of the country's overall trade deficit. The poor performance of Brazilian sales to the U.S. market is not unrelated to the imposition of high duties, duty peaks, phytosanitary restrictions, quotas, and other non-tariff barriers applied to Brazil's exports.

The Policy Report assigns this market share decrease to factors such as loss of competitiveness and low productivity of manpower, a result, in turn, of poor levels of domestic investment and savings. This may be true for some Brazilian industries, but it is certainly not true for all, particularly for agribusiness.

I am not sure that Santiago should mobilize funds to help smaller economies in the region implement the Summit leaders' decisions, as proposed in "Step 2." Smaller economies may benefit even more from special treatment, such as longer terms for implementing tariff reduction schedules. However, implementation of a compensation fund, to which all other countries should contribute, does not seem acceptable.

*Senator José Serra*

# LEADERSHIP COUNCIL FOR INTER-AMERICAN SUMMITRY

**Sergio Aguayo**
El Colegio de México
(Mexico)

**Bernard W. Aronson**
Acon Investments LLC
(United States)

**C. Fred Bergsten**
Institute for International Economics
(United States)

**Charles E. Cobb, Jr.**
Cobb Partners, Inc. and
Pan American Airways
(United States)

**Charles H. Dallara**
Institute of International Finance
(United States)

**Winston Dookeran**
Central Bank of Trinidad and Tobago
(Trinidad and Tobago)

**Richard E. Feinberg**
APEC Study Center
University of California, San Diego
(United States)

**Alejandro Foxley**
Corporation for Latin American Economic Research
(Chile)

**Kathryn Fuller**
World Wildlife Fund, Inc.
(United States)

**Irwin Jacobs**
Qualcomm
(United States)

**Luis Moreno Ocampo**
Transparency International
(Argentina)

**Sylvia Ostry**
University of Toronto
(Canada)

**Sonia Picado Sotela**
Former Ambassador
(Costa Rica)

**Beatrice E. Rangel**
Cisneros Group of Companies
(Venezuela)

**Gonzalo Sánchez de Lozada**
Former President
(Bolivia)

**José Serra**
Senado Federal
(Brazil)

## BIOGRAPHICAL DATA

**Sergio Aguayo, Ph.D.,** has been a professor at the Colegio de México's Center for International Relations since 1977. He received a doctorate from the Johns Hopkins School of Advanced International Studies. In 1990, the John D. And Catherine T. MacArthur Foundation awarded him a Research and Writing Grant to examine national security issues of Mexico and the United States. He has been a visiting Fellow or Professor in several institutions, among others, the Center for U.S.-Mexican Studies at the University of California, San Diego; the Ortega and Gasset Foundation in Madrid; and the New School for Social Research in New York. He is also a member of the National Coordination of Civic Alliance, a coalition of hundreds of non-governmental organizations and thousands of citizens promoting democracy in Mexico. Dr. Aguayo is a founding member and current president of the Mexican Academy for Human Rights. He publishes a weekly column that appears in 14 Mexican newspapers (*la Jornada, El Norte,* and *El Diario de Yucatán,* among others).

**Bernard W. Aronson** is Chairman of Acon Investments and Chairman of Newbridge Andean Partners, L.P. Prior to assuming this position, Mr. Aronson was International Advisor to Goldman Sachs and Co. Mr. Aronson served as Assistant Secretary of State for Inter-American Affairs from 1989-1993, the longest tenure of any holder of that office. In 1993, then-Secretary Aronson was presented with the State Department's highest honor, the Distinguished Service Award. Prior government positions include Deputy Assistant to President Jimmy Carter in the Office of the White House Chief of Staff and Special Assistant to Vice President Walter Mondale. He serves as a Director of Royal Caribbean Cruise Lines, Inc. and Scala Inc., is on the Board of Directors of the National Democratic Institute for International Affairs, and is a member of the Inter-American Dialogue and the Council on Foreign Relations.

**C. Fred Bergsten, Ph.D.,** is Director of the Institute for International Economics, the only major research institution in the United States devoted to international economic issues. Dr. Bergsten has been Chairman of the Eminent Persons Group (EPG) of the Asia Pacific Economic Cooperation (APEC) Forum and of the Competitiveness Policy Council, created by the U.S. Congress. He has served as Assistant Secretary of the Treasury for International Affairs and as Senior Fellow at The Brookings Institution and the Carnegie Endowment for International Peace. He has authored or co-authored 26 books on international economic issues, including *Global Economic Leadership and the Group of Seven* (1996). Dr. Bergsten frequently testifies before congressional committees.

**Charles E. Cobb, Jr.,** is Chairman of the Board of Directors of Pan Am Corporation and Pan American World Airways and the Senior Partner of the investment firm, Cobb Partners, Inc. He served as U.S. Ambassador to Iceland during the Bush Administration. During the Reagan Administration, he was Under Secretary and Assistant Secretary at the U.S. Department of Commerce with responsibilities for the nation's trade development, export promotion, and international travel and tourism. Ambassador Cobb is a former Chairman and CEO of Arvida/Disney Corporation. Prior to that, he was the Chief Operating Officer and a Director of Penn Central Corporation. He is also a former President and General Manager of several subsidiaries of Kaiser Aluminum and Chemical Corporation. Ambassador Cobb earned undergraduate and graduate degrees at Stanford University. He was an officer in the U.S. Navy. He is active in many civic affairs and corporate organizations and currently serves on the Florida Governor's Commission on Education, the Florida Business/ Higher Education Partnership, and the University of Miami Board of Trustees, among others.

**Charles H. Dallara, Ph.D.,** is Managing Director and Chief Executive Officer of the Institute of International Finance in Washington, D.C. The Institute represents more than 275 global financial institutions, including many of the world's largest banks. Before joining the Institute, Dallara was a Managing Director at J.P. Morgan and Co. where he chaired Morgan's Emerging Markets Risk Committee. He has held a number of senior positions in government, including Assistant Secretary of the Treasury for International Affairs in the Bush Administration, Assistant Secretary of the Treasury for Policy Development, and United States Executive Director of the International Monetary Fund. Dr. Dallara is a member of the Board of Directors or Trustees of the German Marshall Fund and has served as a member of the U.S.-Japan Business Council. He holds master's and doctoral degrees from Tufts University and an Honorary Doctor of Laws degree from the University of South Carolina.

**Winston Dookeran,** who holds an honorary Doctor of Laws degree from the University of Manitoba, is Governor of the Central Bank of Trinidad and Tobago. He served as Senior Economist at the Economic Commission for Latin America and the Caribbean. He earned a master's degree from the London School of Economics and Political Science and was a Lecturer in Economics at the

University of the West Indies. Mr. Dookeran was also a Fellow at the Centre for International Affairs at Harvard University, where he edited *Choices and Change: Reflections on the Caribbean* (1996), published by the Inter-American Development Bank. He was Planning Minister in the government of Trinidad and Tobago and on several occasions served as Prime Minister.

**Richard E. Feinberg, Ph.D.,** is Director of the Asia Pacific Economic Cooperation Study Center based at the Graduate School of International Relations and Pacific Studies (IRPS) at the University of California, San Diego. He also serves as Special Advisor to the Chancellor for Pacific Rim Affairs and is responsible for developing a strategic plan for increasing the university's links in the Pacific Rim (including Latin America) and the international community at large. He is former Dean of IRPS at the University of California, San Diego. Dr. Feinberg served as Special Assistant to President Clinton for National Security Affairs and Senior Director of the National Security Council's Office of Inter-American Affairs. He was one of the principal architects of the 1994 Summit of the Americas in Miami and crafted one of the first in-depth analyses of how U.S. foreign policy is made in the Clinton administration. Dr. Feinberg has served as President of the Inter-American Dialogue and Executive Vice President of the Overseas Development Council. He has held positions on the policy planning staff of the U.S. Department of State and in the Office of International Affairs in the U.S. Treasury Department. He has written more than 100 articles and books, most recently, *Summitry in the Americas,* published by the Institute of International Economics, where he was a visiting fellow.

**Alejandro Foxley, Ph.D.,** is Senator-elect in the Chilean Senate and co-Chairman of the Inter-American Dialogue in Washington, D.C. He has served as Minister of Finance to the Republic of Chile, Governor of the Inter-American Development Bank, and Chairman of the Development Committee at the World Bank. Dr. Foxley earned a doctorate in economics at the University of Wisconsin. He has authored or edited 11 books on economics, economic development, and problems of democracy, including *Economía Política de la Transición* (Ediciones Dolmen, 1993).

**Kathryn Fuller, J.D.,** is President and CEO of the World Wildlife Fund based in Washington, D.C. She served previously as Executive Vice President, General Counsel, and Director of WWF's public policy and wildlife trade monitoring programs. Before joining WWF in 1982, Fuller worked at the U.S. Department of Justice as head of the Wildlife and Marine Resources Section. She was a special advisor to the United Nations at the Earth Summit in 1992 and serves on numerous boards, including the Board of Trustees of Brown University and the Board of Trustees of the Ford Foundation. Fuller has received the U.N. Environment Programme's Global 500 Award and is a member of the Council on Foreign Relations, the U.S. Advisory Committee for Trade Policy and Negotiations, the Overseas Development Council, and the World Bank's Advisory Group on Environmentally Sustainable Development.

**Irwin Jacobs, Sc.D.,** is Founder, Chairman, and Chief Executive Officer of Qualcomm Incorporated. He has led the company, which has international activities in digital wireless telephony, mobile satellite communications, and internet software, through a period of rapid growth to over 7500 employees. He is a former President, CEO, and Chairman of Linkabit which he also co-founded. From 1959-1966, Dr. Jacobs served as Assistant/Associate Professor of Electrical Engineering at Massachusetts Institute of Technology and from 1966-1972 was Professor of Computer Science and Engineering at the University of California, San Diego (UCSD). He is co-author of *Principles of Communication Engineering.* Dr. Jacobs is the recipient of many awards including the National Medal of Technology Award bestowed by the President of the United States, the Alexander Graham Bell Medal, the Inventing America's Future Award, and the Albert Einstein Award. He is a member of the California Council on Science and Technology. Dr. Jacobs currently serves or has served on the boards of the National Academy of Engineering Industry Advisory Board, the University of California President's Engineering Advisory Council, UCSD Foundation Board of Trustees, UCSD Green Foundation for Earth Sciences, UCSD Cancer Center, San Diego Symphony, and San Diego Repertory Theater.

**Luis Moreno Ocampo** is Associate Professor of Criminal Law at the University of Buenos Aires Law School, where he received his law degree. In private law practice, Mr. Moreno Ocampo specializes in corruption control programs for large organizations. Through the auspices of the United Nations and the Inter-American Development Bank, he has aided governments in developing corruption control systems, specifically in the Dominican Republic, Bolivia, and Venezuela. Mr. Moreno Ocampo is co-founder of Poder Ciudadano, a non-governmental organization that promotes citizen responsibility and participation. He is also a member of the Advisory Committee of Transparency International, a worldwide organization that reduces corruption in international business transactions, and is President of its division for Latin

America and the Caribbean. His books include *Self Defense: How to Avoid Corruption* (1993) and *When Power Lost the Trial: How to Explain the Dictatorship to our Children* (1996), which explains the functioning of the systems that were the causes of crimes during the Argentine military dictatorship. Mr. Moreno Ocampo also played a crucial role as prosecutor in trials related to Argentina's democratic transition.

**Sylvia Ostry, Ph.D.,** is Distinguished Research Fellow, Centre for International Studies, University of Toronto. She has a doctorate in economics from McGill University and Cambridge University. Dr. Ostry has held a number of positions in the Canadian Federal Government, among them, Chief Statistician, Deputy Minister of Consumer and Corporate Affairs, Chairman of the Economic Council of Canada, Deputy Minister of International Trade, Ambassador for Multilateral Trade Negotiations, and the Prime Minister's Personal Representative for the Economic Summit. Dr. Ostry has written numerous books and papers, most recently, *Who's on First? The Post-Cold War Trading System* (University of Chicago Press, 1997). She has received 18 honorary degrees from universities in Canada and abroad and the Outstanding Achievement Award of the Government of Canada. She is a Companion of the Order of Canada and a Fellow of the Royal Society of Canada. She is a director of Power Financial Corporation; chairman of the International Advisory Council, Bank of Montreal; and a member of many distinguished councils and advisory boards. In 1992 the Sylvia Ostry Foundation annual lecture series was launched by Madam Sadako Ogata, U.N. High Commissioner for Refugees.

**Sonia Picado Sotela** is former Ambassador of Costa Rica to the United States. She has served as Vice President of the Executive Council and Executive Director of the Inter-American Institute for Human Rights (San José). She was a judge in the Inter-American Court of Human Rights at the Organization of American States and was the first Latin American woman to be elected dean of a law school when she served as Dean of the University of Costa Rica School of Law. She has received many awards in recognition of her efforts to promote human rights and women's rights, including an award from the Inter-American Commission on Women, the Max Planc/Humboldt Award, and the United Nations Human Rights Award.

**Beatrice E. Rangel** is currently the Senior Vice President, Corporate Strategy, of the Cisneros Group of Companies in New York. Ms. Rangel's responsibilities include identifying, defining, and implementing business policies and investment projects. She is a personal advisor to the Office of the Chairman and the liaison between the Cisneros Group of Companies and governments and private enterprises for the development stage of projects. Ms. Rangel has served in a number of advisory positions in the private and public sectors of Venezuela. She was Advisor to former President of Venezuela, Carlos Andrés Pérez, and was elected Alternative Deputy of Congress for Miranda State. She served as General Secretary of the Ministry of Education in 1985 and the following year became Executive Secretary of the Presidential Commission in charge of drafting the National Education Reform Project. She later served as Minister of the Secretariat of the President. Ms. Rangel has served as a board member for several large companies and organizations, including Venezuelan Airways, The Vienna Institute for Development, and the Robert Kennedy Foundation for Human Rights. Ms. Rangel holds an M.A. in Public Administration from Harvard University and an M.S. in Development Economics from Boston University. Among her awards are The Order of Merit of May, conferred by the Republic of Argentina; Condor of the Andes Order, by the Republic of Bolivia; the Bernardo O'Higgins Order, by the Republic of Chile; the Order of Boyaca, by the Republic of Colombia; and the National Order of José Matias Delgado, by the Republic of El Salvador.

**President Gonzalo Sánchez de Lozada,** as a Senator and Minister of Planning in Bolivia, gained popular recognition as the author of the 1985 economic "shock therapy" program, which brought Bolivia's 25,000 percent hyper-inflation rate under control and created the foundation for future economic stability and growth. A graduate of the University of Chicago, he was inaugurated as President of Bolivia in August 1993 and served until August 1997. During his administration, President Sánchez de Lozada implemented his "Plan de Todos," based on profound economic, social, and political reforms. The Plan's main elements were administrative decentralization, which strengthened Bolivia's democratic process by transferring decision-making authority and revenue sharing to local regions and communities; popular participation, which allowed all citizens to be included in the process of administering and controlling revenue sharing in their communities; education reform, which incorporated multilingual and multicultural education into the educational system; capitalization, involving equity contributions in state-owned monopolies by strategic foreign partners and the transfer of government-owned shares to privately administered pension funds, which now distribute a yearly lifetime bonus to people over 65 years of age; and judicial reform.

**José Serra, Ph.D.,** was elected to the Brazilian Senate in 1994 and is the current President of the Senate Committee on Economic Affairs. He is a former Minister of Planning and Budget in the Fernando Cardoso Administration. Senator Serra served for many years in the Chamber of Deputies as leader of the Party of Brazilian Social Democracy (PSDB). He was Secretary of Economy and Planning for the State of São Paulo and Coordinator of the Committee for President Tancredo Neves' Administration Program. Senator Serra, who received his doctorate in economics at Cornell University, has been a professor/lecturer at several universities, including the University of Campinas, São Paulo; University of Chile; Latin American College of Social Sciences (FLACSO); Oxford University; and Princeton University. He is the author of numerous articles and books on the Brazilian and Latin American economies.

## RESEARCH AUTHORS

The Leadership Council for Inter-American Summitry acknowledges the research contributions of the following authors in the indicated areas. The original research undertaken by these authors provided an overview and analysis of the implementation of some of the major summit initiatives and helped to inform many of the group's recommendations.

**Felipe Agüero,** Guaranteeing Democracy and Human Rights

**Richard L. Bernal,** Developing and Liberalizing Capital Markets

**Cristina B. Cunico,** Providing Equitable Access to Basic Health Services

**Ana María De Andraca,** Reforming Educational Systems

**Kimberly Ann Elliott,** Combating Corruption

**Marcela Gajardo,** Reforming Educational Systems

**Eduardo Gamarra,** Combating Illegal Drugs and Related Crimes

**Arturo García-Costas,** Building Sustainable Development Partnerships

**Inter-American Dialogue,** Strengthening the Role of Women in Society

**International Center for Research on Women,** Strengthening the Role of Women in Society

**Manuel Lasaga,** Developing, Liberalizing, and Integrating Financial Markets

**Luigi Manzetti,** Combating Corruption

**Colleen S. Morton,** Progress Toward Free Trade in the Western Hemisphere Since 1994

**Sean Neill,** Guaranteeing Democracy and Human Rights

**Jeffrey Puryear,** Reforming Educational Systems

**Robin Rosenberg,** Invigorating Civil Society Participation

**José Salazar-Xirinachs,** Promoting Free Trade in the Americas

**S. Jacob Scherr,** Partnerships for Sustainable Development

**Michael Shifter,** Guaranteeing Democracy and Human Rights

**Justin Ward,** Building Sustainable Development Partnerships

**Robert Watson,** Partnerships for Sustainable Development

To review the full content of research papers, visit the North-South Center's web page at http://www.miami.edu/nsc/

# V. LEADERSHIP COUNCIL FOR INTER-AMERICAN SUMMITRY

*Felipe Agüero is associate professor at the School of International Studies of the University of Miami and a senior research associate of the Dante B. Fascell North-South Center. He is the author of* Soldiers, Civilians, and Democracy: Post-Franco Spain in Comparative Perspective; *co-editor of* Fault Lines of Democracy in Post-Transition Latin America *with Jeffrey Stark; and co-editor of* Fracturas en la Gobernabilidad Democrática *(Universidad de Chile).*

## Democracy and Human Rights Since the 1994 Summit of the Americas

*Felipe Agüero*

### INTRODUCTION: DEMOCRACY AND HUMAN RIGHTS AS SUMMIT GOALS

The December 1994 Summit of the Americas held in Miami was a celebration of the hemisphere's new democratic reality. In fact, without this reality, the Summit probably would not have been conceived. Addressing areas dear to most leaders — such as trade and finance — was greatly facilitated by the fact that all of those present had been elected by the citizenry of their nations. This also facilitated agreement on a diverse array of issues, as reflected in the Summit's *Declaration of Principles* and *Plan of Action*.

The Summit expressed the force of democratic winds that had picked up with the termination of military-authoritarian regimes that dominated the region in the 1970s and 1980s. The removal of Stroessner in Paraguay and the end of autocratic rule in Haiti powerfully signaled the advancement of the democratization wave. Already governments in the hemisphere had manifested a new resolution, expressed in the Santiago Declaration, to secure new democratic achievements with assertive collective action. Presidents Alberto Fujimori in Peru and Jorge Serrano in Guatemala had the opportunity, as later did military conspirators in Paraguay, to experience the vigor of this determination when the inter-American community put pressure on them for a prompt return to, or acceptance of, democratic rule.

However, the 1994 Miami Summit was not satisfied with mere celebration. Its participants willingly committed themselves to "advance...democratic values and institutions," to "strengthen democratic institutions" and "promote and defend constitutional democratic rule." They rightly specified that government responsiveness, transparency, and accountability to its citizens are indispensable to the maintenance and strengthening of democratic institutions. They recognized the complexity of the system they pledged to secure by identifying its essential components in an independent judiciary and an effective legal system and the satisfaction of "the needs of women and the most vulnerable groups, including indigenous people, the disabled, children, and minorities." Components also included the invigoration of civil society and the fight against corruption, crime, and illegal drug trafficking. Leading participants made sure that these goals and commitments were placed at the start of the *Declaration of Principles*, so as to reflect the priority accorded them.[1] There should be no question, then, about the importance the Summit accorded these

---

The author is grateful to Carlos Basombrío, Richard Feinberg, Robin Rosenberg, Jeffrey Stark, and Paulo de Mesquita Neto for their helpful comments on the first version of this manuscript. The usual disclaimer applies.

goals — strengthening democracy, and promoting and protecting human rights — which became items one and two, respectively, of the *Plan of Action*.

"Mindful of the need for practical progress on the vital tasks of enhancing democracy," the Summit committed governments to a number of initiatives that would strengthen the Organization of American States' (OAS) ability to assist in those goals and to foster dialogue, participation, and exchanges for their attainment. In the area of human rights, the Summit encouraged the strengthening of and cooperation with international bodies and compliance with international agreements and instruments. Yet the *Plan of Action* went beyond to outline specific domestic initiatives that would lead to greater protection and enhancement of the rights of women, minorities, people with disabilities, children, indigenous peoples, and migrant workers and to countering inhumane conditions in prisons. It emphasized programs for education in the area of human rights that would inform people of their rights and improve training of law enforcement agents.

## ABSENCE OF MONITORING AGENCIES

The Summit did not produce mechanisms and agencies to monitor the implementation of the plan. Only afterwards did the Summit Implementation Review Group (SIRG) form, with areas of implementation review placed under Responsible Coordinators. The areas of democracy and human rights were placed jointly under the coordination of Brazil, with Canada and the OAS. Nicaragua was assigned the area of women's rights. However, progress in these areas has been hard to determine because of difficulties in the organization, support and actual functioning of the Responsible Coordinators in some cases, and very insufficient flow of information from each government.

Independent assessments made outside the SIRG deemed substantive progress in implementation in the areas of democracy and human rights "slow and uneven at best."[2] Progress in these areas and in the area of women's rights was deemed "modest" and "minor."[3] Because of those difficulties, these assessments refer mostly to initiatives taken in multilateral bodies, but little is known in systematic fashion of progress in the items in the *Plan of Action* within the signatory countries.

It is praiseworthy that Brazil and Canada offered a detailed *Proposal for Implementation* of the *Plan of Action* in the Areas of Democracy and Human Rights, to which countries began reacting in preparation for the April 1998 Summit.[4] Debate and action on all areas addressed by this proposal would provide the foundations for more systematic hemispheric efforts in these areas, in ways that would be transparent and open to accountability and evaluation.

However, as the title of the proposal indicated, it was a plan of action for the *Plan of Action*. Three years after the Summit, there only existed a proposal suggesting ways to implement the plan accorded in 1994. The proposal contained no evaluation of progress attained in the participant countries since the approval of that plan. Countries reacted to this proposal without, at the same time, providing their own assessment of domestic initiatives. Meetings of the SIRG in this area focused more on plans for implementation than on implementation evaluation. Brazil and Canada, as Responsible Coordinators, intended to coordinate the collection of information from governments on this matter before the April 1998 Summit in Santiago, but little of this became available.

Nevertheless, an important and noteworthy effort by the OAS was the *Informe del presidente de la comisión especial sobre gestión de cumbres interamericanas sobre las acciones de la OEA en la implementación y apoyo a la ejecución de los mandatos de la Cumbre de las Américas realizada en Miami, entre el 9 y el 11 de diciembre de 1994,* [5] which contained a detailed account of activities undertaken by the OAS to promote initiatives approved in the 1994 *Plan of Action*. They included the strengthening of the Unit for the Promotion of Democracy, assistance to electoral processes and to enhance the role of legislatures, programs for the exchange of experience in other areas and levels of democratic governance, and programs for the promotion of democratic values and practices.

More specifically in the area of human rights, the report noted that six countries ratified or adhered to the San Salvador Protocol since the 1994 Summit (although not in force, since it requires at least 11 ratifying countries), that the Interamerican Convention on Forced Disappearance of Persons became effective in 1996, that Brazil ratified the Protocol on the Abolition of the Death Penalty, that the Belém do Pará Convention became effective in 1995, with most countries ratifying or adhering after the 1994 Summit. The Convention on the Prevention and Penalization of Torture had not registered, however, any ratification or adhesion since the Miami Summit. The report detailed OAS activities in all other areas contemplated in the *Plan of Action* in the area of human rights of the Miami Summit.

This document was an important step in the attempt to monitor implementation of the Summit agreements and should be followed by similar initiatives specifically focused on monitoring action at the level of individual countries. In the future, monitoring and evaluation should be greatly facilitated with the creation of electronic data banks at the OAS on national and international capacities and programs in Democracy and Human Rights and with the actual submission of reports by all governments, as stipulated in the proposal put forth by Brazil and Canada.

## MONITORING PROGRESS: DEFINING THE SCOPE

In what ways can progress be evaluated in these areas since the last Summit? First, there is the question of scope. Democratic governance is, among others, composed of a number of elements outlined in the *Plan of Action*: clean electoral processes, protection and enhancement of human rights, women's rights, invigoration of civil society.[6] These elements all can be subsumed in the critical features of participation, representation, and accountability that characterize democratic governance. They relate to institutions and initiatives, from civil society and from government's various layers and branches, including, very centrally, the judiciary. All these elements must inform evaluations that should remain broad in scope.

Yet democratic governance also involves subjection of the state's coercive instruments, the armed forces and police, to the authority of elected political officials. It means, in this realm, democratic civilian control of the armed forces and the police and of the behavior of these institutions in accordance with laws and rules that guarantee the rights of citizens and lawfully organized associations. The Summit's *Declaration of Principles* or *Plan of Action* did not specifically address this point. Only implicitly did it take the armed forces into consideration by including the building of mutual confidence through confidence-building measures, a point significantly placed within the chapter on *Preserving and Strengthening the Community of Democracies of the Americas*. The assumption was that the expansion of democracy in the hemisphere provided a basis for the affirmation of regional security based on cooperation and mutual confidence. However, building mutual confidence and eliminating old sources of rivalry and distrust are not only results of the expansion of democracy; they also help strengthen it by facilitating the advancement of civilian control and by contributing to lesser domestic political power for the armed forces. Cooperation in this area between Argentina and Brazil, for instance, or Argentina and Chile, provides ample evidence of the potential that the advancement of mutual confidence holds for security, development, and democracy in the region.[7]

Although the Defense Ministerial of the Americas, held in Williamsburg on July 24-26, 1995, is not organically part of the Summit process, it was led by the principles the Summit inspired. The prevalent topics in the meeting emphasized the ideas of transparency and military confidence, security-building measures, and defense cooperation. It also explicitly advanced the ideas that democracy is the basis for ensuring mutual security in the Americas and that the armed forces should be subordinate to democratically constituted authority and respect human rights.[8]

Clearly the text and spirit of the *Declaration of Principles* and the *Plan of Action* of the 1994 Summit indicated this as a critical area that should be part of the evaluation. Progress in this domain obviously has enormous beneficial effects on democratic governance, just as lack of progress may severely hamper it. This is all the more evident in light of the weight of recent experiences with military authoritarianism in many countries in the region. Although transitions from authoritarian rule were completed at different points, the influence of the armed forces is still widely felt, although with great variation across cases.[9] In fact, many of the human rights problems still haunting the new democracies exist as a result of difficulties and constraints in dealing with the legacy of military-authoritarian rule.

Monitoring progress ought to highlight the actions or inaction of governments both in regard to the specific measures outlined in the *Plan of Action* and the general spirit of the Summit as expressed in the *Declaration of Principles*. Those items in the *Plan of Action* should be examined as well as the general public perception on the advancement of democracy and the protection and enhancement of the rights of its citizens. The actual attitude of governments in regard to respect for the rule of law and its principal institutions and the responsiveness of governments, and their promptness, to demands for compliance with democratic procedures and respect for citizens' rights, whenever they have been manifestly violated, should also be part of the evaluation. In other words, government action to implement particular items in the *Plan of Action* loses much of its meaning if government officials are simultaneously found to sustain activities that, for instance, tinker with the independence of courts and the judiciary.[10] Not only does this undermine the architecture of balanced powers that sustains the democratic arrangement; it also has immediate and direct bearing on the rights, the security, and well-being of individual citizens.

In addition to assessing progress in light of the *spirit* of the 1994 Summit, which must be captured within a larger *scope* than may be derived from a restricted view of the items in the *Plan of Action*, monitoring must be especially rigorous on human rights issues.[11] It is clear that in many cases full justice for past abuses has not been possible simply because of the need to avoid destabilizing conflict with military institutions that exited authoritarian rule in powerful bargaining positions. Governments, however, short of actual justice, can at the very least make sure that the truth of human rights violations is investigated and publicized and reparations made. In addition, and perhaps most importantly, governments constrained in the pursuit of justice in the case of past abuses and crimes should ensure that military or police organizations commit no further violations under the democratic administrations. Punishment for past abuses may be difficult, but continuing violations under democratic government are unacceptable. Putting an end to such violations depends largely on democratic officials' initiative in controlling the public agencies involved; such officials cannot continue to rely on the excuse of "constraints" on their power.

Monitoring must take into account countries' different realities and starting points. Some countries bear the legacy of military-authoritarian rule, which reflects on difficulties in the full institutional expression of civilian supremacy that is a central component of democratic governance and on unresolved cases and consequences of human rights violations.[12] Other countries bear the difficulties of recent termination of protracted and bloody internal wars, while others still continue to confront internal rebellion, or terrorism, and the transnational subversion of state sovereignty and law carried out by drug lords. All these difficulties are faced with different institutional capacities, policies, and intent, which should be borne in mind at the time of assessment.

The assessment conducted in this paper is not intended as an evaluation of the current state of democratic governance in the countries of the region or of the state of human rights. Such a task goes well beyond the possibilities of a report like this and is better left to experienced and reliable non-governmental international organizations, such as Amnesty International and Human Rights Watch, the Inter-American Commission on Human Rights, and the variety of human rights organizations that carry out those tasks within each country. This is, rather, an assessment of the efforts made by governments to improve on those areas, inspired by the spirit expressed at the Miami Summit. Obviously, a deteriorated state of democratic governance and little improvement in the area of human rights must be indications of meager or poorly conceived or implemented official efforts, and attention should be given to this. The majority of countries in the region, all under democratic rule, have been reported as having very grave human rights problems: prisoners of conscience, torture, extra-judicial executions, threats and extortions, in addition to poor prison conditions, ill treatment of prisoners, the well-known problem of "street children," and many more.[13]

Problems in these areas affect, in different degrees, all countries in the Americas, and evaluation ideally should cover the whole region. Here, however, the focus is only on a few cases, as an exercise in evaluation that ought to be applied to all:[14] Brazil, one of the Responsible Coordinators in the area of human rights since the 1994 Summit; Chile, the host of the 1998 Summit; and Peru, one of the countries that have been subjected to complaints at the OAS in this area.

## Brazil

The ascent of Fernando Henrique Cardoso to the presidency of Brazil almost at the same time of the Miami Summit significantly energized this country's commitment to the spirit endorsed in the *Declaration of Principles*. Brazil deposited instruments of ratification of the Convention of Belém do Pará on November 27, 1995, of the Protocol to Abolish the Death Penalty on August 13, 1996, of the Protocol of San Salvador on August 21, 1996, and was signatory to the Inter-American Convention on Forced Disappearance of Persons. An important step by the Cardoso administration was the proposal of legislation, which Congress passed, to provide indemnification to relatives of the victims of forced disappearance under the military-authoritarian regime.[15] In regard to the implementation of Summit agreements, Brazil swiftly took initiative, jointly with Canada, to devise formulas for the carrying out and monitoring of the *Plan of Action* in the areas of Democracy and Human Rights throughout the region.

Internally, major steps were taken, such as the adoption of a comprehensive and ambitious Human Rights National Plan in May 1996 that was to be coordinated by the subsequently created Human Rights Secretariat based in the Ministry of Justice. The Plan was elaborated through the celebration of six regional seminars that convoked the participation of national and regional agencies as well as community and non-governmental organizations. In announcing the Plan, President Cardoso stated that democracy cannot coexist with the violation of human rights that takes place in Brazil and reiterated the government's commitment to the promotion of human rights. As proof of this commitment, Cardoso mentioned the creation of a Human Rights Award, the campaign against sexual violence, the creation of an Interministerial Working Group for the Valorization of the Black Population, and the creation of an Executive Group for the Repression of Forced Labor. These new groups joined existing ones in the promotion of rights, such as the National Council on Women's Rights and the national Council for the Rights of Children and Adolescents.[16] Significantly, the Federal Chamber of Deputies also established a Human Rights Commission to investigate reports of human rights violations and monitor government programs in the area.[17]

The Human Rights National Plan takes a comprehensive view of social, economic, cultural, and collective rights, but, in fact, it emphasizes civil rights most directly related to the physical integrity and citizen rights of individuals. The plan contains short-, medium-, and long-term goals in areas such as protection of the rights to life; freedom and security of individuals, especially those among the most vulnerable groups; fight against impunity; freedom of expression; forced labor; and improvement of prison conditions. The Plan includes the development of data banks on relevant resources and capacities and education and information programs on human rights. It also dedicates programs on children and adolescents, women, the black population, indigenous societies, foreign refugees and immigrants, seniors, and disabled persons.

The Plan requires congressional approval for its most important sections, at federal or state level, and this is likely to slow down its implementation. However, part of the plan itself is the awareness of human rights issues that is aided by debate, and congressional debate will therefore be expected to play a useful role. Some aspects have already been approved, such as the passing of certain cases from military to ordinary justice (cases of intentional homicide perpetrated by members of the military police), and, most importantly, the passing of Law 9455 on April 7, 1997, that defines torture as a crime and penalizes it with prison sentences from two to up to eight years. An authoritative recent report evaluating progress on the Plan concludes that it already has contributed to the promotion of important changes in state and society and their interrelation and that it has resulted in lesser tolerance in society and public agencies at the federal and state level of human rights violations and impunity. Much of this is the result of the unprecedented commitment to such a plan by the federal government, followed by independent initiatives at the state level.[18] Critics, however, point out that the Plan lacks adequate funding and a means to monitor implementation of the Plan through a variegated set of agencies in the state bureaucracy.[19]

Certainly, the level of commitment that the government of Brazil has shown in the promotion and protection of human rights is unprecedented. Unfortunately, the level of violation of human rights has remained high in most areas addressed in the National Plan.[20] The enormous difficulties encountered in the proliferation of police organizations and court systems at the federal and state level may hinder the ability for actual implementation of the National Plan. The combination of well-entrenched habits of violence and brutality by different branches of the police, with very high rates of civilian deaths at its hands,[21] with uneven judicial practices throughout the country, and the existence among some sectors of attitudes that tend to support the practice of "bravery" by the police, complicates the situation as well as the solutions to these problems.[22] Police processes and criminal procedures all conspire to augment the role of impunity in worsening the condition of human rights. Paradoxically, the "decentralized" feature of human rights violations in Brazil, that is, violations that are not the result of intent or policy from the central governmental authorities, makes them much harder to curtail and demands a much more intense and coordinated effort at all levels, within and outside government agencies.[23] It should be noted, however, that decentralized measures, often at the state level, have occasionally succeeded in bringing down the numbers of violations by the police and in subjecting perpetrators of violations to prosecution, highlighting the fact that "the cycle of impunity can be broken."[24] Perhaps the most important accomplishment is represented by the fact that the Cardoso administration has actively engaged the participation of federal agencies in the campaign for human rights and against impunity. It is to be expected that this level of commitment will outlive the tenure of the top officials at the Ministry of Justice that gave birth to the current Plan.

With regard to civil-military relations, Brazil has made important progress. During the early years of the New Republic, the military participated amply in the political process. It decisively helped obstruct the substitution of parliamentarism for presidentialism, the shortening of President José Sarney's term, and the creation of a ministry of defense during deliberations in Congress for the 1988 Constitution.[25] The 1988 Constitution did not innovate much in regard to the role of the armed forces: external defense and the protection of law and order. Before the 1967 Constitution, however, this internal mission was dependent on the authority of the president, with the military constitutionally empowered to interpret the legality of that authority. In the new constitution, the military's internal mission could be called upon by any of the constitutional powers (the executive, the congress, or the judiciary), giving the military room to maneuver among them. It did, however, significantly eliminate the clause that allowed for military discretion in interpreting the president's authority. Furthermore, in 1991 President Fernando Collor de Mello passed a law specifying that the military's internal role may be invoked exclusively by the president; the Congress and the judiciary may only petition the president to do so.[26] Formally, these changes represent an important curtailment of military prerogatives.

Fernando Collor, who took over in 1990 after the first direct presidential elections since military rule, vigorously delivered on his campaign promise to reduce military power. The number of military officers in the cabinet was reduced from six to only the three service ministers. A civilian was appointed to head the newly created Secretariat for Strategic Affairs to replace the old military-led National Information Service (although its records were transferred to the Army's Information Center).[27] Collor disciplined officers who verbally challenged his authority and took other steps that would have been unthinkable a few years earlier: He dismantled a military program aimed at testing nuclear explosives,[28] worked with Argentina to set up a system of international safeguards, and created a reserve in the Amazon for imperiled Yanomami Indians. Furthermore, during the protracted political turbulence that led to Collor's removal by Congress in October 1992 and his subsequent impeachment on corruption charges, the military, breaking with a long tradition of intervention in crises of this nature, stayed on the sidelines and supported the full observance of legal procedures.

The weakening of the presidency resulting from Collor's impeachment, however, led to a reassertion of military influence during the administration of Itamar Franco (1992-1995), the vice-president in Collor's administration who assumed the presidency to finish his term. The military was often put in situations of public disagreement with civilian authorities on issues of corruption and salaries. The armed forces resented the discriminatory treatment given them by Congress compared to the rest of the public bureaucracy, leading President Franco to appease the military by promising major raises[29] and appointing military officials to positions in government agencies and public sector companies.

Expressions of military discontent and influence were again rolled back after the assumption of President Cardoso in 1995. During his presidency, the military budget has continued to decline, and important initiatives have been taken to affirm the leading role of the executive on defense matters, such as the issuing of an official statement on national defense policy that unequivocally grants leadership to the executive[30] and the project to create an intelligence system and agency controlled by a special committee of Congress and under the leadership of the president.[31] Despite the "erosion of military influence,"[32] the military continued to exert influence, insisting, for instance, on an internal mission for the army and delaying the creation of a ministry of defense to substitute for the separate service ministries, although the government had announced its commitment to create such a ministry. Indeed, major responsibility lies with civilian officials in their yet-to-be-tested capacity to lessen the utilization of the military in public security and to advance the demilitarization of the police and internal security system.

## Chile

Chile joined the democratization wave through a process that, among other transition cases in the region, was perhaps the farthest from a *ruptura* with the past. Of all those cases, Chile is the only one whose constitution during the democratic period was conceived and crafted by authoritarian rulers, with a few modifications. The consequence of this transition path has been the incompleteness of its democratization, featured in numerous aspects of the constitution that the new authorities have, on several occasions, tried unsuccessfully to reform. The powers of the president over the armed forces; the powers of the heads of the armed forces in the National Security Council and, through it, on government; the powers and mechanism of selection of the Constitutional Court; the presence of non-elected individuals in the Senate;[33] and the electoral system are the major features inherited from the authoritarian constitution.

This transition path also has resulted in a legacy of unresolved problems in the area of human rights violations, particularly in cases of torture and disappearances during the military-authoritarian regime. Foremost among these problems has been difficulty in investigating the fate of the disappeared and other cases of human rights violations, principally as a result of the amnesty passed during the Pinochet regime and the lack of cooperation from responsible individuals and institutions. A repeal of the amnesty law was never considered by successor democratic governments because it was always deemed politically not feasible.[34] A number of government and congressional initiatives have been offered to put an end to activities of courts on this matter, mostly intending to appease the armed forces, but there has been enough opposition within the government coalition to prevent these initiatives from advancing.[35] Similarly, the Military Prosecutor General petitioned the Supreme Court to instruct courts and judges to close cases of human rights violations that occurred in the 1970s during the period covered by the military government's amnesty law, still in force. In October 1996 the Supreme Court rejected the petition, allowing judges to continue to decide on cases under their jurisdiction.[36]

Despite severe obstacles placed by the military, the government and the courts succeeded in carrying out the sentences against two top army officers in charge of government intelligence under General Pinochet, who were responsible for the assassination of Orlando Letelier in Washington, D.C., in 1976.[37] Human Rights organizations also praised the ability of some judges to pursue their cases, as in the sentence of 20 years given Osvaldo Romo, former DINA informer and torturer, for the charge of kidnapping.[38] Compensation was awarded to victims in some cases, according to procedures established by the National Corporation for Reparation and Reconciliation, a government agency created in 1992 and whose mandate expired in 1996.[39]

The government of Chile has, on those and other issues relevant to this assessment, demonstrated its willingness to honor the spirit of the Summit as expressed in the *Declaration of Principles* and *Plan of Action*. The government deposited on November 15, 1996, the instrument of ratification of the Convention of Belém do Pará. It was one of the signatories of the Convention on Forced Disappearance of Persons (although ratification was pending) and, in the report to the 1995 SIRG meeting, announced that it was considering adhering to the Protocol to the American Convention on Human Rights to Abolish the Death Penalty and the Additional Protocol on Human Rights in the Area of Economic, Social, and Cultural Rights. It also announced legislative initiatives for the protection of the rights of women and the family, indigenous people, and disabled persons, in addition to reforms to the judicial and prison systems.

In the area of women's rights, an important initiative was the constitutional reform passed in 1997 that establishes the equality of men and women before the law. Additionally, the National Women's Service (SERNAM), following guidelines from the Inter-American Convention, successfully submitted Law 19,325 on Domestic Violence (*Violencia Intrafamiliar*). SERNAM has informed of its participation in a number of other initiatives, such as the promotion of a manual on women's rights in thousands of women's centers around the country; a manual to help women search for employment, jointly with organized training programs; and a campaign to monitor working conditions for women. In this area SERNAM announced its intention to submit a bill on pregnancy subsidies for certain categories of female workers and the pursuit of a bill on sexual harassment. In the area of education, SERNAM has participated in the Program for the Improvement of the Quality of Education within the Ministry of Education in order to include gender perspectives in the curricula, aiding the general goal stated in the National Plan for Equality of Opportunities. In this area the goal also is the promotion of nondiscriminatory teaching practices. With the Ministry of Health, SERNAM is implementing a program on prevention of teen pregnancy. Finally, SERNAM is elaborating a draft bill on equal opportunities for women.[40]

Since the resumption of democracy, Chilean governments have been actively seeking to advance judicial reform. In addition to the complete neglect shown by the judiciary in the protection of basic human rights under the dictatorship, the judiciary has become unable effectively to grant the right of access to justice by all, as a consequence of its backward structure and practices. These factors coupled with deficiencies in the penal code and process have resulted, in practice, in severe harms to the institutional guarantees for the protection of human rights. That is, despite government policy and attitudes on human rights, deeply embedded judicial structures end up thwarting those very guarantees. Judicial reform has thus become an indispensable component of very basic policies for the protection and promotion of human rights.[41] Reform of the judiciary, however, has actually remained out of reach due to the lack of support from the opposition, which has held the key to the majorities that in this area the constitution requires, and also by the lack of support from the judiciary itself.

Very recently, however, a number of factors have permitted the resuscitation of government reform plans. On August 30, 1997, the full session of Congress approved by overwhelming majority a constitutional reform that creates the Office of the Attorney General, to enter into force in 2002.[42] The Attorney General will be appointed by the president from a list of five submitted by the Supreme Court and with the approval of two-thirds of the Senate. Attorneys within this new structure will be appointed by the Attorney General from proposals by regional courts. At the same time, the government reached agreement with the opposition in Congress for other major steps in judicial reform, including changes in the mechanisms of designation of Justices to the Supreme Court, an expansion of its members and the setting of a retirement age, the elimination of lawyer members of the Court, and the incorporation of members from outside the judicial career. Although the Supreme Court formally expressed its opposition to the reforms, the Congress approved them. There has already formed, across the political spectrum, a consensus to expand the reforms to include reforms to the Court's Organic Code that dates back to 1875 and the penal processal system.[43] Consensus for these reforms augur success in initiating the modernization of the judiciary and in guaranteeing its independence simultaneously with lessening its corporate autonomy. In addition, there are signs indicating that the momentum attained by the reform initiative may persist enough to advance to a reform of military justice, principally aimed at restricting its jurisdiction and at modernizing its procedures.[44]

There are areas, however, where violations of human rights continue to occur and which observers have noted that a more energetic action by the government would be desirable. Twenty cases of torture and ill-treatment by security forces were reported to the Director General of Carabineros by non-governmental organizations.[45] Moreover, the UN Special Rapporteur on Torture endorsed, after visiting Chile in 1995, a report by the UN Committee against Torture that cited a pattern of police ill-treatment of detainees. "The Special Rapporteur urged the government to bring provisions for incommunicado detention into line with the Body of Principles for the Protection of All Persons under Any Form of Detention or Imprisonment. The Special Rapporteur also recommended prohibiting the blindfolding of detainees and ensuring that all detainees had prompt access to medical examination by an independent physician."[46] Human Rights Watch reported that government officials were unable to show that any security agent had been convicted on the many cases of torture reported.[47]

Regarding civil-military relations, the strong initial tensions and uncertainties on civilian-military accommodation under the democratic regime inaugurated in 1990 have been, eight years after the transfer of power, substantially brushed away. A *modus vivendi* developed between civilian authorities and the military, allowing for the handling of the numerous crises that surfaced in the past seven years without fear of outright authoritarian regression. These crises surfaced from military intolerance to measures taken by civilian officials regarding human rights issues, the pursuit of investigations of irregularities and corruption among army generals, and the ultimately successful move to imprison Pinochet's initial chief intelligence/repression officer for the assassination of an opposition leader in Washington, D.C., during the initial years of his rule. The crises gave way to turbulent episodes of military contestation, orchestrated by General Pinochet or senior officers, involving the mobilization and deployment of troops in flagrant challenge to civilian authority. The second democratic administration, inaugurated in 1994, has for the most part been spared the staging of these military demonstrations, but military chiefs remained outspoken on political issues, contesting government or other civilian parties' views.[48]

There remain the constraints resulting from clauses in the 1980 Constitution and specific organic laws that maintain enhanced military prerogatives. Despite repeated reform attempts by the first and second democratic administrations since 1990, these laws and constitutional clauses remain fully in place. These constraints prevent the president from exercising powers assigned his office in the previous constitution, such as removing and freely appointing the commanding general officers in each of the armed services. Neither of the two democratic presidents since 1990 were, for instance, granted the power to remove the commander-in-chief of the army, who has kept the post since 1973. General Pinochet waited until the last day authorized by the 1980 Constitution to leave his post and then only to assume in March 1998 the position of senator for life. The president cannot remove the armed services' chiefs once appointed for fixed four-year terms and is dependent on these chiefs' proposals for the promotion and assignment of general officers, having no say on promotions and assignments at lower levels. In addition, the president and three other civilian officials sit on equal terms with the heads of the three armed services and *Carabineros* in the National Security Council (NSC), which the military has the power to convene for the debate of issues it deems relevant for national security. The council also appoints four senators and designates two members of the Constitutional Court. Up until very recently, all authorities designated by the NSC were designated before the transfer of power to the first democratic administration and were thus appointed directly by the military. As the tenure of those appointed officials has recently ended, the NSC appointed new members to the Constitutional Court, placing the president and some of the heads of the armed forces in opposite positions[49] and four new members from the military to the Senate. The military also maintains much budgetary autonomy, as a substantial part of its budget is constitutionally mandated not to drop under a certain level, and another part comes as a fixed percent of copper exports, the state's largest source of foreign revenue. Many of these constraints could disappear or be softened with constitutional reform or new bills, but reform attempts have been obstructed by nonelected senators as well as elected representatives in the opposition, even if they do not hold a majority: The constitution sets high minimum vote requirements for such reforms, thus enabling the obstructive stance by the opposition. The elections of December 11, 1997, (with the designation of nonelected senators) yielded a share of seats in Congress that continues to make reforms highly unlikely.[50]

There certainly has been progress during the tenure of democratic administrations, which have attempted to contest military prerogatives.[51] Much progress has been made in diminishing distrust between the military and former opposition leaders and parties now in government, especially as they collaborate on efforts at military modernization. A policy of regional cooperation, which, for instance, has recently led to an agreement between the governments of Argentina and Chile to hold joint military exercises, stands fully in agreement with the Williamsburg principles and helps in the advancement of civilian democratic leadership over the military.

## Peru

Peru was the only case among those that experienced military-authoritarian rule in the 1970s in which gross violations of human rights took place *after* the military's exit. The resumption of civilian democratic rule in 1980 coincided with the powerful emergence of *Sendero Luminoso* and other subversive groups, that led to the activation of norms the military had prepared during the transition to maintain autonomy in the fight against subversion. The counterpart of subversive violence was thus the complete autonomy of the military from civilian-political supervision in the areas declared in state of emergency, which at one point covered one-third of the national territory. The consequence of the states of emergency was increasing violations of human rights by state forces, a situation that was passed on, worsened, to every successor government.

Since the 1994 Summit, after President Fujimori had been led to restore representative institutions following his military-supported break with democracy, there were signs of progress in the promotion of measures in the Summit's spirit, at least in terms of loosening some of the highly restrictive measures that had been adopted in preceding years. Peru deposited the ratification of the Protocol of San Salvador (*Additional Protocol to the American Convention on Human Rights in the area of Economic,* Social and Cultural Rights) on June 4, 1995, and to the Convention of Belém do Pará (*Inter-American Convention on the Prevention, Punishment, and Eradication of Violence Against Women*) on June 4, 1996. In its provisional report, that was to be included in Appendix II of the SIRG report approved on May 26, 1995, the government of Peru announced a number of initiatives that complied with the *Plan of Action*, such as the request to the OAS of an observation mission for the elections of April 1995. In October 1996 the government passed Decree Law 866 that created the Ministry for Women and Human Development with the goal of advancing programs that promote equality of opportunities for women. In June 1997 the government passed Supreme Decree Law on Protection from Family Violence.

Other positive measures were related to the activation of agencies and posts created in the 1993 Constitution, such as the Human Rights Ombudsman, or other organs that had existed before but had ceased to function after Fujimori's break with democracy, such as the Court of Constitutional Guarantees. At the same time, there was evidence of decrease in the number of victims of violence attributed to government security forces and in the number of complaints of human rights violations, as reported by the Attorney General's Office.[52]

The Human Rights Ombudsman, appointed by Congress in March 1996, moved swiftly to right the problem of numerous individuals unjustly sentenced and imprisoned under antiterrorist laws by faceless courts, under procedures that severely undercut due process and the independence of courts. The government admitted to mistakes in this area and endorsed the bill proposed by the Ombudsman that provided for the creation of an Ad Hoc Commission to evaluate cases and recommend pardons.[53] Other positive steps included reforms undertaken in 1995 and 1996 to amend several aspects of the antiterrorist law of 1992[54] and the acknowledgment by the Ministry of Justice of the existence of subhuman conditions in prisons.[55]

Peru also informed the Inter-American Commission on Human Rights that the Attorney General's Office (the *Fiscalía Especial de Derechos Humanos*) set up the

National Register of Detainees intended to prevent arbitrary arrest, the forced disappearance of persons, torture, and extrajudicial executions. However, the Commission noted that the United Nations Working Group on Forced or Involuntary Disappearances found that disappearances still occurred, although at a lesser rate, and that the registry was ineffective in preventing them.[56]

Unfortunately, many other situations and initiatives have undone much of the progress made and created quite a generalized impression that the government is actually not being led by its commitment to the *Declaration of Principles* or the *Plan of Action*. For instance, Law 26,447, cited above, provided for the termination of the faceless court system as of October 15, 1995. However, another law extended the faceless courts for another year, and in October 1996 yet another law, with almost no debate, again extended these tribunals until October 4, 1997.[57]

The reelection of President Fujimori for a five-year term with 64 percent of the vote, and the majority held by the government party in Congress, has made it extremely difficult to check government power on issues relevant to human rights and democracy. With no prior debate on such an important issue, in or outside Congress, the government used its congressional majority to pass legislation (Law No. 26,479) granting general amnesty to military and civilian personnel who were already serving prison sentences for human rights violations committed between May 1980 and June 15, 1995, or who were the subject of a complaint, investigation, indictment, trial, or conviction for such violations. This law, which actually institutionalized impunity, with all its negative consequences for deterring future unlawful behavior, was contested in the judiciary, but the government insisted with a new law (Law No. 26,492) passed by Congress on June 28, 1995, which prohibits the judiciary from ruling on the legality or applicability of the first amnesty law. Experts have judged this legislation as blatantly infringing on judicial independence. It denies the courts the right to interpret the law and review arbitrary acts of government, at the same time that it forces them to apply laws deemed unconstitutional. In addition, this legislation was passed at the time investigations were making progress in cases of torture, forced disappearances, and extrajudicial executions that presumably involved high-ranking officials in the military.[58]

In light of situations like these, the Inter-American Commission on Human Rights noted "scant progress has been made...in restoring the separation of powers among the three branches of government. In addition, the improper influence of the Executive and military in the judiciary persists."[59] Giving credence to this view, Congress approved in June 1996, again with almost no debate, Law 26,623 creating a Council of Judicial Coordination to guide judicial reform. However, with tremendous concentration of power around individuals close to the government and with the ability to fire judges and prosecutors during a transitional period that lasts until December 1998, the Council undermined the reprofessionalization of the judiciary that had been undertaken by the independent National Magistrates Council.[60]

The work of the Constitutional Court's mission of overseeing the lawfulness of bills and other government bodies' actions also has been severely curtailed. The Organic Law of the Constitutional Court (Law 26,435 of January 1995) establishes the requirement of consent of six of its seven members to declare the unconstitutionality of a bill. This requirement in fact allows for just a single one of its members to ratify the constitutionality of a contested bill. This became clear in a statement by the Court in December 1996, in response to a request of unconstitutionality of a law raising the requirements established by the constitution for a citizen referendum, that "this Court is forced, against the stated majority of its members, to declare the demand unfounded."[61] Graver still, in May 1997 Congress ousted three members of the Constitutional Court who had voted for the inapplicability of a law that allowed for yet another reelection of President Fujimori.[62] And, as if these measures were not enough, the government had Congress approve on March 11, 1998, a bill that drastically curtails the powers of the National Magistrates Council in another maneuver aimed at eliminating obstacles for the approval of the possibility of reelection for Fujimori. As a consequence, all seven members of the Council submitted their resignations.[63]

Further evidence of power concentration in the Executive and high military circles was the detention in December 1996 of General Rodolfo Robles, who had denounced military participation in the La Cantuta crimes. The military then forced him to retire and leave for exile. He returned in 1995 but was detained in December 1997, charged with insubordination by a military court, after denouncing that a military death squad had been responsible for blowing up the transmission tower of a television station that had been critical of the government.[64] It took special effort by the president to convince the military to set General Robles free, after asking Congress to pass a law granting amnesty to retired officers who criticize the military.[65] In July 1997, the government revoked the citizenship of an Israeli-born owner of a television station after the latter broadcast reports that government intelligence had wiretapped the phones of prominent citizens and journalists. The action of the government against Mr. Baruch Ivcher, the television station owner, led to the resignation of several cabinet members in protest.[66] Clearly, the government has given no signs that would make it unworthy of the dictum of the Inter-American Commission of Human Rights cited above.[67]

Regarding the military, observers agree that the ascent of Alberto Fujimori to the presidency in 1990 brought about an expansion of the military's legal prerogatives that put them on a par with the actual prerogatives it had accumulated. Through a series of presidential decrees allowed by Congress, the role of the armed forces in internal control and repression was greatly expanded. The Congress elected in 1993 restored all those decrees that a previous Congress had attempted to roll back.[68] Fujimori established a tight alliance with the military hierarchy, particularly with the army chief he appointed in 1990 and who, by presidential approval, remains in charge as of this writing. While the president supports (and protects) through his formal-legal powers the military clique he appointed in 1990, the top military chiefs have given unconditional support to his policies in all areas.[69] The politicization of the military hierarchy has resulted in serious divisions and the desertion of renowned army generals denouncing corruption and complicity in human rights crimes by the top military leadership. This, in turn, has led the president to rely ever more strongly on the national intelligence system to suppress dissent in the ranks. The resulting system is thus one of expanded autonomy for the military in alliance with the president. The president may appoint and dismiss army chiefs, according to the constitution, a fact that has led government apologists to boast of unprecedented levels of civilian control during President Fujimori's tenure. However, the truth is that the military performs its internal functions with little outside controls from Congress or the president, a practice that suits well the alliance between the president and the military clique that has controled the army since 1990.

## PRELIMINARY CONCLUSIONS

There are differences in the level of commitment by high-level government officials to the spirit of the initiatives unleashed in the Miami Summit. Some governments' actions, by undermining the independence and separation of powers or by showing careless disregard for the rule of law, simply subvert whatever progress might have been accomplished in specific areas. No tampering with the independence of the judiciary for personal political purposes, such as observed in some countries in the region, will ever be compatible with the spirit expressed in the Miami Summit. Such disregard permeates all levels of government, which may easily feel that a less zealous attitude in the promotion and protection of human and citizen rights is condoned by complicity from above. Other governments have, instead, shown zeal in the promotion of the principles and actions jointly accorded but face varying levels of resistance from the judiciary, the police, powerful private interests, widespread attitudes among segments of the population, or other institutions. It is clear that, in these cases, violations that do occur are not the product of government policy or intent; they result instead from habits that percolate through government agencies, especially those dealing with internal order and security, and that are resistant to government directives.

Similarly, much variation is found in the area of civil-military relations. Some countries battle with legacies from the past according powers to the military that are at odds with democratic arrangements; other governments face with little assertiveness of their own a military that is to a large extent autonomous. Others still successfully promote the supremacy of democratically elected powers while, nonetheless, facing situations in which military forces are too often employed in internal security missions. The promotion of democratization in this area will certainly have to respond to each country's specific situation; common to all, however, is the need that elected officials both in the executive and Congress advance measures that assert their power over the military, enhance accountability, and lessen the often exceptional status enjoyed by the military in the law and state administration. Also beneficial are measures aimed at promoting international cooperation in the defense area, confidence-building, and control over the spread of weapons.

In the area of human rights, beside the problems evidenced by all countries, monitoring and evaluation of the Summit's *Plan of Action* have been defective. There was no regular reporting by countries of progress made in the items specified in the plan and no clear instance where information should have been processed. In this regard there seems to have existed little connection between the *Plan of Action* and already existing inter-American agencies, such as the Unit for the Promotion of Democracy, the Interamerican Institute of Human Rights, the Interamerican Commission on Human Rights, and the Working Group on Democracy and Human Rights. This is a weakness that must be resolved and that does not require onerous or complex design. The existing inter-American institutions, in the framework provided by the OAS, ought straightforwardly to assume leadership in the monitoring and evaluation of progress, or lack thereof, in the specific areas contained in the *Plan of Action*.

Reinforced international monitoring and coordination within the Americas may act as facilitator of greater progress in cases of governments making real advances and as deterrent in the case of less committed governments. A greater coordinating and monitoring role for OAS organs should facilitate exchange of the substantial experiences accumulated within countries at both government and non-governmental levels, an exchange in both promotion and monitoring of measures in the human rights area. Moreover, improved methods for the collection of information on initiatives in the advancement and protection of human rights at disaggregated levels are necessary. Many actions take place outside government reach or scope that ought to be registered in evaluations. In this connection, greater cooperation and coordination between government agencies and non-governmental organizations of all kinds, including those at the state or regional level, ought to be emphasized. The Summit principles and plans contributed to momentum to national initiatives in this area. Yet, in addition to the energy resulting from the confluence of central government initiatives and those unleashed at the state, regional, or community level by state and non-government organizations, it appears that international coordination and pressure are most necessary. International initiative has the power to foster responsiveness and accountability if maintained persistently.

Initiatives well focused on areas targeted for progress, such as specific measures regarding security agencies, ought to be combined with comprehensive long-term approaches aimed at the reform and improvement of criminal procedures as well as in the capacities and functioning of the judiciary. What is needed is a more efficient and effective translation and implementation of inter-American directives in a persistent and regular manner, through a set of institutions and practices for enforcement and monitoring and for the education and training of the relevant personnel as well as society at large.

# Notes

1. For the process of preparation of the Summit and its deliberations, see the informative account in Richard E. Feinberg, *Summitry in the Americas: a Progress Report* (Washington, D.C.: Institute for International Economics, 1997).

2. See Michael Shifter and Sean Neill, *Implementing the Summit of the Americas: Guaranteeing Democracy and Human Rights*, A Working Paper Series, The North-South Center, November 1996, p. 7.

3. Feinberg 1997, p. 165.

4. See "Plan de Acción de la Cumbre de las Américas: Democracia y Derechos Humanos, Propuesta de Ejecución," propuesta presentada por Brasil y Canadá, Consejo Permanente de la Organización de Estados Americanos, Comisión Especial sobre Gestión de Cumbres Interamericanas, CE/GCI-44/96 rev. 1, 30 enero 1997.

5. See G/GCI-127/97 "Actividades desarrolladas por la OEA en el marco del CIDI en cumplimiento de los madatos de la Cumbre de las Américas realizada en Miami, en Diciembre de 1994."

6. For an evaluation of this area, see Robin L. Rosenberg, *Implementing the Summit of the Americas: Invigorating Civil Society Participation*, A Working Paper Series, The North-South Center, November 1996.

7. See, for instance, Francisco Rojas Aravena, ed. *Medidas de Confianza Mutua: Verificación* (Santiago: FLACSO-Chile, 1996).

8. See the conclusions in the closing statements by the Chair of the meeting, U.S. Secretary of Defense William J. Perry.

9. For a recent review, see Felipe Agüero, "Toward Civilian Supremacy in South America," in Larry Diamond et al., eds. *Consolidating the Third Wave Democracies* (Baltimore: The Johns Hopkins University Press, 1997), and "Las Fuerzas Armadas en una Época de Transición: Perspectivas para el Afianzamiento de la Democracia en América Latina," prepared for the Ford Foundation's project on "La Cuestión Cívico-Militar en las Nuevas Democracias de América Latina" and presented at the workshop held at Universidad Torcuato di Tella, Buenos Aires, May 22, 1997. Also, Carlos Basombrío, "La subordinación de los militares a la democracia en la América Latina de los noventa," paper presented to the international seminar "La cuestión cívico-militar en las nuevas democracias de América Latina," Buenos Aires, Universidad Torcuato di Tella, May 22, 1997.

10. For a broad conceptual view on human rights, see Carlos Basombrío, *Y Ahora Qué? Desafíos para el trabajo de Derechos Humanos en América Latina* (Lima: Diakonía Acción Ecuménica Sueca, 1996).

11. For a view that warns about the need for conceptual disaggregation in this area, see James M. McCormick and Neil J. Mitchell, "Human Rights Violations, Umbrella Concepts, and Empirical Analysis," *World Politics* 49, 4, July 1997, 510-525.

12. In this regard, see Juan Méndez, "Dead Reckoning," *Hemisfile* 7, 2, March/April 1996, 8-9.

13. See, for instance, the country reports in *Amnesty International Report 1997*.

14. As indication that no country is exempt from severe human rights problems, Amnesty International has decided to effect its 1998 international campaign on the case of the United States.

15. The bill did not, however, contemplate mechanisms to investigate the disappearances or to include in the indemnification the relatives of those that were executed for political reasons. See Human Rights Watch/Americas, *Informe Anual sobre la Situación de los Derechos Humanos en el Mundo 1996*. In any case, the commission appointed to examine cases for indemnification, which included representatives of the military and of the families of disappeared persons, granted indemnity in certain cases against the opposition of the military.

16. It is noteworthy that Brazil has attempted to expand women's participation by establishing a quota of at least 25 percent of the candidates of each party or alliance for each sex (Federal Law 9.504/97, September 30, 1997), which improves over previous regulations in force in 1996 that established a 20 percent quota. However, the exact impact of this regulation on actually enlarging women's representation has not yet been systematically assessed.

17. See Francisco Panizza and Alexandra Barahona de Brito, "The Politics of Human Rights in Brazil under Democratic Rule," paper prepared for delivery at the meeting of the *Latin American Studies Association*, Guadalajara, Mexico, April 17-19, 1997.

18. Paulo Sérgio Pinheiro and Paulo de Mesquita Neto, "Programa Nacional de Direitos Humanos: Avaliacao do Primeiro Ano e Perspectivas," Núcleo de Estudos da Violencia, Sao Paulo, Brazil, n.d. This report contains a detailed list of accomplishments under the *Plan*.

19. Pinheiro and Neto.

20. See the yearly reports by Amnesty International and by Human Rights Watch/Americas.

21. See Human Rights Watch/Americas, *Police Brutality in Urban Brazil*, New York, April 1997.

22. Humans Rights Watch/Americas, April 1997.

23. See Panizza and Barahona de Brito 1997.

24. Human Rights Watch/Americas, *Police Brutality in Urban Brazil,* New York, April 1997, 3.

25. Mesquita Neto, Paulo de. (1995). *From intervention to participation: the transformation of military politics in Brazil, 1974-1992*. Ph. D. Dissertation. Columbia University.

26. Zaverucha, Jorge. *Rumor de sabres: tutela militar ou controle civil?*. (São Paulo: Editora Ática, 1994), 228.

27. Zaverucha 1994, 288.

28. Mesquita Neto 1995, 222.

29. *Latin American Weekly Report*, August 14, 1991; January 20, 1994, 17; April 7, 1994, 152.

30. The government issued in 1996 a document officially stating Brazil's defense policy, in which the military's external defense role is emphasized. See "Brasil 1996: la política de defensa nacional," *Paz y Seguridad en las Américas,* No. 10, Diciembre 1996, FLACSO-Chile, Woodrow Wilson Center, Washington, D.C.

31. Eliézer Rizzo de Oliveira, "Política de Defesa nacional e Relacoes Cívico-Militares no Governo do Presidente Fernando Henrique Cardoso," paper presented at the Conference, "Civil-Military Relations in the Americas for the 21st Century," Latin American Institute, The University of New Mexico, Albuquerque, NM, November 3-5, 1997. Control over domestic intelligence gathering has been in dispute between civilian and military agencies. Earlier reports had stated that the head of the president's military household had announced that the *Agencia Brasileira de Inteligencia*, a new national intelligence agency, would be controlled by the military. See *Latin American Regional Reports: Brazil*, May 2, 1996, 3.

32. Hunter, Wendy. *Eroding military influence in Brazil: politicians against soldiers.* (Chapel Hill and London: The University of North Carolina Press, 1997).

33. The Interamerican Human Rights Commission at the OAS acceded to review a presentation by 11 Chilean lawyers stating that the existence of designated and life senators violated the principle of equality of citizen's vote. *La Epoca Internet*, January 25, 1998.

34. The Inter-American Commission of Human Rights has stated that, on the occasion of condemning Peru's amnesty laws, "In cases related to Argentina, Uruguay, and Chile, the Commission has held that as a matter of principle amnesty laws are incompatible with the American Convention, because the Convention imposes on the states the obligation to prevent, investigate and punish all violations of human rights guaranteed by the Convention, and because an amnesty law tends to undercut the state's competence to carry out this obligation." Inter-American Commission on Human Rights, Organization of American States, *Annual Report of the Inter-American Commission on Human Rights 1996*, General Secretariat, Washington, D.C., 1997, 735.

35. See *Amnesty International Report 1997*, 116.

36. A new attempt by the *Ministerio Público Militar* to get the Supreme Court to close human rights cases was being made in September 1997. *La Época (Internet)*, September 24, 1997.

37. *Amnesty International Report 1996*, 116.

38. *Balance de FASIC sobre los derechos humanos en Chile correspondiente al primer semestre de 1997* (Digitalizado por el Equipo Nizkor en Madrid, August 26, 1997).

39. For an excellent analysis of the human rights situation during the transition and the successor government, see *Chile: Sistema Judicial y Derechos Humanos*, Comisión Andina de Juristas, Lima, Mayo de 1995.

40. See SERNAM, *El Fortalecimiento del Papel de la Mujer en la Sociedad: Informe de Chile*, 5 May 1997, submitted to the Summit General Coordination Office in the Ministry of Foreign Affairs, Chile. However, Chile stood out, among the countries compared here, for not having minimum percent set for the inclusion of women in electoral lists or organs of representation. Similarly, Chile stands out in the whole region for the absence of a divorce law.

41. On this see the insightful previously cited report by the Comisión Andina de Juristas.

42. *La Época* (Santiago), August 31, 1997.

43. This information from various days in August of *La Época Internet*.

44. *La Época*, August 18, 1997.

45. See *Amnesty International Report 1997*, 117. More recently, in January 1998, the president of the Chilean Human Rights Commission, Jaime Castillo Velasco, admitted the existence of such a situation of uncorrected "anomalies." *El Mercurio Internet*, February 1, 1998.

46. *Amnesty International Report 1997*.

47. Human Rights Watch/Americas, *Informe Anual Sobre la Situación de los Derechos Humanos en el Mundo 1996*, 24.

48. For recent examples, see "Presidente Frei rechazó declaraciones de Pinochet," *La Época*, Santiago, March 4, 1997, and "General Pinochet expresa rechazo a protestas de los estudiantes," *La Época*, Santiago, June 23, 1997. The occurrence of this kind of episode is likely to decline considerably after the retirement of General Pinochet from his post as head of the army in March 1998.

49. The commanders-in-chief of the army and the navy voted against the president's choice. *La Época,* Santiago, March 8, 1997.

50. Felipe Agüero, "Chile's Lingering Authoritarian Legacy," *Current History* 97, 616, February 1998.

51. See Claudio Fuentes, "Militares en Chile: ni completa autonomía ni total subordinación," *Chile 96: análisis y opiniones*, Santiago, Chile. Nueva Serie FLACSO, 1997, 165-181, and Gonzalo García P. & Juan Esteban Montes I., *Subordinación democrática de los militares: éxitos y fracasos en Chile* (Santiago. Editorial Atena, 1994).

52. See Inter-American Commission of Human Rights, Organization of American States, *Annual Report of the Inter-American Commission on Human Rights 1996*, General Secretariat, Washington, D.C., 733.

53. The bill passed in August 15, 1996, (Law No. 26,556) allows for recommendations of pardons in cases where no connections between individuals convicted of terrorism or treason and terrorist organizations or activities are proved. The Commission began making recommendations in December 1996, which were followed by the granting of pardons, although large numbers still remain in prison. Reference note #52, 741-742. The Commission's mandate was extended in July 1997 until February 1998.

54. For this law and the treason law, see Americas Watch, *Human Rights in Peru One Year after Fujimori's Coup* (New York: Human Rights Watch, 1993). The 1995 and 1996 reforms include a Supreme Decree of January 6, 1995, which prohibits the police from presenting detainees charged with terrorist offenses to the news media, violating the presumption of innocence, although the practice continued for those charged with treason; Law 26,447 (April 21, 1995), which restored the right of access to a lawyer from the moment of detention and mandated the presence of the public prosecutor during police interrogation and raised the age at which juveniles could be charged as adults in cases of terrorism from 15 years to 18. For these and other laws, see *Presumption of Guilt: Human Rights Violations and the Faceless Courts in Peru*, Human Rights Watch/Americas, Vol. 8. No. 5 (b), August 1996.

55. The Ministry then announced works for improvement in 20 prison facilities in the interior areas. However, the *Coordinadora Nacional de Derechos Humanos'* mission to the Challapalca prison, located at an altitude of 5,000 meters where 111 prisoners had been transferred, concluded that the prison and the operating system violated a number of local and international norms, and recommended the suspension of the transfer. *Informe de la Misión de la Coordinadora Nacional de Derechos Humanos a Challapalca*, July 15, 1997.

56. See Inter-American Commission of Human Rights, Organization of American States, *Annual Report of the Inter-American Commission on Human Rights 1996*, General Secretariat, Washington, D.C., 739. For detailed itemized cases of disappearances, torture, extrajudicial executions, see *Informes Sobre la Situación de los Derechos Humanos en el Peru en 1996*, Coordinadora Nacional de Derechos Humanos, Lima, February 1997.

57. Reference note #56, 736.

58. The revelations of General Rodolfo Robles about groups in the military responsible for the execution of a professor and nine students from the University of La Cantuta, and the massacre of Barrios Altos, have been widely reported.

59. Inter-American Commission of Human Rights, Organization of American States, *Annual Report of the Inter-American Commission on Human Rights 1996*, General Secretariat, Washington, D.C., 1997, 739.

60. *Informe sobre la situación de los derechos humanos en el Perú en 1996*, Coordinadora Nacional de Derechos Humanos, Lima, February 1997, 77-80.

61. Reference note #60, 83.

62. *La Época*, (Santiago), May 30, 1997.

63. *El Mercurio* (Santiago), March 21, 1998, D1-D5.

64. *The New York Times*, December 2, 1996, A4.

65. *Amnesty Action* (AI USA), Spring 1997, 3.

66. See *The New York Times*, July 18, 1997, A3; and *La República*, July 19, 1997.

67. Furthermore, the government did not comply with the decision of the Inter-American Court of Human Rights that Peru pay compensation for the violation of the right to life inflicted on three individuals. Inter-American Commission of Human Rights, Organization of American States, *Annual Report of the Inter-American Commission on Human Rights 1996*, General Secretariat, Washington, D.C., 744.

68. These decrees establish, for instance, a National Defense System, which is led by the president but gives ample prerogatives within it to the military; a mobilization system that prescribes that individuals must make information available to the armed forces; a national intelligence system and service that may obtain any information required from public or private agencies; the power of the military to intervene in university locales, prisons, and areas not declared in state of emergency; and the expansion of military prerogatives in areas declared in state of emergency. For a detailed description of these decrees, see Carlos Iván Degregori and Carlos Rivera, "Perú 1980-1993: fuerzas armadas, subversión y democracia," *Instituto de Estudios Peruanos*, Documento de Trabajo No. 53, 1994; and Carlos Basombrío, "La subordinación de los militares a la democracia en la América Latina de los noventa," paper presented to the international seminar "La cuestión cívico-militar en las nuevas democracias de América Latina," Buenos Aires, Universidad Torcuato di Tella, May 22, 1997.

69. See Philip Mauceri, "State reform, coalitions, and the neoliberal *autogolpe* in Peru," *Latin American Research Review* 30, 1995, 7-37.

# V. LEADERSHIP COUNCIL FOR INTER-AMERICAN SUMMITRY

## *Postscript:* Democracy and Human Rights Since the 1994 Summit of the Americas

*Felipe Agüero*

ADDENDUM: THE 1998 SUMMIT IN SANTIAGO, CHILE (APRIL 18-19)

*October 1998*

The Declaration of Santiago is generous in references to democracy and human rights as primary goals and aspirations of the Americas. This time, however, the Summit was much more focused, concentrating, in practice, on deliberations over the ways to promote free trade and emphasizing education as a stepping stone to sustained development and democracy. In this way, the Summit took note of the criticism made of the previous 1994 meeting, which had tried to cover too much. With the focus on trade and education, the concern for human rights suffered. The generosity of the Declaration in this area, therefore, does not reflect the actual deliberations in the meeting nor an actual willingness to concentrate on implementation of specific goals.

The 1998 Summit again asserted the goal of strengthening democracy, and this time it connected it with the goal of strengthening education. It again emphasized respect and promotion of human rights as a primary concern of all governments. The Declaration stated agreement on the need to promote the ratification and implementation of the international agreements aimed at preserving human rights and to strengthen the pertinent national and international institutions. It highlighted the importance of a free press and commended the appointment of a Special Rapporteur for Freedom of Expression within the framework of the Organization of American States (OAS). It continued to underscore the value of an independent, efficient, and effective administration of justice for the consolidation of democracy and decided to support the strengthening of national entities involved in the study of the administration of justice and the establishment of a hemispheric center for studies on this subject.

The *Plan of Action* states that it endorses "new initiatives" that deepen the governments' commitment to the principles of democracy, justice, and human rights. However, except for a few more specific references to the protection of rights of migrant workers, there is really nothing new in the proposed initiatives. Yet the importance of measures to protect the rights of all migrant workers and their families should not be underestimated. The *Plan of Action* lists a number of specific measures that, if implemented, would have significant impact on the lives of thousands of people in this category. They also establish a balance in the assignment of tasks in the area of human rights, as much of the problems in the situation of migrant workers lies with the United States, the largest recipient country of migrant workers. The outlined measures are, in addition, fully consistent with the needs that stem from a critical diagnosis of this situation in the United States, as stated in reports by Amnesty International and other organizations.

The *Plan of Action* also outlines measures aimed at the strengthening of justice systems and judiciaries, with particular emphasis on the protection of the rights of children, youths, and families. In the same direction are placed initiatives for the modernization of the state in labor matters and for the promotion of legal equality and equality of opportunities between women and men. In this area the *Plan of Action* calls for carrying out the commitments undertaken by governments at several world and regional conferences on related matters. The protection of the basic rights of workers and the promotion of greater participation of indigenous populations also support the basic goals contemplated in the promotion and protection of human rights.

In all, the most specific initiatives are the creation of the Rapporteur for Freedom of Expression, previously created in the Inter-American Human Rights Commission, and the call for the creation of a justice studies center of the Americas, which would also help in training officials in the judiciary.

These positive elements notwithstanding, it should be pointed out that Summit debates did not include an evaluation of progress in the areas that had been specified in the 1994 *Plan of Action*. In the absence of such an evaluation, the reiteration of goals and plans in the new *Plan of Action* loses some of its power and credibility. Credibility problems are worsened by the fact that, in addition to lack of evaluation of past plans, no specific follow-up mechanisms for the review of implementation of new or reiterated goals are offered. Orientations for the Summit Implementation Review Group (SIRG) remain very vague and do not follow from any revision of the effectiveness of the SIRG in monitoring progress in previous initiatives.

The Summit's most concrete legacy has been the formation of Free Trade Area of the Americas (FTAA) negotiating groups. However, the "democratic clause" proposed by the Leadership Council for Inter-American Summitry, which would establish an explicit linkage between participation in the FTAA and democratically elected governments, was not adopted by participating governments.

Absence of significantly new initiatives in the area of human rights, the lack of evaluation of previous plans, and the absence of specific review mechanisms for the future underscore the need for continuing and reinforced monitoring by independent organizations. This is especially necessary in the area of human rights, in which verbal generosity is not expression of a real debate and is not turned into accountable initiatives.

# V. LEADERSHIP COUNCIL FOR INTER-AMERICAN SUMMITRY

*Cristina B. Cunico, M.D., University of Brazil, has a master's degree in public health from Johns Hopkins University. Dr. Cunico is an independent public consultant to international organizations, such as the World Bank, the Inter-American Development Bank, the Pan American Health Organization, and the U.S. Agency for International Development, and to private companies.*

# Providing Equitable Access to Basic Health Services

## Cristina B. Cunico

### I. EXECUTIVE SUMMARY

This paper reviews the implementation of Initiative #17, "Equitable Access to Basic Health Services," of the Summit of the Americas, at the regional level and in three countries — Chile, Colombia, and Brazil.

The paper begins by outlining recent profound changes in the region — political, economic, demographic, and epidemiological. These changes have had significant effects on the demand and costs of health care delivery. In addition, these changes represent major challenges to governments in their efforts to ensure equitable access to basic health services and to improve the health and living conditions of their populations.

The paper describes the activities of the technical and financial cooperation agencies in assisting countries to implement Initiative #17. The Pan American Health Organization (PAHO) was the "responsible coordinator" of the implementation of the initiative in the region. In compliance with its mandate, PAHO has been providing direct support for the national health sector reform processes through the promotion of seminars, workshops, and several research projects. Other international organizations, such as the Inter-American Development Bank (IDB), the World Bank, the United States Agency for International Development (USAID) and the United Nations Children's Fund (UNICEF), have also been active in providing technical and financial support to health sector reform and child, maternal, and reproductive health.

On the national level, Initiative #17 translated the commitment of the governments of the region to health sector reform as the mechanism that would guarantee equitable access to basic health services. The three countries reviewed are going through important reforms of their health sectors.

Even though the characteristics of the reform processes are remarkably different from country to country, the long-term objectives are the same, that is, improvement of health conditions, equitable access to health care, better quality of care, and improved efficiency in the financing and delivery of health services.

The paper concludes with a few recommendations for improving implementation of Initiative #17 at the international and national levels.

Although each country in the region has its own process of implementation of Summit commitments, especially regarding the health sector reform, it is possible and necessary to develop indicators to monitor and evaluate the impact of the interventions on some critical issues such as equity, quality, and efficiency.

The establishment of a monitoring mechanism will help to track and to facilitate the implementation of the Summit initiative at the national level, as well as to orient the activities of cooperating agencies that will provide technical and financial support to the countries of the region.

Databases and mechanisms of dissemination of technical scientific information should be created, taking advantage of electronic means of communication, to assist policymakers, institutions, professionals, and cooperating agencies that take part in the reform processes. Similarly, health systems and service research should be promoted as ways to increase knowledge of priority areas and for orientation of future developments.

Countries and agencies should better coordinate technical and financial cooperation in support of the commitments made at the Summit in order to enhance the impact of cooperative activities and adjust those activities to national needs.

## II. INTRODUCTION

The health sector has contributed significantly to the improvement of the health situation in the region over the last few decades. However, in spite of the progress achieved, there are still important problems to be solved: 1) limited access to basic health services, 2) poor quality of services, and 3) unsatisfactory health conditions for large groups of the region's population.

There is a growing recognition among countries and cooperation agencies (also called cooperating agencies) working in the region that appropriate distribution of the benefits of economic growth to all sectors of the population is an essential part of the development agenda. As a result, a consensus was formed on the need to overcome social inequities, especially in the area of health, in order to achieve the goals of growth, human development, regional integration, and consolidation of democracy in the Americas.

This consensus was reflected in the commitments undertaken by the governments of the region at the World Summit for Children in 1990, at the International Conference on Population and Development in 1994, and at the Summit of the Americas, held in Miami in December 1994.

Initiative 17, Equitable Access to Basic Health Services, translates the commitment of the governments of the Americas towards the implementation of a series of actions addressing the most significant health problems in the region.

The initiative includes the endorsement by the governments of the goals set during the 1990 World Summit for Children, the "Nariño" Agreement of 1994, and the International Conference on Population and Development of 1994 of reduction of infant mortality by one-third and maternal mortality by one-half by the year 2000, compared to the rates of 1990. The leaders also endorsed a basic package of clinical, preventive, and public health services to attend to child, maternal, and reproductive health.

The governments of the region expressed their commitment to develop, in accordance with the mechanisms determined by each country, reforms in the health sector designed to meet the targets of child, maternal, and reproductive health; equitable access to basic health services; strengthening of the public health infrastructure; introduction of new alternatives for financing, administration, and delivery of health services; improvement of the quality of health services; and greater participation of social actors.

In addition, the leaders decided to convene a meeting of the governments of the Western Hemisphere with donors and international organizations, in order to establish a framework for health sector reform throughout the hemisphere, define the role of PAHO in regional monitoring of national plans and programs for reform, and plan the strengthening of the Inter-American Network, including contributions from its co-sponsors.

The leaders also endorsed the establishment of programs to prevent the propagation of HIV/AIDS and endemic and transmissible diseases.

## III. BACKGROUND

The economic crisis of the 1980s forced countries in the Americas to introduce economic adjustments. As part of this economic restructuring, significant cutbacks in social spending were introduced. Public health spending in Latin America and the Caribbean decreased from 1.6 percent to 1.4 percent of the regional GDP in the 1980s. One consequence of the adjustment measures was the exacerbation of social inequities, especially in health [2].

In the early 1990s, a process of economic recovery started taking place in the region. However, inequities, poverty, and unsatisfactory living conditions of broad sectors of the population still remain. The available information indicates that 105 million people in the Latin America and Caribbean region do not have regular access to formal health systems [16].

The process of globalization and the advancement of the processes of regional integration have led countries to become more productive and competitive in order to guarantee a privileged position at international markets. In the health sector, those national plans were expressed in health policies that call for greater efficiency in the allocation and use of resources available.

In the political sphere, almost all countries of the region have adopted democratic and participatory models that have led to the redefinition of the role of government and society, with increased participation of the community, private sector, and local governments in the administration and financing of public sector organizations. As societies increasingly include health care among their basic citizenship rights, various sectors of populations have been putting increased pressure on their governments for better and more diversified health services [14].

Other developments affecting the countries of the region in recent years are the demographic, epidemiological, and technological changes. Changes in the age structure of the population, increasing urbanization and industrialization, and changes in the epidemiological profiles of the countries — characterized by the coexistence of transmissible and deficiency diseases with other conditions, such as chronic diseases and accidents — have affected the demand for health services.

These changes along with the incorporation and dissemination of new technologies have had a dramatic impact on costs of health care delivery, generating a pressure over resources allocation between preventive and health promotion programs on the one hand and treatment and rehabilitation services on the other [3].

As a consequence of all of the above, the countries of the region have initiated health sector reforms in an effort to improve the health and living conditions of their populations. The common goals of almost all reform processes, besides promoting equity in health conditions, can be summarized as follow: equity of access to basic services; improvement of the quality of care; increased efficiency in the allocation and management of resources; and promotion of social participation in the planning, management, delivery, and evaluation of health services.

## IV. IMPLEMENTING INITIATIVE 17 IN THE REGION OF THE AMERICAS

The *Plan of Action* of the 1994 Summit of the Americas establishes the responsibility of the Pan American Health Organization (PAHO) as the coordinator of the implementation of Initiative 17. In compliance with its mandate, PAHO has made significant progress in implementing many of the action items of Initiative 17. Many of those actions directed at increasing equitable access to basic health services have already been undertaken by the majority of countries of the region over the last few years. Nevertheless, PAHO, in response to the Summit's's mandates, has decided to strengthen its collaborative efforts with the countries and other agencies and institutions, particularly to reinforce its technical cooperation on national sectoral reform.

Health reform has been an essential part of the action programs of regional cooperating agencies. In fact, technical and financial agencies have been working very close to national governments at all stages of development of health sector reform proposals, from their design to development of mechanisms and instruments for their implementation [17].

By the end of 1994, 24 countries in the region had received technical and financial support for health reform from either bilateral or international agencies [2].

Among the most active cooperating agencies are PAHO, the World Bank, the Inter-American Development Bank (IDB), and the United States Agency for International Development (USAID). Other important bilateral agencies participating in this process are the Japan International Cooperation Agency (JICA), the Swedish International Development Authority (SIDA), Canada's International Development Research Centre (IDRC), and the United Kingdom's Overseas Development Administration (ODA). Some of the donors related only to a single country, but multi-agency cooperation at the country level is the norm in the region [2].

PAHO has been supporting 26 national health sector reform processes in the region through its regional and country structure. This cooperation usually involves direct technical assistance, training, seminars, as well as forums for consensus-building, dissemination of technical information, research activities, and information-sharing of national experiences.

USAID traditionally has worked in the region on family planning for high-risk populations, particularly women and children in rural areas, in partnership with national NGOs. As a direct result of the Summit of the Americas, there has been a shift in emphasis to focus more closely on issues related to health care reform in several countries. Particular emphasis has been given to community participation, especially to groups that have been traditionally marginalized; maternal and child health; improvement in the quality of care and coverage of services, especially in the area of reproductive health; and sustainability of reforms.

The IDB and the World Bank have been providing financial support for several projects on the development and modernization of the health sector.

The *Plan of Action* of the Summit of the Americas established the responsibility of the IDB, the World Bank, and PAHO for the convocation of the "Special Meeting of Ministries of Health on Health Sector Reform in the Region of the Americas" to discuss and design a frame of reference, a monitoring system, and a support network for a regional sectoral reform process.

An interagency committee — composed of PAHO, the World Bank, the IDB, the Organization of American States (OAS), the Economic Commission for Latin America and the Caribbean (ECLAC), the United Nations Children's Fund (UNICEF), the United Nations Population Fund (UNFPA), USAID, the Canadian International Development Agency (CIDA), the Canadian International Development Research Center (IDRC), and government officials from the Western Hemisphere — was responsible for the preparations of the special meeting. Based on the deliberations of this committee, a joint background document on health sector reform was prepared for the special meeting.

The committee was also held responsible for follow-up of the reform mandates of the Summit of the Americas and those of the Special Meeting on Health Sector Reform, in addition to serving as a mechanism for consultation and coordination among agencies working on regional sectoral reform.

The committee was very active during the preparation of the special meeting. Currently, contacts among the agencies that compose the committee have been renewed in order to define the course of action as follow-up to the Summit and the special meeting.

The special meeting was held as a Special Session of the Directing Council of PAHO in September 1995, with the participation of multi-institutional government delegations, representatives of donor agencies, and non-governmental organizations. The conclusions of the Special Meeting on Health Sector Reform have been translated into a conceptual framework to support the actions of the technical cooperating agencies and to orient the analysis of the national processes taking place in the region.

The special meeting also confirmed that health reform processes were taking place in most countries of the region. In a resolution, adopted on the basis of the deliberation of the special meeting, the Direct Council of PAHO requested its member states to give priority to health sector reform as a mechanism to guarantee equitable access to basic health services and to achieve greater efficiency and effectiveness in health sector activities [5].

The Direct Council of PAHO also requested that the cooperating agencies provide greater coordination and increase their support of the Health Sector Reform processes. In addition, it requested that PAHO, together with the countries and cooperating agencies, develop a monitoring mechanism and an inter-American network to support health sector reform.

These mandates were implemented in 1995 through a variety of activities at the country and interagency levels and within the Secretariat itself [5].

In compliance with the mandate of the Summit of the Americas and the Special Meeting on Reform, PAHO was the agency chosen to establish national evaluation mechanisms for monitoring the process of health reform, its results and effects [1].

Currently, PAHO is developing a network for the exchange of experiences and a monitoring mechanism for sectoral reform in the region [1]. PAHO/WHO Representative Offices will be responsible 1) for organizing key partners into an inter-American network to support the reform and 2) for promoting the affiliation with this network of all interested institutions and individuals, such as representatives of the executive and legislative branches of government, universities, NGOs, health care providers and users, and international agencies. PAHO/WHO provided direct support for health sector reform by promoting high-level seminars and workshops for exchange of information, expertise, and consensus-building about national reform processes. Several subregional seminars dealing with reforms were held with the collaboration of the IDB, the World Bank, and subregional integration organizations.

Several research projects and studies on reform processes in general and on special aspects of these processes were conducted and funded by PAHO and other agencies and universities [5]. In 1996, a research competition on Financial and Organizational Aspects of Health Sector Reform was organized by PAHO, and five projects (Brazil, Uruguay, Peru, Colombia, and Costa Rica) were selected from more than 90 proposals. A similar initiative was taken by the Ad-Hoc Committee of the World Health Organization on Health Research, and five projects were also financed in the region. PAHO and the Ad-Hoc Committee are also organizing a clearing house for collection, analysis, and dissemination of scientific literature about health sector reform.

External interagency groups to support the national health sector reforms have been created. The groups comprise representatives of the principal technical and financial cooperating agencies working in the countries of the region. These support groups facilitate the coordination of the cooperation activities of the agencies to national needs [5].

As a consequence of the mandate of interagency collaboration in support of health sector reform efforts in countries of the Americas, PAHO and USAID are working on the identification of areas of regional cooperation in support of the health reform processes in the region and on the evaluation of their impact [10]. A proposed five-year (1997-2001) USAID-funded project on "Equitable Access to Basic Health Services" was executed by PAHO in collaboration with the Partnerships for Health Reform (PHR) Project, Abt Associates, and the Data for Decision Making (DDM) Project, Harvard University [13].

Another mechanism of interagency cooperation that takes part in the sectoral reform process is the Inter-American Network on Health Economics and Financing (REDEFS). REDEFS was established in 1994 by the Economic Development Institute (EDI) of the World Bank, PAHO, and the Inter-American Center for Social Security Studies (CIESS) to promote training, research, and information activities in health, economics, and finance.

Since 1994, REDEFS has rapidly expanded its membership, which is formed by 22 national and/or subregional health economics and financing associations or groups [4]. Its members include government officials, representatives of the private sector, non-governmental organizations, donors, and scholars.

In only a few years, the network has promoted more than 10 training workshops on topics related to the reform, with the support of the EDI, the United Kingdom's Overseas Development Administration (ODA), and the IDRC [5].

The 1994 Summit of the Americas suggested that the Inter-American Network on Health Sector Reform should be based on the experience of REDEFS. At the Summit, the governments of the region endorsed the goals set in previous Summits regarding the reduction of child and maternal mortality and the provision of a basic package of clinical, preventive, and public health services to attend to child, maternal, and reproductive health. In compliance with those mandates and also as part of the plans of action of cooperating agencies working in the region and those of national governments, a series of actions addressing child and maternal health have been taken by the cooperating agencies in support of national governments.

In compliance with the mandate of measles virus eradication in the Western Hemisphere by the year 2000 and that of the Summit of the Americas, PAHO has been supporting the countries of the Caribbean and Latin America in planning mass vaccination campaigns and the establishment of surveillance systems. Starting in 1991, the English-speaking Caribbean region succeeded in interrupting transmission of measles following a month-long mass vaccination strategy. Since then, mass vaccination campaigns have been held in Brazil, Chile, Peru, and Central American countries, among others.

The First Ladies of the Americas, with the technical support of PAHO, have pursued an important hemispheric campaign against measles. They have also committed themselves to work on the problems of reducing maternal and infant mortality and reproductive health.

The World Summit for Children, held in 1990, set the goal of reducing infant mortality by 50 percent by the year 2000. At the Summit of the Americas in 1994, the governments reaffirmed their commitment to reduce infant mortality to one-third, compared with the rates of 1990. PAHO and UNICEF have joined efforts together with other cooperating agencies to implement a new strategy, Integrated Management of Childhood Illness (IMCI), to help reduce infant mortality in the region of the Americas.

The strategy includes educating health workers on how to evaluate major problems and diseases that affect the health of children, educating parents on how to care for children in the home, and preventing illness through vaccinations [11]. In March 1996, the IMCI strategy began to be implemented in Bolivia, Brazil, Ecuador, Peru, and the Dominican Republic. The training of health workers responsible for the care of children less than five years old was already in progress.

Consistent with the mandate of the Summit of the Americas and as part of the Regional Plan (established in 1990 by PAHO for reduction of maternal mortality to one-half of 1990 levels by the year 2000), PAHO, USAID, the Mother Care Project, and the Quality Assurance Project signed an agreement to implement the project "Intensive Implementation of the Basic Obstetric Emergency Care" (BEOC), which is aimed at improving reproductive health services in several countries of the region.

## V. IMPLEMENTATION AT THE NATIONAL LEVEL

The reform of the health sector has been considered a priority on the political agenda of the countries of the Americas since the last decade. The majority of, if not all, countries have been going through some sort of health sector reform. The Summit of the Americas reaffirmed the commitment of the governments of the region to health sector reform as the mechanism for guaranteeing equitable access to basic health services. The agreements reached at the Summit of the Americas, along with those of other international and subregional summits that took place over the last few years, have been expressed in the policies and plans for the health sector in several countries of the region.

The objectives, scope, and characteristics of those reforms are remarkably different from country to country, as are the strategies and mechanisms adopted for its implementation. However, all of the reform proposals recognize the improvement of health conditions as a common goal. Other common goals are to achieve equitable access to health care, better quality of care, and improved efficiency in the financing and delivery of health services.

Some countries are going through comprehensive reforms of their health systems, encompassing the organization of services and the financing of the health sector as a whole. Some of the policies oriented to the area of financing the health sector emphasized the need for efficient allocation and use of resources to address the needs of the most vulnerable segment of the population. In a few countries of the region, those policies aim at achieving universal coverage through the creation of appropriate packages of basic health services and by focusing public expenditures on high-impact, cost-effective health interventions for special groups and programs, such as reproductive health services.

Other countries have undertaken partial reforms, making changes in some health sector institutions or redefining health care models. This redefinition in some cases emphasizes greater participation of the private sector and competition among private providers for public and private financing. It is expected that this network of providers competing among themselves will improve the quality of care in both sectors as well as improve the efficiency of the whole system.

Others redefinitions of health care models emphasize strengthening services at the local level by introducing decentralization strategies and promoting social participation in the management, organization, and planning of services [2].

The decentralization strategy has been adopted for the majority of the countries in the region. It implies the transfer of authority, management of resources, and decisionmaking to the state and local levels. At the central level, the Ministries of Health are strengthening their role in policymaking, planning, and regulation, whereas their responsibility as direct service providers is diminishing.

Special attention has been given to the financial sustainability of the reforms through the promotion of greater efficiency in the management of resources and services, improvement of allocation systems, and improvement of coordination and cooperation between public and private sectors.

Major efforts have been devoted to political support for national Health Sector Reform processes through the establishment of national commissions for health sector reform as consensus-building mechanisms on several aspects of the reform [5]. Usually, these commissions comprise representatives from different agencies of government, groups from civil society interested in health, and cooperating agencies.

Despite the social and economic heterogeneity among and within the countries of the region, reflected in the variety of health care institutions and systems, few challenges can be identified that are common to all reform processes.

First, the reform processes involve a large number of actors from all levels of society. These multiple actors, whose interests do not always coincide, demand a high degree of leadership and negotiation capacity on the part of the government in order to reach a democratic consensus on the nature and substance of reform. To date, few countries have advanced very far in the decision-making process, with some remarkable exceptions, such as Colombia, which is conducting a comprehensive reform of its health system [15].

Another important challenge in the management of the reform processes is to maintain coherence and harmony with different reform processes that are taking place in other sectors and at the government level that will have effects on the health sector and influence the health of populations [1].

There is also a great regionwide concern about the sustainability of the reforms, that is, whether a reform is a state policy. Most of the time, health sector reforms require a period of time prior to implementation that exceeds the period of time of governments in office.

An overview of the implementation of Initiative 17 in Chile, Colombia, and Brazil follows, with particular emphasis on the process of health sector reform as the basic mechanism for the implementation of mandates at the country level called for by the Summit of the Americas.

## Chile

### Overview of the Health System

The health sector in Chile is composed of institutions in the public and private sectors. The public sector comprises the Ministry of Health (Ministerio de Salud — MINSAL), the National Health Care System (Sistema Nacional de Servicios de Salud — SNSS), the municipalities, and the National Health Care Fund (Fondo Nacional de Salud — FONASA). The public sector is financed mostly by social security taxes. Other sources of revenue are transfers from the central government and the sale of "vouchers" to the users of the Preferential System of Providers, a system that allows their insured to be serviced by private providers. MINSAL is the principal provider of health care and is responsible for designing public health care policies and programs; supervising, monitoring, and evaluating health care policies; and coordinating the diverse health agencies that are part of SNSS.

The private sector comprises the financial and health care providers' institutions. In the private sector, health care services are financed through employer-based health insurance, and a larger percentage through the ISAPRE (Instituciones de Salud Previsional — ISAPRE), a pre-paid system to which some employers subscribe on behalf of their employees as an alternative to the public system. The private providers are the not-for-profit institutions such as charitable institutions, Red Cross, NGOs, and others or physicians in private practice, clinics, hospitals, pharmacies, and laboratories.

In terms of coverage, clients from the public sector use 81.4 percent of the beds in the country; 74 percent of those correspond to the National Health Care System. The private sector is concentrated in the metropolitan region. Twenty percent of the population lack any kind of health care coverage [18].

### Health Status Indicators

Health status indicators show that Chile is going through an intermediate epidemiological situation with the coexistence of epidemiological profiles characteristic of both developing and developed countries.

Infant mortality in 1993 was 13.1 per 1,000 live births, and maternal mortality was 0.34 per 1,000 live births. Both are decreasing, due to the implementation of health programs focusing on the child and maternal group, better education of the population, and an increase in per-capita income.

In relation to transmissible diseases, the prevalence of tuberculosis is 33.3 per 100,000 inhabitants in 1993; with striking regional differences (variation between 112 and 23.5 per 100,000 inhabitants). The cholera epidemic that started in 1991 in Peru extended to Chile with an incidence of 66 cases in 1992, 33 cases in 1993, and 1 case in 1994. The decrease in the number of cases is due to an intense education campaign, better sanitary measures regarding food products and epidemiological surveillance. Those measures had a positive effect in the incidence of typhoid and other infection enteric diseases.

On the other hand, HIV/AIDS presents a trend towards increase with concentration of cases in the regions more developed economically. The national rate is 8.2 per 100,000 in 1994. There is a predominance of sexual transmission [91 percent of the cases) and 92.8 percent of cases are male.

In 1992 and in 1996 mass immunization campaigns were held for measles, followed by the implementation of a System of Active Epidemiological Surveillance. Since 1993, there is no death caused by measles. Only 2 cases of the disease were detected in the 1993-1996 period.

### Chilean Health Sector Reform

A new health sector reform in Chile is underway as part of the process of modernization of the State. In the public sector, the objective is to achieve greater efficiency in the management of its resources so that the most vulnerable segments of society will have access to more and better quality services.

The main problems of the Chilean health sector are the inefficiency in the management of public institutions, lack of an adequate legislation to regulate the private insurance market, absence of mechanisms to coordinate the actions of private and public sectors and lack of incentive in the public sector for the recruitment of human resources [6].

The decentralization process in Chile started in 1979 when the Ministry of Health transferred federal resources to regional health services and to the primary health care services entrusted to the municipalities. Both levels were granted financial autonomy. They were financed by either the National Health Care Fund or the ISAPRE. The ISAPREs buy the health services for its affiliates. Until 1987, that strategy, which had already made considerable progress since its implementation, was regarded as a success [12].

Since 1995, new decentralization strategies have been adopted focusing on the redefinition of the role of the central, regional and local governments in the management of the health system and services.

The reform emphasizes the role of the regional health services both as health care providers and as responsible for the establishment of priorities, planning, elaboration of investment projects and implementation of information systems. The strengthening of the managerial capacity at the regional level has been recognized as a condition for an efficient management of the human and financial resources available and of the actions taken at this level.

The Government is planning a closer collaboration between public and private institutions in the health sector as well with other sectors whose actions have an impact on the health status of the population.

Efforts are being made to reorient, based on criteria of equity, the financial resources of the FONASA, which is the public financing agency in charge of the administration of public health insurance. In addition, different forms of payment mechanisms for hospital care are being introduced.

The Chilean government is focusing also on strengthening the leadership and normative capacity of the State to perform regulatory control over the new modalities of social participation in the financing and delivery of services and goods. This includes improving the accreditation process of health facilities, increasing the control of laboratories, reinforcing the minimal standards of technical quality for the provision of health services, reinforcing the control over the ISAPREs and improving the mechanisms of financing and insurance reimbursement of the public health insurance.

Finally, the reform of the health sector in Chile is focusing on the management of human resources with the creation of monetary and non-monetary incentives to improve working conditions and increasing participation of the health personnel in training and performance evaluation. The goal is to strengthen the human resources managerial capacity at the local level and to create new legislation concerning new forms of payment aimed at keeping professionals from being driven out of public service into the private sector.

## External Technical and Financial Cooperation

Chile, due to the level of development of its health system, places more importance on the technical aspects of the cooperation than those of a financial nature. Nevertheless, the country has received financial support from WHO/PAHO in the 1990-1994 and 1995-1996 periods for the prevention of AIDS. Several bilateral agencies (Germany, United States, Holland, Italy, France, Sweden and Japan) provided financial support for development projects in the health sector during the 1994-1995 period for a total amount of around US$24 million. In terms of multilateral cooperation, in the 1994-1995 period, the European Union (EU) has given financial support for a project on prevention of drug use for US$986,440.

In the same period, the World Bank has financed several projects including rehabilitation of hospitals (US$3.3 million), institutional development (US$3.5 million), investment projects at the regional level (US$86.5 million). The BID has financed a project on rationalization of the regional services (US$70 million). The German government has lent US$31.75 million for rehabilitation of hospitals.

## Colombia

### Health Status Indicators

The country is going through demographic and epidemiological transition characterized by a coexistence of transmissible diseases and deficiency diseases and other conditions such as chronic and degenerative diseases and accidents, all of which affect more severely the most vulnerable segments of the population.

There has been a decrease in mortality for transmissible diseases in the 1983-1991 period which is associated with better education, extension of coverage of public health services, rise of public spending in health prevention programs, particularly mass immunization campaigns [7]. On the other hand, there was a considerable rise of mortality for external causes, those related to violence and accidents. In 1991, the rate of homicides was 90 per 100,000 inhabitants (87.9 percent males), compared to 32 per 100,000 in 1983 (82.6 percent males) [7].

Similarly, the decrease of child mortality rates for infectious diseases, especially diarrhea, pneumonia and tuberculosis, are associated with increased urbanization, better access to basic health care services, better quality services, better education, especially of mothers, better income and housing [7]. However, there are considerable disparities between regions, levels of urbanization and socioeconomic groups within regions, which reflect in the health status of the population.

Child and maternal mortality reduced to one-half between 1965 and 1990. In 1994, peri/neonatal mortality represented 43.5 percent of total death rates for children less than one year old which is consistent with problems regarding the assistance to mothers during delivery. One-fifth of pregnant mothers do not receive any kind of health care assistance during their pregnancy [9]. Abortion is the second cause of maternal mortality, representing 15 percent of the total of deaths related to reproductive health. The high number of abortions, which are illegal in Colombia, is due in part to the lack of access to contraceptive methods and health planning services [9].

## Health Sector Reform

Health sector reform in Colombia started in 1991, when a new Constitution was put in place recognizing social security as a right of all Colombians based on the principles of universality, equity, and efficiency.

Moreover, the new Constitution guarantees to all citizens the access to preventive, promotional, and public health services. The State takes the roles of leader, regulator, and policymaker, while the provision of services is the responsibility of either the public or private sector. The organization of services follows the decentralization strategies with increasing participation of the community. The municipalities acquire authority and administrative autonomy to manage the resources transferred from the central level of government.

In 1993, new legislation was created that focuses on reforming the National Social Security System (the System), which now guarantees a Basic Health Care Plan — a package of health services and benefits that includes curative, promotional, and preventive ambulatory care and access to essential drugs.

The whole population will be affiliated to the System through a contributive regime financed by payroll deduction for the higher income population and a subsidized regime for the poor (financed by tax revenues and transfers from the central government to departments and municipalities and to solidarity funds). Currently, only 48.67 percent of the population is affiliated to the System, 33.83 percent to the contributive regime, and 14.84 percent to the subsidized regime [9]. As part of the project of health sector reform, the institutional organization of the services went through a considerable change with the creation of the Health Care Promoting Entities (Entidades Promotoras de Salud — EPS), which are social security entities responsible for the affiliation of the population to the System, as well for the organization and provision of the mandatory health plan to its affiliates. These entities can be either public or private and are mandated by law to serve Colombians and their families under both regimes, contributive and subsidized.

Efficiency of the System is guaranteed by competition between the social security entities and by the fact that each individual is free to choose the entity for his/her affiliation. Furthermore, incentives were created according to the improvement of health indicators of the affiliated population. In addition, resource allocation is based on the demand of the population as opposed to the provision of services by the providers.

The Health Service Provider Institutions (Instituciones Prestadoras de Servicios de Salud — IPS) provide health services to the affiliates of the National Social Security System. The IPS may be associated or not with the EPS. They were granted technical and financial autonomy in order to strengthen their management capacities and efficiency, as well as to improve their capacity to compete with private providers.

The reform is guided by the principle of complementary services between public health services and those non-governmental services aimed at increasing the negotiation power of users and articulating a public/private mix of suppliers.

The public hospitals also were granted administrative, technical, and financial autonomy. In fact, they were turned into public state enterprises.

The progressive autonomy of those public institutions has forced the Ministry of Health to enforce its role as a regulator, resulting in the creation of new mechanisms of control, such as the implementation of a national program of accreditation of the IPS, auditing systems, and implementation of mechanisms of cost control.

The Colombian Ministry of Health is also responsible for setting priorities, policymaking, and formulation of plans and programs. The Ministry is also responsible for the evaluation of quality of care and for the control, orientation, and supervision of the National Social Security regarding such issues as the definition of reimbursement criteria, composition of the basic health and benefits package, amount of subsidies and selection criteria for those entitled to the subsidized regime, and list of essential drugs covered by the mandatory health plan.

## External Technical and Financial Cooperation

International Cooperation Agencies and Investment Banks participated with technical and financial support for several of the reform initiatives taken over the years [9]. In 1995, 56.6 percent of the total technical and financial cooperation given to Colombia, approximately US$80.9 million, was provided by multilateral agencies. The other 43 percent is represented by bilateral cooperation by countries such as Germany, Spain, and Canada. Since 1995, according to the priorities established by the National Plan of Development, social programs have been receiving 47 percent of the total external cooperation entering the country [9].

The Colombian government recognizes that international cooperation is an important support mechanism to its social and economic development in order to comply with the goals established in its Development Plan. Therefore, in March 1995, the government issued a document on international cooperation policies that will guide its national institutions in the establishment of priorities and coordination of the demands for international cooperation [9].

## Brazil

### Health Status Indicators

Brazil is going through a epidemiological and demographic transition, as are the other countries of the region. Recent estimates show that besides the increase in mortality for chronic degenerative diseases, a high prevalence of endemic diseases remains, along with the persistence and even increase of some infectious parasitic diseases such as malaria. In addition, there are cumulative incidences of AIDS affecting all segments of the population. Furthermore, as the urbanization process intensifies, a higher incidence of accidents and violence has been observed.

In 1992, the child mortality rate was 41.9 deaths per 1,000 live births. The rate varies widely, according to the region of the country: in the Northeast region it is 63.8 per 1,000, while in the Southeast region it is 25.9 per 1,000 [8]. There is also wide variation between urban and rural populations; the child mortality rate is twice as high in rural areas as it is in urban areas [8]. A study carried out in 1996 showed that in the last decade, the child mortality rate fell from 56 per 1,000 live births to 39 per 1,000, with significant variations between the two regions and related to mothers' educational levels and rural/urban populations [9].

The rate of maternal mortality fell 26.8 percent between 1982 and 1991. Rates for the year 1989 illustrate the disparity between regions: 153 maternal deaths per 100,000 live births in the Northeast region and 97 per 100,000 in the Southeast region [8]. The most important cause of maternal death is eclampsia (30 percent of the deaths).

In February 1997, 103,262 cases of AIDS were registered since the beginning of the AIDS epidemic in 1980; 74 percent of the cases were concentrated in the Southeast region of Brazil. In the last few years, important changes in the epidemiological profile of the disease were observed: while sexual transmission is predominant (66 percent of cases), there has been a reduction in the number of cases in the homosexual and bisexual groups in contrast with a progressive increase of cases in the heterosexual group, males and females [8]. In 1995, 11 percent of blood transmission cases were due to blood transfusions, compared to 40 percent in 1986; that result is attributed to the improvement of control mechanisms of blood donors in the whole country. On the other hand, in the same year, the number of AIDS cases due to drug use rose dramatically, making drug use now responsible for 87.9 percent of the registered cases through blood transmission [8].

## Health Sector Reform

Health sector reform in Brazil started in the beginning of the last decade. The movement toward reform started within the health sector in response to a health system highly centralized, focusing heavily on curative care and offering little coverage for the majority of the population.

The first actions addressed the issues of integration of health services and universal access to health services and social security. In the 1984-1987 period, as a result of those actions, there was some improvement in terms of the extension of coverage; inter-institutional coordination through the organization of health councils at the central, intermediate, and local levels; and complete utilization of the network of public health facilities. As a result of the extension of coverage, more resources started to be transferred from the central level, via the National Institute of

Health Assistance and Social Security (Instituto Nacional de Assistência Médica da Previdência Social — INAMPS), to the states and municipalities.

In 1987, the Unified and Decentralized Health System (Sistema Unificado e Descentralizado de Saúde — SUDS) was implemented, which represents the initiation of the decentralization process in Brazil — with the transfer of authority, management of resources, and decisionmaking from the federal to the state level; the implementation of health districts; the integration of health services; and the development of a human resources policy. The most remarkable effect of decentralization on the health sector structure was the "dissolution" of the INAMPS, which transferred its decision-making authority to the Ministry of Health and reassigned its state health secretaries to manage its medical assistance units.

The implementation of the SUDS facilitated the introduction of a health amendment to the Constitution of 1988, which, along with two other laws enacted in 1990, provided the legal framework for the current Unified Health System (Sistema Único de Saúde — SUS).

In compliance with the constitutional principles of promotion of equity, integration of services, and universal access, SUS has adopted the goals of decentralization of the health services; public financing; provision of public health services by a network of public and private providers; and community participation.

The decentralization strategies undertaken aimed at the creation of mechanisms and structures to foster the managerial capability of the states and municipalities. For this purpose, commissions were created at different levels of the System, with the participation of representatives of the Ministry of Health and state and municipal health officials, for inter-institutional negotiations and decision-making regarding the operation and implementation of the SUS.

Other mechanisms created concerning the management of the System and services at the national, state, and local levels are the Health Conferences, which are held periodically, and the National Councils. Both mechanisms count on the participation of health officials, members of civil society, and users.

The federal government plays the guiding role through policymaking, regulation, monitoring of the implementation of its national health policies, and the development of projects and programs that aim at sectoral development to ensure equitable access to health services for the whole population.

The municipalities are responsible for the provision of health services according to the needs of their populations, and for this purpose they receive technical and financial support from the central and state levels. Recently, all users of the System were issued a card that allows them to use health services outside the municipality of their residence. This mechanism is regarded as a means of strengthening the link between the SUS and its users [9]. Currently, 75 percent of the Brazilian population is covered by the curative and rehabilitation services of the SUS [8]. The SUS comprises all public health services at central, state, and local levels and those private providers under contract with the public sector.

Public spending in health was 3.3 percent of the GDP in 1989. In the following years, that figure went down to 2.7 percent of GDP in 1995. In the same year, the total spending as a percentage of GDP was estimated to be 4.1 percent when taking into account out-of-pocket spending [9].

The private sector encompasses individuals or groups in private practice and private providers contracted by insurance schemes such as employment-based insurance, prepayment schemes, medical cooperatives, and third-party payment mechanisms. Those insurance schemes are responsible for the coverage of 20 percent of the population, almost all of whom live in large urban centers [8]. All of the insurance schemes except for individual health care reimbursement are not regulated. Currently, the government is involved in a project that addresses the issue of regulation of all insurance schemes.

In its Plan of Action for the 1997-1998 period, the Ministry of Health stated two objectives that will orient its actions: improvement of the health conditions of the population, with emphasis on the reduction of child mortality, and political and institutional restructuring of the health sector, aiming at the modernization and rehabilitation of the operational capacity of the health system [9].

A series of interventions were identified that effectively will contribute to the achievement of those goals: improvement of quality, quantity, and efficacy in the delivery of services through the consolidation of the decentralization process and a balanced mix of preventive, promotive, curative, and rehabilitative programs; strengthening of managerial capacity at central, intermediate, and local levels, including development or restructuring of information systems, regulation and evaluation; reduction of child mortality, with an emphasis on integrated maternal and child health care; reduction of incidence and prevalence of transmissible diseases, through immunization, improvement of epidemiological surveillance, and AIDS prevention programs; strengthening the regulation of inputs to health care, such as drugs and equipment; and improvement of basic sanitation.

Several of the above interventions are being implemented, such as the Health Family Program, created in 1994 as part of the strategy of the reorganization of the basic health services network, with emphasis on health promotion actions at local and state levels. The Program of Community Health Agents is being expanded; in 1996, the program included 45,000 community health workers.

The mass media, particularly radio and television, have been used as important mechanisms for informing the population about health problems and the national government's priorities for acting on them. The so-called "national social communication campaigns" have been an important source for health education messages and health promotion. They have been used widely as part of the AIDS prevention program.

Many other programs have been implemented to address child and maternal health care, among those, the Project of Reduction of Child Mortality, an intersectoral collaboration for improving the articulation between child and maternal health care and basic sanitation. The project was implemented in 1995 and covers 913 municipalities with the highest indexes of poverty in the country [8].

A few municipalities where the decentralization process is more advanced carried out a project with participation of the community in the implementation of several intersectoral actions aimed at health promotion and improvement of the life conditions of the most vulnerable segments of the community. The Health Municipalities Project addressed issues such as housing, sanitation, food processing, job creation, and minimum wage for families [9].

Intersectoral collaboration strategies have also been adopted in the area of control of transmissible diseases. The focus is on sustainable intersectoral actions managed at the local level as opposed to vertical programs administered by the central government. However, the shortage of investment funds in the public sector has limited the implementation of that strategy [9].

## External Technical and Financial Cooperation

International technical cooperation has been playing an important role in the areas of management of health systems and services and quality control. Bilateral technical cooperation is provided by the following sources: Japan, United Kingdom, Canada, France, Germany, United States, Russia, India, China, Spain, and Italy. The cooperation usually consists of supporting either short- or long-term projects in specific areas of interest of both parties.

Brazil has cooperation agreements with several countries in the region, including Bolivia, Colombia, Venezuela, Paraguay, Cuba, and El Salvador. It also has official cooperation arrangements with several international NGOs whose principal interest is the health of indigenous populations.

Multilateral cooperation consists of Brazilian health sector participation in technical commissions of MERCOSUR, the Amazon Cooperation Treaty (Tratado do Cooperação Amazônica—TCA), different regulatory bodies on health care delivery in neighboring countries, and the Community of Portuguese-speaking Countries (Comunidade de Países de Lingua Portuguesa—CPLP).

PAHO's cooperation is based on support of the formulation of policies and programs and the establishment of priorities that are incorporated into the government's plans of action.

Financial cooperation has been provided by FNUAP, which provides considerable financial support for the Women's Health Program; the World Bank, which cooperates with large projects such as the NORDESTE Project, the project for controlling endemic diseases in the Northeast (PCDEN Project), and the project for controlling malaria in Amazonia (PCMAM Project).

The Ministry of Health signed a financial cooperation agreement with the World Bank and the IDB to execute the REFORSUS Project. One objective of the project is the rehabilitation of the infrastructure of health services, with emphasis on maternal health care facilities, emergency services in large urban centers, public health laboratories, and the hemotherapy network. Another objective is the development of the managerial capacity at all levels of the system, including the development of information and evaluation systems, formulation of health policies emphasizing decentralization, and improvement of the quality of health services. The project has an estimated time of three years, starting in 1997, and a total cost of US$650 million, with US$195 million to be applied in the first year [9].

Brazil has progressed in its subregional economic integration through its participation in MERCOSUR along with Argentina, Paraguay, and Uruguay. Currently, there is a proposal for harmonization of national legislation applied to the health sector in order to establish common standards, which would also facilitate economic integration among the participating countries.

A working group on health was set up, in compliance with the recommendation of the Ministries of Health of MERCOSUR, to address the issue of harmonization of standards of quality of services, medical devices, and mechanisms of sanitary control [9].

## VI. RECOMMENDATIONS

Several national and regional forums, seminars, workshops, and recently established national and international commissions for health sector reform have contributed significantly to an increase in information exchange among governments, civil society, and cooperating agencies. There is no doubt that important advances in regional integration were achieved through the mechanisms of consultation and horizontal cooperation — such cooperative efforts should be expanded, carefully respecting the specificity of the processes and national autonomy.

Nevertheless, to avoid the risk of lack of substance, any cooperative efforts should also be strengthened with in-depth systematization and analysis of health sector reform experiences, based on strong scientific and technical grounds.

Databases and mechanisms of dissemination of scientific information must be put in place, taking advantage of modern electronic means of communication and networking. The provision of scientific information will allow for more rational decisions from those actors who have the power to decide upon better courses of action.

There is a clear need to develop indicators to monitor progress and foresee obstacles to national reform processes as well as to evaluate the impact of interventions on some critical issues such as equity, quality, and efficiency.

A monitoring mechanism should be established to track and facilitate the implementation of Summit initiatives at the national level. Monitoring may also help to orient the activities of cooperating agencies providing technical and financial support for countries in the region and may help target those countries with the greatest need for external support.

There is also a need to develop scientific knowledge about organizational, financial, and operational aspects of health systems and services. Research capabilities should be strengthened through support of research groups and institutions, promotion of collaborative research projects, and development of mechanisms for dissemination and utilization of research results.

At the national level, Ministries of Health should strengthen their role regarding the coordination of external cooperation to national needs to avoid duplication of efforts and contradictions among different assistance proposals. In addition, the cooperating agencies should coordinate their support activities to enhance their impact on the countries of the region.

The Summit of the Americas represented an important benchmark in regional integration and served as a conceptual framework for what remains to be done in the countries of the region to achieve the goal of equitable access to basic health services for their populations. It helped to mobilize resources and political support for important issues in the health sector at national and regional levels.

Nevertheless, more could have been accomplished in terms of the implementation process of Initiative 17 on a regional basis if a monitoring system were established. From the beginning of the process, guidelines for monitoring the implementation of the initiative were created, indicators for expected outcomes had been developed, targets were well defined, knowledge of the current status of summit commitments in the countries was available, and available resources for carrying out the activities were known by the various participating actors.

# Notes

Note: Each entry in the list below is numbered. Within the text, the numbers in brackets indicate which sources were consulted for preceding material.

1. Pan American Health Organization. 1997. *Cooperation of the Pan American Health Organization in the Health Sector Reform Processes*. Washington, D.C.: PAHO. (ISBN 9275073740).

2. Pan American Health Organization. 1996. *Reunión Especial sobre Reforma del Sector Salud*. Washington, D.C.: PAHO. (ISBN 9275321981).

3. Panisset, U. 1997. "Armonización de Estandares para Equipos Médicos en el Ambito de los Acuerdos de Integración Regional." Working Paper Research Coordination. Washington, D.C.: PAHO. Mimeo.

4. Economic Development Institute (EDI) of the World Bank, Inter-American Center for Social Security Studies (CIESS), and Pan-American Health Organization. 1994. *Primera Reunión de la Red Interamericana sobre Economía y Financiamiento de la Salud*. Final Report. Mexico City: CIESS.

5. Pan American Health Organization. 1996. *Progress of Activities in Health Sector Reform*. Paper prepared for the XLVIII Meeting of the Directing Council. Washington, D.C.: PAHO.

6. Pan American Health Organization. 1995. *Health Sector Reform in Chile*. Report to the Special Section of the Directing Council. Washington, D.C.: PAHO.

7. Pan American Health Organization. 1995. *Health Sector Reform in Colombia*. Report to the Special Section of the Directing Council. Washington, D.C.: PAHO.

8. Pan American Health Organization. 1995. *Health Sector Reform in Brazil*. Report to the Special Section of the Directing Council. Washington, D.C.: PAHO.

9. Pan American Health Organization. 1997. "Health Conditions in the Americas." Draft for the 1998 edition. Washington, D.C.: PAHO. Mimeo.

10. Pan American Health Organization. 1997. "Health Sector Reform in the Americas: Equitable Access to Basic Health Services." Proposal from Pan American Organization to the United States Agency for International Development. Washington, D.C.: PAHO.

11. Pan American Health Organization. 1997. *UNICEF. TACRO. Interagency Agreement to Support Implementation of the Strategy for Integrated Management of Childhood Illness in the Americas (IMCI)*. Washington, D.C.: PAHO. (PAHO/HCP/HCT/ARI-CDD/96.41.).

12. Medici, André. 1995. "Financiamento da Saúde na América Latina e Caribe (Balanço e Opções para a Reforma)." Preliminary version. Washington, D.C.: IDB. Mimeo.

13. Partnerships for Health Reform (PHR) Project. 1997. *Abt Associates, Inc. PHR Work Plan for the LAC "Equitable Access" Initiative*. Proposal from PHR to the United States Agency for International Development (USAID). Bethesda, Md.: PHR.

14. Londoño, J.L., and J. Frenk. 1995. "'Structured Pluralism': Towards a New Model for Health System Reform in Latin America." The World Bank, Technical Dept. for the LAC Region. Washington, D.C. Mimeo.

15. Londoño, J.L. 1996. "Managed Competition in the Tropics?" Paper presented at the International Health Economics Association Inaugural Conference, Vancouver, in May 1996. Mimeo.

16. Londoño, J.L. 1995. "Is There a Health Gap in Latin America? — A Graphical Exposition." The World Bank, Technical Dept. for the LAC Region. Washington, D.C. Mimeo.

17. Barillas, E. 1997. "Organización, Gestión y Evaluación de los Servicios de Salud: Mas alla de la Reforma Prescrita." Presented at the IV Congreso Latinoamericano de Ciencias Sociales y Medicina, Cuernavaca, México, in June 1997. Mimeo.

18. Londoño, J.L., and O. Icoechea. 1996. "Latin American Health Care Systems: A Simple Description of Their Financing and Organization." The World Bank, Technical Dept. for the LAC Region. Washington, D.C. Mimeo.

# V. LEADERSHIP COUNCIL FOR INTER-AMERICAN SUMMITRY

## *Postscript:* The Summit of the Americas

*Cristina B. Cunico*

At the Miami Summit of the Americas, the governments of the region made a series of commitments that were expressed in Initiative #17, Equitable Access to Basic Health Services. The Initiative included the reduction of child and maternal mortality rates; health sector reform aimed at increasing equity, quality, and efficiency of services; and establishment of programs to prevent the propagation of HIV/AIDS and endemic and transmissible diseases.

The *Plan of Action* of the Miami Summit of the Americas established the responsibility of the Pan American Health Organization (PAHO) for the coordination of the implementation of Initiative #17 as well as Initiative #23, Partnership for Pollution Prevention, and Initiative #18, Strengthening the Role of Women in Society. In my paper I have only commented on Initiative #17 as that was the main core of the health initiative in the Miami *Plan of Action*.

Since the Miami Summit, PAHO, along with other cooperation agencies, has made significant progress in the implementation of several Initiative #17 action items.

The governments of the region continue their efforts to reduce child and maternal mortality rates. PAHO/WHO, the United Nations Children Fund (UNICEF), and the United States Development Agency (USAID), among other cooperation agencies, have been working together on the Integrated Management of Childhood Illness (IMCI) strategy to treat and prevent the leading health problems and diseases responsible for most of the deaths in children younger than five years. The strategy includes educating health workers on how to evaluate major problems and diseases affecting children's health, educating parents on how to care for children at home, and the prevention of illness through vaccination. Between 1996 and 1997, nine countries with the highest child mortality rates have adopted the IMCI strategy and initiated its implementation at the local level of health systems. For the future, there are plans for strengthening the application of the IMCI strategy in health services and extending coverage both at the regional and the country level.

Also in compliance with the mandate of child mortality reduction, the governments have established national surveillance systems for vaccine-preventable diseases (diphtheria, tetanus, pertussis, polio, measles, and tuberculosis). It has been reported by PAHO that at least 80 percent of the children in the region are protected against those diseases. Noteworthy is the hemisphere initiative for eradication of the measles virus by the year 2000. Considerable progress has been made toward achieving that goal; transmission has already been interrupted in many countries of the region, and the number of confirmed cases reported has declined from more than 240,000 in 1990 to 2,109 in 1996.

Efforts to reduce maternal mortality rates have been focused on improvement of emergency obstetric care, improvement in coverage, and quality of reproductive health services in several countries of the region. PAHO and USAID have been active in addressing those issues through the realization of a joint project at the regional level. The Inter-American Development Bank (IDB) and the World Bank have also increased their investments in the maternal health and maternal mortality components of their projects being carried out in several countries of the region.

At the Miami Summit, the governments expressed their commitment to develop, in accordance with mechanisms adopted by each individual country, reforms in the health sector designed to meet the targets of equitable access to basic health services, improvement of quality and efficiency of services, and greater participation of social actors. To date, the majority of countries in the region are going through reforms of their health sector. Moreover, the health sector reform has been an essential part of the programs of action of regional agencies of cooperation.

PAHO was the agency chosen to establish national evaluation mechanisms for monitoring the health reform process, its results and effects. In this regard, PAHO is developing a network for the exchange of experiences and a monitoring mechanism for sectoral reform in the region.

Another development related to the health sector reform mandate and to the interagency collaboration mandate in support of the reform processes was the strengthening of the existing Inter-American Network on Health Economics and Financing (REDEFS). The network has been active in facilitating significant exchanges of knowledge and experience through promotion of seminars, workshops, and training in health economics and finance.

Finally, as a consequence of the mandates for combating endemic and communicable diseases and developing a program to prevent the spread of HIV/AIDS, a Regional Plan was adopted for countering the threat of new, emerging and re-emerging diseases. Besides the measles eradication resolution of September 1994, the hemisphere approved a resolution in September 1996 urging the countries to cooperate in the preparation of a hemisphere-wide plan for the eradication of dengue. In addition, in the 1995-1997 period, PAHO prepared a Regional Plan for HIV/AIDS prevention and control in connection with the new Joint United Nations Program on AIDS (UNAIDS). This plan is being implemented, in coordination with the countries, throughout the region.

Even though many of the activities related to Initiative #17 of the Miami Summit were already part of programs of actions of individual countries and of regional cooperation agencies, the Miami Summit helped foster a regional agenda addressing the most critical health problems and, in the process, encouraged hemispheric cooperation to deal with some of those problems. That common agenda is responsible for successful regional initiatives, such as the Measles Eradication Plan of Action launched in 1995, the strengthening of collaborative efforts of cooperation agencies within the countries of the region, and greater interagency coordination and collaboration in their support and assistance activities.

Notwithstanding the progress achieved by regional governments in the health situation of their peoples since the Miami Summit, important problems still remain of limited access to basic health services, poor quality of services, and unsatisfactory health conditions for large population groups.

At the second Summit of the Americas, held in Santiago, Chile, April 18-19, a very different approach was adopted with regard to the health agenda. Health has been aggregated to several other issues pertinent to the broader context of the development agenda, the focus being on poverty alleviation and equitable distribution of the benefits of economic growth.

The Declaration of Santiago states that overcoming poverty is the greatest challenge facing the hemisphere. The measures adopted to resolve those health problems related to poverty, social inequities, and environmental deterioration focus on efforts to ensure access by the poor to adequate health services, proper nutrition, and a healthy environment as well as access to new health technologies.

The action item "Eradication of Poverty and Discrimination" has two initiatives directly related to health: Health Technologies and Hunger and Malnutrition. Two other initiatives — Women and Indigenous Populations — aim at improving the standard of living of those groups through, among other measures, greater access to health care for the indigenous populations and promotion of policies designed to improve women's health conditions and the quality of health services at every stage of their lives.

At the Miami Summit, health technologies such as sanitation and water supply fell under Initiative #23: "Partnership for Pollution Prevention" and thus were not part of the scope of this paper. Health technologies such as vaccines and health information and surveillance systems fell under Initiative #17.

In addition to the endorsement of the commitment made at the Miami Summit of strengthening the immunizations programs to prevent the propagation of endemic and transmissible diseases, at the Santiago Summit, the governments proposed strengthening their countries' capability for research, development, and production of new and improved vaccines against such diseases as pneumonia, meningitis, measles, rubella, and mumps. Moreover, the governments expressed their commitment to seek, through public and private sectors or partnerships between them, to enhance the availability, access to, and quality and safety of vaccines and essential drugs, especially for the most needy.

One priority of the Miami Summit was regional support for health reform processes. Although the health reform process, underway in the majority of countries in the region, was not part of the Santiago Summit agenda, the governments reaffirmed their commitment toward the development, implementation, and evaluation of need-based health information systems and technology to support the operation and management of health services and programs and the development of surveillance systems.

In my research, I identified the need for the establishment of databases and monitoring mechanisms, taking advantage of electronic means of communication, to monitor and evaluate the impact of health reforms. These databases could also be used as mechanisms of dissemination of technical-scientific information to assist policymakers, health professionals, and managers regarding some of the critical regional health issues. The governments have addressed those same issues at the Santiago Summit, including the use of telecommunications, telemedicine, computer networks for epidemiological surveillance, health education and promotion, and operation and management of health services and programs. Moreover, the governments agreed to make investments in new health technologies to deal with priority health problems in addition to developing mechanisms for evaluating the relevance and cost-effectiveness of those technologies.

The governments have also pledged to make every effort to ensure that the necessary resources are allocated for carrying out the lines of action of the Santiago Summit Plan of Action, with the technical support of the Pan American Health Organization (PAHO).

In my research, I pointed out the importance of collaboration between countries and technical and financial cooperation agencies in support to the commitments made by governments at the Summit of the Americas. In fact, at the Santiago Summit, the governments have pledged to promote bilateral and multilateral collaboration. Furthermore, they requested that the Inter-American Development Bank (IDB) and the World Bank, along with other technical and financial cooperation institutions, support the programs and activities included in the Health Technology initiative.

At the Miami Summit, the governments endorsed the goals set at previous international Summits regarding the reduction of child and maternal mortality through the provision of a basic package of clinical, preventive, and public health services to attend to child, maternal, and reproductive health.

At the Santiago Summit instead, the governments through the initiative Hunger and Malnutrition have placed the highest priority on the reduction of infant malnutrition and on the nutritional and caloric needs of women before and during pregnancy and while breast-feeding. To that end, emphasis was given to health, nutrition, and educational programs for the nutrition of infants and children less than three years-old and promotion of breast-feeding as critical to the nutrition of children in their first four to six months of life. Those activities will be carried out along with greater use of vaccination and immunization and monitoring of child's growth. The governments have also agreed to address the nutritional needs of other high-risk groups, such as the elderly and the disabled.

Regarding the Hunger and Malnutrition initiative, the governments also agreed to explore the application, in their respective jurisdictions, of the measures suggested at the Inter-American Conference on Hunger, held in Buenos Aires in October 1996. Those include the creation of alliances with the private sector to fight hunger and malnutrition, the creation of food bank networks, and the creation of an Honorary Council dedicated to fostering activities to reach Summit objectives in this area.

Even though some of the topics in the Miami Summit Initiative #17 have not even been mentioned at the Santiago Summit, governments have advanced progress on some other activities related to that initiative through specific commitments and implementation mechanisms. It seems that at the Santiago Summit, governments have chosen to adopt a different line of action from that of the Miami Summit. One reason for that might be that the health area was regarded within the context of the "Eradication of Poverty and Discrimination" action item, and therefore, the commitments made by the governments during the Santiago Summit would have to express their concerns for the health problems more closely related to poverty and social inequities, such as hunger and malnutrition and vaccine-preventable diseases.

It is noteworthy that the implementation of the set of initiatives laid out in the Eradication of Poverty and Discrimination action item, not only those concerned with the health area, will have a strong impact on the health conditions of the people of the region to the extent that better income and housing, better education, and reduction of social inequities are by themselves associated with decreases in child and maternal mortality and improvement of the population's health situation.

One should expect that significant progress will be seen in the future regarding the implementation of the Santiago health initiative because, first of all, contrary to Miami Initiative #17, the targets were fewer and more specific, although timetables for each of the activities are still missing. Second, the governments have pledged to make every effort to allocate the resources needed to carry out the activities. Indeed, the World Bank, the IDB, and USAID have already committed $12.5 billion for a period of three years to reducing poverty in the region. Third, there are already regional and national monitoring mechanisms in place or in the process of being implemented to monitor and evaluate the impact of the interventions. Fourth, the governments have pledged to work in collaboration with NGOs, the private sector, the Pan American Health Organization (PAHO), the World Bank, the Inter-American Development Bank (IDB), and other financial and technical cooperation institutions in support to the commitments made at the Santiago Summit.

Finally, the summits have become "institutionalized," which will help foster compliance by governments and cooperation agencies and lay the groundwork for stronger mechanisms for monitoring and evaluating the countries' follow-up on their summit promises. Last but not least, a next Summit of the Americas has already been scheduled for Canada within the next two to three years, and the planned topic is health, which will certainly contribute toward advancing progress in the implementation of the mandates of the Santiago Summit.

# V. LEADERSHIP COUNCIL FOR INTER-AMERICAN SUMMITRY

# Developing, Liberalizing, and Integrating Financial Markets

*Manuel Lasaga*

*Manuel Lasaga, Ph.D. in economics, is an economics and finance consultant and president of Strategic Information Analysis, Inc., Miami. Dr. Lasaga has extensive management and research experience in analyzing Latin American, North American, and global economies and in formulating business strategies. He also is an adjunct professor in the Department of Finance at the University of Miami.*

## SUMMARY

The timing of the Summit of the Americas was ideal in terms of the challenges and opportunities facing the financial environment. The financial sector initiative in the *Plan of Action* is an ambitious agenda calling for the full-scale integration of capital markets in the Americas. The design of the three stages (development, liberalization, and integration) implies that regional financial integration should proceed according to a reasonable sequencing of tasks. The experience with reforms during the past 15 years underscores the importance of a balanced and properly sequenced approach to structural economic and financial sector reforms.

The European experience with a single market can provide valuable insights regarding procedures, sequencing of tasks, and identification of critical issues associated with the regional integration of financial markets. Some of the critical success factors in the formation of the European Community (EC) are as follows:

- Regional integration was a gradual process characterized by the sequencing of goals and objectives.

- Liberalization of capital flows was conditioned on appropriate currency arrangements with safety mechanisms for vulnerable countries. In view of Latin America's chronic currency management problems, much greater attention should be focused on this issue.

- Regional integration was facilitated by emphasis on basic principles. Integration of financial markets involved agreement on market fundamentals; participants thus avoided getting caught up in micro-management of complex issues.

- Regional integration involved all aspects of the financial sector: banking, securities, and insurance.

The capital markets initiative in the *Plan of Action* is a comprehensive mission statement with guidelines for initiating the process of integration. The May 1996 New Orleans Communiqué was a first attempt at verbalizing some action steps in the implementation of that initiative. The New Orleans document thus became the Work Program for the financial sector initiatives. While the Work Program has the potential to move in the right direction, it could benefit from better focus on fewer issues and much greater consultation with market participants in order to facilitate its implementation.

The principal issues regarding the design of the Work Program are as follows:

- As a minimum, the Work Program could have started with just three activities pertaining to the original *Plan of Action*: 1) review of existing hemispheric financial sector agreements, 2) preparation of a comparative analysis of financial sector regulations, and 3) discussion of supervisory practices.
- In view of the complexity of the issues dealing with financial integration, the amount of information that needs to be centralized, and the huge responsibility associated with the monitoring of dozens of initiatives, a fully dedicated institution is necessary.
- In the design of program initiatives, much greater consultation with the private sector would have been useful. A more formal arrangement based on periodic consultations with private sector representatives would enhance the Work Program's effectiveness.
- Although well-intentioned, the emphasis on the training of supervisors may detract from the Work Program's priority of discussing mechanisms for effective integration. Contrary to what the Work Program may imply, the strengthening of regulatory standards is already being handled at the national level. More attention should be given by the CHFI to discussions on appropriate techniques for consolidated supervision in a regional context.
- Two important issues not mentioned in the Work Program are national tax regimes — specifically, the treatment of financial sector operations — and the adequacy of foreign investment laws.
- The initiative to review the problems of debt in our hemisphere is somewhat surprising considering the high degree of success during the 1980s in the debt workout process.

Several conclusions can be drawn from the brief analysis of the experience with financial sector reforms in the four countries selected for this study (Chile, El Salvador, Mexico, and Peru):

- With respect to the development continuum, the four countries are at an advanced stage in terms of development of financial sector legislation and are moderately advanced in terms of liberalization.
- The experience of these countries demonstrates that the design and implementation of their reform agendas occurred independently of the Summit initiatives, although the Summit did provide some external support of existing reform programs.
- All four countries underwent extensive restructuring and modernization of the financial sector in response to major crises.
- The design of new financial sector legislation and the reforms to the regulatory structure reflect a dynamic agenda focused on the globalization of financial markets. At the same time, there is concern on the part of regulators as well as market participants for the vulnerability of their system to external factors.
- In recent years there has been a notable increase in awareness of the importance of adequate supervision to prevent future crises.

Overall, implementation of the Summit's Work Program is considered good. The program needs to focus on fewer issues supported by more aggressive action steps.

Some of the lessons learned from this analysis include the following:

1. It is important to identify the proper sequence for financial sector integration. The Work Program thus needs to identify the appropriate tasks at the national level for regional integration.

2. Among other things, the European experience points to the importance of currency stability and arrangements and to the need for a gradualistic approach to integration.

3. The design of the Summit Work Program for the financial sector should follow the original president's goals more closely. The actual Work Program released at the New Orleans meeting of Finance Ministers diverted attention to some areas that were outside the scope of the original principles. At the same time, the agenda did not address the establishment of a forum to discuss guidelines on capital movements.

4. The design of a Work Program needs to be simple and realistic. Too many tasks can lead to a bottleneck in the implementation process. Ownership of the program by individual players is also key to its effectiveness. A number of countries have not actively participated in this process.

5. In the design of complex financial sector initiatives, it is important to identify the entity charged with its implementation. Because of the multiplicity of Summit initiatives, it would be highly desirable to establish a fully dedicated secretariat.

6. One of the key ingredients missing from the implementation of the Summit initiatives is financial

# V. LEADERSHIP COUNCIL FOR INTER-AMERICAN SUMMITRY

## Developing, Liberalizing, and Integrating Financial Markets

resources. If there is no political will to channel resources, both human and capital, into the integration process, then the framers of the Summit erred on its timing.

7. International conferences provide a good forum to disseminate critical information on issues pertaining to integration and to keep the regional community informed about progress on integration initiatives.

8. Before developing a regional integration strategy, it is important to recognize significant differences across countries in terms of their locations on the financial sector continuum. As mentioned in the analysis of the country experiences, there is a critical mass of reforms that can already serve as a basis for the identification of convergence criteria for financial sector integration. Discrepancies with respect to these core areas need to be examined for relevance; otherwise, they can be left to national preferences. Special issues such as dollarization need to be studied and recommendations provided. The crises experienced by some countries should serve as the basis for the development of adequate safeguard mechanisms.

## BACKGROUND

The timing of the Summit of the Americas was ideal in terms of the challenges and opportunities facing the financial environment. The globalization of financial markets had intensified pressures in the Americas to open up markets, while the successful resolution of the debt crisis of the 1980s had paved the way for new relationships for financial flows within the hemisphere. One of the lessons from the crisis was that greater efforts were needed in promoting domestic savings and in attracting greater foreign investment. However, the Mexican financial crisis in 1995, which broke out only days after the Summit in Miami, and a similar crisis in Venezuela a year earlier pointed to the risks associated with rapid structural changes accompanied by a lack of institutional capacity to assimilate and control the new structures.

The Summit of the Americas held in Miami produced a comprehensive *Plan of Action* for integration in the hemisphere. One of the initiatives in the document dealt with the financial sector. About 18 months later, the Ministers of Finance issued a Work Program for the implementation of the Summit initiatives for the financial sector. This report analyzes these initiatives and reviews the implementation experience. Reference to the financial sector and capital markets as used in this report, and in keeping with the intent of the original Summit document, includes the banking and securities markets but excludes the insurance industry.

## THE FINANCIAL SECTOR MULTIDIMENSIONAL CONTINUUM: DEVELOPMENT, LIBERALIZATION AND INTEGRATION FOR BANKING, INSURANCE, AND EQUITY MARKETS

The financial sector initiative in the *Plan of Action* is an ambitious agenda calling for the full-scale integration of capital markets in the Americas. It is a mission statement for the transition from a disparate, segmented, volatile and from time to time unstable regional environment to an open, efficient, stable, predictable, compatible and dynamic system that supports sustainable economic growth in the region. The action continuum encompasses three essential stages: development, liberalization, and integration. The two dimensions of this system identified in the *Plan* were banking and equity markets; insurance was excluded. By breaking the integration process into three stages, the participants recognized the wide dispersion across the financial sectors in the hemisphere. Even though the goal of full integration at this point is rather ambitious, considering the number of countries involved and their differential stages of development, the emphasis on progressive integration through stages establishes a more realistic agenda.

Banking systems vary considerably in terms of their development. The United States is by far the largest and strongest system, yet it is very restrictive in terms of the separation between commercial and investment banking dating back to the time of the Great Depression. Nevertheless, the banking industry in the rest of the Americas has shown notable progress in terms of institutional development and market liberalization. The debt crisis in the early 1980s led to the realization that the solution to financial sector problems was through structural reforms not through quick-fix stabilization policies.

After the collapse of the banks in Chile, their nationalization in Mexico, a severe crisis in Venezuela, the subsequent nationalizations in Central America and Peru, notable failures in Brazil, and decapitalization in Argentina, many of the countries embarked on a fundamental restructuring process during the latter part of the 1980s supported by the technical advice of the multilateral agencies. This approach achieved notable success. Almost a decade after the crisis, in the early 1990s, most of the countries in the hemisphere had already adopted modern banking legislation. Nevertheless, another important lesson was to be learned by the subsequent banking crises in Venezuela (1994) and Mexico (1995), accompanied by severe liquidity problems in Argentina.

Modern laws by themselves are not a guarantee for a healthy and dynamic financial system. A critical ingredient is the quality of financial management both in the public and the private sectors. In other words, a healthy financial system is dependent on adequate supervision of market players, who, in turn, are inclined to pursue sound management practices. The Venezuelan and Mexican experiences also point to the risk of dramatic and ambitious reform agendas. Without proper sequencing and appropriate timing for implementation, the financial sector reform agenda can become overloaded, even though with well-intentioned measures, and thus short-circuit the whole financial intermediation process.

The design of the three stages (development, liberalization, and integration) implies that regional financial integration should proceed according to a reasonable sequencing of tasks. For example, the recent emphasis on banking system reforms in Latin America has not been to the neglect of the securities markets or insurance. A strong banking system provides a good foundation for development of the securities and insurance markets. Of course, a stable macroeconomic environment is a pre-condition to the sustainability of all reforms.

On the other hand, the sequencing of regional integration initiatives should not be interpreted within a narrow perspective. Since the mid-1980s, there has been ample discussion regarding the appropriate design of structural reforms. As the pioneer in the development of structural adjustment lending, the World Bank has learned many lessons on sequencing and on the speed of reform implementation. One of the basic lessons from their experience has been that initial conditions are critical to the design of an effective reform program, especially in the financial sector.[1] At the same time, the speed of reforms will play a critical role on the quality of the outcome. In this arena, there are two opposite approaches: 1) the Big Bang, which calls for a full-scale all-out dramatic one-time shock treatment, and 2) the gradual approach, which recommends step-wise changes with adjustments along the way. Once again, the experience has demonstrated that initial conditions are critical in defining what approach to take. A country with a long history of stable financial conditions, with a national consensus on reform policies and with a strong institutional framework, would be a good candidate for a Big Bang adjustment. The Big Bang approach also works well in the context of macro policies such as exchange rate liberalization, de-controlling of prices, and tariff reforms; however, it does not work well when applied to the reform of complex institutional arrangements such as public sector management reforms — specifically when it involves downsizing a bloated bureaucracy.

Because of the notable differences between various financial systems in this hemisphere, in terms of development and liberalization and the lack of consensus as to a regional integration agenda, a regional integration strategy for the financial sector based on the sequencing of individual initiatives would produce the best outcome. Of course, this could be accomplished through simultaneous tasks introduced at the appropriate timing. The speed of adjustment would obviously depend on the initial conditions. The disparity between financial systems was evident during the The North American Free Trade Agreement (NAFTA) negotiations. In fact, some of the agreements on market entry were framed in terms of transitional measures, based on a 15-year adjustment period, aimed at giving Mexico time to further develop and liberalize its own markets. On the other hand, the tie-in to policy coordination between the two countries and the almost instant response from policymakers led to Mexico's strong recovery from the peso crisis in 1995.

The challenge facing any regional integration initiative is appropriately to identify each country's progress on the continuum for each of the three major components or dimensions: banking, equities, and insurance. The fact that many countries are still implementing financial sector reforms does not in any way diminish the importance of initiating a dialogue regarding possible formulas for financial markets integration. No two countries will adopt an identical agenda in financial sector development. For this reason, it is imperative to identify a common denominator and then to negotiate a meaningful common ground. One starting point could be the recently negotiated General Agreement on Tariffs and Trade (GATT) agreement on trade in financial services. Another approach that has been suggested by the Working Group on Small Economies is to work within existing subregional accords as a basis to negotiate a critical path to more uniform standards. If key rules and regulations are not in synch, any attempt at integration, no matter how well intentioned, could wreak havoc on individual financial systems as investors redeploy their assets to benefit from blatant arbitrage opportunities arising from such distortions as differential cross-border pricing, taxation, and information requirements.

# V. LEADERSHIP COUNCIL FOR INTER-AMERICAN SUMMITRY

## THE EUROPEAN MODEL FOR FINANCIAL SECTOR INTEGRATION

The Summit of the Americas *Plan of Action* called for the integration of capital markets. The principal action step contained in the *Plan* was to "form a Committee on Hemispheric Financial Issues (CHFI) to examine steps to promote the liberalization of capital movements and the progressive integration of capital markets, including, if deemed appropriate, the negotiation of common guidelines on capital movements that would provide for their progressive liberalization."[2] While there may be differences of opinion among countries about the timing or the degree of integration, the goal of a single hemispheric financial market is clear in the Miami declaration that was signed by the participating presidents.

As a precursor to the Summit initiatives, the experience in Europe with the successful creation of a single market in 1992 is a relevant model for the development of a similar process in the Americas. The European Community (EC) is the first successful multi-country market and currency arrangement. It is the only working model of a formal regional integration mechanism. Obviously, the Europeans were far more advanced than the Americas toward regional integration when their process was first formalized. Nevertheless, the EC experience can provide valuable insights regarding procedures, sequencing of tasks, and identification of critical issues associated with the regional integration of financial markets.

Perhaps the most relevant lesson is that the formation of a single market in Europe was a gradual process that started with the Treaty of Rome in 1957 and culminated 35 years later with a single market. Notwithstanding their impressive accomplishments, the Europeans are still working on the merging of their currencies into the Euro, which is scheduled for 1999 contingent on the compliance by each participant of certain convergence criteria.

As clearly stated by the participants from the outset of the process, a precondition for the creation of a single market in Europe was the liberalization of capital movements between member nations. The European Community took the first step toward the free flow of capital in 1960 with the reduction of some barriers to cross-border movement of funds and securities. The gradual elimination of exchange controls had to incorporate transitional status for certain countries with vulnerable currencies that thus needed the controls as a shield against disruptive capital movements. After several successful steps, an EC Directive in 1988 adopted the complete liberalization of capital flows by 1990.[3]

The sustainability of the free flow of capital hinges on the stability of the currencies, which in turn depends on the quality of monetary and fiscal policies and the success of policy coordination between countries. After the breakdown of Bretton Woods and subsequent decision to allow floating exchange rates in 1973, the EC looked for a mechanism that would assure the stability of their currencies. Thus, in 1979, the European Monetary System was established with member currencies pegged to the European Currency Unit (ECU). Each currency would be allowed to fluctuate in value within a prespecified band with realignments from time to time. In 1989, an agreement was reached that linked the completion of a single market with the move to a single currency.

In tandem with the progressive integration of foreign exchange markets, the creation of a single European market for financial services involved three components: banking, securities, and insurance. The process involved the issuance of numerous Directives by the EC that addressed different aspects of consolidation. One of the principal goals was to establish suitable conditions for the issuance of a single EC license for banking, securities, and insurance. A division of powers was achieved by assigning primary supervisory responsibilities to the home countries and the oversight of financial intermediaries' business with customers to the host countries. A single license offered several advantages to a financial firm, including 1) use of a single capital base, 2) consolidation of management functions throughout the EC, and 3) a more coherent set of regulations and fewer regulators.[4]

The decision to name the home country regulators as the primary supervisor of financial institutions operating across EC countries gave rise to the concept of consolidated supervision. Parallel discussions within the Basle Committee on Banking Supervision also provided essential input in the framing of EC policies, including the development of policies and procedures for consolidated supervision. The Basle Concordat on consolidated supervision was introduced in 1983, expanded in 1990 and again in 1992. The Directive on consolidated supervision issued in 1983 established that the supervisor of a financial institution was required to examine all its operations on a consolidated basis at least yearly. In 1992, a new Directive extended the treatment to holding companies and their affiliates.

One of the key strategic decisions dealing with the integration of various country markets occurred with the White Paper of 1985. The goal was to develop a core of essential regulations and standards. It was decided that no attempts would thus be made to impose community rules beyond a set of core principles. Thus, member countries agreed to the mutual recognition of rules and regulations established by individual countries that went beyond those required for basic harmonization.

For the EC, the process of financial market integration basically involved two stages: first, the liberalization of capital transactions and, second, the deregulation of financial markets. Some of the mechanisms they developed, such as division of labor between regulators across countries and the standards for consolidated supervision, will prove useful in the design of similar efforts in the Americas. In fact, the buzz word in the hemisphere has become effective regulation through consolidated supervision. However, more attention also needs to be paid to the liberalization of capital markets transactions. Some of the critical success factors in the formation of the EC are the following:

1. Regional integration was a gradual process characterized by the sequencing of goals and objectives. Concern about potential destabilizing effects from liberalization of capital flows led to a cautious approach.
2. Liberalization of capital flows was conditioned on appropriate currency arrangements with safety mechanisms for vulnerable countries. In view of Latin America's chronic currency management problems, much greater attention should be focused on this issue. In recent years, a number of Latin American Central Banks have been experimenting with the use of a currency band. This mechanism is similar to that developed by the EMS without the currency matrix that keeps their values within a prespecified range.
3. Regional integration was facilitated by emphasis on basic principles. Integration of financial markets involved agreement on market fundamentals; participants thus avoided getting caught up in micromanagement of complex issues.
4. Regional integration involved all aspects of the financial sector: banking, securities, and insurance.

## THE DESIGN OF THE SUMMIT INITIATIVES FOR THE FINANCIAL SECTOR

The capital markets initiative in the *Plan of Action* is a comprehensive mission statement with guidelines for initiating the process of integration. The goal, as stated in the Summit document, is to work toward integrating capital markets while strengthening the regional regulatory process. The May 1996 New Orleans Communiqué was a first attempt at verbalizing some action steps in the implementation of that initiative (see Annex). The New Orleans document thus became the Work Program for the financial sector initiatives. While the Work Program has the potential to move in the right direction, it could benefit from better focus on fewer issues and much greater consultation with market participants in order to facilitate its implementation.

According to the *Plan of Action*, the governments agreed to 1) form a Committee on Hemispheric Financial Issues (CHFI) to examine steps to promote integration and, if deemed appropriate, to negotiate common guidelines; 2) call on the Interamerican Development Bank (IDB) to prepare a comprehensive list of national capital regulations in order to support the process of negotiations; 3) support the Association of Latin American and Caribbean Bank Supervisors (ALACBS) and the Council of Securities Regulators of the Americas (COSRA) in strengthening the regulatory process in the context of integration; and 4) review the problems of debt in the hemisphere. An earlier version of the initiative presented by the United States contained a more ambitious goal of negotiating a Hemispheric Capital Movements Code that would facilitate the free flow of capital.

The Work Program announced in the New Orleans ministerial meeting assigned the CHFI numerous tasks, including the support of existing national initiatives, the completion of studies and surveys, the organization of conferences, and the development of training programs. The issues to be studied included the relationship between economic performance and financial markets; existing capital markets regulations in each country; ways to improve access to medium- and long-term financing; ways to increase private sector savings, that is, pension funds; and management of the overall debt situation, especially in the poorest countries. Based on these studies, the CHFI was to prepare policy recommendations for a ministerial meeting within two years. As part of this process, the IDB was to organize three meetings to discuss steps governments can take to facilitate financial sector development. In addition, an analysis of laws affecting the financing of private sector activity was to rely primarily on private sector input and to cover the following areas: private property rights, bankruptcy regimes, commercial dispute resolution, and competition policy. The training programs were aimed at banking and securities markets supervisors and at institutions involved in the combating of financial crimes.

# V. LEADERSHIP COUNCIL FOR INTER-AMERICAN SUMMITRY

Because of the multiplicity of interests and the compromises needed to keep all parties satisfied, the design of the financial sector Work Program became too ambitious and suffered from lack of clarity in terms of objectives. This design problem was also identified by Richard Feinberg (1995) in other Summit initiatives. In the case of Europe, the formation of a single market began with modest proposals in the 1960s, and once they gained momentum, the process was accelerated. Simple logical steps have a better chance of achieving a complex goal, at least if they allow time for mid-course adjustments.

One of the key elements in the design of financial sector initiatives is appropriate sequencing of tasks. This does not necessarily mean implementing each initiative separately until completion. Once the process of regional integration gets going, several initiatives can be implemented simultaneously, such as the negotiation of currency targets and the development of currency futures and options markets. On the other hand, it would not make much sense to train supervisors without a banking law that gives them authority to perform their duties. The experience with structural reforms has demonstrated a bias toward an overly ambitious policy agenda. While well-intentioned, policymakers sometimes attempt to accomplish too much too fast, fearing their political window of opportunity will be short-lived. Part of the problem is the mixing of certain macroeconomic reforms such as price liberalization, which can be executed almost instantly, with complex institutional reforms such as administrative reform of the public sector, which takes much time to implement and must overcome great political resistance. In the case of regional integration strategies, policymakers need to be sensitized to the disparities among the financial sectors of various countries. The financial crises of Latin America in the past 15 years demonstrate that a Big Bang approach can lead to a Big Bust of the financial sector.

Focusing on the initial conditions through a comparative analysis of financial systems in the hemisphere is a logical first step in the identification of a feasible agenda for regional integration. For example, the Small Economies Group has been focusing its efforts on two basic areas: 1) the analysis of critical factors in determining the performance of small economies and 2) the identification of technical assistance needs of small economies in preparation for regional integration. The design of any initiatives involving the development, liberalization, and integration of markets for 34 countries requires a gradual approach that starts with a narrow agenda that can then be expanded based on actual results. As a minimum, the Work Program could have started with just three activities pertaining to the original *Plan of Action*: 1) a review of existing hemispheric financial sector agreements, 2) preparation of a comparative analysis of financial sector regulations, and 3) discussion of supervisory practices.

The success of the Work Program will depend critically on the effectiveness of the institution(s) responsible for its implementation. The Interamerican Development Bank (IDB) was prominent in the Summit Declaration dealing with financial sector issues; specifically, it was assigned the task of preparing a comprehensive list of financial sector regulations. From the start, the IDB has been viewed as a temporary secretariat for hemispheric initiatives. In the New Orleans Communiqué, it was assigned a coordinating role in terms of programs with other multilateral agencies. In addition, the IDB was asked to fund the training program for regulators and for entities involved in combating financial crimes. As a regional development bank, the IDB has strong expertise in the financial sector. Nevertheless, its primary function historically has been to serve as a facilitator in the financing of economic development. If the IDB were now to assume a much bigger role in the process of financial integration, it would detract from its principal economic development objectives.

In view of the complexity of the issues dealing with financial integration, the amount of information that needs to be centralized, the huge responsibility associated with the monitoring of dozens of initiatives, a fully dedicated institution is needed to accomplish these tasks. Whether a single entity to handle all Summit accords or just those for the financial sector, the *Plan of Action* and the Work Program should have been more forthcoming in assigning this responsibility to one entity. A more appropriate forum would be a single agency for all Summit initiatives, since this would greatly facilitate the coordination between different areas such as trade and finance. Primary responsibility for the management of a permanent secretariat for financial issues should rest with the Central Banks of the region. Such an agency could be named the Monetary Council of the Americas, the Financial Integration Fund — similar to the Regional Integration Fund proposed by the Small Economies Group — or the Americas Financial Board. This entity would be staffed by individuals with extensive background in economics and finance and with policy-making as well as operational capabilities.

While the IDB could reasonably assume the role of provisional secretariat, more attention needs to be paid to a permanent agency, whether newly created or adapted from an existing organization. The sustainability of a program that involves the development, liberalization, and integration of regional financial markets hinges on the appropriate institutional infrastructure, which in turn requires significant financial resources. Perhaps the question of whether there is sufficient political will to pursue the integration agenda needs to be answered first.

A permanent secretariat would have the additional advantage of in-house resources that could be used to support the smaller economies with their own work programs. Due to resource limitations, Finance Ministries in smaller economies are usually preoccupied with the country's own policy agenda. In addition, they have to respond to commitments with international and multilateral agencies. At the same time, a permanent policy-making body could be more responsive to an overriding concern of small economies that they be assured a level playing field for their own home-grown firms once they open their markets to foreign investors. A fully dedicated secretariat could also provide technical assistance in the formulation of regional integration policies at the national level. The Working Group on Smaller Economies is currently considering a proposal for a Regional Integration Fund that would achieve these objectives.

In the design of program initiatives, greater consultation with the private sector would have been useful. A number of associations, such as the Latin American Federation of Banks (FELABAN) and individual country banking associations as well as regional and national securities dealers associations, can play an important role in the framing of financial sector initiatives. In fact, FELABAN (1995) commissioned a basic study of existing global and regional integration initiatives that already provides the basic groundwork for further discussion. The study points out that with the spread of global, regional (ALADI), and subregional (CARICOM, MERCOSUR, NAFTA) accords, a major challenge is to keep track of all the individual agreements and to resolve conflicting practices between subregional accords.

One of the experiences of financial reforms in the region has been a tendency by governments to make decisions without sufficient consultation with the private sector. For instance, a government may adopt a policy regarding regulatory capital requirements that could in turn jeopardize some financial intermediaries' ability to engage in certain activities even though these transactions would not be detrimental to capital adequacy. For this reason, a practice of circulating proposed changes to rules and regulations to market participants would be highly desirable. Likewise, proposals for regional integration should be circulated to representative private sector working groups whose participants have the technical expertise to analyze the initiatives and to provide useful input. Limiting private sector participation to selected international forums would not take advantage of their valuable experience in the marketplace. A more formal arrangement based on periodic consultations with private sector representatives would enhance the Work Program's effectiveness.

Although well-intentioned, the emphasis on the training of supervisors may detract from the Work Program's priority of discussing mechanisms for effective integration. The need to strengthen regulatory functions is an ongoing process that has gathered much greater attention after the recent banking system crises. The lessons from recent banking system problems have pointed to the quality of management, both in the public and in the private sectors, or the institutional capacity as a key ingredient to the safety and soundness of the financial sector. Even the most advanced and complete financial systems laws cannot prevent bad credit and investment decisions, mismanagement of liquidity, and lack of adequate supervision. A country with sophisticated state-of-the-art banking legislation could experience a major systemic collapse, while a country with an outdated banking law could continue to function with a stable system and a healthy currency. The ideal combination would be modern financial sector law combined with an effective regulatory institution and a level playing field that promotes healthy competition.

Contrary to what the Work Program may imply, the strengthening of regulatory standards is already being handled at the national level. The Work Program initiatives on training of regulators should not be a part of the CHFI's agenda. The Latin American Association of Banking Supervisors and COSRA have been actively involved in disseminating best practices to member countries. The multilateral agencies have also been providing technical assistance in this area. In terms of the *Plan of Action*'s goal of supporting the regulatory process, more attention should be given by the CHFI to discussions on appropriate techniques for consolidated supervision in a regional context. In recent years, policymakers have intensified the application of consolidated supervision standards, and as the European experience demonstrated, this is an important ingredient for effective integration of financial markets. Awareness of this issue in the Americas was heightened with the passage of the U.S. Foreign Bank Supervision Enhancement Act of 1991, which called on the Federal Reserve to grant operational licenses only to those banks whose home country regulators were considered to use the principles of consolidated supervision. In terms of integration priorities, the regulators' training requirements can be better handled by the individual countries who, if necessary, could seek technical assistance from regional associations or the multilateral agencies. Likewise, the agenda on training of agencies involved in the combating of financial crimes could be delegated to a regional association of regulators who could better focus on the specific needs of individual countries.

Two important issues not mentioned in the Work Program are national tax regimes — specifically, the treatment of financial sector operations — and the adequacy of foreign investment laws. One of the principal factors behind the movement of capital to off-shore locations is differential tax regulations. The agenda for financial sector integration should include consideration of uniform taxation. On the other hand, existing foreign investment laws vary considerably across countries. One of the critical factors to the free flow of capital is the development of compatible foreign investment laws at the national level that assure equal treatment to all investors, whether domestic or foreign, and provide investors with basic guarantees. Careful analysis of existing legislation and the identification of common principles governing the treatment of investment should be part of the overall integration agenda.

The initiative to review the problems of debt in the hemisphere is somewhat surprising considering the high degree of success during the 1980s in the debt workout process. The average debt to export ratio of Latin America has fallen from 3.2 times exports in 1990 to 2.3 times exports in 1996. The management of the debt crisis is a tribute to the effectiveness of financial intermediaries, supported by responsive and well-guided officials of various monetary authorities and multilateral agencies. The term Brady Bonds, named after former U.S. Secretary of the Treasury Nicholas Brady, is the epitome of market solutions to financial sector problems: Huge loan syndications from the 1970s and early 1980s were converted into small denomination tradable securities with credit enhancements and after discounting the original face value of the loans. Despite these improvements, external debt continues to be a burden in some countries, particularly some of the smaller, highly indebted countries. However, the issue of additional solutions to high-debt countries might be more appropriate to a small economies group rather than part of the overall regional agenda for financial integration. In fact, the Paris Club continues to play an instrumental role in the management of the external debt of smaller economies.

The design of the financial sector Work Program needed more emphasis on monitoring mechanisms as well as deadlines for each of the major components. This is a weakness that has been commented on by Feinberg (1995) with respect to Summit initiatives in other areas. Having a permanent secretariat would greatly facilitate the monitoring process.

Considering that the goals established in the Summit *Plan of Action* were well thought out, there appears to be lack of ownership in the Work Program. Not all countries have actively participated in this process. The CHFI needs to be more embracing in terms of governmental as well as private sector participation. In the final analysis, the success of a regional integration strategy will hinge on the willingness of each participant to abide by the rules of the game.

## PROGRESS REPORT ON THE IMPLEMENTATION OF THE FINANCIAL SECTOR INITIATIVES

Any review of the Work Program related to the Summit's *Plan of Action* must recognize that for an agenda likely to require decades to implement, it is too soon to reach any definitive conclusions as to the effectiveness of the initiatives much less their sustainability. For that reason, this analysis is limited to an evaluation of incremental measures in the context of the overall goals; thus, it is only a progress report.

The first meeting of the CHFI, which is de facto the implementing agency for the Summit Initiatives relating to the financial sector, was held on July 25, 1995, and since then four additional meetings have been held. The CHFI is co-chaired by the United States and Chile. In addition, a Financial Sector Working Group on Small Economies was created in March 1997 but has not yet met. Based on the summaries of these meetings, the activities appear to have concentrated around the IDB survey of financial systems, the preparation of the Work Program announced by the Ministers of Finance at the New Orleans summit in May 1996, and the discussion of various issues affecting the performance of regional financial systems.

CHFI's Work Program is still at a very basic level in terms of the overall goals and objectives established by the presidents at the Miami Summit. An underlying benefit of this process so far has been the opportunity for Finance Ministers and other economic policy technicians to establish a productive policy dialogue. However, the Work Program needs to be more aggressive and focused on fewer issues.

Independent of the Work Program, the multilateral lending agencies' long-established development financing agenda has been the critical factor to their own positive contribution to the implementation of Summit initiatives. The IDB, International Monetary Fund (IMF), and the World Bank have developed an extensive loan portfolio aimed at supporting financial sector development and liberalization throughout the hemisphere. In fact, all three agencies were instrumental in the resolution of the external debt crisis in the 1980s, and commercial banks relied on their recommendations when making decisions on debt reschedulings. Thus, closer coordination among these agencies and the CHFI could further enhance the Work Program. Nevertheless, as mentioned in the earlier section, it may not be advisable to divert the attention of these agencies away from their lending and policy advice roles to that of facilitator of regional financial markets integration strategies.

As noted in the analysis of its design, the implementation of the Work Program has also been characterized by limited consultation with groups outside the circle of financial sector officials. Early in the process, the multilateral agencies were approached by CHFI representatives to gather information on their activities. On the other hand, very little interaction with private sector representatives has been noted. During the New Orleans Ministerial meetings, several sessions were held with the Latin American Business Council and the Inter-American Council for Commerce and Production. However, the relevant players in this arena are the commercial and investment bankers and securities dealers. Closer communications between the CHFI and the regional banking associations, such as FELABAN (Federation of Latin American Banks), national bankers associations, as well as those of securities dealers would be desirable. For example, there are more than 600 foreign banks in the United States that control about 40 percent of U.S. banking assets. There are several organizations that represent them: the Institute for International Bankers, the International Bankers Advisory Council, the International Bankers Association of California, the Florida International Bankers Association, not to mention the American Bankers Association and the National Association of Securities Dealers. Yet none of these organizations has been actively consulted.

One of the greatest obstacles to the implementation of the Summit initiatives has been a lack of financial resources. Several programs, such as the comparative analysis of financial sectors and the training of regional regulators, have been long delayed, while others, such as the review of critical legislation governing investments, have been eliminated due to a lack of financial resources. The emphasis on macroeconomic stability through sound fiscal policies has resulted in drastic cutbacks in government spending. On the other hand, any progress toward liberalization and integration of regional markets is bound to accelerate the growth of intraregional trade and thus provide tangible economic benefits that could be measured against the initial investment of resources. At the same time, global competition is intensifying, and the ability to sustain job growth will hinge on new mechanisms to enhance regional trade. Without a sizable injection of fresh resources, the Summit's Action Program may lose relevance as an effective vehicle for regional integration. Of course, a realistic assessment of financial costs can only be surmised from detailed plans for each of the initiatives, which is beyond the scope of this analysis. The key point is that lack of resources has so far been a principal deterrent to progress on the Work Program, and it would thus follow that additional resources are needed to enhance the efficacy of the program. Greater outreach to the private sector and to non-governmental organizations could result in additional financial resources, as well as enrich the final product by making it more responsive to market needs.

## Support of Existing National Initiatives

To a large extent, the Work Program defined by the New Orleans Communiqué was a recognition of existing financial sector development and liberalization initiatives that were already adopted by participating countries and supported by the multilateral agencies. In this regard, the Summit initiatives have initially served as an external support platform for compatible national agendas. Independent of the Work Program, the Latin American Association of Banking Regulators had already identified consolidated supervision as a high priority in their issues agenda; thus, the Summit initiatives in this area have helped to strengthen their efforts. Likewise, at this year's annual meeting, COSRA agreed to address the following issues: 1) new standards regarding external auditors, 2) the development of an educational campaign for individual investors, and 3) an assessment of regulations affecting mutual funds. Once again, the compatibility of its work agenda with the Summit initiatives will help COSRA in achieving its objectives.

The Work Program's goal to improve economic and financial information was helpful in providing additional support to the IMF's own agenda in this area. The IMF has been working on homogeneous reporting stan-

# V. Leadership Council for Inter-American Summitry

dards since the early 1950s when they introduced International Financial Statistics (IFS), which is considered an authoritative source of information and is used by financial institutions throughout the world. IMF contributions also include the Balance of Payments Manual and the Fiscal Accounts Manual that have set the standards for reporting by all countries. More recently, the IMF has begun to make available its country reports to outside analysts. To the extent that the CHFI introduces new concepts in financial reporting associated with regional integration efforts, the IMF is bound to be a logical ally in the dissemination of those practices.

## Studies and Surveys

The principal activity in this area, as reported by the CHFI meetings, is the IDB survey of financial sector regulations. While this work has not yet been made available outside the multilateral agencies or the CHFI, it appears to be a very ambitious comparative database of 26 countries. The questionnaire used to survey the countries contained more than 3,000 items. The IDB is putting together a CD ROM with the data and will present the results at the December meeting of the finance ministers. This information could be useful in a subsequent phase to identify common grounds for financial sector integration. The survey should provide a snapshot of practices and procedures. It is hoped the presentation of the survey results will segregate the information along key functional areas in order to facilitate future discussions on integration.

The survey represents an exhaustive list of regulations at one point in time. However, it may need to be converted into a dynamic document that focuses on key areas. Perhaps a less ambitious survey in terms of the number of items covered would have streamlined the process of implementation and contributed to a quicker turnaround in terms of survey responses. The challenge of identifying structural differences in terms of the development, liberalization, and integration continuum at this very early stage of the process could have been addressed within a more simplified framework organized around key areas such as credit limits, permissible activities, capital adequacy, quality of assets, liquidity and market risk, financial conglomerates, corporate governance, supervision, auditing standards, and financial disclosure and then moved on to a more in-depth analysis in a subsequent phase.

The CHFI now needs to consider how to update a smaller version of this survey in order to keep abreast of new country initiatives as the integration process continues. The financial sector is continuously evolving within a dynamic process, and as a consequence, the rules of the game are frequently modified to fit the new financial realities. For this reason, a one-time survey would quickly lose relevance as a dynamic instrument for defining regional integration strategies. The design of the survey may also have benefitted from additional consultations with market participants. For instance, none of the regional banking and securities associations and associations of regulators were consulted in terms of the design of the questionnaire.

One of the initiatives dealing with reviews of national laws affecting the financing of the private sector was dropped from the agenda of the New Orleans Communiqué. The focus of this analysis was to be on the following areas: private property rights, bankruptcy regimes, commercial dispute resolutions, and competition policy; and it was to rely on extensive input from the private sector. Two of the reasons given for not going ahead with this project were the lack of financial resources and that there were no clear ideas on the usefulness of the final product. From the perspective of an over-loaded agenda, this decision was appropriate. However, further consideration might have been given to dropping another initiative instead. At least consultation with market participants might have helped in making the decision. Perhaps one of the greatest impediments to medium- and long-term financing has been the absence of adequate collateral in the form of property rights and ease of foreclosure in the event of insolvency. An alternative approach would have been a less ambitious project on review of the national laws that would have provided some useful information for preliminary discussions on the subject.

## Conferences

International conferences can play a very useful role as a networking opportunity for market participants. Just as industry conferences help to bring together individuals with common business interests to discuss the latest trends and to develop new contacts for future ventures, the conferences hosted by the IDB helped to raise the awareness of the CHFI's work throughout the hemisphere. These conferences can attract reputable experts to discuss issues of relevance to the development of the integration agenda. The proceedings of the conference can serve as a useful reference library for future policy discussions.

The IDB was assigned the task of organizing three conferences. The first, entitled *Building Modern and Effec-*

*tive Banking Systems in Latin America and the Caribbean*, was held on August 8, 1997, in Buenos Aires, Argentina. The second on October 28, entitled *The Development of Securities Markets in Emerging Markets: Obstacles and Preconditions for Success*, was held in Washington, D.C. The third conference is planned for December 1, just prior to the Ministers' meeting in Santiago, Chile. The first two conferences offer a broad variety of perspectives on selected topics. It is hoped more conferences will be offered in the future in order to keep the community abreast of developments with the integration agenda. Perhaps some more attention might be given to private sector participants in future conferences. For instance, out of 31 panelists in the first conference, 20 were government officials, five were from multilateral agencies, three were academics, and three were bankers. For the second conference, out of 28 panelists, the proportions were 15 government officials, six from multilateral agencies, two academics, and five representatives from the securities industry.

## Training Programs

The development of training programs has been spearheaded by the IDB. The goal is to assist in the training of bank and securities supervisors. The IDB has had to allocate internal resources to fund a small pilot program. It has met with banking and securities regulators to assess their training needs. Once again part of the delay in implementation has been the lack of financial resources. The allocation of these limited resources to specific training programs will be made on a needs basis, and the trainers will be chosen according to standard international bidding criteria. In view of its extensive experience with technical assistance programs and in supporting financial sector adjustment operations, the IDB was a good choice for managing the training program. The technical assistance program for combating financial crimes is still in the design stage. The IDB has been coordinating this initiative with the Organization of American States (OAS); however, lack of financial resources once again continues to block further progress.

## Recent Experiences with Financial Sector Development and Liberalization in Chile, El Salvador, Mexico, and Peru

One of the determining factors in the outcome of development, liberalization, and integration initiatives is the initial conditions in each of the countries. The road to convergence and the speed at which it can be accomplished will also depend on the compatibility of national policies and thus the potential for greater policy coordination. Fortunately, economic policy decisions at the national level have already started to approach a common threshold. The success of economic reforms during the past decade is noteworthy in the financial sector where most countries have adopted similar legislative agendas. Where differences do exist across countries along the developmental continuum, a gradual multivariate approach to integration is recommended. In this regard, the CHFI needs to identify a feasible set of conditions that will serve as a common denominator, with appropriate safeguards for vulnerable economies. Once again, attention to appropriate sequencing can avoid perilous consequences.

In order to review recent trends and current status of financial markets, a sample of four countries — Chile, El Salvador, Mexico, and Peru — was chosen on the basis of size, geographical location, and historical experience with financial sector development. This brief analysis attempts to underscore differences in background, recent convergence regarding basic principles of reform (an essential ingredient for successful integration), and the role that the Summit process has played in these developments.[5]

One of the challenges in evaluating the results of the Work Program in terms of individual country experiences is the ability to identify those components of the CHFI program that have had an impact on financial sector development and liberalization programs at the national level. In other words, which national policies have been 1) designed and implemented as a result of the Summit process, 2) redesigned in response to the Summit agenda and also supported by it, 3) designed independently of the Summit agenda but supported by it, and 4) designed and implemented independent of the Summit agenda. A preliminary assessment is provided for each of the four countries.

*Chile*. The financial sector of Chile went through dramatic changes starting in the 1970s, and since the mid-1980s, it has evolved as a model of stability and dynamic growth. In the early 1970s, the Salvador Allende administration nationalized the banking system. Following the 1973 coup, the military government privatized banks and launched a program of deregulation. However, the rapid pace of deregulation and lax supervision, combined with the fixed exchange rate instituted in 1979, eventually led to a commercial banking system crisis in 1982. The authorities had to intervene to avoid a financial sector collapse and have remained extremely cautious ever since.

The Chilean banking system has strengthened considerably since the 1982-1983 crisis. The banking system is one of the most sophisticated in the hemisphere, offering a wide range of products. Competition is fierce, which explains the low interest rate spreads prevalent in the Chilean market. Increasingly, companies are raising equity in the stock market, turning to large investors or tapping foreign financial sources. Most financial institutions have a relatively low-risk portfolio. The percentage of past-due loans to total loans declined from 2.1 percent at the end of 1990 to 0.9 percent at the end of 1995. It is becoming evident that the banking system is outgrowing the relatively small Chilean market, and financial institutions have begun to expand aggressively into neighboring countries. This underscores the importance of regional integration strategies as financial institutions are expanding into other neighboring markets in the hemisphere.

Chile's regulatory environment is compatible with internationally accepted standards and would have no problem in meeting any core principles of prudential supervision that would be established by a hemispheric integration council. The principal supervisors of the financial system are an autonomous Central Bank and the Chilean Banking Supervisory Agency (CBSA). The Central Bank has sole responsibility for the formulation of monetary and exchange rate policies. The Banking Supervisory Agency is a dependency of the Finance Ministry. It is charged with examination and ongoing supervision of banks, which includes overall evaluation of the banks' financial positions, operations and asset quality, and qualification of bank directors. The banks are limited to undertaking only those activities allowed by the CBSA.

Congress recently approved a new banking law, which opens the way for Chilean banks' regional expansion. Under the new law, banks can engage in cross-border lending and leasing. In addition, there is greater flexibility in establishing branches, affiliates, and subsidiaries overseas, including the possibility to invest in other banks, either as a minority or majority shareholder. The Chilean law allows overseas expansion only into those countries where regulators are considered to apply the standards of consolidated supervision. In the securities field, a new law last year established Foreign Investment Funds. These are local investment companies that are authorized to invest their portfolios overseas. The Foreign Investment Funds are expected to derive most of their business from existing pension funds which to date have relied on foreign investment managers. Under review in Congress is a new law to establish an international securities exchange that would allow foreign companies to raise capital in the Chilean market. This will be particularly relevant for the subregional markets of Argentina, Brazil, Bolivia, and Peru. In addition, discussions are being held on draft legislation for an off-shore financial center strictly for nonresidents.

In 1996, Chile agreed to co-chair the CHFI. Based on the above-mentioned accomplishments, their leadership role in the CHFI could add needed dynamism to the Summit process. As for the influence of the *Plan of Action* and Work Program on reforms of the financial sector, it appears that they have been designed and implemented independently of the Summit agenda, although the latter reflects the good policies adopted by Chile.

*El Salvador.* The financial sector of El Salvador was jolted by severe volatility in the 1980s, particularly as a result of the domestic conflict. The banking system in El Salvador was nationalized in 1980, with the government assuming full control of all financial intermediaries. During the 1980s, the financial sector had been extremely repressed, thus experiencing substantial losses that eroded its capital base. The downturn in the economy induced by the civil war made commercial banking operations very difficult. When President Cristiani assumed office in 1990, one of his goals was the restructuring and privatization of the banking system.

A new Central Bank law in 1991 eliminated the old Monetary Board and granted the Central Bank autonomy in the management of monetary policy. It also prohibited the Central Bank from further credit activities. Liberalization of interest rates occurred in 1992, when all deposit and loan rates were made market-determined. The development of open market operations in the early 1990s is proving effective in controlling the monetary aggregates, although the unusually large size of these operations has strained domestic liquidity in recent years.

During 1990-1991, the government approved several laws dealing with the restructuring of the banking system. The legislation set the stage for first reviving and then privatizing the banks. It also strengthened standards with respect to the safety and soundness of the financial system. The government began to privatize the banks in 1991, a process that was completed in 1995. The new legislation was in line with internationally accepted banking practices.

Supervision of banks and finance companies falls under the authority of the Banking Superintendent under a Financial System Superintendency formed in 1991. As part of an innovative approach to supervision, the Superintendency of the Financial System was divided into three sections: 1) financial institutions, 2) securities exchange, and 3) pension system.

The positive trends in the Salvadorean banking sector can be attributed to the favorable environment created by the banking legislation in 1990-1991. Reforms to the banking legislation included raising the minimum capital requirement for banks and reducing the maximum that can be lent to shareholders from 50 percent to 5 percent of total capital, and credit to related parties was limited to 25 percent of capital, down from 50 percent. Greater leniency was introduced in the release of information regarding the identity of stockholders owning more than 1 percent of the shares of a financial institution. Risk-based capital requirements were increased to 10 percent from 8 percent. The reforms also allowed foreign banks to offer a full range of services and facilitated their operations in El Salvador. These features of the legislation could very well form part of a critical mass of financial sector conditions for regional integration.

Prior to 1992, El Salvador had no formal capital market. This situation changed as a result of the government's reform program initiated in 1990. The Securities Exchange (Bolsa) was created in February 1992. The principal instruments traded in the bolsa today are government bonds and bills and Monetary Stabilization Certificates. Most of the paper issued by private sector companies is in the form of investment certificates, which are mostly money market instruments offered by a very select group of large corporations. El Salvador has been an active participant in the Central American Common Market's goal of establishing a regional securities exchange.

Being a small economy, El Salvador has had little impact or participation in the deliberations of the CHFI; nevertheless, its policy reform agenda provides many useful elements that could be applied to the regional integration efforts. In terms of the relationship of the *Plan of Action* and the Work Program, El Salvador's reforms have been designed and implemented independently, although the Work Program reflects similar initiatives.

*Mexico*. Mexico introduced multipurpose banking in the mid-1970s, which explains the high degree of consolidation in the financial system. Under that system, banks could perform the functions of depository institution, savings bank, mortgage bank, and finance company. President Lopez Portillo nationalized the banking system in 1982. In 1990, Congress approved a constitutional reform to privatize the Mexican banks, which were subsequently sold to private investors during 1991-1992.

Under the reforms introduced in 1990, a financial services holding company was allowed to own banks, brokerage houses, insurance companies, and other financial intermediaries. Capital adequacy is based on internationally accepted standards, with the minimum regulatory capital at 8 percent of risk-weighted assets. Lending limits equivalent to 30 percent of capital for corporate borrowers apply to a single borrower as well as to related parties and affiliates. Banks must classify their loans on a quarterly basis, and provisions must be made accordingly. A minimum liquidity coefficient is required according to the type of deposit liability — that is, DDAs, time, savings deposits, and foreign credits. Banks can invest in shares of stock of nonfinancial enterprises up to 5 percent of total stockholders' equity. Mexican banking practices as established in the 1990 reform legislation also conform to internationally accepted standards. Many of these components are compatible with those applied in other regional economies, hence, the appropriateness of initiating discussions on regional integration efforts.

Monetary policy is managed by the Central Bank (Banco de Mexico). The Central Bank regulates the money supply through the setting of reserve requirement rates and through open market operations. It does not set interest rates but allows them to be determined by the market or influenced through its intervention via open market operations. Constitutional changes approved in 1993 gave Central Bank legal autonomy in the implementation of monetary policy.

Supervision of the banking system involves several entities: the Ministry of Finance, which issues regulations governing banks and grants banking licenses; the National Banking and Securities Commission (CNBV), which monitors compliance with laws and regulations and is responsible for bank examinations; and the Central Bank, which acts as lender of last resort and supervises foreign exchange regulations. In the past, supervision had been weak, and financial disclosure requirements were not very strict. The 1995 financial sector crisis has nonetheless triggered new efforts to strengthen banking and securities markets supervision. In a regional context, the lessons from Mexico's crisis could be used by the CHFI in making recommendations on adequate safeguards for other countries.

The banking system suffered sizable losses as a result of the 1995 financial crisis sparked by the devaluation and the consequent deterioration in their loan portfolio. The solvency of a number of institutions was thus compromised as the crisis spilled over into the first half of 1995. Since the financial system had accumulated a huge amount of short-term dollar-denominated foreign liabilities, the government was compelled to negotiate a rescue package from several large industrial countries in the form of special lines of credit. A mechanism was established through the Central Bank and the deposit guarantee fund (FOBAPROA) to provide liquidity assistance to banks. A program was initiated to recapitalize the banks (PROCAPTE) by allowing them to issue subordinated debt. A loan restructuring program was instituted whereby the banks could tap Central Bank funds to restructure their mostly short-term loans into five- to 12-year indexed loans. Finally, the government amended the foreign ownership regulations to allow foreign banks to acquire up to 100 percent interest in Mexican banks.

The Summit process has had little impact on Mexico's financial sector reforms, although the Work Program reflects the basic ingredients. The Mexican experience provides valuable insights into the reform process and the importance of proper design and sequencing. As a participant in NAFTA, it serves as a good model for the design of regional integration initiatives, especially for transitional measures.

*Peru.* The financial sector of Peru has gone through dramatic changes since the crisis of the 1980s. The government used to exert almost total control over the banking system through direct ownership of banks and through regulations. For example, the state still controlled 68 percent of assets and was responsible for 73 percent of employment in the financial sector in 1990.

One of the goals of the Alberto Fujimori administration was to launch a comprehensive financial sector reform program in 1991. The principal elements of this strategy included 1) the closure and downsizing of development banks, with remaining institutions lending only through private sector financial institutions; 2) removal of subsidized lending; 3) privatization of commercial banks; 4) reform of the banking system's regulatory environment; and 5) development of the capital markets and pension funds.

In 1991, new banking legislation was approved. The new legislation adopted the universal-type banking model. Strict rules were approved regarding credit limits to single borrowers, to other banks, and to affiliates and related parties. Loan classifications were made more responsive to potential credit losses. Capital adequacy rules were specified according to the internationally accepted risk-weighted assets standards, and as of 1993, the minimum capital ratio was set at 8 percent of risk-weighted assets. The new law also increased the powers and granted greater flexibility to the Superintendency of Banks. These reforms were within the scope of internationally accepted standards and created a critical mass for the liberalization of the financial sector.

The banking law of 1993 opened new areas of business such as leasing, insurance, and stock brokerage. By expanding into new lines of business, commercial banks have enhanced their profitability. The influx of foreign commercial banks has also contributed to increased competition.

The financial system has a high proportion of assets and liabilities denominated in foreign currency. The fact that the reserve requirement rate on dollar deposits is very high (45 percent) reflects the concern of the monetary authorities over the degree of dollarization of the monetary system. The dramatic opening of the economy since 1990 has aggravated the vulnerability of the financial intermediaries to a sudden outflow of capital. In contrast to the other three countries in this analysis, the Peruvian experience with dollarization of the financial sector introduces a critical issue for discussion of regional integration. Dual-currency regimes accentuate the vulnerability of the financial sector to capital flows. Once again as the EC experience demonstrated, discussion of currency arrangements should be a starting point for the development of any regional strategies.

The Superintendency of Banks and Insurance Companies oversees local banks. The Central Bank manages monetary policy and sets foreign exchange policy. Banking regulators were given broad powers under the 1993 banking law and, more recently, under the revised 1996 banking legislation, which also adopts the standards of supervision recommended by the Basle Agreement. The reforms to the securities law and the pension system have also laid the groundwork for sustainable development of the capital markets.

The equity markets have shown an impressive growth in terms of market capitalization. During 1991-1995, market capitalization increased by a factor of ten times, from $1.118 billion in 1991 to $11.795 billion in 1995, making it one of the fastest growing emerging country equity markets. This bodes well for sustained growth supported by further expansion of the pension funds.

The Peruvian reform agenda once again appears to have been developed and implemented independently of the Summit process. The rapid expansion of its capital market should lead to some consideration of uniform regional standards for securities markets that would allow cross-border expansion of these activities.

*Conclusions from the Recent Financial Sector Experiences.* Several conclusions can be drawn from the brief analysis of the experience with financial sector reforms in the four countries:

- With respect to the development continuum, the four countries are at an advanced stage in terms of development of financial sector legislation and moderately advanced in terms of liberalization. All four countries are active in subregional integration accords: Chile within MERCOSUR, El Salvador within the Central American Common Market, Mexico within NAFTA, and Peru has been seeking greater participation in MERCOSUR and diminishing its role within the Andean Pact.

- The experience of these countries demonstrates that the design and implementation of their development and liberalization agenda occurred independently of the Summit initiatives, although the Summit did provide some external support of existing reform programs.

- All four countries underwent extensive restructuring and modernization of the financial sector in response to major crises. Chile began the reform process in the mid-1980s, although extensive reforms had already taken place in the 1970s, whereas the other three countries achieved a critical mass of reforms at the beginning of the 1990s.

- The design of new financial sector legislation and the reforms to the regulatory structure reflect a dynamic agenda focused on the globalization of financial markets. At the same time, there is concern on the part of regulators and market participants of the vulnerability of their system to external factors.

- In recent years, there has been a notable increase in awareness of the importance of adequate supervision to prevent future crises. Financial sector regulators have been given much greater powers to act before a crisis unfolds.

## LESSONS LEARNED AND RECOMMENDATIONS FOR THE FUTURE

On the basis of the review of the financial sector initiatives, overall implementation of the Summit's Work Program is considered good. The program needs to focus on fewer issues and to be supported by more aggressive action steps. In view of the very good statement of goals contained in the *Plan of Action*, and the tasks already performed by the CHFI, significant progress can be achieved through a restructuring of the Work Program that places more emphasis on specific integration initiatives.

### Table 1. Evaluation of Summit Initiatives in the Financial Sector

| | Very Strong | Very Good | Good | Modest | Minor |
|---|---|---|---|---|---|
| Program Component: | | | | | |
| Design of the Plan of Action | XX | | | | |
| Design of the Work Program | | | | | |
| Comparative Analysis | | XX | | | |
| Country Participation | | | XX | | |
| Impact on National Policies | | | | | XX |
| International Conferences | | XX | | | |
| Public-Private Partnerships | | | | | XX |
| **Overall** | | | XX | | |

Some of the lessons learned from this analysis are as follows:

1. It is important to identify the proper sequence for financial sector integration. The Summit *Plan of Action*, signed by the participating presidents, is a carefully crafted statement that identifies three phases in the financial market continuum: development, liberalization, and integration. The *Plan of Action* also recommended some initial action steps such as assigning the task of implementation to a technical committee comprised of Ministers of Finance. The Work Program thus needs to identify the appropriate tasks at the national level for regional integration.

2. The European experience with the formation of a single market is a good model for similar efforts in the Americas. Among other things, the European experience points to the importance of currency stability and arrangements and to the need for a gradualistic approach to integration.

3. The design of the Summit Work Program for the financial sector should follow the original president's goals more closely. The *Plan of Action* called for the possibility of negotiating common guidelines on capital movements and to support regional regulators associations reaching common grounds on regional integration issues. However, the actual Work Program released at the New Orleans meeting of Finance Ministers diverted attention to some areas that were outside the scope of the original principles. At the same time, the agenda did not address the establishment of a forum to discuss guidelines on capital movements. The training programs for financial sector regulators and for agencies combatting financial crimes went beyond the scope of a regional integration agenda.

4. The design of a Work Program needs to be simple and realistic. Too many tasks can lead to a bottleneck in the implementation process. Ownership of the program by individual players is also key to its effectiveness. A number of countries have not actively participated in this process. A valuable lesson from the European experience in this regard is to start with a focused but relatively simple agenda, then move on to more complex tasks in subsequent stages.

5. In the design of complex financial sector initiatives, it is important to identify the entity charged with their implementation. Because of the multiplicity of Summit initiatives, many of which are linked across functional areas, it would be highly desirable to establish a fully dedicated secretariat to monitor the process and to develop the institutional capacity that will be required in future stages of convergence.

6. One of the key ingredients that is missing from the implementation of the Summit initiatives is financial resources. If there is no political will to channel resources, both human and capital, into the integration process, then the framers of the Summit erred on its timing.

7. International conferences provide a good forum to disseminate critical information on issues pertaining to integration and to maintain the regional community informed about progress on integration initiatives. Conference participation should be balanced in terms of government, non-governmental associations, multilateral agencies, academics, and private sector participants.

8. In view of the impressive progress made at the national level with financial sector development and integration during the 1990s, the introduction of regional integration initiatives is a logical next step in the sequence. Nevertheless, it is important to recognize significant differences across countries in terms of their location on the financial sector continuum. As mentioned in the analysis of the country experiences, there is a critical mass of reforms that can already serve as a basis for the identification of convergence criteria for financial sector integration. Discrepancies with respect to these core areas need to be examined for relevance; otherwise, they can be left to national preferences. Special issues such as dollarization need to be studied and recommendations provided. The crises experienced by some countries should serve as the basis for the development of adequate safeguard mechanisms.

## Notes

1. For extensive discussion of the importance of proper sequencing, see Vittorio Corbo, Stanley Fischer, and Steven B. Webb, 1992, *Adjustment Lending Revisited* (Washington, D.C.: The World Bank); Carl Jayarajah and William Branson, 1995, *Structural and Sectoral Adjustment* (Washington, D.C.: The World Bank); and The World Bank, 1996, *1994 Evaluation Results* (Washington, D.C.: The World Bank).

2. Rosenberg and Stein 1995.

3. See Golbembe 1990.

4. See Fraser 1993.

5. This analysis is based on the corresponding banking and securities laws, financial statements of the banking system, and discussions with supervisors and market participants.

## References

Bernal, Richard L. 1996. *Implementing the Summit of the Americas: Developing and Liberalizing Capital Markets*. Coral Gables, Fla.: North-South Center at the University of Miami, Working Paper, October.

Feinberg, Richard E. 1997. *Summitry in the Americas: A Progress Report*. Washington, D.C.: Institute for International Economics.

Golembe, Carter H., and David S. Holland. 1990. "Banking and Securities." In *Europe 1992: An American Perspective*, ed. Gary Clyde Hufbauer. Washington, D.C.: The Brookings Institution.

Hitiris, T. 1991. *European Community Economics*. New York: St. Martin's Press.

Lindberg, Leon N. 1993. "Financial Deregulation, Monetary Policy Coordination, and Economic and Monetary Union." In *The 1992 Project and the Future of Integration in Europe*, eds. Dale L. Smith and James Lee Ray. New York: M.E. Sharpe.

Maurer, Martin, H. Mora, M. Pardo, and L. Torres. 1995. *Acuerdos de Integracion de Servicios Financieros en America Latina: Perfiles de Negociaciones Hacia el ALCA*, prepared for FELABAN, December.

Rosenberg, Robin, and Steve Stein, eds. 1995. *Advancing the Miami Process: Civil Society and the Summit of the Americas*. Coral Gables, Fla.: North-South Center Press at the University of Miami.

# Annex I

SUMMIT OF THE AMERICAS

*PLAN OF ACTION* — December 1994 — MIAMI

I. PRESERVING AND STRENGTHENING THE COMMUNITY OF DEMOCRACIES OF THE AMERICAS

II. PROMOTING PROSPERITY THROUGH ECONOMIC INTEGRATION AND FREE TRADE

*10. Capital Markets Development and Liberalization*

The availability of capital at competitive rates is essential to finance private sector investment — a vital ingredient in economic development. Developing, liberalizing, and integrating financial markets domestically and internationally, increasing transparency, and establishing sound, comparable supervision and regulation of banking and securities markets will help to reduce the cost of capital by enhancing investor and depositor confidence.

*Governments will:*

- Form a Committee on Hemispheric Financial Issues to examine steps to promote the liberalization of capital movements and the progressive integration of capital markets, including, if deemed appropriate, the negotiation of common guidelines on capital movements that would provide for their progressive liberalization.

- Prepare, in cooperation with the Inter-American Development Bank, a comprehensive list of national capital regulations in order to promote transparency and support the discussions in the Committee on Hemispheric Financial Issues.

- Support the cooperative endeavors of the Association of Latin American and Caribbean Bank Supervisors and the Council of Securities Regulators of the Americas to provide sound supervision and regulation that support the development and progressive integration of markets.

The Committee on Hemispheric Financial Issues should also review problems of debt in the Hemisphere, taking account of ongoing work and drawing, as appropriate, on a broad range of expertise.

# Annexes II and III

## ANNEX A: MANDATES FOR FUTURE WORK

Annexes II and III are the original annexes A and B attached to the Joint Communiqué from the Summit of the Americas Meeting of Western Hemisphere Finance Ministers in New Orleans, Louisiana, on May 18, 1996.

### Committee on Hemispheric Financial Issues:

16. The Committee on Hemispheric Financial Issues meeting at the Deputies level will continue its current mandate to pursue strong, open financial and capital markets consistent with the Summit of the Americas goal of regional integration and to review the problems of heavily indebted countries in the hemisphere. The Committee is specifically directed to:

a. Examine issues that affect the performance of our economies and financial markets, such as improved analysis and dissemination of information concerning national economies by the private sector and international financial institutions, possible ways to improve access to medium- and long-term financing, and the conduct of monetary policy in the context of globalized markets.

b. Oversee and build on the work of the newly established Technical Working Group on National Financial Markets Regulations (see below) and identify priority actions to strengthen and integrate financial markets.

c. Ensure implementation of IMF disclosure standards — as appropriate for each country — and work toward making key economic and financial information available on the Internet.

d. Encourage the adoption and rigorous application of high-quality national accounting and disclosure standards by enterprises.

e. Consider and, as appropriate, endorse recommendations from other sources, including regional associations dealing with financial markets, the Meetings on Financial Market Development, and the reviews undertaken by private sector groups within our countries on laws affecting the financing of the private sector (see Annex B).

f. Work with the Inter-American Development Bank, International Monetary Fund, and the World Bank to develop new programs to strengthen and integrate regional financial markets where needed.

g. Explore ways to increase private sector savings, including private sector options for financing and managing pension funds.

h. Develop new recommendations, where appropriate, to address other financial issues of regional concern — including privatization, infrastructure investment, and microenterprise development.

i. Examine the overall debt situation in the hemisphere and explore new mechanisms to deal with it, in particular, measures to address the multilateral debt obligations of the poorest countries.

j. Complement the ongoing work of the OAS and the hemispheric governments through identification of specific initiatives, where appropriate, that Financial Ministries can pursue to combat money laundering and corruption.

k. Prepare recommendations for future work to be considered by the Ministerial meeting in two years.

17. By affirming the Committee's mandate for future work, we:

a. Strengthen the network of finance officials in the hemisphere, facilitating discussion and consensus on key economic issues in the hemisphere.

b. Provide impetus to other organizations, including multilateral development banks and banking and security regulators, to advance efforts important to the hemisphere.

c. Provide opportunities for mutual support and cross-validation of individual countries' reform efforts.

### Technical Working Group on National Financial Market Regulation:

18. A technical working group on national financial market regulations is to be created to:

a. Complete, in conjunction with the Inter-American Development Bank, compilation of a comprehensive list of national financial market regulations.

b. Determine the best mechanism for making this list publicly available, in order to promote transparency and assist potential investors.

c. Develop procedures for informing and reviewing significant changes in these regulations, to encourage transparency and keep the comprehensive list current.

d. Draw from the experiences of participating countries and policies contained in the list of national financial market regulations to identify policies that encourage the development, liberalization, and integration of the region's financial markets.

e. Identify ways that our countries can cooperate to advance this goal.

19. The working group will be a dynamic vehicle to promote the development, liberalization, and integration of financial markets. It will provide periodic progress reports to the Committee on Hemispheric Financial Issues meeting at the Deputies level and will issue a report of its conclusions to the Committee within 18 months. The working group will be comprised of officials with special knowledge about their country's policies and how they affect financial markets.

## ANNEX B: INITIATIVES

- Training Program for Supervision and Examination
- Identifying Priorities for Financial Market Development
- Reviews of National Laws Affecting the Financing of the Private Sector
- Technical Assistance for Combating Financial Crimes

## Training Program for Supervision and Examination

*Summary:*

The Ministers called on the Inter-American Development Bank to establish a technical training program to help develop and train more highly skilled bank and securities supervisors and examiners as a means of promoting greater safety and soundness in Latin American financial systems.

Currently, no regional training programs of the type described below exist for financial market regulators. The proposed training program will foster development in the region of an expanded cadre of technically skilled bank and securities market regulators and examiners and, by providing common training, will promote regulatory cooperation across countries and across markets. The specific content of the program's courses should be based on an ongoing analysis of training needs in the region.

*Description of Program:*

The program will sponsor short-duration courses in banking and securities market supervision and examination. The courses will include opportunities for banking and securities examiners to focus together on issues of common interest. The program will coordinate these courses with the Association of Latin American and Caribbean Bank Supervisors and the Council of Securities Regulators of the Americas.

Participating countries will send officials from their banking, securities and other financial regulatory offices as appropriate (e.g., bank examiners, securities regulators, pension regulators, and supervisors of operations).

The IDB will be asked to fund the program.

## Identifying Priorities for Financial Market Development

*Summary:*

In order to identify priorities for policy action, the Ministers called on the Inter-American Development Bank to host three meetings between policymakers, regulators, and market participants to identify the main problems in the development of deep, liquid financial markets and to recommend solutions. Key issues to be addressed will include the expansion of long-term financing options and the creation of new opportunities for domestic savings. The Ministers further charged their Deputies to review the recommendations and to propose next steps for action.

*Description of Conferences:*

The IDB will host several hemisphere-wide meetings, including one in the Caribbean, over an 18-month period. Participating countries will send experts from their regulatory agencies that have policy-level responsibility for financial market development. Private sector participants also will be invited and will be asked to present papers on specific topics. The meeting agendas will focus on practical steps that governments can take to facilitate greater depth and liquidity in domestic financial markets. Topics will include:

- Ways to facilitate greater participation by institutional and retail investors in financial markets, with special emphasis on practical steps that governments can take to widen and deepen domestic institutional participation in financial markets.

- Ways to improve the financial, legal, and regulatory environments so as to make the issuance of medium- and long-term debt and equity instruments attractive to both issuers and investors.
- Ways to improve financial market infrastructure (e.g., quicker and more assured payments and settlement systems that use DVP (delivery versus payment); more efficient provision of custodial services; development of computer-based trading systems).
- Ways to improve financial disclosure and transparency on an internationally comparable basis (e.g., issuer disclosure; investment prospectuses; fund management performance data; transparency with respect to market transactions).
- Development of legal infrastructure to establish property rights, the perfection of security interests, and rules governing bankruptcy proceedings.

The IDB will be asked to provide funding for the meetings.

## Reviews of National Laws Affecting the Financing of the Private Sector

*Summary:*

The Ministers encouraged relevant national private sector organizations to propose recommendations for improvements in their national laws, regulations, and implementation that could enhance financing for the private sector and to recommend practical solutions. The Ministers further charged their Deputies to review the reports and recommendations and to propose next steps for action.

National laws and institutions that protect private property rights, including the rights of creditors, and establish the conditions for innovation and competition are essential to a country's ability to provide finance for the private sector and to sustain economic growth. Ministers have identified reviews by national private sector organizations as an effective way to mobilize the private sector's expertise on aspects of national laws, regulations, and implementation that could be improved.

*Description of Reviews:*

The reviews will identify the most important aspects of laws, regulations, and implementation that affect a country's ability to provide finance for the private sector. The areas to be covered will include:

- Protection of private property rights (e.g., secured interests, expropriation issues, policy risk issues)
- Bankruptcy regimes
- Commercial dispute resolutions
- Competition policy.

Finance Ministries encourage appropriate private sector organizations in each country to conduct reviews of these four areas. These organizations might include lawyers associations, accountancy groups, trade unions, employer and business groups, financial markets participants, Chambers of Commerce, and other professional organizations. The completed reviews would then be submitted to the Deputies of the Committee on Hemispheric Financial Issues for consideration in 1997.

## Technical Assistance for Combating Financial Crimes

*Summary:*

The Ministers encouraged the IDB, in conjunction with the OAS, to establish a comprehensive training and technical assistance program to support nations in their implementation of commitments in the December 1995 Buenos Aires Ministerial Communiqué on Money Laundering. The program will improve the integrity of the region's financial systems by addressing key legislative, legal, and law enforcement objectives.

*Description of Technical Assistance Program:*

The program will focus on the three core areas of legislation/regulation, investigation/prosecution, and financial intelligence support. For each country that participates, it will entail the following discrete steps:

Step 1: Training and technical needs assessment. A consultative process incorporating the unique legal, law enforcement, economic, banking sector, and other conditions and needs of each nation would be used to make country-specific recommendations for training and technical assistance.

Step 2: Training and technical assistance tailored to specific country needs. For each country, the range of possible program modules includes:

- Three-week core training program. The program will cover the three core areas of legislation/regulation, investigation/prosecution, and financial intelligence support.

- Train-the-trainer modules. The aim of these modules is to empower nations to undertake the training of their own personnel.
- Consultation modules. International consulting teams will assist with specific problems.
- Self-instruction modules. Interactive computer-based programs will be created to provide self-paced study of a broad range of topics.
- Linkage to other international training programs. The program will support countries' access to non-duplicative training provided by other organizations and initiatives.
- Technology transfer. Where appropriate and subject to resource constraints, the program may provide assistance in developing or procuring computer hardware and software.

The IDB will be asked to fund the training and technical needs assessments and, where appropriate, to fund the training and technical assistance provided to specific countries. Other organizations may also be asked to finance appropriate activities.

# V. Leadership Council for Inter-American Summitry

## *Postscript:* Developing, Liberalizing, and Integrating Financial Markets

*Manuel Lasaga*
OCTOBER 30, 1998

The recent Santiago Summit marked an important step toward the institutionalization of the Summit of the Americas process. The Summit of the Americas comprises many areas ranging from politics to education and the economy. Keeping such a complex and comprehensive agenda on track is a major undertaking, particularly when considering the ambitious deadlines that have been established for the culmination of this process. With the globalization of financial markets, the challenges and opportunities created by an interconnected global network of financial flows, it is more important than ever to continue to work intensively on the integration of regional capital markets. Economic integration and free trade are at the forefront of this process. The financial sector agenda continued to hold prominence in the Santiago Summit. However, its scope has been downsized from the Miami initiatives. The Santiago Summit has, in effect, constrained the domain of the multidimensional financial sector continuum to the development and liberalization of individual markets, while disengaging most of the integration efforts. The new agenda for the financial sector also raises some questions about continuity of the process, adequacy of the implementing entity, and absence of other areas, such as currency management and monitoring of capital flows. With greater focus on the creation of a regional network rather than on individual country initiatives, the new agenda could move the hemisphere closer to its goal of an integrated financial market.

### DOWNSIZING OF FINANCIAL SECTOR INITIATIVES

In contrast to Miami, the Santiago Summit resulted in a downsizing of financial sector initiatives. However, as prior analysis has shown, the Miami Summit's *Plan of Action* was overly ambitious and the subsequent Work Program designed by the Finance Ministers was not well focused on key issues.[1] The Santiago Plan of Action is thus much less ambitious in terms of breadth and depth. In this regard, the new approach will facilitate the achievement of the Plan of Action objectives and allow time to prepare an appropriately sequential agenda for the following Summit.

On the other hand, the Santiago Plan of Action may indeed be too narrow if the initial goal of integrating financial markets is also anticipated by the 2005 deadline agreed to in the Miami Summit. In view of the modest progress in achieving the initial *Plan of Action* goals, the new simplified agenda may also reflect a lack of agreement on the approach to financial sector integration. This is part of the challenge of moving from a national to a regional agenda, from a field of one to many decisionmakers. The financial sector problems encountered by a number of countries during the past several years have drawn the full attention of policymakers to crisis management and may thus have diminished their ability to work on the regional initiatives. Creating a hemispheric common market calls for a new mind-set by policymakers. In the financial arena, regional integration will involve a shift from the traditional, exclusively national orientation of financial sector policies to a more open cooperative approach based on an ongoing dialogue.

The theme of both summits is developing, liberalizing, and integrating financial markets. The Miami Summit was more ambitious in calling for a review of steps to "promote the liberalization of capital movements and the progressive integration of capital markets, including, if deemed appropriate, the negotiation of common guidelines on capital movements." In addition, governments were committed to the support of cooperative endeavors to "provide sound supervision and regulation that support the development and progressive integration of markets." The emphasis in the Miami *Plan of Action* was on regional initiatives aimed at increasing the integration of markets. As discussed in the earlier paper, the Committee on Hemispheric Financial Issues (CHFI) made limited progress toward these goals, although the New Orleans Communiqué provided a satisfactory agenda.

The Santiago Summit has moved away from discussion of regional integration strategies by emphasizing the strengthening of national markets. The principal goal is to strengthen banking supervision through the implementation of the Basle Core Principles of Effective Banking Supervision. The Plan also calls for the establishment of a Working Group to assist countries in this process. In addition, governments have committed to improving "banking and securities market clearance and settlement systems in the hemisphere in order to facilitate the transparency, efficiency, and security of internal and cross-border transactions."

The application of a common framework for banking supervision is a critical component for the integration of financial markets. As an international standard for banking supervision, the Basle Principles address the following areas: 1) licensing and structure, 2) prudential regulations and requirements, 3) methods of ongoing banking supervision, 4) information requirements, 5) powers of the supervisors, and 6) cross-border banking.[2] While these comprise the basic building blocks for an efficient and sound banking system, the Basle Principles are only general statements of policy. The effectiveness of these principles in a regional context will hinge on the ability of banking regulators to develop clear rules of the game that are understood by the supervisors as well as the financial intermediaries and that these rules are equally applicable throughout the hemisphere. For example, it may be feasible to agree on the principle that the minimum capital requirements for banks should reflect their level of risks, but it may be very difficult to reach a common understanding in terms of how that risk is measured and what should be the relationship between capital and risk. Cross-country differences in those risk standards could result in greater risk through distorted financial flows.

The success of the Santiago Summit goal of strengthening banking supervision will depend on the effectiveness of the Working Group in developing a regional-based agenda rather than a country-specific exercise. In other words, the quality of the outcome will be determined by whether the Working Group assumes a proactive or reactive strategy. If its goals are limited to helping each country reach a satisfactory level of sound supervision, then the Santiago Summit agenda will have fallen short of the goal of regional integration. The Working Group has to adopt an aggressive strategy of integration based on an intensive dialogue among banking supervisors. The Association of Latin American and Caribbean Bank Supervisors would be a good forum for the activities of the Working Group. At the same time, the Working Group needs to have a permanent base of operations, such as the Summit secretariat referred to in the earlier paper. Most important, the Working Group needs to receive its authority from the highest levels. In this regard, the Group should be comprised of the Ministers of Finance as the governing body, supported by the Superintendents of Banks who will participate in the development and implementation of the Group's policies.

Fortunately, the CHFI has already prepared some of the work related to the integration of banking supervision practices. One of the tasks identified in the Miami Summit was to prepare a comprehensive list of national capital markets regulations throughout the hemisphere. This project was coordinated by the IDB and completed in 1997. The report contains an excellent description and comparison of different banking practices. This material should be used in the development of regional banking supervision standards. Perhaps a follow-up survey, much less ambitious than the first, could focus on the individual Basle Principles and be updated on a regular basis. Any discussions of regional integration must be supported by comprehensive and reliable information about each country's banking system.

With the failure of a number of banks in the 1970s arising from currency speculation, with the onslaught of the debt crisis in the early 1980s, and with the more recent systemic crises in a number of Latin American banking systems, regulators have been paying closer attention to the integrity of the payments systems (this term includes clearance and settlement). For instance, in the United States, the Federal Reserve constantly monitors the risk profile of the Fedwire; while the member banks of CHIPS and the Society for World Interbank Financial Telecommunications (SWIFT) are also involved in a permanent self-assessment process. The move to electronic banking has made important advancements in the area of payments processing, and the regional economies need to bring their systems up to speed with respect to the global financial network. As stated in the earlier paper, this is an area where many countries are already working at the national level to assure the integrity of their payment systems, and almost all countries are active in the global SWIFT network.

The commitment to support a strengthening of the payments system needs to be brought into focus. Is the Plan of Action recommending this program as part of a regional integration strategy, or is it just another endorsement of the financial sector initiatives that have already been developed at the national level? If the goal is to promote greater regional integration of payments systems, then the proposal needs to be more explicit. The design of regional standards for payments clearing and processing is a highly complex task. Perhaps the design of such a mechanism might involve the creation of a SIIFT (Society for Inter-American Interbank Financial Telecommunications) network. The Plan of Action should also have assigned this task to the Working Group. Banking supervision and payments systems are interrelated, so that a dedicated Working Group could help to move the process forward.

While the emphasis on payments systems is needed to assure the integrity of the individual financial sectors, the Plan of Action's goal may raise a procedural problem. In order for the payments system to facilitate the transparency and efficiency of cross-border transactions, the participating countries need first to agree on how they will liberalize capital flows between countries. In this respect, the Santiago Summit's attention to country-specific initiatives may result in a bottom-up approach to integration, when the process needs to start with a top-down view. It is important first to agree on what types of transactions will be allowed to flow freely between countries and what type of protocol will be used in the settlement of each transaction. In this regard, the Santiago Summit may have lost a bit of the global vision with respect to the financial sector. The payments system initiative as stated in the Plan of Action deals more with individual country mechanisms rather with the development of a comprehensive regional structure.

## ADDITIONAL QUESTIONS RAISED BY THE NEW PLAN OF ACTION

Overall, the Santiago Plan of Action supports additional measures that will enhance future regional integration efforts. However, is the financial sector work program contained in this Plan of Action consistent with the goal of achieving a common market by the year 2005? It is unlikely, based on the current Plan of Action. In order to speed up the process, the Working Group needs to assume a much more aggressive posture in fostering greater dialogue regarding regional integration strategies. This may result in additions to the Plan of Action agenda that would incorporate more elements of the Miami Summit's goal of negotiating common guidelines on capital movements.

The lessons of structural reforms and the recent catastrophic experience in some banking systems have underscored the need for a sequential approach to reforms. In this regard, both Summits have failed to identify one of the key issues in the development of regional integration initiatives. One of the pre-conditions for the success of a common market is the stability of currencies. After the world monetary system adopted floating exchange rates in 1973, the European Economic Community (EEC) established the European Monetary System in 1979 to provide a mechanism whereby the individual member currencies would be held within a pre-specified margin with respect to each other. This facilitated trade between the member countries since importers and exporters were able to negotiate prices within a reasonable degree of uncertainty. The coordination of currency management policies should be a critical component of regional integration. Traditionally, this has been an area where Central Banks in the hemisphere have been most reluctant to negotiate with their neighboring countries. The introduction by some countries of a currency band could mark an initial step toward a common framework. Nevertheless, the wide differences in currency management practices, from fixed to free-floating exchange rates, still presents a challenge to any regional discussions on convergence of currency policies.

The change in the scope of work from the Miami to the Santiago Summit, while simplifying the agenda, does raise some concern about continuity of the process. The key initiative of negotiating common guidelines on capital movements was dropped in the Santiago Summit. This may reflect a lack of agreement on a long-term agenda for integration. Because the process of integration takes many years, and in this case it involves a large number of countries, it is important to develop a long-range plan of how this goal will be achieved. However, the Santiago Summit agenda may be indicative of a different approach, whereby each Summit develops its own short-term plan, and the sequence may not necessarily lead to a smooth path to integration. A long-term plan could be developed as a working document that establishes basic principles and targets that would then be updated at each Summit. The long-term plan would contain the basic ingredients of the strategy and would thus be more conducive to the continuity of the process.

The recent turbulence in the global financial markets provides an important lesson for the integration initiatives in this hemisphere. The market response to the Asian problems and to the crisis in Russia appears to be an overreaction in terms of their impact on Latin America and the Caribbean. The engine of growth for this region, in terms of the external sector, are the U.S. and European economies. As long as the U.S. continues on its present robust expansion, the regional economies will not be adversely affected. On the other hand, the financial market panic also points to a lack of understanding of market fundamentals in Latin America and the Caribbean by the international investment community. In this regard, the CHFI could have seized on the opportunity to organize a meeting of finance ministers to discuss a regional response to global financial tensions. The issuance of a communiqué stating each government's commitment to continued economic and financial reforms, and their willingness to act in a coordinated fashion to support the continued expansion of their economies, could have had a significant impact on market perceptions and thus helped to stem some of the capital outflows from the region. At the same time, the volatility of short-term capital flows triggered by this recent episode points to the need for greater discussion by the governments in this hemisphere on appropriate mechanisms to manage and monitor these flows.

# Notes

1. *Liberalizing, and Integrating Financial Markets* by Manuel Lasaga, November 1997.

2. The Basle Principles were, in fact, developed as a result of the European initiatives in the creation of a single market.

3. The information is available on CD ROM, and the report can be obtained via the Internet at http://www.mercados-financieros.iadb.org.

# V. LEADERSHIP COUNCIL FOR INTER-AMERICAN SUMMITRY

*Jeffrey M. Puryear is director of education programs at the Inter-American Dialogue and co-director of the Partnership for Educational Revitalization in the Americas (PREAL). Ana Maria Andraca is associate researcher in PREAL's Santiago office. Marcela Gajardo is co-director of PREAL.*

# Implementing the Education Recommendations of the 1994 Summit of the Americas

*Jeffrey M. Puryear, Ana Maria Andraca, and Marcela Gajardo*

## INTRODUCTION

This paper documents progress in carrying out the recommendations on education approved at the December 1994 Summit of the Americas in Miami. It is part of a major independent initiative of the North-South Center at the University of Miami to monitor progress on implementing the 23 initiatives approved by the 34 heads of government who signed the *Declaration of Principles* and *Plan of Action* at the Summit of the Americas.

A previous progress report published in October 1996 concluded that the Summit of the Americas had made an important first step in capitalizing on the growing concern for educational reform in the region. This paper builds on that report and examines the transformation of *dichos* into *hechos* (words into deeds). For this purpose, a different strategy was used. We reviewed secondary materials, interviewed government and nongovernment officials and specialists, and reviewed pre- and post-Summit official declarations. We visited several Latin American countries, including the "responsible coordinators" for the area of education — Mexico, Chile, and Argentina — along with two countries, Colombia and the Dominican Republic, selected because they have different degrees of advancement in educational reform and different degrees of linkage with the Summit coordinators. In each of the five countries, we carried out interviews with relevant staff at ministries of education (usually with heads of international relations offices or advisors to the minister) and at ministries of foreign affairs (with officials responsible for following up or implementing the agreements of the Miami Summit). We also interviewed a number of education specialists based at non-governmental organizations (NGOs) in each of the countries, with the goal of gauging their knowledge of the Summit's education initiative and their participation in its implementation.

This paper is divided into several sections. The first reviews the Summit's education recommendations and arrangements for implementation. The second looks at the activities of governments, international organizations, and non-governmental organizations, and the third and fourth discuss obstacles to implementing the recommendations, and provide some concluding observations.

## THE SUMMIT'S EDUCATION RECOMMENDATIONS

Education is one of 23 initiatives developed within the framework of the hemispheric Summit. Each initiative has its own *Plan of Action*, with countries that act as responsible coordinators to ensure that the agreements are implemented. In the case of education, the heads of state approved an initiative entitled "Universal Access to Education," in which they pledged to improve access to quality education and to eliminate illiteracy. More specifically, they agreed to:

- Guarantee universal access to quality primary education and strive for a primary completion rate of 100 percent by the year 2010, a secondary enrollment rate of at least 75 percent, and the development of programs to eradicate illiteracy, prevent truancy, and improve human resources training;

- Promote worker professional training and encourage adult education that is more relevant to the needs of labor markets;

- Improve human resources training and technical, professional, and teacher training;

- Increase access to and strengthen the quality of higher education and promote cooperation in producing scientific and technological knowledge;

- Support strategies to overcome nutritional deficiencies of primary school children;

- Support decentralization that includes adequate financing and broad participation by civil society in decisionmaking about education;

- Review existing regional and hemispheric training programs and make them more responsive to current needs;

- Urge the March 1995 World Summit for Social Development and the September 1995 Fourth World Conference on Women to address the issue of universal access to education; and

- Create a hemispheric partnership, working with existing organizations to provide a consultative forum for governments, non-governmental actors, the business community, donors, and international organizations in order to reform educational policies and focus resources more efficiently.

The government of Mexico agreed to act as the responsible coordinator for the education initiative and to work with the governments of Argentina and Chile on promoting the implementation of the education recommendations. They formed part of a system of responsible coordinators established by the Summit Implementation Review Group (SIRG) — an executive committee representing all the ministries of foreign affairs and several multilateral organizations — which was to meet periodically to monitor and guide implementation of the plans of action of the several Summit initiatives.

At their own initiatives and under the leadership of Richard E. Feinberg, former senior director for Inter-American Affairs at the National Security Council and one of the architects of the Summit of the Americas, the North-South Center at the University of Miami and the Institute of International Economics have decided to monitor efforts to implement the Summit agreements. In 1995, they contracted a group of reports, and the results were presented on May 29, 1996, in a workshop in Washington, D.C. The reports have since been revised and published as a set of separate working papers by the North-South Center. Feinberg has also published an analysis of the 1994 Summit of the Americas and subsequent efforts to implement its *Plan of Action*, drawing heavily on those papers (Feinberg 1997).

In late 1996, the North-South Center contracted a second series of reports to document the degree to which there was movement from *dichos* to *hechos* in the diverse agreements signed by the 33 governments of the region. In preparing these reports, they asked the authors to assess progress, report on mechanisms designed to implement actions, look at the role of the responsible coordinators, and gauge the involvement of the private sector and non-governmental organizations in the implementation process.

## TRANSFORMING *DICHOS* INTO *HECHOS*

In his report on the 1994 Summit of the Americas, Feinberg constructed a table that summarized progress on each of the 12 initiatives as of mid-1996, placing them in one of six categories: strong, very good, good, modest, minor, and little or no movement (Feinberg 1997, 165). Efforts to implement the education initiative were given a rating of "modest" compared with other initiatives, noting that there had been slow movement on several fronts but little effort by national governments or international organizations to provide strong leadership (Feinberg 1997, 170).

Our review of activities over the past year suggests that a rating of "modest" continues to be appropriate. Government efforts are reflected in a draft *Plan of Action* prepared in early 1996 by the government of Mexico and circulated to the other responsible coordinators for comment. A later version of the plan (July 1997) was shared with all the region's countries for comment. A definitive version and activities that derive from it will be made public prior to the 1998 Hemispheric Summit in Santiago.

## Government Initiatives

As mentioned, the government of Mexico agreed to act as the responsible coordinator for the education initiative, with assistance from the governments of Argentina and Chile. In early 1996, Mexico prepared a draft background document and circulated it to other governments (via their ministries of education) for comment. In that document, Mexico proposed

- that each country identify the specific shortcomings of its educational systems as well as the groups most affected by those shortcomings and fix goals for progressively expanding access to education;
- that each country share a set of common principles and goals and adopt strategies of hemispheric collaboration so as to achieve equitable, quality education for all by the year 2010; and
- that priority be given to strategies at preschool, primary, and secondary levels, focusing attention on those groups that are most vulnerable, such as indigenous peoples, geographically dispersed populations, migrants, incapacitated students, urban marginals, those over 35 years of age, illiterates, and poor women who lack primary education.

Mexico's draft document emphasized guaranteeing universal access to education through improvements in the internal efficiency of educational systems. Strategies included the following:

- Compensatory programs;
- Initial and preschool programs using nonformal approaches that involve mothers;
- Programs to strengthen basic skills in reading, writing, and arithmetic;
- Validation of workplace skills;
- Methods and practices for self-learning; and
- Distance education.

The proposal recommended targeting vulnerable groups, in accord with the priorities, needs, and characteristics of each country. These groups include indigenous peoples, geographically dispersed populations, migrants, incapacitated students, urban marginals, those over 35 years of age, illiterates, and poor women who lack primary education.

Viewed from the perspective of current debates in Latin America and the Caribbean on educational reform, several omissions in the document are worth noting. No references were made to the following:

- Existing analyses and recommendations (such as those prepared by the World Bank; the United Nations Educational, Scientific and Cultural Organization [UNESCO]; the United Nations Economic Commission for Latin America and the Caribbean [ECLAC]; and the Inter-American Development Bank [IDB]) designed to promote educational transformation in the region's countries, nor was there any reference to the policy options that derive from them;
- Structural reforms that might make the educational system an instrument for achieving these objectives;
- Actors other than those in the education sector;
- The potential of public-private partnerships for promoting reforms needed to improve the quality of teaching and for overcoming obstacles to more modern and efficient management of educational systems;
- Existing regional initiatives to develop management and information systems that would make it easier to decentralize educational systems, target the disadvantaged, make schools more accountable for what students learn, create collaborative networks, and identify new sources of financing;
- Possible actions that would integrate themes slated for attention in the upcoming 1998 Summit in Santiago, Chile — themes such as sustainable development, health, gender, economic integration and international relations, trade, the strengthening of democracy, citizen participation, human rights, and peace.

Some of those interviewed criticized the initial document as "a plan that does not sufficiently take into consideration the differences in educational advancement among the countries of the region — particularly those that are more developed.... The document implies that a policy vacuum exists, and proposes to fill it.... [But] what about those countries that have already established their priorities?" Another government official observed that "the plan does not reflect the great capacity of the education specialists that the three responsible coordinators have. ... It uses very official, ministerial language, and most countries are already addressing those problems."

The document has been extensively revised, and its contents have been modified to correspond more closely with the range of views and conditions that characterize the countries of the region.

In July 1997, the responsible coordinators met in Mexico to review the draft and decided to redefine the proposed lines of strategy for hemispheric cooperation. The group introduced two criteria — equity and quality — for new lines of action. They urged priority for strategies that promote equal opportunity to obtain quality education. Lines of action discussed were more directly relevant to current problems; they included literacy and adult education programs, bilingual preschool and primary education programs for indigenous children, compensatory strategies for vulnerable and underserved groups, teacher training, distance learning that incorporates new technologies, certification of job skills, the establishment of national standards in primary and secondary education, and education for democracy. As will be seen later, these proposals influenced the final version of the *Plan of Action*.

At the same time, the government of Chile, which will host the 1998 Summit, asked its Ministry of Education to begin pulling together possible recommendations and established an ad-hoc committee, composed of staff from the ministry, multilateral organizations, and nongovernmental organizations, to review the document prepared by the responsible coordinators. The committee observed that the draft did not take sufficient advantage of the region's enormous experience in developing policies designed to promote equity in education, focus attention on what children learn, devise more effective systems of management, strengthen the leadership capacity of schools, link education to work, strengthen the teaching profession, and expand resources allocated to education. The committee also noted the importance of drawing more systematically on the analyses and recommendations produced by the World Conference on Education in Jomtien, Thailand; the Latin American Regional Office of UNESCO; ECLAC; the DeLors Commission on Education; the annual meetings of ministers of education (PROMEDLAC); the World Bank; and the IDB.

Chile's ministry of foreign affairs also expressed its hope that the emphasis on education proposed by the heads of state would be converted into a concrete plan of cooperative activities. They felt that these activities should be implemented using instruments already in existence, together with support from the Organization of American States (OAS) and the IDB.

In August 1997, the responsible coordinators held a meeting in Santiago, to which they invited representatives of other governments interested in the education recommendations. The results of that meeting, combined with the work of the responsible coordinators, established the base for the last technical meeting, which took place in Mexico City, in November 1997. Financed by the OAS and convened by the responsible coordinators, this meeting included participation by a greater number of countries (although very few from the English-speaking Caribbean), with representation by officials from ministries of education and several ambassadors. Representatives of several international organizations (the OAS, UNESCO, and the United Nations Children's Fund [UNICEF]) were also on hand. No one attended from the World Bank or the IDB. The revised document was approved by the group and is expected to be signed — with few changes — by the heads of state at the Santiago Summit.

The November 1997 meeting also sought to review national progress in carrying out the recommendations of the 1994 Summit. Countries were asked to fill out a form registering education initiatives undertaken since the Miami Summit; however, only some six or seven countries provided the information requested.

The revised *Plan of Action* includes several proposals suggested in earlier meetings, as mentioned above. It expressly reiterates the commitment at the Miami Summit to achieve universal access to quality primary education, a secondary enrollment rate of at least 75 percent, and opportunities for continuing adult education. With respect to quality and equity, it incorporates two additional principles:

- *Relevance*, understood as the capacity of educational systems to respond to the needs and aspirations of society, in all its social, cultural, ethnic, and linguistic diversity, and

- *Efficiency*, understood as the provision of sufficient resources, utilized properly to achieve better educational outcomes.

The new plan proposes the following courses of action for achieving quality and equity in education:

- Compensatory and intersectoral educational policies, with compensatory programs for vulnerable and educationally disadvantaged groups.

- Systems for assessing educational quality, paying special attention to standards in language, mathematics, and science. These systems should permit measurement of the performance of educational agents, the outcomes of innovations, and factors related to successful learning.

- Programs to professionalize teaching and educational administration, with institutions of higher education playing an active role.

- Strengthening of educational management and institutional capacity at the national, regional, local, and school levels, with progress toward decentralization and promotion of community and family involvement.

- Stronger programs of education and vocational training, incorporating new technologies and emphasizing the certification of job skills.

- Strategies for intercultural, bilingual education, introducing respect and appreciation for cultural diversity into basic education.

- Strategies that contribute to the formation of ethical values, including such aspects as democratic principles, human rights, gender equity, peace, tolerance, and respect for the environment.

- Greater access to and use of information and communication technologies, along with updated teaching methods and training for teachers in the use of these technologies. Emphasis should be on using these technologies to serve the most vulnerable groups through distance education and the establishment of information networks; increasing the quantity of teaching materials; and linking schools and communities.

- Scholarships and exchange programs for students, teachers, researchers, and administrators, designed to make innovative teaching and management methods known throughout the hemisphere.

In general, the revised plan overcomes several shortcomings in the original document by

- Mentioning explicitly the participation of other social sectors (business leaders, universities, and the mass media) in improving schools;

- Including educational administrators and researchers in reform initiatives;

- Incorporating the possibility of formulating intersectoral plans to achieve the goals proposed;

- Alluding – although weakly – to the other Summit initiatives (democracy, human rights, gender, the environment) in proposing efforts to teach values; and

- Specifying possible actions and responsibilities for international organizations such as the OAS, the IDB, and the World Bank.

Nonetheless, several deficiencies remain:

- The channels through which the different actors and organizations of civil society might participate are not specified.

- No concrete programs are proposed.

- Even though the revised plan proposes that heads of state provide adequate financing to carry out the proposed objectives, it does not identify possible sources of funds.

In general, government efforts to develop follow-up activities have been characterized by relatively restricted mechanisms of participation. Deliberations have involved principally the coordinating countries (Mexico, Argentina, and Chile). Other countries have been asked to provide written comments on preliminary documents. Only government officials have been invited to participate, through ministries of education and foreign affairs, along with a few officials from international organizations. Non-governmental organizations, the business sector, and other representatives of civil society have not been systematically involved. A comment by one representative of an NGO working on education appears to be typical: "We've heard very little about the Summit.... Only those directly involved in the process know about the specific agreements."

Follow-up and monitoring of the implementation of the education recommendations appears to constitute a delicate issue in the eyes of the governments. No agreement was reached on the topic during the Miami Summit. In fact, the issue was not addressed in the written agreements signed there. Some mention was made in the March 1997 meeting to the effect that the follow-up should be the responsibility of a multinational institution such as the OAS.

The most recent version of the plan proposes a more active role for the OAS, assigning to it the responsibility for promoting, articulating, and facilitating collective action, and for carrying out a technical consultation among countries, in collaboration with the responsible coordinators. This version also charges the OAS with convening a meeting by August 1998 of ministers of education in Brazil to develop implementation plans. The revised plan asks the OAS, in collaboration with the IDB, to develop and strengthen regional programs in distance education, short courses and study tours, and creation of centers that can provide information and technology for updating statistical systems and evaluating educational quality. Finally, the revised plan makes the OAS, IDB, and World Bank responsible for supporting programs and initiatives compatible with Summit commitments.

It is difficult for the governments to understand that follow-up and monitoring could be handled by an academic institution (such as the North-South Center) or by a non-governmental organization. Because the issue was not properly addressed in Miami, however, they recognize the interest by non-governmental groups in carrying out studies on progress in implementation and obstacles encountered.

Overall, the governments have established few channels for collaboration with the organizations of civil society in following up and implementing the education agreements. Responsibility for planning and executing the activities is assigned to the international relations departments of the ministries of education, who, in turn, report through the foreign ministries. Developing the agenda for the 1998 Summit is the responsibility of the foreign ministries, and in none of the countries visited had they convened civil society groups to participate. This situation may be changing somewhat. Conversations about broadening participation have taken place in Argentina and Chile. As mentioned above, the Chilean government has created an ad-hoc committee composed of several civil society groups to advise it on preparations for the education portion of the Santiago Summit, thus offering new opportunities for public-private cooperation.

Some of those interviewed expressed concern about government initiatives in the process and about the results. One of the responsible coordinators observed that "the Summit mechanisms are difficult to operate, often involving professionals from the ministries of foreign affairs who are not experts in the themes." Others made the following observations:

- Few initiatives are being recommended that would commit governments to make immediate, fundamental, and easily measurable changes in their educational policies.
- Although the organizations of civil society are interested in participating, no formal mechanisms have been established to incorporate their contributions.
- Governments are willing to accept input from NGOs with respect to nonformal education but see the formal educational system and its reform as the exclusive responsibility of ministries of education.

Our interviews also revealed concern about the nature of the education recommendations approved at the 1994 Summit. As one of those interviewed put it: "The Summit's education recommendations are very broad and target so many themes that I doubt that we'll achieve much.... New paradigms and new challenges have appeared that enable us to transcend the old schemes." The vagueness of many of the recommendations makes it difficult for the responsible coordinators to identify a few key activities that might produce real change.

Also of concern was the relationship between the Miami Summit and other regional initiatives. One interviewee observed, "Countries are asked to meet on many occasions, by the OAS, the Ibero-American Summit, and others.... Each meeting seems to be totally distinct with respect to the theme [education]." Another noted, "There is a succession of regional meetings on the same topics ... many parallel initiatives ... which require extraordinary effort. When you consider the limited personnel available,... the demands that these meetings imply are perceived almost as a nuisance." Clearly, the number of regionwide governmental education initiatives underway make it difficult for most ministries of education to participate actively in each one.

In terms of activities, it is difficult to identify any governmental mechanisms that were created for implementing the recommendations of the Miami Summit or any concrete actions that have been undertaken. To date, efforts have been concentrated on developing a document that outlines next steps and will feed into the 1998 Summit in Santiago.

Of course, quite apart from the efforts of the responsible coordinators to establish a *Plan of Action*, most of the region's countries are undertaking activities that can be defined as concrete efforts to achieve universal access to quality education by 2010. Over the past several years, education has moved steadily up the list of priorities for most governments. Most countries have in place a significant program of educational reform aimed at improving both quality and equity, and most are moving to expand access to education at all levels, decentralize decisionmaking, and increase investments in human capital. Overall, educational reform is a dynamic topic in the region.

These national initiatives, however, have little to do with the Summit. They are responses to the educational realities and internal dynamics of the individual countries and are based on national development priorities and plans that would exist with or without the Summit.

Our interviews confirmed this impression. One government representative said, "There is a correspondence between the recommendations of the Summit and our plans, but in no way has [the Summit] been the motor that has caused the changes." Another said, "We are working in all these areas but independent of the Summit recommendations." A third representative said, "I don't think the Miami recommendations have had any influence on the changes in education that are underway here. Those have been the fruit of our needs and a very rich process of dialogue and consultation regarding our problems."

The Summit's call to achieve universal access to quality education by 2010 is, therefore, probably more an expression of the region's growing political will to invest in education as a means of reducing poverty and inequity than it is a cause of those efforts. "We think that the value of the Summit is to raise the profile of some themes ... so the heads of state will value them and provide political support. The Summit serves, in the words of a Chilean government official, 'more to legitimate than to inspire.'"

## International Organizations

The *Plan of Action* of the Miami Summit called for the OAS and IDB to support countries in implementing the initiative through technical assistance and financial aid. Other organizations, such as the World Bank and the European Community (EC) were also mentioned as key supporters for implementing actions in all the areas alluded to at the Summit. Several other organizations, such as UNESCO, although not mentioned, are potentially important actors in implementing recommendations.

In general, neither the OAS nor the IDB has been very active in providing specific support for the Summit's education initiative. The OAS is in the process of redefining its mission and has significantly reduced its education staff, as part of a larger commitment to reconcentrate its efforts in areas where it believes the OAS has a comparative advantage. In mid-1997, the OAS commissioned a paper by Ernesto Schiefelbein, former regional director of UNESCO and Chilean minister of education, reviewing the problems of education in the region and laying out recommendations for reform. That paper was subsequently presented to the organizers of the 1998 Santiago Summit.

The IDB, for its part, has given increasing priority to education in its lending programs and has been particularly willing to provide support to countries that are far from achieving 100 percent enrollment in primary and 75 percent in secondary — two of the most important goals in the Summit's *Plan of Action* for education. The IDB's actions appear to be part of its ongoing institutional strategy, rather than a deliberate attempt to generate activities based on the Summit.

It is worth noting, however, that both institutions lately have shown a growing interest in increasing their participation in the Summit's education initiative. The OAS played a more active role in the Mexico meeting, providing some financial resources. The IDB participated in discussions and helped prepare the revised *Plan of Action*. Specific responsibilities were assigned to both, along with the World Bank, in the revised document.

The regional office of UNESCO, which has long made a special effort to promote better educational policy and the exchange of experiences and information — all objectives similar to those of the Summit's education initiative — has not articulated its actions with the Summit. Its participation in the Mexico meeting, however, suggests that a closer relationship may emerge in the future. The same is true of UNICEF, which also attended the Mexico meeting.

The World Bank, although deeply committed to lending in support of educational reform in the region, has not specifically keyed its work to Summit recommendations. The Andres Bello Pact, a consortium of eight Andean countries that aims to improve education, reports no involvement in the Summit process: "We don't have much information about the Summit, even though we have underway a four-year program on educational reform."

## Civil Society

We indicated earlier that participation by NGOs in the Summit follow-up on education has been quite limited, particularly with respect both to decisionmaking regarding next steps in follow-up activities and to the formulation of recommendations for the agenda of the 1998 Summit in Santiago. The limited nature of non-governmental participation can be explained by various factors:

- Because the Summit is a meeting of heads of state, the chief role and formal representation falls logically to the foreign ministries, who, in turn, convene other actors to take responsibility for the specific themes. In the case of education, this task has been given to ministries of education — usually to the departments responsible for international relations within those ministries, which the foreign ministries see as the legitimate agents for such work in the field of education.

- Some government officials actively resist the idea of non-governmental involvement in public educational policy.

- Few channels have been established to incorporate non-governmental actors in the Summit process, and few NGOs have taken the initiative to act on their own. In only two of the five countries we visited had NGOs approached their governments with specific proposals for monitoring activities in the field of education.

- NGOs have little information regarding the objectives, progress, and procedures related to implementation of the Summit's education recommendations, and they have shown little interest in the issue beyond recognizing the value of the Summit in drawing attention to education.

- The situation of most NGOs in Latin America and the Caribbean is one of precarious subsistence. Recent changes in the policies of foreign donor institutions have deprived them of significant financial resources and have made them increasingly dependent on government contracts for survival. This makes it difficult for them — on their own initiative and without adequate financing — to play a significant role in monitoring or implementing Summit follow-up activities.

- In contrast to North America and Europe, Latin America and the Caribbean have virtually no tradition of citizen participation in following up events such as the Summit. This is particularly true of formal education, which has long been assumed to be the exclusive responsibility of the state. Citizen participation is much more frequent in initiatives such as human rights, women's rights, democracy, and sustainable development, which have become clearly identified with civil society.

The chief exception to this relative absence of non-governmental participation has been the Partnership for Educational Revitalization in the Americas (PREAL) – a public-private partnership established by the Inter-American Dialogue to promote educational reform. PREAL is based on a program established in 1995 by the Inter-American Dialogue in Washington and the Corporation for Development Research (CINDE) in Chile, which sought to build a broad and active constituency for educational reform in many countries and to push education to the top of the policy agenda. That program garnered substantial support from the IDB, the U.S. Agency for International Development (USAID), the Canadian International Development Research Centre (IDRC), and the GE Fund.

Because the original program was so similar to the hemispheric partnership called for in the education recommendations of the Summit, the Inter-American Dialogue decided to build on its installed capacity, broadening activities in response to significant new support by USAID and modifying the program's structure so as to create a hemispheric partnership to help governments, non-governmental actors, the business community, donors, and international organizations to focus on educational reform and allocate resources more efficiently. PREAL receives major support from USAID — some $1.1 million annually over five years, since September 1996 — and has support as well from IDRC and the GE Fund.

Today, PREAL seeks to promote informed debate on policy alternatives, identify and disseminate the best educational practices emerging in the region and elsewhere, and monitor progress toward improving educational policy.

From the standpoint of Summit recommendations, PREAL's work over the past two years has been a good fit. Activities include regional working groups on key policy issues, workshops and conferences, research on relatively neglected policy issues, advocacy groups in nine countries working to organize and lead a sustained process of national debate and discussion on educational reform, state-of-the-art analyses of key educational policy issues, a series of policy papers, professional exchanges, and a web site on the Internet. Specific activities include the following:

- Three major subregional meetings. The first of these took place in mid-1996 in Managua, Nicaragua, on the topic of decentralization of education. The second was held in December 1996, in Rio de Janeiro, Brazil, on the topic of national educational standards and educational assessment; it brought together many of the region's leading specialists to discuss advances in establishing educational objectives and the measurement of progress toward achieving them. A third conference, held in July 1997 in Colombia, brought experts from Latin America, North America, and Europe to discuss recent advances in educational finance. Proceedings from all three meetings have been published recently.

- Nine working papers in English and Spanish on a variety of educational reform issues, including early childhood education, effective schools, national standards and performance assessment, regional trends in educational reform, new teaching and learning techniques, and decentralization. In addition to the working paper series, PREAL also publishes a quarterly Spanish-language journal, *Formas y Reformas de la Educación*, which deals with current reform issues throughout the region.

- A special Task Force on Education, Equity, and Economic Competitiveness in the Americas, which held its first meeting in January 1997. The Task Force is composed of more than a dozen distinguished private leaders from throughout the hemisphere, working to formulate concrete proposals for improving education in the region and to bring those proposals to the attention of national decisionmakers. The group is now reviewing a draft report that it plans to release early in 1998.

- The design of several regionwide working groups — on a politics of educational reform, national educational assessment systems, and teachers' unions.

- The establishment, in collaboration with the regional office of UNESCO in Santiago and with the Andres Bello Pact in Bogotá, of a program to identify best educational practices being developed in Latin America and to disseminate them to practitioners and researchers throughout the region.

- Collaboration with two consortiums of Latin American business leaders — the Chairman's International Advisory Council of the Americas Society and the Latin American Business Council — to generate private sector interest and involvement in educational reform. An edited volume of case studies of business-education partnerships in 11 countries in Latin America has been published, and national meetings of business leaders are being organized in several countries to discuss educational reform.

## OBSTACLES TO BETTER IMPLEMENTATION

Our review suggests that several obstacles to better implementation have emerged from the experience of the past 12 months:

- *The public monopoly syndrome.* Implementation of the education recommendations is often viewed by the governments as their exclusive responsibility, rather than as a task to be shared with all members of civil society. As a result, deliberations and information are restricted to a small group of public officials; non-governmental groups have almost no involvement; proposals do not benefit from the considerable energy and expertise that resides in the private sector; and there is little public awareness of the issues or their possible resolutions.

- *Absence of a reform mentality.* Most of the proposals emerging so far from the work of the responsible coordinators call upon countries to improve the quality and equity of their schools in various ways. Almost none of the proposals call for the fundamental systemic reforms that will be necessary in most of the region's educational systems in order to make schools better. This conservative approach may be due to the fact that the deliberations are monopolized by ministries of education, which traditionally have not been advocates of major reform.

- *Tepid Summit recommendations.* In general, the education recommendations approved at the Miami Summit reflect neither the best thinking of the region's education specialists nor the dynamic policy innovations underway in many countries. Key concepts, such as school autonomy, national testing regimes, competition, and parental choice, were not mentioned. In addition, the sheer number of recommendations makes it difficult for countries to mount a serious effort to carry them out, and progress on most of the recommendations is difficult to measure.

- *The absence of a mandate to involve the organizations of civil society* in Summit deliberations and the nonexistence of clear channels for their participation.

## FINAL CONSIDERATIONS

The education initiative of the Summit is an ongoing process. Although the impact so far has been modest, most countries of the region are genuinely interested in improving the quality of their educational systems. A new set of agreements, concerning lines of action, strategies for hemispheric cooperation, and collaborative projects, will be reached during the 1998 Summit in Santiago. However, it is not clear whether or how those agreements will be implemented, nor whether the Summit's education initiative will come to have a greater impact than in the past.

Achieving real impact will depend first on establishing a set of Summit recommendations that represent major reform and include concrete measures. We offer the following list of possible recommendations for the countries:

- Establish a high-profile national commission on educational modernization. The commission should be composed of leaders from the diverse social and economic sectors — business, media, churches, political parties, parents, unions, and professional associations — that have a stake in the country's educational systems and wield political power. The commission should be designed to draw attention to educational shortcomings, develop broad support for reform, and generate consensus on a national strategy for educational improvement.

- Develop a world-class system of educational statistics and indicators. The goal would be a system that emphasizes educational outcomes, rather than inputs, and is compatible with the system of international education indicators used by the Organization for Economic Cooperation and Development (OECD).

- Develop content and performance standards for education, and establish a national system of assessment based on the new standards. The standards should specify what students should know and be able to do in order to be successful in the global economy and in democratic citizenship. The tests should be administered to all students at specific points in the primary cycle and perhaps eventually in the secondary cycle.

- Lengthen the school year to at least 1,200 hours, making it comparable with public schools in OECD countries.

- Restructure educational systems to give schools more authority in managing their affairs and to make them more accountable to parents and local communities. Central and provincial governments should no longer directly run individual schools and should concentrate instead on setting standards, evaluating results, and promoting equity. School directors and local communities should be given control over budgets and personnel. New approaches should be devised to give parents choices about what schools their children attend and to promote competition among schools.

- Establish a program to strengthen the teaching profession by reforming training, establishing competitive salary levels, linking salaries to performance, and requiring teachers to take responsibility for the quality of their work.

- Commit to increasing gradually investment in primary and secondary education with the goal of doubling spending per student by 2005.

- Substantially expand preschool education, making it readily available to the children of families that cannot afford to pay for it themselves. Emphasis should be on encouraging diverse approaches, reaching the poorest families, and promoting private-public partnerships. Countries should enroll 30 percent of age-cohorts by 2000, and 50 percent by 2005.

The monitoring and follow-up of the Summit's education recommendations has considerable potential for raising the profile of educational reform and promoting debate on reform alternatives. Transforming *dichos* into *hechos* will work much better only if activities are linked more directly to national efforts to promote educational reform, if they include a sustained process of national debate on educational policy, and if they seek to develop a broader and more sophisticated constituency for better schools.

# References

Álvarez, Benjamín. 1996. *Informe sobre la revitalización de la educación en las Américas*. Working Paper No. 11. U.S. Agency for International Development, Education and Human Resources Division, Bureau for Latin America and the Caribbean. Washington, D.C.: Academy for International Development.

*Cumbre de las Américas, plan de acción para lograr el acceso universal a la educación básica de calidad para el año 2010*. 1997. (Coordinador: México, co-coordinadores: Argentina and Chile.) April.

Feinberg, Richard. 1997. *Summitry in the Americas. A Progress Report*. Washington, D.C.: Institute for International Economics.

Government of Chile, Ministry of Foreign Relations. 1997. *Plan de Acción Hemisférico Sobre Educación*. November.

Government of Chile, Ministry of Foreign Relations. N.d. *Declaraciones: Cumbre de las Américas; Conferencia sobre Medio Ambiente y Desarrollo; Cumbre Mundial sobre Desarrollo Social; Compromiso de Santiago con la Democracia; Cumbre sobre Desarrollo Sostenible; Declaraciones de Santiago sobre medidas de fomento de la confianza y de la seguridad*. Mimeo.

Insulza, José Miguel (Minister of Foreign Relations, Chile). 1997. Keynote address at international conference on "Educación, Democracia y Desarrollo Sustentable," August 7. Mimeo.

Puryear, Jeffrey. 1996. *Implementing the Summit of the Americas: Reforming Educational Systems*. Working Paper Series of the North-South Center at the University of Miami. Coral Gables, Fla.: North-South Center. This paper was prepared for a conference organized by the Institute of International Economics, Washington, D.C., and the North-South Center at the University of Miami.

# V. Leadership Council for Inter-American Summitry

## *Postscript:* Education and the Summit

*Jeffrey M. Puryear*
*The Inter-American Dialogue*

At the April 1998 Summit of the Americas in Santiago, Chile, the assembled heads of state renewed their commitment to revitalizing education and making it a sustained force for economic development and social equity. They placed education at the top of the agenda, calling it "The Key to Progress." They agreed to a plan of action that reaffirmed the 1994 Summit objectives in education and established 11 measures designed to achieve those objectives. Significantly, three of these measures placed on the agenda themes not mentioned at the 1994 Summit:

- Standards and evaluation,
- Teacher training and incentives, and
- The involvement of parents and local communities in school management.

These themes are important. They begin to address the institutional and systemic problems that have plagued schools in Latin America and the Caribbean for decades and are crucial to making them better. By placing them on the agenda, the Santiago summit took a real step forward in getting governments to recognize officially what most analysts agree are fundamental causes of the region's long-standing educational crisis.

Equally noteworthy, however, is what the discussion of education in the Santiago Plan of Action leaves out. It is oriented strongly toward ends and says little or nothing about the means needed to achieve those ends. It emphasizes access to education and says little about educational quality. It does not mention the magnitude of existing inequities in school systems and says little about how those inequities might be reduced. On key issues, such as decentralization, school autonomy, school choice, accountability, and national testing, the Summit document either conditions statements with "where appropriate" or is silent. The document makes only occasional reference to the role of nongovernmental actors in education. It avoids committing governments to increased education spending. The focus is much more on strengthening existing institutions than on reforming them.

### *More specifically, the Plan of Action*
- Urges only "special attention" to education standards rather than stating forcefully that governments should establish such standards as soon as possible.

- Makes no mention of the need to make teachers more accountable to principals, parents, and local communities and does not address the question of salaries.
- Does not recommend giving schools more decision-making authority or giving the private sector a greater role in school management.
- Does not recommend greater national investment in education nor experimentation with new finance mechanisms.

In sum, this document is a real, but small, step forward. It does not acknowledge the major failures of Latin American education. Nor does it call for fundamental, systemic change.

The 1998 Santiago Summit Plan of Action also established a more detailed process for implementing the education recommendations than did the *Plan of Action* approved at the Miami Summit in 1994. Multilateral organizations were asked to intensify their work in education and, specifically, to support initiatives based on the Summit recommendations. The Organization of American States (OAS) was charged with convening "technical consultation forums" to develop implementation plans and with bringing together the ministers of education to discuss them. Subsequent to the Summit, government representatives have met in Mexico, Washington, and Brazil (the latter, a ministerial meeting). A series of governmental working groups were established to promote work on the specific recommendations and are expected to develop proposals for funding by late 1998. The Inter-American Development Bank (IDB) and the World Bank have announced that they are significantly increasing funds earmarked for lending in education over the next several years.

Whether these initiatives will blossom into sustained and effective agents of change remains to be seen. They are composed exclusively of government representatives, having so far made little effort to involve nongovernmental organizations. They have yet to produce concrete action plans, and it is not clear how much importance the region's governments will give them. Yet they go well beyond the weak and ineffective follow-up efforts that were developed after the Miami Summit.

What would it take for these initiatives to have a truly positive impact? Governments need to take another critical step. They need to make a formal commitment to a sustained process of change that has measurable goals and a timetable.

The model for doing so has already been established by the hemisphere's efforts to build a Free Trade Area of the Americas (FTAA). FTAA-like machinery now needs to be organized and put into operation to create quality education throughout the Americas.

As in the pursuit of free trade, governments should establish a series of issue-specific working groups that engage every country of the Americas and together address all the key challenges to education reform. Specialized working groups might, for example, be established on these priority issues:

- Finance, aimed at setting targets for investments in each level of education and at exploring new sources of funds
- Teacher preparation and motivation, designed to identify ways to strengthen the teaching profession, including attention to standards, salaries, training, and accountability to parents and local communities
- Measurement and evaluation, including the setting of national and perhaps regional content and performance standards and establishing national and regional tests to measure progress
- Decentralization, aimed at developing effective approaches to giving schools more responsibility and making them accountable to parents and local communities.

The set of governmental working groups established after the Santiago Summit touch on just some of these issues, and there is no indication that they will address the crucial issues of accountability, incentives, investment, and strengthening the demand for education.

As ministers of trade do, ministers of education from every nation should assemble once a year to gauge the progress of the working groups, consider proposals, and set the agenda for the coming period. Business forums, scheduled in tandem with the ministers' meetings, should bring together corporate and financial leaders from throughout the hemisphere and involve them in the planning of programs for improving education. A small secretariat for the process should be created, perhaps by pooling the resources of regional institutions, such as the IDB, the OAS, and the UN Economic Commission for Latin America and the Caribbean (ECLAC), just as was done in the case of trade. Resources should also be made available to provide technical assistance to those countries that need it.

Most important, the governments should set concrete goals for education and ensure useful monitoring of each country's progress toward meeting those goals. Our own program—the Partnership for Educational Revitalization in the Americas (PREAL)—recommends that, by 2005, every government have established the following:

- A modern system of education statistics and indicators (for example, one that is compatible with the Organization for Economic Cooperation and Development OECD system of education indicators)
- National and regional content and performance standards that outline what students should know in math, science, and language when they complete each grade
- A regional testing system that generates comparable information on student performance in mathematics, science, and reading
- A substantial increase in per student investment in preschool, primary, and secondary education.

This approach would require every government to collect information and report on the details of their educational systems, thereby creating comparative data on educational laws and policies, teacher training and salaries, budgets and expenditures, performance, and other key issues. It would also require them to involve non-governmental stakeholders in their plans and to incorporate their concerns. Over time, the working groups, with the aid of the secretariat, would begin to propose standards against which nations should judge and compare their performance and to develop norms and guidelines for carrying out educational reform efforts. Later on, a common test for school children of all nations would allow for comparative evaluations of performance. These initiatives would be reviewed and approved at the annual meetings of education ministers and perhaps reviewed by finance ministers at their meetings. The idea is to make educational performance in every country open to regional review and judgments, as well as to stimulate hemispheric support to promote improvements. Only if education is transformed into a fully hemispheric issue will it get the attention and resources it needs.

# V. LEADERSHIP COUNCIL FOR INTER-AMERICAN SUMMITRY

## Monitoring Implementation of the Summit of the Americas: Partnerships for Sustainable Development

*S. Jacob Scherr and Robert K. Watson*

*The Natural Resources Defense Council, Inc. (NRDC) is a 290,000-member national environmental organization that promotes protection of the natural environment and public health. It has four offices in the United States and a staff of 150 lawyers, scientists, and environmental specialists.*

*S. Jacob Scherr is senior attorney with the NRDC and director of its International Program. He has worked with the NRDC since 1975 on a broad range of international environmental and nuclear issues. Mr. Scherr's projects include the global phase-out of leaded gasoline, the preservation of a gray whale nursery on the Baja Peninsula of Mexico, and the shutdown of dangerous Soviet-era nuclear power plants. He also serves as president of Earth Summit Watch, an organization he founded to monitor national implementation of commitments to sustainable development made at the 1992 Earth Summit.*

*Robert K. Watson is a senior energy resource specialist with the NRDC and the director of its International Energy Project. Mr. Watson, who joined NRDC in 1985, has worked on a wide range of issues related to energy policy and conservation efforts, including utility issues and building energy conservation. He is a board member of the U.S. Green Building Council and has also worked on projects in Russia, Belarus, Chile, Cuba, Mexico, Sri Lanka, and Ukraine. Mr. Watson works with a number of international financial institutions and U.S. government agencies to promote sustainable energy policies and programs in the developing world.*

### INTRODUCTION

Our Declaration constitutes a comprehensive and mutually reinforcing set of commitments for concrete results. In accord with the appended *Plan of Action,* and recognizing our different national capabilities and our different legal systems, we pledge to implement them without delay.

Summit of the Americas *Declaration of Principles*, Miami, 1994

The 1994 Miami Summit of the Americas produced agreement among the 34 leaders to establish three Partnerships for Sustainable Development: 1) the Partnership for Sustainable Energy Use, 2) the Partnership for Biodiversity, and 3) the Partnership for Pollution Prevention. Under each Partnership, the governments committed to 10 or 11 actions. These commitments varied widely in focus and scope. Some were directed toward actions to be taken by governments at the national level and others to be carried out cooperatively on a regional level. Some were extraordinarily broad; others were very specific.

In a working paper prepared in 1996, we described the genesis of the partnerships and intergovernmental efforts to implement the partnerships.[1] We noted the lack of a governmental effort to collect systematically information on the *national* implementation of the Partnership promises. We described our plans to conduct our own national-level implementation survey focusing on a number of the key commitments made in the Miami *Plan of Action* on energy and biodiversity. At that time, we remained hopeful that this gap would also be addressed by the December 1996 Summit of Americas on Sustainable Development in Santa Cruz, Bolivia. The leaders had explicitly agreed in Miami that the Bolivia Summit would discuss national progress on the implementation of the partnerships on biodiversity and pollution prevention.[2]

Starting in the summer of 1996, we began intense efforts to obtain responses to our implementation questionnaires. We repeatedly solicited responses from government officials, non-governmental organizations (NGOs), and the private sector throughout Latin America to report on actions taken by each nation. We reviewed materials and documents generated by the Summit Implementation Review Group. Natural Resources Defense Council (NRDC) staff were actively involved in the implementation processes for the Partnership for Sustainable Energy, the leaded gasoline phase-out project under the Partnership for Pollution Prevention, and, to a lesser extent, the Partnership for Biodiversity. We participated fully in the preparatory process for the Bolivia Summit. More recently, we have also discussed the implementation process with numerous officials, diplomats, and experts.[3] Our experience has been that it is very difficult to obtain information about national-level implementation.[4]

Overall, our conclusion is that while there is more talk now about the importance of implementation of the sustainable development partnerships, governments do not appear to take their commitments seriously or take the necessary measures to fulfill them. Our greatest disappointment was the total failure of the Bolivia Summit to fulfill the objective the leaders established for the gathering two years earlier. The December 1996 Summit did virtually nothing to assess progress that had been made on the partnerships over the last two years. Instead, it generated another 65 initiatives contained within five broad substantive areas.[5]

In this paper, we describe intergovernmental implementation efforts and review the results of our national implementation survey on energy. We then describe the limited hemispheric-level work underway and summarize our efforts to assess national activities to protect biodiversity. Next, we provide a case study that analyzes the success of the leaded gasoline phase-out initiative within the Partnership for Pollution Prevention. We conclude with a discussion of the negotiation process and provide some recommendations to improve implementation.

## TRANSFORMING *DICHOS* INTO *HECHOS*

In December 1994, President Bill Clinton proclaimed that the purpose of the Summit of the Americas in Miami was "to create a whole new architecture for the relationship between the nations and the peoples of the Americas, to ensure that *dichos* become *hechos*, that words are turned into deeds."[6] We have chronicled the numerous regional activities — additional conferences, plans of action, and reports — initiated in response to the Summit of the Americas Partnerships. However, despite concerted and prolonged labor to gather empirical evidence, we found it impossible — with the exception of the phase-out of leaded gasoline — to find a causal link between the Partnerships and actions by governments on the national level. This is not to suggest that many governments did not already have significant efforts underway related to biodiversity, pollution prevention, and sustainable energy. We were just not able, as a general matter, to demonstrate that these efforts were in fact stimulated, advanced, or even significantly supported by the process of Summit of the Americas implementation.[7]

## PARTNERSHIP FOR SUSTAINABLE ENERGY USE

### Hemispheric Energy Steering Committee

On both the international and the national level, the Partnership for Sustainable Energy Use has shown a fair amount of activity, though measurable progress at the country level has been modest to date. In part, this can be attributed to the fact that nearly 10 months passed without any action before energy officials from 26 nations gathered in Washington, D.C., for the Hemispheric Energy Symposium (HES).

Despite the fact that the meeting had been called for in two separate Miami Summit initiatives,[8] the October 1995 Symposium generated a new action plan that only partially addressed the Miami commitments, while adding new substantive commitments in Petroleum and Natural Gas.[9] A Hemispheric Energy Steering Committee (HESC) was created to coordinate implementation of the HES Plan of Action.

Margaret Mead once attributed all progress to a handful of dedicated people. As the following case studies illustrate, this maxim certainly holds with regard to the implementation of the Miami and Bolivia Summit sustainable development commitments, both at the national and the international level. While presidential-level agreement and institutional engagement are essential ingredients, what is critical to real progress is individuals, often at lower levels in national and regional agencies, who have been committed to finding the financial and human resources necessary to get the job done. NRDC has been a nongovernmental participant in the HES process since its inception. We have observed firsthand how the dedication of a few individual "champions" in the seven lead countries has been responsible for driving the process forward, despite a serious lack of budgetary or administrative support.

The private sector has been actively participating in this process from the outset. Opinions and support have been solicited on everything from the wording of specific initiatives in each of the Summits to sharing responsibility for implementing key projects. This should not be too surprising since energy is clearly the most commercial of the three Partnerships. The degree to which NGOs have participated in the development of energy initiatives ranges from extensively in the case of the United States, to moderately as in the cases of Chile and Canada, to not at all for most of the rest of the hemisphere. As the Hemispheric Energy Steering Group process has matured, greater participation of NGOs has been sought, but the reality is not many groups in the hemisphere focus on this issue and only a few, relatively wealthy, northern NGOs can afford to participate in the process with any regularity.

The first HESC meeting, in February 1996, organized the 40 Symposium actions into eight working areas and selected volunteer countries to coordinate each task.[10] The eight "outcomes" agreed upon at the Santiago, Chile, meeting were 1) Increased Investment in the Energy Sector of the Hemisphere (Coordinating country: United States), 2) Promote Clean Energy Technologies in Restructured Power Markets (OLADE[11]), 3) Advance Regulatory Cooperation in the Hemisphere (Argentina), 4) Regional Oil Integration (Venezuela), 5) Advance New Opportunities for Natural Gas (Bolivia), 6) Promotion of Energy Efficiency in the Hemisphere (Brazil), 7) Develop Strategies for Rural Electrification in the Hemisphere (Chile), and 8) Workplan for Establishing a Framework for Information Exchange (USA).

As can be seen, the activity supported by these eight outcomes consists of gathering data and information at the hemispheric level for exchange between countries, rather than supporting specific national actions to promote sustainable energy as was originally envisioned in the Miami Energy Partnership.

Brazil hosted the second HESC meeting in April 1996, where workplans for the eight outcomes were approved and preparations for the July 1996 Energy Ministers Meeting in Santa Cruz, Bolivia, were begun, including a preliminary agenda and a draft communiqué. The meeting also discussed possible energy initiatives for inclusion in the Bolivia Summit on Sustainable Development.

The third HESC meeting was held in Buenos Aires, Argentina, in October 1996 where the participants updated progress to date, continued work on energy initiatives for the Bolivia Summit, and discussed the need to locate a permanent secretariat for the HESC. Participants determined that the level of coordination and communication necessary to maintain the level of activity required that an administrative apparatus be set up.

Miami was the venue for the fourth meeting in March 1997. Several of the Outcome groups had work products completed or nearing completion, and discussions centered around how to make them useful at the national level. Project financing and the need for administrative help at the Working Group level were identified as priority items. Work products to date include the following:

- A portfolio of sustainable energy project financing mechanisms has been created.
- A White Paper on Innovative Financing for sustainable energy projects has been prepared.
- A hemispheric Energy Mix Baseline and Projections to 2000 and 2010 has been developed.
- Twelve "Fast-Track" clean energy projects have been identified.[12] These options will be entered into a "Clean Energy Database" for countries to evaluate.
- A database of Regulatory Training Needs and Resources has been prepared.
- Over a dozen international conferences and workshops on issues linked to the HES process have been held.
- A minimum standard fuel product specification has been developed.
- A White Paper on "Promoting Investment in the Petroleum Refinery Sector of the Americas" has been completed and made available on the Internet.
- A draft White Paper on a "Comprehensive Strategy for Natural Gas in the Western Hemisphere" has been circulated for comment.
- An Internet site on energy efficiency has been established.
- A cooperative plan has been developed for implementing energy efficiency financing in the hemisphere through the Inter-American Development Bank.[13]
- A report and analysis of the present status of rural electrification programs in the hemisphere has been prepared and distributed.

In addition to the HESC process, two Energy Minister meetings have occurred. The first meeting was the HES itself, and the other was held in Santa Cruz, Bolivia, in July 1996 in anticipation of the Summit later that year. A third gathering is proposed for early 1998 in preparation for the Santiago Summit.

## COUNTRY-LEVEL ACTIONS

At the national level, NRDC surveyed the progress made in implementation of four of the action items under the Partnership for Sustainable Energy Use.[14] Below, we describe the information gathered on the efforts of 23 nations, representing 98 percent of the population in the region. Our research focused on national governmental actions in four key Miami energy commitments: 1) the development of least-cost national energy plans, 2) the adoption of market-oriented energy pricing, 3) the development of sustainable energy projects for priority financing, 4) the undertaking of rural electrification programs, and 5) international cooperation in energy ventures outside the Summit process.

Our survey revealed that there was a lot of activity that was consistent with furthering the commitments made in Miami. Once again, we were unable to find evidence to show that these actions were started or furthered in any way as a result of the Summit of the Americas implementation process.

## COMMITMENT #1: INTEGRATED LEAST-COST ENERGY STRATEGIES

> "Governments will pursue, in accordance with national legislation, least-cost national energy strategies that consider all options including energy efficiency, non-conventional renewable energy (i.e., solar, wind, geothermal, small hydro and biomass) and conventional energy resources"[15]

Only six nations (Colombia, Costa Rica, Jamaica, Nicaragua, St. Lucia, and the United States) have what could be called an integrated least-cost national energy plan. These countries' plans assess and compare opportunities for meeting energy service needs through demand-side and supply-side measures and make policy recommendations to facilitate the capture of the most cost-effective and environmentally beneficial measures first. Another eight countries (Bolivia, Canada, Ecuador, El Salvador, Honduras, Mexico, Panama, and Paraguay) indicated that they had developed or are developing elements that begin to address this commitment. The remaining nine countries (Argentina, Belize, Brazil, Chile, Guatemala, Haiti, Peru, Uruguay, and Venezuela) either had no national energy strategy or did not submit information on it.

## COMMITMENT #2: MARKET-ORIENTED PRICING

> "Governments will emphasize market-oriented pricing, which discourages wasteful energy use."[16]

Five nations (Argentina, Canada, Chile, Ecuador, and the United States) either have completely deregulated or minimally regulated market pricing or are strongly moving in that direction. It is worth noting that while competitive pressures have increased the efficiency of energy production, costs to consumers have been driven down in many cases, resulting in higher energy consumption. For example, the energy intensity of the Chilean and Argentine economies has increased significantly over the last few years, while there has been no appreciable growth in the energy efficiency industry, and Canada still has the highest per capita energy consumption in the hemisphere.

Twelve countries (Belize, Bolivia, Brazil, Costa Rica, El Salvador, Jamaica, Mexico, Nicaragua, Panama, Paraguay, Peru, and Venezuela) have incorporated some element of market-based pricing. These nations are either moving toward marginal-cost pricing under a regulatory schema or are eliminating cross-subsidies between different classes of energy consumers or have recently opened up the market for generation for sale to the national grid to private concerns. The remaining six countries (Colombia, Guatemala, Haiti, Honduras, St. Lucia, and Uruguay) have not incorporated or did not report on efforts to move to market-oriented pricing.

It has been somewhat more difficult to remove or reduce subsidies for diesel for transportation, kerosene for lighting and heating for the poor and in rural areas, and heavy oil for power generation, which still remain in several countries, including Bolivia and Costa Rica.

## COMMITMENT #3: PRIORITY FINANCING FOR SUSTAINABLE ENERGY PROJECTS

> "Governments will identify for priority financing and development at least one economically viable project in each of the following areas: non-conventional renewable energy, energy efficiency, and clean conventional energy."[17]

In terms of the number of individual projects, this Partnership commitment resulted in the most activity, though sustainable energy projects are still far from the mainstream. We found many more renewable energy than energy efficiency projects being demonstrated (Jamaica and the United States are exceptions); few nations reported on clean conventional energy projects. In addition, almost all countries profiled have undertaken or have underway one or more studies of sustainable energy project potential or feasibility.

The majority of the countries in the hemisphere have several renewable energy projects going, particularly in conjunction with rural electrification programs. Most of the projects at this stage are relatively small: at the pilot or demonstration scale. But several countries have committed to making energy efficiency or renewable energy a significant part of the national resource portfolio. Ten countries (Argentina, Brazil, Canada, Colombia, Costa Rica, Honduras, Jamaica, Nicaragua, St. Lucia, and the United States) are seriously studying and demonstrating sustainable energy projects with the intent of making them a major part of their national or rural energy development plans.

Another eight countries (Belize, Bolivia, Chile, Ecuador, El Salvador, Mexico, Panama, and Paraguay) have begun development and implementation of sustainable energy programs and projects but at a very low level compared to the need or potential. Although many of these programs have not yet borne fruit, they may begin to show better results soon. Only five countries surveyed (Guatemala, Haiti, Peru, Uruguay, and Venezuela) do not have or did not report on sustainable energy projects under development.

## COMMITMENT #4:
## RURAL ELECTRIFICATION PROGRAMS

> "Governments will promote, in cooperation with the private sector and rural and isolated communities, rural electrification programs which take into account where appropriate the utilization of renewable energy resources, in accordance with the domestic regulatory framework."[18]

The Western Hemisphere's population is predominantly located in urban areas. As a consequence, many countries do not have or did not report having formal rural electrification programs, although several countries have developed innovative programs that combine government and private sector participation in appropriate-scale sustainable energy projects. Canada and the United States completed their rural electrification programs over the last decade or two, so this question is not applicable to them.

Six countries (Argentina, Brazil, Bolivia, Chile, Colombia, and Mexico) all have active rural electrification programs that emphasize sustainable energy sources for remote, stand-alone applications or for use in microgrids. Seven nations (Belize, Costa Rica, Ecuador, Jamaica, Nicaragua, Paraguay, and St. Lucia) have modest programs that address rural energy issues but do not have a significant sustainable energy component. The rest of the hemisphere's countries (El Salvador, Guatemala, Haiti, Honduras, Panama, Peru, Uruguay, and Venezuela) either do not have a rural energy program or did not report on it.

## INTERNATIONAL COOPERATION

Bilateral and multilateral efforts are key to moving the hemisphere toward a sustainable energy path. NRDC wanted to gauge the amount of international cooperation on energy occurring outside the scope of the Partnership for Sustainable Energy Use.

All of the hemisphere's nations except two (Haiti and St. Lucia) reported on international cooperative efforts. The Central American nations (Costa Rica, El Salvador, Guatemala, Honduras, and Panama) developed the CONCAUSA alliance with the United States to cover sustainable energy and joint implementation issues. The European Union and Spain have programs with Bolivia, El Salvador, Panama, and Paraguay. Canada, Mexico, and the United States have bilateral agreements with several other hemispheric nations. In addition, some countries are working jointly on international power development projects, for example, Mexico with Belize and El Salvador with Honduras.

## PARTNERSHIP FOR BIODIVERSITY

The Partnership for Biodiversity generated the least immediate intergovernmental follow-up of the three Miami Partnerships. This was due in part to the lack of strong continuing support for the initiative from any domestic agency of the U.S. government. In our last Working Paper, we described an effort supported by AID to resuscitate the Partnership in advance of the Bolivia Summit.[19] By the time of the December 1996 Summit, some biodiversity advocates were characterizing the Partnership as "dead in the water."

Hemispheric activity in biodiversity has been resuscitated somewhat in the aftermath of the Bolivia Summit. In large measure this is due to the official designation of the Organization of American States (OAS) as the principal coordinator for implementation of the Bolivia Summit initiatives. The OAS has some modest funding to play a catalytic role in the development of the Inter-American Biodiversity Information Network (IABIN).[20] The OAS has established a working group that includes officials from the U.S. Department of Interior and their counterparts in government and NGOs in the region and worldwide. Two important meetings to discuss the structure and content of the IABIN are scheduled for October and November of this year.

The Bolivia meeting appears to have renewed interest in biodiversity-related issues.

The first Latin American Congress on National Parks and Protected Areas released a series of recommendations for how the Santa Cruz *Plan of Action* should affect Parks and Protected Areas as fundamental repositories for protecting biodiversity. What is interesting about this series of recommendations is that they are specific to areas in Central and South America.[21]

At the national level, NRDC in 1996 surveyed country implementation, compiling information on the Summit of Americas implementation in 16 countries — including six case studies — on three priority issues: 1) public participation, 2) conservation funding, and 3) sustainable forestry incentives.[22] In addition, NRDC and its partners identified "biodiversity flashpoints" in 20 countries around the hemisphere as test cases for countries' commitments to biodiversity protection and sustainable development.[23]

Our work on the "flashpoints" pointed to the existence of another serious disconnect: that is, between national commitments and their implementation. Many of our flashpoints involved the failure of governments to assure the preservation of legally protected areas. National parks, biosphere reserves, and other such areas in Bolivia, Ecuador, Honduras, Uruguay, and elsewhere are being invaded and degraded. Also, some of the last remnants of northern, temperate, ancient forests in Canada and the United States are not being preserved for future generations.

## COUNTRY LEVEL SURVEYS

We found once again that while there were some encouraging actions in a number of countries on biodiversity, there was no evidence that the international commitments at the Summit had in any way been responsible for precipitating these national actions.

## Public Participation

"Governments will support democratic mechanisms to engage public participation, particularly including members of indigenous communities and other affected groups, in the development of policy involving conservation and sustainable use of natural environments. The forms of this participation should be defined by each individual country."[24]

There is little evidence that countries have made substantial progress in providing public notification and comment on government regulations and policies, opening government meetings and documents to the public, and enabling members of the public to challenge government decisions through impartial administrative and judicial processes. While many countries engage public participation through Environmental Impact Assessment (EIA) procedures that seek to identify and mitigate potential damages from development activities, NRDC's research revealed a number of troubling lapses in implementation of EIA requirements in countries such as Chile, Honduras, Mexico, and the United States. In a related area, six of the 16 country profiles indicated that public participation has been engaged through various forms of national planning for land and resource management.

We found it difficult to separate biodiversity concerns from indigenous peoples' rights and environmental democracy. In spite of a growing recognition of the rights of indigenous people, they and the lands that they have traditionally inhabited are being exploited indiscriminately. As highlighted by the Nicaraguan case study, governments need to do much more to support democratic mechanisms to enable meaningful participation by indigenous communities in decisions on land and resource management. The case study focusing on indigenous efforts in the Darien Gap region of Panama provides a precedent-setting model for the kind of local community participation that is needed before major infrastructure projects are undertaken. In Peru, areas designated for oil and gas development are demarcated without regard to indigenous lands. Despite some citizen and indigenous rights groups' protests, we found that there is still reluctance in some countries to speak out on controversial issues. This reluctance to speak out belies an eagerness to work constructively in finding "on-the-ground" solutions to protect biodiversity and move toward sustainable development.

## Conservation Funding

"Governments will review the regulatory framework for non-governmental actors with a view to facilitating their operations and promoting their ability to receive funds. This review will emphasize the management and oversight of resources as well as transparency and the accountability to society of said actors." [25]

There is only limited evidence that governments have followed through with this explicit Summit commitment This implementation shortfall remains a significant impediment to improved financing of NGO activities for biodiversity conservation. However, one bright spot emerging from the study is the growing international support among policymakers for innovative financing mechanisms such as National Environmental Funds (NEFs). More than 25 NEFs and similar mechanisms have been established or are being created throughout the Western Hemisphere.

Most often, NEFs manage capital investment funds or endowments, using the proceeds, and sometimes part of the principal, to make grants supporting sustainable development and environmental activities. A well-managed and adequately capitalized NEF can help build a nation's capacity to achieve biodiversity conservation objectives by providing dependable financing to cover operating and infrastructure expenses for NGOs. NRDC found that sustaining the necessary political support for NEFs remains a significant challenge in many countries.

## Sustainable Forestry Incentives

"Governments will seek to ensure that strategies for conservation and sustainable use of biodiversity are integrated into relevant economic development activities including forestry, agriculture, and coastal zone management, taking into account the social dimension and impact of these activities."[26]

and

"Governments will develop and implement the policies, techniques, and programs to assess, conserve, and sustainably use terrestrial, marine, and coastal biodiversity resources."[27]

NRDC's study found little overall movement toward reform of tax, credit, and agricultural policies to encourage forest conservation. In many countries throughout the Americas, national policies have historically created incentives for land conversion to crop and livestock production at the expense of biologically rich forest cover.

The information compiled for this report showed that a number of countries have recently enacted, or are in the process of developing, new forestry legislation with conservation provisions. However, enforcement of forestry laws remains a serious problem in many parts of the hemisphere. Examples from the survey responses include inconsistent enforcement of forest practice regulations in the Brazilian Amazon, legal loopholes undermining the effectiveness of the forestry statute in El Salvador, and the government's failure to promulgate regulations implementing forestry law reforms in Jamaica.

There have been a number of developments throughout the Americas on forest certification, which has been identified as a promising tool for conservation and sustainable use of biodiversity. Examples of certification efforts can be found in Bolivia, Costa Rica, and Canada. At the hemispheric level, significant progress and broad-based public support is being achieved on forest certification under the auspices of the Forest Stewardship Council (FSC), which is a multi-stakeholder international organization that accredits certification bodies. The FSC approach features independent, third-party certification of well-managed forests, with measurable performance standards and labeling of products that verifiably come from certified forests.

Some countries provide various forms of financial and technical assistance for forest management activities. Examples we uncovered in our research include Mexico's "PRODEFOR" program, low interest loans in El Salvador, and forestry incentive payments in Colombia.

Finally, the study did not reveal significant progress toward reform of environmentally damaging timber concession policies. The study findings highlight the continuing urgent need for governments to end the practice of opening forest areas to logging companies without safeguards for indigenous peoples' rights and the environment.

## PARTNERSHIP FOR POLLUTION PREVENTION: THE PHASE-OUT OF LEADED GASOLINE

In accordance with the Miami *Plan of Action*, a technical meeting was held in November 1995 to develop specific initiatives in response to the Summit's general guidance. At that meeting held in Puerto Rico, an interagency task force headed by the OAS and including the

World Bank, the Inter-American Development Bank, and the Pan-American Health Organization was created to oversee working groups convened around the four topic areas: phase-out of leaded gasoline, water resources, pesticides, and sustainable tourism.[28] A working group on the development of a legal experts support network also was created as a first-step response to the call for creation of environmental policies and laws and the call to "strengthen and build technical and institutional capacity to address environmental priorities." A number of countries have reported on creating a basic environmental legal framework, as called for in the Partnership.[29] As often as not, however, these same reports cited *Agenda 21* as the impetus for this action. Thus, while it is apparent that countries are engaging in the implementation of elements of the Partnership, it is not clear to what degree they have been spurred by the Summit of the Americas process.

Although the hemispheric implementation process for the Pollution Prevention Partnership started off reasonably well, it soon lost momentum. According to participants, the interest and energy that had been generated at the Puerto Rico meeting was diverted by the Santa Cruz process; the result was a lack of progress in moving forward the Partnership activities, with the exception of the lead phase-out, as described below.

Perhaps the greatest success story to emerge from the Miami Summit involves efforts on the phase-out of leaded gasoline. Lead compounds have been added to gasoline since 1923 to increase octane and enhance performance. The dangers of lead, particularly to children, are well recognized and accepted. Exposures from leaded gasoline can result in impaired growth, mental retardation, and blood-related diseases. Also, unleaded gasoline is required for catalytic converters, which are essential for reducing a range of other auto emissions. Prior to the Miami Summit, a number of countries in the hemisphere had already eliminated lead from their gasoline supply, including Brazil, Canada, Colombia, Guatemala, and the United States.[30]

The Miami *Plan of Action* called on governments [to] "[d]evelop and implement national action plans to phase out lead in gasoline."[31] Then, just a few months after the Miami Summit, the U.S. Environmental Protection Agency (US EPA) and the Mexican Ministry of Environment, Natural Resources, and Fisheries co-hosted an "International Workshop on the Phase-out of Lead in Gasoline" in Washington, D.C.[32] The March 1995 meeting was also sponsored by the Pan-American Health Organization (PAHO) and the World Bank. It was the first large international gathering ever to address specifically this issue and feature reporting from governments around the world on their experiences in phasing out leaded gasoline.

Subsequently, in November 1995, a meeting of technical experts was convened in Puerto Rico under the auspices of the Partnership for Pollution Prevention to "identify priority projects," as had been agreed to in Miami. A Working Group focused on Lead Risk Reduction. It proposed a project to facilitate the development of national plans to phase out leaded gasoline, for presentation at the December 1996 Bolivian Summit on Sustainable Development.[33] The Working Group recommended that governments complete the phase-out by January 1, 2001. It called upon each government to identify a focal point responsible for information and statistical data relevant to the national effort to phase out leaded gasoline. It also identified the World Bank — which already was developing a regional project on leaded gasoline phase-out — or the Inter-American Development Bank as potential institutions to manage the project.

A consultation starting shortly after the Puerto Rico meeting led to the launching in January 1996 of a program led by the World Bank to

- assist the Governments of the Americas in their formulation and implementation of National Plans for the phase-out of leaded gasoline,
- exchange information and experiences during this planning process, and
- provide technical assistance on a country-by-country basis.[34]

An informal Steering Committee was created to oversee the implementation of this project chaired by the Oil and Gas Division of the World Bank. The other members of this committee included representatives of the Organization of American States (OAS), Inter-American Development Bank (IDB), PAHO, US EPA, U.S. Department of Energy (U.S. DOE), U.S. Agency for International Development (USAID), and the Natural Resources Defense Council (NRDC).

The World Bank had already identified potential financial support for this effort from the European Union and the Canadian International Development Agency. The Steering Committee recommended that each government in the region designate a National Focal Point to coordinate projects and implement National Leaded Gasoline Phase-out Plans and to serve as liaisons between the Steering Committee and the various organizations within their countries. In February 1996, OAS Secretary-General

César Gaviria sent formal diplomatic letters at the ministerial level requesting that each country identify its Focal Point. After significant prodding by the OAS, 25 countries had responded and identified their focal points by July.

In spite of the success of this initiative, the Bolivia Summit did not review — as had been hoped — the progress made in implementing this or other Pollution Prevention Partnership commitments made in Miami. Nor did the subject receive any discussion at the meeting. Indeed, the final declaration of the Bolivia Summit included weaker language on leaded gasoline phase-out than that agreed to in Miami.[35]

In April, 1996, the World Bank and ARPEL (Reciprocal Assistance of Latin American Oil Companies), with assistance from the Committee on Cooperation, initiated a regional Inventory Diagnostic survey.[36] A detailed questionnaire, sent to all of the countries in Latin America and the Caribbean, covered motor fuel production and consumption, vehicle fleets, regulations, environmental and health issues, and opportunities for cooperation and technical assistance. The responses to this survey were collated into a report for review and comment.

In September 1996, the National Official's Seminar on the Elimination of Lead in Latin America and the Caribbean was held in Santiago, Chile, with 23 countries and eight international organizations represented. The "Santiago Seminar" evaluated the results of the draft Alconsult report.[37] Attendees discussed the difficulties and successes of their phase-out efforts, and identified specific needs for technical assistance.

Following this seminar, the World Bank has been involved in carrying out national-level "case studies" on leaded gasoline phase-out in a number of countries, including Peru, Trinidad, Jamaica, Chile, El Salvador, and the Dominican Republic. These studies involve technical aid to develop national phase-out plans, a workshop on a specific aspect of the phase-out problem, and a review of the successful experience of one nation in moving quickly to eliminate lead from its gasoline fuel supply. More recently, with financial support from the European Union, the Bank worked with OLADE on "studies" in Ecuador, Panama, and Paraguay.[38]

In February 1997, the United States Environmental Training Institute (USETI) — with financial support from U.S. EPA — carried out a very innovative project in Lima, Peru, on leaded gasoline phase-out. USETI combined a two-day "executive seminar" and a three-day training program. It brought together the entire range of "stakeholders" from the Prime Minister to industry and NGO representatives. It appears to have improved the political will and enhanced the technical capabilities to phase out leaded gasoline.

This initiative has produced real results in encouraging nations to move more quickly to reduce and eliminate leaded gasoline. Bolivia phased out leaded gasoline in 1995, and Argentina completed its phaseout in 1996. That same year, all of the Central American countries became lead gasoline-free with the sole exception of Panama. Since 1994, Mexico has cut leaded gasoline use by some 30 percent and Ecuador by more than 50 percent. Both expect to eliminate all leaded gasoline use by the year 2000.

While unwilling to set a target date, Chile is now in the process of reducing the use of lead in its gasoline supply and of upgrading its refineries. Peru has set 2009 as its target date for phase-out, although there are indications that it will accelerate the phase-out. The biggest holdout is Venezuela, the only country in the hemisphere where unleaded gasoline is not made available to domestic consumers.[39] This is particularly galling since Venezuela refines and exports significant amounts of unleaded gasoline to the United States and other countries.

The use of lead in gasoline in Latin America has decreased from 27,400 tons in 1990, to 10,300 tons in 1996, and is expected to decrease to 6,400 tons by the year 2000. In Latin America, the percentage of unleaded gasoline consumed in 1996 was 68 percent. By 2000, 83 percent of the gasoline consumed will be unleaded.[40]

What made implementation of this initiative so successful? The initiative was sharply focused, and there was a continued resistance to efforts to expand the scope of the effort. The issue was one that was accessible and understandable to the general public and thus attractive to political leaders. It already was the subject of public and technical debate and discussions in a number of countries. The World Bank had already identified leaded gasoline phase-out as a priority, had personnel dedicated to work, had a project to focus on the Latin American region, and was able to provide real leadership. There was financial support available, most importantly from the Canadian government. The initiative went beyond general regional discussions to include targeted assistance at the national level. Finally, there was an effort to engage a range of stakeholders — political, technical, industry, financial, and the public — necessary to move forward on this matter.

At the Bolivia Summit, the OAS was given a number of new responsibilities for ensuring the fulfillment of sustainable development commitments. These new responsibilities include coordinating the efforts of an international ad hoc group that includes multilateral development banks, national government agencies, and other international organizations.

There are five working groups the OAS is involved with coordinating: 1) Energy, 2) Legal Network for the Environment, 3) Sustainable Cities, 4) Financing Sustainable Development, and 5) Clean Water for Urban Populations. The most successful to date appears to be the Energy working group, which identified a single project — the Bolivia-Brazil natural gas pipeline — on which to concentrate its efforts. Through the working group, the WB, IDB, and Andean Development Corporation (CAF) were able to collaborate intensively with the project sponsors on a well-defined and specific goal. Within three months, each of the multilateral development banks was able to commit $200 million to the project, while attracting seven other international finance agencies. The collaboration has been so successful, the working group is looking to develop it as a case study and disseminate its findings.

## IMPROVING THE SUMMIT PROCESS

Not surprisingly, there was near unanimity about the top constraints to the implementation of the Miami and Bolivia Summit Partnerships for Sustainable Development. We heard complaints about failures in content, as well as failures in intent, on the part of governments to craft workable initiatives with adequate resources to fulfill them. We would argue that these problems are endemic to the Summit process itself, and frankly we are not sure they are soluble given the current structure.

The failure to implement negotiated commitments stems from the interaction of four principal areas: 1) a negotiating process that emphasizes "sounding presidential" over crafting workable initiatives, 2) a lack of commitment and leadership on the part of countries actually to undertake the agreed-upon activities, 3) an international coordinating structure that is ill-equipped to support national-level implementation, and 4) international institutions that are ill-equipped to support international coordination efforts.

## IMPROVING THE NEGOTIATION PROCESS

One of the largest barriers to implementation of the Summit sustainable development commitments is the initiatives themselves. The failure to have workable commitments is a result of the Summit negotiating process.

The major constraint is the need to "sound presidential." To get around this constraint, we recommend that the vision and soaring rhetoric that characterize Summit documents should be confined to the *Declaration* portion of the statement, while the *Plan of Action* should contain specific, achievable, and measurable outcomes that include deadlines.

The drive for consensus and the short time horizon over which accord must be achieved result in enormous leverage for countries wishing to incorporate their pet interest in the hemispheric agenda. All participants in the agenda-setting process — governments and nongovernmental stakeholders alike — are guilty of succumbing to the path of least resistance, which is to accept someone else's initiative in exchange for support of their own — the "Christmas Tree" effect. This results in the second major constraint to implementation: an excessive number of overly broad initiatives already committed to. This problem also is exacerbated by the fact that countries want to be seen as progressive, so they commit to activities that are above their technical, fiscal, and political capability to implement.

We recommend that the hemisphere engage in a process to consolidate, simplify, and adopt no more than a total of 10 high-priority Partnership for Sustainable Development action items. They should be drawn from the Miami and Bolivia meetings in full consultation with civil society and responsible national and international institutions. These 10 priority initiatives would become, in a sense, the hemisphere's "To Do List" for the next few years. Each initiative should be very specific and achievable. Each should have a deadline and include measurable outcomes. To ensure this, primary responsibility for negotiating details of each action item should be given to the national agencies that would be required to implement them. They know what their legal requirements, interests, capabilities, and budgets are; thus, they are more unlikely that presidential representatives or diplomats to make commitments that are really difficult or impossible to implement at the national level.

The current approach to Summit negotiations consists of two separate elements that often do not combine very well. What appears to be missing is an opportunity for all of the key participants in making meaningful national commitments to meet and reach agreement. These participants are the national implementing, finance, and diplomatic agencies and the multilateral and bilateral development, financing, and assistance institutions.

As a general matter, the process of creating Summit sustainable development proposals generally involves a set of international expert meetings and consultations. These meetings will involve the relevant implementing and international agencies and private and NGO stakeholders, more often from wealthier countries that possess greater resources to develop and implement programs. This technical process often results in solutions that are well thought-out, specific in nature, and even include deadlines.

These proposals are then taken up in more traditional diplomatic negotiations involving officials from foreign ministers and representatives of the leaders. Unfortunately, much of the effort and expense associated with coming to technical consensus ends up being wasted because the final negotiators either have not been involved in the technical discussion leading up to the specific proposals or are not well-versed in the issues. In any case, the tendency is to avoid deadlines and specificity. These negotiations will often be more reflective of international and national political concerns. At this stage, there is little or no attention paid to whether the national governments have any real interest or intent in carrying out the resulting mandates. The outcome is a lot of beautifully expressed but hopelessly unworkable commitments that satisfy the need of saying something without actually committing to anything concrete.

## IMPROVING NATIONAL IMPLEMENTATION

There are a number of steps that national governments should take to improve the implementation of Summit commitments. As a first step, each government must assign a specific official and agency with responsibility for implementation. It is critical that such a "focal point" be identified for each Summit commitment. Otherwise, there is a likelihood that no one within government will be responsible or accountable, and nothing will be done. The focal point should also be responsible for coordination among the implementing, financing, and diplomatic agencies and for reporting on implementation. Each national government must devote sufficient resources to maintain a viable level of activity in each priority area.

Finally, the private sector, NGOs, other nongovernmental stakeholders, and the public should be full participants in the implementation processes. Many governments made efforts to solicit the views of civil society in the process of developing initiatives for the Miami and Bolivia Summits. Governments should also assure that such stakeholders are also involved in the process of implementation.

On the hemispheric level, governments must report periodically to one another and the public about the progress they are making to fulfill their Summit promises. As indicated earlier, there has been little or no national reporting in the Summit of the Americas process; as a result, we found it almost impossible to document that there were indeed national actions initiated or furthered by the Summit process. Without such actions, there will never be progress toward sustainable development, the broad goal now embraced by all governments in the hemisphere. Nor is it clear that the Summit process would remain vibrant or even viable if it cannot show results. At the Bolivia Summit, the OAS has been given a very important role in coordinating and collecting information on national-level implementation activities. We hope that the effort results in a clearer picture on sustainable development activity in the hemisphere.

## IMPROVING INTERNATIONAL IMPLEMENTATION MECHANISMS

The Miami Summit *Plan of Action* vested international coordination of each of the partnerships with national governments. The United States and Venezuela shared responsibility for the Energy Partnership. The Partnership for Biodiversity was supposed to be coordinated by the leader of SICA (Central American Integration System),[41] with Ecuador and Peru acting as co-coordinators. The Pollution Prevention initiatives were chaired by Ecuador, along with SICA and Peru in the role of co-coordinators. In practice, we saw two models emerge: 1) the government-led efforts and 2) an ad hoc process described below that relied on existing international institutions, such as the World Bank and the OAS.

In general, the Energy Partnership coordinators received high marks from participating governments for their roles in moving the process forward. Due to the early and consistent support for the Hemispheric Energy Symposium (HES) process, the United States and Venezuela were able to generate sufficient momentum that allowed other countries to become invested in the process. As a result, the HES is now ready to move to the next level with a permanent secretariat, not only for the overarching process but for many of the sub-processes as well. Although the Hemispheric Energy Symposium process has resulted in a fairly effective international mechanism, it can only be considered a qualified success because it has yet to facilitate significant efforts on the ground in individual countries.

Participants in the Biodiversity and Pollution Prevention Partnerships generally agreed that the responsible coordinators had inadequately discharged their duties. One problem with the Biodiversity Partnership coming out of Miami was that the government responsible for overseeing the initiatives rotated every few months, not allowing sufficient time for anyone to get invested in the task and exercise the necessary leadership.

Similarly, the Pollution Prevention Partnership had several countries involved in a coordinating capacity, which made it easy to assume that someone else was going to take primary responsibility for the work. In addition, some participants felt that the Responsible Coordinator was attempting to dictate the agenda rather than build consensus among countries on specific actions, which resulted in a loss of momentum after the Puerto Rico meeting. Because little action was being taken by the Responsible Coordinator, international organizations such as the OAS and World Bank stepped into the breach to allow some progress to continue. In addition, when it came time to begin preparing for the Bolivia Summit, government attention was diverted from other issues except the phase-out of leaded gasoline.[42]

## IMPROVING INTERNATIONAL FINANCIAL SUPPORT

Governments must assure that the multilateral agencies do in fact play a role in providing support for Summit initiatives. National governments serve on the governing boards of, for example, the World Bank, Inter-American Development Bank, and the Organization of American States and have the theoretical ability to set the agenda for these institutions. However, our interviews with a number of government and multilateral development bank officials indicate that the Summit of the Americas process has had a very limited impact on the agendas of these institutions. More often than not, existing initiatives developed independently by these organizations are merely repackaged so as to appear to be responding to Summit *Plans of Action*.

The priorities of the World Bank and the Inter-American Development Bank (the "MDBs") are established in processes quite separate from those of the Summit of the Americas. The agendas of the MDBs are principally set 1) through the replenishment process or 2) in bilateral interactions with borrowing countries. Generally, representatives of ministries of finance sit on the boards of the MDBs or take the lead responsibility in relations with these institutions. As noted above, these finance agencies are almost never involved in the negotiations of sustainable development initiatives. Even if they are, budgeting and appropriation processes are subject to domestic politics, which may or may not be responsive to the particular political imperatives that led to the adoption of the Summit initiatives. To avoid this disconnect, we recommend that specific initiatives be designed to be more closely in tune with existing government and MDB agendas and that national finance ministries be integrated more fully into the Summit negotiation process.

## CONCLUSION

The Summit of the Americas raised expectations throughout the hemisphere that national governments would move forward with concrete steps toward sustainable development through three Partnerships. Our research finds that these hopes remain unfulfilled. We have put forward a series of relatively simple, straightforward recommendations for improvement of the Summit process to help assure that more of the "words" of the leaders actually are transformed into "deeds."

# Notes

1. Justin Ward, Arturo Garcia-Costas, S. Jacob Scherr, and Robert Watson, 1996, *Implementing the Summit of the Americas: Building Sustainable Development Partnerships* (Coral Gables, Fla.: North-South Center Press).

2. At the July 1996 Energy Ministers meeting in Santa Cruz, Bolivia, the Ministers also agreed to report on progress at the Summit on Sustainable Development later that year.

3. Because of the very frank assessments given, many of these officials did not wish to be identified or quoted, and we have respected these requests.

4. For example, it was not possible to get a list of country focal points for the Partnerships for Sustainable Development from the Summit Coordinating Office at the U.S. Department of State. Nor does this information exist on any of the Internet sites devoted to the Summit of the Americas.

5. They are 1) Health and Education, 2) Sustainable Agriculture and Forests, 3) Sustainable Cities and Communities, 4) Water Resources and Coastal Areas, and 5) Energy and Minerals. In addition, 16 other initiatives in the institutional, financing, technology, and cooperation aspects of sustainable development also were agreed upon.

6. Remarks delivered by President Clinton at the Miami Summit.

7. For example in December 1994, USAID compiled a 100-page report, *New Partnerships in the Americas,* that regarded the Miami Summit initiatives on sustainable development as an extension of the Agenda 21 process launched at the 1992 Rio conference.

8. Initiative #12: Energy Cooperation and Initiative #21: Partnership for Sustainable Energy Use.

9. See Table 1 from Ward, *et.al.*, note 1, above.

10. There have been over 15 international meetings of the various Outcome working groups to date.

11. *Organizacion Latino Americano de Energía* — The Latin American Energy Organization.

12. Projects include Natural Gas in Argentina; Wind and Cleaner Coal in Brazil; Biomass in Colombia; Hydro, Biomass, Solar, and Wind in Mexico; Energy Efficiency in Peru; Geothermal in St. Vincent; and Cleaner Fuel in the United States.

13. The Sustainable Markets for Sustainable Energy (SMSE) program.

14. Watson, R. K., A. Garcia-Costas, A., Mary Anne McConnel, S. Jacob Scherr, December 1996. *The Road to Enlightened Energy in the Americas* (Washington, D.C.: Natural Resources Defense Council).

15. Initiative #21: Partnership for Sustainable Energy Use, Summit of the Americas *Plan of Action*, December 1994.

16. Ibid.

17. Ibid.

18. Ibid.

19. Ward, *et. al.*, Note 1, above.

20. Initiative #31: Sustainable Agriculture and Forests, *Declaration of Santa Cruz de la Sierra and Plan of Action for the Sustainable Development of the Americas*, December 1996. It could be argued that this Bolivia Summit commitment has its origin in the "Decade of Discovery" action item from the Miami Partnership, which called upon governments to "facilitate the exchange of information relevant to conservation and sustainable use of biological diversity."

21. *Actividad Especial: Coordinación del Seguimiento del Plan de Acción de las Américas para el Desarrollo Sostenible— Iniciativas sobre Biodiversidad.* Primer Congreso Latinoamericano de Parques Nacionales y Otras Áreas Protegidas, Santa Marta, Colombia, May 21-28, 1997.

22. Justin Ward, Arturo Garcia-Costas, S.. Jacob Scherr, Thomas Butler, and Mary Anne McConnell, *Falling Trees and Fading Promises*, Natural Resources Defense Council, Washington, D.C., December 1996.

23. NRDC, *et.al. Biodiversity Flashpoints in the Americas: Test Cases for Sustainable Development*, Natural Resources Defense Council, Washington, D.C., December 1996.

24. Partnership for Biodiversity, Summit of the Americas *Plan of Action*, December 1994.

25. Invigorating Society/Community Participation, Summit of the Americas *Plan of Action*, December 1994.

26. Initiative #22: Partnership for Biodiversity, Summit of the Americas *Plan of Action*, December 1994.

27. Ibid.

28. The water quality issue and the legal experts network received additional support from the Bolivia meeting and have been revived, though no concrete proposals have yet emerged. A number of bilateral efforts regarding legal experts network have been underway, particularly in Central America.

29. At the domestic level, Chile, Colombia, Nicaragua, and Paraguay all reported progress in developing a national environmental framework without mentioning the impetus. Ecuador and Uruguay, on the other hand, made it clear that *Agenda 21* was the initiating event.

30. The United States began to phase in the use of unleaded gasoline in 1973; and by 1993, 99 percent of all gasoline sold in the United States was unleaded. As of January 1, 1996, the sale of leaded gasoline was banned.

31. Initiative #23: Partnership for Pollution Prevention, Summit of the Americas *Plan of Action*, December 1994.

32. The impetus for this workshop was the call for a global phase-out of leaded gasoline issued by U.S. EPA administrator in April 1994 at the United Nations Commission on Sustainable Development.

33. The Working Group also proposed a project to establish national inventories of lead and its impact on the environment and the development of national plans aimed at reducing lead exposures.

34. Energy Sector Management Assistance Program (ESMAP), Oil and Gas Division, Industry and Energy Department, The World Bank, 1996, *Elimination of Lead in Gasoline in Latin America and the Caribbean* (Washington, D.C.: The World Bank) at 2.

35. Santa Cruz Initiative #46 in Sustainable Cities and Communities calls for "Improve[d] cooperation in order to continue the development and execution of national plans for the gradual elimination of leaded gasoline." *Declaration of Santa Cruz de la Sierra and Plan of Action for the Sustainable Development of the Americas*, December 1996.

36. The survey was carried out by Alconsult International Ltd., a Canadian consulting firm.

37. This report is included in ESMAP 1996, 23-82.

38. There were also a number of related supporting efforts undertaken by PAHO, U.S. AID, and other agencies. Two examples are a study on the creation of monitoring blood-lead levels as lead in gasoline is phased out and EPA-WHO regional workshops.

39. Also some of the small island states in the Caribbean have still not adopted national plans to phase out leaded gasoline.

40. Energy Sector Management Assistance Program (ESMAP), Oil and Gas Division, Industry and Energy Department, The World Bank, 1996, *Elimination of Lead in Gasoline in Latin America and the Caribbean* (Washington, D.C.: The World Bank) at 24.

41. "Sistema de Integración para Centro América." Headquartered in El Salvador, leadership of this body rotates every six months, and with it, the responsibility to coordinate the Biodiversity Partnership.

42. Momentum has been revived in clean water issues and a legal experts network because coordination responsibility has been vested with the OAS.

# V. LEADERSHIP COUNCIL FOR INTER-AMERICAN SUMMITRY

*Colleen S. Morton is vice president and director of research at the Institute of the Americas, La Jolla, California.*

# Progress Toward Free Trade in the Western Hemisphere Since 1994

*Colleen S. Morton*

## EXECUTIVE SUMMARY

The purpose of this paper is to evaluate progress on trade liberalization in the Western Hemisphere, focusing particularly on those activities resulting from commitments made at the 1994 Summit of the Americas in Miami. Five different types of activities are examined: unilateral policy changes; developments in existing subregional arrangements; the negotiation of new subregional arrangements, whether bilateral or regional; the Free Trade Area of the Americas (FTAA) process itself; and the implementation of commitments under the Uruguay Round of multilateral trade negotiations. In addition, we analyze the economic and political forces driving decision-making in key countries: the United States, Brazil, Canada, and the smaller countries taken as a group.

Based on this examination, two long-term trends in trade policy can be identified in the region. The first trend is toward the adoption of further liberalizing policies, however unevenly implemented, at all levels – unilateral, bilateral, subregional and regional. The second trend is toward increasing politicization of trade policy as awareness of the impact of globalization on microeconomic factors continues to grow. This second trend, which has served to block or retard efforts toward effective implementation of liberalizing policies, portends serious challenges for the FTAA effort.

In addition to identifying long-term trends, this analysis raises several critical short-term policy questions. The first is the degree of linkage between trade policy and other macroeconomic and social policy concerns such as labor rights, environmental protection, and currency and market volatility. Linking progress on trade to progress on these other policy issues clearly complicates the politics of the entire process, from the fight over fast-track authority in the United States to the implementation of the final accord. Nevertheless, linkage is a direct result of the increasing awareness of the impact of globalization on domestic economies and is therefore likely to increase in scope and political salience rather than the reverse.

A second critical short-term policy question is the relationship between the evolving FTAA process and a multitude of other planned or possible trade initiatives, including the launch of a new multilateral round under the auspices of the World Trade Organization (WTO), which is desired by many countries; the initiation of sectoral talks in APEC (Asia-Pacific Economic Council); investment negotiations in the Organization for Economic Cooperation and Development (OECD); and the continuation of a variety of bilateral negotiations and unilateral decisions. The coherence of trade policy is being called into question by the proliferation of overlapping initiatives, resulting in a complex patchwork of different standards, rules, schedules, and responsibilities. Such complexity of arrangements detracts from the ability of businesses to respond effectively to new opportunities and diminishes the economic results that might have been anticipated.

Finally, the FTAA process needs analysis from the point of view of regional costs and benefits, taking into account the effort required to implement multiple competing commitments and the political will needed to counteract anti-globalization sentiment. How will an FTAA really affect the economies of the region, individual sectors, and individual firms? Cost-benefit analysis must take into account not only the existing situation, but also the situation that will arise after implementation of Uruguay Round commitments and related follow-up negotiations. If fully implemented, these commitments will have a significant impact on this hemisphere, particularly on tariff rates in developing countries – thereby diminishing the benefits one could expect from a preferential regional agreement.

Many governments doubt that an FTAA will significantly benefit their economies, but instead are convinced that it will hurt their most sensitive industries. The economic analyses conducted so far on the costs and benefits of hemisphere-wide free trade have been relatively superficial and do not address the specific concerns of many Latin American and Caribbean nations. While it is intuitively obvious that freer trade in the hemisphere would benefit the most open economies in the region (i.e., Canada and the United States) by leveling the playing field, it is also clear that serious adjustments would have to be made within a circumscribed period of time in all the other countries. Since many countries in the region do not have economic or social safety nets in the form of unemployment insurance or adjustment assistance, it is easy to understand politicians' reluctance to accelerate the adjustment process any more than is absolutely necessary.

When combined with the continuing volatility of financial markets and unease over current account deficits (witness the recent emergency package adopted in Brazil), it is perhaps easier to foresee a retrenchment on the trade front in some key countries rather than an enthusiastic embrace of free trade, particularly if the leading economy in the region, the United States, remains incapable of offering anything more than rhetorical support.

That being said, there has developed a certain amount of political momentum around the FTAA through the annual trade ministers' meetings, business forums, and technical working groups. Whether this momentum will survive if the United States cannot provide leadership for a formal launch of negotiations in 1998, as agreed in Belo Horizonte (the location of the 1997 trade ministerial meeting), remains to be seen.

## INTRODUCTION

The broad objective of this paper is to provide an overview of progress on trade liberalization in the Western Hemisphere since the 1994 Summit of the Americas. More specifically, it looks at trends toward consolidation of subregional trade agreements and at the progress to date in the pre-negotiation phase of the Free Trade Area of the Americas (FTAA) talks. In this regard, it should be noted that tariff reductions and commitments under the Uruguay Round, which will have a significant impact on trade in the hemisphere, are not examined in detail, being outside the scope of this particular exercise. However, the FTAA negotiators will be starting in 1998 from a post-WTO context and will be able to build on that framework.

Since the 1994 Summit of the Americas in Miami, significant technical progress has been made toward defining negotiating issues, identifying commonalities and divergences, and consolidating existing subregional and bilateral agreements. The trend in most countries in the hemisphere is toward more liberalization and toward the adoption of stronger disciplines on tariff and nontariff barriers. Some subregional groups are also beginning to deal with issues such as services, intellectual property protection, and macroeconomic coordination. The governments of the region have taken the difficult initial step of committing to begin actual negotiations for a Free Trade Area of the Americas in 1998, and they have initiated the necessary political, administrative, and conceptual processes to make this possible.

The North American Free Trade Agreement (NAFTA), while still not overwhelmingly popular in any of the three member countries, has nevertheless proved to be a positive economic experience. Trade is growing rapidly among the three members, and most of the commitments that were made have been adhered to with relatively little controversy.

The Common Market of the Southern Cone (Mercado Commun del Sur – MERCOSUR), though subject to the centrifugal forces of volatile exchange rates, has held together well and since 1994 has made major strides both in consolidating its internal regime and toward expanding its regional scope through agreements with other Latin American countries (with Chile and Bolivia to date).

Progress in the smaller regional groups has been less dramatic, but still visible. The Caribbean Community and Common Market (CARICOM) has begun to reach out to the larger Caribbean community through the Association of Caribbean States (ACS). The Central American Common Market (CACM) has moved ahead on a variety of non-trade related infrastructure projects, which should bring good economic results by helping to integrate physically the small economies of that region.[2] The Andean Community, meanwhile, had temporarily lost one of its members, Peru, but is now seeking ways to accommodate Peru's reentry at the same time as it negotiates with MERCOSUR.

Bilateral agreements continue to proliferate. In 1994, there were 26 bilateral or trilateral free trade agreements or customs unions in the hemisphere, not to mention a large number of bilateral investment treaties.[3] By the beginning of 1997, several more had been added, including the Bolivia-MERCOSUR agreement, the Chile-MERCOSUR agreement, and the Canada-Chile bilateral agreement. Discussions are ongoing between Chile and CARICOM, Chile and CACM, CACM and MERCOSUR (starting in September 1997), the Andean Community and MERCOSUR, Venezuela and MERCOSUR, Mexico and MERCOSUR (a transitional agreement only); Mexico and the northern triangle countries in Central America, Mexico and Nicaragua[4], Mexico and CACM as a whole, Mexico and Peru, and Mexico and Ecuador. Trinidad and Tobago has expressed interest in joining the North American Free Trade Agreement (NAFTA). In addition, Chile and Mexico are exploring the possibility of deepening their bilateral agreement to make it NAFTA-plus. (See Appendix E for a complete list of agreements signed or under negotiation.)

The nature, depth, and extent of these agreements vary. Analysts at the Inter-American Development Bank (IDB) have categorized them as either first generation agreements (relatively simple tariff elimination agreements) or "new" generation agreements (agreements having more complex objectives with a "selective-strategic character").[5] First generation agreements in force at the end of 1994 will eliminate almost all tariffs for members by the end of the 1990s. New generation agreements will "eliminate virtually all tariffs on trade among member countries for about 95 percent of the items by the year 2004, and the rest will be eliminated shortly thereafter."[6] The IDB further points out that in the next five years, customs unions currently being perfected will create integrated markets with common external tariffs and only limited exceptions for certain categories of goods.

All these trade agreements and arrangements have contributed to a dramatic increase in intra-hemispheric trade. Trade data for 1995 and 1996 demonstrates rapid growth in intraregional trade, with trade diversion from other regions occurring on a relatively small scale and in just a few sectors.[7]

Table 1. Exports by Destination[8] – 1996 (partial)

| Destination | MERCOSUR | Andean Community | G-3 | ALADI | CACM | Latin America | NAFTA | Hemisphere |
|---|---|---|---|---|---|---|---|---|
| MERCOSUR | 12.2 | 0.3 | 6.1 | 9.7 | -2.9 | 9.7 | 6.8 | 8.1 |
| MERCOSUR-Bolivia-Chile | 10.9 | 3.1 | 14.6 | 9.8 | -11.1 | 9.8 | 7.7 | 8.2 |
| Andean Community | -8.5 | -0.6 | 0.5 | -2.8 | 5.3 | -2.7 | -0.7 | -2.0 |
| CACM | -13.5 | 10.7 | 11.8 | 11.0 | 4.6 | 8.0 | 5.1 | 4.8 |
| CARICOM | -4.9 | 5.0 | 6.4 | 4.8 | 46.8 | 5.5 | 5.9 | 5.5 |
| NAFTA | 9.7 | 19.5 | 20.2 | 18.1 | 12.8 | 17.9 | 10.0 | 10.4 |
| G-3 | -17.4 | -2.4 | -2.8 | -6.9 | 37.1 | -6.2 | 15.5 | 13.2 |
| ALADI | 9.1 | -0.1 | 5.4 | 6.7 | 22.9 | 6.8 | 12.4 | 10.7 |
| Latin America[10] | 9.0 | 1.4 | 6.8 | 7.2 | 8.9 | 7.2 | 11.3 | 9.9 |
| Latin America/Caribbean[11] | 8.9 | 1.9 | 6.8 | 7.2 | 9.4 | 7.2 | 11.1 | 9.8 |
| Hemisphere | 8.4 | 13.6 | 18.5 | 14.8 | 10.4 | 14.7 | 9.3 | 9.4 |
| World | 6.6 | 10.3 | 16.4 | 11.4 | 5.7 | 11.2 | 7.4 | 7.4 |

Source: Inter-American Development Bank

Meanwhile, some countries, such as El Salvador and Nicaragua, have continued to reduce tariffs unilaterally, and many have begun to attempt to address the administrative and bureaucratic problems affecting their ability efficiently and competitively to engage in global trade. With the help of the IDB and the Organization of American States (OAS), efforts also are underway to expand technical trade knowledge in order to better implement, monitor, and enforce compliance with regional and subregional trade agreements.

This generally positive hemispheric picture is counterbalanced by a number of worrisome trends. Of particular concern since 1994 has been the severe macroeconomic instability of several parts of the hemisphere, most notably in Mexico but also affecting several countries in South and Central America. While most economies have recovered almost completely from the Mexican peso crisis and the so-called "tequila effect", a number of economic warning signs remain on the horizon, particularly with respect to balance of payments issues, exchange reserves, debt service levels, domestic savings rates, and unemployment. The impact of the recent volatility in Asian markets provides another illustration of the fragility of Latin American economies. Nevertheless, many economists predict fairly robust, if uneven, economic growth in Latin America over the next few years.

Politically, the case for more unilateral or regional liberalization has been undercut somewhat by the numerous and deep commitments made under the Uruguay Round, most of which are just beginning to be implemented in Latin America. This is particularly true for Brazil as well as for the very small states; neither feels particularly prepared to move ahead on both multilateral and regional fronts at the same time.

In the United States, the political situation remains cloudy following the postponement of a vote on fast track until early 1998. It remains to be seen whether the full-employment economy underway in the United States will persist until a vote occurs and whether it will convince a majority of Congressmen that they can afford to be pro-free trade in the face of strong labor opposition and other objections to fast track, regional free trade, and free trade in general. Postponement means the vote will occur in an election year, giving unions and environmental groups more time to work the hustings against the fast-track bill. In view of these difficulties, the administration appears to be quietly floating the idea of dropping the FTAA from the fast-track request, limiting the bill to multilateral and perhaps bilateral negotiations.

The U.S. business community is largely supportive of fast track, both for the FTAA and for other multilateral and bilateral trade initiatives currently under discussion. However, for a variety of reasons, they remain skeptical about the administration's chances of winning the battle in Congress for new authority. NAFTA has soured many in Congress on trade agreements, despite its positive trade results and minuscule labor impacts. The Democratic Party is deeply divided over trade, particularly over linkage to labor and environmental issues. In turn, the Republican Party is ready to bolt if it appears that President Bill Clinton is caving in to demands for stronger labor or environmental provisions. While the initial bill passed by committees in both houses contains only the most lukewarm language on the disputed topics (promising to take them up in the WTO), the final bill to be passed by Congress could conceivably incorporate different and possibly stronger language if Democrats are able to convince some moderate Republicans to side with them to save the bill.

In Brazil, the business community is still struggling to adapt to a noninflationary economy and to the substantial liberalization that has occurred over the past four years. According to Brazilian businesspeople, the transition to an open economy has been too rapid, and the government has not done enough to build the export-oriented infrastructure that would help firms become more competitive. In particular, they cite what they call "Brazil costs," or the costs of inefficient ports, roads, railways, bureaucracies, and markets, as major impediments to competitiveness. The Brazilian business community is supportive of government efforts to postpone any market access negotiations until the very end of the negotiating process, even though, no matter when market access negotiations are started, the resulting agreement will certainly provide for an extended period of at least ten years duration for the phase-in of tariff and nontariff reductions.

The most important political challenge being mounted against the FTAA in the United States and in Brazil comes not from embattled businesses, but from labor. This challenge has much less to do with free trade than with income inequality; differential rates of growth in wages for blue-collar and white-collar workers; the shifting of the economy toward services and away from traditional assembly-line jobs; and the fragmented and inadequate state of education, training, placement, and retraining services. In Brazil, as in most of Latin America, the lack of any real "safety net" or unemployment insurance makes decisions that may increase unemployment significantly more costly in a political sense than they are even in the United States.

To go back to the wage issue, wages for blue collar and middle-income workers in the United States clearly have been stagnating for several years.[12] The reason for this is unclear. Is it due to greater competition from overseas suppliers relying on cheaper labor? Is it a result of technological change? Or is it primarily due to the weakening of unions and of labor's bargaining power in a service-oriented economy? Opponents of trade liberalization argue that large multinational corporations are benefiting from liberalization at the expense of workers and small businesses. Despite the strong economy, Congress remains susceptible to these arguments.

In Brazil, income inequality has been worsening, leaving Brazil with the worst income distribution in the world, according to some estimates. Again, the trend is clearer than the causes, but left-leaning politicians have been quick to identify foreign competition and foreign "exploitative" companies as culprits. In general, the notions of "liberal economic policy" and "globalization" have come under attack in these circles as not sufficiently taking into account the social costs of openness and change. These are difficult assertions to counter effectively, particularly in an era of governmental budget stringency.

Thus, by the end of 1997, we were left with a mixed picture concerning progress on free trade in the region and the outlook for the future. On one hand, the concrete results of trade liberalization have been impressive and positive at the macroeconomic level. On the other hand, a growing unease about microeconomic and social costs, as well as the pace of change, belies the otherwise optimistic picture. Looking ahead, the prospects for an official launch of the FTAA negotiations in 1998 have been hurt by the Clinton administration's failure to acquire fast-track negotiating authority and by the economic crisis in Brazil, which has forced a retrenchment on market liberalization in that country.

## UPDATE ON COUNTRY-BY-COUNTRY READINESS INDICATORS SINCE 1994

If one were to utilize the 1994 Hufbauer/Schott readiness indicators in 1997 to evaluate the readiness of individual countries and groups to participate in a regional free trade agreement, significant improvements in readiness would be visible in a number of countries, particularly Brazil. However, as we have discussed above, readiness does not necessarily indicate willingness.

What this table summarizes is the view that although readiness has improved almost everywhere in the hemisphere, the desire to participate – i.e., the desire to undertake negotiations for an FTAA and to implement additional reforms and liberalization – varies considerably around the region. A particular problem is that the United States and Brazil, the hemisphere's pacesetters, are so far only providing cautious leadership, the U.S. for lack of fast track and Brazil for internal political reasons. Internal politics will continue to dictate the speed and vigor of their efforts.

Domestic politics are no less important for the rest of the hemisphere, and balance of payments, fiscal considerations, and entrenched interest groups will have to be factored into any cost/benefit calculation.[14] Downturns in the region's macroeconomic picture probably have the greatest potential to skew calculations against FTAA negotiations and could even set back implementation of pre-agreed commitments under subregional arrangements and the WTO.[15]

If the hemispheric trade liberalization process were to stumble on the basis of any of the difficulties identified above, a wide variety of outcomes would be possible, all of them suboptimal for the region.[16] Some have proposed that in light of the complex set of collective action problems implied by an FTAA negotiation, it will be necessary to buy support for the FTAA by setting up mechanisms (based on the IDB, the UNDP (United Nations Development Program), and the North American Development Bank – NADBANK) to "multilateralize" the benefits of liberalized trade, i.e., to tax trade and redistribute the revenues to those most requiring "adjustment assistance."

However, it is doubtful that such a redistribution would mitigate the political economy problems faced by countries like the United States and Brazil; it could actually worsen them. A debate in the U.S. Congress over the collection and transfer of trade tax revenues to other countries in the region – whether through multilateral or supranational means – could not possibly be any less combative or controversial than the vote over fast track (or implementing legislation); it would probably be much worse. What criteria would be established, and by whom, for determining how much revenue various countries would get and which ones were deserving and which ones not? While such a transfer might help buy support from the smaller economies that ostensibly would be the major

Table 2. Readiness and Willingness Table

| Country/Group | Readiness 1994 | Readiness Gain/Loss to 1997 | Desire to Participate in FTAA[13] |
|---|---|---|---|
| **North America** | 4.4 | + | **Medium** |
| U.S. | 4.7 | + | Medium |
| Canada | 4.6 | + | High |
| Mexico | 3.9 | + | Medium |
| **Chile** | 4.4 | + | **High** |
| **MERCOSUR** | 3.1 | + | **Medium** |
| Argentina | 2.6 | + | Medium |
| Brazil | 2.3 | + | Low |
| Paraguay | 3.7 | + | Medium |
| Uruguay | 3.7 | + | Medium |
| **Andean Community** | 3.4 | + | **High** |
| Bolivia | 3.7 | + | High |
| Colombia | 3.7 | - | High |
| Ecuador | 3.4 | + | Medium |
| Peru | 2.1 | + | High |
| Venezuela | 3.9 | - | Medium |
| **CACM** | 2.7 | + | **High** |
| Costa Rica | 3.3 | - | High |
| El Salvador | 3.7 | + | High |
| Guatemala | 2.6 | + | High |
| Honduras | 2.6 | + | Medium |
| Nicaragua | 1.6 | No change | Medium |
| **CARICOM** | 3.7 | + | **Low** |
| Bahamas | 3.6 | No change | Medium |
| Barbados | 4.1 | No change | Medium |
| Guyana | 2.4 | No change | Low |
| Jamaica | 3.7 | - | Low |
| Trinidad and Tobago | 4.4 | No change | Medium |

Source for readiness figures: Hufbauer and Schott 1994, 102.

recipients, they are not really at the heart of the collective action problem facing the hemisphere.

Thus, one may hope that the modest political momentum built up over the last three years, described in more detail below, and the obvious benefits of trade liberalization to the economies of the entire region will carry the day. If not, the likely alternative is not degeneration into competing subregional blocs, but rather a call for a new global trade round that would mitigate some of the uncertainties faced by the hemisphere's multilateral traders and raise the stakes for the entire global trading community.

## CONSOLIDATION OF SUBREGIONAL AGREEMENTS SINCE 1994

### Andean Community

Perhaps the most visible development in the Andean region has been the changing institutional structure and membership issues. "In 1996, the [Andean] countries focused on reforming the institutions which support their internal integration process – agreeing to transform the Andean Pact institutions created in 1969 by creating the 'Andean Community,' with a single Secretary-General to replace the current five-member Junta."[17]

Changes to the institutional structure include the following:

- Formally incorporating the Andean Presidential Council into the Community
- Formally incorporating the Andean Council of Ministers of Foreign Relations (Consejo Andino de Ministerios de Relaciones Exteriores – CAMARE) into the Community
- Subordinating the Andean Commission to CAMARE
- Replacing the three-member Junta with a single Secretary-General who will manage the General Secretariat of the Andean Community
- Making the Andean Tribunal of Justice a more active and effective jurisdictional organ of the Community.[18]

In consolidating its internal and external trade policies, the Andean Community has faced a number of problems stemming from differential treatment provided for Bolivia and Peru and, to some extent, from the centrifugal pull of MERCOSUR. The internal free trade area has been in force since 1993 among Bolivia, Colombia, Venezuela, and Ecuador. Bilateral agreements and partial implementation of the internal free trade area continue to govern trade with Peru. A four-tiered Common External Tariff (CET) was in place between 1995 and 1997 among Colombia, Venezuela, and Ecuador, but it is riddled with exceptions. A five-tier structure has been adopted recently, with levels at 5, 10, 15, 20, and 35 percent. Until the end of 1998, Venezuela, Colombia, and Ecuador are exempt from applying the CET on 230, 230, and 400 items, respectively. In addition, one critical sector remains completely outside the CET, namely, automotive industry products, which are subject to tariff rates as high as 40 percent.[19]

Bolivia has its own 5 and 10 percent flat-tariff rate structure, which it continues to exercise on non-Andean products, and Peru maintains a two-tier national tariff level (12 percent and 20 percent). After an on-again, off-again relationship with the Group over the last few months, Peru once again rejoined the Group as of June 1997 under an agreement that allows Peru to retain tariffs until 2006 on some 40 to 50 sensitive regional agricultural products and phases in free trade with Colombia, Venezuela, and Ecuador until 2003. Peru's bilateral agreement with Bolivia will continue to govern trade between those two countries, and Peru will not be bound by the CET, but rather will continue to impose its two-tier structure.[20]

The Andean Community countries adopted a common intellectual property rights policy in 1993, and they have begun trying to harmonize policies on foreign investment. They have initiated a number of liberalizing steps in surface, air, and maritime transportation, with a dramatic impact on commercial and passenger traffic and shipments in the region. Their efforts toward macroeconomic coordination have been notably less successful.[21]

The Andean Community, including Peru, initiated joint negotiations with MERCOSUR in December 1997, hoping to reach an agreement before the preferences they receive under ALADI expired. However, these proved very difficult and have not so far resulted in an agreement.[22] Progress could perhaps have been more rapid if the Bolivia-MERCOSUR agreement could have been adopted as a model for larger Andean Community negotiations. Both Venezuela and Peru, individually and separately, have discussed negotiations with MERCOSUR, and if the Andean Community talks do not succeed soon, such unilateral efforts are likely instead.

Andean Community members are also involved in a series of other agreements around the hemisphere, most importantly perhaps with Mexico and CARICOM. The Group of Three arrangement among Colombia, Venezuela, and Mexico, in force since January 1, 1995, has imposed important new NAFTA-like disciplines on trade among those countries. The effects will gradually become more noticeable to the respective business communities over the next eight years, as tariffs are phased out and macroeconomic stability is restored in the subregion.

Internal trade within the Andean Community grew dramatically between 1990 and 1994. During this period, non-oil exports from members to each other grew from 8 to 17 percent of total exports. Over the same period, imports from all sources increased at an average annual rate of 12.5 percent, while imports from the subregion grew at an annual average of 33.4 percent.[23] More recently, however, between 1995 and 1996, the rate of growth in intra-subregional trade declined dramatically to -0.6 percent due to a variety of economic factors affecting Colombia, Venezuela, Peru, and Ecuador.

The decision to attempt to reintegrate Peru in order to carry out a unified negotiation with MERCOSUR is encouraging. Such a negotiation, if eventually successful, would set the stage for a major realignment of trade orientation for most of the Andean countries, away from North America to their neighbors in South America. To avoid significant disruptions in trade patterns, it would be preferable for an Andean Community-MERCOSUR agreement to take place in the context of ongoing FTAA liberalization involving North America. However, the timing of the latter effort may not come soon enough to suit some Andean nations.

## CENTRAL AMERICAN COMMON MARKET (CACM)

CACM, established in 1961, is composed of Guatemala, Honduras, El Salvador, Nicaragua, and Costa Rica. Since 1993, the CET has been set with a floor at 5 percent and a ceiling of 20 percent. The CET will be phased in gradually with specific targets for individual countries; the average external tariff is now 15 percent.[24] Panama, which has never been part of CACM, remains the most protected market in the region with a tariff ceiling of 40 percent. In 1995, Panama became a signatory of the Tegucigalpa Protocol establishing the Central American Integration System.

Severe macroeconomic imbalances in Costa Rica, Honduras, Guatemala, and Nicaragua have created obstacles both to implementation of the CET and to further liberalization. Both Costa Rica and Nicaragua actually increased tariffs in recent years (Costa Rica increased tariffs in 1995, then reduced them in 1996; Nicaragua increased tariffs in 1993). On average, more than 20 percent of federal tax revenues in the region come from import tariffs.

Since the March 1995 San Salvador Summit, CACM governments have reasserted their commitment to regional integration and to modernization of regional institutions. Some 57 regional organizations and bodies now comprise the Central American Integration System (SICA), but the ability of these institutions actually to implement policy decisions has been very limited. The IDB and the United Nations Economic Commission for Latin America and the Caribbean (ECLAC or CEPAL) are involved in efforts to increase the efficiency and effectiveness of these organizations.[25]

Central America also is afflicted by the continued existence of strong entrenched import-substitution interest groups, such as freight carriers and agricultural producers. The agricultural sector is characterized by a series of only partially implemented agreements to liberalize and deregulate the sector. Import licenses, quantitative barriers, tariffs, phytosanitary certifications, border delays, and red tape still create major obstacles to an integrated regional market for agricultural goods.[26]

To date, services have not been included in the CACM framework, although the so-called "northern triangle countries" – Guatemala, El Salvador and Honduras – have adopted agreements to facilitate the movement of capital and labor. The lack of liberalization and integration of freight services is particularly damaging to the goal of expanded trade in the region.

CACM readiness for the FTAA negotiations is thus relatively low in both services and agriculture.[27] Many nontariff barriers are still in place; they include unreasonably stringent and selectively enforced sanitary, safety, and quality standards, as well as import licenses for sensitive items. According to United States Trade Representative (USTR), "Ongoing discussions to remove these barriers have not been widely successful, as CACM members have only limited leverage for reform in the absence of dispute settlement and enforcement provisions. In addition, recent discussions have not produced a consensus with respect to the protection of intellectual property rights, foreign direct investment, and services (especially banking and telecommunications) in the context of regional integration."[28]

More fundamentally, there is an urgent need at the national level for an adequate legal and institutional environment that guarantees property rights, including intellectual property rights and contract validity, in order to provide an attractive climate for foreign investment. National governments are moving at different speeds to make these reforms. El Salvador, for instance, has made dramatic strides in privatizing industries such as telecommunications. Panama, a CACM observer, completed its accession to the WTO in 1997.

To attempt to remedy some of these gaps, CACM countries in 1995 agreed to a common agenda of microeconomic reforms, including:

- deregulation;
- steps to attract investment;
- pension reform;
- construction of infrastructure links.

In keeping with this commitment, the Council of Ministers Responsible for Central American Economic Integration and Regional Development in 1996 approved new regulations on rules of origin, unfair trade practices and safeguard clauses. Also, the Secretariat of the Treaty on Central American Economic Integration (SIECA) is working on a series of regulations and new instruments, including technical standards, plant and animal health standards, a customs code, and trade in services. New versions of the Single Customs Form and the International Transit Guide aimed at facilitating trade in the region have also been approved.

However, the first priority for most countries in the region will continue to be to get their fiscal houses in order and to improve the overall macroeconomic picture. While progress has been made in reducing inflation levels, current account deficits and large external debt loads undermine the regional commitment to and ability to implement true economic integration. A further indication of this lack of commitment came in early 1997, when CACM countries decided to postpone for two more years the reduction in the CET ceiling from 25 percent to 15 percent. This step ostensibly was taken to protest the lack of any real proposal for NAFTA parity by President Clinton during his trip to the region. However, given the fiscal climate, the decision was probably a foregone conclusion.

## CARICOM

CARICOM was founded in 1973 and, with the addition of Surinam in 1995, it now includes 14 countries: Antigua and Barbuda, the Bahamas, Barbados, Belize, Dominica, Grenada, Guyana, Jamaica, Montserrat, St. Kitts and Nevis, St. Lucia, St. Vincent and the Grenadines, Suriname, and Trinidad and Tobago. The Dominican Republic and Haiti are not members, although they have a larger population than the rest of the region combined. CARICOM's internal market is about 6.3 million people with an average GDP of $2,500 per capita. Members are gradually moving toward a common external tariff of 40 percent for agricultural products and 5 to 20 percent for nonagricultural products by the year 1998 for a few countries, and by 2000 for the rest. Ninety-five percent of intraregional trade is now free of illegal restrictions although member states are allowed to retain their own import surcharges, licenses, quotas, and prohibitions.

That being said, there is very little intraregional trade and almost no intraregional investment. Most of the economies in the region rely on the same export base, with the partial exception of Trinidad and Tobago's oil exports. Excluding petroleum and petroleum-based products, intraregional exports accounted for only 5 to 8 percent of total exports through 1994. Besides the similarity of production structures, several other factors have been blamed for the low level of intra-CARICOM trade; these include high production costs, the persistence of trade barriers, the absence of a trade payments mechanisms, high transportation costs, limited knowledge of product availability, marketing shortcomings, and negative consumer perceptions.

An important feature of CARICOM is the bifurcation of benefits between the More Developed Countries (MDCs) and the Least Developed Countries (LDCs). Under CARICOM rules, LDCs can suspend common market tariff treatment on products from MDCs in order to develop an industry. According to the terms of the Colombia-CARICOM agreement, the LDCs never have to offer reciprocal tariff privileges. Many of the LDCs belong to the OECS (Organization of Eastern Caribbean Countries). These countries share a common currency, the EC dollar, which is managed by the Eastern Caribbean Central Bank. They are strongly reliant on bananas, sugar, and tourism.

This division between larger and smaller economies has created obstacles to rapid liberalization and integration, particularly because of CARICOM's requirement for unanimity in all regional decision-making. As a result, the Dominican Republic is negotiating with the CACM rather than CARICOM, and Trinidad and Tobago and Jamaica, frustrated with the slow pace of change in the region, have started to strike out on their own in discussions with the rest of the hemisphere, including NAFTA. They feel that gaining access to NAFTA, or at least to U.S. markets, on the same terms that Mexico enjoys is critical to avoid trade and investment diversion away from CARICOM.

This view is not commonly shared by the smaller CARICOM economies:

"... the smaller countries are more reticent to join NAFTA, even through they have signed on to the Miami/Denver/Cartagena hemispheric process aimed at creating the Free Trade Area of the Americas (FTAA). They see little advantage to be gained since manufacturing is underdeveloped, inefficient, very narrowly based, and heavily dependent on imported inputs, while agriculture is generally also not competitive and dependent on trade preferences. Their exports are mainly commodities that are sold on the European market. In their view, NAFTA and the FTAA bear little relevance to the vitally important tourism sector. By contrast, they fear the obligations involved and the impact of external competition."[29]

In general, the effectiveness of CARICOM has been thwarted by non-implementation of decisions due to a lack of political will and deficient local infrastructure. Particularly serious for the FTAA enterprise is the serious shortage of legal drafting capacity[30] caused by the extremely small-scale bureaucracies found in most member states. "The shortage of trained personnel and the limited range of available skills both have a major bearing on the capacity of small CARICOM countries, singly and collectively, to undertake more far-reaching commitments such as are involved in a NAFTA-type agreement."[31]

To begin to redress this situation, the governments decided in July 1995 to establish a Technical Action Service Unit to help governments with training and implementation. With IDB and ECLAC help, CARICOM also is trying to modernize and strengthen its secretariat. CARICOM countries also recently agreed to parcel out responsibility for individual FTAA working groups and presumably will continue to divide responsibility for the actual negotiating sessions.

With respect to the various issues that presumably would be negotiated under an FTAA, most CARICOM countries still have a long way to go before they could be deemed "ready" to participate. Regarding standards, for instance, only 97 regional standards have been promulgated, of which 27 are mandatory. Even of these, "... there is widespread non-application of regional standards. Administrative capacity is limited in most Member States for the management of a national standardization program, in terms of both implementing standards and monitoring compliance, even where the establishment of a national standards organization has been effected."[32]

Sanitary and phytosanitary standards are already quite similar due to a common regional legal inheritance (except for Surinam), but there has been no effort to coordinate or consolidate national laws beyond this. Rules of origin in CARICOM are very complex and are imposed in a variable manner that can create additional barriers to trade.

Agriculture continues to receive special treatment, which is understandable due to the very significant share of export revenues and employment generated by bananas, particularly in Dominica, St. Lucia, and St. Vincent.

Services are not covered by any CARICOM agreement, nor is national treatment provided for CARICOM investors. Intellectual property protection is not coordinated regionally, and many countries are not signatories of the major multilateral conventions.[33]

There are no regionally established rules either for government procurement or for dumping and subsidies, and while arbitration panels are provided for the settlement of disputes, members tend to prefer politically mediated settlements. Finally, there are no regional environmental or labor agreements, although CARICOM committees have been established on each issue.

In light of these various weaknesses, CARICOM heads of government decided in 1994 to establish a new organization, the Association of Caribbean States (ACS), to promote economic cooperation in trade-related areas such as tourism, transport, and agriculture, inter alia. The ACS is composed of the 25 states and territories in the Caribbean Sea and on the Caribbean littoral, with a population of 200 million consumers. The ACS includes members of CARICOM, CACM, Andean Pact, and NAFTA (Mexico), plus European dependencies. Due to the inclusion of Cuba in the ACS, the United States has not recognized it as a new regional entity. For this and other budget-related reasons, the ACS has gotten off to a slow start.

In 1996, the heads of government reaffirmed their commitment to the establishment of a Single Caribbean Market and Economy, including the implementation of the CET and elimination of nontariff barriers. The summit also approved a plan to improve currency convertibility, which remains a problem among some of the member states. Implementation will continue to be the main challenge facing CARICOM as it tries to become more engaged in the FTAA process while simultaneously seeking to reinforce group decisionmaking within CARICOM and now the new ACS.

## MERCOSUR

On January 1, 1995, a customs union among Brazil, Argentina, Paraguay, and Uruguay entered into force. The customs union provides for the free movement of a high percentage of tradable goods originating in the area, a common external tariff (with some exceptions), and a common tariff code. MERCOSUR's common external tariff, with 11 levels varying from 0 to 20 percent, covers 85 percent of all tariff items. The average external tariff is 11.4 percent.[34]

A number of important items are exempted from internal free trade, including the following:

- (Argentina) iron and steel, textiles and shoes, paper
- (Brazil) textile products, rubber
- (Paraguay) textiles and shoes, food, paper, iron and steel
- (Uruguay) textiles, food, chemical products, iron and steel, paper

These exceptions must be eliminated by January 1, 1999, for Brazil and Argentina and by January 1, 2000, for Paraguay and Uruguay.[35]

All automotive and sugar products were excluded from internal free trade, although automotive trade is governed by bilateral agreements,[36] and internal trade in sugar should be liberalized by the year 2001.

In addition to the tariff reductions and establishment of common external tariffs, many nontariff measures also were eliminated or harmonized in 1995. The MERCOSUR standards committee has carried out extensive work on harmonization of national standards in the areas of information technology, telecommunications, transport, construction, pharmaceuticals, and foodstuffs. A subgroup is also working on an agreement on testing and certification procedures and common conditions and codes of practice for laboratories and certification bodies.[37] MERCOSUR has adopted WTO rules on sanitary and phytosanitary measures.

Exceptions to the CET are as follows:

- Up to 300 domestic exceptions are allowed per country (399 for Paraguay) for sensitive products.
- Tariffs on capital goods will converge at 14 percent by the year 2000 for Brazil and Argentina and by 2006 for Paraguay and Uruguay.
- Tariffs on informatics and telecommunications products are scheduled to converge to 16 percent by 2006.
- Tariffs in the automotive sector will begin to fall under the CET in the year 2000.
- Sugar will be covered by the CET in 2006.

The internal and external investment regimes are broadly similar except for the automotive sector, where Brazil and Argentina have retained the option of requiring otherwise prohibited performance requirements. All four countries have taken a number of exceptions to the investment regime, but these are to be eliminated "as soon as possible."[38]

Exceptions to MERCOSUR investment regime include:

- (Brazil) mineral prospecting and mining, hydraulic power, health services, broadcasting and telecommunications, rural property, financial intermediation, insurance, shipping
- (Argentina) real estate in border areas, air transport, ship-building, nuclear plants, uranium mining, insurance, fishing
- (Uruguay) electricity, petroleum and natural gas, financial intermediation, railways, telecommunications, broadcasting, the press
- (Paraguay) real estate in border areas, information media, transport, public utilities, petroleum and natural gas

With respect to the services sector, a framework agreement was scheduled to be submitted to the Common Market Council before the end of September 1997. In Ouro Preto, the members adopted a Multi-modal Transportation Agreement governing trade operations under a single contract involving more than one transport mode, as well as a Hazardous Merchandise Transportation Agreement. At present, transport of goods and persons across frontiers is allowed, but internal cabotage is not.

The 1991 Treaty of Asunción provided for very weak central institutions that have since been strengthened and given formal juridical status by the Ouro Preto Protocol, signed on December 17, 1994, and ratified in 1995. These institutions are:

1. *The Common Market Council (CMC)* (foreign affairs and economy ministers). This body has legal authority to act on behalf of the group.

2. *The Common Market Group.* This is the principal body responsible for proposing draft resolutions to the CMC and for implementing CMC decisions with the support of 11 technical working subgroups (communications, mining, technical rules, financial matters, transport and infrastructure, environment, industry, agriculture, energy, labor and social security, and health). There are also specialized meetings on science and technology and tourism, as well as ad hoc groups on services, institutional matters, MERCOSUR-LAIA, MERCOSUR-WTO, and sugar.

3. *The Trade Commission.* This entity is responsible for coordinating common trade policy and for supervising implementation of the CET, the Joint Parliamentary Commission, the Economic Consultative Forum, and the Administrative Secretariat. Ten technical committees advise the Commission: tariffs, nomenclature and the classification of goods, customs matters, rules and trade disciplines, public policies which distort competitiveness, defense of competition, unfair practices and safeguards, consumer protection, nontariff restrictions and measures, the automotive sector, and the textile sector.

These bodies are all specifically designed as intergovernmental rather than supranational agencies, which is understandable given the history of supranational organs in Latin America but perhaps a long-term weakness, particularly in the areas of investment and services.[39]

There is still no supranational court through which either a member state or the Secretariat can enforce treaty obligations on another member or a private party. There is a provision for arbitration under the Brasilia Protocol, but trade disputes are typically solved by negotiation.[40]

Intra-MERCOSUR trade has been growing rapidly since 1991. With the introduction of free internal trade and the CET in 1995, trade growth continued to accelerate. In 1996, intra-MERCOSUR exports accounted for 21.5 percent of total exports, up from under 9 percent in 1990. When Chile and Bolivia trade is factored in, the percentage rises to 26.5 percent. Intraregional investment has also grown substantially, largely due to unilateral liberalization and privatization programs, but also due to MERCOSUR reductions of foreign investment barriers. Internal trade growth would have been even higher had it not been hampered by continuing administrative problems relating to the collection of duties at internal frontiers and the imposition of rules of origin.[41] Unlike the EU (European Union), MERCOSUR is not intended to become a single market, and thus these types of administrative problems at internal borders (mostly with Paraguay, which is landlocked) could continue indefinitely.

Soon after the entry into force of the customs union at the beginning of 1995, MERCOSUR faced a major challenge both to the CET and to internal free trade. In April 1995, facing a cumulative trade deficit of US$4.4 billion between November 1994 and April 1995, Brazil raised tariffs, added new exceptions, and imposed quotas on a number of products – primarily automobiles and durable goods. These measures were supposed to be discontinued as of April 1996. However, in December of 1996, Brazil initiated a new auto regime offering auto manufacturers reduced duties on imports of assembled cars and other benefits if they would export sufficient quantities of parts and vehicles and promise to meet local content targets in their Brazilian plants. (Argentina has had investment incentives in place for the automotive sector for some years.) In 1997 Brazil eliminated the tariff preferences on parts but retained the rest of the regime, arguing that it is aimed at helping to develop the impoverished northeastern part of the country.

The United States has requested a number of consultations with Brazil on this matter under the WTO, and apperntly the negotiators are now close to an agreement.[42]

Due to the sensitivity of the automobile sector in MERCOSUR trade, Brazil has pushed for an acceleration of negotiations to bring the sector under common rules. Meanwhile, in January 1996 Brazil and Argentina negotiated a bilateral agreement on the automotive sector revising the text signed in Ouro Preto in 1994. Under this agreement, "Each partner agrees to recognize the validity of the automotive regime of the other country until December 31, 1999."[43] Also under the agreement, imports from third countries are treated less favorably than intraregional trade, and the location of assembly operations in Brazil is favored. Brazil recently persuaded its MERCOSUR partners to raise tariffs (CET) across the board; internally, Brazil adopted a series of additional taxes on autos.

The United States continues to express concerns about MERCOSUR's treatment of intellectual property rights. This concern is focused more on Argentina than on Brazil, since Brazil accelerated its implementation of key TRIPs (Trade Related Intellectual Property Agreement) provisions in 1996 and committed to enact a package of other protections in 1997. MERCOSUR's Common Market Council has adopted a Protocol on the Harmonization of Rules on Intellectual Property that covers marking and origin, but so far, only Paraguay has ratified it. Likewise, a Protocol on Trade Marks, Indications of Source and Appellations has been adopted but is awaiting ratification by Argentina, Brazil, and Uruguay. The Council approved an Agreement on Copyright and Related Rights, but the governments have returned this to the working group for further study.

With respect to government procurement, MERCOSUR members thus far have opted not to join the WTO government procurement agreement and have deferred a decision on whether to establish an ad hoc group on the subject, as proposed by Argentina. The Trade Commission has proposed a common statute on competition policies to the Common Market Council, and a decision on approval is pending.[44] Because the public sector still plays such a large role in the economies of MERCOSUR countries, it would be advantageous to have strong government procurement and competition policy frameworks in place at the regional level to ensure transparency and an even playing field for internal and external investors.

## NAFTA

NAFTA came into force on January 1, 1994, in Canada, the United States, and Mexico. This agreement builds on the Canada-U.S. Free Trade Agreement that entered into force in 1989. NAFTA has become a model in the hemisphere for so-called "new generation" agreements that purport to deal with many trade-related issues other than tariffs and nontariff barriers. The issues covered under NAFTA, in addition to basic market entry, customs procedures, standards, and rules of origin, include investment, services, intellectual property protection, government procurement, competition policy, and, in side agreements, environment and labor.

Assessments carried out in 1997 by the U.S. International Trade Commission (USITC) and the United States Trade Representative (USTR) conclude that in the United States, NAFTA has had a modest positive impact with very minimal job losses. The impact on Mexico has been much greater in two respects: (1) The United States was convinced to provide Mexico with a $10 billion stabilization loan after the 1994 peso crisis largely because of the existence of NAFTA, without which the crisis would have resulted in an even sharper and more sustained drop in Mexico's GDP; and (2) Mexico's exports to other NAFTA members have grown dramatically in the past two-and-one-half years. Also, the greatest regulatory and administrative change has occurred in Mexico, since the United States and Canada were relatively more open economies to begin with.

The NAFTA partners continue to experience a number of serious disputes on various long-standing trade issues; these now are frequently referred to the NAFTA dispute settlement process. However, because of the highly political nature of some of these disputes (for instance, the dispute with Canada over softwood lumber), the dispute settlement mechanism is sometimes superseded by a political agreement between the disagreeing countries (at times through negotiated deals such as the recent softwood lumber agreement, and at times through the Extraordinary Challenge mechanism).

As of December 1996, 25 cases had been accorded panel reviews under the NAFTA dispute settlement mechanisms in either Chapter 19 or 20. Of those, 24 were reviews of Mexican, Canadian, or U.S. antidumping or countervailing duty decisions – eight reviews of U.S. decisions, seven reviews of Mexican decisions, and nine reviews of Canadian decisions.[45] While these numbers demonstrate that the dispute settlement mechanism has been used relatively evenly among the three countries, strong opposition has grown up in the United States to the extension of the Chapter 19 AD/CVD (antidumping/countervailing duty) panel review process to any other country in the hemisphere. This opposition is coming from citizens' groups, business groups, lawmakers, and trade court officials who feel that the process is unconstitutional, as well as unnecessary. They reference recent agreements, signed by Mexico, Canada, and Chile, which do not incorporate a Chapter 19-like mechanism.

Aside from AD/CVD disputes, the implementation of NAFTA and its side agreements has been relatively smooth, with one glaring exception, namely, liberalized access for Mexican truck operators to the U.S. market. The United States decided not to implement an opening of the border in December 1995, as had been required under the NAFTA, due to pressure from the International Teamsters Union. Subsequently, the union has taken its case to various courts and it continues to be successful in barring increased Mexican truck traffic on safety grounds. The U.S. and Mexican Departments of Transportation have begun to work on a number of steps to improve coordination on driver and truck safety, but the final resolution of this problem will certainly be political, and possibly at the presidential level.[46]

Trade growth in the NAFTA region has been strong since 1994, although the ITC, in its analysis of the impact of NAFTA, estimates that a fairly small percentage of that growth is actually attributable to the NAFTA itself.[47] According to the USTR's report,

> "exports of U.S. goods to Mexico grew by nearly 37 percent (or $15.2 billion) in the three years after NAFTA went into effect, to a record high of $56.8 billion. This large increase came during a three-year period when Mexico experienced a 3 percent decline in total domestic demand. At the same time, the United States widened its lead over its trade rivals in sales into the Mexican market – increasing its share of Mexico's imports from 69 percent in 1993 to 75 percent in 1996 and displacing imports, particularly from Asia."[48]

The IDB notes that:

> "trade figures show that from 1990 to 1994, intra-NAFTA merchandise exports grew by 54 percent while NAFTA countries' merchandise exports to the rest of the world grew by only 18 percent. In the case of Canada, exports to Mexico and the United States rose by 53 percent and 35

percent respectively, compared to a decline of 2 percent to the rest of the world. U.S. merchandise exports to Canada and Mexico increased by 38 and 79 percent respectively, while exports to the rest of the world improved by 20 percent. The case of Mexico is even more impressive; its exports to Canada and the United States increased 1,350 percent and 160 percent respectively."[49]

This rapid intra-NAFTA trade growth implies that trade diversion did occur, as argued in the USTR report.

The services trade picture is quite different, with two-way services trade between the United States, Canada, and Mexico growing only by about 1 percent between 1993 and 1995. This is partly explained by the sectoral variations within the services account, where large offsetting fluctuations occurred in tourism and financial services.

## THE FTAA PROCESS

In the interim since the 1994 Miami Summit, the formal intergovernmental trade process has consisted primarily of the work of 12 technical working groups and the decisions reached by ministers at the annual trade ministerial meetings. The Tripartite Committee, composed of the Inter-American Development Bank, the Organization of American States, and the United Nations Economic Commission for Latin America and the Caribbean, has staffed the working groups. According to the terms of reference established by the ministers, these working groups have undertaken analyses of the state of trade law in the region and have made comparisons of differing subregional and national regimes. These analyses, while not all complete, have contributed enormously to an appreciation of the degree of commonality that exists in the hemisphere on these 12 critical sets of issues. For this reason, I will briefly examine the progress made in each working group, noting instances in which experts previously commissioned by the Institute of the Americas have provided specific advice to ministers on how some of these topics could be handled in an actual FTAA negotiation.

The most useful finding so far is the high degree of commonality among countries, policies, and practices in the region. This was expected in investment, but in intellectual property rights (IPR), the degree of commonality is somewhat surprising, as is the lack of acrimony in the working group. In the competition policy working group, there are different dynamics because most countries in the hemisphere do not have competition policies. The question is therefore whether they should adopt individual national policies or whether there should be a regional agreement that sets the principles for everyone. In the area of competition policy, the WTO is watching what is happening at the FTAA level, rather than vice-versa, as in most other groups.

In the services group, there are essentially two different approaches, the NAFTA approach and the WTO or GATS approach; the basic difference is between positive and negative listing approaches. Brazil and MERCOSUR seem to prefer the GATS approach because it will make it easier to proceed more slowly.

In general, the working group process has been characterized by huge differences in terms of timeliness, quality, transparency, and accessibility of work. This is primarily due to differences in the way the chairs utilize the support staffs. Three different approaches have been observed:

1. An OECD-type relationship where the staff is fully consulted and is an active player
2. A WTO-type relationship where the staff is fully consulted
3. A model in which the staff is not consulted, just informed

The unevenness might be improved through the following mechanisms:

1. More transparency in information sharing among the Tripartite Committee staff
2. Greater availability of databases to all the staff
3. Regular meetings of the support staff
4. Greater responsiveness to requests from governments

That being said, the vice ministers have not seemed to be particularly unhappy about any aspect of the working group process or the functioning of the Tripartite Committee. The vice ministers have not felt the need to consider the working group papers in detail (although they have approved reports from 11 of the 12 groups), instead preferring to focus on specific areas where disagreements arise or where rapid progress is possible. The vice ministerial meetings usually have had representation from 25 to 28 countries; of those 25 or so, half have been regular attendees. NAFTA is always well represented, along with Brazil, Argentina, El Salvador, Costa Rica, Jamaica, and Colombia. Chile has been surprisingly inconsistent.

Once the vice ministers had assumed the role of a preparatory committee, each working group was requested to submit recommendations on negotiating structures and issues by the time of the October 1997 vice ministerial meeting in Costa Rica. The working groups were largely able to agree on common objectives and principles for the negotiations, but fell short of agreeing on a common negotiating structure. The agreed objectives and principles, as well as any contested language, are incorporated in Appendix B, which also describes the terms of reference for each working group.

Negotiations in Costa Rica in October on the structure of the negotiating groups revealed not only significant differences of approach between the United States and MERCOSUR, but also some significant differences between the United States and Canada. Without going into too much detail, these differences relate to the following issues:[50]

- the importance of agricultural in the negotiations (MERCOSUR wants a separate agricultural negotiating group, the United States does not.)
- the feasibility of including "study" groups on labor and the environment (The United States wants them, but no one else does, at least at this point.)
- nuances in the language for market access talks implying either faster or slower negotiations (The United States and Canada want faster negotiations; MERCOSUR wants more "gradual" negotiations.)
- the date for implementation of the agreement (MERCOSUR does not agree to the year 2005; Canada is pushing strongly for implementation to begin January 1, 2005, which would imply that negotiations have to conclude in 2003 or 2004 at the latest.)
- the degree of special and differential treatment to be accorded to the smaller economies (Canada is siding with the smaller economies, while the United States wants to keep special language out of the market access and rules of origin negotiations unless it is absolutely necessary to include it.)
- the coverage and scope of intellectual property negotiations (Canada wants to be able to take exceptions; United States does not want any, nor does the United States like the concept of applying IPR principles by "thematic area.")
- the degree to which trade remedy rules (i.e., AD/CVD) should be fundamentally renegotiated to reflect the existence of a free trade area (The United States is opposed; everyone else is in favor.)

- the degree to which federal countries should be expected to negotiate government procurement disciplines that apply to subfederal government levels (The United States and most federal countries are opposed, although the United States has negotiated such commitments in past agreements including NAFTA, but Chile and other unitary governments favor this approach.)
- the interpretation of the concept of "single undertaking" (MERCOSUR believes it means that "nothing is agreed until everything is agreed"; the United States, Canada and several other countries adhere to the view that it means that you can have interim or partial agreements and even begin implementation, yet these agreements could be viewed as part of an overall deal to be signed at the end of the negotiations as a package.) (See Appendix F for current Chairman's draft of proposed Ministerial Declaration for Costa Rica meeting.)

## PROGRESS ON THE TECHNICAL ISSUES

*Competition Policy.* The working group on competition policy was established at the ministerial meeting in Cartagena. The main division that evolved in the working group was between trade people and competition policy agency people, rather than on a subregional or north-south basis.

The work of the group was made more difficult by lack of experience with competition policies in the region. Only 12 countries in the hemisphere currently have competition policy laws. The 10 Latin American countries have very similar policies, all having been enacted between 1992 and 1996. These countries have little or no experience with implementation.

As noted earlier, in December 1996 MERCOSUR signed a new protocol on competition that is more comprehensive than NAFTA. This protocol, designed more along the lines of the Australia-New Zealand Closer Economic Relations agreement (CER), tries to harmonize competition policies in order to deal with the Brazil-Argentina antidumping problem. The Andean Community also is in the very early stages of trying to harmonize competition policies.

Unfortunately, WTO work on this topic has not progressed very far. In fact, it is likely that WTO is watching the FTAA process for clues about how to proceed.

The working group has launched a study on convergence and divergence among competition policies in the hemisphere that may result in the defining of some principles and the building of a bridge between antidumping and competition policy.

So far, the consensus that appears to be developing in the group is that harmonizing competition policies is a non-starter and that instead different laws and policies should be allowed as long as they accomplish the same objectives, among which increasing transparency is paramount.[51]

In a recent study prepared for the Institute of the Americas by Sarath Rajapatirana and Luis Guasch of the World Bank, the authors argue that competition policy should replace antidumping regimes in an FTAA.

"Further fine tuning and refining of antidumping policy is not the answer to prevent the slippage into protection with the use of this instrument. The antidote is competition policies. The current efforts should be directed toward the implementation of comprehensive competition policies and credible enforcement agencies. They should also be aimed toward the phasing out of most of the trade policy instruments, such as antidumping, countervailing duties and safeguards and their replacement by a broader application of competition policies and of extraterritorial jurisdiction.[52] Competition policies, when broadly used, can effectively substitute for most trade instruments. The competitive merits, if any, of any antidumping request can and should be evaluated by the competition (antitrust) agency, using the same standards and framework of competition policies, and not discriminate against the source from which competition arises, whether it be domestically or from abroad."[53]

Unfortunately, antidumping laws are so popular in the United States and elsewhere, among both politicians and distressed industries (and even prospering industries) that it is hard to imagine any major changes coming about in a regional context in the foreseeable future. Perhaps the best hope for progress in this regard is the WTO's work on competition policy and a new multilateral round.

*Dispute Settlement.* The dispute settlement working group, chaired by Uruguay, met for the first time in early July 1997, and had for its consideration a document prepared by the OAS comparing the region's dispute settlement procedures. However, MERCOSUR "refused to recognize the validity of the matrix," and instead proposed an alternative set of guidelines for preparing a comparative matrix. MERCOSUR also argued that this working group did not have the mandate to prepare recommendations on technical alternatives, as required from the other working groups. Non-MERCOSUR countries apparently disagreed with this approach and were hoping to make more progress at the early October 1997 meeting.

Based on the disputed matrix, the OAS had found broad similarities in the dispute-settlement mechanisms incorporated in most regional agreements. MERCOSUR's mechanism stands out because of the additional layers of review at the ministerial level prior to sending a dispute to arbitration.

In an earlier Institute of the Americas study on the successes and failures of the dispute settlement mechanism in place between Canada, the United States, and Mexico, Daniel Schwanen concluded that:

"Despite the strains which inevitably accompany dispute settlement in high-profile cases, it remains the case that a dispute settlement mechanism which is seen to be impartial is probably useful in most cases and could be the key to the success of any trade agreement between countries that have 'free trade' but wish to retain the ability to impose contingent protection on their partner. Indeed, for a country not to subscribe to a DSM when others already do would put that country at a disadvantage, because such mechanisms do, overall, increase market access for one's own producers."[54]

However, he also concluded that:

"A cloud will hang over any work towards extending a NAFTA-like DSM for antidumping and countervailing duties as long as the issue of the constitutionality of such mechanisms has not been resolved. If these challenges succeed, the system will explode. A radical (but inevitable in the long term) solution would be to severely curtail the use of AD and CVD within the hemisphere, at least between countries that have met certain criteria with respect to competition policy and public subsidization of industries."[55]

In the United States, recent challenges to NAFTA's dispute settlement mechanism on constitutional grounds remain unresolved. Opponents cite the fact that Canada, Chile and Mexico have not included such provisions in any of their bilateral arrangements and instead rely upon WTO mechanisms and international arbitration. However, regardless of the constitutionality of the mechanism in the United States, there is strong opposition in the United States to the extension of the arrangement beyond the current three NAFTA members.

*Government Procurement.* The working group on government procurement has so far prepared two documents on government procurement in the region, one on national legislation and rules and the other on trade agreements.

The latter document points out that:

"Among the integration arrangements in the region, currently only NAFTA, the Group of Three Accord and the bilateral agreements of Mexico with Costa Rica and Bolivia contain provisions governing purchases by government entities. Consequently, of the 34 countries that will comprise the FTAA, only six countries have signed subregional agreements of this type. Nonetheless, the rest of the integration arrangements such as MERCOSUR, the Andean Community, the CACM, and CARICOM are currently contemplating the inclusion of government procurement provisions in their agreements."[56]

On the basis of these two inventories, the working group is now preparing two additional documents, one on barriers to access to government procurement and one on commonalities and divergences. The United States, as chair of the working group, has expressed the opinion that information and transparency agreements in the area of government procurement may be possible early on in the FTAA process as part of the governments' business facilitation efforts. A U.S. priority in these negotiations is to encourage countries in the region to accede to the WTO Government Procurement Agreement (GPA), or at the very least to negotiate FTAA provisions at least as strong as the WTO's GPA. So far, only the United States and Canada are members from this hemisphere. In the 1996 National Trade Estimate Report, USTR singled out Brazil, Colombia, Honduras, and Venezuela as having serious barriers that hinder foreign access to government procurement opportunities.

*Intellectual Property.* This working group, chaired by Honduras, is currently reworking an extensive inventory of national and international intellectual property rights (IPR) commitments that have been assumed by the countries of the region. In addition, an effort is underway to begin identifying commonalities and divergences.

The working group has held several seminars on various IPR-related topics, including the implementation of TRIPS and the application of IPR to new technologies, specifically biotechnology. Several countries have requested technical assistance in this area, and the working group is exploring with WIPO the possibility of providing training on these and other issues.

In a study done for the Institute of the Americas, Carlos Primo Braga and Robert Sherwood recommended that substantial technical assistance be provided to promote adequate enforcement of IPR. They conveniently summarize the current state of play on IPR in the hemisphere in the following excerpt:

"Many countries in the Western Hemisphere are upgrading their IP systems for a variety of reasons. Some are implementing these reforms in response to competitiveness concerns, some are responding to new types of technology, some as the result of external pressure, and almost all, of course, have committed to the standards of the TRIPS Agreement.[57]

"Among recent examples, El Salvador recently improved its patent and copyright laws in parallel with an Investment Sector Loan operation of the Inter-American Development Bank. Mexico revised its IP system in stages between 1987 and 1994, partly in anticipation of the North American Free Trade Agreement (NAFTA) negotiations. Chile adopted a more modern system, partly in response to external pressure and partly for competitive reasons.

"Most recent regional trade agreements in the Western Hemisphere address 'behind-the-border' impediments to trade and investment, incorporating IP issues under their coverage. NAFTA, for example, explicitly covers IP, expanding the reach of its forerunner, the Canada-United States Free Trade Agreement. In the same vein, the Argentina-Brazil Economic Cooperation Agreement (1986) had no IP provisions in its origins. Its expanded successor (MERCOSUR, the Southern Cone Common Market), however, has been addressing issues of harmonization of IP protection. Colombia, Mexico, and Venezuela incorporated IP commitments into their Group of Three accord. It is also worth noting that the Andean Common Market (ANCOM) countries addressed the issue of a common IP regime for their trade pact as far back as the 1970s."

They conclude by recommending a more ambitious objective for the FTAA's IPR negotiations:

"Finally, we suggest that although not enough is yet known about the conditioning effect of intellectual property protection on technology enhancement, investment promotion, and economic development, enough is known to encourage analysis of a level of IP protection which rises above the limited ambition of eliminating trade frictions. The leading challenge for the countries of the hemisphere is to shake the image of intellectual property protection as purely a rent transfer mechanism, viewing it instead as an effective instrument for technological development in a global environment of intensifying competition and opportunity."[58]

*Investment.* The investment working group, chaired by Costa Rica, has produced two compendia, one entitled "Investment Agreements in the Western Hemisphere," produced by the OAS, and one entitled "Investment Regimes in the Americas," produced by the IDB. These two compendia not only list agreements and national legislation, but also outline areas of commonality and divergence.

The OAS found in its survey of 35 bilateral investment treaties (BIT) that only three countries in the region have not signed one, and of the 34 countries, 24 have BITs with other countries in the region. These agreements vary on several important characteristics:

- degree of national treatment
- pre-clearance versus national treatment with exclusions approach
- inclusion of performance requirements and/or incentives

All the Western Hemisphere BITs and investment agreements include dispute settlement mechanisms between the members and procedures for referring "investment disputes" between private parties and states to existing arbitral bodies.

The investment group has agreed on a list of "key topics" to be included in any FTAA investment agreement, including basic definitions, scope of application, national treatment, MFN (most-favored nation status), fair and equitable treatment, expropriation, compensation, top managerial personnel, transfers, performance requirements, general exceptions, and dispute settlement.[59]

In 1996, the working group began to discuss specific issues such as:

- definition of investment
- definition of investors
- how to deal with different admissions rules.

According to officials and representatives of the tripartite committee (OAS, IDB, ECLAC), this working group has progressed farther than any other and is now ready to begin negotiations. Many observers expect an investment agreement to be one of the first products of the FTAA negotiations.

*Market Access.* The market access working group, chaired by El Salvador, has had a difficult time assembling its hemispheric database of market access barriers. As of February 1997, only 19 countries had submitted the required information on tariff measures and 17 on nontariff measures. Of the 17 submitting nontariff measures data, only 10 provided the data in a usable format.[60]

Rene León, formerly El Salvador's vice minister for trade and now ambassador to the United States, has pointed out that if each country submits a separate tariff offer for every other country, over 500 proposals will have to be considered. On the other hand, if most of the subregional groups made one offer on behalf of their members, this process would be streamlined considerably.

The pace of market access negotiations has been a controversial point in discussions regarding the launching of negotiations in 1998. MERCOSUR has insisted, at least until recently, that tariff reductions be discussed only at the very end of the negotiations, starting in 2003, while the rest of the hemisphere would prefer to have all topics start simultaneously.

Recently, however, both Brazilian and Argentine diplomats have hinted that negotiations on market access could be launched simultaneously with everything else, as long as the principle that "nothing is agreed until everything is agreed" is strictly adhered to. They argue that this is the correct interpretation of the term "single undertaking" which has been agreed to by the ministers as one of the critical characteristics of the FTAA.[61]

USTR officials have disagreed publicly with this interpretation of the "single undertaking" concept, arguing that if the ministers have succeeded in negotiating an agreement in a particular area, it does not really make sense to postpone implementation until 2005.

*Rules of Origin and Customs Procedures.* In a study prepared for the Institute of the Americas by Simão Davi Silber of Brazil,[62] it was recommended that FTAA negotiators attempt to replace as many sectoral rules of origin as possible with a common external tariff, as was adopted under NAFTA for some electronics products. This approach has a number of significant advantages, not least of which is that rules of origin negotiations among 34 countries would not be required for many products. Certification procedures also would be inherently much simpler.

This approach has also been advocated by John Simpson, Deputy Assistant Secretary, Regulatory, Tariff, and Trade Enforcement, U.S. Treasury Department, who made the following argument earlier this year:

"The administrative complexity of the NAFTA may make it unsustainable if we attempt to go beyond Chile and expand the NAFTA to a hemispheric scale. NAFTA's shortcomings result largely from well-intentioned efforts to respond to the requirements of various groups, without adequate consideration of the consequences for NAFTA's functioning as an agreement to liberate and stimulate trade. While some of the NAFTA's flaws can be corrected, a customs union is an inherently superior arrangement. But it cannot be achieved quickly. In designing a hemispheric free trade agreement that could serve as a transition to a customs union, the following objectives should be pursued.

"1. Reduce Red Tape – The final [U.S.] rule implementing the North American Free Trade Agreement, as it was submitted to the Federal Register, was almost 500 pages, not including the preamble and analysis of comments received in response to an earlier public notice in the Federal Register.

"A free trade agreement that requires almost 500 pages of rules is, *a fortiori*, not an agreement that meets the needs of business, especially small business. As a result, in 1994 the U.S. Customs Service NAFTA Help Desk received over 21,000 inquiries from confused importers and exporters. Many companies have chosen not to use the NAFTA owing to its complexity.

"2. Eliminate RVC Requirements – The chief cause of red tape and record keeping requirements in the NAFTA is the so-called regional value content requirement, which is Byzantine in its complexity. In addition, the NAFTA value content rules require companies to maintain records that they never kept before, to require information from suppliers that they never needed to give before, and to provide certifications about the origin and regional content of goods shipped to customers. Even after the greatest care, companies, their suppliers, and their customers may all have to undergo a long and arduous audit by any one – or even more than one – of the three governments involved.

"3. Use Simplified Tariff Change Rules of Origin as a Transition – Partly to assure national legislatures that the benefits of NAFTA would stay in North America, but mostly to prevent individual companies in each of the three countries from jumping into the camp of NAFTA opponents, the tariff shift rules of origin in Chapter 4 of the NAFTA are gerrymandered to meet the demands of industry sectors, subsectors, and individual companies. The result is an unlovely set of rules that reflect commercial and political interests more than any sort of rational, consistent principle. Moreover, in order to accommodate all the special needs the United States had to create 392 new tariff breakouts, which made the tariff schedules even fatter and more prolix. To the extent it can be done without jeopardizing sacred interests, future agreements should avoid tariff shift origin rules that go below the 6-digit level at which the tariff is internationally harmonized. Wherever possible, consideration should be given to using rules being developed by the WTO for non-preferential use. Using the WTO rules for a new free trade agreement will produce the delightful result that a product's country of origin for all purposes, preferential and non-preferential, will be the same.

"4. Create Sectoral Customs Unions – Better yet, begin to move away from rules of origin altogether. If by the year 2004, when Uruguay Round tariff reductions are complete, the duty difference among all parties to an Americas free trade agreement is less than, say 2.5 percent, rules of origin can be dropped to create what is in effect a sectoral customs union, with a common rate of duty harmonized at the lowest level in effect in any of the parties. As long as each member of the Agreement undertakes to collect the common rate of duty and not to refund it, an article imported from outside the free trade area can be allowed to move freely throughout the free trade area, for further manufacturing or for sale, with all parties secure in the knowledge that it was subjected to the same duty that would have been imposed had it initially entered their own country. This is an important step in paving the way to a customs union."[63]

Unfortunately, many in the United States automatically associate the term "customs union" with the European Union, which, while it is a customs union, goes well beyond the minimum requirements of a common external tariff to dictate many social, political, industrial, and economic policies to its members. Such wide and deep integration is not a necessary characteristic of a customs union, nor does it necessarily naturally follow from the establishment of one.

*Sanitary and Phytosanitary Standards (SPS).* Work is proceeding in this working group on an inventory of all SPS agreements in the hemisphere. The working group, chaired by Mexico, has made a series of recommendations to the vice ministers, most of which are aimed at assisting countries in the adoption and implementation of WTO's SPS standards and at providing training and technical assistance. The working group also has recommended that an electronic data exchange system be implemented in the region to facilitate the transfer of information about existing and planned standards.[64]

In 1997 meetings and correspondence among the members of the group, disagreements emerged over the degree of institutionalization or formalization of the harmonization process that should take place prior to the completion of FTAA negotiations. Some officials close to the process have identified the source of the groups' difficulties as a conflict between the chairman and the rest of the members of the group.

*Services.* The work of this group has been similar to the work carried out in the investment working group, namely, identifying barriers to services trade and identifying commitments on services undertaken by various countries. The OAS has prepared and published a compendium entitled *Provisions on Trade in Services in Trade and Integration Agreements of the Western Hemisphere*, which finds that:

"NAFTA and the Group of Three contain extensive commitments and provisions for the liberalization of services and well as disciplines for trade in services, as do the bilateral free trade agreements between Mexico/Bolivia, Mexico/Costa Rica and Canada/Chile. The other trade and integration arrangements contain no provisions specific to services or to the liberalization of trade in services, although definitions on services are set out in the annex to the CARICOM and services are mentioned within the general objectives of MERCOSUR, which is also in the process of elaborating a Framework Agreement for Trade in Services. A project of the agreement should be ready by September 30, 1997. Chile/MERCOSUR and Bolivia/MERCOSUR agreements include a short chapter on services, with a few provisions."[65]

The two models for an FTAA services agreement are deemed to be NAFTA and GATS. MERCOSUR has so far been reluctant to accept NAFTA as a model since it would require dramatic and rapid changes in MERCOSUR members' services regimes.

In a recent report to the vice ministers, the services working group outlined some areas where agreement had been reached on approaches to services negotiations in FTAA:

- Coverage of the commitments: The working group has agreed that no sector should be excluded *a priori* from coverage of liberalization commitments. Alternatives include the following approaches: sectoral, positive list, negative list, and universal.

- Liberalization principles and standards: These include most-favored-nation treatment, national treatment, market access based on all modes of supply, quantitative nondiscriminatory restrictions, and denial of benefits.

- Depth of commitments: The approaches include transparency, ceiling bindings, freeze on existing nonconforming measures, 'ratcheting,' and 'list or lose.'"[66]

*Small Economies.* OAS, the Sistema Economico Latinoamericano (SELA - Latin American Economic System), and World Bank have been working with this working group to try to define "small economy" and to identify which characteristics of "smallness" matter in trade negotiations. They have identified the following factors that characterize many of these countries:

1. small size of population and territory
2. small size of GDP and GDP per capita
3. high dependence on external trade
4. high levels of imports
5. high vulnerability to fluctuations in world prices and demand for their exports
6. high dependence on trade taxes for government revenues
7. limited human resources and technical expertise
8. high unit costs for infrastructure and public administration
9. relatively undiversified economic base
10. small size of domestic markets

11. heavy reliance on primary commodities
12. extreme vulnerability to external shocks
13. vulnerability to natural disasters

Within the working group, CARICOM has tended to act as a bloc with the CARICOM secretariat making a number of proposals. Somewhat surprisingly, the CACM has not acted as a bloc in this context. Instead, Honduras, for one, has worked closely with the CARICOM group.

Of the larger countries, Canada, in particular, has recognized the need to give smaller economies special attention and extra time to adjust to the rigors of a non-preferential, reciprocal arrangement. The existence of this working group has also given these countries an opportunity to talk to the United States as a group, which has been beneficial psychologically, if nothing else.

Jamaica's Ambassador to the United States, Richard Bernal, who chairs the working group, recently commissioned a report on a regional integration fund to be carried out by CEPAL and presented in October. This idea has not found great favor with the larger countries and has tended to alienate them a bit from the work of the group. Potentially, this could have negative repercussions in other areas such as technical assistance, where there is some resistance to providing "training on how to negotiate."

The larger economies would prefer to see technical assistance aimed at improving the capacity of the smaller states to implement agreements in the trade and investment area. Toward that end, the working group has commissioned and received a series of studies from SELA on the technical assistance needs of smaller economies.

*Standards.* Within this working group, which is chaired by Canada, the United States and Canada have staked out a position of wanting to go beyond the WTO standards agreements. However, it would appear that developing countries in the region need time to fully implement WTO first. For this to happen, there is a critical need for infrastructure development, both technical and human. One partial answer would be for the IDB to provide funding for training of national and regional standards officials by COPANT, the regional standards organization.

The working group has agreed that a hierarchy needs to be established among the various bodies of standards from which governments can choose. This hierarchy should put international standards first, then regional standards (COPANT), subregional standards, and, finally, national standards.

Given the current variation in standards around the hemisphere, harmonization in an FTAA is probably not feasible. The only feasible short- and medium-term approaches are equivalency and mutual recognition, with the eventual goal of convergence toward multilateral standards.

Even this objective will be challenging for many countries, as implementation of national, subregional, and regional standards will require the establishment and enhancement of national standards setting and enforcement agencies around the region. According to the compendium published by the OAS for the working group, of the 34 participants in the FTAA process, 22 have a national standardizing body or bodies. Of those, 10 are government entities, while 9 are private entities and 3 are mixed bodies. Seventeen countries have metrology laboratories.[67]

In a recent paper for the Institute of the Americas, Sherry Stephenson, OAS Senior Trade Specialist, argued that standards is an area where a lot of work already has been done, but where commitments far outpace implementation.[68]

"… It is evident that a considerable amount of common background already exists in the standards area in terms of multilaterally agreed, legally binding rules and disciplines under the WTO, as well as a large amount of voluntary activity for the development of international standards and international guidelines on standardizing activities under the ISO/IEC and others. Hemispheric-wide standards-related activities already take place under COPANT, the Inter-American Metrology System and the Inter-American Accreditation Cooperation.

"However, a note of caution must be sounded before going further. What is equally true is that this potentially rich common base is, in fact, far from universal, since many countries in the region have not been able to fully implement the disciplines of the WTO TBT Agreement. Much remains to be done in the most fundamental areas. Nor have most countries of the hemisphere been active participants in either the international standardizing activities or the regional standardizing activities described earlier, though this is a subject too detailed for the purposes of this paper.[69] Recent efforts to bring about greater compliance with multilateral disciplines or to adopt international standards has been slow, at best."

She further argues that it will not be enough to negotiate standards agreements without establishing the capacity for implementation at the national and sub-regional level.

> "… In the standards area, common disciplines and approaches towards the elaboration of standards and mutual recognition of conformity assessment procedures do not yet exist for the majority of the FTAA participants for various reasons. *These have to do with the costly nature of the infrastructure necessary for the development of a proficient and reliable system of metrology and laboratory testing, the long-term nature of the creation of human resources necessary to carry out such functions (emphasis added)*, and the relative lack of prominence which this area has received until recently by national policy makers. The task in the standards area is therefore not only to determine how to negotiate within the FTAA process, but to devise incentives and policies that will permit countries of the hemisphere to implement already-existing disciplines and to participate in multilateral and regional standards-related activities that are essential in developing a common approach toward trade facilitation in this area."

The likely result of FTAA negotiations on technical standards will be relatively rapid progress in those sectors where business associations can agree on common international standards for voluntary compliance. More difficult will be the establishment of credible standards certification bodies, unless this task is undertaken by regional trade blocs rather by than individual countries.

*Subsidies, Dumping, and Countervailing Duties.* The AD/CVD working group has prepared a compendium of antidumping and countervailing duty laws in the hemisphere, but the group decided not to prepare a study on commonalities and divergences on grounds that these practices may not be desirable at all, even if they are harmonized. What the compendium demonstrates is that while almost every country in the hemisphere has adopted AD/CVD legislation (23 out of 34), only a few countries make frequent use of these laws.

One of the interesting developments in this group is the distinction that has been drawn between subsidies (primarily agricultural export subsidies) and dumping. As a result, the discussions have tended to go in two different directions, either focusing on the disciplines to be applied to export subsidies or on the appropriate conditions for utilizing trade remedies such as antidumping duties. There is little commonality between these two discussions, particularly since the United States has become somewhat isolated on the issue of export subsidies, which are rarely used elsewhere in the hemisphere.

The previously referenced study by Rajapatirana and Guasch attempts to identify some areas of common ground or useful overlap between competition policy and antidumping law, which could be utilized by the negotiators to establish a new, more procompetitive trade regime for the region.

As we know, Latin American countries have begun to imitate developed countries in their use of antidumping as the trade weapon of choice, once tariffs and other protective barriers have declined. Such tactics are as popular within trade blocs as between them. While the LAC has adopted (General Agreement on Tariffs and Trade) GATT/WTO-consistent antidumping laws, this unfortunately does not eliminate their essentially anticompetitive nature, nor their negative impact on general economic welfare. Rajapatirana and Guasch argue that in the context of moving toward an FTAA, history indicates that the Americas should rather adopt an entirely different approach, as follows:

> The principle behind free trade arrangements is to integrate markets so that domestic and foreign (those of treaty members) markets are considered one and the same with equal treatment. That allows for no room for antidumping actions. If indeed there are anticompetitive actions, and dumping is generally not one of them, competition (antitrust) policies and the corresponding agency are perfectly entitled to oversee and police them. Yet, there has been little interaction or coordination between competition and antidumping agencies. Domestic and supranational (when existing) competition legislation can very appropriately deal with genuinely unfair trade practices and anticompetitive behavior by domestic and foreign companies alike.[70]

Given that it is highly unlikely that competition laws will replace antidumping laws in the near future, the authors offer an interim suggestion, which is to promote cooperation between the two sets of agencies in each country, thereby helping to balance competitive and anticompetitive interests in the economy.

# V. LEADERSHIP COUNCIL FOR INTER-AMERICAN SUMMITRY

## PROGRESS IN DEVELOPING A CONSENSUS FOR SANTIAGO

*Operation of Blocs in Pre-negotiation Process – Commonalities and Divergences.* The ability of the subregional blocs actually to negotiate as blocs is being increasingly tested as the moment to launch formal negotiations draws closer. From observers close to the process, one gets the distinct impression that the various subregional blocs have not been operating very efficiently to put forward common positions or strategies in either the working groups or at the vice ministerial or ministerial levels. However, other analysts argue that the FTAA process has provided additional impetus to MERCOSUR, CARICOM, and the Andean Community to solidify their bloc status, as indicated by papers submitted to the 1997 Belo Horizonte ministerial meeting.

From the outset, NAFTA members have stated that they would negotiate individually since NAFTA itself, as a free trade area, has no common external trade organs or policies. So far, the Andean Community has not been very successful at coordinating positions, although they have produced some common discussion papers and they are beginning to coordinate. Central American countries are coordinating but not acting as a bloc.

There has also been a visible degree of tension in the MERCOSUR bloc between Brazil and the other members, although positions seem to be starting to coalesce, though not necessarily around Brazil's position. This should not be surprising; although MERCOSUR countries have a common external tariff policy, very little else has been commonly decided, including positions on competition policy, government procurement, and intellectual property. MERCOSUR institutions also are relatively weak insofar as they are intergovernmental rather than supranational. All MERCOSUR positions have to be negotiated with all four parties (six, if one includes Chile and Bolivia), a process that may lead MERCOSUR to negotiate only select sectors together and others individually.

Interestingly, it appears that these subregional trading blocs are not lining up along a north-south axis in either the working groups or the ministerial meetings. Instead, in services for instance, there are basically two blocs, the NAFTA approach bloc and the GATS approach bloc. The GATS approach bloc is limited to MERCOSUR, while the NAFTA approach bloc includes the NAFTA countries plus Bolivia, Costa Rica, Chile, Colombia, Venezuela, and Peru.

*Structure of Secretariat and Negotiations.* What kind of secretariat will be required for these complex negotiations? So far, the governments have indicated that they are interested in a strictly administrative secretariat. However, the Tripartite Committee will need to continue to be available to do technical, factual background work upon the request of the governments. In addition, the smaller economies will need some technical assistance to bring their negotiators up to speed on some topics.

At some point, there will probably develop an FTAA technical secretariat like the GATT secretariat, but this will take time. The various support institutions need to develop credibility and trust with governments in order to carry out objective technical and legal work.

One area that will require action by the governments soon is the question of technical assistance for the smaller economies. There are three areas where it will probably be required:

- to improve negotiating capabilities in all the new trade disciplines
- to improve implementation
- to increase capacity to evaluate impacts (modeling, etc.)

There is some concern about the extent to which the small economies can actually absorb such training effectively, since appropriate incentive structures and political backing must be in place before technical training will stick.

Questions about negotiating groups and about how to restructure the working groups will require careful consideration not only of the issues, but also of the human resource limitations of many countries in the hemisphere (not just the so-called small economies). While not commonly thought of as a negotiating group, the topic of small economies, technical assistance, and implementation needs to have a home during the negotiations and should continue to receive attention in its own right, if only to ensure that the views of the smaller economies are regularly and consistently heard.

Other questions that will need to be addressed early on include:

1. What will be the role of the private sector?
2. What role will labor play?

*Role of the Private Sector and Labor.* There is a strong sentiment among U.S. and Canadian negotiators that the Latin American private sector must be actively engaged in the advisory process, if possible in a fashion similar to the manner in which Canadian and U.S. companies are represented. They offer Costa Rica as an example of a private sector that has organized itself similarly to the U.S., Canadian, and Mexican private sectors. Some governments in the region seem to be uncomfortable with this open approach and are moving very slowly, if at all, to institutionalize private sector involvement in their countries.

Brazil has seen a dramatic increase in activity by its private sector as a result of the Belo Horizonte meeting, but on a hemisphere-wide basis, experience has been mixed. Some countries in the region have problems with including private sector advice because it creates an asymmetry with the treatment labor is receiving. To date, the labor issue has not been dealt with coherently. A number of different formula have been proposed, but there is little agreement among governments, between governments and the business community, or between governments and labor about the appropriate role for labor representatives, or about discussions of labor issues. The Mexican government has been particularly adamant that labor not be included or linked to the trade negotiations, while Brazil and the United States seem to share the opinion that if an appropriate format can be devised, labor should have the same right to submit suggestions and recommendations as the business sector.

A first, necessary step toward establishing an appropriate format will be to identify labor unions in each country that might be able and willing to work with trade negotiators. A repeat of the experience in Belo Horizonte with the so-called Labor Forum, which presented the ministers with a series of ideological demands, should be avoided at all costs. While some of labor's recommendations will probably not be granted a serious hearing, others should be given a hearing, both for the sake of the negotiations and for the eventual political acceptability of the accord.

*WTO, APEC, OECD Talks and the FTAA.* As pointed out in the introduction to the proposed fast-track legislation, the Clinton administration wants new negotiating authority primarily to be able to participate in a series of sectoral market access negotiations the United States would like to see launched under the auspices of the WTO and within APEC. The administration is predicting large positive results from the 1996 Declaration on Trade in Information Technology Products and the subsequent implementing agreement signed in March 1997 (which brings tariffs down to zero for a wide range of computer, telecommunications, and information technology products among the 25 signatories, including the EU), [71] and would like to replicate this experience in as many sectors as possible. The U.S. administration is particularly interested in initiating negotiations in the wood, pulp, and paper sectors; chemicals; energy equipment and products; environmental technologies and products; and oil seeds.

In addition to these new proposals, a list of sectors to be discussed under the WTO built-in agenda for market liberalization was agreed to at the end of the Uruguay Round (the last GATT trade round); these include services and agriculture and a series of trade reviews, including intellectual property implementation.

APEC has prepared an impressive list of sectors to be considered for sectoral "0 for 0" negotiations for which the United States would also like to have fast-track negotiating authority. Also mentioned in the context of opportunities for new agreements are bilateral agreements with New Zealand, Australia, and Singapore.

Clearly, part of the purpose of delineating this laundry list of trade agreement objectives is to demonstrate to Capitol Hill that there is an important and growing set of trade opportunities to be taken up, if only the administration had the authority to negotiate.[72] More importantly, USTR and others in the administration view these initiatives as being mutually reinforcing, particularly if talks are progressing in the same sectors in several different arenas. While they recognize the danger that some countries may not have the resources to engage in both global and regional negotiations simultaneously, they do not see this as presenting a major problem for most Latin American countries, most of whom sat out the Information Technology Agreement (ITA) negotiations in any case. However, the new sectors being proposed for global talks, particularly agriculture, are of central interest to most of Latin America and the Caribbean and will also certainly be included in the FTAA. Many LAC countries will probably need to "beef up" their negotiating resources in this sector in the near future to deal with the prospect of simultaneous WTO and FTAA agriculture talks.

Were a comprehensive new multilateral round of negotiations to be launched before the year 2000, as some are calling for, it is hard to imagine an FTAA negotiation proceeding. Such a round would consume enormous resources and would ostensibly deal with all remaining tariff issues as well as with several of the most contentious "new" issues, such as competition policy and environment and trade. Does the United States commitment to the FTAA kill the chances for a new multilateral round before

2005? Will limited sectoral negotiations be sufficient to keep the multilateral trading system "bicycle" moving? Or will the United States decide to try to ride both the WTO and FTAA bicycles at once?

## POLITICAL REALITIES AND PERCEPTIONS OF RISK

### The United States

Leading up to the ministerial meeting in San José and the hemispheric summit in Santiago next year, the most critical questions will be not substantive, but political, and many of them revolve around the objectives and strategies of the United States and Brazil. Will the Clinton administration have fast track by April 1998? What is the degree of U.S. business community commitment to the concept of an FTAA, and will business be willing to take the initiative to support or speed up the process? Will Brazil and the United States come to an understanding on pace and timing of negotiations?

All these questions are critical to decisions on the shape and pace of the negotiations, and to the long-term success of the negotiations, and to the FTAA itself, since they describe, fundamentally, the depth of political will behind the effort. At this point, prior to the granting of fast-track negotiating authority by Congress, significant uncertainty persists about whether the United States will be in a position to provide real leadership at either the Costa Rican or the Chilean meeting, particularly on such critical issues as the pace and structure of FTAA negotiations. If an agreement is not struck soon, it will be difficult, the U.S. will cede its role in defining the negotiating agenda and page to Brazil.

*The Official Position of the U.S. Administration.* The Clinton administration appears to be strongly committed to the concept of a free trade area of the Americas. Then-Under Secretary of Commerce Stuart Eizenstat (now under secretary of state) argued forcefully in March 1997 that the United States not only was committed to the FTAA but also was committed to getting fast track in 1997 so that formal negotiations could be launched in 1998 in Santiago.

Eizenstat mentioned that the primary reason for such a strong and aggressive stance was the huge potential for economic growth, both in the United States and in the region, if trade were to become free of all tariff and nontariff barriers. He cited the statistic that an FTAA could add at least 1.5 percent to the region's annual growth rate. He also cited numerous statistics regarding the rapid growth of U.S. trade with the region and cited as a precedent the strong positive impact NAFTA has had on U.S. trade with Mexico and Canada. In particular, he mentioned that since tariffs are still quite high in many countries in the region, U.S. exporters could expect to make real gains relatively rapidly under an FTAA. This is the basis for the U.S. position that market access talks need to be started simultaneously with the rest of the negotiations in order to be completed in 2005.

In a more defensive sense, it is clear that the United States is worried about directions trade in the region (particularly in MERCOSUR countries) might take, if not linked, at least informally, with NAFTA or a larger FTAA. The administration would not like to see an EU-MERCOSUR deal with discriminatory or preferential provisions, since this could have serious and large trade impacts on a variety of U.S. firms. The administration may also be concerned about the prospects for a Mexico-MERCOSUR deal or a Canada-MERCOSUR deal that leave out the United States. These concerns point to an additional defensive rationale for early engagement in FTAA negotiations on the part of the United States. As USTR Charlene Barshefsky pointed out in her testimony to the Senate upon the introduction of the fast-track legislation proposal, the rest of the hemisphere is not waiting for the United States to join the game.[73] More recently, both Secretaries Albright and Rubin have stressed the Administration's view that an FTAA serves significant U.S. foreign policy and economic interests. And, of course, President Clinton, in his State of the Union Address, argued for embracing globalization rather than running away from it, saying that the Administration was committed to free trade and would seek fast track this year (1998).

*U.S. Congressional Position and Fast-track Authorization.* The U.S. Congress has an opportunity to derail the entire FTAA process by not providing the administration with negotiating authority. Unfortunately, the debate on fast track has turned into a debate on whether the measure should contain environmental and labor provisions, and it is being used as a litmus test for Congressional commitment to those ideals, rather than to the issues of economic growth and free trade. In the bill introduced by the administration on September 16, 1997, the language relating to environmental protection and labor rights was extremely mild, yet some Democrats considered it a sell-out while Republicans considered it a dangerous loophole.[74]

Under any realistic scenario, fast track will be passed only with a significant number of Democratic votes, which is problematic to say the least. Environment and labor issues top the list of issues, but the whole question of how or whether to link social justice to preferential trade access is much more difficult for Democrats than for Republicans. The fact that the AFL-CIO has launched an all-out war on fast track will have a serious impact on Democratic support for the measure. Also, although the Republican leadership has expressed confidence that their membership will support a fast-track bill without objectionable labor and environmental provisions, there is no guarantee of solidity in Republican ranks, particularly if the administration tries to strengthen the language in bills passed by Senate and House committees referencing sustainable development, environmental protection, and workers' rights. One wing of the Republican party recalls with trepidation the popularity of Ross Perot's nationalistic, anti-trade rhetoric during the last two presidential elections and may be tempted to court the same groups with an anti-fast-track vote.

At the same time, there are a number of factors working in favor of passage, including strong export growth to the region; continuing problems with market access in other parts of the world; solid economic growth in most countries of the region; demonstrably good trade results from the NAFTA; the prospect of lost sales and markets, particularly from a EU-MERCOSUR agreement; and strong private sector interest in having fast-track authority in place. The recent decision by MERCOSUR to raise its common external tariff across the board to compensate for Brazil's economic woes indicates of the importance of having agreements in place to prevent this type of action from having a disproportionately negative impact on U.S. exporters.

Perhaps most importantly, the current robust state of the U.S. economy would seem to augur well for more, rather than less, trade, particularly since the United States has been one of the most open economies in the world for the past 20 years and has seen growth rates and employment rise, rather than fall, as a result.

Summing up, one has to conclude that the odds for fast track are about 50-50, but could succeed if most of the following conditions are met:

- Strong, unified, persistent, and well-crafted pressure is exerted by the White House.
- The Clinton administration remains domestically popular and the economy stays strong.
- Nothing goes severely wrong on the foreign policy front that would undermine Clinton's improving foreign policy profile.
- On the environmental and labor provisions, some deal can be worked out that does not alienate critical Democratic congressmen, on the one hand, or key Republican and business leaders on the other.
- The business community can demonstrate losses due to lack of access to preferential terms in one or another of the existing subregional agreements, and it remains committed to the inclusion of FTAA in the fast-track request.

Given the specific bill the administration introduced last year, one can imagine a number of different scenarios developing over the next two to three months. The first is that the Republican-dominated Congress will strip out or weaken any references to environment and labor in the bill and attempt to get it passed with almost no Democratic support. This is unlikely to occur, since it would not fit well with House Minority Leader Gingrich's desire to put House Democrats on the spot with a trade vote in an election year. Also, this would not appeal at all to the Gore faction of the administration.

The second scenario is that with insufficient enthusiasm among Republicans for the current or stripped-down bills, the measure will fail and Clinton will have to go to Santiago with empty hands.

The third and most likely scenario is that in order to keep the minimum number of votes required for passage, the bill will become a "Christmas tree" loaded with enough provisions on labor and environment to satisfy a few Democrats and with enough enforcement and "fair-trade" language to satisfy the Perot wing of the Republican party, so the majority of pro-free trade Republicans will hold their noses and vote for it anyway. This is apparently what began to happen prior to the decision to pull the bill, with the administration making a variety of commitments of all sorts (from agriculture to uranium) to buy votes. Evidently, those were not sufficient, and the administration is now looking to beef up its commitments on labor training and retraining, in particular.[75]

A fourth scenario would involve changes to the coverage of the bill, perhaps limiting it to just WTO and APEC sectoral talks or to bilateral talks only, but leaving out the FTAA.

With respect to the launching of FTAA, the most positive result obviously would be the first scenario, and the most negative, the fourth. However, the third scenario also could be quite chilling, as too many extraneous conditions would undermine Latin American enthusiasm for a negotiation with the United States. With regard to the second scenario, it is conceivable that the United States could still participate in FTAA negotiations without fast track, though admittedly in a much weaker position, and the administration could go back to Congress for authorization closer to the completion date in the hope of getting a clean bill. It is also conceivable that the rest of the hemisphere could refuse to discuss environmental and labor issues in the context of FTAA, but it is not clear what impact this would have on the ability of the United States to negotiate on trade matters.

*U.S. Business Community.* In view of the foregoing analysis, the U.S. business community remains skeptical about the prospects for getting fast track as well as about the 2005 deadline for the completion of FTAA talks. However, since the Clinton administration has assembled such a long list of potential new agreements that would be made possible by fast-track authorization, some attention has been diverted from FTAA. It remains to be seen whether the business community will aggressively fight for the inclusion of either Chile or the FTAA if Congress tries to limit fast track to WTO and APEC initiatives.

## THE CANADIAN PERSPECTIVE

Canadian government and majority business positions, which are identical for all intents and purposes, are aimed at achieving the broadest possible liberalization in the shortest possible time. This is no doubt due to the fact that fully half of Canada's annual production is exported, while for the United States only 30 percent of GDP is generated by trade (notwithstanding the fact that this is significantly higher than the 13 percent share in 1980).

Canada's position also is certainly due to the positive experience Canada has had so far with both the Canada-U.S. FTA and NAFTA. Canada's exports to both the United States and Mexico have grown dramatically over the last three years. Canada also perceives Latin America as largely virgin territory, since Canadian trade with most of Latin America has been extremely small compared to trade with Asia, Europe, and the United States. Thus, Canadians see the potential for significant growth being driven, as it was in the case of the NAFTA, by an agreement which helps Canadians "discover" the region.

Meanwhile, Canada remains devoted to the idea of multilateralism, as well as to the APEC process, but contrary to the situation in the mid-eighties, Canadians do not now seem to have any problem in reconciling their preference for multilateralism with serious engagement on a regional and subregional basis.[76] What Canada has discovered is that the FTA and NAFTA have made Canadian producers more competitive globally, not just regionally. As a result, Canada has hitched its wagon to the star of trade liberalization in any way, shape, or form it can be achieved – the faster, the broader and the deeper, the better.

Canada's stance is a logical one for a relatively small, trade-dependent economy, and indeed, it resembles closely the position of Chile, New Zealand, Singapore, and Hong Kong in other forums. It contrasts sharply, however, with positions of larger countries with large domestic markets, particularly those that do not have the infrastructure in place for rapid expansion of their exporting sector. Still, if a multilateral trade round were launched soon, Canada would surely put the lion's share of its resources into that effort.

## THE BRAZILIAN PERSPECTIVE

Brazil represents perhaps the opposite extreme from Canada with respect to its export orientation, its attitude toward trade liberalization, and its commitment to the FTAA process. Traditionally a highly protected internal market, Brazil has only in the last six years embarked on trade liberalization within the context of MERCOSUR and the WTO. The trade liberalization that has occurred has been unsettling for Brazilian firms, both large and small, and has resulted in something of a backlash against any further rapid opening.

Part of the reason for the negative reaction by Brazilian business is that at the same time that trade liberalization was occurring, the Brazilian government was also undertaking a number of other serious structural reforms, including redesigning its currency in order to reduce inflation dramatically. Profits and losses are now measured in real money, which has meant significant changes in accounting and managerial practices in the Brazilian private sector. These changes, along with continuing efforts to lower tariffs for Argentina, Paraguay, and Uruguay, have caused, in the words of one private sector representative, "wrenching dislocations" in the Brazilian economy. Furthermore, the Brazilian private sector perceives itself as being badly hampered by the lack of an export-oriented infrastructure, either physical or bureaucratic, that would support them in their efforts to become globally competitive.

The Cardoso administration is also concerned both about the impact of further dislocations and unemployment caused by import competition on political support for his broader program of reforms, including privatization of government corporations and assets, social security and pension reform, health reform, and education reform, and, of course, about the impact on his prospects for re-election in 1998.

Unemployment is an even more serious political problem in Brazil than in the United States because of the lack of any real safety net for the unemployed. Furthermore, since political support is weak for some of the hard political and economic reforms the Cardoso administration is seeking, escalating unemployment could provide the ammunition to sink them. In other words, moving too quickly towards additional market opening would have real and very serious economic and political consequences for the current Brazilian regime.

Despite everything, official Brazilian policy is to support the concept of an FTAA, but to move cautiously on any additional market opening for the foreseeable future; hence Brazilian proposals for business facilitation talks to precede market access talks, and for talks on agriculture to be given the highest possible priority. While this stance has changed recently, perhaps due to pressures from its MERCOSUR partners, Brazil continues to advocate a "gradualist" approach to the negotiations.

MERCOSUR interests are essentially multilateral, so a new WTO round is seen as more beneficial than a preferential arrangement with North America. However, due to the pressures alluded to above, Brazil is unlikely to be enthusiastic about another multilateral trade round in the near future, possibly except for sectoral negotiations in agriculture.

## THE SMALL, LESS DEVELOPED COUNTRY PERSPECTIVE

The most serious problem facing small and less-developed countries in the hemisphere is also a problem for all countries in the region that would like to export more textile goods and shoes to the United States. Time and again, the U.S. Congress has refused to consider granting parity with NAFTA access provisions to the Caribbean Basin Initiative (CBI) countries because of labor opposition in the domestic textile and apparel industry and, to a lesser extent, in the shoe industry. The political costs and benefits for most members of Congress of granting such parity do not seem to be balanced in the direction of the CBI countries. This was demonstrated again recently when the U.S. domestic textile and apparel industry leaders actually crafted a piece of legislation favoring the extension of limited NAFTA parity to CBI countries that they tried to have passed as part of the budget deal. It foundered once more on labor opposition and uncertainties about reciprocity.

The best remedy for small, textile-dependent countries is to build coalitions within a new global trade round. An FTA with the United States with an extended phase in of reciprocal obligations would be the second-best solution for most of these economies; third best would be an FTAA. Under any of these formulations, these countries will have to continue to liberalize their own markets and, while this should not be a problem for countries like Trinidad and Tobago, which have relatively competitive export sectors, other CARICOM and some CACM countries may have second thoughts about accepting WTO-plus obligations.

## NEGOTIATING STRATEGIES AND PRIORITIES

Given this widely divergent set of economic and political interests, is it realistic to assume that an FTAA can be negotiated by the year 2005, or even to believe that the negotiations can be launched by March 1998? What are the central questions that need to be answered before San José and Santiago for the process to proceed? Some of these have already been mentioned:

1. Will all the countries of the region have negotiating authority, and, in particular, will the United States be in a position to provide leadership for the process?

2. What exactly will be negotiated – a free trade agreement, a customs union, or some sort of sector-by-sector hybrid?

3. Will the negotiation be a "single undertaking," or will there be sectoral or regional carve-outs? Can we expect so-called "early harvest" results in certain sectors, and, if so, which ones?

4. Is the target to be very aggressive and achieve at least WTO-plus, if not NAFTA-equivalent commitments for almost every sector? Or is the goal to provide a generic, hemispheric umbrella agreement over several disparate regional agreements? In which sectors can we expect the most aggressive results?

5. How will the negotiation proceed? Will the currently comprised working groups become negotiating groups? Will groups be collapsed, combined, expanded, eliminated? Where will the negotiations take place, and what precisely will be the role of the secretariat?

6. How much linkage will or should be allowed between the trade negotiations and other hemispheric discussions on labor rights, environmental protection, macroeconomic coordination, infrastructure development, etc.?

7. How will LAC countries handle the simultaneous launch of several new global sectoral negotiations? Should agriculture be carved out of the FTAA and dealt with only at the global level?

## TRADE LIBERALIZATION OR SOCIAL TRANSFORMATION?

The fact that these questions are still unresolved going into the March 1998 San José meeting is indicative of two underlying weaknesses in the FTAA process. The first and most serious is that *there is no clear shared vision of what the hemisphere should look like in 2015 or 2020 if the free trade negotiations are successful.* In other words, there is little common agreement about the depth or breadth of commitments that ought to come out of the negotiations. While the ministers have agreed to cover many of the so-called "new" areas, such as intellectual property, government procurement, and services, MERCOSUR countries, in particular, seem to have continuing difficulties with the language of WTO-*plus*, given that they and many other countries in the region are just beginning to try to implement the last WTO agreement.

While some would argue that it is clear that the common objective is to form a free-trade area incorporating all the countries of the Americas, i.e., eliminate all tariffs, and most, if not all, nontariff barriers to trade, others (particularly in the U.S. Congress) argue that the FTAA should be utilized to accomplish a much larger set of social and political goals.

According to the most extreme version of this idea, the end result of such a negotiation would be a radically transformed social, legal, and political contract in the hemisphere along North American lines, one that would be enforced by trade sanctions. Clearly, this is not a vision that Latin American leaders can share, nor is it one that makes sense in the medium or probably even long term.

However, there are many shades of gray along this continuum, and it is likely that U.S. politicians, at least, will continue to skirmish for the duration of the negotiations to push their social reform agenda using the "trade stick." It will be up to the U.S. administration to clearly, firmly, and consistently draw the line with Congress.

The administration can do this in a number of ways, first of all by reminding U.S. congressional leaders through the consultation process that to link too many U.S. foreign policy goals to the FTAA is likely to endanger valuable achievements on trade. A single trade negotiation cannot possibly deal with every item on the regional agenda. The size and complexity of the trade negotiation is daunting enough without adding to it a raft of extremely complex and politically controversial issues. Even if every country in the region agreed to the addition of an extraneous issue such as money laundering, for instance, would it actually make sense to increase the workload of the trade negotiators in order to handle such an issue, or would it be more efficient to establish a separate and more focused parallel negotiation?

In addition, of course, many things the United States would like to see happen in the region do not lend themselves to negotiation. Instead, they are processes that must evolve out of the particular political, social, and economic culture of each country. For instance, how does a country negotiate a decline in income inequality or improvements in women's' rights, particularly if it is not willing to devote large sums of capital to the effort?

The U.S. administration will have an excellent opportunity to make these points (probably many times) to Congress during the course of the fast-track debate that will soon begin again.

## LEADERSHIP VERSUS BRINKMANSHIP

The fast-track problem raises the second serious problem with the FTAA process, which is that the United States and Brazil are, by virtue of their size and role in subregional groupings, the pacesetters for the process.

The internal political dynamics of free trade in the United States are of Byzantine complexity, as illustrated by the need for fast track. Other complications are Congress's excessive attachment to U.S. antidumping and countervailing duty legislation, and the tendency to utilize trade sanctions to accomplish a wide variety of foreign policy objectives, as illustrated by the Helms-Burton legislation. Nor are congressional politics particularly susceptible to rational economic argumentation, as illustrated by the seemingly never-ending debate over the impact of NAFTA.

As U.S. trade policy has come to be determined less by the Executive and more by Congress, short-term, domestic economic considerations and misperceptions about bilateral trade balances have badly distorted the debate. Thus, Congressional concerns about illegal immigration, drug interdiction, political and economic stability, human rights, income inequality, judicial reform, rebel insurgencies, air safety, and any number of other unrelated issues will be drawn into the debate on fast track and into the final approval of any FTAA.

Brazil also tends to be a problem insofar as its business community has concluded that enough liberalization has occurred for the time being. Brazil's response to the development in 1994-95 of a trade deficit for the first time in recent history was not reassuring. Increasing tariffs, imposing quotas, establishing discriminatory investment regimes, and cutting credit for imports are not policies calculated to bolster a country's reputation as a free trader.

Complex internal politics, dealing with the fallout from the "Asian flu," an upcoming election, concerns about consolidating MERCOSUR, and other relationships in South America all will further complicate Brazil's decision on how to proceed vis-à-vis the launching of FTAA talks.

Given that Brazil and the United States need to come to some sort of accommodation in order to make a negotiation successful, one can be only cautiously hopeful that by the end of April, both governments will have decided that an FTAA is still worth the inevitable short-term political pain.

## BUSINESS FACILITATION AND EARLY HARVEST MEASURES

The Institute of the Americas has earlier identified regulatory, judicial, and administrative reform, as well as capacity building as among the top priorities for the hemisphere. This agenda was widely supported at Cartagena, and more recently in the Brazilian position paper for Belo Horizonte, which emphasizes the need for rapid progress on business facilitation and the elimination of administrative, bureaucratic, and logistical obstacles to trade.

I have elsewhere argued that in order for the United States to achieve its goal of markedly better access for small- and medium-size firms, LAC countries would need to commit to serious and sustained *administrative, judicial, and regulatory reform*. Reforming customs enforcement, implementation, and interpretation of trade law and of technical standards should precede harmonization in these areas. Reform and harmonization, together, will dramatically enhance the ability of small- and medium-size firms to take advantage of opportunities in regional markets, and larger companies will also benefit, particularly in the services and investment areas.

The difficulty for LAC countries will be to decide how large a reform effort they can afford to make, either politically or economically. For, while it is relatively easy to identify inefficiencies and problems in administrative, judicial, or regulatory matters, to eliminate them will be a costly and long-term process. To address these problems, many of the governments of the region would need to make significant investments in training and professionalization of bureaucrats and judges; this includes raising salaries, reorganizing bureaucracies, increasing legislative oversight, reforming the legal system, and improving institutional capacity.[77]

Consequently, one of our strongest recommendations issuing from the 1996 Hemispheric Policy Forum was that countries with strong technical competence in the application and administration of technical standards should actively assist smaller countries and countries with less sophisticated expertise to devise and implement clear, transparent, and easily administered rules. Such technical assistance should be brokered by the IDB and the OAS to assure impartiality. Countries should also establish exchange programs to encourage cross-fertilization among themselves, particularly within the public-sector segment that will be responsible for implementing the FTAA. The IDB, OAS, U.S. Agency for International Development (USAID), Canadian International Development Agency (CIDA), U.S. Information Agency (USIA), and other federal, provincial, state, and nongovernmental organizations can help organize and fund such exchanges.[78]

In our view, and we believe this reflects the attitude of many in the private sector, business facilitation and administrative capacity building should not wait for formal negotiations to be completed, but should form the backdrop for further integration efforts.

## CONCLUSION

This survey of progress since 1994 on trade liberalization in the Western Hemisphere has served to highlight two diverging trends in the region. The first, toward the consolidation of subregional agreements and even toward some additional unilateral trade liberalization, is generally a positive development that has already had a significant impact on economic growth and intraregional trade patterns. The second trend, toward greater politicization of trade policy, is occurring everywhere in the region and is more and more frequently accompanied by strenuous debates over labor, environmental, legal, political, and social issues.

Unfortunately, answers to many questions about the impact of trade on economies at various levels of development are not readily available from the economics literature. Economists and policy makers disagree emphatically about many of the most critical issues, including the impact of trade liberalization on low and unskilled workers, on income disparity, on the relationship between trade liberalization and technological change, and on appropriate policy responses to trade-related job or wage dislocations. The business and labor communities, meanwhile, have not made much of a contribution to consensus building, instead devoting almost all their energies to supporting ideological positions for or against some short-term political objective.

It would seem that for future liberalization efforts to succeed in such a political climate, governments must begin a broader debate about the costs and benefits of globalization, technological change, and free trade. Such a dialogue will need to encompass a much larger portion of civil society than the usual trade policy clique sitting in Washington, Brasilia, Ottawa, or Santiago. The upcoming debate about fast track in the United States should be the first step.

# Notes

1. Ms. Morton is the Vice President and Director of Research for the Institute of the Americas in La Jolla, California.

2. CACM has hired Jeffrey Sachs and Michael Porter to help them analyze the competitiveness of their manufacturing sectors and recommend regional policy changes.

3. IDB, Integration, Trade and Hemispheric Issues Division and ECLAC.

4. Agreement signed in January 1998.

5. Luis Jorge Garay and Antoni Estevadeordal, 1996, "Protection, Preferential Tariff Elimination and Rules of Origin in the Americas," *Integration and Trade* (0) 11.

6. Garay 1996, 12.

7. For a thorough discussion of the MERCOSUR trade creation versus trade diversion debate, see Robert Devlin, "In Defense of MERCOSUR," (Washington: Inter-American Development Bank) and Inter-American Development Bank 1996, *Periodic Note,* December.

8. Estimates produced on the basis of data available by November 23, 1996.

9. Compares partial data for 1996 with the corresponding period of 1995.

10. Includes ALADI Countries, CACM and Panama.

11. Includes Latin America plus Bahamas, Barbados, Belize, Guyana, Jamaica, Surinam and Trinidad and Tobago.

12. It is too soon to tell whether the small recent reversal is a trend or just a temporary improvement.

13. Based on official pronouncements, as well as own assessment of political and economic costs & benefits. Also see: Anthony T. Bryan, 1997, "Trading Places: The Caribbean Faces Europe and the Americas in the Twenty-first Century," *The North-South Agenda Papers,* 27(June).

14. Raúl A. Hinojosa-Ojeda, Jeffrey D. Lewis and Sherman Robinson, 1997, "Simon Bolivar Rides Again? Pathways Toward Integration between NAFTA, MERCOSUR, and the Greater Andean Region," *Integration and Trade.,* 1 (Jan-Apr.): 95, 112.

Hinojosa, et.al., summarize the factors going into LAC calculations as follows:

> Latin American countries face major tradeoffs in opening to trade with a much more economically advanced market in exchange for potential access to the U.S. market and reduction in "risk premiums" for foreign investors. The economic significance of this bargain will depend on the relative importance of links with the United States for each LAC economy. For these countries, the potential benefits of the WHFTA include: greater guaranteed access to the U.S. market through rules-based procedures, and insurance against future trade restrictions; cheaper inputs and access to technology that might increase productivity; and a lock-in effect on reforms as countries seek a reduction in investment discount rates. The WHFTA can make large countries more attractive for FDI by offering possible economies of scale and scope to multinational investors. Moreover, all countries will be attracted to a WHFTA for defensive purposes, trying not to be left out of any potential arrangement.
>
> These benefits have to be balanced with costs associated with the WHFTA: the politics of displacing domestic labor and exposing local firms to competition from global firms that are bigger and have more resources; imposing large tariff reductions and undertaking financial liberalization that, in the short run, could exacerbate trade deficits and macroeconomic risks; limitations on the flexibility of short-term policymaking, as well as losing the use of certain industrial and development policy tools; and possible geopolitical problems or even retaliation by third-party trading partners."

15. Sarath Rajapatirana, 1995, "Trade Policies, Macroeconomic Adjustment, and Manufactured Exports: The Latin American Experience," *Policy Research Working Paper* #1492 (Washington: World Bank). And Rajapatirana 1995, "Post Trade Liberalization Policy and Institutional Challenges in Latin America and the Caribbean," *Policy Research Working Paper.* #1465 (Washington: World Bank).

Rajapatirana warns against underestimating the impact of macroeconomic distress on trade liberalization efforts.

16. Hinojosa 1997, 114.

17. Office of the United States Trade Representative, 1997, *Report on the Impact of NAFTA.*

18. Inter-American Development Bank, 1996, *Periodic Note,* (August) 18.

19. Jorge G. Vega, 1997, "Foreign Trade Policy and Economic Integration Policy in Peru: Analysis of a Dilemma." In *Integrating the Americas,* eds. Ana Julia Jatar and Sidney Weintraub (Washington: Inter-American Dialogue), 49.

20. *Americas Trade* 7, 24: 14.

21. Miguel Rodriguez, 1997, "The Andean Group's Integration Strategy." In *Integrating the Americas,* eds. Ana Julia Jatar and Sidney Weintraub (Washington: Inter-American Dialogue), 16.

22. *Americas Trade* 6, 26: 4.

23. Rodriguez, 1997, 17 & 19.

24. Eduardo Lizano and José M. Salazar-Xirinach, 1997, "The Central American Common Market and Hemispheric Free Trade." In *Integrating the Americas,* eds. Sidney Weintraub and Ana Julia Jatar (Washington: Inter-American Dialogue), 125.

25. Inter-American Development Bank, 1996, *Periodic Note,* (August), 22.

26. Lizano 1997, 126.

27. Lizano 1997, 134.

28. Office of the United States Trade Representative, 1996, *Annual Trade Report - Enforcement of Trade Agreements* (Washington), 8.

29. Gill, Henry S. 1997. "Caricom and Hemispheric Trade Liberalization." In *Integrating the Americas,* eds. Ana Julia Jatar and Sidney Weintraub (Washington: Inter-American Dialogue), 103.

30. Gill 1997, 101.

31. Gill 1997, 101.

32. Gill 1997, 105.

33. Gill 1997, 105.

34. Organization of American States, 1997, *Trade and Integration,* See Section II.

35. Arocena, Martin. 1997. "MERCOSUR." In *Integrating the Americas,* eds. Ana Julia Jatar and Sidney Weintraub (Washington: Inter-American Dialogue), 156.

36. Arocena 1997, 157.

37. Sam Laird, 1997. "MERCOSUR: Objectives and Achievements." paper prepared for the Annual World Bank Conference on Development in Latin America and the Caribbean, July 1, Montevideo, Uruguay. 22.

38. Arocena 1997, 170-1.

39. Laird 1997, 6.

40. Laird 1997, 5.

41. Laird 1997, 16.

42. *Americas Trade* (1/22/97): 7.

43. Laird 1997, 21.

44. Laird 1997, 24.

45. *Inside Nafta* (1/8/97): 10.

46. *Americas Trade* (2/5/98), 1.

47. U.S. International Trade Commission, 1997, The *Impact of the North American Free Trade Agreement on the U.S. Economy and Industries: A Three-Year Review,* Investigation No. 332-381, 14-15.

The results indicate, after controlling for changes in income, prices, and exchange rates, that the volume of U.S. imports from Mexico increased by 1.0 percent in 1994 as a result of NAFTA. In addition, U.S. imports from Mexico are estimated to be 5.7 and 6.4 percent higher in 1995 and 1996, respectively. Similarly, the results indicate that the volume of U.S. exports to Mexico increased by 1.3 percent in 1994 as a result of NAFTA, and increased by 3.9 and 2.9 percent in 1995 and 1996, respectively. Two important points emerge from these estimates. First, in 1994, the only year in which NAFTA was in place and the peso devaluation does not confound the estimates, the increased volume of exports from the United States to Mexico outpaced the increased volume of U.S. imports from Mexico. Second, during 1995 and 1996, the estimated simultaneous increase in import and export volumes demonstrates the high degree of integration between U.S. and Mexican bilateral trade flows.

48. Office of the United States Trade Representative, 1997, *Report on the Operation and Effect of the NAFTA,* (Washington) 1.

49. Inter-American Development Bank, 1995, *Periodic Note* (First Quarter - Downloaded 8/5/97) 3.

50. See *Americas Trade,* 1997: November 4 and 13, for detail on the different structural proposals.

51. *Americas Trade* 7, 24: 16.

52. An innovative and welcome step in that direction is the institutional design of Peru's competition enforcement agency, INDECOPI. It has been given jurisdiction to enforce both trade and competition policies.

53. Rajapatirana and Guasch 1997, 21.

54. Daniel Schwanen, 1996, "Dispute Settlement in the Americas: The Lessons of Canada-U.S. Relations under Free Trade 1989-1995," in *Outlook for Free Trade in the Americas,* ed. Colleen Morton (La Jolla, Calif: Institute of the Americas), 69.

55. Schwanen 1996, 69.

56. Inter-American Development Bank, 1996, *Comparative Analysis of Government Procurement Rules in Integration Agreements in the Americas.* (Washington), 5.

57. All countries in the Western Hemisphere but Ecuador and Panama signed the Uruguay Round agreements in Marrakesh in April 1994. Since then both have become members.

58. Robert Sherwood and Carlos Primo Braga. 1996. "Intellectual Property, Trade, and Economic Development: A Road Map for the FTAA Negotiations," in *Outlook for Free Trade in the Americas,* ed. Colleen Morton, ( La Jolla, Calif: Institute of the Americas).

59. *Americas Trade* 5, 12: 19.

60. *Americas Trade* 5, 12: 17.

61. *Americas Trade* 7, 24: 2.

62. Simão Davi Silber, 1996, "Rules of Origin in Preferential Trade Agreements: The case of the Free Trade Agreement of the Americas," In *Outlook for Free Trade in the Americas,* ed. Colleen Morton (La Jolla, Calif.: Institute of the Americas).

63. Institute of the Americas, 1997, *Transcript of the Hemispheric Policy Forum Proceedings,* (La Jolla, Calif.).

64. *Americas Trade* 5, 12: 25.

65. Organization of American States, 1997, *Provisions on Trade in Services in Trade and Integration Agreements of the Western Hemisphere,* 2.

66. *Americas Trade* 5, 12: 21.

67. Organization of American States, 1997, *National Practices on Standards, Technical Regulations and Conformity Assessment in the Western Hemisphere* (Washington), 1-2.

68. Sherry Stephenson, 1997, "Standards, the Environment and Trade Facilitation in the Western Hemisphere: Negotiating in the FTAA," *Occasional Paper Series* (La Jolla, Calif.: Institute of the Americas). 19.

> It has earlier been pointed out in this paper that implementation of the basic disciplines of the WTO TBT Agreement has been very poor in the hemisphere, and that less than one-third of FTAA participants have complied with two or more of the three basic multilateral obligations of the Agreement, though these should have been implemented by all countries since 1995. And, while the membership of the WTO now includes all FTAA participants, only 22 countries of the hemisphere are members of the ISO. This number is misleading, however, since it does not give an accurate idea of the actual participation by national standards bodies in the numerous ISO committees and working groups where international standards are actually drafted. Coincidentally, only 22 countries are members of COPANT, and the activities of the latter in developing hemispheric-wide approaches to the elaboration of standards have been limited. Most recently, only nine countries signed the IAAC Memorandum of Understanding as full members, pledging to promote mutual recognition of conformity assessment certificates among themselves. Clearly the implementation of multilateral disciplines is not yet in place in the hemisphere, and participation in international and regional or hemispheric-wide standardizing activities is far from universal for FTAA participants.

69. Sherry M. Stephenson, 1997, "Standards, Conformity Assessment and Developing Countries," *Working Paper Series,* (Washington: The World Bank).

70. Luis Guasch and Sarath Rajapatirana, 1997, "Antidumping and Competition Policies in Latin America and Caribbean: Total Strangers, Rival Siblings or Soul Mates?" *Occasional Paper Series* (La Jolla, Calif.: Institute of the Americas), 20.

71. Costa Rica is the only signatory in Latin America.

72. *Americas Trade* (2/5/98), 5.

73. United States Senate Finance Committee hearings, 1997, CSPAN televised report, September 17.

74. White House, *Export Expansion and Reciprocal Trade Agreements Act of 1997,* Section One, Paragraph (b)(7).

75. *Americas Trade,* 1997, November 11.

76. During the FTA debate, a regional agreement with the United States was widely viewed in Canada as having the potential to undermine the global trading system and global trade liberalization, as well as further intensifying an unhealthy dependence on the U.S. market.

77. Colleen Morton, ed. 1996. *Outlook for Free Trade in the Americas* (La Jolla, Calif.: Institute of the Americas).

78. Morton 1996, 8.

# References

Americas Business Forum III. 1997. *Workshops: Working Documents.* Meeting of the Americas: One Continent. One Market. Belo Horizonte, Brazil (May).

*Americas Trade* (previously *Inside Nafta*), 1997: various issues.

Arocena, Martin. 1997. "Common Market of the Southern Cone: MERCOSUR." In *Integrating the Americas,* eds. Ana Julia Jatar and Sidney Weintraub. Washington: Inter-American Dialogue.

Bouzas, Roberto. 1996. MERCOSUR's Economic Agenda: Short- and Medium-term Policy Challenges. *Integration and Trade.* 0.

Bryan, Anthony T. 1997. "Trading Places: The Caribbean Faces Europe and the Americas in the Twenty-first Century." *The North-South Agenda Papers,* 27(June).

da Motta Veiga, Pedro. 1997. "Brazil's Strategy for Trade Liberalization and Economic Integration in the Western Hemisphere." In *Integrating the Americas,* eds. Ana Julia Jatar and Sidney Weintraub. Washington: Inter-American Dialogue.

Devlin, Robert. 1997. "In Defense of MERCOSUR," Washington: Inter-American Development Bank.

Devlin, Robert, and Luis Jorge Garay. 1996. "From Miami to Cartagena: Nine Lessons and Nine Challenges of the FTAA." *Working Papers 211.* Washington: Inter-American Development Bank (July).

Garay, Luis Jorge, and Antoni Estevadeordal. 1996. "Protection, Preferential Tariff Elimination and Rules of Origin in the Americas." *Integration and Trade.* 0.

Gill, Henry S. 1997. "Caricom and Hemispheric Trade Liberalization." In *Integrating the Americas,* eds. Ana Julia Jatar and Sidney Weintraub. Washington: Inter-American Dialogue.

Guasch, J. Luis, and Sarath Rajapatirana. 1997. "Antidumping and Competition Policies in Latin America and Caribbe: Total Strangers, Rival Siblings or Soul Mates?" La Jolla, Calif.: Institute of the Americas.

Heads of State. 1994. "Declaration at Miami Summit." Miami.

Hinojosa-Ojeda, Raúl A., Jeffrey D. Lewis, and Sherman Robinson. 1997. "Simon Bolivar Rides Again? Pathways Toward Integration between NAFTA, MERCOSUR, and the Greater Andean Region." *Integration and Trade.* 1 (Jan-Apr.): 95.

Hufbauer, Gary Clyde, and Jeffrey J. Schott. 1993. "Western Hemisphere Economic Integration: Subregional Building Blocks." *Occasional Paper 10b.* Washington: Inter-American Development Bank.

Hufbauer, Gary Clyde, and Jeffrey J. Schott. 1994. *Western Hemisphere Economic Integration.* Washington: Institute for International Economics.

Iglesias, Enrique. 1997. "Free Trade Area of the Americas: From Miami to Belo Horizonte." *Speech at Belo Horizonte Business Forum.* Washington: Inter-American Development Bank (May 14).

Inter-American Development Bank. 1996. *Comparative Analysis of Government Procurement Rules in Integration Agreements in the Americas.* Washington (September).

Inter-American Development Bank. 1996. "Integration and Trade in the Americas - A Preliminary Estimate of 1996 Trade," *Periodic Note.* Washington. (July).

Inter-American Development Bank. 1996. "Integration and Trade in the Americas." *Periodic Note.* Washington. (August).

Inter-American Development Bank. 1996. *National Legislation, Regulations and Procedures Regarding Government Procurement in the Americas.* Washington (October).

Inter-American Development Bank. 1996. "A Preliminary Estimate of 1996 Trade." *Periodic Note.* Washington. (December).

Jatar, Ana Julia, and Sidney Weintraub, eds. 1997. *Integrating the Americas,* Washington: Inter-American Dialogue.

Laird, Sam. 1997. "MERCOSUR: Objectives and Achievements." paper prepared for the Annual World Bank Conference on Development in Latin America and the Caribbean, July 1, Montevideo, Uruguay.

Lizano, Eduardo, and José M. Salazar-Xirinachs. 1997. "The Central American Common Market and Hemispheric Free Trade." In *Integrating the Americas,* eds. Ana Julia Jatar and Sidney Weintraub. Washington: Inter-American Dialogue.

Meller, Patricio. 1997. "An Overview of Chilean Trade Strategy." In *Integrating the Americas,* eds. Ana Julia Jatar and Sidney Weintraub. Washington: Inter-American Dialogue.

Michaely, Michael. 1996. "Trade Preferential Agreements in Latin America — An Ex-Ante Assessment." *Policy Research Working Paper #1583.* Washington: The World Bank (March).

North-South Center at the University of Miami and the Institute of the Americas, 1997. *Free Trade in the Americas: Policy Recommendations and Issue Papers.* Miami: North-South Center.

Office of the United States Trade Representative. 1996. *Annual Trade Report - Enforcement of Trade Agreements,* Washington.

Office of the United States Trade Representative. 1996. *National Trade Estimate.* Washington.

Office of the United States Trade Representative. 1997. *National Trade Barriers Estimate Report.* Washington.

Office of the United States Trade Representative. 1997. *Report on the Operation and Effect of the NAFTA.* Washington.

Organization of American States. 1997. *Compendium of Antidumping and Countervailing Duty Laws in the Western Hemisphere.* Washington.

Organization of American States. 1997. *Investment Agreements in the Western Hemisphere: A Compendium.* Washington.

Organization of American States. 1997. *National Practices on Standards, Technical Regulations and Conformity Assessment in the Western Hemisphere.* Washington.

Organization of American States. 1997. *Provisions on Trade in Services in Trade and Integration Agreements of the Western Hemisphere.* Washington.

Organization of American States. 1997. *Small and Relatively Less Developed Economies and Western Hemisphere Integration.* Washington (April).

Organization of American States. 1997. *Trade and Integration Arrangements in the Americas: An Analytical Compendium.* Washington.

Rajapatirana, Sarath. 1994. "The Evolution of Trade Treaties and Trade Creation: Lessons for Latin America." *Policy Research Working Paper* #1371. Washington: World Bank (October).

Rajapatirana, Sarath. 1995. "Post Trade Liberalization Policy and Institutional Challenges in Latin America and the Caribbean." *Policy Research Working Paper.* #1465. Washington: World Bank (May).

Rajapatirana, Sarath. 1995. "Trade Policies, Macroeconomic Adjustment, and Manufactured Exports: The Latin American Experience." *Policy Research Working Paper* #1492. Washington: World Bank (August).

Rodriguez, Miguel. 1997. "The Andean Group's Integration Strategy." In *Integrating the Americas,* eds. Ana Julia Jatar and Sidney Weintraub. Washington: Inter-American Dialogue.

Schwanen, Daniel. 1996. "Dispute Settlement in the Americas: The Lessons of Canada-U.S. Relations under Free Trade 1989-1995." in *Outlook for Free Trade in the Americas.* ed. Colleen Morton, La Jolla, Calif: Institute of the Americas.

SELA, 1997. *Boletín sobre Integración de América Latina y el Caribe.* 5(Junio) and 1(Febrero). (Downloaded August 8, 1997).

Sherwood, Robert, and Carlos Primo Braga. 1996. "Intellectual Property, Trade, and Economic Development: A Road Map for the FTAA Negotiations." in *Outlook for Free Trade in the Americas.* ed. Colleen Morton. La Jolla, Calif: Institute of the Americas.

Stephenson, Sherry M. 1997, "Standards, Conformity Assessment and Developing Countries", *Working Paper Series,* Washington: The World Bank.

Stephenson, Sherry M. 1997. "Standards, the Environment and Trade Facilitation in the Western Hemisphere: Negotiating in the FTAA." La Jolla, Calif.: Institute of the Americas.

*The Economist.* 1996. Special Issue on MERCOSUR. October 12.

*The Economist.* 1997. "Central America Opens for Business." June 21.

U.S. General Accounting Office. 1997. *Trade Liberalization - Western Hemisphere Trade Issues Confronting the United States.* Report to the Chairman, Subcommittee on Trade, Committee on Ways and Means, House of Representatives. Washington (July).

U.S. International Trade Commission. 1997. *The Impact of the North American Free Trade Agreement on the U.S. Economy and Industries: A Three-Year Review,* Investigation No. 332-381.

United States Senate Finance Committee hearings, 1997, CSPAN televised report, September 17.

Vega, Jorge G. 1997. "Foreign Trade Policy and Economic Integration Policy in Peru: Analysis of a Dilemma," In *Integrating the Americas.* eds. Ana Julia Jatar and Sidney Weintraub. Washington: Inter-American Dialogue.

White House, *Export Expansion and Reciprocal Trade Agreements Act of 1997.*

# Appendix A - FTAA Negotiating Priorities - Areas of Convergence and Divergence[1]

| Issue | Related and Underlying Issues | Degree of Convergence | Early Harvest Opportunities |
|---|---|---|---|
| Investment | Dispute Settlement, Judicial Capacity Building | High convergence | Identification of impediments; agreement on arbitration tribunals; technical assistance with infrastructure project finance |
| Standards | Regulatory and Administrative Capacity Building | High convergence on need for clearer and more easily administered standards (only medium convergence on types of standards and on sectors of interest) | Technical cooperation on standards development and application |
| Services | Investment and Regulatory Capacity Building | Low convergence | Cooperation on regulatory harmonization in financial services and telecommunications sectors |
| IPR | Dispute Settlement and Judicial Capacity Building | Medium convergence | Identify ways to lower enforcement and implementation costs. Cooperation on developing monitoring and enforcement capacity. |
| Rules of Origin | Administrative Capacity Building (computerization, standardization, simplification techniques) | Medium convergence | Jointly explore alternatives to rules of origin. Explore the possibility of establishing a commission to carry out reviews of regional rules and to encourage harmonization. |
| Dispute Settlement | Judicial and Administrative Capacity Building | Medium convergence on different sectors, high convergence on necessity | Identification of major sources of disputes; development of dispute avoidance mechanisms |
| Market Access | Administrative Capacity Building | Medium convergence (on different sectors) | Identification and reduction of tariff peaks; simplification of customs procedures; coordination of customs practices |

# Appendix B - Terms of Reference and Negotiating Objectives and Principles for FTAA Working Groups

## COMPETITION POLICY

### Competition Policy Terms of Reference (Cartagena):

- Promote understanding of the objectives and operation of competition policy.
- Compile an inventory of domestic laws and regulations that exist in the Hemisphere that deal with anti-competition conduct and, on the basis of that information, identify areas of commonality and divergence.
- Create an inventory of the competition policy agreements, treaties and arrangements existing in the Hemisphere.
- Identify cooperation mechanisms among governments in the Hemisphere aiming at ensuring the effective implementation of competition policy laws.
- Recommend ways to assist members to establish or improve their domestic competition policy regimes, as they may request.
- Exchange views on the application and operation of competition policy regimes in the countries of the Hemisphere and their relationship to trade in a free trade area.
- Make specific recommendations on how to proceed in the construction of the FTAA in this area.

### Competition Policy Objectives (San José):

*General Objectives:*

- to guarantee that the benefits of the FTAA liberalization process not be undermined by anti-competitive business practices.

*Specific Objectives:*

- to advance towards the establishment of juridical and institutional coverage at the national, sub-regional or regional level, that proscribes the carrying out of anti-competitive business practices;
- to develop mechanisms that facilitate and promote the development of competition policy and guarantee the enforcement of regulations on free competition among and within countries of the Hemisphere.

### Competition Policy Negotiating Principles:

Among the negotiation principles in the issues area, the Working Group identified two categories of principles, general and specific, and in this sense agreed that the negotiations should develop based on the following principles:

*General Principle:*

- Strict adherence to the Joint Ministerial Declaration of Belo Horizonte and in particular to paragraphs 5, 10 and 12.

Specific Principles:

- to consider the differences between existing legal systems and traditions in countries of the Hemisphere;
- to consider the distinct degrees of development and enforcement of competition policies;
- to consider the differences in the development and size of the economies of the Hemisphere.

## DISPUTE SETTLEMENT

Dispute Settlement Terms of Reference (Belo Horizonte)

- Compile an inventory of dispute settlement procedures and mechanisms included in agreements, treaties and arrangements of integration existing in the hemisphere and those of the WTO, appending the legal texts.
- On the basis of this inventory, identify areas of commonality and divergence among dispute settle-

ment systems in the hemisphere, including with respect to the extent to which these systems have been employed.

- Exchange views, following internal consultations with the private sector, regarding mechanisms to encourage and facilitate the use of arbitration and other means of alternative dispute resolution for the settlement of international commercial disputes.
- Recommend methods to promote understanding of the procedures under the WTO Understanding on Rules and Procedures Governing the Settlement of Disputes.
- In the light of the various subjects to be covered by the FTAA agreement and other relevant factors, exchange views on possible approaches to dispute settlement under the FTAA agreement, in line with the World Trade Organization understanding on Rules and Procedures Governing the Settlement of Disputes.
- Make specific recommendations on how to proceed in the construction of the FTAA in this area.

Dispute Settlement Objectives (San José)

Dispute Settlement Principles (San José)

## GOVERNMENT PROCUREMENT

### Government Procurement Terms of Reference (Cartagena):

- Collect, systematize and create an inventory of the legislation, regulations, and procedures in the countries of the Hemisphere regarding government procurement, starting at the central government level, including, among other, state-owned enterprises. On the basis of that inventory, undertake a study of barriers to access to procurement by the public sector.
- Create an inventory and analysis of regulations on government procurement included in integration schemes and other existing agreements to which countries in the Hemisphere are signatories.
- Compile available data on purchases of goods and services by central governments, including, among others, state-owned enterprises, in the Hemisphere.
- Identify areas of commonality and divergence among government procurement systems in countries of the Hemisphere.

- Recommend methods to promote understanding of the WTO Government Procurement Agreement.
- Recommend methods to promote transparency in government procurement.
- Make specific recommendations on how to proceed in the construction of the FTAA in this area.

### Government Procurement Objectives (San José):

The broad objective of negotiations in government procurement is to expand access to the government procurement markets of the FTAA countries.

More specifically, the objectives of the negotiations are:

- to achieve a normative framework that ensures openness and transparency of government procurement processes, without necessarily implying the establishment of identical government procurement systems in all countries;
- to ensure non-discrimination in government procurement within a scope to be negotiated; and
- to ensure impartial and fair review for the resolution of procurement complaints and appeals by suppliers and the effective implementation of such resolutions.
- [Negotiations shall not exclude trade in goods and services, investment and government procurement at any levels of the political-administrative structure of the countries negotiating the Agreement.]
- [Negotiations shall include trade in goods and services, investment and government procurement at all levels of the political administrative structure of the countries negotiating the Agreement.]
- [The scope of government procurement shall be subject to negotiation.]

### Government Procurement Principles (San José):

- Compatibility with the multilateral development and disciplines of the topic of government procurement in the World Trade Organization (WTO);
- Non-discrimination within the negotiated scope of the agreement; and
- facilitation of the integration of the smaller economies and their full participation in the process

leading to the FTAA in the area of government procurement, bearing in mind the wide differences in levels of development and sizes of economies.

## INTELLECTUAL PROPERTY

### Intellectual Property Protection Terms of Reference (Cartagena):

- Create an inventory of the intellectual property agreements, treaties and arrangements that exist in the Hemisphere, including all international conventions to which countries are parties.
- Compile, in the most efficient manner, an inventory of intellectual property protection laws, regulations and enforcement measures in the Hemisphere and, on the basis of this information, identify areas of commonality and divergence.
- Recommend methods to promote the understanding and effective implementation of the WTO Agreement on the Trade-Related Aspects of Intellectual Property Rights (TRIPs).
- Identify possible areas for technical assistance, which countries may request, involving both the administration and enforcement of intellectual property rights.
- Analyze the implications of emerging technologies for intellectual property rights protection in the FTAA.
- Make specific recommendations on how to proceed in the construction of the FTAA in this area.

### Intellectual Property Protection Objectives (San José):

In the framework of the general objective of the FTAA to construct a free trade area, the objective of the negotiations in the area of intellectual property shall be to achieve an agreement or common understanding that reduces distortions in trade in the Hemisphere and promotes and ensures adequate and effective protection to intellectual property rights.

*[The agreement shall take into account changes in technology.]*

### Intellectual Property Protection Principles (San José):

Consistent with the framework of the general principles of the Belo Horizonte Declaration and the WTO Agreement on Intellectual Property Right Trade Related Aspects, the following specific principles were identified:

- National treatment
- most-favored nation
- [principles of intellectual property applicable by thematic area]
- [not diminishing the level of protection to the countries during negotiations in accordance with [their] [existing] international obligations.]
- to cover all areas of intellectual property rights, including enforcement.]

The provisions of paragraph b shall not prevent some countries being granted specific privileges or facilities within the framework of bilateral or sub-regional agreements beyond FTAA.]

Canada accepts the national treatment and MFN principles with exceptions.

## INVESTMENT

### Investment Terms of Reference (Denver):

- Create an inventory of investment agreements and treaties, and the protection therein, that exist in the region.
- Compile in the most efficient manner possible an inventory of investment regimes in the region and, on the basis of this information, determine areas of commonality and divergence and make specific recommendations.
- Publish a guidebook on investment regimes in the Hemisphere.
- Promote accession to existing arbitral conventions.
- Publish the inventory of investment agreements and treaties in the region.

### Investment Objectives (San José):

- To establish a fair and transparent legal framework that leads to a stable and predictable environment that protects investors, their investment and related flows; and stimulate the development of investment opportunities, without creating improper obstacles to extra-hemisphere investments, in accordance with paragraph 2 of the Cartagena Declaration and paragraph 2 of the Belo Horizonte Declaration.

## Investment Principles (San José):

The negotiation shall provide for transparency and the protection of investors and their investments. This negotiation shall be based, at least, on the following principles:

- Principle of non-discrimination;
- National Treatment;
- Most-favored nation treatment;
- Fair and equitable treatment.

## MARKET ACCESS

## Market Access Terms of Reference (Denver):

- Construct and organize in the most efficient manner possible a comprehensive data base on market access barriers (tariffs and nontariff measures as required for the WTO Integrated Data Base) in the Hemisphere covering all industrial and agricultural products, using the format of the WTO Integrated Data Base;
- Make specific recommendations for conducting market access negotiations;
- Keep data bases current;
- Make them public, once contents have been approved by governments.

## Market Access Objectives (San José):

*General Objective:*

- To build a Free Trade Area in the Americas, by means of elimination of barriers to trade of goods.

*Specific Objectives:*

- Consistently with article XXIV of GATT 94 and its understanding, to progressively eliminate, *[starting in the year 2005]*, tariffs, and nontariff barriers, *[for the substantial trade] [for all trade]* as well as other measures with equivalent effects, which restrict trade between participating countries, in accordance with the provisions of the WTO.
- All tariffs will be subject to negotiation.
- *[Different trade liberalization time tables can be drawn up which could include special treatment for countries, sectors and products.]*
- to facilitate the integration of smaller economies and their full participation in the FTAA negotiations.

## Market Access Principles (San José):

The general principles for the FTAA negotiations included in the Belo Horizonte Ministerial Declaration.

- Consistency with WTO disciplines, in particular, with Article XXIV of the General Agreement on Tariffs and Trade (GATT 1994), and with the Understanding pertinent to the Interpretation of Article XXIV of GATT 1994.
- Transparency in the trade negotiations.
- To recognize the wide differences in the level of development and size of economies existing among FTAA participants, as it is stated in paragraph 3 of the Declaration of Belo Horizonte.
- Coexistence with bilateral and sub-regional agreements, as long as the rights and obligations under such agreements are not covered or exceed the FTAA rights and obligations.
- *[The negotiations shall be rules by the following principles; they should be balanced, gradual and simultaneous.*
- *Balance as it refers to the negotiation process and to the results of this negotiation, which shall contemplate the objectives and interests of all parties.*
- *Gradual as it regards to the development and process of the negotiations, in accordance with the sequence demanded by thematic area.*
- *Simultaneous in the implementation different partial understandings that are reached, which must be part of a general agreement, in accordance with the commitment of "single undertaking."]*

## RULES OF ORIGIN AND CUSTOMS PROCEDURES

### Rules of Origin and Customs Procedures Terms of Reference (Denver):

- Compile in the most efficient manner possible a comprehensive inventory of Hemisphere customs procedures and determine the feasibility of publishing a Hemisphere Guide to Customs Procedures.
- Develop features that are fundamental to an efficient and transparent system of rules of origin, including nomenclature and certificates of origin.
- Identify areas for technical cooperation in customs operation, such as connections among computerized systems and the prevention of fraud.
- Recommend a specific approach for Hemisphere-wide simplification of customs procedures.
- Make specific recommendations for conducting negotiations on rules of origin.

### Rules of Origin and Customs Procedures Objectives (San José):

#### *Rules of Origin*

- To develop an efficient and transparent system of rules of origin, including nomenclature and certificates of origin, in order to facilitate the exchange of goods, without creating unnecessary obstacles to trade.

#### *Customs Procedures*

- to simplify customs procedures, in order to facilitate trade and reduce administrative costs.
- to create and implement mechanisms to exchange information in customs issues among FTAA countries.
- to design effective systems to detect and combat fraud and other illicit customs activities, without creating unnecessary obstacles to foreign trade.

### Rules of Origin and Customs Procedures Principles (San José):

The guiding principle for negotiations should be consistency with the obligations under the World Trade Organization (WTO).

Rules of origin and customs procedures should be elaborated and administered in an objective, transparent, coherent and predictable manner. *[With the aim that its implementation would give equal opportunities to all FTAA members.]*

Technical assistance and cooperation may be requested and provided by the countries, both on rules of origin and customs procedures, in accordance with the modalities to be defined.

#### *Rules of Origin*

The regime of rules of origin should provide for mechanisms to update the system on the basis of technological changes and other requirements.

*[Rules of origin shall take into account the specific commercial interests of all countries of the Hemisphere, including those of the smaller economies].*

For the elaboration of this system, the nomenclature of the Harmonized commodity Description and Coding System will be adopted (HS).

#### *Customs Procedures*

With the purpose of attaining the proposed objectives in this matter, the customs procedures should:

a) Be clear and precise;

b) Only require the necessary information for the efficient performance of customs functions.

As well, develop mechanisms for the exchange of the information regarding progress of the agreed upon simplification, and of the adoption of mechanisms to detect and combat fraud and other illicit customs activities.

The modalities of the implementation of the simplified customs procedures, by Customs Administrations, should be determined during the negotiations.

## SANITARY AND PHYTOSANITARY STANDARDS (SPS)

### Sanitary and Phytosanitary Standards Terms of Reference (Denver):

- Create an inventory of all agreements on the SPS in the Hemisphere and compile in the most effective manner possible an inventory of SPS regimes in the region;

- Recommend ways to enhance transparency and information-sharing and improve understanding of laws and regulations that affect trade flows in the region.
- Identify practices that may need improvement, and make recommendations for their improvement.
- Promote understanding of the WTO Agreement on Sanitary and Phytosanitary Measures, including through technical assistance, and recommend measures for the effective implementation of this Agreement.
- Enhance mutual understanding of the scientific basis for SPS certification procedures, with a view to recommend ways to promote recognition of certificates among countries of the Hemisphere.
- Compile by the most efficient means possible the methods used for risk assessment in the Hemisphere, with a view to work toward common approaches.
- Develop proposals on ways to promote the recognition of sanitary and phytosanitary certificates among countries in the Hemisphere.

(No agreement was reached in San José. Working group has until the next vice ministerial meeting in February 1998 to produce its recommendations.)

## SERVICES

### Services Terms of Reference (Cartagena):

- Undertake conceptual background work on the nature of trade in services, including the relationship to other working groups, including investment.
- Compile a comprehensive inventory of agreements accords and other arrangements covering trade services in the Hemisphere and determine areas of commonality and divergence.
- Create a comprehensive inventory of measures affecting trade in services within the Hemisphere and identify steps to enhance transparency and facilitate trade.
- Create a statistical database of trade flows in services in the Hemisphere.
- Recommend methods to promote understanding and effective implementation of the WTO General Agreement on Trade in Services (GATS), including technical assistance.
- Make specific recommendations on how to proceed in the construction of the FTAA in this area.

### Services Objectives (San José):

- Establishment of an agreement containing disciplines for trade in services, to permit the achievement of a hemispheric free trade under conditions of certainty and transparency;
- ensure the integration of smaller economies into the FTAA process.

### Services Principles (San José):

- Taking into consideration the provisions set forth by WTO and, in particular full consistency with Article V of GATS to deepen in the FTAA the level of commitments undertaken by the countries in the GATS.
- Disciplines established in the hemispheric agreement on services will apply to all service sectors and to all modes of supply, under conditions of non-discrimination;
- The needs of the smaller economies shall be taken into account to ensure their ability to fully participate in the negotiations and derive maximum economic benefits.

## SMALL ECONOMIES

### Small Economies Terms of Reference (Denver):

- Identify and assess the factors affecting the participation of smaller economies in the FTAA and the expansion of trade and investment stimulated therefrom.
- Identify and examine ways to facilitate the adjustment of the smaller economies to the FTAA process, including the promotion and expansion of their trade, and provide recommendations on measures and issues to be taken into account in the negotiations of the FTAA.
- Request the IDB, ECLAC, the OAS and other relevant institutions to provide pertinent information on their activities to facilitate integration of the smaller economies in the Hemisphere.
- Make recommendations on measures, including technical assistance, to facilitate the integration of smaller economies into the FTAA.

### Small Economies Objectives (San José):

As stated in the Summit of the Americas Declaration of Principles, and reiterated in the Denver Ministerial Joint Declaration, one of the main objectives of the FTAA negotiations should be "to provide opportunities to facilitate the integration of the smaller economies and to increase their level of development."

In this context, the Working Group, recognizing the wide differences in level of development and size of the economies participating in the FTAA process, agreed that one of the objectives of the negotiations should be to facilitate the effective participation of smaller economies in the FTAA process and to maximize their opportunities.

It was also agreed that measures that may be accorded or negotiated to facilitate the participation of the smaller economies in the FTAA process, should be transparent, simple and easily applicable, yet should recognize the degree of heterogeneity among them.

### Small Economies Principles (San José):

The general principles that will guide negotiations in all areas under consideration in the FTAA shall include the following:

1. all the negotiating groups should be open to all 34 countries;
2. the negotiations should be carried out in a transparent manner;
3. consensus should continue to be the fundamental principle of decision making;
4. the outcome of the negotiations will constitute a comprehensive single undertaking which embodies the rights and obligations mutually agreed upon;
5. the FTAA negotiations should be consistent with the WTO;
6. countries may negotiate and join the FTAA individually or as members of a sub-regional integration group negotiating as a unit;
7. special attention should be given to the needs, economic conditions (including transition costs and possible internal dislocations) and opportunities of the smaller economies to ensure their full participation in the FTAA process;
8. the rights and obligations of the FTAA will be shared by all countries. In the negotiation of the various thematic areas, measures such as technical assistance in specific areas and longer periods for implementing the obligations could be included on a case by case basis, in order to facilitate the adjustment of smaller economies.

## STANDARDS AND TECHNICAL BARRIERS

### Standards and Technical Barriers Terms of Reference (Denver):

- Recommend specific ways to enhance transparency, especially in standards development;
- Compile information on the bodies that exist which are charged with conformity assessment to technical regulations in the Hemisphere, and those organizations which accredit such bodies;
- Recommend methods to promote understanding of the WTO Agreement on Standards and Technical Barriers to Trade, including through technical assistance;
- Make recommendations on product testing and certification with a view to mutual recognition agreements.
- Develop proposals on mutual accreditation of testing facilities.
- Prepare an inventory of standards and related measures.

### Standards and Technical Barriers Objectives (San José):

The working Group agreed the main objectives are:

- To strive for the elimination and prevention of technical barriers to trade in the Western Hemisphere;
- To ensure consistency with the provisions of the WTO.

An elaboration of objectives and principles is contained in the Common Objectives Paper attached.

### Standards and Technical Barriers Principles (San José):

Standards, technical regulations and conformity assessment procedures should not create unnecessary barriers to trade.

Other principles are set out in greater detail in the Common Objectives Paper attached.

## SUBSIDIES, ANTIDUMPING AND COUNTERVAILING DUTIES

### Subsidies, Antidumping and Countervailing Duties Terms of Reference (Denver):

- Identify agricultural export subsidies and other export practices with similar effects on Hemispheric trade.
- Recommend ways to address all trade-distorting practices for agricultural products that are traded in or with the Hemisphere.
- Promote understanding of WTO obligations in the area of subsidies, and begin to compile an inventory of subsidies practices in the Hemisphere.
- Review information on the dumping and subsidies laws of countries in the Hemisphere.
- Exchange views on the application and operation of trade remedy laws regarding subsidies and dumping and develop recommendations for further work.
- Release the compendium of the Hemispheric trade laws and procedures being compiled by the OAS.

### Subsidies, Antidumping and Countervailing Duties Objectives (San José):

1. Eliminate agricultural export subsidies affecting trade in the Hemisphere.
2. Identify other trade distorting practices for agriculture products including those that have an effect equivalent to agricultural export subsidies and bring them under greater discipline.
3. Examine ways to deepen, if appropriate, existing disciplines provided for in the WTO Agreement on Subsidies and Countervailing Measures and enhance compliance with the terms of the WTO agreement on subsidies and countervailing measures.
4. Achieve a common understanding with a view to improving, where possible, the rules and procedures regarding the operation and application of trade remedy laws in order to ensure transparency and [due process] [fairness] in the use of those instruments and in order not to create unjustified barriers to trade in the Hemisphere.

*[Members of the Working Group disagree on the appropriate scope of the above objective. One view is that, given the existence and nature of multilateral rules, negotiations, should focus exclusively on identifying potential improvements in the ways in which greater transparency and due process are assured in the process of applying such rules. Another view is that negotiations should fully examine the use of trade remedies in the hemisphere and engage in substantive negotiation aimed at improving the operation and application of these laws consistent with the objectives of a free trade area.*

*Some countries consider that the following would also be objectives:*

- *Establish and improve existing trade rules that would be conducive to the attainment of fair trade in agricultural products.*
- *Assess the feasibility of eliminating the use of antidumping measures within the Hemisphere once free trade has been achieved.*
- *Provide for special and differential treatment for the smaller economies.]*

### SUBSIDIES, ANTIDUMPING AND COUNTERVAILING DUTIES PRINCIPLES (SAN JOSÉ):

The negotiations shall:

- Be conducted in a transparent manner ensuring that progress is made in a balanced and gradual manner with respect to the treatment of the subjects.
- Be consistent with WTO disciplines and obligations and shall improve upon WTO rules and disciplines wherever possible and appropriate.
- To the extent applicable, build upon existing regional and sub-regional trade and integration arrangements in the Hemisphere.
- Allow a Hemisphere agreement to co-exist with bilateral and sub-regional agreements to the extent that rights and obligations under these agreements are not covered by or go beyond the rights and obligations agreed to in the Hemisphere.
- Take into account the special concerns of the smaller economies and the issue of special and differential treatment for developing countries.
- Provide for predictability when organizing the negotiations so as to ensure the full participation of the smaller economies.
- Take into account the role of non-FTAA trading partners.
- Require that countries avoid adopting, to the greatest extent possible, policies that adversely affect trade in the hemisphere.

# Appendix C - The Miami Summit Declaration

## TO PROMOTE PROSPERITY THROUGH ECONOMIC INTEGRATION AND FREE TRADE

Our continued economic progress depends on sound economic policies, sustainable development, and dynamic private sectors. A key to prosperity is trade without barriers, without subsidies, without unfair practices, and with an increasing stream of productive investments. Eliminating impediments to market access for goods and services among our countries will foster our economic growth. A growing world economy will also enhance our domestic prosperity. Free trade and increased economic integration are key factors for raising standards of living, improving the working conditions of people in the Americas and better protecting the environment.

We, therefore, resolve to begin immediately to construct the "Free Trade Area of the Americas" (FTAA), in which barriers to trade and investment will be progressively eliminated. We further resolve to conclude the negotiation of the "Free Trade Area of the Americas" no later than 2005, and agree that concrete progress toward the attainment of this objective will be made by the end of this century. We recognize the progress that already has been realized through the unilateral undertakings of each of our nations and the subregional trade arrangements in our Hemisphere. We will build on existing subregional and bilateral arrangements in order to broaden and deepen hemispheric economic integration and to bring the agreements together.

Aware that investment is the main engine for growth in the Hemisphere, we will encourage such investment by cooperating to build more open, transparent and integrated markets. In this regard, we are committed to create strengthened mechanisms that promote and protect the flow of productive investment in the Hemisphere, and to promote the development and progressive integration of capital markets.

To advance economic integration and free trade, we will work, with cooperation and financing from the private sector and international financial institutions, to create a hemispheric infrastructure. This process requires a cooperative effort in fields such as telecommunications, energy and transportation, which will permit the efficient movement of the goods, services, capital, information and technology that are the foundations of prosperity.

We recognize that despite the substantial progress in dealing with debt problems in the Hemisphere, high foreign debt burdens still hinder the development of some of our countries.

We recognize that economic integration and the creation of a free trade area will be complex endeavors, particularly in view of the wide differences in the levels of development and size of economies existing in our Hemisphere. We will remain cognizant of these differences as we work toward economic integration in the Hemisphere. We look to our own resources, ingenuity, and individual capacities as well as to the international community to help us achieve our goals.

# Appendix D - Belo Horizonte Ministerial Declaration

• We, the Ministers responsible for Trade, representing the 34 countries that participated in the Summit of the Americas in December 1994, met in Belo Horizonte for the Third Trade Ministerial Meeting, in pursuance of the mandate issued by our Heads of State and Government during the Summit of the Americas, held in Miami. We reviewed the results of the work program to which we unanimously agreed at our previous Ministerial Meetings in Denver and Cartagena, to prepare for negotiations on the Free Trade Area of the Americas (FTAA). We reiterate our commitment to conclude negotiations no later than 2005, and to make concrete progress towards the attainment of this objective by the end of this century.

• We also reviewed the substantial progress that has been achieved in trade liberalization in the hemisphere since the Miami Summit of the Americas. We note that such progress is being reflected in the increasing widening and deepening of existing sub-regional and bilateral agreements; the implementation of our countries obligations under the Uruguay Round; the negotiation of new bilateral and sub-regional free trade agreements in the hemisphere; the participation of some Western Hemisphere countries in the negotiation of sectoral trade liberalization agreements in the World Trade Organization (WTO); and the autonomous trade liberalization measures adopted by individual countries. We reiterate our commitment to ensure that all our efforts to promote free trade in the hemisphere shall be consistent with our obligations in the WTO, in particular with Article XXIV of GATT 1994 and its Uruguay Round Understanding and Article V of the GATS. We also reiterate the principle previously adopted that the construction of the FTAA will not raise barriers to other countries. We will avoid adopting, to the greatest extent possible, policies that adversely affect trade in the hemisphere.

• At the Second Summit of the Americas, to be held in Santiago, in March 1998, our Heads of State and Government will have the opportunity to review the implementation of the broad social and economic agenda contained in the Miami Declaration of Principles and Plan of Action, aiming at the prosperity of our peoples. We are aware that the FTAA should be negotiated taking into account those broad objectives. To this end, we recognize the wide differences in the level of development and size of economies existing in our hemisphere and we will remain cognizant of these differences as we work toward building the FTAA.

• We reviewed the work undertaken by the Vice Ministers regarding the various approaches for the construction of the FTAA, building upon the existing sub-regional and bilateral agreements. We agree that the FTAA negotiations should be initiated at Santiago, in March 1998, and we will recommend to our Leaders that they do so at that time. To this end, at the Fourth Ministerial Meeting in San Jose, Costa Rica, in February 1998, we will formulate how the negotiations will proceed, including such features as their objectives, approaches, structure and venue. We instruct our Vice Ministers to maintain the practice of holding three meetings before the next Trade Ministerial Meeting and to make recommendations to us on those issues for our decision at our San Jose Meeting.

## AREAS OF COMMONALITY AND REMAINING ISSUES

• Vice Ministers had, at our request, extensive discussions on the scope and timing of the negotiations. We welcome the specific proposals tabled by delegations and after comprehensive discussions, we agreed that there is a significant measure of convergence on key principles and issues:

1. Consensus constitutes the fundamental principle of decision making in the FTAA process, which seeks to preserve and promote the essential interests of our 34 countries in a balanced and comprehensive manner;

2. The outcome of the negotiations of the Free Trade Area of the Americas will constitute a comprehensive single undertaking which embodies the rights and obligations mutually agreed upon. The FTAA can co-exist with bilateral and sub-regional agreements, to the extent that the rights and obligations under these agreements are not covered by or go beyond the rights and obligations of the FTAA;

3. The FTAA will be consistent with the WTO agreements;

4. Countries may negotiate and joint the FTAA individually or as members of a sub-regional integration group negotiating as a unit;

5. Special attention should be given to the needs, economic conditions and opportunities of the smaller economies to ensure their full participation in the FTAA process;

6. The need for establishing a temporary administrative Secretariat to support the negotiations;

7. The year 2005 as the date for concluding negotiations, at the latest;

• We hereby establish a Preparatory Committee consisting of the 34 Vice Ministers responsible for trade. We instruct them to intensify their efforts to build consensus and to complete recommendations on the remaining issues which they will submit for our decision at the San Jose Meeting. We further instruct Vice Ministers to continue to direct, evaluate and coordinate the work of all Working Groups.

## WORKING GROUPS

• We thank the Chairpersons of the Working Groups for the work they have completed thus far. We direct our Vice Ministers at their next meeting to review the reports of the Working Groups and approve as appropriate their recommendations on work programs, areas for immediate action and business facilitation measures. We also took note of the documents listed in Annex I which have been proposed by the Working Groups and approved by Vice Ministers for publication as official documents of the FTAA; as such, they are already available for the public and constitute a concrete result of the ongoing preparatory work for the FTAA negotiations. We instruct the Working Groups to continue their tasks according to their agreed terms of reference. We further instruct them to submit to Vice Ministers at the second meeting under Costa Rica's Chairmanship different technical alternatives on possible issues and negotiating approaches in their respective disciplines which should be considered by Vice Ministers as they prepare recommendations for our decision at our San Jose meeting.

• In accordance with our agreement at Cartagena, we have set up the Working Group on Dispute Settlement, whose terms of reference are to be found in Annex II. The Working Group will take into account the compilation of information prepared by the OAS, as requested at Cartagena, on the existing mechanisms for dispute settlement in the sub-regional and bilateral agreements in the hemisphere.

• We approved the list of countries that will chair the twelve Working Groups, until our next meeting in Costa Rica (Annex III). They shall be responsible for the coordination and programming of the Working Groups' meetings, in consultation with the representatives of participating countries, and ensure fulfillment of their respective terms of reference. We remind the Chairpersons of the Working Groups that consensus remains the operating principle of the FTAA process. After diligent efforts have been made to reach agreement on controversial issues, different positions should be remitted to Vice Ministers for their decision.

• We are in receipt of the report of the Working Group on Smaller Economies and have taken note of the range of factors identified which could constrain the effective participation of the smaller economies in the FTAA. We have studied the recommended measures to facilitate their integration into the FTAA, including the need for appropriate internal policies, technical assistance and cooperation in order to facilitate the effective participation of these economies in the FTAA process. We encourage the Working Group on Smaller Economies to advance its ongoing work and urge it to make specific suggestions to the Vice Ministers as to measures that would allow their effective participation in the FTAA process. We call upon other Working Groups to take into account, in their deliberations, the findings and recommendations of the Working Groups on Smaller Economies in order to realize the opportunities of those economies in the FTAA and to increase their level of development.

• We ask Vice Ministers to recommend to us, by our next meeting, how the Working Groups could be reconfigured into negotiating groups, taking into account the need for efficiency and the complementarity of subject matters.

## OTHER REPORTS AND CONTRIBUTIONS TO ECONOMIC INTEGRATION

• We acknowledge and appreciate the technical and logistical support provided to the Working Groups by the Tripartite Committee, as well as the contribution received from regional, sub-regional and multilateral organizations. We request that the Tripartite Committee continue to provide analytical support, technical assistance and related studies, as requested by the respective Working Groups. We also request the member institutions of the Tripartite Committee to provide assistance to individual member countries, on request, in accordance with the procedures of the respective institutions. We encourage further contributions in support of those tasks, within their areas of expertise, from relevant regional, sub-regional and multilateral institutions as may be requested by the Working Groups.

• Moreover, we agreed to ask the Tripartite Committee to undertake a feasibility study on alternatives for establishing a temporary administrative secretariat to support the FTAA negotiations, based on the terms of reference in Annex IV, and to report their findings to Vice Ministers in time for them to issue recommendations for our decision at our meeting in Costa Rica.

• We received with interest the contributions for the Third Business Forum of the Americas relating to the preparatory process for the FTAA negotiations, which we consider may be relevant to our future deliberations. We acknowledge and appreciate the importance of the private sector's role and its participation in the FTAA process. We reiterate our commitment to transparency in the FTAA process. In this sense, we consider the inputs from stakeholders of our civil societies to be important to our deliberations, including those from the labor sectors, and we encourage all countries to take them into account through mechanisms of dialogue and consultation.

• The issue of the environment and its relation to trade has been considered by our Vice Ministers since the Cartagena meeting and is the subject of ongoing discussions within the WTO and within the FTAA process. We will keep this issue under consideration, in light of further developments in the work of the WTO Committee on Trade and Environment.

• We take note of the "Declaration of the Tenth Inter-American Conference of Ministers of Labor", presented at the Meeting of the Ministers of Trade, Belo Horizonte (Brazil), May 1997. We reaffirm paragraph 4 of the Singapore Ministerial Declaration of the WTO.

## NEXT MINISTERIAL MEETING

• We reiterate our decision, adopted at Cartagena, to hold the Fourth Ministerial Meeting and the Fourth Business Forum in Costa Rica, both of which are to be held in February 1998. We therefore accept with appreciation the offer extended by the government of Costa Rica to host those two meetings. We request the host country of the 1998 Trade Ministerial Meeting to chair the Vice Ministerial Meetings to be held until then.

• We wish to express our appreciation to the Government of Brazil for its significant contribution throughout the past year in hosting and chairing the four meetings of Vice Ministers in Florianópolis, Recife, Rio de Janeiro and Belo Horizonte, as well as this Ministerial Meeting, also held in Belo Horizonte.

# Appendix E - Table of Agreements

| Country/Group | ACS | Andean Group | Antigua | Argentina | Bahamas | Barbados | Belize | Bolivia | Brazil | CACM | Canada | CARICOM | Chile |
|---|---|---|---|---|---|---|---|---|---|---|---|---|---|
| ACS | 1995 | | 1995 | | 1995 | 1995 | 1995 | | | 1995 | | 1995 | |
| Andean Group | | 1969 | | | | | | | | | | | |
| Antigua | ✔ | | | | | | | | | | | | |
| Argentina | | | | | | | | 1992 | 1990 | | | | |
| Bahamas | ✔ | | | | | | | | | | | | |
| Barbados | ✔ | | | | | | | | | | | | |
| Belize | ✔ | | | | | | | | | | | | |
| Bolivia | | | | 1992 | | | | | | | | | 1993 |
| Brazil | | | | 1990 | | | | | | | | | |
| CACM | | | | | | | | | | 1961 | | | |
| Canada | | | | | | | | | | | | | 1995 |
| CARICOM | ✔ | | | 1973 | 1973 | | | | | | 1973 | | |
| Chile | | | 1991 | | | | | 1994 | | | OG | OG | |
| Colombia | ✔ | | 1991 | | | | | | | | 1994 | | 1993 |
| Costa Rica | ✔ | | | | | | | | | 1961 | | | |
| Cuba | ✔ | | | | | | | | | | | | |
| Dominican Republic | ✔ | | | | | | | | | | | | |
| Ecuador | | | | | | | | | | | | | |
| El Salvador | ✔ | | | | | | | | | 1961 | | | |
| G3 | | | | | | | | | | | | | |
| Guatemala | ✔ | | | | | | | | | 1961 | | | |
| Guyana | ✔ | | | | | | | | | | | | |
| Haiti | ✔ | | | | | | | | | | | | |
| Honduras | ✔ | | | | | | | | | 1961 | | | |
| Jamaica | ✔ | | | | | | | | | | | 1973 | |
| MERCOSUR | | OG | | 1991 | | | | 1996 | | | OG | | 1996 |
| Mexico | ✔ | | | | | | | 1994 | | | OG | 1993 | 1991 |
| Nicaragua | ✔ | | | | | | | | | | | | |
| NAFTA | | | | | | | | | | | | | |
| Panama | ✔ | | | | | | | | | | | | |
| Paraguay | | | | | | | | | | | | | |
| Peru | | 1997 | | | | | | 1992 | 1993 | | | | |
| Santa Lucia | ✔ | | | | | | | | | | | | |
| St. Vincent | ✔ | | | | | | | | | | | | |
| Suriname | ✔ | | | | | | | | | | | | |
| Trinidad and Tobago | ✔ | | | | | | | | | | | | |
| U.S. | | | | | | | | | | | | | |
| Uruguay | | | | | | | | | 1991 | | | | |
| Venezuela | | | | 1992 | | | | | | | | | 1994 |

Continued on next page

Progress Toward Free Trade in the Western Hemisphere Since 1994

# V. LEADERSHIP COUNCIL FOR INTER-AMERICAN SUMMITRY

Continued from previous page

| Country/Group | Colombia | Costa Rica | Cuba | Dominican Republic | Ecuador | El Salvador | G3 | Guatemala | Guyana | Haiti | Honduras | Jamaica | MERCOSUR |
|---|---|---|---|---|---|---|---|---|---|---|---|---|---|
| ACS | 1995 | 1995 | 1995 | 1995 | | 1995 | | 1995 | 1995 | 1995 | 1995 | 1995 | |
| Andean Group | | | | | | | | | | | | | OG |
| Antigua | | | | | | | | | | | | | |
| Argentina | 1991 | | | | 1993 | | | | | | | | |
| Bahamas | | | | | | | | | | | | | |
| Barbados | | | | | | | | | | | | | |
| Belize | | | | | | | | | | | | | |
| Bolivia | | | | | | | | | | | | | |
| Brazil | | | | | | | | | | | | | |
| CACM | | 1961 | | | | 1961 | | 1961 | | | 1961 | | OG |
| Canada | | | | | | | | | | | | | |
| CARICOM | | | | | | | | | 1973 | | | 1973 | |
| Chile | 1993 | | | 1994 | | | | | | | | | 1996 |
| Colombia | | | | | | | | | | | | | |
| Costa Rica | | | | | | | | | | | | | |
| Cuba | | | | | | | | | | | | | |
| Dominican Republic | | | | | | | | | | | | | |
| Ecuador | | | | | | | | | | | | | |
| El Salvador | | | | | | | | | | | | | |
| G3 | | | | | | | 1994 | | | | | | |
| Guatemala | | | | | | | | | | | | | |
| Guyana | | | | | | | | | | | | | |
| Haiti | | | | | | | | | | | | | |
| Honduras | | | | | | | | | | | | | |
| Jamaica | | | | | | | | | | | | | |
| MERCOSUR | | | | | | | | | | | | | 1991 |
| Mexico | | 1994 | | OG | | | OG | | | | | | OG |
| Nicaragua | | | | | | | | | | | | | |
| NAFTA | | | | | | | | | | | | | |
| Panama | | | | | | | | | | | | | |
| Paraguay | | | | | | | | | | | | | |
| Peru | | | | | | | | | | | | | |
| Santa Lucia | | | | | | | | | | | | | |
| St. Vincent | | | | | | | | | | | | | |
| Suriname | | | | | | | | | | | | | |
| Trinidad and Tobago | | | | | | | | | | | | | |
| U.S. | | | | | | | | | | | | | |
| Uruguay | | | | | | | | | | | | | |
| Venezuela | | | | | | | | | | | | | OG |

Continued on next page

Continued from previous page

| Country/Group | Mexico | Nicaragua | NAFTA | Panama | Paraguay | Peru | Santa Lucia | St. Vincent | Suriname | Trinidad & Tobago | U.S. | Uruguay | Venezuela |
|---|---|---|---|---|---|---|---|---|---|---|---|---|---|
| ACS | 1995 | 1995 | | 1995 | | | 1995 | 1995 | 1995 | 1995 | | | |
| Andean Group | | | | | | 1997 | | | | | | | |
| Antigua | | | | | | | | | | | | | 1992 |
| Argentina | | | | | | | | | | | | | |
| Bahamas | | | | | | | | | | | | | |
| Barbados | | | | | | | | | | | | | |
| Belize | | | | | | | | | | | | | |
| Bolivia | 1994 | | | | 1994 | 1992 | | | | | | 1991 | |
| Brazil | | | | | | 1993 | | | | | | | 1994 |
| CACM | OG | 1961 | | | | | | | | | | | |
| Canada | | | | | | | | | | | 1988 | | |
| CARICOM | | | | | | | | | | 1973 | | | |
| Chile | 1991 | | | | | | | | | | | | 1993 |
| Colombia | | | | | | | | | | | | | |
| Costa Rica | 1994 | | | | | | | | | | | | |
| Cuba | | | | | | | | | | | | | |
| Dominican Republic | | | | | | | | | | | | | |
| Ecuador | OG | | | | | | | | | | | | |
| El Salvador | | | | | | | | | | | | | |
| G3 | | | | | | | | | | | | | |
| Guatemala | | | | | | | | | | | | | |
| Guyana | | | | | | | | | | | | | |
| Haiti | | | | | | | | | | | | | |
| Honduras | | | | | | | | | | | | | |
| Jamaica | | | | | | | | | | | | | |
| MERCOSUR | | | | | | | | | | | | 1991 | |
| Mexico | | 1998 | | OG | | OG | | | | | | | |
| Nicaragua | 1998 | | | | | | | | | | | | |
| NAFTA | | | 1993 | | | | | | | | | | |
| Panama | | | | | | | | | | | | | |
| Paraguay | | | | | | | | | | | | | |
| Peru | OG | | | | | | | | | | | | |
| Santa Lucia | | | | | | | | | | | | | |
| St. Vincent | | | | | | | | | | | | | |
| Suriname | | | | | | | | | | | | | |
| Trinidad and Tobago | | | ? | | | | | | | | | | |
| U.S. | | | | | | | | | | | | | |
| Uruguay | | | | | | | | | | | | | |
| Venezuela | | | | | | | | | | | | | |

# Appendix F - Chair's Proposal for a Draft Ministerial Declaration at San José, Costa Rica, 1998

The Ministers Responsible for Trade of the 34 countries that participated in the I Summit of the Americas, held in Miami on December 1994, held in the IV Ministerial Meeting on Trade, according the mandate received in the Declaration of the Americas and its accompanying Plan of Action and according to the work program agreed to in previous Ministerial Meetings, hereby recommended to our Heads of State and Government the launching of the negotiations to build the Free Trade Area of the Americas (FTAA), in conformity with the present Declaration.

## PART I

### Objectives and Principles of the Negotiations

We have agreed that the negotiations for the establishment of the FTAA will be guided by the following General Objectives and Principles:

### 1. General Objectives

a) To promote prosperity through economic integration and free trade among the countries of our hemisphere, as key factors for raising standards of living, improving the working conditions of people in the Americas, and better protecting the environment.

b) To establish a Free Trade Area, in which barriers to trade and investment will be progressively eliminated, concluding negotiations no later than 2005 and achieving concrete progress toward the attainment of this objective by the end of this century.

c) Encourage investment, aware that it is the main engine growth in the Hemisphere, by cooperating to build more open, transparent and integrated markets, creating strengthened mechanisms that promote and protect the flow of productive investment and promote progressive integration of capital markets.

d) Maximize market openness through high levels of disciplines through balanced and comprehensive agreements, including among others: Market access; customs procedures and rules of origin; investment; norms and technical barriers to trade: sanitary and phytosanitary measures, subsidies, antidumping and countervailing duties; government procurement; intellectual property rights; services; competition policy and dispute settlement.

e) To provide opportunities to facilitate the integration of the smaller economies in the FTAA process, to maximize their opportunities and to improve their level of development.

### 2. General Principles

a) Negotiations will be held in a transparent manner, based on the consensus of participating countries for decision-making in the FTAA process, in order to preserve and promote the essential interests of all parties.

b) The FTAA Agreement will be consistent with the rules and disciplines of the World Trade Organization, WTO. With this purpose, the participating countries reiterate their commitment with multilateral rules and disciplines, in particular with Article XXIV of GATT-1994 and its understanding of the Uruguay Round, and Article V of General Agreement of Trade in Services, GATS. As well, we endorse rapid and full implementation of the Uruguay Round, as well as active multilateral negotiations in the World Trade Organization.

c) The agreements reached will be balanced and comprehensive in scope, considering the interests of all countries and covering the areas specified in Objective 1.d).

d) Negotiations in all issue areas will be held simultaneously, under the agreement that all the agreements reached constitute a single undertaking which embodies the rights and obligations mutually agreed upon.

f) The FTAA will coexist with bilateral and subregional agreements.

h) The agreements reached shall not result in the imposition to barriers to trade and investment with countries outside the hemisphere.

i) Starting on the beginning of the negotiations, countries will avoid the adoption of policies that adversely affect trade in the hemisphere.

j) Special attention will be given to the special needs, economic conditions (including transition costs and possible internal imbalances) and opportunities of smaller economies, actively looking for ways to facilitate the integration of smaller economies, as a key factor for increasing their level of development.

k) The rights and obligations of the FTAA will be shared by all countries. In the negotiation of the various thematic areas and longer periods for implementing the obligations could be included on a case by case basis, in order to facilitate the adjustment of smaller economies.

l) The measures that may be accorded or negotiated to facilitate the integration of smaller economies in the FTAA process should be transparent, simple and easily applicable, yet should recognize the degree of heterogeneity among them.

## 3. Objectives and Principles by Issue Area

We have agreed that the negotiations of the FTAA, in each issue area, will be guided by the following Objectives and Principles:

### Market Access

The Objectives of the negotiations are:

• To progressively eliminate, **(starting in the year 2005)**, tariffs, and non tariff barriers, **(for the substantial trade) (for all trade)** as well as other measures with equivalent effects, which restrict trade between participating countries, Consistently with the provisions of the WTO, including article XXIV of GATT 94 and its understanding.

• All tariffs will be subject to negotiation.

• **(Different trade liberalization time tables can be drawn up which could include special treatment for countries, sectors and products).**

To facilitate the integration of smaller economies and their full participation in the FTAA negotiations.

The principles of the negotiations are:

• Consistency with WTO disciplines, in particular, with Article XXIV of the General Agreement on Tariffs and Trade (GATT 1994), and with the Understanding pertinent to the Interpretation of Article XXIV of GATT 1994.

### Rules of Origin

The Objectives of the negotiations are:

• To develop an efficient and transparent system of rules of origin, including nomenclature and certificates of origin, in order to facilitate the exchange of goods, without creating unnecessary obstacles to trade.

The principles that will govern the negotiation are:

• Rules of origin should be elaborated and administered in an objective, transparent, coherent and predictable manner, **(with the aim that its implementation would give equal opportunities to all FTAA members).**

• Technical assistance and cooperation may be requested and provided by the countries on rules of origin in accordance with the modalities to be defined.

• The regime of rules of origin should provide for mechanisms to update the system on the basis of technological changes and other requirements.

• **(Rules of origin shall take into account the specific commercial interests of all countries of the Hemisphere, including those of the smaller economies).**

• For the elaboration of this system, the nomenclature of the Harmonized Commodity Description and Coding System will be adopted (HS).

### Customs Procedures

The objectives of the negotiations are:

• To simplify customs procedures, in order to facilitate trade and reduce administrative costs.

• To create and implement mechanisms to exchange information in customs issues among FTAA countries.

• To design effective systems to detect and combat fraud and other illicit customs activities, without creating unnecessary obstacles to foreign trade.

The principles that will govern the negotiations are:

• Customs Procedures should be elaborated and administered in an objective, transparent, coherent and predictable manner, **(with the aim that is implementation would give equal opportunities to all FTAA members).**

• Technical assistance and cooperation may be requested and provided by the countries' customs procedures in accordance with the modalities to be defined.

• With the purpose of attaining the proposed objectives in this matter, the customs procedures should be clear and precise and only require the necessary information for the efficient performance of customs functions.

• Develop mechanisms for the exchange of the information regarding progress toward the agreed upon simplification, and toward the adoption of mechanisms to detect and combat fraud and other illicit customs activities.

• The modalities of the implementation of the simplified customs procedures, by Customs Administrations, should be determined during the negotiations.

## Investment

The objectives of the negotiations are:

• To establish a fair and transparent legal framework that leads to a stable and predictable environment that protects investors, their investment and related flows; and stimulate the development of investment opportunities, without creating improper obstacles to extra-hemispheric investments, in accordance with paragraph 2 of the Cartagena Declaration and paragraph 2 of the Belo Horizonte Declaration.

The principles that will govern the negotiations are:

• The negotiation shall provide for transparency and the protection of investors and their investments. This negotiation shall be based, at least, on the following principles: Non-discrimination, National Treatment, Most-favored-nation treatment, Fair and equitable treatment.

## Standards and Technical Barriers to Trade

The objectives of the negotiations are:

• To strive for the elimination and prevention of technical barriers to trade in the Western Hemisphere;

• To ensure consistency with the provisions of the WTO. An elaboration of objectives and principles is contained in the Common Objectives Paper attached.

The principles that will govern the negotiations are:

• Standards, technical regulations and conformity assessment procedures should not create unnecessary barriers to trade.

Other principles are set out in greater detail in the Common Objectives Paper attached.

## Subsidies, Antidumping and Countervailing Duties

The objectives of the negotiations are:

• Eliminate agricultural export subsidies affecting trade in the Hemisphere.

• Identify other trade distorting practices for agriculture products including those that have an effect equivalent to agricultural export subsidies and bring them under greater discipline.

• Examine ways to deepen, if appropriate, existing disciplines provided for in the WTO Agreement on Subsidies and Countervailing Measures and enhance compliance with the terms of the WTO agreement on subsidies and countervailing measures.

• Achieve a common understanding with a view to improving, where possible, the rules and procedures regarding the operation and application of trade remedy laws in order to ensure transparency and **(due process) (fairness)** in the use of those instruments and in order not to create unjustified barriers to trade in the Hemisphere.

• **(members of the Working Group discharge on the appropriate scope of the above objective. One view is that, given the existence and nature of multilateral rules, negotiations should focus exclusively on identifying potential improvements in the ways in which greater transparency and due process are assured in the process of applying such rules. Another view is that negotiations should fully examine the use of trade remedies in the hemisphere and engage in substantive negotiation aimed at improving the operation and application of these laws consistent with the objectives of a free trade area.**

• **Some countries consider that the following should also be objectives.**

• **Establish and improve existing trade rules that would be conducive to the attainment of fair trade in agricultural products.**

• **Assess the feasibility of eliminating the use of antidumping measures within the Hemisphere once free trade has been achieved.**

• **Provide for special and differential treatment for the smaller economies).**

The principles that will govern the negotiations are:

- Negotiations shall improve upon WTO rules and disciplines wherever possible and appropriate.
- To the extent applicable, negotiations shall build upon existing regional and sub-regional trade and integration arrangements in the Hemisphere.
- Negotiations shall take into account the role of non-FTAA trading partners.
- Negotiations shall require that countries avoid adopting, to the greatest extent possible, policies that adversely affect trade in the Hemisphere.

## Government Procurement

The objectives of the negotiations are:

- The broad objective of negotiations in government procurements is to expand access to the government procurement market of the FTAA countries.
- To achieve a normative framework that ensures openness and transparency of government procurement processes, without necessarily implying the establishment of identical government procurement systems in all countries;
- To ensure non-discrimination in government procurement within a scope to be negotiated;
- To ensure impartial and fair review for the resolution of procurement complaints and appeals by suppliers and the effective implementation of such resolutions.
- **(Negotiations shall not exclude trade in goods and services, investment and government procurement at any levels of the political-administrative structure of the countries negotiating the Agreement).**
- **(Negotiations shall include trade in goods and services, investment and government procurement at all levels of the political-administrative structure of the countries negotiating the Agreement).**
- **(The scope of government procurement shall be subject to negotiation).**

The principles that will govern the negotiations are:

- Non-discrimination within the negotiated scope of the agreement.

## Intellectual Property Rights

The objectives of the negotiations are:

- In the framework of the general objective of the FTAA to construct a free trade area, the objective of the negotiations in the area of intellectual property shall be to achieve an agreement or common understanding that reduces distortions in trade in the Hemisphere and promotes and ensures adequate and effective protection to intellectual property rights.
- **(The agreement shall take into account changes in technology).**

The principles that will govern the negotiations are:

- Consistent with the framework of the general principles of the Belo Horizonte Declaration and the "Agreement on Trade Related Aspects of Intellectual Property Rights" of the WTO, the following specific principles were identified:

    a) National treatment

    b) Most favored nation

    **(Principles of intellectual property applicable by thematic area)**

    d) **(Not diminishing the level of protection to the countries during negotiations in accordance with (their) (existing) international obligations).**

    e) **(To cover all areas of intellectual property rights, including enforcement).**

- **The provisions of paragraph b shall not prevent some countries being granted specific privileges or facilities within the framework of bilateral or sub-regional agreements beyond FTAA).**
- Canada accepts the national treatment and MFN principles with exceptions.

The objectives of the negotiations are:

- Establishment of an agreement containing disciplines for trade in services, to permit the achievement of a hemisphere free trade area under conditions of certainty and transparency;
- Ensure the integration of smaller economies into the FTAA process.

The principles that will govern the negotiations are;

- Taking into consideration the provisions set forth by WTO and, in particular full consistency with article V of GATS, to deepen in the FTA the level of commitments undertaken by the countries in the GATS.
- Disciplines established in the hemispheric agreement on services will apply to all service sectors and to all modes of supply, under conditions of non-discrimination.

*Competition Policy*

The objective of the negotiations are:

• To guarantee that the benefits of the FTAA liberalization process not be undermined by anti-competitive business practices.

PART II

Structure of the Negotiations

### 1. Structure of the Negotiations

We agree on the following structure for the negotiations:

Number and issues for Negotiating Groups to be defined.

### 2. Functions:

The functions of each of the previous instances of the negotiation process are the following:

*Ministers Responsible for Trade:*

The Meeting of Ministers is the instance of higher level in the conduct of the process of negotiations. Its functions will be:

a) To assess the advance of the negotiations in the Ministerial Meetings and approve negotiated matters submitted for their consideration by the Trade Negotiations Committee.

b) Select the country that will hold the Presidency of the FTAA process.

c) Select the Presidents and Vice Presidents of the Negotiations groups.

They will meet every 18 months on the following dates: late 1999, mid 2001, early 2003 and mid 2005.

• To advance towards the establishment of juridicial and institutional coverage at the national, sub-regional or regional level, that proscribes the carrying out of anti-competitive business practices:

• To develop mechanisms that facilitate and promote the development of competition policy and guarantee the enforcement of regulations on free competition among and within countries of the Hemisphere.

The principles that will govern the negotiations are:

• To consider the differences between existing legal systems and traditions in countries of the Hemisphere.

• To consider the distinct degrees of development and enforcement of competition policies.

*Committee of Trade Negotiations:*

The Committee of Trade Negotiations (CTN) is formed by the Vice-Ministers Responsible for Trade of the countries of the Hemisphere. It will be in charge of carrying the negotiations process. Its functions will be:

a) To coordinate the tasks of the Negotiation Groups. Receive the reports submitted by the Presidents of the negotiation groups and define the substantive negotiation issues in the periods between ministerial meetings.

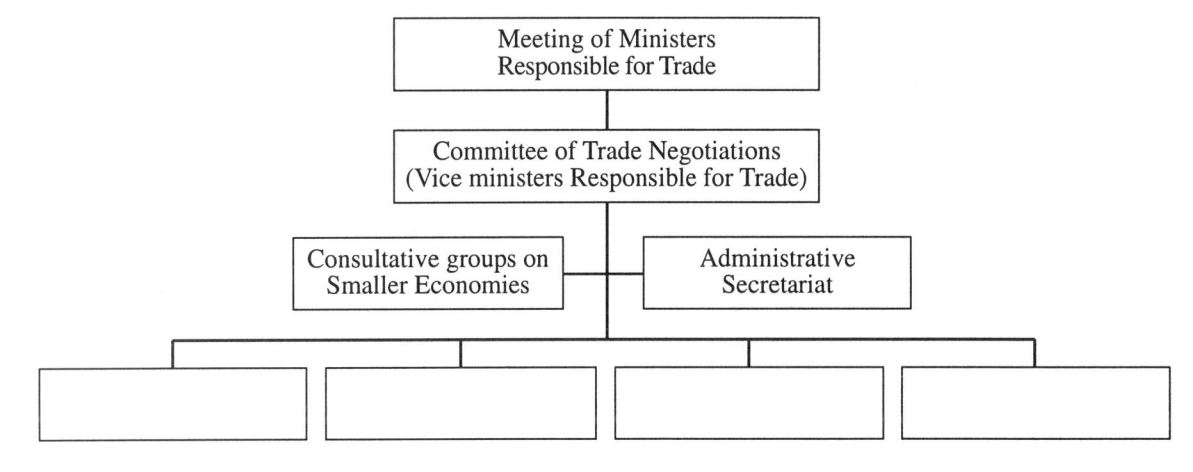

```
                 ┌──────────────────────────┐
                 │   Meeting of Ministers   │
                 │   Responsible for Trade  │
                 └──────────────┬───────────┘
                 ┌──────────────┴──────────────────────┐
                 │    Committee of Trade Negotiations  │
                 │  (Vice ministers Responsible for Trade) │
                 └──────────────┬──────────────────────┘
         ┌──────────────────────┴──────────────────┐
  ┌──────┴───────────────┐              ┌──────────┴─────────┐
  │ Consultative groups on│              │   Administrative   │
  │   Smaller Economies   │              │     Secretariat    │
  └───────────────────────┘              └────────────────────┘
         │                │                │                │
     ┌───┴──┐       ┌─────┴───┐      ┌─────┴────┐     ┌─────┴───┐
     │      │       │         │      │          │     │         │
     └──────┘       └─────────┘      └──────────┘     └─────────┘
```

(Number and issues for Negotiating Groups to be defined.)

b) To create, dissolve or merge negotiation groups according to the necessities of the process.

c) To report to the Meeting of Ministers Responsible for Trade.

d) To name the Presidents and Vice Presidents of the negotiation groups provisionally, in the periods between ministerial meetings.

e) To meet at least twice a year.

*Negotiation Groups:*

The negotiation groups are responsible for holding negotiations in each one of the technical issues. They will meet the times they consider necessary, or by mandate of the Committee of Trade Negotiations.

*Presidents of the Negotiation Groups:*

The negotiation group has a President, whose responsibility is to steer the work of the Group, according to the instructions received from the Committee of Trade Negotiations. The presidents of the negotiation groups are named by the Ministers Responsible for Trade, considering the need for a geographical balance, as well as the personal and professional qualities of the candidates. They can be confirmed for their positions for subsequent periods.

*Vice Presidents of the Negotiation Groups:*

They assume the presidency of the Group in case the President cannot continue exercising its charge. They will not be selected from the same country of origin than the President of the Negotiation Groups.

*Consultative Group on Smaller Economies:*

It is integrated to give special attention the needs, economic condition and opportunities of the smaller economies, actively seeking the means to facilitate their integration to the FTAA process.

## 3. Venues of Negotiation:

*Options:*

a) To establish a unique site for the Negotiation Groups and the Administrative Secretariat.

b) To establish two sites for the negotiations groups, in one of which the Administrative Secretariat will be established.

c) To establish two sites for the negotiations groups, with the Administrative Secretariat established in a third place.

d) To establish three or more venues for the negotiation groups.

Elements to be considered:

- Easy access (Cost, time, frequency of flights)
- General conditions of local infrastructure, security and managerial capacity.
- Political and geographical balance.
- Offers of countries that are proposing candidacy (physical space, logistical support, personal support)

## 4. Administrative Secretariat:

We have agreed on creating a Administrative Secretariat of the process of negotiations of the FTAA, to give logistical and administrative support to the negotiations process, to facilitate the translation services during the meetings and of official documents, to keep the official documents of the FTAA process and to be in charge of the distribution and publication of the documents (Belo Horizonte Declaration).

## 5. Tri-partite Committee:

We request to the Tri-partite Committee to continue providing analytical support, technical assistance and related studies, as required by the negotiation groups. Also to provide technical support to member countries individually, at their request, according to the procedures of the institutions (Ministerial Declaration of Belo Horizonte).

## Other Issues

*Trade and Environment*

Free trade and increased economic integration are key factors for sustainable development. This will be furthered as we strive to make our trade liberalization and environmental policies mutually supportive, taking into account efforts undertaken by the GATT/WTO and other international organizations (Plan of Action of the Summit of the Americas). We will keep this issue under consideration, in light of further developments in the work of the WTO Committee on Trade and Environment (Belo Horizonte Ministerial Declaration).

*Trade and Labor Rights*

We renew our commitment to endorse the fundamental labor norms internationally accepted. The International Trade Organization (ITO) is the instance competent to establish these norms and their observance, and we reaffirm our support to its role in promoting them. We consider that economic growth and development, fostered by trade growth and further trade liberalization, will contribute to the promotion of these norms. We reject the use of these norms for protectionist purposes, and agree that comparative advantage of the countries should not be questioned, in particular that of low wages developing counties. As we advance in economic integration, we support a higher level of observance and promotion of worker rights, such as defined in pertinent international treaties. (WTO Ministerial Declaration of Singapore, Plan of Action of the Declaration of the Americas, Belo Horizonte Ministerial Declaration).

## Civil Society

In order to guarantee the participation and commitment of individuals, we invite the private sector, labor political parties, academics, and other non-governmental actors and organizations to cooperate and participate in our national and regional efforts, thus strengthening liaisons among governments and Societies. (Plan of Action of the Summit of the Americas)

## PART IV

## Business Facilitation

We have agreed to instruct the Trade Negotiations Committee to define a group of business facilitation measures, based on the documents raised by the FTAA process, for the countries to adopt before the year 2000.

## Ministerial Resolutions:

We have agreed to instruct the Trade Negotiations Committee to define a group of business facilitation measures, based on the documents raised by the FTAA process, for the countries to adopt before the year 2000.

## Ministerial Resolutions:

We have agreed the following:

- To name _____ as the country that will hold the Presidency of the FTAA negotiations process from now and until the next Ministerial Meeting, that will be celebrated in 1999 in _____.

- To name the following persons as Presidents and Vice-Presidents of the Negotiation Groups: _____.

- To instruct the Trade Negotiations Committee to approve a detailed program of trade negotiations before June 19, 1998, in which the terms of reference for the negotiation groups and the date for ending their mandates will be defined.

- To instruct the Trade Negotiations Committee to advance in their first meeting in the mechanisms of business facilitation to be adopted in the short term.

# V. LEADERSHIP COUNCIL FOR INTER-AMERICAN SUMMITRY

## *Postscript:* Update on Progress Toward Hemispheric Free Trade

*Colleen S. Morton*

Three globally significant events have occurred since the drafting of the original paper, which have affected the efforts toward hemispheric economic integration: first, the decision by the heads of state in April to formally launch free trade negotiations in 1998 and conclude them by the year 2005; second, the negative vote in the U.S. House of Representatives in September on giving the U.S. president the so-called "fast-track" authority to carry out these negotiations; and third, the worsening and spreading of the global financial crisis which began in Asia to Russia, Latin America (particularly Brazil), and recently to the United States.

On a regional scale, political trends are, for the moment at least, still conducive to integration. President Henrique Cardoso was relected handily as Brazil's president in October, and it is clear that he remains committed to a vision of Brazil becoming more integrated into the global economy, rather than retreating into the deceptively peaceful arena of a huge domestic market.[1] Caribbean and Central American governments have continued to draw closer together in their integration attempts, as have the Andean and MERCOSUR countries. Several additional bilateral agreements have been signed among countries or groups of countries, and others are still under negotiation.

At the same time, we see worrying political trends in Venezuela, where a populist military man is running in the presidential race on a backwards-looking platform arguing for more state control of the economy and now unaccountably enjoys a slim majority in the polls.

On the economic front, the global financial crisis is providing additional ammunition to political foes of globalization in the United States and elsewhere, who argue that less rather than more exposure to global markets is a surer route to economic development. Many countries in the region have begun to experience severe balance of payments problems, although only a few have slowed down, stopped, or reversed liberalization efforts.[2]

Another, though different, problem continues to challenge all the economies of the region, but particularly the smaller ones, namely, the scarcity of resources to negotiate, much less implement, trade agreements and obligations. In recent meetings, many governments have pointed to the need for more technical resources even to implement the obligations already undertaken in the Uruguay Round multilateral negotiations. Concerns have been raised about the viability of launching or re-launching negotiations on the Uruguay Round's unfinished agenda at the same time that FTAA negotiations are underway. This, added to the fact that several groups of countries are also negotiating agreements with the European Union, raises the obvious question about priorities and the allocation of scarce resources in the trade arena, particularly over the next two or three years. While some analysts have argued that there is no real shortage of resources (at least in the larger countries that actually intend to participate in all these negotiations), that it is simply a matter of juggling them effectively, one wonders about the degree of political commitment and support that negotiators can expect when pursuing so many potentially divergent goals simultaneously. Also, the fact that countries themselves are worried about the situation should give us pause. Fortunately, there are a number of ameliorative measures being put in place in a subregional context, where the smaller economies in the Caribbean and Central America, as well as the countries of the Andean Group and the MERCOSUR, are working out how to pool their negotiating resources more effectively. Second, regional economic institutions (IDB, OAS, ECLAC, SELA, ALADI, and the World Bank) are aware of the problem and are studying ways to increase their financial, training, and technical assistance to governments to enhance their performance in this arena.

Most encouraging, perhaps, is the continued strong support for economic liberalization and integration evinced by the documents and language coming out of recent meetings of trade and financial ministers, as well as out of the second Summit of the Americas in Santiago, Chile, in April. A significant percentage of political and business leaders throughout the hemisphere support the FTAA and continue to support the move toward economic integration into the global economy despite the recent economic turmoil. Most countries in the hemisphere are holding the line on raising tariffs, although Brazil has enacted a number of steps to "toughen" its tariff regime, and Colombia has devalued its currency.

Given the expected trade impact of the current crisis, we should expect existing disagreements over the pace and scope of the negotiations (e.g., should the FTAA be WTO-Plus or just WTO compliant?) and on the modalities for the negotiations, including the role of "civil society"[3] to worsen. While the official position of the U.S. government remains that the negotiators should seek to conclude preliminary, or interim, agreements by the year 2000, many in Congress, and their labor and environmental supporters, remain unconvinced. Meanwhile, the Brazilian private sector continues to face the strain of astronomical interest rates and an overvalued currency, leading many to argue for the slowest possible pace of liberalization. Some Brazilian commentators have noted that without fast track, the United States will be unable to push its agenda for preliminary or interim agreements.

The hemisphere's corporate leaders have also had their attention diverted somewhat from the FTAA negotiations by the current financial crisis. Nevertheless, U.S. corporate lobbyists staged a convincing, if doomed, show of support for fast track legislation over the summer and into September, despite the fact that literally no one in Washington gave the bill better than a 25 percent chance of success. For U.S. businesses, the FTAA and global trade negotiations remain important because they see such agreements as the best chance for achieving better protection for intellectual property rights, standards harmonization or mutual recognition, tariff reductions and elimination of contingent protection in certain sectors (particularly agriculture), investment reform, market access for service providers, regulatory transparency, and enforcement of competition policy. The test of how deep U.S. corporate support is for the FTAA negotiations will come in and after the year 2000, when the unfinished business of the Uruguay Round is taken up, the FTAA negotiations begin to get serious, and the business community has to start making judgments about where to expend its limited political capital. In the meantime, they will have little difficulty monitoring the slow progress of the nine negotiating groups and making selective input through industry advisory groups or the civil society committee.[4]

Labor and environmental groups have been buoyed by the recent defeat of the fast track legislation in the U.S. Congress and are likely to continue to hold the upper hand in the next Congress, if only because there continue to be substantial Republican defections from the cause of free trade. Republican disunity has unfortunately left a badly splintered Democratic caucus as the final arbiter of U.S. trade policy. Furthermore, predictions of large Republican gains in the House now seem to have been premature, as Clinton's poll numbers remain solid and Congress's slide. Thus, the stalemate over trade policy (among other things) is likely to continue until the 2000 presidential elections, by default leaving the regional initiative with the Canadians and the Brazilians, both of whom recognize that not much will be achieved without strong and consistent U.S. participation. One can take heart, perhaps, in noting that even with relatively consistent U.S. leadership, the Uruguay Round agreement took eight years to conclude, and the president did not have fast track at the beginning of that process either. A 2005 deadline for the FTAA negotiations should give the United States plenty of time to get its trade policy house in order and still have a chance to influence the final agreement. It is certainly not an ideal situation, but politics, and particularly trade politics, seldom is.

Postscript: Update on Progress Toward
Hemispheric Free Trade

# V. LEADERSHIP COUNCIL FOR INTER-AMERICAN SUMMITRY

**Trade Agreements Signed or Initiated in 1998**

| Countries/Groups | Type of Agreement | Date Signed or Initiated |
| --- | --- | --- |
| Andean Community | Deepening and broadening existing commitments to establish a common market by the year 2005 | Signed at Guayaquil Summit, April |
| Andean Community – MERCOSUR | Framework Agreement signed in April to initiate Free Trade Negotiations | Talks were to have been initiated in October, but the ALADI historic tariff preference renegotiations (which come first) will now not be completed until March 1999. |
| Canada – MERCOSUR | Cooperation Agreement on Trade and Investment and Action Plan | Signed June |
| Central America – MERCOSUR | Framework Agreement for Free Trade Negotiations | |
| Chile-Peru | Economic Complementation Agreement (limited liberalization of market access) | Entered into force on July 1 |
| Domincan Republic – Central America | Free Trade Agreement | Signed in April |
| Dominican Republic-CARICOM | Free Trade Agreement | Signed in August |
| European Union – Mexico | Free Trade Negotiations | Initiated in July |
| Mexico and Venezuela – Central America and the Caribbean | Renewed the San Jose Agreement providing oil supplies to Central America and the Caribbean | |

## Notes

1. "Brazil will not curb imports, capital flows in response to crisis," AmericasTrade, 9/17/98, 3.

2. "El embajador de Colombia en el Perú, Luis Guillermo Grillo, señaló estar 'totalmente de acuerdo' con el Secretario General de la CAN, Sebastián Alegrett, en el sentido de que se deben tomar las medidas necesarias para darle al proceso de integración hemisférica una dinámica mucho mayor. 'Desafortunadamente la crisis internacional incide en el atraso de las negociaciones para llegar a una integración mayor. Es mucho más fácil integrarse con economías fuertes en buenos momentos. La actual coyuntura, en cambio, dificulta bastante la integración', señaló." GESTION, Lima, Perú (quoted from the Internet).

3. "Industry Says FTAA Civil Society Panel to Complement Current Process," Americas Trade, 9/3/98, 30.

4. "FTAA Services, Investment Groups get off to Slow Starts in Miami," and "FTAA Trade Remedy Group cuts Short Meeting, Decides on Followups," Americas Trade, 9/17/98, and "first FTAA Market Access Talks Produce Work Program, Few Specifics," Americas Trade, 9/3/98.

# V. LEADERSHIP COUNCIL FOR INTER-AMERICAN SUMMITRY

# Combating Corruption

*Luigi Manzetti is associate professor of political science at Southern Methodist University and visiting associate professor of political science at Duke University. Among his recent publications are* Privatization South American Style; Institutions, Parties, and Coalitions in Argentine Politics; *and* Regulatory Policy in Latin America: Post-Privatization Realities, *North-South Center Press (forthcoming 1999).*

*Luigi Manzetti*

## INTRODUCTION

Corruption is a problem that in Latin America can be traced back to the Spanish and Portuguese conquests. Analyses of its nature and pernicious consequences abound, yet we have seen very little practical action to combat it until the early 1990s. In the 1980s, most of the region adopted democratic forms of government that were followed, in the 1990s, by market-oriented economic reforms. These rapid transformations have produced tangible economic progress, but they have also exposed the inadequacies of the socioeconomic environment in which they were introduced: an environment, particularly in the political realm, still characterized by a lack of transparency and accountability and within which many politicians still behave as if the corrupt practices of old are still compatible with the functioning of an economy inserted in competitive world markets. However, as the world economy has pushed forward, so has the need for a more efficient way of doing business. Thus, as of late, government corruption has come to be regarded as an obstacle to business transactions. This trend has also coupled with increasing demands from society at large to make politicians accountable for their actions. As a result, since the mid-1990s, a series of unprecedented initiatives have been taking place, both regionally and internationally, aimed at tackling the corruption issue.

The goal of this paper is not to present a theoretical argument about corruption in the 1990s, which I have done elsewhere (Manzetti and Blake 1994). Rather, my aim here is to evaluate the implementation to date at the international level of initiatives to combat corruption in Latin America. The first section briefly outlines why the fight against corruption has recently come to be part of the political agenda of several governments, international organizations, and non-governmental organizations (NGOs). In the second section, I will pay particular attention to the Foreign Corruption Practices Act that the U.S. Congress passed in 1977. In the third, I will describe the 1994 Summit of the Americas *Plan of Action* against corruption, including the Organization of American States (OAS) Convention Against Corruption. In the fourth, I will examine other initiatives that several multilateral organizations and NGOs have recently undertaken. In the fifth, I will assess the progress made by several Latin American countries in the fight against corruption. The sixth and last section will summarize the findings.

---

(*) Paper prepared for the conference "Monitoring the Summit of the Americas," Washington, D.C., September 1997.

# I. THE PERILS OF CORRUPTION IN A GLOBAL ECONOMY

Huntington (1968) long ago pointed out that corruption tends to increase when countries experience rapid economic transformations and modernization as a result of the combination of new social values and sources of political power and wealth. This statement is still valid today.

The demise of communism, the globalization of the world economy, and market reforms were all welcomed events in the late 1980s. In Latin America, these events opened great opportunities for democracy to take root and for private business to flourish as the state retreated to a more subsidiary role. Indeed, according to the World Bank, between 1990 and 1996, Latin America was the world leader in privatization policies, which generated $82 billion.

However, as billions of dollars started pouring into the region to take advantage of new business opportunities, international investors started to notice that the stakes of corrupt deals were taking unprecedented proportions. In an interview with *The Wall Street Journal*, a banker described corruption in these terms, "Nowadays, it's more opportunistic, institutionalized and very close to the style of organized crime. It's very, very large because the stakes are very large."[1]

As most Latin American nations started to embrace market reforms in the early 1990s, their efforts were actively supported by the International Monetary Fund (IMF) and the World Bank. However, while the latter institutions were willing to look the other way in the past to achieve higher goals, today such tolerance is running thin. At the 1996 IMF/World Bank meeting, the directors of these institutions have publicly stated that countries receiving their funds will be held accountable for their behavior.

The new stance of the IMF and the World Bank mirrors the changed attitude on corruption taking place in Washington. While corruption was hardly mentioned in public forums until 1990, it has recently become a hotly debated issue, to the point that the Clinton administration has made the fight against corruption one of its top priorities in foreign policy starting with the Miami Summit of 1994. In 1996, the countries of the Western Hemisphere subscribed to the Inter-American Convention Against Corruption, the first attempt to combat this phenomenon on a regional scale.

The activism of the Clinton administration on this front was prompted by a score of complaints by U.S. firms. The U.S. Foreign Corrupt Practices Act of 1977 is the only legislation in the world barring companies from bribing abroad. As competition for new markets is becoming increasingly fierce, U.S. companies have found themselves at a disadvantage since they cannot provide bribes as Japanese or European companies can. Not surprisingly, in a recent poll commissioned by the Bank of Boston surveying 303 chief officers or presidents of Fortune 1000 companies, commercial banks, and debt investment firms, political corruption was cited as the most significant problem in Latin America.[2] According to a 1996 U.S. Commerce Department report, of the business transactions involving corruption in which U.S. firms were competing, an estimated 80 percent of those contracts were won by foreign firms paying bribes. This situation has cost U.S. concerns an estimated $100 billion in lost business since 1994.

# II. U.S. INITIATIVES IN PREVENTING CORRUPTION

By far, the United States has been the most active country in preventing corruption. In the mid-1970s, a Securities and Exchange Commission (SEC) inquiry found that more than 450 U.S. companies had paid bribes to foreign officials in excess of $450 million (Cruver 1994). The public outcry that these results created in the United States, which was still reeling from the effects of the Watergate scandal, prompted Congress to pass the Foreign Corrupt Practices Act (FCPA) in 1977. Based upon the SEC's investigation, the FCPA made it illegal for U.S. companies to bribe government officials abroad. Violating FCPA rules may result in fines of up to $2 million for firms and up to $100,000 for individuals, and jail terms for up to five years.[3] The FCPA's provisions that amended section 13 of the 1934 Securities and Exchange Act consequently now apply to all companies regulated by the SEC. The first part of the FCPA focuses on accounting procedures and internal control requirements to prevent the hiding of illegal payments. The second part identifies under which circumstances individuals and companies are subject to the FCPA's sanctions. The legislation distinguishes between bribe "issuers" and bribes instigated by "domestic concerns." The FCPA applies to individual officers, employees, managers, and representatives of U.S. firms as well as to joint ventures, unincorporated associations, and similar business entities.[4] The FCPA forbids

Combating Corruption

# V. LEADERSHIP COUNCIL FOR INTER-AMERICAN SUMMITRY

1. the use of an instrumentality of interstate commerce (such as the telephone, telex, telecopies, air transportation, or the mail) in furtherance of
2. a payment of, or even an offer to pay, "anything of value," directly or indirectly
3. to any foreign official, foreign political party, or foreign political candidate,
4. if the purpose of the payment is the "corrupt" one of getting the recipient to act (or to refrain from acting)
5. in such a way as to assist the company in obtaining or retaining business or in directing business to any particular person (Slocum 1996,45-46).

As noted earlier, the 1988 amendment tries to clarify some uncertain aspects of the FCPA. For instance, they added prohibitions regarding third parties who knowingly make payments directly or indirectly benefitting a foreign official.[5] However, they allowed for "grease payments" if the payment is a "facilitating or expediting payment to a foreign official, political party, or party official, the purpose of which is to expedite or to secure the performance of a routine governmental action."[6]

Currently, there is no legislative action pending on the FCPA. Breaching the FCPA anti-bribery clauses "may give rise to a private cause of action under the Racketeer Influenced and Corrupt Organizations Act (RICO), by a plaintiff competitor who alleges that the defendant won a foreign contract due to bribery. Such a precedent exists under a similar criminal RICO case, where the FCPA violations were allowed to serve as the basis for the Travel Act violations, which in turn were alleged to be predicates for RICO violations. In a private court action under RICO for conduct that was alleged to violate FCPA, the court denied a motion to dismiss, thereby allowing the plaintiff's claims of a FCPA violation (coupled with a Travel Act claim) to serve as a predicate offense under RICO."[7]

Later on, the 1988 Trade Act added some amendments that 1) clarified issues related to the illegality of payments to intermediaries, 2) stipulated exceptions and affirmative defenses, 3) stiffened penalties, and 4) added governmental civil and injunctive sanctions. Title VII of the 1988 Trade Act also requires the president to brief Congress annually on the discrimination suffered by U.S. companies abroad in government procurement. Title VII also provides for consultations with countries that are singled out in the report. If a country fails to address the discriminating situation suffered by U.S. companies within a specified period of time, actions should follow. Moreover, Title VII forbids U.S. procurement, under some circumstances, from those countries that are listed in the presidential report.

The Uruguay Round Agreement Act, "requires the President also to identify under Title VII, countries from which the United States procures significant amounts of goods and/or services, that are not signatories of GATT (General Agreement on Tariffs and Trade) Procurement Code and that fail to maintain and enforce effective prohibitions against bribery in government procurement."[8]

Admittedly, the enforcement of the FCPA provisions was neglected during the Reagan administration, but under the Bush administration and more so under the Clinton administration, U.S. government efforts to investigate possible offenders have stepped up. Nonetheless, since 1977 a handful of U.S. companies have actually been fined.

A major scandal has recently involved International Business Machines (IBM) in Argentina. In 1996, Argentine tax auditors found that IBM had paid $37 million to two local software companies that, in turn, had not reported such revenues. The $37 million that IBM had paid was part of a $249 million government contract that the U.S. firm had won in 1994 to modernize the computer system of the state-owned Banco Nación, the country's largest bank. Argentine auditors accused IBM of overcharging Banco Nación an amount ranging between $70 million to $120 million. Shortly thereafter, a federal judge indicted 30 IBM and Argentine government officials, and Banco Nación requested IBM to reimburse the $82 million that it had already disbursed to the computer giant.

However, IBM's problems in Argentina have taken a new twist. Shortly after the Banco Nación scandal, a federal judge began to investigate alleged irregularities in the 1995 computer contract award that Argentina's tax collection agency, DGI, had signed with IBM. The probe came after accusations of wrongdoing from an IBM competitor, Canadian SHL Systemhouse, that had bid for the same contract $177 million, as opposed to IBM's $425 million. The Argentine press also published reports which stated that in the last two decades IBM had such an "inside track" on government contracts that other computer companies often failed to compete. As a result of these scandals, IBM removed the managers of its Argentine branch, citing that their behavior had been inconsistent with company policy, but insisted that it had not engaged in any wrongdoing.

The U.S. government has also increased pressure upon some foreign governments where alleged cases of corruption have been taking place. One main reason is that more and more companies are unofficially denouncing illegal acts, but still very few of them actually file formal charges for fear of exposing themselves to legal suits or loss of future business. Corruption abroad is fueled by the lack of transparency in government procurement contracts. According to the 1995 Title VII report, "the lack of a comprehensive national system of transparent and competitive procurement procedures multiplies the opportunities for awarding contracts in exchange for bribes and conclud[ed] that anticorruption laws and enforcement should be coupled with transparent and competitive procurement systems."[9]

In March 1995, Senator Feingold introduced a bill that would forbid trade assistance to foreign companies and their U.S. subsidiaries that lack effective mechanisms to prevent the disbursement of bribes. Bill S. 576, "would prohibit TDA, OPIC, EX-IM Bank, and A.I.D. from providing economic support to a corporation unless the head of these agencies certifies to Congress that the corporation has adopted and enforces a corporate-wide policy that prohibits the bribery of foreign public officials in connection with the corporation's international business transactions."[10] The bill was referred to the Senate Foreign Relations Committee, which has commissioned the State Department to perform a study on the impact that corruption abroad has on U.S. business.

## III. THE 1994 SUMMIT OF THE AMERICAS AND SUBSEQUENT INITIATIVES

In its first two years in office, the Clinton administration was very active in pressuring fellow member states of the Organization of Economic Cooperation and Development (OECD) to take concrete action against corruption abroad (more later), but the inclusion of corruption in the 1994 Summit of the Americas' agenda was possible because of the insistence of some Latin American countries, like Ecuador and Venezuela (Elliot 1996). The Summit *Declaration of Principles* eventually stated that "effective democracy requires a comprehensive attack on corruption as a factor of social disintegration and distortion of the economic system that undermines the legitimacy of political institutions." In the section "Combating Corruption," the Summit *Plan* laid out a "Plan of Action" urging governments to 1) promote discussion of the most significant corruption problems and elaborate reforms to tackle them; 2) strengthen internal control mechanisms within the public administration and allow meaningful outside review; 3) establish standards of conflict of interest for public employees and other measures penalizing illicit enrichment; 4) urge other governments around the world to cooperate against illicit financial and commercial transactions when affecting the Western Hemisphere; 5) improve cooperation in the judicial and financial realms to quickly pursue internal investigations; 6) improve regulations on government procurement, tax collection, and the administration of justice; and 7) develop a regional approach in the fight against corruption under the auspices of the Organization of American States (OAS).

The most tangible result of the Summit *Plan* has indeed come so far from the last point involving the OAS. Following the Miami Summit, Venezuela presented a draft of the Inter-American Convention Against Corruption (IACAC) in 1995. In March 1996, 21 countries from the Western Hemisphere convened in Caracas where the final draft of the convention was signed. The IACAC identifies acts of corruption and contains articles that create binding obligations under international law as well as hortatory principles to fight corruption. The convention also provides for institutional development and enforcement of anticorruption measures, including the criminalization of specified acts of corruption and provides procedures for extradition, seizure of assets, mutual legal assistance, and technical assistance where acts of corruption occur or have effect on one of its parties. In addition, subject to each party's constitution and the fundamental principles of its legal system, the convention requires parties to criminalize bribery of foreign government officials. The convention also contains a series of "preventive measures" that the parties agree to consider establishing to prevent corruption, including systems of government procurement that assure the openness, equity, and efficiency of such systems.

The most controversial part of the IACAC is Article IX where the concept of "illicit enrichment" is discussed. The article reads, "...each State Party that has not yet done so shall take the necessary measures to establish under its laws as an offense a significant increase in the assets of a government official that he cannot reasonably explain in relation to his lawful earnings during the performance of his functions." In other words, the burden of proof is no longer with the prosecution but instead with the defendant. This provision goes against the constitution of the United States and creates problems for the applicability of the convention in U.S. courts. Thus, the U.S. government obtained that it would not be required to adopt the concept of illicit enrichment in its criminal justice system. Consequently, the rather tough language of the convention allows for some room of maneuvering since a country can defer to its own legislation (Slocum 1996, 30). Now the convention must be ratified by the legislatures of each member country of the OAS.

To date, Argentina, Bolivia, Colombia, Costa Rica, Ecuador, Honduras, Mexico, Paraguay, Peru, and Trinidad and Tobago have ratified the convention, but only Bolivia and Paraguay have submitted the instruments of ratification to the OAS. Presently, the convention is undergoing a "Language Discrepancy Reconciliation Process," which is expected to be finalized by summer 1997. Upon such completion, the convention should be sent to the U.S. Senate for "Advice and Consent."

With respect to the other points spelled out in the *Plan of Action*, progress has been negligible for the most part. However, the Inter-American Development Bank (IDB), which was mentioned in the Summit of the Americas Action Plan as a means of technical and financial assistance to support Latin American governments' efforts toward the improvement of tax collection, government procurement and regulations, and the administration of justice, has become more active since 1994 in all the policy areas just mentioned. For instance, the IDB is currently providing financial assistance to the Dominican Republic to improve its judicial system and establish criteria of transparency and accountability of the public administration.

## IV. INITIATIVES BY MULTILATERAL ORGANIZATIONS

In 1976, the Organization of Economic Cooperation and Development (OECD) issued a Declaration on International Investment and Multinational Enterprises whose Guidelines for Multinational Enterprises states that such enterprises should "not render and they should not be solicited or expected to render any bribe or other improper benefit, direct or indirect, to any public servant or holder of public office." These guidelines were periodically updated. The 1988 Trade Act directed the U.S. government to negotiate an agreement with the OECD on corruption practices. In 1994, the OECD council recommended that its members had to take concrete measures in order to prevent the bribery of foreign officials.

After years of lobbying, in June 1997 the United States finally succeeded in having the OECD, which includes the 29 most industrialized countries of the world, start negotiations in order to draft a treaty that would hopefully commit its member states to 1) eliminate tax deductibility of bribes by national companies, 2) impose stricter guidelines for companies in terms of financial disclosure, 3) eliminate government subsidies known to be used by corrupt exporting firms, 4) create transparency in banking transactions, 5) reform commercial and civil law to penalize corruption, and 6) make a criminal offense the payment of bribes paid abroad by national companies. On December 17, the OECD issued its own convention against corruption that included the points mentioned above. Its member countries pledged to have it approved by their respective legislatures shortly. However, the ratification process is likely to take some time. In fact, the convention does not come into effect until five of the 10 countries with the largest share of exports (or 60 percent of total exports of the 10 most important countries in this regard) within the OECD will approve it.

In the U.S. government view, many European companies have used their national legislation (i.e., Germany and France) to gain an unfair advantage over their U.S. competitors. Not surprisingly, both Germany and France have tried first to block and later delay any binding agreement on this issue. However, the globalization of the world economy and diminished economic protectionism seem to have convinced many governments and transnational corporations that in an increasingly competitive business environment, it makes more sense to cut the transaction costs involved in corruption practices rather than abiding to their rules that, by their very nature, are often unclear and unpredictable.

As for other organizations, the 1979 General Agreement on Tariffs and Trade (GATT) Agreement on Trade in Civil Aircraft (Article 4) stipulates that "Signatories agree to avoid attaching inducements of any kind to the sale or purchase of civil aircraft from any particular source which would create discrimination against suppliers from any Signatory." In 1992 the U.S.-European Union (EU) Agreement concerning the application of the GATT Agreement on Trade in Civil Aircraft strengthened the language of the original document.

In January 1996, the World Trade Organization (WTO) Agreement on Government Procurement went into effect for the United States, Japan, Canada, Norway, South Korea, Israel, and the EU. It includes procurement of goods and services by central governments and their entities, government agencies, government-owned utilities, and a range of institutions and companies partly owned by the government.

The WTO agreement spells out in detail the procedures in government procurement that, in theory, should promote transparency and curtail the opportunities for illicit payments. However, the agreement's main problem is that it was undersigned by a limited, although economically very powerful, group of nations. Thus, the Clinton administration:

> has proposed negotiation of a framework of transparent and competitive procurement procedures in the context of the Summit of the Americas. For those countries that adopt such a framework and also agree to maintain and enforce effective anticorruption measures, the President has the authority to waive the purchasing prohibition that applies under the Trade Agreement Act of 1979 to products of countries that are not members of the WTO Code (Slocum 1996, 15).

The European Union has stepped up its initiatives since 1994. The European Council formed a Multi-Disciplinary Group on Corruption to generate guidelines and a plan of action. In January 1996, the Italian Presidency of the EU drafted a convention dealing with corruption in general, rather than with EU's financial interests as in the past. The original proposal, the first one of its kind, commits member states to take the necessary measures in order to sanction the corrupt activities of foreign officials operating within EU boundaries.

In terms of multilateral lending agencies, since James D. Wolfensohn took World Bank leadership, this institution has become more and more sensitive to the corruption issue. The World Bank has changed its loan and procurement guidelines in order to disqualify companies and consultants that engage in corruption. Under the new rules:

1. The Bank may reject a proposal for the award of a contract by the borrower upon the determination that the bidder recommended for the award has engaged in corrupt or fraudulent activities in competing for that contract.

2. The Bank will cancel a corresponding amount of a loan if it determines that corrupt or fraudulent practices were engaged in by representatives of the borrower or a beneficiary of the loan during the procurement process or the execution of any contract under the loan without the borrower having taken action satisfactory to the Bank to remedy the situation.

3. The Bank will declare ineligible to be awarded a contract for a specific time or indefinitely any supplier/contractor/consultant who is found by it to have engaged in a corrupt or fraudulent practice.

4. The Bank has the right to inspect accounts and records of contractors/suppliers/consultants engaged in Bank-financed contracts.

5. Contractors/suppliers/consultants have to disclose any commissions or other payments paid to local or foreign agents in the context of the procurement or execution of Bank-financed contracts (Shihata 1996, 9-10).

Of course, this is not a small change for an institution that in the past, when recipient countries openly misused funds, had a tradition of ignoring such matters for fear of creating a political backlash (Celarier 1997). This tough stand is having some encouraging effects. Some African countries have recently submitted to the World Bank loan requests conforming to that institution's anticorruption clauses for procurement contracts.

The International Monetary Fund (IMF) has recently stepped up its effort to thwart corruption. In July 1997, the Washington-based organization issued new guidelines stating that:

> Financial assistance from the IMF...could be suspended or delayed on account of poor governance, if there is a reason to believe it could have significant macroeconomic implications that threaten the successful implementation of the programme, or if it puts in doubt the purpose of the use of IMF resources.[11]

In a public statement, the IMF managing director, Michel Camdessus, explained his institution's new policy stand in these terms, "...increasingly we find that much broader range of institutional reforms is needed if countries are to establish and maintain private sector confidence and thereby lay the basis for sustained growth [and] every country that hopes to maintain market confidence must come to terms with the issues associated with good governance."[12]

The new emphasis on good governance focuses on three main policy areas: 1) management reform of public resources (i.e., taxation, audit and accounting procedures, and budget preparation); 2) the establishment of a transparent and stable regulatory environment in commercial and tax law; and 3) the strengthening of judicial systems. From now on, Article 4, which the IMF employs to assess a country's progress toward macroeconomic goals (i.e., inflation, balance of payments, trade barriers) will also include governance criteria.

The first casualty of the new good governance guidelines was Kenya which, in August 1997, saw the suspension of a $220 million loan program due to the serious corruption problems plaguing the government of its country.[13] The degree to which the IMF will pursue similar actions in the future remains to be seen. One, however, should not be overly optimistic. In July 1997, the IMF decided to enhance Argentina's credit line because of that country's "good governance" record. However, this is a bit surprising since that country, as shall be seen in a moment, has been in the headlines due to alleged corruption cases involving high government officials.[14]

Nonetheless, the good governance approach is a major step forward. The IMF has already announced that it intends to collaborate with other multilateral institutions, and in particular with the World Bank, to make this new policy more credible and far-reaching. Indeed, as former U.S. Secretary of State Robert McNamara pointed out, the fight against corruption not only has to be internationalized, but it also requires close cooperation among multilateral institutions, governments, and the private sector.

As for the Inter-American Development Bank (IDB), unfortunately it is behind both the World Bank and the IMF. At present, the IDB is revising its procurement guidelines, which are not as strict as the ones of the World Bank, to deter corruption in its assistance programs.

When it comes to the role of non-governmental organizations (NGOs), Transparency International (TI), created in 1993 by Peter Eigen, a former World Bank official, has been on the forefront in the fight against corruption. It has established numerous national chapters throughout Latin America that have taken several initiatives to promote greater government accountability and public awareness throughout the Western Hemisphere. TI has been recently involved in a series of activities, ranging from seminars to consulting jobs, with the OAS, the World Bank, and the OECD. Several Latin American chapters contributed to the 1994 Miami Summit and to the OAS Convention Against Corruption. Yet TI's greatest impact so far has been its "corruption index," which despite its methodological limitations has served as a rule of thumb to identify those countries (the index covers 50 nations) that are still most at risk when it comes to corruption practices. TI-USA has recently contributed to the revision of the International Chamber of Commerce Rules of Conduct to Combat Extortion. TI also had some input in the revision of the World Bank's procurement guidelines examined earlier. The TI chapters in Latin America are actively lobbying their respective legislatures to ratify the OAS Convention Against Corruption. For example, in September 1998, TI-Argentina signed an agreement with the City of Buenos Aires to assist in the monitoring of the public hearings for the renewal of the leasing contracts of the subway lines.

## V. NATIONAL CASES IN LATIN AMERICA

If attention shifts to improvements at the national level, the picture is quite disturbing. Despite much phamphare on supposed campaigns against corruption, some of the most important countries in the region have shown no tangible willingness to make any concrete steps. Let us briefly analyze some bench-mark cases.

### Argentina

Under the presidency of Carlos Saúl Menem (1989-present), Argentina has experienced the most radical market reform program of Latin America, which has been instrumental in defeating inflation, reviving economic growth, and bringing back foreign investments to the country in such a dramatic fashion that many observers began to talk about the "Argentine miracle" by the mid-1990s. However, the Menem administration has been marred by over three dozen corruption scandals at the highest levels of government. The press, NGOs, and opposition parties have repeatedly denounced scandals affecting privatization, economic deregulation, tax collection, and government procurement, but to no avail. President Menem's strategy has been systematically to defend the accused only to sack them later on when things became untenable. To save the reputation of his administration, the president has repeatedly announced anticorruption legislative initiatives, which never got off the ground.

In August 1995, Economy Minister Cavallo, widely credited for the so-called "Argentine miracle," accused old-style Peronist politicians of derailing his market reform policies to favor "mafia-like cartels." More specifically, Cavallo claimed that many legislators, along with prominent administration officials, were trying to change the privatization bill of the national post office that was being discussed in Congress so that the only possible bidder could be Alfredo Yabram, a businessman and a personal friend of Menem's, who already controlled 70 percent of the private couriers working in Argentina. If passed in the amended form, the bill would not only allow Yabram to acquire a virtual monopoly of mail service but would also enable him to ship items in and out of the country without any control from law enforcement officials. For Cavallo this was most disturbing as he claimed to have evidence that Yabram was involved in narcotrafficking. A year later Menem sacked Cavallo who is now facing a barrage of judicial inquiries by judges that the former minister described as being manipulated by his political enemies, among whom Justice Minister Elías Jassan and Interior Minister Carlos Corach topped the list. Jassan always denied that he was protecting Yabram or had ever spoken to him, but in the summer of 1997, investigative reporters found that the Justice Minister had indeed spoken to Yabram on numerous occasions via phone. As a result, Jassan was forced to resign.

To this day, no high-ranking official of the Menem administration, save for Cavallo who blew the whistle, has faced any judicial prosecution largely because many judges and state prosecutors have failed to act. Not surprisingly, in 1994 a Gallup survey found that 84 percent of the respondents believed the judiciary to be politically manipulated by the government.[15] The problem has become so alarming that a new Gallup survey in January 1996 recorded that the most important problem facing the country was the corruption among politicians and public officials (47.6 percent of all respondents).[16]

However, in the October 1997 mid-term congressional elections, these misgivings turned into votes. Menem's Peronist Party suffered a burning defeat at the hands of Graciela Fernández Mejide, the leader of the *Alianza* coalition who "repeatedly accused Mr Menem of corruption" and had campaigned strongly on that issue.[17] *The Wall Street Journal* explained the electoral results in this way:

> the public widely perceives that the country's progress is undermined by government graft, organized crime, cronysm and a broken judicial system. Mr. Menem claimed there is nothing wrong with the judicial system and this was not the right time to take on corruption. This attitude clearly contributed to his party's defeat.[18]

## Brazil

While Argentina is a typical case, it is not an isolated one. Brazil is another case where much official rhetoric about the fight against corruption has actually met with repeated attempts to cover up scandals (Fleischer 1997). For instance, in 1988, a congressional investigative committee (CPI) recommended that impeachment procedures be initiated against President José Sarney for corruption charges. Inexplicably, the President of the Chamber of Deputies, Innocêncio de Oliveira, decided to close the case and refused to allow the chamber to debate the issue. The impeachment of President Fernando Collor de Mello in 1992 came only after a reluctant Congress was forced by the media and an outraged public opinion to act. A year later, the Supreme Court found Collor de Mello not guilty primarily because most of the evidence gathered against him had been acquired by the federal police without a warrant.

In 1993, Congress set up another CPI to investigate a massive scandal involving federal legislators of the Joint Budget Committee, which was quickly dubbed "Budgetgate." As the hearings began to unravel a massive corruption scandal that potentially involved up to one-third of the members of Congress, many governors, and administration officials, the CPI decided to hurriedly close the inquiry. Preliminary findings showed that up to 40 percent of public funds for public works and infrastructure projects went astray.[19] Of the 43 members of Congress investigated, the CPI recommended the sacking of 17. In 1994, Congress absolved six, ousted seven, while four resigned voluntarily. A separate committee set up to inquire of the public officials involved in the scandal had several of them fired and transmitted the whole documentation to federal prosecutors to start criminal procedures. This, however, was not the case for the legislators involved, as Congress refused to pass the evidence to the judiciary for fear of having the scandal take a new, and possibly more damaging, spin.

Upon taking office in 1995, President Fernando Henrique Cardoso promised to put an end to the "looting" of public funds. However, in a surprise move, he decided to disband the CPI that President Itamar Franco (who had taken over after Collor's impeachment) had appointed to investigate corruption scandals. All the evidence gathered by the CPI was transferred to the justice and finance ministries, which failed to produce any meaningful investigations thereafter. By contrast, several high-profile members of the Cardoso administration were implicated in corruption scandals and, as in Argentina, none of them subsequently were indicted as their resignations were regarded as sufficient punishment. The first such case involved Cardoso's Chief-of Staff, Clóvis Carvalho. Shortly after assuming office, Carvalho forced the Brazilian Central Bank (that had ruled against it) to provide a soft loan to a company for which he had worked that was facing bankruptcy. In 1995, Carvalho also convinced Cardoso to abolish the special investigative commission of the executive branch that was investigating important corruption charges in the public administration.

In May 1997, new charges emerged in the press according to which the Cardoso administration had paid off some legislators in order to vote for an amendment that would allow President Cardoso to seek a consecutive second term (the 1988 Constitution prevents such an option) in 1998.[20] Although during his first term Cardoso sponsored the OAS convention against corruption and has proposed to Congress a bill to fight money laundering, under U.S. and European Community pressure, when it came to fight corruption at home, he has distinguished himself at best for lack of action. As Fleischer (1997,16) pointed out, "the new internal control agency...was not given political autonomy, nor adequate funding and staff. Finally, the Ministry of Administration and Reform of the State..has proposed major changes on the 1988 Procurement Law, which would 'streamline' bidding processes, but which most observers feel would facilitate corruption."

## Mexico

In Mexico, the Ernesto Zedillo administration has launched a seemingly ambitious anticorruption campaign that, however, seems to focus on the wrongdoing that occurred under his predecessor, Carlos Salinas de Gortari, rather than on scandals that have been denounced since he took office. For instance, the current administration is now reviewing a number of privatizations completed by Salinas. The suspicion is that many sales were manipulated to favor domestic investors close to Salinas. Some of these deals involved AeroMexico and the national telephone company. Gerardo de Prevoisin, who in 1989 put together the consortium that bought AeroMexico, is now accused by the same company of having embezzled $72 million. De Prevoisin, for his part, told a Texas court that he paid $8 million to Salinas and Zedillo's Institutional Revolutionary Party (PRI).[21]

Corruption rumors started in 1993, when the press uncovered the so-called "billionaires' banquet" to which Salinas had invited the beneficiaries of the privatization process. Allegedly, the former president requested individual donations of $25 million to fund PRI expenses for the 1994 presidential elections. Charges of corruption have also been a commonplace at the local government level.

Even at the local levels, where governments are ceding many functions to the private sector, astounding sums can flow into campaign coffers. In the rural Mexican state of Tabasco, federal authorities are investigating contributors to the governor's $70 million election campaign.[22]

Nonetheless, after the initial statements, no true headway has been made to uncover the suspect corrupt activities of the largest Mexican economic groups since such groups still fund the campaign of Zedillo's party. The biggest case to date that Mexican prosecutors are putting together involves Raúl Salinas, the brother of the former president. In the early 1990s, one of Citibank's top private bankers, Amy Elliott, began to move millions of dollars out of Mexico on behalf of Raúl Salinas. Raúl Salinas is now in jail in Mexico and, among other things, is accused by Mexican state prosecutors of having stashed abroad $120 million. If, as the Mexicans believe, some of the money that Ms. Elliott took out of Mexico was the result of criminal activities, Raúl Salinas may be convicted on a variety of counts, while Ms. Elliot may face federal money-laundering charges in the United States.

However, aside from these sporadic instances, no tangible progress has been made on the corruption front. The investigation on the assassination of Luis Donaldo Colosio, the official candidate who was supposed to succeed President Carlos Salinas, has not produced meaningful results. The connection between the ruling and Mexican drug lords remains an untouchable issue.

The good news is that the opposition parties, now in control of the Mexican lower house, have demanded that the government disclose information with regard to key policies that in the past, when the PRI was in complete control of Congress, were simply rubber-stamped. Recently, opposition parties have tried to expose the close links existing between the PRI and big business. In fact, they have refused to approve the bailout of many bankrupt financial institutions, whose estimated cost is around 77 billion pesos, unless a "truth commission" is appointed to investigate where the money went. There is strong suspicion that the same bankers, who are now asking the taxpayer to foot the bill, spent large sums to finance the PRI electoral campaigns. So far talks in Congress have stalled, but pressure is mounting on the government after the opposition published 310 names of the beneficiaries of a possible bailout, which include some of Mexico's richest people.

## Peru

President Alberto Fujimori has often portrayed himself as a corruption fighter. During his first term in office, he instructed the judiciary to investigate alleged cases of corruption involving his predecessor, Alan García, and some Italian companies for a suburban railway contract. In 1992, Fujimori closed the Peruvian Congress citing, among other things, that corruption was widespread among legislators. However, Fujimori in recent times has dismissed supreme court judges who were unwilling to bend the law to satisfy his demands. Equally troubling, the president in 1997 revoked the citizenship of Baruch Ivcher, an Israeli businessman, whose television station disclosed documents showing how Fujimori's intelligence adviser, Vladimiro Montesinos, had a very high income that was inexplicable given his government salary. In short, while Fujimori has been quite active in using the judicial system to attack his political enemies, he has been equally swift in covering up scandals within his administration and in harassing the independent media (Weyland 1998).

## Chile

Chile proudly considers itself immune to the corruption excesses affecting other Latin American countries. Yet, according to both opposition and government backers, in recent years it has experienced an increase of reported corruption cases at the municipal level.[23] Moreover, press reports have underscored a growing collusion between businessmen and politicians. Concerned with these developments, in 1994 President Eduardo Frei appointed a commission to make recommendations on how to improve ethical standards in the public administration and regulate political parties' campaign financing (currently, there is no norm forcing parties to disclose their campaign contributions). After several months of hard work, the commission sent to the legislature a draft bill for approval. However, to date, legislators of different political persuasions have not shown much interest in discussing the bill. According to some members of Frei's commission, this lack of action rests on the fact that many members of Congress see the bill as detrimental to their campaign finances.[24] Thus, although Chile remains a relatively corruption-free country, Frei's good intentions to bring transparency to campaign financing have met with disappointing results.

## VI. OBSTACLES AND INCENTIVES IN CONTROLLING CORRUPTION

How can "dichos" turn into "hechos"? In order to respond to this question, we must distinguish between efforts within individual countries (micro-analysis) and those at the international level (macro-analysis).

As far as the first type of analysis is concerned, the frequent anticorruption crusades launched so far in the countries discussed above have not turned into a "Mani Pulite" political revolution because those at the helms have much to lose if serious action is taken in this regard. It also must be stressed that the argument that Latin American countries lack ethical and criminal codes to go after corrupt officials is simply a myth in many cases. These countries and many others in the region do possess rather sophisticated legal instruments to pursue criminal and administrative sanctions. Thus, focusing on whether OAS member states have passed new laws or enacted new legal practices will simply miss the point. The problem is that the judiciary and internal control mechanisms in the public administration do not have the political independence to act independently in Latin America. Multilateral agencies and foreign governments can spend a fortune helping these countries to improve the technical aspects linked to judicial and government auditing inquiries, but if the public officials who are in charge of such investigations are either politically manipulated or prevented from doing their jobs when it affects politically powerful individuals, we simply go back to square one.

What is missing here is a clear breakthrough within the highest levels of government to produce any true change. In this regard, progress has been slim at best. The proof rests on the fact that while some presidents have publicly declared their commitment to champion the anticorruption crusade, in practice they have been intimidating (i.e., Argentina, Peru, Panama, and Venezuela) the independent media that pursued corruption allegations involving government officials. This is because some members of the media have been willing to find out what a politically coopted judiciary is reluctant to even consider. Another example of the lack of progress is the fact that genuine reform toward public disclosure of governmental information and greater transparency in government action is nowhere noticeable.

Thus, legislatures may pass state-of-the-art anticorruption laws, and governments may sign OAS-patterned conventions to fight illicit behavior, but they will all amount to much ado about nothing if they are not actually implemented. Many governments, legislatures, and bureaucracies, not just in Latin America, operate within a code of unwritten and often illegal norms. As Reisman (1978) put it, the law amounts to a mythical code; that is, it establishes the difference between what is allowed and what is not and is used publicly. However, there are "secret" operational rules that define who, how, and when something is done that contradicts the mythical code and against which no punishment is applied. Unfortunately, these operational rules are often more important than the mythical code. As Blum (1997,13) pointed out in analyzing Mexico, "as long as the purpose of those [operational] norms of the political system remain the control of Mexico's population and resources by a small elite, complicity and corruption are ineradicable." The same conclusion could be easily applied to a host of other countries.

To be sure, these few cases that I have outlined are only the tip of the iceberg and came to light because of fortuitous lobbying or infighting within the governing political coalition. Yet their significance does not rest just on the damage that they bring to the reputation of the firms and governmental officials involved. When high-profile public officials and corporations portray themselves as bringing a new era of economic prosperity only to be caught in illicit activities behind the scene, the damaging effects they produce are more long-lasting. This is because through corrupt activities they undermine the hope held by many people in developing countries around the globe that democratic forms of government fostering market-oriented policies are the best means to promote economic progress and transparency. Indeed, privatization, deregulation, trade liberalization are theoretically means of promoting greater transparency in the marketplace and reducing the politicians discretionary role that so often has been used to pursue illegal ends.

However, if such policies are actually decided and implemented in a non-transparent fashion, they can actually end up in opening new windows of opportunity for corrupt politicians. Allegations of wrongdoing in carrying out market reforms in recent years have surfaced in many Latin American countries, often casting a doubt regarding who is really benefitting from such policies, which in the short run usually carry a high social cost particularly with respect to employment.[25]

One should not be surprised then if a recent poll taken by the Latinobarometro shows that dissatisfaction and pessimism about socioeconomic issues are on the rise in Latin America. Synthesized in a few words, democracy and market reforms in Latin America have not yet delivered the expected goods to the poorer sectors of the population. If cases like the ones just mentioned proliferate, there is a real danger that the trend toward greater openness in trade relations may be jeopardized. After all, one has only to go back to the impeachments of President Fernando Collor de Mello in Brazil and Carlos Andrés Pérez in Venezuela to see how corruption scandals can almost bring to a halt a market reform agenda.

If the analysis is shifted at the macro level, some major obstacles are also political in nature. Japan, the EU, and many countries in other parts of the world have been so far unwilling to comply with legislation similar to the FCPA until the OAS sponsored the IACAC in 1996. Some see in the U.S. government effort an attempt to impose moral standards alien to many cultures. The extraterritoriality of the FCPA provisions also infringes upon the national sovereignty of individual countries (Jacoby et al. 1977). Some scholars also argued that the application of the FCPA has been uneven over the years.

Some object to the adoption of FCPA-like legislation on the grounds that it is inconsistent with local jurisprudence. Indeed, negotiations over incorporating the GATT 1992 agreement (cited above) into the WTO have stalled over Article 4 that reads, "signatories shall refrain from the use of negative or positive linkages between the sale or purchase of civil aircraft and other government decisions or policies which might influence such a sale or purchase."

However, the major obstacles, according to many analysts, are based on economic calculations. Imposing and enforcing legislation similar to FCPA would automatically affect negatively the business of many companies in Europe and Japan with very close ties to government officials. It is plausible to suppose that were such companies to compete without using bribes, they would find it difficult to develop business outside their countries. In other words, those corporations that are less competitive in the marketplace are more likely to lobby their governments against any legislation tying their hands because this could spell financial disaster.

Thus, we are in a catch-22 situation. As long as there is no mutual trust among the industrialized nations on how to tackle the problem, it is rational for a given country to allow its companies to engage in corruption, and even encourage them to do so through tax breaks, because otherwise there would be a financial loss. This is precisely what U.S. companies consistently complain about with their government when they see their business prospects evaporating because of unfair practices adopted by foreign competitors that do not face FCPA-like sanctions.

However, continuing in this state of affairs is likely to increase business costs even for those who bribe. Once one subjects oneself to paying a bribe, he puts himself at the mercy of politicians and civil servants who may change the rules of the game at any time. So we are back to square one.

The WTO has no real power to produce such an agreement at this time, but even if it could, who would enforce it? Enforcement is crucial to deter corruption from taking place. The answer rests with the individual countries. However, who can assure us that, in the hypothetical situation where the United States, the EU, and Japan come to an agreement, penalties will actually be enforced? Suppose such group of countries would abide by the spirit of the agreement. Who can assure the compliance of countries that did not sign an international convention to combat corruption?

The litigious world of international trade can provide an example of how difficult it is to enforce rules when too many players are involved and sanctions for noncompliance are ineffective. Much greater difficulties should be expected in achieving a cross-national agreement in as sensitive a topic as corruption where evidence is usually hard to find and the mere fact of denouncing comes attached with a high personal risk in many countries.

What are, then, the incentives to cooperate on this issue? First, as mentioned earlier, a primary incentive stems from the fact that were all the players involved playing honestly, transaction costs would be reduced significantly. Second, the disclosure of massive corruption scandals in many countries has created a low tolerance for briberies. This is a fact with which politicians must reckon. Third, the threat that drug money poses to the political stability of many nations as well as to the international financial markets is finally forcing many political leaders to conclude, albeit slowly, that something must be done. Fourth, the democratization process that took place in many countries around the world has allowed the emergence of an independent media that, spurred by competition, is for the first time keeping a close eye on what their political and economic elites are doing. Hiding corrupt deals is becoming increasingly difficult.

What can be done then? Realistically, we should acknowledge that corruption cannot be eliminated but advances can be made to curb it. The FCPA, according to both government officials and business leaders, has been instrumental in improving the ethical conduct of U.S. companies operating abroad. However, the possibility that far-reaching legislation can be adopted by the most advanced industrial nations is very small. It is instead more realistic to aim for a minimum winning strategy attacking the problem from several fronts.

First of all, there must be political leadership from the major industrial countries to start working on this problem in a concerted manner. The OECD recent decision to devise a treaty to criminalize corruption and eliminate the tax-deductibility of bribes is a first important step in this direction, but it must be followed by facts. What remains to be seen is whether there is a political commitment by the ruling elites of the OECD countries to agree on such a treaty and then enforce its content.

As it was noted elsewhere, "The North is tightening the control on billions of dollars of development aid and technical assistance and is demanding adequate control of whether the money is used for its exact purpose. So it is hard to understand why the same donor countries support their own industries in bribing the same civil servants receiving the donor aid" (TI 1996, 3). As long as developing countries see the leaders of industrial powers preaching one thing and doing just the opposite, it is hard to imagine that anything will ever happen to curtail corruption.

Second, there should also be an effort from the bottom up. NGOs, societal organizations, and interest groups should keep pressure on their leaders to keep the commitment alive and well. This is not easy. Even in Italy, where scandals generated strong public support for anticorruption initiatives, politicians from the right to the left have dragged their feet to promote meaningful change. However, the continued effort of the Italian judiciary in this task has received renewed support from good part of the media and societal groups, which in turn have kept the heat on the political leadership to act.

Third, wherever this is not true, there should be an effort to strengthen or create institutions capable of implementing and enforcing anticorruption measures. The judiciary should be made independent from political interference. Institutions like ombudsmen, anticorruption commissions, and inspectors general should be created, and where they already exist, they should be made as sheltered from political interference (World Bank 1997). Whistleblowers should be encouraged and protected by the promulgation of new statutes. The civil service should be reformed by combining a carrot-and-stick means to prevent corruption. The first goal could be reached by granting higher pay levels and generous benefits as a means to diminish the incentives to enter corrupt deals. The second goal should emphasize effective sanctions. Penalties "should be tied to marginal benefits of the payoff received. The probability of detection and punishment and the level of punishment, given conviction, should increase with the level of peculation" (Rose-Ackerman 1996, 1).

Fourth, we should push whenever possible for public disclosure and free flow of information across countries (Shihata 1996; Rose-Ackerman 1998). Corrupt deals thrive upon secrecy. This entails an effort to make government action accountable to the public as well as to Congress and the judiciary. Politicians should be held accountable for wealth that they accrue while in public office. Moreover, restrictive libel laws and other measures that many governments adopt to intimidate the press should be resisted at all costs. Indeed, the press has played a key role in uncovering corruption scandals, and therefore it is often subject, particularly in developing countries, to heavy pressure to refrain from reporting illicit behavior.

Fifth, it would be desirable that international agencies and multinational corporations develop similar procedures to prevent corruption. This can be achieved through the device of comparable ethic standards as well as sophisticated financial management systems that can make a strong contribution in detecting corrupt practices.

These again are some suggestions, many of which can be regarded as just an exercise in wishful thinking. However, it may not be so in the long run. Only a few years ago, corruption was hardly a topic debated both in political and business circles. Today it makes headlines all over the world. A great deal of this openness is owed to the media and NGOs like TI that have worked hard not only to create public awareness about the issue but also to encourage citizens to make their politicians accountable for their actions at the ballot box if everything else fails. In this realm, we have seen some of the most encouraging progress. Nonetheless, grassroots movements and media campaigns can only go so far, as the Italian experience demonstrates. For this debate to turn into an actual plan of action, international cooperation and the leadership of the United States, the EU, and Japan are essential. Unless the fight against corruption is internationalized, progress will be piecemeal. Whether this leadership will materialize though remains to be seen. In the last few years, people around the world have been increasingly outraged by corruption scandals involving politicians and businessmen alike. As Maingot (1995, 21) aptly put it, "that outrage can be converted into action only by a worldwide, coordinated set of rules and the mechanisms for enforcing them. This means more government involvement...not less."

# Notes

1. *The Wall Street Journal*, July 1, 1997, 1.

2. Data gathered by Whirthlin Worldwide Bank of Boston. Data released on March 17, 1997.

3. 15 U.S.C. §§78dd-2(g)(2)(A-B), 78ff(c)(2)(A-B) (1988).

4. 15 U.S.C. §78dd-1(a) and 78dd-2(a) (1988).

5. 15 U.S.C. §78dd-1(a)(3) (1988).

6. 15 U.S.C. §§78dd-1(b), 2(b) (1988).

7. Office of the Chief Counsel of International Commerce (OCC-IC) of the U.S. Department of Commerce. *The Anti-Corruption Review*, February 21, 1996, 6.

8. Ibid., 7.

9. Ibid.

10. Office of the Chief Counsel of International Commerce (OCC-IC) of the U.S. Department of Commerce. *The Anti-Corruption Review*, February 21, 1996, 7.

11. Quoted from the *Financial Times*, August 7, 1997, 4.

12. *Accountability*, Special Edition, September 1997, 1.

13. *Financial Times*, August 1, 1997, 12.

14. *The Wall Street Journal*, July 23, 1997, A18.

15. Cited in *Poder Ciudadano* (Buenos Aires), May 1994, 8.

16. Data provided by Gallup Argentina.

17. *Financial Times*, October 28, 1997, 7. The *Alianza* comprises the left-wing Frepaso party and the centrist Radical Civic Union.

18. *Wall Street Journal*, November 4, 1997, A22.

19. *Latin American Regional Reports: Brazil*, January 12, 1995, 7.

20. *The New York Times*, May 22, 1997, A3.

21. *The New York Times*, July 1, 1996, A1-7.

22. Ibid., A7.

23. Alfredo Rehren, "Corruption and Local Politics in Chile," *Crime, Law, and Social Change*, vol. 25, no. 4 (1996/1997): 323-334.

24. Interviews with committee members Oscar Godoy and Alejandro Ferreiro. Santiago de Chile, August 1996.

25. *Newsweek*, November 14, 1994, 14 and *The Wall Street Journal*, July 1, 1996, A1.

# References

Blum, Roberto. 1997. "Corruption and Complicity: Mortar of Mexico's Political System?" Paper prepared for the conference The Challenge of Corruption, Colima, Mexico, March 6-9.

Celarier, Michelle. 1997. "Corruption: The Search for the Smoking Gun," *Public Fund Digest*, Vol. VIII, No. 1, 37-45.

Cruver, Donald. 1994. "Complying with the Foreign Corrupt Practices Act: A Guide for U.S. Firms Doing Business in the International Marketplace," Mimeo.

Huntington, Samuel. 1968. *Political Order in Changing Societies*. New Haven, Conn.: Yale University Press.

Jacoby, Neil H. et al. 1977. *Bribery and Extortion in World Business: A Study of Corporate Political Payments Abroad*.

Maingot, Anthony. 1995. "Offshore Secrecy Centers and the Necessary Role of States: Bucking the Trend," *Journal of Interamerican Studies and World Affairs* 37, 4 (Winter):1-24.

Manzetti, Luigi, and Charles Blake. 1996. "Market Reforms and Corruption,' *Review of International Political Economy*, 3: 671-682.

Murphy, Mark J. 1995. "International Bribery: An Example of An Unfair Trade Practice?" *Brooklyn Journal of International Law* 21, 385-391.

Reisman, W. Michael. 1978. *Folded Lies: Bribery, Crusades, and Reforms*. New York: Free Press.

Rhodes, Jill. 1995. "The Foreign Corrupt Practices Act." Mimeo, World Bank, Operation Policy Department.

Rose-Ackerman. 1996. "Redesigning the State to Fight Corruption," *Viewpoint*. Washington, D.C.: World Bank.

Rose-Ackerman. 1998. "Corruption and Development," *Annual World Bank Conference on Development Economics 1997*. Washington, D.C.: World Bank.

Shihata, Ibrahim. 1996. "The Role of the World Bank in Combating Corruption," paper prepared for the conference "After Caracas: Anti-Corruption Strategies in Latin America," Woodrow Wilson International Center, Washington, D.C., September.

Slocum, Deanna. 1996. "International Approaches to Combating Corruption." Mimeo, Southern Methodist University.

*TI Newsletter*, September 1996.

Weyland, Kurt. 1998. "The Politics of Corruption in Latin America," *Journal of Democracy* 9, 2 (April): 108-121.

World Bank. 1997. "Restraining Arbitrary State Action and Corruption," *World Development Report 1997*. Washington, D.C.: World Bank.

# V. Leadership Council for Inter-American Summitry

## *Postscript:* Combating Corruption

*Luigi Manzetti*

In April 1998, the second Summit of the Americas convened in Santiago de Chile. During the Miami Summit of 1994, corruption was one of the most debated issues as it followed the impeachments of Fernando Collor de Mello in Brazil and Carlos Andres Perez in Venezuela. By 1998, there were still plenty of scandals to go around but none could capture the imagination, nor the sense of urgency, of the early 1990s. Yet, 1998 presented an opportunity for policymakers to go beyond the rhetoric of the Miami Summit and translate some "dichos" into "hechos."

Not surprisingly, in Santiago, corruption occupied a relatively minor role in the discussions held by the heads of states and their staffs. This not only resulted from the fact that corruption had somewhat subdued as a "hot" topic but also from the realization that the OAS-sponsored Inter-American Convention Against Corruption, the major outcome of the Miami Summit in this regard, presents a large amount of legal and political problems that need to be addressed in order to make it a meaningful tool in the fight against corruption. In point of fact, the Santiago Plan of Action, while reaffirming its support for the OAS anticorruption convention, explicitly calls for a strategy to quicken its ratification as only half a dozen of the OAS members have so far done so. Moreover, the Plan of Action endorses the drafting of domestic ethic codes for public officials and the organization of information campaigns on government transparency and democratic values as well. By the same token, the Plan of Action calls for the enactment of legislation forcing senior public officials and politicians to disclose their assets and liabilities. On a more practical side, the same document sets up the holding of a symposium, by August 1998, to assess the implementation progress of the convention, as well as the discussion of ways to overcome the socioeconomic and legal obstacles encountered so far.

However, by themselves, these are enormous tasks, and little progress, if any, should be expected in the near future. The organization of a few symposia to monitor the implementation process may result in sensible recommendations but have no bearing on policy action. The problem is that the OAS convention, while being a well-intentioned document, sets up goals that are unlikely to be achieved. The convention contains very little in the way of how to enforce it. Negotiations to make domestic criminal and administrative codes compatible may take decades. Also missing in the Santiago Plan of Action is any timetable for international negotiations to start. Perhaps the core of the problem rests on the simple fact that, as pointed out by Michael J. Hershmann of Decision Strategies/Fairfax International consulting group, there is no driving force behind the implementation of the convention. The campaign financing scandals that have affected the Clinton administration have substantially undermined the U.S. leadership role in this regard, and no other country, including Venezuela that was instrumental in bringing up the corruption issue at the Miami Summit, has the political clout to keep the initial momentum alive.

This is not to say that there is no hope in sight. In the middle 1990s, Poder Ciudadano, an NGO that has been on the forefront in Latin America in creating public awareness on the corruption issue, asked Argentine politicians running for mid-term congressional elections to disclose their assets, as proposed in the Santiago Summit. Quite a few candidates surveyed actually responded and some later used the same survey to defend themselves from charges of illicit enrichment (i.e., Domingo Cavallo did so in February 1988). However, even if similar legislation were to be passed by all OAS member states, income registration of public officials would amount to nothing if governments fail to act when suspicious situations call for an inquiry.

The Santiago Summit makes no headway in clarifying the role of civil society in combating corruption. This is because the OAS convention is a top-down document that perceives corruption strictly as a legal and administrative problem. Yet, whenever corruption scandals were able to produce some change in the status quo, it was primarily through the pressure that the press and citizens' associations were able to mount (i.e., Collor de Mello's impeachment). It would be a welcome change if the OAS convention would institutionalize the input of NGOs like TI in providing practical solutions.

Likewise, the Santiago Summit ignores the role of judicial reform with regard to corruption. The few available examples of successful cases in the fight against corruption point to the pivotal role that a fairly independent judiciary played in bringing up charges against politicians (i.e., United States, Italy, and France). Unless countries in the Western Hemisphere promote substantial reform toward the creation of a skillfully trained, well paid, and politically independent judiciary, it is doubtful that those in charge of upholding the law will go against the politicians from whom they depend.

Given this persisting limitation, some initial progress on the corruption issue is more likely to come from the enforcement of international standards by multilateral agencies. I am referring here to the recent World Bank and IMF good governance requirements for the disbursement of loans. Both the World Bank and the IMF have the power to induce cooperation for non-complying countries by simply refusing to provide financial assistance. If the country in question is unable to secure such assistance from other sources, good governance standards may induce some cooperation. Likewise, were the WTO and OECD able to adopt similar rules, they could turn into international means to penalize guilty parties, similar to what is actually taking place in the WTO when it comes to the resolution of international trade disputes.

The key question is whether politicians in the Americas have the political will to address this problem that touches the vested interests of too many constituencies. Despite much fanfare about campaign reform, the Republican-dominated U.S. Congress was unable to pass any legislation on this campaign reform, the Republican-dominated U.S. Congress was unable to pass any legislation on this issue in 1998 because there was no political will to promote meaningful change. The OAS convention, which aims at much more profound structural and behavioral changes, may never be put into effect if the leaders of the Western Hemisphere are not committed to its spirit.

# V. LEADERSHIP COUNCIL FOR INTER-AMERICAN SUMMITRY

# Combating Illegal Drugs and Related Crimes

*Eduardo A. Gamarra*

*Eduardo A. Gamarra is professor of political science at Florida International University, where he is the Director of the Latin American and Caribbean Center.[1] The author, coauthor, or coeditor of several books, including* Bolivia: Revolution and Reaction *(1998),* Latin American Political Economy in the Age of Neoliberal Reform *(1994), and* Entre la Droga y la Democracia *(1994), and dozens of articles on his native Bolivia and Latin America, Gamarra is also the editor of* Hemisphere.

## 1. INTRODUCTION

Unlike during any previous period, today illegal drugs and related crimes are at the core of inter-American relations. Combating narcotics trafficking is at the center of U.S. relations with nearly every nation of the hemisphere, especially with the Andean region but increasingly with Mexico, the Caribbean, and Central America. The Summit of the Americas process, which was launched by the United States in December 1994 in Miami, Florida, has also adopted drugs and related crimes as a key component of a broader agenda that includes the establishment of a Free Trade Area of the Americas by the year 2005. In April 1998, at the Second Summit of the Americas in Santiago, Chile, narcotics became one of the four significant topics discussed by the leaders of the hemisphere. Moreover, the final document committed the 34 nations attending the Summit to the development and implementation of a multilateral process to combat drugs and related crimes.

This essay evaluates progress on combating drugs and related crimes in the Americas within the goals and benchmarks established by the Summit of the Americas process. It is important to note at the outset that the Summit of the Americas process constitutes a celebration of democracy, and the continuity of democratic rule in the region is clearly threatened by both the proliferation of drug trafficking and unaccountable counternarcotics policies. The first threat is obvious and is the one that most often receives attention. No one questions the fact that large criminal organizations have the capacity to undermine, corrupt, and even take over entire nations in the hemisphere.

Many current efforts, however, lack accountability mechanisms that could insure that the struggle against drug trafficking and related crimes does not undermine democratic rule in the region. Along these lines, the trend toward greater military involvement and the militarization of police structures is an item of critical concern. Democratic governments in the Americas, at this juncture, lack both the tradition and the capacity to effectively oversee the role of these institutions.

In a previous effort, the road from Miami was analyzed in detail, noting progress on a range of issues including the signing of agreements pledging to curb money-laundering, to control precursor traffic, to eradicate crops, and other dimensions of the problem.[2] This essay provides an update, relying primarily on a review of government and multilateral agency documents as well as interviews with policymakers, law enforcement and military officials. In general, the interpretation that follows is based on a combination of official information available from multilateral agencies, U.S. congressional testimony, and U.S. government agencies. The analysis is supplemented with interviews of senior law enforcement officials in several countries including Bolivia, Brazil, Colombia, Dominican Republic, Ecuador, Panama, Peru, United States, and Venezuela.

Overall, the picture that emerges is quite mixed. It is evident that some progress has been achieved, at least in what may be termed the political will of the countries of the region to combat illegal drugs and related crimes. Political will is evidenced by the fact that all countries of the region have become signatories of the 1988 United Nations convention and numerous other agreements that have followed, including those on money-laundering, precursor control, crop eradication, and the like. Political will is also evidenced by concrete figures provided by the U.S. State Department.[3] In some measure, this trend reveals a growing realization by most nations of the hemisphere that drug trafficking and related crimes impact the polities, economies, and societies in a number of complex ways. Few reasons exist to doubt the sincerity of the region to seriously engage in combating illegal drugs and related crimes.

Political will, in this sense, refers to country responses to international pressures brought on by both other governments, especially the United States, and to some extent, multilateral agencies such as the Organization of American States (OAS) and others. A striking conclusion derived from interviews with government and law enforcement officials in the aforementioned countries is that without a degree of international pressure, countries appear less likely to abide by the terms of the international agreements they have signed. Government officials argued that in some instances, international conditions, such as certification, have become important tools that they can use for domestic negotiations.[4] Put another way, without intensive international pressure, the governments of the region may pursue other avenues to combat drugs. This is an important consideration for the U.S. and other nations, especially as they ponder alternatives to the current Washington-based Unilateral Certification Process.

The political will question has to do mainly with the types of domestic constraints that each country faces in attempting to implement the terms of international accords. Hard political domestic facts, such as dealing with opposition parties and coca growers, have an important bearing on the decision-making process of the democratic governments of the region. While this view does not satisfy international actors interested in resolving this significant issue, it is increasingly clear that what governments have in will they lack in capacity. Stated more clearly, in general, governments have found it necessary to sign international agreements pledging cooperation in this area to prevent international isolation and critique. At the same time, however, they have discovered that they lack the capacity (institutional and material) to implement the full range of international commitments they have subscribed. A more cynical description may be the old Spanish saying *obedezco pero no cumplo*.

Moreover, governments have found themselves pledging to carry out unrealistic policies largely to satisfy international pressures to demonstrate degrees of commitment to the War on Drugs. One example is noteworthy. Bolivia's highly praised "Plan por la Dignidad," which pledges to extricate the country from the coca/cocaine circuit in a five-year period, is an extreme example of this situation. To demonstrate that it is not under the total influence of politicians accused of having linkages to narcotics traffickers, the government of retired General Hugo Banzer Suarez has put forth a policy that commits Bolivia to yearly record-breaking quotas of crop eradication and to develop alternatives for displaced coca growers. While the new government may be genuinely committed to this objective, history and Bolivian politics tells a different story. Moreover, despite certification in March 1998, Bolivia will continue to face yearly threats of cutbacks in U.S. assistance.[5] Pledges such as Bolivia's may be simple broken electoral promises, but the record reveals that the international community, especially the U.S., takes these seriously and expects governments to meet their obligations.

A tendency exists to question the motivations and sincerity of the governments of the region.[6] Competing international and domestic pressures account for the apparently contradictory behavior of the governments of the region. At the core, the problem has to do with age-old questions of governability and political stability. And this reality presents the nations of the Americas with a serious dilemma: relentlessly pursuing the implementation of international counterdrug accords could have serious repercussions for the political stability of individual countries. In some places, the very survival of countries and their governments may be threatened. Moreover, enforcing pre- and post-Miami counterdrug accords implies having in place effective enforcement mechanisms. Apart from the long stick of U.S. decertification and threats of economic sanctions, no effective mechanisms exist to coerce the countries of the region to abide by the terms of agreements the governments of the Americas have signed.

In late 1998, the momentum toward a multilateral approach that was to flow from the Santiago Summit appeared to have stalled. Nevertheless, as this essay will show, progress has been achieved at least in terms of the commitments made by the 34 nations of the hemisphere. Given this context, while many agreements have been signed since Miami and Santiago, it is difficult to conclude that *dichos* have become *hechos* on the counternarcotics front. Congressional testimony by U.S. officials reveals a very somber panorama.[7] No matter how much effort, resources, and time are dedicated to this phenomenon, it appears to grow larger and to become increasingly more sophisticated. As things currently stand, an extremely large, sophisticated, and transnational bureaucratic counternarcotics apparatus has been created. Yet, drugs continue to flow, money-laundering increases, and criminal enterprises become more complex.

Finally, one of the principal obstacles to achieving any type of success is the proliferation of corruption. It is increasingly evident that drug-related corruption has penetrated nearly every government in the region and that this affects the degree of trust that the international community has regarding specific officials. In the bizarre world of drugs, it is possible to complain about corruption in governments while also praising the will of the same governments to sign money-laundering legislation and other agreements.[8] This is not necessarily contradictory. Corruption becomes a major problem, however, when the agreements are only *dichos* and the laundering of money and the trafficking of drugs are the only *hechos*.

This essay is divided into three sections and an Annex. Section one provides a brief historical narrative of the Miami process. In the second section an evaluation of the Action Plans of the Miami and Santiago Summits is presented with a focus on the central objective of establishing an alternative multilateral strategy. In the conclusion, some final thoughts on the process after the Santiago Summit are presented. The Annex provides statistics on the counternarcotics battle and summaries of the Summit of the Americas agreements.

## 2.0 FROM MIAMI TO SANTIAGO

Building hemispheric consensus on the need to fight drug trafficking and related crimes has been a long and tedious process. It has involved building domestic coalitions, combating corruption, overcoming bureaucratic politics, establishing international alliances, and consolidating trust among transnational law enforcement and military institutions. Following the Santiago Summit, a hemispheric consensus may have been established, but it is fragile and extremely shallow and threatened by the same forces that have made difficult the establishment of a hemispheric consensus. The process of building this consensus is discussed in this section.

## 2.1 The Road to Miami

At least in terms of establishing a hemispheric counternarcotics front, the road to Miami was not easy.[9] For years, debate and confrontation on the ways to fight drug trafficking prevented the achievement of any viable common strategy. Even the negotiations leading to Miami were difficult and at times tumultuous. December 1994 reflected the best and the worst of times to seek the implementation of a hemispheric counternarcotics agreement.

December 1994 constituted the best of times because the leadership of the nations of the region had reached an apparent consensus regarding the nature of the drug industry and its impact on their respective countries.[10] The basic elements of this *Counternarcotics Consensus* are noteworthy. The democratically elected heads of state of the hemisphere recognized that drugs constituted a serious threat to both democracy and the consolidation of market-oriented reforms. The leadership of the region also noted the transnational characteristics of the drug industry and realized that alone few nations could combat drug trafficking and related crimes. Moreover, in several nations, the power and influence of transnational organized crime were affecting traditional power relations. Leaders were less enthusiastic about the notion that drug-related money-laundering was a threat to the economies of the region. Additionally, rising crime rates and increasing social costs of addiction were no longer limited only to the United States but were showing up throughout the region.

Bolivia, Colombia, and Peru were at the forefront in the negotiations with the United States that led to the aforementioned consensus. Several multilateral meetings, including the 1988 United Nations Convention, the 1989 Cartagena Accord, and the 1992 San Antonio Declaration, helped forge an agreement around the notion that producer, trafficker, and consumer nations alike "shared responsibility" in fighting a common threat.[11] Shared responsibility was defined as a balanced counternarcotics approach that combined interdiction efforts with adequate doses of alternative development and demand reduction strategies.

The overarching goal at the Miami Summit was to encourage the implementation of previous agreements rather than promote new initiatives. The agreements signed prior to Miami were significant because they gave credence to the idea of an emerging "Inter-American Counternarcotics Consensus." To many, the Miami Summit of the Americas represented the culmination of a process that had begun a decade earlier during the most intense and violent days of the drug war. Nevertheless, the U.S. did put forth a new strategy that was discussed by several Latin American and Caribbean countries.

December 1994 also represented the worst of times for the signing of yet another counternarcotics agreement. In the context of severe economic crises and the transition to democracy, the battle against drugs was not a priority item for any country but the United States. Even within the Clinton administration, few of the actual negotiators wanted drugs to take away the spotlight from what was supposed to be a free trade show.

With only a few notable exceptions, the leaders of the Americas were unwilling to include the problem of drugs as a principal element of discussion during the Summit of the Americas. After all, the Summit was supposed to be about trade integration, and they had been invited to discuss trade not to be lectured to about the evils of drug trafficking. Just as there was good will about the establishment of a Free Trade Area of the Americas (FTAA), with the exception of a few countries, there was also resistance to the inclusion of the U.S. drug agenda. Many leaders complained about the insistence by U.S. State Department officials to sign a counternarcotics annex that was allegedly, as one Andean governmental representative described it, "twenty pages longer than the proposed Action Plan for the entire Summit of the Americas."[12]

In general, the mixture of counternarcotics programs and free trade policies was potentially explosive, and the Summit of the Americas could have served as the catalyst. Counternarcotics programs could ostensibly contradict the thrust of market-oriented reforms that call for the dismantling of the state and the relaxation of border controls. Two basic elements characterize counternarcotics programs: They increase the role of the state, especially its security apparatus; and they aim to tighten border controls. Prior to Miami, U.S. policy had taken an interest in conditioning free trade on compliance with counterdrug initiatives. In the context of expanding markets and trade, an argument could be made that counterdrug measures constitute non-tariff barriers.

An argument could also be made that as market-oriented reforms relax border controls and dismantle states, drug trafficking and related crime will increase. Evidence from Eastern Europe and the increasing flow of narcotics through Mexico might be used to suggest that this has occurred. The nature of narcotics trafficking in Latin America today is different from that of the early 1980s before the democratization of the region and before the adoption of neoliberalism. Similarly, democratization in Eastern Europe and Russia has provided a number of avenues and opportunities for the emergence of drug trafficking and other forms of transnational crime.[13]

While U.S. relations with the Americas in terms of commerce and trade issues were at a very good moment in December 1994, discussions over narcotics trafficking and related crimes were not. Beneath the official rhetoric of an Inter-American Counternarcotics Consensus raged charges and countercharges about who was performing well and who was misbehaving. U.S. accusations that Colombia was doing little to combat the Cali cartel and money-laundering abounded. Added to these were laments about President Ernesto Samper's alleged close ties with the Cali cartel. Samper, in turn, sought to demonstrate his innocence and appease the U.S. by launching an offensive against the Cali cartel and proposing a far-reaching anti-money-laundering scheme.

Similarly, Bolivia failed to meet coca leaf eradication targets for a third year in a row, thus violating the terms of a bilateral agreement with the United States. Moreover, the government of Bolivia charged former President Jaime Paz Zamora, —the signatory of the Vienna Convention, the Cartagena Accord, and the San Antonio Declaration— with having received contributions from a trafficker to fund his 1985 and 1989 electoral campaigns.

Paraguay consolidated its position as a crucial transhipment point for traffickers while its government stood by. Peru also failed to meet U.S. eradication and other demands. Panama and Mexico continued to launder drug proceeds, and their governments appeared to do little against these crimes. New trafficking networks evolved linking Bolivia and Peru directly with Mexico. More ominous was the growing internationalization of the drug industry as Latin traffickers became increasingly linked with European, Russian, and Nigerian organized crime.

The controversy over the significance of Mexican cartels raised the level of distrust between Latin America and the United States, as Washington insisted on decertifying Colombia while Mexico was cleared each year despite major signs of drug-related corruption in very high places. Suffice it to say that the U.S. appeared to be committed to its own certification policy only insofar as it did not get in the way of its free trade agenda or other foreign policy priorities. Certification will be discussed in more detail below.

That these trends were evident in Latin America and the Caribbean does not mean that U.S. trends were impressive. While spending more on fighting drugs domestically, economic assistance and counternarcotics assistance for the region declined. Under President Clinton, the focus on interdiction in the Caribbean shifted toward the source countries of the Andes. More significantly, there appeared to be little progress in terms of reducing demand for drugs in the United States.[14]

President Clinton's strategy to increase spending on demand reduction programs came under attack from the Republican-controlled Congress that insisted on interdiction efforts. In 1995, for example, the House of Representatives eliminated all funding for the White House Office of National Drug Control Policy (ONDCP), which is charged with designing and coordinating all counternarcotics efforts. Although the Senate restored funding, these actions sent a clear message that efforts aimed at demand reduction were not politically popular.[15] Faced with severe criticism of his conduct of the War on Drugs, Clinton named General Barry McCaffrey, a highly decorated Vietnam veteran and former Commander-in-Chief of the U.S. Southern Command, to head up the ONDCP. In the next section, McCaffrey's strategy is discussed in more detail.

Thus, a consensus on counternarcotics was fragile and lacked depth. Beyond the hollow declarations of the leadership, there was little action that might have led to more effective regional cooperation. Nevertheless, the Summit of the Americas served to prop up this weak consensus in the midst of the free trade enthusiasm. The issue of illegal drugs was not allowed to take center stage; it was a sideshow buried behind the limelight of the pledge to extend NAFTA to Chile and the promises of a free trade area of the Americas by the year 2005.

## 2.2 The Miami Summit's Counternarcotics Agreements and the Road to Santiago

In Miami, the 34 heads of state agreed on the basic notion that drug trafficking poses a threat to societies, polities, and economies and that all efforts must be underway to prevent its expansion. The leaders called for the establishment of a "new hemispheric strategy for the 21st Century" that would reduce drug use and production and would develop enforcement methods to combat trafficking and money-laundering.[16]

The majority of agreements had to do with combating money-laundering. Apart from the standard statements about criminalizing laundering proceeds, the Summit of the Americas *Plan of Action* called for a working conference to be followed by a ministerial level conference where an Inter-American Convention to combat laundering would be considered. Concern for money-laundering was a rather novel development and was pushed significantly by the Colombians. The Ernesto Samper government correctly noted that its proposal formed the basis of the laundering agreements of the Action Plan.

Two observations are important about the Miami agreements. First, the objective agreed to in the initiative was a hemispheric-wide ratification of regional and/or bilateral agreements of the past decade. In this sense, the *Plan of Action* was an important development, as the agreements signed by the U.S. and the Andean nations achieved a new hemispheric dimension. Second, the initiative integrated diverse views and committed the U.S. and the region to a common set of guidelines. The U.S. appeared committed to the Latin view that demand control is as or more significant than supply reduction. Most other countries appeared wedded to the view that interdiction and law enforcement efforts are essential.

While the Miami *Plan of Action* on drugs appeared to give a sense of regional consensus, very little that occurred thereafter suggested that the leaders of the hemisphere were on the same page. Instead, the entire region appeared headed for a confrontation over the drugs issue, especially after the U.S. announced its decertification decisions in early March 1995, less than three months after the Miami ceremony. Moreover, for at least two years, few inside and outside the law enforcement community appeared to notice any linkage between the Summit of the Americas *Plan of Action* and the fight against narcotics trafficking.[17] When plans were announced for a Second Summit of the Americas to be held in Santiago, Chile, in 1998, few expected that counternarcotics would be a central theme. Surprisingly, when the Santiago agenda was announced, one of the principal items was combating illicit drugs and related crime.

Many reasons account for this transformation. First is the overall negative experience that the entire region had with unilateral certification measures on the part of the United States. Second is the growth of the size and impact of the industry in nearly every country of the hemisphere and the growing realization that multilateral efforts had to be undertaken. Third is the gradual acceptance on the part of the U.S., especially the ONCP under General McCaffrey, that the only way to guarantee collaboration in the Americas in this area is through serious multilateral efforts. Fourth was the momentum generated by the negative reactions to U.S. certification policy. In particular, the anti-certification sentiment contributed to the adoption of the OAS/CICAD's Hemispheric Anti-

Drug Strategy. Finally, although perhaps cynically, the fact that the U.S. Congress refused to grant the Clinton administration fast-track authority to negotiate the expansion of NAFTA to Chile played an important part in the setting of the Santiago agenda. Without any serious offer from the U.S. on extending free trade, education, narcotics, and other items came to dominate the agenda.

As the following section will demonstrate, before Santiago and after Miami, the region as a whole embarked on an ambitious schedule of ministerial summits, conferences, and meetings on the broad areas established by the First Summit. The most noteworthy accomplishment was the ratification of the OAS/CICAD-guided Hemispheric Anti-Drug Strategy in 1997, which for most of the leaders of the region demonstrated their will and commitment to combat narcotics trafficking and related crimes.[18]

The Santiago *Plan of Action* built on these objectives; however, as can be seen in Figure 6, the Plan retains the flowery language of all Summit documents and provides no real guidelines for implementation. Nevertheless, the region as whole was, at a minimum, very active on the counternarcotics front. Progress toward fulfilling the agenda, however, does not mean the resolution of the problems associated with narcotics trafficking. It simply signifies that, at least formally, the region complied with most of the pledges to host meetings, develop conventions, and sign more agreements.

The one clear advancement from Miami was a proposal to "develop, within the framework of the Inter-American Drug Abuse Control Commission (CICAD-OAS), a *singular and objective* process of multilateral governmental evaluation to monitor the progress of their individual and collective efforts in the Hemisphere and of all the countries participating in the Summit, in dealing with the diverse manifestations of the problem." As shall also be seen below, because it is intended to eventually replace the annual U.S. certification process, this objective became the single most important and controversial part of the entire Santiago *Plan of Action*.

## 2.3 Ratification of 1988 United Nations Convention: A Hidden U.S. Certification Agenda?

To understand the Santiago *Plan of Action*'s call for a multilateral strategy, it is important to first review the situation generated in the Americas by the unilateral U.S. decision to impose annual certifications on several nations of the region. A first step to understand certification is to review one of the principal objectives of the Miami *Plan of Action*: the ratification of the 1988 United Nations Convention.

Since December 1994, every country of the Americas has ratified or acceded to the Convention. Although it is not a party to the Summit of the Americas process, Cuba ratified the Convention in June 1996.[19] In ratifying the Convention, the leaders of the Americas have agreed to carry out some rather bold steps towards combating drug trafficking. As Table 5 shows, these include several steps that were reiterated by the agreements signed in Miami and Santiago. Ratification of the UN Convention is one thing; carrying out the letter of the agreement has proven to be quite another. The Convention did not establish any firm mechanisms for the enforcement of each article. In a vague way, the UN is the only organization that can call into question a country's non-compliance with the terms of the Convention.

Any discussion of the UN Convention and its application in the Americas must include some reference to the annual U.S. certification process, which since 1986 has filled the enforcement gap of its provisions. Each year following a congressional requirement, the U.S. president certifies —with the recommendation of the Department of State— that the drug producing or transit countries of the Americas "have cooperated fully with the United States." Following Vienna, the U.S. Congress added "or taken adequate steps on their own, to achieve full compliance with the goals of the 1988 United Nations Convention Against Illicit Traffic in Narcotics Drugs and Psychotropic Substances."[20] As Elizabeth Joyce notes, the certification process has "achieved a weight in bilateral relations that placed it firmly at the heart of U.S. foreign drug policy."[21] In this sense, all other counternarcotics processes, especially the 1994 *Plan of Action,* have been secondary foreign policy instruments in the Americas. At least for the countries that yearly await the sentence (Bolivia, Belize, Colombia, Jamaica, Paraguay, Peru, Mexico), certification has determined the nature and direction of their relations with the United States.[22]

U.S. decertification policy has been a source of great controversy in the Americas; many law enforcement officials interviewed for this project believe Washington assigned itself the role of sole judge and enforcer of the 1988 Convention.[23] In their view, it is one thing to certify compliance with U.S. efforts; it is quite another to become the sole enforcer of a UN Convention. Much confusion exists over just exactly what "decertification" means for a country. Under the terms of the law, a decertified country may become ineligible for most U.S. economic

# V. Leadership Council for Inter-American Summitry

## Combating Illegal Drugs and Related Crimes

assistance, and it could lead to a U.S. boycott on loans from the International Monetary Fund (IMF), the World Bank, and the Inter-American Development Bank (IDB).[24] Decertification, however, does not signify the suspension of counternarcotics or humanitarian assistance to the affected country.

While the U.S. pushed a counternarcotics drug agenda in Miami, the State Department's Office of International Narcotics and Law Enforcement Affairs (INL) proceeded with harsh recommendations about its South American partners. In March 1995, it called for a "national interest waiver" certification for Bolivia, Colombia, Peru, and Paraguay. Then, it secretly enforced an ultimatum on Bolivia that forced the Sanchez de Lozada government to comply with the terms of a bilateral agreement before June 30, 1995, or face a suspension of U.S. assistance.[25] In March 1996, and again in March 1997, Colombia was decertified but only some elements of a boycott on loans to that country were imposed.

The February 1998 decisions again showed the complexity and the contradictions of certification. Colombia and Paraguay were granted a national interest waiver certification, while Bolivia, Peru, and Mexico sailed through. The explanations about each case are noteworthy. Secretary of State Albright argued, for example, that Colombia was granted the national interest waiver to allow the country to hold congressional and national elections. Every year, the discussions surrounding the Mexican case have revealed the degree to which other non-objective criteria determine which country is fully certified.[26] As General Barry McCaffrey described it, by 1997, certification had become a process of "creative hypocrisy."[27]

The arrival of General Barry McCaffrey to the Office of National Drug Control Policy (ONDCP) brought with it an important process of rethinking the certification process. Nevertheless, McCaffrey and others in the executive branch charged with carrying out counternarcotics policy realize that certification is a congressional law and that only an act of Congress can eliminate its provisions. Moreover, while a few members have expressed their disagreement with the process, it is unlikely that it will be repealed in the near future. For many in Congress, certification has in fact worked by forcing countries in the region to carry out policies they might not have if this instrument were not available. The U.S. Congress has also not shown too much interest in the Summit of the Americas process and has been reticent to endorse any efforts to multilateralize counternarcotics efforts.

General McCaffrey along with the INL put forth an initiative entitled "Enhancing Multilateral Drug Control Efforts." McCaffrey discussed this proposal with most countries in the hemisphere and allowed the proposal to be examined in the CICAD's annual meeting held in Lima, Peru, in November 1997. The Summit Implementation Review Group (SIRG) which met in December 1997 and again in March 1998 also examined the proposal. The Santiago *Declaration* and any subsequent multilateral agreement will carry the imprint of McCaffrey's rethinking of the certification process.

The key idea behind McCaffrey's proposal was to grant the CICAD broad powers to become a hemispheric drug conscience. Under the terms of the proposal, the CICAD would convoke a group of experts to serve on a type of certification board, evaluating country national plans and handing down recommendations. Unlike certification, however, it would not have the power to impose sanctions or suspend assistance.

As noted earlier, the Santiago *Plan of Action* calls for the development of a singular and objective process of multilateral evaluation. But achieving this goal may prove more elusive than any hemispheric leader expected in Santiago. Many reasons exist to be skeptical of not only the multilateral nature of this initiative but also of the ability of the region to agree on the elements that would define a singular and objective process. First, the OAS/CICAD has never been adequately funded. Past experience shows that without larger doses of U.S. funding, this institution will be unable to carry out its new mission. It is even more unlikely that any Latin American or Caribbean nation will increase its own share of funding to satisfy CICAD's new needs. Second, although theoretically a panel of independent experts is to be in charge of handing down recommendations, it is unlikely that any single nation will be severely admonished. It is important to recall that the OAS is above all a political body that may not have the wherewithal to condemn any single member.

Third, the most important reason to be skeptical of the proposed Counternarcotics Alliance is domestic opposition within the U.S. When the heads of state met in Santiago, Chile, in April 1998, the stage was set for the launching of a multilateral effort. Hemispheric leaders, however, were rudely awakened in Santiago by the distribution of a republican view on the matter. Noting the Summit's goal to empower the OAS to monitor and assess drug policies of the hemisphere, Representatives Ben Gilman (R-NY) and J. Dennis Hasten (R-IL) argued that

Under this scenario, the OAS could also become yet another forum for drug producing and transiting nations to join those who blame the problem solely on U.S. demand, ignoring the effect that massive amounts of cheap, pure drugs from their own countries have on that very same demand.

At the same time, President Clinton would be freed from the annual certification process and the "painful" decisions it requires. Many in Congress are committed to prevent that from happening. The [Counternarcotics] alliance while welcome could not become a substitute for certification....

For our friends here in the Americas and those in Washington who think that the U.S. annual certification process is headed for the dustbin of history, we regret to disappoint them.[28]

In summary, even under the best of circumstances, if the Counternarcotics Alliance directed by the OAS works, it will not replace the annual certification process. Instead, the nations of hemisphere will continue to note an obvious and apparent contradiction in U.S. hemispheric counternarcotics policy. On the one hand, it will participate in a diplomatic evaluation exercise, and on the other, it will continue to enforce a law of the U.S. Congress that seeks to punish and embarrass non-complying nations.

## 2.4 Demand Reduction

In Santiago, nearly one-third of the Action Plan dedicated to narcotics is directed at demand reduction programs. This is remarkable since until recently, the nations of the Americas involved in producing and trafficking drugs did not recognize that drug use was a problem that had to be dealt with on a multilateral basis. Even after the signing of the UN Convention, Cartagena, and San Antonio, there was little recognition of this problem. Recent figures reveal alarming growth rates in drug use in trafficking nations (Brazil, Colombia, and Panama, especially) and significant levels in producing countries (Bolivia and Peru). The reality is that countries involved in the production or trafficking will inevitably face a consumption problem. At the same time, however, the available figures on drug abuse are new and unreliable. Since 1994, U.S. officials have mentioned specifically the proliferation of drug consumption in the Americas. These claims have been interpreted by many as a way to avoid recognizing its own failure at reducing drug consumption in the U.S. Nevertheless, some success has been achieved as nations gradually begin to face severe drug addiction problems.[29]

It is not surprising, therefore, that some progress has been made on developing programs to prevent and reduce the demand for illicit drugs. The major problem throughout the region, however, is the lack of adequate funding for these programs. Government funds are small or non-existent in the majority of countries in Latin America and the Caribbean. U.S. assistance has been important in smaller nations, but these funds appear to be drying up in the context of budget reductions.

Non-governmental institutions represent the largest growth sector in the development of prevention and reduction programs. Still their role is limited. Significantly, the Inter-American Development Bank (IDB) and the United Nations Drug Control Program (UNDCP) have been active in funding some programs in response to requests from Bolivia, Colombia, and Peru. The Organization of American States (OAS) through its CICAD has also been involved in promoting these initiatives.

The U.S. continues to be the world's largest consumer market of drugs. Statistics related to drug use in the U.S. are illustrative of the problem: Approximately 72 million Americans have experimented with illegal drugs; in 1993, Americans spent an estimated $49 billion on illegal drugs; the rate of drug use among youth has climbed; past month use of all drugs among youth aged 12 to 17 increased by 50 percent between 1992 and 1994; among youth aged 12 to 17, the use of marijuana almost doubled between 1992 and 1994; one out of every four drug users is a hardcore abuser; hardcore abusers consume the majority of the illegal drugs and commit a disproportionate number of drug-related crimes; in the 1990s, there have been 100,000 drug-related deaths in the United States; drug-related hospital emergencies are at record levels, over 500,000 annually; each year over one million persons are arrested on drug-related charges.[30]

The U.S. government claims some success in reducing demand. The ONDCP states that since 1985 illegal users have declined from 22.3 to 12.2 million; new cocaine users have declined from 1.5 million in 1980 to .5 million in 1992; between 1975 and 1992, new heroin users have dropped by 25 percent; drug use among U.S. workers decreased from 19 percent in 1979 to 8.1 percent in 1993; and three out of four companies with more than 250 employees have formal antidrug programs in place.

These figures may not reflect the efforts that have been underway since December 1994 to reduce demand in the United States. But they could reflect that not enough has been done, as some Latin Americans have charged. Or perhaps they reflect that the current demand reduction programs are overrated and have performed poorly. The U.S. spends approximately $2 billion on prevention programs, although the effectiveness of many of the programs has not been carefully evaluated. Some programs, such as the DARE school program, have been shown to have little or no impact on demand reduction. Funding for treatment programs, on the other hand, is quite scarce. At the same time, they have little public support and are unlikely to be popular for funding by the U.S. Congress.[31]

While the U.S. continues to be the principal market, it is incorrect to assume that the drug abuse problem is not widespread in the Americas and elsewhere in the world. The United Nations Drug Control Program calculates that 3.4 to 4.1 percent of the world's population is involved in illicit drug consumption; about 140 million consume marijuana; 13 million, cocaine; and over 8 million, heroin. Moreover, there has been significant increase in the use of synthetic amphetamine-type stimulants. Approximately 30 million people consume ATS in the world. The perception that drug abuse is only a developed nation phenomenon is quickly giving way to more informed views on the impact of drugs throughout the developing world.

Following the mandate of the Antidrug Strategy in the Hemisphere, the OAS/CICAD established a Group of Experts on Demand Reduction with the mandate of developing a line of action to reduce drug abuse in the Americas. The Group of Experts has been responsible for developing a strategic plan for the hemisphere and for each country to include prevention, treatment, re-incorporation into society, and program development. As part of a recent U.S. strategy, the State Department has released information on drug consumption patterns in the Americas. In its 1997 report, the INL notes that Colombians consume about two metric tons of cocaine per year.

> New users are found in the areas with the highest population density and where economic development is greater. These include the coffee-producing regions and the areas surrounding large cities such as Bogota, Medellin, and Cali. The Colombian government's priority target groups for prevention programs on the use of psychoactive substances include males ages 12–17 who are studying and whose level of education is high school.[32]

Citing the U.S./Mexico Bi-National Drug Threat Assessment, General Barry McCaffrey pointed out recent trends in Mexico before a Senate committee.

> [Mexico's] 1993 Second National Survey of Addictions (ENA) reported that 3.9 percent (1.6M people) of the 12-65-year-old urban population reported having used an illegal drug. The 1993 Northern Border Survey found that overall consumption rates in the four main cities (Matamoros, Monterrey, Ciudad Juarez, and Tijuana) were significantly higher (5.3 percent) than the national average. ENA also reported that cocaine had recently gained importance in the epidemiological scenario of drug use in the country. National surveys undertaken among the student population also showed a significant increase, rising from 0.5 percent in 1976 to 0.83 percent in 1991.

In summary, while some progress has been achieved on the establishment of demand reduction programs, the results are mixed in the U.S. If the CICAD's Group of Experts can complete its diagnosis, a clear sense will exist of the state of drug abuse in the hemisphere. U.S. efforts to get an accurate measure of the state of drug abuse in the hemisphere will help. In FY 1999's drug control budget, approximately $7.2 million are included for international demand-reduction efforts. This budget will fund among other initiatives the expansion of multilateral cooperation in demand reduction through participation in summits on drug abuse issues in Central and South America and through collaboration with CARICOM nations, OAS/CICAD, UNDCP, and the European Commission. These summits provide opportunities to strengthen the gathering, analysis, and dissemination of demand reduction information, such as results of needs assessments, identification of at-risk populations, obstacles to prevention and treatment, and emerging regional trends in drug abuse.

## 2.5 Crop Reduction

New crop reduction programs in the Americas have not been designed or implemented. For the better part of the past three decades, crop substitution programs have been essentially the same. There have been a few significant modifications including the alternative development concept that now characterizes all debate on this issue. The main point of contention has been whether crop-producing nations could implement those programs already on the books. The record on established crop reduction programs is not good.

Crop reduction programs have achieved few significant gains in the last two years. Overall, crops have increased and governments have been incapable of making any real progress on reducing the availability of crops. Progress in this area continues to be determined by the specific circumstances of crop cultivation in each country. In Bolivia, Colombia, and Peru, crop reduction carries with it broader and very complex situations for national leaders. Most often it involves difficult negotiations with the cultivators and, in some instances, confrontation with traffickers.

The situation with crop cultivation in the Americas in 1997 is described in the tables provided in the Annex. The INCSR summary provides a detailed account of the mixed record of crop reduction in the past decade and since the Summit of the Americas. In Colombia and Mexico, estimates of poppy cultivation have decreased and, after an eradication campaign in the early 1990s, Guatemalan production has not returned. The situation with coca, however, is different. A new cultivation record of 214,800 hectares under cultivation was established in 1995. Colombia experienced a noticeable increase and has relegated Bolivia to second place. Yet Colombia eradicated nearly 65,000 hectares in 1998. In 1998, Bolivia eradicated a record 12,000 hectares of coca, leaving over 30,000 hectares under cultivation.

One of the key issues in reducing crop cultivation concerns the method. Involuntary eradication programs have generated a tension with coca growers. In Bolivia, for example, these tensions have repeatedly escalated into violent confrontations that have left some coca growers dead. In the past two years, the Bolivian government has initiated forceful eradication procedures and has for the first time admitted that the coca grown in the Chapare region is exclusively cultivated to service the narcotics industry. The resolve to carry out involuntary (forceful) eradication will inevitably pit government forces against growers and lead to human rights violations and government charges that peasants are knowledgeably linked to the narcotics industry.[33]

Unlike Bolivia and Peru, Colombia has employed aerial spraying to reduce crops and has entered into direct confrontation with coca growers. But Colombia had its own set of problems as coca growers, guerrillas, and paramilitary groups have violently resisted crop reduction programs. The difficulties associated with crop reduction programs were highlighted in August 1996 in the Putumayo region of Colombia where cultivators and eradicators clashed violently leaving several dead and wounded and forcing the government to rethink its strategy of forced eradication and aerial spraying. The situation in 1998 is even more complex as the new government of President Andrés Pastrana attempted to negotiate with guerrillas in the coca growing regions of the Guaviare and Caquetá regions.

Crop eradication cannot be discussed without mentioning its impact on thousands of individuals who make a living from the cultivation of coca in particular. Both the Miami and Santiago Plans of Action called on leaders to seek national and international support for "development programs that create viable economic alternatives to drug production." Alternative development programs have been around for nearly a decade. In general, they have received a great deal of rhetorical support both nationally and internationally.

Beyond positive declarations in support of alternative development, the same basic set of problems prevails. First, few funds are available for alternative development despite the promise of those few programs that functioned in the Bolivian Chapare. U.S. government funds for alternative development have decreased (although Peru received $44 million in 1996), and these have not been replaced by funds from other donors. The UNDCP has provided some funding but not enough to make any real difference. In March 1996 at the Rio Group meeting held in Cochabamba, Bolivia, leaders of the European Union pledged to provide funding for alternative development programs in coca growing areas. Some hope exists that funding levels will increase and alternative development programs will be in place. U.S. government officials believe that the Summit Plan of Action broke new ground by calling on international financial institutions and multilateral development banks to provide new funds for alternative development. They also admit, however, that convincing these institutions has been a slow process. Only the Interamerican Development Bank (IDB) has agreed to include counternarcotics objectives in its programs for Bolivia, Peru, and Colombia.[34] More recently, U.S. government officials claimed that the World Bank had been drafted to join in this effort.[35] As of this writing, however, the World Bank had no serious counterdrug or crop reduction effort underway.

Second, a discussion of alternative development strategies is warranted that extends beyond the funding dimension. Success has been elusive because markets are not available for alternative products. Moreover, technical support is rarely available to peasants who wish to switch to legal crops. Finally, the fact remains that no other crop has been identified that can provide the income derived from coca.

The Clinton administration has made efforts to link alternative development with crop reduction programs and to recognize its importance to the overall U.S. counternarcotics strategy. These programs, however, have been assailed in the U.S. Congress, and by some specialists, as ineffective and as a complete waste of scarce resources that could be used more effectively to pursue interdiction.[36] The fact remains that while alternative development programs have not had the overnight success some may expect, it is still the only scheme around to deal with the hundreds of thousands of Andean coca and poppy seed growers. It is also evident that alternative development's chances of success have been minimized by the absence of technical assistance, the development of markets for products, and the uneven flow of funds.

Defending alternative development does not mean that enforcement efforts should be forgotten or vice versa. The U.S. government's position is that the Summit of the Americas Plan of Action provides a way to integrate alternative development programs with law enforcement strategies.[37] A more accurate characterization would be to state that the Summit of the Americas process calls for the development of an integrated policy that combines law enforcement with alternative development but does not provide the way.

A final observation on alternative development is that for nearly two decades the focus on crop substitution in coca growing areas has negated a broader approach. If anything has been learned over the last few years, it is that alternative development programs have indeed served to elevate the standard of living of farmers in coca growing regions. They have been the net beneficiaries of better roads, improved infrastructure, electricity, and the like, while other rural areas, which expel population to coca growing areas, have regressed. Peru has been at the forefront in recent years in attempting alternative development strategies in population expelling zones in an attempt to draw migrant labor back to their home areas. These attempts hark back to integrated rural development strategies that paradoxically may be do a better job than the current policies in coca growing areas.

## 3.0 CONCLUSION

Success in the realm of fighting drug trafficking and related crimes has been defined primarily as the ratification of the Plan of Action of Miami and Santiago. Defined in such a manner, the issue is not whether the region is actually making any significant inroads into fighting drugs but the degree to which the leadership of the Americas has committed to combating drugs. The Santiago Summit reflected the degree to which the leaders of the Americas have accepted the language and the extent to which they have agreed to sign agreements in this area. At least in the view of the United States, this is significant progress, as the leadership of the region is now utilizing the same language and is supporting many initiatives that were previously contested as U.S. imposed. This commitment at the head of state level is important, but at least two observations made in the introduction must be reiterated.

First, the willingness on the part of governments of the Americas to sign pledges and international agreements that were not readily subscribed prior to December 1994 reflects some degree of commitment on the part of Latin American and Caribbean regions to combat drug trafficking and related crimes. Until recently, Latin American nations were in a state of denial, failing to recognize the threat drug trafficking posed. As violence escalated, corruption became pervasive, mass addiction became problematic, and transnational criminal organization threatened national sovereignty, the countries of the hemisphere opted to support a position the U.S. had held for many years.[38] It also demonstrates U.S. leverage.

Most of the items in the Miami and Santiago Plans of Action and in subsequent meetings have been part of the U.S. counternarcotics agenda for a long time. It is not surprising that most policies in place in drug producing and trafficking countries are also U.S. inspired, if not designed. Beyond the calls for a multilateral approach and the Latin American rhetoric of achieving a legitimate alternative, the Santiago Plan of Action represents the triumph of U.S. counternarcotics initiatives. A careful survey of the agreements reveal that, in some ways, the multilateral approach may simply have multilateralized a unilateral (U.S.-designed) strategy. Cloaked in the language of multilateralism, it may indeed be easier for the nations of the hemisphere to sell interdiction and crop reduction programs domestically.

Second, the last statement raises the issue of the political will and the capacity to pursue counternarcotics arrangements. The fact that they have signed numerous agreements, some of which are not necessarily in their best domestic interests, reveals political will. Political capacity entails having the institutional wherewithal to implement international agreements. Most drug producing and trafficking nations lack the capacity to implement agreements such as the Miami or Santiago Action Plans because they also suffer from tremendous institutional weakness and few resources.[39] Nevertheless, as former Bolivian President Gonzalo Sánchez de Lozada noted, proportionally, even Bolivia spends more of its resources combating drugs than the U.S.[40] The same situation applies in nearly every country of the region that is afflicted by the problem.

It is clear that one of the main issues is the lack of funds and other resources to implement multilateral strategies. At least this is the principal complaint of nearly every law enforcement official interviewed for this project. The Santiago Action Plan provides no resources, or anything else, to support institutional strengthening. The bulk of institutional strengthening efforts remain at the national and bilateral level. Nearly all counternarcotics efforts in the hemisphere are also at these levels. As long as this is the case, few reasons exist to assume that in the short to medium term, multilateral efforts will displace bilateral and national strategies.

This raises questions regarding the relevance of summits. It is important to note that a generalized perception among law enforcement officials was that these gatherings are of little importance and that grand declarations do little to assist in the day-to-day battle against large trafficking organizations. In this sense, summits only serve heads of state in their quest to obtain international credibility. The Santiago Action Plan and the calls for a multilateral approach are seen as rhetorical and symbolic statements that will have only a marginal impact on the course of the drug war.

At the same time, the region as a whole may be suffering from summit burnout. In addition to the Summit of the Americas process, other summit processes have added to the generalized view that these gatherings provide little beyond rhetorical declarations. Even the much anticipated UN General Assembly Special Session on the World Drug Problem held in June 1998 generated little enthusiasm. Consider the following declaration emanating from the Special Session.

> [the Session is the first time] national leaders from throughout the world gathered together to agree to the first truly global strategy to control drugs; the first international agreement on demand reduction; and the goal of substantially reducing the illicit cultivation of opium, coca, and other narcotic crops in the next 10 years. They also agreed to find solutions to the problems posed by amphetamines and stimulants and to identify specific timetables to strengthen and harmonize member states' laws on money-laundering, extradition of drug traffickers, and the sharing of information on drug cartels.

Declarations such as these are undoubtedly important, but their unachievable objectives render them to the long heap of discarded and hollow rhetorical statements made by heads of state and other officials at gatherings on the drug problem over the course of the last two decades. This is what troubles those who are at the operational level.

Notwithstanding this sentiment and the overwhelming significance of bilateral and national approaches, it is important to analyze the capacity of the multilateral institutions charged with implementing the Santiago counterdrugs agreements. It has become quite popular to discredit the OAS and its CICAD unit, the agencies that have the mandate to pursue the most significant dimensions of the narcotics dimension of the Santiago Action Plan. Many of the criticisms are accurate: lack of funds and specialized personnel in this area, the politicization of the institution, and the weak support the institution receives from the largest countries in the hemisphere. Some reasons exist to be optimistic about the positive role that CICAD in particular can play in promoting the hemispheric strategy and the development of a multilateral approach. With few exceptions, CICAD is perceived as impartial and, as such, has become an important balancing force to the overwhelming U.S. presence in this area. Law enforcement officials interviewed for this project ratify the view that the OAS/CICAD has provided an important balancing role that could foster the development of a significant multilateral approach.

The problem, however, has to do mainly with the declining momentum of this specific area of the Summit of the Americas process. Since Santiago, the OAS/CICAD has made the effort to develop and specify the broad mandate of the Action Plan. Several meetings have been held since Santiago with this objective in mind. Interviews with participants in the process, however, reveal that the momentum has slowed down and that the prospects for a multilateral strategy are not good.

Finally, it is important to discuss a few of the major concerns about the future of the battle against drugs in the

Americas expressed by those in the field. Their concerns are primarily operational, relating more to questions such as better international and national coordination of specific operations. Their concerns focus on the significance of better training and equipment. And their worries focus on specific issues such as sharing of information, which is often the key problem in any law enforcement effort across borders and in which multiple nation institutions participate. Numerous efforts are underway to build the confidence levels of law enforcement institutions in the region so that coordination of efforts can be improved.[41]

Nevertheless, while efforts at the operational level boost confidence and summits have led to greater political will, the situation in the region leaves much room for improvement. At one level, suspicion of the U.S. continues. In the past year alone, for example, efforts to build a Multilateral Counternarcotics Center failed as U.S. and Panamanian officials could not agree on the terms of any such arrangement. This failure has sent the U.S. on a difficult task of negotiating with several nations of the region landing rights for U.S. airplanes involved in counterdrug missions. Already the revelation of such negotiations has prompted cries of U.S. expansionism and base building.

At the same time, despite the rhetoric of collaboration, deep suspicion prevails among countries of the region. Telling instances, such as the absence of any significant collaboration in counterdrug matters between rival countries (Bolivia-Chile, Peru–Ecuador, Colombia-Venezuela), suggest that summits could do more. Consider the case of Venezuela, which refuses to allow U.S. planes pursuing suspect small engine planes to enter Venezuelan airspace as long as a Colombian national is a rider, or the absence of non-U.S. mediated direct lines of communication between Bolivian and Peruvian officials in counterdrug missions, or the refusal on the part of U.S. agencies, such as DEA, to share information with countries of the region for fear of compromising operations. This is where and how the drug war is being fought. Until summits can figure a way to deal with such issues, their credibility and relevance will remain in question.

# Notes

1. Joseph Rogers, Diego Ferreyra, Manuel Hidalgo, and Robert Simpson at the Latin American and Caribbean Center at Florida International University provided research assistance.

2. Eduardo A. Gamarra, *Implementing the Summit of the Americas: Combating Illegal Drugs and Related Crimes* (North South Center, 1996).

3. On March 12, 1997, in testimony before the Subcommittee on the Western Hemisphere, Peace Corps, Narcotics, and Terrorism of the Senate Foreign Relations Committee, Robert Gelbard, former Assistant Secretary for International Narcotics and Law Enforcement Affairs noted that Mexico, Colombia, Venezuela, Ecuador, and Peru "are jailing more notorious criminals than ever. Coca production in Peru has been reduced by 18%, the lowest in 10 years. New extradition treaties with Bolivia, France, Poland, Cypress, and Spain signal new willingness to cooperate with the U.S...."

4. Interviews with former President Gonzalo Sánchez de Lozada of Bolivia (July 1997) and President Leonel Fernández, Dominican Republic (September 1997).

5. Statement of Jane Becker, Acting Assistant Secretary of State, Office of International Narcotics and Law Enforcement Affairs, July 16, 1997. See República de Bolivia, *!Por la Dignidad! Estrategia Boliviana de la Lucha Contra el Narcotráfico: 1998-2002*.

6. Interviews with presidential candidate Alfonso Valdivieso (Bogotá, June 1997) and Vice President Jorge Quiroga (La Paz, July 1997) revealed the frustration felt by policymakers whose commitment to counternarcotics policies are constantly questioned by international actors.

7. See, for example, statement by Donnie Marshall, Chief of Operations, Drug Enforcement Administration, before the Subcommittee on National Security, International Affairs, and Criminal Justice, July 9, 1997, on Cooperative Efforts of the Colombian National Police and Military in Anti-Narcotic Efforts, and Current Initiatives DEA has in Colombia; statement by Thomas A. Constantine, Administrator, Drug Enforcement Administration, before the House Judiciary Committee, April 3, 1997, regarding Puerto Rico and Law Enforcement Efforts in the Caribbean Region; statement by Thomas A. Constantine, Administrator, Drug Enforcement Administration, before the Senate Foreign Relations Committee, March 12, 1997, on Mexico and the Southwest Border Initiative; and statement by James Milford, Drug Enforcement Administration, before the Subcommittee on the Western Hemisphere of the House International Relations Committee, July 16, 1997. These testimonies reveal a somber view of the current narcotics situation in the hemisphere. Milford noted, for example, that Mexican and Colombian traffickers are more resourceful, wealthy, and powerful than any law enforcement has encountered in the past.

8. See Stanley Meisler and Faye Fiore, "White House Report Cites Corruption but Notes New Laws Against Moneylaundering," *Los Angeles Times*, September 16, 1997.

9. For an overview of the road to Miami, consult William O. Walker III, *Drugs in the Western Hemisphere: An Odyssey of Cultures in Conflict*, (Wilmington: Jaguar Books, Scholarly Resources, Inc. 1996) and Bruce Bagley and William O. Walker, eds., *Drug Trafficking in the Americas* (Coral Gables, Fla.: North-South Center, 1994).

10. This was the official view of the majority of the heads of state who were in Miami for the Summit. It was also the U.S. official view as is evidenced in several government documents. The elements of the consensus are not in doubt; what is questionable is the level of capacity to carry out the consensus in each nation.

11. For a discussion of these, see Eduardo A. Gamarra, *Entre la droga y la Democracia* (La Paz: ILDIS, 1994).

12. Interview with Colombian law enforcement official, December 9, 1994, Miami, Fla. U.S. officials note, however, that this characterization was inaccurate. The counternarcotics annex, which became the basis for the current OAS/CICAD Counternarcotics Strategy for the 21st Century, was less than 15 pages. Moreover, U.S. officials note that while the annex was a U.S. initiative, approximately seven countries in the region had some input into the final version. No agreement was reached on the document, and it was not discussed at the Summit in Miami. After a very intense but unproductive process of revisions following the Miami meeting, the U.S. State Department's INL turned the document over to the OAS/CICAD. This document is discussed later.

13. This argument was used by opponents of the NAFTA agreement. While more drugs are arriving in the U.S. from Mexico since the approval of the agreement, there is no data to support the argument that NAFTA has led to greater narcotics movements across the border.

14. Some debate exists on this front, but overall there is agreement that casual use has declined in the U.S. while addiction rates have reached the highest in history. Consult Drug Strategies, *Keeping Score: What We Are Getting for Our Federal Drug Control Dollars 1995* (Washington, 1995). In any event, the point is that Latin Americans still perceive that not enough is being done in the U.S. to prevent drug consumption.

15. This is not to say that the Republican Congress was willing to spend more money on interdiction programs. Instead, the Clinton counternarcotics strategy faced cuts in 1995 and threatened cuts in 1996. Especially unpopular with the Republican Congress are crop eradication and substitution programs, otherwise known as alternative development.

16. Robin Rosenberg and Steve Stein, eds., 1995, *Advancing the Miami Process: Civil Society and the Summit of the Americas* (Coral Gables, Fla.: North-South Center Press at the University of Miami), 15.

17. Interviews with law enforcement officials from throughout the hemisphere confirmed the almost complete lack of

knowledge of the Miami accords and/or their significance. This raises an important issue: Law enforcement officials who are faced with the daily task of combating drug trafficking give little significance to agreements signed by heads of state or other high-ranking officials. In their view, most are photo opportunities that have little impact on how the war on drugs is fought in the field.

18. A summary of the Hemispheric Strategy is provided in the Annex.

19. Speculation about Cuba's role in the narcotics trade has increased in the last few years. In several interviews with the author, DEA, Coast Guard, and U.S. law enforcement officials point to numerous instances of cooperation by Cuban authorities. General Charles Wilhelm, the Commander-in-Chief of the U.S. Southern Command told *The Miami Herald*'s Andres Oppenheimer that there was no evidence linking the Cuban government to narcotics trafficking and reiterated that authorities there cooperate with U.S. law enforcement efforts. See also Eduardo A. Gamarra and Joseph Rogers, "Perverse Integration in the Caribbean: Cuba, the Dominican Republic and Haiti," in Wilfredo Lozano ed.

20. The U.S. Congress requires certification by the president based on the UN Convention criteria. Many members of the U.S. Congress believe that Latin America is not serious about fighting drugs and are extremely reluctant to provide more funding for any counternarcotics efforts. For a summary of the 1996 certification process, consult Bureau for International Narcotics and Law Enforcement Matters, *International Narcotics Strategy Report*, March 1996 (Washington: United States Department of State, 1996), p. xii.

21. Elizabeth Joyce, "Packaging Drugs: Certification and the Acquisition of Leverage," paper presented to the Study Group on U.S. Relations with Latin America and the Implications for Europe, Institute for Latin American Studies, University of London, March 13, 1998, p. 4.

22. For a recent treatment of U.S.-Andean relations, see Andrés Franco, ed. *Estados Unidos y los países andinos, 1993-1997: poder y desintegración*. (Bogotá: CEJA, 1998).

23. This view prevailed in interviews held over the past two years with government officials of the Andean nations of Bolivia, Ecuador, Colombia, and Peru.

24. As Joyce (1998, 26) notes, "a complete cut-off of sales or financing under the Arms Export Control Act, non-food assistance under Public Law 480, financing by the Export-Import Bank, and most assistance under the FAA with the exception of specified types of humanitarian assistance and counternarcotics assistance. In addition, the United States must vote against any loans from six multilateral banks to the country concerned. The president also has the discretion during the year to impose trade and other economic sanctions under Section 802 of the Narcotics Trade Control Act."

25. The Bolivian situation in 1985 showed how the Summit process did not coincide with the counternarcotics agenda of the United States. While Bolivia faced the ultimatum, the Sanchez de Lozada government meticulously planned the Summit/Conference on Sustainable Development. The planning of the Santa Cruz, Bolivia, Summit/Conference also brought to the surface tensions between the U.S. and Latin America. See Eduardo Gamarra, "Las relaciones entre Estados Unidos y Bolivia durante el gobierno de Gonzalo Sánchez de Lozada," in Andres Franco ed., *Estados Unidos y los paises andinos, 1993-1997: poder y desintegracion*. (Bogota: Pontificia Universidad Javeriana, 1998).

26. In 1996, for example, Mexico was certified despite revelations that the director of Instituto Nacional Contra las Drogas (INCD), General Jesus Gutierrez Rebollo had been accused of taking bribes from Amado Carrillo Fuentes, the boss of the Juarez cartel. Gutierrez Rebollo was subsequently fired. Numerous other allegations linking Mexican public officials to narco-traffickers have also surfaced in the past three years. Members of the U.S. Congress, such as Senator Diane Feinstein (Democrat, California) and Representative Richard Gephardt (Democrat, Missouri) have also headed efforts to decertify Mexico and to apply the law equally to all countries. It has become increasingly clear, that as long as NAFTA is around, the U.S. cannot afford to decertify Mexico.

27. *The Economist,* March 8, 1997, 47, cited by Elizabeth Joyce (1998, 30).

28. Ben Gilman and J. Dennis Hasten, "Media Alert:Drug Certification, A U.S. Congressional Republican View on Drug Certification. A U.S. Congressional Republican Alternative Response to President Clinton's Counternarcotics Alliance Proposal," (mimeo).

29. Personal conversations with law enforcement officials in Chile, Brazil, Panama, Bolivia, Colombia, Peru, and Ecuador reveal that drug abuse is now a significant security issue, especially in urban areas throughout the Americas. In Santiago, Chile, for example, one law enforcement official explained that drug abuse was responsible for the proliferation of urban crime.

30. *The National Drug Control Strategy: 1996*, (Office of National Drug Control Policy):pp 11-13.

31. See *Keeping Score: What We Are Getting for Our Federal Drug Control Programs (1995)*.

32. *1997 International Narcotics Control Strategy Report,* cited in Statement by Barry R. McCaffrey, Director, Office of National Drug Control Policy, before the Senate Caucus on International Narcotics Control, June 18, 1998.

33. For a thorough survey of the human rights dimension of U.S. and Bolivian counternarcotics efforts in Bolivia, see Human Rights Watch Americas, *Bolivia: Human Rights Violations and the War on Drugs,* (New York: July 1995).

34. Comments by Ambassador Jane E. Becker at the Institute for International Economics, May 29, 1996.

35. Report on Counternarcotics by the United States at the May 1996 SIRG meeting.

36. See, for example, Patrick L. Clawson and Rensselaer W. Lee III, *The Andean Cocaine Industry* (New York: St. Martin's Press, 1996).

37. Ambassador Becker's comments as cited in note 34.

38. Robert Gelbard speech, Miami, May 4, 1996. According to Ambassador Gelbard, criminal organizations have become global and have formed transnational alliances. The Cali cartel has established links with Italian and Russian mafias; there is a significant Polish, Hungarian, Brazilian, Colombian link; and Nigerian traffickers dominate the heroin trade and have been moving into the Latin American cocaine business.

39. The profound crisis of the Colombian state is a classic example of the institutional incapacity to carry out counternarcotics programs. The same could be said about Bolivia and Peru. For a superb account of the Colombian situation, see Francisco Thoumi, *The Political Economy of Drug Trafficking in Colombia* (Boulder: Westview Press, 1995).

40. Interview June 14, 1998, Miami, Florida.

41. The OAS and the U.S. Southern Command, for example, have collaborated on an annual exercise that brings together key law enforcement and military personnel. These efforts have, at a minimum, familiarized operators from each country with each other. The expectation is that personal contact will facilitate interagency and international cooperation in drug enforcement efforts.

# VI. Education: The Key to Progress

# VI. EDUCATION: THE KEY TO PROGRESS

# The Future at Stake:
## Report of the Task Force on Education, Equity, and Economic Competitiveness in Latin America and the Caribbean

*The **Inter-American Dialogue** is the premier center for policy analysis and exchange on Western Hemisphere affairs. The Dialogue's select membership of 100 distinguished private citizens from throughout the Americas includes political, business, academic, media, and other non-governmental leaders. Seven Dialogue members served as presidents of their countries and more than a dozen have served at the cabinet level.*

*The Dialogue works to improve the quality of debate and decisionmaking on hemispheric problems, advance opportunities for regional economic and political cooperation, and bring fresh, practical proposals for action to governments, international institutions, and non-governmental organizations. Since 1982 — through successive Republican and Democratic administrations and many changes of leadership in Latin America, the Caribbean, and Canada — the Dialogue has helped shape the agenda of issues and choices on inter-American relations.*

*The **Partnership for Educational Revitalization in the Americas** (PREAL) is jointly managed by the Inter-American Dialogue based in Washington, D.C., and the Corporation for Development Research (CINDE) in Santiago, Chile. PREAL is a hemispheric partnership of public and private sector organizations seeking to promote informed debate on policy alternatives, identify and disseminate best education practices emerging in the region and elsewhere, and monitor progress toward improving education policy. PREAL includes actors from civil society, governments, universities, political leaders, the business community, international organizations and churches.*

*The partnership seeks to help improve the quality and equity of education by promoting better education policy. It pursues three intermediate objectives:*

* *build public and private sector support for educational reform*
* *strengthen public and private sector organizations working for educational improvement and*
* *identify and disseminate best education policies and practices.*

## THE MISSION

In 1996, the Inter-American Dialogue and the Corporation for Development Research (CINDE) established the Task Force on Education, Equity and Economic Competitiveness in Latin America and the Caribbean.

The Task Force was the central element of a broader program—the Partnership for Educational Revitalization in the Americas (PREAL)—that the Inter-American Dialogue and CINDE established in 1995. The Task Force is composed of distinguished citizens from throughout the region who are concerned about issues of school quality. Its members include leaders in the fields of industry and commerce, government, higher education, law, and religion. Although few of them have previously participated in the education policy debate, all have extensive experience in public policy, and share a strong conviction that schools must be made better.

The Task Force was asked to examine the state of education, and to present its findings and recommendations in a non-technical, policy-oriented report. Task Force members were particularly concerned with reaching leaders from outside the education sector, whose support would be crucial to achieving fundamental institutional change. The Task Force sought to promote consensus among diverse sectors of society regarding the need for fundamental education reform, and to create new alliances in support of that reform; broaden the constituency for reform, by involving leaders from outside the education sector; identify new and modern approaches to education policy emerging in the region and elsewhere; and monitor progress toward improving education policy.

Task Force members met in Santiago, Chile, in January 1997 to discuss the content and structure of the report and to establish a work plan. Subsequently, staff at the Inter-American Dialogue and CINDE, with the help of several consultants, drafted a report which was discussed and revised at a second meeting in Washington, D.C., in December 1997.

The report that resulted from these deliberations is attached. It reflects the consensus of the members of the Task Force on Education, Equity and Economic Competitiveness. Not every signer agrees fully with every phrase in the text, but—except as noted in individual statements—each of the members endorses the report's overall content and tone, and supports its principal recommendations. All subscribe as individuals; institutional affiliations are for purposes of identification only.

We are convinced that better schools are crucial to generating economic growth, promoting equity, and sustaining democratic government. The report proposes a series of practical steps for addressing the serious shortcomings we have detected in the region's schools. We believe that these recommendations provide a firm base for moving forward. We urge every nation in Latin America and the Caribbean to give education reform top priority, to work systematically to develop a broad consensus on the changes needed, and to exercise the political leadership that is essential to achieving fundamental institutional reform.

José Octavio Bordón, co-Chair<br>John Petty, co-Chair

## ACKNOWLEDGEMENTS

This report is based on the deliberations of the Task Force on Education, Equity and Economic Competitiveness at its two meetings in 1997. The first was held in Santiago, Chile, under the auspices of the Corporation for Development Research (CINDE). The second was held in Washington, D.C., under the auspices of the Inter-American Dialogue. It draws on documents produced by a variety of education experts. Many people have contributed to the report through informal discussion, commissioned papers, and advice. We particularly want to thank Cecilia Braslavsky, Gloria Calvo, Gustavo Cosse, Cristián Cox, E. Mark Hanson, Nancy Morrison, Robert G. Myers, Diane Ravitch, Robert E. Slavin, and David N. Wilson, all of whom prepared PREAL working papers that informed our deliberations. Michelle Miller played a crucial role in taking the analysis we produced and turning it into a coherent draft report. Patricia Arregui, José Joaquin Brunner, Ernesto Ottone, José Angel Pescador, and Larry Wolff provided important comments on preliminary versions. Marcela Gajardo and Jeffrey Puryear coordinated the preparation of the report, and revised each draft for submission to the Task Force.

The preparation of the report was a collective effort that involved staff from the Inter-American Dialogue and CINDE. Tamara Ortega Goodspeed, Paul Kantz, Sandra Forero, and Carlos Rosales played important roles in generating information, organizing meetings, and reviewing documents at the Dialogue, as did Ana María Andraca and Nelson Martínez at CINDE.

This report would not have been possible without the sustained support of the Inter-American Development Bank, the Canadian International Development Research Centre, the U.S. Agency for International Development, and the GE Fund. Their willingness to provide steady and flexible funding to the Partnership for Educational Revitalization in the Americas (PREAL) over several years has been crucial in developing the information and institutional networks necessary to the project.

We particularly want to offer a special tribute to Francisco J. Garza, a well-known and respected Mexican business executive, who served on the Task Force until his death in October 1997.

## MEMBERS

**José Octavio Bordón,** Co-Chair - Argentina
**John Petty,** Co-Chair - United States
**Roberto Baquerizo** - Ecuador
**Patricio Cariola,** S.J. - Chile
**Juan E. Cintrón Patterson** - Mexico
**Jonathan Coles** - Venezuela
**José María Dagnino Pastore** - Argentina
**Nancy Englander** - United States
**Peter Hakim** - United States
**Ivan Head** - Canada
**Rudolf Hommes** - Colombia
**Emerson Kapaz** - Brazil
**Jacqueline Malagón** - Dominican Republic
**José Mindlin** - Brazil
**Roberto Murray Meza** - El Salvador
**Manuel Fernando Sotomayor** - Peru
**Osvaldo Sunkel** - Chile
**Celina Vargas do Amaral Peixoto** - Brazil

## EXECUTIVE SUMMARY

No one disputes that education is vital for economic growth, social advance, and democratic progress. Yet most children in Latin America and the Caribbean are today deprived of a decent, high-quality education. Indeed, Latin America's schools are in crisis. They are not educating the region's young. Instead of contributing to progress, they are holding back the region and its people—reinforcing poverty, inequality, and poor economic performance. Students from the region's top private schools perform at levels comparable to schools in the industrialized countries. Public school students, in contrast, perform dismally by any standard. Latin America's future will be bleak until all its children are provided real opportunities for decent education.

Our Task Force offers parents, governments, educators, the business community, political leaders, private

# VI. Education: The Key to Progress

citizens, and international financial agencies four key recommendations to make schools better. These recommendations are designed to work together. The problems that plague the region's schools are systemic, and must be addressed along several dimensions at once.

## Recommendation #1

*Set standards for the education system and measure progress toward meeting them.*

Governments should establish clear education standards, introduce national tests, and use the results to revise programs and reallocate resources. Latin American and Caribbean nations should have their students participate in international tests so they can compare the quality of their schools with those of other countries.

## Recommendation #2

*Give schools and local communities more control over —and responsibility for— education.*

Centralized education systems deny school principals, teachers, and parents the authority they need to improve school performance. Central governments should develop a new role—withdrawing from directly running schools and concentrating instead on generating funds, setting standards, promoting equity, monitoring progress, and evaluating results. They should give school directors, parents, and local communities greater responsibility for school management, including authority over teachers. Parents should have choices among competing schools.

## Recommendation #3

*Strengthen the teaching profession, by raising salaries, reforming training, and making teachers more accountable to the communities they serve.*

Teachers in the public schools are often underpaid, underprepared, and poorly managed. Governments should take firm steps to make teaching a stronger and more attractive profession. School principals and the local community should have the authority and resources to reward good teachers.

## Recommendation #4

*Invest more money per student in preschool, primary and secondary education.*

The changes required in Latin America's schools (as spelled out in recommendations 1-3) cannot be provided at present levels of expenditure. Expenditures per pupil in public schools lag far behind those in private schools, and in the public schools of other regions. Governments will have to invest significantly more if they are to increase the quality and equity of basic education. More money alone, of course, will not solve the problem. New funds will be wasted unless they are coupled with the major institutional reforms we are recommending. Both fundamental change and additional resources are needed.

## A REGION IN PERIL

> All over the world it is taken for granted that educational achievement and economic success are closely linked — that the struggle to raise a nation's living standards is fought first and foremost in the classroom. — *The Economist,* March 29, 1997

Education throughout Latin America and the Caribbean is in crisis. Enrollments have expanded rapidly and dramatically over the past three decades, but quality has eroded just as dramatically. Language, mathematics, and science teaching is dismal in most places. Few students develop strong skills in critical thinking, problem-solving, or decision-making. Only the small number of children attending elite private schools get an adequate education. The vast majority attend weak and under-funded public schools, where they fail to acquire the knowledge and skills needed for economic success or active citizenship. At a time when good schools are increasingly crucial to economic growth, Latin America is falling behind.

Indicators of the region's educational crisis include:

### Low test scores.

International comparisons underscore the poor performance of Latin American schools. Only two countries from Latin America chose to participate in a worldwide test of fourth grade math and science skills in 1996. One of them—Colombia—ranked fortieth out of the forty-one countries surveyed, below every participating Asian, Eastern European, and Middle Eastern country. The other—Mexico—refused to allow its scores to be published. An earlier cross-national test of reading ability among nine-year-olds produced no less troubling results. Venezuela—the only Latin American country in the study—scored the lowest of the twenty-seven participating countries, well below Hong Kong, Singapore, and Indonesia. In a 1992 study of math and science skills, Brazilian thirteen-year-olds from Sao Paulo and Fortaleza scored below all but one of the nineteen participating countries. We commend these few countries for making their schools compete internationally, but their performance highlights the educational crisis in Latin America and the Caribbean. The reluctance of most Latin American countries to take part in cross-national testing is a strong indictment of the failure of education in the region.

### Table 1. Gaps in Education for Latin America and the Caribbean, 1995

|  | Latin America | Countries at similar levels of economic development |
|---|---|---|
| Percent completing fourth grade | 66% | 82% |
| Average years of schooling for labor force | 5.2 | 7.0 |

Source: Inter-American Development Bank, *Economic and Social Progress in Latin America, 1996 Report* (Washington, DC: Inter-American Development Bank, 1996).

### Poor educational attainment.

Latin American and Caribbean students enter the labor force with less education than their counterparts in Asia and the Middle East—and the gap is increasing. On average, Latin American workers have nearly two years less schooling than workers in other countries with similar incomes (Table 1).

The comparison with the high-growth economies of Southeast Asia is particularly striking. Latin America's labor force has less education today than any country of that region, and appears to be steadily falling further behind (Figure 1).

More Latin American children are entering primary school than ever before, but few get very far. Roughly half of all students fail the first grade. Nearly a third repeat whatever grade they are in. In Honduras, Guatemala, El Salvador, and Nicaragua, the average student takes 10 years to complete six years of primary school (Figure 2). High repetition is usually associated with inadequate learning, and the problem is most severe for poor, rural, and indigenous children. As Table 2 indicates, a few countries do better than the dismal average.

The cost of teaching children who are repeating a grade was recently estimated at $3.3 billion—nearly one-third of public spending on primary education in the region.

### Figure 1. Educational Level of the Labor Force
Latin America and Southeast Asia, 1950-90

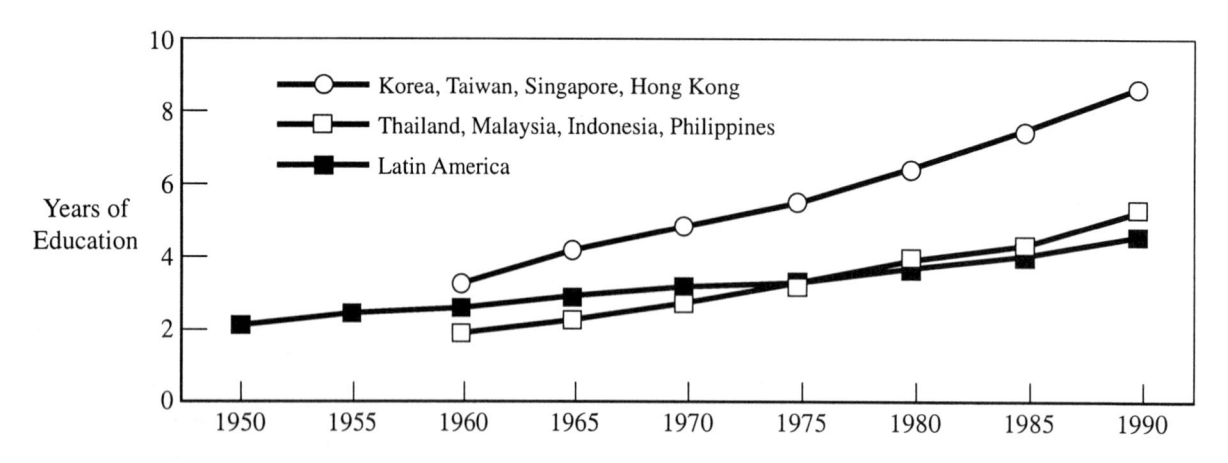

Source: Juan Luis Londoño, *Poverty, Inequality, and Human Capital Development in Latin America, 1950-2025* (Washington, DC: World Bank, 1996).

# VI. EDUCATION: THE KEY TO PROGRESS

**Figure 2. Average School Years Per Sixth-Grade Graduate**
1988-92

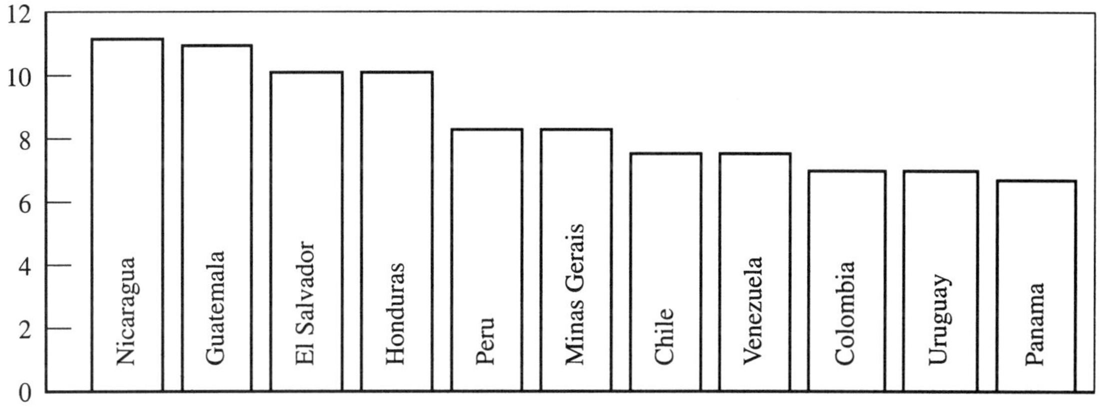

| Country | Years |
|---|---|
| Nicaragua | ~11.2 |
| Guatemala | ~11.0 |
| El Salvador | ~10.2 |
| Honduras | ~10.2 |
| Peru | ~8.3 |
| Minas Gerais | ~8.3 |
| Chile | ~7.5 |
| Venezuela | ~7.5 |
| Colombia | ~7.0 |
| Uruguay | ~7.0 |
| Panama | ~6.7 |

Source: Inter-American Development Bank, *Economic and Social Progress in Latin America, 1996 Report* (Washington, DC: Inter-American Development Bank, 1996).

**Table 2. Primary School Repetition and Completion**
Latin America and the Caribbean, 1989

| | First grade repetition rates | % graduating from 6th grade without repeating any grade |
|---|---|---|
| Jamaica | 6 | 52 |
| Chile | 10 | 41 |
| Uruguay | 15 | 54 |
| Costa Rica | 22 | 31 |
| Peru | 28 | 21 |
| Venezuela | 28 | 14 |
| Argentina | 31 | 17 |
| Colombia | 31 | 26 |
| Bolivia | 33 | 9 |
| Ecuador | 33 | 34 |
| Mexico | 33 | 23 |
| Panama | — | 33 |
| Paraguay | 33 | 20 |
| Brazil | 53 | 1 |
| Honduras | 53 | 12 |
| El Salvador | 54 | 4 |
| Guatemala | 55 | 9 |
| Dominican Republic | 58 | 3 |
| Haiti | 61 | 1 |
| Weighted average for Latin America/Caribbean | 42 | 10 |

Source: Laurence Wolff, Ernesto Schiefelbein and Jorge Valenzuela, "Improving the Quality of Primary Education in Latin America and the Caribbean: Toward the 21st Century," World Bank Discussion Paper No. 257 (Washington, DC: The World Bank, 1994).

One out of two students in Latin America never finishes the sixth grade (although there are wide variations among countries). The contrast with the newly industrialized countries of East Asia is striking. In Korea and Malaysia, more than 95 percent of students graduate from primary school; in Sri Lanka and Thailand, more than 80 percent; and in China, about 70 percent.

Latin America's record at the secondary level is no better. Only one out of three children attends secondary school, compared to over 80 percent in Southeast Asia. Most of those who enter never graduate. They drop out to take jobs, but they lack the language, math, science, and problem-solving skills necessary for success in modern economies.

The gap in educational attainment between Latin America and East Asia is getting worse. The average East Asian child will soon be going to school for as many years as in Europe, Japan, and the United States. Latin American and Caribbean children are left out of this progress.

## Inequity.

Education may be the single most important mechanism to reduce income inequality. In Latin America today, however, education is doing just the opposite: it is exacerbating inequality.

Nothing illustrates better the problem of inequity in Latin America than the enormous chasm between private and public schools. Virtually all families with the resources to do so send their children to private primary and secondary schools. Virtually all poor families—by necessity—send their children to public schools. While not all private schools are of high quality, the best schools in the region are private—and many of these are on a par with the best schools worldwide. Most private schools invest significantly more money per pupil, enabling them to pay teachers higher salaries and provide more teaching materials. Private schools, on average, offer 1,000 hours or more of instruction yearly, while public schools offer 500 to 800 hours. Students in private schools routinely cover 100 percent of the official curriculum, while the average public school student covers just 50 percent. Private school students score significantly higher on achievement tests than do those who attend public schools (Table 3). Not surprisingly, the vast majority of repeaters attend public schools.

**Table 3. Achievement in Mathematics and Science in Five Countries by Type of School**
The TIMSS Pilot Study of Achievement of Thirteen-year-old Students, 1992

|  | Elite Private | Lower Class Private or Upper Class Public | Lower Class Public | Rural Public |
|---|---|---|---|---|
| **Mathematics** | | | | |
| Argentina | 50 | 41 | 33 | 29 |
| Colombia | 66 | 32 | 27 | 35 |
| Costa Rica | 72 | 59 | 44 | 43 |
| Dominican Republic | 60 | 41 | 29 | 31 |
| Venezuela | 44 | 29 | 55 | 33 |

*National Average for Thailand: 50*
*National Average for USA: 52*

| **Science** | | | | |
|---|---|---|---|---|
| Argentina | 45 | 43 | 37 | 28 |
| Colombia | 47 | 29 | 36 | 37 |
| Costa Rica | 66 | 59 | 50 | 50 |
| Dominican Republic | 52 | 38 | 29 | 29 |
| Venezuela | 55 | 38 | 37 | 35 |

*National Average for Thailand: 55*
*National Average for USA: 55*

Source: Ernesto Schiefelbein, "Education Reform in Latin America and the Caribbean: An Agenda for Action," in *The Major Project of Education in Latin America and the Caribbean* 37 (Santiago, Chile: UNESCO, 1995).

Rural schools are the most deprived. Teachers have far less training than in urban settings, funding is lower, and fewer grades are offered. Distance makes it even more difficult for children to complete their primary education, and basic materials, such as libraries and textbooks, are often not available.

In the important area of gender equality, Latin America and the Caribbean outperform other developing regions. By the early 1980s, in fact, more than 50 percent of all students in the region were female. The challenge now is to treat girls equally once they are in school, by eliminating gender stereotypes and making sure that girls receive the same encouragement to excel in difficult subjects, such as mathematics and science, as do boys.

Latin America has the most unequal distribution of income in the world. Much of that inequality reflects a failure to invest in quality education for its children.

## WHY EDUCATION MATTERS

High quality education contributes to economic growth, social equity, and democracy. It provides children with skills that are crucial to social and economic success. Education helps reduce fertility and improve health. It makes workers more flexible, better able to learn on the job, and more capable of making good decisions. It encourages entrepreneurial activity. It prepares citizens for responsible participation in the institutions of democracy and civil society.

Historically, education has always gone hand-in-hand with economic growth. No country has made significant economic progress without expanding and improving its schools. Virtually all of the fast-growth economies of East Asia achieved universal primary enrollment by 1965, and then improved school quality by setting high standards and steadily increasing per-pupil investments. Those efforts have endowed East Asian workers with more cognitive skills than workers in Latin America, enabling them to more easily acquire technological capability. Education is estimated to account for nearly 40 percent of the growth differential between East Asia and Latin America. The most important contributor to that difference has been the expansion of high-quality primary schools.

Today, education is more important than ever for the countries of Latin America and the Caribbean. Open economies, global competition, and the shift to technology-based production have expanded the demand for workers who understand mathematics and science, and who can adapt to rapidly changing conditions. Democratic government and state decentralization require citizens who can take on greater responsibility for problem-solving and decision-making. The demand for education is changing rapidly in Latin America and the Caribbean. The supply of education must change as well.

## DIAGNOSING THE PROBLEM

Four linked factors explain the region's educational crisis: inadequate evaluation of student learning and school performance, limited school authority and accountability, poor teaching, and too little investment in primary and secondary schools.

### Failure to evaluate student learning and school performance.

The countries of Latin America and the Caribbean seldom evaluate their schools systematically—nor do they set goals against which progress can be measured. Most countries rely on education statistics that emphasize physical inputs, such as spending, enrollment, and the number of teachers and schools. The school's most important output—learning—is not measured in any reliable way. Neither is the availability of textbooks, teaching methods, and libraries. Existing systems of education statistics are unreliable, and fail to incorporate modern indicators that have become common in the industrialized countries.

Most countries refuse to take part in cross-national tests that would compare national performance with schools in other countries. Only a few countries have established national tests designed to measure progress against a clear performance standard, and several others are beginning their own experiments. But resistance—from teachers unions, bureaucrats and even politicians—has been strong.

The absence of system-wide evaluations remains a major obstacle to improving schools. An organization that cannot measure the quantity and quality of its most important product—learning—stands little chance of success.

### Schools lack authority and accountability.

Genuinely local schools are rare in Latin America and the Caribbean. Education has traditionally been managed centrally, by national ministries or state-level education departments. They make critical decisions about hiring and firing teachers, choosing textbooks, allocating resources, and organizing teacher-training programs. Ministries appoint teachers and principals, whose salaries are determined by rigid formulas related mainly to seniority rather than performance. Teachers unions and ministries negotiate national contracts. School principals have limited authority.

The result is that schools are more likely to serve the interests of those who supply education than those who consume it. Schools are not accountable to their local communities. The consumers of education—students, parents, local communities and employers—have almost no influence.

Many countries have launched innovative decentralization programs designed to redress the balance of power. Most commonly, they have placed authority for school management in the hands of municipal governments. Several countries, notably El Salvador and Nicaragua, have gone further, transferring key management tasks to school principals and local community councils. But few of them have decentralized all the way to the school level. (The promotion of local school autonomy in the Brazilian state of Minas Gerais is discussed in Box 1.)

### Teaching is poor.

The problem with teaching quality begins outside the classroom. In most countries, the teaching profession has been allowed to decline—the victim of inadequate salaries, low standards, and poor management. These deficiencies have lowered the prestige of teaching, making it difficult to attract top candidates.

Salaries vary widely, but are generally too low to attract, motivate, and maintain a superior teaching corps. Many teachers hold second jobs in order to make ends meet. Research suggests that low salaries translate directly into teacher candidates with weaker qualifications.

More importantly, teachers face few incentives—monetary or non-monetary—to perform at high professional levels. Salaries, promotions, and working conditions are negotiated nationally in most countries, rather than being pegged to performance. Performance evaluations are uncommon. Teachers have little control over teaching materials and school management. They are not directly accountable to parents and local communities for their work.

Teacher training is deficient. On average, one-quarter of Latin American and Caribbean teachers lack a professional degree or certificate. Training programs do

> **Box 1. Increasing School Authority: Empowering Local Communities in Minas Gerais**
>
> Beginning in 1991, the Brazilian state of Minas Gerais decentralized its educational system. Boards made up of teachers, parents, and students over the age of sixteen were elected for each school and were made responsible for financial, administrative, and pedagogical decisions concerning their school. The state provides funds for purposes other than paying salaries; it is up to the board to decide how to spend these resources as well as others raised locally. To overcome the longstanding problem of patronage in appointments, principals are elected by the entire school community. Voting is by secret ballot from among those candidates who scored highest on a series of examinations. The educational reform also includes standardized tests for students and preparation of a development plan by each school. The state government has retained some functions, such as bargaining with the teachers union. The results have been good. Between 1990 and 1994, the percentage of children completing primary school rose from 38 percent to 49 percent, while the percentage of those needing to repeat a grade fell from 29 percent to 19 percent. Officials say they expected the strongest community participation in middle-class areas, but it is in the poorer communities that participation has been greatest. It is also in these schools where students have shown the most improvement.
>
> Source: Adapted from Edward B. Fiske, *Decentralization of Education: Politics and Consensus* (Washington, DC: The World Bank, 1996); Interview with Ana Luiza Machado Pinheiro, *UNICEF Education News* No. 17 and 18 (February 1997); Inter-American Development Bank, *Economic and Social Progress in Latin America, 1996 Report* (Washington, DC: Inter-American Development Bank, 1996).

not provide enough subject matter expertise, and stress theory over practice. Their pedagogical methods are out of date. Far too many teachers simply present material for students to memorize—an approach that tends to discourage problem-solving and critical thinking. They do not apply flexible teaching styles, such as personalized instruction and teaching in small groups, that are necessary to help students with different skills. And they fail to teach students how to learn on their own.

The combination of centralized administration, inadequate salaries, and low job satisfaction has made teachers unions one of the dominant forces in Latin American education. They constitute, in many countries, a national monopoly on the supply of teaching, and have power comparable to that of ministries of education. Unfortunately, that power has mainly been mobilized to resist efforts to establish local control, greater accountability, and incentives for performance. Teachers unions have concentrated almost entirely on raising wages. They have not played an important role in efforts to improve learning.

These problems have seriously weakened the profession of teaching in Latin America and the Caribbean, reducing prestige, weakening morale, and generating mediocre performance.

## Investment in primary and secondary education is too low.

The crisis of public education in Latin America and the Caribbean is a crisis of investment, at least in part. From one perspective, Latin American governments do well, investing 4.5 percent of GNP in education each year—above the developing country average of 3.9 percent (Table 4). But these figures are misleading. Because of Latin America's high fertility and low economic growth, funds invested per student have remained low. By contrast, in East Asia declining fertility and expanding economies have led to steadily increasing public investments per pupil, particularly at the primary level. For example, in 1970 public spending per primary student in Korea was only one-third higher than in Mexico. By 1989 it was nearly four times as high. It is often misleading to report educational investments as a percentage of GNP. What counts are per-student investments. On this score, primary and secondary students in Latin American and Caribbean public schools are being given short shrift.

East Asian countries allocate more of their public education spending to primary and secondary schools. In East Asia only 15 percent of education spending between 1960 and 1990 went to higher education. In Latin America, almost one quarter did. Latin America and the Caribbean spend only 1.1 percent of GDP on primary education, compared to 1.5 percent in the high-growth East Asian economies. For each dollar spent per primary student, Latin American governments spend nearly seven dollars on university students. The ratio in the OECD countries is less than one to three (Table 5).

The funding shortfall is damaging in multiple ways. The school day in Latin America and the Caribbean is far

The Future at Stake: Report of the Task Force on Education, Equity and Economic Competitiveness in Latin America and the Caribbean

# VI. EDUCATION: THE KEY TO PROGRESS

**Table 4. Public Expenditure on Education**
Latin America and the Caribbean, 1980-1994

|  | Year |  |  |  |
|---|---|---|---|---|
|  | 1980 | 1985 | 1990 | 1994 |
| Public Expenditure (Billions of $US) | 33.5 | 27.9 | 44.6 | 72.8 |
| Public Expenditure as % of GNP | 3.8 | 3.9 | 4.1 | 4.5 |
| Public Expenditure Per Capita ($US) | 93 | 70 | 102 | 153 |
| Developed Countries: Public Expenditure as % of GNP |  |  |  | 5.1 |
| Developing Countries: Public Expenditure as % of GNP |  |  |  | 3.9 |
| Developed Countries: Public Expenditure Per Capita ($US) |  |  |  | 1211 |
| Developing Countries: Public Expenditure Per Capita ($US) |  |  |  | 48 |

Source: United Nations Educational, Scientific and Cultural Organization, *UNESCO Statistical Yearbook 1997* (Paris: UNESCO and Lanham, Maryland: Bernan Press, 1997).

shorter, on average, than in other regions of the world. Public schools average between 500 and 800 hours per year, compared with approximately 1,200 hours for private schools and schools in the industrialized countries. Some schools run double or triple shifts because of overcrowding. Schools are poorly built, badly equipped, and often unrepaired. Most governments devote less than five percent of education spending to teaching materials, such as texts, workbooks, and rudimentary school libraries. Many schools have no teaching materials at all. Primary school teachers are usually underpaid. Preschool programs are largely funded by parents, leaving the poor at a significant disadvantage.

**Table 5. Annual Spending per Pupil by Level of Education**
1992

|  | Latin America & Caribbean | OECD Countries |
|---|---|---|
| Pre-primary & primary* | $252 | $4,170 |
| Secondary | $394 | $5,170 |
| Tertiary | $1,485 | $10,030 |

*primary only for OECD countries
Source: United Nations Educational, Scientific and Cultural Organization, *World Education Report, 1995* (Paris: UNESCO, 1995); Centre for Educational Research and Innovation, *Education at a Glance: OECD Indicators* (Paris: Organization for Economic Cooperation and Development, 1995).

Two recent developments provide some hope, however. First, Latin America and the Caribbean are emerging from the economic crisis of the 1980s with stronger economies and healthier public finances, opening the way for countries to expand primary and secondary education budgets, should they choose to do so. Second, demographic change in many countries will reduce the number of children reaching school age over the next fifteen years, allowing funds to be used for improving quality rather than for accommodating ever-rising numbers of students.

## RECOMMENDATIONS AND IMPLEMENTATION

The governments of the hemisphere face no more important challenge than improving their nations' educational systems and making them effective contributors to economic growth, social equality, and democracy. Changing just one part of the system will not lead to success, however. The problems that plague the region's schools are systemic, and must be pursued along several dimensions at once. Accordingly, we call on the nations of the hemisphere to embark on a broad and profound reform of their education systems.

The task is immense and will take time. But it must be started now. We offer four inter-linked recommendations on how to begin.

## Recommendation #1

*Set standards for the education system and measure progress toward meeting them.*

Governments should establish clear education standards, introduce national tests, and use the results to revise programs and reallocate resources. Latin American and Caribbean nations should take part in international tests so they can compare the quality of their schools with those of other countries.

There is no way to know whether schools are improving unless the performance of their students can be measured and analyzed. To accomplish this, governments should:

- Develop a world-class system of education statistics and indicators. The goal should be a system that emphasizes educational outcomes, rather than inputs, and is compatible with the OECD system of international education indicators.

- Establish national content and performance standards that outline what students should know when they complete each grade. The standards should be keyed to the requirements of the global economy and of democratic citizenship.

- Establish a national testing system that measures progress toward achieving the new educational standards. The tests should initially be administered to all students at specific points in the primary cycle, and eventually in the secondary cycle.

Most countries now have some experience with national education assessments, but the level of commitment is weak and few full-blown systems are in place. Governments and leaders from civil society should make a strong political commitment to meaningful measurement and evaluation, and work together to develop a robust system.

The results of national assessments must be made public, so that the consumers of education—parents, local communities, and employers—can evaluate how well their schools are doing. Moreover, results must feed back into educational policy and practice, so that they change what goes on in the classroom for the better.

Assessments can also help target resources to the neediest schools (as was done in Chile; see Box 2); identify highly effective schools so that their characteristics can be replicated; and shift the curriculum, textbooks, and teaching practice in the direction of more realistic goals. National assessments also can help parents decide

---

**Box 2. Targeting Schools at Risk: The Use of Assessments in Chile**

In Chile, the results of nationwide testing are used in part to target resources to the neediest schools. Each school receives a score based on its students' average performance on Chile's national assessment test, the school's socioeconomic level, whether it is located in a rural or urban location, and the number of grades it offers. On the basis of this score, schools are rated as high, medium, or low risk. More than 90% of the resources available for improving schools go to those in the high- and medium-risk categories. Within each category, schools compete for funds by proposing school improvement activities to be supported. These activities are evaluated to see if they succeed in raising students' test scores.

Source: Adapted from the World Bank, *Priorities and Strategies for Education: A World Bank Review* (Washington, DC: The World Bank, 1995).

---

which schools they want their children to attend, thereby increasing school accountability.

Governments, while relinquishing control over school administration, should retain a role in implementing standards and evaluating performance in order to ensure that minimum quality levels are met across the nation.

## Recommendation #2

*Give schools and local communities more control over—and responsibility for —education.*

Centralized education systems deny school leaders, teachers, and parents the authority they need to improve school performance. Central governments should withdraw from directly running schools and instead concentrate on generating funds, setting standards, promoting equity, monitoring progress, and evaluating results. They should give school directors, parents, and local communities greater responsibility for school management, including authority over teachers in personnel decisions. Parents should have choices among competing schools.

Governments should allow individual schools increasingly to manage their own affairs. They should give principals greater power to determine how resources are allocated, and how classrooms are organized. Governments should give parents and local communities a say in school management and enable them to hold schools accountable for the educational performance of their students. They should establish incentives that reward good professional performance. Experiments in delegating greater authority to schools and local communities are underway in several countries, and initial results are encouraging (Box 1).

National or state-level ministries of education should continue to take principal responsibility for financing education, and should see to it that funds are allocated in ways that address geographic and cultural disparities. But they should withdraw from directly running schools and concentrate instead on developing a new role. They should set goals, generate funds, promote equity, monitor progress, and evaluate educational results. They should adapt salaries and benefits to local circumstances. They should give schools and local communities authority over teachers in personnel decisions, including salaries, evaluations, promotions, hiring and firing. Day-to-day management of schools should be handled by school principals and local communities as much as possible.

Central governments should experiment with new financial arrangements—such as the private management of public schools, financing the demand for education through vouchers or capitation grants, incentives for greater private investment in education, and promoting competition among schools—that give consumers more power and make schools more accountable. Chile and Colombia, for example, have used vouchers to give parents the option of sending their children to private schools (Box 3). Under these systems, schools—public or private—receive government funds based on the actual number of students who attend. These programs—and others like them—have helped expand the choices facing parents, and have injected an element of healthy competition into the school system. Central governments should also establish incentives for greater private investment, via tuition payments, in education.

## Recommendation #3

*Strengthen the teaching profession, by raising salaries, reforming training, and making teachers more accountable to the communities they serve.*

Teachers in the public schools are often underpaid, underprepared, and poorly managed. Governments should take firm steps to make teaching a stronger and more

---

**Box 3. Demand-Based Financing in Chile and Colombia**

In Chile, public and private schools at both the primary and secondary level have competed since 1980 to attract and keep students. The schools are financed by central government transfers based on the actual number of students who attend. In 1996, 57 percent of students attended municipal schools, 33 percent attended state-funded private schools, and 8 percent attended fee-paying private schools. This financing system has forced public schools to compete with private schools and has given parents the power to choose what school their children will attend. It did not by itself, however, lead to improvements in children's learning. One reason is inadequate funding. Per-pupil spending declined during the 1980s and, in 1990, was only 77 percent of 1982 levels. The government has increased spending since 1990, to the point that per-pupil expenditure now amounts to almost double the level of a decade ago. Much of this increase has gone to higher salaries and better training for teachers. Policymakers hope that higher levels of spending and new incentives for teachers, coupled with school choice, will have positive results in terms of children's learning.

Source: Adapted from Inter-American Development Bank, *Economic and Social Progress in Latin America, 1996 Report* (Washington DC: Inter-American Development Bank, 1996); Cristián Cox, "La Reforma de la Educación Chilena: Contexto, Contenidos, Implementación," PREAL Occasional Paper No. 8 (Washington, DC, and Santiago, Chile: Partnership for Educational Revitalization in the Americas, August 1997).

In 1991, Colombia began an experimental voucher program for secondary education. The program is aimed at low-income families whose children have received their primary education in public schools; the vouchers are used to allow them to attend private secondary schools. The program began with 18,000 vouchers, and by 1995 had grown to 88,000—or about 4 percent of secondary school enrollment.

Source: Adapted from Inter-American Development Bank, *Economic and Social Progress in Latin America, 1996 Report* (Washington, DC: Inter-American Development Bank, 1996).

attractive profession. School principals and the local community should have the authority and resources to reward good teachers.

Countries should make a special effort to raise the status of the teaching profession. Governments should provide scholarships and loans to encourage bright students to become teachers. They should set salaries high enough to give increased prestige to the profession, and to attract and hold teachers with talent. Governments should establish incentives—monetary as well as non-monetary—for good professional conduct. They should tie bonuses, promotions, and public recognition to performance. They should make teachers directly accountable to school directors and parents.

Teacher training should be fundamentally reorganized, placing greater emphasis on substantive expertise and practical experience. Training should help teachers master techniques that promote critical thinking, problem-solving, and cooperative learning. Special initiatives are needed to improve the quality of teaching in rural areas. Colombia's Escuela Nueva program is an example of an initiative started by teachers to increase their ability to handle multi-grade classes at small rural schools (Box 4).

Governments should experiment with different approaches to evaluating performance, and involve local communities in the process. They should also give teachers greater authority and autonomy in determining how and what to teach, and offer them direct participation in education planning.

Teachers should take full advantage of every opportunity to enhance their professional status. They should agree to spend more hours teaching, adopt new methods, and regularly upgrade their skills. They should accept greater accountability to the schools and communities they serve as an essential step in professional advancement.

## Recommendation #4

*Invest more money per student in preschool, primary and secondary education.*

Most of the region's future labor force—and nearly all of its poor—are concentrated at the lower levels of the system, and will go no further. Their skills are the foundation for national economic growth. Countries that fail to invest properly in this crucial human resource will not realize their economic potential.

---

**Box 4. Improving Teaching in Rural Schools: Colombia's Escuelas Nuevas**

The Escuela Nueva reform began in the mid-1970s as an experiment by a group of teachers with financial support from NGOs. Since then, it has become an official government program serving 17,000 schools—almost half the rural schools in Colombia. The program objective is to expand access to primary education in Colombia's rural areas and to raise quality. Participating schools seek to provide a complete five-year primary education in areas where there are not enough students to justify a separate teacher for each grade. Most schools operate with only one or two teachers who use a flexible, multi-grade teaching approach. Students complete academic units at their own pace and work individually or in small groups, with older students helping younger students. Self-paced learning guides and accompanying teachers manuals are provided to the schools, along with a small library. An important part of the program is teacher training. Teachers receive in-service training at demonstration schools that are thought to be good examples of the Escuela Nueva approach and at follow-up workshops. Evaluations indicate that Escuela Nueva students do better than those in traditional rural schools, and that the program enjoys the strong support of teachers and the local community.

Source: Adapted from Martin Carnoy and Claudio de Moura Castro, *Improving Education in Latin America: Where to Now?* (Washington, DC: Inter-American Development Bank, 1996).

---

Good public education cannot be provided at present levels of expenditure. Latin America's top private schools perform at levels comparable to schools in the industrialized countries. Public school students, in contrast, perform dismally by any standard. Experimental schools in several countries have demonstrated that the performance of children can be brought up to acceptable levels—but only by managing schools differently and providing resources that significantly exceed those currently being invested in public schools. The gap between public and private education will only get worse unless more money is invested in public schools.

Accordingly, we urge governments to sharply increase their investment per student in preschool, primary, and secondary education. It doesn't matter whether the funds come from reallocating the education budget, draw-

# VI. EDUCATION: THE KEY TO PROGRESS

ing on other areas of government spending, or from new sources. What is important is that additional investment be generated, and deployed in tandem with the major institutional reforms we are recommending. Both fundamental change and additional resources are needed.

## A CALL TO ACTION

The recommendations of this task force pose a challenge to business as usual in the region. Powerful vested interests and bureaucratic inertia have made public schools seem impervious to change. Governments have failed to make education a top political priority and to put political muscle behind reform. Ministries are jealous of their power and patronage. Teachers unions have resisted efforts to make teachers more accountable to the communities they serve. University students have fiercely defended tuition-free higher education. Parents and community leaders have not stepped up to demand higher quality primary and secondary schools.

These are fundamentally political problems. The consensus on education is a false consensus. Everyone favors better schools, but few are willing to make the hard decisions that better schools require. The key actors—ministries, parents, teachers, and employers—disagree on key issues—money, control, accountability, choice, and jobs. Those disagreements are very difficult to resolve.

It is essential, therefore, that the task of improving the quality of education become everybody's business. To date, responsibility for educational reform has been confined to a small group of players. Technocrats have proposed reforms, and governments have attempted to enact them. The key stakeholders in education—parents, teachers, and employers—have not been consulted. That approach does not work. Instead, people from all parts of society must participate in efforts to improve public education. Parents, business leaders, political parties, churches, the media, labor unions, and professional associations should help set goals for the educational system, discuss policy options, and press for change. Teachers, who have long been excluded from reform planning, should play an important role.

The task force calls on individuals throughout Latin America and the Caribbean to recognize their role in educational reform and work to bring it about.

### To political leaders:

Many of you have made commitments to improving education. Now is the time to deliver on these promises. Make education a top priority and give it the attention and money it requires. Work to build a multi-party consensus on reform that will shield education from the destructive effects of political patronage and partisan advantage. As your nation's leaders, you are in a position to make the case to the public that a strong education system is essential to economic success, to the functioning of democratic institutions, and to a healthy civil society. And you alone can address the formidable political obstacles to change.

### To business leaders:

Throughout the world, business leaders have come to recognize the importance of high-quality primary and secondary schools for productivity, international competitiveness, and economic growth. But these changes will not be made without the help of the business community. You have an important role to play—through your expertise in management and finance, through your seed capital that can support new and innovative programs, and—most of all—through your political backing for reform-minded politicians. Only by intervening now will you have the employees you need to make your businesses competitive in the years to come.

### To parents:

Without your attention and support, educational reform is meaningless. It is essential that you become more deeply involved in your children's education. This means working with community leaders, teachers, and schools to demand excellence from the educational system and contributing your own effort and enthusiasm to bring it about.

### To teachers:

For too long you have been shut out of efforts to plan and carry out educational reform. You must be brought into the process—but, in exchange, you must take greater responsibility for your performance. We call on you to work with policymakers and local communities to establish a new educational compact that makes schools accountable to the children and families they serve.

## SUPPLEMENTAL COMMENTS
## by Members of the Taskforce

### José María Dagnino Pastore

I agree with the report in general, but would like to point out what I consider to be omissions and, in some cases, misplaced emphasis.

Education faces two challenges. It is fundamentally inefficient, producing visibly poor results, and its productivity is improving only slowly—which means it is becoming more costly over time. But globalization forces efficiency on governments, which limits the expenditures that they can make, and places serious restrictions on social policies. This in turn means that education will change profoundly—and those changes are already underway. The only question is whether change will come from without, through inadequate financing, segmentation, and de facto privatization, or from within, through proposals that respond to the demands of globalization.

Successful reform must meet the following requirements:

- an emphasis on the successful insertion of individual into society, and society into the world, along with teacher and student evaluations;
- a "leap" in the productivity of the education sector, correcting the chief inefficiency factors, for example, the low number of school days worked by the teachers, the lack of order in private education;
- the design, testing and extension of institutional and pedagogical experiments, usually by private, non-profit entities, aimed at improving the cost-benefit ratio of education with funds saved through the above measures; and
- increased financing based on the above, which improves the relative cost and equity of education.

## ABOUT THE MEMBERS OF THE TASK FORCE

### Co-Chairs

### José Octavio Bordón

(Argentina) is president of the Andean Foundation. He was governor of the province of Mendoza, Argentina, from 1987 to 1991, and also served in the senate, where he chaired the foreign relations committee. He is a former president of the Peronist Party, and has been a visiting professor at Georgetown University. He is a member of the Inter-American Dialogue.

### John Petty

(United States) is former chairman and chief executive officer of Marine Midland Bank. He also served as U.S. assistant secretary of the treasury for international affairs and chairman of the High Level Review Committee of the Inter-American Development Bank. He currently is chairman of Federal National Services, and is a member of the Inter-American Dialogue.

## MEMBERS

### Roberto Baquerizo

(Ecuador) is president of Banco Unión S.A. and of Multiplica, Consulting Company of Economic Studies, based in Quito. He is a member of the Chairman's International Advisory Council of Americas Society and the Inter-American Dialogue. He served as president of Fruit Shippers-Pacific Fruit in New York until 1996 and prior to that was head of the Central Bank of Ecuador.

### Patricio Cariola, S.J.

(Chile) is former director of the Center for Education Research and Development (CIDE) in Santiago. He represented private schools at the ministry of education and has served as president of the Federation of Secondary Education Institutes. He is a member of the International Development Research Centre's Research Review and Advisory Group and was a member of the board of directors of Georgetown University, Washington, D.C., and of the steering committee of the World Conference on Education for All (WCEFA).

### Juan E. Cintrón Patterson

(Mexico) is president of Consultores Internacionales CLB. He serves on the boards of numerous corporations in the United States and Mexico, including Grupo Modelo, Grupo Financiero Serfin, and the International Advisory Council of the University of Notre Dame, Indiana. He is president of the Mexican chapter of the World Presidents Organization, Junior Achievement-Mexico, the board of trustees of the Monterrey Institute of Technology, and the Cuernavaca Cultural Institute.

# VI. Education: The Key to Progress

## Jonathan Coles

(Venezuela) is chairman of the board of directors of Mavesa S.A., one of Venezuela's largest agribusiness conglomerates. He served as minister of agriculture of Venezuela, as presidential commissioner for emergency food supply and distribution, and as director of the Central Bank of Venezuela. He belongs to the Inter-American Management Education Foundation, the International Agribusiness Management Association, Inter-American Dialogue and the Yale Club of New York. He received his B.A. in philosophy from Yale University and his master's in business administration from IESA in Venezuela.

## José María Dagnino Pastore

(Argentina) is a professor of economics at the Catholic University of Argentina. He served as minister of finance, minister of economy and labor, and ambassador-at-large in Europe. He has also served as an advisor to the governments of four Latin American countries and has authored numerous books and articles on economics and finance. He served as governor of the International Monetary Fund, the World Bank, and the Inter-American Development Bank and chairman of the IMF Annual Meeting in 1969. He is a member of the Inter-American Dialogue.

## Nancy Englander

(United States) is vice president of Capital International, Inc., in Los Angeles, California, and president and director of the Emerging Markets Growth Fund, an equity fund with substantial investments in Latin America. She is chairman of the board and a trustee of New World Investment Fund, director of a number of capital funds investing in Latin America, and a member of the Inter-American Dialogue.

## Peter Hakim

(United States) is president of the Inter-American Dialogue, the leading U.S. center for policy analysis and exchange on Western Hemisphere affairs. The author of a regular column for the *Christian Science Monitor,* Mr. Hakim speaks and publishes widely on U.S.-Latin American relations. He serves on boards and advisory committees for the World Bank, Inter-American Development Bank, International Center for Research on Women, Carnegie Endowment for International Peace, and Human Rights Watch/Americas.

## Ivan Head

(Canada) is a past president of the International Development Research Centre of Canada. From 1968 to 1978 he was special assistant to the prime minister for foreign policy issues. He is an officer of the Order of Canada and a federal queen's counsel. He is professor of law and director of the Liu Centre for International Studies at the University of British Columbia, and a member of the Inter-American Dialogue.

## Rudolf Hommes

(Colombia) was rector of the University of the Andes in Bogotá. He has served as minister of finance, director of public credit, and advisor to the monetary board of Colombia, and at the World Bank as chairman of the Development Committee and president of the Group of Twenty-Four. He is a director of the Colombian business journal *Estrategia* and holds a Ph.D. in business administration from the University of Massachusetts.

## Emerson Kapaz

(Brazil) is chairman of the board of Elka Plásticos Ltd., a major toy manufacturer, and former president of the Brazilian Association of Toy Manufacturers and the Pensamento Nacional das Bases Empresariais (PNBE), an organization of Brazilian businessmen. He has also served as president of the administrative board of ABRINQ Foundation, which defends children's rights, and on the board of directors of the International Council of Toy Industries.

## Jacqueline Malagón

(Dominican Republic) is executive director of Action for Education and Culture (APEC), a non-governmental organization working to promote education reform in the Dominican Republic. She previously served as her country's minister of education and representative to the United Nations International Research and Training Institute for the Advancement of Women (INSTRAW), and as director of the non-governmental organization EDUCA. She has been named "Woman of the Year" by the Association of Secretaries and Businessmen of the Dominican Republic.

*José Mindlin*

(Brazil) is the founder of Metal Leve S.A., a leading Brazilian manufacturing company. He serves as vice president of the Federation of Industries of the State of São Paulo and is a member of the National Council of Scientific and Technological Development. He is chairman of the Advisory Board of the *Estado de São Paulo,* one of the leading Brazilian newspapers. Mr. Mindlin is also an honorary member of the International Council of the Museum of Modern Art in New York and a book collector for many years, owning a library of more than 30,000 volumes, and has been awarded an honorary degree of doctor of humane letters by Brown University, in Providence, R.I.

*Roberto Murray Meza*

(El Salvador) is president of La Constancia, S.A., a leading brewery and beverage distributor, Credomática (Salvadoran representative of Visa and MasterCard), and Bienes y Servicios. He previously served as president of the Central Reserve Bank of El Salvador. He sits on the boards of Taca International Airlines and Cemento de El Salvador, and is involved in the Salvadoran Foundation for Economic and Social Development (FUSADES), the Business Foundation for Educational Development (FEPADE), the Salvadoran Social Investment Fund, and the Foundation for Integral Education in El Salvador (FEDISAL). He is a member of the Inter-American Dialogue, the Chairman's International Advisory Council of the Americas Society, Caribbean/Latin American Action, and the Young Presidents Organization, and served on the Commission for the Reconstruction and Development of Central America (Sanford Commission). He holds a bachelor's degree in economics from Yale, a master's degree from Middlebury College, and an MBA from Harvard.

*Manuel Fernando Sotomayor*

(Peru) is president of Productos Pesqueros Peruanos, S.A., one of Peru's largest fish-processing corporations. He is president and founding member of Peru 2021, a business organization that promotes sustainable development projects, second vice president of the National Confederation of Private Business Institutions (CONFIEP), vice president of the Peru-Japan Business Council, and past president of the National Fisheries Society and the Fishmeal Exporters Organization. In 1992 he was named "Businessman of the Year" by *América Economía,* a leading Latin American business magazine. He is a member of the Group of 50.

*Osvaldo Sunkel*

(Chile) is president of the Corporation for Development Research (CINDE), senior fellow of the Center for the Analysis of Public Policies at the University of Chile, special advisor to the UN Economic Commission for Latin America and the Caribbean (ECLAC), and director of the magazine *Pensamiento Iberoamericano.* He is a member of the Academy of Social Sciences of the Chile Institute and of the Colombian Academy of Economic Sciences. In 1994 he received the Kalman Silvert Prize of the Latin American Studies Association. He has authored several books published in a number of countries and languages. His most recent publications include *Debt and Development Crises in Latin America* (1986) and *Environmental Sustainability of Chilean Economic Growth* (1996).

*Celina Vargas do Amaral Peixoto*

(Brazil) was general director of the Getulio Vargas Foundation in Brazil. She is a member of the Brazilian State Reform Council, the Commission on Global Governance, and several national commissions on cultural, historical and technological issues. She served as director of Brazil's National Archives from 1980 to 1990 and has written extensively on Brazilian political and social history.

## SUGGESTED READINGS

**Birdsall, Nancy, David Ross and Richard Sabot.** 1997. "Education, Growth, and Inequality" in *Pathways to Growth: Comparing East Asia and Latin America.* Nancy Birdsall and Frederick Jaspersen (eds.). Washington, D.C.: Inter-American Development Bank.

**Economic Commission for Latin America and the Caribbean (ECLAC) and UNESCO Office for Latin America and the Caribbean.** 1992. *Education and Knowledge: Basic Pillars of Changing Production Patterns with Social Equity.* Santiago, Chile: ECLAC. (Also available in Spanish.)

**Inter-American Development Bank.** 1996. "Education: The Dynamics of a Public Monopoly," in *Economic and Social Progress in Latin America, 1996 Report.* Washington, D.C.: Inter-American Development Bank, chapter 4. (Also available in Spanish.)

**Lockheed, Marlaine E., Adriaan M. Verspoor and associates.** 1991. *Improving Primary Education in Developing Countries.* London: Oxford University Press.

**Organization of American States.** 1998. *Education in the Americas: Quality and Equity in the Globalization Process.* Washington, D.C.: Organization of American States. (Also available in Spanish.)

**Puryear, Jeffrey** (ed.). 1997. *Partners for Progress: Education and the Private Sector in Latin America and the Caribbean (Second Edition).* Washington, D.C.: Inter-American Dialogue, Chairman's Advisory Council of the Americas Society, and Latin American Business Council (CEAL). (Also available in Spanish.)

**Schultz, Theodore.** 1961. "Investment in Human Capital." *American Economic Review* 51 (March).

**The World Bank.** 1995. *Priorities and Strategies for Education: A World Bank Review.* Washington, D.C.: The World Bank. (Also available in Spanish.)

## PREAL OCCASIONAL PAPERS

All papers in this series are available in Spanish and Portuguese, and most are available in English. They can be accessed through the PREAL web page at http://www.preal.cl.

**No. 1.** Robert G. Myers. "Preschool Education in Latin America."

**No. 2.** Robert E. Slavin. "Salas de Clase Efectivas, Escuelas Efectivas: Plataforma de Investigación para una Reforma Educativa en América Latina."

**No. 3.** Diane Ravitch. "National Standards In Education: A 'State of the Practice'" (a summary of Diane Ravitch, *National Standards in American Education: A Citizen's Guide,* Washington, D.C.: The Brookings Institution, 1995; summary prepared by Nancy Morrison.)

**No. 4.** David N. Wilson. "Reform of Vocational and Technical Education in Latin America."

**No. 5.** Cecilia Braslavsky and Gustavo Cosse. "Las Actuales Reformas Educativas en América Latina: Cuatro Actores, Tres Lógicas y Ocho Tensiones."

**No. 6.** Gloria Calvo. "Enseñanza y Aprendizaje: En Busca de Nuevas Rutas."

**No. 7.** Jeffrey M. Puryear. "Education in Latin America: Problems and Challenges."

**No. 8.** Cristián Cox. "Education Reform in Chile: Context, Content and Implementation."

**No. 9.** E. Mark Hanson. "Educational Decentralization: Issues and Challenges."

**The Partnership for Educational Revitalization in the Americas (PREAL)** is a hemispheric partnership of public- and private-sector organizations seeking to promote informed debate on policy alternatives, identify and disseminate best education practices emerging in the region and elsewhere, and monitor progress toward improving education policy. PREAL is jointly managed by the Inter-American Dialogue, based in Washington, D.C., and the Corporation for Development Research (CINDE) in Santiago, Chile. It includes actors from civil society, governments, universities, political leaders, the business community, international organizations, and churches.

PREAL is a response to the growing importance of education to economic growth and social development. Open economies, democratic politics, and decentralized government have placed new demands on schools, requiring that they produce a flexible work force, foster technological change, prepare people for democratic citizenship, and expand social opportunities.

PREAL seeks to help improve the quality and equity of education in Latin America and the Caribbean by promoting better education policy.

It pursues three intermediate objectives:

1. build public- and private-sector support for educational reform;

2. strengthen public- and private-sector organizations working for educational improvement; and

3. identify and disseminate best education policies and practices.

PREAL operates through a network of associated centers based in countries throughout Latin America and the Caribbean. They work with key policy and opinion leaders from business, labor, political parties, churches, the media, and government to strengthen public debate on education, and to identify promising policy options for reform.

PREAL receives financial support from the U.S. Agency for International Development, the Canadian International Development Research Centre, the Inter-American Development Bank, and the GE Fund. Through its associated centers, PREAL also receives support at the national level from a variety of public and private institutions.

The **Inter-American Dialogue** is the premier U.S. center for policy analysis, communication, and exchange on Western Hemisphere affairs. The Dialogue's select membership of 100 distinguished citizens from throughout the Americas includes former presidents and cabinet-level officials as well as business and other private-sector leaders. The Dialogue seeks to promote informed debate on hemispheric problems, advance opportunities for regional economic and political cooperation, expand channels of communication among the countries of the Americas, and bring fresh, practical proposals for action to the attention of governments, international institutions, and private organizations. Since 1982, throughout successive Republican and Democratic administrations, the Dialogue has helped shape the agenda of issues and choices on inter-American relations.

**The Corporation for Development Research (CINDE)** is a private, non-profit institution based in Santiago, Chile. Founded in 1968, CINDE provides a non-partisan academic environment for interdisciplinary research on national and international development issues.

# VI. EDUCATION: THE KEY TO PROGRESS

*The Partnership for Educational Revitalization in the Americas (PREAL)*

## *Postscript:* Improving Education

A COMPARISON OF RECOMMENDATIONS ON EDUCATION IN THE PLAN OF ACTION FROM THE SANTIAGO SUMMIT AND THE REPORT OF THE PREAL TASK FORCE ON EDUCATION, EQUITY, AND ECONOMIC COMPETITIVENESS IN THE AMERICAS

Overall, the two reports cover similar subject areas but with different emphases. The Summit Plan of Action has as its primary objective increased *access* to quality education. On key issues, such as decentralization, school autonomy, school choice, accountability, and national testing, the Summit document either conditions statements with "where appropriate" or is notably silent. The focus is on strengthening existing institutions rather than reforming them. Changes are phrased in terms of ends, without specific reference as to the means that will be used to accomplish those ends. As a document of governments, its focus is on what governments will do, with only occasional reference to cooperation with other actors. The document also carefully avoids committing governments to increased educational spending.

By contrast, the Task Force report calls for specific structural changes and suggests means for improving the quality of education. It places responsibility for change on all stakeholders, calling on politicians, businesses, communities and teachers alike to cooperate in making reforms happen. For the Task Force, the problems of education reform are fundamentally political. The consensus on education is a false one. Although everyone favors better schools, few actors are willing to make the hard decisions that better schools require. The Task Force report realistically points out that increased per-pupil spending, along with structural reform, will be required.

| Topic Area | Santiago Summit Declaration | PREAL Task Force Report | Analysis |
|---|---|---|---|
| Mission | Ensure access to and improve the quality of education, based on the principles of equity, quality, relevance, and efficiency. | Improve school quality in order to better generate economic growth, promote equity and sustain democratic government. | **Summit Declaration** includes access.<br><br>**PREAL Task Force** makes quality the chief issue and ties it to equity, economic growth, and democracy. |
| Objectives | • Provide for universal access to and completion of quality primary education for 100% of children by the year 2010.<br>• Provide access for at least 75% of young people to quality secondary education, with increasing percentages of young people who complete secondary education by the year 2010.<br>• Assume responsibility for providing the general population with opportunities for life-long learning. | • Promote consensus and create new alliances among diverse sectors of society regarding the need for fundamental education reform.<br>• Broaden the constituency for reform by involving leaders from outside the education sector.<br>• Identify new and modern approaches to education policy merging in the region and elsewhere.<br>• Monitor progress toward improving education policy. | **Summit Declaration** is oriented strongly toward ends, defined entirely in terms of access.<br><br>**PREAL Task Force** emphasizes means that will promote reform and monitor its progress, including development of a broad coalition of leaders pressing for better schools.<br><br>**Summit Declaration** objectives are identical to 1994 Summit objectives. |
| Equity | • Implement targeted and inter-sectoral educational policies, as necessary, and develop programs that focus specifically on groups at a disadvantage in the areas of education, functional illiteracy, and socio-economic conditions, with attention to women, minorities, and vulnerable populations.<br>• Inter-sectoral programs in education, health and nutrition, as well as early childhood educational strategies, will be priorities inasmuch as they contribute more directly to plans to combat poverty. | • At present, schools are exacerbating inequality instead of reducing it. Major quality differences between public and private schools illustrate the problem. Gender equity in terms of access is commendable, but the need now is to treat girls equally once they are in school.<br>• Much of the income inequality in Latin America reflects a failure to invest in quality education for the region's children. | **Summit Declaration** does not mention the magnitude of existing inequities in school systems and relies entirely on "targeted and inter-sectoral policies" to achieve equity.<br><br>**PREAL Task Force** declares that inequity in education is a major problem and that current school systems are making the problem worse. It argues that the disadvantaged cannot be served unless the system is fundamentally reorganized. |
| Education Standards and Evaluation | • Establish or strengthen systems to evaluate the quality of education which permit assessment of the performance of various educational actors, innovations, and factors associated with achievements in learning. | • Set standards for the education system and measure progress toward meeting them.<br>• Develop a system of education statistics and indicators which emphasizes educational outcomes, not inputs, and is compatible with the OECD system. | Both documents strongly urge establishing national systems to evaluate performance of schools. |

*Continued on next page*

# VI. EDUCATION: THE KEY TO PROGRESS

Postscript: PREAL — Improving Education

| Topic Area | Santiago Summit Declaration | PREAL Task Force Report | Analysis |
|---|---|---|---|
| Education *continued* | • Indicators will be made available that can be used to design, carry out, and evaluate equitable quality improvement programs.<br>• Standards for reading, writing, mathematics, and science shall receive special attention.<br>• Where appropriate, data will be collected that permits comparison of educational indicators across countries. | • Establish national content and performance standards that outline what students should know when they complete each grade.<br>• Establish a national testing system that measures progress toward achieving the new educational standards.<br>• Use the results of national tests to revise programs, reallocate resources, and inform the public about school performance. | **PREAL Task Force** states clearly that countries should "establish national content and performance standards," whereas **Summit Declaration** makes a weaker statement, urging only "special attention" to standards.<br><br>**Summit Declaration** makes no mention of reforming systems of education statistics and making them compatible with the OECD.<br><br>**Summit Declaration** does not advocate releasing evaluation results to the public, nor using them to reallocate funds.<br><br>**PREAL Task Force** urges countries to participate in international tests, whereas **Summit Declaration** makes cross-national comparison of indicators optional. |
| Teaching Profession | • Develop comprehensive programs to improve and increase the level of professionalism among teachers and school administrators. The program should combine pre-service and in-service training, exploring incentive mechanisms tied to updating their skills, and meeting such standards as may have been agreed upon.<br>• Higher education must collaborate in this endeavor through research and pedagogy, both of which should be strengthened. | • Strengthen the teaching profession, by raising salaries, reforming training, and making teachers more accountable to the communities they serve.<br>• Take firm steps (scholarships, attractive salaries, incentives, performance-based promotion, etc.) to make teaching a stronger and more attractive profession.<br>• Give school principals and the local community the authority and resources to reward good teachers. Teachers should be accountable to the communities they serve.<br>• Fundamentally reorganize teacher training, placing greater emphasis on substantive expertise and practical experience.<br>• Give teachers greater autonomy in determining how and what to teach. Involve them directly in education planning. | Both documents focus on strengthening the profession of teaching, via improving training and establishing performance incentives.<br><br>**PREAL Task Force** urges that teachers be paid competitive salaries, given greater autonomy in the classroom, and made more accountable to principals and consumers; **Summit Declaration** mentions none of these. |

*Continued on next page*

| Topic Area | Santiago Summit Declaration | PREAL Task Force Report | Analysis |
|---|---|---|---|
| Institutional Change | • Strengthen education management and institutional capacity at the national, regional, local, and school levels, furthering, where appropriate, decentralization and the promotion of better forms of community and family involvement.<br>• Encourage the mass media to contribute to bolstering efforts being made by educational systems. | • Give schools and local communities more control over—and responsibility for—education.<br>• Give school directors, parents and local communities responsibility for school management, including resource allocation, classroom organization and authority over teachers in personnel decisions such as salaries, evaluations, promotions, hiring and firing.<br>• Parents should have choices among competing schools.<br>• Schools should experiment with private management.<br>• Central governments should develop a new role, withdrawing from directly running schools and instead concentrating on generating funds, setting standards, promoting equity, monitoring progress, and evaluating results. | Both documents emphasize greater involvement by parents and the local community in education, and **Summit Declaration** singles out mass media.<br><br>**PREAL Task Force** strongly advocates fundamental institutional reform, placing responsibility and authority in the hands of the school and the community. Specific mention of giving schools authority to hire and fire teachers.<br><br>**Summit Declaration** urges strengthening capacities at local level, but does not recommend giving schools more decision-making authority, promoting choice and competition among schools, involving the private sector, or establishing a new role for central governments. Local participation is conditional ("where appropriate"). |
| Preparation for the World of Work | • Strengthen preparation, education, and training for the world of work so that an increasing number of workers can improve their standard of living and, together with employers, have the opportunity to benefit from hemispheric integration.<br>• Adopt new technology as appropriate, based on different options and alternatives, ranging from specific occupational training to strengthening general employability competencies.<br>• Establish or strengthen mechanisms that permit workers to obtain certification of job-related competencies acquired through formal education and work.<br>• Include actions that take into account the development of entrepreneurial skills involving the different sectors and offering various options and alternatives. | • The poor educational attainment of Latin American workers is cited as major hurdle confronting the region. Latin America's labor force has less education today than any country in Southeast Asia and appears to be falling further behind. On average, Latin American workers have nearly two years less schooling than workers in other countries with similar incomes.<br>• Secondary students drop out to take jobs, but they lack the language, math, science and problem-solving skills necessary for success in modern economies.<br>• The Task Force calls on business leaders to support innovation reform programs and provide political backing for reform-minded politicians in order to ensure having employees qualified to meet future needs. | Both documents emphasize providing students with the skills and problem-solving abilities necessary for a changing job market.<br><br>**Summit document** calls for certification of job-related skills and adoption of new technology.<br><br>**PREAL Task Force** stresses involvement of business community in decisions on education policy as means of better connecting education to the demand for skills. |

*Continued on next page*

# VI. Education: The Key to Progress

| Topic Area | Santiago Summit Declaration | PREAL Task Force Report | Analysis |
|---|---|---|---|
| Multi-culturalism | • Establish or improve, according to their internal legal framework, educational strategies relevant to multi-cultural societies, so as to shape, with the participation of indigenous populations and migrants, models for bilingual and inter-cultural basic education.<br>• Enhance the content of basic education, together with respect and appreciation for the cultural diversity of peoples, and expand the knowledge of the different languages spoken in the hemisphere, where resources and possibilities permit. | No specific mention. Emphasis is on all the poor. | |
| Values | • Develop, within and outside schools, with the assistance of families and other actors and social organizations, educational strategies that foster the development of values, with special attention to the inclusion of democratic principles, human rights, gender-related issues, peace, tolerance and respect for the environment and natural resources. | No specific mention. | |
| Technology and Distance Education | • Promote access to and use of the most effective information and communication technologies in education systems. Emphasis on the use of computers, in combination with revised pedagogical methods and proper training for teachers in the use of these technologies.<br>• Strengthen distance education programs and information networks established.<br>• Use technology to link schools and communities to establishing ties in the hemisphere and encourage the participation of higher education institutions that have advantages in this field. | No specific mention. | |

*Continued on next page*

| Topic Area | Santiago Summit Declaration | PREAL Task Force Report | Analysis |
|---|---|---|---|
| Teaching Materials | • Make efforts to increase the availability of teaching materials in collaboration with official institutions and, depending on the specific conditions in each country, with the private sector. | • Lack of teaching materials is cited as one side effect of inadequate investment in education. Most governments devote less than five percent of education to teaching materials, such as texts, workbooks, and rudimentary school libraries. Many schools have no teaching materials at all. | **Summit document** assumes that teaching materials are the responsibility of central governments.

**PREAL Task Force** assumes that if schools have the power to allocate their budgets, they will invest more in teaching materials. |
| Exchange Programs | • Further scholarship and exchange programs for students, teachers, researchers, and educational administrators using strategies including institution-to-institution ties, communications technology, and internships which permit exposure to pedagogical and management innovations in the hemisphere. This will strengthen the institutional capacity of Ministries or Departments of Education, decentralized administrative entities, and centers of higher learning. | No specific mention. | |
| Finance | • The IDB is encouraged to work with member countries to substantially increase the share of new lending for primary and secondary education, by more than doubling the quantity over the next three years, compared to the previous three years.
• We also request that the IDB establish a special regional fund for education in the hemisphere, utilizing the existing resources of this institution. This fund would support efforts to raise educational standards and performance throughout the region.
• OAS, World Bank, and IDB, and other national and multilateral agencies are requested to provide support for programs and initiatives consistent with their own areas of action and the goals/objectives of the Plan of Action. | • Invest more money per student in preschool, primary, and secondary education.
• National or state-level ministries of education should continue to take principal responsibility for financing education and should see that funds are allocated so as to address geographic and cultural disparities.
• It doesn't matter whether the funds come from reallocating the education budget, drawing on other areas of government spending, or from new sources. What is important is that additional investment be generated and deployed in tandem with the major institutional reforms recommended.
• Governments should also establish incentives for greater private investment, via tuition payments, in education.
• Governments should experiment with financing the demand for education (vouchers, capitation grants, etc.). | Both documents acknowledge that additional resources are needed to implement change.

**PREAL Task Force** strongly urges countries to invest more in education, in tandem with institutional reforms, and to experiment with new approaches to finance, such as financing the demand and establishing incentives for greater private funding.

**Summit Declaration** focuses entirely on increasing lending for education by development banks. It does not recommend greater national investments in education nor experimenting with new approaches to finance. Only mention of private sector is in terms of regional cooperation and "contributions." |

*Summit Declaration* focuses entirely on increasing lending for education by development banks. It does not recommend greater national investments in education, nor experimenting with new approaches to finance. Only mention of private sector is in terms of regional cooperation and "contributions."

# VI. EDUCATION: THE KEY TO PROGRESS

*The **Caribbean/Latin American Action (C/LAA)** is a non-profit organization governed by an international Board of Trustees that promotes private sector generated economic development in the Caribbean and Latin America. C/LAA has played an active role engaging the business community in the move toward a Free Trade Area of the Americas by serving as a vehicle for private sector input at each of the major FTAA meetings, including the Summit of the Americas and subsequent business forums in Denver, Colorado (1995); Cartagena, Colombia (1996); and Belo Horizonte, Brazil (1997). (C/LAA's) program of work is divided along a sectoral basis, where business teams of company representatives from each sector come together to identify public policy actions that governments could take to increase regional prosperity through trade and investment liberalization.*

*This report was presented to the Roundtable on Education at the Informatics 2000 Exhibition, sponsored by the Inter-American Development Bank, at the Summit of the Americas in Santiago, Chile, April 1998. The report was prepared by Caribbean/Latin American Action and Bellcore International, with support from Informatics 2000 Initiative – Inter-American Development Bank; Global Information Infrastructure Commission; and The International Institute for Educational Excellence.*

# Hemisphere at a Crossroads: Education and Human Capital for the Information Age

## 1. INTRODUCTION / EXECUTIVE SUMMARY

Recent shifts in global economic patterns driven largely by the information technology revolution are changing the nature of competition among nations. Comparative advantages are increasingly based on innovation and knowledge rather than traditional factors of land, capital, and cheap labor. These charges are dramatically rewarding countries whose education systems are able to produce workers with the technical and learning skills needed to compete within the global economy.

This new environment places Caribbean and Latin American countries at a crossroads, where investments in education have enormous implications for their future role in the global economy. How effectively nations of Latin America and the Caribbean respond to the human capital development challenge posed by this new paradigm will determine their competitive role among nations of the world for many years to come.

Investments in education and human capital are proven to yield returns equal to or higher than many other government infrastructure investments. Economists from the Inter-American Development Bank, the World Bank, and the Organization of American States, among others, have developed sophisticated models, which confirm a clear and direct correlation between investments in education and levels of economic competitiveness and growth.

Many Caribbean and Latin American governments have not adequately considered these economic findings on returns to investment in education and human capital as they design national strategies for competition within the new global economy. These countries have failed to make the connection between education programs and national policies which strengthen economic stability and attract foreign investments.

There is a need, therefore, to translate the message contained in these economic analyses into a language that is both meaningful and compelling to local businesses and community members. These economic findings must be harnessed to generate public support and the political will needed to drive increased government investments in education. Policy-makers who recognize the impact of technology and are willing to make needed investments in education must be able to count on support from a public that understands the value of education and votes accordingly.

This paper is the first step in a process aimed at generating support for the greater and more effective investments in education and human capital. The paper begins by highlighting economic evidence documenting the relationship between education levels and economic performance and proposing ways of using this information to leverage additional support for effective human capital development programs. The paper then identifies a process by which governments are able to determine investments in education and human capital development, which provide the greatest possible return to societies. Emphasis is placed on the development of technology skills and on the importance of identifying and meeting urgent local needs. The paper strongly advocates the use of business-education partnerships to ensure that education investments are effective, sustainable and responsive to workforce requirements.

The paper concludes with recommendations based on analytical findings for the public and private sector. Recommendations will be formally presented to Heads of State during the Second Summit of the Americas in Santiago, Chile, and to the region's business community through the efforts of Caribbean/Latin American Action's Telecommunications Business Team and Board of Trustees.

## 2. HEMISPHERE AT A CROSSROADS: THE URGENCY OF PREPARING FOR THE 21ST CENTURY

The combined effects of market integration, democratization, and the new Information Age are creating a greater urgency to the need for nations of the region to prepare for the competitive challenges of the 21st Century.

In response to global integration and reform, the "continents" of the 21st Century are forming strategic economic partnerships rather than physical and geographical barriers. The Americas are integrating economically, Western Europe is formalizing the development of the European Community, and the Far East continues to consolidate its role as an economic powerhouse.

Expanding information networks are changing the nature of business and society through low-cost Internet applications such as electronic commerce, telemedicine, distance education, just-in-time learning, on-the-job performance support, electronic global marketing, telecommuting, and virtual communities. These technologies are becoming the most critical, most pervasive, most rapidly developing factors of competitive advantage in the world today. Nonetheless, outdated regulatory frameworks and inadequate human resources prevent many countries from using these technologies effectively. These countries must respond aggressively to develop both the human resources and regulatory frameworks that support the use of modern information and communications technologies.

If nations of the region fail to develop the capacity to utilize these powerful information tools, the gap with respect to the industrialized world will widen to a point at which the social, political, and economic structures of the region will be seriously at risk.

## 3. HUMAN CAPITAL DEVELOPMENT: THE KEY INGREDIENT FOR SUCCESS

The critical factor for competing within this changing global economic arena is a human resource pool with technical competence and adaptive learning skills to support the use of modern technologies. The technological shifts described above are generating a critical shortage of workers and managers with the skills needed for the technology and telecommunications age. Caribbean and Latin American countries must respond aggressively by developing the human capital needed for both traditional and knowledge-based services and industries.

Reducing this shortage of skilled and educated workers requires a strong education system that continuously re-evaluates coursework and curriculum to ensure that the skills being developed are relevant to emerging workforce requirements. Re-evaluation of teacher training programs is also necessary to ensure that technology tools are being used within the education process by teachers who are competent in the use of these tools. Education programs must be complemented by effective programs in health, community, family, and civil society, and by private sector initiatives that provide on-the-job training in areas such as organizational development, systems thinking, technical know-how, specialized knowledge, and management competence.

## 4. HIGH RATES OF RETURN ON INVESTMENTS IN HUMAN CAPITAL: CITING THE EVIDENCE

The findings of studies in the economics of human capital in this analysis provide a basis for quantifying anticipated returns to additional investment in education. Because of the magnitude of these returns relative to returns on physical capital infrastructure investments, these analyses provide economic justification for greater government expenditures on human capital development in preparation for the 21st Century.

# VI. EDUCATION: THE KEY TO PROGRESS

## A. Returns on Investment in Education

The countries of Latin America and the Caribbean have extraordinary opportunities to benefit from additional investment in the human capital of their nations. According to the Inter-American Development Bank, one additional year of average education in a nation is estimated to increase real economic output from 5% to as much as 20%.[1] Figures from the 1970s and 1980s demonstrate that a one-year increase in a nation's average level of education increases real economic output by as much as 20%, although a minimum average education of 3 to 4 years may be necessary as a foundation before this improvement is noted, thus generating an average 5% per year for the first four years.[2,3] Recognizing the implications of these figures, the Inter-American Development Bank (IDB) currently allocates 40% of its lending to social and human capital development programs.

These estimates are supported by World Bank statistics for average social returns (benefits to society as a whole) to investment in education for different developing regions, with Latin America and the Caribbean estimated at 17.9%; Asia at 19.9% and Sub-Sahara Africa at 24.3%, as shown in Graph 1 below.[4]

Investments in education have been shown to have different rates of return for society and for individuals. For a representative sample of 32 countries, the average social rate of return for primary education is 19.4%, for secondary education 13.5% and for higher education 11.3%.[5] Rates of return for individuals (benefits to the individual and their families) are somewhat higher. For those attending primary education, the return on personal investments is 23.7%, for those attending secondary education it is 16.3%, and for higher education 17.5%. In developing nations, individual rates of return exceed these international averages, reflecting greater education subsidies to schools and universities in these nations.[6] This underscores the importance of scholarship programs to promote equity within the region.

Rates of return to society for education investments in skilled professions are particularly large. In the United States, the social rate of return for an associate degree for electrical technicians was 41.3%, a bachelors degree in architecture was 23.6%, and an associates degree in accounting was 23%.[7]

For industries in Brazil, workers with higher levels of education receive proportionally higher wage markups due primarily to their education rather than other factors including tenure and experience.[8] These findings are especially important to the region's information technology industry, because of the greater economic benefits that could be derived from investments made for information technology careers.

**Graph 1.**
**Average Returns to Investment for Developing Countries by Region**
**(as percentage increase over original investment)**

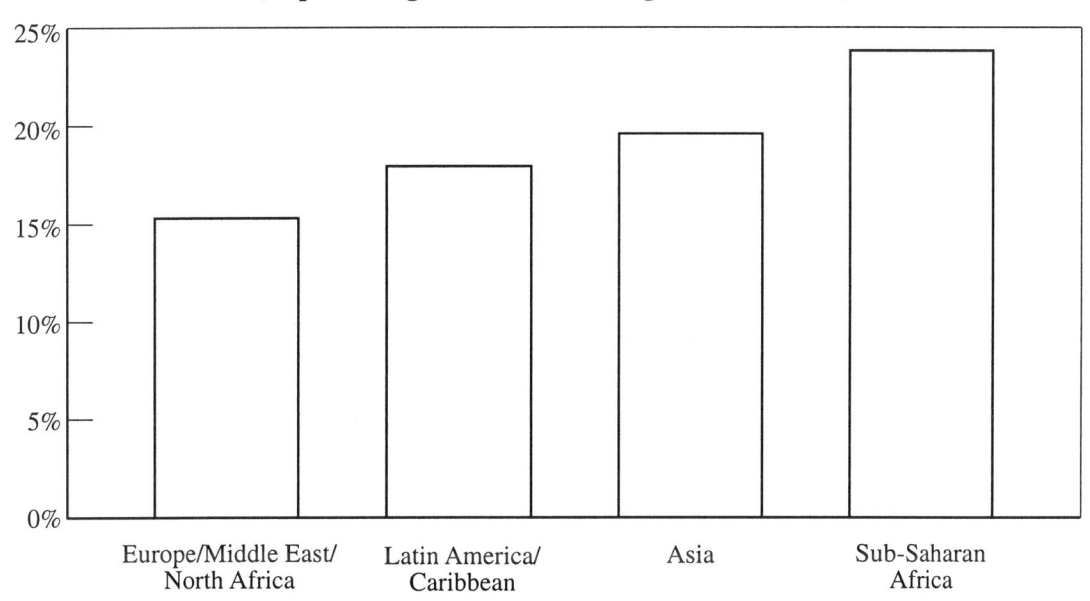

Source: George Psacharopoulos, *Returns to Investment in Education: A Global Update,* Washington, D.C.: The World Bank, 1994.

*Human Capital and Economic Growth: Comparing the Americas and Asia*

Statistical analyses indicate that countries with a higher level of human capital relative to physical capital are likely to benefit from faster economic growth. Many economists believe this was a factor in East Asia's success: in the early 1960s the Asian tigers had relatively well educated workforces and low levels of physical capital. Broader policies of encouraging education, opening the economy to foreign technologies, promoting trade and keeping taxes low are cited as the determining factors in the Asian region's high level of economic growth.[9]

Analyses reveal striking figures to support these claims: if Korea had been limited to the lower enrollment rates for secondary schools which were experienced in Brazil during the 1970s, there would have been an 8.3% reduction in Korea's per capita GDP by the year 1985.[10]

In Korea, Taiwan, Singapore, and Hong Kong between 1960 and 1990 the average educational level rose from 3.5 years to almost 9 years, while in Latin America the average rose from 2.8 years to 4.8 years.[11] Around the same time, the percentage of the population of East Asia living below $1 per day dropped from 24% in 1987 to 14% by 1993, while the percentage in Latin America and the Caribbean increased from 22% to 24% during the same period.[12] These figures show that:

- Korea's educational attainment was an increase of 5.5 years, while Latin America's was only 2 years.
- High levels of social inequality in the delivery of education in Latin America compared to Asia which explain why the average educational level in Latin America increased at the same time that the level of poverty in the region also increased (see graphs 2 and 3).

*Human Capital and Physical Capital: Comparing Rates of Return*

The extremely favorable rates of return on human capital development ranging from 11% to 40% compare favorably with anticipated rates of return for capital infrastructure projects. Depending on the economic risk, electrical generation projects are often approved with rates of return ranging from 15% to 22%, electrical transmission and gas pipeline projects of 10% to 12%, and roads and other physical capital investments of 12% to 30%. This comparison highlights the opportunity for greater return on investments in human capital.

In addition to returns on investment in education, there is substantial evidence of the potential for high returns to other key components of human capital development in Latin America and the Caribbean, an example of which is the effective delivery of healthcare. Economic analyses by the World Health Organization document sizable economic returns on healthcare investments across the globe in the range of 16% to 1500%. The following examples reveal the opportunity to dramatically increase the human capital of a nation through carefully evaluated investments in healthcare:

- A recent study in Israel estimated the costs and benefits that would result from a viral hepatitis B prevention program, including the indirect benefits of reduced work absences and mortality, would provide a return on investment of 41%.[13]

- In addition to being a public health problem, blindness and visual impairment have important socioeconomic implications. The costs of rehabilitation and care may be the most apparent. Equally important are the indirect costs resulting from the loss of productivity. A South Asian study revealed that not only did 85% of the men and 58% of the women who regained their sight return to work, but that there was also a financial return of 1500% on the expense in the year following surgery.

- In many developed countries, diabetic retinopathy, the most common cause of vision loss in the working population, can be effectively prevented by adequate control of diabetes and through periodic examination and laser surgery when required. In a study in the USA, the annual savings of welfare benefits per patient with severe visual loss caused by diabetes was estimated to be nearly seven times the cost of examination and treatment.[14]

## B. Qualitative Returns on Human Capital Investments

The benefits of human capital development are multifaceted and far-reaching. While we have described many qualitative returns to investment in education, there are extraordinary qualitative societal benefits, which cannot be mathematically measured. These include:

Social Benefits

- Higher levels of education, training, and computer literacy alleviate poverty.
- Education adds value to basic human rights, promises equal opportunity for all citizens, and alleviates

# VI. EDUCATION: THE KEY TO PROGRESS

**Graph 2.**
**Educational Level of the Labor Force**
Latin America and Southeast Asia

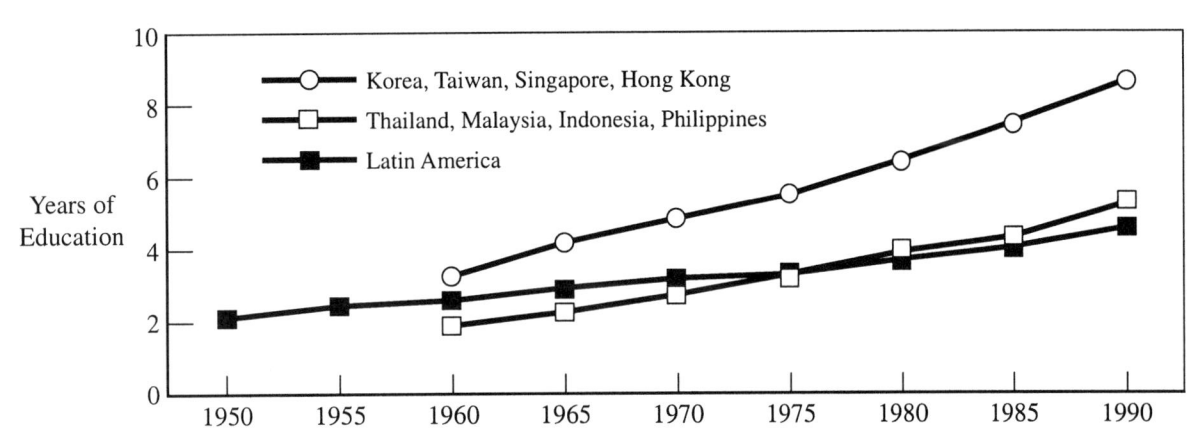

- ○ Korea, Taiwan, Singapore, Hong Kong
- □ Thailand, Malaysia, Indonesia, Philippines
- ■ Latin America

Source: Juan Luis Londoño, *Poverty, Inequality, and Human Capital Development in Latin America, 1950-2025.* Washington, DC: World Bank, 1996.

**Graph 3.**
**Incidence of Poverty**
1987 — 1992

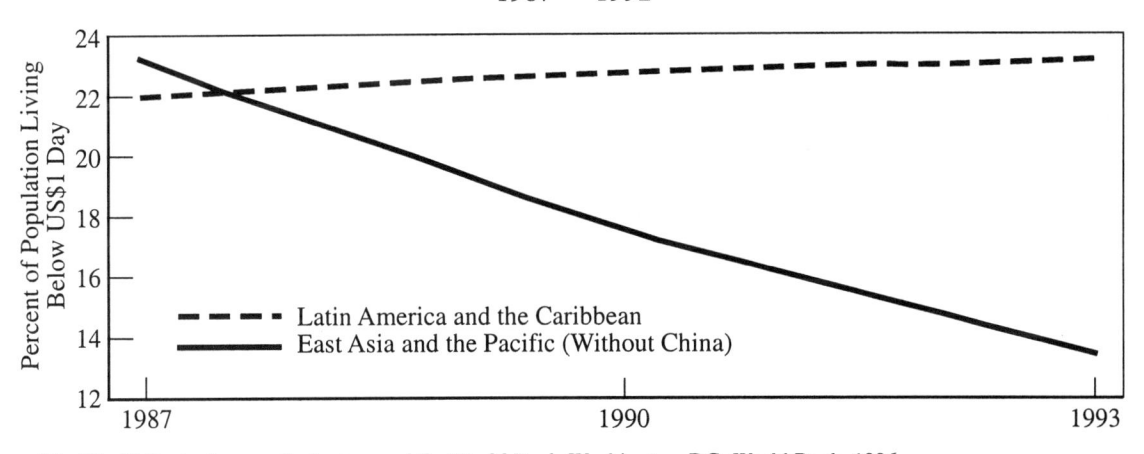

- - - - Latin America and the Caribbean
——— East Asia and the Pacific (Without China)

Source: The World Bank, *Poverty Reduction and the World Bank.* Washington, DC: World Bank, 1996.

the intensity of traditional socioeconomic and racial divisions.

- Access to information and training through electronic networks allows all levels of society to more effectively participate in both local and global economies.
- Better educated individuals are more able to participate as contributing members of society and of families, and to provide guidance for future generations.

- Skills developed through effective training decrease unemployment resulting in reduced need for government spending on subsidies, welfare programs, and crime prevention.

Political Benefits

- Democratic values and stability are strengthened by educated, literate, and empowered populations.
- Empowered and educated citizens and public figures raise standards for civil responsibility and community participation, thus gradually eliminating political favors and corruption.

- Skilled and educated populations take responsibility and initiative for their own economic health, diminishing the need for government intervention.
- Effective education programs increase personal income, widen the tax base and increase tax revenues.
- Education builds increased political participation and transparency, which strengthens public perception of Latin economies.

Business Benefits
- An educated, skilled workforce attracts foreign and local investment and development of human capital intensive industries and service sectors.
- Education promotes increases in the standard of living resulting in new domestic markets for products and expansion of international trade.
- Management and worker training increases corporate profitability and strength.

## 5. STRENGTHENING THE HUMAN CAPITAL INFRASTRUCTURE

Education is one of several key components which enables optimal development of a nation's human capital in support of long-term, sustainable economic development. Creating a full human capital infrastructure also requires support for a network of governmental, health, social services, community, business, and family institutions through which all components of human capital are developed.

In the same way that roads, railways and airports are key components of transportation infrastructures, components of the human capital infrastructure described below prepare the labor force for the global economy of the Information Age.

- Educational Institutions – at all levels, including primary, secondary, college and university, adult and organizational education and training, with a high priority for professional development of teachers and other human capital professionals.
- The Culture of the Workplace – building a strong culture of quality and productivity attitudes and skills through management training and mentoring programs, and company-wide quality programs.
- Technology – including computer-based training, telecommunications networks (distance education, Internet access, radio and TV), on-the-job performance support systems, and state of the art learning and teaching methodologies.
- Governmental, Regulatory, and Union Considerations – legal reforms, government regulations, and union contracts—need to redress constraints on investment in human capital.
- Civil Society – protection of democratic equality for all citizens and guaranteed mechanisms for citizen participation in the political, civil, and electoral process.
- Other Social Factors – including health, nutrition, social services, and personal safety.

## 6. FOCUSING INVESTMENTS TOWARDS THE AREAS OF GREATEST RETURN

Currently, significant portions of national budgets and international loans are being disbursed for educational programs. In general, investments have not been successful in achieving the necessary workforce development. To improve educational investment results, changes in the political decision-making process regarding investment priorities are needed. Governments must strengthen the role of local communities and private sectors in shaping education and human capital development programs, and must ensure that technology tools are fully utilized to improve workforce information technology skills.

### A. Meeting Urgent Local Needs

In the developing nations of Latin America and the Caribbean, scarce resources require educators to be highly discerning in choosing options for educational investments. For example, in some educational settings, urgently needed items such as desks, blackboards, teacher training and textbooks may yield a higher benefit than information technology tools.

It has been generally recognized in education reform that grassroots efforts are more effective than a top-down approach. The most successful projects in the region have been started at the grassroots level by individuals with substantial knowledge and experience of local circumstances.[15] This approach, as exemplified in business-education partnerships, relies on greater leadership by the individuals who will be responsible for program implementation, resulting in higher motivation to achieve ultimate success.

# VI. EDUCATION: THE KEY TO PROGRESS

## B. Developing Skills for the Information Age

The curriculum of the 20th Century school is becoming obsolete as the world enters into the Information Age. Rote learning, drill and practice lessons, memorization, and teacher-centered education were requirements of the Industrial Age. These skills were necessary for assembly line work and other types of manual labor. The Information Age and technology that accompanies it requires advanced skills in the creation and use of knowledge. These knowledge-based skills are developed through the classroom application of the latest technological advances in information systems and the design of curriculum and instruction based on new theories in cognitive science.

In classroom settings, information tools must be included as integral components of educational programs to develop a highly skilled workforce for the rapidly expanding information technology economic sector, to furnish the skill sets required for the Information Age:

- Basic literacy
- Computer literacy
- Researching, assimilating and synthesizing information
- Working in groups (synchronously or asynchronously)
- Working with other cultures, races, and languages
- Critical and independent thinking

Over time, representatives of the private sector, in collaboration with educators and constituencies, can assist in defining the information technology workforce requirements of their communities and developing funding proposals to obtain the relevant IT tools.

## 7. ENSURING RESULTS THROUGH BUSINESS – EDUCATION PARTNERSHIPS: GETTING THE BUSINESS COMMUNITY INVOLVED

Since productivity of the region's private sector depends on a more highly educated workforce, a clear incentive exists for the private sector to encourage investment in the development of human capital. Involving local and international business communities in education efforts is a critical factor in channeling of investments to ensure the highest returns. The private sector business community with Latin America and the Caribbean Basin must assume a greater role in achieving reform of the education system.

On a local level, partnerships with schools often include corporate citizen advocacy for needed changes in curriculum, teacher preparation, quality of instruction and choice of course materials. While most small businesses in the region cannot contribute technology or equipment to schools, they can make a difference by demanding better education services from national and local government leaders. Larger and mid-sized companies should take a more active role by generating partnerships for teacher training, student internships, shared training facilities, and curriculum development that targets industry-specific skills.

Multinational level business-education partnerships have also emerged as positive forces supporting education in the region and improving the allocation of resources to schools, universities, and training centers. Private sector investments, if properly focused, can help to provide the infrastructure, equipment, content and training needed to extend quality education services into rural areas. Through distance-learning techniques and information exchange, schools and local companies can benefit from training services developed by companies with far greater resources for these critical investments.

Business-education partnerships are particularly effective because they:

- Create valuable linkages between the business community and the education sector.
- Encourage creative, focused training programs tailored to meet labor force demands.
- Apply private sector management skills to innovative educational projects.
- Facilitate the problem definition process to derive locally defined solutions.
- Reinforce local institutions in their efforts to obtain funding.[16]
- Encourage public sector officials and community members in the field to assess educational and social needs in local areas.
- Provide input on use of economic models which quantify the benefits of education.
- Work with national governments to prepare new plans for business-education partnerships.

Business partnerships with schools, government leaders and parents strongly support community efforts in achieving results. As the benefits of these partnerships to companies, the education community, and society become apparent, additional partnerships must be formed to support educational innovation and improvement, to provide human and financial resources, and to support systematic reform of the education system.[17]

## 8. CONCLUSIONS

This white paper presents a comprehensive approach to addressing workforce challenges facing Latin America and the Caribbean as the region enters the 21st Century. This paper's analysis concludes that governments must partner with both local and multinational business communities to ensure the development of the human capital needed for competition in an aggressive global economy. The following conclusions summarize our findings:

1. The nations of Latin America and the Caribbean are at an important crossroads due to the combination of market liberalization and technological advancement. The need to respond to workforce challenges posed by these changes is urgent and vital to the region's future.

2. The response to this challenge demands human capital development focused on ensuring new and advanced workforce skills and knowledge.

3. Developing human capital requires excellent education and training institutions for students of all ages. However, in addition to improving schools and training centers, the entire human capital development infrastructure must be strengthened to ensure that all components complement each other to yield maximum results.

4. Investments in human capital development must be carefully chosen to maximize the return on investment. These choices must assess local needs and national workforce strategies and, where possible, incorporate use of information technologies to increased value and effectiveness of investments.

5. These investment choices require suppliers and employers of human capital to join together in partnerships to develop improved educational plans which also maximize use of scarce resources. These partners include teachers, administrators, government officials, business leaders, community members, and parents.

6. Business-education partnerships in the hemisphere are proven engines of change which should be encouraged.

## 9. RECOMMENDATIONS

Based on these findings, *governments* are urged to undertake the following reforms:

- *Develop a clear national education strategy* with input from businesses, teachers, parents and local community leaders.

- *Give greater authority to local governments to develop their own education strategies* with input from businesses, parents and community leaders.

- *Place greater emphasis on teacher training programs* by developing programs for formal training and information exchange among education professionals.

- *Establish national education standards* along with mechanisms for measuring and reporting performance levels.

- *Provide universal access to standard levels of education services* by increasing investment in primary and secondary education and making use of information and communications technologies to reach rural areas.

- *Acknowledge the importance of telecommunications infrastructure and technology applications as part of national education strategies* – by supporting efforts to expand telecommunications networks and develop applications for K-12 and continuing education.

- *Provide incentives for private sector investment* to address social needs in education and human capital development. Recognizing that market forces alone may not achieve universal access to education services, provide incentives for the use of information technology to:

  - Expand national information infrastructure (NII) and establish community centers to provide access to technology for education, health, social and commercial sectors.

  - Link universities, libraries and museums together by digitizing their information collections and making them available via the Internet.

  - Enable networking among teachers to accelerate the spread of best practices in education.

  - Expand the availability of education materials and resources for primary and secondary education as well as workforce training.

- *Establish partnerships with local and international business communities* to leverage their support and expertise in achieving educational reform. Provide incentives for the private sector to:
  - Identify human resources and skills needed in their particular industry sector.
  - Identify education investments which yield the greatest return on investment.
  - Provide teachers with training to foster computing and technology skills.
  - Generate practical experiences for students through internship programs.
  - Develop information resources with useful information of a local / regional nature.
  - Build shared training facilities for companies, students and educators.
  - Participate in programs to increase formal continuing education of the workforce.
- *Broaden the national approach to education to include a more comprehensive development of human capital infrastructure*, including health and social services.

To support government efforts, the *private sector* is urged to:

- **Identify** human resources and skills needed in their industry.
- **Work** with governments to develop short- and long-term strategies for education reform. Ensure that these strategies produce an education system that is able to respond to the workforce requirements of a competitive economy.
- **Assist** governments in focusing investments efficiently by targeting local priorities and identifying technologies which can help to increase returns.
- **Contribute** to the education process by providing computer and technology training for teachers; by developing curriculum and information resources based on industry needs; by supporting shared training facilities for use by companies, students and educators; and by developing programs to increase formal continuing education of the workforce.

## 10. APPENDICES

## A. Case Studies

The urgent human capital requirements of the region that we have described in this White Paper have prompted multilateral development banks, governments, local communities and private sector organizations to review ways to improve the quality, equity and efficiency of educational delivery systems. This process is exemplified in several case studies reflecting effective private/public sector partnerships to foster IT training, industry skills development, and cultivation of innovative teaching methods and problem-solving skills for students. Examples of projects of the Inter-American Development Bank which have been initiated or proposed to integrate business/education solutions include:

### Barbados Education Sector Improvement Program

This sector reform program is addressing four key components related to human resource development, training and the use of IT software and hardware to facilitate improvement of learning skill development. The objective of this program is to stimulate innovation in learning best practices through private sector incentive-based systems. Key elements of the program include:

1. Human resource skills training, problem solving and applications of IT education tools.
2. Integration of technology hardware and software applications with curriculum development.
3. Upgrade primary and secondary school facilities to accommodate computer networks.
4. Strengthen institutional capacity and outreach to local communities.

### Colombia Technical Training for the Paper Industry

This program will assist the Corporacion Centro de Capacitacion y Desarrollo Tecnologico para la Industria Papelera to help institutions develop industry-specific skills training related to the pulp and paper industry. It represents a unique joint-venture partnership between education and business partners. Key elements of the program include:

1. Curriculum enhancements for industry-related fields, standards and training.

2. Promotion of private sector participation in financing training design and supervision.
3. Facilitation of specialized seminars and workshops hosted by international industry experts.
4. Tracking industry trends in human resource development through employment trends.
5. Setting up a data bank on standards developed by key international industry competitors.
6. Technology exchange between Colombian and foreign counterpart firms.

## Costa Rica Modernization of Technical Education

This program is designed to improve the effectiveness and availability of training in formal and non-formal technical skills through establishment of a close partnership between the Instituto Nacional de Aprendizaje and various private sector groups. The program is intended to enhance youth's access to jobs through technology training by converting 10 of the formal Ciclo diversificado colleges into regionally specialized technologists' training centers. The remaining 70 colleges would continue to offer widespread academic curricula. Key elements of the program include:

1. Improve information about quality, relevance and costs of training.
2. Promote private sector involvement in articulation and definition of training needs.
3. Develop regional training and industry boards to create incentives for student learning.
4. Improve exchange of labor market information related to placement and job opportunities.
5. Expand innovative non-formal youth training programs with public/private sector inputs.

## B. Sponsoring Organizations

This analysis is a result of a joint research effort spearheaded by Caribbean/Latin American Action (C/LAA) and Bellcore International, with additional support from the Inter-American Development Bank's Informatics 2000 Initiative, the Global Information Infrastructure Commission (GIIC), and The International Institute for Educational Excellence (IE).

## Caribbean/Latin American Action

Caribbean Latin American Action (C/LAA), headquartered in Washington, D.C., is an independent, private non-profit organization that promotes private sector-oriented economic development in the countries of the Caribbean and Latin America. Founded in 1979 as a not-for-profit 501(c)(3) educational corporation, C/LAA focuses its programs primarily in the smaller economies of the region by encouraging U.S. and local governments and private sectors to address the economic and social needs of the region. C/LAA's Board of Trustees represents over 85 of the leading private sector companies in the U.S., Caribbean and Latin America, and works in Business Teams focused in the areas of education, agribusiness, apparel and textiles, energy, financial services, telecommunications, tourism and transportation. C/LAA will serve as a catalyst to involve its member companies in mobilizing and strategically focusing available resources toward high value educational opportunities.

## Bellcore International

Bellcore International is a wholly owned subsidiary of Bellcore. Bellcore, based in Morristown, New Jersey, USA, is a leading provider of communications software, engineering and consulting services based on world-class research. Bellcore provides business solutions that help information technology work for telecommunications carriers, businesses, and governments worldwide. Bellcore is a wholly owned subsidiary of Science Applications International Corporation (SAIC). The combined SAIC and Bellcore companies have estimated annual revenues for the current year of nearly $4 billion and more than 30,000 science, engineering, software, and administrative professionals.

## C. Supporting Institutions

### Informatics 2000 Initiative – Inter-American Development Bank

The Inter-American Development Bank has established the Informatics 2000 Initiative to encourage the deployment of significant information technology applications by the year 2000, which will support economic growth and social development throughout Latin America and the Caribbean. The Bank has drafted a plan to: identify information products and services with widespread demand in the region; develop strategies of policy reform and market development to enable their rapid introduction; arrange for policy advice, technical assistance, and funding to facilitate their implementation by the year 2000.

### Global Information Infrastructure Commission

The Global Information Infrastructure Commission (GIIC) is an independent, non-governmental initiative involving leaders from developing as well as industrialized countries. The GIIC Commissioners, representing leading international IT and telecommunications companies and organizations, agree on the need to accelerate the evolution of the Global Information Infrastructure (GII) or Global Information Society (GIS). Since 1995, the GIIC has been working to enhance development of a GII by strengthening the role of the private sector, promoting the involvement of developing countries, and facilitating activities and policy options that foster effective information infrastructure applications. The GIIC has identified education as one of the key needs in the development of the Global Information Infrastructure.

### The International Institute for Educational Excellence

The International Institute for Educational Excellence, Inc. (IE) is a not-for-profit educational corporation with offices in New York City. IE works with corporations, universities, and school districts to accomplish projects in support of education reform including policy analysis, comprehensive educational planning, development of grant applications, and design and delivery of training programs. The organization's special interest is the design of training using new approaches for human capital development to prepare educators for expanded roles required to prepare learners for the global economy and to facilitate education's culture shift to the Information Technology Educational Paradigm.

# Notes

1. Birdsall, Nancy and Sabot, Richard H., eds., *Opportunity Forgone: Education in Brazil*, Inter-American Development Bank, Washington, DC, 1996, page 110.

2. Birdsall, Nancy and Sabot, Richard H., eds., *Opportunity Forgone: Education in Brazil*, Inter-American Development Bank, Washington, DC, 1996, page 110.

3. Lau, L.J., D.T. Jamison, and F.F. Louat, 1990. "Education and Productivity in Developing Countries: An Aggregate Production Function Approach." Working Paper WPS 612, World Bank, Washington, DC, 1990.

4. Psacharopoulos, George, *Returns to Investment in Education: A Global View*, Washington, DC, The World Bank, 1994.

5. Psacharopoulos, George, *Returns to Education: An International Comparison*, Jossey-Bass, San Francisco, 1973, pages 5-6.

6. Psacharopoulos, George, 1973, pages 5-6.

7. McMahon, W.W. and Geske, T., eds., *Financing Education: Overcoming Inefficiency and Inequality*, University of Illinois Press, Urbana, Illinois, 1982, Chapter 7 (and in Psacharopoulos, G., (ed.) *Economics of Education: Research and Studies*, Pergamon Press, New York, 1987, page 192).

8. Birdsall and Sabot, 1996, page 230.

9. Barro, Robert, "The poor and the rich," *The Economist*, 1996.

10. Birdsall, Nancy and Sabot, Richard H., eds., *Opportunity Forgone: Education in Brazil*, Inter-American Development Bank, Washington, DC, 1996, page 31.

11. Londono, Juan Luis, "Poverty, Inequality, and Human Capital Development in Latin America, 1950-2025," World Bank, Washington, DC, 1996.

12. "Poverty Reduction and the World Bank," World Bank, Washington, DC, 1996.

13. Ginsberg G., Berger S., Shouval D., *Bulletin of the World Health Organization*, 1992.

14. "Blindness and Visual Disability." Fact Sheet N 145, part IV of VII: Socioeconomic Aspects, World Health Organization, February 1997.

15. "Education in the Information Age Conference Summary," July 11, 1997, Inter-American Development Bank, page 4.

16. In Latin America, many such programs have already experienced success, and findings are compiled in an edited volume of case studies of business-education partnerships developed by the Americas Society, the Latin American Business Council (CEAL), and Inter-American Dialogue, as cited in, *Partners for Progress: Education and the Private Sector in Latin America and the Caribbean*, Puryear, Jeffrey M., Second Edition, Inter-American Dialogue, Washington, DC, 1997.

17. Puryear, Jeffrey M., ed., "Partners for Progress: Education and the Private Sector in Latin America and the Caribbean," Inter-American Dialogue, Washington, DC, 1996.

# VII. Preserving and Strengthening Democracy and Human Rights

# VII. PRESERVING AND STRENGTHENING DEMOCRACY AND HUMAN RIGHTS

# Establishing an Effective Government-Civil Society Dialogue

*Civil Society Task Force — Washington, D.C.*

*Esquel Group Foundation (EGF), a non-profit, private foundation created in 1984, provides a variety of services to non-governmental organizations, foundations, private corporations and international development agencies working in Latin America and the Caribbean. Its membership in the Grupo Esquel network of entities in Argentina, Bolivia, Brazil, Chile, Ecuador, Peru and Uruguay enhances the expertise it draws upon to provide quality services. It promotes alternative policies and programs that incorporate social equity and environmental concerns and strengthen the role of civil society. In addition, EGF works in collaboration with private sector entities to improve public policy for sustainable development, paying attention to political, economic, social, as well as natural resource considerations. Services include research, advocacy, technical cooperation and extensive advice regarding development in Latin America.*

## I. INTRODUCTION

Esquel Group Foundation (EGF) currently coordinates the Civil Society Task Force. The Task Force exists as a collaborative group of representatives from a broad range of organizations concerned with issues relative to the advancement of active citizen participation in the hemisphere, especially within the framework of the Summit of the Americas Process, which emphasizes a sustainable and inclusive development process. Participants include U.S. and international non-governmental organizations (NGOs), government agencies, multilateral institutions, foundations, academics, associations, and private for-profit organizations. The meetings have been remarkably successful —"the best briefing in town" according to one participant—as a clearinghouse as well as a vehicle to coordinate civil society input and monitoring action on the Summit of the Americas (Miami, 1994), the Hemispheric Summit for Sustainable Development in Santa Cruz, Bolivia (December 1996) and the Santiago Summit held in Chile (April 1998).

As "summitry in the Americas has become the predominant institution driving relations between the United States and its neighbors,"[1] it is crucial to now ensure civil society participation in the process itself as well as using it to promote openings at the national level. Exceptional opportunities now exist for civil society to contribute to the design of the next Summit of the Americas, to be held in Canada in the year 2001, and to assure effective implementation of key provisions of the previous summits. Notable among the results of the summits are these specific directives relating to civil society:

- Mandate to the Organization of American States to assist governments in increasing citizen participation. Particularly important will be the implementation of the Interamerican Strategy for Public Participation in Sustainable Development now being developed at the Organization of American States (OAS).

- Formalization of the Dominican Republic and Jamaica as Responsible Coordinators for the Civil Society Initiative of the Summit.

Additionally, the Task Force has been an important venue to debate a broader range of issues which, even if outside the immediate scope of the Summits, are linked to its objectives of promoting an active and engaged civil society in the Americas. Some examples include the OAS Anticorruption Convention, innovative funding mechanisms for civil society, lessons learned from the European Convention on Access to Information, Public Participation in Decision-Making and Access to Justice in Environmental Matters, and the role of the private sector in strengthening civil society.

We believe the Task Force has made an important contribution to enhancing the role of civil society in the Summit Process and, thus, will ultimately impact citizen participation throughout the region by "raising the floor" of acceptable participatory practices. It has achieved this through a long and consistent process of building relationships between interested parties, evolving on its own more than by design. This article is an attempt to share that experience in the hope that it can assist others as they seek to establish similar dialogues in their own countries.

## II. HISTORY OF THE TASK FORCE

The Task Force, initiated in 1994 in the Latin America and Caribbean Bureau of the United States Agency for International Development (USAID) as a means of providing civil society input for the Miami Summit Process, has evolved into a broadly participative forum that continues to focus on the summit process and at the same time allows for interchange of information and views on many aspects of civil society development in Latin America.

While Deputy Director at the Latin American and Caribbean Bureau at USAID, Ramón Daubón initiated the Summit of the Americas Civil Society Task Force. It began as an ad hoc consultation group to promote a "civil society initiative" in the 1994 Miami Summit of the Americas, and afterward its first charge was to follow up on the commitments to civil society made at the Summit. The Miami Declaration, which states that "...a vigorous democracy requires broad participation in public issues" committed governments to review the regulatory framework for non-governmental actors and to "... take steps [to improve] society and community participation." USAID, which was put in charge of chairing this civil society initiative as a result of its advocacy and planning role throughout the Summit planning, institutionalized follow-up by consolidating and expanding the informal consultative group of governmental and non-governmental organizations involved in the initiative's development. The Task Force, officially launched in February 1995 as the implementing "arm" of USAID's coordination effort, became an important venue for communicating with the State Department's Summit Coordinating Office on implementation efforts. The Task Force's working relationship with the Department of State has persisted to this day.

While under the aegis of USAID, the Task Force was, to a great extent, responsible for the inclusion of the "Civil Society Initiative" in the Miami Declaration, and worked closely with representatives from country coordinators Jamaica and Uruguay to accomplish the following tasks:

1. to draft and include the report mandated in Miami into the Bolivia Agenda (albeit as part of an adjunct reporting session on Miami topics and not as an integral part of the agenda itself); and

2. incorporate citizen participation as a unique hemispheric strategy into the Bolivia Agenda, directly as a result of the Montevideo Conference, described below.

Task Force collaboration in this effort was critical in defining the U.S. position for Summit negotiations–that citizen participation be one of the institutional lenses for addressing environmental issues. The Task Force was also involved in the U.S. national consultation on the Bolivia Agenda, sponsored by the Technical Advisory Commission to the Bolivian Government, of which Task Force Coordinator Daubón was a member, and the hemispheric wrap-up presented to the official negotiating delegations at the OAS in August 1996.

A key event preliminary to the Bolivia Summit was the Montevideo Hemispheric Conference on Citizen Participation in Decision-making for Sustainable Development, organized by the Task Force under official sanction of the OAS and the Technical Advisory Committee for the Bolivia Summit, with added support from USAID's Latin America and Caribbean Bureau, the Inter-American Foundation and the Canadian International Development Research Centre (IDRC). The conference was a resounding success. With the participation of twenty-nine official delegations and forty-five regional NGOs, it drafted a clear recommendation to the Summit—that the Heads of State authorize within the OAS the creation of an institutional space and strategy to promote and systematize such citizen participation. This recommendation survived intact the arduous negotiations and was signed as part of the Plan of Action of the Bolivia Summit.

In September 1996, because of its active participation and reputation as an outstanding advocate for civil society in the hemisphere, EGF assumed leadership of the Task Force. Ramón Daubón, originator and coordinator of the Task Force at USAID, was incorporated as EGF's Civil Society Program Coordinator. Upon taking charge of Task Force Coordination, EGF expanded the invitation list, in an attempt to broaden the spectrum of participation, adding, for example, representatives from labor, academia, international development banks, other governmental agencies, and the private sector.

# VII. Preserving and Strengthening Democracy and Human Rights

In February 1997, members of the Task Force were invited to join the OAS at the North-South Center of the University of Miami to develop the proposal on the Inter-American Strategy for Public Participation (ISP). Funding for the proposal was subsequently approved by the Global Environment Facility (GEF) and the OAS has continued to update and consult the Task Force regarding its development and implementation. Particularly relevant was Task Force participation in the definition of a mechanism to select civil society representatives to the ISP's Project Advisory Committee.

The Task Force has continued to participate in related efforts to implement the Bolivia Plan of Action. The U.S. State Department has been permanently involved with the Task Force, updating members on actions and intentions as well as receiving feedback on possible next steps through representation by the Advisor to the Under-Secretary for Global Affairs, the Summit Coordinating Office, the Bureau of Oceans and International Environmental and Scientific Affairs, and the U.S. Mission to the OAS. After attending, in February 1997, the *Briefing on Priorities for Implementation of Agreements from Santa Cruz Summit on Sustainable Development* with the Honorable Timothy Wirth, then Under-Secretary of State for Global Affairs, EGF's President summarized Task Force suggestions on how the U.S. Department of State could contribute to Bolivia implementation.

Throughout 1997 Task Force participants were systematically updated on developments at the Inter-Agency Working Group (IAWG) and Summit Implementation Review Group (SIRG), as well as consulted on U.S. proposed language for civil society in the Summit Process. As part of the U.S. consultation process for Santiago, Ambassador Richard Brown, Senior Coordinator for the Summit of the Americas up to August 1998, addressed the Task Force on 18 April 1998 regarding the efforts of his office and solicited input from participants.

Several Task Force members attended the *Workshop on the Role of Public Participation in Development Actions and Eradication of Poverty Within the Framework of the Summit of the Americas* coordinated by PARTICIPA in Santiago at the behest of the Chilean government during November 1997, which drafted a document submitted to the SIRG. This document was also discussed with several civil society organizations to be incorporated into the U.S. delegation's position at a meeting coordinated by USAID on November 17, 1997.

In June 1998, EGF submitted a letter on behalf of the Task Force to the Prime Minister of Jamaica commending the efforts of that Government, in the person of Ambassador Ellen Bogle, as the responsible co-coordinator of the Civil Society Initiative in the Hemispheric Summit Process. The letter also invited the new Summit Ambassador to meet with the Civil Society Task Force, to which the Ambassador has responded positively. EGF has also entered into conversations with Amb. Flavio Dario Espinal, Permanent Representative of the Dominican Republic to the OAS, who has now replaced Uruguay as co-coordinator of the initiative.

Both ambassadors joined the Summit coordinators of the governments of Canada, Chile, and the US at the September meeting of the Task Force to discuss the process for civil society input for the Summit to be held in Canada in 2001. This special session of the Task Force was organized as a dialogue with knowledgeable parties to: (a) briefly cover the history of the civil society involvement with the summits; and (b) suggest priorities for the Civil Society Initiative, with a view to the year 2001 Summit to be held in Canada.

Concrete activities undertaken as a result of summit mandates were reviewed as were specific cases indicating possible models for civil society coordination with governments. Leaders of civil society, the business sector and local government highlighted how they have achieved results consistent with the mandates of the summits. In addition, participants offered suggestions by way of open discussion as to the priorities the Responsible Coordinators of the Civil Society Initiative might consider, regarding implementation of existing mandates and in the shaping of the Year 2000 summit. A document summarizing the meeting is in the process of being circulated to all participants, indicating the ideas discussed during the event. The document also identifies priorities about which there is consensus, possible obstacles to be overcome, and suggestions for follow-up activities.

Other interesting windows are opening up for increased civil society participation within the broader Summit process:

- Because of its broad responsibilities for implementing summit agreements, the OAS has established in recent months a new Summit Coordination Office. The office has indicated strong interest in communicating with and receiving contributions from civil society, and the newly appointed Director of this office participated also in the September Task Force briefing.

- The Government of Canada, through both its mission to the OAS and the Canadian International

Development Agency (CIDA) has expressed interest in broadening communication with the civil societies of Latin America and the Caribbean, as part of the prelude to the year 2001 Summit that country will host.

- The Mission of the United States to the Organization of American States is promoting new processes that will provide opportunities for participation and direct access for civil society organizations within the OAS. The Mission is looking to consult with different organizations, particularly regarding the effectiveness of systems currently in use at the United Nations to give accreditation to civil society groups. The U.S. Ambassador to the OAS was also present at the September Task Force Briefing.

- The OAS has recently created its Trust for the Americas, an office particularly interested in strengthening the organization's ties to the private sector of the region. The main role of the Trust will be to become a resource for parties interested in collaborating around key issues for the area's development.

- The Free Trade Area of the Americas has recently established its Committee of Government Representatives, which in turn is laboring to devise procedures governing discussions with civil society. The Civil Society Co-coordinators are exploring possible ways to connect their work to the CGR. The prospects, the Dominican Republic and Jamaica, are interesting for a long-term undertaking to bring together the civil society actors of different key areas of summit implementation.

## III. PARTICIPATION AND DISSEMINATION

Notice of Task Force meetings are circulated by electronic mail and fax to a broad list of individuals associated with international agencies, diplomatic missions, U.S. government offices, civil society organizations throughout the region (development NGOs, labor organizations, policy groups, etc.), and consultants, among others. The list, with more than 250 names, includes numerous persons and organizations in Latin America (the Esquel network, the Inter-American Democracy Network, and participants in the OAS Public Participation Initiative, among others). The invitation list continually expands and usually thirty or more persons are present at each meeting. The special meeting in September drew over sixty registrants.

By way of example, the U.S. private organizations involved in the Task Force, in addition to those mentioned in the previous paragraph, include but are not limited to the following: Transparency International, Washington Office on Latin America, Point of Lights Foundation, Church World Services/Lutheran World Relief, the Episcopal Church, the Inter-American Dialogue, Environmental Law Institute, The Nature Conservancy (International), and the Organization of Africans in the Americas, and the AFL-CIO Solidarity Center. Non-U.S. organizations involved include all Esquel sister organizations, PARTICIPA and REDESOL in Chile, Fundación Carvajal in Colombia, GADIS in Argentina, the Dispute Resolution Foundation in Jamaica, and Participación Ciudadana in the Dominican Republic. Official Organisms represented include the Embassies of Chile, Jamaica and Uruguay, as well as the Organization of American States, the Inter-American Development Bank, the World Bank, and the U.S. Agency for International Development.

Visitors from Latin America frequently come to Task Force meetings and brief the group on developments in their particular country. Often these visitors are here to work with U.S.-based development organizations such as Partners of the Americas, Esquel and the Kettering Foundation, to indicate some examples. Other visitors may be in Washington for dealings with the international finance institutions or the OAS.

Task Force meetings are summarized in writing and circulated by electronic mail to the entire list of invitees (not just participants at the particular meeting). In this way the main points of information are brought to the attention of many persons throughout the region.[2] In addition, many of the recipients of these notices forward the information to their respective list of subscribers, thus expanding rapidly the scope of the audience in both North America and Latin America.

The minutes and other information relevant to the Task Force are also posted for access to the general public on the world wide web. They can be accessed at EGF's home page, www.esquel.org, as well as at the official Summit of the Americas site, http://fiu.americas.net/.

## IV. ACCOMPLISHMENTS

The Task Force has contributed to the participation of U.S.-based and Latin American Civil Society Organizations in the Summit Process. This has, in turn, resulted in the incorporation of explicit supportive language in the Declarations as well as specific initiatives in the Plans of Action of Miami, Santa Cruz and Santiago which continue to "raise the floor" of participation in the region. The development of the Task Force during the last four years, as a result of its broad appeal and consistent participation, has contributed to the opening up of windows for increased citizen participation while also offering critical opportunities to pursue questions of effective implementation. The Task Force hopes to make a similar contribution to Canada 2001.

The second interesting accomplishment of the Task Force related to the summit is the sensitization of actors to each other. As representatives from civil society and government interact on a consistent basis, they become more aware of each others' needs and limitations. In this way, civil society actors come to realize what is viable and how to best communicate their interests while government representatives start to more fully understand these demands and even adopt them as their own.

Another important result of the task force mechanism is the continual flow of information to and from a wide audience concerned with the strengthening of civil society in Latin America. In addition, a number of specific results have been achieved by the Task Force itself or because the Task Force has served as a point of convergence of like-minded persons and organizations. For example:

- Task Force participants are coordinating efforts to provide the OAS with orientation relating to the governance of the Inter-American Strategy for Citizen Participation, particularly with regard to formation of a civil society advisory panel.

- Meetings have encouraged outreach to other venues regarding the importance to civil society of new international agreements such as the Anticorruption Convention sponsored by the OAS and the UN Convention to Combat Desertification (a landmark agreement for promoting citizen involvement).

## V. LESSONS LEARNED

The basic lesson we can draw from the experience of the Task Force is that it is possible to develop long-term, comfortable relations between civil society and the government. However, these will require sustained efforts at collaborating constructively and cannot be expected to develop in the absence of an interactive process of cooperation.

The Summit processes are useful media for developing these relations. However, Summits are meetings of governments and proponents of these better relations should approach Summits as opportunities to improve governments' receptiveness to citizens not as mechanisms *per se* to strengthen civil society. Most governments will welcome opportunities to receive constructive inputs from citizens, but will be less receptive upon perceiving open undue influence from organized interest groups. It is a subtle yet significant distinction that should help frame the approach to governments by civil society groups. A key element in the development of these relationships will be identifying those members of government which are most receptive to participatory ideas and nurturing a mutually rewarding relationship with them. The Civil Society Task Force has offered a forum to identify such members of governments.

Civil society will be most strengthened, however, by the interaction among and between citizen groups. This can occur as they prepare to talk to governments, as in the context of the Summits, but also as they address public issues on their own. Networking among civil society groups to learn from each other and to construct common, cross-sectoral agendas (particularly in the face of conflicting interests) is perhaps the strongest tonic for civic life. The Civil Society Task Force has offered such a forum and has served as catalyst for interest in such fora in other countries (Canada, Jamaica, and the Dominican Republic, for instance).

Finally, we have learned to make a distinction between working with governments to help make them more receptive to their own citizens' input, and working in international fora such as the Summit processes or the OAS to give non-governmental actors a voice in framing the international agenda. The Task Force has worked at both levels, in being instrumental in proposing institutional and regulatory frameworks for civic-government relationships, and in creating a venue for non-governmental citizens to interact responsibly and constructively in international processes.

## ANNEX I
## CIVIL SOCIETY TASK FORCE MINUTES

### Friday, 17 July 1998

Ramón Daubón welcomed the participants and introduced Atziri Ibaóez of National Wildlife Federation for an update on the last Trade Ministerial of the Free Trade Area of the Americas (FTAA), held in Buenos Aires June 17 and 18. Ibaóez informed that the Ministers were unable to select a chair for the Committee of Government Representatives (CGR) from the four proposals received (United States, Mexico, Canada and MERCOSUR). This will be decided in the committee's first meeting, scheduled for October 1998. It is unclear how exactly the committee will operate, but apparently the only agreement reached was that it was to gather feedback for specific topics and report back to the Trade Ministers. Ibañez confirmed that the US Government Office of the Trade Representative will be receiving comments on the general objectives of the country for all negotiating groups, including the CGR, until July 29, which NWF will coordinate through a sign-on letter. She noted that most Latin American groups with which NWF has spoken are concerned that the CGR will not fulfill their expectations and are thus looking to create avenues to impact upon the specific negotiating groups, which are to meet next September again. Ibañez concluded expressing NWF's commitment to working with Latin American groups on this issue and was optimistic in that the debate over CGR has substantively impacted National Processes of Participation by triggering a discussion of such issues among Foreign Ministers. Eric Dannenmaier of USAID's Environmental Law Program emphasized the importance of working through other delegations (in addition to US and Mexico) in emphasizing the need for an active CGR role. Ibañez concurred, noting that NWF was to act more as a coordinator, lowering its profile while increasing that of the Latin American NGOs. For such purposes, they will be setting up a listserve, the address of which she will make available to interested parties. Paula Coke Hamilton of the Embassy of Jamaica commended NWF's work and emphasized the Caribbean's commitment to the notions of CARICOM's Civil Society Charter. She explained that Jamaica and its new Summit Ambassador were promoting increased civil society participation across Summit Issues as well as co-coordinators of the Civil Society Initiative.

(Note: Mark Wells was unable to attend but kindly offered the following information for the Task Force members.) The Foreign Ministers met in Caracas on June 1 to discuss implementation of the Santiago Summit, which occurred in April 1998. The meeting was chaired by the foreign ministers of Chile, Canada, and the U.S., representing the new "troika" leadership of the Summit Implementation Review Group (SIRG). The troika issued a statement which laid out the work program for the SIRG in the coming year (see attached). Governments were also asked to identify those initiatives for which they were interested in being "Responsible Coordinators." This was the occasion for the Dominican Republic volunteering to take over coordinating duties for the civil society initiative from Uruguay, which will now join Argentina as a fellow Responsible Coordinator for judicial reform. Plans are already underway for the next SIRG meeting, which will take place in the Dominican Republic in late October. Meanwhile, the SIRG troika has been consulting with heads of international organizations (OAS, IDB, PAHO, ECLAC, World Bank) to identify senior officials of those organizations who will handle Summit issues. Response so far has been good, and the Government of Chile plans to convene regular meetings between the troika and these officials to coordinate the various Summit follow-up activities carried out by the organizations.

Zoila Girón, of the Regional Economy and Environment Department of the Organization of American States (OAS) informed the group that they were in the midst of preparing a proposal on Trade and Environment that would build upon the mandate from the Bolivia Summit. In this effort, she noted, they were looking to collaborate closely with the Governments of Jamaica and the Dominican Republic as co-coordinators of the Civil Society Initiative. Girón also updated the group on the Inter-American Strategy for Citizen Participation (ISP), noting that they were developing several of its components: (a) the basic legal framework; (b) technical assistance component (given that National Councils on Sustainable Development are doing little on participation), with seminars to be held in the Caribbean (September), South America (October), and Central America (November); and (c) the information network, which is in place with a roster of 28 focal points and over 200 civil society organizations. Girón briefed the group and handed out literature on the Fourth Ministerial Conference on Environment for Europe, which she attended, noting that it could provide important insights for the ISP. She highlighted that the Conference assigned particular importance to access to information and participation. The ISP team is developing guidelines for the next two years and will take into account lessons learned from this European experience.

Martha Cecilia Villada explained that Partners of the Americas (POA), where she directs the Civil Society Program, is the largest volunteer organization in the United States, assisting cross-border communities with their development by linking them to sister-cities within the US. Through its Citizen Participation Program, started in 1993 with funds provided by USAID, POA has developed 60 partnerships through 120 NGOs. Villada explained that in order to build upon the relationships developed between POA and several Latin American

# VII. Preserving and Strengthening Democracy and Human Rights

## Establishing an Effective Government – Civil Society Dialogue

NGOs, the Inter-American Democracy Network (IADN) was formed. Robert Asselin, who directs the IADN for POA, explained the program areas of the network: (a) shared learning; (b) local participation; (c) social responsibility; (d) capacity-building; and (e) advocacy. He noted that shared learning and capacity building were the most important components of the network, and that advocacy represented less than 5% of the work undertaken. Asselin provided examples of projects under each program area and handed out literature which explains POA's general activities as well as IADN's mission and programs (all available through EGF or at Partners' website, www.partners.net). He said that future development of the network will center around thematic areas. Villada expressed Partners' desire to expand the work of the Network, noting that a major challenge will be developing appropriate evaluation and monitoring systems. Madeline Williams of USAID commented on that Agency's satisfaction with the work of the Network, which has surpassed their expectations in such a short time.

Eric Dannenmaier of the Environmental Law Program (ELP) of USAID inquired about the participation of Caribbean and North American partners in the network's activities, emphasizing that they have much to contribute to such an undertaking. Daubón informed him of a recent seminar on deliberative methodologies held in Jamaica and an upcoming one in St. Vincent. Villada recognized the network had not successfully integrated the Caribbean, particularly as a result of the language problem, but that it was an issue they were increasingly concerned with. She did clarify that POA has extensive activities in the Caribbean through other programs.

Arturo Garcia Costa of the Alliance to End Childhood Lead Poisoning (AECLD) briefed the participants on that organization's recent efforts to phase out leaded gasoline throughout the hemisphere. He explained that the World Bank took leadership of this effort under the Pollution Initiative of the Miami Summit, assisting in the formulation of National Action Plans to Phase Out Leaded Gasoline. The successful implementation of this initiative could provide important lessons for Summit follow-up as well as illustrate how international commitments can facilitate or even accelerate national progress in key issues, Garcia Costa stated. He noted that, unfortunately, in some countries there has been discontinuity between progressive elements within the government and interested civil society actors—all of which emphasizes the need for the promotion of consistent dialogue such as the one fostered by the Task Force. He concluded with an important lesson from this experience that public awareness and access to information are critical to the success of this process.

Eric Dannenmaier of ELP presented the book *Guía Practica sobre Derechos y Responsabilidades Ambientales en Nicaragua,* a practical guide to citizen rights and responsibilities in that country sponsored by ELP, CIEL, Cedaprode and the Ministry of the Environment. The team in charge of this initiative is currently developing similar projects in Guatemala, Panama and Ecuador. Dannenmaier explained that the book is part of a year-long project inspired by the ISP and that it could serve as a model of a very practical way of educating citizens on their rights.

Bill Millan of The Nature Conservancy informed that the Tropical Forest Conservation Act was passed by Congress, authorizing $325 million in subsidies for debt-for-nature swaps. The money freed from bilateral debt would go into National Tropical Forest Funds similar to, but distinct from, those established through the Enterprise for the Americas Initiative.

## Friday, 19 June 1998

Marisol Pagés of EGF informed the group that Atziri Ibañez of National Wildlife Federation was on her way to the press conference on the Trade Ministerial held in Buenos Aires June 17 and 18, having informed her that the Ministers were unable to select a chair for the Committee of Government Representatives (CGR). This will be decided in the first meeting, scheduled for October 1998. It is unclear how the committee will work, but apparently the only agreement reached was that it was to gather feedback for specific topics and report back to the Trade Ministers. Ibañez will provide more thorough information once she returns from Argentina, which will be disseminated to participants.

Scott Hamilton, a political officer with the US Mission to the Organization of American States (OAS), informed the group on the results of the OAS General Assembly (GA), held in Caracas during June 1 and 2 in conjunction with the Summit Implementation Review Group (SIRG). He explained that the format of the GA was modified to allow the Secretary of State to attend, resulting in a shorter (3-day) meeting addressing only three topics: (1) strengthening of the Inter-American System; (2) cooperation for development; and (3) strengthening justice systems. Hamilton noted that discussions around (3) included the proposal of a regional training center for judges and prosecutors, the issue of corruption and the scarcity of resources. Issue (2), he added, focused mostly on the concern of the smaller Caribbean states with shielding themselves from the effects of global and regional integration, particularly being left out of the Free Trade Area of the Americas (FTAA) process. Hamilton expanded on the issue of strengthening the Inter-American System, which he perceives as the most important to the United States and other countries of the region. The group agreed on the creation of a Joint Committee of Permanent Council members and technical experts from the Inter-American Council for Integral Development (ICID) that would focus, in the first few months, on the needed internal restructuring of the OAS and, later, on its relationship with other regional entities (including Civil Society). This body, he explained, will be in charge of addressing the mandates on citizen participation received from the Region's Heads of State at Santa Cruz and Santiago, the first step of which is the resolution entitled the OAS and Civil Society approved at the May 26 meeting of the Permanent Council (available from EGF at your request). Hamilton clarified that there is still resistance from many governments that are concerned with an increased role for civil society. He anticipates the creation of a working group with a strong US role for September of this year charged with suggesting mechanisms for the OAS to become more participatory. He invited the group to submit ideas to him within the next 4-6 weeks and expressed Ambassador Marrero's interest in addressing the Task Force. He placed particular emphasis on evaluations of the experience of the United Nations' Economic and Social Council, the creation of which Amb. Marrero witnessed and was planning to use as a model. In response to Ken Cole of EGF, Hamilton clarified that this was an invitation for feedback from the US delegation in particular, but that the working group would most likely contain representatives from other areas of the OAS, including the office of the Secretary General.

Hamilton spoke briefly on the SIRG, noting that it was mostly an administrative session. Pagés noted that Mark Wells, of the State Department, announced a possible transfer from Uruguay to the Dominican Republic of co-coordinator responsibility for the civil society initiative. Though the decision is not yet official, the Task Force has offered to host and brief Amb. Flavio Dario Espinal (Dominican Mission to the OAS). Amb. Juan Felipe Yriart of Esquel commented on the political implications of the civil society issue within the OAS, expressing concern that it could create a negative backlash from some Governments. Hamilton concurred but was optimistic given current restructuring efforts, including the spin-off of ICID as a technical cooperation unit a la UNDP.

Eric Dannenmaier of the Environmental Law Program of the US Agency for International Development presented on advancements towards the establishment of a Regional Network of Professionals in Environmental Law, called for in the Bolivia Plan of Action and undertaken by the OAS. The team in charge of this initiative is currently developing an action plan for the formulation of the Network's blueprint. Their intention is to do it through a process of openness and collaboration, Dannenmaier explained. In that spirit, he handed out a survey to be filled out by those interested in this process, which will continue through the summer. The blueprint, which should allow the network to complement existing work, will be presented to the appropriate body (most likely ICID) once finalized. Daubón noted that environmental activities have been one of the most important catalysts for developing a sense of civic responsibility and participation. Daubón proceeded to confirm that the letter to the Prime Minister of Jamaica commending their role as responsible co-coordinators of the civil society initiative had been drafted and granted participants the opportunity to sign-on as individuals or on behalf of their organizations.

Rolf Lipton of the National Conference of States on Building Codes and Standards (NCSBCS) handed out literature on the Caribbean Basin/Central America Forum on Building Codes and Economic Development. The conference will explore common building codes, public health and safety needs, resources and cooperative approaches enhancing economic development and is scheduled for October 2 in San Juan, Puerto Rico (call 703-437-0100). David Ruhala of the Conference of World Regions (CWR) announced the First Global Regional Leaders Forum (GRLF), to be held in Brussels during September and handed out the preliminary program. The GRLF is the first meeting of high-level sub-national leaders from around the world to discuss regional issues and the promotion of sustainable economic growth, investment, mutual security, health and safety, educational and technological development while remaining sensitive to civil society and environmental needs (see www.cwr.org).

Aaron Zazueta briefed participants on the Quito-based Corporación para el Desarrollo y la Responsabilidad Social en América Latina (CDR), an effort to promote and strengthen a movement of social and environmental responsibility among the business sector in the region. CDR has the support of important business leaders in the region and working relationships with the Prince of Wales Business Leaders Forum as well as with Business for Social Responsibility (BSR), a group of prominent US businesses that supports leadership among the private sector

# VII. Preserving and Strengthening Democracy and Human Rights

for public issues based in San Francisco. Zazueta explained that in contrast to previous similar attempts such as the Business Councils for Sustainable Development, CDR seeks to strengthen existing movements in Latin America and to work with groups in the United States and others to adapt the methodologies they have developed. Another important aim of CDR is to link those hemispheric efforts. He cited some examples of the efforts currently under way: Peru 2021 and an effort in Venezuela by over 200 corporations focused on bringing the educational system to developed country standards by the year 2010. Zazueta explained the two-tier nature of social responsibility: (a) responsible business practices, including the internalization of costs such as environmental impact, safe and fair working conditions, and the provision of services to poor or marginalized areas currently underserved; and (b) social investments, meaning contributions (whether they be financing, in-kind donations or human resources) in areas that ultimately affect their long-term sustainability, such as better education and combating corruption. In response to Daubón, Zazueta clarified that the emphasis was not necessarily financial, but doing business differently. Amb. Yriart noted that collaboration with civil society was a critical factor in legitimizing the efforts of the corporate world to undertake a broader public role just as it was important for governments to do so if they intend current reforms to be sustainable.

Cole inquired about the current political situation in Ecuador. Zazueta expressed his optimism, particularly given that for the first time in the country's history a joint effort of civil society actors was able to peacefully push out the undesired Bucharam government under the respectful watch of the military. He noted that many people see presidential candidate Novoa as a façade for the ousted party. Finally he expressed his optimism about a possible victory for Maguat, who has 32% of the votes.

Vera Weill-Hallé of the International Fund for Agricultural Development (IFAD) briefed the group on the results of its 20th Anniversary event, which took place June 4th on Capitol Hill and focused on the central theme Partners for Prosperity, analyzing successful experiences in the areas of Micro-credit, Alleviation of Hunger and Combating Desertification. She noted that recommendations from working sessions on each of these topics would be formally submitted to the US Congress.

## Friday, 15 May 1998

Mark Wells reported on the Santiago Summit, stating that the US Government considered it a pretty good Summit and informed the group that the next Summit will be hosted by Canada in 2000/2001. Wells explained that the Hemispheric Leaders charged their Foreign Ministers to come up with recommendations on strengthening the Inter-American System. Accordingly, one special session of the Summit Implementation Review Group (SIRG) will be dedicated each year to Summit follow-up, most likely to be held in conjunction with the General Assembly of the Organization of American States (OAS), as is the case with the upcoming meeting in Caracas (June 1-2). Wells noted that at Caracas, the new and continuing responsible coordinators will be assigned to each initiative. He added that the US Government will design its internal implementation strategies on each initiative, including follow-up issues.

Tim Mahoney of the US Agency for International Development (AID) concurred that the Santiago Summit was a success, characterizing it as a development summit for its focus on what have been called the second-generation reforms. He explained that this meant a shift of emphasis from growth to poverty reduction in the economic area, as well as from elections to more substantive political issues (i.e., judicial reform, freedom of the press, corruption and civil society). Mahoney emphasized the importance of education in complementing efforts to achieve these new priorities. In terms of civil society participation, his opinion is that formal representation at the SIRG is less important than pushing for what the Plan of Action calls an enabling environment throughout the hemisphere. He also highlighted the role that civil society can play in other Summit Initiatives, particularly through the Committee of Government Representatives created within the Trade Ministerial. The specifics of how the Committee will go about fulfilling its responsibility to receive input from civil society have yet to be negotiated.

Bruce Jay of the AFL-CIO noted that his organization has drafted some suggestions as to how the Committee should function. He noted that the draft is not meant to define a position regarding the Committee, but rather a discussion paper on which they would be interested in receiving feedback from interested organizations. Jay highlighted that one of the key recommendations in the paper is the need to have balanced access for all of civil society, which would imply the merging of all other privileged access mechanisms such as the Business Forum.

Zachary Teich from the Organization of American States informed the group that the OAS was assigned 22 lead agency responsibilities as well as 9 cooperative ones. Of the main 22 assignments, two are in the area of civil society. Teich highlighted the fact that the OAS has only recently taken a welcoming view on civil society participation, particularly after the Bolivia Summit mandate that it should assist member states in becoming more participatory. So that the OAS can effectively implement this and the new mandates it has received from Santiago, Amb. Victor Marrero (US Permanent Representative) has submitted a proposal to the upcoming General Assembly (GA) that would result in concrete mandates to incorporate civil society into OAS operations, Teich informed. The speech and draft resolution, kindly provided by Mr. Teich, are available from the Esquel Group Foundation. Finally, Teich announced that he will be leaving the US Mission to the OAS for another position within the administration. We wish him the best and send our sincere gratitude for his continued cooperation with the Task Force.

Ramón Daubón of the Esquel Group Foundation consulted the group on sending a letter on behalf of the Civil Society Task Force to the Prime Minister of Jamaica (via the Embassy in Washington) commending their role as responsible coordinators of the civil society initiative, particularly the efforts of Amb. Ellen Bogle. The letter would also express hope that the new Summit Representative will continue to play such an important role and invite him to address the Task Force should he be in Washington, D.C. The group endorsed the idea EGF will request organizations to specify if they are interested in being listed as signatories.

Janine Perfit of the Inter-American Development Bank (IDB) briefed the group on the seminar entitled Social Programs, Poverty, and Citizen Participation held in March 1998 in conjunction with the Annual Meeting of the Board of Governors in Cartagena, Colombia. At the seminar, 32 case studies of public-private collaboration in 16 countries were analyzed, spanning across eight programmatic areas: (a) descentralization; (b) health; (c) education; (d) urban infrastructure and services; (e) productive sectors; (f) environmental protection; (g) vulnerable groups; and (h) philanthropy and social responsibility. Perfit noted that over 800 individuals involved in social sector activities through the public and private (for-profit and not-for-profit) sectors participated. Though there was no single set of conclusions from the discussions, she noted some recurring themes:

- Citizen Participation as increasing efficiency, both political and economic, through the mobilization of resources (human and financial), the promotion of equity and the strengthening of the democratic system.
- Citizen Participation as a central element of the formulation and implementation of social policies.
- Dialogue can increase cooperation around shared interests, thus benefiting all actors.
- The need to promote a culture of social responsibility through the incorporation of the private for-profit sector.
- Importance of volunteerism in addressing serious social problems, particularly those of the most vulnerable sectors of the population.
- The key role of decentralization in strengthening participation, particularly at the local level.

Perfit noted that the seminar underscored the work undertaken by the State and Civil Society Division to assist the Bank in this respect, which can be categorized into four core areas: (1) The promotion of consensus-building between the state, the private sector and civil society in order to form strategic alliances in the social area; (2) the inclusion of a participation component in the project cycle including a separate and specific evaluation of the impact of participation; (3) study and design of alternative financing mechanisms for increased civil society activity and autonomy; and (4) capacity building for civil society organizations in the areas of management, negotiating skills, etc. She explained that the efforts of the Division need to continue being fine-tuned, particularly as the lessons from the seminar are more thoroughly digested. A summarizing document due out shortly and the planning of a public event in D.C. as follow-up to the seminar should assist in this process. Perfit concluded that she believes the Divisions and the Bank's efforts will continue to focus on: a) promoting dialogue; b) training and professionalization of civil society; c) learning and information sharing; d) agile lending procedures, and e) legal and fiscal frameworks.

Eric Olson from the Washington Office on Latin America (WOLA) commented on the IDB Seminar, which he attended. He agreed on the success of the seminar, emphasizing that it provided strong political support for the notion of participation within the Bank and with the attending Government Ministers by explaining how it can contribute to higher efficiency and effectiveness of development efforts. Olson also expressed some critiques he would like to bring to the Bank's attention: (a) the seminar was preaching to the choir in that most attendees were supporters of citizen participation; (b) it did not go into a real debate of how to handle the conflicts and challenges that emerge when you try to increase participation; (c) he is unsure of how the Bank (and other institutions) will go about learning and implementing lessons from these experiences. Perfit acknowledged these drawbacks, explaining that they result from the fact that the Bank is in the early stages of dealing with these issues and needs to be educated slowly. She also expressed that the Division has struggled with the question of how to move these ideas forward and would welcome the assistance of organizations such as the ones attending this meeting. Finally, Perfit emphasized the need to educate the Bank's Board, who are the ultimate owners of the institution, on the need to move further along these lines.

Vera Weill-Hallé of the International Fund for Agricultural Development (IFAD) invited the group to join that organization in the celebration of its 20th Anniversary. The event will take place June 4th on Capitol Hill and will center around the main theme partners for Prosperity, analyzing successful experiences in the areas of Micro-credit, Alleviation of Hunger and Combating Desertification.

## Friday, 17 April 1998

Mark Wells reported on the telephone from Santiago that the US Government was happy with the final language of the Declaration, as it contains references to key deliverables. In terms of the Plan of Action, he said the US would have preferred less action items (now 170). Wells informed the group on changes to the Declaration and Plan of Action as compared to the final versions approved at the last Summit Implementation Review Group (SIRG):

A subsection on Sustainable Development was added under Eradication of Poverty and Discrimination (Section IV, page 34 of the Plan of Action) endorsing the Bolivia Summit and OAS efforts for its implementation, as well as requesting support from the entities of the Inter-American System and the United Nations. According to Wells, the Bolivians did not succeed in their attempt at including a complete section on Sustainable Development. A request for a joint Trade and Environment meeting was not successful either.

A section on cooperation which charges donor agencies (of the governments of Argentina, Brazil, Canada, Colombia, Chile, Mexico, the United States and Venezuela) with supporting the Plan of Action with specific programs and projects. It also requests similar support from the multilateral cooperation institutions.

A final, fairly concrete, section on Summit of the Americas Follow-Up (page 38 of the Plan of Action). It consolidates the SIRG as the mechanism for Summit Implementation, falling under the responsibility of Foreign Ministries, and supported by an OAS Secretariat. The SIRG will meet two to three times a year, chaired by the current Summit Coordinating Country and co-chaired by previous hosts. Representatives from the OAS, the IDB, the Pan American Health Organization (PAHO) and the United Nations Economic Commission on Latin America and the Caribbean (ECLAC) will be invited to join the SIRG. To further enhance coordination, a representative from the World Bank will also be invited.

Wells explained that in addition to these changes, the Hemispheric Leaders charged their Foreign Ministers to come up with recommendations on strengthening the Inter-American System.

Eric Dannenmaier of the Environmental Law Program/USAID inquired about civil society representation in the US delegation as well as the committee setup at the last Trade Ministerial in Costa Rica charged with listening to input regarding other issues such as labor and environment. Wells answered that Mack McLarty was under pressure to limit the size of the delegation, but he invited four prominent people, among them Ambler Moss (North-South Center). Wells also told the group that references to this committee are included in the document and that references were included in other sections, such as Basic Rights of Workers.

In response to Bill Millan, of the Nature Conservancy, Wells lamented that the endorsement of bi-national parks did not survive the negotiations. He noted that the Declaration contains general language on protecting natural resources. Susan Bass of the Environmental Law Institute inquired about the Parallel People's Summit and whether they would have the opportunity to address the Heads of State. Wells noted that there was no official position on the People's Summit as of yet, but that his impression from reading their daily newsletter is that it is mostly in opposition to FTAA. He clarified that there is no official time allotted to them at the Summit. In response to David Jessup of AFL-CIO's Solidarity Center, Wells explained that there were two groups from Congress—the Official Presidential Congressional Delegation (Portman, Hamilton, Levin, Hinojosa, Rodriguez) as well as an additional delegation that was to focus on Drug issues, particularly the Multilateral Monitoring Process.

Robin Rosenberg of the North-South Center was also reached in Santiago for his impressions on the Summit. He noted that President Clinton had been very well received and that over 3,000 media representatives were in Santiago. He explained that there was no official civil society representation in the US delegation, but that McLarty had asked a group of wise men to assist the President. He also noted that according to his conversation with Andrea Sanhueza of PARTICIPA, the Chilean Delegation had no representation either. Rosenberg was under the impression that civil society representatives had been included in the Canadian and Jamaican delegations, however. In terms of the Follow-Up mechanism, Rosenberg noted the explicit endorsement of the Foreign Ministries as responsible under the SIRG mechanism, which he perceives as problematic. He highlighted the formal invitation to the entities of the Inter-American System as well as the request that they give financial support to the initiatives of the Plan of Action, albeit there were no specifics on amounts or mechanisms. Rosenberg also noted his disappointment with the lack of institutionalization of civil society participation in the monitoring and implementation of the Summits. Asked by Ramón Daubón about any opposition activities taking place in Santiago, Rosenberg expressed that they had not received much attention from the media and had suffered from poor planning. In response to Bass he noted that there was very little impact of the Parallel People's Summit, mostly due to the strongly anti-FTAA nature of the groups involved.

Daubón presented Dante Pesce, currently a Senior Fellow in Philanthropy at Johns Hopkins University. Pesce is a member of REDESOL, a network of social service non-profit organizations in Chile. He noted that Chile is a middle-income developing country with a long tradition of community participation (30% of all adults belong to some type of community organization). Pesce explained that the third sector expanded rapidly during the 1970s and 1980s as it became a space for academics and politicians opposed to the Pinochet Regime. During that time, most NGOs worked on issues of Human Rights, Democracy and other sometimes underground political activities, he noted. After the transition to a democratic regime, Pesce highlighted, the situation has changed dramatically as many of those who were in the third sector have moved to government positions. As a result, the nature of the work performed by NGOs has changed, and a redefinition of the sector is now in order. At the same time, civil society-business sector relations have historically been confrontational as opposed to cooperative.

Pesce cited some lessons drawn from the Chilean experience: he believes that one of the biggest challenges to Chilean civil society organizations today is to keep their own mission given their new dependency on the government as they have become contractors for the delivery of social services, over 50% of their budgets comes from the state. Another big challenge will be to maintain their long-term commitment in the communities they serve, in spite of their role as short-term government contractors. To meet these challenges and opportunities, Pesce said, it will be essential for Chilean NGOs to develop their own capacity, particularly in the area of advocacy. One key element in achieving this will be their ability to raise funds to invest in institutional and professional development.

Mario Marcel, Executive Director for Chile at the Inter-American Development Bank, commented on Pesce's presentation. He highlighted a recent survey where 69% of Chileans expressed that they thought the society was becoming too individualistic and 80% thought people were becoming more aggressive. He mentioned that the transition to democracy had not led to the expected upsurge in civil society activity. Among reasons for that, Marcel emphasized the recent authoritarian experience and a long-standing tradition of a presidential, centralized state. He noted also that the Chilean State has always been very effective and, as such, has attempted to develop civil society in a very patronizing way. He explained that the Chilean state has devised many mechanisms to involve civil society within specific scopes of public policy, but that this has many times been counterproductive, as it feeds back into the top-down tradition. He thus emphasized the need to break this self-perpetuating cycle through a system of checks and balances on policy-making. There needs to be an effort at strengthening civil society from within and to view the reform of the state not as a matter of efficiency (internal to government) but as a matter of redefining the roles of the state and the citizen, Marcel concluded. David Valenzuela of the Inter-American Foundation added the need for effective decentralization, particularly in Chile which is one of the few countries regressing in this area. Marcel responded that, in theory, the situation is not so bad: approximately 30%-35% of financial resources are transferred to regional governments and, as of 1992, local councils are regionally elected (soon, the Mayor will be as well). However, he noted, the lack of democratic institutions and accountability at the sub-national level translates into a very powerful local executive. Millan clarified that despite this high level of resource transfers to regional governments, decision-making still takes place at the center as most of those funds are earmarked. Daubón highlighted the fact that the Association of Mayors has brought to light this lack of autonomy and is actively seeking the transfer of decision-making power to local institutions.

## THE CIVIL SOCIETY TASK FORCE DIALOGUE WITH THE RESPONSIBLE COORDINATORS OF THE CIVIL SOCIETY INITIATIVE OF THE SUMMIT OF THE AMERICAS

September 18, 1998 — 8:30 a.m. to 12:00
The Washington Club, 15 Dupont Circle, NW

Ramón Daubón welcomed the participants, noting that it was a privilege to be holding this special session with the Co-Coordinators of the Civil Society Initiative of the Summit of the Americas on the fourth anniversary of the Task Force and the second since being coordinated by the Esquel Group Foundation (EGF). He introduced Ambassador Juan Felipe Yriart, member of the Board and former Chairman of EGF.

Amb. Yriart expressed his gratitude for everyone's presence on behalf of EGF's President, Kenneth Cole. He noted that Grupo Esquel has been intimately involved in advocating the importance of civil society in Latin America and the Caribbean (LAC). Amb. Yriart explained that the great changes taking place in the region—market reforms, globalization, redefined states—have caused much confusion and misunderstanding as the traditional roles of different societal actors are necessarily questioned and realigned. In the midst of such change and confusion, he said, Esquel has come to the conclusion that the participation of civil society—by providing an umbrella under which such issues can be digested in their cultural, social, political and economic dimensions—has become even more critical for the sustainability of the processes of democratization and development. In that context, he welcomed the decision of Ambassadors Espinal and Thompson to seek this dialogue and offered the Task Force as a venue for continued exchange.

Ambassador Flavio Darío Espinal of the Dominican Republic expressed his country's commitment to their new role as co-coordinators of the Initiative, and their sense of pride in sharing this responsibility with Jamaica. He highlighted that having civil society included in Summit language is an important accomplishment that responds to a new reality in which political opening and participation are increasingly important. In this sense, he noted, the strengthening of civil society is part of a general process of democratic consolidation which also requires institutional reform, tolerance, renewed judicial systems, a free press, the rule of law and pluralism. A variety of issues need to guide our efforts to move forward this Initiative, Amb. Espinal stated:

1. This does not imply the search for a uniform model or a generalized prescription, as each society has its own specific characteristics. Therefore, we need to promote substantive discussion that will allow us to understand those different realities and define alternatives that take them into account.

2. The issue of civil society has caused a political division along the lines of "good" (promoting its development) and "bad" (resisting its promotion). We need to seek a positive environment that promotes advancements in this area, acknowledging that no country is totally open or closed.

3. We need to ensure the participation of a broad range of groups and prevent the development of an "elite" group of organizations with access to these processes.

4. We need to create new possibilities and open new doors for keeping the momentum of the initiative.

Amb. Espinal concluded by inviting all participants to voice their suggestions on how to move forward the Civil Society Initiative.

Amb. Arthur Thompson of Jamaica thanked the organizers and participants, noting that he would try to complement the introduction of Amb. Espinal. He agreed on the need for pragmatism regarding uniform models and solutions, while emphasizing that there are common problems and key issues we should be addressing. He warned about resurfacing skepticism by some governments in Santiago to recognize civil society. Finally, Amb. Thompson called upon the participants to work for the integration of civil society vis-à-vis the governments of the region, explaining that the pressures of reduced budgets threaten the ability of bureaucracies to deal with a growing number of civil society groups.

Daubón introduced Amb. William Walker as the first speaker of the next session, "Negotiating the Civil Society Initiative: Miami to the Present." Amb. Walker introduced himself to the group, as he has recently replaced Amb. Richard Brown as US Senior Summit Coordinator. He explained that he has spent two-thirds of his 37-year foreign service career in LAC-related issues, including assignments in Argentina, Brazil, Bolivia, El Salvador and

Honduras. Most recently, Amb. Walker was directing a USAID-funded project on Administration of Justice throughout the region. He noted that as Summit Coordinator he plans to continue his predecessor's commitment to the promotion of civil society in the Hemisphere.

Daubón explained that reaching a consensus on the Civil Society Initiative at the Miami Summit in 1994 was very hard, as a result of the reluctance of many governments to accept the importance of the topic. He highlighted the role of the Government of Jamaica along with other supporters that insisted on including civil society language in Summit documents. Miami has undoubtedly provided a good foundation, but it was in the Summit on Sustainable Development held in Santa Cruz, Bolivia that the Initiative really "raised the floor" of minimally accepted participatory practices, Daubón mentioned. A key step in that process was the officially sanctioned conference of civil society held in Montevideo before the Summit. He explained that the meeting produced recommended language on civil society which had been drafted by 45 NGOs and 28 official representations. This language was ultimately approved by the Heads of State and included in toto in the Santa Cruz Declaration and Plan of Action.

Mr. Sergio Jáuregui, who came in representation of Minister Eric Reyes of Bolivia, explained that his country has approached participation in a serious and systematic way through its Popular Participation Law and its practical implementation.

Robin Rosenberg of the North-South Center of the University of Miami was a member of the US Delegation to the Santiago Summit. He noted that the Civil Society Initiative was advanced only marginally by the language at Santiago, and this after very difficult negotiations. Such advances included the following:

a. Program to fill the gaps of Miami in terms of promoting an enabling environment for CSOs, including the issue of financing.
b. Commitment to the promotion of Civil Society-Government partnerships.
c. Positioning of the OAS as a focal point in these discussions and eventual programs.
d. Endorsement of ongoing projects such as the Inter-American Strategy for Public Participation.
e. Promoting the adoption of work plans for the establishment of legal and institutional frameworks for civil society that can be implemented at the national level.

Rosenberg believes that the challenge is now to ensure that the initiative moves forward by preventing the lowest common denominator from becoming the norm. This will be critical for the success of the Inter-American system, he noted, and will require the continued institutionalization of the Summit Process in Canada and beyond.

Chilean Summit Coordinator Ambassador Carlos Portales highlighted the fact that in the Santiago Summit, civil society participation was seen as a cross-cutting theme running through the four baskets—education, democracy, poverty and economic integration. He also noted that the challenge of building civil society in the region goes beyond raising demands, but should necessarily include an active participation in seeking solutions to our pressing problems.

Jaime Aparicio, the new Coordinator for Summit Follow-up at the OAS, introduced the next section on concrete activities affecting civil society development in the region. He stressed that the Miami Summit marked the realization by governments that the incorporation of civil society is critical if the region is to accomplish the mandates of the new Inter-American Agenda. Aparicio explained that the OAS has had a positive evolution in the last couple of years with regards to civil society:

a. the celebrations for the organizations' 50th Anniversary included, for the first time in its history, many civil society representatives on its panels;
b. during the Bolivia Summit Process, over 60 civil society organizations addressed the Permanent Council of the OAS;
c. emerging out of Santa Cruz, the Inter-American Strategy for Public Participation (ISP) was conceived at the OAS and is now developing the pilot projects which will allow it to assist governments in becoming more participatory on issues related to sustainable development;
d. during the last General Assembly, the Ministers of Foreign Affairs directed the Permanent Council to design ways by which the OAS could involve civil society in its operations as well as assist member governments in becoming more participatory; and
e. it has recently created the Office of Summit Follow-up, which will work closely with civil society in assisting and monitoring.

Eric Dannenmaier of USAID's Environmental Law Project explained that the ISP is a 1.5-year project designed to identify key elements of a strategy for participation that will be presented to governments in July 1999. The strategy has seven key components—six consist of information gathering and the seventh is the technical report containing strategic recommendations. One of the components of the project, entitled the "Legal and Institutional," is an empirical review of the regulations that govern public participation and how they work in practice. This component consists of a study, which is already under way, of legislation in 12 countries based on 21 indicators of participation. Dannenmaier shared some preliminary findings with participants:

- Aggregated figures indicate that less than 50% of the laws do not allow participation.
- The three types of "access" studied include access to process (most important in Latin America), access to justice and access to information.
- They noted a regional difference between Central and South America in terms of a distinct bias towards participation being an obligation of government (CA) vs. a right of the citizen (SA). This conceptual difference has implications for policy choices affecting participation.
- Less than 25% of the laws provide the necessary financing for activities related to participation (i.e., staff time, resources for meetings and information dissemination, etc).
- In terms of trends over time, there has been a consistent increase in the level of sensitivity of environmental laws to participation. In contrast, general legislation excluding participation increased until 1990 and has evened out since then.

He noted that in the last organizational meeting of the ISP held in Jamaica, three major conclusions were reached regarding the strategy to be formulated:

1. that it be geographically balanced (taking into account the particular needs of small island states);
2. that it focus on sustainable development as defined by the Santa Cruz Declaration and Plan of Action;
3. that it ensure sectoral diversity.

Anne Marie Blackman of the Unit for the Promotion of Democracy (UPD) at the OAS informed the group of efforts that Unit is undertaking to promote citizen participation. She noted that as the Unit mandated to provide support to Member States in consolidating their democratic systems and institutions, participation permeates all activities of the UPD. Particularly relevant is the "Program of Cooperation in Decentralization, Local Government and Citizen Participation," currently being undertaken and which focuses simultaneously on strengthening decentralization efforts and the functioning of local government as well as on opening space for citizen participation at the municipal/local/community levels. The program has four general objectives to be implemented across six program areas:

## Objectives

a. Contributing to policy debate and serving as a forum for creation, dissemination and exchange of information;

b. Supporting institution-building in central, local government and civil society, principally through "horizontal cooperation" approaches among countries of the region;

c. Enhancing the democratic legitimacy of local governance through increased citizen access and participation;

d. Collaboration with other agencies and institutions.

## Program Areas

1. Legal and regulatory frameworks
2. Institutional development
3. Relations between central and local government authorities
4. Relations between legislatures and local authorities
5. Aspects of economic and social development relating to local governance
6. Information systems to support decentralization, local government and citizen participation.

Blackman also mentioned that the UPD is planning to hold a "Democratic Forum" specifically on the topic of civil society before the end of the year.

Stahis Panagides of Fundação Grupo Esquel Brasil (FGEB) and Esquel Group Foundation gave an overview of new proposed legislation to modernize the regulation of civil society organizations in Brazil. He emphasized that this is one of the most participatory legislative efforts, resulting from extensive analysis and dialogue conducted by senior public officials together with leaders of civil society. Accordingly, the proposed legislation is expected to produce a legal framework conducive to the expansion and strengthening of the third sector. Luis Danin Lobo, also of FGEB, stressed the importance of the new legislation in the context of the process of decentralization.

Nelson Stratta of Grupo Esquel Uruguay informed the group of recent events in Uruguay. He explained that one of the objectives of the process of modernization of the state in Uruguay was to "bring the state closer to the people" in response to a heightened awareness regarding the importance of civil society. This is conceived as increased openness and cooperation in the definition and implementation of social policy, including subcontracting of civil society organizations. In the reform of the state loan from the Inter-American Development Bank, he noted, are funds to be used in the setup of an Institution that would assist in the modernization of civil society so that it can effectively take on this enhanced role. Stratta mentioned that the Institution is currently bringing together interested parties in Government and both the private for-profit and non-profit sectors to explore cooperation in social investment—a win-win situation from a practical standpoint for all three actors: (a) for the state, it could mean increased impact for its social expenditures; (b) for the business sector, increased impact and recognition of their social investments; and (c) for CSOs, increased participation in social policy design, implementation and monitoring, including financial transfers. Stratta concluded by emphasizing that civil society needs to focus on modern approaches based on concepts of social capital and to seek cooperation with the for-profit sector in thinking and addressing social problems.

Martha Cecilia Villada of Partners of the Americas introduced participants to the Inter-American Democracy Network, a coalition of civil society organizations working together to promote citizen participation and strengthen democracies in the hemisphere. The network currently consists of 80 non-governmental organizations in sixteen countries and works across six program areas: (a) deliberation for citizen participation; (b) mobilizing citizens for community action; (c) civic and voter education; (d) social responsbility; (e) organizational capacity building; and (f) advocacy. Villada explained that most members are very experienced in transitions from authoritarian rule and are now exploring how to move into democracy-building and deepening. She said that the network has been successful at allowing for information exchange among members. The network also provides support that enhances the local advocacy efforts of members, she concluded.

Aparicio closed the section and invited participants to enjoy a short coffee break. Upon return from break, Daubón introduced Amb. Peter Boehm of Canada to kick off the next section on the future of the Civil Society Initiative.

Amb. Boehm, who has been Summit Coordinator for Canada for the last three years, confirmed his country's commitment to enhancing a broader role for civil society in the hemisphere. He explained that the first step in expressing that commitment is ensuring a broad and open consultative mechanism for the Summit in Canada in 2001. This openness should be ecumenical, avoiding domination by certain groups and ensuring space for all. In terms of Canada 2001, Amb. Boehm called upon the participants to focus on a few tangible and realistic issues. He cited the Parliamentary Network of the Americas as a positive example of efforts that create opportunities for learning, modernizing and strengthening through the Inter-American Summit Process. He emphasized the need for the OAS to put a structure in place that allows it to play a major role in the Summit Process and the promotion of civil society within it. He concluded reiterating his interest in receiving feedback from participants.

Daubón opened up the floor for feedback from participants. Bruce Jay of the AFL-CIO Solidarity Center thanked and congratulated the organizers of the meeting, noting that it stimulated an open debate while allowing for useful information exchanges. He agreed with Amb. Beahm's comment on the need for broader access—which he and many others feel is not the case. Many groups feel their views are not well represented and are calling for greater receptiveness from governments, he commented.

Amb. Yriart highlighted the need to distinguish between citizens participating and organizations of civil society engaging in advocacy. He stressed the need for a transformation of passive citizenship to participatory citizenship in Latin America, noting that a key aspect of that transformation is education because it is the means by which citizens will (or will not) be prepared to live in a globalized world.

Atziri Ibañez of the National Wildlife Federation urged the Co-Coordinators to link their efforts with other Summit initiatives in which citizen participation is critical. She mentioned specifically the recently created Committee of Government Representatives within the process of the Free Trade Area of the Americas (FTAA), noting that it would be useful for the Co-Coordinators to offer their assistance in ensuring that it fulfill its role of allowing for participation. There is much they can do for this and other initiatives to enhance citizen participation in those specific contexts, she stressed. Rosenberg agreed, adding that it will be very hard to establish a mechanism for involvement of civil society in negotiations at the Summit Level but that perhaps the sector should focus on monitoring and implementation. Michael Franklin of the Organization of Africans in the Americas brought to light the point of accountability by governments of the commitments made at Summits. Citing a case in Argentina, he asked for advice on actions that could be taken to increase the implementation of these participatory practices at the national level. Carlo Dade of the Enterprise Research Foundation commented on the need to incorporate the business sector into this process, a sector that is already involved extensively in social issues at the local and regional level.

Amb. Boehm emphasized the need to accept that when 34 countries are working together, it will be hard to reach agreement on certain topics. He clarified that currently the Summit Process has two separate tracks—the FTAA negotiations and the Summit Implementation Review Group (SIRG) which deals with all other initiatives—that will ultimately have to come together. He noted that Canada was very interested in seeing the CGR move ahead.

Amb. Thompson reminded the group that ultimately, it is governments that will decide on implementation within their own countries, as the SIRG does not have enforcement capabilities. In light of this, civil societies must work with their governments and make sure that they group themselves so that the consultative mechanism is both manageable and accountable. He and Amb. Espinal thanked the participants for their attendance and comments, stating that they look forward to continued exchanges.

Amb. Yriart thanked the participants and the members of the Diplomatic Corps on behalf of Esquel. Daubón invited all to join us for the next session of the Civil Society Task Force, to be held Friday, October 23rd from 8:30 to 10:00 a.m.

## Notes

1. Richard Feinberg, *Policy Brief* of the Institute on Global Conflict and Cooperation (University of California-San Diego, May 1988).

2. For minutes from April to July 1998, see Annex 1.

# VII. PRESERVING AND STRENGTHENING DEMOCRACY AND HUMAN RIGHTS

*Nola-Kate Seymoar, Ph.D., is Deputy Director of the International Institute for Sustainable Development.*

*The mission of the **International Institute for Sustainable Development (IISD)** is to promote sustainable development in decisionmaking internationally and within Canada. We contribute new knowledge and concepts, analyze policies, identify and disseminate information about best practices, demonstrate how to measure progress, and build partnerships to amplify these messages. Our audiences and clients are businesses, governments, communities and concerned individuals.*

*Through Internet communications, working groups and project activities, we create networks designed to move sustainable development from concept to practice. Action must address the differing views and needs of both developing and industrialized nations. IISD bridges these concerns in its six program areas and through membership on its international board.*

*IISD was established in 1990 with continuing financial support from Environment Canada, CIDA, and the Province of Manitoba. It also receives revenue from foundations and other private sector sources.*

## Civil Society Participation in the Summit of the Americas, Santiago, Chile

*Nola-Kate Seymoar*

### A REPORT ON THE PEOPLES' SUMMIT AND VARIOUS OTHER FORA FOR PARTICIPATION

The Santiago Summit was the third meeting of the democratically elected Heads of State of the Americas. The first was convened in 1994 in Miami and a second meeting was held in 1996 in Bolivia on the theme of Sustainable Development. The Bolivia Summit was never given the same recognition as the Miami and Santiago Summits, partly because it was on a specific theme and did not attract all of the Heads of State (the Presidents of the USA and the Prime Minister of Canada, for example, were not in attendance). For all of the Summits, the involvement of civil society organizations was a subject on the agenda and action plan and was part of the process of preparations. I have described elsewhere the Bolivia process. This report will consider only my experience as it relates to the Santiago Summit. By "civil society organizations" or CSOs, I refer to the voluntary associations, organizations, movements, and networks that live and work in the space outside of the state and the private sector.

There were four major tracks for involvement of civil society organizations in the recent Summit.

### 1. CONSULTATIONS

Corporación PARTICIPA from Chile, with financial assistance from the Organization of American States (OAS), the IDB, and the Governments of Canada and Chile, organized a series of consultations on topics relevant to the formal agenda. One focused on education and another on "The Role of Public Participation in Development Actions and the Eradication of Poverty in the Framework of the Summit of the Americas." The purpose was to formulate recommendations to be presented to the preparatory bodies of the Santiago Summit.

These consultations organized by Corporación PARTICIPA brought together CSOs from throughout the hemisphere, along with some government representatives (the national focal points for the Interamerican Strategy for Public Participation, for example, attended the final consultation). The CSOs attending were approved by and quite closely aligned with their governments and for the most part they were not the same CSOs as were involved with the "People's Summit." The results of these consultations were forwarded to the OAS and to the participants and were brought forward to the preparatory meetings by Jamaica and Uruguay (the countries responsible for this item on the Summit agenda). Thanks to the efforts of the Ambassador from Jamaica, these discussions did have some influence on the wording of the documents later discussed at the SIRG (Summit Implementation and Review Group). The recommendations were affected by the inclusion of government representatives. Some government delegates, for example, could not endorse a recommendation regarding the inclusion of civil society in the FTAA process without instructions from their governments.

In Canada, FOCAL, with financial support from Canadian International Development Agency (CIDA), DFAIT, and the John Holmes Fund, organized a series of regional workshops on the Summit topics. The results of these consultations were brought to the PARTICIPA meetings by the FOCAL Coordinator and were forwarded to Ministers and officials of DFAIT and CIDA. Representatives of the key groups involved in the FOCAL consultations also met with Ambassador Boehm, and later with Ministers Axworthy and Marlowe prior to the Santiago Summit. In addition, the Canadian Centre for Foreign Policy Development held a roundtable of NGOs and others on the subject of Education and brought the recommendations forward to the DFAIT officials preparing Canada's position. The Canadian position regarding the education basket seemed to be consistent with these recommendations.

## 2. FORMAL DELEGATIONS

Some countries, such as Canada, Chile, and the USA, included representatives of CSOs on their country delegation to several meetings of the SIRG (Summit Implementation and Review Group). (CSOs could participate in the SIRG process only as members of their country's formal delegation.) As members of the delegation, CSO representatives received the briefing book and participated in the delegation deliberations and in the negotiations with other delegations. Like other delegates, they were restricted to speaking within their countries' positions and operated within the norms of confidentiality of the negotiation process. Due to the last minute arrival of the working papers, CSO representatives were not able to consult with their constituents about particular wording prior to the negotiations. The United States included a CSO representative in its delegation to the official Summit in April. Canada did not.

Canada invited three CSO representatives to the 13th SIRG meeting (the third of the Santiago process), where we learned a good deal about the negotiation process. There were several issues on which the CSO representatives attempted to gain stronger or different wording. On some we were unsuccessful in persuading the other members of the Canadian delegation or the other countries to adopt our proposals; on some we were successful. This is part and parcel of the normal give-and-take that occurs in such negotiations. Our ability to be effective was limited by the concern for confidentiality and the lack of time to review documents or consult with key groups on particular issues. Canada did press actively for wording in the Santiago Action Plan on civil society.

As well as participation in formal delegations for the SIRG, CSOs were included in the delegations to a few of the Ministerial meetings that preceded the Summit. I believe that this was true for the Mining and the Education Ministerials. The Trade Ministerial did not include CSOs on the delegations, although private sector representatives have a formal channel of input to the discussions. In addition to meetings that officials (Kathryn McCallion) had with CSO representatives, Minister Marchi met with CSOs prior to the San José Trade Ministers Meeting. One of the outcomes was Canada's support for the recommendation that a committee of government representatives be formed to seek, assess, and bring forward the views of CSOs in the negotiations for the FTAA. This recommendation fell short of the proposals of CSOs for a full social/labour forum or joint working group.

The issues of selection of CSO members on the national delegation became the subject of discussion among DFAIT officials and CSOs. There was agreement that this issue would be addressed as soon as possible after the Summit.

## 3. THE OAS INTER-AMERICAN STRATEGY FOR PUBLIC PARTICIPATION (ISP)

The ISP is a 22-month project that came out of the Bolivia Summit on Sustainable Development and is supported by the OAS, the Global Environmental Facility (GEF), U.S. Agency for International Development (USAID), and Scientific and Cultural Organization (UNESCO). It will make recommendations to the formal OAS and SIRG process in 1999. It has a Project Advisory Group (PAC) with seven elected representatives of CSOs (representing women, indigenous, minorities, labour, environmental, economic and social interests). The PAC also includes seven national focal points and three donor representatives. I sit on the PAC as an elected representative of CSOs representing economic interests within the context of sustainable development.

CSOs can make their views about public participation processes known to their government focal points or to the elected CSO representatives for consideration in the formulation of the ISP. To its credit, the ISP has attempted to use a democratic and open process of election and has mounted all of its documents on a web page. However, there has not yet been an effective system set up for the PAC to solicit and report back to CSOs on views or positions. At present, the communication system is limited to the web site and contact numbers. The PAC is budgeted to meet only twice, and the agenda is dominated by three demonstration projects funded by the GEF. The largest influence on the content of the ISP comes from a very competent and committed Technical Advisory Committee that serves as an unpaid kitchen cabinet to the OAS staff person responsible for the project. The challenge for the ISP may be to figure out how to encourage effective participation in its own process and not just present draft material and seek input in traditional ways.

## 4. THE PEOPLE'S SUMMIT

The People's Summit was the alternative forum created by and for NGOs in parallel to the Summit of the Americas. The People's Summit was in fact a number of concurrent workshops and events that began early in the week and culminated in a declaration that was presented to the governments on Saturday afternoon.

The People's Summit was organized by a coalition of NGOs and Labour groups from the region. The Canadian participation was led by four organizations: the Canadian Labour Congress (CLC), the Confederation des Syndicats Nationaux (CSN), Common Frontiers, and the Réseau Québécois sur l'Intégration Continentale (RQIC). Of the approximately 60 Canadian participants, well over half were from the labour movement. The others represented human rights, poverty, social justice, environmental, and women's groups (or academics) active nationally or internationally. One of the significant achievements of the Santiago meeting over a previous one held in Belo Horizonte was the coming together of labour, environmental, and social groups in a cooperative partnership. Preliminary meetings and papers had been developed in preparation for the Forum in Santiago. Approximately 2,000 people attended, mostly from southern NGOs and labour groups. The People's Summit was free. It received financial support from the labour movement, governments, and NGOs.

The overriding agenda of the People's Summit was a critique and resistance to the Free Trade Area of the Americas (FTAA) as it is presently portrayed. There was a deep and widely shared concern about the impacts of unfettered trade and market forces. In a very few cases this was based on a lack of information or knowledge about how the multi-lateral system works, but in most cases the concern reflected a thoughtful critique and the real experiences of workers and communities who have born the brunt of changes wrought by the North American Free Trade Agreement (NAFTA). So while on the surface the themes and workshops were devoted to the environment, economic, and social issues, underneath the issue was a concern about how the FTAA would impact upon environmental conservation, human rights, labour standards, cultures, and communities. The Multilateral Agreement on Investment (MAI) and the NAFTA were used as concrete reference points to raise awareness about how trade negotiations have been carried out in the past (in private and with private sector but not civil sector input). The discussions included a knowledgeable assessment of the strengths and weaknesses of the NAFTA sub-agreements on labour standards and environment.

This FTAA priority at the People's Summit actually paralleled the priority at the Heads of State Summit, although President Clinton's lack of fast track authority changed the discussions somewhat. Education, drugs, and other items that were less controversial were of significant importance to several countries, including Mexico, Brazil, and Canada. It is important to keep in mind that both Summits were pursuing several parallel agendas.

The FTAA priority was a reflection of the nature of the organizing groups and the participating delegates. The vast majority of the 2,000 participants at the People's Summit were from networks of grass-roots organizations or labour unions, or from academic institutions or think tanks working in the region. There was very little overlap between the participants in the People's Summit and the groups that had participated in the PARTICIPA-sponsored consultations for the Santiago Summit or the NGOs gathered in various meetings in 1996 prior to the Bolivia Summit. Likewise, in the Canadian delegation to the People's Summit there were few who had been involved in the Bolivia process, in the "official" Summit preparatory processes, or in OAS processes. The majority of the Canadians at the People's Summit knew one another from their history of working together on the NAFTA and MAI campaigns. Those of us who had been working on other issues or in the "official" process were welcomed with mixed feelings. On the one hand, there was a genuine desire to widen the constituency of those who share a critique of the FTAA agenda and, on the other hand, there was a mistrust of those who cooperate with governments and the private sector – particularly in Latin America.

I participated in the Environmental Forum (April 15, 16), in the Forum on Social and Economic Alternatives (April 17), and the plenary sessions (April 18). The Environmental Forum included papers and panel discussions on Trade, Biodiversity, Forests, Energy, and Civil Society Participation. The session was well organized and the papers that had been prepared were useful in focusing the panel discussions. The "Winnipeg Principles for Trade and Sustainable Development" were included in the paper on trade, and the Inter-American Strategy for Public Participation (ISP) was referred to in the paper on civil society. The debates that ensued were between those who were most concerned about getting the critique understood and communicated and those who were interested in moving on to examining options and proposing alternatives. My impression in this workshop was that the "protesters" were definitely in the majority. The Winnipeg Principles were not discussed. On the issue of civil society participation, some of the material presented was outside of the context of the lengthy discussions that have gone on at the OAS, the IDB, and during the Bolivia process. Further in reporting back on this topic, two separate sets of conclusions were reached – one on the broad issues that included attempts to build on the existing mechanisms and a second that focused entirely on the FTAA issue. The election of representatives for the Project Advisory Committee to the ISP was criticized due to the lack of time and the narrow group of organizations polled. Concern was also expressed about how to make the representatives accountable and the discussions responsive and transparent to those who are not part of the Advisory group.

The tone of the Forum on Social and Economic Alternatives was very different. The focus was on moving from the critique of unfettered trade into issues of how to participate in trade in ways that share the benefits among people more equitably, respect cultural diversity, and sustain the environment. A lengthy paper had been drafted and was circulated to participants. The key issues were presented by panelists, and participants were invited to send further comments to the authors. In my perception, the groups involved with this panel hold the best chance of influencing the FTAA agenda in the mainstream process. Other groups, of course, will exert influence in other ways.

The plenary sessions were characterized by speeches that were critical of governments and transnational corporations and made many demands. Perhaps this is the inevitable outcome of a structure that leads to resolutions and declarations on the part of 2,000 people. The event concluded with the presentation of the Declaration [1] to the President of Chile, with a few other countries (including Canada) in attendance. There was also a public demonstration in a park. The police were in evidence, but there was no attempt to interfere with the event.

The People's Summit was held immediately prior to the Heads of State meeting; thus it did not (and could not) influence the discussions or negotiations of that particular meeting. Furthermore, it was not able to garner the kind of media attention that it might have if it were held at a different time.

During the People's Summit, Ministers Axworthy and Marchi and Ambassador Boehm met with 16 representatives of the Canadian CSOs attending the People's Forum. Those participating reported that the meeting was useful, and on the issue of civil society participation, it reaffirmed the Ministers' commitment to further discuss the involvement of CSOs in both the FTAA and Summit process.

In general, it would be easy to dismiss the People's Summit as being predictable. A group of unions and NGOs with a critique of the free trade agenda, getting together to talk among themselves and condemn governments and business and the market economy. Indeed, that does describe a stereotype of the event. At a deeper level, however, there were many signs of significant areas for possible engagement between civil society actors in Canada and Latin America and the official Summit, OAS, and FTAA processes. It is important to highlight the incredible amount of work that groups in the hemisphere are putting into proposing concrete alternatives and mechanisms to the current system to build a better and fairer trade agenda.

## RESULTS ACHIEVED

It is very difficult to trace the impact of civil society input on the Summit and FTAA processes. In general, it seems that Canadian officials believe they have incorporated many of the ideas and suggestions from the various meetings and consultations, and many NGOs believe that the gains were few.

Regarding the specific issue of civil society participation in the Americas, the result of the Santiago Summit fell short of civil society's objectives as identified in the consultations.

The final declaration states:

*"Governments will:*

• Promote, with the participation of civil society, the development of principles and recommendations for in-

# VII. PRESERVING AND STRENGTHENING DEMOCRACY AND HUMAN RIGHTS

stitutional frameworks to stimulate the formation of responsible and transparent, non-profit, and other civil society organizations, including, where appropriate, programs for volunteers, and encourage, in accordance with national priorities, public sector-civil society dialogue and partnerships in the areas that are considered pertinent in this Plan of Action. In this context, the Organization of American States (OAS) may serve as a forum for the exchange of experiences and information.

• In this process, draw upon existing initiatives that promote increased participation of civil society in public issues, such as relevant successful experiences from the National Councils for Sustainable Development and the Inter-American Strategy for Public Participation, among others. As soon as possible, governments will adopt work plans to implement legal and institutional frameworks based on the principles and recommendations in their respective countries.

• Entrust the OAS to encourage support among governments and civil society organizations, promote appropriate programs to carry out this initiative, and request that the Inter-American Development Bank (IDB) develop and implement, along with interested states and other inter-American institutions, hemispheric financial mechanisms specially devoted to the implementation of programs oriented toward strengthening civil society and public participation mechanisms."

This is a weaker formulation than that contained in the Bolivia Summit Declaration in which the Heads of State and Government supported: *"broad participation by civil society in the decision-making process, including policies and programs and their design, implementation and evaluation."* The Bolivia Action Plan states: *"In order to support the specific initiatives on public participation contained in the Plan of Action, [we] entrust the OAS with assigning priority to the formulation of an Inter-American strategy for the promotion of public participation in decision-making for sustainable development, taking into account the recommendations of the Inter-American Seminar on Public Participation held in Montevideo in 1996."*

With regard to participation in the FTAA, the creation of a committee of government representatives to receive contributions from CSOs, analyze them, and present a range of options to ministers to consider is certainly less than the goal of active participation in the negotiations. It is also less than the fall-back position of having two tracks: a private sector forum and a civil sector forum that both have the opportunity to present their views to the ministers during the meetings and negotiations.

Clearly on this issue, the OAS and its member states remain less advanced than the UN system or many other multilateral fora.

## OBSERVATIONS AND IMPLICATIONS

I will use the *Self Empowerment Cycle*[2] as a framework to analyze my experience of these various events. In brief, the Cycle characterizes four phases of empowerment, including "powerlessness," "protesting," "proposing," and "partnering." It is important to recognize that different activities are appropriate on different issues at different times, and that this is a cycle not a straight linear progression from powerlessness to a fixed or better state of partnering.

In my perception, most Latin American CSOs attending the People's Summit were involved in various forms of advocacy on behalf of the poor, indigenous, or marginal peoples. On most issues, they were actively protesting injustices and using consciousness raising to move people from powerlessness to action. A smaller number of groups at the People's Summit and those involved in the mainstream consultation process focused their attention on "proposing" alternatives. Common Frontiers, for example, had taken the lead in preparing a paper outlining alternative economic and social measures to support trade within a context of principles that ensure greater equity. Few of the discussions were about "partnering," partly because the proposals were not yet well enough formulated and accepted within the CSO community. The reality of dealing with CSOs is that different groups are actively involved with different phases of the Empowerment Cycle and tend to see things through their own prisms. One of the characteristics of the cycle is that, typically, groups do not get to the partnership phase without experiencing the protest and proposal phases. Thus, it is difficult to imagine a set of meetings alongside the Trade Ministerials or the Canadian Summit in 2000 or 2002 that will not involve all three activities (protesting, proposing, and partnering). The question then becomes how can Canada best react to this and how can we explain it to the public so as to support the groups that have a legitimate need and desire to express their critique. The recent experience of the APEC Summit was not a happy one for any of those concerned.

My second observation relates to the preeminent role that Canada is starting to play in the hemisphere. The Canadian Mission is perceived as central to reform of the OAS. Large numbers of Canadian CSOs have been involved in development, human rights, and environment projects in Latin America and the Caribbean, in the People's Summit, and in the various OAS-related meetings. CIDA and International Development Research Centre (IDRC) have a long history of involvement in the hemisphere. We have the lead on the Trade Ministerial, the GA in the year 2000, the Pan Am Games, and the next Summit. Thus, it is reasonable to expect Canada to be in the forefront for the next five years. To assert our leadership responsibly and effectively, we need to work together with the private, government, and civil sectors. This involves understanding and respecting our different needs and agendas and finding those areas where we can cooperate on common objectives. It is also a question of timing our interventions and contributions to facilitate forward movement.

The third observation I would make on the process is the need to expand the range of opportunities for interaction across sectors and into the official Summit and trade negotiations process. Elsewhere, I have made recommendations about some of the ways in which that objective might be achieved. Suffice it to say that, in my opinion, real dialogue and negotiation, not just "consultation," is needed. If we cannot reinvent Summitry, we will continue to have two parallel processes with little synergy between them. If there is no change on the part of governments, the OAS, and civil society organizations, the situation will become more contentious, and greater polarization will occur.

## RECOMMENDATIONS FOR ACTION

### 1. Consultations

Ministers Axworthy and Marchi have indicated their willingness to discuss the involvement of CSOs in the official fora (the OAS, the trade talks, and the Summit process). There is a concern on the part of CSOs that such discussions will be held among only a small group of organizations selected by DFAIT. It is important that these discussions be as open and inclusive as possible if they are to build trust between the government and civil sectors. A regular and on-going process is needed – preferably one designed and implemented jointly by CSOs and government officials. Thus, it is recommended that the Centre for Foreign Policy Development support a series of regional and national workshops on the subject of civil society participation in national and international fora related to foreign policy, in general, and in the hemisphere, in particular. The workshops should be open to any CSOs or individuals who wish to attend or participate in person, by conference call, or electronically. It would be useful to circulate a working paper in advance of the meetings, identifying the various ways in which civil society has been involved in the past, providing an assessment of the effectiveness of this participation, identifying the issues involved, and proposing options for discussion.

A similar series of workshops should be held specifically to focus on CSO involvement in the FTAA process. Ideally, these meetings should be held in conjunction with one another so as to avoid two distinctly different approaches.

### 2. Delegations

It should be a matter of explicit policy and accepted practice to include CSO and private sector representatives in Canadian delegations to the SIRG, ministerial meetings, summits, and other multi-lateral fora and their preparatory meetings. Such practice, if consistently followed, demonstrates a commitment to participation that words alone cannot do.

### 3. The Inter-American Strategy for Public Participation (ISP)

The ISP needs to be strengthened by building a broader research component on the range of ways to facilitate public participation and by bringing forward examples of success from throughout the hemisphere. A structure to improve responsiveness and accountability needs to be built into the PAC. Canada needs to put some money on the table to encourage movement in this direction.

### 4. The People's Summit

If a People's Summit is planned for the next Heads of State Summit, it should be held sufficiently in advance of the formal Summit to allow the issues raised and the recommendations made to be considered and addressed in the preparatory process and the SIRG negotiations. Holding the Alternative Forum in advance would also increase the likelihood of media coverage of the event.

## 5. Overall Strategy for Canadian Leadership

The results of the preliminary discussions led by the Center for Foreign Policy Development regarding an overall strategy for the "Year of the Americas" should be discussed as quickly as possible and as widely as possible with government, private, and civil society representatives. This would allow the best ideas to come forward, build synergy among the activities proposed, and use limited resources as efficiently and effectively as possible.

## Notes

1. See <<http://ourworld.compuserve.com/homepages/oca_chile_rm/>>.

2. See *Creating Common Community,* edited by Nola-Kate Seymoar and Juana Ponce de León, Friends of the United Nations, (Calgary: Weigl Educational Publishers), 1997.

# VII. PRESERVING AND STRENGTHENING DEMOCRACY AND HUMAN RIGHTS

## Social Capital and Civil Society

*Damián J. Fernández*

*Damián J. Fernández is Chair of and Associate Professor in the Department of International Relations at Florida International University. His research interests include the international relations of Latin America and Cuban politics. Dr. Fernández has two books forthcoming:* Cuba and the Politics of Passion *(University of Texas Press) and* Cuba, the Elusive Nation: Interpretations of National Identity *(University Press of Florida).*

*The three papers by Florida International University Professors Damián J. Fernández, Kathleen R. Martín, and Patricia L. Price were presented on February 5, 1998, at the First Academic Consultation on the Presidential Summit of the Americas, sponsored by the Latin American and Caribbean Center (LACC) at Florida International University, the Facultad Latinoamericana de Ciencias Sociales (FLACSO), and the Ministry of Foreign Affairs of the Republic of Chile.*

The title of the Second Summit of the Americas "Hacia una comunidad hemisferica" presents one of the principal sociopolitical challenges for the integration of regions as well as for the creation of national polities: the establishment and maintenance of community. At the end of the Twentieth Century across the globe countries as distinct as the United States and Algeria, Brazil and Honduras, Italy and Russia are wrestling with the breakdown of the civic community. Economic modernization and the dislocations associated with it have been one of major causes of this problem, but not the only one. The depersonalization of politics, the widespread reporting of corruption and the accompanying loss of faith in government, anomie and weak civic traditions have also contributed to the erosion of communal bonds and civic engagement. Despite the vitality of democratic forms of government, the rise of social movements and the newfound dynamism in civil society throughout the region, the Americas are not the exception to this worldwide issue.

An engaged civic community is difficult to sustain due to the disintegrating factors typical of modern society. Clearly integrative forces are also at play. For example, the interamerican effort to build community is important both at the international and national levels. Precisely due to the relevance and timeliness of the effort, we should identify the underpinnings of a civic community. Once we locate those building blocks of civil society and civic participation we will be better suited to invest in them.

The concern for civility and civic traditions is not new; on the contrary it has a long tradition. Neither is the argument that civic engagement has a positive impact on economic performance and institutional efficiency and accountability. What is new is the realization that in the same way that societies can lose some of the foundations that support civic behavior, they can also attempt to secure those foundations to further community goals and institutional performance at the local and national levels.

The Summit of the Americas process has directed its attention, if not as many resources as some would like, to the strengthening of civil society. Civil society participation is recognized as a linchpin in democratic governance, in sustainable development, and in the eradication of poverty. Civil society is one of the ways that communities manifest themselves and in the process communal ties are extended and deepened. But, what makes a civil society civil? What helps generate its civility? What can be done to reproduce civic involvement over time and help magnify the economic and political benefits that can be accrued?

In the numerous volumes written as a result of the Miami process, civil society is perceived as an output— something that is produced or has been produced and that will contribute to other social goods. The focus has been on the dynamics of civil society. Much less attention has been paid to the quality of civil society. Why are some organizations more effective than others? What are some more democratic? Why are some regions and localities richer in these types of associations? Although the Summit has engaged in discussions regarding how to increase participation in civic tasks and in public decision-making and has invested in training leaders of nongovernmental organizations, much less consideration has been given to the inputs necessary to the formation of a civil society. An analysis of the factors that give civil society its qualitative dimensions has been largely absent. Furthermore, the connection between civil society, eradication of poverty, sustainable development, education, and democratic governance— key goals of the Summit — has not been articulated clearly. The links between all these factors are not integrated explicitly. The expectation is that all good things will come together. What is missing is the logical connection between these social, economic and political goals through integrative concepts that will help shape policies. Social capital is one of the concepts that can provide the missing link and at the same time help us rethink public policy from an alternative perspective that can contribute to the goals of the Summit.

Social capital "refers to features of social organization, such as networks, norms, and trust, that facilitate coordination and cooperation for mutual benefit. Social capital enhances the benefits of investment in physical and human capital." (Robert Putnam, "The Prosperous Community" The American Prospect No. 13 Spring 1993, pp.35-42). Social capital helps resolve many of the conflicts inherent in community building: how to guarantee cooperation for mutual benefit without resorting to the creation of an authoritarian state.

Social capital is a common good that has individual and group dimensions and repercussions at both levels as well. The factors of social capital include networks and associations that facilitate civic engagement. These organizations, based on solidarity, reciprocity and trust, enhance collaboration and coordination and provide valuable information. Social capital has an impact on the type of democracy and on the economic achievement of a nation. In short, social capital contributes to mutual gains for the community and the nation at large.

The concept of social capital helps us think about and act upon the interrelated factors of civil society, democracy and economic growth from an integrative perspective. In addition to establishing an explicit relationship between economic growth, participation and effective institutions, social capital can help us craft policies to further economic growth and democratic governance. Several social scientists have concluded that social capital is a precondition for prosperity and good democratic governance. Prosperous communities had dense patterns of civic engagement, but a rich endowment of social capital is not a substitute for good public policy rather a prerequisite and a consequence of it.

If we agree with this conclusion, the policy implications are worth considering. In fact, many of the initiatives proposed by the Summit of the Americas in the area of civil society have been concerned with the enhancement of social capital, without labeling as such. Making the concept explicit will facilitate appropriate policy responses in a number of areas.

The Summit of the Americas II should introduce the notion of social capital in its vocabulary and direct resources, first, to study the different aspects of the concept and, second, to find practical ways to invest in it. The promotion of community associations and programs that cut across racial, ethnic and regional divides is one of the ways to capitalize on social capital. In terms of sustainable development, social capital can be a practical yardstick to measure, as well as predict, success of development programs. Recently the Interamerican Foundation has adopted a model called the Grassroots Development Model that does exactly that. It takes into account the effect of social capital formation on development, and vice-versa. For policymakers, the realization that social capital matters in tangible ways can help design policies that would contribute to its formation; for instance, policies that balance individual with communal interests and at the same time enhance the social capital of a community. Education programs that encourage participation of parents, students, and other members of the community and also transmit civic values can contribute to social capital. The possibilities are many as are the challenges in this area.

Social capital is a slippery concept for a number of reasons. It might raise sensitive issues as well. But if it is approached from the perspective that social capital can increase or decrease over time (like in the case of the United States), it is made responsive to appropriate public policy and not essential to one region or another. The multiple benefits warrant an effort in this direction. Such an attempt would entail talking explicitly about a community's values, attitudes, and norms as well as its organizational culture and personal capacity. The purpose is to magnify those aspects that can contribute to collaboration and thereafter to participation, government accountability, institutional performance and economic well-being. Thereafter, we need to explore how policy can foster the formation of social capital.

# VII. PRESERVING AND STRENGTHENING DEMOCRACY AND HUMAN RIGHTS

# The Indigenization of Latin America

*Kathleen R. Martín*

*Kathleen R. Martín is an associate professor in the Department of Sociology/Anthropology at Florida International University. Her main research area is Mexico, and her major research topics are women, indigenous peoples, and politics. Dr. Martín's most recent publication is "From the Heart of a Woman: Yucatec Maya Women as Political Actors," in the journal, Sex Roles 39, nos. 7/8, Dec. 1998. This article won the 1999 Sturgis Leavitt Award for the best article published by a member of the South East Council of Latin American Studies (SECOLAS).*

*The three papers by Florida International University Professors Damián J. Fernández, Kathleen R. Martín, and Patricia L. Price were presented on February 5, 1998, at the First Academic Consultation on the Presidential Summit of the Americas, sponsored by the Latin American and Caribbean Center (LACC) at Florida International University, the Facultad Latinoamericana de Ciencias Sociales (FLACSO), and the Ministry of Foreign Affairs of the Republic of Chile.*

Despite 506 years of conquest, discrimination and the imposition of non-indigenous cultures into their homelands, the indigenous peoples of the Americas have neither been eliminated nor absorbed by Latin American cultures. It is more accurate to say that the indigenous peoples of the Americas have become active participants in the evolving democracies and market economies of the region.

In their societal participation indigenous peoples are taking elements of non-indigenous cultures and reformulating them to fit indigenous cosmovisions, i.e., a process of "indigenization." Consequently, mechanisms must be found that assist the already underway successful participation of indigenous peoples in a democratic, market-oriented Latin America. Their unique heritage must also be acknowledged and their continued distinctiveness as peoples respected.

The following are issues to be addressed to achieve the goal of the successful participation of indigenous peoples in a changing Latin America. (In the order listed on the "Proposed Agenda for the Summit of the Americas".)

## EDUCATION:

Educational reform is critical to assure the successful participation of indigenous peoples and to respect their cultural uniqueness. Indigenous peoples must have access to education which grants them not only literacy but also includes them in the end-of-millennium communications revolution. Indigenous peoples must also have access to an education appropriate to assure their economic well-being and intellectual development. Bi-lingual education must be guaranteed for all indigenous groups who choose to maintain their own language. Special effort must be made to assure the education of indigenous women who have often been bypassed in educational reform.

In addition, the national educational curriculum must be redrawn to include an accurate and respectful depiction of indigenous cultures and the inclusion of indigenous peoples into the national history. Education must seek to preserve indigenous peoples' unique cultural heritage in contradistinction to the trend toward global cultural conformity.

## PRESERVING AND STRENGTHENING DEMOCRACY AND HUMAN RIGHTS:

Many Latin America nations have laws in place which guarantee basic human rights and outline democratic principles. The proper enforcement of such laws needs to be ensured as applying to all citizens. In addition, indigenous peoples must be allowed self-determination in decisions regarding the means and degrees of integration and articulation with the state. The use of violence as a means to resolve conflict between indigenous peoples and the state must be permanently renounced.

To assure the human rights of indigenous peoples as indigenous peoples within the context of democratic societies their unique patrimony and continuing cultural distinctiveness must be honored. To this end indigenous archaeological sites and indigenous sacred places must be repatriated and allowed to remain within the domain of indigenous control.

The rituals sacred to indigenous peoples as part of their spiritual and intellectual patrimony must be respected by allowing their continued practice. Also the value of indigenous cultures and their relevance for contemporary society must be recognized. At the very least indigenous peoples have much to offer non-indigenous peoples in teaching cultural resilience and alternative cosmo-visions. There must be a guarantee of pluri-ethnic societies in Latin America and a recognition that cultural diversity is wealth.

## ECONOMIC INTEGRATION AND FREE TRADE:

In addition to the educational reforms suggested earlier in this paper that would assist indigenous peoples in obtaining the skills needed to participate in market-oriented economies, indigenous peoples should be permitted to control their own patrimony and especially any economic development of it. The development of eco-tourism and ethnic tourism has had a marked impact on indigenous peoples. The development of these kinds of tourism especially should be determined by indigenous peoples themselves.

Careful consideration of the consequences to indigenous peoples of any kind of economic development must be made with indigenous peoples actively participating in this discourse.

Indigenous peoples should have the final determination in any economic decisions that affect them.

## ERADICATION OF POVERTY AND DISCRIMINATION:

The most basic and obvious means to eradicate poverty and discrimination is to allow all citizens functional access to education, health care and necessary public services. In addition a healthy economy and a public consciousness respectful of cultural differences are also necessary components of eradicating poverty and discrimination.

Within any plan to end poverty and discrimination the special concerns of indigenous women must be confronted. Many indigenous women are poor and thus suffer from a triple discrimination as women, indigenous people and low-income individuals.

In the case of indigenous peoples the special characteristics of rural poverty must also be addressed. Conflicts over land ownership, disputes about resource management and inter-ethnic struggles must be resolved to allow indigenous peoples to leave behind the assaults of poverty and discrimination. Creating a just distribution of land and a fair sustainable development of the natural environment plus a changed public consciousness about indigenous identity and indigenous heritage will do much to end poverty and discrimination.

## SUSTAINABLE DEVELOPMENT:

Indigenous peoples have long been associated with the natural world. Given that many indigenous peoples live in rural areas where they are dependent on the natural world for their livelihood, their special knowledge of the environment and their dependency on it should permit them a central role in determining environmental policy and the structure of sustainable development. Their technical and scientific knowledge should be at the core of any plans for sustainable development.

Religious and spiritual beliefs of indigenous peoples are intimately intertwined with their knowledge of the natural world. These beliefs must be respected and viewed as alternative cosmo-visions to the world views that prevail in Western thought and practice. The knowledge that indigenous peoples possess to teach to non-indigenous peoples is based on the indigenous understanding how to live with this planet rather than merely on it.

# VII. Preserving and Strengthening Democracy and Human Rights

*Patricia L. Price is an assistant professor of geography in the Department of International Relations at Florida International University. Her ongoing research interests merge an empirical focus on gender, poverty, and development across the Americas with theoretical work on borders and the spatiality of human agency in late modernity. Among Dr. Price's recent publications are "Bodies, Faith, and Inner Landscapes: Rethinking Change from the Very Local," Latin American Perspectives 26 (3), 1999; and "No Pain, No Gain: Bordering the Hungry New World Order," forthcoming in Environment and Planning D: Society and Space, early 2000.*

*The three papers by Florida International University Professors Damián J. Fernández, Kathleen R. Martín, and Patricia L. Price were presented on February 5, 1998, at the First Academic Consultation on the Presidential Summit of the Americas, sponsored by the Latin American and Caribbean Center (LACC) at Florida International University, the Facultad Latinoamericana de Ciencias Sociales (FLACSO), and the Ministry of Foreign Affairs of the Republic of Chile.*

# Signposts Toward Building a Hemispheric Community

*Patricia L. Price*

## I. INTEGRATING THE ISSUES

There is nothing more profoundly indicative of the emerging world order than the promotion of a freer flow of goods, services, money and ideas across national borders. Success, indeed survival, requires an increasingly nimble choreography which is able to respond to ever-changing economic, social, and political conditions. Ensuring effective competitiveness requires both the vision to think regionally and the drive to make integration a reality. In our hemisphere, this union is expressed most fully in the ongoing negotiation of a Free Trade Area of the Americas. However, through the legislation and implementation of NAFTA and MERCOSUR, sub-regions of the Americas have already begun to experience the benefits, as well as the complex issues, involved in regional integration.

These statements are compelling. Yet the recognition that formal integration on a world regional level provides the framework for investment and trade flows of the future must be refined along two points. First, globalization — however important — constitutes only half the story of the late 20th Century. For even as "the global" emerges as ever-more central, "the local" is also becoming increasingly important for understanding international dynamics. Indeed, the idea of the nation-state and the national boundaries that have shaped international relations for roughly the last 200 years no longer provides the pre-eminent organizational framework that it did up to the beginning of the 1990s. The period from the oil crisis in 1973-74, through debt crisis in Latin America, and up until the collapse of the Soviet Union in 1991 signaled the end of the bipolar geopolitical order of the Cold War. More generally, the rise of the global-local interplay has emerged as the crucial taxonomy for the future. As the leaders of the Americas face the Summit Meeting in mid-April, they must bear in mind the importance of the local level as well as the centrality of the global scale. Particularly in the Americas, local reconfiguration of state-society relations, local mediation of economic change, and local understanding of cultural identity constitute currents of change which are every bit as central as (and, indeed, inextricably connected to) change at the global level.

Second, it has become quite commonplace to mention "free trade" and "democratization" in the same breath. Indeed, many would have us believe that an outward-focused market economic system in fact *causes* political democratization. It is indeed true that the majority of the repressive military rulers in this hemisphere have retreated to the barracks. But democracy is more than simply the absence of military rule. While fair elections provide a step in the right direction, the deeper issues dividing the hemisphere stem from the ongoing (and indeed, growing) gap between the region's haves and have-nots. This inequity constitutes the most serious limit to a real and lasting democracy in the

Americas. Ongoing instability in Chiapas, Shining Path and Tupac Amaru activity in Peru, outbreaks of preventable infectious diseases like cholera, and widespread civil violence linked specifically to drugs (and more-generally to poverty) are striking reminders that many Americans have yet to enjoy meaningful democracy in their daily lives.

It is unclear that simply relying on free trade to solve these problems will prove to be effective. In this regard, we would do well to recall the words of Peter Hakim:

*Whatever progress has been made in Latin America toward consolidating democratic politics, restoring economic dynamism, and building toward an economically integrated hemisphere has been tarnished and jeopardized by the mass poverty and profound inequalities of wealth that plague most nations of the region. It is not only that glaring income disparities and extreme poverty are morally offensive. It is also that their persistence could defeat the region's struggle for sustained economic growth and undermine prospects for a stable democracy.*

## II. DISCUSSION OF SUMMIT AGENDA

### 2.1 Democracy and Human Rights

There is a tenuous link — if any at all — between free market reforms and democratization. Indeed, nurturing fledgling democracies in the region may well require rethinking the trajectory of free market reforms. Empirical evidence has repeatedly revealed that free market reforms undertaken in the 1980s have weighed most heavily on the poorest Americans. Whether increased hardship and inequality attributed to economic reforms is really simply a harsh period of "crossing the desert" soon to be overcome (as proponents of welfare reform in the United States argue), or whether the horizon of improvement will be indefinitely delayed (as the recent round of instability in Mexico suggests) is still open to question. What is clear is that, for the 44% of Latin Americans officially considered "poor" (and their counterparts in the U.S. and Canada), this long period of flux and uncertainty has forced significant reconfigurations in state-civil society relations and has brought issues of human rights and democracy to the forefront of the region's agenda.

So-called "new social movements" provide one illustration of locally-based, "grassroots" responses of civil society to the changing role of the Latin American state. In some cases, those most affected by growing hardship stemming from economic reform take to the streets to protest the high cost of food, housing, and lack of services. In others, issues formerly considered non- or a-political — the environment, indigenous identity, domestic violence — become intensely politicized. In still others, human rights abuses running the gamut from the intimidation of journalists, police abuses, and kidnapping provide rallying points for citizen organization. In all cases, these locally-based mobilizations present the region with a new way of doing politics and a kaleidoscope of new political actors. They have the potential to open new channels of dialogue, to define new ways of conducting politics, and give rise to novel transnational coalitions of interest.

The role of religion, in particular, appears to be a central dynamic of new stances toward democracy and human rights. Activist Catholicism has certainly played an important role in calling world attention to abuses of human rights and demanding their widespread fulfillment. Evangelical Protestantism, while on one hand challenging the hegemony of traditional Catholicism in Latin America, will most likely lead to still different ways of defining civil society and citizen participation in local, national, and regional communities.

### 2.2 Eradication of Poverty and Discrimination

The ability of America's leadership to close the gap between the hemisphere's haves and have-nots is the biggest challenge facing Summit participants. Education is the single most important avenue out of poverty, yet Latin America's wide educational coverage must be backed up with meaningful employment opportunities. In the context of a streamlined state, creative public-private ventures can be supported in order to deepen secondary educational opportunities in the Americas and tie these to post-graduation employment opportunities.

While advocates of regional integration celebrate increased cross-border exchange of goods, money, and ideas, the increased volume of transnational flows in the Americas is not always desirable. Some have pointed to the increasing "Colombianization" of Latin American countries (particularly with regard to Mexico). In this view, drug production, traffic, and use threatens to increasingly dominate the national, and perhaps international, balance of power. Profound alterations of the regional tissue are implicated: rising gang and mafia-related violence, significant underground shifts in monetary flows, family breakdown, and a redistribution of authority from licit to illicit spheres. Without a doubt, drug-related activity is an important security issue. At a deeper level, however, poverty (not security) emerges as the most important driving force behind regional "Colombianization."

Thus any attack on drug activity must focus on addressing deeper issues of poverty. In particular, the production and consumption of illicit drugs appears to be founded in lack of viable alternatives. Drug production is strongly rooted in an eroded ability to engage in remunerative licit cash cropping. Drug consumption, while constituting an activity which cuts across class divides, involves America's poor in its most dangerous manifestations (adulterated, inexpensive, deadly "crack"-type concoctions). Neither production nor consumption is limited to any one geographic area or one social group. My research in an impoverished Mexican urban neighborhood, for example, reveals high numbers of young men and women taking drugs which range from glue-sniffing and marijuana smoking through a range of injectibles, as well as being involved in the most precarious aspects of local drug distribution.

The reconfiguring hemispheric order involves not just regional economic integration, but also the widespread breakdown in old systems of reward and punishment. America's leaders must ensure that new systems of reward and punishment — systems outside the purview of licit activity, such as gangs, drug lords, and underground violence — do not emerge to take the place of old systems. Particularly urgent in this regard are what appear to be links of persons and institutions of authority, in some cases, to illicit drug activity. These links serve to both to entrench and legitimate this activity.

## 2.3 Human Capital

The decade of the 1980s in Latin America was referred to as the "lost decade" and this label is not without justification. Regional debt crisis and economic adjustment in the short- to mid-term did force useful reconfigurations in many arenas of social, political, and economic life. However, the setbacks to Latin America's human capital stock, particularly in its most basic dimensions — health care and education — have negatively affected a whole generation of young people. Indeed, a new and more insidious "domino effect" in the Americas may involve the intergenerational transmission of disadvantage. Nutritional deficiencies, low skill levels, and educational shortfalls which accrued to the "lost-decade cohort" must, where at all possible, be addressed. If Latin American workforces are underskilled, uneducated and malnourished, Latin American countries will be at a disadvantage when competing for global capital and export opportunities.

Yet while addressing shortcomings of the recent past is important, a forward-looking focus must also be adopted. Nowhere is the gap between the "haves" and the "have-nots" expressed more clearly, or more ominously, than between those who have access to information and can understand and manipulate it, and those who do not. Thus a vital component of educational provision in the Americas involves closing the gap between "information haves" and "information have-nots."

## III. TOWARD NEW SPACES

Like it or not, the economic future of this hemisphere is one of increasing interdependence. National borders provide a less relevant organizational framework, and footloose capital and fluid trade patterns provide new pivot-points of power in the Americas. Map distance has become ever-more a fiction of the past, while virtual proximity is of the essence. Increased dialogue about the contours of the Americas in the 21st Century is an example of the benefits of interdependence. Yet the spectacular financial collapse in Mexico, and the reverberating "tequila hangover" of 1995, provide another, less upbeat illustration of the ramifications of integration.

At the same time, local communities, alliances, and understandings of these broader changes provide a counterbalance to the blind logic of globalization. Grassroots politics, religion, and community participation in overcoming poverty are a vital component of change in the Americas. Strengthening local endeavors holds forth the potential for crafting a more-inclusive model of development which avoids the destiny of placeless power and powerless places.

The Summit of the Americas Agenda has the potential to chart such a course.

# VII. PRESERVING AND STRENGTHENING DEMOCRACY AND HUMAN RIGHTS

## Recommendations Concerning Corruption to the SIRG Ministers for the Summit of the Americas
### April 18, 1997 – Santiago, Chile

*Transparency International (TI), a non-profit, non-partisan NGO headquartered in Germany, is the leading advocate of action to curb corruption. TI national chapters in over seventy countries, including seventeen in the Americas, are coalitions of leaders from major business enterprises, the legal and development communities, academia, and civic organizations. Some have held high public offices.*

*They are building public understanding of the adverse impact of corruption on open markets, democracy, and sustainable and equitable development. They are forging partnerships in support of constructive action by the public and private sector in both industrialized and developing countries around the world. To promote best practices by the private sector in foreign markets, TI chapters supported the recently signed OECD Convention on Combating Bribery of Foreign Public Officials, which criminalizes bribery of foreign public officials. Several countries in the hemisphere are signatories, including Argentina, Brazil, Canada, Chile, Mexico, and the United States. TI also contributed to the 1996 adoption of the International Chamber of Commerce Rules of Conduct on Extortion and Bribery, voluntary rules which would prohibit bribery for any purpose.*

*In the Americas, TI chapters encouraged the adoption of important anticorruption commitments by the leaders of the hemisphere at the 1994 Summit of the Americas in Miami. They have worked since that time for the implementation of those commitments through systemic reform at the national level. TI commends the OAS and the leaders for concluding the InterAmerican Anticorruption Convention, an important milestone.*

Considering the commitments made to combat corruption in the Action Plan of the 1994 Summit of the Americas,

### I. UNDER THE AGENDA HEADING, "DEMOCRACY AND HUMAN RIGHTS: ACTIONS TO COMBAT CORRUPTION":

A) Before the Organization of American States (OAS) General Assembly Meetings in 1999, governments will ratify the InterAmerican Convention Against Corruption and agree to an effective monitoring process with adequate resources from the Inter-American Development Bank (IDB) and national governments to promote region-wide implementation.

B) Before December 31, 1999, governments will:

i) Promote legislation to establish and enforce rules regarding conflict of interest on the incompatibility of public office and private interests, requirements for public disclosure of assets of high level public officials and their families, in the executive, legislative and judicial branches, and to create national organizations for oversight of such laws.

ii) Promote legislation requiring the timely publication of information regarding government activities, including budgets and expenditures, public access to information, and public hearings for expression of the opinion of citizens.

### II. UNDER THE HEADING OF THE AGENDA: "ECONOMIC INTEGRATION AND FREE TRADE," GOVERNMENTS WILL:

A) Conclude negotiation of a regional agreement on transparency in procurement for approval and implementation before December 31, 1998 and encourage the use of "no bribe commitments" and corporate codes of conduct that prohibit bribes in public bidding as well as in projects financed by the IDB.

B) Instruct the Interamerican Development Bank to adopt regulations, procedures, and policies of the highest standard for public bidding.

# VII. PRESERVING AND STRENGTHENING DEMOCRACY AND HUMAN RIGHTS

*Transparency International (TI) USA*

## Workshop on the Role of Public Participation in Development Actions and Eradication of Poverty Within the Framework of the Summit of the Americas
### November 4-7, 1997

### RECOMMENDATIONS ADOPTED BY CONSENSUS ON TRANSPARENCY AS A MEANS OF COMBATING CORRUPTION

Considering the commitments made to combat corruption in the *Plan of Action* of the 1994 Summit of the Americas,

A. Under the Agenda Heading "Democracy and Human Rights: Actions to Combat Corruption":

*Before December 31, 1998, governments will:*

i) Encourage ratification of the Interamerican Convention Against Corruption and take concrete steps to implement the commitments, including the establishment of mechanisms that promote civil society participation in an effort to prevent, detect, sanction and eradicate corruption.

ii) Promote legislation to establish and enforce standards of conduct, rules regarding conflict of interest and the incompatibility of public office and private interests, requirements for public disclosure of assets of high level public officials and their families, in the executive, legislative and judicial branches, and legislation to create national organizations for oversight of such laws.

iii) Promote and finance education to strengthen ethical values and behavior and encourage the communications media to support such programs.

iv) Establish an Organization of American States (OAS) secretariat (similar to the CICAD model) with adequate resources from Inter-American Development Bank (IDB) and national governments to promote the implementation of the convention and to monitor progress, including by mutual evaluation, with annual reports to ministers.

v) Create an interamerican network of governmental and civil society institutions under the OAS Secretary General to cooperate in the struggle against corruption through, among others, the exchange of information and experiences and horizontal cooperation.

## B. Under the Agenda Heading "Democracy and Human Rights: Actions Destined to Strengthen Civil Society Participation":

*By December 31, 1998, governments will:*

i) Promote legislation requiring the timely publication of information regarding government activities, including budgets and expenditures, public access to information, and public hearings for expression of the opinion of citizens.

## C. Under the Agenda Heading "Democracy and Human Rights: Actions in the Area of Strengthening the Judicial System":

*By December 31, 1999, governments will:*

i) Concerning judges, promote merit selection, train in the highest ethical standards, and create oversight mechanisms, and strengthen the role of public prosecutors, in order to promote independence, integrity and transparency in the administration of justice.

## D. Under the Agenda Heading "Economic Integration and Free Trade":

i) Conclude negotiation of a regional agreement on transparency in procurement for approval and implementation before December 31, 1998.

ii) Encourage the use of "no bribe commitments" and corporate codes of conduct that prohibit bribes in public bidding as well as in projects financed by the IDB.

iii) Instruct the Interamerican Development Bank to adopt regulations, procedures, and policies of the highest standard for public bidding.

iv) Take immediate measures to eradicate corruption in customs offices.

# VIII. Economic Integration and Free Trade

# VIII. ECONOMIC INTEGRATION AND FREE TRADE

*National Wildlife Federation (NWF) focuses its efforts on five core issue areas (Endangered Habitat, Water Quality, Land Stewardship, Wetlands, and Sustainable Communities) and pursues a range of educational projects and activist, advocacy, and litigation initiatives within these core areas.*

*The Chilean Ecological Action Network **(Red Nacional de Acción Ecológica — RENACE)** is the main environmental organization in Chile. RENACE was created in 1988 and currently provides a link for 154 regional organizations.*

*RENACE's main activities involve providing information, education and environmental training, organization of campaigns to solve environmental problems, and promotion of alternatives for sustainable development at the local, regional, and national levels. RENACE organizes annual national meetings for analysis, discussion, and planning of campaigns and activities.*

# Foro Ambiental - Cumbre de los Pueblos de América (Santiago, abril 1998) Comercio y Desarrollo Sustentable:
## Recomendaciones de la Sociedad Civil para la Integración Hemisférica

*Redactado por Atziri Ibáñez y John Audley, National Wildlife Federation (EUA), integrando recomendaciones hechas por Eduardo Gudynas, Centro Latino Americano de Ecología Social (Uruguay); Sara Larraín, Chile Sustentable (Chile); Patricia Gay, Consultora; Gustavo Alanis, Centro Mexicano de Derecho Ambiental (México); Franklin Paniagua, Centro de Derecho Ambiental y de los Recursos Naturales (Costa Rica); Mario Gerardo Galindo, Centro de Derecho Ambiental de Honduras (Honduras). Este documento se apoya, en principio, en la Declaración de las Organizaciones No Gubernamentales con motivo de la IV Reunión Ministerial del Area de Libre Comercio de las Américas, que tuvo lugar el 15-16 de marzo, 1998, en San José, Costa Rica.*

## INTRODUCCIÓN

La creación del Area de Libre Comercio de las Américas (ALCA) no constituye solamente otra de las 23 iniciativas encaradas por la Cumbre de las Américas (Miami, 1994). Representa la base, el fundamento del proceso de integración hemisférica contenido en la visión de la Cumbre de Miami de 1994 que vincula la promoción de la prosperidad de los pueblos con tres principios fundamentales: el progreso social, la prosperidad económica y un medio ambiente saludable. Aunque el ALCA constituye el fundamento de este proceso de integración hemisférico, no ha logrado adelantar estas metas.

En la sección titulada «Pacto para el Desarrollo y la Prosperidad: Democracia, Libre Comercio y Desarrollo Sustentable en las Américas», los funcionarios gubernamentales destacaron claramente que estos tres principios deberán respetarse para que los pueblos puedan gozar de los beneficios prometidos por la integración hemisférica. Citando la Declaración de Miami,

El progreso social y la prosperidad económica sólo se pueden mantener si nuestros pueblos viven en un entorno saludable y nuestros recursos naturales se utilizan cuidadosamente y de manera responsable...Fomentaremos el bienestar social y la prosperidad económica en formas que tomen plenamente en cuenta el impacto que producimos sobre el medio ambiente.

En el Plan de Acción de la Cumbre se han identificado los siguientes proyectos como prioridades regionales que promoverían la conservación de los recursos naturales para las futuras generaciones a través de acciones cooperativas regionales:

• La energía sustentable. El desarrollo y el uso de la energía sustentable, incluyendo la promoción de tecnologías energéticas eficientes y no contaminantes. Además, se identificaron el financiamiento y el desarrollo prioritarios de por lo menos un proyecto económicamente viable en energía renovable no convencional, en eficiencia energética y en energía convencional no contaminante.

• La conservación y el uso sustentable de la biodiversidad. Uno de los principales objetivos del Plan de Acción de la Cumbre fue la integración de estrategias para la conservación y el uso sustentable de la biodiversidad en las actividades de desarrollo económico.

• La creación de una alianza para la prevención de la contaminación.

Los gobiernos participantes también reconocieron la importancia que revisten los numerosos acuerdos internacionales, como el compromiso de apoyar la Alianza Centroamericana para el Desarrollo Sustentable, la Agenda 21, y la Conferencia Mundial sobre los Pequeños Estados Insulares en Desarrollo.

En toda la Declaración de Miami los gobiernos expresaron su convencimiento de que un elemento clave en el plan general para la integración hemisférica es el fortalecimiento de las democracias. Como señala la Declaración de Miami,

...la democracia representativa es indispensable para la estabilidad, la paz y el desarrollo de la región. La democracia es el único sistema político que garantiza el respeto de los derechos humanos y el estado de derecho; a la vez, salvaguarda la diversidad cultural, el pluralismo, el respeto de los derechos de las minorías y la paz en y entre las naciones.

La expansión del nivel de participación pública en las actividades gubernamentales es fundamental para el objetivo de la integración hemisférica. Las partes han formulado planes específicos de acción para fortalecer el diálogo entre los grupos sociales y reforzar la participación de la sociedad y la comunidad en el gobierno. Creemos firmemente que el gobierno democrático y el estado de derecho son componentes esenciales de los esfuerzos nacionales e internacionales para proteger el medio ambiente. Es por eso que aplaudimos el compromiso de nuestros gobiernos en favor de esa participación y de los mencionados principios.

Desafortunadamente, las negociadores comerciales de la Cumbre de Miami no tomaron medidas concretas para asegurar que el progreso social y un ambiente saludable estuvieran garantizados por el ALCA. Por el contrario, ha crecido una resistencia a integrar el comercio y el desarrollo sustentable como parte de la agenda negociada. La mayor parte de los países sostienen que la inclusión del medio ambiente crea obstáculos para acceder a los mercados, y que las vacilaciones violan el derecho de un país a utilizar sus recursos naturales. No fue sorprendente que los funcionarios del ALCA hayan rechazado las primeras propuestas de los Estados Unidos para crear un Grupo de Estudio sobre Comercio y Medio Ambiente, presentadas en la Segunda Declaración Ministerial, en Cartagena, Colombia, en 1996. Debido a esto, los funcionarios comerciales han relegado los aspectos ambientales de las negociaciones comerciales al Comité de Comercio y Medio Ambiente de la Organización Mundial del Comercio (OMC, CTE). De todas formas, considerando las circunstancias y con cierta reserva, nosotros consideramos que el recientemente creado Comité para la Sociedad Civil (4ta. Declaración Ministerial, San José, Costa Rica) tiene el potencial para reintegrar en el comercio las prioridades del desarrollo sustentable.

Reconocemos que el Comité para la Sociedad Civil tiene el potencial para desempeñar un papel clave en la definición de la relación que existe entre el sistema de comercio del hemisferio occidental y el medio ambiente. El desafío que enfrentan los jefes de estado es establecer una conexión entre los objetivos del desarrollo sustentable y las propias negociaciones comerciales.

Ahora bien, antes de entrar a las recomendaciones presentamos a continuación una lista de principios que se incluyen con el propósito de orientar las políticas, las prácticas y los acuerdos de comercio relacionados con el comercio y el desarrollo, para asegurar el logro de un desarrollo sustentable.

Las medidas comerciales aplicadas al nivel nacional y los acuerdos multilaterales de comercio deben contribuir a la internalización de los costos ambientales a través del uso combinado de instrumentos económicos y reglamentaciones ambientales. Al mismo tiempo, deben fortalecerse y modernizarse las capacidades institucionales para garantizar su aplicación y vigilancia.

# VIII. ECONOMIC INTEGRATION AND FREE TRADE

Foro Ambiental - Cumbre de los Pueblos de América (Santiago, abril 1998) Comercio y Desarrollo Sustentable: Recomendaciones de la Sociedad Civil Para la Integración Hemisférica

Apoyar un proceso de integración hemisférica justo y equitativo que mejore la calidad de vida, reduzca la pobreza, reconozca el valor intrínseco de la naturaleza y promueva el desarrollo sustentable para todos los individuos y las naciones sin excepción.

El comercio y el desarrollo deben respetar y ayudar a mantener la integridad ambiental. Esto comprende el reconocimiento del impacto de las actividades humanas sobre los sistemas ecológicos y el respeto por su capacidad regenerativa.

La subsidiaridad reconoce que la acción ocurrirá a diferentes niveles de jurisdicción dependiendo de la naturaleza de los temas.

El desarrollo sustentable requiere el fortalecimiento de los sistemas internacionales de cooperación a todos los niveles, abarcando el medio ambiente, el desarrollo y las políticas comerciales. Esto evitará conflictos y permitirá adelantar iniciativas sobre el intercambio tecnológico, la formación de capacidades, las transferencias de recursos, el alivio de la deuda o la creación de nuevos mecanismos para tratar los problemas ambientales.

Adoptar el principio precautorio así como los principios de prevención ambiental y responsabilidad legal y financiera de los contaminadores por los daños producidos al medio ambiente.

Apoyar el máximo acceso a la información y a la participación pública en el proceso de toma de decisiones.

Exhortamos a los gobiernos del hemisferio occidental a que acepten las siguientes recomendaciones:

## RECOMENDACIONES GENERALES PARA LOS GOBIERNOS DEL HEMISFERIO OCCIDENTAL

Creemos que las siguientes recomendaciones ayudarán a formular un plan de trabajo que promueva una agenda del hemisferio occidental en materia de comercio y desarrollo sustentable. Con este fin, los gobiernos deben:

1. Promover la investigación para poder comprender mejor los beneficios y los impactos derivados de las políticas o las medidas de comercio (dentro del contexto local, nacional, regional) y el medio ambiente.

2. Desarrollar un sistema nacional de contabilidad que incluya todos los aspectos ambientales, y que promueva un sistema adecuado para administrar esos costos de una manera que se asegure que no sean resignados directamente o indirectamente a la sociedad, sino que sean internalizados por las empresas.

3. Los gobiernos producirán un inventario de experiencias específicas de las industrias nacionales y sectores en las que la internalización de los costos ambientales crea una ventaja competitiva, reduce los costos y/o es ambientalmente seguro. El propósito de este ejercicio es el de compartir estas experiencias entre los gobiernos del hemisferio y desarrollar marcos comunes de política.

4. Los gobiernos deberían procurar desarrollar medidas concretas para mejorar la capacidad de los gobiernos nacionales de mantener un diálogo interno constructivo y crear sus propios programas en materia de comercio y medio ambiente. También deberían promover relaciones de trabajo entre los ministros de comercio y medio ambiente, así como entre sus propios organismos nacionales.

5. Los gobiernos deberían procurar reducir y eliminar patrones insostenibles de producción y consumo, dentro y entre los países, reconociendo las presiones sobre el medio ambiente debido al consumo desproporcionado de recursos por parte de muchos países industrializados.

6. Crear Grupos Consultivos Nacionales que faciliten la participación que incorpora los miembros de la sociedad civil, los organismos gubernamentales, las universidades, los profesionales, las asociaciones industriales y empresariales, los sindicatos, y los expertos, con el objetivo de identificar las necesidades de investigación, recopilación de información y evaluar los aspectos intergubernamentales e intersectoriales. Los informes de cada Grupo Consultivo Nacional sometidos al TNC permitirían el establecimiento de un Grupo Consultivo sobre Comercio y Desarrollo Sustentable sobre el ALCA encargado del análisis hemisférico de estos informes nacionales y de efectuar recomendaciones acorde con esto. Estos Grupos Consultivos Nacionales deberían establecer una ventana de información para la sociedad civil. Pero, al mismo tiempo las oficinas coordinadoras de los tratados como el Mercosur, el TLC, el Pacto Andino, deberían proveer el mismo tipo de servicio.

7. Los gobiernos también deben fortalecer la participación de la sociedad civil en los procedimientos judiciales y administrativos dentro de un marco jurídico ambiental interno y en la formulación, negociación e implementación de políticas y acuerdos de comercio e inversión.

8. Los gobiernos deben armonizar estándares mínimos consistentes con cada ecosistema, que aseguren la protección de la salud humana y la integridad ambiental. Al mismo tiempo, deben incluir mecanismos económicos

y cooperativos que aseguren la transferencia y la creación de tecnologías apropiadas, incluyendo tecnologías endógenas, esenciales para la implementación y el mejoramiento sostenido de las normas ambientales.

9. Los gobiernos deben comenzar por intercambiar información sobre medidas regulatorias y de política en un esfuerzo por alcanzar la estandarización de normas regionales ambientales efectivas y establecer mecanismos para actualizar y mejorar periódicamente las normas ambientales con la participación de todos los interesados (ONG, empresas, sindicatos, académicos, etc). Los gobiernos deben también asegurar que las naciones, en su capacidad regulatoria, mantengan la habilidad de fijar normas ambientales más altas.

## RECOMENDACIONES ESPECIFÍCAS PARA EL COMITÉ SOBRE LA SOCIEDAD CIVIL

a) Este comité debe otorgársele el mismo nivel de prioridad que al comité de negociaciones comerciales, el comité sobre economías pequeñas y los grupos negociadores. Es esencial la rápida elección de un presidente y de un plan de trabajo para el comité sobre la sociedad civil.

Debido a que vemos a este comité como el vehículo a través del cual la sociedad civil comunicará nuestras recomendaciones al comité de negociaciones comerciales, los grupos negociadores y el grupo consultivo sobre economías pequeñas, éste deberá comprometerse a:

b) Establecer un procedimiento transparente que asegure que la información proporcionada por las organizaciones no gubernamentales sea analizada y comunicada al comité de negociaciones comerciales, los grupos negociadores y al grupo consultivo sobre pequeñas economías.

c) El comité sobre la sociedad civil debe garantizar la oportuna difusión de informaciones como el orden del día, los puntos de discusión y los horarios de los puntos en consideración.

d) Establecer un procedimiento transparente para responder a las recomendaciones de las organizaciones no gubernamentales y otros sectores de la sociedad civil.

## 5. Iniciativas para el Comité sobre la Sociedad Civil

1. Convocar diálogos regionales entre los organismos no gubernamentales, el gobierno y el sector empresarial para hablar sobre los temas sustantivos que caracterizan al comercio y desarrollo sustentable. Hasta la fecha, diferencias políticas sobre las posturas ambientales y las prioridades de desarrollo han impedido el desarrollo de una agenda de comercio y desarrollo sustentable en el proceso del ALCA. Las posiciones en el actual acerca de los efectos potenciales del libre comercio sobre el medio ambiente son muy divergentes. Es preciso iniciar discusiones sobre el conflicto «producto versus proceso», en cuanto se relaciona con sanciones comerciales, aspectos de soberanía nacional y formas disfrazadas de proteccionismo.

2. Este Comité, junto con la secretaría administrativa, debe coordinar la información existente y hacerla más fácilmente accesible a la sociedad civil. Debe autorizar la revisión y la publicación de las condiciones de acuerdo a la perspectiva de las leyes y sus prácticas laborales de cada país del ALCA; de sus leyes y prácticas ambientales; el sistema jurídico; la situación y las políticas macroeconómicas; leyes comerciales y otras condiciones relevantes. Estas evaluaciones deben estar terminadas para el 30 de junio de 1999.

3. El presidente puede invitar a expertos para que presenten información al comité y puede crear subcomités o grupos de estudio para revisar e informar a los ministros sobre aspectos de desarrollo sustentable. Los subcomités pueden incluir personas que no sean miembros del comité y deberán estar balanceados en términos de los intereses representados.

4. El Comité tiene luego que negociar los términos de referencia de las evaluaciones conjuntas de impacto ambiental para junio de 1999, que serán usadas para evaluar el impacto potencial de los acuerdos de comercio. Las partes llevarán a cabo las evaluaciones con fondos provenientes del Banco Interamericano de Desarrollo (BID).

5. El comité tendría que desarrollar e implementar una asociación con el Banco Interamericano de Desarrollo (BID) para proveer los suficientes recursos financieros que aseguren que las recomendaciones anteriores se hagan realidad, pero en particular para asegurar la participación de la sociedad civil en las negociaciones sobre comercio e inversión.

6. El Comité sobre la Sociedad Civil debe explorar el papel de las instituciones paralelas, con el fin de desarrollar una capacidad nacional para establecer e implementar políticas ambientales nacionales.

Foro Ambiental - Cumbre de los Pueblos de América (Santiago, abril 1998) Comercio y Desarrollo Sustentable: Recomendaciones de la Sociedad Civil Para la Integración Hemisférica

# VIII. ECONOMIC INTEGRATION AND FREE TRADE

## RECOMENDACIONES ESPECIFÍCAS PARA EL COMITÉ SOBRE NEGOCIACIONES COMERCIALES

Reconocemos que el comité de negociaciones comerciales (CNC) es crítico para las negociaciones del ALCA. En consecuencia, ofrecemos las siguientes recomendaciones al mismo tiempo que se desarrolla un programa de trabajo para los grupos negociadores:

1. Formula términos de referencia para asegurar la incorporación de los objetivos de medio ambientales estipulados en la Cumbre de Miami: energía, biodiversidad y la prevención de la contaminación.

2. Alentamos al CNC que explore el uso apropiado de grupos negociadores ad-hoc autorizados por la Declaración de San José para desarrollar estos términos de referencia.

## DECLARACIÓN DE ORGANIZACIONES NO GUBERNAMENTALES CON MOTIVO DE LA IV REUNIÓN MINISTERIAL DEL AREA DE LIBRE COMERCIO DE LAS AMERICAS

Nosotros, representantes de las organizaciones de la sociedad civil abajo firmantes, provenientes de distintos países del hemisferio, reunidos el 18 de Marzo de 1998, en San José, Costa Rica:

Reconocemos que los Gobiernos están concluyendo sus discusiones informales con respecto a la integración económica del hemisferio en esta Cuarta Reunión Ministerial de Comercio de las Américas, y que están por iniciar una negociación formal para llegar a un Area de Libre Comercio de las Américas (ALCA), después de la Cumbre de Jefes de Estado en Santiago, Chile;

Apoyamos un proceso de integración hemisférica justa y equitativa que mejore la calidad de vida, reduzca los niveles de pobreza, reconozca el valor intrínseco de la naturaleza y promueva el desarrollo sustentable para todas las personas y naciones sin excepciones;

Reconocemos que nuestros gobiernos se han comprometido con los principios del desarrollo sustentable, que incluye la protección ambiental, la reducción de la pobreza y la democratización, tal como se estableció en la Cumbre de Miami de 1994 y se reafirmó en Santa Cruz, Bolivia, en 1996;

Reconocemos que los acuerdos comerciales, si están estructurados apropiadamente, pueden ser compatibles con los principios del desarrollo sustentable;

Estamos preocupados porque el avance de la integración económica se ha realizado sin incorporar de manera efectiva los componentes ambientales, laborales, sociales, culturales y políticos, los cuales son indispensables para alcanzar el desarrollo sustentable;

Reconocemos que la competencia justa no puede estar basada en la competitividad espurea, que no toma en cuenta los costos ambientales y sociales, y reconocemos también que existen costos durante la transición que tienen que ser tomados en consideración;

Por lo tanto, solicitamos atentamente que nuestros gobiernos establezcan un plan de acción así como mecanismos formales para incorporar dentro del proceso de integración económica los principios del desarrollo sustentable, incluyendo un grupo de negociación en comercio, medio ambiente y desarrollo sustentable, con igual rango a otros grupos de negociación establecidos en el proceso del ALCA. Mas aún, la protección y el mejoramiento de la calidad ambiental debe ser parte de los objetivos de negociación en todos los grupos del ALCA.

## PARTICIPACIÓN PÚBLICA

La participación pública es fundamental para el desarrollo sustentable del hemisferio, y como tal debe ser ubicada al mismo nivel de los demás objetivos de las negociaciones.

Con este propósito, apelamos a los gobiernos para que en el diseño del ALCA:

1. Fortalecer la participación de la sociedad civil en procedimientos judiciales y administrativos dentro del marco de la legislación nacional ambiental, así como en la formación, negociación e implementación de políticas y acuerdos sobre comercio e inversión.

2. Facilitar el acceso oportuno a información relativa a políticas así como acuerdos comerciales y procesos de integración.

3. Establecer procesos formales que oportunamente permitan y estimulen contribuciones de un amplio espectro de la sociedad civil, en el desarrollo del ALCA. Estos deben incluir el derecho a hacer presentación verbales y escritas, y a participar en reuniones nacionales y hemisférica que traten de sobre la liberación.

4. Implementar mecanismos de solución de controversias y otros procedimientos que permitan la participación pública.

5. Proveer los recursos financieros adecuados para lograr los fines anteriores.

6. Permitir el acceso público a documentos con respecto al proceso de integración interamericano mientras se circulan entre los gobiernos, para asegurar la participación temprana y significativa del público en esas deliberaciones; estos no deben tener costo alguno y deben estar en una variedad de formatos, incluyendo medios impresos y electrónicos, y también la creación de un centro de datos sin costo alguno.

7. Establecer comités nacionales de asesoría que incluyan representantes gubernamentales y no gubernamentales que, entre otros objetivos, promueven el diálogo multisectorial y sean responsables por desarrollar recomendaciones concretas para las negociaciones, así como respuestas a las recomendaciones ofrecidas por otros países.

8. Promover la investigación, la capacitación y el fortalecimiento institucional en el área del desarrollo sustentable.

9. Financiar la participación de la sociedad civil en las negociaciones sobre comercio e inversión.

## COMERCIO, INVERSIÓN Y DESARROLLO SUSTENTABLE

También apelamos a los gobiernos para que:

1. Implementen medidas nacionales y regionales que aseguren que la integración económica promovera la conservación de la diversidad cultural y biológica, y la integridad de los ecosistemas del hemisferio.

2. Aseguren que el Grupo de Negociación sobre Derechos de Propiedad Intelectual garantice que los derechos de acceso y los beneficios derivados sean distribuidos de manera equitativa.

3. Aseguren que se llevan a cabo investigaciones sobre los efectos ambientales y sociales del comercio y la inversión, y que sus resultados sean distribuidos de manera oportuna y efectiva a todos aquellos interesados.

4. Implementen y hagan cumplir políticas y regulaciones que aseguren la protección del medio ambiente, incluyendo la cooperación para asegurar la armonización de estándares tendiendo a su mejoramiento.

5. Implementen y hagan cumplir políticas y regulaciones que promuevan una distribución equitativa de los beneficios del comercio y la inversión.

6. Reduzcan y eliminen patrones insustentables de producción y consumo, dentro y entre los países, reconociendo las presiones sobre el ambiente debido al consumo desproporcionado de recursos por parte de muchos países industrializados.

7. Eliminen los subsidios que favorecen el uso insustentable de los recursos naturales y aseguren simultáneamente la internalización de externalidades ambientales. De igual manera se deben promover incentivos para la producción y el consumo sustentable, incluyendo el desarrollo de sistemas nacionales de contabilidad ambiental.

8. Aseguren que los Acuerdos Multilaterales sobre el Medio Ambiente y sus sistemas de solución de controversias tengan al menos igual estatus que los acuerdos comerciales. Las controversias derivadas de amenazas ambientales deben resolverse en negociaciones multilaterales.

## ESTÁNDARES AMBIENTALES Y COMERCIO

Apelamos a los gobiernos a que, en las negociaciones del ALCA:

1. Incorporen los principios de precaución, prevención y responsabilidad legal y financiera del contaminador por los daños al medio ambiente.

2. Establezcan y fortalezcan mecanismos administrativos y judiciales para la implementación de leyes y políticas ambientales, así como mecanismos para la denuncia ante la falta de aplicación de las normas ambientales nacionales e internacionales.

3. Armonicen estándares mínimos, de acuerdo a cada ecosistema, que aseguren la protección de la salud de la población y la integridad ambiental. Al mismo tiempo se deben incluir mecanismos financieros y de cooperación que aseguren la transferencia y generación de tecnologías apropiadas, incluyendo tecnologías endógenas, esenciales para la implementación y el mejoramiento sostenido de los estándares ambientales.

4. Establezcan mecanismos para la actualización periódica y el mejoramiento de los estándares ambientales, con la participación de todos los sectores (ONGs, empresarios, sindicatos, académicos, etc.).

5. Aseguren que los países, en su capacidad regulatoria, mantengan la postestad de fijar estándares ambientales más rigurosos.

6. Como se acordó en la Cumbre de las Américas celebrada en Miami en 1994, establezcan mecanismos de cooperación entre organismos gubernamentales para el intercambio de información, capacitación, transferencia de tecnología y formulación de políticas, así como la creación de mercados verdes.

Foro Ambiental - Cumbre de los Pueblos de América (Santiago, abril 1998) Comercio y Desarrollo Sustentable: Recomendaciones de la Sociedad Civil Para la Integración Hemisférica

# VIII. ECONOMIC INTEGRATION AND FREE TRADE

Participaron en la redacción del documento IBDPA (Brasil), Canadian Institute for Environmental Law and Policy (Canadá), Red Nacional de Acción Ecológica y Corporación Participa (Chile), Fundación Natura (Colombia), CEDARENA (Costa Rica), PRONATURA (Rep. Dominicana), Centro Ecuatoriano de Derecho Ambiental, CLD, Fundación Natura y Fundación Futuro Latinoamericano (Ecuador), IDEADS (Guatemala), CEMDA y Red Mexicana Acción Frente al Libre Comercio (México), Fundación M. Bertoni (Paraguay), Fundación ECOS y CLAES (Uruguay), National Audubon Society, National Wildlife Federation, Environmental Law Institute y Center for International Environmental Law (Estados Unidos), International Institute for Sustainable Development (Suiza).

# Participación Ciudadana:
## 10 Iniciativas Prioritarias de la Sociedad Civil Para la Integración Hemisférica

*Redactado por Brennan Van Dyke, Center for International Environmental Law (USA) y Claudio Torres Nachon, Centro de Derecho Ambiental y Desarrollo Sustentable del Sur, DASUR (México), con apoyo de Steve Suppan, Institute for Agriculture and Trade Policy, IATP (USA); Ken Traynor, Canadian Environmental Law Association, CELA (Canadá); Rafael Friedmann, National Resources Defence Council, NRDC (USA); Jean Pierre Leroy, FASE (Brasil); James Love (USA); Maude Barlow, Council of Canadians (Canadá); Rosa Virginia Suárez, Probioma (Bolivia); Karin Nansen, Red de Ecología Social de Uruguay, REDES (Uruguay); Walter Miglionico, PIT-CNT (Uruguay); Manuel Baquedano, Instituto de Ecología Política, IEP (Chile); Wilfredo Marcelo, Instituto de Ecología Política, IEP (Chile); Patrice Laguerre, Centre Quebeçois du Droit de L'Environment (Canadá); Yves Corriveau, Centre Quebeçois du Droit de L'Environment (Canadá); Roxana Salazar, Fundación Ambio (Costa Rica); Hilda Salazar, Desarrollo, Ambiente y Sociedad, DAS (México).*

## INTRODUCCIÓN

En diciembre de 1994 en Miami, Florida, se lanzó el Proceso Interamericano de Integración (PI-AI) con el objetivo de forjar una relación nueva y cooperativa entre las naciones del Hemisferio Occidental (con excepción de Cuba). Las 34 naciones participantes en la Cumbre de Miami se comprometieron con un Plan de Acción para alcanzar los siguientes cuatro objetivos: Preservar y Fortalecer las Democracias en las Américas; Promover la Prosperidad a través de la Integración Económica y el Libre Comercio; Erradicar la Pobreza y la Discriminación en el Hemisferio; y Garantizar el Desarrollo Sustentable y Conservar el Medio Ambiente Natural para Futuras Generaciones.

A pesar de los ostentosos ideales del PI-AI para intensificar la democracia en la región, el proceso de elaboración de políticas se ha conducido con una mínima participación de la sociedad civil. La ironía de la disonancia entre retórica y practica es más puntual en la implementación del plan para la integración económica del PI-AI: la creación de un Area de Libre Comercio de las Américas (ALCA). Las políticas económicas que se están negociando en el ALCA pueden impactar significativamente las leyes y políticas a nivel nacional y la vida cotidiana de la población. Las negociaciones comerciales deben conducirse bajo un sistema abierto, transparente y democrático para asegurar que los beneficios que fluyan de la reestructuración radical de los sistemas políticos y económicos sean distribuidos equitativamente.

Posteriormente, los presidentes de las Américas se reunieron en Bolivia en 1996 y acordaron, en la Declaración de Santa Cruz de la Sierra de 1996 y en el Plan de Acción para el Desarrollo Sustentable de las Américas:

Apoyar y promover, como requisito fundamental del desarrollo sostenible, una amplia participación de la sociedad civil en el proceso de toma de decisiones, incluyendo políticas y programas y su diseño, implementación y evaluación. Declaración de Santa Cruz (Principio 8) así mismo, promover mayores espacios para la expresión de las ideas y el intercambio de información y de conocimientos tradicionales sobre el desarrollo sostenible entre grupos, organizaciones, empresas e individuos, incluidas las poblaciones indígenas, así como para su efectiva participación en la formulación, adopción y ejecución de las decisiones que afectan sus condiciones de vida. Declaración de Santa Cruz [Principio 10 (d )] también acordaron, promover el perfeccionamiento de los mecanismos institucionales de participación pública. Declaración de Santa Cruz (Principio 8).

Para apoyar las iniciativas específicas sobre participación pública contenidas en el Plan de Acción, los gobiernos confiaron a la Organización de Estados Americanos (OEA) la responsabilidad de formular una «Estrategia interamericana para la promoción de la participación pública en la elaboración de políticas para el desarrollo sustentable». La Estrategia interamericana para la Participación Pública (ISP) contiene tres elementos básicos: permitir la participación responsable, fortalecer las instituciones representativas y expandir los mecanismos y canales para la participación.

Sin embargo, la participación de la sociedad civil no puede estar limitada a las oportunidades presentadas en la Estrategia interamericana para la Participación (ISP). El proceso de la OEA y de la USAID debe entenderse simplemente como un primer paso hacia la meta de alcanzar una participación totalmente democrática y abierta para la sociedad civil en el hemisferio occidental en los niveles regional, nacional y subnacional. La actual Estrategia Interamericana para la Participación (EIP). No apunta, por ejemplo, a facilitar la participación de la sociedad civil en el PI-AI en sí mismo. Aún más, la EIP será completada después de que la mayoría del PI-AI concluya. Consecuentemente, es necesario crear mecanismos adicionales para analizar y solventar la necesidad urgente de participación de la sociedad civil en el Proceso Interamericano de Integración en curso.

Para obtener legitimidad ante los ciudadanos y el escrutinio publico, el PI-AI debe desarrollarse con transparencia que permita la activa participación de la sociedad civil en el proceso de elaboración de políticas. De hecho, la credibilidad de las instituciones internacionales depende en alto grado del apoyo de la opinión pública en los estados miembros. Los negociadores internacionales no son funcionarios electos directamente, sin embargo tienen la capacidad de ignorar y excluir estándares legales establecidos nacionalmente bajo principios democráticos. Lo cual amenaza la justicia y equidad de los principios y políticas que resulten de las negociaciones. Sin participación ciudadana directa en el proceso de elaboración de políticas internacionales, la legitimidad de las reglas y políticas internacionales se tornan aún más cuestionables. La participación pública aumenta la probabilidad de que las decisiones disfruten un amplio apoyo de la sociedad civil.

Además, en los regímenes internacionales de elaboración de políticas públicas, la participación ciudadana asegura que las mismas consideren una perspectiva global. Los gobiernos nacionales no pueden lograrlo aisladamente; es decir, el amalgamar distintas posiciones de estados-naciones obedientes a sus particulares intereses, no reflejaría una perspectiva global. Cuando las políticas transcienden las fronteras nacionales, se vuelve menos relevante el que las personas afectadas residan en estados-naciones. Entonces, se vuelve realidad la noción de una comunidad internacional. Así las políticas bien formuladas deben forzosamente responder a las necesidades de tal comunidad internacional. En este contexto, es importante el aporte de las organizaciones no-gubernamentales (ONGs) y de otros actores independientes de los gobiernos, ya que esas organizaciones no están limitados a los asuntos nacionales. De hecho, el afán de la sociedad civil de operar a nivel internacional refleja el reconocimiento genuino de que algunos asuntos son intrínsecamente multilaterales, y como tales, es apropiado que se aborden a ese nivel.

Las ambiciosas metas del Plan Interamericano de Integración (PI-AI) sobre las políticas regionales de comercio e inversión, enfatizan la importancia de garantizar que el PIAI sea transparente y participativo. Se pretende establecer una zona de libre comercio e inversión en el hemisferio occidental, es decir, una Area de Libre Comercio de las Américas (ALCA). Las políticas de liberalización comercial y de inversión limitan un amplio rango de iniciativas legislativas en los niveles nacionales. Por esto, es crucial proveer a los ciudadanos de oportunidades genuinas para comprometer a sus representantes a debatir franca y totalmente tales asuntos.

La sociedad civil posee una gran experiencia y conocimiento. Los encargados de diseñar las políticas comerciales necesitan este conocimiento. La diversidad de opiniones y puntos de vista, como factores fundamentales en el diálogo político, son de un valor inestimable para la toma de decisiones en el desarrollo de políticas ambientales y de desarrollo. Al adoptar un sistema participativo, los creadores de políticas pueden evitar enormes desperdicios de tiempo y energía negociando o estableciendo políticas, reglas, derechos y obligaciones inefectivas o inaceptables desde un punto de vista ambiental o de desarrollo. Los ministros de comercio y sus representantes operan como parte de un gran sistema internacional de producción de leyes y políticas. De esta manera, deben asegurar que las políticas y prácticas que

Foro Ambiental - Cumbre de los Pueblos de América (Santiago, abril 1998) Comercio y Desarrollo Sustentable: Recomendaciones de la Sociedad Civil Para la Integración Hemisférica

# VIII. ECONOMIC INTEGRATION AND FREE TRADE

promueven sean consistentes y coherentes con el derecho y las políticas internacionales en otras materias, por ejemplo el derecho y la política internacional ambiental, laboral, de desarrollo y del fomento democrático.

La Segunda Cumbre de las Américas a realizarse en Santiago, Chile, en abril de 1998, representa una oportunidad única para ambos, estados y sociedad civil, para avanzar en la participación directa de las organizaciones ciudadanas, incluyendo a la mujer, los pueblos indígenas y las personas en condiciones económicas de pobreza del hemisferio occidental. Las siguientes iniciativas reflejan las prioridades de las organizaciones ciudadanas del Hemisferio para integrar a la sociedad civil en el diseño y toma de decisiones sobre el proceso de integración hemisférica.

## 10 INICIATIVAS PARA PROMOVER LA PARTICIPACIÓN PÚBLICA

Prioridad N°1: Asegurar a la sociedad civil un rol protagónico en el desarrollo de políticas del Proceso de Integración Interamericana (PI-AI) que sea equivalente, o de mayor alcance, que el papel otorgado a la sociedad civil bajo las Reglas del Consejo Económico y Social EcoSoc.

Las actuales decisiones para intensificar la participación de la sociedad civil en todo el hemisferio no están enfocadas hacia la creación de oportunidades en el mismo proceso de integración PI-AI. La Declaración de Santa Cruz llama a los países signatarios a «apoyar ... una amplia participación de la sociedad civil en el proceso de toma de decisiones,» lo cual debe incluir las actividades de toma de decisiones llevadas a cabo por los gobiernos en el PI-AI. El Plan de Acción para el Desarrollo Sustentable de Santa Cruz identifica iniciativas específicas para alcanzar las amplias metas del PI-AI respecto del desarrollo sustentable. El Plan de Acción asigna como mandato la participación activa de la sociedad civil en cada una de las cinco iniciativas substantivas de acción hemisférica. Además, el Plan instruye a la OEA a apoyar en la implementación de estas iniciativas específicas para la participación de la sociedad civil mediante la formulación de una Estrategia interamericana para la promoción de la participación pública en la toma de decisiones para el desarrollo sustentable (EIP). Entre otras metas, el EIP debe «establecer procesos de consulta a nivel regional.»

Sin embargo, el EIP ha sido enfocado principalmente hacia la creación de canales para la participación de la sociedad civil al nivel nacional, excluyendo y de hecho ignorando la elaboración de políticas del Proceso Interamericano de Integración, particularmente en las discusiones relacionadas con el ALCA. De esta manera, las discusiones sobre participación pública en el PI-AI han sido limitadas al proceso de desarrollo de la Estrategia interamericana EIP. Una nueva discusión deberá desarrollarse durante la Segunda Cumbre de las Américas, enfocada a integrar la participación de la sociedad civil en el PI-AI.

Mínimamente los gobiernos deben acordar que se apliquen las reglas sobre participación ciudadana del EcoSoc de las Naciones Unidas. Todos los países involucrados en el PI-AI son miembros de las Naciones Unidas y por lo tanto han aceptado estas reglas en foros similares. Las reglas EcoSoc proveen la acreditación de los grupos de la sociedad civil. Los grupos acreditados pueden observar y participar en actividades de toma de decisiones de las Naciones Unidas, sujetas a ciertas limitaciones.

Prioridad N°2: Desarrollar a nivel nacional e internacional mecanismos formales para facilitar la participación de la sociedad civil en el Proceso Interamericano de Integración, PI-AI.

La creación de un mecanismo formal y de acuerdo a normas preestablecidas, para apoyar la participación de la sociedad civil en el PI-AI ayudará a estructurar dicha participación de manera que asegure la recepción de las propuestas de los ciudadanos sin impedir el buen funcionamiento del PI-AI. Para asegurar un proceso abierto de toma de decisiones, los mecanismos formales deben concentrarse dos puntos focales: la deliberación de las políticas y la información. Estos mecanismos deben operar a los niveles nacional y regional. La participación a nivel nacional podría ser inadecuada pues se le ha dado a una agencia regional, la OEA, la responsabilidad de las primeras etapas de deliberación política.

El establecimiento de canales formales para distribuir la información facilitará enormemente la participación de las ONGs en las deliberaciones del PI-AI. Para dar oportunidad a la sociedad civil para preparar contribuciones y propuestas significativas para los procesos deliberativos, los documentos y toda la información relevante deberá circularse con tiempo suficiente. La existencia de canales formales de comunicación garantizarían que el flujo de información entre los negociadores no excluya a la sociedad civil. Estos canales deben asegurar que el público tenga acceso a la información al mismo tiempo que esa información llegue a los gobiernos. Sólo cuando parte o la totalidad de un documento contenga una excepción específica, tal

433

documento o parte de él puede excluirse de la circulación pública. Esta presunción de disponibilidad, que sujeta solamente a excepciones específicas y claramente definidas, forma la base de los actuales mecanismos de acceso a la información en otros regímenes internacionales, tales como el Banco Mundial y el Programa de Naciones Unidas para el Desarrollo, PNUD.

Similarmente, mecanismos formales para asegurar la comunicación entre los gobiernos y la sociedad civil a los niveles nacional y regional ayudará a incorporar diferentes puntos de vista a las deliberaciones y el desarrollo de políticas en el PI-AI. Una vez que la sociedad civil esté al tanto de los tópicos bajo consideración a través de la diseminación de la información, entonces serán capaces de presentar ideas y comentarios al respecto. Este intercambio de puntos de vista debe elaborarse de una manera que garantice que ninguna agrupación relevante quede fuera del proceso y de la misma manera asegure que ningún grupo de intereses específicos tengan un mayor acceso al proceso deliberativo.

Para avanzar en esta dirección, será útil examinar algunos de los mecanismos nacionales y regionales en el hemisferio para la diseminación de información y la participación pública en los procesos de elaboración de políticas.

Prioridad N°3: Asegurar, en particular, a la sociedad civil un rol activo en el desarrollo de las estrategias para la participación pública (EIP).

Un Area particularmente propicia para que la sociedad civil se beneficie con el establecimiento de mecanismos formales para institucionalizar y organizar los canales para las propuestas ciudadanas, es precisamente el desarrollo de la Estrategia interamericana para la Participación Pública (EIP) de la OEA. Sería absurdo que este proceso se diera de una manera que no fuera transparente y participativa. Los gobiernos del hemisferio necesitan establecer en forma inmediata canales que permitan a un amplio espectro de la sociedad civil enriquecer, modificar y dar un efectivo seguimiento a la EIP. El Comité Asesor de Proyectos (CAP) representa un primer paso, sin embargo, se deben establecer nuevos mecanismos para asegurar que los procesos sean tan abiertos y transparentes como sea posible.

Prioridad N°4: Asegurar que la Estrategia Interamericana de Participación, EIP, abarque todos los aspectos de la participación pública en la elaboración de políticas.

La OEA presentará a los países del hemisferio en la Cumbre de Santiago, una Propuesta para una Carta interamericana de la Participación Pública. Tal documento intenta alcanzar acuerdos sobre los principios y prácticas para fortalecer la participación pública en la toma de decisiones. Para ser aceptable, la Carta debe intensificar la participación de la sociedad civil en tres Areas específicas: información, deliberación de las políticas y resolución de controversias. Por otro lado, los mecanismos establecidos en la Carta deberán operar en los niveles nacional y regional. A nivel nacional, la participación podría ser inadecuada pues la responsabilidad de las primeras etapas de la deliberación de las políticas se lo ha dado a la OEA que es un organismo regional. Por otro lado, a escala regional de las deliberaciones del Proceso de Integración justifican la formación de redes regionales de organizaciones ciudadanas, cuya participación sería más adecuada a nivel regional.

Prioridad N°5: Desarrollar e implementar, conjuntamente con el Banco Interamericano de Desarrollo (BID) y otras instituciones financieras multilaterales, regionales y subregionales, mecanismos financieros para facilitar y fortalecer la participación de la sociedad civil.

El BID y otras instituciones financieras que se han comprometido a apoyar el Proceso de Integración deberán dirigir parte de sus recursos para permitir a grupos de la sociedad civil prepararse y asistir a las reuniones del PI-AI. La participación pública de los ciudadanos en la elaboración de las políticas presupone la existencia de una sociedad civil bien informada y con recursos adecuados para dedicarse de lleno al proceso participativo.

Prioridad N°6: Crear a través de estos mecanismos financieros, una red hemisférica de organizaciones e individuos de la sociedad civil, para alcanzar una participación y una coordinación más amplia y efectiva.

Una precondición para la efectiva participación ciudadana es el suministro de recursos adecuados para que la sociedad civil se involucre en el debate. Esto significa que los países tendrán que proveer los recursos necesarios para permitir a los ciudadanos del hemisferio comunicarse efectivamente entre ellos. A través del intercambio de información, los ciudadanos podrán intensificar su capacidad para comprometerse decididamente a dialogar sobre los asuntos de interés. Muchas veces las organizaciones ciudadanas poseen perspectivas únicas que podrían ampliar o profundizar los razonamientos de los negociadores sobre temas particulares. Al mismo tiempo también, distintos individuos tienen experiencias en común, que al ser analizadas conjuntamente, entregan argumentos o apoyos más convincentes, a favor o en contra de determinada política.

# VIII. ECONOMIC INTEGRATION AND FREE TRADE

Una sugerencia sobre como los gobiernos podrían ayudar a diseminar efectivamente la información, sería apoyar la fundación de una organización, para distribuir información sobre la elaboración de políticas comerciales. Una organización regional de este tipo, apoyaría los esfuerzos de las organizaciones de la región para lograr relaciones de trabajo más cercanas con los actores locales en el hemisferio.

Prioridad N°7: Asegurar específicamente a través de dichos mecanismos, la participación de los pueblos indígenas en los procesos de elaboración de políticas integrando su visión y posición única en la sociedad.

De particular interés es el asegurar la participación activa de los pueblos indígenas en el Proceso de Integración, PI-AI. Esta participación no debe limitarse a las discusiones de los pueblos indígenas. Muchos de los temas considerados en el PI-AI implican impactos directos en poblaciones minoritarias las que no son tomadas en cuenta por los negociadores. Las discusiones sobre minería, por ejemplo, se beneficiarían con la contribución de las tribus que históricamente han sido gravemente afectadas por las actividades mineras.

Recordemos que el Convenio 169 de la Organización Internacional del Trabajo (OIT) consagra en su Artículo 6 que los gobiernos deberán «establecer los medios a través de los cuales los pueblos interesados puedan participar libremente en todos los niveles de decisión», así mismo establece que deberán crear los canales necesarios para el completo desarrollo de las iniciativas de los pueblos indígenas, pero no se ha avanzado mucho en su implementación.

Complementariamente, la Declaración Americana sobre los Pueblos Indígenas, en su Artículo 15, dice: «Las poblaciones indígenas tienen el derecho de participar sin discriminación, si así lo deciden, en la toma de decisiones, a todos los niveles, con relación a asuntos que puedan afectar sus derechos, sus vidas y destino.» Los gobiernos deben encontrar mecanismos precisos para pasar del discurso a la acción en este tiempo.

Prioridad N°8: Promover a través de estos mecanismos el rol de la participación de la mujer en el proceso de elaboración de políticas y tomas de decisiones.

La mujer constituye un grupo de especial interés que merece un tratamiento particular en el Proceso Interamericano de Integración. Su participación es fundamental y deben seguirse los preceptos establecidos en la Convención de las Naciones Unidas sobre la Eliminación de Todas las Formas de Discriminación contra la Mujer, en especial en su Artículo 7. Allí establece que los gobiernos deberán eliminar todas las formas de discriminación en la vida política y que las mujeres deberán participar en la formulación de políticas gubernamentales y su implementación en todos los niveles de gobierno. De la misma manera protege el derecho de la mujer a participar activamente en agrupaciones ciudadanas orientadas a acciones políticas.

Por otro lado, la Convención Interamericana para Prevenir y Erradicar la Violencia contra la Mujer, establece en sus Artículos 4 y 5 el derecho de la mujer de participar en los asuntos públicos y en la toma de decisiones, así como el acceso a funciones públicas. Los Estados reconocen que la violencia contra la mujer impide el pleno ejercicio de tales derechos.

Prioridad N°9: Asegurar la participación de representantes de la sociedad civil en futuras Cumbres Hemisféricas y en los Grupos de Negociaciones.

La representación de la sociedad civil en futuras reuniones del Proceso de Integración establecerá la oportunidad ideal para que los gobiernos obtengan comentarios y aportes de los sectores más interesados respecto de los temas a discutir. Adicionalmente, mantendría al público informado de las negociaciones regionales. Existen muchos precedentes de coordinaciones entre gobiernos y ONGs. Por ejemplo, la mayoría de los regímenes ambientales, como el Protocolo de Montreal o la Convención sobre Biodiversidad, han permitido la inclusión de representantes de la sociedad civil en las delegaciones gubernamentales, para el beneficio de tales acuerdos. Con el fin de generar una relación cada vez más cercana entre los gobiernos nacionales y sus grupos de interés público, se debería alentar a los gobiernos a invitar representantes de la sociedad civil debidamente elegidos a formar parte de sus delegaciones, o darles apoyo y garantías para la asistencia y seguimiento del Proceso.

Prioridad N°10: Poner a disposición de los ciudadanos en forma inmediata los documentos de trabajo de los grupos de negociación del Proceso de Integración hemisférica, PI-AI.

La disponibilidad oportuna, con tiempo suficiente, de los documentos del PI-AI es un requisito imprescindible para dar a la sociedad civil la oportunidad de contribuir con aportes de alta calidad a los procesos de negociación, tanto a nivel nacional como al nivel regional. Es simple retórica sin contenido declarar que los gobiernos del hemisferio querrían ver una cooperación más cercana entre la sociedad civil y sus gobiernos al nivel nacional, si los ciudadanos no tienen acceso oportuno a toda la información relevante, con suficiente tiempo, para meditar y preparar adecuadamente sus respuestas, sugerencias e ideas.

Muchos gobiernos se beneficiarían enormemente con una sociedad civil informada y activa. El contar con el consejo de las ONGs ampliaría rápidamente los recursos analíticos de los ministros de las naciones en vías de desarrollo, permitiendo a los ministros de medio ambiente intensificar su participación en las discusiones sobre liberalización económica, por ejemplo. Los expertos ambientales frecuentemente sobrecargados de trabajo podrían incrementar su capacidad y competencia para participar en el proceso del ALCA si contaran con miembros de la sociedad civil que les ayudarán a eliminar lo superfluo y a identificar lo crucial de la información respecto de los asuntos de mayor importancia para sus gobiernos y así contextualizar efectivamente tal información.

Sin embargo, para que la sociedad civil sea útil para sus gobiernos, debe de ser una sociedad civil bien informada. Se requiere un flujo abierto y oportuno de información. Un paso importante sería que el PI-AI operará bajo la presunción de que todos sus documentos estarán a disposición del público, a menos que se acuerden determinadas excepciones de restricción en casos particulares.

Reconocer y analizar profundamente a las democracias de diverso nivel y tipo que coexisten en el Hemisferio Occidental es un desafío fundamental para desarrollar al interior de ellas iniciativas que promuevan y fortalezcan la participación ciudadana en el PI-AI.

Hacemos un llamado a todos los sectores, organizaciones, instituciones académicas e individuos a participar en este decisivo proceso, que sin duda le dará forma a las inter-relaciones económicas y ambientales de los pueblos de las Américas.

# Bosques:
Antecedentes y Recomendaciones de la Sociedad Civil en el Contexto de la Integración

*Redactado por Martha Núñez (Ecuador), Red Latinoamericana de Bosques, y Pablo Ospina (Ecuador), Fundación Natura, con apoyo de Ricardo Carrere (Uruguay), Movimiento Mundial por los Bosques Tropicales, WRM; Adriana Hoffmann (Chile), Defensores del Bosque Chileno; Carlos Leal (Chile), Sustenta XXI; María Luisa Robleto (Chile), Greenpeace; Jim Jontz (USA), Western Ancient Forest Campaign, WAFC; Ivan Basso (Chile), Sustenta XXI; Victor Menotti (USA), International Forum on Globalization, IFG; Dan Seligman (USA), Sierra Club; James Langman, Western Ancient Forest Campaign, WAFC; Hernán Verscheure (Chile), CODEFF; Pat Rasmussen, Western Ancient Forest Campaign, WAFC; Silvia Ribeiro (Uruguay), Red de Ecología del Sur, REDES; Valerie Langer (Canada), Friends of Clayoquot Sound; Lizbeth Espinoza (Costa Rica), CEDARENA; Hilda Salazar (México), Red Mexicana de Acción Frente al Libre Comercio, RMALC; Chris Willie (Costa Rica), Rainforest Alliance; Paige Fischer (USA), Pacific Environment Resource Center, PERC; Brian Staszenski (Canada), Canada Environment Resource Center, CERC; Randy Hayes (USA), Rainforest Action Network; Geraldine Patrick (Chile), Chile Sustentable; Yolanda Kakabadse (Ecuador), Fundación Futura Latinoamericana, UICN-Sur; Rosa Roldan (Brazil), IBASE; Ivonne Yánez (Ecuador), Acción Ecológica; Cecilia Cherres (Ecuador), Acción Ecológica; Paulo Adario, (Brazil), Greenpeace Brazil Amazon Campaign; Flavia Liberona (Chile), Renace; Sara Larraín (Chile), Chile Sustentable.*

Foro Ambiental - Cumbre de los Pueblos de América (Santiago, abril 1998) Comercio y Desarrollo Sustentable: Recomendaciones de la Sociedad Civil Para la Integración Hemisférica

# VIII. ECONOMIC INTEGRATION AND FREE TRADE

## ANTECEDENTES

En la Cumbre Hemisférica sobre Desarrollo Sustentable realizada en Santa Cruz, Bolivia, en 1996, los gobiernos del Hemisferio se comprometieron débilmente con la solución de los problemas ambientales que enfrenta el continente (ver anexo). Aunque la declaración de Santa Cruz contiene algunas importantes propuestas, estas pierden fuerza al ser presentadas como sugerencias que no obligan a ningún compromiso o decisión expresa. Este tipo de declaraciones, hacen muy difícil la implementación de medidas concretas y tampoco permiten evaluar los progresos existentes.

En marzo de 1998 en la reunión ministerial para la negociación de ALCA, los ministros de Comercio de las Américas dieron un significativo paso atrás: se desechó la constitución de Grupos de Trabajo sobre temas ambientales y laborales que examine las implicaciones de la zona de libre comercio y proponga disposiciones para considerarlos adecuadamente en los acuerdos regionales.

En el mes de abril de 1998 con motivo de la II Cumbre de Presidentes y Jefes de Gobierno de las Américas, la sociedad civil representada a través de Organizaciones Locales y No Gubernamentales que trabajan en las Américas por la conservación y el manejo sustentable de los bosques, considera importante recordar a los gobiernos que su agenda de integración económica debe evaluar los riesgos que el modelo vigente significa para la conservación de sus bosques, los cuales son depositarios de la mayor parte de la biodiversidad terrestre existente en el hemisférico.

Muchas de las principales amenazas a los bosques provienen, en realidad, de políticas y modelos de explotación de recursos distintos a los forestales. En especial las políticas de extensión de la infraestructura vial, grandes e irreflexivos proyectos mineros y energéticos o la expansión de la frontera agrícola en tierras ineptas por campesinos expulsados de las mejores tierras. Todo ello, que se suele identificar con el "desarrollo", ha promovido y promueve en verdad la destrucción de los bosques a cambio de beneficios sociales y económicos mínimos.

Por ello es imprescindible que se reconozca la existencia de una serie de causas «subyacentes» o «indirectas» que destruyen y/o contribuyen a la degradación de los ecosistemas forestales en las Américas, presentes tanto a nivel nacional como internacional. Entre estas, cabe destacar la promoción del comercio internacional y la liberalización económica, cuyas reglas de funcionamiento se basan exclusivamente en la ampliación de los mercados, desestimando consecuencias ambientales, especialmente en el largo plazo. Por tal razón, las organizaciones ambientalistas del hemisferio consideran necesario promover urgentemente en toda negociación internacional, bilateral o multilateral, el respeto por algunos principios básicos en relación a los bosques, teniendo presente que:

1. Que los bosques son ecosistemas variados y complejos; poseedores de una importante biodiversidad, por tanto, deben utilizarse respetando el equilibrio del conjunto de factores bióticos y abióticos que los componen. En las Américas, los bosques son el hogar de múltiples pueblos, en especial indígenas, pueblos dependientes de los bosques y otras comunidades tradicionales. Se deben garantizar sus derechos territoriales, sociales y culturales, sus formas de vida y civilización y el uso de sus recursos naturales, pues es condición indispensable para construir sociedades más justas y sostenibles y asegurar la conservación de los bosques y los servicios ambientales que brindan.

2. Que la conservación de los bosques debe ser un objetivo prioritario del proceso de integración hemisférica y por lo tanto, la integración comercial debe subordinarse a los acuerdos ambientales internacionales, y las políticas y legislaciones nacionales, regionales y locales pertinentes.

3. Que deben promover y apoyar una amplia y efectiva participación ciudadana en la toma de decisiones que afectan a los bosques.

4. Que deben diseñar e implementar sistemas de ordenamiento territorial que contribuyan a vincular las políticas agrarias con las políticas forestales incorporando las necesidades de las poblaciones locales.

5. Que deben adoptar criterios e indicadores que permitan comprobar si el uso de los bosques es sostenible en sus respectivos territorios y evaluar si la integración comercial los afecta negativa o positivamente.

6. Que deben eliminar los subsidios ambientales y económicos existentes que favorecen el uso insustentable de los bosques y aceleran su destrucción y crear subsidios para tecnologías ambientalmente beneficiosas, prácticas sustentables y en particular reforestación con especies nativas. En especial es necesario remover los subsidios existentes para plantaciones de monocultivos de árboles a gran escala.

7. Que es necesaria una profunda reforma institucional que subordine los servicios forestales a las instituciones ambientales nacionales y que asegure así una más eficaz aplicación de las leyes de protección de los bosques y provea recursos económicos suficientes para ello.

8. Que deben incluir disposiciones para que aquellas inversiones que puedan afectar a los bosques contemplen evaluaciones previas de sus posibles impactos ambientales y sociales donde todos los grupos interesados y en especial las poblaciones locales puedan intervenir en la decisión final.

9. Que los bosques deben ser protegidos de la explotación forestal a gran escala y debe evitarse toda sustitución de bosques nativos por plantaciones.

10. Que se debe prohibir la exportación de productos no procesados, en especial la madera rolliza y las astillas.

## COMERCIO INTERNACIONAL Y LOS BOSQUES

### Criterios Generales

La discusión en torno al comercio internacional de productos forestales es uno de los principales ejes del debate internacional sobre los bosques. La mayor parte de gobiernos del mundo, liderados por los principales exportadores de productos forestales (Canadá, Finlandia, Malasia, Brasil e Indonesia entre otros) están especialmente preocupados por asegurar un adecuado acceso a los productos forestales (casi exclusivamente de madera) en mercados abiertos y desrregulados.

Las negociaciones que resulten de este nuevo escenario no pueden ser exclusivamente lideradas por el Acuerdo sobre Obstáculos Técnicos al Comercio de la OMC, cuyo objetivo es incrementar el volumen del comercio mundial, sino que debe incorporar el marco de los Acuerdos Internacionales y la acción de organizaciones locales y no gubernamentales, cuyo objetivo común es la conservación y el uso sustentable de los bosques.

La experiencia enseña que los acuerdos de liberalización comercial que no incluyen salvaguardas ambientales y sociales tienen mas efectos negativos que positivos. El Tratado de Libre Comercio entre Estados Unidos, Canadá y México ha debilitado las medidas y estándares de protección de los bosques, a la pérdida de empleos en el sector forestal norteamericano, a ampliar la explotación de los recursos forestales en los bosques nativos de Canadá sin mejorar los sistemas de extracción forestal ineficientes y destructivos que imperan en ese país y ha llevado a México, por su parte, a trabajar en clara desventaja con sus socios comerciales. Así pues, no es posible asumir como un supuesto, tal como lo están haciendo los gobiernos de la región, la mutua relación beneficiosa entre liberación comercial, ampliación de mercados y sustentabilidad del uso de los bosques. En muchos casos el comercio internacional ha sido percibido como una «oportunidad» para apoyar la conservación de los bosques en el supuesto de que al aumentar su valor comercial se harán esfuerzos para conservar los recursos. Aunque el incremento del comercio internacional de madera y otros productos forestales puede contribuir parcialmente a mejorar la "valoración económica" de los bosques, en las condiciones actuales, basadas en explotaciones insustentables, dicho comercio constituye un grave riesgo para los ecosistemas boscosos, porque no representa una mayor valoración ecológica-ambiental y promueve la sobreexplotación de recursos escasos, así como la sustitución de bosques naturales por plantaciones de especies exóticas.

No será posible avanzar en el manejo sustentable de los bosques mientras se los considere exclusivamente como fuentes de productos madereros, desconociendo las posibilidades de uso múltiple que ofrecen. Es indispensable que al momento de establecer acuerdos comerciales, se tomen en consideración su valor biológico, científico, social y cultural, representado por la biodiversidad existente, el material genético, el potencial educativo y turístico, su rol en la generación y protección de los suelos, su rol como regulador de los cursos de agua y los ciclos de nutrientes y demás servicios de los bosques.

No podemos tomar los medios como si fuera fines. El desarrollo del comercio y la ampliación de las inversiones productivas debe subordinarse a los objetivos del mejoramiento de la calidad de vida de todos sus hambientes y de la conservación a largo plazo de los sistemas naturales que la soportan. En efecto ampliar las inversiones y entregar amplias concesiones de tierras forestales a grandes empresas multinacionales, sin modificar sustancialmente los modelos actuales de uso y las capacidades estatales de control, sólo puede ampliar la escala de la destrucción de los bosques de las Américas. Por ello es indispensable incluir los temas ambientales y sociales como parte esencial de la agenda de negociación de ALCA.

Por ello es necesario promover una negociación global sobre comercio internacional de todos los productos que se transan en el mercado (agrícolas, mineros, forestales, entre otros) de modo que se consideren no sólo los impactos directos sino también los impactos indirectos que su extracción o producción tiene sobre los ecosistemas forestales. Desde este ángulo, es evidente que la Organización Mundial del Comercio (OMC) debe considerar, en relación a estos temas, su compatibilidad con acuerdos ambientales internacionales y en especial la Convención de Diversidad Biológica y las recomendaciones del Panel Intergubernamental sobre los Bosques. Las negociaciones de la OMC y de ALCA no pueden continuar aisladas de los debates e imperativos ambientales mundiales, así como no debieran ser vistas por los gobiernos como el único camino para otorgar pautas a los acuerdos internacionales de comercio, porque tales acuerdos, al no incorporar la dimensión ambiental apropiadamente, tendrán efectos devastadores sobre los bosques.

# Anexo

## COMPROMISOS SOBRE BOSQUES Y DIVERSIDAD BIOLÓGICA ADQUIRIDOS POR LOS GOBIERNOS DE LA REGIÓN EN SANTA CRUZ DE LA SIERRA, BOLIVIA.

### DICIEMBRE DE 1996 (PLAN DE ACCIÓN PARA EL DESARROLLO SUSTENTABLE DE LAS AMÉRICAS INICIATIVAS 17 A 31)

Iniciativa 17. Continuar participando activamente en el dialogo internacional sobre cuestiones forestales iniciado por el Grupo Intergubernamental de Expertos sobre Bosques bajo los auspicios de la Comisión de Desarrollo Sostenible de las Naciones Unidas. Al respecto es necesario prestar la mayor atención a todos los elementos del programa incluidos en los términos de referencia aprobados por el Grupo de Expertos.

Iniciativa 18. Procurar establecer, implementar y controlar, según corresponda, los planes y programas nacionales para la conservación y ordenación forestal sostenible.

Iniciativa 19. Desarrollar mecanismos apropiados para promover las oportunidades de la participación pública en la ordenación forestal sostenible, incluyendo la de las comunidades indígenas y locales, cuyos valores culturales y necesidades deberán ser apoyados y respetados.

Iniciativa 20. Cooperar en la formulación de políticas y estrategias globales para lograr la ordenación forestal sostenible, bilateralmente y a través de programas, tales como la Red Internacional de Bosques Modelo, así como considerar formas y medios para abordar las áreas críticas relacionadas con la transferencia y desarrollo de tecnologías ambientalmente sanas, en condiciones favorables y mutuamente acordadas.

Iniciativa 21. Apoyar criterios e indicadores a nivel regional, subregional y nacional como instrumentos para evaluar el progreso hacia la ordenación forestal sostenible. Continuar participando, cuando proceda, en las iniciativas en marcha relacionadas con la formulación de criterios e indicadores para la ordenación forestal sostenible, tales como los procesos de Tarapoto y Montreal.

Iniciativa 22. Definir claramente, de conformidad con el sistema jurídico de cada país y cuando sea necesario, la tenencia y los derechos de propiedad de la tierra, incluso con respecto a las comunidades indígenas y otras comunidades locales, e identificar medidas adicionales que puedan resultar necesarias para mejorar la ordenación forestal sostenible bajo distintos regímenes de tenencia de la tierra, teniendo en cuenta el interés de todas las partes interesadas.

Iniciativa 23. Procurar, según corresponda, la ratificación de la Convención sobre la Diversidad Biológica, la Convención sobre el Comercio Internacional de Especies Amenazadas de Fauna y Flora Silvestres y la Convención de las Naciones Unidas de Lucha contra la Desertificación, y la adopción de medidas legislativas y administrativas y otras medidas de política para implementar las disposiciones de estas convenciones y promover sus objetivos.

Iniciativa 24. Desarrollar, según corresponda, políticas y normas nacionales sobre el acceso a los recursos genéticos y su protección, incluidas las reservas genéticas endémicas, y promover la investigación sobre la identificación y la valoración económica de la diversidad biológica.

Iniciativa 25. Promover, según corresponda y de acuerdo con la legislación y los acuerdos vigentes, y con el aporte correspondiente de las partes interesadas, la identificación de áreas protegidas transfronterizas y parques nacionales que los países vecinos respectivos consideren fundamentales para la conservación de la biodiversidad. Fomentar, además, la cooperación entre dichos países con el fin de mejorar la gestión sostenible de dichas áreas.

Iniciativa 26. Promover programas de investigación y capacitación sobre la conservación y el uso sostenible de la diversidad biológica.

Iniciativa 27. Promover el intercambio de experiencias innovadoras sobre alianzas de cooperación para la gestión de áreas protegidas.

Iniciativa 28. Considerar, conforme a los términos de la Convención sobre la Diversidad Biológica, los medios y arbitrios para la protección y el uso eficaces de los conocimientos tradicionales, las innovaciones y las prácticas de las poblaciones indígenas y otras comunidades locales, relevantes a la conservación y el uso sostenible de la diversidad biológica, así como para una distribución justa y equitativa de los beneficios derivados de dichos conocimientos, innovaciones y prácticas.

Iniciativa 29. Promover, conforme a los objetivos de la Convención sobre la Diversidad Biológica, debates sobre biodiversidad a nivel interamericano para proponer estrategias sustantivas con miras a superar los desafíos relacionados con la conservación, el uso sostenible y la participación justa y equitativa de los beneficios derivados de la utilización de la diversidad biológica en el Hemisferio.

Iniciativa 30. Promover la cooperación técnica y financiera continua a nivel multilateral, bilateral y nacional, y la creación y el desarrollo de instrumentos financieros y mecanismos de financiamiento que respalden las mencionadas convenciones. Promover al nivel nacional, multilateral o internacional, según corresponda, inter alia, el incremento de las inversiones nacionales de los sectores público y privado, fondos de capital de riesgo, mecanismos de recuperación de costos y fondos nacionales para el medio ambiente.

Iniciativa 31. Procurar el establecimiento, de una Red de Información Interamericana sobre Diversidad Biológica, principalmente a través de la Internet, con el fin de promover medios compatibles para la recolección, comunicación e intercambio de información relevante para la toma de decisiones y educación en materia de conservación de la diversidad biológica, según corresponda, partiendo de iniciativas tales como el Mecanismo de Cámara de Compensación previsto en la Convención sobre la Diversidad Biológica, la Red de las Américas sobre el Hombre y la Biosfera (MABNET Américas) y el Sistema de Información sobre la Conservación de la Diversidad Biológica (BCIS), iniciativa de nueve programas de la Unión Mundial para la Naturaleza (UICN) y organizaciones homólogas.

# Biodiversidad y Derechos de Propiedad Intelectual Principios y Recomendaciones de la Sociedad Civil para la Integración Hemisférica

*Redactado por Silvia Ribeiro, Red de Ecología Social, REDES (Uruguay), con la colaboración de Steve Suppan, Institute for Agriculture and Trade Policy, IATP (USA); Adriana Hoffmann, Defensores del Bosque Chileno (Chile); Hernán Verscheure, Comité Nacional Pro Defensa de la Flora y Fauna, CODEFF (Chile); Martha Núñez, Red Latinoamericana de Bosques (Ecuador); Karen Lehman, Kristin Dawkins, Institute for Agriculture and Trade Policy, IATP (USA); Jim Jontz, Western Ancient Forest Campaign (USA); Victor Menotti, International Forum on Globalization (USA); Valerie Langer, Friends of Clayoquot Sound (Canada); Jean Pierre Leroy, FASE (Brasil); José Augusto Padua, FASE (Brasil); David Hathaway, AS-PTA/Rio (Brasil); Camila Montecinos, Centro de Estudios de Tecnología, CET (Chile); Sergio Schlesinger, PACS (Brasil); Lizbeth Espinoza, CEDARENA (Costa Rica); Margarita Flores, ILSA (Colombia).*

## INTRODUCCIÓN

La diversidad es la base del equilibrio y sustentabilidad de todos los sistemas biológicos, es decir de las especies, los ecosistemas y sus múltiples interacciones. La biodiversidad para el sustento, — incluyendo cultivos, animales domésticos, pesca, hierbas medicinales, bosques y otros recursos silvestres—, interactuando

# VIII. Economic Integration and Free Trade

permanentemente con la diversidad cultural, son la base misma de nuestra sobrevivencia en el planeta.

Desde hace miles de años, y a partir de diferentes culturas, las comunidades locales (indígenas, pescadores, agricultores) fueron descubriendo y adaptando, a partir del conocimiento de su medio, miles de cultivos alimentarios y recursos para la salud, la vivienda, la vestimenta, los utensilios y las artesanías. Para ello utilizaron recursos silvestres y desarrollaron múltiples variedades adaptadas localmente, para su consumo propio y para el de los animales que iban domesticando. Esta creación de diversidad 'domesticada' es, y siempre ha sido, dependiente de su interacción con la biodiversidad silvestre.

En un proceso lento y continuo se fueron desarrollando sistemas de sustento donde las comunidades locales han sido la piedra fundamental del mejoramiento genético y la conservación y estímulo de la biodiversidad, aumentando así la base de recursos disponibles para el sustento y los usos rituales y estéticos, no sólo de las generaciones protagonistas de estos cambios, sino también de las futuras.

El libre flujo de conocimientos asociados al uso de estos recursos se fue trasmitiendo sin fronteras y de generación en generación, como un bien común sobre el que asentaron formas sociales locales, regionales y a veces nacionales. Hoy incluso, la base alimentaria y farmacéutica de pueblos del mundo entero está íntimamente vinculada a recursos genéticos generados por comunidades locales en otros rincones del planeta. Pero los beneficios de este intercambio son distribuidos de manera cada vez más injusta, y el uso de los recursos es orientado cada vez más por un interés puramente comercial y no por las necesidades vitales de los pueblos.

Contrariamente a los que están acostumbrados a que los alimentos vienen de un supermercado, o los medicamentos de una farmacia, la mayoría de la humanidad depende directamente de la biodiversidad para su sustento: Se calcula que la población rural del Tercer Mundo depende directamente de los recursos biológicos para suplir un 90% de sus necesidades. Un 60% de la población mundial depende esencialmente del autosustento para su alimentación. Un 80% de esa población hace un uso importante de plantas medicinales para el cuidado de la salud.

Sin embargo, la diversidad biológica para el sustento está seriamente amenazada, tanto la diversidad cultivada como la silvestre con la que ésta interactua permanentemente. Según estimaciones de la FAO, desde principios de este siglo se ha perdido hasta el 75% de la diversidad genética en los cultivos agrícolas. Además, una tercera parte de las 4000 razas de animales domésticos utilizadas en el planeta para la agricultura o la alimentación están en peligro o amenazadas de extinción. La deforestación y degradación de los ecosistemas naturales producto de su destrucción y explotación cortoplacista, en función de intereses mercantiles, ha llevado a un nivel de erosión genética nunca antes conocido. Se calcula que a principios de siglo se perdía una especie por año. En la actualidad es posible que estemos perdiendo 100 especies por día, un ritmo que aparentemente no se ha dado en la Tierra desde hace 65 millones de años, el período crítico de extinción de los dinosaurios.

De continuar los patrones actuales de distribución de la biodiversidad para mediados del próximo siglo, habremos perdido un 25% de las especies hoy existentes.

Otro elemento importante a tener en cuenta es que la mayor diversidad no se encuentra en los países industrializados del Norte, sino en los territorios de los países -paradójicamente llamados pobres- del Tercer Mundo. El cinturón tropical y subtropical del planeta, debido principalmente a condiciones climáticas a través de los siglos, ha dado lugar a una enorme riqueza genética en plantas y animales. A modo de ejemplo, un 7% de la superficie del planeta, aquella cubierta por los bosques tropicales, es el hogar de más de la mitad de la biodiversidad estimada.

Conjuntamente, en este proceso de pérdida de biodiversidad, los actores principales para su conservación, las comunidades locales, incluidos agricultores, indígenas, pescadores y habitantes de los bosques, están siendo eliminados como tales, expulsados de sus territorios y del acceso a los recursos que ellos mismos han creado, y que ha sido la base de sus culturas, su sustento y de la humanidad.

Sus conocimientos ancestrales están siendo despojados, fragmentados y transformados en mercancías para el lucro, a través de la bioprospección y el patentamiento. Incluso partes de seres humanos están siendo patentadas y vendidas.

Este proceso de destrucción ecológica, cultural, social y de los sistemas económicos locales, tuvo un impulso definitivo a partir de la industrialización en este siglo, particularmente de la agricultura; de la expansión sucesiva, de la agricultura química, de los híbridos «modernos» y de las nuevas biotecnologías; y de la apropiación de los recursos, conocimientos y sistemas de sustento por parte de las empresas transnacionales, para su utilización en mercados crecientemente globalizados.

Actualmente, el 45% de la economía mundial -contabilizada- se basa en biotecnologías. La industria de semillas mueve actualmente unos 15.000 millones de dólares anuales, y las diez compañías mayores de semillas acaparan el 37% del mercado. Se estima que solamente para el mejoramiento de variedades de maíz cultivadas en EE.UU., el aporte de material genético procedente del Sur supone un valor añadido que ronda los 7.000 millones de dólares. El mercado mundial de productos farmacéuticos asciende a unos 197.000 millones de dólares y entre las diez compañías más grandes acaparán el 43% del volumen total. El mercado mundial de farmacéuticos derivados de plantas se calcula en 43.000 millones de dólares anuales. El valor de las plantas medicinales del Sur para la industria farmacéutica del Norte se calcula en 32.000 millones de dólares anuales. (RAFI)

Mas del 90% de las patentes biotecnológicas y derechos del obtentor son poseídas por empresas transnacionales y/o instituciones gubernamentales de los países industrializados.

## Privatización de las bases del sustento

A partir de la finalización de la Ronda Uruguay del GATT (ahora Organización Mundial de Comercio, OMC) todos los países signatarios quedaron obligados por las cláusulas de los Acuerdos sobre Propiedad Intelectual Relacionados al Comercio (TRIPs por su sigla en inglés) a implementar sistemas de propiedad intelectual sobre seres vivos y conocimiento asociado al uso de estos. Estos acuerdos surgen a partir de las presiones, fundamentalmente de la industria biotecnológica, para proteger sus intereses e inversiones en todo el planeta. Existen en estas cláusulas algunas excepciones, para el caso de plantas y animales que no sean microorganismos y para procesos esencialmente biológicos. Para las variedades de plantas agrícolas hay una formulación que permitiría la implementación de 'sistemas sui generis', es decir que los países podrían tener sistemas de propiedad intelectual que, aunque no fueran leyes de patentes, sean igualmente «eficaces» en términos de protección que las patentes de las corporaciones.

Pero todas las posibles excepciones han resultado una quimera, dando origen a legislaciones que provocan el mismo efecto que el patentamiento.

En nuestra región, todos los industrializados y varios del Sur ya han ido incluso más lejos que las reglamentaciones exigidas por la OMC, implantando leyes de patentes. En varios países esto ha incluido también la legalización del patentamiento de material genético humano, y existen casos donde ya se está practicando.

Simultáneamente, países como Argentina, Chile, Colombia, Ecuador, México, Paraguay, Trinidad y Tobago y Uruguay- han firmado y ratificado el Convenio de la Unión de Protección de Nuevas Variedades Vegetales (UPOV). Este es un mecanismo, que obliga a los países a aceptar como válidos en su territorio, los derechos de propiedad intelectual de todos los países miembros de UPOV, que son prácticamente todos los países industrializados. El sistema UPOV ha sido interpretado por algunos como una forma más permisiva de patentamiento, pero en la práctica y sobre todo a partir de las propuestas de su re-formulación de 1991, legaliza igualmente la biopiratería de las corporaciones y conlleva graves restricciones a la circulación e intercambio de recursos genéticos y conocimiento, tanto a nivel de los agricultores como de las instituciones de investigación.

## El precio que estamos pagando

Para los "actores de la biodiversidad" -agricultores, campesinos, pueblos indígenas, artesanos, pescadores artesanales- el avance de los sistemas de propiedad intelectual está significando limitaciones importantes para conservar y para acceder a sus propios recursos genéticos. En forma acelerada se acrecienta la uniformización de los campos y bosques, la erosión genética, la desaparición de la biodiversidad y junto con esto, de la base del sustento de las comunidades locales rurales e indígenas.

Los territorios de los países del Sur, también están siendo usados como base experimental de las transnacionales, para liberar en campo organismos manipulados genéticamente (OMG), aprovechando la falta de normativas de bioseguridad. Esto no sólo sucede con ensayos de laboratorio, sino también con cultivos industriales de escala, donde se aprovechan los vacíos legales y la falta de controles para introducir OMGs, — que no tienen evaluación de impacto ambiental en ninguna parte del mundo. Además de intensificar el uso de tóxicos en la mayoría de los casos, puede significar la transmisión de características modificadas a parientes silvestres de esos mismos cultivos, desplazan a las variedades locales. Estas situaciones, si bien afectan directa y cruelmente a las comunidades locales, es en alto grado un tema con consecuencias para todos los ciudadanos de nuestros países. Conlleva severas limitaciones al acceso a alimentos sanos, sin químicos, variados, con acentos locales y a la utilización no mercantilizada de muchos recursos para la salud y otros aspectos del sustento.

# VIII. Economic Integration and Free Trade

Foro Ambiental - Cumbre de los Pueblos de América (Santiago, abril 1998) Comercio y Desarrollo Sustentable: Recomendaciones de la Sociedad Civil Para la Integración Hemisférica

Los sistemas de investigación locales, regionales y nacionales sobre recursos genéticos, también han sufrido impactos negativos debido a las limitaciones de uso e intercambio de recursos y conocimientos. Esto está llevando a la desaparición de los institutos públicos, puesto que en general se convierten en subsidiarios de laboratorios de las empresas multinacionales cuyas prioridades de investigación están exclusivamente guiadas por el fin de lucro, sin consideraciones sociales, ambientales o éticas.

No significa tampoco ventajas, ni aún en términos macroeconómicos o de países, para los gobiernos del Sur, ya que la cantidad de patentes extranjeras que deben aceptar es mucho mayor que las que algún día, superando sus limitaciones tecnológicas, podrían llegar a obtener.

Actualmente, un 95% de las patentes biotecnológicas en el mundo pertenecen a empresas transnacionales o a instituciones de gobiernos del Norte. El 99% de las patentes y derechos de obtentor sobre vegetales, pertenecen a instituciones y empresas de los países del Norte.

Durante el período previo a las negociaciones hacia un tratado de libre comercio para las Américas, EE.UU. ha anunciado en el grupo de trabajo sobre Propiedad Intelectual del ALCA, que las cláusulas ya existentes en la OMC son suficientes, y exige reglamentaciones más estrictas.

La creación y los aspectos más vitales de la conservación de la biodiversidad siempre han sido un fenómeno local, responsabilidad de miles de comunidades que cultivan o utilizan sus recursos por razones muchos más vitales que el interés de lucro. El intercambio internacional de los recursos de la biodiversidad ha beneficiado históricamente a muchos pueblos, aunque de manera cada vez más desigual en las ultimas décadas. La conservación de nuestros recursos genéticos en centros «científicos» lejos de sus lugares de origen se ha combinado hoy con los sistemas de propiedad intelectual (patentes y UPOV) para institucionalizar el robo y la monopolización de recursos ajenos.

Frente a la ofensiva de privatización, monopolización y mercantilización de la vida que estos acuerdos significan, es necesario que nos replanteemos claramente cuáles son nuestros desafíos y qué queremos lograr. En ese sentido, proponemos los siguientes principios y objetivos como puntos de partida para nuestra actividad a nivel local e internacional.

## PRINCIPIOS Y OBJETIVOS

### 1. Derechos colectivos sobre biodiversidad

• Reconocer, defender, afirmar y proteger el protagonismo y los derechos colectivos —inalienables e inapropiables— de las comunidades locales agrícolas, indígenas, pescadoras y habitantes de los bosques, en la conservación, cuidado y cría de la biodiversidad para el sustento; y el derecho al libre uso e intercambio de los recursos genéticos para el sustento y del conocimiento asociado a estos (limitado solamente en términos de conocimientos rituales o religiosos de voluntaria circulación restringida).

• Exigir y garantizar el reconocimiento a priori y la primacía de estos derechos, frente a cualquier forma de propiedad intelectual sobre seres vivos y conocimiento asociado.

### 2. Soberanía alimentaria

• Lograr que la soberanía alimentaria, incluyendo el control local de la producción, el acceso al consumo, el cuidado y conservación de la biodiversidad para el sustento, el acceso a la tierra y a alimentos sin químicos, sea un derecho humano fundamental, real, efectivo y para todos. Debe primar frente a cualquier acuerdo comercial.

• Restablecer simultáneamente el derecho a elegir qué queremos consumir y cómo queremos producirlo.

### 3. Derecho a la tierra, al territorio y los recursos.

• Lograr el pleno acceso, derecho y control de las comunidades rurales e indígenas sobre los recursos existentes para la satisfacción de sus necesidades, incluyendo el derecho a la tierra, al territorio y a mantener sus sistemas productivos.

### 4. Sistemas justos de distribución de recursos

• Exigir que las comunidades rurales e indígenas sean los primeros beneficiados de los recursos por ellos creados, promoviendo también la creación de mercados locales y relaciones más directas y solidarias entre productores y consumidores.

### 5. Sistemas locales de innovación

• Asegurar que las comunidades locales puedan mantener sus sistemas de innovación y creación de conocimientos, para que los produzcan e intercambien de acuerdo a sus necesidades.

• Defender la libre circulación de conocimientos y el acceso a los recursos genéticos para la investigación al servicio de las necesidades de las poblaciones y de los centros de investigación públicos locales y nacionales.

### 6. Diversidad cultural

• Resguardar y defender la diversidad cultural, los valores y las visiones de mundo no determinadas por la globalización de los mercados.

### 7. Protagonismo de la mujer

• Reconocer y reafirmar el papel fundamental de la mujer en la cría, cuidado y desarrollo de la biodiversidad para el sustento.

### 8. Impedir el patentamiento de la vida

• Rechazar al patentamiento de formas de vida, incluyendo las diversas formas de propiedad intelectual sobre seres vivos y conocimientos asociados.

## ESTRATEGIAS Y DEMANDAS INMEDIATAS:

### 1. Defender y proteger los derechos colectivos sobre biodiversidad

• Reconocer y afirmar de los derechos colectivos de las comunidades locales sobre la biodiversidad, sus recursos y conocimientos sobre cualquier acuerdo comercial.

### 2. Primacía de la soberanía alimentaria y del sustento

• Obtener el reconocimiento de la soberanía alimentaria y del sustento como derecho humano, por sobre los acuerdos comerciales y de inversión.

### 3. Excluir la agricultura y la biodiversidad de los tratados comerciales

• Excluir a la agricultura, biodiversidad y propiedad intelectual sobre recursos genéticos, procesos y conocimientos asociados a ellos, del ámbito de la Organización Mundial del Comercio (OMC) y de los tratados comerciales.

### 4. Moratoria a la bioprospección

• Detener el despojo genético en las Américas a través de una moratoria a la bioprospección.

### 5. Evaluar los impactos de la aplicación de los sistemas de propiedad intelectual.

• Producir y difundir públicamente, información sobre las consecuencias de la entrada a la Unión para la Protección de Nuevas Variedades Vegetales (UPOV) y la aprobación de leyes de patentes en los países latinoamericanos. Difundir los impactos sociales, ambientales, económicos y científicos de la implementación de los Derechos de Propiedad Intelectual Asociados al Comercio (TRIPS).

### 6. Establecer normas de bioseguridad

• Prohibir la entrada y liberación al ambiente de organismos manipulados genéticamente. Establecer claras normativas vinculantes -nacionales e internacionales- de bioseguridad.

### 7. Reconocimiento de la deuda ecológica

• Reconocer el aporte histórico de los pueblos y comunidades que crean y conservan las bases de la biodiversidad para el sustento, incluyendo los recursos genéticos, el conocimiento asociado a ellos y la relación sustentable con la tierra, los ecosistemas y las generaciones futuras, y promover sean compensados por la deuda ecológica que hemos generado.

# Energía: 10 Iniciativas Prioritarias de la Sociedad Civil para la Integración Hemisférica

*Redactores: Rafael Friedmann and Robert Watson, NRDC. Colaboraron en la elaboración del documento: organizaciones nombradas en Anexo.*

Foro Ambiental - Cumbre de los Pueblos de América
(Santiago, abril 1998) Comercio y Desarrollo Sustentable:
Recomendaciones de la Sociedad Civil Para la Integración
Hemisférica

# VIII. ECONOMIC INTEGRATION AND FREE TRADE

## INTRODUCCIÓN

Durante la Segunda Cumbre de las Américas el 18 y 19 de abril de 1998 en Santiago, Chile, presidentes del Hemisferio se congregarán para discutir iniciativas nacionales relacionadas con educación, integración económica, gobierno, y desarrollo. Independiente a la Cumbre, organizaciones de la sociedad civil del Hemisferio, se reunirán en la Cumbre de los Pueblos para desarrollar una agenda basada en un consenso sobre desarrollo y medio ambiente, la cual será considerada por líderes de gobierno. Aunque el enfoque del documento presentado a continuación trata iniciativas ciudadanas sobre el sector energético, debe considerarse que es una parte de una visión más amplia sobre el futuro desarrollo del hemisferio, tal como queda expuesto en otros documentos de la Cumbre de los Pueblos.

Este documento presenta cuatro metas que deberían ser guía para políticas y programas en el sector energético del hemisferio. Para respaldar y lograr estas metas, se presentan también una lista de 10 iniciativas prioritarias para el sector energía.

Estas iniciativas provienen de una amplia lista inicial de propuestas que cubrían toda la gama de elementos necesarios para una estrategia de desarrollo sustentable del sector energético del hemisferio. Más de 135 expertos de 21 países fueron consultados en dos rondas en el desarrollo de estas metas e iniciativas prioritarias. Estos expertos energéticos provenían de muchas disciplinas, incluyendo organismos no-gubernamentales, la academia, sector privado, y agencias multilaterales. Hemos incorporado comentarios sustantivos de unos 55 expertos. Veintisiete de ellos son latinoamericanos, 22 de Norteamérica, y seis de otros países. La lista de personas contactadas y aquellos que respondieron ha sido incluida en un anexo, junto con la metodología utilizada para derivar la priorización de las iniciativas. También se incluye en los apéndices una declaración que prioriza objetivos y acciones en el sector energético y propuestas por una de las organizaciones.

Algunas de las iniciativas propuestas ya están incorporadas en los acuerdos alcanzados en Miami y Santa Cruz, mientras que otras todavía no se están llevando a cabo. De hecho, existe bastante concordancia entre la agenda actual del Grupo de Trabajo Hemisférico de Energía, y las iniciativas que hemos desarrollado en este esfuerzo. Lo novedoso es que estas iniciativas han sido priorizadas para guiar el orden de acción. El grupo de expertos consultados aquí, cree que un Plan de Acción hemisférico para el sector energético debe concentrarse en las prioridades que hemos elaborado, antes de involucrarse en otras Areas.

La actual implementación de políticas energéticas en el hemisferio avanzan lentamente y no son consistentes con la necesidad imperiosa de mejorar significativamente el rendimiento económico y reducir el impacto ambiental. Por esta razón, pedimos a los presidentes que adopten esta agenda prioritaria y logren avances mensurables en su implementación, para luego dedicarse a otras Areas. Hemos incluido fechas específicas para implementar las iniciativas propuestas, para que los países sepan que su avance en la implementación de éstas será juzgado en términos de lo que hacen y no por Declaraciones o Planes de Acción.

Creemos que las metas y medidas propuestas permitirán al sector energético del hemisferio proveer los servicios requeridos por la creciente población, a menor costo y con significativamente menos impactos ambientales. También incrementarán el empleo y convertirán al sector energético en un proveedor neto de servicios para otras necesidades del desarrollo. Esperamos que notarán los Ministros de Hacienda y Finanzas que hoy lideran la toma de decisiones en el hemisferio incorporan estas iniciativas. Las acciones propuestas están basadas en las experiencias exitosas de muchos programas y políticas ya complementadas en el mundo. Pensamos que estas metas y acciones deberían ser los componentes principales de las políticas y programas de los gobiernos del hemisferio, en su búsqueda por facilitar el desarrollo de la región con el menor costo económico, político, y ambiental, y con el mayor potencial para aumentar la equidad.

Metas Hemisféricas Para el Sector Energético

La agenda ciudadana para la integración hemisférica en el sector energético se encuentran las siguientes metas:

1. Lograr que la producción y consumo de energía, tanto actual como futura, sean sustentables, es decir, más eficientes económica y energéticamente, renovables, limpias, y menos intensivas en combustibles fósiles.

2. Incrementar el acceso y facilitar la adquisición de servicios energéticos a sectores de la población que todavía no cuentan con ellos o que reciben un servicio insuficiente.

3. Minimizar el costo de la energía para la sociedad, basando el futuro desarrollo del sector energético en una combinación óptima de menor-costo durante el ciclo de vida, de opciones de expansión de recursos y gestión de la demanda en usos-finales, en donde se incorporen los costos debidos a externalidades ambientales y sociales.

4. Identificar y eliminar las causas de mercados imperfectos, y asegurar que las condiciones institucionales, estructurales, hábitos, e incentivos, favorezcan el desarrollo sustentable del sector energético.

Las 10 Iniciativas Energéticas Hemisféricas Prioritarias

## Prioridad N°1: Adoptar Políticas y Programas de Transporte Sustentable

*Los gobiernos:*

• Incorporarán decisiones sobre uso de suelo en el proceso de planificación del transporte a través de la inclusión de medidas de planificación territorial en los modelos de transporte y asegurando que haya conexiones intermodales entre vehículos personales, transporte público, y transporte no-motorizado.

• Adoptarán medidas para reducir el consumo de combustibles incluyendo: 1) normas económicamente rentables de eficiencia mínima de combustibles para nuevos vehículos personales y comerciales, antes del año 2003; 2) medidas de mercado que premien a los vehículos que son más eficientes o menos contaminantes que lo estipulado por la normas, y penalizarán aquellos vehículos que no cumplan con las normas, antes de año 2004; 3) convocarán a un grupo de trabajo para explorar tecnologías emergentes que incorporen conceptos de bajo peso y baja resistencia al aire, tanto en la locomoción privada como la pública.

• Adoptarán incentivos para promover patrones de planificación territorial que generen una reducción en la dependencia del transporte privado, incluyendo desarrollo de usos múltiples, y financiamientos suaves para desarrollos que promuevan densificación en las urbes para el año 2001.

• Adoptarán incentivos para desarrollar alternativas de transporte no-motorizado, incluyendo infraestructura para peatones y bicicletas para el año 2001.

• Financiarán con fondos de la banca multilateral y nacional una Iniciativa de Transporte Urbano para el Siglo XXI cuyo objetivo será implementar, al año 2005, el uso de autobuses con combustibles alternativos y el desarrollo de infraestructura de transporte público tipo Curitiba en todas las ciudades del hemisferio de más de medio millón de habitantes

• Adoptarán medidas para reducir las emisiones contaminantes, incluyendo que: 1) eliminarán la venta de gasolina con plomo y el diesel de alto contenido de azufre para el año 2000; 2) desarrollarán normas de emisiones máximas permisibles para nuevos vehículos personales y comerciales, y centros de pruebas, para fines del año 2003; 3) establecerán programas obligatorios de inspección para asegurar que los vehículos cumplan con las normas mínimas ambientales y de seguridad; 4) promoverán el uso de combustibles renovables basados en biomasa, económica y ambientalmente viables.

## Prioridad N°2: Crear una Base Legislativa e Institucional para las Estrategias de Energía Sustentable

*Los gobiernos:*

• Desarrollarán para fines de 1998 una entidad regional para la diseminación de información sobre estrategias regulatorias y legislativas para la promoción del desarrollo energético sustentable.

• Desarrollarán -preferentemente a través de la expansión de responsabilidades de instituciones ya existentes- instituciones independientes, profesionales, expertos en política y regulación energética con claro mandato legislativo y suficientes recursos financieros para fines del año 2000.

• Desarrollarán para fines del año 2000 estrategias energéticas nacionales de menor costo durante el ciclo de vida, que incluyan la eficiencia, fuentes de energía renovables, además de tecnologías convencionales limpias, que incorporen los costos ambientales y sociales en los análisis.

• Adoptarán una metodología para calcular los costos ambientales y sociales para fines del año 1999.

• Identificarán antes del año 2001, barreras legales y administrativas para la concreción de estrategias energéticas sustentables y desarrollarán propuestas de política energética y financieras que eliminen las barreras.

## Prioridad N°3: Promover el Desarrollo Rural Sostenible

*Los gobiernos:*

• Identificarán el potencial de vinculación entre el desarrollo energético rural (incluyendo el uso eficiente de la biomasa para la cocción, calefacción, y electrificación rural) con los proyectos y programas de desarrollo económico y social para el sector rural.

• Incluirán a las poblaciones que carecen de servicios energéticos, en el diseño e implementación de los programas energéticos rurales, para sus comunidades.

- Considerarán en el diseño e implementación de los programas de desarrollo energético rural, toda la gama de servicios energéticos requeridos por las comunidades: cocción, calefacción, bombeo de agua y su purificación para uso doméstico y agrícola, almacenamiento y procesamiento de productos agrícolas, refrigeración de comida y medicinas, iluminación entre otros.

- Implementarán estrategias energéticas rurales de menor costo durante el ciclo de vida, que incluyan los costos de las externalidades en los análisis.

- Promoverán el incremento en la eficiencia de uso, comercialización, y disponibilidad de combustibles de biomasa para usos rurales energéticos y no-energéticos.

- Proveerán acceso a servicios energéticos comerciales al 95% de la población rural de cada país para el año 2005.

- En las estrategias de electrificación, utilizarán las opciones de menor costo durante el ciclo de vida, incluyendo alternativas renovables independientes de los sistemas de interconexión nacional para comunidades aisladas y peri-urbanas.

## Prioridad Nº4: Asegurar la Participación Democrática en la Toma de Decisiones del Sector Energía

*Los gobiernos:*

- Crearán antes del año 2000 mecanismos para la participación democrática de representantes de la sociedad civil y del sector privado en los procesos de toma de decisiones sobre aspectos regulatorios e institucionales del sector energía, para permitir la consideración de los diversos puntos de vista. Entre estos mecanismos se debe considerar: tiempos para comentarios públicos, consultas ciudadanas y colaborativas, oportunidades para apelaciones legales y de procedimientos, y la creación de una institucionalidad formal que asegure la participación formal y el involucramiento de los ciudadanos en instituciones regulatorias y en la toma de decisiones.

## Prioridad Nº5: Implementar Mecanismos que Estimulen Inversiones en Eficiencia Energética y Recursos Renovables de Energía.

*Los gobiernos:*

- Crearán incentivos regulatorios, de mercado, y fiscales para que los ciudadanos, el sector productivo, las compañías eléctricas, de servicios energéticos, u otros, inviertan en eficiencia energética y suministro con recursos renovables de energía para el año 2000. Se debe de dar prioridad a los recursos renovables disponibles localmente y de larga tradición de uso y desarrollo.

- Eliminarán antes del año 2001 las políticas reguladoras y de precios de la energía que subsidian, promueven y favorecen el aumento de las ventas, el consumo o uso dispendioso de la energía y el uso de combustibles fósiles.

## Prioridad Nº6: Desarrollar Mercados de Energía Sustentable

*Los gobiernos:*

- En el actual contexto hemisférico en el cual aumenta la privatización y reestructuración de los sistemas nacionales eléctricos, recomendarán reglas y procedimientos de competencia que no discriminen a fuentes privadas o de potencia intermitente o a agentes del lado de la demanda, para el año 1999.

- Generarán para el año 2000, mecanismos para que los precios de la energía reflejen los costos sociales y ambientales y valor de mercado, manteniendo tarifas que aseguren el acceso a la energía a la población de bajos recursos.

- Introducirán en el año 2001 mediciones netas de consumo para usuarios que generen su propia energía con recursos renovables de energía.

- Basarán la competencia nacional del mercado eléctrico en la internalización del costo de contaminación ambiental, los impactos culturales, y explotación de los recursos naturales para el año 2003.

- Se comprometerán a que la integración energética de países de hemisferio esté condicionada a los objetivos del desarrollo social y ambientalmente sustentable.

## Prioridad Nº7: Establecer un Fondo Para la Promoción de la Eficiencia Energética y los Recursos Energéticos Renovables

*Los gobiernos:*

- Crearán para fines de 1999, un fondo rotatorio con recursos nacionales y/o de la comunidad financiera internacional. Esto podría incluir una versión aprobada internacionalmente del Mecanismo de Desarrollo Limpio propuesto en el Protocolo de Kyoto de Cambio Climático Global.

• Promoverán la utilización de los recursos este fondo, entre entidades públicas y privadas, para financiar programas piloto, demostrativos, y más adelante, programas a gran-escala, o programas de investigación, con desarrollo y demostración tecnológica.

## Prioridad N°8: Promover la Producción y Adquisición de Tecnologías Energéticas Renovables y Eficientes

*Los gobiernos:*

• Identificarán para fines de 1998 equipos fabricados en la región cuya eficiencia energética sea peor a la tecnología disponible a nivel internacional y que conlleva a grandes consumos de energía.

• Diseñarán incentivos fiscales y financieros para promover y apoyar el mejoramiento de la eficiencia energética de los equipos que producen las industrias de la región para fines de 1999.

• Promoverán proyectos conjuntos entre industria, sector público, e instituciones de investigación aplicada para acelerar la producción de equipos eficientes o renovables para surtir mercados nacionales y regionales, y a la vez, aumentar la capacidad humana nacional para fines de 1999. Esto incluye paquetes de tecnologías eficientes y renovables en las que se aproveche la economía lograda al combinar equipos eficientes y renovables.

• Creerán «cooperativas de compradores de tecnologías sostenibles» nacionales o regionales, compuestas de empresas eléctricas, agencias gubernamentales, instituciones financieras nacionales y extranjeras, y empresas privadas, para fines del 2000.

## Prioridad N°9: Adoptar Normas de Mínima Eficiencia Energética, Etiquetas de Energía, y Certificación Para Edificios y Equipos

*Los gobiernos:*

• Acordarán antes del 2000, métodos nacionales de pruebas de eficiencia energética y evaluación para edificios y enseres.

• Certificarán y homologarán un número adecuado de centros de pruebas nacionales y regionales para evaluar enseres para fines de 2001.

• Promulgarán para el año 2001, normas de eficiencia energética mínima, etiquetas, y protocolos de certificación de edificios y enseres.

• Desarrollarán un plan hemisférico para la armonización de normas de eficiencia energética mínima para nuevos edificios y enseres para fines de 1999. El proceso de armonización deberá tomar en cuenta condiciones locales climáticas, así como prácticas de construcción y manufactura.

• Acordarán para fines del 2003 un primer nivel de normas regionales o hemisféricas de eficiencia energética mínimas para nuevos edificios y enseres.

## Prioridad N°10: Creación de «Centros de Excelencia Energética» a nivel Hemisférico

*Los gobiernos:*

• Identificarán las necesidades de capacitación en energía sustentable en el hemisferio a través del Grupo de Trabajo Hemisférico de Energía antes de fines del año 1998.

• Identificarán durante 1999 «Centros de Excelencia» potenciales en cada país y solicitarán propuestas para concretarlos a nivel nacional o regional, incluyendo presupuestos y recursos existentes durante 1999.

• Seleccionarán suficientes «Centros de Excelencia energética» y creerán una red de enlace entre ellos, para cubrir las necesidades de entrenamiento planteadas, para fines del año 1999.

• Desarrollarán un currículum para los profesionales, en aspectos analíticos y metodológicos relacionados al desarrollo energético sustentable.

• Desarrollarán programas de entrenamiento en estas metodología y en la instalación, operación y mantenimiento de equipo y materiales energéticamente eficientes o renovables.

• Empezarán a entrenar especialistas analíticos y de campo para fines del año 2000.

# VIII. ECONOMIC INTEGRATION AND FREE TRADE

Foro Ambiental - Cumbre de los Pueblos de América (Santiago, abril 1998) Comercio y Desarrollo Sustentable: Recomendaciones de la Sociedad Civil Para la Integración Hemisférica

## Anexo
## Propuesta Hemisférica Sobre el Sector Energético para la Cumbre de la Américas

*Redacción: Esperanza Martínez, Oilwatch, Ecuador.*

Considerando:

• Que la integración deber ser entendida como un proceso que permita el crecimiento de las potencialidades de los distintos países en relaciones de equidad. Las políticas deben basarse en una política de microregiones en las que se tomen en cuenta las características ambientales y culturales de cada una.

• Que el tratamiento hemisférico de las políticas energéticas podrían implicar que la desigualdad entre los países sean aun mayor, y que en América Latina y el Caribe, se desatiendan las necesidades y demandas internas de los países por atender a los mercados internacionales.

• Que ningún tema ambiental puede ser tratado de manera homogénea a nivel hemisférico puesto que venimos de realidades diferentes y las causas del deterioro ambiental y sus efectos son distintas en los países industrializados y en el resto del continente.

• Que el problema energético parte del hecho de que hay países que consumen demasiada energía, como es el caso de los Estados Unidos (que tiene el más alto consumo per capita de energía en el mundo) y que hay países tropicales que están sacrificando sus bosques o sus mares por aumentar la producción de petróleo, o por construir grandes represas. Que hay países que están importando tecnología nuclear para aumentar su capacidad energética.

Proponemos impulsar una agenda desde la sociedad civil tendiente al logro de los siguientes objetivos:

1. Iniciar una transición energética de toda fuente de energía intensiva, centralizada y de alto riesgo ambiental, a fuentes de energía sustentables, a fin de lograr que la producción y el consumo de energía sean sustentables; es decir, limpias, eficientes, de fuentes renovables y descentralizados, de acceso democrático y que sus costos reflejen los impactos sociales y ambientales.

2. Desarrollar políticas nacionales para fomentar las energías sustentables, particularmente aquellas dirigidas a satisfacer las demandas de energía de los sectores más empobrecidos.

Para lograr estos objetivos, se propone a los gobiernos:

1. Declarar una moratoria a toda nueva exploración de carbón, petróleo y gas, enmarcada en los compromisos frente al Cambio Climático y como pasos inmediatos hacia una transición energética.

2. Desarrollar estrategias para la recuperación de la capacidad de sustentación de los países de la región. Esto incluye la cancelación de proyectos poco eficientes, la modernización de la tecnología en operación, la restauración de las Areas intervenidas para la extracción de energía fósil y de grandes represas, bajo la responsabilidad de las empresas que las operaron.

3. Suspender todo préstamo, crédito y otras formas de subsidios provenientes de agencias extranjeras de desarrollo multilateral y bilateral para proyectos de extracción de combustibles fósiles, grandes represas o energía nuclear y aquellos relacionados con estos. Estos prestamos e inversiones en el sector energético deberían ser reorientados hacia energías sustentables (solar, eólica, miró centrales hidroeléctricas, biomasa, etc.)

4. Crear garantías para la participación democrática en la toma de decisiones de los sectores energéticos. Evaluen todo proyecto energético actual y futuro con completa consulta a las comunidades afectadas por el proyecto, respetando su derecho a rechazar aquellos que puedan impactarlos negativamente.

5. Desarrollen una base legislativa e institucional para el fomento de las energías sustentables. Esto implica un soporte a la capacidad de investigación de los países, la creación de instancias de difusión de energías limpias y la eliminación de los subsidios directos e indirectos a la energía basada en combustibles fósiles.

6. Desarrollar propuestas de transporte publico sustentable y des-incentiven el transporte privado. Eliminen la importación de motores usados e implementen un estricto control sobre los vehículos en circulación. Como parte del transporte público se debe desarrollar propuestas de planificación, que a través de la descentralización, reduzcan la necesidad de desplazarse.

7. Adoptar, para todos los proyectos energéticos, los estándares que ofrezcan las mayores garantías ambientales y sociales. Apliquen el principio precautorio el cual sostiene que la falta de evidencia científica no es razón para dejar de tomar acciones para prevenir daños ambientales.

8. Aplicar el principio de prueba de cargo mediante el cual la responsabilidad de probar los impactos ambientales y sociales es de los que ejecutan un proyecto y no de los afectados.

9. Garantizar que en la implementación de estudios de impacto ambiental de todo proyecto de energía sea obligatorio examinar formas de reducir el consumo y opciones de energía limpias y renovables.

10. Impulsar el reconocimiento de la Deuda Ecológica que los países del Norte industrializado han asumido con los países del sur, por la utilización de recursos naturales, la degradación ambiental y el uso de la capacidad de absorción de $CO_2$ emitido por los países industrializados y de alto consumo de energía. Se comprometan a incluir este concepto en todas las negociaciones hemisféricas e internacionales.

# VIII. Economic Integration and Free Trade

# Free Trade in the Americas: Fulfilling the Promise of Miami and Santiago

*Ambler Moss and
Stephen Lande*

## ABOUT THE NORTH-SOUTH CENTER

For over a decade, the North-South Center has been dedicated to the intensive study of complex global problems, with special emphasis on the Western Hemisphere. As an independent research and educational organization, it produces policy-relevant research aimed at facilitating the resolution of the most critical issues in the region. The Center's research, cooperative study, education, and training have benefited citizens of the Western Hemisphere by supplying significant knowledge and expertise relevant to an inter-American agenda that grows more pressing each year.

Among the crucial international issues that challenge the Americas are the search for freedom and democracy, the economic crises that divide rich and poor, the pursuit of a path toward sustainable development, and the construction of trade partnerships that cross international borders.

The Center engages and informs government and private sector opinion leaders throughout the Americas by means of conferences, public affairs activities, and research resulting in timely publications. A valuable national and global resource, the Center has become a focal point for cooperative study, a respected clearinghouse for ideas, and an adept coordinator of international projects.

Strategically located in Miami, the natural gateway between the United States and most of Latin America and the Caribbean and a key metropolis for Europe in the region, the Center hosts leaders and scholars who value opportunities for dialogue, study, and exchange in an ambience free of partisan agendas. The Center is bound only by a commitment to democracy, economic progress with sustainable development, and the free interchange of ideas.

The North-South Center benefits from its congenial home adjacent to the campus of the University of Miami, an institution that has always provided international contacts in commerce, the arts and sciences, and international studies, among many other areas. The University of Miami is distinguished in the nature and extent of its international activities, particularly its study of the culture, politics, history, language, and development of Latin America and the Caribbean — all of which are complemented and reinforced by the North-South Center.

The Center welcomes a collegial relationship with organizations and citizens concerned with these issues.

---

*The mission of the **Dante B. Fascell North-South Center** is to promote better relations and serve as a catalyst for change among the United States, Canada, and the nations of Latin America and the Caribbean by advancing knowledge and understanding of the major political, social, economic, and cultural issues affecting the nations and peoples of the Western Hemisphere.*

© *1998 North-South Center
Agenda Papers • Number Thirty*

# Moving Toward a Free Trade Area of the Americas:
## An Overview

*Ambler Moss*

The bold centerpiece of the Summit of the Americas (Miami, December 1994) was the commitment by the 34 heads of state and government there assembled to create a Free Trade Area of the Americas (FTAA) by the year 2005. Integration efforts were already in place; at least 30 trade agreements were in effect in the Western Hemisphere even before the completion of the North American Free Trade Agreement (NAFTA) in November 1993. Yet the FTAA would be a gigantic project to overshadow the others. To guard against undue delay or backsliding, the leaders stipulated that substantial, concrete progress should be achieved by the end of the century, and they set a specific calendar of trade ministerial meetings.

The calendar proved to be of critical importance. The Mexican peso crisis, following directly on the heels of the Summit, might have stopped the process but for the obligation of the trade ministers to meet in Denver a few months later. As it happened, progress toward the FTAA has continued almost unabated. In the process, the Western Hemisphere has learned some valuable lessons in fiscal management and rapid response to crisis in a global economy.

It is valuable, at this juncture, to look at the FTAA process and to assess its chances for success within the accepted time frame. The North-South Center has published a paper before each trade ministerial to reflect particular viewpoints of the private sector, non-governmental organizations (NGOs), and other civil society actors.

### THE SAN JOSÉ TRADE MINISTERIAL

The private sector has a vital economic interest in the FTAA process and, in fact, has led the way in the entire integration process. Therefore, a series of measures known as "business facilitation," which could be implemented before the year 2000, have come into focus as high-priority steps along the way. The North-South Center asked Stephen Lande (adjunct senior research associate of the Center and president of Manchester Trade) to review the status of and possibilities for these measures. Published in this White Paper, they were offered as the Center's principal contribution to the Americas Business Forum at San José. Excellent studies on the subject have also been made by Jorge Ramírez Ocampo (organizer of the Cartagena Americas Business Forum in 1996) and the National Association of Manufacturers.

Initiation of the negotiations toward achieving the FTAA was recommended by the San José trade ministerial on March 19, 1998, the final meeting held before the Summit of the Americas (Santiago, April 1998). The ministers at San José recommended that FTAA negotiations begin by mid-1998. As with the previous ministerials (Denver, Cartagena, Belo Horizonte), a large business forum took place at San José accompanied by meetings of environmental NGOs.

Even while making appropriate allowances for the problems inherent in such an ambitious undertaking, the fact is that economic integration in the Americas has progressed well in a short time. It took decades to create a European common market. It is not far-fetched to think that the economies of the Americas, although far more disparate than those of European countries, are coming together more quickly. A newly formed private group of eminent persons, the "Leadership Council for Inter-American Summitry," has gone so far as to call for the completion of the FTAA by the year 2002 and to institutionalize the summits with biannual meetings and a "summit secretariat."

### THE SANTIAGO SUMMIT

The Santiago Summit was not, of course, just about the FTAA. In fact, over 150 action items were set into motion by the Miami Summit in its *Plan of Action,* and many of these were on center stage at Santiago. The agenda at Santiago was divided into four general headings — Education, Preserving and Strengthening Democracy and Human Rights, Economic Integration and Free Trade, and Eradication of Poverty and Discrimination. Each contains an abundance of subheadings; the second area, for example, gets into such issues as migrant workers,

---

Ambler Moss is director of the North-South Center and professor of International Studies at the University of Miami and of counsel to the law firm of Greenberg Traurig in Miami. He is a former U.S. ambassador to Panama.

# VIII. Economic Integration and Free Trade

municipal and regional administration, corruption, illicit drug trafficking, and the strengthening of judicial systems. Even within the economic area, the Summit examined investment, transportation, energy, and telecommunications as well as trade.

Progress on the social, political, and environmental initiatives of the Summit is crucial. Cooperation among governments on these "non-economic" issues is precisely what is needed to address the concerns of many groups who see trade negotiations as the "only game in town" and the most productive arena for their issues.

## THE RIGHT MOMENT TO PROCEED

Despite downward revisions in estimates of growth rates because of the Asian financial crisis, an underlying sense of optimism pervaded Santiago. First, the meeting was composed of, just as at Miami, 34 freely elected leaders (the whole hemisphere except for Cuba). Moreover, the notion that the FTAA must be a "democratic club" was even more firmly entrenched at Santiago than it was at Miami. Cherished traditional principles of absolute sovereignty and non-interference, while not altogether gone, have given way to a collective sense of institutionalizing democracy as a *sine qua non* of participation in the inter-American system, including the FTAA.

Second, the economic statistics in Latin America are basically good. The UN Economic Commission for Latin America and the Caribbean (ECLAC), in its report for 1997, showed that growth in the region was 5.3 percent that year, as opposed to an average of 3.2 percent for 1991-1996. The average inflation rate was less than 11 percent and into single digits in 13 of the 22 countries surveyed. The region had an average current account deficit of 3 percent of GDP but experienced an inflow of US$70 billion in new capital, about two-thirds of which represented direct investment. Foreign direct investment in Brazil alone was in excess of $16 billion and is expected to be substantially greater in 1998. The effects of the Asian crisis on growth will be felt, but even conservative analysts such as Enrique Iglesias, president of the Inter-American Development Bank, predict a figure of 3 percent for 1998, not bad given the magnitude of the crisis. Latin America is prepared to avoid some of the worst problems of Asia. It already has had extensive experience in recent years with domestic fiscal stabilization and the rehabilitation of its banking systems.

The Santiago Summit took into account, of course, the understanding that while trade and economic growth are essential engines of change and improvement, they do not exist in a vacuum. Huge problems beset the hemisphere, subjects of the Miami and Santiago summit agendas. Unemployment, poverty in a large segment of the population, corruption, the weakness of civil society, growing inequality in income distribution, inadequate health systems, the failure of schools and universities, and environmental degradation are generalized problems which, if left to fester, challenge the political sustainability of positive economic reforms.

In regional economic integration, of course, the FTAA is not the only game in town, so to speak, a point sometimes lost in Washington circles. Subregional integration continues at a lively pace, notably the increase in intra-regional trade within the Southern Cone Common Market (MERCOSUR — Argentina, Brazil, Paraguay, and Uruguay) and the addition of trading relationships with associate member countries (Chile and Bolivia). Haiti joined the Caribbean bloc Caribbean Community and Common Market (CARICOM) in July 1997. Canada and Chile established a free trade agreement in 1997. The Andean Pact of countries may yet, despite setbacks, associate with MERCOSUR to form a sort of South American free trade area ("SAFTA"), a dream of some Brazilians, which, they feel, positions the South better to negotiate with their strong neighbors in NAFTA.

Moreover, as affirmed by all Western Hemisphere leaders on many occasions, the FTAA process is an "open regionalism," not a trading bloc to compete against the other great economic "spaces" in the world, Europe and Asia. Two Latin American countries, Mexico and Chile, are members of the Asia-Pacific Economic Cooperation (APEC) and three others, Peru, Colombia, and Panama, wish to join.

The European Union (EU), as well, has long been engaged in deepening its trade relationships with Latin America. It has framework agreements with MERCOSUR and Chile and, as of December 1997, with Mexico. The EU has bilateral economic development accords with every Latin American country except Cuba. In Panama on February 11-12, 1998, the EU and the Rio Group of Latin American democracies celebrated their Eighth Institutionalized Meeting of Foreign Ministers. The meeting dealt with such topics as economic cooperation, the strengthening of democratic regimes and institutions, advancement of sustainable development, social progress, and cooperation against illegal drug trafficking, among others. It was the prelude to a full-scale Heads of State Meeting between EU and Latin American and Caribbean countries that will take place in Rio de Janeiro in 1999.

In fact, the coexistence of these subregional, regional, and intercontinental arrangements is perfectly compatible with the global trading system established within the context of the World Trade Organization (WTO), which serves as the basis for all of them. In the past, if some countries feared the creation of competitive, mercantilistic trading blocs, by now those fears should have been allayed.

## MOVING AHEAD ON THE MIAMI SUMMIT PROCESS

What were the problems faced at the time of the Miami Summit relative to the completion of the FTAA? The immediate one, of course, was the Mexican peso crisis, already cited. On a broader scale, four others seemed to be present:

1. The lack of a comprehensive plan or blueprint to create the FTAA;
2. The absence of an organizing entity around which to build the FTAA;
3. The lack of a specific role for the private sector in the process; and
4. Increasingly, after Miami, doubts in Latin America as to the commitment of the United States in leading the process.

Looking at these one by one,

The *blueprint* was scarcely discernible at the beginning but is beginning to come into better focus. The agenda of the Miami Summit was put together too quickly to try to define a blueprint, and it would have been premature to attempt it. There were really two unstated blueprints, a NAFTA one and a MERCOSUR one. The first assumed that the most logical way to construct an FTAA was to envisage a gradual expansion of NAFTA, beginning with Chile, a step originally promised by President George Bush and actually announced by the three NAFTA members immediately following the Miami Summit. Caribbean and Central American countries thought they should be next, and the presidents of Colombia and Venezuela expressed their countries' interest in joining NAFTA. For several years, Chile continued to be the most logical choice for fourth member. NAFTA never added members because of the inability of the United States to enact fast track legislation; the political mood in Washington clearly was not favorable to enlarging NAFTA, though Congress appears to be undergoing a mood swing in Spring 1998.

Meanwhile, the MERCOSUR concept, as noted above, was to strengthen and consolidate its own trading system and businesses within the bloc, expand its trading relationships with a group of countries in the region, and enter into trading arrangements with Europe. As time passed, MERCOSUR advocated a more gradual approach to achieving the FTAA (but still within the 2005 time frame). Led by Brazil, its approach was to emphasize "business facilitation" measures and defer negotiating the harder issues, such as government procurement and intellectual property, until the final stages.

A process has emerged through the trade ministerials that points the way to eventual success of FTAA negotiations. At the Denver, Cartagena, and Belo Horizonte trade ministerials, working groups were established in 11 substantive areas and one on dispute resolution mechanisms. They were supported by the "Tripartite Committee" established at Miami — the Organization of American States (through its Special Trade Unit), the Inter-American Development Bank, and ECLAC. These groups have essentially completed their necessary initial missions of compiling and documenting information in their respective areas and are now ready to constitute themselves into negotiating groups.

The number of such negotiating groups and their chairmanships were set by the San José ministerial. There will be nine groups, as follow:

| Negotiating Group | Chair | Vice Chair |
|---|---|---|
| Market Access | Colombia | Bolivia |
| Investment | Costa Rica | Dominican Republic |
| Services | Nicaragua | Barbados |
| Government Procurement | United States | Honduras |
| Dispute Settlement | Chile | Uruguay-Paraguay |
| Agriculture | Argentina | El Salvador |
| Intellectual Property Rights | Venezuela | Ecuador |
| Subsidies, Antidumping and Countervailing Duties | Brazil | Chile |
| Competition Policy | Peru | Trinidad and Tobago |

# VIII. Economic Integration and Free Trade

Following the Santiago Summit, the trade ministerials will take place only every 18 months, but more frequent meetings of vice ministers will, in the form of a Trade Negotiating Committee (TNC), supervise the work of the Negotiating Groups. The chairs of those groups will remain the same until the next ministerial.

The San José ministerial also directed that overall chairmanship of the FTAA process rotate among different countries at the end of each ministerial meeting. The country that will chair the FTAA process will also host the ministerial meetings and will chair the TNC. The chair rotation for the FTAA process is as follows:

| Dates | Chair | Vice Chair |
|---|---|---|
| May 1, 1998 to Oct. 31, 1999 | Canada | Argentina |
| Nov. 1, 1999 to April 30, 2001 | Argentina | Ecuador |
| Nov. 1, 2002 to Dec. 31, 2004 | co-chair between Brazil and the United States | |

The ministerial declaration states that Brazil and the United States will continue to act as co-chairs until the end of the negotiations.

An *organizing entity* around which to build the FTAA, something that might correspond roughly to the European Commission, was never established at the Miami Summit. This was certainly not an oversight but acknowledged that the political reality of the hemisphere would not accept any entity that might even seem to take on attributes of supranational authority. The *pro tempore* site of the FTAA was, therefore, each ministerial host country in turn (the United States, Colombia, Brazil, Costa Rica) with the background assistance of the Tripartite Committee. Yet, it has been understood progressively at the ministerial and vice-ministerial meetings that when the working groups became negotiating groups, some form of administrative secretariat would have to develop. At the Belo Horizonte meeting, the members of the Tripartite Committee were commissioned to study the comparative advantages of various cities in the Americas that had announced their aspirations to be the "Brussels of the Americas." The candidates were Bogotá, Lima, Kingston, Mexico City, Miami, Panama, and Rio de Janeiro. While not taking sides in favor of any candidate, the Tripartite Committee published its results, taking into consideration such factors as ease of transportation and communications, hotel costs, overall cost of living, contributions to the operation of the secretariat, and secretarial infrastructure available (translators, interpreters, and others).

The ministers at San José did not decide upon a permanent site for FTAA negotiations and for an Administrative Secretariat but mandated three successive sites from May 1998 until December 2004. The site will begin at Miami for the first three years, then shift to Panama for the next two years, and finally move to Mexico City until the end of negotiations. Future ministerial meetings, however, will be held in the country that holds the chair at the time.

The *role of the private sector* has been recognized as essential ever since the Miami Summit's *Declaration of Principles* recognized it explicitly. Nevertheless, it has still not been specifically defined in the FTAA process. Private sector leaders were invited to certain events of the Miami Summit but did not meet to discuss it, before or afterward. The United States, as host of the first ministerial at Denver in March 1995, organized a business forum, but following the ministerial itself. Colombia and Brazil corrected this mistake, and the Americas Business Forums, organized by their private sectors, took place before the ministerials of Cartagena and Belo Horizonte, as was also the case at San José. These forums are useful in offering recommendations to the ministerials, although their input is obviously not timely enough to impact directly on the results. Nevertheless, position papers prepared for the business forums by private sector groups in various FTAA countries are released in advance of the meetings and known by government delegations.

Direct private sector input to government negotiators does take place at a national level in some countries, the United States being a good example. In others it does not, nor does it at the FTAA level except for the business forums. An idea put forward by some private sector groups but never implemented is for meetings to be held between interested business groups with members of the official working groups, at least in informal, face-to-face encounters. This idea is also in keeping with the business facilitation measures under discussion, in which the private sector has a direct and immediate interest.

Host governments of the FTAA ministerials can also help generate more public support for economic integration by finding ways to incorporate the perspectives of non-governmental actors that are not necessarily private business groups. The inclusion of input from environmental and labor organizations, for example, can help build powerful constituencies for free trade in such countries as the United States, where environmental and labor issues are given high priority.

## FAST TRACK OR SLOW TRACK?

In November 1997, the Clinton administration, faced with a negative vote in the Congress, withdrew fast track legislation. The event called into question the *United States' commitment* to the free trade process in the minds of many Latin Americans. What does it really mean in terms of the U.S. role in creating that as centerpiece of the 1994 Miami Summit? Has Washington opted out?

Economic integration and free trade arrangements will continue in the hemisphere, of course, with or without the United States. There are even more than the 30 free trade agreements in the hemisphere that existed before NAFTA. Yet, it would be a strange paradox to see an FTAA built to include the entire hemisphere except for two countries, the United States and Cuba (the latter has not been a part of the Summit process because of incompatible political and economic systems). Despite the failure of fast track legislation, however, that is not going to happen. In a way, it is a shame that passage of fast track became such a litmus test of U.S. political will both here and in Latin America.

Nor is the fast track rebuff a sign that the United States is headed for a new historical era of protectionism. The Congress is not talking about raising tariffs or undoing NAFTA and U.S. participation in the World Trade Organization (WTO). Since Franklin Roosevelt began in 1934 to lower the major trade barriers imposed in 1930, this country has been moving in a free trade direction. Congress may have slowed that process but has not reversed it. However, recently congressional support for fast track appears to be increasing.

Admittedly, the rebuff weakens, in foreign eyes, the image of this country as a leader. That is why Secretary of State Madeleine Albright urged the passage of fast track as a "foreign policy imperative." In a world where economic power has substantially replaced military power as the criterion of leadership, it means a major loss of prestige. Fast track had a significance beyond just trade, particularly in inter-American relations. If the United States cannot come through on trade, it can expect less cooperation on other issues it wishes to pursue with Latin America.

U.S. failure is also seen by others outside the hemisphere as an opportunity. The day after fast track failed, the EU announced that it would seek to accelerate by one year, from 2001 to 2000, its free trade arrangements with MERCOSUR. Discussions between the two common markets began in 1994.

Within the United States, we may see more industries moving production into such trade areas as MERCOSUR with direct investment. They will not be willing to wait for the FTAA to break down tariff barriers. This is ironic, as saving U.S. jobs was an argument used by opponents of fast track. Nor will environmental protection necessarily be enhanced by the outward migration of U.S. industries.

From a technical standpoint, the fast track failure does not change the world in some practical terms. If an FTAA is to materialize, its text will not take form for several more years, time enough for the United States to revisit the issue. Meanwhile, nothing prevents the United States from entering into negotiations for the FTAA. It did so without fast track authority at the beginning of the Tokyo Round and the Uruguay Round of the General Agreement on Tariffs and Trade (GATT). Many people, including (and perhaps especially) those in the United States think that lack of fast track authority prevents the United States from negotiating. It does not; it only refers to the way in which a trade agreement is handled by the Congress, with an up-or-down vote and no amendments allowed.

Similarly, progress can proceed within the working groups already set up by the trade ministers with negotiations of essential topics such as customs procedures, rules of origin, market access, intellectual property rights, government procurement, and the others. The United States has been and will be a vigorous participant in these forums. No fast track authority is needed to make progress in these areas; doing so will enhance trade and capital flows across borders.

Business, in any event, is global and does not wait for government. It will make its own plans to move ahead. Existing major trading arrangements through the WTO provide infrastructure enough to move boldly in world markets. Latin America is increasingly important to U.S. business. The region will continue to offer great opportunities, with or without fast track. By the first decade of the next century, it is expected to become the world's major market for U.S. products and services, greater than Europe and Japan combined.

# VIII. Economic Integration and Free Trade

## IS THE UNITED STATES ENGAGED IN LATIN AMERICA?

It is often thought that the United States, with respect to Latin America, oscillates between periods of active engagement and "benign neglect." There was reason to hold such a view during the Cold War, when security objectives along the East-West axis dominated U.S. policy in the region. Today, however, the policy agenda, as characterized in the agendas of the two Summits, gives a permanency and stability to U.S. objectives.

## Ten Latin American Policy Successes

In fact, it is no exaggeration to claim 10 U.S. successes in its Latin American policies during just the last five years:

1. Enactment of the NAFTA (1993).
2. Approval of legislation for the WTO (1994; with a significant impact on U.S.-Latin American relations).
3. The Miami Summit of the Americas and its commitment to the FTAA (1994).
4. Rapid and successful response to the Mexican peso crisis, along with international financial institutions (1995).
5. A steady, collegial course with other countries on the workout of the Haitian crisis and the aftermath to the Guatemalan peace process.
6. The Santa Cruz Summit of the Americas on Sustainable Development, with its 65 action items (1996).
7. President Clinton's Latin American and Caribbean trips and more than 40 missions by the First Lady and the President's Special Envoy to the Americas, Mack McLarty.
8. Vigorous leadership and high representation in the Trade Ministers' meetings, in the Finance Ministers' meetings, and in other Summit follow-up forums.
9. Orderly and successful planning and leadership in the transfer to Panama of the Panama Canal by the year 1999.
10. President Clinton's solid commitment to the Santiago Summit (1998) and to following up the FTAA commitment by the year 2005 with concrete progress by 2000.

The processes now taking place in the Americas reflect a new and different era in inter-American relations. Their beginning cannot be pegged to one significant event, such as the fall of the Berlin Wall in Europe. Nor, at this stage, can all of the hopeful trends toward democratic consolidation, economic growth, and social advancement be guaranteed to be irreversible. Nevertheless, the commitment to the process around the Americas offers reason for optimism. The recent Santiago Summit of the Americas has added a deeper level of hemispheric solidarity that reinforces commitment to the FTAA, now an attainable goal for the near future.

# Free Trade in the Americas:
## Launching Negotiations and Concrete Progress by the Millennium

*Stephen Lande*

### SUMMARY AND INTRODUCTION

By launching negotiations, the second Summit of the Americas of April 18-19, 1998, in Santiago, Chile, brought the goal of creating the Free Trade Area of the Americas (FTAA) much closer to fruition. These negotiations are targeted to end by the year 2005 with concrete progress to be attained by the year 2000. The chiefs of state at the Summit accepted the recommendations from the successful fourth Trade Ministerial[1] held in March 1998, which had worked out details for the launch.

The hemisphere's private sector noted two other achievements of the Trade Ministerial.

1. An agreement to develop a package of business facilitation measures to be adopted by the year 2000, which would put flesh on the Miami Summit commitment that the process would make concrete progress by that date. It was left to future negotiations to work out the composition of the package. However, if the magnitude of the package is reflective of the areas of consensus reached by the private sector at the fourth Americas Business Forum (ABF) coinciding with the Trade Ministerial, trade flows would be significantly enhanced. Various studies have shown that effective streamlining and simplification of customs procedures alone is equivalent to wiping out 15 percentage points of duties, whereas average duty rates in hemispheric countries today are less than 15 percent.

2. Opportunities for continuous business participation beyond the sporadic meetings of the Americas Business Forum were agreed. First, an outreach group was established to receive, analyze, and transmit views from various sectors of civil society, including the business sector. Second, a Committee on Electronic Commerce was established to make recommendations on how to increase and broaden benefits to be derived from the electronic marketplace. It is significant that this group may be the first official body created in any trade negotiation consisting of government and private sector representatives.

The significance of the decision to launch the negotiation at the second Summit of the Americas is that it deepens the hemispheric commitment to the process. Many chiefs of state attending this meeting were not present at the original 1994 Miami Summit that started the process, and thus their commitment to its launch is a strong reaffirmation of each country's policy and makes it even more difficult for leaders in power in 2005 to miss the goal without losing face. Also, the fact that the launch occurs after the Mexican peso crisis, during both the current Asian crisis and a period when the United States is without fast track is very positive. Any of these factors could have been used as an excuse to forestall the negotiations. In fact, the three leading countries in the hemisphere — the United States, Brazil, and Mexico — are particularly committed to a successful conclusion to the negotiations. Since the United States and Brazil will co-chair and Mexico will be hosting the concluding phase, they will all share the blame for any failure.

However, do not expect significant progress until later in the process. Negotiations do not reach the decisive point until late in the process unless there are intermediary deadlines or required benchmarks before then. The only deadline before the year 2005 is to the aforementioned commitment for business facilitation measures to be adopted by the turn of the century. With hemispheric leaders still having more than six-and-one-half years to

---

Stephen Lande is an adjunct senior research associate of the North-South Center at the University of Miami; an adjunct professor in the School of Foreign Service at Georgetown University; and president of Manchester Trade, a Washington-based consulting firm. He has been intimately involved in hemispheric trade matters for more than 30 years and is considered one of the visionaries behind the present movement toward hemispheric free trade by the year 2005.

1. Although referred to as a Trade Ministerial in this paper, to be accurate, representation is by Ministers responsible for Trade; for example, in Brazil, Foreign Minister Lampreia is responsible for FTAA trade negotiations.

# VIII. Economic Integration and Free Trade

conclude the negotiations and the repeated determination of Brazil not to agree on significant liberalization until the concluding phase of the negotiations, it is difficult to foresee the pace of negotiations picking up in the near future. In fact, a large and significant package of business facilitation measures may be necessary to prevent a flagging of interest in the process.

The hemispheric business community convened the fourth Americas Business Forum (ABF) in San José to coincide with the Trade Ministerial. At earlier ABFs, the private sector engaged in spirited debate over how far to pursue liberalization in the FTAA process. This business forum was more focused since its major goal was to identify business facilitation measures for early implementation. In this regard, the meeting was successful. According to Marco Vinicio Ruiz, chairman of the ABF, of the 250 recommendations on which there was a consensus, about 80 addressed facilitation issues that could be implemented in the near future.

This paper was commissioned by the North-South Center at the University of Miami[2] to review the operation of the FTAA process through the Chilean Summit and to serve as a reference paper thereafter. It reviews the more important details of the agreement to launch the negotiations and establishes a list of possible measures to include in the year 2000 agreement on business facilitation.

The paper offers two major recommendations. The first recommendation is that to restore credibility to the U.S. negotiating approach, the U.S. President who succeeds President Clinton must either win fast track or convince U.S. hemispheric trading partners that existing conditions do not require fast track for approval of trade agreements. During the interim, to maintain a more credible trade profile, the administration should negotiate relatively noncontroversial subregional agreements (for example, an FTA with Chile or some of the beneficiaries of the Caribbean Basin Initiative (CBI) or a WTO-based agreement to eliminate duties in a non-import-sensitive sector such as chemicals) that can pass Congress without fast track.

Its second recommendation is that over the next 20 months, the major preoccupation of the FTAA process should be to develop a comprehensive and significant package of business facilitation measures to maintain momentum in the negotiations process. In fact, the first order of business of the Trade Negotiating Committee (TNC), composed of vice ministers, in organizing the negotiations should be to begin development of wide-ranging options for business facilitation for adoption by the ministers at the end of 1999. If there are no significant results in 2000, four years after the FTAA process was launched with five years still remaining to negotiate, the public and government leaders will have a hard time maintaining interest in FTAA negotiations.

Consensus on acceptable hemisphere-wide measures reached by the private sector at the 10 workshops making up the fourth Americas Business Forum demonstrates business support for a significant package. This package could allow for concrete results through agreements in at least 14 of the following areas — customs procedures, standards, professional accreditation, electronic commerce, generally accepted accounting principles (GAAP), world-class standards on telecommunications, financial services, information technology, investment and government procurement, courier and express mail services, alternative dispute settlement mechanisms, data and other materials of interest to business, improved efficiency of business, double taxation, business travel, select standstills, and implementation of Uruguay Round obligations and concessions.

Thereafter, FTAA negotiators periodically should develop additional packages of concrete results — business facilitation as well as intermediary agreements if the pace of negotiations permits. This should both inspire interest by the business community in the process and allow the participants to meet one of the goals of the 1994 Miami Summit of the Americas.

The private sector can play a major role in the development of this package. It can follow up and deepen ABF recommendations and transmit them to the new outreach group established by the ministers to receive, review, and analyze submissions from civil society (consisting of representatives from business and other productive sectors, labor, environment, and academic groups) and then to present the range of views to the ministers.

---

2. In 1997, the North-South Center organized private sector Shadow Group workshops that submitted recommendations to the ABF. Of the 120 recommendations formulated by the Shadow Groups, more than one-half were reflected in the conclusions of the 1997 ABF. (See Summary of Recommendations in Annex I of this paper, which is the executive summary of the Shadow Groups' recommendations as presented in the publication, *Free Trade in the Americas: Policy Recommendations and Issues Paper,* prepared jointly by the North-South Center and the Institute of the Americas.) As these recommendations are still current, the North-South Center did not believe it was necessary to develop new recommendations. In 1998-1999, the Shadow Groups will be reactivated if FTAA negotiations gain some momentum.

The only business group addressing FTAA issues on a hemispheric level is the Business Network for Hemispheric Integration (BNHI). The BNHI can maintain pressure on government negotiators to make progress on business facilitation, act as a transmission belt for national submissions, pressure negotiators to incorporate these suggestions into their consideration, and keep the private sector informed of progress.

The BNHI will be convening a special assembly on June 5, 1998, when it is expected that decisions will be made on how to adapt to the opportunities for private sector input on business facilitation provided by the ministers. The assembly should review ideas for meaningful facilitation measures recommended by the San José ABF (see below); by the Colombian Chairman of the second ABF held in Cartagena, Jorge Ramirez-Ocampo, in a February submission to the vice ministers (Annex II); and by the National Association of Manufacturers (NAM), the only submission to the ABF specifically focusing on facilitation (Annex III).

## FAST TRACK AND THE PACE OF NEGOTIATIONS

Well before the year 2005, the U.S. administration will have to resolve the issue of fast track. In fact, to prevent FTAA negotiations from languishing, fast track should be passed or a decision made to forgo this authority for the FTAA. The latter would involve convincing U.S. trading partners that fast track is no longer absolutely necessary to pass trade agreements. In fact, changes in U.S. trade law and the political setting in the United States actually have reduced chances that in approving trade agreements, Congress will force their renegotiation. Even if doubts remain, given the attraction of U.S. markets, the hemisphere may have no choice but to negotiate without fast track.

If U.S. hemispheric negotiating partners knew that uncertainties surrounding fast track were resolved or accepted the fact that fast track, although convenient, was not absolutely necessary, they probably would be willing to give the negotiations a higher priority, agreeing at the next ministerial meeting to establish intermediary deadlines.

Enthusiasm surrounding the launch is not noticeable largely due to perception that, without fast track, the United States can not be considered a credible negotiating partner. Whereas trade was the clear centerpiece of the first Summit, organizers of the second Summit focused on other issues as well as trade. These issues included instilling more confidence into the hemispheric monetary system, adopting measures for improved education and training programs, insuring greater security using confidence-building measures, and combating narco-trafficking.

There is a nagging fear among negotiators that, without fast track in place or expected to be in place in the near future, negotiations will not go very far. The absence of fast track does not prevent negotiation from being undertaken; it is well understood in the hemisphere that the United States needs fast track only to present trade agreements for congressional approval. However, given five years of failure to pass fast track legislation, the United States may never succeed in enacting fast track for the FTAA process. The Southern Cone Common Market (MERCOSUR) and the World Trade Organization (WTO) offer alternative negotiating forums to the FTAA process if the United States is perceived as unable to negotiate seriously. Chances of congressional passage of fast track during the remaining years of the Clinton administration are slight to nonexistent for the following reasons:

- There is a lack of consensus over whether the United States is a net winner from liberal trade, especially since many liberal groups such as labor, environmentalists, and church groups are harping on the losers from trade.

- Little progress is being made in resolving the major obstacle to passage — the current U.S. domestic imbroglio over the relationship of social issues to trade concessions. The absence of a consensus on this issue, especially in the Democratic party, makes it increasingly unlikely that the stalemate will be overcome over the next several years.

- At least for the moment, fast track and trade relations within the Western Hemisphere are taking second place to U.S. efforts to help resolve the Asian monetary crisis by replenishing depleted International Monetary Fund (IMF) reserves and to a much lesser extent, to efforts for passage of the African Growth and Opportunity Act.

- Some profess a belief that fast track is an antidemocratic procedure, as it allows members of a previous Congress (many of whom will not be in office when future decisions are made) to limit the ability of future members to exercise their normal parliamentary prerogatives.

- And, there is disagreement as to whether free trade provides undue benefits to large corporations and businesses at the expense of labor and environmental concerns.

Without fast track, the U.S. negotiating position in the hemisphere is weakened to the extent that it is not able to overcome resistance to moving faster. Brazil, in particular, seems concerned about prematurely opening its markets to competition from the United States and also has hemispheric and extraregional priorities that are of more immediate concern than the FTAA negotiations. Other countries also may want to move cautiously on negotiations due to the lingering threat from the late 1997-1998 Asian monetary crisis. With fast track in place, there is no question that the lure of the U.S. market would enable the United States to overcome this resistance.

## UNTHINKABLE THOUGHT: FAST TRACK UNNECESSARY FOR U.S. IMPLEMENTATION OF FTAA

A way out of this situation might be for U.S. negotiators to decide not to pursue fast track but to allow the results of the FTAA negotiations to be considered under normal legislative procedures. Deep-seated philosophical differences among U.S. citizens and their governmental representatives, such as those described above, make passage of fast track highly questionable even after the year 2000.

If the Clinton administration or its successor were to decide that fast track could not be enacted in the foreseeable future or that the political price of enactment were too high, would that doom hemispheric trade negotiations? Probably not, if the decision were to be made in the next few years. In that case, U.S. negotiators could credibly argue that fast track is not indispensable for passage of legislation implementing trade agreements. Fast track is convenient for negotiators because it provides more certainty as to congressional passage. Fast track authority also protects the implementing legislation from being subjected to delaying tactics and killer amendments and, thus, reduces the chance that Congress will mandate that the United States must return to the negotiating table to demand more concessions.

At one time fast track negotiating authority may have been necessary to expedite passage of trade agreements, but this may not be the case today. Fast track was originally passed in the 1974 Trade Reform Act as an inducement for the European Community to participate in the Tokyo Round of multinational negotiations. The Community was incensed that the U.S. Senate Finance Committee had modified provisions on dumping and customs valuation, specifically as they affected the import-sensitive chemical industry, in legislation implementing the previous round of multilateral trade negotiations — the Kennedy Round in the mid-1960s. These modifications had forced renegotiations of this agreement.

This occurred more than 30 years ago. Since then, new, improved consultation procedures have been put into place between the U.S. executive with both the Congress, especially the trade oversight committees (Senate Finance and House Ways and Means), and the private sector. Since the Kennedy Round, the Office of the U.S. Trade Representative (USTR) has emerged as a cabinet-level agency with extraordinary power in trade negotiations. Unlike traditional agencies, the USTR is a creature not only of the administration but also is reliant on Congress. Today, it is difficult to imagine a situation in which the administration would bring back an implementing bill to Congress without some assurance that the oversight committees would accept it and the leadership would work with the administration to assure passage.

To be enacted, legislation implementing a free trade agreement must be passed by both the House of Representatives and the Senate. Fast track does not add much certainty to legislation being considered in the House, as that body already operates under generic rules similar to fast track procedures. The House leadership, working through its rules committee, requires that any bill coming to the floor be debated under a rule that limits the time for debate and the number and type of amendments allowed to be considered. The House rules are crafted in ways that prevent any bill implementing a trade agreement from being subject to amendments that would require the agreement to be renegotiated (so-called killer amendments) or subject to tactics forestalling or delaying a timely vote. For example, the most recent piece of controversial trade legislation — the African Growth and Opportunity Act— was considered under a closed rule with a time limit on debate and prohibitions on amendments. Opponents of the bill could only offer a motion to recommit, which was turned down. Despite being able to muster 194 votes for this motion, only 30 votes short of a majority, they were not able to alter the bill.

Although harder to bring into play, procedures in the Senate for overcoming delaying tactics and killer amendments do exist. The Senate, with a majority of three-fifths of its membership, can close debate and shut off amendments. In fact, even with fast track in place, the need to seek an exemption in the Senate from certain budget funding requirements required 60 votes for both the North American Free Trade Agreement (NAFTA) and the Uruguay Round implementing bills. The necessary votes were forthcoming.

One should also remember that in ratifying treaties negotiated by the President, the Senate operates under open rules and requires a two-thirds vote for approval compared with implementing legislation for trade agreements that require only a majority vote. These procedures for approving treaties have operated since the founding of the United States in 1789. Many controversial treaties have been approved by the required two-thirds majority without the addition of killer amendments requiring renegotiation.

This is not to deny that a determined minority opposed to implementation of any agreement could wreak havoc on the bill. However, the opposition must number at least two-fifths of the whole Senate, which means without vacancies, they must be able to garner 41 votes. Fortunately, only from the House of Representatives, not the Senate, has President Clinton confronted serious opposition to fast track renewal. In fact, the Senate demonstrated in a procedural vote on fast track legislation that enough votes exist not only to pass the legislation but to turn off debate, if necessary.

Approval of a bill to implement a specific trade agreement may indeed be easier to secure than passage of fast track, which would cover all trade agreements. Implementing legislation for trade agreements includes specific provisions that can be constructed so that special interests are balanced. Trade negotiating authority (fast track) is more difficult for Congress to deal with because it is not being asked to approve specific provisions. Instead, Congress is being asked to approve procedures for expediting passage of the implementing bill before anyone knows what the agreement's provisions will be. Naturally, it is more difficult to deal with unknown contingencies than to pass an implementing bill for an agreement whose provisions are already known.

The fast track, if renewed as currently proposed in the Ways and Means version of the bill, will exclude any provision from the implementing bill not directly related to the functioning of the trade agreement. This prevents the type of parliamentary maneuvering in which non-germane provisions are included to gain votes for an agreement from those who put a higher priority on inclusion of their amendment than on their opposition to the trade agreement. Past fast track legislation did not have this limitation. For example, passage of the Uruguay Round and NAFTA was helped materially by inclusion on the legislation of vote-attracting, non-germane amendments.

Another point to remember is that fast track does not guarantee that renegotiations will not occur. Even with fast track in place, Mexico was forced to renegotiate provisions on sugar and fresh vegetables in NAFTA and to add side letters on labor and the environment.

The reason a decision must be made early in the administration of the next President is that some time will be needed either to enact fast track, once introduced, or to convince Latin America and the Caribbean that the United States can proceed to negotiate without this authority. Until now, the administration has had to emphasize its need for fast track with its trading partners so as to maintain pressure on Congress to enact fast track. If it was to argue that fast track was not necessary for passage of the agreement, Congress would rapidly lose interest in even considering this political "hot potato." However, if the United States decides to proceed without fast track, it could make a credible argument to the hemisphere. Unfortunately, it cannot play it both ways. Convince the hemisphere that fast track is not necessary for conclusion of an agreement — but continue to argue with Congress that it is necessary.

A possible middle ground could be explored. Fast track could be enacted for multilateral but not for bilateral agreements. Even today, Congress probably would be willing to grant fast track negotiating authority for multilateral negotiations under the WTO, such as for a new round of multilateral negotiations or for sectoral talks.

Fortunately, negotiating authority is more necessary for multilateral than for bilateral agreements. Whereas modification of a bilateral or subregional agreement would involve renegotiations with no more than a few countries, modification of a multilateral agreement would involve more than 100 participants. As demonstrated by NAFTA, it was possible to modify the agreement to meet President Clinton's requirements even though this involved reopening controversial questions that were resolved by his predecessor. It would have been much more difficult to reopen the Uruguay Round, since renegotiation would have involved more than 100 countries. To prove that fast track is not necessary, it has been suggested that sometime before the turn of the century, less controversial sectoral agreements covering phase II of Information Technology or non-import-sensitive chemicals or subregional FTAs with Chile or select CBI countries be brought back without fast track.

Under the current situation, Congress would probably not be willing to approve fast track for FTAA talks since they smack too much of NAFTA. If this were to continue into the administration of Clinton's successor, could the then-existing administration develop some assurance that the FTAA would pass Congress with only so-called water-edge amendments included or accepted? Water-edge amendments are those that may limit administration discretion in interpreting provisions but not require renegotiation. They are often used in approving treaties such as a Cold War disarmament agreement with the Soviet Union. So-called "killer" amendments that would have required renegotiations were not attached, although many water-edge amendments were accepted. A commitment by the administration and the Senate leadership to follow this approach could possibly work with U.S. Latin partners, particularly if Congress had passed less controversial accords without fast track.

## BASIC ORGANIZATION OF NEGOTIATIONS AGREED UPON

The trade ministers were able to reach an understanding on the basic organization of the negotiations. It was a classic negotiation with the usual late-night compromises required for final approval of the communiqué.

The ministers established a three-level negotiating structure.

1. Ministers will provide political direction to the process. They will meet, at least initially, only once every 18 months to oversee the negotiations.

2. Their vice ministers will compose the TNC. The TNC will meet probably more often than the required two or three times a year to supervise the day-to-day progress of the negotiations. The TNC is designed to make political decisions in the absence of the ministers. The ministers mandated the TNC to develop a work program for the negotiating groups at their first meeting in order to ensure that each of the negotiating groups begin their work no later than September 30, 1997.

Two groups will be reporting to the TNC:

- A small Administrative Secretariat will be limited to facilitating the negotiations through

    a. logistic and administrative support of the negotiating groups;
    
    b.. translation of documents and interpretation during deliberations; and
    
    c. maintenance, distribution, and selective publication of official negotiating documents.

- A Consultative Group on Smaller Economies will be open to all participating countries. Its terms of reference are limited to "following the FTAA process by keeping under review the concerns and interests of smaller countries" and "bringing to the attention of the TNC issues of concern and interests of smaller economies." The consultative group, however, will not be able to negotiate or make proposals, a serious limitation on its role. The chair of the group will be Jamaica; its vice chair, Guatemala.

3. The principal engine of the negotiations will be the negotiating groups. Nine negotiating groups were established covering market access, agriculture, investment, services, government procurement, intellectual property, subsidies and countervailing and antidumping duties, competition policy, and dispute resolution. This division is without prejudice to future decisions by the TNC to dissolve, establish, or merge groups. Likewise, the negotiating groups may establish ad hoc working groups.

Although a Mexican proposal to link formally the groups looking at antidumping with competition policy was not accepted, the ministers recognized the work in different groups may be interrelated. A specific mandate was provided to study the interaction between trade and competition policy as well as between market access and agriculture in order to identify any areas that may merit further consideration. The fact that this issue was left open is of great significance because an effective way to limit the protectionist effects of antidumping laws is to incorporate within these laws definitions of market concentration and motivations that are part of antitrust law.

## FTAA LAUNCH IS SIGNIFICANT

Probably, the most significant aspect of the launch was that it was agreed to despite the host of obstacles described above (for example, absence of fast track, Asian Flu, and so on). There were a number of pretexts that countries could have invoked to delay the launch but did not. The willingness of the negotiating partners to agree to the launch reflected a significant reaffirmation commitment to the process throughout the hemisphere, which augurs well for the timely conclusion of the talks. Countries also agreed to the negotiations launch since it provided their chiefs of state with positive publicity, without committing any country to consider offering controversial trade liberalizing concessions until much later in the process.

1. In fact, the Brazilian team under the overall direction of its Foreign Minister Luis Felipe Lampreia and

under the day-to-day direction of Jose Gonçalves Botofogel until he became Minister of Trade and Commerce played the usual skillful Brazilian game. The Brazilians effectively maintained their position against moving forward quickly while exhibiting just enough flexibility to meet the minimal U.S. demands required for them to agree to the launch.

2. However, negotiating laurels go to the USTR, Ambassador Charlene Barshefsky, and her new Deputy Richard W. Fisher as well as day-to-day negotiators, Associate USTR Peter Allgeier and his deputy for the FTAA Karen Lezny. Despite being hobbled by the absence of fast track since the FTAA process began, they were able to see the negotiations launched while protecting priority U.S. interests — definitive early concrete results and keeping the labor/trade linkage alive — in the Ministerial Declaration. Also by agreeing to co-chair the final negotiating phase with Brazil, USTR may have assured the success of this venture. Brazil would not want to be overseeing negotiations that fail.

3. Despite the small size of the Costa Rican economy, the Costa Rican chairmen of the process, Minister of Foreign Trade Jose Manuel Salazar and his Vice Minister Carlos Murillo, were able to exert enough pressure to keep the process moving ahead throughout the 10 months from Belo Horizonte to San José. Salazar received positive reviews for his decision to have the negotiations assigned to a small group of countries representing the key players meeting late into the night to reach a final agreement on the key points.

4. An unexpected surprise of the FTAA preparatory stage so far has been the strength and professionalism of the technical support provided by the tripartite group — the Economic Commission for Latin America and the Caribbean (ECLAC), the Inter-American Development Bank (IDB), and the Organization of American States (OAS). All three of these agencies were thrown into an unaccustomed role of providing technical support for trade negotiations. Largely as a result of their work in developing compilations of trade measures in the hemisphere, it is generally agreed that the technical basis for these negotiations is stronger than for any previous plurilateral or multilateral negotiations including the Uruguay Round.

The ministers reaffirmed the principles and objectives that have guided FTAA work since Miami. They included that the agreement would be balanced, comprehensive, WTO-consistent, and a single undertaking. It will take into account the needs, economic conditions, and opportunities of smaller economies. The negotiations will be transparent and build on consensual decisionmaking. The FTAA can coexist with subregional agreements to the extent that the rights and obligations under these agreements are not covered by or go beyond those in the FTAA.

The ministers also agreed on certain housekeeping elements of the negotiations including the venue and the chair and vice chair of the negotiations as well as the chair and vice chair of the nine negotiating groups.

## VENUE

Miami      From May 1, 1998, to February 8, 2001

Panama City      From March 1, 2001, to February 28, 2003

Mexico City      From March 1, 2003, to December 31, 2004.

## CHAIR AND VICE CHAIR OF THE FTAA PROCESS

Canada and Argentina
     From May 1, 1998, to October 31, 1999

Argentina and Ecuador
     From November 1, 1999, to April 30, 2001

Ecuador and Chile
     From May 1, 2001, to October 31, 2002

Brazil and the United States
     From November 1, 2002, to December 31, 2004, or until negotiations conclude

## NEGOTIATING GROUPS' CHAIR AND VICE CHAIR

*Market Access:* Colombia, Bolivia

*Investment:* Costa Rica, Dominican Republic

*Services:* Nicaragua, Barbados

*Government Procurement:* United States, Honduras

*Dispute Settlement:* Chile, Uruguay-Paraguay

*Agriculture:* Argentina, El Salvador

*Intellectual Property Rights:* Venezuela, Ecuador

*Subsidies, Antidumping and Countervailing Duties:* Brazil, Chile

*Competition Policy:* Peru, Trinidad and Tobago

# VIII. Economic Integration and Free Trade

## HOWEVER, NEGOTIATIONS PROCEEDING SLOWLY

Despite this launch, numerous elements can impede or slow down negotiations.

1. Since the FTAA process requires unanimity in decisionmaking, any participating country can forestall agreement and thereby slow progress.

2. Although ministers have agreed on the structure of negotiations, they have not agreed on a timetable for carrying them out. Since negotiations are not to conclude until the year 2005 — more than six years from now — there is no pressure to enter serious negotiations immediately. There are enough outstanding technical issues to allow delays in controversial decisions for a number of years. Well before the year 2005, the term of every incumbent chief of state in the hemisphere will have expired. Therefore, it is very likely that they will instruct their ministers to move slowly, leaving the tough decisions to their successors.

3. Many political decisions necessary to begin the negotiations were not made by the ministers in San José and require sorting out by the vice ministers in June. Most important is that, whereas the general principles and objectives for the negotiations and specific objectives for the negotiating groups were agreed, the actual negotiating modalities were not discussed. For example, the Hemispheric Working Group (HWG) on Services could not agree on the modality for negotiating services. Many countries favored the NAFTA negative list, in which all services are covered except those that gain a special derogation. MERCOSUR advocates a positive list, which would mean that only those services identified and agreed upon in the negotiations would be covered.

Even though the TNC is supposed to make these and other decisions in the absence of the ministers, it is not clear that the vice ministers will have the political authority or will to do so. If that is true, these decisions will have to wait until late 1999 at the earliest, as the ministers are not scheduled to meet before then. In fact, ministerials are foreseen to be held at 18-month intervals, not a schedule prone to accelerate the pace of negotiations.

4. Some of the modalities that have already been addressed by the HWGs will have to be reviewed in light of the fact that the negotiating groups are being organized along lines different from those used for the HWGs. For example, the market access negotiating group will encompass the work of at least three HWGs — market access, customs valuation and rules of origin, and industrial standards and regulations.

5. MERCOSUR is arguing that negotiations should proceed more or less simultaneously, gradually, and in a balanced fashion. If this principle remains operative for MERCOSUR (acknowledging that any country can impede or stop progress), the slowest negotiating group may well determine the pace of negotiations.

6. Some countries will slow negotiations until the United States has fast track or decides that fast track is not necessary for passage of the FTAA and demonstrates this fact to them.

7. There is no agreement yet on whether Uruguay Round commitments should be the starting point of negotiations in each of the groups or should simply be factors to be taken into account. This issue will have to be resolved in a number of groups before serious negotiations can begin.

8. Countries may hold back on concessions until they know whether plans for another round of multilateral trade negotiations will materialize. A "Millennium Round," beginning shortly after the turn of the century, has been suggested by Sir Leon Brittan, EU Commissioner for External Relations. The annual WTO Trade Ministerial meeting in fall 1998 will provide some indication of whether these negotiations will take place.

9. There is no consensus yet on how to treat trade-related environmental and labor matters. Disagreement in these areas could stall negotiations in other areas.

10. There is no agreement yet on whether, and if so how, to incorporate the views of business, labor, and environmental groups into the negotiations once they have been analyzed by the outreach group and transmitted to the ministers.

## "CONCRETE PROGRESS" BY 2000 ONLY PARTIALLY DEFINED

At the Miami Summit, the heads of state agreed to make *concrete progress* toward the attainment of the objective of an FTAA by the end of this century. The heads of state, in calling for concrete progress, were anxious to avoid a damaging (and potentially fatal) fall-off in interest in the FTAA process over the course of a protracted, 11-year negotiating process.

The San José Ministerial reaffirmed their commitment to concrete progress. It directed the negotiating groups to achieve considerable progress by 2000 and instructed the TNC to agree on specific business facilitation measures to be adopted before the end of the century. However, the ministers avoided any definition of "business facilitation," leaving this decision to the TNC and the negotiating groups. The *Declaration,* in recognizing the rapid expansion of Internet usage and electronic commerce, welcomed the offer of the Caribbean Common Market (CARICOM—Barbados) to lead a joint government-private sector committee of experts that will make recommendations to the next ministerial. However, there was no commitment whether the work of this group would become part of the package of early concrete progress.

Vice ministers at their first meeting in June will confront the task of beginning to define the extent of business facilitation measures. As in other areas, the positions of Brazil and the United States differed widely during the prenegotiating phase, and it is unclear whether they are fully reconciled now.

## BRAZIL ARGUED FOR LIMITING EARLY CONCRETE RESULTS TO BUSINESS FACILITATION

During the prenegotiation process, Brazil argued that the concept of the FTAA as a single undertaking with negotiations means that sectoral and other substantive issues cannot be resolved in an early harvest. Progress, Brazil maintains, should be balanced with negotiations in the different groups, all moving forward gradually and simultaneously. Thus, Brazil opposes the early conclusion of any intermediary accord as well as implementation of these measures because to do so would compromise the final package to be concluded in the year 2005. At that time, negotiators should preserve their abilities to engage in cross-sectoral tradeoffs, necessary components of any negotiation, according to Brazil.

Brazil also argues that MERCOSUR's businesspeople need time to adjust to increased competition from the United States. Businesspeople are faced with adjusting to liberalization from internal Brazilian market reforms and from commitments undertaken by MERCOSUR to its free trade partners and to the WTO. Thus, Brazil opposes implementing or, for that matter, even negotiating liberalization until much later.

After fast track legislation was withdrawn by the Clinton administration, a number of Latin American countries, including Chile and Mexico, expressed concern about "cherry-picking." They were concerned that concrete results would be implemented in areas of high priority to the United States that do not require congressional approval or are so noncontroversial that congressional approval would not be a problem. Once the United States received satisfaction, there would be less inducement to fight the battle for fast track or otherwise stay at the table.

Brazil contended that a literal reading of the Miami *Declaration of Principles* demonstrates that there is no specific requirement for implementation of actual measures. The launching of the negotiations and work undertaken before and after the launch will certainly be, according to Brazil, concrete progress as foreseen in the *Declaration.*

Brazil supported business facilitation measures as ways to lower the cost of doing business, provided that the measures do not involve concessions that would weaken its future negotiating position or subject its businesspeople to increased competition in the short term. Until now, Brazil has insisted on a narrow definition of business facilitation.

## UNITED STATES ARGUED FOR WIDE-RANGING PACKAGE OF EARLY CONCRETE RESULTS

The United States did not accept the argument that the requirements of a single undertaking would prevent a substantive early harvest. U.S. negotiators pointed out that there were early, substantive, concrete results in the Uruguay Round despite the existence of a single undertaking rule in those negotiations. The 1986 Punta del Este Ministerial Declaration, which launched the Uruguay Round of the General Agreement on Tariffs and Trade (GATT), stated that agreements reached at an early stage may be implemented on a provisional or definitive basis prior to the formal conclusion of the negotiations.

There were even interim agreements in the Round's midterm review. These agreements endorsed some changes to dispute settlement and initiated interim trade policy reviews for assessing on a regular basis the degree of openness of member state economies. Ministers also agreed on a framework for tariff and services negotiations and on the base date for calculating the extent and value of tariff reduction offers. The latter encompassed an agreement on how to credit participants for their voluntary or IMF-sanctioned liberalizations that were not bound in the GATT.

The office of the USTR argued that there can be three forms of early concrete results by the year 2000:

1. Participating countries' implementation of legislation and regulations and establishment of all institutions required by the Uruguay Round agreements.

2. Negotiation of interim agreements. Such interim pacts might include transparency and due process agreements on government procurement as a step toward a full-scale, WTO-like procurement package; mutual recognition of agreements for the certification of some telecommunications equipment; and a code of conduct for customs officials in accordance with declarations from the Customs Cooperation Council.

3. Business facilitation measures developed in concert with the private sector. A solid source for such advice would be recommendations resulting from the 1998 San José Americas Business Forum.

The United States further argued that agreements reached at an early stage should be implemented on a provisional or on a definitive basis prior to the formal conclusion of negotiations. Early agreements, of course, should be taken into account in assessing the overall balance of the negotiations.

Acceptance of too restrictive a definition of concrete results, especially one limited to narrow business facilitation, will not accomplish the objectives agreed upon at the 1994 Summit. The leaders in Miami called for concrete progress in order to maintain the interest of the public and the involvement of high government officials during what promised to be a relatively arduous process that would last until 2005.

The United States argued that it is a wasteful exercise to debate what are business facilitation measures and what are not. One should simply focus on agreeing to a significant package of measures for early implementation. If there is a consensus for specific measures, no one is going to object that they go beyond business facilitation.

## INITIAL INTERPRETATION OF THE COMPROMISE

Brazil and the United States both gained from the compromise. Brazil was successful in limiting the request to the TNC to business facilitation measures. Brazil avoided U.S. wording that would have included in the instruction to the TNC intermediary agreements as well as business facilitation and commitments to implement rather than simply adopt measures.

The United States was successful in instructing the TNC to agree on specific measures that went beyond the ministerial wording calling for early concrete progress by the year 2000. By leaving the definition of business facilitation open, the United States may prove successful in eventually gaining a more comprehensive package. The United States argues that it is not important at this stage whether early concrete results are defined as business facilitation or include intermediary agreements also. If there is a consensus to implement any measures by the year 2000, one can assume that no one will object on the grounds that they are inconsistent with the definition of business facilitation.

Thus, the most important issue left open was how or even whether to define business facilitation. There seems to be little controversy that business facilitation measures should not upset the final balance of concessions. However, there is no agreement on whether they should be limited to technical matters between governments and voluntary undertakings by the private sectors or whether they could encompass official government agreements needing legislative approval.

## OTHER IMPORTANT ISSUES

There are a number of other issues worth mentioning. Given the breadth of coverage of the FTAA, the emphasis on business facilitation measures, and the demands that rapid technological changes are imposing on the regulatory and rule-making processes in all countries, it is probably advisable to plan for several periodic packages of early concrete results, beginning with the one at the end of 1999. In the 1999 report to the ministers, the vice ministers could make suggestions as to elements that might constitute a package for the end of the year 2000 and include additional measures to be implemented between the years 2000 and 2005.

Additionally, a package of early harvest measures can be developed outside the FTAA forum. Such measures can be developed at the national level or in subregional groupings and then be generalized to apply to the entire hemisphere. For example, at the Ministerial, the United States agreed to establish with Central America and the Dominican Republic a Trade and Investment Forum (TIF) to replace the present system of bilateral forums with the United States. The United States has expressed unhappiness with the current reliance on nonreciprocal agreements; Central America and the Dominican Republic are also concerned about so-called nonreciprocal agreements since they give the appearance of allowing them a free ride while subjecting them to unilateral U.S. conditions without allowing them resort to dispute settlement. These forums can provide an opportunity to move into reciprocal relationships, perhaps by focusing on measures considered for inclusion in the early concrete results package suggested by the United States.

Measures can also be drawn from experiences outside the hemisphere. For example, the FTAA can benefit from adopting measures similar to those being developed in the Asia-Pacific Economic Cooperation (APEC) forum and in the Transatlantic Dialogue between the United States and the European Union. The private sector can develop such measures themselves. In fact, private sector groups probably can identify, better than government officials, measures that would facilitate their operations.

## PRIVATE SECTOR WELL-POSITIONED TO INFLUENCE BUSINESS FACILITATION PACKAGE

Until now, business has been limited to a single opportunity (when ministerials are convened) to present its views to the ministers. Also, the requirement that there be consensus on issues before they are recommended to the ministers means that many ideas are dropped from the final document or appear as areas of divergence. Unfortunately, until now there is little indication that even those measures where there has been a consensus have been considered by government representatives, nor has there been any reaction to these recommendations.

The outreach group established by the ministers can provide a vehicle for continuous inputs from the private sector. The fact that the new outreach group will be opened to representatives from all FTAA participants and will be meeting between ministerials to receive private sector views, to analyze recommendations, and to present the whole range of views to the ministers opens up new possibility for the private sector. A concern of this approach is that it is not clear whether the private sector can make inputs directly to the TNC and negotiating group in between the trade ministerials. If not, will the outreach group be able to transmit private sector inputs to them? If not, their ideas will languish until the next ministerial at the end of 1999.

The Business Network for Hemispheric Integration (BNHI) consists of key national umbrella, sectoral, and regional groupings and trade associations located throughout the hemisphere. However, until now it has suffered from lack of a regular work plan, a clearly defined mission, and financial commitments. Funding has been the exclusive responsibility of Costa Rica. A regular work plan and a clearly defined mission can be developed if members wish BNHI to become a regular communicant with the new outreach group. Fund raising would be facilitated if the national private sector can be convinced that BNHI has a legitimate and productive role to play in working with the outreach group.

Let us be clear! We do not expect the hemispheric private sector to arrive at a consensus on any issue where Brazil and the United States disagree — specifically on the extent of concrete progress and what to include in the final package. However, there should be consensus on the need for effective, cost-saving measures to be put into effect by the year 2000 or as soon thereafter as practical. The private sector through the BNHI can first of all exert pressure on the FTAA process, together with national members exerting pressure on their governments, to assure that the outreach group becomes an effective transmission belt for private sector views to be considered by decisionmakers at the TNC and in the negotiating groups. If a clear private sector consensus exists behind any recommendation, the BNHI can be requested to push the proposal actively on the hemispheric level in concert with national efforts by its members.

## SPECIFIC FACILITATION MEASURES

A careful review of the recommendations agreed to at the fourth ABF reveals that there exists enough consensus for a significant package of early harvest. Thus, we have drawn heavily on this list in identifying 14 issues where private sector consensus exists.

However, this process involved some editing of the recommendations. Each workshop in San José was requested to develop business facilitation issues going beyond recommendations made at the third Americas Business Forum, which met last May in Belo Horizonte. Some workshops, unfortunately, did not break out recommendations for business facilitation from general recommendations. Others listed measures that were not germane to their subjects; for example, the Workshop on Market Access recommended infrastructure needs; tighter IPR rules were recommended by a number of workshops not only the one on IPRs. The groups used different definitions of business facilitation. Sometimes it was difficult to define the borderline where an agreement on business facilitation becomes an agreement that could upset the current balance of concessions.

Some workshops, especially three of the seven services subsectors covering information technology, telecommunications, and financial services, went into great detail. In fact, their recommendations were as detailed as provisions in recent WTO agreements on these subjects.

Other groups simply identified areas for business facilitation measures without details. In these cases, recommendations considered too detailed were not included. Finally, recommendations, not drafted in a way where their thrust was clear, were rewritten to clarify their meaning.

## POSSIBLE COMPONENTS OF BUSINESS FACILITATION PACKAGE

Below is a possible package of business facilitation measures grouped into 14 recommendations drawn from the ABF supplemented by suggestions from the National Association of Manufacturers to the Forum and by Ramirez Ocampo to the vice ministers.

One recommendation on which there was a consensus in a number of the workshops was for a large package of business facilitation measures. Indeed, the ABF recommended that developing such a package be a high priority of the trade negotiators when the TNC convenes again in June.

A package based on these 14 private sector recommendations, if adopted by trade ministers, would not only satisfy the private sector but would fulfill the Miami expectation of a package of early concrete results that maintain the interest of the hemisphere in the process.

1. *Streamlining and Simplifying Customs Procedures* — Suggestions for harmonization and simplification of customs procedures include adoption of common forms, introduction of special carnet procedures for temporary imports, introduction of electronic paperless clearance, hemisphere-wide implementation of WTO customs valuation procedures, adoption of common procedures for private sector appeals of customs rules, and a code of conduct for customs officials modeled after the World Customs. Many of these recommendations go beyond those required in the Uruguay Round Agreement on Customs Procedures.

2. *Identifying Targets for Harmonization and Mutual Recognition Agreements* — The ABF identified a number of areas going beyond earlier recommendations for mutual recognition agreements. It specifically recommended that, in cases where harmonization is appropriate, consideration be given to applying of the principle "One Standard-One Test," Supplier's Declaration of Conformity, (or a third-party certification).

Although the workshops did not identify specific sectors or products for such agreements, there is no question that the private sector supports pilot sectors. The United States has already indicated that it believes that computers may be an appropriate sector for harmonization and telecommunications for MRAs. Also, the European Union and the United States have already agreed on seven sectors for MRAs. Thus, at a minimum by the year 2000, the TNC should agree on pilot sectors with a target date to complete harmonization or MRAs for them. A more ambitious goal would be actually to complete a number of such agreements by then. It may be necessary to develop subregional agreements first and then expand to the hemispheric level.

3. *Developing Common Criteria for Accrediting Professionals* — The conclusion to the ABF workshops was that since limiting factors existing in industrial sectors do not exist in the professional services sector, liberalization should proceed in this sector expeditiously and promptly. A comparative study and analysis of regulations governing the practice of each major professional service should be carried out on a national basis. This should serve as a preliminary step before starting any type of negotiations on minimum standards. Existing models for harmonization such as those maintained by the Inter-American Bar Association should be reviewed. Specific ABF workshop recommendations would grant national and MFN treatment to foreign professionals, eliminate citizenship/residency requirements, and encourage collaboration among national professional associations for accreditation and for exchanging data to verify credentials, titles, and background.

Negotiators may decide to choose one or two professions for establishing common accreditation requirements and procedures. One area where there was support for accepting common criteria was for the professionals in construction and engineering.

4. *Promoting the Expansion of Electronic Commerce and Introduction of Information Technologies* — ABF recommendations in this area included no restrictions being placed on the free flow of information on the Internet, including encryption of data, and privatization not allowing monopoly concessions to replace state bureaucracies. Lists of specific subjects for negotiations should be developed, prioritized, and made available to officials.

Steps should be taken to assure the availability of infrastructure and human resources to support the following:

a. High-quality telecommunication media

b. Interconnections with the network of international services

c. Product and services database
d. Wide-band facilities
e. Nonconventional technical services.

5. *Gaining Hemispheric Recognition of Generally Accepted Accountancy Principles (GAAP)* — The report on the conclusions of the workshops called for the adoption of GAAP on a hemispheric basis for financial statements, customs documentation, payment procedures, supply of financial information, and incorporation of hemisphere-wide databases. This is similar to a so-far unsuccessful attempt to agree on Generally Accepted Accounting Principles (GAAP) in the WTO.

6. *Adopting on a Binding or Nonbinding Basis World Class Norms for Government Procurement, Telecommunications, Financial Services, Information Technology, and Investment* — The forum could not agree on hemisphere-wide acceptance of recently concluded agreements on telecommunications, financial services, and information technology. Similarly, there was no consensus in favor of negotiating, as part of business facilitation, hemispheric agreements on transparency in government procurement and a preliminary investment agreement. On the other hand, the workshops did support incorporation into the FTAA of a number of liberalizing and market-opening measures and commitments drawn from the WTO agreements on telecommunications, financial services, and information technology; proposals for a WTO agreement on procurement transparency; and the draft Organization for Economic Cooperation and Development (OECD) Multilateral Agreement on Investment.

Acceptance of these measures and commitments would facilitate investment and productive activity in the hemisphere. An interim step could be to include in the business facilitation package acceptance of a number of these principles (full transparency, inviolability of contracts, and so on). A less binding alternative could be an understanding or undertaking to accept these principles as a goal or objective not as a full commitment.

7. *Liberalizing Courier and Express Mail Services* — The workshop recommendations reflected a consensus to remove restrictions in the services subsector of integrated express transportation services and international deliveries of goods and services (couriers and express mail). This subsector can be identified as a pilot sector for implementing hemispheric norms by the year 2000. If there is opposition to this idea as premature, nonbinding provisions similar to recommendation 6 above can be agreed upon.

8. *Promoting Alternative Dispute Settlement Procedures* — The Dispute Settlement working group suggested consideration be given to developing alternative dispute resolution that avoids more formal court and government-to-government procedures. By the year 2000, governments could develop mechanisms for utilizing such alternative facilities in state-state, state-private party, and private party-private party disputes.

9. *Improving Efficiency of Business Establishment* — There were a large number of proposals to develop programs to facilitate business entities in the hemisphere in their integration into the global economy. There was an emphasis on assisting micro, small, and medium-sized enterprises.

Specific suggestions included organization of a structure for technological cooperation, introduction of preferential lines of credit to facilitate the absorption and transfer of technology, creation of multilateral funds to invest in or guarantee investments in business entities and to support training in starting and operating businesses, construction of a website on the Internet to provide information about sectoral business opportunities, and development of a mechanism to promote joint international production and strategic alliances.

Members of the Tripartite Group could be requested to develop data on official, non-governmental, and private sector groups with expertise in these areas. Members can also determine the availability of funding for such projects. Agreement on implementation of programs to prepare small and medium-sized enterprises for FTAA implementation can be included in the package of early concrete results.

10. *Incorporating Procedures for Developing and Disseminating Information to the Private Sector to Facilitate Adjustment to Free Trade* — The workshops identified information and data not prepared during the preparatory phase that would contribute both to the negotiations of the FTAA and the ability of the private sector to adjust. Recommendations included detailed comparative studies on regulations for professional accreditation, rules against consumer fraud and money laundering, and government policies in sectoral or functional areas such as tax policies. In addition, the recommendations called for a listing of responsible agencies and officials for specific policies; reports on the progress of FTAA negotiations; compilations of private sector recommendations, including those made at the ABFs, and any responses to them; and updates on hemispheric progress in implementation of Uruguay Round commitments. Other recom-

mendations called for updating the compendia of trade, services, and investment measures and the data on trade flows completed during the preparatory stage.

Ministers can agree on creation of a single website with appropriate linkages to provide this information on a regular basis. Organizations could be tasked with responsibility for collecting, analyzing, and placing the information and data on the website.

11. *Eliminating Double Taxation* — Hemispheric taxation policy was also addressed, particularly the avoidance of double taxation and regularization of social benefits. Regional agreements should eliminate double social security taxation and at the same time facilitate the movement of resources within the region. Countries were asked to sign agreements that eliminate double taxation in relation to professional honoraria or profits of professional services companies. In fact, in cases involving situations where more than one country received social security taxes for the same worker, labor legislation could allow for the deposit of social security and health care contributions in countries of origin. Finance officials should be asked to work with trade officials to establish guidelines for harmonizing these policies.

12. *Facilitating Business Travel* — Visa and entry requirements, especially for business travelers, should be eliminated or, if not possible, simplified. An ABF recommendation was that hemispheric agreements should be reached allowing for free movement of professionals between firms. It is of critical importance that governments eliminate their restrictions on the mobility of personnel between countries of the hemisphere by providing temporary work visas in conjunction with the terms of consulting contracts. In addition to the visa requirements, introduction of expeditious entry procedures for frequent business travelers should be considered.

Immigration and trade officials should work together to develop hemispheric norms for business travel by the year 2000.

13. *Implementing Selective Standstills* — Standstill means an agreement not to increase protection, wherever possible. There is an understanding that sometime during the negotiations, some type of standstill will be implemented, but exactly when is unknown. However, given the fact that all countries in the hemisphere, with the exception of the United States and Canada, maintain the flexibility to raise duties by applying duty rates below WTO bound or contractual levels and the U.S. insistence of being able to increase duties under trade remedy procedures, an effective standstill on products is difficult to foresee. There was a suggestion for standstills outside of the product area that may be easier to agree upon over the next few years. These standstills could a) preclude new restrictions on foreign and domestic investment, b) protect from government interference the free flow of information through the Internet and other electronic networks, and c) assure that regulations protecting privacy and consumer rights not create unnecessary barriers to free trade and to the free flow of information.

14. *Implementing Uruguay Round Commitments* — Countries have resisted U.S. proposals to agree to implement all Uruguay Round commitments fully as part of the package of early concrete results. The ABF agreed on implementing obligations in a number of areas that appear to be less controversial and more related to business facilitation. These included obligations associated with customs, standards and non-tariff barriers, sanitary and phytosanitary (SPS) measures, dispute settlement, and competition policies.

## CONCLUSIONS

The TNC, together with the negotiating groups, will be preparing business facilitation measures to be adopted and probably implemented before the year 2000. It is important that these measures be wide-ranging and significant if only to keep momentum alive in the process.

Negotiators should not forget that the main objective of negotiations is to provide opportunities for their countries' businesses to increase sales and lower costs as soon as possible. Close consultation with the private sector in the development of these measures is necessary. Businesspeople are better able than government officials to determine the types of measures that will most stimulate business activities and increase productivity. For example, if Brazilian producers believe they benefit from early implementation of agreements in the areas of agriculture and industrial standards, then Brazilian negotiators should be amenable to agreeing — even if this means that they have to give up a little of their negotiating leverage.

# Annex I:
## Executive Summary of Recommendations for the May 1997 Hemispheric Trade Ministerial in Belo Horizonte, Brazil

The May 13-16, 1997, Hemispheric Trade Ministerial and Americas Business Forum in Belo Horizonte, Brazil, marked another milestone in the process of implementing a Free Trade Area of the Americas (FTAA) by the year 2005.

As it had done before the Cartagena Ministerial of March 1996, the North-South Center organized private sector contributions to the process through the creation of "shadow groups," so named because of their private sector members' expertise in areas covered by the government-only Hemispheric Working Groups (HWGs). The private sector shadow groups generated a full set of policy recommendations, which are recapitulated in summary form below.

## MARKET ACCESS

A continued policy of structural adjustment throughout the hemisphere would help overcome current problems of market access. FTAA market access negotiations should involve immediate publication of the market access data bases constructed by the HWGs to allow private sector input, to facilitate trade, and to provide early identification of products of special interest to hemispheric suppliers. To ensure that this information is updated, the private sector should have the confidence to ask for a formalized review process. Attention should also be given to the following specific suggestions: 1) earliest possible elimination of duties applicable to products included in the "zero-for zero" tariff liberalization package of the Uruguay Round of the General Agreement on Tariffs and Trade (GATT) and subsequent agreements (such as the Information Technology Agreement); 2) special staging schedules for market access concessions by the smaller economies; 3) establishment of a negotiation modality that would facilitate exchanging market access liberalization for products, in return for concessions on services and investment; and 4) tariff negotiating modalities that would also address product-specific nontariff barriers, such as certain disputed sanitary-phytosanitary (SPS) measures and manufacturing standards.

The private sectors throughout the hemisphere should cooperate in publicizing the job creation and growth stimulation provided by enhanced market access.

## CUSTOMS PROCEDURES AND RULES OF ORIGIN

Customs procedures should be scrutinized by corporate traffic managers and customs administrators and by the transportation, freight forwarding, and brokerage communities responsible for the movement and clearance of cargo. By contrast, rules of origin are of principal concern to material managers and production specialists. As the issues within the competence of the HWG for Customs Procedures and Rules of Origin must draw from such distinct groups in the private sector, it is very important for this HWG to establish a mechanism for its consultations with private sector actors.

There must be concerted action regarding the training of a sufficient number of customs officials to handle the increased volume and complexity of customs transactions, utilization of the information superhighway for customs clearance, and maximum use of electronically transmitted documentation.

Work should be undertaken to harmonize rules of origin, wherever possible, among subregional groupings. However, the best way to simplify the administrative complexity of origin rules is to eliminate the need to use them. Origin rules are not necessary in cases for which countries agree on a common external tariff.

## INVESTMENT

A coordinated approach by the hemisphere's Finance Ministers and Trade Ministers is critical. Finance Ministers should be focusing on 1) self-sustainable growth and exchange rate policies, 2) ways to encourage the growth of domestic savings, and 3) expanding access to global capital markets. Specific agenda items should also include elimination of taxes that unduly discourage foreign investment, particularly discriminatory withholding taxes; reduction of the role of state-owned banks operating on noncommercial principles; and the best mix of asset-based, income, sales, and profit taxes for encouraging investment.

The HWG on Investment should develop model hemisphere-wide investment provisions covering the issues of transparency, nondiscriminatory most favored nation (MFN) treatment, national treatment, expropriation, transfer of funds and capital movement, performance requirements, and investment incentives.

Public policy actions aimed at improving poorly developed infrastructures are of the utmost importance as well.

## STANDARDS AND TECHNICAL BARRIERS

Policymakers in the Western Hemisphere should be able to draw conclusions about the trade effects of standards and standards-making and to monitor the evolution of the standards-making process from information contained in a central registry of existing and proposed standards in the hemisphere. The central registry should make it possible to determine whether standards-making is in fact achieving the three-fold purpose of protecting the end user and the public, rationalizing and harmonizing standards, and providing for a system of mutual recognition of testing and certification procedures. A hemispheric system, which could be included as part of the FTAA, should recognize the regional and cultural differences involving health, safety, and security.

Countries should consider privatization of government-owned testing and certification entities. This would reduce one of the most costly fiscal burdens of free trade, while using the profit motive to accelerate work on mutual recognition agreements (MRAs).

## AGRICULTURAL SUBSIDIES, ANTI-DUMPING AND COUNTERVAILING DUTIES

The FTAA negotiations should take existing WTO commitments as a starting point, since all FTAA participants (with the exception of Panama) are WTO members. Current WTO disciplines on agricultural subsidies limit — but do not prohibit — their use. Outlawing hemispheric agricultural subsidies could be undertaken in sectors where third countries play a small role in hemispheric trade. A hemispheric position for future WTO talks in this area could also lead to important enlargements of existing WTO obligations.

Unfair trade remedies — anti-dumping and countervailing duties — could be reduced in frequency and made less disruptive of trade through increased understanding of conditions where dumping and subsidies are likely to have a deleterious effect on domestic producers and workers. Opportunities for sectoral agreements, advanced consultations before actions are brought, and government mediation of disputes could combine to provide alternatives to trade-suffocating anti-dumping and countervailing cases.

A specific method for linking competition policy to anti-dumping action could be for national authorities to be required to take into account similar factors to those considered in the enforcement of competition law. For example, national authorities could take into account existing competition in domestic and international markets, perhaps as measured by the degree of concentration in a specific industry. Dumping laws could be modified so that remedies are less likely to be imposed when the degree of concentration is low.

## COMPETITION POLICY

Beyond market opening measures, the best way to facilitate the flow of goods, services, and investment in the Western Hemisphere would be harmonization of governments' rules affecting competition. The early work of this HWG indicates the need to develop a basis for applying agreed-upon principles of competition policy that are compatible with and equally applied under two different legal systems: *common law,* used by the United States, Canada, and the English-speaking Caribbean; and *Roman (or civil) law,* used by the Latin American countries.

Consideration should be given to providing mechanisms for increased cooperation among competent authorities in competition policy. Such cooperation could be the forerunner of the development of hemispheric norms in this area.

Ministers at the Belo Horizonte meeting, or at the next Trade Ministerial in San José, Costa Rica, in February 1998, should authorize establishment of a new HWG on "Government Ownership and Deregulation." Such a group could develop general principles but not consider specific disciplines. These principles could include openness of decisionmaking, due process, nondiscrimination, and proportionality (that is, the cost of a regulatory measure should be proportional to the benefits it is expected to bring to society in general and should cause the minimum distortion of trade, consistent with carrying out its objectives).

Hemispheric norms related to competition, no matter how constructive, will not allow countries to renounce the use of unfair trade remedies. A more limited solution might be to require that national authorities, in the course of applying anti-dumping law, take into account the same factors as those considered in the enforcement of national competition law. For example, national authorities could take into account existing competition in domestic and international markets, as measured by various factors, inter alia, the degree of concentration in a specific industry. Dumping laws could be modified so that remedies are less likely to be imposed when the degree of concentration is low.

The FTAA process should concentrate on education and information dissemination, as few countries have experience with competition law. The private sectors should develop information jointly with the HWG on the effects of government ownership and regulatory policy on free competition overall and in major sectors.

## GOVERNMENT PROCUREMENT

National governments and the private sector should work to remove restrictions that tend to favor local manufacturers and service providers over their foreign counterparts. Related to this, governments should focus on ways to fight corruption. They could design and accept uniform bidding documents and clear, practical rules that promote efficiency and guarantee transparency; eliminate or significantly reduce preferences favoring domestic firms; reform legislation so that parties to a government contract agree to resolve their disputes outside the judiciary; set up procedures so that contractor protests are resolved promptly and effectively by an agency other than the government agency calling for bids; and ensure that government agencies that frequently procure goods from the private sector develop a cadre of procurement experts who are part of the permanent civil service. These obligations should be phased in over time.

The private sector must develop the technical capacity to analyze the implications of accession to the WTO Government Procurement Agreement and the assumption of NAFTA-type government procurement obligations during the FTAA negotiations.

## INTELLECTUAL PROPERTY RIGHTS (IPR)

The absence of strong IPR protection restricts technology transfer, investment in manufacturing, and the development of a pool of skilled workers familiar with world-class technologies.

Hemispheric countries should fully implement the provisions of the WTO Agreement on Trade Related Intellectual Property Rights (TRIPS), if possible on an accelerated basis. TRIPS obligations should be the starting point of FTAA negotiations on intellectual property; entering into a TRIPS-plus agreement also should be considered. FTAA nations should develop cooperation among patent offices and trademark registries through consultations and memoranda of understanding.

To make IPR protections meaningful, a significant upgrading of technical and judicial resources needs to be undertaken. Specific actions suggested include mechanisms for the validation of patents granted elsewhere, as well as bringing in technical aids (such as online services, scanners, and advanced software) to conduct registry functions.

## SERVICES

As a basic principle of the FTAA negotiating modalities, governments should affirm that all service sectors will be covered by agreed-upon rights and obligations, unless other participants receive notification of specific exceptions and these exceptions are accepted by them. The agreement should include provisions on MFN treatment for FTAA providers, national treatment, transparency, progressive liberalization, clear rules and disciplines, and dispute settlement procedures.

FTAA obligations should cover the 12 sectors covered in the General Agreement on Trade in Services (GATS). Governments should consider privatization, deregulation, and market opening in the context of FTAA negotiations.

FTAA work in services should be carried out in concert with work in related areas, such as investment, government procurement, and standards and technical barriers. Because of the mutual benefits inherent in the ability of qualified professionals to obtain work permits and professional certification on a hemispheric basis, immediate action in the liberalization of professional qualification requirements is also highly desirable.

# VIII. Economic Integration and Free Trade

# Annex II:
## FTAA Business Facilitation Proposals for Actions To Be Implemented before Year 2000

*This Annex was prepared by Jorge Ramírez Ocampo, Chairman of the Second Americas Business Forum (1996) and consultant to the government of Costa Rica for the San José Trade Ministerial.*

## SCOPE AND DEFINITION

The scope of this work is to propose Business Facilitation (BF) initiatives, that is, those that participating countries can carry out unilaterally or in coordination with other governments by the year 2000, so as to expedite and simplify trade and investment transactions in the hemisphere, through the reduction of costs and risks or the simplification or elimination of red tape.

## TYPES OF PROPOSALS
- Transparency and Information
- Education
- Customs and Procedures
- Other

## INFORMATION AND TRANSPARENCY
- To create a new FTAA Home Page or to use the existing OAS Page to transmit the conclusions and recommendations of the Hemispheric Working Groups (HWGs).
- To request to the Ministerial and the HWGs that they officially react to the proposals of the business fora, following the procedures suggested by the Business Network for Hemispheric Integration (BNHI).
- To recommend the advanced publication of proposed changes in regulations for comment by interested parties.
- To publish the following information with the authorization of the HWGs and the Vice Ministers (VMs):

  A guide for customs procedures

  A guide to sources on demographic and market data

  An inventory of laws and regulations regarding competition

  An inventory of regulations and a list of agencies responsible for public sector procurement

  A list of goods and services frequently purchased by governments

  An inventory of regulations and a list of agencies responsible for subsidies and dumping and countervailing duties

  An inventory of regulations and a list of agencies responsible for foreign direct investment

  An inventory of regulations and a list of agencies responsible for industrial standards and health and phytosanitary regulations

- To create data banks coordinated by the Tripartite Commission covering the following:

  Hemispheric Trade Flows

  Foreign Direct Investment Flows

  Tariffs

  Non-Tariff Barriers

  National Payment Instruments for Commercial Transaction

  Infrastructure Projects and Invitations to International Tenders

## EDUCATION
- To promote a symposium on business facilitation (BF) with international organizations, governments and the private sector to update the participants on developments and present recommendations.
- To promote cooperation and exchange information among sister agencies, such as customs, standards certification, and others.
- To invite the Chairs of the HWGs to participate in the workshops of the Americas Business Forum (ABF) and regional seminars on relevant issues

with public and private sector representatives. As an alternative, private sector representatives could be invited to presentations before or after the meeting of the HWGs.

## CUSTOMS PROCEDURES

- To establish simplified customs procedures for promotional material, low cost shipments, personal software, and professional documents.
- To recommend to the relevant HWGs the harmonization and simplification of customs procedures on the basis of the Kyoto Convention.
- To implement the Agreement on Interpretation of Article VII (Customs Valuation) of GATT 1994, which establishes that valuation of imported merchandise should be the transaction value, unless circumstances clearly require an alternative valuation. Valuations should not be based on the value of comparable domestically produced goods nor on constructed or fictitious values. They should take into account that the use of transaction value has limitations when dealing with trade-marked goods.
- To recommend the elimination of consular services. The compulsory utilization of private value certification agencies for imports should also be avoided, unless there may arise exceptional circumstances that will justify it. In these cases, the number of imports subject to this requirement should be restricted to the minimum possible, and importers should be allowed to choose freely among several alternatives previously approved by the respective government.
- To recommend that governments sign the ATA Carnet Convention (The Istanbul Convention) for temporary duty-free admission of goods.
- To recommend that participating countries adhere to the UN Electronic Data Exchange System (EDE) that includes the exchange of structured message EDIFACT/UN. The system has developed a complete set of rules and procedures in order to encode all levels of commercial information. Each element of information has an icon. The system has also developed the "EDIFACT Syntax," which establishes the order in which icons should be placed within each message. The EDIFACT Syntax has been standardized as ISO 9735.
- To adopt the forms and procedures established by the UN/Economic Commission for Europe.
- To effectively apply the WTO Harmonized System (for classifying goods).

## OTHER

- To recommend the simplification of visa issuing procedures for business travelers, including among other regulations, multiple entry business visas and not requiring business visas for short visits.
- To expedite immigration procedures for business visitors.
- To simplify and harmonize industrial standards, specifications, and technical requirements.
- To promote the acceptance of Standard Conformity Certificates among signatories of Recognition Agreements by applying the principle: "Once tested, accepted every time."
- To request the Inter-American Association of Chambers of Commerce to propose legal adjustments that may be necessary for the facilitation of electronic trade.
- To create national agencies for BF and deregulation.
- To adopt the OECD Bribery Control Protocol and to reinforce the OAS declaration on corruption.
- To adjust incentives for attraction of International Direct Investment (IDI) to those accepted by the WTO.
- To apply to IDI the fair and equitable treatment foreseen in the Multilateral Agreement on Investment.
- To promote the application of International Accounting Standards.
- To recommend that the international transfer and processing of financial data be authorized.
- To request that the Inter-American Development Bank (IDB) prepare a "White Book" showing the deficiencies of existing hemispheric infrastructure and the investment necessary to solve them. The White Book should include a description of the proposed "hemispheric integration corridors." In the future, governments should take this information into account for the preparation of their national infrastructure programs.
- To recommend the adjustment of national legislation in order to allow the use of the "Principles for International Contracts" developed by the Interna-

tional Institute for the Unification of Private Legislation (UNIDROIT).
- To promote agreements for mutual recognition in licensed professions.
- To promote the nonjudicial settlement of disputes by utilizing the existing mechanisms at Chambers of Commerce.
- To promote participation of member countries in international organizations, such as ISO, the Pacific Economic Consultation Council (PECC), or the CODEX Alimentarius.
- To strengthen institutional consultation mechanisms of HWGs and Ministerials with the private sector, by channeling information through an organization such as the BNHI, which acts as an information catalyst without assuming the representation of those who originate it.

## IMPLEMENTATION

- To recommend to the Ministerial that it adopt these BF recommendations and instruct the VMs, acting as the Trade Negotiating Committee, to supervise the implementation of these initiatives and develop new ones.
- To transmit to the private sector through the BNHI the BF recommendations adopted, as well as information on progress in their implementation.

## CONCLUSION

These proposals may not seem very ambitious, but they fall within the scope of this document, which is to present only proposals for BF applicable by the year 2000. Nonetheless, I believe that they do contribute to the improvement of the business environment in the hemisphere, as shown in the following examples:

- Texas Instruments has saved US$50 million through the introduction of EDE.
- Volkswagen expects to reduce costs by 1 percent by utilizing EDIFACT/UN.

# Annex III:
## NAM (National Association of Manufacturers)

*The National Association of Manufaturers was founded in 1895 to advance a pro-growth, pro-manufaturing policy agenda. More than a century later the NAM continues to be the leading voice for manufacturers in the USA.*

*The purposes of NAM are to enhance the competitiveness of manufacturers and improve living standards for working Americans by shaping a legislative and regulatory environment conducive to US economic growth and to increase understanding among policy-makers, the media, and the general public about the importance of manufacturers to America's economic strength.*

### COMMENTS OF THE NATIONAL ASSOCIATION OF MANUFACTURERS REGARDING AN FTAA EARLY HARVEST STRATEGY

Provided for the IV Business Forum of the Americas

*March 16-18, 1998*

### INTRODUCTION

The National Association of Manufacturers (NAM) supports the goal of attaining a Free Trade Area of the Americas (FTAA), as first set forth at the Miami Summit of the Americas in January 1995.

At the Miami Summit of the Americas, it was not only agreed to target the conclusion of negotiations for 2005, but the 34 participating countries also collectively agreed "to make concrete progress toward the attainment of ... [a Free Trade Area of the Americas] by the end of this century." In order to maintain the momentum of long-term negotiations and to achieve interim concrete results, the notion of attaining an FTAA "early harvest" has been discussed.

The NAM supports the concept of an early harvest, as set forth below. Moreover, NAM strongly recommends that the Ministers at the March 1998 San José Ministerial formally agree to pursue an early harvest strategy and that they make the issues listed below part of the formal FTAA early harvest agenda.

### EARLY HARVEST GENERALLY

"Business facilitation issues" have been a central theme of early harvest discussions. These proposals are considered realistic and achievable as they do not require formal negotiation or legislation, but instead lend themselves to voluntary adoption unilaterally or collectively by businesses and governments alike. Even if negotiations or legislation are required, these issues are generally not considered controversial and thus implementation should not be hindered. In fact, their implementation is key to the facilitation of international business transactions and the NAM urges that they be pursued with vigor. NAM-supported business facilitation issues are detailed below.

An early harvest strategy should definitely focus on more than just business facilitation, however. For example, to advance concrete and integrated economic development in the region, transparent investment rules, regulations, and practices are a must. Latin America should not be painted with the "Asian flu" brush, but must demonstrate discipline and transparency in this area to assure its trading partners of liquidity, stability, and predictability.

In order to anchor actual trade negotiations, a formal Standstill Agreement should be reached immediately to ensure there is no backsliding as formal negotiations begin in earnest. In addition, de minimis duties (2 percent or lower) could be eliminated as a show of good faith. Finally, hemispheric adoption of multilaterally agreed zero-for-zero commitments, as well as a balanced and early duty reduction and elimination package, would be instrumental in shoring up FTAA progress. (See further details below.)

As transparency is one of the most important issues for trading partners, one goal might be to agree to hemispheric adoption of an FTAA provision mandating transparency in all participating countries' administrative and regulatory procedures (for example, something striving to encompass such core principles as those embodied in the US Administrative Procedures Act).

Another early harvest item might include a hemispheric agreement regarding public procurement that incorporates the core elements of the WTO Government Procurement Agreement and the NAFTA Chapter 10 government procurement provisions. Adoption of the Reference Paper on Basic Telecommunications would be another important step towards early liberalization in the hemisphere. Finally, recognition and ratification of the OAS convention, and adoption of the OECD convention (following the example set by Argentina, Brazil, and Chile) on anti-bribery would be a key hemispheric early harvest item.

A defined and useful role for the Private Sector should be set forth as soon as possible. The business sector obviously has the hands-on experience of hemispheric transactions and has much to contribute to the process. Furthermore, formal and productive hemispherically integrated discussion and submission of business proposals will not only strengthen the content of any final FTAA agreement but produce its own early harvest of closer hemispheric business ties.

## BUSINESS FACILITATION ISSUES

The following is a non-exclusive list of business facilitation issues that U.S. manufacturers would like to see pursued in an FTAA early harvest:

## Distribution of Information

NAM supports the compilation and publication of as much information as possible to enhance the ability to conduct free and fair hemispheric transactions. That information should be made available through a myriad of mediums, including an FTAA homepage. The information should be as comprehensive as possible and updated regularly to make it useful. Information to be disseminated should include:

- data regarding hemispheric trade flows, foreign direct investment flows, tariffs (for individual countries and for hemispheric regional blocs), non-tariff barriers, subsidies, and national payment instruments for commercial transaction;
- guidelines for customs procedures;
- an inventory of hemispheric laws and regulations regarding competition;
- an inventory of regulations, a list of agencies responsible for public sector procurement, and a list of goods and services frequently purchased by governments;
- an inventory of hemispheric consumer-based market research and market-needs analysis for goods and services;
- an inventory of regulations and a list of agencies responsible for administering dumping and countervailing laws and regulations;
- an inventory of regulations and a list of agencies responsible for intellectual property rights;
- an inventory of regulations pertaining to, and a list of agencies responsible for, electronic commerce;
- an inventory of regulations and a list of agencies responsible for industrial standards and sanitary and phytosanitary regulations;
- an inventory of regulations and a list of agencies responsible for foreign direct investment;
- an inventory of corporate tax policies, updated regularly to reflect any changes made thereto;
- an inventory of regulations and a list of agencies responsible for environmental policies, updated regularly to reflect any changes made thereto;
- a progress report on WTO rules compliance by the 34 participating countries within the hemisphere;
- a continually updated inventory of infrastructure projects and invitations to international tenders;
- official written comments on the progress, including recommendations and conclusions of, the governmental Hemispheric Working Groups (HWGs) as they proceed with formal negotiations and in response to proposals of the Business Forum of the Americas; and
- the effective date and details for operation of any business facilitation measures generally agreed to.

## Education

U.S. manufacturers support the promotion of a symposium on business facilitation with international organizations (including the UN), governments (including customs agencies), and the private sector to update the participants on developments and present suggestions on business facilitation, and to promote increased cooperation between sister agencies such as customs and standards certification entities.

## Customs Procedures

NAM supports a harmonized, efficient, hemispheric customs system. To that end, NAM supports early hemispheric agreement on the following:

- collective adoption of the WCO Harmonized System;
- collective adoption of internationally accepted customs forms and procedures;
- agreement to harmonize and simplify customs procedures on the basis of the Kyoto convention;
- collective adherence to the UN Electronic Data Exchange System (EDE) that includes the exchange of structured message EDIFACT/UN;
- collective adoption of an advanced classification ruling system providing certainty regarding classification information prior to importation;
- collective adoption of customs rules and procedures to speed processing and effectively facilitate voluntary compliance, including electronic filing and pre-shipment clearance;
- the establishment of simplified customs procedures for low-cost shipments;
- collective adoption of simplified customs procedures, including the ATA Carnet Convention, for temporary duty-free importation of products;
- adoption of the principles of the WTO Intellectual Property Agreement (TRIPS) to implement border enforcement of standard procedures for administering intellectual property rights;
- agreement to implement the Agreement on Interpretation of Article VII (Customs Valuation) of GATT 1994 to prevent against the burgeoning of differing import-price determining regimes;
- collective agreement to facilitate the creation and use of free trade zones and bonded warehouses; and
- collective adoption of a clear appeals provision to provide a means for business to challenge Customs decisions which they feel are erroneous or inequitable.

## Public Procurement

Government procurement practices throughout the hemisphere should be non-discriminatory, transparent in their administration, and free from corrupt practices. To that end, the NAM strongly urges:

- adequate notice for evaluating projects and preparing bids and, in large or complex contracts, pre-qualification of bidders;
- the use of neutral or internationally recognized standards wherever possible and the use of performance standards to ensure that equivalent products are treated equally;
- that objective criteria should be specified, as should be the formula by which they will be applied, which formula should be ascertainably followed in the selection process;
- that bids should be opened in public in the presence of all bidders;
- that contracts should be awarded to the lowest compliant bidder on the basis of objective criteria or, in appropriate sectors (for example, control processes, measurement and medical equipment), on the basis of a "best overall value" approach anchored by transparent criteria and evaluation procedures;
- that contracting agencies should provide unsuccessful bidders access to independent review of the bid process and its compliance with these principles, including adequate remedies for non-compliance by such agencies with such principles; and
- that the rights of the seller in its technical data and patents be considered and respected as is necessary in any fair and open government procurement process.

## Standards, Testing and Conformity Assessment

NAM supports:

- where applicable or appropriate (for example, the computer industry), promoting regulatory structures that reference: internationally accepted standards or suite of standards; one test or suite of tests to meet those standards; acceptance of a supplier's or third-party's test results; and acceptance of a supplier's declaration of conformity, without precluding the supplier from choosing the third-party certification route;
- the adoption of international standards, where they exist, or standards widely accepted within an industry;
- pursuit of sector-specific hemispheric Mutual Recognition Agreements (for example, telecommuni-

cations), not as an end in themselves, but as an interim step towards regional harmonization;

- basing all standards on sound scientific research and evidence;

- the establishment of a hemispheric central registry to which existing, proposed, and newly created standards would be notified; and

- the reduction of product marking/labeling requirements to a single hemispheric system for demonstrating conformity.

## Services

NAM supports the following:

- collective adoption of international accounting standards for use in the preparation of financial statements;

- improved hemispheric securities market clearance and settlement procedures;

- streamlined procedures for the unrestricted provision of financial information, particularly on a cross-border basis;

- streamlined procedures for the approval of foreign mutual fund investment;

- eliminating economic means tests and publishing clear, transparent rules for the establishment of financial entities;

- increasing the number and types of financial services that can be provided or consumed on a cross-border basis; and

- open participation in distribution services within and between countries.

## Other

NAM supports early hemispheric agreement on the following:

- simplification of visa issuing procedures for business travelers, including not requiring visas for short visits;

- the expedition of immigration procedures for business visitors;

- hemispheric participation in institutions such as ISO, Codex Alimentarius, and the Pacific Economic Consultation Council (PECC);

- the adoption of "Principles for International Contracts" developed by the International Institute for the Unification of Private Legislation (UNIDROIT);

- the adoption of informal mechanisms to mediate and arbitrate trade disputes;

- requesting the Inter-American Development Bank (IDB) to prepare a "White Book" showing the deficiencies of existing hemispheric infrastructure, including regional transportation difficulties and energy integration issues, outlining the investment needed to solve them, and listing the agencies responsible for project management and construction; and

- strengthening institutional consultation mechanisms between the HWGs and Ministerials and the private sector, by channeling information through a formal organization such as the BNHI.

## ADDITIONAL DETAILS FOR EARLY HARVEST ISSUES

### Investment

It is critical that Western Hemispheric investment regimes be non-discriminatory and transparent. Financing strategies must be based upon sound investment criteria. To avoid unfair competition in the attraction of international direct investment, there should be hemispheric agreement to only use incentives accepted by the WTO. Finally, intra-hemispheric investment flows should be supported by principles of MFN, national treatment, fair and equitable treatment, and impartial and fair dispute settlement.

### Tariff and Non-Tariff Measures

As was suggested in the Business Forum recommendations from Belo Horizonte, a hemispheric Standstill Agreement, covering both tariff and non-tariff measures, should be reached as soon as possible. Additionally, NAM urges early commitment to duty elimination through the adoption of GATT "zero-for-zero" packages (currently in effect for medical devices and semiconductor fabrication equipment). Such agreement could be part of a larger balanced duty reduction or elimination package comprised of the following types of concessions: undertakings to consider reducing high tariffs to levels that do not exceed a maximum duty rate or to levels to at least allow a minimal amount of trade to flow; elimination of "nuisance duties" (de minimis duties of 2 percent or below); and hemispheric adoption of multilaterally agreed zero-for-zero commitments. An early package could tackle tariffs in each of the three categories and seek to achieve hemispheric results modeled after agreements such as the ITA.

Such an early package could be agreed to on a non-contractual basis, providing that the country be bound only in the final FTAA package. The major contributions of countries such as the United States and Canada would be in the elimination of nuisance duties. The major contributions of countries such as Brazil would be in reducing some of their high duties. If actual implementation were prevented by the free rider problem associated with MFN requirements, it could be agreed early on that such reductions would be implemented as soon as the FTAA went into effect or as soon as third countries agreed to pay for their implementation.

## Role of the Private Sector

Establishing the role of the private sector should be done as soon as possible. It is important to define specific mechanisms for full private sector participation that provide a regular, predictable and useful framework for input. While it is recognized that formal trade negotiations are conducted on a government-to-government basis, parallel business community input will enhance both the content and the implementation of an FTAA.

To that end, at the national level, the NAM endorses regular and continuous briefings for the business community on the status of FTAA negotiations and recommends that the views of all private sector advisors, official and otherwise, be taken into consideration. At the hemispheric level, the NAM endorses the continuation of the Business Forum of the Americas, understanding that it may have to be modified to reflect that the FTAA process is entering the formal negotiating stage. NAM would be interested in seeing procedures for formal government responses to consensus forum recommendations, perhaps through set briefings from, or meetings with, Chairpeople of the HWGs, and at intervals of less than 12 months.

## CONCLUSION

The NAM supports the launching of formal hemispheric trade negotiations at the second Summit of the Americas to be held in Chile in April 1998. It is hoped that such negotiations will be based upon WTO disciplines and agreements as the floor for further progress.

The NAM strongly supports the concept of an FTAA early harvest to move the region concretely and progressively toward the goal of hemispheric trade integration. To that end, NAM urges the Ministers to explicitly direct the Vice Ministers to define and pursue an early harvest agenda by mid-1998, with first concrete results to be achieved by 2000 at the latest. Should early harvest issues be achievable before and after the year 2000, NAM supports a "rolling harvest" scenario as well.

It is hoped that all 34 participant countries will be diligent and creative in pursuing business facilitation and other easily achievable early harvest items. Hemispheric private sector participation is crucial to this goal, and the NAM stands ready to assist in the endeavor.

---

This paper was prepared by Dianne Sullivan, director of international trade policy of the NAM's Economic Policy Department, in close coordination with the NAM's member companies and the following associations: American Electronics Association, American Forest and Paper Association, American Iron and Steel Institute, Chemical Manufacturers Association, Coalition of Service Industries, Distilled Spirits Council of the United States, Grocery Manufacturers Association, Information Technology Industry Council, JBC International, Motor and Equipment Manufacturers Association, National Electrical Manufacturers Association, Telecommunications Industry Association, Transparency International USA, and the United States Council for International Business.

This paper was also prepared closely in conjunction with the North-South Center at the University of Miami and its Adjunct Senior Research Associate, Stephen Lande.

# VIII. Economic Integration and Free Trade

## Santiago: Launching the FTAA: Report to the San José Trade Ministerial

*The Council of the Americas Chamber of Commerce of the U.S. Association of American Chambers of Commerce in Latin America (AACCLA). The text (with input from member companies) was written by Ambassador Julius L. Katz, President, Hills & Company, and Robert C. Fisher, Managing Director, Hills & Company, February 1998.*

**The Council of the Americas** *is dedicated to promoting economic integration, free trade, open markets and investment, and the rule of law throughout the Western Hemisphere. Council members include approximately 250 leading manufacturing and services companies representing a broad spectrum of U.S. industry.*

*AACCLA is the umbrella group for 23 American Chambers of Commerce in 21 Latin American/Caribbean nations. Representing over 16,600 companies and individuals managing the bulk of U.S. investment in the region, AACCLA advocates trade and investment between the United States and the countries of the region through free trade, free markets, and free enterprise.*

**The United States Chamber of Commerce** *is the world's largest business federation representing an underlying membership of more than three million businesses and organizations of every size, sector, and region.*

The Council of the Americas, the U.S. Chamber of Commerce and the Association of American Chambers of Commerce in Latin America have sponsored and developed the enclosed paper for presentation at the IV Americas Business Forum in March 1998.

This paper, drafted by former Deputy U.S. Trade Representative Julius Katz and Robert Fisher, with input from our combined memberships, is intended to guide the development of private sector recommendations to Americas Business Forum leaders and Western Hemisphere Trade Ministers when they meet in San José, Costa Rica this March. The paper cogently restates the need to move forward on free trade and, as with similar documents presented at previous Business Fora, offers specific recommendations to advance the process of hemispheric trade liberalization as agreed to at the 1994 Miami Summit of the Americas. With negotiations scheduled for launching at the Santiago Summit in April, these recommendations which reflect the practical experiences of U.S. businesses in Latin America as well as of American Chambers of Commerce in the region, are designed to achieve substantial progress toward hemispheric integration by the year 2000.

As we continue to pursue the Summit of the Americas' vision of hemispheric trade liberalization, we look forward to successful meetings in San José. We hope that our suggestions help lay the groundwork for substantive progress towards advancing the goal of a Free Trade Area of the Americas.

Sincerely,

| *Everett Ellis Briggs* | *Thomas Donohue* | *Charles Preble* |
|---|---|---|
| President | President and CEO | President |
| Council of the Americas | U.S. Chamber of Commerce | AACCLA |

### EXECUTIVE SUMMARY

The Council of the Americas, the Chamber of Commerce of the U.S.A., and the Association of American Chambers of Commerce in Latin America believe that the effort to create a Free Trade Area of the Americas (FTAA) is at a critical milestone. In April 1998, hemispheric leaders are set to meet in Santiago, Chile, and are expected to launch negotiations for completing the FTAA by the year 2005.

Trade ministers will gather in Costa Rica in March to lay the groundwork for the Santiago Summit. They will focus on the goals, principles, and objectives for the negotiations, as well as matters related to organization, logistics and timing. Ministers also will consider how to fulfill the commitment made at 1994's Miami Summit to make "concrete progress" toward attainment of the FTAA by the end of this century.

Despite uncertainty over whether President Clinton will have new fast-track negotiating authority prior to Santiago, he and other hemispheric leaders should initiate FTAA negotiations when they meet in April. The launching of negotiations would be strengthened if the leaders also give clear instructions to trade ministers to reach interim arrangements that would make substantive progress toward the FTAA by the year 2000.

**The start of FTAA negotiations must be accompanied by a strong, sustained effort to mobilize public support on behalf of the FTAA.** Our political and business leaders need to get out the facts about the FTAA and trade: that expanded trade will promote economic growth and improve the standard of living of all our peoples. And we must find ways to address the legitimate concerns of those adversely affected by changing economic conditions.

## PRINCIPLES FOR THE NEGOTIATIONS

Beyond the principles already agreed to at the 1997 Belo Horizonte trade ministerial, we urge that governments agree that the FTAA:

- **Provide for full tariff elimination on all goods, and that all other restrictions on goods, services and investment will be eliminated unless specifically exempted.**
- **Contain disciplines of the highest order on all covered areas, exceeding those of the WTO where possible.**
- **Ensure that governments cannot derogate from existing environmental, health, safety, or labor measures as an encouragement to gain competitive advantage in trade or investment.**

Governments also should agree at the outset of negotiations not to raise or impose new tariffs, nor to impose new non-tariff barriers to trade in goods and services during the talks.

## RECOMMENDATIONS FOR EARLY ACTION

There are numerous steps that trade ministers could take at San José to help deliver on the commitment to substantial progress toward the FTAA by the year 2000, including commitments to:

- Increase transparency in the formulation and administration of government policies and practices in all areas affecting business, including standards and regulatory requirements and government procurement.
- Seek opportunities to eliminate tariff barriers on a sectoral basis, reduce tariff peaks, and eliminate "nuisance" tariffs.
- Enact customs facilitation and simplification measures.
- Simplify the creation and administration of standards and regulatory requirements.
- Reduce barriers to trade in services, including harmonization and mutual recognition of professional standards, simplifying procedures for business travel, and adherence to recent WTO agreements on telecom and financial services.
- Conclude a hemispheric convention on investment.
- Improve protection of intellectual property rights, including full implementation of the WTO's TRIPs agreement by the year 2000.
- Adhere to Organization of American States (OAS) and OECD accords combating corrupt business practices.

## ROLE OF THE PRIVATE SECTOR

More than ever, the private sector is committed to helping governments realize the goal of the FTAA, both by helping to mobilize public support for the agreement and through specific negotiating advice. Much of this assistance would be through efforts at the national level.

Work also should proceed at the multilateral level through the Americas Business Forum, in which business representatives from all nations involved in the FTAA can meet to develop common positions and recommendations. **The Forum should continue to meet with Trade Ministers on an annual basis and mechanisms should be established so that the Forum is kept abreast of the status of the negotiations and given feedback on the Forum's recommendations.**

## CONCLUSION

The time has come to make the vision of the FTAA a reality. The recommendations in the attached paper are intended as a guide to help translate political commitments into concrete achievements delivering early real benefits.

# Santiago: Launching the FTAA

The effort to create a Free Trade Area of the Americas (FTAA) is approaching a critical milestone. In April 1998, the leaders of the 34 democratically elected governments of the hemisphere are scheduled to meet in Santiago, Chile. There they are to launch the final negotiations for the FTAA, which are to be completed no later than the year 2005.

Trade Ministers of the 34 nations will gather at San José, Costa Rica, in March to lay the groundwork for the Santiago Summit. Among the decisions to be reached are those related to the goals, principles, and objectives that will guide the negotiations. Decisions also will be required about the timetable, as well as organization and logistics, including location (site or sites) and secretariat support facilities. Ministers also should recommend how to carry out the commitment made at 1994's Miami Summit to make "concrete progress" toward the attainment of the FTAA by the end of this century.

The United States private sector, as represented by the Council of the Americas, the Chamber of Commerce of the U.S.A., and the Association of the American Chambers of Commerce in Latin America, has endeavored to support this effort through the presentation of constructive recommendations. Once again, these organizations wish to take the opportunity to present their views on the major substantive issues to be faced by the ministers at San José and the heads of state at Santiago. In particular, they wish to recommend how concrete progress can be achieved in the period immediately ahead.

## LAUNCHING THE NEGOTIATIONS

Despite the uncertainty over whether the U.S. Congress will authorize new fast-track negotiating authority prior to the Santiago Summit, there is no legal reason why President Clinton should not be able to agree on behalf of the United States to initiate FTAA negotiations. An agreement to begin talks would allow negotiating groups to begin preliminary work – analysis of the issues, the formulation of conceptual approaches for the dismantling of restrictions surrounding the most difficult and most highly regulated sectors, discussion of the institutional arrangements for the FTAA, and preparation of initial texts of the agreement. None of this work would require advance legislative authority.

The agreement to launch the negotiations should be accompanied by instructions from the leaders to ministers to search for interim agreements and arrangements that would give expression to the Miami Summit's commitment to make substantive progress toward the FTAA by the turn of the century. Promising areas for early action include business facilitation, transparency, and harmonization of government procedures and policies. Bearing in mind the agreement of ministers at Belo Horizonte "to preserve and promote the essential interests of our 34 countries in a balanced and comprehensive manner", it should be possible to reach agreement on matters of common interest. Such agreements could be freestanding subjects that would not entail loss of bargaining position by participants in the more comprehensive FTAA negotiations.

## MOBILIZING PUBLIC SUPPORT

Underlying the challenge of creating the FTAA is a far more difficult task – mobilizing public support on behalf of the effort. It is clear that public support for free trade has eroded to varying degrees in a number of countries since the first Summit of the Americas at Miami. This is reflected most dramatically by the failure of the U.S. Congress to enact fast-track legislation and by increasing calls for protection in a number of countries, including Argentina, Brazil, and Mexico.

There are several reasons for the decline of support for free trade. There is a lingering reaction to the Mexican peso crisis in late 1994 and early 1995 and the contagious effects it caused. Increasing current account deficits in certain countries and the recent financial crisis in Southeast and East Asia are other major factors. These specific problems serve to exacerbate concerns over job security and stagnant wages that arise from the dislocations sometimes caused by change.

The fears and concerns over what is loosely described as "globalization" need to be attacked at two levels. First, the ability of nations to adopt and maintain free-trade policies depends on complimentary macroeconomic policies. Without sound fiscal and monetary policies, an open investment regime, and non-burdensome regulation, free trade cannot be sustained. In addition, as the financial crises in this hemisphere and in Asia have demonstrated, it is necessary to have strong prudential regulation, accompanied by full disclosure of financial and economic data to provide a sound underpinning to investor confidence. Pro-competitive policies and a fair, effective judicial system also bolster investor confidence and lead to more choice at lower cost for the consumer.

Perhaps most importantly, popular backing of free trade requires strong and continuing leadership. Support for free trade does not well up from the grass roots. The many benefits our economies derive from globalization – lower priced, higher quality goods and services; better paying jobs; increased economic efficiencies – often are diffused throughout society and are overlooked or undervalued by many people. But economic dislocations – whether or not the result of globalization – provide graphic illustrations and instant sound bites for those promoting misguided protectionist policies.

We therefore need strong leadership at the top to increase public awareness of the importance of trade and its benefits. The primary responsibility for leadership rests with governments, supported by the private sector, both of which need to educate the public. Expanded trade promotes economic growth, which in turn improves conditions of life and standards of living. It is only by means of economic growth that nations can afford all of the things their people need and desire, including education, public infrastructure, health care, safety net, a clean environment, and above all economic opportunity.

But education alone is not enough. We need to find ways to address the legitimate concerns of those adversely affected by change. Globalization is but one of many factors that cause change. But in the final analysis, it matters little whether the dislocation is the result of technology, immigration, migration from rural to urban areas, or increased imports. Whatever the cause, the proper answer will rarely be to attempt to turn back the clock. The more sustainable approach will be to promote alternative opportunities through better education and higher or different skill levels for workers, and policies that encourage investment.

In this century, the alternatives to free trade and open economies have been tried and found wanting. Over the past decade, most nations of the world have thrown off the failed policies of protectionism, excessive regulation and state control of economies in favor of trade expansion, deregulation, and privatization. The painful lessons of economic mismanagement are too fresh in memory to permit a return to the failed policies of the past.

It is encouraging that most governments have not yielded to reverse course. On the contrary, they have realized that the Asian financial crisis calls for greater openings of their economies, rather than their closing.

This is reflected in the decisions of the APEC leaders to continue on the path toward trade liberalization and economic cooperation. Nothing less should be expected of hemispheric leaders.

But our political leaders need to do more than to agree among themselves; they need to persuade their constituents of the stake they all have in free trade and thereby help assure domestic support for trade. Our collective stake was clearly expressed in the statement in the Declaration of Principles from the Miami Summit of the Americas:

> "Our continued economic progress depends on sound economic policies, sustainable development, and dynamic private sectors. A key to prosperity is trade without barriers, without subsidies, without unfair practices, and with an increasing stream of productive investments. Eliminating impediments to market access for goods and services among our countries will foster our economic growth. A growing world economy will also enhance our domestic prosperity. Free trade and increased economic integration are key factors for raising standards of living, improving the conditions of people in the Americas and better protecting the environment."

As we look to begin the process of negotiating the FTAA, there is perhaps no more important mission for government and the private sector alike than that of education.

## THE GOALS OF THE FTAA

FTAA negotiators should seek a single agreement providing for elimination over a reasonable time period of all tariff and non-tariff restrictions on trade in goods and services; rules that facilitate the free flow of investment, and full protection of intellectual property rights. Fundamental to the free trade area are provisions assuring most-favored-nation treatment within the region; national treatment for goods, for firms, and investors; rights of establishment, transparency of national laws and regulations, and freedom of movement of business-related information and business personnel.

# VIII. ECONOMIC INTEGRATION AND FREE TRADE

## PRINCIPLES FOR THE NEGOTIATION

At Belo Horizonte, trade ministers agreed that there was "a significant measure of convergence on key principles" for the FTAA. These include:

- Consensus constitutes the fundamental of decision-making, "which seeks to preserve and promote the essential interests of our 34 countries in a balanced and comprehensive manner".
- The FTAA will constitute a single undertaking embodying all rights and obligations agreed upon.
- The FTAA will be consistent with the WTO agreements.
- Countries may negotiate and join the FTAA individually or as members of a sub-regional group.
- The needs, economic conditions and opportunities of smaller economies of the region should receive special attention; and the negotiations should be concluded by the year 2005, at the latest.

We concur with these principles and would add others. First, from the date of the formal initiation of the negotiations, **governments should pledge not to raise existing tariffs or impose new tariffs, nor to impose new non-tariff barriers to trade in goods and services.**

**Secondly, it should be agreed that the FTAA will provide for full tariff elimination on all goods, and that all other restrictions on goods, services, and investment will be covered unless specifically exempted from the agreement.**

**Finally, with respect to all areas to be covered by the FTAA, governments should strive for disciplines of the highest order, exceeding those of the WTO where possible.**

## TIMING AND PROCESS OF THE NEGOTIATION

It is well known that there is an unresolved issue regarding the timing and process of the negotiations, with the MERCOSUR countries, on the one hand, seeking a slower pace, with closer linkage and simultaneous resolution of issues. The United States, Canada, and others, on the other hand, prefer to make progress more rapidly and to resolve issues sequentially.

**We believe that the negotiations should move forward deliberately and as quickly as circumstances permit.** There is no need now to prescribe linkage among issues. Since, in the end, nothing will be agreed unless all is agreed, balance and comprehensiveness are assured. **The pace of work should therefore depend on the ability of the participants to agree upon specific issues, rather than seeking simultaneous agreement on all issues.**

The establishment of a fixed timetable would be unrealistic at this time. However, **Ministers should schedule review sessions between the launch of the negotiations and the year 2000 to serve as mileposts, at which there can be reviews and assessments of the progress of the negotiations.**

## MAJOR RECOMMENDATIONS

### Market Access for Goods

Eliminating all tariff and non-tariff barriers to trade at the earliest feasible time is one of the main goals of the FTAA. Most leaders in the hemisphere understand that the expansion of trade that results from eliminating trade barriers can provide a major stimulus to economic growth and improve living standards. How to achieve full elimination is the major challenge facing the negotiators. In many instances, appropriate transitional arrangements can alleviate the anxieties and opposition of those accustomed to existing in protected environments. At the same time, achieving early progress where possible in particular sectors or on specific issues of benefit to all parties would create momentum and provide confidence in the liberalization process.

**We therefore recommend that Ministers instruct negotiators to seek interim agreements to:**

- Support and participate in efforts in the WTO to eliminate tariffs and non-tariff measures on a sectoral basis.

Asia-Pacific Economic Cooperation (APEC) leaders at their Vancouver meeting identified 15 sectors that could be fully liberalized on a multilateral basis. Many of these should be of interest to countries of this Hemisphere, whose support could assure adoption in the WTO. Achievement of this volume of trade liberalization would constitute a major building block for the FTAA. As a first step, we urge those nations that have not signed on to the Information Technology Agreement to do so.

- Reduce tariffs within the hemisphere to levels not to exceed 10 percent where barriers cannot be eliminated quickly.

Since such action would be in the interests both of individual countries and in furtherance the goal of the FTAA, we encourage governments to avoid exceptions. Countries taking such action could be given credit in the final balancing of commitments for elimination of all trade barriers.

- Eliminate immediately tariffs below five percent.

Such tariffs frequently have nothing more than a nuisance value. Their elimination would have a positive economic effect and, again, would give impetus to the larger FTAA negotiations.

## Customs

Among the subjects for potential early agreement are trade facilitation measures. None are more significant than customs harmonization and simplification. Agreement in this area would benefit all and involve no loss of negotiating position for anyone. **Our specific recommendations are that:**

- **Early agreement be reached on the harmonization of customs systems based on the Harmonized Tariff system, the World Trade Organization (WTO) Valuation Agreement and the revised Kyoto Customs Convention;**
- **Customs procedures throughout the region be simplified through the adoption of common forms and increased use of technology; and**
- **Agreement be reached to increase transparency in customs rule-making and procedures.**
- **Governments that have not already done so sign on to the ATA Carnet Convention (the Istanbul Convention) for the temporary duty-free admission of goods.**
- **Nations adopt the APEC Sub-Committee on Customs Procedures (SCCP) plan for customs harmonization, with two additional provisions for measuring customs release times and compliance with customs measures.**
- **Governments implement the June 4, 1996, Cancun Memorandum of Obligation to harmonize customs procedures for express shipments.**

## Standards and Regulatory Requirements

We believe that technical and sanitary and phytosanitary standards and regulatory requirements provide another area where early agreement would make a positive contribution to facilitating trade. As we have done previously, **we recommend an agreement that would provide for:**

- Rules on transparency assuring publication of regulations in readily accessible official journals, advance notice of proposed rule-making, with opportunity for public comment and advance notice of final rules and regulations;
- Simplification and harmonization of standards and specifications, technical requirements, and regulatory procedures, including promotion of the use of applicable international, regional, or widely accepted industry standards;
- Establishment of mutual recognition agreements for conformity assessment and certification, laboratory accreditation, and product markings that would promote regional adoption of the principles of *"approved once, accepted everywhere"*;
- Adoption of the approach of "One Standard-One Test, Supplier's Declaration of Conformity" in developing regulations to implement internationally agreed technical standards;
- Establishment of a central registry to which existing and proposed standards would be notified; and
- A dispute resolution mechanism to assure that technical and sanitary and phytosanitary standards are based on legitimate health and safety requirements and are not disguised barriers to trade.

## Services

Services represent a dominant portion of the economies of the region and are growing rapidly. Trade in services to date is for the most part concentrated in the fields of retail, tourism, transportation, and travel. Financial services, telecommunications, information technology, professional services and transportation remain highly regulated and restricted. If countries in the hemisphere are to become more competitive globally, it is essential that they accelerate the deregulation and privatization of the services sector. Such measures can, of course, be undertaken unilaterally in each country's self-interest, but an agreement in the context of the FTAA can provide a catalyst for action and investment and growth.

Recognizing that the negotiation of such an agreement will be integral to the larger FTAA negotiations, we believe that certain interim steps can be taken to facilitate trade in services. **We recommend that early agreements be reached to provide for:**

# VIII. Economic Integration and Free Trade

- Simplified procedures for business travel;

Current laws and regulations in many countries are burdensome, time-consuming and costly to business enterprises. The rapid growth of trade requires that firms be able to serve their customers and train employees by quickly moving professional and technical personnel between countries for temporary periods of time. The simplification of the granting of visas and work permits would be a significant facilitator of trade.

- **Adoption of the OECD Guidelines Governing the Protection of Privacy and Transborder Flows of Personal Data;**

These guidelines are widely employed by companies and nations globally. They are an essential element of the global information infrastructure on which electronic commerce will be based.

- **Adherence to and implementation of the WTO agreements on basic telecommunications and financial services;**

- **Clear, transparent professional qualification requirements and procedures, technical standards and licensing requirements based upon objective criteria such as professional competence and ability to provide the service;**

- **Transparent rules and regulations governing the provision of a particular service, with advance notice and the opportunity for public comment on such rules and regulations; and**

- **Harmonization or mutual recognition of professional services standards.**

These measures would contribute significantly to the facilitation and expansion of trade in services as well as to the negotiation of the eventual services component of the FTAA.

## Investment

Economic problems in Asia have caused some observers to question the wisdom of allowing investment to flow freely. We therefore are extremely heartened that the nations of this Hemisphere remain committed to continuing a process of deregulation and privatization that has encouraged hundreds of billions of dollars in foreign capital to flow to the region.

We believe the time has come to formalize on a hemispheric basis the unilateral measures taken by countries to privatize and deregulate their economies and open them to foreign investment. This view has been endorsed by each of the Business Forums.

**As a first step toward negotiating a comprehensive investment accord within the FTAA, we urge countries to reach agreement on a hemispheric Convention on Investment to take effect by the year 2000.** The Convention would require that where nations already have opened their markets to foreign investment, they agree to provide for the following:

- National treatment;
- The right of establishment in sectors now opened to investment;
- Full and free repatriation of capital, profits, and dividends;
- Protection against expropriation, and fair, adequate, and effective compensation in cases where expropriation occurs; and
- A prohibition against performance requirements.

The Convention in essence would commit countries to maintain their current level of openness to investment as an initial step toward a comprehensive agreement on investment. In so doing, it would reassure domestic and foreign investors about the stability of the investment regimes in the hemisphere. Future liberalization, including an effective dispute settlement mechanism, would be left to the FTAA negotiations.

## Government Procurement

Despite the large-scale privatizations that have occurred in the hemisphere, government purchases account for a significant share of economic activity in many countries. Just as in private economic activity, the public sector should avail itself of the opportunity to purchase the highest quality goods and services at the lowest price, and the private sector should have the opportunity to sell to the public sector on a fair, transparent, and nondiscriminatory basis.

**Increasing the transparency of government procurement rules, procedures and practices is an area in which governments should reach a trade-enhancing early agreement.**

This action was recommended by the Business Forum of the Americas in 1997 and remains a high-priority business facilitation objective for U.S. companies. Such an agreement would help ensure that government purchases are carried out in an open and transparent process.

**As an additional step toward the negotiation of government procurement within the FTAA, we urge governments that have not already done so to become signatories of the WTO's Government Procurement Agreement.** While the FTAA's provisions on government procurement ultimately should provide for greater discipline and broader coverage than the WTO agreement, the latter would significantly advance the process of achieving a hemispheric agreement on government procurement.

## Intellectual Property Rights

In recognition of the key role that intellectual capital can play in the transfer of technology which enhances economic development, the nations of the Western Hemisphere have made tremendous progress in the protection and enforcement of intellectual property rights (IPR) – patents, copyrights, trademarks, and trade secrets. With many of the higher value-added economic activities increasingly dependent on IPR, it is essential that the FTAA set a new standard for IPR protection, going beyond the levels contained in any existing multilateral or regional trade agreement.

We believe that governments should take steps now to facilitate the transition toward new hemispheric disciplines governing intellectual property rights by:

- Accelerating their implementation of the WTO's Agreement on Trade-Related Aspects of Intellectual Property Rights (TRIPS) accord so that all commitments are fully implemented and enforced by the year 2000, including: restricting compulsory licensing, providing a 20-year patent term; protecting confidential data for 10 years; abolishing local manufacturing requirements; and fully implementing exclusive marketing rights.
- Ratifying the World Intellectual Property Organization (WIPO) Copyright Treaty and the WIPO Performances and Phonograms Treaty by the year 2000, while taking into account the need to address the scope of liability for any copyright infringement.

## Corrupt Business Practices

A free market works best to the extent that all distortions to trade and investment are eliminated. Bribery is among the worst of all distortions. It is inherently non-transparent, discriminatory, and costly to companies that unfairly lose business and societies whose institutions are undermined.

The Organization for Economic Cooperation and Development (OECD) recently concluded a strong anti-bribery convention that will criminalize foreign commercial bribery. The pact is due to enter into force by early 1999. Non-OECD members such as Argentina, Brazil, and Chile already have indicated that they intend to sign the convention.

**We urge every nation in the Hemisphere to sign, implement and enforce the OECD anti-bribery convention, so that it applies throughout the hemisphere by the year 2000. In addition, governments that have not done so should ratify and enforce the Organization of American States (OAS) Inter-American Convention Against Corruption.** Such actions would send a clear signal to the rest of the world that bribery and corruption have no place in modern society and would encourage other nations to join the accords.

## Labor and the Environment

The issue of whether to require enforceable provisions in trade agreements on labor and environmental standards has caused serious contention domestically and in international trade fora, such as the WTO, APEC and the FTAA.

We believe that expanded trade, through the negotiation of new trade agreements, stimulates increased wages, improved standards for workers, and job creation. Similarly, the economic growth stimulated by trade enables societies to dedicate additional resources to protecting the environment.

There is a clear consensus among business organizations that it is neither reasonable nor acceptable to link trade agreements to labor and environmental standards in other countries. We will continue to oppose fast track legislation that requires the enforcement of non-trade issues in trade agreements.

But we believe that labor and environmental concerns are needed to be considered. There are a number of existing multilateral fora where governments and private sectors can and should work together to address these issues. And we encourage hemispheric labor and environmental officials to continue their efforts to advance labor and environmental protections in conjunction with the Summit process.

There is, moreover, growing support for the idea that governments should not lower standards or derogate from regulations with the direct purpose of distorting trade or investment patterns. Provisions to address labor and environmental issues that are directly related to trade have been part of previous trade agreements. Such provisions were in draft fast-track legislation reported out of the House Ways and Means Committee that was strongly supported by the U.S. business community.

**We could support inclusion in the FTAA of a provision that governments not derogate from existing environmental, health, safety, or labor measures as an encouragement to gain competitive advantage in trade or investment.**

## Role of the Private Sector

The private sector is committed to helping the governments of the hemisphere realize the goal of the FTAA. It can do so by providing governments invaluable advice about the impact of trade and investment barriers on the conduct of business. The private sector also can help to mobilize public support within nations for the FTAA and for the legislative and policy changes that are necessary to bring it into being.

The private sector's participation in the FTAA process should take place at two levels. First, at the national level the private sector can contribute most directly to the negotiating process by providing guidance to the negotiators. In the United States and several other countries, advisory committees have been established under law to assist trade officials. Other nations might well consider emulating this arrangement, the effectiveness of which has been proven over the course of more than two decades.

Second, at the multilateral level, the creation of the Americas Business Forum after the Miami Summit has contributed to the formation of the negotiating agenda for the FTAA and to the activities of the Hemisphere Working Groups. The Business Forum enables representatives from all nations involved in the FTAA to exchange views on the many issues that will be encountered in the negotiations and to seek to develop common positions and collective recommendations to governments.

To make effective the work of the Americas Business Forum, **the Forum should continue to meet annually with ministers, and governments should establish mechanisms for providing to the Forum on a timely basis appropriate information on the progress of the negotiations, including feed-back on recommendations submitted by the Forum.**

## CONCLUSION

The time has come to make the vision of the FTAA a reality. While much useful preparatory work has been accomplished since the first Summit of the Americas, government declarations of support for the FTAA are no longer enough. Such declarations must be translated into concrete achievements.

There is a serious risk that without such achievements, the pendulum will tilt away from trade liberalization and integration toward policies of protection and restriction. The recommendations contained in this paper are intended as a guide to advance a process that will end in the realization of the Free Trade Area of the Americas.

For more information, please contact the following organizations…

**Council of the Americas**
1310 G Street, NW   Suite 690
Washington, DC  20005
Tel: (202) 639-0724   Fax: (202) 639-0794

**The U.S. Chamber of Commerce**
1615 H Street, NW
Washington, DC  20062
Tel: (202) 463-5485   Fax: (202) 463-3126

**The Association of American Chambers of Commerce in Latin America**
1615 H Street, NW
Washington, DC  20062
Tel: (202) 463-5485   Fax: (202) 463-3126

**The Council of the Americas** is dedicated to promoting economic integration, free trade, open markets and investment, and the rule of law throughout the Western Hemisphere. Council members include approximately 250 leading manufacturing and services companies representing a broad spectrum of U.S. industry.

**AACCLA** is the umbrella group for 23 American Chambers of Commerce in 21 Latin American/Caribbean nations. Representing over 16,600 companies and individuals managing the bulk of U.S. investment in the region, AACCLA advocates trade and investment between the United States and the countries of the region through free trade, free markets, and free enterprise.

**The United States Chamber of Commerce** is the world's largest business federation representing an underlying membership of more than three million businesses and organizations of every size, sector, and region.

The Council and AACCLA, together with the U.S. Chamber of Commerce in Chile, organized a highly successful and well-attended colloquium for public and private sector leaders in Santiago on the morning of April 17. Council Chairman Robert Mosbacher's speech outlining the goals of U.S. business in expanding free trade was well received and elicited many questions from the audience. Chairman Mosbacher also participated in a panel with Presidential Envoy Mack McLarty, Commerce Secretary Daley, U.S. Trade Representative Barshefsky, and Chilean Minister of Trade Alvaro Garcia.

# VIII. ECONOMIC INTEGRATION AND FREE TRADE

*This declaration was made by NGOs at the IV Ministerial of the Free Trade Area of the Americas on March 16-18, 1998, in San Jóse, Costa Rica.*

*The following organizations participated in the drafting of this document: Instituto Brasileiro de Direito para um Planeta Verde (IBDPV), Brazil; Canadian Institute for Environmental Law and Policy, Canada; Red Nacional de Acción Ecológica (RENACE), y Corporación Participa, Chile; Fundación Natura, Colombia; Centro de Derecho Ambiental y de los Recursos Naturales (CEDARENA), Costa Rica; PRONATURA, Rep. Dominicana; Centro Ecuatoriano de Derecho Ambiental, Corporación Latinoamericana para el Desarrollo (CLD), Fundación Natura y Fundación Futuro Latinoamericano, Ecuador; Instituto de Derecho Ambiental y Desarrollo Sustenable (IDEADS), Guatemala; Centro Mexicano de Derecho Ambiental (CEMDA) y Red Mexicana Acción Frente al Libre Comercio, Mexico; Fundación M. Bertoni, Paraguay; Fundación ECOS y Centro Latinoamericano de Ecología Social (CLAES) Uruguay; National Audubon Society, National Wildlife Federation, Environmental Law Institute and Center for International Environmental Law, United States; International Institute for Sustainable Development, Canada.*

# Declaration by Non-Governmental Organizations of the Hemisphere on the Occasion of the IV Ministerial of the Free Trade Area of the Americas

We, the undersigned representatives of civil society organizations from countries throughout the hemisphere, gathered here today, March 18, 1998, in San José, Costa Rica:

Recognize that our governments are concluding their preliminary discussions on hemispheric economic integration here at the Fourth Trade Ministerial of the Americas, and are about to launch formal negotiations for a Free Trade Area of the Americas (FTAA) at the Second Summit of the Americas in Santiago, Chile;

Support a just and equitable hemispheric integration process that improves the quality of life, reduces poverty, acknowledges the intrinsic value of nature and promotes sustainable development for all people and nations without exception;

Recognize that our governments have committed to the principles of sustainable development, including environmental protection, poverty alleviation and democratization, as established at the Miami Summit of 1994 and reaffirmed in Santa Cruz, Bolivia in 1996;

Recognize that trade agreements, when properly structured, can be consistent with the principles of sustainable development;

Are concerned that economic integration has advanced without effectively integrating environmental, labor, social, cultural and political components which are indispensible to achieving sustainable development;

Recognize that fair competition cannot be based on spurious competition that does not take into account environmental and social costs and recognize that there are transition costs associated with economic integration that must be taken into consideration.

Therefore, we call on our governments to establish an action plan and formal mechanisms to integrate the principles of sustainable development, including a formal negotiating group on trade, environment and sustainable development with equal status to other negotiating groups established in the FTAA process. Moreover, the protection and enhancement of environmental quality must become part of the negotiating objectives of all FTAA negotiating groups.

Public participation is fundamental to the sustainable development of the Hemisphere, and as such must be placed on the same level as the other negotiation objectives. To that end, in the design of the FTAA we call on governments to:

1. Strengthen the participation of civil society in judicial and administrative proceedings within a domestic environmental law framework and in the formation, negotiation, and implementation of trade and investment policies and agreements.

2. Provide timely access to information, relating to trade policy as well as trade agreement and integration processes.

3. Establish formal processes to permit and encourage timely contributions of a broad spectrum of civil society in the development of the FTAA. This must include the right to make verbal and written submissions and attend national and hemispheric meetings involving policy deliberations.

4. Implement dispute settlement mechanisms and other proceedings that allow for public participation.

5. Provide access to adequate financial resources to achieve the the above goals.

6. Make available Inter-American integration process-related documents to the public at the same time as they are circulated to governments to ensure timely and meaningful participation of the public in policy deliberations; these should be at no cost and in a variety of forms, including printed and electronic formats, and should also include the creation of a Data Center, at no cost.

7. Establish National Advisory Committees, with governmental and non-governmental representatives, that, among other objectives, should promote cross-sectoral dialogues and that are responsible for developing concrete recommendations for negotiations, and responses to recommendations offered by other countries.

8. Promote research, training and capacity building in the area of sustainable development.

9. Finance the participation of civil society in the trade and investment negotiations.

We further call on governments to:

1. Implement national and regional measures to ensure that economic integration in the Western Hemisphere promotes conservation of cultural and biological diversity and ecosystems in the hemisphere.

2. Ensure that the Negotiating Group on Intellectual Property Rights provides guarantees that rights, access and benefits are shared in an equitable manner.

3. Ensure that research on environmental, social and other effects of trade and investment is undertaken and that the results are distributed in a timely and effective manner to all interested parties.

4. Implement and enforce regulations and policies that ensure environmental protection, including cooperation to ensure the upward harmonization of standards.

5. Implement and enforce regulations and policies that ensure equitable distribution of benefits from trade and investment.

6. Reduce and eliminate unsustainable patterns of consumption and production within and among countries, recognizing the strains placed on the environment by the disproportionate consumption of resources by many industrialized countries.

7. Remove subsidies that encourage the unsustainable use of natural resources, as well as ensure the internalization of environmental externalities and promote incentives for sustainable production and consumption, including the development of national environmental accounting systems.

8. Ensure that Multilateral Environmental Agreements (MEAs) and their dispute resolution mechanisms have at least equal status to trade agreements in the conduct of international trade and in dispute resolution. Environmental disputes arising out of trade agreements should be resolved in multilateral negotiations.

As part of the FTAA negotiations we call on governments to:

1. Incorporate the precautionary principle, as well as the principles of environmental prevention and legal and financial responsibility of polluters for damages to the environment.

2. Create and strengthen administrative and judicial mechanisms for implementing environmental laws and policies, as well as mechanisms to denounce cases where national and international environmental norms are not applied.

3. Harmonize minimum standards, consistent with each ecosystem, that assure the protection of human health and environmental integrity. At the same time, include financial and cooperative mechanisms to ensure the transfer and creation of appropriate technologies,

including endogenous technologies, essential for the implementation and sustained improvement of environmental standards.

4. Establish mechanisms to periodically update and improve environmental standards with the participation of all interested parties (NGOs, business, labor, academics, etc.).

5. Ensure that nations, in their regulatory capacity, maintain the ability to set higher environmental standards.

6. As agreed to in the 1994 Miami Summit of the Americas, establish mechanisms for intergovernmental cooperation for the exchange of information, training, technology transfer and policy formulation; as well as the creation of greenmarkets.

# VIII. Economic Integration and Free Trade

*This position paper on the FTAA Process and the Role of the Private Sector was presented at the IV Americas Business Forum, March 16-18, 1998, in San José, Costa Rica.*

*Caribbean/Latin American Action (C/LAA) is a non-profit organization, governed by an international Board of Trustees, that promotes private sector-generated economic development in the Caribbean and Latin America. C/LAA has played an active role in engaging the business community in the move toward a Free Trade Area of the Americas. By serving as a vehicle for private sector input at each of the major FTAA meetings, including the Summit of the Americas and subsequent business forums in Denver, Colorado (1995); Cartagena, Colombia (1996); and Belo Horizonte, Brazil (1997). C/LAA's program of work is divided along a sectoral basis, where business teams of company representatives from each sector come together to identify public policy actions that governments could take to increase regional prosperity through trade and investment liberalization.*

## Launching Negotiations for the Formation of a "Free Trade Area of the Americas"

### I. BACKGROUND

Caribbean/Latin American Action (C/LAA) is a non-profit organization, governed by an international Board of Trustees, that promotes private sector generated economic development in the Caribbean and Latin America. C/LAA has played an active role engaging the business community in the move toward a Free Trade Area of the Americas by serving as a vehicle for private sector input at each of the major FTAA meetings, including the Summit of the Americas and subsequent business forums in Denver, Colorado (1995); Cartagena, Colombia (1996); and, Belo Horizonte, Brazil (1997). C/LAA's program of work is divided along a sectoral basis, where "business teams" of company representatives from each sector come together and identify certain public policy actions which governments could take to increase regional prosperity through trade and investment liberalization.

To focus on the issues addressed in the FTAA Business Fora, C/LAA asked each Business Team to prepare a set of recommendations, place them within the context of an actual problem that is impeding trade or investment in the region, and provide an example of that problem, where useful. For the 1998 Costa Rica Business Forum, the Business Teams separated these recommendations into groups according to the 10 workshops under which the Business Forum is organized.

Throughout 1997, C/LAA circulated its **Business Team Sectoral Papers "Moving Towards Free Trade for the Americas"** to over 200 companies in the hemisphere for contributions, commentary and follow-up work. More than 75 hemispheric companies and private sector institutions responded and provided input to the sectoral documents. As the papers incorporate the views of a large number of companies, they include a very broad range of concerns and, in some instances, reflect dissenting views.

In addition, much of this work and the input from these collaborating partners was incorporated into a variety of discussions at the **1997 Miami Conference on the Caribbean and Latin America: "The Americas 1997 - A New World for Business."** In close collaboration with these counterparts, with the organizers of the IVth Business Forum of the Americas and the Ministry of Foreign Trade of Costa Rica, and with the assistance of Manchester Trade, Ltd., C/LAA has been able to advance on many of these proposals regarding the FTAA process, focusing primarily on the fundamental issue of the participation and role of the private sector in the hemispheric free trade and integration process. This document is a reflection of that collaboration.

Recognizing that FTAA leadership must come from within each country, C/LAA encourages participation from throughout the region and will coordinate a delegation of C/LAA Business Team Members and Trustees to present the recommendations outlined below at the Business Forum workshops and panels in San José.

## II. PREFACE

Through its **1997 Miami Conference "The Americas 1997: A New World for Business,"** C/LAA offered an opportunity for our private sector Business Teams to prepare contributions to the IVth Americas Business Forum, held in San José), Costa Rica from March 16-18, 1998. Through both public and private sector Conference Sessions on the FTAA process, and with additional sectoral Business Team Meetings, C/LAA was able to provide a medium for private sector dialogue and recommendations regarding the FTAA process. This has now resulted in C/LAA's Position Paper to the IVth Americas Business Forum, and seeks to provide the foundation for C/LAA's work and contribution to the Business Forum meetings of San José). The C/LAA Position Paper has been designed to accomplish four (4) objectives.

### A. Put forth some general private sector principles that ought to be observed throughout the FTAA negotiations.

To reiterate the importance of launching FTAA negotiations in April. To emphasize the importance of early concrete results, consistent with the work program agreed at the San José) Trade Ministerial and formally ratified in Chile at the IInd Summit of the Americas. Early results should be geared toward both (i) facilitating ongoing hemispheric business; and (ii) choosing key negotiating approaches to difficult issues. The Statement reflects the private sector's expectations that the FTAA negotiations should go beyond the results of the Uruguay Round and any further progress made in the World Trade Organization (WTO) during the eight year time frame for FTAA negotiations.

### B. Establish some benchmarks for what should be viewed as the "full participation" of the private sector in the negotiation process.

To address the type of mechanisms necessary to allow full private sector input into the process. This input must take place both on the national and hemispheric levels. It must allow for input with respect to general rules governing hemispheric integration, specific measures for trade liberalization, and sectoral programs designed to increase the overall competitiveness. Trade Ministers at San José must not only recognize the importance of private sector involvement but must agree on the specific mechanisms for its participation.

### C. Confirm full private sector support for both the FTAA and non-FTAA initiatives of the Summit process.

To recognize that the FTAA process is part of the overall hemispheric integration process launched in Miami in 1994, and to therefore emphasize that the process must contribute to goals beyond free trade, including the goals of education, democracy, and self-sustainable economic growth, among others. C/LAA reaffirms the need for private sector participation in the IInd Summit of the Americas of Santiago, Chile in April 1998, thus allowing for greater input of the business community into specific non-trade areas of the hemispheric integration agenda. Not allowing for a private sector role in the Summit would serve to weaken the hemispheric integration process as there is no meaningful linkage between the Heads of State/Government and the civil societies which they seek to integrate.

### D. Affirm the importance of the United States passing fast track and other countries eschewing the adoption of protectionist measures to deal with any possible economic crisis.

To address the importance of passing fast track with a bipartisan majority early in 1998. To emphasize the need for commitments to pass fast track legislation even if it means eschewing short term political gains. It will also urge any country in the hemisphere faced with economic pressure from the spread of the so-called Asian Flu to deal with their problem through market liberalization, and not return to protectionist instruments.

## III. C/LAA RECOMMENDATIONS: THE FTAA PROCESS

**The Trustees, Contributors, and Business Team Members of C/LAA:**

A. Voice their strong support for the efforts of the 34 democratically elected Governments of the Western Hemisphere, the private sectors of the participating countries, and the many international non-governmental organizations (NGOs) (most particularly the Economic Commission for Latin America and the Caribbean, the Inter-American Development Bank, and the Organization of American States) to be prepared to formally open negotiations for the formation of the "Free Trade Area of the Americas" (FTAA) at the IInd Summit of the Americas (SOA) of Hemispheric Heads-of-State, scheduled for April, 1998.

B. Anticipate an FTAA negotiation whose results, achieved no later than 2005, would link all the participating countries in a "Free Trade Area" in which the movement of all goods and services would be subject to rules and practices which, in a number of areas, would be more liberal than provided for under the World Trade Organization (WTO).

C. Call on the negotiators of the FTAA to produce agreements or understandings which would facilitate hemispheric trade and investment, and for which it is realistic to expect implementation by all participants by the year 2000. Examples of the type of agreements or understandings include:

1. A hemispheric Customs Code
2. Adherence to mutual recognition arrangements and conformity agreements
3. Harmonization of agricultural sanitary and phytosanitary standards (SPS), industrial standards (SPS)
4. Rules governing the supply of services
5. Hemispherically accepted documentation for business travellers
6. Requirement that consultations precede any government action which raises levels of protection
7. Elimination of nuisance duties, i.e. duties below 1.0 percent

D. Urge the negotiating Governments to agree by the end of 2000 on the key objectives for each of the negotiating topics (e.g. intellectual property rights,) and on negotiating approaches.

E. Agree that decisions on negotiating approaches should always take into account the special needs of the smaller economies. The participants recognized that accommodations for the smaller economies would vary, depending on the topic under discussion.

F. Request negotiators and Negotiation Groups to give consideration to the special situation of micro, small and medium-size businesses on a cross-national basis.

G. Reiterate the intention of the private sector to fully participate in the process of hemispheric integration. In this regard, urged the negotiating Governments to make provision for the full participation of the private sector and other stakeholders in the negotiating phase. Such participation should be realized at the national and subregional level, as well as in framework of a hemispheric-wide process.

H. Recommend that at the national level, Governments and members of the private sector should be free to establish consultation procedures which are best suited to their local situation. However, guidelines, especially for organizing the consultation process in smaller economies should be made available. For example, one model of an organizational framework is provided by the Private Sector Commission for International Negotiations (CENI), created by the Dominican Republic business community with the support of the government. To increase its effectiveness, the Commission is organized to assure the following:

1. Comprehensive representation of established business groups, thus fostering sufficient technical competence in the private sector so as to be in position to advise on all technical issues under negotiation;
2. Recognition by the Dominican Government that CENI is the spokesperson for the private sector in matters of FTAA negotiations;
3. Development within the private sector, and between the private sector and the government of consensus positions on trade policy principles;
4. That CENI would receive a steady flow of information about the negotiations; and,
5. Provision of a special facilities to involve micro, small and medium-sized companies.

I. Acknowledge Guatemala as providing an additional model of private - public sector collaboration. Similar advances have been made by Guatemala's public and private sectors preparation for trade negotiations under the aegis of the Business Commission for International Trade Negotiations (CENCIT).

J. Advise that at the subregional level, private sector participation may not require development of new entities. Effective mechanisms have been based on both formal and informal coordination of the views between national organizations.

K. Suggest that at the hemispheric level, the Business Forum of the Americas has shown that it is a suitable means for the national private sectors, meeting together, to provide thoughtful advice to Governments, and to collaborate on measures which could be implemented by Governments without entering into the formal negotiation of the FTAA.

- While C/LAA Trustees, Contributors, and Business Team Members endorse the continuation of the Business Forum of the Americas, we also recognize that the Forum format may have to be modified to reflect the fact that the FTAA process is entering the negotiating stage. In this regard, C/LAA welcomes the decision of the organizers of the Americas Business Forum-San José) '98 to treat the subject of Services in the FTAA through sectoral workshops on Telecommunications Services, Information Technologies and Electronic Commerce Services, Financial Services, 'Professional Services, Courier Services, Engineering and Construction Services, and Tourism Services.
- C/LAA recommends modifying the Business Forum to ensure that it meets more often than once a year, that procedures are established to ensure that governments respond to consensus Forum recommendations at intervals of less than 12 months, and that Forum procedures recognize that private sector entities representing groups of businesses reflect a broader consensus than individual companies.

L. Reflect the view that "full participation" by the private sector and other stakeholders should mean that Governments have taken into account these groups' advice and recommendations covering i) general rules governing trade and investment measures under subregional integration schemes; ii) specific measures for trade and investment liberalization; and iii) sectoral initiatives designed to increase the competitiveness of hemispheric exporters.

M. Affirm that the FTAA negotiations were mandated in the context of a vital and continuing process of hemispheric integration and reform, as reflected in the Summit Action Agenda agreed to by the Heads of State at the Ist Summit of the Americas of December 1994 in Miami.

N. Recognize the essential relationship between the goals of the FTAA and those of the other Summit Action topics, including the goals of education, democracy, and self-sustaining economic growth.

O. Express an interest in exploring ways in which this relationship could be reflected in the overall Summit Action Plan, to be agreed at the Santiago Summit.

P. Appeal to the United States to demonstrate support for the FTAA negotiations by early passage of "fast-track" legislation covering all aspects of the agreed FTAA negotiating framework.

Q. Strongly urges Governments participating in the FTAA to avoid the adoption of any protectionist measures, and proposes that under the current international economic system, there are available many effective ways to deal with financial and monetary problems other than the raising of barriers to trade in goods and services, or to foreign investment and investors.

## IV. C/LAA RECOMMENDATIONS: THE PRIVATE SECTOR FOCUS

Many private sector businesses from throughout the hemisphere approach their work within the framework of a particular sector (i.e., energy, transportation, agribusiness, telecommunications, etc.) This focus limits the capacity to envision the entire FTAA process, and how it affects individual companies doing business in the region.

The private sector has a common interest in receiving better access to information about *existing tariff and non-tariff barriers,* and about the *schedule and parameters of FTAA negotiations* so that they can more effectively express their concerns and positions within the process.

Lack of information is a critical barrier towards effective private sector participation in the FTAA process. The release of information about existing trade barriers and about the parameters of negotiations should not be treated by governments as a subject for negotiation. The private sector must have access to information in order to have a fair and effective participation in the process.

Organizations like Caribbean/Latin American Action should encourage their constituencies to think broadly about the concept of a Free Trade Area of the Americas, and urge them to actively participate in the future Business Fora and Trade Ministerials.

Governments should encourage organizations like C/LAA that successfully coordinate private sector input for the FTAA meetings. The role of the private sector in government-led negotiations is becoming increasingly important and critical to the successful negotiation of trade agreements. Countries that have advanced on incorporating private sector and other civil society participation on their negotiations have benefitted enormously from these new resources. Critical examples of this are the national negotiation bodies of Guatemala and the Dominican Republic, to name but two, in their negotiations at the sub-regional level in Central America and the Caribbean.

The business community should attend C/LAAs annual Miami Conference on the Caribbean and Latin America, as this conference is an official Summit follow-up event that incorporates sessions on FTAA progress, and offers a venue for business leaders from throughout the hemisphere to come together and address important issues facing the region.

## V. RESPONSIVENESS TO PRIVATE SECTOR INPUT

FTAA Working Groups should respond in a timely manner to recommendations and concerns raised in the annual Business Fora. Presentations at the Business Fora should be used to engage an ongoing discussion and dialogue between the public and private sectors of the hemisphere.

Governments in each country must establish a means for ongoing consultation with the local private sector. Likewise, governments must develop a credible and reliable mechanism for disseminating information to local businesses and associations. Specifically:

- Governments should notify the private sector of who represents the country in FTAA negotiations and Working Group meetings;
- Working Groups should release agendas in advance of meetings so that the business community may contact their government representatives to express their positions, and should consider releasing minutes of meetings to the private sector for comment;
- Private sector advisory groups should be established in each country as part of the FTAA process and should have direct input to the negotiating parties.

Governments should ensure transparency not only in the FTAA negotiation process, but also in the process by which national policies are developed.

Information sharing between all parties involved must improve. Better information must be supplied to the negotiators involved in the FTAA process from both the private sector and the scientific community in each country. There must be greater efforts at mobilization of the private sector in order to generate improvement in this area.

## VI. SMALL ECONOMY ISSUES

Small economy issues should be addressed by all working groups and during all negotiations, while at the same time allowing for specific FTAA discussions on the question of small economy needs and requirements, as well as capabilities to engage the full commitments of the FTAA. Future business fora and trade ministerials should integrate discussion of small economies within each of the other technical areas involved in the creation of an FTAA. This allows and encourages advocates of small economies to be represented throughout the process. In this regard, C/LAA supports the proposal to incorporate a Small Economies Working Committee with participation permeating all Negotiation Groups.

In addition to focussing on the participation and special circumstances of small economies in the FTAA process, C/LAA Business Teams have identified the need for special focus on the role and participation of micro, small, and medium-sized firms — on a cross-national basis — in the FTAA process and the special requirements for their effective participation and access to the benefits of hemispheric integration. The Working Committee on Small Economies should expand its focus to include this special and unique aspect of small size in the FTAA process.

Functional guidelines are required regarding the availability of and access to technical assistance (TA) resources which would enable small economies to maximize their role and participation in the FTAA process. Given the critical importance of small firms, as well as small economies, as key actors in the process of free trade and hemispheric integration, private sector input and participation in the TA process should be ensured in order to allow and provide for practical business experience and resources in support of the process.

C/LAA endorses the recommendations of the FTAA Working Group on Small Economies and supports the findings and recommendations of the Independent Group of Experts on Smaller Economies and Western Hemispheric Integration (c. May 1997), with particular emphasis on the following issues:

- The FTAA should recognize that smaller economies face particular policy concerns and limitations with regards to facilitating their effective participation in the FTAA. As such, the development of appropriate mechanisms and measures to facilitate their participation in the FTAA must be a joint effort of the hemispheric community as a whole.

- Various technical trade issues need to be given special attention with regards to the participation of small economies, such as:
- Trade frictions and their impact on the FTAA process
- Investment and capital flows measures
- Comprehensive services negotiations, especially regarding tourism
- Labor mobility
- Tariff liberalization and its impact on fiscal revenues
- Facilitation of technical and financial assistance mechanisms
- Trade negotiation compatibility with the Lomé Convention

## VII. ADVANCING FREE TRADE THROUGH BUSINESS FACILITATION

Through the various Business Forums to-date, C/LAA has continuously supported initiatives to advance **Business Facilitation** at the level of unilateral and/or coordinated/multilateral agreements between governments, seeking to advance and simplify trade, investment, and other business transactions by reducing business costs and risks and/or by simplifying the administrative practices regulating business. More often than not, these are understood to be measures which target certain domestic policies or practices without necessarily requiring major changes in the legislative and regulatory frameworks in place.

Through the temporary and partial implementation of some of these measures, the FTAA process should seek to advance business, trade, and/or commercial initiatives and policies which promote business facilitation. Despite an initial focus on "concrete progress" initiatives, hemispheric disillusionment remains with these measures as they have not resulted in meaningful and tangible measures for advancing business at the hemispheric level.

Advancing specific and implementable "Business Facilitation Measures" has become a central theme for San José '98 at the IVth Americas Business Forum. The main concern for the private sector remains whether or not such initiatives would actually result in direct benefits to the private sector engaged in regional and hemispheric business. To encourage concrete results, C/LAA supports various business facilitation measures identified by its Business Teams and by other organizations providing input to the FTAA process[1]

- *Investment-related measures* centered on "fair and equitable treatment", as per the Multilateral Agreement on Investment, and promotion of the usage of international accounting standards.

- Effective compilation, publication, circulation and distribution of national and regional *trade information* for usage in advancing the FTAA: trade regimes, tariffs an non-tariff barriers, customs regulations and procedures, trade and investment flow data, consumer market research and market analyses of goods and services, as well as information, regulations and guidelines concerning the negotiation themes of the FTAA (intellectual property rights, standards, sanitary and phytosanitary measures, investment, environmental policies, procurement, etc.). Updated reports and results of the FTAA Working Groups should be made available by the governments for the private sector, especially as they advance with FTAA negotiations.

- Advancing on streamlining and facilitating national and regional *customs procedures*, including the elimination of duties and cumbersome bureaucratic "red tape", and the effective implementation of internationally-agreed customs agreements, conventions, and treaties.

- Facilitation of *temporary entry of business people* (professional, technical and managerial personnel), via the use of standardized application forms and procedures for business visas, establishing multi-year, multiple-entry business visa as the norm for the region, and eliminating visa requirements for business visits of less than 30 days.

- Strengthening the national and regional implementation of *transparent business practices* in legal systems, customs procedures and policies, procurement regulations and systems, public information mechanisms, and conflict of interest standards, and

---

1. E.g., Coalition of Services Industries, "The FTAA: Services Sector Recommendations on Negotiation Structure, the Role of the Private Sector, and Business Facilitation Measures" (Mimeo., February 1998); National Association of Manufacturers, "Comments of the National Association of Manufacturers Regarding an FTAA Early Harvest Strategy" (Mimeo, February 1998).

# VIII. ECONOMIC INTEGRATION AND FREE TRADE

through the implementation of international anti-corruption agreements.

- Similar measures in the area of *standards*, testing, and conformity assessment and harmonization of regulatory structures and internationally-accepted standards and measures.

- *Electronic commerce* initiatives to advance measures such as the development of a harmonized legal framework for e-commerce contracts, guaranteeing ease of transborder data flow, facilitating the cross-border trade and consumption of services through electronic means; and harmonized regulations for electronic commerce. Regulations and policies should include fraud, loss, theft and disputes; disclosure requirements; deposit insurance and other guarantees; privacy; anti-money laundering measures; prudential requirements for issuers; examinations, internal controls and information systems security; and licensing, by country where applicable.

## VIII. BUSINESS SECTOR PERSPECTIVES

Through the work of its sectoral Business Teams, C/LAA has been able to provide a unique contribution to the FTAA private sector participation process, particularly insofar as specific sectoral business proposals. As Business Forum meetings have advanced since the 1994 Summit of the Americas and the hemispheric commitment to a FTAA, C/LAA's contributions have sought to prepare contributions and recommendations which provide a business-specific addition to the work of the Business Forum. For 1998 these contributions have focussed on developing a private sector agenda and contribution to the negotiation process to be launched in April 1998.

## C/LAA's Agribusiness Team

C/LAA's Agribusiness Team has focused its past FTAA input on the primary recommendation that the FTAA be compatible with and go further than the rules of the WTO, and that governments prepare for the FTAA by placing top priority on the implementation of measures previously agreed upon through the Uruguay Round of the GATT. The Agribusiness Team believes that great benefit would result from a greater commitment to implementing these previous agreements, and that the hemisphere's business community is willing to assist with resources and expertise needed to strengthen the regulatory and enforcement capabilities of governments toward this end.

The Agribusiness Team's input to previous FTAA fora has included specific recommendations which emphasized the following main issues:

- Improving market access by: 1) reducing incentives for contraband, 2) identifying and eliminating discriminatory internal taxes which distort competitive advantage, 3) harmonizing existing tariff structures in order to prevent tariff escalation for value added products, and 4) implementing reform for products which remained protected after the Uruguay Round such as sugar and dairy products.

- Reducing market distortion by: 1) identifying and eliminating both direct and indirect subsidies provided by governments in order to reduce the threat of countervailing duties, 2) reforming competition policies in order to reduce anti-dumping concerns, and 3) eliminating the use of state trading enterprises and other state monopolies in agricultural production and trade.

- Facilitating product distribution by: 1) improving customs enforcement procedures, 2) simplifying product classification norms, 3) guaranteeing transparency in publication of the fees collected at ports of entry, 4) improving the dependability and continuity of pre-clearance facilities.

- Reducing technical barriers to trade by: 1) creating mechanisms to leverage public and private sector support in helping governments implement the Uruguay Round agreement on sanitary and phytosanitary (SPS) measures, 2) 'developing procedures by which to address emerging controversial issues such as food safety and the use of genetically modified organisms.

- Improving the trade environment for agribusiness by: 1) strengthening intellectual property legislation and enforcement, 2) providing the tax and regulatory environment which would attract private investment needed to modernize and strengthen local agricultural production as well as physical infrastructure.

## C/LAA's Energy Business Team

C/LAA's Energy Business Team believes that private sector energy companies, working under appropriate government regulations, can produce clean, affordable energy which will support broad-based sustainable economic development. Starting with a set of core values which define a clear and important role for government, the C/LAA Energy Business Team focused on the importance of transparency and consistency between a country's laws and regulations, the importance of trade in the energy sector which could be encouraged by appropriate standards and regulations that support cross border transactions and integrated projects, and finally, the important role for government in helping the poor have access to basic energy needs. C/LAA Energy Business Team has noted that most of the actions required to facilitate energy integration do not demand hemispheric wide agreements under the FTAA, but rather they require basic good government in the area of laws and regulations. This is not to take away from the extra support for private sector led energy development which will result from a hemispheric agreement and uniformity in investment codes, standards, services, subsidies, and the other areas which will make up the Free Trade Area of the Americas.

The C/LAA Energy Business Team recognizes the critical role the energy sector plays in economic development. Thus, in order to improve social well being through sustained economic growth, governments must create conditions under which the private sector can invest and compete. Utilizing private enterprise in a free market is the best way to assure the customer receives reliable, cost-effective energy supplies and related services. To meet the requirements for private energy investors to participate, governments should:

- Maintain independent and transparent legal systems,
- Ensure the existence of free markets where prices are established and contracts awarded competitively,
- Provide national treatment for foreign investors,
- Reduce or eliminate trade barriers to allow for the free flow of competitive energy, and energy-related equipment, between countries,
- Regulate rather than compete with private business, privatizing government companies where these currently exist,
- Ensure free convertibility to/from the national currency,
- Enact flexible labor legislation that respects market-oriented compensation and enhances salary growth in hand with productivity growth,
- Allow competition to fuel economic growth by acting forcefully to end existing situations of corruption, conflict of interest or unlawful monopoly, and
- Adopt workable environmental laws and regulations.

These "Core Values" were adopted to provide a framework for recommendations for a diverse set of energy issues. The I Energy Americas Business Forum held in Caracas, Venezuela January 14-15, 1998 brought together 250 private sector energy company representatives to reflect on how energy could be integrated in this Hemisphere. In the **"Summary of Key Conclusions"** paper, this Forum adopted these core values as the principles upon which energy trade and investment liberalization should take place. The Forum also noted the importance for multinational energy companies to utilize local service and manufacturing companies as a way to provide technology transfer and improve local employment conditions.

The I Energy Americas Business Forum was held in conjunction with the III Meeting of the Hemispheric Energy Ministers. This was the first time that the Hemispheric energy private sector formally worked with the Hemispheric energy public sector. The striking fact which emerges when one studies the public and private sector documents, is the uniformity of views on how energy markets should be liberalized throughout the Hemisphere, whether from the private or public sectors. Because of this fact, many changes in the energy sector could be treated under business facilitation with the goal to have concrete results by the year 2000. Since the energy sector is fundamental to the process of economic development, its early coordinated liberalization would have a major positive influence on growth in the Hemisphere which would make other, more difficult areas for liberalization, easier to attain.

Based on the above discussion, the C/LAA Energy Business Team recommends that the IV Americas Business Forum strongly recommend to the Trade ministers that the energy sector be pulled out as a special negotiating subgroup, probably under the market access negotiating group. By highlighting the energy sector in this way, many of the political obstacles for this liberalization can be minimized. Based on work carried out by the C/LAA Energy Business Team, the Team recommends that this subgroup examine some of the political obstacles for liberalization, particularly the erroneous view that energy pricing liberalization necessarily hurts the poor. The Team feels strongly that the poor should be protected to a degree, but that this can be done by methods other than through energy pricing restrictions.

Launching Negotiations for the Formation of a "Free Trade Area of the Americas"

# VIII. ECONOMIC INTEGRATION AND FREE TRADE

There is a strong case to be made for identifying many of the liberalizing actions in the energy sector as business facilitation. First, since the energy sector is fundamental to the process of economic development, its early coordinated liberalization would have a major positive influence on growth in the Hemisphere which would make other, more difficult areas for liberalization, easier to attain. Second, there is a relatively high degree of public/private sector uniformity and consensus of views on how the energy markets could be liberalized. C/LAA urges the Trade Ministers to single out the energy sector for special consideration as the negotiating process for the FTAA is formulated. By establishing a special energy negotiating subgroup, probably under the market access negotiating group, clear concrete progress could be attained by the year 2000.

## C/LAA's Financial Services Business Team

Increasing trade in the Americas depends on significant infrastructure investment, including the priority allocation of financial resources, in accordance with national legislation and with the participation of both the public and private sectors. C/LAA's Financial Services Business Team views the availability of capital at competitive rates as essential to the financing of private sector investment -- a key ingredient in economic development. Developing, liberalizing and integrating financial markets domestically and internationally, increasing transparency, and establishing sound comparable supervision and regulation of banking and securities markets are necessary business facilitation measures for supporting commerce.

Currently, the growth of official sources of capital is failing to keep pace with the region's needs. The Business Team will continue working with multilateral, regional and sub-regional banks to strengthen the flow of private productive capital to economically and environmentally sound projects. Through our work in developing capital markets, we will encourage legislation, regulations and electronic formats for the establishment of an over-the-counter stock exchange in the Caribbean and facilitate stock exchange integration within the Caribbean Basin.

## C/LAA's Telecommunications and Information Technology Business Team

C/LAA's Telecommunications / Information Technology Business Team has provided substantial input to past FTAA fora, focusing primarily on the linkages between progress in the telecommunications sector, the ability of countries to compete within an FTAA, and the achievement the goals outlined by the President's of the Hemisphere in the Summit of the Americas process.

Since the inception of the FTAA process, many Latin American and Caribbean countries have committed to reform their telecommunications systems. In most of the markets today, telecommunications is now in private hands, and attention is focused on liberalization. Demonstrating their commitment to reform, many countries from the region participated in the WTO negotiations on basic telecommunications services that concluded on February, 15, 1997. As part of their commitments in the negotiations, many of the region's leading economies guaranteed market access to international telecommunications services and facilities, committed to permit foreign ownership or control of all telecommunications services and facilities, guaranteed market access for services and facilities (domestic and international) and guaranteed to implement pro-competitive regulatory principles. These commitments extended international guarantees to the liberalization now underway in many countries.

Although not all countries of the Western Hemisphere made commitments in the negotiations, the agreement provides a framework by which these other countries may approach liberalization of their telecommunications industries. C/LAA urges countries who have not yet done so to agreement agree to the WTO Agreement on Basic Telecommunications Services.

In past FTAA Business Fora, the Business Team has outlined specific recommendations highlighting the following main issues:

- Improving market access through the development of: 1) an independent regulatory agency and transparent terms of competition, 2) clear interconnection regulatory frameworks, 3) spectrum allocation regulations that allow wireless solutions in harmonized spectrum bands, 4) competition policies that enable movement towards full liberalization as quickly as appropriate.

- Reducing barriers to trade and investment by: 1) developing of interoperability standards, 2) intervening in regulated, franchised markets in cases where there is no incentive for opening proprietary product/service interfaces, 3) streamlining and liberalizing conformity assessment processes for equipment certification, 4) avoiding rules of origin provisions related to telecommunications equipment, and 5) treating products from different countries equally when standards are the same, 6) strengthening intellectual property legislation and enforcement, including TRIPS.

- Reducing market distortion and promoting investment by rebalancing telecommunications rates between local and international services as local economic conditions permit.

Recognizing the central importance to countries of developing clear and transparent regulations and an independent regulatory body, the Business Team also strongly endorses the establishment of specific processes and mechanisms by which governments could draw on private sector resources and expertise in developing the procedures and institutions needed for regulatory reform. These mechanisms should offer the training and education needed at both national and regional levels to facilitate coordinated regulatory frameworks.

To facilitate the development of these processes and mechanisms, C/LAA urges governments to: (1) collaborate at the regional level in order to support cross border ties and coordinated regulatory frameworks, and to enable the potential implementation of common tariffs that are cost based, and to enable operators to cooperate in coordinating plans, building alliances and negotiating settlement rates with foreign carriers; and, (2) work in close collaboration with the local and international private sector by drawing on their resources and expertise through meetings, seminars, and specific regulatory consultations on a country by country basis.

As the private sector will play an essential role in facilitating progress in the telecommunications sector, governments are encouraged to work actively and on an on-going basis with companies and private sector industry groups (e.g. Chambers of Commerce, TIA, C/LAA, AHCIET) to ensure that all interested parties' positions are taken into account, and to include them in the preparations for CITEL and ITU meetings and delegations.

## C/LAA's Transportation Business Team

Realizing that an efficient and integrated transportation industry is key to enhancing economic development within the Hemisphere, the Transportation Business Team (TBT) previously drafted a white paper which focused on issues affecting transportation competitiveness. The *1994 Summit of the Americas Transportation White Paper*, offered recommendations to the Hemisphere's leaders, suggesting ways in which strong leadership can remove the impediments to competitive transportation which presently hinder economic development in the Caribbean and Latin America. The White Paper has been officially endorsed by 11 of the Hemisphere's governments. A follow-up document was prepared for the 1997 Belo Horizonte Business Forum as a continuation of the Business Team's White Paper process. Keeping with the Business Forum's "early harvest" objectives, this document draws from C/LAA's *Transportation White Paper*, offering specific recommendations for reforms in the transportation sector.

Vessel seizures, customs delays and underutilized port infrastructure are all factors which impede a country's ability to compete in today's global marketplace. Fortunately, there are a variety of low cost policy reforms that can be implemented over the next year which will greatly enhance hemispheric transportation competitiveness. These recommendations require a reassessment and modification of current policies to take full advantage of existing resources.

**Capricious Vessel Seizure.** Arbitrary vessel seizures cause major disruptions to vessel schedules. Such delays can cost many thousands of dollars to importers and exporters, cause the loss of future cargo for the carrier and disrupt trade. To assure that vessel seizure is not a barrier to trade, governments must decree:

- all carriers with regular service to the country in question can post a bond precluding vessel seizure as collateral for any claims against the carrier;
- a vessel cannot be seized unless the claimant provides funding for the immediate delivery of all the cargo on board the vessel in question.

**Burdensome Customs Documentation.** International trade is severely delayed in many countries because original documentation is required to process shipments at customs. Although electronically transmitted documents are accepted as viable substitutes for original documents elsewhere in the world, this has not yet become a hemispheric practice. To facilitate customs procedures, the Hemisphere's governments should mandate the following:

- electronically transmitted documents (e.g., fax invoices, computer transmissions) must be accepted at customs in lieu of original documentation.

**Transportation Infrastructure.** Many governments have invested heavily in infrastructure and cargo handling equipment which is grossly under-utilized. To enhance efficiency and port utilization, the Hemisphere's governments should follow the example they have set for most of their airports by assuring the following:

- port working hours must be expanded to support operations 24 hours per day, seven days per week;
- ports must be equipped with appropriate navigational aides, buoys and lights; proper lighting systems for piers, docks, wharfs, terminals and warehouses must be available for night operations.

# VIII. Economic Integration and Free Trade

# Promoting Transparency Through the FTAA Process

*This position paper by Transparency International was presented at the IV Business Forum of the Americas, San José, Costa Rica, March 1998.*

**Transparency International (TI)**, *a non-profit, non-partisan NGO headquartered in Germany, is the leading advocate of action to curb corruption. TI national chapters in over seventy countries, including seventeen in the Americas, are coalitions of leaders from major business enterprises, the legal and development communities, academia, and civic organizations. Some have held high public offices.*

*TI's chapters are building public understanding of the adverse impact of corruption on open markets, democracy, and sustainable and equitable development. They are forging partnerships in support of constructive action by the public and private sectors in both industrialized and developing countries around the world. To promote best practices by the private sector in foreign markets, TI chapters supported the recently signed OECD Convention on Combating Bribery of Foreign Public Officials, which criminalizes bribery of foreign public officials. Several countries in the hemisphere are signatories, including Argentina, Brazil, Canada, Chile, Mexico, and the United States. TI also contributed to the 1996 adoption of the International Chamber of Commerce Rules of Conduct on Extortion and Bribery, voluntary rules which would prohibit bribery for any purpose.*

*In the Americas, TI chapters encouraged the adoption of important anticorruption commitments by the leaders of the hemisphere at the 1994 Summit of the Americas in Miami. They have worked since that time for the implementation of those commitments through systemic reform at the national level. TI commends the OAS and the leaders for concluding the InterAmerican Anticorruption Convention, an important milestone.*

## INTRODUCTION: AGENDA FOR THE YEAR 2000

At the Santiago Summit in April 1998, the leaders are scheduled to launch the final negotiations for the Free Trade Area of the Americas (FTAA). Trade Ministers, convening in March 1998 in Costa Rica should recommend that leaders commit to steps that will yield concrete progress in creating the environment of transparency and predictability in which free trade will flourish by 2000. In an ever more competitive global economy, bribery and other corruption have become a powerful deterrent to trade and investment. Rapid progress in eliminating them can be a powerful tool to enhance economic growth, creating jobs and raising the standard of living. Such progress would also constitute the early harvest results that are key to maintaining momentum in the FTAA process.

The leaders made a good beginning in 1994 when they brought the issue of corruption out of the shadows and gave it a prominent place on the Miami Summit agenda. The Summit was a watershed in confronting the issue with a new frankness. The leaders adopted a *Declaration* and *Plan of Action* that recognized that prosperity depends on economic integration and free trade and that this objective would be undermined if corruption were not reduced. Therefore, they committed to create open and transparent markets and specifically to launch a "comprehensive attack on corruption."

### The 1994 Summit *Plan of Action* laid out the fundamental changes necessary to defeat corruption:

1. Reforms to make government operations transparent and accountable;
2. Facilitating public access to information necessary for meaningful outside review;
3. Conflict of interest standards and effective measures against illicit enrichment;
4. Strengthening procurement;
5. A hemispheric approach to acts of corruption through negotiation of a new hemispheric agreement.

These commitments are of great significance to the business community. They are the basic building blocks that will create a favorable investment climate and generate economic growth. All the FTAA working groups should recognize that corruption and lack of transparency threaten to undermine progress whether on investment, government procurement, intellectual property rights, services, customs, or market access.

Transparency International (TI) submits the following comments and recommendations to the IV Americas Business Forum as part of its ongoing support for the Summit process. The Business Forum's recommendations to the ministers are important to securing the requisite elements of an environment conducive to trade and investment, one where transparency, accountability, and predictability are the norm. The Business Forum and the FTAA working groups should consider these realistic, achievable, concrete steps to create this environment. There is already consensus among governments, the private sector, NGOs and aid donors for these steps.

The following recommendations, prepared by Transparency International - USA, in consultation with the other Transparency International national chapters in the Americas, are intended to provide concrete steps to implement the 1994 Summit *Plan of Action* commitments.

## RECOMMENDATIONS

### Issue #1: Ratification and Implementation of the OAS Convention

• The Inter-American Convention Against Corruption, signed in May 1996, is the first regional agreement of its kind. It provides for greater mutual assistance to enable countries to enforce existing laws and to criminalize transnational bribery and illicit enrichment. It also encourages action on the other agenda items from 1994, including transparency in procurement. If fully implemented, this Convention could contribute significantly to creating an environment in which business can flourish and would constitute a key hemispheric early harvest. While many countries have signed the Convention, it is necessary for more to ratify it in order for it to succeed.

*Recommendation #1:*

The Americas Business Forum should encourage ministers to promote the ratification and implementation of the Convention by the year 2000 as a priority and should require annual progress reports.

### Issue #2: Transparent Legal Systems

• Concrete steps are still needed to make government operations transparent and accountable. The 1994 Summit *Plan of Action* states that "[A]ll aspects of public administration in a democracy must be transparent and open to public scrutiny."

*Recommendation #2:*

All FTAA working groups should encourage independent and transparent legal systems that provide for fair competition in their area of competency. This includes transparency and impartiality in participating countries' administrative and regulatory procedures.

### Issue #3: Public Hearings and Access to Information

• Lack of information can be a critical barrier to fair competition. Business competitors and citizens should be able to easily determine the legal rules and relevant information that will be applicable.

*Recommendation #3:*

All FTAA working groups should take steps to promote the incorporation of provisions to ensure adequate disclosure, public access to information and legal standards, and public hearings and review processes.

### Issue #4: Conflict of Interest Standards

• The public good and not private interests should govern public sector decisions on such issues as procurement and privatization. Fair and equitable treatment and impartial, non-discriminatory public administration should be the norm.

*Recommendation #4*

Participating governments should promulgate, and public employees should be informed of and subject to, codes of conduct and conflict of interest standards with effective sanctions for noncompliance.

### Issue #5: Procurement

• Since the 1994 Summit, when leaders agreed to give priority to strengthening government procurement systems, the FTAA working group on transparency in procurement has made progress toward a regional agreement.

*Recommendation #5:*

Early conclusion of such an agreement should be a high priority business facilitation early harvest objective. The agreement should require best practices including providing bidders with adequate notice; establishing open meetings among all bidders to review or discuss bid specifications; publishing bid documents and specifications in widely accepted terms; spelling out in bidding documents the objective criteria on which awards will be based and providing other open opportunities to obtain relevant information; adopting sealed tender procedures; providing adequate transparency in the award process to demonstrate that those criteria governed the award; and providing bidders with access to independent review and remedies for non-compliance with these requirements.

• The importance of the highest standards in public procurement has been underscored by the World Bank and Inter-American Development Bank (IDB), which have adopted anticorruption provisions in their procurement guidelines, including requirements for disclosure of commissions paid to agents, provisions for the Bank to conduct audits, procedures for investigating bribery allegations and for declaring corrupt contractors barred from future bidding, and provisions for the use of antibribery pledges on Bank-financed projects.

*Recommendation #6:*

The IDB should encourage the use of antibribery pledges on bank-financed projects with commitments by bidders not to pay bribes, to adopt compliance programs, and to report commission payments. They should also encourage bidders to have corporate compliance programs to promote best practices in IDB-financed projects.

• The World Bank and the IDB can play a leadership role by applying a single set of consistent rules to ensure adequate anticorruption controls.

*Recommendation #7:*

The World Bank and the IDB should take steps to standardize rules, forms, and procedures to pave the way for universal agreement on transparency in procurement at the World Trade Organization (WTO).

## Issue #6: Customs

• In customs matters, corruption in under- and non-invoicing, bribery, and a lack of transparency have been long-standing problems which, if unchecked, can seriously discourage trade, diminish governmental revenue and impair benefits of trade liberalization negotiated under an FTAA. This is an important area for early action.

*Recommendation #8:*

Customs conventions, procedures, and policies should be harmonized and simplified in the region and world-wide. Information on customs laws, regulations, administrative guidelines, procedures and rulings should be transparent and accessible to users. A transparent, independent, and timely appeals procedure should be available for erroneous or inequitable customs decisions.

## Issue #7: Civil Society Participation

• The Summit *Plan of Action* calls for more open discussion, public access to information and review of regulations to facilitate the operation of non-governmental actors. Civil society played an important role in formulating the commitments undertaken by the leaders in Miami and in preparation for the Bolivia Summit on Sustainable Development.

*Recommendation #9:*

Ministers should recommend the opportunity through specific, clearly defined mechanisms, for civil society organizations to be constructive partners with the private and public sectors by providing a regular channel for input and opportunity to be present at proceedings.

## ABOUT TRANSPARENCY INTERNATIONAL

Transparency International, a non-profit, non-partisan NGO headquartered in Germany, is the leading advocate of action to curb corruption. TI national chapters in over seventy countries, including seventeen in the Americas, are coalitions of leaders from major business enterprises, the legal and development communities, academia, and civic organizations. Some have held high public offices.

They are building public understanding of the adverse impact of corruption on open markets, democracy, and sustainable and equitable development. They are forging partnerships in support of constructive action by the public and private sector in both industrialized and developing countries around the world. To promote best practices by the private sector in foreign markets, TI chapters supported the recently signed OECD Convention on Combating Bribery of Foreign Public Officials, which criminalizes bribery of foreign public officials. Several countries in the hemisphere are signatories, including Argentina, Brazil, Canada, Chile, Mexico, and the United States. TI also contributed to the 1996 adoption of the International Chamber of Commerce Rules of Conduct on Extortion and Bribery, voluntary rules which would prohibit bribery for any purpose.

In the Americas, TI chapters encouraged the adoption of important anticorruption commitments by the leaders of the hemisphere at the 1994 Summit of the Americas in Miami. They have worked since that time for the implementation of those commitments through systemic reform at the national level. TI commends the OAS and the leaders for concluding the InterAmerican Anticorruption Convention, an important milestone.

# VIII. Economic Integration and Free Trade

*Transparency International (TI) USA*

# The Importance of Transparency in Government Procurement

Consumers, businesses and governments throughout the Western Hemisphere should agree on the need to maintain open and transparent government procurement practices. Such measures have already been called for in the Inter-American Convention Against Corruption and should be adopted as rapidly as possible. The Free Trade Area of the Americas (FTAA) process provides an ideal mechanism for completing work on such an agreement as a business facilitation measure by 2000.

## RATIONALE

1. **Transparency is fundamental to public confidence.** Transparency in public sector procurement results in public sector accountability by demonstrating that government officials are spending public funds responsibly.

2. **Transparency promotes sustainable economic growth.** An open and transparent procurement process gives new entrants confidence to compete for public contracts. This creates fair and healthy competition, leading to higher quality levels and reduced costs. This efficiency, in turn, supports rational economic growth.

3. **By contrast, non-transparent procurement costs countries and companies needlessly and is incompatible with the realities of today's global sourcing.**

4. **Transparency in procurement is the current standard.** The Inter-American Development Bank (IDB) and World Bank have adopted stringent anticorruption procurement guidelines. An FTAA agreement would provide consistent rules for non-bank-financed procurement.

Proposal: A hemispheric agreement on transparency in public procurement should be concluded by 2000, providing for:

5. **Adequate Notice.** Timely notice of opportunities to allow bidders to properly evaluate projects and prepare bids. Invitations should be published internationally and should establish a minimum term of 60 days from publication for proposal submission.

6. **Neutral Standards.** The broadest possible scope should be applied to technical specifications to insure that all qualified bidders have an opportunity. Bid specifications should be stated in terms of internationally recognized standards, and performance standards should be used to ensure equivalent products are treated equally.

7. **Specifications Development.** All qualified suppliers should be invited to participate in the development of specifications prior to the issuance of requests for proposals. Specifications developed should be widely disseminated with a request for public comment to ensure requirements adopted for a procurement can be met by the widest possible range of competitive suppliers.

8. **Objective Criteria.** Bidding documents should specify the relevant factors in addition to price which are to be considered in the bid evaluation and the formula by which they will be applied.

9. **Public Tenders and Bid Openings.** Tender or bidding documents should be made publicly available in the country of procurement, and all bids should be opened in public, in the presence of all bidders.

10. **Award of Contracts.** Contracts should be awarded to the lowest compliant bidder or to the bid offering the best overall value (as specified in advance) on the basis of objective criteria. Awards, including the total amount of the award, should be internationally published.

11. **Dispute Settlement with Impartial and Fair Review.** Contracting agencies should provide unsuccessful bidders access to an impartial, fair and independent review of compliance with the bid process. Standard written procedures for lodging a protest and adequate remedies for non-compliance should exist.

12. **Protection for Intellectual Property.** Bidders' rights to their technical data and patents must be protected in the procurement process. Technical submissions should be treated as proprietary and confidential. Inappropriate transfer of proprietary technical information should be sanctionable.

**Background:** At the 1997 Americas Business Forum in Belo Horizonte and in 1998 in San Jose, private sector representatives from around the hemisphere reached consensus on the need for an agreement on transparency in procurement and on the elements of such an agreement. The only disagreement concerns the timeframe for implementation. The timing issue appears to be related not to the merits of a procurement transparency agreement, but to more generalized concerns about the timing of FTAA agreements. This issue, however, is in the interest of all countries of the Americas and should not be delayed because of perceived tradeoffs with other FTAA issues.

## ACTION ITEMS:

13. The Trade Negotiation Committee (TNC) will accept proposals for early concrete progress until mid-September 1998 and will decide which will be considered for early progress in December. Supporters should submit the above proposal to their national TNC representative.

14. Contact with other relevant government representatives should be made.

15. Efforts should be made to place the issue on the agenda of private sector and professional association meetings to build private sector support.

16. Results of government contacts should be reported back to US.

# VIII. Economic Integration and Free Trade

*Transparency International (TI) USA*

# Universal Elements of Sound Procurement Systems

There is broad agreement on the characteristics of a sound public procurement system. Rules should be clear and fair, the process transparent, and the results predictable. The following are the main elements in a competitive, transparent bidding process, as reflected in the best practices of the major multilateral development banks, the APEC Government Procurement Experts Group recommendations, and the private sector recommendations of the 1998 Americas Business Forum, among others.

**Regulatory Transparency.** Laws, regulations, and policies related to the government procurement process should be readily available to the public.

**Adequate Public Notice.** Timely public notice of opportunities to allow bidders to properly evaluate projects and prepare bids is essential to transparent procurement. Invitations should be published internationally and should establish a minimum term of 60 days from publication for proposal submission. In large or complex projects, pre-qualification of bidders is advisable.

**Neutral Standards.** All interested parties should have the opportunity to contribute and comment on the preparation of national standards for materials, goods, works and services. Draft standards should be widely disseminated with a request for public comment. The standards should be clear and specific and reflect international experience and practice. There should be no unnecessary requirements, while comprehensively treating the requirements essential to the purchaser's needs.

**Specifications.** Bid specifications should be stated in terms of internationally recognized standards. The specifications should be broadly defined to ensure that the requirements adopted can be met by the widest possible range of competitive suppliers and should set out the neutral selection parameters in a clear, specific and objective manner. Performance standards should be used whenever appropriate and feasible to ensure equivalent products are treated equally.

**Objective Criteria.** Bidding documents should specify the relevant factors in addition to price which are to be considered in the bid evaluation and the formula by which they will be applied, as well as describing the bidding process. All bidders should be able to determine whether the objective criteria have been followed in the final award.

**Public Tenders and Bid Openings.** Tender or bidding documents should be made publicly available in the country of procurement, and all bids should be opened in public, in the presence of all bidders.

**Award of Contracts.** Competent evaluators should conduct an impartial comparison and evaluation of bids without influence or interference by bidders or other parties. Contracts should be awarded to the lowest compliant bidder or to the bid offering the best overall value (as specified in advance) on the basis of objective criteria. Awards, including the total amount of the award, should be internationally published.

**Dispute Settlement with Impartial and Fair Review.** Contracting agencies should provide unsuccessful bidders access to an impartial, fair and independent review of compliance with the bid process. Standard written procedures for lodging a protest and adequate remedies for non-compliance should exist.

**Protection for Intellectual Property.** Bidders' rights to their technical data and patents must be protected in the procurement process. Technical submissions should be treated as proprietary and confidential. Inappropriate transfer of proprietary technical information should be sanctionable.

# IX. Eradication of Poverty and Discrimination

# IX. ERADICATION OF POVERTY AND DISCRIMINATION

*This proposal was presented at the Summit of the Americas by the **Organization of Africans in the Americas (OAA)** at the workshop on Public Participation for Developing Actions for the Eradication of Poverty and Discrimination.*

*The OAA seeks to empower communities of African descent in the Americas by assisting these populations in the exercise of their social, political and economic privileges and responsibilities, in the expressions and acknowledgment of their cultural heritage and contributions, and of their past and current conditions.*

*The mission of the OAA is established for charitable and educational purposes to improve the life chances and conditions of communities of African descent with special regard for those populations who speak Spanish and Portuguese. Through involvement and promotion of cooperative efforts among diverse Black communities, OAA functions as a resource and referral center of data, service, support, and empowerment of Africans in the Americas.*

## Propuesta de Afroamérica XXI ante el Taller de Participación Pública en Acciones de Desarrollo de la Erradicación de la Pobreza y la Discriminación en la Cumbre de las Américas

Michael John Franklin, Presidente de La Organización Pro-Avance de los Pueblos de Ascendencia Africana (OAA) en Washington, D.C, y Gregoria Flores Martínez, Presidenta de la Organización Fraternal Negra Hondureña (OFRANEH), La Ceiba, Honduras, Vice-Presidenta de la Confederación de Pueblos Autóctonos de Honduras (CONPAH), delegados oficiales en representación de las organizaciones delegadas de AFROAMERICA XXI:

CONSIDERANDO que la población de personas de ascendencia africana alcanza a un tercio de la población total de América Latina, entre ellos un grupo de tez oscura que constituye noventa millones de personas o veinte (20%) por ciento de la población total:

CONSIDERANDO que este veinte (20%) por ciento representa aproximadamente un cuarenta (40%) por ciento de los pobres de América Latina:

CONSIDERANDO que los afrolatinoamericanos no están considerados como grupo vulnerable a pesar de sus circunstancias de extrema pobreza y marginación, y a su vez exclusión de los beneficios de cooperación internacional:

ATENTO A ESTAS CONSIDERACIONES nos permitimos poner a consideración de los honorables Líderes de Gobierno de las Américas y a sus ministros:

1. Visibilizar la población afroamericana en América Latina:
   a) acreditando sus contribuciones históricas al desarrollo de las naciones
   b) como parte de las poblaciones viviendo en pobreza crónica
   c) como poblaciones vulnerables en las cuales el desarrollo no las ha tocado en una forma significativa y positiva.

2. Compromiso de los estados a entrar en un proceso colaborativo de desarrollo en las comunidades afroamericanas organizadas y la cooperación internacional.

3. Acordar que el objeto de esta colaboración es generar un proceso de desarrollo afroamericano autogestionario que resulta en una mejor calidad de vida y en aportes culturales, espirituales, morales, etc., y ciudadanía a la vida latinoamericana.

4. Dar prioridad en ese proceso colaborativo al desarrollo de políticas, programas y acciones para remover las barreras sistémicas que enfrenta esas poblaciones toda la región.

   a) Incorporar toda su historia, cultura, lengua, en los currículum de todos los niveles de la educación formal, con la intención de generar una sociedad latinoamericana que valore la etno-cultura, especialmente la afroamericana.

   b) Orientar inversiones de desarrollo que proporcione toda la infraestructura necesaria para generar economías locales en sus zonas rurales y urbanas-marginales. Esto incluye carreteras y caminos accesibles todo el año, fuentes de energía eléctrica, medios de comunicación, transportes públicos permanentes, sistemas de agua potable y saneamiento básico.

   c) Incorporar a estas poblaciones, como sujetas de su desarrollo, en todos los planes de desarrollo nacional, visibilizándolos en los mapas de pobreza, en planes de descentralización y en programas de desarrollo humano/capacitación.

   d) Incorporar la identificación etno-cultural en los datos de censos y encuestas de hogar usados en la programación para el desarrollo social y económico.

   e) Como medida inmediata, dar prioridad a incorporar las poblaciones afroamericanas como sujeto de programación de alivio y erradicación de la pobreza en todos los países y trabajar en colaboración con las ONG's afroamericanas involucradas en el proceso de AFROAMERICA XXI, para que estas informen/sensibilicen a los funcionarios estatales de desarrollo para abrir oportunidades de financiamiento a proyectos de las comunidades afroamericanas y usar las arterias de desarrollo propuestas por AFROAMERICA XXI para seleccionar.

   f) Asegurar el funcionamiento de los programas estatales más relevantes al desarrollo afroamericano para participar en el proceso de AFROAMERICA XXI nacional/regional para formular planes de acción que el estado y las comunidades puedan ejecutar/financiar.

   g) Requiere que las agencias de cooperación, instituciones bilaterales y multilaterales sean también partícipes del proceso de AFROAMERICA XXI, como socios financieros en ese proceso.

   h) Considerar el proceso/estrategia AFROAMERICA XXI como una experiencia piloto de etno-desarrollo orientada a apoyar grupos vulnerables a sobrepasar la pobreza que enfrentan y a generar en ellas capacidad en sí mismas de fortalecer sus destrezas, habilidades, conocimientos, además de un sentimiento emprendedor que sostendrá el proceso de desarrollo a través del tiempo.

## CONSIDERANDO LO ANTERIOR EXPUESTO, AFROAMERICA XXI ESTABLECE QUE LAS INSTITUCIONES DE COOPERACION Y MULTILATERALES:

1. Den prioridad a las comunidades afrolatinoamericanas como grupo vulnerable, y las seleccione para programas de desarrollo institucional y organizativo.

2. Den prioridad al fortalecimiento de capacidad microempresarial a las comunidades.

3. Den prioridad de desarrollo turístico en las comunidades afroamericanos.

4. Den prioridad a que los afroamericanos sean sujetos de programas en medios de comunicación.

5. Den prioridad que los gobiernos subscriban y apliquen el Convenio 169 de la OIT afroamericanos.

6. Den prioridad en países relevantes en el proceso de titulación de tierras a las comunidades afroamericanas.

7. Implementen programas específicos de derechos humanos de los países de AFROAMERICA XXI.

## FIRMAS OFICIALES POR AFROAMERICA XXI:

**Gregoria Flores Martínez** — Presidenta, OFRANEH
Apartado Postal 341
La Ceiba, Atlántida, Honduras
Tel/Fax: 504-43-24-92

**Michael John Franklin** — Presidente, OAA
1234 Massachusetts Avenue, NW, Suite C-1007
Washington, DC 20005, USA
Tel: 202-638-1662    Fax: 202-638-1667

# IX. Eradication of Poverty and Discrimination

# Communiqué: To the Second Summit of the Americas in Santiago, Chile

*The **Inter-American Dialogue** is the premier center for policy analysis and exchange on Western Hemisphere affairs. The Dialogue's select membership of 100 distinguished private citizens from throughout the Americas includes political, business, academic, media, and other non-governmental leaders. Seven Dialogue members served as presidents of their countries and more than a dozen have served at the cabinet level.*

*The Dialogue works to improve the quality of debate and decisionmaking on hemispheric problems, advance opportunities for regional economic and political cooperation, and bring fresh, practical proposals for action to governments, international institutions, and non-governmental organizations. Since 1982–through successive Republican and Democratic administrations and many changes of leadership in Latin America, the Caribbean, and Canada — the Dialogue has helped shape the agenda of issues and choices on inter-American relations.*

*The **International Center for Research on Women (ICRW)** is a private, nonprofit organization dedicated to promoting economic and social development with women's full participation. ICRW conducts policy-oriented research and provides technical assistance on women's economic activity, their reproductive and sexual health and rights, their leadership in society, and their management of environmental resources. ICRW advocates with governments and multilateral agencies and engages in an active policy communications program. It collaborates with other non-governmental institutions to advance women's economic opportunities and rights. Founded twenty years ago, ICRW focuses principally on women in developing and transition countries. It is supported by grants, contracts, and contributions from international and national development agencies, foundations, corporations, and individuals.*

## FOREWORD

The Women's Leadership Conference of the Americas (WLCA) is pleased to present its recommendations for action to enhance opportunities for women in the hemisphere. These are intended for consideration by the heads of state when they meet for the second Summit of the Americas in Santiago, Chile, on April 17 to 19, 1998. Our document points to a decided lack of progress on women's issues since the Miami Summit in December 1994. We urge the heads of state to reaffirm their broad commitment to advancing women's equality—but also to develop a practical plan for proceeding. We propose focusing on a small number of high priority concerns—domestic violence, education and employment, and women in private and political leadership. We also call on governments to establish mechanisms to monitor, measure, record and report on actual improvements in women's status over time, so they are publicly accountable for the international commitments they have made to women.

Our analysis and recommendations reflect the consensus of the members of the Women's Leadership Conference of the Americas. Not every participant agrees fully with every phrase in the text, but each endorses the overall content and tone and supports its main recommendations. WLCA members subscribe in their individual capacity; institutional affiliations are provided for purposes of identification only.

The Women's Leadership Conference of the Americas is a hemispheric network of 100 outstanding women leaders who have decided to work together to: (1) expand the number and enhance the contribution of women in top leadership positions in Latin America and the Caribbean; (2) promote policy and institutional changes that will improve opportunities for all women in the region; and (3) strengthen other non-governmental initiatives that advance women's equality and facilitate their access to policy officials. The members bring experience in politics and government, business, civic organizations, and scholarship.

The WLCA network, coordinated by the Inter-American Dialogue and the International Center for Research on Women (ICRW), got its start in October 1994 when a diverse group of 35 women leaders from thirteen countries of the hemisphere met in Washington to discuss the key issues confronting the Americas, and to explore how they affect women. It was the recommendations of this group that led to the inclusion of a women's initiative in the 1994 Miami Summit of the Americas' *Plan of Action*.

We would like to thank the Inter-American Dialogue and ICRW who serve jointly as secretariat to the WLCA, under the direction of Joan Caivano.

Anne-Marie Smith prepared the Rapporteur's Report of the WLCA's first plenary in July 1997. Sandra Forero and Samuel Robfogel collaborated on the preparation of this publication. We are especially grateful to the WLCA members who contributed to our conclusions. We also wish to express our appreciation to the Ford, Kellogg and MacArthur foundations and the Inter-American Development Bank for their support of the WLCA, and to the Miranda Foundation for a special grant that made this publication possible.

*Jan Meyers, Co-Chair - United States*
*Sonia Picado, Co-Chair - Costa Rica*

## COMMUNIQUÉ TO THE SECOND SUMMIT OF THE AMERICAS IN SANTIAGO, CHILE

At the Summit of the Americas in Miami in December 1994, the heads of state of this hemisphere committed to a series of principles and actions to bolster the role of women in society. Every nation in the hemisphere reaffirmed these commitments at the UN Fourth World Conference on Women in Beijing in September 1995. The proposals set out in the Miami *Plan of Action* are well conceived and, if implemented, would go a long way toward achieving the Summit goals to "strengthen policies and programs that improve and broaden the participation of women in all spheres of political, social, and economic life and that improve their access to the basic resources needed for the full exercise of their fundamental rights." The pace of progress has been slow, however. Despite their pledge, six countries still have not signed the Inter-American Convention on the Prevention, Punishment and Eradication of Violence Against Women, and many that have signed have not passed national implementing legislation. The Inter-American Commission of Women has not yet become a minimally effective institution. We now challenge our countries' leaders to reaffirm their commitments and to do more to turn those commitments into reality.

We also think that the proposals regarding women in the Miami Summit *Plan of Action*, while all of them valuable, are somewhat vague. We call on the presidents and prime ministers to focus on enhancing the equal oportunity of all women to contribute to development by investing in anti-poverty policies and programs that enhance women's productivity and income. The issues that particularly demand vital attention are: 1) increasing women's opportunities in the workforce by strengthening education, particularly by ending tracking; 2) advancing women to positions of power and influence in their workplaces, their communities, and their nations; 3) stopping the brutality of violence against women at home, at work, and in the streets; 4) making the Organization of American States (OAS) Inter-American Commission of Women a real bastion for protecting women's rights. Furthermore, it is vital that governments monitor, measure, record and report on their successes and failures in these areas. This is the greatest weakness of the last Summit's recommendations. There is nothing to force governments to face up to their failure to produce concrete results.

### Increase women's opportunities in the workforce by strengthening education

In Miami, governments pledged to "...enhance [women's] productivity through education..." and "adopt appropriate measures to improve women's ability to earn income beyond traditional occupations...." This time around, governments must commit themselves to increase the quality of schooling to all, especially to girls, and to stop the de facto tracking of girls into courses of study that lead to low-paying, low-prestige occupations. Educational tracking has the single most devastating effect on women's professional opportunities. While in many countries girls have achieved parity with boys in school enrollment and performance, obstacles still impede women from translating these gains into decent jobs, especially in the fields of business management, science and technology.

### Advance women to positions of power and influence in their workplaces, their communities, their nations

In Miami, governments pledged to "Promote the participation of women in the decision-making process in all spheres of political, social and economic life." We note that women have occupied leadership roles at lower rates in Latin America than in most other parts of the world. Only 11% of elected legislators in the region are women. With few exceptions, this does not represent a significant improvement from ten years ago. We propose as a target that by the year 2002, 25% of parliamentary representatives and cabinet-level leaders be women. In the private sector, the numbers are even more disappointing. We call for a region-wide conference among government and business leaders to develop strategies for promoting women into the highest levels of corporate leadership.

# IX. Eradication of Poverty and Discrimination

## Stop the brutality of violence against women at home, at work, and in the streets

In Miami, governments pledged to "Undertake appropriate measures to address and reduce violence against women." Meanwhile, as many as forty percent of women in the hemisphere suffer physical domestic violence at some point in their lives. Domestic violence perpetuates the general level of violence in a society. The response to the appalling prevalence of domestic violence has been weak and largely in the area of rhetoric. We call on all governments to implement a range of initiatives that will both prevent and treat domestic violence. For example, judicial systems should adopt proven mechanisms—such as specially trained police officers and family courts to litigate cases of domestic violence—to ensure women's basic human right to be free from violence.

## Make the OAS Inter-American Commission of Women (CIM) a real bastion for protecting women's rights

In Miami, governments pledged to "Further strengthen the Inter-American Commission of Women." We see no evidence that this has happened. Women's rights are human rights and they deserve the same quality of attention. We call on governments to put in place a strategy to transform the Inter-American Commission of Women into as relevant and potent a mechanism as the Inter-American Commission on Human Rights. We recommend a blue ribbon group be appointed to propose a reorganization of the CIM.

## Monitoring

If governments seriously carried out what they committed to in Miami, there would be considerable change in the numbers of women in public and private decision-making positions, new laws in place guaranteeing women full legal and civil protection, a higher percentage of women studying traditionally male fields in universities and vocational schools, and other concrete, measurable changes in the status and condition of women. This has not happened.

A crucial element is missing from the good principles espoused in the 1994 *Plan of Action*. There is no mechanism by which to measure the status and condition of women in the areas where commitments were made—leadership, legal equality, educational equity, economic opportunities, and protection against violence—nor results by which to judge countries. Governments must improve opportunities for women in every sphere of activity. If there is no evidence of an equality of results, then governments are clearly failing to implement the right policies to provide equal opportunities.

We call on all governments to put in place a transparent, standardized process to collect statistical data on women's position in society. Governments should commit to establish a hemispheric mechanism to measure actual improvements in women's status over time. A prominent non-governmental commission should be created to oversee this process and report the results on a regular, comparative basis. This commission should be established under the auspices of an international institution—like the Inter-American Development Bank in coordination with the OAS Inter-American Commission of Women—and receive the necessary resources to function effectively. Findings of the commission should be disclosed and made readily available on the Internet, as the International Monetary Fund does with macroeconomic data.

## Signatories of the Communiqué

Co-Chair
**Jan Meyers**
United States

Co-Chair
**Sonia Picado**
Costa Rica

**Mariclaire Acosta Urquidi**
Mexico

**Beverley Anderson-Manley**
Jamaica

**Peggy Antrobus**
Barbados

**Carmen Barroso**
Brazil/USA

**Maria Antonietta Berriozabal**
United States

**Charlotte Bunch**
United States

**Kim Campbell**
Canada

**Mercedes Pimentel de Canalda**
Dominican Republic

**Patricia Carney**
Canada

**Elisa Carrió**
Argentina

**Margaret Catley-Carlson**
Canada

**Violeta Barrios de Chamorro**
Nicaragua

**Piedad Cordoba**
Colombia

**Gisèle Côté-Harper**
Canada

**Maria Isabel Cruz Velasco**
Colombia

**Susana de la Puente Wiesse**
Peru

**Vivian Lowery Derryck**
United States

**Cecilia Dockendorff**
Chile

**Peggy Dulany**
United States

**Joan Dunlop**
United States

**Patricia Ellis**
United States

**Graciela Fernández Meijide**
Argentina

**Azucena Ferrey**
Nicaragua

**Pia Figueroa Edwards**
Chile

**Lourdes Flores Nano**
Peru

**Rossana Fuentes-Berain**
Mexico

**Amalia García Medina**
Mexico

**Magdalena García Hernández**
Mexico

**Ana Milena Gaviria**
Colombia

**Dale A. Godsoe**
Canada

**Margarita Guzmán**
Colombia

**Antonia Hernández**
United States

**Adriana Hoffman Jacoby**
Chile

**Ana Julia Jatar**
Venezuela

**Monica Jiménez**
Chile

**Clara Jusidman**
Mexico

**Yolanda Kakabadse**
Ecuador

**Ruth de Krivoy**
Venezuela

**Audrey Langworthy**
United States

**Thérèse Lavoie-Roux**
Canada

**Mirna Liévano**
El Salvador

**Cecilia Loria Saviñón**
Mexico

**Beatriz de Majo**
Venezuela

**Barbara J. McDougall**
Canada

**Daisy May McFarlane-Coke**
Jamaica

**Juliette C. McLennan**
United States

**Patricia Mercado**
Mexico

**Beatriz Merino**
Peru

**Lourdes R. Miranda**
United States

**Sonia Montaño**
Bolivia

**Michelle Montas**
Haiti

**Maria Eugenia Morasso Nikken**
Venezuela

**María de los Ángeles Moreno**
Mexico

**Diana Natalicio**
United States

**Laura Novoa**
Chile

**Milagros Ortiz Bosch**
Dominican Republic

**Sylvia Ostry**
Canada

**Maria Otero**
United States

**Maria Elena Ovalle**
Chile

**Marta Oyhanarte**
Argentina

Communiqué: To the Second Summit of the Americas

# IX. Eradication of Poverty and Discrimination

**Nina Pacari Vega**
Ecuador

**Dulce Maria Pereira**
Brazil

**Jacqueline Pitanguy**
Brazil

**Pilar Ramírez**
Bolivia

**Beatrice Rangel**
Venezuela

**Rozanne L. Ridgway**
United States

**Reyna Rincón de McPeck**
Venezuela

**Rosa Roa Peguero**
Dominican Republic

**Cira Romero Barboza**
Venezuela

**Maria Antonieta Saa**
Chile

**Gloria Salguero Gross**
El Salvador

**Elizabeth Sanders**
United States

**Margaret Schuler**
United States

**Helga Stephenson**
Canada

**Paula Stern**
United States

**Marta Suplicy**
Brazil

**Rosalina Tuyuc**
Guatemala

**Virginia Vargas Valente**
Peru

**Ximena Alexandra Verdesoto**
Ecuador

**Rocío Villanueva Flores**
Peru

**Elena Viyella de Paliza**
Dominican Republic

**Carmen Delgado Votaw**
United States

**María Soledad Weinstein**
Chile

**Claudette Werleigh**
Haiti

## WOMEN'S LEADERSHIP CONFERENCE OF THE AMERICAS SUMMARY OF RAPPORTEUR'S REPORT

The Women's Leadership Conference of the Americas (WLCA) held its first full meeting on July 10 and 11, 1997, in Washington, D.C.

Convened by the Inter-American Dialogue and the International Center for Research on Women, the meeting brought together more than 60 women leaders from the United States, Canada, and 19 countries of the Caribbean and Latin America. The participants represented a broad array of fields—government, law, education, business, banking, health, and international development. The group, chaired by Amb. Sonia Picado of Costa Rica and Rep. Jan Meyers of Kansas, discussed the challenges related to expanding women's leadership—getting more women into politics, improving educational opportunities for women, and supporting women in multilateral development bank programs and the private sector. Regional efforts to prevent and punish violence against women were another major concern. A final item on the meeting's agenda was how to monitor countries' compliance with international commitments to women and to incorporate women's concerns into the Santiago Summit upcoming in April 1998.

One important theme that recurred in the two days of meetings was the need to remain aware of larger goals. For example, getting women into elected office is not an end in itself, but a step toward attaining fair and equal representation for all women. A second recurring theme was that strategies to advance women's leadership should not generate permanent special treatment for women or keep them on the sidelines of mainstream activity. Finally, throughout the discussions, the women recognized that their diversity of experience and perspectives could enrich their shared efforts to further women's status both as leaders and in society overall.

The following were the main conclusions of each session:

## Women's Access to Political Leadership

The discussion of increasing women's access to political leadership centered on the use of quotas in electoral systems—i.e., reserving places on ballots for women candidates. The consensus was that quotas are never an optimal solution, but many participants agreed that they may be essential to fight discrimination in politics under current circumstances. Participants' concerns about quotas included their lack of effectiveness if political parties themselves remain discriminatory; their potential stigmatizing effect on women office-holders; and their failure to fix fundamentally flawed political systems.

Quotas should be used to work for the day when quotas will not be needed. They must be combined with provisions for campaign financing and legislative training, so that women can not only win but also be effective.

Also, quotas should only be advocated in the context of other political reforms that create more representative democracies.

## Access to and Benefits from Education

Women's access to education in the Americas has improved markedly. But several participants expressed concerns that curricular materials are laden with gender stereotypes, and teaching methods may favor boys' participation in the classroom. The major concern is the channeling of women into traditional female occupations characterized by low pay and little opportunity for advancement. Better occupational counseling and training is needed for women to step into the more challenging occupations. The discussion continually returned to the larger purposes of women's education, including employment in the changing global economy, full participation in existing societies, and transformation of those societies.

Investment in education for women produces results—increasing per capita GNP overall, expanding women's life opportunities, and improving the health and education of their children. Government investment is not always correlated with better quality education, but lack of resources tends to be a widespread problem. The group discussed various proposals including private management of schools, making schooling compulsory through secondary grades, and providing childcare for teen mothers.

## Opportunities to Expand Women's Leadership

The Program for the Support of Women's Leadership and Representation, of the Inter-American Development Bank (IDB), will make $3.8 million available to organizations that promote women's civic participation and access to leadership positions. A representative of the IDB requested assistance in identifying possible grant recipients; WLCA participants urged that the allocation of program funds remain agile and free of politicization or government control. The group also encouraged women's participation in all aspects of multilateral development bank lending and grant programs, not only the small portion dedicated to women.

The group discussed the social responsibilities of business and women's leadership in the private sector, noting some gains. Many argued the corporate sector should have codes of conduct regarding women, human rights, and labor standards. One suggestion was to publicly recognize businesses when they provide training for women or promote women to important leadership positions. Another idea was to push corporations to exercise leadership on such issues as domestic violence.

## International Efforts to Stop Domestic Violence

According to the Inter-American Development Bank, as many as forty percent of women in the hemisphere suffer physical domestic violence at some time in their lives. Participants were briefed on the activities of the IDB, United Nations Development Fund for Women, Pan American Health Organization, and the Organization of American States, including public awareness campaigns, community-based projects, databanks, and training programs.

Some participants recommended that the WLCA endorse the "The Inter-American Convention on the Prevention, Punishment, and Eradication of Violence Against Women" and encouraged all countries to sign it (only 27 of 34 have done so). Others felt that a strong judiciary is more important for progress against domestic violence. Formal ratification of the convention may have little relevance without implementing legislation and training for judges, lawyers, health workers, and police. Suggestions included building a databank of laws on domestic violence and models for community-based prevention, and training law students about the problem of domestic violence.

Poverty is an important component to any discussion of domestic violence. Many participants believed ombudsmen can play an important role to ensure that police, judges, and doctors carry out their obligations within the law, regardless of the economic resources of the perpetrators and victims. Others argued that victims of violence also need viable economic alternatives: not just a safehouse for the night, but a job and access to credit that will enable them to be independent. Finally, participants discussed the need to encourage broader cultural change, to assure that domestic violence is not considered acceptable behavior.

## Monitoring International Commitments

In a series of international conferences—notably Vienna, Copenhagen, Cairo, and Beijing—countries have signed numerous commitments to improve the status of women. The challenge is to close the gap between language and reality—to demand compliance with the content of international agreements.

The current agenda for the Santiago Summit includes four topics: education, trade and economics, poverty and discrimination, and human rights. There was a lively discussion about whether it would be best to have a separate agenda item addressing the status of women, or whether women should be cited throughout the agenda, in each category, as appropriate.

To monitor implementation of agreements, participants suggested working with research groups, identifying indicators of progress, and then developing a report which would assess the performance of each country in the region. Such a report could be a valuable means to demand accountability, permit recognition of accomplishments, and condemn failures to advance the status of women.

## Conclusions and Action Items

The conference concluded with a review of the actions that the WLCA should undertake. Some of the discussion, as on quotas, did not necessarily yield consensus on further collective actions by the WLCA, but might inform participants' decisions and actions as leaders within their own countries. Other discussions served to make the leaders aware of opportunities and shortcomings presented by programs of international organizations and development banks. Influencing the Santiago Summit was one immediate, time-sensitive objective, but not the sole focus for action.

## Specific action items included:

- Monitor Government Compliance of International Agreements: Using available data and working with other women's organizations, analyze the status of women in the region today. Identify indicators of progress and set up mechanisms to measure and report on the successes and failures of governments in meeting their commitments to women.
- Issue a Statement for Santiago Summit: Based upon commitments from the Miami Summit, write a communiqué that urges governments to produce concrete results in priority areas for women.
- Form Working Groups: Create subgroups to discuss and design further initiatives for the WLCA. Some suggested areas are education and labor markets, women's leadership, corporate and multilateral bank responsibility, and domestic violence and judicial reform.
- Develop Communications and Outreach Strategy: Promote the work of the WLCA throughout the hemisphere. Strategy will target decision-makers at all levels, popular media, private sector, and the general public. It will also build ties to other women's organizations.
- Endorse Continued Secretariat Role of ICRW and Inter-American Dialogue.

## BIOGRAPHICAL SKETCHES OF THE SIGNATORIES OF THE SANTIAGO COMMUNIQUÉ

*Co-Chair*
**Jan Meyers — United States**

Meyers was a Republican congresswoman representing the state of Kansas. A member from 1985 to 1997, she chaired the Committee on Small Business and served on the International Relations Committee, the Subcommittee on International Economic Policy and Trade, and the Economic and Educational Opportunities Committee.

*Co-Chair*
**Sonia Picado — Costa Rica**

Sonia Picado is congresswoman from San José for the National Liberation party. She was Costa Rican ambassador to the United States, executive director of the International Institute of Human Rights, a justice on the Inter-American Court of Human Rights, co-chair of the International Commission for Central American Recovery and Development, and dean of the University of Costa Rica Law School.

**Mariclaire Acosta Urquidi — Mexico**

Acosta is president of the Mexican Commission for the Defense and Promotion of Human Rights, and founder of the Mexican Academy for Human Rights. She was president of Amnesty International in Mexico.

**Beverley Anderson-Manley — Jamaica**

Anderson-Manley was first lady and representative to the UN Commission on the Status of Women and the Inter-American Commission of Women of the OAS. Ms. Anderson-Manley is currently co-producer and co-host of the weekday radio program, The Breakfast Club. She is a motivational speaker and has been a consultant on gender, communications, and Third World development issues for the UN, the IDB, the World Bank, and CIDA.

**Peggy Antrobus — Barbados**

Antrobus was head of the Women and Development Unit at the University of the West Indies and Development Alternatives with Women for a New Era. She is a member of the Inter-American Dialogue.

**Carmen Barroso — Brazil/United States**

Barroso is the Director of the Population Area of the Program on Global Security and Sustainability at the John D. and Catherine T. MacArthur Foundation. She has a wide range of experience related to population and women's health: from university teaching and research, to the development of educational materials, to writing a guest column for a major newspaper. She has served as chairperson of the Committee of Reproductive Rights of the Brazilian Ministry of Health, was a member of the National Council on Women's Rights (appointed by the President of Brazil), and has been a consultant to several international organizations.

**Maria Antonietta Berriozabal — United States**

Berriozabal is a founder and former chair of the National Hispana Leadership Institute and served as U.S. Representative to the Inter-American Commission of Women of the OAS. Berriozabal was councilwoman for the City of San Antonio, Texas, from 1981 to 1991. She is currently a candidate for the U.S. Congress from Texas.

**Charlotte Bunch — United States**

Bunch is Executive Director of the Center for Women's Global Leadership at Douglas College and is a professor in the Bloustein School of Planning and Public Policy at Rutgers University. Bunch has edited seven anthologies and two books on feminist issues and is a founder of the movement for women's human rights. In 1996 she was inducted into the National Women's Hall of Fame.

**Kim Campbell — Canada**

Campbell was prime minister of Canada and is now Consul General of Canada to the United States.

**Mercedes Pimentel de Canalda — Dominican Republic**

Canalda is the founder and member of the board of directors of the Dominican Association for Women's Development (ADOPEM). She is a member of the executive committee of Women's World Banking (WWB) in New York, and she was elected chairperson of the board of directors of WWB. She is the president of the Council of American Foundations for Development (Solidarios).

**Patricia Carney — Canada**

Carney was appointed to the Canadian Senate in 1990. From 1984-1988, she held a number of federal cabinet posts, including minister of energy, mines, and resources, minister for international trade, and president of the Treasury Board. She served as a member of parliament in the House of Commons from 1980-1988.

**Elisa Carrió — Argentina**

Carrió is a member of the Argentine Congress (term from 1995-99). In 1994, she was a member of the constitutional congress. She is a tenured professor of constitutional law at the Universidad Nacional del Nordeste (UNNE) and is the author of several legal works.

**Margaret Catley-Carlson — Canada**

Catley-Carlson is President of the Population Council. She was Deputy Minister for Health and Welfare in Canada and President of the Canadian International Development Agency. Catley-Carlson also served as Assistant Under Secretary in the Department of External Affairs and as Deputy Executive Director of UNICEF with the rank of Assistant Secretary General of the United Nations. She is a member of the Inter-American Dialogue.

**Violeta Barrios de Chamorro — Nicaragua**

Chamorro was president of Nicaragua from 1990-1996. Under her leadership, Nicaragua passed from war to peace, from a centralized to a free market economy, and from a dictatorial and totalitarian government to a democratic one. She reduced the size of the military and was the first Nicaraguan president to transfer power to a freely elected successor.

**Piedad Cordoba — Colombia**

Cordoba is a senator and is president of the Senate's legal commission on human rights. She has authored several laws to promote women's political participation and to protect the rights of black minorities. In addition, she authored Colombia's law protecting women and children from domestic violence. She is a member of the commission for peace and the commission to reform political parties. She was the chamber representative from Antioquia and the alternate director of the Colombian Liberal Party.

**Gisèle Côté-Harper — Canada**

Côté-Harper is a barrister and teaches law at Laval University in Quebec City. She is a member of the board of directors of the Inter-American Institute of Human Rights in Costa Rica and founding chair of the board of directors of the International Centre for Human Rights and Democratic Development. She is a member of the Inter-American Dialogue.

**Maria Isabel Cruz Velasco — Colombia**

Cruz Velasco has been a member of the Senate since 1991 and has served as its vice president. From 1986-1991, she was a congresswoman for the Conservative Party and from 1980-1986, she was a member of the city council of Cali.

**Susana de la Puente Wiesse — Peru**

De la Puente is the country manager for Peru and a managing director of the Latin American Investment Banking Group of J.P. Morgan in New York. She has been responsible for the bank's most important clients in Mexican and Peruvian privatization deals.

**Vivian Lowery Derryck — United States**

Derryck is currently a senior vice president at the Academy for Educational Development. From 1989-1996, she served as president of the African-American Institute. From 1984-1988, she was vice president of programs for the National Democratic Institute (NDI). She served as a deputy assistant secretary of state in the Carter and Reagan administrations.

**Cecilia Dockendorff — Chile**

Dockendorff is the founder of SOLES (Solidarity and Spirituality), a professional society dedicated to promoting social development through cultural change.

**Peggy Dulany — United States**

Dulany is president and founder of the Synergos Institute. Dulany was senior vice president of the New York City Partnership, where she headed the youth employment and education programs; directed a Boston public high school program for drop-outs; and has consulted for the United Nations and Ford Foundation on health care and family planning in Brazil and elsewhere. She is a member of the Inter-American Dialogue.

**Joan Dunlop — United States**

Dunlop is president of the International Women's Health Coalition. She was an associate to John D. Rockefeller 3rd. She has worked for the City of New York under Mayor John Lindsay, at the New York Public Library under Dr. Vartan Gregorian, at the Ford Foundation and the Metropolitan Applied Research Center under Dr. Kenneth B. Clark.

**Patricia Ellis — United States**

Ellis is executive director of the Women's Foreign Policy Group, which promotes the leadership, visibility and participation of women in international affairs professions. Previously she taught at American University, specializing in news coverage of foreign affairs, and covered foreign affairs for the MacNeil-Lehrer Newshour and the Canadian Broadcasting Corporation. She was a fellow at Harvard's Center on the Press, Politics and Public Policy and a founding member of the International Women's Media Foundation, and is a member of the Council on Foreign Relations.

**Graciela Fernández Meijide — Argentina**

Fernández Meijide became national deputy representing the province of Buenos Aires for the Alianza in 1997, where she previously served from 1993 to 1995. She was elected to the Argentine Senate, representing the Federal Capital, for the Bloque FREPASO in 1995. She has been a member of the president's council of the Permanent Assembly for Human Rights since 1977. Fernández Meijide is a member of the Inter-American Dialogue.

**Azucena Ferrey — Nicaragua**

Ferrey was a national deputy and former leader of the Contras. She played a role in promoting an alliance between Contra and Sandinista women, to push through progressive legislation in favor of women. She is currently the director of Fundación Mujer Nicaraguense.

**Pia Figueroa Edwards — Chile**

Figueroa is an international consultant on the environment and is a member of several corporate boards. Figueroa was under-secretary of national assets during the Aylwin government and has been active in the Humanist Party in Chile, which she helped to create. She has also served as President of the Laura Rodriguez Foundation.

**Lourdes Flores Nano — Peru**

Flores Nano is a member of congress and served as a national deputy of the lower house of Congress from 1990 to 1992. She was also secretary general of the Popular Christian Party (PPC) of Peru. Flores Nano is a member of the board of directors of the Inter-American Dialogue.

**Rossana Fuentes-Berain — Mexico**

Fuentes-Berain has been the special assignment managing editor for *Reforma/El Norte* since August 1997. Prior to that she served as a reporter for the paper. From 1991 to 1994, she wrote and edited for *El Financiero,* and from 1988 to 1991, she wrote for the Mexican wire service *Notimex.* From 1983 to 1985, she was an analyst in the international press section of the Foreign Ministry.

**Amalia García Medina — Mexico**

García was elected to the Mexican Senate in 1997. She is a founding member of the Democratic Revolutionary Party (PRD) and as part of its national executive committee, she has served as the Party's secretary of communication, of international relations, and of political alliances.

**Magdalena García Hernández — Mexico**

García Hernández is an economist and has been a professor and researcher at UNAM, ITAM and the Universidad Autónoma de Puebla. She has served as executive director of economic studies at Banco Mexicano Somex, as a founding member and coordinator of the Women's Association for the Defense of Civil Rights (AMDEC), as a founder of the Agrupación Política Nacional Causa Ciudadana and of the National Assembly of Women. She is candidate for the legislature of the Federal District and currently serves as the Federal District's Director General for Social Policy.

**Ana Milena Gaviria — Colombia**

Gaviria is an economist and was first lady of Colombia. During her tenure as first lady she initiated various educational, health, recreational and cultural programs—including Banco Social, "Es Rico Leer", FAMI, and others—designed to incorporate young people, women and vulnerable groups into a range of development activities. She is a member of the board of ICRW.

**Dale A. Godsoe — Canada**

Godsoe is vice president external of Dalhousie University and director of numerous organizations including: Maritime Telegraph and Telephone Company, Viacom Canada, Women's Television Network Foundation, and Hambros Bank of Canada. From 1987-96, she was the director, and later national president, of YWCA Canada.

**Margarita Guzmán — Colombia**

Guzmán is an economist and independent consultant in the financial sector. She was vice president of the Corporación de Ahorro y Vivienda, a private bank and worked in the Coffee Federation for nearly ten years. She was the general manager of ten Women's Rural Factories and worked for the Inter-American Development Bank as a consultant on micro credit and women's issues. She founded the first affiliate of Women's World Banking in Cali and served as a member of its board of directors and executive committee for several years.

**Antonia Hernández — United States**

Hernández is President and General Counsel of the Mexican-American Legal Defense and Educational Fund in Los Angeles. She is a member of many boards including the Innovations in State and Local Government, National Endowment for Democracy and Council on Foreign Relations. She is a member of the Inter-American Dialogue.

**Adriana Hoffman Jacoby — Chile**

Hoffman is a biologist and botanist. She helped create the non-profit organization, Defenders of the Chilean Forest (Defensores del Bosque Chileno). Since 1979 she has worked with the Claudio Gay Foundation of the *El Mercurio* company in botanical and ecological research. She has written more than ten books on the flora and environment of Chile. In 1995 she won the Chilean Peace Prize from the World Peace Project Foundation and in 1997 the UNEP Prize Eyes on the Environment.

**Ana Julia Jatar — Venezuela**

Jatar is a senior fellow at the Inter-American Dialogue. She served as superintendent for the promotion and protection of free competition (the Venezuelan anti-trust agency); professor at the Institute for Advanced Administrative Studies; general director for the Venezuelan Institute of Planning; and financial analyst at VALIVENCIA investment bank.

**Monica Jiménez — Chile**

Jiménez is the executive director of PARTICIPA, an organization which promotes democratic civic participation. She is also an international consultant on citizenship and women's political leadership, for the UN, the Ford Foundation, the Inter-American Institute for Human Rights, the International Foundation for Electoral Systems, the National Democratic Institute and the Inter-American Foundation, in addition to being a member of the Board of Directors of the International Institute for Democracy and Electoral Assistance. Jiménez was executive director of the civic education campaign leading up to the 1988 plebiscite in Chile and was a member of the Truth and Reconciliation Commission.

**Clara Jusidman — Mexico**

Jusidman, an economist, is the Secretary of Education, Health and Social Development of the Federal District. She headed the Federal Electoral Register for the 1997 elections. Her other positions have included: coordinator of the Interdisciplinary Group for Women, Work and Poverty (GIMTRAP), Undersecretary of Fishery

Planning and Development and Director General of the National Consumer's Institute. She is a member of the Advisory Councils of the National Program of Women in Mexico and of the Women in Development (WID) program of the Inter-American Development Bank.

**Yolanda Kakabadse — Ecuador**

Kakabadse is executive president of Fundación Futuro Latinoamericano and president of the World Conservation Union (IUCN). She is counselor to the vice president for environment and sustainable development at the World Bank and senior advisor to UNDP's Global Environmental Facility. Kakabadse is a member of the boards of directors of the World Resources Institute and The Ford Foundation.

**Ruth de Krivoy — Venezuela**

Krivoy was president of the Central Bank of Venezuela and is currently president of Síntesis Financiera, a financial consulting firm. She was also director of the presidential commission for industrial competitiveness; member of the advisory commission for public sector debt refinancing; and member of the board of the Institute for Advanced Studies.

**Audrey Langworthy — United States**

Langworthy has been a Kansas state senator since 1984. She serves on the Executive Committee of the National Conference of State Legislatures and has been on the National Board of Governors of the American Red Cross. She is active in numerous community development organizations.

**Thérèse Lavoie-Roux — Canada**

Lavoie-Roux has been a senator since 1990 and was chairman of the Senate Committee on Internal Economy, Budgets and Administration. She is a member of the Committee on Social Affairs, Science and Technology and the Committee on National Finance. Lavoie-Roux was first elected to the Quebec National Assembly in 1976 and re-elected twice. She was minister of health and social services and the minister responsible for family policies and the office of the handicapped.

**Mirna Liévano — El Salvador**

Liévano is president of the School for Higher Education on Economics and Business. She was minister of planning and coordination of economic and social development; president of the Social Investment Fund; and governor to the World Bank and Inter-American Development Bank.

**Cecilia Loria Saviñón — Mexico**

Loria is a psychoanalyst, currently serving as president of the Popular Education Group for Women (GEM) and of Causa Ciudadana. She was president of the coordinating committee of the national coordination of NGOs "Toward Beijing in 1995/Hacia Beijing '95"; a member of the coordinating committee for the "Ganando Espacios" (1993-1994) and "Espacio Civil por la Paz" (ESPAZ, 1994-1995) campaigns; a member of the organizational group for the National Assembly for Women, the National Feminist coordinating committee and of the consultative council of the National Program for Women.

**Beatriz de Majo — Venezuela**

Majo is the president of Petroquímica Trasandina. She is also a member of the editorial board and columnist for the newspaper *El Nacional* and director of the Venezuelan Free Drug Foundation. She was president of the consulting firm CIEN and vice president of the Grupo Beracasa. Majo founded the Latin American Economical System, SELA, in 1976.

**Barbara J. McDougall — Canada**

McDougall is Chairperson of AT&T Canada Long Distance Services and a director of several other major Canadian corporations. She is an international business strategist. McDougall was Secretary of State for External Affairs, Minister of State (Finance), Minister of Privatization, and Minister of Employment and Immigration. She is a member of the Inter-American Dialogue.

**Daisy May McFarlane-Coke — Jamaica**

McFarlane-Coke is senior partner of Coke & Associates (Consulting Actuaries); Chairman of First Equity Corporation of Florida, and Director of Trafalgar Development Bank. She also serves as a member of the Council of the University of the West Indies and is Chairman of the Public Service Commission.

**Juliette C. McLennan — United States**

McLennan was U.S. ambassador to the UN Commission on the Status of Women and has represented the United States at various UN meetings. McLennan is a member of the board of ICRW, U.S. Friends of the UN World Food Program, and the Chesapeake Bay Maritime Museum.

**Patricia Mercado — Mexico**

Mercado is the Executive Director of Equidad de Genero: Ciudadania, Trabajo y Familia (Gender Equity: Citizenship, Labor and Family). She is a member of the directive council of DIVERSA, a feminist political association, and a member of the Executive Committee of the National Forum of Women and Population Policy.

**Beatriz Merino — Peru**

Merino is a congresswoman, elected in 1995. She was president of the Congressional Women's Committee in 1997 and is currently a member of the Environmental Committee and the Permanent Committee. A Harvard Law graduate, she is senior partner of Merino, van Hasselt & Morales, a corporate law firm. In 1990, Merino was elected to the Senate and in 1991 she chaired the Senate's Environmental Committee. She is a member of the Inter-American Dialogue.

**Lourdes R. Miranda — United States**

Miranda is president of the Miranda Foundation. For over twenty years she was chief executive of her own company, Miranda Associates, Inc., which provided international training and technical assistance. She has served as president of the National Association for Women Business Owners and the National Conference of Puerto Rican Women and as director of numerous organizations, including Amnesty International USA, the Puerto Rico Community Foundation and the Center for Women's Policy Studies.

**Sonia Montaño — Bolivia**

Montaño is a consultant on social policy, community development, governance and women's participation, and teaches for the graduate program in gender at the Universidad Mayor de San Simón de Cochabamba. From 1993-1995, she was the country's first under-secretary for gender in the Human Development Ministry. Montaño founded one of Bolivia's first feminist centers, Center for Information and Development of Women (CIDEM), in 1982.

**Michelle Montas — Haiti**

Montas is news director of Radio Haiti. Her work at the station has symbolized the struggle for press freedom and democratic gains in Haiti. She has worked as a journalist for 25 years, including nine years as a radio producer and writer for the United Nations Radio and eight years as chief editor of *Conjunction,* a magazine on social and economic issues.

**Maria Eugenia Morasso Nikken — Venezuela**

Morasso is Vice President of Empresas 1BC, a media communications conglomerate. She is a member of the executive committee of Gems Television in Miami and Coral International TV, a cable channel dedicated to Hispanic women.

**María de los Ángeles Moreno — Mexico**

Moreno is a national senator elected in the Federal District. She serves on the Foreign Affairs and Finance commissions and presides over the commission for the Federal District. She was head of the Under Secretariat of Planning and Budget for Social and Regional Development; Secretary of Fisheries; Deputy and President of the government body in the Lower Chamber; and President of Mexico's Institutional Revolutionary Party (PRI).

**Diana Natalicio — United States**

Natalicio is president of the University of Texas at El Paso. She has served on numerous boards and commissions, including the National Science Board, NASA Advisory Council, U.S.-Mexico Commission for Education and Cultural Exchange, the Advisory Commission on Educational Excellence for Hispanic Americans, and she chaired the American Association for Higher Education board.

**Laura Novoa — Chile**

Novoa is president of the board of PARTICIPA and a member of the law firm Philippi, Yrarrázaval, Pulido & Brunner, involved in mining, corporate and financial business. She was appointed to the National Commission on Truth and Reconciliation of Chile and served on the high-level advisory board for sustainable development of the United Nations.

**Milagros Ortiz Bosch — Dominican Republic**

Ortiz Bosch is a member of the National Council of the Magistrate. In 1994, she was Senator for the federal district. In 1992, she was the president of the eastern national district and the president of the southern national district in 1991.

**Sylvia Ostry — Canada**

Ostry is Distinguished Research Fellow, Centre for International Studies, University of Toronto. She has held several federal government posts including Chief Statistician, Deputy Minister of Consumer and Corporate Affairs, Chairman of the Economic Council, Deputy Minister of International Trade, Ambassador for Multilateral Trade Negotiations and the Prime Minister's Personal Representative for the Economic Summit. From 1990 to 1997 she was Chairman, Centre for International Studies. She is a member of the Inter-American Dialogue.

**Maria Otero — United States**

Otero is executive vice president of Acción International and chair of the Inter-American Foundation. She chaired the board of Bread for the World for six years, was a program officer for Acción International in Honduras, and worked in the women in development office of the U.S. Agency for International Development. She has published several monographs and edited a book on microenterprise. She was born and raised in La Paz, Bolivia.

**Maria Elena Ovalle — Chile**

Ovalle became a member of the board of the Central Bank of Chile in December 1995, having worked there from 1960-1978. From 1988-1995, she was president of the Chilean affiliate of Women's World Banking. She was the general manager of the Banking and Financial Institutions Association, alternate governor of the Latin American Federation of Banking ("FELABAN"), and general director of the Institution of Banking Studies.

**Marta Oyhanarte — Argentina**

Oyhanarte was elected as a representative to the Buenos Aires legislature in 1997. Prior to that, she was director of the Center for Citizen Participation and Control. She was co-founder and president of Poder Ciudadano Foundation, a non-profit citizens' group for democratic change. Currently, she is a member of the Academic Council of the Institute for the Promotion of Human Rights, the Advisory Council of the Inter-American Association of Mediation, the Center for Alternative Conflict Resolution, and the Society of Professionals in Dispute Resolution.

**Nina Pacari Vega — Ecuador**

Pacari is a representative to the National Constituent Assembly charged with drafting a new constitution for Ecuador and is a legal advisor for the Confederation of Indigenous Nationalities of Ecuador (CONAI). She is a member of the Inter-American Dialogue.

**Dulce Maria Pereira — Brazil**

Pereira is the president of the Palmares Cultural Foundation of the Ministry of Culture. She also directs and anchors the radio show, "The Black World: Brasilamefricaribe" and is the owner of VENUS Cinevideografia. She serves on the Interministerial Working Group for Valorization of Black People. She has worked on city planning in the Ministry of the Interior.

**Jacqueline Pitanguy — Brazil**

Pitanguy is the founding president and director of CEPIA (Citizenship, Studies, Information, and Action), which conducts research and advocacy on gender issues. She is a member of the board of directors of the Commission on Citizenship and Reproduction, the Institute for Education of UNESCO (Scientific and Cultural Organization), and the Inter-American Dialogue and was president of the National Council for Women's Rights.

**Pilar Ramírez — Bolivia**

Ramírez founded the Center for the Promotion of Economic Initiatives (FIE), a non-profit microenterprise-lending organization, which is creating a private financial fund of which she will be the first president.

**Beatrice Rangel — Venezuela**

Rangel is the Senior Vice President for Corporate Strategies for the Cisneros Group of Companies.

**Rozanne L. Ridgway — United States**

Ridgway was assistant secretary of state for European and Canadian affairs. She holds a variety of corporate and non-profit directorships. In addition, Ridgway is a member of the Inter-American Dialogue.

**Reyna Rincón de McPeck — Venezuela**

Rincón is developing an executive search practice through her own firm, McPeck & Associates. She was executive director of international operations for Grupo Zoom, a courier and transportation company. She is a licensed insurance broker, sits on two corporations' boards and consults with Grupo Zoom on new projects and development.

**Rosa Roa Peguero — Dominican Republic**

Roa Peguero is a member of the women's advisory commission to the Chamber of Deputies. She was her country's delegate to the Inter-American Commission of Women (CIM) of the Organization of American States as well as the general director of the national policy for the promotion of women.

**Cira Romero Barboza — Venezuela**

Romero formed two of her own consulting firms, Estrategias Empresariales 1A and Consultores ARIC. She has advised and served on the board of directors of both public and private sector institutions including Venezuelan Airmail Line, Industrial Bank of Venezuela, and the Ministry of Development.

**Maria Antonieta Saa — Chile**

Saa is a deputy in the Chilean Legislative Assembly.

**Gloria Salguero Gross — El Salvador**

Salguero is a deputy in the Salvadoran Legislative Assembly.

**Elizabeth Sanders — United States**

Sanders advises executive management on the implementation of people-centered leadership practices. She is the director of several national and international organizations, both profit and non-profit. From 1978-1990, she was the vice president and general manager of Nordstrom.

**Margaret Schuler — United States**

Schuler is founding executive director of Women, Law and Development International. From 1979-1992, she worked for OEF International on issues such as women's rights, civic education, and Central America. She was the national coordinator of the Federation for Economic Democracy and director of the Hispanic Women's Center.

**Helga Stephenson — Canada**

Stephenson is chair of Viacom Canada Ltd. She was executive director of the Festival of Festivals/Toronto International Film Festival and executive director of Cinematheque Ontario. Stephenson is on several boards of directors, including FOCAL Canadian Foundation for the Americas.

**Paula Stern — United States**

Stern is president of The Stern Group, an economic analysis and trade advisory firm. She was chairwoman of the U.S. International Trade Commission. Stern is a member of the President's advisory committee for trade policy and negotiations and chairwoman of the advisory committee of the U.S. Export-Import Bank. She is a senior fellow at the Progressive Policy Institute. She is a member of the Inter-American Dialogue.

**Marta Suplicy — Brazil**

Suplicy was elected to Congress, representing the Workers' Party, in 1995. She coordinated the Campaign for Women without Fear of Power, which promoted a 20% quota system for women candidates to elective posts, and organized a post-Beijing meeting of women parliamentarians and women's social movements in São Paulo.

**Rosalina Tuyuc — Guatemala**

Tuyuc is a vice president of the Guatemalan congress, representing the Frente Democrática Nuevo Guatemala (FNDC). She is also president of CONVIGUA, an association of Guatemalan widows.

**Virginia Vargas Valente — Peru**

Vargas is part of the World Bank's advisory board on gender, a Co-Chair

**Ximena Alexandra Verdesoto — Ecuador**

Verdesoto is coordinator of the Corporacion Andina de Fomento's United Technical Cooperation. Prior to that, she worked with the Swiss Embassy on a technical assistance project and at the International Bank of Reconstruction and Development as a consultant on adult education.

**Rocío Villanueva Flores — Peru**

Villanueva is the Peruvian ombudsman for women's affairs. She is a lawyer and has written and spoken extensively on human rights and domestic violence. She has worked for the women's organization, Movimiento Manuela Ramos, and taught at the University Castilla La Mancha in Toledo, Spain. Villanueva is also consulting for the Academy of Magistrates on the training of judges and public defenders.

**Elena Viyella de Paliza — Dominican Republic**

Viyella de Paliza is executive vice president of Fertilizantes de Santo Domingo and Sacos Agro-Industriales. She is a board member of several banks and corporations and is also on the board of the American Chamber of Commerce, the Dominican Development Foundation, and the Economic and Development Foundation. Viyella de Paliza is a member of the Group of Fifty and the Inter-American Dialogue.

**Carmen Delgado Votaw — United States**

Delgado is Director of Public Policy of United Way of America. She was president of the Inter-American Commission of Women (OAS) and co-chair of the presidentially appointed U.S. National Advisory Committee on women. She was director of government relations for Girl Scouts of the U.S.A. and an UNA/NCA (United Nations Association/National Capital Area) board member. Her most recent book is *Puerto Rican Women*.

**María Soledad Weinstein — Chile**

Weinstein is coordinator of the Center for Information and Documentation of Isis International, and co-founder of Isis in Chile. She is a member of the Chilean Committee of Women for Leadership a member of the Advisory Council of the National Women's Service (SERNAM) in Chile, and director of the Family Foundation.

**Claudette Werleigh — Haiti**

Werleigh is the president of the Women's Power League (Lig Pouvwa Fanm). She has held many public offices in the Haitian government including prime minister, minister of foreign affairs, chief of staff for the prime minister, and minister of social affairs.

# IX. Eradication of Poverty and Discrimination

# Women's Rights and Opportunities in Latin America: Problems and Prospects

*Mala N. Htun*

*Issue Brief, April 1998*

## FOREWORD

In July 1997, the Inter-American Dialogue and the International Center for Research on Women (ICRW) convened the first meeting of the **Women's Leadership Conference of the Americas (WLCA)**, a network of 100 women leaders from nineteen countries in North, Central and South America and the Caribbean—including former presidents, prime ministers, business executives, women's rights activists, and other non-governmental leaders. The group has decided to work together toward three goals: expand the number and enhance the contribution of women in top leadership positions; promote policy and institutional changes that will improve opportunities for all women in the region; and strengthen other non-governmental initiatives that advance women's equality, and facilitate their access to policy officials.

In accord with decisions reached at the first meeting of the Women's Leadership Conference of the Americas, members of the WLCA network formed a task force to monitor the status of women in the hemisphere and the extent of progress being made by governments to fulfill their international commitments to women. We are pleased to present this preliminary report on the status of women prepared under the auspices of the **WLCA Task Force on Monitoring**.

This report provides a snapshot of the condition of women in Latin America now, underlining the advances women have made and the obstacles they still face in the areas of political leadership, legal rights, domestic violence, health, economic opportunities, and education. Over the next six months, building on this report, the Task Force will set out to design a methodology for governments of the hemisphere to monitor, measure, record and report on the progress they have made toward fulfilling commitments to women undertaken at the two Summits of the Americas, in Miami and Santiago, and at other international forums. The blueprint will lay out how existing data on the status

---

*The **Women's Leadership Conference of the Americas (WLCA)** is a hemispheric network of 100 women leaders from throughout the hemisphere, drawn from 20 different countries and diverse political and professional perspectives. These outstanding women have decided to work together to expand the number and enhance the performance of women in top leadership positions in Latin America and the Caribbean, promote policy and institutional changes to improve opportunities for all women in the region, and reinforce other non-governmental initiatives to advance women's equality and access to power. They are focusing priority attention on four issues as they relate to women in the region: leadership, domestic violence and judicial systems, education for the workplace, and corporate and multilateral bank social responsibility. The membership includes former presidents and prime ministers, business executives, parliamentarians, scholars, activists, and other civil society leaders. The WLCA is co-sponsored by the Inter-American Dialogue and the International Center for Research on Women.*

*The **Inter-American Dialogue** is the premier center for policy analysis and exchange on Western Hemisphere affairs. The Dialogue's select membership of 100 distinguished private citizens from throughout the Americas includes political, business, academic, media, and other non-governmental leaders. Seven Dialogue members served as presidents of their countries and more than a dozen have served at the cabinet level.*

*The Dialogue works to improve the quality of debate and decisionmaking on hemispheric problems, advance opportunities for regional economic and political cooperation, and bring fresh, practical proposals for action to governments, international institutions, and non-governmental organizations. Since 1982–through successive Republican and Democratic administrations and many changes of leadership in Latin America, the Caribbean, and Canada–the Dialogue has helped shape the agenda of issues and choices on inter-American relations.*

*The **International Center for Research on Women (ICRW)** is a private, nonprofit organization dedicated to promoting economic and social development with women's full participation. ICRW conducts policy-oriented research and provides technical assistance on women's economic activity, their reproductive and sexual health and rights, their leadership in society, and their management of environmental resources. ICRW advocates with governments and multilateral agencies and engages in an active policy communications program. It collaborates with other non-governmental institutions to advance women's economic opportunities and rights. Founded twenty years ago, ICRW focuses principally on women in developing and transition countries. It is supported by grants, contracts, and contributions from international and national development agencies, foundations, corporations, and individuals.*

---

Mala N. Htun is a graduate student associate and Ph.D. candidate at the Weatherhead Center for International Affairs, Harvard University. Beginning in January 2000, she will assume a position as Assistant Professor of Political Science at New School University.

of women should be assembled, evaluated, and linked to policy. It will also point out where information is deficient, and call on governments and international institutions to put in place a region-wide system of monitoring that will allow citizens to hold their governments accountable.

On behalf of the WLCA, we wish to thank the members of the Task Force for their guidance in this endeavor. They are Co-Chairs Juliette C. McLennan (United States) and Jacqueline Pitanguy (Brazil); Mayra Buvinic (United States/Chile); Margaret Catley-Carlson (canada); Lourdes Flores Nano (Peru); Monica Jimenez de Barros (Chile); Clara Jusidman de Bialostozky (Mexico); and Sonia Montaño (Bolivia). We are particularly grateful to Mala N. Htun for her extensive field research and the sustained quality of her writing of the report. Special thanks are also due to Samuel Robfogel for his skillful management of the monitoring project overall, and for the production of this report. We also wish to thank Sandra Forero, Kara Krolikowski, and Ben Smith for their research and editorial assistance. Special thanks go to Co-Chairs of the WLCA, Jan Myers (United States) and Sonia Picado (Costa Rica) for their unflagging leadership. Finally, we wish to express our appreciation to ICRW and the Promoting Women in Development (PROWID) program of the United States Agency for International Development for providing the financial support for this project.

Joan Caivano
Director, WLCA

---

This report was made possible through support provided by the International Center for Research on Women (ICRW) through the Office of Women in Development, Global Bureau, United States Agency for International Development (USAID), under the terms of Cooperative Agreement FAO-0100-A-00-5030-00. The opinions expressed herein do not necessarily reflect the views of USAID, ICRW, Inter-American Dialogue, or the members of the WLCA.

# IX. ERADICATION OF POVERTY AND DISCRIMINATION

## INTRODUCTION

This brief analyzes the status of women in Latin America in six thematic areas: political leadership, legal rights, domestic violence, health, economic opportunities, and education. These six areas correspond to the commitments made by governments at the 1994 Summit of the Americas in Miami, and the priorities established by members of the Women's Leadership Conference of the Americas (WLCA). The brief aims to describe some of the legal changes and policy initiatives being introduced in various countries to improve women's position and analyze their effects.

Although new laws have been passed and new public policies adopted, the commitment of most governments to improving the status of women is primarily symbolic. Women's participation has increased and there is more official attention to creating equal opportunities; yet, too often new policy initiatives and institutions lack the political will and the resources to carry out their mandate.

The analysis presented here is preliminary. It takes an anecdotal approach, highlighting the experiences of a few countries that may suggest general tendencies in the region as a whole. A more comprehensive report will be published later this year by the Women's Leadership Conference of the Americas (WLCA). In addition, the WLCA will design and promote a strategy for monitoring the status of women throughout Latin America and the Caribbean.

## POLITICAL PARTICIPATION, REPRESENTATION, AND LEADERSHIP

Women's presence in power in Latin America and the Caribbean has increased significantly, but is still low relative to women's share of the electorate and participation in political parties. Only about 9 percent of cabinet level posts and 15 percent of the seats in the national legislature are held by women (IPU 1998, UN 1996). Women's participation in decisionmaking and leadership lags behind women's gains in education, their contributions to the workforce, and their participation at the middle and bottom of organizations.

Today, women's opportunities to participate in decisionmaking tend to be greatest outside of the main centers of power. The proportion of women in leadership roles is greater at lower levels of the organizational hierarchy and in less prestigious and less powerful government agencies. Women are more likely to succeed in politics outside of major cities. According to a survey of 133 Latin American women parliamentarians published in 1993, 64 percent came from outside of capital cities (Rivera-Cira 1993). In Mexico, data from 1995 show that there were 101 women mayors (4.2 percent of a total of 2,395 municipalities), but that only nine of these governed municipalities with more than 50,000 inhabitants, and none with more than 100,000 residents (Massolo 1995). In Brazil, the wealthier, more developed southeastern region tends to elect fewer women mayors (four percent were women in 1997) than the poorer north and northeastern regions (nine percent) (Martins Costa 1997).

Although it is likely that cultural changes produced by women's presence in the workforce and at the middle and bottom of organizations will help to erode discriminatory barriers, this will happen only in the long term. To help women gain access to power on an equal basis in the short and medium-term, many Latin American governments are experimenting with affirmative action policies.

The most popular affirmative action mechanisms in Latin America today are quota rules establishing a minimum level of women's participation in national elections. To date, Argentina, Bolivia, Brazil, Costa Rica, the Dominican Republic, Ecuador, Panama, Peru, and Venezuela have passed national laws requiring political parties to reserve 20 to 40 percent of candidacies for women [see box]. No consensus exists, however, that quotas are the best policy tool. Furthermore, the effectiveness of quotas in helping more women get elected depends on additional factors, such as the country's electoral system and the support political parties give to women candidates.

Once in power, women politicians in Latin America have been able to bring about legislative and policy changes when they have united into broad, multi-partisan alliances (called a *bancada feminina*). These *bancadas* are particularly effective when supported by linkages with women's movements and NGOs in civil society. Women's organizing of this nature has led to the approval of domestic violence and quota laws in Argentina, the Dominican Republic, Mexico, and Peru.

Most countries have created agencies for women charged with proposing legislation, advising other ministries on public policies related to women, and serving as an advocate of women's interests within the state. The power, institutional position, resources, and legitimacy of these agencies varies dramatically among countries. A preliminary analysis of successes and failures reveals that their success depends on several factors: the personal interest of the president and other senior leaders; a favorable relationship with other ministries; stable budgets; and credibility with the organized women's movement. Without these conditions, women's agencies can become ghettos that isolate women's issues away from the mainstream of state action, or instruments to promote the interests of the ruling party and not of women.

Congressional commissions on women have also been established. The structures and powers of these commissions vary. In Brazil, for example, the national commission was created to study legislative implementation of the Platform for Action that emerged from the UN Fourth World Conference on Women in Beijing, and has no other powers. The Peruvian Commission, on the other hand, is a regular commission with powers to propose legislation. It has sponsored four successful pieces of legislation promoting women's interests, including the quota law of 1997.

At the sub-national level, there are an increasing number of women's agencies in state and municipal governments. One notable example is the state of São Paulo's Council on the Condition of Women, which promoted new policy measures in the areas of violence and women's health, and secured the approval of the Paulista Convention on the Elimination of All Forms of Discrimination against Women.

---

## Quotas

One of the most interesting new trends in Latin American democracies is the creation of quota laws intended to increase women's representation in political office. The movement toward quotas is gaining momentum (see table).

The quota debate in national legislation has been spurred by the fact that several major political parties already use quotas in elections for internal leadership posts. Parties with women's quotas include: Mexico's PRD (30 percent) and PRI (30 percent); Chile's Partido Socialista (30 percent), Partido por la Democracia (40 percent), and Democracia Cristiana (20 percent); Costa Rica's PUSC (40 percent); Brazil's PT (30 percent); Venezuela's Acción Democrática (20 percent); El Salvador's FMLN (35 percent); Nicaragua's FSLN (30 percent); and Paraguay's Partido Colorado (20 percent) and Partido Revolucionario Febrerista (30 percent).

The case for quotas centers on two themes. First, because discrimination is deeply ingrained in organizational practices and everyday assumptions, more gradualist forms of affirmative action will only produce results in the long-term. Quotas are an effective way of getting women into power in the immediate term. Second, the presence of women in decisionmaking positions is expected to change policy outcomes, since women leaders will be more likely to represent women's interests. The experience of Argentina supports some of the arguments in favor of quotas. One study shows that Argentine women legislators are more likely to sponsor pieces of legislation dealing with women's rights and families than men are (Jones 1996).

Opponents of quotas argue that they discriminate against men, will elevate underqualified women to power, and above all, are unnecessary, since qualified women will rise to power on their own merits. They are also concerned that women beneficiaries of a quota will be stigmatized for owing their position to the quota and not to their own efforts.

The outcomes of quotas are dramatically different depending on a country's particular electoral institutions. In Argentina, national congressional elections are conducted according to a closed party list system, and the law requires that women be placed in electable positions on the list. The results of quotas have been spectacular. Women's representation in Congress was 5 percent before the quota law took effect, and is now 28 percent.

In Peru and in Brazil, electoral rules are different, and there is no party list. In national legislative elections, voters vote in huge, multi-member districts for individual candidates. Although quotas require that women be named to 25 percent of party spots, women candidates complain that sex discrimination within parties means that their campaigns receive little publicity and little support. Brazil's first experiment with quotas took place in the 1997 municipal elections where a quota of 20 percent applied to candidates for city council positions (vereadores). Before the elections, women amounted to 8 percent of the total number of vereadores in the country, and after, women's representation climbed to 11 percent nationwide. In the 1998 national elections, women's presence in Congress decreased from 7 to 6 percent.

# IX. ERADICATION OF POVERTY AND DISCRIMINATION

**Countries with Quota Laws**

| Country | Date of Law | Requirement for Women's Participation | Women's Representation in Congress |
|---|---|---|---|
| Argentina | 1991 | 30% of places on closed party lists for elections to Lower House of Congress | 28% (from 5% before the law) |
| Bolivia | 1997 | 30% of closed party lists used to elect half of Lower House of Congress | 12% (from 7%) |
| Brazil | 1995; modified in 1997 | 25% of candidates in legislative elections (to increase to 30% in 2000)[‡] | 6% (from 7%) |
| Costa Rica | 1996 | 40% of candidates for internal party elections and among candidates for general elections | 19% (from 16%) |
| Dominican Republic | 1997 | 25% of candidates | 16% (from 10%) |
| Ecuador | 1997 | 20% of candidates | 17% |
| Panama | 1997 | 30% of candidates for internal party elections and among candidates for general elections | no data |
| Peru | 1997 | 25% of candidates in general elections | 28% of municipal councilors in metropolitan Lima (from 21%) |
| Venezuela | 1998 | 30% of candidates for PR list seats | 13% |

[‡] In the 1996 municipal elections, a women's quota of 20 percent was in effect. In 1997, the law was changed to establish a quota of 25 percent for the 1998 national elections, and 30 percent for the 2000 municipal elections.

## LAW AND THE JUDICIARY

When it comes to women, Latin America's laws are both progressive and reactionary. On the one hand, Latin American countries have made major advances toward legal equality in recent years with respect to domestic violence, political participation, family law, and basic rights. In the region's labor codes, women have long enjoyed mandatory maternity leave and protection of pregnancy.

On the other hand, laws persist in many countries that are completely antithetical to women's equality. Women in all countries except for Chile, Cuba, Mexico, and Venezuela, are prohibited from certain types of work including working at night, at dangerous or unhealthy jobs, from lifting heavy objects, from working in mines, and/or from distilling or manufacturing alcohol (FLACSO 1995). In some countries rapists can be acquitted by marrying their victims, and rape is considered a crime against custom, not against a person [see box]. A woman commits adultery when she has sexual relations with any man other than her husband, but a man engages in adulterous behavior only by having a long-term extramarital relationship (UNIFEM 1996).

Yet, the central problem with women's legal rights in Latin America is not always the lack of legislation and regulation, rather, it is its uneven application. In order for the equal rights women enjoy in written law to be put into practice, three factors are important: women must bring suits based on those rights into court, lawyers must base their arguments on women's rights, and judges must be sensitive to such arguments.[1]

In the past, these three factors combined negatively. Today, however, the scene is different, largely due to the effort of women's movements to increase women's knowledge of their rights and to train lawyers and judges to be sensitive to gender prejudice. Women are also entering into the legal profession in greater numbers. The proportion of students enrolled in law school who are women is climbing to nearly or above half in many countries. Women's representation among trial court judges in the region is around 45 percent. Nonetheless, women's growing presence at lower levels of the judiciary is not duplicated at higher levels. Regionwide, women comprise 20 percent of appeals court judges, and their presence is virtually zero at the Supreme Court level (FLACSO 1995).

Fifteen Latin American countries have human rights ombudsman offices, and in six of these (Colombia, Costa Rica, El Salvador, Guatemala, Mexico and Peru) there is a specific institution charged with working with women.[2] The "women's rights ombudsman" agencies receive complaints about human rights violations, investigate cases, work to train and sensitize judges and law enforcement personnel, and have challenged the constitutionality of discriminatory laws in court.

Finally, international conventions, which in theory are binding on member states, have contributed to changing legal culture in the region. The U.N. Convention on the Elimination of all Forms of Discrimination against Women (CEDAW) has been ratified by all but one of the Organization of American States (OAS) member states (the United States), and the Inter-American Convention to Prevent, Punish, and Eradicate Violence against Women (Belém do Pará) has been ratified by all but six OAS member states.

Other international documents such as the Beijing Platform for Action are statements of principles, and not binding on member states. In a legal sense, the documents may influence jurisprudence if judges consider them to be "general principles of law." More importantly, they serve as rallying forces for women's movements seeking reform, and as instruments to measure governmental progress and hold governments accountable to their commitments.

---

### Rape

In many countries, rape is considered a crime against custom, not against a person. This means that the goal of the law is to protect good customs, not the person who is raped (Linhares 1994; UNIFEM 1996). In all but three Latin American countries, charges can only be pressed against a rapist through a private suit initiated by the victim or her legal representatives; state authorities on their own initiative cannot prosecute rapists (FLACSO 1995). A private suit, however, exposes women to threats by the rapist and pressure from family and peers to drop the charges (Linhares 1994).

In Guatemala, rape and other sex crimes can only be committed against "honest women." According to the law, dishonest women and men (usually prostitutes) are incapable of being raped (Mijangos 1998).

An important advance in some countries has been the definition of marital rape as a crime. Colombia's Intra-family Violence Law of 1996 defined and penalized marital rape. In December of 1997, a political alliance of women in the Mexican Congress and civil society secured approval of a law that defined marital rape as a serious crime. The bill generated enormous controversy and debate, yet was eventually approved due to the pressures and threats advanced against recalcitrant male legislators by a united front of women.[3]

Even in countries where advances in the formal laws have been made, law enforcement authorities remain insensitive to victims of sexual violence. The Peruvian *Defensoría del Pueblo* (or human rights commission), for example, has been investigating complaints that judges are more favorable toward women who were virgins prior to the rape, and that they frequently blame victims for provoking rape. Rape victims have also complained that medical examiners question them extensively about their sexual histories (US Department of State 1998b). In Mexico City, in spite of the creation of a unit in the public prosecutor's office to receive victims of sexual and domestic violence, the prosecution of rapists has steadily decreased over the last twenty years. In 1971, 37 percent of presumed rapists were prosecuted. This decreased to 24 percent in 1980, 19 percent in 1990, and 14 percent in 1994 (Acosta 1997).

## Abortion

With the exception of Cuba, abortion is considered a crime in all Latin American countries. Many countries permit "therapeutic abortion," or abortions performed to save the life of the mother (Argentina, Bolivia, Brazil, Costa Rica, Ecuador, Guatemala, Panama, Paraguay, Uruguay, Venezuela, and Peru). Some countries also permit abortions if the pregnancy results from a rape (Mexico, Bolivia, Brazil, Panama, and Uruguay) (UNIFEM 1996). In Panama, abortions may be performed in the case of serious fetal abnormalities (Bermúdez 1993). In other countries where non-therapeutic abortions are illegal, the penalties for abortion are reduced when the abortion is performed after a rape (Peru, Colombia), to hide a woman's "dishonor" (Argentina), or when there are fetal abnormalities (Peru). In Uruguay, abortions are not punished when performed for reasons of economic hardship or anxiety (UNIFEM 1996).

Legal abortions are rarely performed in public health facilities. Middle class women who can afford private doctors and clinics have safe access to legal abortions, but poor women do not.

Although few women are prosecuted by the state for having an abortion, the fact that abortion is considered a crime pushes the practice underground. The millions of women who undergo abortion every year in Latin America must do so in unregulated and often dangerous circumstances. Women who undergo clandestine abortions are at risk of infection, hemorrhage, damage to the uterus or cervix, and adverse reactions to drugs. Abortion accounts for a high proportion of maternal mortality. In Bolivia, for example, studies show that 27 to 35 percent of maternal deaths result from abortions (Montaño 1998).

## VIOLENCE AGAINST WOMEN

Although violence against women is an ancient problem, it has emerged on the political agenda of Latin American countries only recently. This is largely due to the efforts of women's movements to call attention to the problem of violence and demand government action. In the 1990s, lobbying by women's movement groups from civil society and women in elected office has led to the adoption of measures to address violence, including new legislation, police stations for women, shelters and counseling centers, and training courses for law enforcement officers.

Domestic or intra-family violence is widespread. Surveys show that around one-half of women have suffered violence at the hands of their husbands or partners. The following table, adapted from a 1994 World Bank document, summarizes the results of studies conducted across Latin America on the prevalence of domestic violence.

Many women tolerate violence in the home because their unequal position in economy and society allows them few other options. Women have fewer opportunities than men in the labor market, receive lower wages, and are subject to family and social pressures. This makes exiting abusive relationships appear unviable, both to women victims and to their male abusers. In this sense, violence against women is related to women's weaker position in the social structure at large.

The victims of violence are disproportionately poor. A study conducted by the Inter-American Development Bank in Nicaragua found that 41 percent of non-wage-earning women are victims of violence, compared to 10 percent of women holding salaried jobs outside of the home (IDB 1997).

Twelve Latin American countries have adopted new laws on domestic violence (GPI 1997). Governments have established shelters, launched educational campaigns, and created centers to counsel women victims of violence and offer legal advice. They have also created women's police stations [see box] and given judges and prosecutors increased powers to issue protective orders. Inadequate resources, however, have resulted in poor enforcement of new laws and incomplete implementation of preventative and treatment programs. Moreover, most efforts to date have focused on urban areas, leaving women in rural areas with little recourse.

One major obstacle to effective investigation and prosecution of domestic violence is obtaining medical evidence. For many women, medical exams are problematic due to scarce facilities, few female personnel at those facilities, and demeaning treatment.

NGOs have led efforts to combat domestic violence, often implementing programs that serve as models for governments. Because of the unevenness of governmental action, NGOs have been forced to play a crucial role in filling communities' needs.

Data suggest that new laws, women's police stations, and increased public awareness of domestic violence have led to an increase in the number of cases reported to the courts. In Chile, for example, there were 13,834 cases reported to the Court of Appeals of Santiago in 1997, up from 1,419 in 1994 when the new law on violence was introduced (Bilbao 1997). However, the number of prosecutions remains low. In Chile, the government estimates that only one in five suits actually lead to a judgement. Out of the cases that are decided by a court, only one in 20 lead to a sentencing (SERNAM 1997).

**Results of Studies on the Frequency of Violence Against Women in Latin America**

| Country and year of study | Sample type | Findings |
| --- | --- | --- |
| Chile (1993) | Random sample of 1000 Santiago women, aged 22 to 55, involved in a relationship for at least 2 years | 60 percent have been abused by a male intimate; 26 percent have been physically abused. |
| Colombia (1990) | National random sample of 3,272 urban women and 2,118 rural women | 20 percent have been physically abused; 33 percent psychologically abused; 10 percent have been raped by their husband. |
| Costa Rica (1990) | Convenience sample of 1,388 women at a child welfare clinic | 54 percent have been physically abused. |
| Ecuador (1992) | Convenience sample of 200 low-income women in Quito | 60 percent had been beaten by a partner. |
| Guatemala (1990) | Random sample of 1000 women in Sacatepequez | 49 percent had been abused, 74 percent of these by a male partner. |
| Mexico (n.d.) | Random household survey of 1,163 urban and 427 rural women on DIF register in Jalisco | 57 percent of urban and 44 percent of rural had experienced interpersonal violence. |
| Mexico (1992) | Random sample of 342 women in Mexico City | 33 percent had lived in a violent relationship; 6 percent had experienced marital rape. |

Source: Heise (1994).

## Women's Police Stations

The first women's police stations in the world were created in 1985 in the state of São Paulo, Brazil. Since then, women's police stations have been established in the rest of Brazil and other countries of Latin America. Created to facilitate reporting, investigation, and prosecution of cases of domestic violence, these stations are largely staffed by women police officers who have been specially trained to handle cases of domestic violence and rape. Today, there are hundreds of women's police stations all over Latin America.

The women's police stations have greatly improved the state's treatment of victims of violence. In Brazil, prior to the creation of the women's stations, police rarely investigated incidents of violence against women and treated victims with indifference. Often, they failed to inform victims of the proper procedures for reporting violence, which involve getting an official medical exam and returning to the station to provide formal testimony (Nelson 1996; Thomas 1991).

*Continued on next page*

# IX. Eradication of Poverty and Discrimination

## Women's Police Stations
*Continued from previous page*

The stations have also helped communities to recognize domestic violence as criminal behavior constituting a violation of human rights. Following establishment of the stations, reporting of domestic violence and rape has increased on an annual basis. However, the stations have not created a significant increase in investigations and prosecutions of perpetrators of violence in the region.

In the first half of 1994, roughly one-third (16,219) of a total of 54,472 incidents reported in the state of São Paulo, Brazil, resulted in a police investigation. Far fewer than these actually led to prosecution or conviction (Nelson 1996). Of the 4000 complaints received by the women's station in the northern Brazilian city of São Luis, Maranhão between 1988 and 1990, only 300 ended up in court, and only 2 perpetrators were convicted (Thomas 1991). Out of the 300 cases of domestic violence investigated by the Support Center for Rape Victims in Mexico City, only 15 percent of offenders were sentenced (Acosta 1997).

The fact that investigation, prosecution, and sentencing rates remain low suggests that while victims of violence feel increasingly empowered to seek help, perpetrators continue to enjoy impunity.

## WOMEN'S HEALTH

The situation of women's basic health has improved in the region as a whole, although there are still major gaps in the area of reproductive and sexual health. Data on life expectancy demonstrate that women in Latin America have gotten steadily more healthy over the past several decades. In the region as a whole, women's life expectancy was 54 years in the 1950s, 64 years in the 1970s, and is now 71 years. Figures for individual countries range from a high of 79 years in Costa Rica to a low of 61 years in Bolivia (FLACSO 1995). Yet, in some countries there have been alarming increases in rates of breast and cervical cancer, heart disease, and AIDS.

The United Nations Conference on Population and Development held in Cairo in 1994 urged governments to approach women's health in an integral manner. The integral approach represents a major advance over past policies, which tended to treat women exclusively in their roles as mothers and reproducers.[4]

Brazil was a pioneer in approaching women's health from an integral perspective. In 1984, the government introduced a Program for Integral Assistance to Women's Health (PAISM), designed on the recommendations of experts and activists from the women's movement. However, the program has still not been implemented in the vast majority of cities and states around the country. The Brazilian example reveals that women's health programs often lack sufficient funding and the political will to seriously implement them.

Women's access to pre-natal care and obstetric services has increased in most countries. In Mexico, for example, women's access to public and private health care has grown significantly in the past decade. In 1987, 45 percent of women giving birth were serviced by the public sector, and 18 percent by the private. By 1994, public coverage had increased to 64 percent of women giving birth, and private to 22 percent. Whereas in 1987, 33 percent of mothers gave birth in their own homes, by 1994 this had decreased to 10 percent (INEGI 1997).

Increased access is reflected in lower rates of maternal mortality since the 1970s, although the variation among countries is substantial (see table).

In general, the coverage and quality of health care remains inadequate, a situation reflected in the low frequency of screening for cervical cancer [see box]. Although preventable if caught early, cervical cancer remains the greatest cause of cancer death among women. Low access to health care is also reflected in high unmet demand for modern contraceptives.

**Maternal Mortality: rate per 100,000 live births.**

| Country | 1990 |
| --- | --- |
| Argentina | 100 |
| Bolivia | 650 |
| Brazil | 220 |
| Chile | 65 |
| Colombia | 100 |
| Costa Rica | 60 |
| Cuba | 95 |
| Dominican Republic | 110 |
| Ecuador | 150 |
| El Salvador | 300 |
| Guatemala (1998) | 248 |
| Honduras | 220 |
| Mexico | 110 |
| Nicaragua (1996) | 198 |
| Panama | 55 |
| Paraguay | 160 |
| Peru | 280 |
| Uruguay | 85 |
| Venezuela | 120 |

Source: UNDP (1997); Pizarro (1997); Alvarado, et. al. (1998).

Government-run family planning programs frequently have low coverage, so many women have no access to safe and reliable contraception, or they self-medicate, without good information and at some risk. As a result, illegal abortions are frequent, and many poor women suffer complications due to dangerous and unsanitary conditions [see box above].

Sterilization is among the most widely used methods of family planning in Latin America, except in countries like Argentina and Chile where it is illegal or access is restricted. High rates of sterilization are common to developing countries around the world: the percentage of contraceptive users who are sterilized is twice as high in developing countries than in developed countries (22 versus 11 percent) (Berquó 1994). Latin America is no exception. In 1990, the percentage of women contraceptive users who were sterilized was 38 percent in Mexico, 44 percent in Brazil, and 69 percent in El Salvador (Ross 1991). Data from Brazil show that there is a high correlation between low levels of economic development and the frequency of sterilization: in 1991 there was a much higher proportion of sterilized female contraceptive users in the poorer Northeast (63 percent) than in the wealthier city of São Paulo (36 percent). This suggests that sterilization is seen as the cheapest option for women who have little money to buy other methods or lack information about their options and proper usage.

Many women are sterilized without receiving prior information about the procedure or giving their consent. A study from Mexico found that one-quarter of women sterilized were not informed about the consequences of the procedure beforehand (UN/CEDAW 1998). Nationwide family planning targets in Peru have created incentives for public health officials to coerce women into the procedure, leading to widespread abuses that have been documented by women's organizations, members of the Peruvian Congress, and the Roman Catholic Church (Sims 1998).

In Argentina and Chile, while improved economic conditions have led to improvements in women's health generally, there has been a severe lack of attention to reproductive health. This has contributed to a high rate of abortions: in 1990, there were 4.5 abortions per 100 women aged 15-49 in Chile, compared with 2.7 in the US, 2.3 in Mexico and 1.2 in canada (Alan Guttmacher Institute 1994). The widespread practice of abortion in Chile is in part a consequence of the lack of comprehensive diffusion of information about contraception and lack of access to sterilization. In Mexico, Colombia, and Brazil, where the state has assumed the responsibility for family planning and approved of private suppliers of contraceptives, the rate of abortion is lower.

In many countries, women's NGOs have begun to fill the gap left by inadequate state action in family planning and women's health. The Nicaraguan non-governmental health clinic, Sí Mujer, services 18,000 women clients in Managua.

Many Latin American governments hesitate to take measures in the area of women's reproductive health because of pressure from the Roman Catholic Church. Yet, the consequences of this inaction are increasing problems for women's health.

> ### Cervical Cancer
>
> One consequence of inadequate health care coverage is the high rate of cervical cancer throughout the region. Cervical cancer is preventable by regular pap smears and effective laboratory analysis, but few women have access to prevention and treatment options. In most countries, cervical cancer is the most common form of cancer death in women. Yet, in Mexico a survey of 4,000 women done in the Federal District and the state of Oaxaca found that 42 percent were unaware of the purpose of a pap smear, and that 97 percent had never had one (CRLP/GIRE 1997). In Peru, one study estimated that merely seven percent of Peruvian women had undergone pap smears; another study found that Peruvian laboratories were generating a high proportion of false negatives when analyzing pap smears (Grupo Impulsor 1997).
>
> Women's movement organizations in some countries have provoked state action on cervical cancer prevention. Several years ago, upon learning that the Brazilian city of Recife had the third highest incidence of cervical cancer in the world, a women's NGO, SOS Corpo, launched a campaign in prevention. Their aim was to enlarge the state's capacity to conduct pap smears and perform laboratory tests, to train medical personnel, and then to educate the public about the importance of regular screening. The campaign was so successful that the state health department adopted it as its own, and the experience became a model for a national campaign launched by the National Cancer Institute.[5]

## WOMEN AT WORK

One of the most salient trends in Latin America over the past several decades has been the increasing participation of women in formal economic activities. Women make up one-third of the labor force in the region as a whole. Yet, women continue to participate on unequal terms with men.

*Women are more likely to be unemployed than men.* In 1990, the rate of unemployment for women in the region as a whole was 8.3 percent; for men, it was 7 percent (FLACSO 1995). Women's rates of economic activity are lower than men's: in the region as a whole in 1990, women's economic activity rate was 27 percent while men's was 70 percent (FLACSO 1995).

*Access to microenterprise credit has expanded, but there is still much unmet demand.* Microenterprise credit is widely seen as an effective way to increase women's income-generating capacities. Both governments and private organizations offer credit to low-income women at reduced interest rates. One promising model is Women's World Banking (WWB). WWB was created in 1979 with support from the United Nations, and has 47 affiliate chapters around the world, including 19 in Latin America. In 1990, WWB had 12 million dollars in loan guarantees outstanding, mostly ranging from $150 to $600.

*Women's salaries are consistently lower than men's.* In Latin America, women's average wages were between 20 and 40 percent lower than men's in 1992, a gap comparable to those in industrialized countries. Since the 1970s, income differentials between men and women have generally decreased, particularly in urban areas. The gap is smaller for younger women than for older women. In 9 out of 12 countries surveyed by the UN Economic Commission on Latin America and the Caribbean (ECLAC), women aged 25 to 34 earned between 80 and 90 percent of men's income in 1992 (UN ECLAC 1995).

In Brazil, the average income of women employees in 1990 was 60 percent that of men (FLACSO 1995). In Colombia in 1990, women's earnings were 76 percent of men's in the formal sector (FLACSO 1993a); women employees earned 74 percent of male wages in Argentina in 1989 (FLACSO 1993b); in Venezuela, 1989 data show that women's earnings amounted to 78 percent of men's (Winter 1992). In Canada women earn 63 percent of men's salaries; in Switzerland, 68 percent; in the U.K., 70 percent; and in the United States and Germany, 75 percent (UNDP 1995).

*Women are clustered in particular occupations, that tend to offer lower status and lower pay.* In Brazil, 50 percent of women work in occupations where one finds only 5 percent of the male labor force; equally, 50 percent of men work in areas where only 5 percent of the female labor force works (Lavinas and Perira 1996). More than 80 percent of tailors, primary school teachers, secretaries, telephone or telegraph operators, nurses, and receptionists are women (Lavinas and Perira 1996).

The need to reconcile work and family often leads women to pick jobs with particular characteristics, such as less demanding hours or proximity to day care. This contributes to the segregation of women into less prestigious occupations from which promotions are rare.

*Gender roles are profoundly consequential for women's opportunities in the workplace.* Gender roles assign women primary responsibility for raising children, caring for the home, and looking after sick and elderly relatives. Expectations about women's gender roles affect their individual choices about family and career; the same expectations inform employer decisions and peer judgments that govern women's mobility in the labor market. Women register lower rates of economic activity than men because they tend to work within the home. Educational tracking and occupational segregation cluster women into fields such as social welfare, service industries, or communication and client-relations departments that often seem to be a logical extension of their roles as wives and mothers.

Much of the discrimination encountered by women can be traced to gender roles. Employers seek to justify paying women lower wages than men on the grounds that women's wages serve to complement a male breadwinner's earnings, rather than sustain a family on their own (Bruschini 1996). Furthermore, to many companies, laws protecting pregnancy and maternity serve as a deterrent to employing women and paying them salaries equal to men's [see box].

*Many women work in the informal sector, where they have no legal protection and no social benefits.* In the early 1990s, two of every five women working in urban areas in Latin America were in the informal sector. The figures are over 50 percent in Bolivia and Guatemala, and around 35 percent in Argentina, Chile, Uruguay, and Venezuela. In Costa Rica and Panama, the figure is less than 30 percent (FLACSO 1995).

*Women's presence at the executive level is low,* much lower than their representation in political decisionmaking. In Chile's 500 biggest companies, there are 50 women in a total of 2,500 decisionmaking positions (two percent) (SERNAM 1997). A 1994 survey of Argentine industrial companies found that only two of a total 83 company presidents, and only 23 out of 291 director generals were women. In the financial sector, women held only one presidency out of a total of 42, one vice presidency out of 59, and three director generals out of 164 (Consejo Nacional de la Mujer 1994). In Brazil, 3 percent of executive positions in the 400 largest companies are held by women (Avelar 1996). In Mexico, a survey of the 600 largest companies revealed that women occupy a total of 5.5 percent of executive posts. Fully 45 percent of these women executives (88 of a total of 194) are in charge of human resources (Zabludovsky 1997).

Virtually no companies in Latin America have contemplated affirmative action policies to promote more women to leadership positions. Even multinational companies that practice affirmative action at home do not replicate these practices in their Latin American offices. The reluctance of private businesses to provide information about the gender breakdown of their personnel makes designing and proposing affirmative action strategies doubly difficult. Advocates lack the basis upon which to identify and diagnose mechanisms of discrimination. A first step in promoting women's leadership in private businesses is therefore to install a mechanism requiring or encouraging companies to collect and publish tabulated data on the presence of women.

---

## Pregnancy, Maternity & Discrimination

### The Law

Laws in Latin America in theory demand that employers protect the rights of pregnant women and new mothers to care for their babies and retain their jobs. Labor laws designed to protect women include mandatory maternity leave, protection from being fired for getting pregnant, prohibitions in some countries against the administration of pregnancy tests, and requirements that businesses with a certain number of women workers provide day care services on the premises and allow women to take breaks to nurse their babies. Many countries forbid companies from firing workers during their maternity leave, and others protect new mothers from dismissal for a set period of time following their return to work (ILO 1998). Women are often allowed to take a paid leave to care for young children who are sick.

### *Businesses avoid costs of hiring pregnant workers and mothers*

In practice, however, employers go to great lengths to avoid situations where the law is applied in order to cut costs. Some companies are reluctant to employ women full-time, and resort to strategies like sub-contracting, part time employment, and paying for piece work done at home. Others pay women less than men to compensate for non-salary costs.

*Continued on next page*

*Continued from previous page: Pregnancy, Maternity & Discrimination*

In Chile, many executives believe that women are more expensive to hire than men because they are likely to take leaves related to maternity and to be absent from work to fulfill family obligations (Lerda and Todaro 1996). Since such leaves are paid by the social security system, they do not produce direct costs to the business. However, employers claim that the leaves disrupt production and reduce total output (Lerda and Todaro 1996). Executives also complain of the high cost of creating day care centers.

Even when child care facilities do exist, many women find that commuting to work with children in tow is time-consuming and unpleasant for the child, and prefer instead to use childcare that is close to home. Most mothers working outside the home rely on family members or domestic employees to care for their children.

Measures to facilitate working motherhood, such as flexible scheduling and job sharing to reduce workloads, are rare in Latin American workplaces. In Mexican companies where these practices do exist, the presence of women executives is higher than in other companies (Zabludovsky 1997).

*Pregnancy screening*

Some companies require a pregnancy test or a sterilization certificate as a condition of employment, or fire women workers once they become pregnant. In Chile, it is not illegal to require that prospective workers take pregnancy tests as a condition of employment, and the practice is common. Pregnancy tests are widespread in the maquiladoras and factories in the export processing zones of Mexico, Central America and the Dominican Republic (Human Rights Watch 1996), in spite of the fact that national laws prohibit them. In Colombia, a 1994 resolution issued by the Ministry of Labor prohibits businesses from requiring pregnancy tests from job applicants. Nevertheless, pregnancy tests are frequently administered as part of the basic medical exams used to evaluate workers' health, in clear violation of the law (National Directorate 1998).

Explicit discrimination against women of childbearing age continues in the maquiladoras of Mexico for several reasons. First, local governments have been unable and unwilling to force businesses to obey the law, even though they are aware of violations. Maquiladoras are valuable sources of foreign currency and generate tremendous employment for local economies (Human Rights Watch 1996). Half a million Mexicans (half of whom are women) work in the sector (Human Rights Watch 1996). Second, many women workers are unaware of the rights granted them in the labor laws, and do not know that pregnancy testing, for example, is illegal—often because it is so ubiquitous. Those who do know of their rights are unwilling to seek recourse because they frequently lack other employment options (Human Rights Watch 1996).

## EDUCATION

Improving women's opportunities in education and transforming the content of educational materials are critical tools for achieving gender equality in Latin America. Today, there are substantial variations among countries in women's access to the educational system, women's levels of educational attainment, and women's choices in school. Countries have made progress to varying extents on reforming their curriculum to reduce sex stereotypes and emphasizing themes like women's rights and human rights.

*Literacy has improved over time, but there are substantial gender differences.* Latin Americans have become steadily more literate since the 1970s. Yet, in the majority (approx. 60%) of the countries in the region, a greater percentage of women are illiterate than men. The situation is most acute in rural areas (see table) and among older populations.

**Illiteracy rates according to sex and zone**

| Country (year) | Women | | Men |
|---|---|---|---|
| Guatemala (1990) | Rural | 60 | 46 |
| | Urban | 27 | 17 |
| Bolivia (1992) | Rural | 50 | 23 |
| | Urban | 15 | 4 |
| Peru (1991) | Rural | 46 | 10 |
| | Urban | 6 | 2 |

Source: FLACSO (1995)

Although these countries have succeeded in reducing their overall illiteracy rates by as much as two-thirds, the decline for rural women has been less dramatic. Gender inequalities in literacy are particularly acute in

Peru. Whereas in 1940, there were approximately two illiterate women for every illiterate man, by 1993 this had increased to a ratio of three to one (Grupo Impulsor 1997).

*Women's enrollment in education has advanced.* UNESCO (Scientific and Cultural Organization) reports that in 1995 females were 48 percent of primary level students and 52 percent of secondary level (including vocational and training programs) students in Latin America and the Caribbean (UNESCO 1997). Yet, there is tremendous variation among countries. In Guatemala, in spite of the fact that primary school education is obligatory, only 45 percent of school-age girls are enrolled (Alvarado, et. al. 1998). In general, women in poor, rural settings are least likely to be enrolled in schools at all levels.

The percentage of women enrolled in universities in the region has climbed steadily: in 1970, women were 35 percent of enrolled university students; in 1980, 43 percent; and in 1995, 49 percent (UNESCO 1997). In Brazil, Colombia, Cuba, Panama, Uruguay, and Venezuela, women outnumbered men in university enrollment in 1990 (FLACSO 1995).

In terms of gender equity, enrollment rates offer some encouragement, but need to be carefully examined among other trends. Women are enrolled at higher rates than men in several countries, and women tend to repeat fewer grades than men. However, because of labor market discrimination, women are in practice required to have higher levels of education than men to compete in the workforce on equal terms. ECLAC found in 1995 that women needed to have four more years of schooling in order to compete for similar salaries as men (Stromquist 1996).

School drop out rates are highly correlated with poverty and maternity. Families who take children out of school generally cite lack of economic resources as the reason. Forced to pick between keeping a son and a daughter in school, families generally choose the son on the assumption that he will be a more profitable investment in the family's future.

Adolescent pregnancies also keep women from completing their education. Data from Peru show that 84 percent of girls attend school, yet only 72 percent of school-age mothers do. Combined with poverty, the situation gets even worse. Only 10 percent of young mothers from poor homes, and only 7 percent of those from extremely poor homes attend school (Grupo Impulsor 1997).

*Certain fields of study remain predominantly masculine or feminine.* Women are underrepresented in fields related to science and technology, but overrepresented in lower paying occupations such as education, nursing and library science. However, business administration and law are becoming integrated (FLACSO 1995).

*School textbooks and curriculum content tend to reproduce gender stereotypes.* Women appear less frequently than men in images and references in school textbooks. A 1995 FLACSO study of textbooks in five Latin American countries found that on average women appeared in only 18% of titles, 23% of figures, and 20% of text. When women do appear in textbooks, they are frequently depicted in traditional roles, cooking or cleaning in the home (FLACSO 1995). A study from Colombia that analyzed 50 school textbooks found that when generic references are made to the human body, illustrations show the male body. The female body only appears when the text makes references to reproduction (National Directorate 1998). These studies show that textbooks reproduce gender ideologies that assign women to private, domestic activities and preserve the public sphere of work and politics for men.

School curricula around the world has historically contributed to sex discrimination by using terms like "men" and "man" as generic references and failing to emphasize women's contributions to economic, political, and social development. Topics taught in school generate the impression that men have been the motor of history while women have been passive participants.

Some countries have incorporated material on sex equality and discrimination into school curriculum. In Peru, the secondary school course on "Family Education" discusses sex roles and equality comprehensively (Grupo Impulsor 1997). However, in spite of general acknowledgment that a problem exists, gender equality has not been adopted as a matter of general educational policy. Educational officials say that without strong political will and outside pressure, it is unlikely that current practices will change (Grupo Impulsor 1997).

*Women and gender studies programs are increasing in number, but have made few inroads into university curriculum.* Women and gender studies have slowly consolidated into a reputable field of study and research. Brazil was one of the first countries in the region to develop women's studies programs and today there are more than 20 university centers dedicated to the field around the country (Navarro and Barrig 1994). These programs and institutes have spearheaded the production of knowledge about women and spawned new research agendas.

The field of gender studies has made fewer inroads into university curriculum at the undergraduate level, although post-graduate courses and certificates are offered (Navarro and Barrig 1994). Yet, teaching courses in women and gender studies to undergraduates is a crucial mechanism for passing values about women's rights and equal opportunities to future generations.[6]

## CONCLUSION

The analysis presented in this brief suggests that women's rights and opportunities are increasing in Latin America. Some progress is attributable to governmental efforts in reforming laws, creating new mechanisms for the representation of women's interests, and adopting gender-specific public policies, particularly in the areas of health and violence prevention. These advancements, however, have been brought about only by steady pressure from women politicians, women's movements, and international organizations.

In a global climate where discourse on women's rights and equal opportunities is gaining momentum, governments have been compelled to assume the goal of promoting women. In some important cases, constant vigilance and monitoring by women's movements has succeeded in translating formal goals and commitments into policy moves with concrete results for women's lives.

The central objective of the Women's Leadership Conference of the Americas (WLCA) is to increase the capacity of individuals and groups in civil society to continue with their vigilance. The WLCA's monitoring project is elaborating a system of quantitative and qualitative indicators to measure progress in individual countries and to compare across countries. The monitoring will focus particularly on the implementation and results of formal policies.

In the final analysis, the current configuration of international norms, formal commitments, increasing women's participation, democratic consolidation, and an increasingly active civil society provides an unprecedented opportunity for women to make gains in the economy, society, and politics. The WLCA aims to help women capitalize on this opportunity.

## Notes

1. I am grateful to Comba Marques Porto for making this point.

2. Based on conversation with Gilda Pacheco Oreamuno of the Inter-American Institute for Human Rights, March 12, 1998.

3. Interview with Senator Amalia García Medina, Mexico City: January 27, 1998.

4. I am grateful to Bonnie Shepard for helping me to see the importance of this point.

5. Interview with Ana Paula Portella, SOS Corpo, Recife: November 1997.

6. I am grateful to Sonia Alvarez for making this point.

# References

Acosta, Mariclaire. 1997. "Vencer la discriminación de la mujer en México es una tarea para Sisifo." In: *Memorias. Primer Taller sobre Derechos Humanos de las Mujeres y el Acceso al Sistema Interamericano de Protección.* México: Comisión Mexicana de Defensa y Promición de los Derechos Humanos.

Alan Guttmacher Institute. 1994. *Aborto Clandestino: Uma Realidade Latinoamericana.* New York: The Alan Guttmacher Institute.

Alvarado, Manuela; Dalila de la Cruz Alvarez; Telma Duarte de Morales; Victor Hugo Fernández; Blanca Guerra de Nicol; Berta Hilda Marroquín; Eugenia Mijangos; Nineth Montenegro; Zury Ríos; and Alicia Rodríguez. 1998. "Situación real de la mujer en Guatemala." Paper presented at the Inter-American Dialogue/WLCA conference "La situación de la mujer en Centro América: una evaluación al umbral del siglo XXI," Managua: March 12-13.

Avelar, Lucia. 1996. *Mulheres na Elite Política Brasileira.* São Paulo: Fundação Konrad-Adenauer-Stiftung.

Bermúdez, Violeta. 1993. "Abortion: the Debate and Strategies in Latin America. The Peruvian Case." In: *Women: Watched and Punished.* Lima: CLADEM.

Berquó, Elsa. 1994. "Brasil, um caso exemplar. Anticoncepção e parto ciúrgico. A espera de uma ação exemplar." *Direitos Reprodutivos: uma Questão da Cidadania.* Brasilia: CFEMEA.

Bilbao, Josefina. 1997. "Minuta conferencia de prensa ministra: 3o aniversario de vigencia de la Ley de Violencia Intrafamiliar." Mimeo.

Bruschini, Cristina. 1996. "Algumas Reflexões sobre o Uso de Estatísticas Sensíveis à Questão de Gênero." Paper prepared for conference of the Brazilian Institute for Geography and Statistics (IBGE), Rio de Janeiro, May 27-31.

Camacho, Rosalía. 1998. "Las cuotas de participación política de las mujeres." Paper presented at the Inter-American Dialogue/WLCA conference "La situación de la mujer en Centro América: una evaluación al umbral del siglo XXI," Managua: March 12-13.

Centro Legal para Derechos Reproductivos y Políticas Públicas y Grupo de Información en Reproducción Elegida (CRLP/GIRE). 1997. *Derechos reproductivos de la mujer en México: Un reporte sombra.* Mexico: CRLP/GIRE.

Consejo Nacional de la Mujer. 1994. *Informe nacional: situación de la mujer en la última década en la República Argentina.* Buenos Aires: Consejo Nacional de la Mujer.

Díaz, Ximena and Rosalba Todaro. 1997. Personal interview at the Centro de Estudios de la Mujer, Santiago, Chile. November 1997.

Dirección General de la Promoción de la Mujer (DGPM). 1998. Personal communication from Patricia Solano. Santo Domingo, Dominican Republic.

FLACSO. 1995. *Latin American Women. Compared Figures.* Santiago: FLACSO.

FLACSO. 1993a. *Mujeres latinoamericanas en cifras: Colombia.* Santiago: FLACSO.

FLACSO. 1993b. *Mujeres latinoamericanas en cifras: Argentina.* Santiago: FLACSO.

Grupo Impulsor. 1997. *Del compromiso a la acción.* Lima: Grupo Impulsor Nacional/Mujeres por la Igualdad Real.

Grupo Parlamentario Interamericano (GPI). 1997. *Módulo legislativo sobre violencia contra la mujer.* New York: GPI.

Heise, Lori L. et al. 1994. *Violence against Women: the Hidden Health Burden.* World Bank Discussion Papers 255. Washington: The World Bank.

Human Rights Watch. 1996. *No Guarantees: Sex Discrimination in Mexico's Maquiladora Sector.* Washington, DC: Human Rights Watch.

IDB. 1997. *Domestic Violence.* Washington: Inter-American Development Bank (IDB).

Instituto Nacional de Estadística (INEGI). 1997. *Mujeres y hombres en México.* Aguascalientes: INEGI.

International Labor Organization (ILO). 1998. "More than 120 Nations Provide Paid Maternity Leave." Press Release: February 16, 1998.

Inter-Parliamentary Union (IPU). 1998. "Women in National Parliaments" [Online]. Available: http://www.ipu.org/wmn-e/classif.htm.

Jones, Mark P. 1997. "Cupos de Género, Leyes Electorales y Elección de Legisladoras en las Américas." *Revista de Ciencia Política* 1 (noviembre).

Jones, Mark P. 1996. "Gender and Legislative Policy Priorities in the Argentine Chamber of Deputies and the United States House of Representatives." Paper presented at the Annual Meeting of the Midwest Political Science Association.

Lavinas, Lena and Hildete Pereira. 1996. *Mulheres sem Medo do Poder: Chegou a Nossa Vez. Cartilha para Mulheres Candidatas a Vereadoras 1996.* Rio de Janeiro: DIPES-IPEA.

Linhares Barsted, Leila. 1994. *Violência contra a Mulher e Cidadania: uma Avaliação das Políticas Públicas.* Rio de Janeiro: CEPIA.

Lerda, Sandra and Rosalba Todaro. 1996. "¿Cuanto cuestan las mujeres? Un analise de los costos laborales por sexo." Santiago: Centro de Estudios de la Mujer.

Martins Costa, Delaine. 1997. "Ampliação da participação feminina no governo local: um trabalho de Sísifo?" In: *Participação Feminina no Governo Local: Construindo a Democracia. Um Levantamento do Resultado das Eleições Municipais de 1992 e 1996.* Rio de Janeiro: IBAM.

Massolo, Alejandra. 1995. "Mujeres en el espacio local y el poder municipal." In: Rodríguez, V. E. et al., *Memoria of the Bi-National Conference: Women in Contemporary Mexican Politics*. The Mexican Center of ILAS, University of Texas at Austin, 7-8 April 1995.

Mijangos, Eugenia. 1998. "Centro de acción legal en derechos humanos: Area de derechos de la mujer." Paper presented at the Inter-American Dialogue/WLCA conference "La situación de la mujer en Centro América: una evaluación al umbral del siglo XXI," Managua: March 12-13.

Montaño, Sonia. 1998. Personal interview.

National Directorate of Equity for Women, Presidency of the Republic of Colombia. 1998. Personal communications.

Navarro, Marysa and Maruja Barrig. 1994. "Consultants' Report on the Status of Women's Studies in Brazil for the Ford Foundation." August/December 1994.

Nelson, Sara. 1996. "Constructing and Negotiating Gender in Women's Police Stations in Brazil." *Latin American Perspectives* 23:1 (Winter).

Pizarro, Ana María. 1997. *Atención humanizado del aborto y del aborto inseguro*. Proyeto de Seguimiento de la Conferencia Internacional sobre Población y Desarollo - Nicaragua. Managua: SI Mujer.

Puppim, Andréa. 1994. "Mulheres em Cargos de Comando," in *Novos Olhares: Mulheres e Relações de Gênero no Brasil*. São Paulo: Fundação Carlos Chagas.

Rivera-Cira, Teresa. 1993. *Las Mujeres en los parlamentos latinoamericanos*. Valparaíso: Universidad Católica.

Ross, J. 1991. "Sterilization: Past, Present, Future." Working Paper no. 29. New York: The Population Council.

SERNAM. 1997. *Cumbre de las Américas. Tema 18. Sistema de Indicadores*. Santiago: Servicio Nacional de la Mujer.

Sims, Calvin. 1998. "Using Gifts as Bait, Peru Sterilizes Poor Women." *The New York Times*. February 15.

Stromquist, Nelly P. 1996. "Gender and Democracy in Education in Latin America." New York: Council on Foreign Relations Working Group on Educational Reform.

Thomas, Dorothy. 1991. *Criminal Injustice: Violence against Women in Brazil*. New York: Human Rights Watch.

UN. 1996. "Statistics and Indicators on the World's Women" [Online]. Available: http://www.un.org/womenwatch/amestat.htm.

UN/CEDAW Committee. 1998. "Progress in Advancement of Mexican Women, but Changes not yet "Radical," Anti-Discrimination Committee Told." United Nations: Press Release WOM/1020, January 30.

UN ECLAC. 1995. *Social Panorama of Latin America*. Santiago: United Nations Economic Commission for Latin America and the Caribbean.

UNDP. 1997. *1997 Human Development Report*. New York: Oxford University Press.

UNESCO. 1997. *Statistical Yearbook 1997*. Lanham, MD: Bernan Press.

UNIFEM. 1996. *La mujer en los codigos penales de América Latina y el Caribe Hispano*. Quito: UNIFEM.

US Department of State. 1998. *Peru Country Report on Human Rights Practices for 1997*. Released by the Bureau of Democracy, Human Rights and Labor, January 30, 1998.

Van Cott, Donna Lee. 1998. "Constitution-Making and Democratic Transformation: The Bolivian and Colombian Constitutional Reforms." Ph.D. dissertation. Georgetown University.

WEDO. 1998. *Mapping Progress*. New York: WEDO.

Winter, Carolyn. 1992. "Female Earnings, Labor Force Participation and Discrimination in Venezuela, 1989." In George Psacharopoulos and Zafiris Tzannatos, eds. *Case Studies on Women's Employment and Pay in Latin America*. Washington, D.C.: The World Bank.

Zabludovsky, Gina. 1997. "Presencia de las mujeres ejecutivas en México." *Sociológia* 12:33 (enero-abril). Mexico.

# X. General Proposals

# X. GENERAL PROPOSALS

*Odette Langlais is the Project Officer for FOCAL.*

*The **Canadian Foundation for the Americas (FOCAL)** is an independent, non-profit organization. FOCAL deepens the knowledge of Canadians and Canadian institutions about Latin America and the Caribbean and contributes to a better understanding of Canada's role in the Americas. Through its conferences and seminars, networking, internships, policy research, reports, and media outreach activities, FOCAL fosters debate on issues of strategic importance within the hemisphere.*

# Toward the Santiago Summit of the Americas:
## Policy Options Resulting from Regional Civil Society Consultations

*Prepared by Odette Langlais*

## INTRODUCTION

This paper presents the results of five regional civil society consultations on what Canada's position should be with respect to the upcoming Santiago Summit of the Americas. The consultations took place in Edmonton, Vancouver, Fredericton, Toronto and Montreal between October 17th and 31st, 1997, in which some 140 individuals from civil society participated. Each consultation resulted in a report on recommendations raised by the respective participants which appear below. The consultations covered all four baskets of the Summit agenda: Basket I. Education; Basket II. Preserving and strengthening democracy and human rights; Basket III. Economic integration and free trade; and Basket IV. Eradication of poverty and discrimination. There was, however, an emphasis on Baskets II and III in the background and discussion papers, in the structure of the consultations and in the allocation of time for discussion.

We begin by presenting key issues and the recommendations that gathered the most support. Each basket is then introduced, with a brief presentation of the main themes. A list of policy options divided by baskets follows. We chose not to include the context of the discussions which can be found in each consultation report. Recommendations which were addressed to sectors other than government are included under Annex 1. Additional recommendations which were not strongly pursued by participants (i.e., there was little or no debate of the proposal), or did not fit in either of the baskets, are listed separately under Annex 2. A calendar of the consultations, the partner organisations and the list of participants are included under Annex 3.

Please note that this report and all five consultation reports are posted on the FOCAL website, as well as the Summit agenda, a description of the consultation process, and other relevant information. The sites address is: http://www.focal.ca/santiago

## KEY ISSUES AND AREAS OF CONVERGENCE

In taking a step back and looking at the five consultations from an overall national perspective, one can make the following remarks.

## A. Labour and social protection in trade agreements

Of all the baskets of the Santiago Summit, *Basket III. Economic Integration and Free Trade* by far led to the most debate, discussion and recommendations. For many participants, the issues of poverty alleviation, human rights and democratic development correspond more to their professional objectives and priorities for the hemisphere. However, the issue of economic integration is the one that attracts the most attention. Canadians (those consulted) are concerned, and in some cases deeply concerned, with the possible impact of a new trade agreement. They are worried about the potential disruption in the lives of Canadians and of other citizens of the Americas. They want future trade agreements to include strong measures to enforce and strengthen workers rights, to guarantee social and economic rights, especially for vulnerable groups in society, and to protect the environment. They want the FTAA to be negotiated and concluded through a process which respects Canadian democratic values. While a minority of participants reject economic integration as a whole, most participants see it as inevitable and strongly believe in the need for a containment of the FTAA within the bounds prescribed by the needs of labour and disadvantaged groups and by environmental concerns. Some participants envision the economic future of the hemisphere as one based on fair trade, partnerships and sustainable development.

*The following recommendation represents a main area of convergence:*

The following core labour standards of the International Labour Organization (ILO) must be enshrined in trade agreements: freedom of association, freedom to form unions, right to collective bargaining, the prohibition of child labour and forced labour, equal remuneration for equal work and the banning of employment discrimination on the basis of sex, race or religion.

## B. Opposing views on multilateralism

Two opposing tendencies are reflected in the policy options. Many participants express the need for strong labour and social protection in trade agreements. They argue that legislation with teeth is needed, as opposed to parallel agreements, to have compliance mechanisms and strong modalities for economic and political sanctions in place. Some call for very tough deals which impose standards to nation states at all levels. For example, a nation would need to achieve a certain literacy rate or a certain distribution of wealth in order to remain in the trade block.

However, some participants express serious concerns about Canadian sovereignty and believe that nations should remain able to pursue their environmental and social programs without being constrained by free trade agreements. They argue that nations should have the freedom to derogate from trade agreements if needed. They also raise a concern that hemispheric agreements will allocate too much power to appointed civil servants as opposed to elected officials.

## C. Consultation of civil society in Canada

Participants are critical of the process used for these consultations. They feel that the timetable was too tight, that documents were available too late, that the debate must be much deeper and wider. Some participants worry that the consultations could be used to legitimize government policy.

*The following recommendations represent a main area of convergence:*

Civil society participation in decision-making must be strengthened. The government of Canada must hold open, ongoing, meaningful and legitimate consultations coupled with the provision of resources to promote the participation of civil society. Civil society organizations should be represented, and not just individuals. Relevant issues should be integrated rather than compartmentalized (e.g., focus consultations on trade policy rather than on trade aspects of APEC, FTAA, WTO, etc.). Consultations must give more time and space to civil society and permit internal debate and discussion within organizations. Consultations should be interactive processes of exchange with elected and government officials, rather than a one-way flow of recommendations which do not get a response. They must not become a limited process which legitimizes government positions or simply a closed debate between experts.

In order to make the official Canadian delegation to the Santiago Summit more balanced and representative, delegates from NGOs, the labour sector and other civil society representatives should be appointed, as well as provincial governments officials, as full-fledged members.

# X. GENERAL PROPOSALS

## D. Views from women's organizations and First Nations

Representatives from women's organizations participated in the Vancouver (National Action Committee on the Status of Women), Toronto (National Action Committee on the Status of Women) and Montreal (Federation des femmes du Quebec) consultations. These organizations are very critical of neoliberalism and argue that women, in particular, pay the price of growing social and economic inequities. Economic globalization has meant worsening working conditions for women, cuts in public health and education, and increasing power enjoyed by multinational corporations. Measures must be taken to protect the rights of workers in free trade agreements, and to prevent the exploitation of women's work now taking place. Human development indicators must be put in place and gender-sensitive data must be accessible to analyze the complex reality faced by women. Women across the hemisphere must have better access to credit, land, micro-entreprise training and genuine political power.

Although efforts were undertaken by organizers across Canada to encourage the participation of First Nations representatives in the consultations, only the Montreal meeting had a first Nations participant. Their relative absence is in itself telling, considering that Canada is the country coordinator responsible for the sub-theme of indigenous populations under the poverty and discrimination basket. In Montreal, several recommendations for the Canadian proposal were made regarding the need to recognize ancestral rights and the right to self-government. It was also noted that a First Nations Forum should be created with the power to make recommendations during the Summit. Finally, the perspective taken at the Summit on economic integration should be based on sustainable development, fair trade and partnership.

## COMMENTS ON EACH BASKET

### Basket I. Education

This basket led to the least debate. In some meetings, the discussion did not result in specific recommendations. While many participants had comments to make about the other baskets, in general only representatives of educational institutions commented on this one. The goals of 100% enrollment rate for primary school and 75% for secondary school were seen as obvious (like motherhood and apple pie as was said in Edmonton).

Nevertheless, Canadians seem to perceive this basket as a primary channel for hemispheric cooperation and as an important tool for coming closer to their neighbours from across the Americas. They are supportive of exchanges of all kinds. They are concerned about access to education for disadvantaged groups in Latin America and the Caribbean. They believe that Canada has a contribution to make in the fields of distance education and access to knowledge using new technologies.

### Basket II. Preserving and Strengthening Democracy and Human Rights

This basket was seen as very important and in some cases as the repository of all the issues. Two specific proposals on human rights were: the need to include social, economic and cultural rights in the Brazil/Canada proposal to the Summit on this issue, and to ratify the Inter-American Convention on Human Rights. On the theme of democracy, participants would like CIDA to expand its democratic development and human rights programs in the Americas. The Brazil/Canada proposal was criticized as being too restrictive. As explained in the previous section "Key issues and areas of convergence," many participants expressed the need for a more elaborate process of consultation and future civil society involvement in hemispheric decision-making.

### Basket III. Economic Integration and Free Trade

As mentioned before, this basket led to the most debate, the longest discussions and the largest number of recommendations. Many recommendations contain specific policy options, such as adherence to ILO conventions, the need for a social clause, the official recognition of the parallel process, the need to assess NAFTA and to closely monitor the impact of the FTAA. Predictably, participants use their experience with NAFTA to evaluate and analyze a potential FTAA. They advocate a soft and slow approach with careful consideration of the possible impact of the agreement on all segments of the population. They do not see the need to rush the process and instead want to ensure full debate of all the issues and democratic processes of ratification in Canada and elsewhere.

## Basket IV. Eradication of Poverty and Discrimination

This basket as defined in the Summit agenda includes a long list of sub-themes and can be seen as a grab bag or catch all. It is not surprising then that the related discussions and policy options were somewhat scattered and lacked cohesion. The issue of poverty reduction remains a primary concern for many of the participants. They raised urgent poverty issues such as human resources development, food security, water and sanitation services, the situation of the indigenous peoples, micro-industry development and the role of women. They advocate increasing budget allocations for Overseas Development Administration (ODA) in Latin America and the Caribbean.

## LIST OF POLICY OPTIONS

## Basket I. Education

### General

- Canada should maintain its strong advocacy role and its commitment to advance Latin American education at all levels through enhancing CIDA and other programs.
- Canadian governments and universities supported by the public and private sectors should expand and develop programs and scholarships to assist Latin Americans with university education, trade and technical training.
- Access, equity, participation and relevance of curricula must be addressed throughout the Americas including Canada, using a multidisciplinary approach.

### Access

- Access to elementary, secondary and post-secondary schooling must become more equitable and include disadvantaged classes and women, in all fields of studies.
- About the goal of secondary enrolment rate of 75% as stated in the draft proposal from Mexico, the rate used should be the success rate and not the enrolment rate, since the former is more representative of the health of a school system.

### Distance education

- Canada should make available its technical and curriculum knowledge to expand internet, satellite systems and television training programs in the field of distance education. Special attention should be given to the education of girls and women, indigenous and the poor.
- Programs must be developed to promote technology management, quality control and long-distance teaching.

### Exchanges

- Exchanges should be promoted and scholarships made available for Latin Americans to study in Canada and for Canadians to study in Latin America.
- Opportunities to study in the developed countries should be open to all students and not just to the elite of the South.

### Others

- Canada should urge Latin American governments to follow-up their commitments to educational reform by announcing specific budget levels devoted to this area.
- A hemispheric conference on education should take place and should address issues such as decentralization, public funding and distribution.
- Canada should act as a leader in supporting the teaching of human rights issues through public education systems across the Americas.
- Post-secondary education in Canada should critically review its curriculum regarding Latin America, and be more committed to providing sound knowledge to Canadian students on the cultures of the South.

## Basket II. Preserving and Strengthening Democracy and Human Rights

### Human rights

- All basic human rights to subsistence, security, participation and mobility should be advanced while trade and economic goals are pursued.
- The draft proposal on human rights and democracy as well as the draft workplan (Brazil-Canada initia-

tive) focus exclusively on civil and political rights and disregard economic, social and cultural rights. This must be changed.

- Canada should ratify the American Convention on Human Rights. This will enhance its credibility as an advocate of international human rights abroad, and expand the rights of Canadian citizens. (two examples: prohibition against monopolization of the media which is not protected under the Canadian Charter; article 26 which commits the state to promote and enact legislation to enhance economic, social and cultural rights).
- Summit participants should go beyond defending certain human rights and engage in the promotion of all human rights.
- The Canadian government must defend the need for coherence between positions and agreements taken at the international level and those taken at the hemispheric level (reference to ILO and UN Conventions). Other international commitments made by Canada must be reviewed to understand their impact on human rights.
- Canada should put more emphasis on human rights observance and compliance (e.g., Universal Declaration of Human Rights) and less on institutions.

### Democratic development

- The Declaration of Principles and Plan of Action from the Miami Summit are consistent with Canadian views of government and society and should continue to be supported.
- The Canadian government should increase funding to CIDA for expanded projects related to investment in democracy and the advancement of human rights in Latin America.
- There needs to be a more global approach to democracy in the Brazil-Canada proposals. It is now reduced to electoral processes and bypasses democratic institutions within the state and civil society. The issue of the administration of justice is presented from a technical perspective and should focus instead on central issues such as the independence of the judiciary and access to justice by marginalized populations.

### Public participation

- Civil society participation in decision-making must be strengthened. The government of Canada must hold open, ongoing, meaningful and legitimate consultations coupled with the provision of resources to promote the participation of civil society. Civil society organizations should be represented and not just individuals. Relevant issues should be integrated rather than compartmentalized (e.g., focus consultations on trade policy rather than on trade aspects of APEC, FTAA, WTO, etc.). Consultations must give more time and space to civil society and permit internal debate and discussion within organizations. Consultations should be interactive processes of exchange with elected and government officials, rather than a one-way flow of recommendations which do not get a response. They must not become a limited process which legitimizes government positions or simply a closed debate between experts.
- In order to make the official Canadian delegation to the Santiago Summit more balanced and representative, delegates from the NGOs, the labour sector and other civil society representatives should be appointed, as well as provincial governments officials, as full-fledged members.

### Cuba

- Cuba should be included in all discussions and negotiations, and be invited to participate in the Santiago Summit.

## Basket III. Economic Integration and Free Trade

### Labour issues

- The following core labour standards of the International Labour Organization (ILO) must be enshrined in trade agreements: freedom of association, freedom to form unions, right to collective bargaining, the prohibition of child labour and forced labour, equal remuneration for equal work and the banning of employment discrimination on the basis of sex, race or religion.
- Canada should take the lead in advocating core labour standards.

- A tri- or multi-national commission on North American or American labour rights should be formed.
- There should be mechanisms for sharing information on labour codes and regulations at a hemispheric level.
- Multilateral mechanisms to control labour codes must be efficient, operational and ensure effective compliance. They should be based on existing international legislation.
- The issue of child labour should be on the Summit agenda.
- Provisions must be included in free trade agreements for fair wages, regulating the contracting out of work and work done in the informal sector.

## Social clause
- Core labour standards should form part of a Charter of Social and Economic Rights for the Citizens of the Americas.
- A priority must be to include a social clause within trade agreements, using the European community as a model. The clause must be included as an integral part of trade agreements and not in a parallel agreement. To be effective, the clause must include mechanisms for economic and political sanctions as well as autonomous verification mechanisms.

## Environmental impact
- Mechanisms for environmental protection must be created and included in trade agreements to regulate the action of corporations and governments.

## Parallel processes
- The Canadian government must publicly recognize the importance of a social dimension to trade agreements and support the civil society parallel summit.
- The Labour and Social Forum must be officially recognized and a working group on labour protection must be established as one of the FTAA working groups.

## Assessment of NAFTA
- The Canadian government should commission evaluative studies on the real impact, benefits and detriments of NAFTA that will assist planning for future initiatives toward economic integration.

## Preparing for the FTAA
- The Canadian government must undertake a global analysis of the impact of a possible economic integration accord on fundamental rights, in particular social and economic rights. Indicators of human development should be used as evaluation tools.
- A hemispheric institution must be created to collect and analyze data, and to produce detailed evaluations of the impact of economic integration, in particular on issues such as income, distribution of wealth, school enrolment rates and environmental sustainability.
- An economic and social development fund should be created to compensate for the negative impact of economic integration, such as in the European community.

## Negotiation and ratification processes
- There must be a gradual negotiation process, allowing each country to adopt transitional policies. Progressive negotiations will allow better identification of opportunities and threats faced by different economic sectors.
- There must be democratic means of ratifying an agreement such as FTAA in each country of the Americas.
- A national referendum should be held on any new free trade agreement, thus facilitating open debate, enhancing the democratic process and serving as a means of educating Canadians about any new accord (as happened in Europe after the Traite de Maastricht was signed).

## Capital controls
- People must be protected from the vulnerability and instability caused by speculative capital. Measures must be taken to strengthen domestic regulations and review, particularly, short-term investments. Measures affecting banking, tax systems and the regulation of profit must be considered.

# X. GENERAL PROPOSALS

*Sovereignty issues*
- Investor-state dispute mechanisms, staffed by appointed trade officials, should not be empowered to make decisions affecting health care and the environment or deal with questions of expropriation. Nations should remain able to pursue their environmental concerns and social programs without being constrained by mechanisms included in a free trade agreement.
- The ability to derogate should be included in any free trade agreement, thus enabling elected, rather than appointed officials, to deal with social issues, expropriation and the environment.

*Code of ethics*
- In order to combat charges that some processes take place in secrecy, the Canadian government should establish a code or charter of ethics for businesses investing in Latin America. And, codes of conduct should be included in any free trade agreement.

*Others*
- The debt situation must be resolved in order to have negotiations among equals.
- The US proposal on labour rights must include compliance mechanisms and be clearer regarding core labour standards.
- It is very important to include First Nations in the economic integration process. A Forum of First Nations should be created, officially recognized and mandated to formulate proposals at the Summit.
- A tri- or multi-national equitable growth board should be established as part of free trade agreements.
- Binding stipulations should be included in any free trade agreement mandating as a basis for continuing participation in the agreement a certain distribution of wealth, the reaching of an agreed-upon literacy rate, and/or the reduction of the infant mortality rate to an agreed-upon level.
- Economic integration should be envisioned from the perspective of sustainable development and in the spirit of fair exchanges and partnerships.

## Basket IV. Eradication of Poverty and Discrimination

- Canada should continue to support the ideas and concepts of the Miami Declaration of Principles.
- The struggle against poverty must be the cornerstone for the whole debate on integration and must be linked to the promotion of human rights within the wide context of economic integration and its perverse effects on populations.
- Canada should increase its ODA budget, with the perspective of decreasing the dependency of the South vis-à-vis the North. Technology transfer and democratization of knowledge are crucial to this end.
- All governments in the Americas should give strong support to human resource development and stop slashing social programs. Social development is as important as economic development. Canada should encourage greater sectoral involvement with the private sector playing a more important role in the promotion of the social agenda.
- Canada should support initiatives to protect the production of food, and watch over land tenure issues, agrarian reform, ways to ease debt repayments, sustainability of the land, and security for agrarian peoples of the Americas.
- Agrarian reform must be implemented in order to improve the quality of life of the rural population.
- Through CIDA programs, Canada should continue to assist with projects to provide potable water and basic sanitation services.
- Increased support should be given to Canadian programs that advance the living standards, education, economic endeavour and political participation of indigenous communities throughout the Americas. The work of Canadian NGOs in these areas should be supported.
- In its proposal for the Summit, the Canadian government should recognize the ancestral rights of First Nations and their right to self-government. In doing so, it should be guided by the Universal Declaration of the Rights of Indigenous Peoples and the Royal Commission on First Nations (Erasmus-Dussault).

- The issue of racism as distinct from discrimination should be addressed during the Summit.
- Canada should develop programs to advance women's education and health in Latin America. The work of Canadian NGOs in these areas should be supported.
- On sustainable development, an Environment Charter should be adopted during the Santiago Summit. The basis of the charter should be the conclusions of the Rio Summit to which Canada has already signed on.

## FINAL WORD

This report was submitted to the Department of Foreign Affairs and International Affairs on December 4th, 1997. A copy was sent to each of the approximately 140 civil society representatives across Canada who participated in the regional consultations. The report is posted on the FOCAL website mentioned in the introduction. FOCAL will undertake efforts to promote and disseminate the results of the consultations and ask for a government response before the Summit. It will attempt to organize a meeting of representatives of the regional forums with key ministers of the Canadian government in the early months of 1998.

The organizations and individuals that met in Toronto expect to hear back from the Department of Foreign Affairs and International Trade regarding the use and impact of, and follow-up to, their recommendations. They expect to be informed by the government about what it will do to encourage ongoing civil society participation in the process leading to, and following up, the Summit as well as the forthcoming FTAA negotiations.

# Annex 1.
## Recommendations Addressed to Sectors Other than Government

### BASKET II. PRESERVING AND STRENGTHENING DEMOCRACY AND HUMAN RIGHTS

- Civil society must participate in the Summit and FTAA processes through various means, such as seeking formal representation in the negotiations as well as pursuing alternative civil society networks to expand hemispheric social alliances and to present alternative proposals to the neoliberal model.

### BASKET III. ECONOMIC INTEGRATION AND FREE TRADE

- We should work in Canada to put in place a parallel social forum in order to support, strengthen and deepen the efforts at the hemispheric level.

- Corporations must adhere to what is now a voluntary code of conduct of international business.

# Annex 2.
## Other Recommendations

- Promote and develop training programs which will contribute to the technical and professional upgrading of workers in Free Trade Zones, whenever this is required.

- Comply with the legal provisions on occupational health and safety in Free Trade Zones.

- There should be total freedom for the mobility of labour, and the distinction between the rights of temporary and permanent residents should be eliminated.

- Existing CIDA structures could be used to promote micro-industry or enterprise development. For the oil industry of Bolivia, for example, local people could be encouraged to represent foreign suppliers of products, establish repair facilities, and manufacture required products using a blend of local and imported primary materials. CIDA could provide connections to both Canadian suppliers and local end users, and work with local banking institutions to provide small amounts for financing. This same approach could be used for other industries.

- Measures must be taken to help ensure freedom of the press.

- Canada should pursue global harmonization of environmental standards.

- Canada should support attempts to demilitarize the drug trade.

- Intellectual property rights should not be privatized.

- Canadians, as consumers, should be educated as to the impact of their buying habits.

- Human security should be made a priority.

# Annex 3.
## Calendar of Consultations, Partner Organisations and List of Participants

| Date of Consultation | Location | Partner Organisation |
| --- | --- | --- |
| October 17th, 1997 | Edmonton | FOCAL-West and the University of Alberta |
| October 21st, 1997 | Vancouver | FOCAL-West and the University of British Columbia |
| October 21st, 1997 | Fredericton | FOCAL-Atlantic |
| October 24th, 1997 | Toronto | Center for Research on Latin America and the Caribbean (CERLAC), York University |
| October 31st, 1997 | Montreal | Groupe de recherche sur l'integration continentale (Gric) of the University du Quebec à Montreal |

# X. General Proposals

## LIST OF PARTICIPANTS

Acuna, Ricardo
Change for Children Association, Edmonton

Alderman, Peter
St. Thomas University, Fredericton

Angel, Barbara
University of Manitoba, Winnipeg

Antipan, Ramon
Alberta Federation of Labour, Edmonton

Archer, Christon
The University of Calgary, Calgary
Director of FOCAL-West

Atack, Peter
Carleton University, Ottawa

Bakvis, Peter
CSN, Montreal

Barr, Gerry
United Steelworkers of America, Toronto

Bartram, Trevor
LL.B. Counsel, Emerging Markets, Toronto

Bayles, Jim
MacMillan Bloedel, Vancouver

Begin, Bertrand
Canadian Labour Congress, Moncton

Benessaieh, Afef
GRIC-UQAM, Montreal

Benmergui, Marlene
Journalist CBC, Thornhill

Besabe, Omar
University of St. Thomas, Fredericton
Black, William
University of British Columbia, Vancouver

Blais, Lise
Solidarite populaire Quebec, Montreal

Bleyer, Peter
Council of Canadians, Ottawa

Boyce, Susan
St. Thomas University, Fredericton

Brock, Michael
Department of Foreign Affairs and International Trade, Ottawa

Brunelle, Dorval
GRIC-UQAM, Montreal

Campbell, Bruce
Canadian Centre for Policy Alternatives, Ottawa

Carter, Terry
New Brunswick Federation of Labour, Chatham

Chambers, Ted
University of Alberta, Edmonton

Clark, Jeffrey
Human Rights Research and Education Centre, University of Ottawa, Ottawa

Close, David
Memorial University of Newfoundland, St. John's

Cooney, James P.
Placer Dome Inc., Vancouver

Cote, Lise
Federation des travailleurs et travailleuses du Quebec, Montreal

Craig, Robert
CUSO-Quebec, Montreal

Cromwell, Jim
Advanced Education and Labour, Fredericton

DeBlock, Christian
GRIC-UQAM, Montreal

de Sousa-Shields, Mark
Centro de Encuentros y Dialogos, Toronto

Dean, Elsie
National Action Committee on the Status of Women, Vancouver

Deonandan, Kalowatie
University of Saskatchewan, Saskatoon

Dickerson, Mark
University of Calgary, Calgary

Dillon, John
Ecumenical Coalition for Economic Justice, Toronto

Drache, Daniel
York University, North York

Dussault, Manuel
Alliance des manufacturiers et exportateurs
du Quebec, Montreal

Einegel, Susanne
B.C. Casa, North Vancouver

Elwell, Christine
Queens University, Toronto

Escudero, Monica
Simon Fraser University, Burnaby

Foster, John W.
University of Saskatchewan, Saskatoon

Galan, Manuel
Malaspina International, Calgary

Garon, Muriel
Commission des droits de la personne du Quebec, Montreal

Grant Cummings, Joan
National Action Committee on the Status of Women, Toronto

Grenier, Carl
Ministere de l'Industrie et du Commerce, Montreal

Grinspun, Ricardo
York University/CERLAC (Centre for Research on Latin America and the Caribbean), North York

Guay, Lorraine
Federation des femmes du Quebec, Montreal

Gunn, Joe
Canadian Conference of Catholic Bishops, Ottawa

Handy, Jim
University of Saskatchewan, Saskatoon

Hennessy, Dean
York University/CERLAC (Centre for Research on Latin America and the Caribbean), North York

Hernandez, Marina
University of New Brunswick / FOCAL - Atlantic Fredericton

Hinds, Robert
N.B. Agriculture and Rural Development, Fredericton

Houle-Courcelles, Mathieu
GRIC-UQAM, Montreal

Ingersoll, Gerald
NB Community College, St. Andrews

Irwin, Rosalind
York University, North York

Jamieson, Sharon
University of Alberta, Edmonton

Jankowski, Christopher K.
Universite de Moncton, Moncton

Jaschke, Bill
Province of Alberta, Edmonton

Judson, Fred
University of Alberta, Edmonton

Katz, Sheila
Canadian Labour Congress, Ottawa

Koth, Karl B.
Okanagan University College, Kelowna

Laberge, Louise
Conseil central de Montreal, Montreal

Lachance, Daniel
Centrale de l'Enseignement du Quebec, Montreal

Lachapelle, Rene
Conseil central de la Monteregie, St-Hubert

Langlois, Richard
Centrale de l'Enseignement du Quebec, Montreal

Laquerre, Patrice
Centre Quebecois du droit de l'environnement, Montreal

Leaman, Hayden
University of New Brunswick, Fredericton

Leclerc, Andre
Federation des travailleurs et travailleuses du Quebec, Montreal

Legg, Philip
B.C. Federation of Labour, Burnaby

Legler, Tom
York University, North York

Levac, Raymond
Developpement et paix, Montreal

Little, Jennifer
Department of Foreign Affairs and International Trade, Ottawa

Loyola, Rodrigo
Edmonton

Macdonald, Laura
Carleton University, Ottawa

MacIsaac, Michael
Canadian Labour Congress, Don Mills

Maclauchlan, Wade
University of New Brunswick, Fredericton

Martinez, Juan Carlos
University of Mount Allison, Sackville

Mason, Steve
Fredericton

Matwychuk, Margot
University of Victoria, Victoria

McWilliams, Cal
Canadian International Development Agency, Hull

Melaneon, Claude
Association des avocats en droit du travail, Montreal

Milner, Rick
Nova Gas International, Calgary

Moore, Stan
Canadian International Development Agency, Hull

Moore, Roger
St. Thomas University, Fredericton

Moore-Kilgannon, Bill
Centre for International Alternatives, Edmonton

Muratorio, Blanca
The University of British Columbia, Vancouver

Navratil, Steven
University of Calgary, Calgary

Nef, Jorge
University of Guelph, Guelph

Noel, Dexter J.
University of New Brunswick, Fredericton

North, Liisa L.
York University, North York

Olson, Kathryn
Earthkeeping, Edmonton

Otero, Gerardo
Simon Fraser University, Burnaby

Paponnet-Cantat, Christiane
University of New Brunswick, Fredericton
Director FOCAL-Atlantic

Paquette, Pierre
CSN, Montreal

Paradis, Andre
Ligue des droits et libertes, Montreal

Passaris, Constatine
University of New Brunswick, Fredericton

Pereira-Tatenburg, Gloria
Comite pour la justice sociale, Montreal

Perez, Marco
University of Calgary, Calgary

Picard, Ghislain
Assemblee des Premieres Nations du Quebec et du Labrador, Village Huron (Wendake)

Picard, Claire
Ministere des relations internationales du Quebec, Montreal

Piper, Stephen
University College of the Fraser Valley, Abbotsford

Proudfoot, Jennifer
Canadian Council for International Cooperation, Ottawa

Rader, Jim
CoDevelopment Canada, Vancouver

Ramos, Duberlis
Hispanic Development Council, Toronto

Randall, Stephen James
University of Calgary, Calgary

Recalde, Andres
World Vision Canada, Mississauga

Riddell, Norman
University of Alberta, Edmonton

Robinson, David
Canadian Center for Policy Alternatives, Vancouver

Rochlin, James F.
Okanagan University College, Kelowna

Rothschild, Jonathan
Canadian International Development Agency, Hull

Routledge, Marg
Oxfam, Fredericton

Roy, Marianne
Solidarite populaire Quebec, Montreal

Rumsey, Suzanne
Inter-Church Committee on Human Rights in Latin America, Toronto

Sagebien, Julia
Dalhousie University, Halifax

Sanmiguel, Olga
York University, North York

Saucier, Roger
CISO-Quebec

Schacter, Noel
Ministry of Employment and Investments, Victoria

Schenk, Chris
Ontario Federation of Labour, Don Mills

Schmidt, Bob
Canadian Catholic Organization for Development and Peace, Edmonton

Schnied, Syd
Telecommunications Workers Union, Burnaby

Seymoar, Nola-Kate
International Institute for Sustainable Development, Winnipeg

Simmons, Alan B.
York University, North York

Spence, Rhonda
Trade Union Group, Vancouver

St. John, Cameron
Teck Corporation, Vancouver

Stedman, Charles
Strategic Intell.-Nova Gas International, Calgary

Taylor del Cid, Alex
University of Calgary, Calgary

Tellier-Cohen, Lorraine
Montreal International, Montreal

Thede, Nancy
Centre international des droits de la personne et du developpement democratique, Montreal

Tonge, Barry
University of Alberta, Edmonton

Torres, Marta
Christian Task Force on Central America, Vancouver

Torres, Carlos
CERLAC(Centre for Research on Latin America and the Caribbean), North York

Traynor, Ken
Canadian Environmental Law Association, Toronto

Trudel, Clement
Le Devoir, Montreal

Trumper, Ricardo
Okanagan University College, Kelowna

Trumper, Camilo
University of British Columbia, Vancouver

Vallee, Emile
FTQ, Montreal

Welton, Larry
Community College Saint John, West Field

Young, Richard
The University of Alberta, Edmonton

Young, Bill
Canadian International Development Agency, Hull

# X. GENERAL PROPOSALS

# Partnership Between Government and Civil Society: The Summit of the Americas

*La Corporación PARTICIPA is one of the most active NGOs in Chile. The mission of PARTICIPA is to promote individual and collective participation as fundamental to the integral and sustainable development of the country, its public and private institutions, and its people in all aspects of life. PARTICIPA encourages the values of social coexistence, particularly the responsible exercise of rights and responsibilities, tolerance, and the capacity for dialogue, and promotes a culture in favor of sustainable development for present and future generations.*

*PARTICIPA seeks to achieve these goals by working in an ideologically open, nonpartisan fashion and seeks to make an effective contribution to social integration and the vanquishing of poverty as ethical imperatives for peace among nations.*

*PARTICIPA's educational and training services, offered in Chile and internationally, provide participatory projects in the areas of organizational management and development that focus on the civic, political, social, economic, and environmental aspects of living in society.*

## INTRODUCTION

This publication provides information on the consultation process organized by PARTICIPA during 1997 in preparation for the Summit of the Americas to be held in Santiago, Chile, on April 18-19, 1998.

For the Miami Summit in 1994 and the Summit Conference on Sustainable Development in Santa Cruz de la Sierra in 1996, mechanisms of citizen participation were implemented, led by the North-South Center in Miami and by the Fundación Futuro Latinoamericano, based in Quito.

These processes of civil society consultation strengthen the democratic system in the Americas as well as governability. To advance in the processes of hemispheric integration and to fulfill the action plans committed to at the Summits, it is important to lay the foundation for a relationship between government - civil society in decision-making processes and in the adoption of measures that allow for a contribution to the well-being of our societies. In addition, citizen participation ensures that people are responsibly committed to reaching the established goals.

As one way of advancing in the process of citizen participation, in March 1997 PARTICIPA presented a proposal to the Government of Chile, through the Ministry of Foreign Affairs, regarding the need to continue with the process of citizen participation that had been initiated in Miami. PARTICIPA's proposal was readily accepted by the Chilean government.

In this context, PARTICIPA held two meetings during the months of August and November in Santiago, Chile, with the support of the Organization of American States, the Inter-American Development Bank, the Government of Canada and the Government of Chile.

The August meeting called "Education, Democracy and Sustainable Development" was held on August 7-8, 1997, and brought together 55 representatives of civil society organizations from 22 countries of the continent. During this meeting, recommendations relating to three aspects of education were formulated: education for democracy, education for hemispheric integration and education for sustainable development. Later, these recommendations were presented by PARTICIPA in a governmental meeting held on August 11, 1997, to discuss the item of education in preparation for the X Summit Implementation Review Group (SIRG) meeting held on October 1-2 at the World Bank offices in Washington, D.C.

The second meeting titled "The Role of Public Participation in Development Actions and Eradication of Poverty in the Framework of the Summit of the Americas" was held on November 4-7 in Santiago, Chile. The main objective of this meeting was to involve the participants (governments and civil society) in a participatory process of formulating recommendations to the preparatory bodies of the 1998 Santiago Summit on initiatives concerned with mechanisms to strengthen civil society, the role of women in the eradication of poverty and discrimination and the strengthening of actions to combat corruption.

The participants also had the opportunity to discuss mechanisms to promote dialogue between governments and civil society to develop and strengthen permanent alliances on the issue of sustainable development and to contribute to the preparatory processes of the Hemispheric Summits, especially the Santiago Summit. In addition, the Inter-American Strategy for Public Participation (ISP) of the Organization of American States (OAS) was discussed as a framework for government - civil society alliances. Seventeen of the focal points of the ISP met to review the goals and activities of the strategy, the role of the focal points, the implementation plan and preliminary budget. The organization Afroamerica XXI also presented their action proposal to be presented to governments on issues of promoting greater participation of indigenous and afroamerican populations.

One hundred thirty-one people attended the second meeting, from 30 countries of the Americas. There were 70 representatives from civil society organizations, 51 governmental representatives (Focal Points of the Inter-American Strategy for Public Participation and SIRG Coordinators and Advisors) and 10 representatives of international and/or regional organizations. Governmental representatives of the coordinating countries for the following topics also attended: Amb. Ellen Bogle, Ministry of Foreign Affairs, Jamaica and Gustavo Alvarez Goyoaga, Ministry of Foreign Affairs, Uruguay in relation to "Actions Destined to Strengthen Civil Society Participation"; Ms. Rosargentina Lopez Prado, Instituto Nicaragüense de la Mujer in relation to "Actions to Strengthen the Role of Women in the Eradication of Poverty and Discrimination"; and Mr. Roque Diaz, Oficina del Comisionado de la Presidencia de la República para la Vigilancia de la Administración Pública de Venezuela in relation to "Transparency as a Means of Combating Corruption."

PARTICIPA was invited by the Chilean Government to participate in the official Chilean delegation in the XI Meeting of the Summit Implementation Review Group, held on December 9-11, 1997 in the offices of the OAS in Washington, D.C. Through this invitation, Andrea Sanhueza was able to actively participate in the working group on the item of strengthening civil society.

This publication includes the recommendations produced from the process of consultation on issues relating to education, strengthening civil society, the role of women in the eradication of poverty and discrimination and actions to combat corruption. One thousand copies of this document will be produced to serve as a contribution to the process of participation of civil society organizations in the context of the discussions for hemispheric meetings.

We would like to express our sincere appreciation for the support and confidence placed in us by the Chilean Ministry of Foreign Affairs in general and especially Ambassador Juan Martabit, Coordinator General of the Summit of the Americas and his team, Raúl Fernández, Rodrigo Fernández and Eduardo Escobar. Without their support, a productive and positive dialogue would not have been possible.

Finally, we would also like to thank Walter Arensberg, Vladimir Radovic and Rolando Castañeda of the Inter-American Development Bank, Zoila Girón of the Organization of American States, Francisco Vio of the Chilean Agency for International Cooperation and Lise Filiatrault and Claude Beausejour from the Canadian Embassy in Chile for the support they provided us. Without their support this consultation process would not have been possible.

## EDUCATION, DEMOCRACY AND SUSTAINABLE DEVELOPMENT

1. Democracy today constitutes a life style that must be strengthened and internalized by people of all countries, in the conviction that it is the best political system.

2. The Summits of the Americas have progressively established themselves as a coherent process towards progress and the strengthening of democracy and should respond to the needs and concerns manifested by all of the countries of the hemisphere, both by governments as well as civil society.

3. Globalization presents a challenge for education. If values are not incorporated into education, true social and economic integration in democracy will not be achieved.

4. In this context, education requires the recovery of human values, social integration, recognition of differences, overcoming prejudices, and the promotion of a culture of respect for the rights of all

people. Hemispheric integration must be accomplished without compromising cultural diversity and the uniqueness of local identity. All of the above ought to be in accordance with the principles established by UNESCO (Scientific and Cultural Organization) regarding the freedom to learn how to know, the freedom to learn how to make, the freedom to learn how to live together peacefully, and the freedom to learn how to be.

5. Education for the next century ought to develop the spirit of the person and train that person to be master of his/her own destiny.
6. To contribute to the development of these principles, the First International Seminar on "Education, Democracy and Sustainable Development" was held in Santiago, Chile in order to formulate recommendations for the next Summit of the Americas from the perspective of members of civil society.

# Recommendations to the Governments of the Americas from the Perspective of Members of Civil Society

## I. EDUCATION FOR HEMISPHERIC INTEGRATION

### Governments should:

- Establish mechanisms that allow all of the countries of the continent to be effectively incorporated in the process of hemispheric integration, assuring that this process will not be limited only to the economic sphere, but that it will also include social and cultural dimensions, using education as a fundamental tool for achieving this holistic integration.

- Favor educational reforms which benefit the processes of hemispheric integration. These reforms should have a long-term perspective, in order to minimize the delays that may be generated as a result of rotation of the government in power.
- Promote continental integration, with special emphasis on ensuring the full regional integration of the Caribbean by means of exchanges of planning experiences and educational programs.

## II. EDUCATION FOR DEMOCRACY

### Governments should:

- Promote, strengthen, and create programs for education in democracy and human rights, at all levels of both formal and informal education, by drawing on expertise from the public, private, and civil society sectors, with regard to curriculum development and reform.
- Present a mandate to regional organization such as the Organization of American States, Inter-American Development Bank and others so that in consultation with civil society organizations, they develop a Hemispheric Strategy for Education for Democracy within one year and within the following two years thereafter, ensure the existence of a curriculum for education for democracy to which all member countries have free access.
- Promote that educational reforms incorporate: a) the participation of all actors involved in the educational process (students, parents and guardians, teachers, business people, etc.), both in the schools as well as the policy-making realms; and b) the democratic leadership of the corresponding educational areas.
- Design mechanisms for follow-up and evaluation of the adopted accords regarding education, both on the part of governments and civil society, as well as establish measures that allow for their disclosure.

## III. EDUCATION FOR SUSTAINABLE DEVELOPMENT

### Governments should:

- Reaffirm their support for Initiative #5 of the Action Plan of Santa Cruz de la Sierra [Bolivia] in 1996, which states:

- "—to stimulate changes in the rules and regulations of educational and communications policies and study plans in order to include in these policies instruction in sustainable development adapted to the different needs and realities of the hemisphere, taking special account of the pluri-cultural and multi-lingual realities of the region, always assuring that these educational policies assure the creation of a social conscience for sustainable development. To achieve these ends, it is important to push for networks and related mechanisms for an interchange of experiences, teaching materials, and educational innovations and communications about this theme." *(unofficial translation)*
- Create and strengthen formal and informal educational systems that promote the practice of a global citizenship that enables every citizen to understand their rights and responsibilities, emphasizing the role played by women, especially in relation to responsible consumption.
- Adopt as basic legislation, that which promotes responsible consumption according to the United Nations Guidelines for Consumer Protection (1985), including subsequent amendments and additions.

## IV. ACTIONS TO STRENGTHEN CIVIL SOCIETY AND PUBLIC PARTICIPATION

### 1. Proposed Actions to Strengthen Civil Society Participation

*Action Proposal:*

Governments will develop, within one year of the date of this Plan of Action, modalities governing the formation and operation of non-profit civil society organizations and model mechanisms for establishing government-civil society partnerships in development decision-making. These modalities and mechanisms will be developed with the support of the OAS and other relevant regional organizations and in consultation with civil society, building upon initiatives underway in the hemisphere, such as the Inter-American Strategy for Participation in the area of sustainable development (ISP). Additionally, during the second year following the date of this Plan of Action, governments will develop a work plan to adapt and implement these modalities and mechanisms in their respective countries in order to optimize public participation in all spheres of national life. Finally, governments call upon the Inter-American Development Bank (IDB) to develop and implement, within one year, hemispheric financial mechanisms to strengthen the capacity of civil society to participate as fully effective and responsible partners, and to broaden and deepen mechanisms for government-civil society partnership.

*Rationale:*

Governments of the hemisphere, through recent global and regional summits, have recognized that strong civil society engagement in decision-making is fundamental for enhancing democracy, promoting sustainable development, achieving economic integration and free trade, improving the lives of all people, and conserving the natural environment for future generations. Important progress has been made since the Miami Summit of the Americas and the Bolivia Summit on Sustainable Development in addressing the need for public participation in decision-making and in identifying and developing the means to strengthen civil society. For example, the Organization of American States, in compliance with the Bolivia Summit mandate, is presently formulating an Inter-American Strategy for Public Participation (ISP) to identify concrete mechanisms for securing the universal rights and obligations of individuals, civil society and governments recognized in previous summits, and to promote participatory decision-making in environmental and sustainable development issues. This strategy is being formulated by conducting demonstration studies, analyzing relevant legal and institutional frameworks and mechanisms, sharing information and experiences, and establishing a basis for long-term financial support for public-private alliances. The proposed action would complement ongoing work undertaken pursuant to prior hemispheric summits and expand the scope of this work to include all relevant areas of development. The action would rely upon creating and strengthening partnerships between government and all sectors of society as a means to secure meaningful participation in decision-making. The action would also advance existing hemispheric commitments by moving toward concrete and realizable goals.

*Measures:*

- Entrust Jamaica and Uruguay, along with other interested states, to comply with the mandate to coordinate this initiative, provide support among governments and members of civil society, and to follow up with the OAS and the IDB to assure that appropriate programs to carry out this initiative are established and supported.

- Develop, strengthen and expand, within one year of the date of this Plan of Action, building on initiatives already underway, modalities permitting the formation and operation of non-profit and other civil society organizations and model mechanisms for establishing government-civil society partnerships in decision-making and policy implementation. These modalities and mechanisms will be developed with the support of the OAS, IDB and other organizations relevant at a regional level, and in consultation with civil society. Further, within two years, the countries will adopt a work plan to implement these modalities and model mechanisms.

- Urge the IDB to develop and implement, along with interested states, hemispheric financial mechanisms specially devoted to the implementation of programs oriented toward strengthening civil society and public participation mechanisms.

## 2. Actions Proposed for Strengthening Civil Society and To Be Inserted in the Agenda of the Santiago Summit

We further would recommend that the SIRG integrate civil society participation as a preferred mechanism in each of its substantive areas of the Summit document, and to that end we recommend that language be inserted as appropriate into relevant sections of the Summit documents, including language committing the governments to:

*Item: Education; Preserving and Strengthening Democracy and Human Rights; Economic Integration and Free Trade; Eradication of Poverty and Discrimination*

- Formulate in the second year a work plan for implementing these mechanisms and regulations in their respective countries.

*Item: Education:*

- Include in the educational curriculum themes relevant to building and educating for peace (peaceful resolution of conflicts, collective responsibility, non-violence, respect for life and dignity, etc.).

*Item: Preserving and Strengthening Democracy and Human Rights*

- Promote consultations on the preparation and implementation of policies designed to optimize the participation of civil society in the various spheres of their national life.

- Ensure that all citizens, women and men, are incorporated in all spheres of public and political life and ensure that their gender interests are taken into account in the promulgation of public policies and programs.

- Develop jointly with all members of civil society, as soon as practical, model mechanisms and regulations to secure full and responsible participation of civil society. In so doing, Governments will seek the cooperation, both technical and financial, of the organizations in the hemisphere (OAS, IDB), and other interested members of the international community.

- Encourage the expression and forms of participation appropriate for indigenous and Afro-American peoples to assert their cultural identity on the basis of respect and guarantee of their rights.

- Aid the decentralization of local governments/municipalities to ensure that communities can participate in decisions which directly affect their environment, productivity and livelihoods.

*Item: Economic Integration and Free Trade*

- Support the efforts of NGOs to develop integrated approaches to capital investment and community development. In particular, Governments should support the initiatives which utilize an integrated approach to community development in the inner cities.

*Item: Eradication of Poverty and Discrimination*

- Encourage the expression and forms of participation appropriate for indigenous and Afro-American peoples to assert their cultural identity on the basis of respect and guarantee of their rights.

## 3. Additional Actions Proposed for Strengthening Civil Society and To Be Inserted in the Agenda of the Santiago Summit

### Item: Preserving and Strengthening Democracy and Human Rights

- Actions in the area of education for democracy and in full respect of human rights of indigenous and Afro-American populations.

- Analyze and support present cultures to reinforce their national identity so that it serves as a foundation for national development.

- Actions aimed at enhancing the participation of indigenous peoples, Afro-Americans, women, peasants and children in civil society.

### Item: Economic Integration and Free Trade

- Promote consultations with civil society and governments on a hemispheric level to formulate and establish positions related to the Free Trade Area of the Americas in accordance with the priorities of civil society.

### Item: Eradication of Poverty and Discrimination

- Actions in support of micro-enterprises and small businesses in Afro-American communities as a way of promoting the creation of new jobs through access to sources of credit, the development of vocational training, programs designed to obtain an increase in productivity and the introduction and application of new and more advanced technologies.

- Actions aimed at promoting greater participation of indigenous and Afro-American populations through adequate access to education, health and vocational training.

### Item: Other Recommendations Proposed for Strengthening Civil Society

- In recognition of the importance placed on alliances between government and civil society organizations, as one form of participation, and conscious of the role and responsibility of civil society in making the initiatives included in the Plan of Action in this summit and the Summits of Miami in 1994 and Santa Cruz in 1996 a reality, the governments should commit to propagate in diverse ways those plans of action in a broad and understandable manner, among citizens and organized civil society. Likewise, they should recognize that civil society organizations are convenient and necessary channels for the effective implementation of this initiative.

- The recognition that without effective citizen participation, there cannot be sustainable development should be introduced into the mention of sustainable development.

- Promote mechanisms that allow for the generation of information and that facilitate follow-up and monitoring of public and private actions that affect the well-being of communities.

- Enable individuals to have fluid access to information on issues of a public nature.

- Promote the elaboration of legal frameworks that allow the institutionalization of public participation through the Permanent Forum of Regional Parliaments. Carry out this analysis with civil society.

- Analyze and reinforce legal mechanisms in the different powers of State to make public participation in decision-making more effective. The first action in this direction would be to elaborate a report/inventory on existing mechanisms.

## V. THE ROLE OF WOMEN IN THE ERADICATION OF POVERTY AND DISCRIMINATION

## 1. Actions for Strengthening the Role of Women in the Eradication of Poverty in the Agenda of the Summit of the Americas

### Political Declaration:

It is the responsibility and obligation of the States to ensure economic, political, social and cultural equality among women and men, as the foundation of human rights, a requirement for the strengthening of democracy and the attainment of social justice, development and peace.

### Initiatives for the Plan of Action:

### Governments should commit to:

- Strengthen politically, administratively and financially where they exist, or create where they do not exist, national mechanisms and governmental organizations responsible for ensuring equality between women and men, as well as their regional and sub-regional networks so that these organizations promote and coordinate public policies that guarantee that the States fulfill their commitments made regarding women in world summits and international conventions, especially in the Action Platform of the United Nations IV World Conference on Women (Beijing) and the Summit of the Americas.

- Impel the revision and creation of laws and any necessary institutional reform to eliminate all forms of discrimination and violence against all women, independent of their ethnic origin.

- Guarantee that the Inter-American Commission on Women (ICW)/Organization of American States (OAS) actively contributes, on a regional and national level, to the monitoring of the commitments on the situation and position of women, made in the Summit of the Americas. This monitoring should be carried out through the instruments established for that purpose, in coordination with the designated country. To fulfill this purpose, the ICW should be provided the necessary financing and international organizations and cooperation agencies should be incorporated into these efforts.

- Designate the heads of governmental institutions for the promotion of women as representatives to the ICW.

## 2. Actions To Strengthen the Role of Women in the Eradication of Poverty and To Be Incorporated in the Agenda of the Summit of the Americas

### Item: Education:

- Offer quality education for the entire population, giving special attention to the education of girls in order to end the de facto segregation that confines them to programs of study that lead to low paying and low prestige occupations.

- Reduce the illiteracy rate to 50% of the current statistics within the next 5 years and encourage international organizations to finance educational programs for adults between the ages of 18 and 40.

- Given the wide gender gaps existing in scientific, technical and management training and in the access to technologies, substantively increase the number of women and girls in training and access to these areas.

- Guarantee gender equality in academic or educational exchange programs.

- Develop within all levels of the educational system a training program for equal opportunities.

### Item: Preserving and Strengthening Democracy and Human Rights

- Develop training programs to build and strengthen women's political and leadership skills in democracy.

- Significantly increase the proportion of women in elected office and in State decision-making positions.

### Item: Eradication of Poverty and Discrimination

- Incorporate reliable mechanisms in the process of official land registry and entitlement that recognize women's right to land.

- Stop the increase of poverty and decrease it by no less than 5% of the current statistics. Develop programs especially aimed at improving the situation of female headed households in poverty.

- Guarantee gender equality in access to financing programs for micro, small and medium enterprises and when necessary, develop initiatives to expand access to credit for women owners of micro enterprises.

- Guarantee the effective fulfillment of the international conventions related with equal pay for equal work among men and women.

- Given the complexity of Afro-American issues and the invisibility to which they have been subject, we propose that the governments include the Afro-American issue in the point of Eradication of Poverty and Discrimination in the sixth paragraph "Actions aimed at promoting greater participation of indigenous *and Afro-American* populations through adequate access to education, health and work training."

## VI. TRANSPARENCY AS A MEANS OF COMBATING CORRUPTION

### 1. Actions to Combat Corruption in the Agenda of the Summit of the Americas

Considering the commitments made to combat corruption in the Action Plan of the 1994 Summit of the Americas, Under the Agenda Heading, "Democracy and Human Rights: Actions to Confront Corruption":

*Before December 31, 1998, governments will:*

- Encourage the ratification of the Inter-American Convention Against Corruption and take concrete steps to implement the commitments, including the establishment of mechanisms that promote civil society participation in an effort to prevent, detect, sanction and eradicate corruption.

- Promote legislation to establish and enforce standards of conduct, rules regarding conflict of interest on the incompatibility of public office and private interests, requirements for public disclosure of assets of high level public officials and their families, in the executive, legislative and judicial branches, and to create national organizations for oversight of such laws.

- Promote and finance education to strengthen ethical values and behavior and encourage the communications media to support such programs.

- Establish an OAS secretariat (similar to the CICAD model) with adequate resources from IDB and national governments to promote the implementation of the convention and to monitor progress, including by mutual evaluation, with annual reports to ministers.

- Create an Inter-American network of governmental and civil society institutions under the OAS Secretary General to cooperate in the struggle against corruption through, among others, the exchange of information and experiences and horizontal cooperation.

### 2. Actions to Combat Corruption and To Be Incorporated in the Agenda for the Summit of the Americas

*Item: Education:*

Promote legislation requiring the timely publication of information regarding government activities, including budgets and expenditures, public access to information, and public hearings for expression of the opinion of citizens.

*Item: Preserving and Strengthening Democracy and Human Rights*

To promote independence, integrity and transparency in the administration of justice, by December 31, 1999, concerning judges, promote merit selection, training in the highest ethical standards, and the creation of oversight mechanisms, and strengthen the role of public prosecutors.

*Item: Economic Integration and Free Trade*

- Conclude negotiation of a regional agreement on transparency in procurement, for ,approval and implementation before December 31, 1998.

- Encourage the use of "no bribe commitments" and corporate codes of conduct that prohibit bribes in public bidding as well as in projects financed by the IDB.

- Instruct the Inter-American Development Bank to adopt regulations, procedures and policies of the highest standard for public bidding.

- Take immediate measures to eradicate corruption in customs offices.

## VII. PROPOSAL OF AFROAMERICA XXI TO THE WORKSHOP ON PUBLIC PARTICIPATION IN DEVELOPMENT AND THE ERADICATION OF POVERTY IN THE FRAMEWORK OF THE SUMMIT OF THE AMERICAS

Michael John Franklin, President of the Organization of Africans in the Americas (OAA) in Washington, D.C., and Gregoria Flores Martínez, President of the Organización Fraternal Negra Hondureña (OFRANEH), La Ceiba, Honduras, Vice-President of the Confederación de Pueblos Autóctonos de Honduras (CONPAH), official delegates in representation of the organizations that are delegates of AFROAMERICA XXI:

Considering that the population of African ancestry reaches one third of the total population of Latin America, among them a group with dark skin that constitutes ninety million people or twenty (20%) of the total population:

Considering that this twenty (20%) per cent represents approximately forty (40%) per cent of the poor in Latin Amerca:

Considering that Afrolatinamericans are not considered a vulnerable group in spite of their circumstances of extreme poverty and marginalization, and at the same time their exclusion from the benefits of the International Cooperation:

In regards to these considerations we put under the consideration of the honorable Leaders of the Governments of the Americas and their ministers:

- To make visible the Afroamerican population of Latin America:
    a) crediting their historical contributions to the development of their nations
    b) as part of the populations living in chronic poverty
    c) as vulnerable populations that development has not touched in a significant or positive manner.
- Commitment from the States to engage in a collaborative process of development with organized Afroamerican communities and the international cooperation.
- Agree that the objective of this collaboration is to generate a process of Afroamerican development that is self-generated and that results in a better quality of life and in cultural, spiritual, moral, etc. contributions and citizenship to Latin American life.
- To give priority in this collaborative process to policies, programs and actions to remove the systemic barriers that are faced by these populations in the whole region.
    a) Incorporate all their history, culture, language to the curriculae for all levels of formal education, with the intention of generating a Latin American society that values ethnocultural diversity, especially the Afroamerican.
    b) Direct development investment to provide the necessary infrastructure to generate local economies in their rural and urban-marginal zones. This includes highways and roads accessible year-round, sources of electric energy, means of comunication, permanent public transport, potable water systems and basic sanitation.
    c) To include these populations, as subjects of development, in all the national development plans, making them visible in the poverty maps, in the decentralization plans and in programs for human development/training.
    d) To include ethno-cultural identication in the data from census and household surveys used in programming for social and economic development.
    e) As an immediate measure, to give priority to including Afroamerican populations as target groups in programs for poverty alleviation in all the countries, and to work in collaboration with the Afroamerican NGOs involved in the process of AFROAMERICA XXI so that they inform/sensitize government officials in development to open opportunities for funding projects from the Afroamerican communities and to use the development priorities proposed by AFROAMERICA XXI to select them.
    f) To ensure the operation of the government programs more relevant to Afroamerican development to participate in the process of AFROAMERICA XXI nationally/regionally to formulate plans of action that the State and the communities can execute and fund.
    g) To require that the agencies of cooperation, bilateral and multilateral institutions, also be participants of the process of AFROAMERICA XXI, as financial partners in this process.
    h) To consider the process/strategy of AFROAMERICA XXI as a pilot experience in ethno-development directed to support vulnerable groups to overcome the poverty they face and to generate within them the capacity to strengthen their skills, abilities, knowledge, in addition to a feeling of entrepreneurship that will sustain the process of development through time.

Considering what is presented above, Afroamerica XXI establishes that the multilateral and international cooperation institutions:

- Assign priority to the Afrolatinamerican communities as a vulnerable group, and select them for programs of institutional and organizational development.
- Assign priority to the strengthening of micro-entrepreneurial capacity to the communities.
- Assign priority to tourism development in Afroamerican communities.
- Assign priority to Afroamericans as target groups for programs in Media Communications.
- Assign priority to Goverments subscribing and applying Convention 169 of the International Labor Organization (ILO).
- Assign priority, in relevant countries, in the process of land titling to Afroamerican communities.
- To implement specific programs of human rights in the countries of AFROAMERICA XXI.

# X. GENERAL PROPOSALS

*This summary is the product of the international conference, "Globalization, Latin America and the Summit of the Americas II," organized by FLACSO-Chile, the Latin American and Caribbean Center at Florida International University, the Latin American Program of the Woodrow Wilson Center, and supported by the Chilean Ministry of Foreign Affairs, March 30-April 1, 1998, Santiago, Chile.*

*The Woodrow Wilson International Center for Scholars was established by the U.S. Congress in 1968 as an international institute for advanced study, "symbolizing and strengthening the fruitful relationship between the world of learning and the world of public affairs." The Center is a nonprofit, nonpartisan organization, supported financially by annual appropriations from the U.S. Congress and by the contributions of foundations, corporations, and individuals.*

## Globalización y Orden Internacional

*Francisco Rojas Aravena*
*Director, FLACSO-Chile*

La globalización es un hecho. Afecta al sistema internacional y a las distintas naciones más allá de la voluntad o deseos de los actores. La globalización genera consecuencias de distinto tipo y diferente orden en las diversas áreas del mundo. El fenómeno de la globalización debe ser identificado esencialmente en dos dimensiones: las de carácter comercial y financieras; y el impacto de la mundialización de los medios de comunicación y la instantaneidad para cubrir los hechos locales con una dimensión global.

Al finalizar el siglo XX la globalización ha tenido como expresión una crisis financiera global cuyas consecuencias en el ámbito social han sido tremendamente graves en Asia y en Rusia, lo que ha afectado a sus sistemas políticos. La globalización ha mostrado las vulnerabilidades de los Estados nacionales para enfrentar las nuevas formas del desarrollo capitalista mundial.

En este marco de crisis y de falta de diseños compartidos para enfrentar las tendencias fragmentadoras producto de la globalización, se evidencia un déficit de liderazgo global capaz de mostrar derroteros para superar los obstáculos y aprovechar las oportunidades que la globalización presenta para una mejor integración de los distintos países al sistema internacional. El rol de la II Cumbre de las Américas fue precisamente establecer un liderazgo multilateral en el hemisferio occidental. La gestación de un liderazgo de nuevo tipo en las Américas posibilitará desarrollar mejores alternativas de cooperación.

El sistema capitalista se encuentra en transición, como lo ha señalado Alain Touraine,[1] quien ha indicado que se requiere construir una salida desde una forma neoliberal extrema, de alto costo social y humano. Al finalizar el siglo se evidencia una crisis en el denominado "consenso de Washington" que apuntaba esencialmente a una liberalización completa, sin marcos reguladores y sin preocupación por los efectos sociales y las consecuencias políticas de una forma particular de desarrollo capitalista.

En los principales organismos financieros y en los centros de decisión mundiales se debate sobre la arquitectura futura del sistema internacional, con el fin de vincularla al impacto de la globalización. En la búsqueda de alternativas aparecen distintas opciones, que van desde una mayor liberalización hasta el establecimiento de marcos regulatorios supranacionales. En el primer caso se expresa en recomendaciones tales como eliminar las instituciones que cumplieron un rol importante en el período de posguerra, como el Fondo Monetario Internacional. En el segundo, se señala la urgente necesidad de regular las transacciones financieras internacionales y proceder a una remodelación de la arquitectura del sistema económico internacional.[2]

El nuevo consenso internacional en construcción apunta hacia una mayor regulación. Desarrollar capacidades para establecer marcos regulatorios —a transacciones financieras que se movilizan como intercambios de dinero electrónico— aparece con una alta prioridad. En este sentido, se ha sugerido el repensar el rol del Estado. En reforzar las capacidades de éstos para diseñar, decidir y aplicar normas que posibiliten enfrentar los retos derivados de la situación de transición en el sistema capitalista internacional. Re-estatizar el Estado para restablecer sus capacidades regulatorias en el nuevo marco internacional.

La crisis del Estado se evidencia en un aspecto esencial, su soberanía. La pérdida de control del Estado para regular aspectos esenciales de la economía internacional, está produciendo un cambio en las configuraciones político-económicas del poder. La territorialidad de la economía global se expresa en grandes ciudades: Nueva York, Londres, Tokio, París, Los Angeles, Hong Kong, Sidney, Sao Paulo y algunas otras. Es en estas ciudades donde se toman las decisiones sobre la circulación de activos internacionales ejecutadas por medios computacionales. Las capacidades de los Estados nacionales para controlar estas transacciones son muy limitadas.[3] Aun las capacidades para construir diagnósticos comunes es limitada. En la perspectiva de Kenichi Ohmae[4] se está formando un nuevo tipo de Estado: los estados-región. Señala que éstos no son ni tienen por qué ser enemigos de los gobiernos centrales. Pero para ello se deberá gestionar una forma flexible de relación de estos Estados regionales (grandes ciudades o federaciones de ellas) con el resto del Estado nacional. Se destaca que los puntos de entrada a la economía mundial son estas ciudades estados. La globalización por su parte, ha generado un nuevo marco de regímenes internacionales de carácter privado. Las regulaciones y las normas que posibilitan estas transacciones han sido establecidas como parte de los arreglos entre empresas privadas. Aún no existe un derecho internacional de la globalización. Se hace cada vez más necesario. Para establecerlo se requiere liderazgo y capacidades efectivas de los Estados que conformen este marco regulatorio.

Los mandatarios del hemisferio occidental destacaron la necesidad de establecer formas de regulación frente a la volatilidad del sistema financiero internacional. En efecto, en la Declaración de Santiago señalaron "la volatilidad de los mercados de capitales confirma nuestra decisión de fortalecer la supervisión bancaria en el hemisferio, así como establecer normas en materias de divulgación y revelación de información para bancos".[5]

La intensidad de las transacciones globales, el aumento del comercio internacional y las tendencias simultáneas a la integración y la fragmentación demandan grados mayores de certidumbre. Para ello es necesario generar estabilidad, lo que se logra con capacidades de gobernabilidad. Esto se alcanzará en la medida en que el Estado sea capaz de accionar de manera adecuada en lo nacional y en la concertación internacional para adoptar medidas supranacionales.

Es desde esta perspectiva que se debe entender el significado de los párrafos establecidos en la Declaración de Santiago de la II Cumbre de las Américas, cuando los presidentes señalaron "la globalización ofrece grandes oportunidades para el progreso de nuestros países y abre nuevos campos de cooperación para la comunidad hemisférica. Sin embargo, puede también incidir en un aumento de las diferencias entre los países y al interior de nuestras sociedades. Firmemente decididos a aprovechar sus beneficios y a enfrentar sus retos, otorgaremos especial atención a los países y grupos sociales más vulnerables de nuestro Hemisferio".[6]

Enfrentar los retos con una propuesta de acción tendiente a reafirmar las tendencias integradoras es la propuesta que emerge de la II Cumbre. Ella se expresa en la construcción de un liderazgo hemisférico que se construye en un marco asociativo multilateral. La institucionalización de la diplomacia de cumbres en las Américas, con un seguimiento adecuado por parte de los Ministerios de Relaciones Exteriores y otras entidades nacionales e internacionales, permitirá el cumplimiento de las metas establecidas.

En este trabajo destaco los principales temas del debate del seminario internacional "Globalización, América Latina y la II Cumbre de las Américas", efectuado en Santiago en los días previos al encuentro de los Jefes de Estado y de Gobierno del hemisferio. Este encuentro académico, intelectual y de decisores de política posibilita tener una mirada sobre el impacto de la globalización en América Latina y los esfuerzos por avanzar hacia la construcción de una comunidad hemisférica. De alguna manera el encuentro académico hemisférico contribuyó al objetivo señalado por los Presidentes: "un proceso de integración en su concepto más amplio, permitirá, sobre la base del respeto a las identidades culturales, configurar una trama de valores e intereses comunes, que nos ayude en tales objetivos". Los resultados del seminario y la conformación de una red académica de carácter hemisférico que pueda dar seguimiento a los acuerdos, son una contribución a los objetivos señalados.

Los temas que analizo corresponden a las perspectivas globales debatidas: globalización; ALCA versus MERCOSUR; la construcción de liderazgo; el

# X. GENERAL PROPOSALS

peso de lo subregional; los temas de seguridad internacional; la diplomacia de cumbres; y, la institucionalización.

## GLOBALIZACIÓN

Los cambios globales derivados del fin de la guerra fría, conjuntamente con los procesos de globalización y de cambio tecnológico, han generado una expansión financiera acelerada y una confluencia e incremento del comercio creciente. Los procesos de acercamiento van más allá de lo financiero-comercial y se expresan de manera asociativa en distintas áreas. La inercia, el empuje y el dinamismo de la convergencia económica, de la coincidencia valórica, y los acercamientos comunes en ciertas áreas de la seguridad internacional, le otorgan un fuerte impulso al proceso en su conjunto. Todo ello se traduce en una mayor interdependencia global.

Dada la magnitud de los procesos involucrados, éstos no tienen un solo cauce, ni un solo canal de expresión. Son procesos abiertos, no consolidados. Su orientación es hacia un incremento de la interrelación. El peso de las variables externas es cada vez mayor. Estableciendo condicionalidades globales sobre las decisiones del desarrollo nacional. De allí la importancia de generar orientaciones sobre este conjunto de acelerados cambios.

La importancia de la institucionalización radica precisamente en la capacidad de establecer cauces que permitan orientar positivamente estos cambios sobre la base de la acción concertada en el ámbito multilateral. Lo anterior conlleva la necesidad de efectuar un proceso de monitoreo y evaluación permanente de los cambios y de las consecuencias que en cada una de las áreas está produciendo en los distintos países, subregiones, el hemisferio y en el conjunto del sistema global. Esta evaluación permitirá detectar la intensidad, amplitud y variedad de los efectos en cada uno de los sectores analizados, que poseen efectos significativos para la sociedad y el desarrollo nacional.

La globalización es un proceso segmentado que hoy día afecta esencialmente al ámbito financiero-económico y que se expande a través de la constante revolución tecnológica. De allí que sus efectos posean una alta heterogeneidad. Si bien ningún sector se escapa a los efectos de los procesos globales, no todas las áreas tienen un grado de interrelación nacional-internacional equivalente. La diferenciación sobre la intensidad y amplitud sectorial de la globalización, posibilita mejorar las políticas nacionales, tendientes a optimizar los aspectos positivos y a generar los resguardos sobre los negativos.

La globalización no elimina la necesidad de adoptar decisiones nacionales cruciales. Por el contrario, ellas facilitan o dificultan la incorporación sectorial y nacional en la inserción global. Dado el carácter heterogéneo de los efectos que produce la globalización, se requiere incrementar las capacidades para concertar políticas públicas en el nuevo contexto internacional. Ello significa dimensionar los efectos nacionales, subregionales, hemisféricos e internacionales en cada materia. La necesidad de concordancia y de asociación muchas veces se ve dificultada por los efectos de la propia globalización segmentada. De allí la necesidad de superar la visión estrictamente financiero-comercial para abordar los análisis con perspectivas políticas integradoras del conjunto de variables.

Los desafíos definidos por CEPAL son: la globalización no asegura que los procesos se expresen en un mayor crecimiento y que, por otro lado, la globalización, unida a procesos de expansión, no significa necesariamente un mayor grado de equidad. La resolución de estas carencias reafirma, con mayor fuerza, la necesidad de establecer regulaciones internacionales que puedan expresarse en normas globales de protección social. Se trata de producir las reformas que permitan el crecimiento económico, pero a la vez, evitar un incremento de la pobreza y la inequidad como resultado no deseado del proceso.

Dada la magnitud de los cambios es fundamental encontrar espacios de diálogo para intercambiar puntos de vista y concordar acciones que faciliten un diagnóstico compartido y la asociación en la acción. Convenir medidas que prevengan frente a situaciones que afecten los intereses vitales de los diversos actores involucrados será uno de los objetivos a ser alcanzados en estos espacios de diálogo. Dadas las características de los fenómenos, no se perciben salidas unilaterales. El nivel de consenso alcanzado en el diagnóstico, si bien es importante, debe profundizarse y afinarse aún más. Ello permitirá generar planes de acción más ajustados a cada una de las prioridades. El diálogo y la construcción de una forma de pensar común, permitirá un mayor grado de concertación. Esta es la gran importancia de la II Cumbre de las Américas, su agenda y definiciones sobre el plan de acción.

El grado de institucionalización alcanzado es aún muy débil para la importancia y magnitud de los procesos en curso. Los instrumentos institucionales tradicionales, más allá de sus carencias evidentes, no son ocupados de la manera más adecuada ni más eficiente. Como contrapartida es necesario indicar que tampoco las instancias generadas en torno a las Cumbres Presidenciales, aseguran el grado de institucionalidad requerido. Institucionalizar significa esencialmente generar una visión de futuro, establecer proyectos para alcanzar las metas definidas y asignar los recursos humanos y materiales necesarios para el éxito de los diversos proyectos.

La II Cumbre de las Américas destacó la comunalidad de valores que permite construir una nueva institucionalidad. Es así como los Jefes de Estado señalaron que "el fortalecimiento de la democracia, el diálogo político, la estabilidad económica, el progreso hacia la justicia social, el grado de coincidencia en nuestras políticas de apertura comercial y la voluntad de impulsar un proceso de integración hemisférica permanente, han hecho que nuestras relaciones alcancen mayor madurez". A partir de estas coincidencias reafirmaron la voluntad para desarrollar reformas y otras medidas que permitan alcanzar una "comunidad solidaria". El plan de acción establece metas específicas a ser alcanzadas en torno a cuatro grandes áreas temáticas que requerirán cada una de ellas el desarrollo de regímenes internacionales funcionales, de tratados específicos o de la profundización e implementación de acuerdos ya establecidos. Estas áreas son: educación; democracia, justicia y derechos humanos; integración económica y libre comercio; y erradicación de la pobreza y la discriminación. El principal hecho en la perspectiva institucional es la voluntad política de continuar con el proceso de Cumbres hemisféricas periódicas cuyo fin es profundizar la cooperación y el entendimiento. Así lo señalaron los mandatarios en el primer punto referido al seguimiento.

Por medio de los Ministerios de Relaciones Exteriores, a través del "Grupo de Revisión de la Implementación de Cumbres" (GRIC), se establecerán los canales para supervisar el proceso. Este grupo tendrá un sistema de reuniones periódicas de dos o tres veces al año. Contribuirán al seguimiento las organizaciones de carácter regional, en especial, la Organización de Estados Americanos. Esta organización tendrá un rol central en el seguimiento de las Cumbres.

Por su parte, la OEA, para desarrollar su cometido en esta significativa misión entregada por los mandatarios del hemisferio, requerirá de recursos humanos y materiales para establecer mecanismos efectivos de seguimiento y tomar las oportunidades que se presenten en su marco institucional propio.

## ALCA VERSUS MERCOSUR

Los avances en el proceso de complementación e integración hemisférica fluyen al ritmo de las necesidades y perspectivas subregionales. La agregación de carácter hemisférico presenta complejidades que son propias de la diversidad de entes nacionales, capacidades y recursos de los Estados y de las facilidades de comunicación en las Américas. Desde el punto de vista de la marcha del proceso de complementación hemisférica, que posee un fuerte énfasis en lo comercial, aparecen algunos imponderables que son necesarios considerar; en especial en relación a cierta polarización en torno a los dos diseños más significativos por su peso económico, dimensiones poblacionales involucradas y áreas geográficas vinculadas. Nos referimos a las potencialidades y vulnerabilidades que presenta el accionar del ALCA y el MERCOSUR.[7] La perspectiva brasileña puede ser vista en el capítulo de Helio Jaguaribe, "MERCOSUR y las alternativas al orden mundial", en este libro. En el primer caso, el peso central lo tiene Estados Unidos y en el segundo, los países sudamericanos con énfasis en Brasil.

Una primera tensión aparece en torno a la carencia de una política consistente expresada en instrumentos adecuados por parte de Estados Unidos. El hemisferio cada vez es más interdependiente. La importancia relativa de la región, en términos comerciales, se ha incrementado considerablemente. El Canciller Insulza ha destacado que en el año 1997, Brasil compró más productos estadounidenses que China. Argentina ha comprado más en Estados Unidos de lo que compra Rusia. Chile compra más que la India y los países de América Central superan con creces lo que compra Europa Central.

Así también, el hemisferio concuerda en valores esenciales como son la democracia y el respeto y promoción de los derechos humanos. La mayor relación comercial y coincidencia valórica, deberían llevar a una reevaluación del espacio que ocupa América Latina en el diseño estadounidense. Sin embargo, Estados Unidos sigue teniendo una mirada esencialmente eurocéntrica, lo que unido al bajo peso burocrático que posee América Latina, reafirma un sentido de marginalidad en las principales decisiones estadounidenses en relación a la región. Lo anterior se traduce en una inercia que recurre al unilateralismo como diseño básico de política.

Es necesario generar certidumbre y mayor transparencia en una perspectiva asociativa. Sin ella no será posible profundizar los grados de interrelación y complementación.

Por otro lado, la falta de decisión del MERCOSUR de asumir un rol más proactivo en la actual coyuntura, también constituye una incertidumbre. El MERCOSUR posee un importante espacio de acción en el ámbito subregional sudamericano. Este espacio puede desarrollarse de manera amplia y concertada sin que signifique establecer privilegios o generar contradicciones con un proyecto de desarrollo hemisférico. No obstante lo anterior, tanto en América Latina como en los Estados Unidos, hay actores que ven esta situación como de suma cero entre el MERCOSUR y el ALCA. Colocado en esta perspectiva, el resultado será necesariamente una pérdida para el conjunto. Los proyectos del MERCOSUR y del ALCA poseen importantes áreas de superposición en las cuales confluyen intereses, pero tienen un carácter distinto. El MERCOSUR desde su génesis va más allá de lo comercial; el proyecto del ALCA es esencialmente un acuerdo de libre comercio.

Ambas situaciones generan dificultades para un liderazgo eficaz, capaz de orientar el proceso a través de una visión de futuro y de pasos concretos para alcanzarla. Para la construcción de este liderazgo, una cuestión clave es resolver los temas de la institucionalidad que permiten diseñar un espacio de diálogo para resolver diferencias y una arena para desarrollar acciones cooperativas.

La construcción de una agenda latinoamericana/ hemisférica no encuentra los incentivos suficientes para concertar esfuerzos de manera adecuada. En el posicionamiento de importantes actores lleva a privilegiar el espacio nacional de acción. Un liderazgo eficaz conlleva visiones con una perspectiva más global, el definir de manera clara las metas a ser alcanzadas y los costos que deberán ser superados por los distintos actores para el logro de los objetivos propuestos.

La globalización y los procesos de asociación que se desarrollan en el hemisferio, no pueden ser ubicados sólo en una perspectiva económica. El dinamismo de la integración no depende exclusivamente de los avances en la expansión financiera o de la complementación comercial, aunque ello sea una condición necesaria.

## LIDERAZGO Y CONSTRUCCIÓN DE PROYECTOS

La fuerza de las tendencias hacia la convergencia y la complementación en el hemisferio occidental, deriva de su perspectiva política, del sentido estratégico que posee la asociación en el hemisferio occidental. Para que este sentido se exprese de manera plena, debe manifestarse con una perspectiva de construcción de una comunidad. La construcción y sentido de una comunidad de intereses se manifiesta en una proyección de futuro en la cual se alcanza la satisfacción de los valores compartidos. Los valores esenciales que comparte el hemisferio occidental son el de la democracia y el de la protección de los derechos humanos.

El sentido de la comunidad, no se crea sobre la base de un mayor o menor intercambio; o solamente de un aumento del libre comercio, aunque este elemento sea importante. El sentido de comunidad se desarrolla en la co-responsabilidad de promocionar y defender los valores compartidos. En la construcción de bienes internacionales y en la formalización de mecanismos operativos que posibiliten preservarlos, como resultado de este proceso. Sus definiciones conceptuales y su formalización jurídica permitirán el disfrute general por parte de la comunidad en formación. La construcción de una comunidad requiere de un liderazgo que señale el camino, los objetivos y los cursos de acción para alcanzar las metas comúnmente definidas. Al momento de la II Cumbre de las Américas se pueden constatar una gran cantidad de iniciativas de carácter subregional y hemisféricas que buscan esta gran meta; sin embargo, les falta coherencia. La coherencia será alcanzada cuando se exprese un liderazgo efectivo y un sólido soporte multilateral. Ambos aspectos determinarán la velocidad y rumbo de los procesos de interdependencia.

En este contexto, el liderazgo está directamente vinculado a la capacidad de generar ideas y construir consensos. Las posibilidades de liderazgo en la región, en el momento actual, son más homogéneas y dependen, en lo esencial, de la voluntad política de los hombres que quieran emprender este liderazgo y perspectiva de asociación regional y continental que promuevan.

La globalización, si bien tiende a uniformar el uso de tecnologías, los tipos de consumo, tanto materiales como de ideas, puede llevar a una conclusión errónea; señalar que la globalización es equivalente al monopensamiento. La globalización contribuye a una difusión rápida, amplia y profunda de determinadas perspectivas y valores —en especial, los derechos humanos, la democracia, el libre mercado— pero no cierra el debate. Por el contrario, el análisis efectuado muestra que existen formas muy diversas de inserción internacionales. No hay una forma única de inserción exitosa en el sistema global, tanto económico como político. No hay una forma unívoca para acceder al desarrollo tecnológico. Este es un factor clave. Uno de los ejes centrales del cambio se vincula al acelerado desarrollo de la tecnología, en especial, la de las comunicaciones. El uso de las tecnologías modernas abre mayores posibilidades de equidad. Su efectivización dependerá de un liderazgo capaz de asumir los costos de decisiones cruciales en el ámbito de la educación, la democratización y la búsqueda de erradicación de la pobreza. Los riesgos que un liderazgo moderno debe asumir son muy altos dado el impacto precisamente de las propias tecnologías de comunicación. Sin embargo, el riesgo de decisiones parciales o que miren más el rating, es quedar rezagados en el acceso a las nuevas tecnologías y la modernización.

La globalización no ha cancelado el debate sobre el tipo de comunidad que debemos construir. Tampoco define las claves esenciales para establecer los consensos que den estabilidad y proyección a cada una de las sociedades nacionales en su inserción internacional. Sigue siendo una tarea del liderazgo político definir las formas de concertación regional y hemisférica. Continúa siendo una cuestión política esencial articular los valores que conforman las bases para la cooperación y proyectar los intereses compartidos en una asociación de futuro. De igual forma, es una responsabilidad central del liderazgo establecer mecanismos de resolución de conflictos que viabilizando acuerdos superen las dificultades. El rol político del liderazgo se expresará en la construcción de regímenes internacionales vinculantes.

## EL PESO DE LO SUBREGIONAL

La subregionalización es lo que caracteriza el actual proceso de relacionamiento en el sistema internacional. Son las regiones las que articulan de mejor manera los intereses económicos, políticos, culturales y otros. Las regiones también se expresan con fuerza en el hemisferio occidental.

Dada la diversidad de territorios, poblaciones, recursos, tipos de producción y otros, los agrupamientos se han producido sobre la base de la vecindad y la complementariedad de intereses, afianzada por lazos culturales. Es en los contextos subregionales donde se ha avanzado, de manera acelerada, en procesos de complementación y asociación. Estos se han fundado en el concepto del regionalismo abierto que vincula lo económico con la proximidad geográfica y la cercanía cultural. El regionalismo abierto genera una búsqueda conjunta de oportunidades, una promoción de intereses y la construcción de propuestas que reafirman el multilateralismo. Por ello las subregiones avanzan rápidamente en la complementación en diversas áreas. Ello se evidencia con claridad en el Sistema Económico Centroamericano (SICA), en el Mercado Común del Sur (MERCOSUR), en la Comunidad Andina, en el CARICOM, en el NAFTA y en el ALCA.

Sin embargo, también es posible diseñar metas que focalizadas en lo comercial permitan arreglos más globales. Este es el caso de las negociaciones para el Acuerdo de Libre Comercio de las Américas (ALCA). La liberalización comercial subregional facilita el encontrar arreglos y acuerdos a nivel hemisférico.

El mapa geográfico ha sido cambiado por la globalización y por el desarrollo tecnológico en cuestiones sustantivas. En la actualidad, es factible establecer proximidades y afinidades comerciales, políticas e incluso culturales, entre países o subregiones distantes. Ello potencia el proceso de interdependencia global. La subregionalización o el agrupamiento de comunidades valóricas y de percepciones, pueden no vincularse estrictamente a ámbitos geográficos próximos aunque dicha condición lo favorece significativamente. En este sentido, tenemos una subregionalización compleja, que va más allá de la estricta proximidad geográfica. Este es un factor extraordinariamente positivo de los procesos de asociación global en curso; pero a la vez, genera incentivos para superar las dificultades de operación práctica más aún su superación posibilita grados de acercamiento mayor y más intensidad en la relación.

## DEFENSA Y SEGURIDAD

Los grados de avance no son simétricos ni equivalentes en distintas áreas. En algunas es preciso reconocer las dificultades para alcanzar perspectivas hemisféricas: el caso de la seguridad es el que hace más evidente esta situación. El hemisferio no comparte un concepto común de seguridad. Además, la forma de organización del uso de la fuerza de los Estados es muy diversa, y los riesgos definidos por cada uno de ellos son muy diferentes. La II Cumbre de las Américas al analizar este tema e incluirlo en el plan de acción, lo ubicó dentro de los instrumentos para la preservación y fortalecimiento de la democracia, la justicia y los derechos humanos. Las actividades principales están focalizadas en torno al fomento de la confianza y la seguridad interestatales, para lo cual los Jefes de Estado reafirmaron los compromisos asumidos en esta materia en las reuniones regionales de la OEA sobre medidas de fomento de la confianza y la seguridad, celebradas en Santiago de Chile en 1995 y en El Salvador en 1998.

En el ámbito de la seguridad se expresa con gran fuerza la diversidad de las Américas. Fue así como los

Jefes de Estado diferenciaron los problemas y preocupaciones especiales de los pequeños Estados insulares.

La meta esencial, que se alcanzará a través de los avances que logre la Comisión de Seguridad Hemisférica de la OEA, se expresarán en los resultados de la Conferencia Especial sobre Seguridad, que se efectuará a más tardar a comienzos de la próxima década.

El caso particular del narcotráfico debe ser abordado desde una perspectiva global. Lo anterior no significa narcotizar el conjunto de la relación, lo que constituiría un serio peligro para establecer relaciones maduras entre la potencia hegemónica y el conjunto de los países del hemisferio.

La forma y el grado en que el narcotráfico afecta a todos y a cada uno de nuestros países es diversa. Se requiere de un constante seguimiento y capacidad de observatorio de la situación para definir políticas multilaterales, subregionales, bilaterales y unilaterales en este campo.

La asociación y la vinculación global de políticas es esencial, sin ello no habrá capacidad de éxito. De igual forma, es necesario establecer políticas de carácter recíproco respecto a las responsabilidades que deben ser asumidas. A la vez, se deben buscar formas de compensar los costos que el enfrentamiento de este tema conlleva para los países con menores recursos.

Sobre este tema los Presidentes y Jefes de Gobierno de las Américas adoptaron 17 resoluciones y recomendaciones tendientes a una prevención y control del consumo indebido y del tráfico ilícito de estupefacientes y otros delitos conexos.

## LA DIPLOMACIA DE CUMBRES

La Diplomacia de Cumbres es la forma de expresión actual del multilateralismo al más alto nivel. Las Cumbres Presidenciales deben mantener su sentido político, de diseño de una Gran Estrategia. Sin embargo, su rutinización y su multiplicación en diversas Cumbres (de Naciones Unidas, de las Américas, Iberoamericanas, del Grupo de Río, de cada uno de los grupos regionales) obliga a que las más altas autoridades y los principales líderes del hemisferio, deban atender en muchas oportunidades cuestiones sectoriales. Para el tratamiento de éstas pueden haber otras instancias más adecuadas, por ejemplo, el multilateralismo tradicional de carácter técnico posee una importante experiencia en este campo.

La Diplomacia de Cumbres cumple un importante papel. En lo fundamental expresa la posibilidad de un alto grado de efectividad en la generación de acuerdos, normas, regulaciones en áreas fundamentales para el desarrollo nacional e internacional. A la vez, posibilitan colocar el conjunto de la energía burocrática detrás de la voluntad política expresada en la cúspide del proceso decisorio, los Jefes de Estado y los Jefes de Gobierno. El éxito de esta forma diplomática depende de la capacidad de implementación y permanencia que le otorguen las burocracias permanentes de cada país y el sistema de organismos multilaterales.

La rutinización puede hacer perder el foco del sentido político y estratégico que debe asumir el diálogo presidencial: definir las bases y la gran estrategia para construir una comunidad sustentada en la democracia con sentido de equidad.

La orientación, por lo tanto, debe estar puesta en la institucionalización. Allí se expresará la voluntad política de los Estados para construir un futuro distinto. La voluntad política es la que posibilita articular soluciones cooperativas multilaterales. La sola voluntad política no es suficiente, es necesario que ella se manifieste institucionalmente para generar capacidades de operacionalizar los acuerdos. Sin institucionalización no habrá un proceso sostenido que permita satisfacer los intereses compartidos.

## LA INSTITUCIONALIZACIÓN

El énfasis fundamental y la perspectiva de futuro está dado por la institucionalización y la capacidad de construcción social y política en este campo. El 50 aniversario de la OEA es una buena oportunidad para reflexionar y reafirmar las necesidades de institucionalización hemisférica.

El sistema internacional alcanzará estabilidad en la nueva etapa de posguerra fría sobre la base de su construcción institucional y el desarrollo de formas de gestión internacionales que sean capaces de resolver los grandes problemas de la humanidad, aunque éstos necesariamente se expresan localmente. La globalización posee un carácter fragmentado y se concentra en los aspectos financieros y comerciales. Del proceso de globalización no se desprende la necesidad de construir un "gobierno mundial". Sin embargo, los procesos de globalización, unidos al desarrollo instantáneo de las comunicaciones, evidencia necesidades de gobernabilidad que superan las fronteras de los Estados nacionales. La necesidad de normas y regulaciones en los distintos campos de acción contribuye a la estabilidad global. Un aporte sustantivo de la diplomacia de cumbres es el alto grado de atención que las más altas autoridades nacionales demandan sobre áreas cruciales, generándose oportunidades de regulación que poseen importantes grados de consenso y evidencian una fuerte voluntad política de implementación. Por ello la cooperación política y diplomática constituyen la esencia de esta diplomacia de alto nivel.[8]

La creación de marcos regulatorios y de regímenes con capacidades de resolución de conflictos establecen áreas de concertación que potencian un trabajo de largo plazo en el cual la institucionalización juega un rol esencial, posibilitando pasar de eventos de alto contenido coyuntural a acuerdos de largo plazo que otorgan certidumbre a las relaciones de cooperación.

El establecimiento de metas, de los proyectos y planes de acción correspondiente, deben basarse en capacidades efectivas de cumplimiento. La dilación en la ejecución de los compromisos, el no cumplimiento de las metas trazadas, el regateo de la voluntad de ejecución, tienen un efecto negativo muy superior al grado de avance en la propia meta. El no cumplimiento erosiona algo más sustancial: erosiona la confianza. Lo anterior tiende a agotar el proceso muy rápidamente.

La II Cumbre de las Américas constituyó una instancia crucial para orientar los distintos procesos hemisféricos. Para reafirmar las tendencias a la integración y la cooperación, a la vez que se generan mecanismos de alerta temprana para analizar las situaciones de riesgo.

La institucionalización que surja de la ejecución de los compromisos de la II Cumbre de las Américas será definitoria en el tipo de multilateralismo y en tipo de cooperación que establezcan las Américas al iniciarse el siglo XXI.

# Notas

1. Alain Touraine, "El capitalismo de fin de siglo: dónde está el piloto". En *Clarín*, Buenos Aires, 6 de septiembre, 1998.

2. Richard N. Haas y Robert E. Litan, "Globalization and Its Discontents. Navigating the Dangers of a Tangled World". En *Foreign Affairs*, mayo - junio, nueva york, 1998.

3. Saskia Sassen, *Losing Control? Sovereignty in an Age of Globalization*. Columbia University Press, nueva york, 1995.

4. Kenichi Ohmae, *El fin del estado-nación*. Editorial Andrés Bello, Santiago de Chile, 1997.

5. Declaración de Santiago. Declaración de principios de la II Cumbre de las Américas. Santiago de Chile, 19 de abril de 1998.

6. Op. cit.

7. Bernard K. Gordon, "The Natural Market Fallacy. Slim Pickings in Latin America". En *Foreign Affairs*, mayo - junio, nueva york, 1998.

8. Ulrich Beck, *¿Qué es la globalización? Falacias del globalismo, respuestas a la globalización*. Editorial Paidós, Buenos Aires, 1998. El autor señala la importancia de abrir un debate sobre la configuración política de la globalización. Propone como la principal respuesta incrementar la cooperación internacional.

# X. GENERAL PROPOSALS

*This Declaration was prepared by the following organizations: Common Frontiers-Canadá; Alliance for Responsible Trade (ART)-Estados Unidos; Red Mexicana de Acción frente al Libre Comercio (RMALC); Red Quebecois sobre la Integración Continental (RQIC); AFL-CIO; CIOSL-ORIT; CUT-Brazil; Canadian Labor Congress; Iniciativa Civil por la Integración Centroamericana (ICIC); Associación Brasileña de ONGs (ABONG); Red Chile de Acción por una Iniciativa de los Pueblos (RECHIP); Movimiento Unitario Campesino y de las Etnias de Chile (MUCECH); y Colegio de Profesores de Chile AG.*

## Final Declaration of the Summit:
### Peoples' Summit of the Americas

### APRIL 18-19, 1998

In the Peoples' Summit of the Americas— a gathering of union, social, environmental, women's, native, human rights, educational, and parliamentary organizations— we have taken a united stand in favour of economic, social, and cultural integration, but one that truly benefits the people of the Americas, not the one set up within a trade framework, directed by corporations and applied by governments. The priorities of our integration proposals are participatory democracy, sustainable development, and cultural and ethnic diversity.

We have no reason to believe in the fulfilment of the social commitments signed by governments. Most of the recommendations from the Round of Social Conferences of the United Nations still have not been implemented. The social concerns proclaimed at the First Summit of the Americas in Miami have not been acted upon either. We believe that governments will go on using these proclaimed social concerns as bargaining chips in their trade negotiations. In practice, these declarations contradict their own policies which result in the deterioration of public services. In most of the continent's countries, programs to privatize education and social security continue.

We are convinced that the Americas does not need free trade. It needs fair trade, regulated investment, and a conscious consumer strategy which privileges national development projects.

We call governments' attention to the priorities which our people have set and which have not been taken into consideration in their official conferences. We place emphasis on the following priorities which were debated at the Peoples' Summit:

- Human, social, labour, environmental, and citizens' rights
- Aboriginal peoples
- Sustainable development
- Alternatives to socioeconomic integration
- Farm workers and agrarian reform
- Ethics in the political process.

All of these topics were amply discussed and debated by representatives and members of the organizations which are most representative of civil society in the countries of our hemisphere who met in 10 different forums from April 15 to 18 in the city of Santiago. Our debates reflected the richness, diversity and plurality of our peoples, as well as our ability to formulate proposals. Under the criteria of inter-sectoral discussions, the forums analyzed the following issues:

- Globalization and integration
- Development and sustainability
- Investment
- Employment and quality of life
- Follow-through of the Summit.

We made a commitment to work for the demands which came out of the forums and to pressure government authorities of our respective countries on our conclusions and on the plan of action which we have adopted.

We reject the anti-democratic character of agreements such as the FTAA. Organizations which represent distinct segments of civil society in our continents are excluded from the process. Not even legislators are consulted, thus restricting even more the limits of democratic representation. We do not accept that any more of these kinds of agreements, which have negative repercussions for the population as a whole, be signed at the cost of our peoples.

We demand that the fundamental negation of our economic sovereignty implied by carrying out accords such as the Free Trade Area of the Americas or the Multilateral Agreement on Investment be directly and ultimately decided upon by the citizens of the Americas, by plebiscite, preceded by fully informed national debates.

Our Summit's goal is to call attention to the inequalities which the official meetings insist upon ignoring.

- Increased unemployment, informal work situations, precarious labour relations, intensification of work rhythms, and salary reductions.

- Increased female and child poverty, along with forms of overexploitation such as forced labour, child labour, and discrimination against women.

- Continuous degradation of our peoples' environment and quality of life.

- Increased migration, xenophobia, and the lack of recognition of the rights of migrant workers.

- Permanent and increased violations of the rights of our indigenous peoples to their life, land, and cultural values.

- Concentration of rural property, growing conflicts over land ownership, murder of farm worker activists, and impunity for their murderers.

- Urban violence, insecurity, and social exclusion.

The Peoples' Summit of the Americas was a milestone in the process of hemispheric articulation of a united strategy which we have called the Hemispheric Social Alliance to fight against neoliberal trade integration.

Free trade rhetoric is inconsistent with the trade blockade of Cuba.

The Peoples' Summit of the Americas reaffirms that continental integration processes must be built upon the principles of participatory democracy, equality, social justice, respect for cultural and ethnic diversity, social development, and ecological sustainability.

# X. GENERAL PROPOSALS

*This document is Discussion Draft #2 prepared in November 1998 by the following organizations: Alliance for Responsible Trade (United States); Common Frontiers (Canada); Red Chile por una Iniciativa de los Pueblos (Chile); Red Mexicana de Acción Frente al Libre Comercio (Mexico); and Réseau Québécois sur l'Intégration Continentale (Quebec).*

# Alternatives for the Americas:
## Building a Peoples' Hemispheric Agreement

### ACKNOWLEDGMENTS

This document draws upon the contributions of individuals too numerous to name. Over the course of many years, hundreds of people have participated in discussions, helped draft documents, or conducted educational or organizing activities around an alternative vision for our hemisphere. To a large extent, this paper is a culmination of all of these efforts.

Individuals primarily responsible for writing, editing, and coordinating the development of this document include:

Sarah Anderson (Institute for Policy Studies, USA)

Alberto Arroyo (RMALC, Mexico)

Peter Bakvis (CSN, Quebec)

Patty Barrera (Common Frontiers, Canada)

John Dillon (Ecumenical Coalition for Economic Justice/Common Frontiers, Canada)

Karen Hansen Kuhn (Development GAP, USA)

David Ranney (University of Illinois/Chicago, USA)

The following individuals also made significant contributions to the writing and editing:

Quebec: Marcela Escribano (Alternatives/ RQIC), Dorval Brunelle (Groupe de Recherche sur l'Integration Continentale-UQAM), Luc Brunet (CEQ), Robert Demers (FTQ), France Laurendeau (FTQ), HÈlËne Lebrun (CEQ).

United States: John Cavanagh (Institute for Policy Studies), Terry Collingsworth (International Labor Rights Fund), Rob Scott (Economic Policy Institute), Lance Compa (Cornell University).

Mexico: Andres Penaloza (RMALC), Teresa Gutierrez, Luz Paula Parra R and the Comision Mexicana de Defensa y Promocion de los Derechos Humanos (CMDPDHAC), Hilda Salazar (Desarrollo, Ambiente y Sociedad/ RMALC), Alejandro Villamar (RMALC), Bertha Lujan (FAT/RMALC), Juan Manuel Sandoval and the Seminario Permanente de Estudios Chicanos, Matilde Arteaga Zaragoza (FAT/ RMALC) and all those who made proposals to the Women's Forum at the Santiago Summit.

Canada: Sheila Katz (Canadian Labour Congress), Ken Traynor (Canadian Environmental Law Association), John Foster (University of Saskatchewan/ Common Frontiers), Tony Clarke (Polaris Institute), Bruce Campbell (Canadian Centre for Policy Alternatives), Carlos Torres, Daina Z. Green, the Ecumenical Coalition for Economic Justice and the Common Frontiers Steering Committee.

Central America: Raul Moreno and Alberto Enriquez (Funde de San Salvador).

We would also like to thank: Renato Martins (CUT Brasil), Coral Pey and RECHIP (red Chile por una Inciative de los Pueblos), CETES (Centro de estudios sobre Transnacionalizacion, Economia y Sociedad, Chile). And our translators: Daina Z. Green (English and Spanish), Philippe Duhamel (French), and Vincente Di Melo (Portuguese).

## SUBMITTING COMMENTS

This is a living document that will be updated and re-distributed in the years ahead.

Please submit comments to the following:

email: ecoalt@web.net

postal: Common Frontiers, 15 Gervais Drive, Suite 305 Don Mills, Ontario, M3C-148, CANADA

fax: 416/441-4073 (attention: Patty)

## PREFACE

On April 15-18, 1998, about 1,000 men and women from nearly every nation of the hemisphere gathered for a Peoples Summit of the Americas in Santiago, Chile. We gathered to express our collective rejection of the dominant "neoliberal" agenda that promotes trade and investment liberalization, deregulation, privatization, and market-driven economics as the formula for development. The Peoples Summit focused on building a hemispheric social alliance around concrete, viable alternatives. Meanwhile, the Presidents and Prime Ministers of our nations were also meeting in Santiago, attempting to negotiate a Free Trade Area of the Americas (FTAA). It is expected that the FTAA will follow the pattern of existing agreements like NAFTA and expand neoliberalism throughout the hemisphere. This document expresses our determination to construct an alternative to the FTAA based on the proposals described herein.

Driving this effort on alternatives is the sense that the neoliberal economic model has been a disaster for most of the peoples of the hemisphere.

Peasants whose labor once fed their nations and themselves are forced to export risky "cash crops" to bring in foreign currency and to provide the well-to-do in the North with meat and fresh produce throughout the year. This has resulted in hunger for many and reduced food quality for others, and has driven hundreds of thousands of small farmers from their lands.

This growing export dependency has added to the plight of landless peasants, particularly in countries where the ownership of the bulk of agricultural land is concentrated in a small number of hands. In Brazil, for example, despite decades-long promises of land reform, one percent of land owners control 44 percent of the lands. Over the past decade private militias and police have killed several hundred landless peasants participating in peaceful occupations of idle or underused lands belonging to wealthy landowners.

With the decline of subsistence agriculture, young women and indigenous peoples have often been forced into our hemisphere's export processing zones, particularly in Mexico and Central America. Paid less than a living wage, they are forced to live in squalor and often subjected to sexual harassment. Long working hours strain their family ties and limit their educational opportunities.

Peasants forced to abandon their lands sometimes come to the cities of our hemisphere to seek work. But what many find is unemployment and poverty and a life in the "informal economy," as much domestic manufacturing has been eliminated by the penetration of transnational corporations and rules which prohibit efforts to strengthen the domestic economy.

Other displaced peasants come north and are met by the militarization of the U.S. border with Mexico, new laws that violate their civil rights, and racist hysteria promoted by right-wing politicians and their constituencies.

Neoliberal rules to deregulate capital markets, combined with new telecommunications technologies, have opened our nations to the vagaries of hot money. Speculators pull their money in and out of our nations at will, leaving misery in their wake as usurious interest rates and currency devaluations slash the buying power of our wages and drastically reduce opportunities for livable wage work.

U.S. and Canadian workers have felt the pain of the elimination of hundreds of thousands of living wage manufacturing jobs. Many have been unable to find comparable work and their sons and daughters are facing the prospect of either no work at all or jobs that are temporary or part time with pay below what it takes to live a decent life in these countries.

In the U.S. and Canada, the governments are destroying publicly subsidized housing and housing programs as the ranks of the homeless soar. This has had a disproportionate effect on women, especially poor women.

# X. GENERAL PROPOSALS

Public funds for basic subsistence living — food, clothing and medical care — programs won by workers' struggles of the past, are being eliminated, and people are told to find non-existent jobs. Meanwhile in both the U.S. and Canada, the call to balance budgets is further straining workers and the poor as programs in health care, education and public transportation are privatized, eliminated or seriously cut back.

Throughout the hemisphere, there is a stratum of society that is doing very well by neoliberal policies. The speculators, the transnational corporations and those in their service proclaim the wonders of the market. But for most of us, the past 25 years have meant declining living standards and in many cases abject poverty.

The birth of neoliberalism in our hemisphere came out of the bloody, U.S.-backed coup in Chile that put General Augusto Pinochet in power. In the wake of that coup, Pinochet invited U.S. economists from the University of Chicago to impose rules on Chilean development that were in line with the interests of those who financed the coup. Pinochet used state-sanctioned terror to make those rules stick. A quarter of a century later, U.S. President Clinton came to Santiago for the launching of FTAA negotiations and proclaimed Chile to be "the model for the hemisphere." His praise reveals the intent of the most powerful government of the Americas to use the FTAA to promote the most extreme form of neoliberalism. By contrast, Luis Anderson, President of the Interamerican Regional Workers' Organization (ORIT), stated at the Peoples Summit the very next day, "when young children must come and beg for food we must be clear that Chile is no model."

Neoliberalism entails the imposition of a set of rules that govern not only the economy but also the social fabric of our societies. The issue for us, therefore, is not one of free trade vs. protection or integration vs. isolation, but whose rules will prevail and who will benefit from those rules.

The Peoples' Summit in Santiago brought to the light of day the fact that there is a rising movement of resistance. This movement is one of the peoples of the Americas telling those political leaders, financial speculators and the transnational corporations who promote neoliberalism that their agenda is unacceptable. It is a movement of the peoples of the Americas demanding their very humanity. They do so by stating that nutritious food, a comfortable place to live, a clean and healthy environment, health care and education are human rights. And they declare that respect for the rights of workers, women, indigenous peoples, black peoples, and Latinos living in the U.S. and Canada must be central to any process of integration.

Supporters of neoliberalism are attempting to counter the resistance of the peoples of the Americas in a number of ways. In the United States, corporate giants have launched a massive propaganda campaign to "educate" the public on the benefits of free trade. In many countries, an extreme response has been to utilize the nation state as an instrument of terror against its own peoples —a return to neoliberalism's birth in Pinochet's bloody dictatorship. Under the guise of a "war against drugs," counter-insurgency efforts, often fueled by U.S. funds, training and military hardware, have become a plague in our hemisphere. Furthermore, the suppression of the popular movements throughout Mexico, Central and South America attempts to limit the demands of the peoples of our nations. At times, this suppression has taken the form of brutal terrorism, such as the Acteal massacre in Mexico, the assassination of thousands of Colombian union and popular-sector leaders over the past several years, and the savage assassination of Bishop Gerardi of Guatemala. Although our leaders publicly condemn this violence, we wonder if they might be secretly breathing a sign of relief because these abominable acts serve to silence those who have and will continue to challenge neoliberalism's onslaught.

While transnational corporations, speculators and their government sponsors will continue to act in their self-interests, we now are beginning to unite across borders and across sectors in order to oppose these self-interests with those of the vast majority of the residents of our hemisphere. While the building of such a social alliance is in its early stages, this urgent task has begun.

History teaches many things. One lesson can be found in the words of the great African-American emancipator, Frederick Douglass,

"If there is no struggle there is no progress... Power concedes nothing without a demand; it never has and it never will...Find out just what any people will quietly submit to and you have found the exact measure of injustice and wrong... The limits of tyrants are prescribed by the endurance of those whom they oppress."

Another lesson of history is that no amount of oppression can stop people from declaring their own humanity and acting on that declaration.

The Summit of the Peoples of the Americas did not stop with the negation of the neoliberal rules; it began a dialogue about alternatives. This document, a product of the dialogue, is thus rooted in the aspirations of the peoples of our hemisphere to live and develop as full human beings. These aspirations to build a more egalitarian and respectful society throughout the hemisphere transcend national boundaries and have a long historical tradition in the Americas. They go back at least as far as the struggles to create free and independent countries in the American hemisphere. Almost two centuries ago Simón Bolivar, who led the movement to liberate a large part of South America from colonialism, declared:

> "Yo deseo mas que otro alguno ver formar en América la mas grande nación del mundo, menos por su extensión y riquezas que por su libertad y gloria."

> ("I wish, more than anything else, to witness the creation in America of the greatest nation in the world, not so much because of its immense territory or wealth, but rather because of its freedom and glory.")

Alternatives for the Americas is not solely an economic doctrine, but is rather an approach to social integration through which the ideas, talents and wealth of all of our peoples can be shared to our mutual benefit. It is a living document that will be altered and expanded as we exercise our rights to continue the debate and discussion.

## INTRODUCTION AND SUMMARY

This document reflects an ongoing, collaborative process to establish concrete and viable alternatives, based on the interests of the peoples of our hemisphere, to the Free Trade Area of the Americas (FTAA). It is the second draft of a document initially prepared for the April 1998 Peoples Summit of the Americas—a historic gathering of activists determined to change the prevailing approach to trade and investment policy in the Western Hemisphere.

This is a working document, designed to stimulate further debate and education on an alternative vision. The paper focuses on positive proposals, while dealing only implicitly with the impact of "neoliberalism" and free trade agreements on our countries. At this stage of the struggle, it is not enough to oppose, to resist and to criticize. We must build a proposal of our own and fight for it.

The document addresses the major topics on the official agenda of the FTAA negotiators (investment, finance, intellectual property rights, agriculture, market access and dispute resolution), as well as topics that are of extreme social importance but which governments have ignored (human rights, environment, labor, immigration, the role of the state, and energy). Issues concerning two other important groups—women and indigenous peoples—have been incorporated throughout the document. The paper begins with a chapter on the general principles underlying an alternative vision, followed by chapters that lay out more concrete proposals. The topics and chapters are complementary. Therefore, the paper is to be viewed and discussed as a whole.

## SUMMARY

General Principles: Trade and investment should not be ends in themselves, but rather the instruments for achieving just and sustainable development. Citizens must have the right to participate in the formulation, implementation, and evaluation of hemispheric social and economic policies. Central goals of these policies should be to promote economic sovereignty, social welfare, and reduced inequality at all levels.

Human Rights: Countries of the Americas should build a common human rights agenda to be included in every hemispheric agreement, along with mechanisms and institutions to ensure full implementation and enforcement. This agenda should promote the broadest definition of human rights, covering civil, political, economic, social, cultural, and environmental rights, gender equity, and rights relating to indigenous peoples and communities.

Environment: Hemispheric agreements should allow governments to channel investment towards environmentally sustainable economic activities, while establishing plans for the gradual "internalization" (taking into account) of the social and environmental costs of unsustainable production and consumption.

Labor: Hemispheric agreements should include provisions that guarantee the basic rights of working men and women, ensure proper assistance for adjustment as markets are opened up, and promote the improvement of working and living standards of workers and their families.

Immigration: Economic and financial agreements should include agreements regarding migrant workers. These agreements should recognize the diversity in immigration-related situations in different countries by allowing for variation in immigration policies but also facilitating funding for programs designed to improve employment opportunities in areas that are major net exporters of labor. At the same time, governments should ensure uniform application of their national labor rights for all workers—regardless of immigration status— and severely penalize employers that violate these rights.

Role of the State: Hemispheric agreements should not undermine the ability of the nation state to meet its citizens' social and economic needs. At the same time, the goal of national economic regulations should not be traditional protectionism, but ensuring that private sector economic activities promote fair and sustainable development. Likewise, agreements should allow nation states to maintain public sector corporations and procurement policies that support national development goals while fighting government corruption.

Investment: Hemispheric rules should encourage foreign investment that generates high-quality jobs, sustainable production, and economic stability, while allowing governments to screen out investments that make no net contribution to development, especially speculative capital flows. Citizens groups and all levels of government should have the right to sue investors that violate investment rules.

Finance: To promote economic stability, agreements should establish a tax on foreign exchange transactions that would also generate development funds, while allowing governments to institute taxes on speculative profits, require that portfolio investments remain in the country for a specified period, and provide incentives for direct and productive investments. To help level the playing field, low-income nations should be allowed to renegotiate foreign debts to reduce principal owed, lower interest rates, and lengthen repayment terms.

Intellectual Property: Agreements should protect the rights and livelihoods of farmers, fishing folk, and communities that act as guardians of biodiversity and not allow corporate interests to undermine these rights. Rules should exclude all life forms from patentability and protect the collective intellectual property of local communities and peoples, especially with regard to medicinal plants. Rules should also ensure that copyright laws protect artists, musicians and other cultural workers, and not just the publishing and entertainment industries.

Sustainable Energy Development: A hemispheric agreement should allow members to file complaints against countries that try to achieve commercial advantage at the expense of sustainability. International agencies should cooperate to create regulatory incentives for energy efficiency and renewable energy and promote related technologies, while eliminating policies that subsidize or encourage fossil fuel sales, consumption and use.

Agriculture: To ensure food security, countries should have the right to protect or exclude staple foods from trade agreements. Hemispheric measures should also support upward harmonization of financial assistance for agriculture (as a percentage of GDP), strengthened protections for agricultural laborers, and traditional rights of indigenous peoples to live off ancestral lands.

Market Access: Access for foreign products and investments should be evaluated and defined within the framework of national development plans. Timetables for tariff reduction should be accompanied by programs to ensure that domestic industries become competitive during the transition. With regard to nontariff barriers, measures are necessary to ensure that they reflect legitimate social interests rather than protections for specific companies.

Enforcement and Dispute Resolution: If the proposed rules and standards are to be meaningful, they must be accompanied by strong mechanisms for dispute resolution and enforcement that are focused on reducing inequalities and based on fair and democratic processes. Agreements may also include special safeguards for countries suffering as the result of surges in imports.

## I. GENERAL PRINCIPLES

### Background

No country can nor should remain isolated from the global economy. This does not mean, however, that the current "neoliberal" or free market approach to globalization is the only, much less the best, form of economic integration.

This dominant free market approach (embodied in the North American Free Trade Agreement, large multinational corporations' negotiating agenda for the Free Trade Area of the Americas, and the temporarily stalled Multilateral Agreement on Investment) argues that the global market on its own will allocate and develop the best possibilities for each country. Thus, free trade does not simply involve opening ourselves to global trade; it also entails renouncing our role as active subjects in determining our future, and instead allowing the market to decide the future for us. According to this view, it is unnecessary for us to envision the kind of society we want to be or could be. We only need to eliminate all obstacles to global trade, and the market itself will take on the task of offering us the best of all possible worlds.

The difference between this dominant approach and the alternative vision presented in this document lies not in whether we accept the opening of our economies to trade. The two fundamental differences are the following: 1) whether to have a national plan we can fight for or let the market determine the plan, and 2) whether capital, especially speculative capital, should be subject to international regulation. The recent trend has been to allow all capital, even speculative capital, free rein, and let the world follow capital's interests. We argue that history has demonstrated that the market on its own does not generate development, let alone social justice. In contrast, we propose a world economy regulated at the national and supra-national levels in the interest of peace, democracy, sustainable development and economic stability.

Our position in this regard is very clear: we cannot remain on the sidelines but must claim our role as valid stakeholders in the globalization dialogue. We must refuse to accept the current neoliberal form of globalization as irreversible. We must not only reduce its negative consequences, but put forward a positive alternative.

We must find ways to take creative advantage of globalization and not passively submit to it. As citizens of the Americas, we refuse to be ruled by the law of supply and demand and claim our role as individuals rather than simple commodities governed by the laws of the market.

Free trade has produced social and economic exclusion. This has resulted in the creation of a social stratum of citizens devalued by the current economic system and the societies that support it. Exclusion renders people unable to enter or re-enter the economic circuit, leading to a process of social "disqualification" and the loss of active citizenship. Anyone who has felt the negative effects of the transition to free trade, has become chronically unemployed, or whose job is precarious, lives and knows this exclusion.

We are not opposed to the establishment of rules for regional or international trade and investment. Nor does our criticism of the dominant, externally imposed form of globalization imply a wish to return to the past, to close our economies and establish protectionist barriers, or to press for isolationist trade policies. But the current rules have not helped our countries overcome, nor even reduce, our economic problems. We propose alternative rules to regulate the global and hemispheric economies based on a different economic logic: that trade and investment should not be ends in themselves, but rather the instruments for achieving just and sustainable development. Our proposal also promotes a social logic that includes areas such as labor, human rights, gender equity, the environment, and minorities—that is, previously excluded issues and people.

While our critique and proposal have a technical basis, they also spring from an ethical imperative. We refuse to accept the market as a god which controls our lives. We do not accept the inevitability of a model of globalization which excludes half or more of the world's population from the benefits of development. We do not accept that environmental degradation is the inevitable and necessary evil accompanying growth.

A profound ethical imperative pushes us to propose our own model of society, one supported by the many men and women united in hope for a more just and humane society for themselves and future generations.

## GUIDING PRINCIPLES:

### 1. Democracy and participation

Debates, decision making, and framework building in matters of economic integration have mostly been dominated by financial, corporate, and political elites. Greater democratization in trade and investment decision making must be introduced. International agreements should be ratified by citizens through direct consultation, for example, through plebiscite or national referendum.

The democratization of debates and decision making is a necessary precondition, but not sufficient in itself for the development of new just and sustainable rules on investment, environment, and labor. Citizens must not only approve economic and social policies, but also participate in their formulation, implementation, and evaluation. Furthermore, they must be able to change or modify these policy directions. In order to realize this goal, it may be necessary to implement special initiatives to guarantee access to debate for marginalized or oppressed social groups, including women.

Global corporations have grown so large that they can no longer be effectively controlled by our governments. We need new instruments to reassert public control and citizen sovereignty over these firms.

The political stability needed for sustainable development requires agreements on economic integration to include mechanisms to ensure democratic security. Stability should be based on democratic participation and not on coercion. Any agreement should promote democracy in the Americas, without being interventionist in internal affairs. Democratic and non-coercive security entails

# X. GENERAL PROPOSALS

civilian monitoring (accountable to citizens) of the forces of law and order. Civilian control is required, for example, to halt the arms race and the militarization of broad areas of the Americas which is currently being conducted under the pretext of fighting arms and drug trafficking and drug production.

International democratization requires the reform of United Nations institutions, including the Security Council, as well as international financial and trade institutions. The reforms must be based on consultation in every country and should be oriented to serving humankind's objectives: sustainable development and democracy and peace based on justice and respect for human dignity. Such institutions should not continue to be the tools of large multinational corporations and nuclear powers. The democratization of the world and inter-American system must also stop the exclusion of countries for ideological or political reasons, as is currently the case with Cuba.

All integration agreements must ensure that the defence and promotion of human rights, taken in the broadest sense, is also globalized. That is, not only civil and political rights and individual protections should be included, but also the collective rights of peoples and their communities: economic, social, cultural, and environmental. Special attention should be given to the rights of indigenous communities and peoples, and mechanisms put in place to eliminate all forms of discrimination and the oppression of women.

## 2. Sovereignty and social welfare

The rules flowing from agreements should preserve the power of individual countries to set high standards of living, valuing dignified work, the creation of enough good jobs, healthy communities, and a clean environment within their borders. There should be no limitations on the sovereignty of peoples, expressed at the state, provincial or local levels.

In today's world, economic sovereignty, stability and social welfare require making productive economic activities a priority, while discouraging speculative investment and regulating the free flow of footloose capital. Corporate interests should not undermine the economic sovereignty of our countries.

Economic integration should represent a commitment to improve the quality of life for all. Our countries should not be promoted on the basis of low wages, systematic discrimination against women or other groups, lack of social protections or lax enforcement. National competitiveness cannot be rooted in the deterioration of standard of living and/or the environment. Equalization of standards should be achieved through upward harmonization. Trade and integration accords, as well as domestic economic policies, should include social objectives, time tables, indicators of social impact and corrective remedies.

National governments must protect local efforts aimed at achieving viable, economically sustainable and food self-sufficient communities, both urban and rural.

Giving priority to welfare in international agreements means reducing military budgets and allocating resources to people's education and health. Money saved through military reductions in powerful nations should be channeled toward an international war on poverty.

Combating drug production, trafficking and consumption should be an element of integration accords. Rather than taking a purely military approach, however, this should be achieved through mass educational campaigns, the elimination of the poverty driving this lucrative business, fighting against corruption and the involvement in the drug trade of high-level authorities, and other measures aimed at the root causes of the problem. International agreements must preserve the sovereignty of nation states over domestic matters and in the application of their own laws. They should not allow for the presence of armed troops or foreign police forces within the borders of a sovereign nation.

## 3. Reduce inequalities

A main objective of any agreement should be the reduction of inequalities within and among nations, between women and men, and among races.

A) Among nations: The rush toward the integration of highly unequal economies without social protections is creating a climate in which large corporations can reduce the standard of living and wages in all regions of the world. The new rules should include mechanisms to reduce imbalance among nations through raising living standards in the poorest countries. This would not only be a step toward meeting the demands for justice and equity in these countries. It would also reduce the power of corporations to take advantage of such inequalities to weaken standards and wages everywhere by threatening to move production to areas where labor costs and environmental protections are lower.

B) Within nations: Inequalities and extreme poverty have been on the increase for more than a decade in the Americas. The new rules should reduce these inequalities, encouraging redistribution of income, land and natural resources.

C) Between women and men and among races: Women, people of color, and indigenous people have had to shoulder a disproportionate share of the economic and social decline caused by neoliberal policy. The cuts to public sector services and employment and the reduction of secure employment and democratic structures have personally affected more women then men and have hit girls harder than boys. When resources are scarce, decisions made by many families and societies, consciously or unconsciously, favor males. On top of this, as society's traditional care-givers, women end up with the responsibility to help others whose access to jobs or publicly funded programs have been cut. This burden comes in addition to existing disparities in the economic, legal, social, and political position of women in countries throughout the hemisphere. Discrimination must be ended by implementing new strategies and economic models to reverse the effects of current policies. Countries should also meet existing international obligations to achieve equity and implement social programs and intensify international cooperation toward this end.

## 4. Sustainability

Along with the war on poverty, sustainability and protection of the environment are the fundamental challenges for any economic strategy or integration agreement. Trade agreements should give priority to the quality of development, which implies establishing social and environmental limits to growth. Sustainability and the welfare of the population should take precedence over short-term profits.

The new rules on integration should allow for more democratic control of land and natural resources and genuine respect for indigenous rights and land. Rich countries and major corporations have accumulated an ecological debt and occupy an ecological footprint far greater than their population and territory warrants. (The term "ecological footprint" refers to the amount of land required to support present consumption levels of materials and energy.) New agreements should allocate the costs of transition towards a sustainable model based on principles which recognize common concerns and different responsibilities. A truly sustainable alternative agreement would also include a comprehensive restructuring of incentives and rules designed to ensure that industrial production reflects its true, long-term costs.

Finally, efforts to promote sustainability should go beyond the natural world to include social sustainability, including the protection of the welfare of girls and boys, as well as family groups, and minority rights. This requires the creation of effective sanctions against policies which attract investment through promises of low wages, super-exploitation of workers, especially women, or a free hand in exploiting natural resources in areas where the population is under the control of local elites.

## II. HUMAN RIGHTS

### Background

Over the past three generations, international conventions and declarations have established an increasingly detailed definition of human rights. In the first generation, civil and political rights were recognized; in the second, economic, social and cultural rights; and in the third generation, environmental rights, and the rights of peoples and communities.

Meanwhile, global as well as hemispheric economic integration have proceeded at a quick pace with no consideration for human rights, especially those associated with economic, social, and environmental rights and those of indigenous peoples and communities. In fact, the recent wave of free trade and trade-related agreements, both in the North and in the South, have shown that economic integration has detrimental effects on many sectors of society, jeopardizing human rights as a whole.

The "neoliberal" approach to free trade and hemispheric economic integration sanctions corporate rights old and new. There are oblique references to workers' rights but almost no mention of the social rights of any other sector of the population. Worse, there is no connection established between these types of rights. In the past, the issue of human rights including gender equity, was incorporated into many regional and international accords. Now these rights are subjected to a barrage of criticism aimed at showing that they are nothing more than an impediment to unhindered trade. This strategy is aimed exclusively at furthering economic growth at the expense of the economic and social welfare of large sectors of the population.

Governments are increasingly adopting a uniform approach, often ignoring past commitments on rights or treating past human rights commitments separate from economic issues. In some extreme cases, they have pushed for collective, social and labor rights to be excluded from constitutional protection. Frequently, free trade negotiations end up affecting amendments to domestic social pacts, making the weakest social partners bear the brunt of concessions made to transnational corporations. These strategies have put human and social rights in jeopardy and have led to the deterioration of protections as well as the weakening of domestic and international enforcement mechanisms.

In the face of a globalization process that marginalizes broad sectors of the population, three basic points must be considered: 1) Democracy is closely linked to human rights. States and authorities can only be considered legitimate if they enforce, promote and guarantee these fundamental rights, broadly defined. 2) Without justice, no government is guaranteed the ability to govern. 3) Human rights must never be sacrificed to a model of development that threatens human dignity.

The countries of the Americas should build a common human rights agenda to be included in every economic, financial, and trade agreement within the hemisphere, along with mechanisms and institutions to ensure full implementation and enforcement.

## Guiding principles:

1. Governments should reaffirm their responsibility for the implementation and protection of human rights, with special focus on economic, social, and environmental rights and those of peoples and communities.

2. All nations which have not already done so should sign and ratify the international human rights instruments listed below:

- a) Universal Declaration of Human Rights of the United Nations
    1) International Convention on Civil and Political Rights
    2) International Convention on Economic, Social and Cultural Rights
- b) International Convention on the Elimination of All Forms of Discrimination Against Women (CEDAW)
- c) International Convention on the Elimination of All Forms of Racial Discrimination
- d) Declaration on the Right to Development (December 4, 1986)
- e) Core Conventions of the International Labor Organization (ILO) including Convention 169 on the rights of Indian communities and peoples; those relating to migrants and their families; and provisions calling for the elimination of discrimination against women.
- f) Draft Declaration on the Rights of Indigenous People
- g) American Convention on Human Rights
- h) Additional protocol to the American Convention on Economic, Social and Cultural Rights, known as the Protocol of San Salvador, signed but as yet not implemented due to outstanding ratifications by certain countries.

The recognition of existing obligations and the ratification of pending accords are only the first step toward the full implementation of human rights. This will bring into effect the Right to Development as a universal and inalienable right and as an integral part of fundamental human rights as declared by the General Assembly of the UN in 1986.

3. Governments should prohibit all forms of discrimination based on gender, sexual orientation, race, ethnicity, religion, membership in any social or cultural group, nationality, or political views. They should establish effective domestic and international measures to eradicate "ethnic cleansing" which includes physical extermination or marginalization of and attacks on any social groups that experience discrimination within society, including gays and lesbians, persons with HIV/AIDS, street children, black people, prostitutes, and indigenous communities.

4. All trade, economic and financial agreements should include a "democracy clause" guaranteeing complete democracy within institutions of the state with unlimited protection of broadly defined human rights. All treaties must also effectively ensure participation of civil society in their development, adoption and implementation, clearly setting out transparent participation and accountability mechanisms for the various parties.

5. The Inter-American System of human rights should be reformed and strengthened in the following ways:

- a) increase effectiveness in the system and of the process for public review of the human rights situation.
- b) strengthen the Commission and the Inter-American Court as well as preventive provisional measures for the system through the recognition of the jurisdiction of every country in the hemisphere.

c) establish an independent, international body to protect internal displaced persons. The effective implementation of the right to asylum and or refugee status in states which have not adopted this right, with domestic regulations in accordance with the relevant international instruments.

d) include in the Inter-American Court's procedures a mechanism for victims or their representatives to participate, and transparency in criteria and procedures.

e) recognize nongovernmental organizations as advisory bodies to the Organization of American States (OAS) and the adoption of an Inter-American Declaration of Protection for Human Rights Defenders.

f) The governments of the Americas should support an international system for the protection of human rights, through allocation of sufficient resources to ensure their effective operation.

g) The process of evaluating the Inter-American Human Rights System should encourage broad discussions with nongovernmental organizations, experts and governments, with the joint aim of proposing reforms which benefit the victims of human rights violations, as well as general human rights promotion and defense activities.

6. In order to implement these international commitments, all parties should ratify the principles of cooperation and coordination among international, regional and national human rights protection instruments. Mechanisms to ensure the enforcement of such rights should be enacted through inclusion of all human rights in all trade, economic and financial agreements. Moreover, the economic components of these agreements should not take precedence over human rights.

## Specific Objectives:

1. Ensure the promotion, enforcement and enforceability of human rights, defined broadly and inseparably (the right to gender equity, civil and political, economic, social, cultural, environmental rights and those relating to peoples and communities) within national borders and in the international sphere, as part of integration and globalization processes.

2. Expand the number of recognized rights universally to all citizens of the Americas.

3. Ensure the right to communication, research and access to information and opinions, taking into account groups which currently and historically have less access. Establish the obligation of member states to repeal all official censorship measures.

4. Ensure all affected individuals' right to pursue justice, including restitution, compensation, rehabilitation, satisfaction, and the guarantee that the offending acts will not be repeated, according to basic guiding principles of the rights of victims of human rights violations and the international humanitarian right to reparation (UN document E/CN.4/1997/104). Affected individuals should also have the right to their choice of mechanism to achieve the most timely and effective response.

5. Implementation by governments of the observations and recommendations developed by the various agencies of the Universal and Regional Human Rights Protection System.

6. Promotion of reforms and programs aimed at achieving autonomy, impartiality and professionalization of judiciary power. Ensure the right of speedy, simple and effective access to the recourse of habeas corpus and court protection in the defense of fundamental rights.

7. End the impunity or exemption from punishment in crimes of strong political or economic importance that may deter investigation or prevent impartiality of the justice system.

8. Initiate human rights and gender equity awareness training programs for civilian authorities responsible for the armed forces and law enforcement. Incorporate human rights into the curriculum of formal and informal education from pre-kindergarten through higher education.

## III. ENVIRONMENT

### Background

Liberalization of investment and the opening of trade through the free trade agreements signed to date, especially the North American Free Trade Agreement, have had severe social and environmental impacts on peoples and workers. The peoples of the Americas aspire to an international economy based on different principles—an economy that makes sustainability a priority.

The problems with classic trade and investment policy from an environmental perspective are that it "externalizes" (does not account for) environmental and social costs and fosters more intense energy use, overexploitation of natural resources, and damage to biodiversity, all of which erodes the underlying basis of the economy and society. Such policies intensify the expropriation of genetic resources, the destruction of natural ecosystems, environmental degradation in agricultural and urban areas, environmental deregulation, and the violation of the individual and collective civil rights of generations present and future. Environmental degradation has also had a disproportionate effect on people living in poverty, especially women, as these groups tend to live with the impact of contaminated habitats and resources in places where there is less political will to improve conditions. Supporters of these policies view components of sustainable development as limitations to trade (e.g., food security, the protection of collective wisdom about and use of biodiversity, the sustainable use of ecosystems and the existence of fair and equitable ways of sharing the benefits of natural resources). Governments for the most part have rejected these ideals, yielding instead to international market pressures.

Environmental concerns cut across all topics. Therefore the points set out below are taken up more concretely or complemented in other chapters, such as those on energy and intellectual property rights.

## Guiding Principles:

1. The precedence of environmental accords signed by the governments of the Americas should be established in the negotiations around, and agreements on, investment and trade. Environment and sustainability should not be limited to a single area of economic-financial accords, but rather be addressed as an overarching dimension and perspective throughout any such agreements.

2. Quality of development should be a key priority. Governments should establish social and environmental limits to growth on the basis of environmental sustainability and social equity.

3. International trade agreements and nation states should establish plans to gradually internalize environmental and social costs arising from unsustainable production and consumption. If this leads to higher prices, governments should conduct awareness-raising campaigns to encourage high-income consumers to purchase goods produced in a sustainable way.

4. The costs of transition to trade and investment practices that are fair and environmentally sustainable should be dealt with equitably, acknowledging that the parties to an agreement may have different responsibilities for achieving common goals.

5. Governments should recognize that there is an existing ecological debt among nations. This has resulted from richer nations occupying an "exaggerated environmental space," meaning that they utilize and exploit a share of the world's natural resources that is disproportionate to their population and territory.

6. Governments should establish strict timelines to end international trading of products that harm the environment. During the transition period, tariffs should be imposed to discourage trade in such products and prevent their use.

7. Environmental regulations should be governed by the principle of precaution (i.e., the principle that, when in doubt, we should take the most environmentally cautious course of action), rather than risk assessment (which applies economic cost-benefit analysis to environmental resources).

8. Trade should be accompanied by incentives for the conservation of soil and natural resources and to reduce and move towards the elimination of chemicals that damage the environment. It should encourage sustainable development and production close to the place/site of consumption.

9. Social and ecological dumping should be rejected.

10. Trade liberalization must not hinder countries' capacity to channel foreign investment toward those sectors in which sustainable development can be strengthened.

11. Trade and investment liberalization must not hinder the regulation and control of companies and investors to ensure compliance with a country's sustainable development objectives.

12. Foreign companies and investors should be held to the highest environmental standards and share technologies that preserve the environment and create jobs.

13. Countries should maintain their sovereignty over the right to restrict investment that aggravates social or environmental problems and their disproportionate impact on the most vulnerable sectors of society, such as women and indigenous peoples.

## Specific Objectives:

### Forests and Sustainable Energy

Sustainable energy development is predicated on respect for the right of communities, energy savings, and the fight against excessive energy consumption. Energy sources should be renewable, clean and low-impact, and equitable, democratic access to them must be ensured.

Energy integration should be a process that allows for the growth of potential and for cooperation among different countries under equitable conditions that reflect each nation's economic, social and cultural characteristics.

## Therefore, the following are proposed:

1. Redirect investment, loans and subsidies toward clean-energy projects and energy efficiency based on equity of access and national priorities, including sustainable transport; giving precedence to public over private, and democratic access to energy for residential, craft, business and industrial use.

2. Eliminate direct and indirect subsidies for fossil-fuel energy.

3. Develop a legislative and institutional base for the promotion of sustainable energy production. This entails support for clean energy research and dissemination capacity.

4. Declare a moratorium on coal, natural gas and oil exploration in new areas as part of the transition to clean, renewable and low environmental impact energy sources.

5. Respect the right of communities in areas affected by energy production, especially indigenous communities.

6. Enforce the use of environmental impact studies for all energy-related projects.

## Mining

Mining in the Americas has involved many decades of heavy metal pollution and the destruction of land and sea habitats, as well as threats to the health and safety of mine workers and their families, who often live near hazardous work sites and suffer effects to their physical and reproductive health due to contact with such contamination. These conditions are present throughout the hemisphere and reflect the inability of the public sector to control effectively the environmental impact of this activity.

The accelerated expansion of mining carried out by international companies has not been accompanied by stronger controls, regulations or safeguards for human or environmental health. Rather, it has generated a demand for greater use of resources such as water and energy.

Therefore, the governments of the Americas must ensure the following:

1. The development of mining must be approved in advance by the communities that will be affected, especially when it would have an impact on other production or soil use. The land rights of indigenous communities must be respected.

2. Implement and enforce the highest health and safety standards for workers and environmental protection as conditions for mining development.

3. Declare a moratorium on mining exploration and development in ecologically and culturally significant areas.

4. Establish priorities and incentives in mining aimed at reducing consumption and increasing the efficiency of mineral processing.

5. Revisit the recommendations presented by non-governmental groups at the Sustainable Development Summit held in Santa Cruz in December 1996.

## Biodiversity and Intellectual Property

Conservation of biodiversity has been the responsibility of thousands of communities which use and cultivate resources for subsistence rather than for profit. The international exchange of the resources of biodiversity has historically been of benefit to many peoples, although benefits have been distributed less equitably over the last decades. Conservation and development of genetic resources in "scientific" centers, combined with institutionalized intellectual property systems, has caused looting and monopolization of genetic resources.

The hemisphere of the Americas currently faces enormous threats to its biodiversity from international trade liberalization treaties and the actions of multinational corporations. This creates a tremendous challenge to citizens, leading to the following demands (for a broader discussion of proposals on intellectual property, see Chapter 9):

1. Reject intellectual property claims over life forms and associated knowledge.

2. Recognize and protect collective rights of local communities in the conservation and raising of species

within biodiversity. This requires collective rights to community property (which in many communities is the historic knowledge transmitted by women) to take precedence over the provisions of any trade treaty or intellectual property instrument.

3. Based on ILO Convention 169, ensure the inalienable right of peoples and "traditional black and indigenous communities" to full autonomy in decisions over their traditional habitats and the biodiversity associated with them, and the use and management of same, according to their cultural systems and traditional rights.

4. Ensure the precedence of the Biological Diversity Convention over trade agreements.

5. Guarantee free circulation of knowledge and access to genetic resources for research in the service of the needs of local communities and residents as well as to public research centers.

6. Recognize and compensate communities that create and conserve biodiversity for the historical ecological debt owed them because of profits made by others through genetic resources and associated knowledge. Trade and investment accords must incorporate international cooperation for the preservation of biodiversity.

7. Promote joint accords between governments and civil society over a country's right to discover, conserve and have primary use and benefit of the biological and genetic properties of plants and animals in the region where they are found.

## IV. LABOR

### Background

Working people in the Americas believe that a just trading system is one that recognizes that basic labor standards and other measures for improving the welfare of working people cannot be left exclusively to markets. The future hemispheric accord must include provisions that guarantee basic worker rights, that ensure proper assistance for adjustment as markets are opened up, and that promote the improvement of working and living standards of workers and their families.

There exists a long tradition within the international community recognizing the necessity to apply and respect basic international labor standards. This recognition led to the creation in 1919 of the International Labor Organization (ILO), an institution that survives to this day as a UN agency that has the specific mandate of defining and monitoring international labor standards. All 35 countries of the Americas are members of the ILO and have ratified ILO conventions. Current trade agreements within the hemisphere, such as the MERCOSUR and NAFTA (more precisely, the NAFTA side agreement on labor, officially called the North American Agreement on Labor Cooperation or NAALC) state that fundamental principles regarding labor conditions should be respected within all member countries and that the agreements should contribute to a general improvement of the living standards of workers.

However, not even the most optimistic analyst of the impact of trade agreements such as NAFTA and the MERCOSUR would claim that these agreements have contributed to a general improvement of working conditions in member countries. On the contrary, the introduction of these agreements has led to greater instability of jobs and insecurity in the workplace. This has been the case most dramatically in Mexico since NAFTA came into effect in 1994. The specific provisions on labor standards, such as NAFTA's NAALC, tend to be strong on principles but weak on any specific mechanisms that can have a real impact on working people. Moreover, it is a recognized fact that even the most basic labor standards agreed upon at the ILO are regularly flouted by employers throughout most countries of the Americas, more often than not in attempting to obtain a competitive advantage over other employers. This takes place in spite of the fact that all countries of the hemisphere are members of the ILO, thus endorsing in principle the respect of international labor standards.

### Guiding Principles:

1. Working people and their organizations have the right to participate in decision making at the national and international level regarding the hemispheric integration process in order to ensure that this process contributes to improving the living standards of workers.

2. The commitment to apply and respect basic workers' rights should be included in any hemispheric agreement as an obligatory requirement for membership in the accord. An appropriate and effective enforcement mechanism should also be included.

3. An appropriate adjustment mechanism must be included to ensure that those workers who find their jobs rendered redundant by the opening up of markets are provided with the opportunities to find other employment, through measures such as skills retraining, infrastructure development and specific job-creation schemes.

4. The hemispheric accord must include mechanisms to promote and improve the living standards of workers through legal norms and social programs in countries participating in the accord. As a basic principle, these mechanisms should strive to establish basic social programs in countries where they do not presently exist and to raise standards towards the highest standards existing in member countries.

## Specific Objectives:
## 1. Worker Rights Clause

Since the early 1990s, the international labor movement has promoted the inclusion in international trade agreements of a "Workers Rights Clause," which would force employers and governments to deal with the frequent and repeated violation of fundamental workers' rights. Within the Americas, the Inter-American Regional Organization of Workers (ORIT), which represents a large majority of unionized workers in the Americas, has proposed the creation of a working group on labor and social issues as part of the FTAA negotiating structures which would have the mandate to negotiate basic labor standards for the Americas. Trade unions of the Americas would have direct participation in this working group.

Our proposed clause in the hemispheric accord for the Americas could result in certain producers losing the privileges accorded by the trade agreement, i.e., tariff-free access to foreign markets included in the free-trade zone, if fundamental workers' rights are not respected. The fundamental rights are defined as those covered by seven core Conventions of the ILO (among the total of 182 that have been adopted between 1919 and 1998), namely:

- Conventions 29 and 105 on the abolition of forced labor;
- Conventions 87 and 98 on the rights to freedom of association, to collective bargaining, and to trade-union action, including the right to elect trade union representatives without employer or government interference, and the right to strike;
- Conventions 100 and 111 on equal pay for work of equal value and on the prevention of discrimination in the work-place;
- Convention 138 on the minimum working age (i.e., prevention of child labor).

All countries of the Americas have ratified one or more of these so-called "core conventions" of the ILO. Moreover, virtually all governments of the countries of the Americas have stated that they respect and strive to apply the principles contained in these Conventions even when they have not yet ratified them formally. Despite these assurances, the rights to freedom of association and collective bargaining are routinely violated by a vast number of countries in the hemisphere, and child labor is endemic in several countries as is work-place discrimination against women and specific racial or ethnic groups.

For these reasons we propose that the seven fundamental workers' rights Conventions of the ILO as described above be included in a hemispheric agreement, meaning that employers and governments would be obliged to respect these Conventions as a condition of access to the benefits of the agreement.

## 2. Monitoring and Enforcement

Naturally, such a worker rights provision would be effective only to the extent that it were accompanied by an effective monitoring and enforcement mechanism. We propose that the monitoring function as well as that of making recommendations regarding the application of specific enforcement measures be delegated to the ILO, whose expertise in the field of monitoring the application of international labor standards is universally recognized. The complaints-based procedure that the ILO currently uses for keeping track of the respect of the freedom of association Conventions would be used for the Americas' workers rights clause. That is to say that unions or other non-governmental organizations (NGOs) could initiate an examination procedure by the ILO by lodging a complaint to the latter when fundamental rights contained in the core Conventions are violated.

The ILO would, at a first stage, carry out an investigation to verify whether or not the Conventions have in effect been violated. In cases where the Conventions are confirmed to have been violated, the ILO would, at a second stage, formulate recommendations to the country to assist it in complying with the Conventions which have not been respected. Only if this second stage were unsuccessful would the enforcement mechanism be applied, which is to say that the direct perpetrator of the violations would be deprived of specific benefits of the accord, i.e., trade sanctions.

To the extent that the perpetrator of the violation was a specific company, any specific sanctions would be directly targeted at that company. For example, if an auto-parts manufacturer in Country A were found to have violated the rights of freedom of association of its workforce, the exports coming from that particular manufacturer in Country A would no longer benefit from tariff-free access to all other countries party to the accord. Regular customs duties would be applied, in accordance with WTO agreements, as if the particular export came from outside of the Americas' free-trade area. More generalized sanctions, that is sanctions which would apply to all exports from a particular country, would only be administered if the country's government were shown to be an active and repeated accomplice in the violation of fundamental workers' rights in that country.

If both countries and companies were obligated to respect and apply fundamental workers' rights, this would help to establish and generalize workplace practices throughout the Americas in which:

the most extreme forms of labor exploitation would be eliminated,

workers could, without suffering threats to their jobs and their physical well-being, strive to improve their wages and working conditions, and

workers and employers could resolve their differences through peaceful means.

## 3. Mechanisms for Adjustment and Job Creation

The elimination of tariff barriers and other forms of protection will inevitably lead to the elimination of certain people's livelihoods in industries unable to meet the challenges of increased competition. If hemispheric free trade does contribute to greater economic efficiency and thus a general improvement of economic welfare, as its proponents claim it will, there should be no hesitation in assuring that the "losers" are compensated. Failure to do so could entail the marginalization of vast numbers of workers and agricultural producers through the process of hemispheric integration.

For this reason it is important that the future hemispheric agreement include a mechanism for allowing national economies to adjust to the impacts of economic integration, namely in the areas of skill retraining, infrastructure development and specific job-creation programs. Compensatory financing would obviously be necessary in order to take account of the unequal levels of development and capacities to adjust of different national economies and, as well, specific regions within countries. Specific funds would be provided for adjustment programs specifically targeted to assist those women and men working in industries or living in areas that suffer job losses through economic integration.

The European Union (EU) has established precedence for such financial support by providing structural development aid to the lower-income countries in the Union and also to specific geographic regions within higher-income member countries that have suffered from a decrease in protection or otherwise have not been able to reap the benefits of the integrated market. In a similar fashion, a structural development fund should be created as part and parcel of the agreement for the Americas to provide financial support for worker training, infrastructure development and job creation in lower-income countries and in designated regions within countries. Such a fund could be financed either through levies paid by countries on a scale which varies with the per capita income level (as is the case in Europe), or through a specific financing mechanism such as a Tobin Tax (i.e., a tax on international financial transactions) applied in the Americas.

## 4. Basic Labor Standards and Social Programs

In addition to the inclusion of a workers rights clause and appropriate adjustment mechanisms, we believe that the hemispheric agreement must include mechanisms for improving basic labor standards and social programs so that the agreement contributes to a betterment of working and living conditions for working people and a more equalized distribution of income within countries. Given the vastly different levels of development between countries of the Americas, we do not envisage developing anything like a common minimum wage throughout the hemisphere. However, it would certainly be within the scope of the agreement to establish guidelines, for example in relation to defined levels of subsistence, in setting minimum wages in the national context. Guidelines could also be established in the area of hours of work, rules on overtime pay, rest periods and vacations. As a first step, there would be a process for meeting minimum ILO standards and, subsequently, harmonizing upwards in order to move towards the highest existing standards within the hemisphere. A more rapid process of harmonization would be put in place regarding the definition of hemispheric norms for the prevention of workplace accidents and work-related disease, based on the highest existing standards in the Americas. These processes would be established with the full participation not only of governments but also of representative trade-union and employers' organizations.

There currently exist enormous differences between the countries of the Americas in the area of social and income-support programs, although there is a general tendency throughout the hemisphere for a serious deterioration of these programs as a result of government cutbacks. Even Canada, which used to pride itself on according a level of social protection that put it in the same league as Western European countries, currently has fallen behind all member countries of the European Union in terms of income maintenance for unemployed men and women. In other countries, universal State pension schemes are being privatized or otherwise eroded, leading to greater inequality of income for retired workers, especially women. If economic integration of the Americas is to contribute to a generalized improvement of living standards in the hemisphere, the rapid erosion of social protection that has taken place over the past decade obviously has to be reversed. Specific targets for basic social and income-support programs should therefore be included in the agreement, including unemployment insurance, compensation for injured workers, and pensions for retired workers.

In addition, financing through the hemispheric agreement must be provided to countries that, because of low per capita income levels, do not have the means to finance such schemes entirely on their own. A financing mechanism, perhaps modeled on the EU's social fund, could provide the necessary financial support. Hemispheric economic integration can be expected to make capital even more mobile than it already is and, subsequently, lead to greater job instability. The hemispheric agreement should provide for protection of workers against increasing job instability, especially respecting employers who may seek to avoid their obligations with regards to their employees by transferring their production to another country. All employers would be required to adhere to nationally administered funds ensuring the payment of all due wages and other indemnities employees are entitled to in case of job termination. Basic hemispheric standards regarding advance notice of layoffs and protection for part-time and sub-contracted labor would also be put in place.

## V. IMMIGRATION

### Background

International migration has increased over the last number of decades, accelerated by the process of globalization. There are currently about 125 million immigrants (people who have moved from one country to another) in the world, 80 million of whom are considered "recent" immigrants. The growing population of immigrant men, women and children has serious impacts for the countries they leave as well as for the countries which receive them. However, despite the demands of numerous nongovernmental organizations, officials have refused to address this issue in the negotiation of trade and investment liberalization agreements. Such agreements only deal with the free movement of capital, goods, and their agents, but exclude the mobility of workers.

The forces driving people to migrate are many. After political violence, the leading reason is the problem of unemployment. Immigration affects not only those who migrate. It has major consequences for the economic and social relationships between countries involved. It is therefore necessary to agree on international rules to address not only the human and labor rights of migrants but also to regulate the flow of labor.

The impacts of immigration are complex. Developing nations have become exporters of workers who are often vulnerable to exploitation. Corporations have taken full advantage of this situation, contributing to the lowering of wages for some workers in host countries. At the same time, the money remitted by the immigrant workers to family members in their homeland plays a major role in reducing problems in the current account balance in developing economies and cushioning social problems and extreme poverty.

The International Organization for Migration estimates that approximately 30 million immigrant workers send a total of nearly US$67 billion a year back to their countries. Many studies show that such remittances are the second leading source of foreign exchange in the world, after petroleum. In fact, for some countries in the Americas (such as El Salvador), remittances are the main source of foreign currency. In Mexico, despite an export-oriented economy and a well-developed maquiladora sector, remittances from workers outside the country remain the fourth-largest source of foreign currency. These remittances count for many governments' lack of interest in regulating the mobility of labor.

The United States, the largest host country for immigrant labor, has hardened and to a great extent militarized its immigration policy. It has also pressured other countries such as Mexico to create a retaining wall against the flow of people from Central America and the Caribbean. However, the rest of the continent is not impervious to the serious border problems linked to the flow of migrant labor.

In the future, trade and investment liberalization agreements must address both the human rights concerns related to immigration (in the broad sense discussed in the chapter in on human rights) and regulations on cross-border labor mobility.

## Guiding Principles:

1. All governments should sign and/or ratify the "International Convention on the Protection of the Rights of All Migrant Workers and Members of Their Families" (1990) and a similar instrument should be created for the Americas. This convention, like all those legal instruments referred to in the chapter on human rights, must be part of the international legal framework for all trade and financial negotiations.

2. The extra-territorial application of any immigration policy not developed democratically among affected nations should be banned. This would mean the banning of certain current practices such as the demand by some countries that individuals entering their territory first obtain a visa for entry into the United States. It would also ban pre-inspection facilities such as those that the U.S. is attempting to institute in certain airports and at borders (and which already exist in Canada).

3. Governments should prohibit the use of violence or excessive force in the implementation of national immigration laws and policies and establish binational commissions, with the participation of nongovernmental organizations in the monitoring of national immigration laws, to ensure strict adherence to human rights.

4. Strengthen the mechanisms for diplomatic protection of migrants.

5. Enact humane national immigration laws, with participation of migrants' and other nongovernmental organizations and experts in the development, implementation and evaluation phases.

6. Immigrant workers should have the same rights and working conditions as the workers in their host country, regardless of their immigration status. Employers taking undue advantage of the workers' immigration status by imposing working conditions and wages below legal requirements should be severely penalized.

7. Trade and investment agreements should include international support for specific development programs designed to improve employment opportunities in areas that are major net exporters of labor.

8. There is tremendous diversity in the immigration-related problems and situations in different countries of the hemisphere. For example, in some countries an open-door policy is both practical and desirable while in others it is not. Hence, the framework for negotiations within the Americas should provide for binational or subregional agreements on immigration in countries or areas with significant flows of migrants. Such covenants should equalize labor rights and social security systems upwards while making the scope of coverage international.

## VI. THE NATION STATE

### Background

The role of the state in leading hemispheric economic integration is irreplaceable if this process is to promote social justice, equity among regions and social groups, and sustainability. The democratic state should be a tool for society to use to address the economic and social problems the market cannot solve. Hence, this discussion should not be framed in terms of a polarization between state and market.

Historical experience shows that the state is necessary to deal with the flux of the market. Furthermore the economy is broader than the market, encompassing all production (not just what is traded), and requires the involvement of the state to establish adequate conditions for stable, sustainable growth and social well-being. Opening up economies internationally does not necessarily mean they have to be left to the vagaries of international markets. There is no such thing as the free market, because of the large corporations which dominate and drive the market. Opening markets actually means letting these corporations drive and dominate the market to suit their own interests. Historically, there is no evidence that the market can achieve general equilibrium within the economy, let alone sustainability and social justice.

The key is for nations to open themselves to the world based on their own plans for fair and sustainable development led by democratic governments, rather than leaving the future of such development to market forces. Economies that are open are all the more reliant on regulation at the national and international levels and require a state strong enough to promote and enforce them.

Under the prevailing dominant economic model, state intervention in the economy is reduced, except in the promotion of the export sector and finance capital. By favoring exports, workers and most of the population cease to be seen as valued consumers since their impoverishment no longer affects the top strata of capital.

The dominant discourse demonizes government and assumes that the market does everything better. Adjustment programs imposed by the World Bank and the IMF increase this pressure, leading to a growing trend toward privatization. Governments see privatization as a short-term remedy for financial crisis and unbalanced budgets. It can also be a mechanism for the illegal transfer of wealth or favoritism toward certain economic interests.

There are three problems inherent in privatization: 1) it reduces the state's ability to lead the process of sustainable and fair development; 2) over the long term, government revenues fall, which normally results in reductions in public spending; and 3) serious injustices are created in public services, with a disproportionate burden of such cuts affecting women and people who are poor. Privatization is also used to lower wages and benefits for organized workers, as the sale of services usually results in the replacement of collective agreements by more "flexible" working conditions entailing fewer rights, less negotiating power, and lower benefits.

We propose a fully democratic state, economically and socially accountable to its citizens, which radically challenges corruption at every level: a state with a qualitatively new role within the economy. We are not proposing an oversized state burdened by huge, inefficient enterprises. The number and size of public corporations is less important than the role they fulfil. Society, not only governments, should make decisions relating to industries in the public realm.

The goal should not be traditional protectionism, but building a state accountable to society that can implement a democratically established national development plan. This may involve the protection of certain sectors considered strategic within a country's plan, but more importantly, it means promoting forward-looking development. Regulation does not imply inhibiting private initiative. On the contrary, it means establishing clear rules balancing rights and obligations, and ensuring that both national and international capital promote a country's fair and sustainable development.

This renewed role for the state implies international regulations which must be determined democratically and through consultation with citizens. Sovereignty belongs to the people, who may decide to submit to international regulations if it is in the collective interest. International regulations are becoming increasingly necessary in the face of the supra-national power of certain corporations which operate within our economies and the weight and mobility of footloose capital.

This new and strategic role for the state in the economic and social spheres requires integrated fiscal reform favoring economic activity and redistribution, coupled with the ability to raise revenue at a level which avoids deficits so large that they impede development.

Nothing in an international agreement should constitute a renunciation or reduction of the state's ability to meet the economic and social demands of its citizens. This principle must take precedence if the state's capacity to meet these demands is diminished by such agreements.

## 1. Guiding Principles:

### Economic and Social Responsibilities of the State

A. The first role of the state is to facilitate debate and establish permanent consultation mechanisms with respect to domestic and international policies.

B. It is the state's responsibility to lead a consensual economic strategy and enact related social policies which strengthen the well-being of citizens. The state should spare no effort to promote the creation of well-paid jobs, which are the best vehicle for achieving that well-being.

Participation in the global economy entails a strong export sector, but this should not be pursued to the neglect of the domestic market. The strength of the export market should be measured not in the volume of exports but in the sector's ability to generate high-quality jobs and foster economic growth. The focus on strengthening the domestic market would mean that citizens would be viewed as valued consumers. Thus, raising standards of living would become an economic necessity for market expansion rather than merely a social justice issue.

Competition punishes corporations with low levels of productivity, but it does not necessarily increase productivity. The state has the inescapable responsibility to create conditions which favor competition among domestic companies in the international as well as internal markets. To achieve this, the promotion of technological research and development as well as education is indispensable to each country's viability. An explicit industrial policy must be established which includes building infrastructure, access to credit, education and research for the promotion of appropriate technology and integration of productive linkages.

C. The social role of the state is a democratic requirement of society and cannot be evaded. However, the economic role cannot be separated from the social role. There is no better social policy than an economic policy that favors the well-being of all men, women, and children. However, even the best political policies must be supplemented by social policies, since the market always generates inequities.

The social role of the state entails public services, public security and the well-being of all. This requires specific policies aimed at each of the most vulnerable sectors of the population. These policies should be translated into laws which create rights, not policies of patronage or favoritism. The state's core aim should be just and sustainable development for all, while not excluding emergency or compensatory aid for particular groups.

D. Education. States should fully take up their responsibilities for financing education, for sharing resources equitably, and for the establishment of a common basic curriculum. However, decentralization necessary for the autonomy of educational programs in specific communities should not lead states to abandon their responsibility for the cost of education and the equitable distribution of resources. Access to education is a right which should not be subject to the ability to pay.

Improving the quality of education and access to it requires new sources of funding. Part of tax revenues accruing from international financial transactions should be allocated to increased investment in education in countries with the smallest budgets (see Chapter 8).

In all countries of the Americas, education should favor a holistic approach. Educational systems should therefore do a better job of balancing utilitarian visions of education to meet the market's needs and humanistic approaches that allow individuals to participate actively and fully in the societies in which they live.

Priority should be given to literacy and basic education for all. Access to secondary and post-secondary education should be improved to allow all societies of the Americas to participate fully in the "globalization of knowledge" without this resulting in a homogenization of this knowledge.

The use of new technologies should favor the access to knowledge and allow for the circulation of the diverse forms of knowledge in all cultural communities. New technologies such as computers should be used in schools, but not as a substitute for teachers. New information and communication technologies must not be converted into yet more tools of exclusion and discrimination.

Any education action plan must contain measures directed toward improving the living standards for children and youth within the family. Especially important are education and mass campaigns to help children avoid drugs. Financial, psycho-social, and public health service supports are necessary. Adult education must not be neglected.

E. Health. As with education, access to health is a fundamental right which should not be subject to the ability to pay. It should be considered the responsibility of the state to provide high quality health care to all. Specific international funds should be set aside for this purpose, including a portion of revenues accruing from speculative financial transactions in the international sphere (see Chapter 8).

Access to health care services should be universal and not limited to those with jobs in the formal sector, since in most countries in the Americas, the majority of people experience unemployment, often turning to precarious employment in the informal sector. Health services should include those specially related to women and be designed with concern for women's access to such services.

Access to public health care services for indigenous communities and peoples should be guaranteed. At the same time, they should be based on the development and increased availability of traditional medicine and the age-old knowledge held in these communities, often by women.

Social security systems (including pensions) should be under the state's jurisdiction, and the savings funds used to finance them should be managed by the state and invested in high-priority national development projects. The funds should not be used as speculative capital, which would only serve to concentrate social wealth in a few hands.

## 2. Criteria for Economic Regulations:

- be clear and explicit and designed to prevent bias on the part of officials whose job it is to apply them.
- be decided democratically.
- be simple and easy to apply.
- be kept to the minimum needed to achieve their objectives.
- preserve the sovereignty of provinces, regions or states to make their own regulations within their areas of competence as long as they act for the good of their communities and not to perpetuate individual privilege, or gender- or race-based discrimination.

*Areas for Special Regulation*

Each country may establish special regulations for sectors it deems to be especially important for its national development such as the following:

- The exploitation of natural resources.

- Financial and monetary policy, especially the management of its payment system and short-term investment.

- Basic food production and/or agricultural production by small family farms.

- Strategic sectors linked to national sovereignty or national economic stability.

The intention should not be to protect or block certain sectors from foreign investment or external trade but to recognize those sectors that need special regulation.

## 3. Public Sector Corporations

Corporations known as "state-owned enterprises" in fact belong to society and are only administered by the state. These public sector corporations are not established for personal profit, but are vehicles for healthy economic development, safeguards of sovereignty, and instruments of social and environmental justice.

Nevertheless, states should ensure that public sector corporations are sound and efficient. Corruption should be avoided by legislative and societal checks. Their preservation, creation or privatization should be decided by legislatures representing the popular will. In the case of strategic enterprises, laws should require broad and direct consultation with the public.

*General provisions*

A. Some public sector corporations may exercise exclusive management, production, transportation or sales rights over specific goods and services where national laws so provide.

B. Public sector corporations should not be treated as monopolies or subject to anti-monopoly laws.

C. The administration and evaluation of public sector corporations should not be based solely on considerations of price and quality but also on their achievement of the specific objectives for which they were created.

## 4. Government Procurement and Public Works Contracts

Government purchasing and public works contracts have a significant influence in some productive sectors. They are carried out with taxpayers' money and should therefore continue to be instruments of economic policy for national development. They should accordingly be subject to the following criteria:

Government procurement of goods and services should be subject to open and transparent competition to avoid corrupt practices in their allocation, with specific exceptions discussed below.

Criteria for competition need not be based exclusively on price and quality, but may also include the following:

A. National content for the good or service involving some degree of integration into the domestic productive economy.

B. Kinds of technology used and their environmental effects.

C. Transfer of technology.

D. Number of jobs created and wages paid.

E. Special safeguards to support medium, small and micro domestic enterprises.

F. Prohibition against conditions requiring the letting of a contract for purchase or a public project to a particular supplier or contractor.

Countries may establish lists of high-priority suppliers whose development they consider strategic for reasons of national development (such as the development of appropriate technology, spin-off effects on other economic sectors or the number of jobs they generate or on the achievement of gender or racial equity) and give them priority over foreign suppliers. To ensure that the priority given to nationals does not protect inefficiencies or place an excessive burden on public resources, suppliers should be required to offer bids within a certain percentage of competing foreign bids, comply with other criteria of the tendering process, and receive privileged status for a limited time. These preferential terms will be negotiated in conjunction with the supports necessary to bring the domestic suppliers up to the international competitive standard within a set timeframe.

Government procurement should also be used to protect and benefit groups affected by discrimination and marginalization, such as certain ethnic groups, cooperatives or producers in particularly depressed regions or those with high levels of extreme poverty.

Disputes over government procurement should be based explicitly on the above criteria, and be dealt with first by mechanisms within a country, and proceed only to international arbitration after recourse to national processes has been exhausted.

## VII. FOREIGN INVESTMENT

### Background

The Director General of the World Trade Organization (WTO), Renato Ruggiero, has compared the negotiation of international investment agreements to "writing a constitution of a single world economy." Indeed the investment rules written into the North American Free Trade Agreement (NAFTA) and the proposed Multilateral Agreement on Investment (MAI) are like constitutions that determine what governments can and cannot do.

Both NAFTA and the draft MAI build on the principle of "national treatment" which requires treating foreign investors "no less favorably" than domestic firms. Although negotiations on the MAI appear to have stalled within the OECD, the draft proposal is clearly intended as the basis for any investment chapter within the Free Trade Area of the Americas (FTAA). Proponents of the MAI also want to incorporate its measures into a revision of the Trade-Related Investment Measures (TRIMs) code within the WTO.

All of these investment agreements are biased in favor of maximizing the ability of transnational investors to move freely around the globe with minimum interference from national governments or international regulatory bodies.

In this chapter we counterpose an investment code based on principles that are fundamentally different than those in the MAI and NAFTA.

### Guiding Principles:

1. Foreign investment is welcome in our countries provided that it adheres to regulations that enforce the economic and social rights of citizens and environmental sustainability.

2. Regulations must be democratically determined by governments in consultation with their people.

3. In the event of a conflict, internationally recognized human, labor and environmental rights must take precedence over investors' rights. At a minimum the signatories must ratify the following international treaties and agreements: Universal Declaration of Human Rights; International Labor Organization conventions concerning trade union freedom, collective bargaining, child labor, forced labor and workplace discrimination; the United Nations Convention for the Elimination of All Forms of Discrimination Against Women and the Covenant on Economic, Social and Cultural Rights; the San Salvador Protocol; and international environmental agreements including the Montreal Protocol on Substances that Deplete the Ozone Layer; the Basel Convention of the Control of Trans-boundary Movements of Hazardous Wastes and their Disposal; and the Kyoto agreements on greenhouse gas emissions.

4. Regulations must be agreed upon multilaterally so as to prevent unfair competition between countries. Competition that results in a lowering of standards in a race to the bottom is by definition unfair. For example, if a government were to lower its standards or refuse to enforce minimum labor and environmental laws in order to attract foreign investment it would be guilty of unfair competition.

5. International agreements on investment regulation must take into account the asymmetries of power and different levels of development that exist between countries.

6. Agreements must also respect the diversity of political jurisdictions {e.g., states, provinces, municipalities and aboriginal governments} that exist within some countries.

### Specific Objectives:

Investment regulation should not mean imposing excessive controls on investors or establishing protections for inefficient industries. Rather, it should involve orienting investment and creating conditions to enable investment to serve national development goals while obtaining reasonable returns.

### Governments should have the power to:

1. implement viable national development policies appropriate to their peoples' goals, while remaining open to the world economy.

2. encourage productive investments that increase links between the local and the national economy and screen out investments that make no net contribution to

development, especially speculative or very short-term portfolio investments that lead to rapid capital outflows, creating instability and economic crises.

3. make foreign investment play an active role in the creation of macroeconomic conditions for development.

4. protect small, local, family and community enterprises from unfair foreign competition.

5. allow for legal measures that preserve public or state ownership in some sectors {e.g., petroleum}; exclusive national ownership in other sectors {e.g., broadcasting} and obligatory national participation in the ownership of other sectors {e.g., finance}.

## Performance Requirements

Performance requirements need not be protectionist measures. Rather they should be a means through which host countries share the benefits of corporate investment. The prohibitions on performance requirements in NAFTA and the MAI prevent national and local communities from implementing economic development policies that utilize investment for the benefit of ordinary people.

Governments should have the power to impose performance requirements on investors such as are necessary to accomplish the following goals:

a) integrate foreign investment into local development plans by requiring investors to achieve a given percentage of national, regional or local content and requiring enterprises to purchase inputs locally. This would prevent foreign enterprises from becoming enclaves that only appropriate natural resources and exploit workers.

b) give preference to hiring local personnel.

c) achieve a minimum level of local equity participation in an investment.

d) respect labor standards that are at least as high, but never lower, than those set by International Labor Organization conventions on trade union freedom, collective bargaining, child labor, forced labor and workplace discrimination against women and minority groups.

e) implement the United Nations Convention to Eliminate All Forms of Discrimination Against Women.

f) fulfill international environmental treaties such as the Montreal protocol on ozone depletion or the Kyoto agreements on greenhouse gas emissions.

g) achieve the transfer of appropriate technology.

h) avoid the destabilizing effect of simultaneous and massive withdrawals of fly-by-night portfolio capital by requiring that portfolio investments or investments in the financial market remain in place for a minimum period. One way to achieve this goal is to require that a portion of portfolio investments (e.g., 20% to 30%) be deposited for a time (e.g., one year) with the central bank.

i) give adequate notice to local communities of intent to shut down or move; and provide adequate compensation to the local community, in conformity with minimum labor standards and payment for any environmental clean-up. In addition, governments should have the right to freeze the assets of a corporation until it adequately indemnifies workers and communities affected by the withdrawal of an investment, violation of a collective agreement or environmental damage.

j) limit the amount of assets that can be repatriated in a given year and the kind of financial investment that can be transferred through such measures as taxation of financial transfers.

k) license technology for others to use when justified for social or humanitarian purposes as in the case of compulsory licensing of generic medicines.

l) provide incentives for the reinvestment of profits.

m) require local permission for the exploitation of natural resources, such as fish or forestry products, for purposes of ecological conservation.

n) contribute to workers' pension funds, health and unemployment insurance benefits and pay their fair share of taxes to support economic {e.g., roads} and social {e.g., education} infrastructure.

## Dispute Resolution

Citizen groups, indigenous peoples, local community development organizations and all levels of government should have the right to sue investors for violations of this investment code. All judicial and quasi-judicial procedures, such as arbitration, shall be fully transparent and open to public observation. Intervenor funding shall be made available to groups such as indigenous communities and environmental groups to enable their participation in legal proceedings.

### Expropriation

The expropriation of corporate assets to serve vital community needs should be permitted. Compensation for expropriated resources shall be determined by national law with due regard to the value of the initial foreign investment; the valuation of properties for tax purposes and the amount of wealth taken out of the country during the duration of the investment. Investors should have the right of appeal to national courts in cases where they deem compensation to be inadequate. Appeal to international tribunals should only occur after all national procedures have been exhausted.

## VIII. INTERNATIONAL FINANCE

### Background

The international financial system must be reformed. We cannot go on lurching from crisis to crisis with ever larger bailouts that benefit the rich at the expense of the poor.

The burden of external debt must be lifted as it continues to cause a perverse transfer of wealth from impoverished peoples to their creditors. Over the years 1981 through 1987 less developed countries paid US$1.5 trillion more in debt service than they received in new loans. In 1995, the countries of Latin America had a total external debt burden of more than $600 billion.

These debt payments and the structural adjustment conditions imposed by creditors exacerbate inequalities among nations and distort development.

The rise in financial speculation at the expense of investment in production threatens the well-being of working people everywhere, North and South. NAFTA's investment rules, the proposed MAI and proposals for changing the articles of agreement of the International Monetary Fund are all designed to allow investors to take any kind of capital in or out of member countries in any amount at any time. We can only expect that FTAA negotiators will pursue similar proposals.

Our vision of international financial regulation has a different logic.

### Guiding Principles:

1. The international financial system should ensure stability and allocate capital for productive purposes.

2. National and international measures must be taken to minimize the disruptive consequences of speculation and fly-by-night capital flows.

3. International financial institutions must promote sustainable economic and social development instead of austerity and structural adjustment policies that impoverish peoples and erode health care, education and the environment.

4. External debts contracted by repressive military dictatorships are illegitimate, "odious debts" that should be written off.

5. The remaining debt for many nations is so high that it renders sustainable development impossible. Unsustainable external debts that accumulated due to high interest rates must be renegotiated and partially written off with the remainder payable over longer terms at low interest rates.

### Specific Objectives:

1. New ways of regulating speculative capital should be agreed upon multilaterally to avoid the instability and vulnerability for national economies and for the international financial system.

2. Inasmuch as the International Monetary Fund and World Bank have failed to oversee the international financial system in a manner that supports sustainable and productive development, they should either be fundamentally restructured or new institutions put in their place.

3. National authorities must have the ability to regulate flows of "hot" money into and out of their countries. There are a wide range of proposals at the international level for confronting this problem that should be evaluated and discussed. At the same time there is a consensus on the need to give priority to direct and productive investments, assure that investments are long-term, and prevent instability that can cause their rapid flight. Such measures should include taxes on speculative profits, laws requiring portfolio investments to remain within the country for a minimum period and incentives for direct and productive investments.

4. Any agreement in the Americas must include provisions to allow governments to channel foreign investment into productive purposes instead of speculation. The North American Free Trade Agreement must be amended to this end. Any other agreement for the Americas or under the World Trade Organization, where they

may attempt to integrate the worst aspects of the proposed Multilateral Agreement on Investment, must also share this orientation.

5. A tax on foreign exchange transactions, as proposed by James Tobin, a prominent monetary economist and Nobel Laureate, should be instituted to slow down currency speculation and enable national governments to exercise more control over their monetary policies. The revenues from a Tobin tax (conservatively estimated at US$302 billion a year for a 0.25% tax) should be administered by an independent United Nations agency and used for social and economic development.

6. Every agreement between countries at different levels of development must include compensatory financing to allow for achieving the competitiveness that integration implies and to fund social programs. This approach has been followed within the European Union, where the richer countries have funneled development aid into Spain, Portugal, Greece, and Ireland to lift up their living standards closer to the level of other EU nations. In the Western Hemisphere, the most effective way to level the playing field would be through a substantial reduction of the debts owed by low-income countries. Therefore the FTAA should include the negotiation of a reduction of the principal owed, lower preferential interest rates, and longer repayment terms.

7. Orthodox Structural Adjustment conditions demanded by the World Bank and the IMF should be abandoned as they have manifestly failed to resolve the debt crisis and have caused enormous hardship for the poorest sectors of the population. Instead countries should adopt economic development policies like those proposed by the UN Economic Commission for Africa in its African Alternative Framework to Structural Adjustment Programmes for Socio-Economic Recovery and Transformation.

8. Central banks and other national regulatory bodies should be strengthened to assure that they are not subordinate to national and international banking oligopolies. Central banks and monetary authorities should be free from the short-term electoral interests of parties or groups. Therefore they must have a certain autonomy from the executive branch of government. However, in no way should these financial institutions be completely autonomous bodies free from social control through democratically elected congresses and legislatures.

9. Central banks and national monetary authorities must take concerted international action to lower interest rates, stimulate demand for goods and services and investment in production instead of speculation. International cooperation is also necessary to combat money laundering.

10. No international agreement should diminish the capacity of states to establish monetary and financial policies for the development and well-being of their peoples.

## IX. INTELLECTUAL PROPERTY RIGHTS

### Background

Intellectual property rights are theoretically intended to provide recognition for all products of the mind, such as inventions, music, or books. However, the recent wave of trade agreements have established intellectual property rights provisions that are biased towards protecting and compensating corporate-sponsored activity. A particular concern has been the emergence of intellectual property rights in products derived from biodiversity. Under these provisions, corporations have the right to patent products that have traditionally been treated as common property of local communities.

### Guiding Principles:

1. The intellectual property provisions of trade agreements such as NAFTA, the WTO and the FTAA should be limited to matters directly related to trade, such as trade in counterfeit goods. These provisions should not be extended to authorize trade sanctions that force individual countries to adopt measures that subordinate the interests of the national population to those of transnational corporations or to their national subsidiaries. For example, no trade or investment agreement should be allowed to supercede national laws requiring foreign investors to transfer appropriate technology to the host country.

2. Before granting private companies legal protection privileges for intellectual property, governments should ensure that obligations to society at large (e.g., patented products should be made available at affordable prices) and to certain social groups (e.g., stewards of biodiversity) will be met.

3. While each country has the sovereign right to establish its own patent and trademark laws, international agreements on intellectual property should also be established through bodies such as the World Intellectual Property Organization (WIPO) and the United Nations Conference on Trade and Development. Such agreements should facilitate the transfer of technology in order to reduce the

enormous gap in technical and scientific knowledge, and the gap in benefits derived thereof, between nations.

## Specific Objectives:

1. Exclude all life forms, including plant and animal species, biological and genetic material and processes and combinations thereof, including that derived from the human body, from patentability. Assert the primacy of international agreements on biodiversity over trade agreements such as the Trade-Related Intellectual Property (TRIPs) code under the WTO in disputes involving conflicts between biodiversity use and conservation and the interests of holders of patent privileges.

2. Require the owners of pharmaceutical patents to grant compulsory licenses to producers of generic medicines. Compulsory licensing does not abolish patent rights but it does oblige patent holders to allow others the right to produce copies in return for payment of royalties. (Generic medicines typically sell at lower prices than brand name pharmaceuticals.)

3. Protect the rights and livelihoods of farmers and communities (and especially indigenous communities) that act as the guardians of biodiversity. Support the Thammasat Resolution (signed in December 1997 by representatives of more than 40 NGOs) to reinforce "the defense mechanisms of local communities that are vulnerable to 'bio-prospecting' and to the introduction of genetically altered organisms." The term "bio-prospecting" refers to the practice of pharmaceutical firms sending scientists into natural habitats to gather samples for the purpose of testing to determine whether they have properties that may be patented for a profit.

4. Support the February 11, 1998 call by the Consultative Group for International Agricultural Research (CGIAR) for a moratorium on the patenting of all germplasm held by CGIAR research centers.

5. Support calls by local communities for a moratorium on bio-prospecting and encourage the development of national legislation to determine the terms of any bio-prospecting as local communities may decide to allow. Support the negotiation of the Convention on Biological Diversity's Protocol on Biosafety to require terms of liability and sanction for the illegal transboundary movement of genetically engineered organisms.

6. Defend indigenous peoples' rights in the face of genetic research that uses tissue, blood or DNA samples without their permission or knowledge of the purposes of the research, as well as appropriation of their craft designs and techniques.

7. Intellectual property related contracts that prohibit the saving of seed or allow the burning of crops as punishment for violating the terms of such contracts, should be superceded by "ordre public." This is an international law term that refers to the ability of governments to take measures for the general public benefit and public health considerations relating to food security.

8. Adopt specific measures to enhance the transfer of appropriate technology to less developed countries according to each country's development priorities. In particular, promote the sharing of energy-efficient and renewable technologies.

9. Ensure that copyright laws protect artists, writers, musicians, crafts producers, and other cultural workers and not just publishers and the motion picture and recording industries as occurs under NAFTA's Article 1705. Such protections would be of special value to indigenous and female crafts producers.

## X. SUSTAINABLE ENERGY DEVELOPMENT

### Background

International agreements can play an important role in making the transition from fossil fuels and nuclear energy to conservation and use of clean, renewable sources of energy. In addition to being indispensable for economic development, energy is vital for sustaining human life. Meeting essential human needs must be the central aim of an energy plan based on equity between peoples and generations.

### Guiding Principle:
Integrated Resource Planning

Integrated Resource Planning (IRP) allows for the best usage of the most appropriate form of energy taking into account social and environmental factors. IRP responds to several criteria, not just market costs, in deciding how to use resources. It makes room for renewable resources because it employs "full cost accounting," taking into account social and environmental costs when evaluating options. IRP includes energy-saving measures and energy efficiency planning as a way of minimizing new construction of generating facilities and use of raw materials. Demand management is an essential feature of IRP. Similarly, IRP requires public consultation as a prerequisite for building a social consensus for every stage of reorienting the energy market.

We propose that the principles of IRP be included in Inter-American integration agreements.

## Specific Objectives:

### *Hemispheric*

1. Make energy consumption and production sustainable, i.e., more efficient, renewable and clean and less carbon intensive;

2. Enhance access to affordable energy services to those who are without or are underserved;

3. Minimize society's energy costs by applying "life-cycle" accounting to a mix of resource and end use options. Life-cycle accounting incorporates the full environmental and social costs involved in the choice of a particular technology. Thus, for example, windpower still has a low life-cycle cost even after taking into account the initial cost of producing, transporting and constructing windmills.

### *National*

Energy policy decisions must be guided by credible mechanisms for evaluating environmental impacts and for public participation. In order to promote optimal use of resources from a social and environmental perspective, national public agencies should be established to oversee environmental assessments and efficient management of energy resources.

### *Supranational*

The right to pursue policies of national development and resource management must be coupled with collective responsibilities.

Thus, each country should have the right to manage its own renewable and non-renewable resources without being obliged to continue to export those resources even in times of national shortages (as currently is the case for Canada under NAFTA's proportional sharing clauses, Articles 315 and 605, but not for Mexico, which has an exemption).

At the same time, countries endowed with non-renewable hydrocarbon resources should minimize their exploitation, to avoid contributing to greenhouse gas emissions causing global climate change and depleting the resource base for future generations. Governments should also support a moratorium on exploration in new areas for coal, natural gas and oil as a step towards the transition to clean and renewable energy sources.

An international agreement should allow members to make complaints against countries that try to achieve commercial advantage at the expense of sustainability. National and International agencies should co-operate to:

1. create regulatory incentives for investment in energy efficiency and renewable energy;

2. eliminate pricing and regulatory policies which subsidize or encourage increased sales, consumption and use of fossil fuels;

3. create an Energy Efficient and Renewable Technologies Consortium to promote such technologies.

## XI. AGRICULTURE

### Background

The pursuance of trade and investment liberalization within the FTAA process is likely to cause serious social and economic problems for the agricultural sector. Likely consequences include the acceleration of migration from rural to urban areas and the growth of poverty zones and increased marginalization both within cities and within rural regions, creating more pressure on local governments for basic services. In several countries, large corporations are pressing for the sale of agricultural land to be converted into forestry plantations, resulting in a decrease in agricultural employment and the loss of basic agricultural capital. These phenomena would make our countries' food security increasingly dependent on volatile international market prices.

In light of these threats, agriculture should be given special treatment in trade and investment liberalization agreements, rather than being considered an economic sector like any other. Agriculture is a sector which fulfils a series of essential functions for the stability and security of nations: to preserve the cultural richness and multi-ethnicity of societies, to preserve bio-diversity, to generate employment and sustainability (as much in agriculture as in related economic activities), to maintain the population of rural areas, to ensure basic food security and to contribute to a sustainable development with more economic, social and political stability.

Therefore, to respond to the impacts of hemispheric integration, the development of a long-term rural development strategy and the adoption of an integrated agricultural policy within the FTAA are urgently needed.

# X. General Proposals

## Guiding Principles:

1. Countries should assume the responsibility to ensure food security. In the negotiation of international trade agreements, they should have the right to protect or exclude foods, such as corn, which form the basic diet of their people.

2. Almost everywhere in the Americas, agricultural markets are open to increased national and global economic exchange, resulting in an even further concentration of land ownership in the hands of a small number of persons or companies. This opening is one of the main causes of migration to large urban centers. An agrarian reform is needed that legitimizes property rights of small producers, including women, and landless rural workers. In particular the traditional rights of indigenous peoples to live off their ancestral lands must be respected.

3. Governments should address the particular environmental and economic issues associated with the agroforestry sector. While recognizing the different levels of development among the nations of the Americas, governments should establish the necessary incentives to allow for secure and sustained advancement towards sustainable agroforestry development.

4. Countries should work to strengthen the organization of its rural sector to ensure that this population is duly represented, both in its relations with the state and with the market. For example, small-scale farmers and their organizations, who have been previously excluded, should be allowed to play an active role in trade negotiations. This ongoing process of modernization of the rural sector must take into consideration the most vulnerable sectors of the society and safeguards should be adopted to protect cultural minorities and social groups that do not have the means to adequately and efficiently integrate into the market.

5. In order for integration to take place in a state of equal conditions, an efficient state which defines policies and generates options that guarantee equity and transparency, is necessary. Support for family enterprises and co-operatives engaged in processing commodities produced by small-scale farmers is a part of this challenge. Governments should also recognize that small-scale farming requires special policies concerning land conservation, appropriate technology (including biotechnology), agricultural research, credit and subsidies.

6. In addition to the large differences in levels of agricultural development that exist among the hemisphere's diverse countries, there are huge differences in the amount of subsidies and other assistance that governments give to agriculture. Therefore, any trade liberalization agreement for agriculture must include concrete measures for the upward harmonization of financial assistance for agriculture with the eventual goal of spending similar amounts expressed as a percentage of GDP.

7. The insertion of a country in the global economy requires the modernization of its agricultural productive capacity, management skills, distribution and commercialization networks, technological innovation and scientific research, and the handling of information.

8. Laws and regulations designed to guarantee sanitary and phytosanitary standards to ensure high quality produce and protection for consumers and the environment should be arrived at through wide consultation with citizens. These standards need to take into account the diversity of different countries' national capacity and establish realistic schedules for their upward harmonization.

9. Agricultural laborers are frequently subjected to abuses and injustices. The main demands of the labor movement as well as of the campesino organizations of the hemisphere are the following:

   a) Guarantee the protection of trade union freedoms that allow for the constitution of a union structure in the rural sector.

   b) The promotion of norms that allow the negotiation of wages and other working conditions, through an efficient system of collective bargaining.

   c) The recognition of the needs of women in waged and unwaged work, taking into consideration the unequal share of responsibility assigned to most women for child-rearing, care for family members, and domestic labor.

   d) The consideration of specific health and safety standards linked, for instance, to the effects of chemicals on campesino workers.

10. Sustainable development and the protection of the environment can only be promoted through the best use possible of natural resources and through a proper monitoring of productive activities, especially of those activities that have a significant impact. In this regard, the pursuance of agrarian reform is indispensable, and the demand in favor of agrarian reform in Latin America and in the Caribbean should receive the broadest support.

## XII. ACCESS TO MARKETS AND RULES OF ORIGIN

### Background

The goal of the recent wave of free trade agreements has been the reciprocal lifting of trade barriers among nations, regardless of the countries' level of development or particular national interests. The dominant principle of these deals has been the concept of "national treatment," which means that governments should be required to treat foreign investors, investments, and products the same as their national counterparts. This chapter, while not criticizing international trade, argues that trade liberalization should not be an end in itself for which everything else must be sacrificed. Instead, market access for foreign products and investments should be evaluated and defined within the framework of national development plans.

### Guiding Principles:

The complex process of reconciling national development plans with international trade rules should take the following matters into account:

1. The differing levels of development among countries are a justification for allowing non-reciprocal and preferential treatment in market access. Articles 2, 4, 17 and 18 of the United Nations Charter of Economic Rights and Duties of States (1974) establish the legal and socio-economic bases for demanding equitable (not equal) treatment. Equal treatment among unequals leads to inequality.

2. A development strategy should be multifaceted and must not treat the external market as the only influence over demand. Domestic markets must be appropriately valued for their role in generating a "virtuous cycle" of raising the population's standard of living and increasing economic growth. By linking economic development to per capita consumption, standard of living for the majority inevitably rises. Fighting poverty and the pursuit of social justice cease to be just ethical demands; they become levers for development.

3. When internal markets are strong and economic activity is not dependent solely on external markets, the conditions exist for negotiating an opening to external trade without adopting a stance of appeasement.

4. Permanent and predictable access to foreign markets is important for advancing growth of productive capacity and securing a healthy balance of payments. That is, necessary imports are financed through a strong and competitive export sector. However, market action only works to eliminate non-competitive producers; trade liberalization does not itself create a strong and competitive productive capacity. Development and competitiveness require concrete policies with clear objectives, goals and instruments. States have a responsibility to meet this challenge. Agreements must not impair the ability of states to set policy for the promotion and even the protection of certain strategic industries to achieve just and sustainable national development.

5. At the present time, the fundamental obstacles to access to developed countries' markets are not tariff barriers but so-called "technical barriers to trade." Trade negotiations should address this issue.

6. The goal of negotiations should be to establish clear and fair rules for permanent and predictable access to markets which benefits consumers, creates jobs and well-being for the population, strengthens productive capacity and protects the environment.

### Specific Objectives:

*Tariffs*

1. Producers and society in general should agree on a transparent and widely participatory process for establishing a timetable and choosing products to be subject to lower duties.

2. Internal timetables for trade liberalization and tariff reduction should be accompanied by coordinated programs to ensure that national industries become competitive during the transition. These programs should include access to consultants and training, technological research and development and long-term credit. Sectoral programs should be accompanied by a national development plan including commitments from the state to create the macro-economic conditions that enhance competitiveness. For developing countries, trade liberalization without an industrial policy is suicidal.

3. An even-handed tariff policy must be implemented to ensure linkage between productive sectors so that no sector is disadvantaged. This could occur if tariffs on an end product were eliminated without a corresponding reduction of duties on imports of its intermediate inputs.

4. The right to impose clear, transparent and agreed-upon performance requirements in conjunction with programs of tariff reduction must be preserved.

# X. GENERAL PROPOSALS

## Non-Tariff Barriers and Standards

1. Non-tariff barriers increasingly take the form of standards of various kinds: quality standards, processing standards, fulfillment of phyto-sanitary specifications (relating to the absence of agents of infection or disease in plants), certificates of origin, organic product standards (e.g., certification of production without toxics or chemical fertilizers), environmental standards, and labor standards, including minimum wage, prohibition of child and forced labor.

These standards, necessary to ensure that such matters as quality, health and environmental protection and workers' rights are taken into account, have also been used as hidden obstacles to the free flow of trade from developing to developed countries. They are imposed unilaterally, and may reflect the interests of corporations and their lobbyists to get governments to impose protectionist sanctions on foreign goods and/or services.

The challenge then is to eliminate bias and arbitrariness from the imposition of such standards to ensure they reflect legitimate interests and are not hidden protectionist measures to benefit specific companies.

2. Laws, regulations, guidelines and standards for guaranteeing the quality of goods and services for consumer and environmental protection should be arrived at through broad public consultation. They should take into account the range of conditions prevailing in different countries and include realistic timetables. They should be written into wide-ranging agreements on scientific and technical cooperation and industrial development. These agreements, reinforced by adequate resources and specific sectoral accords, should raise standards by international consensus, especially for developing countries and for socially owned enterprises (such as cooperatives) and micro, small, and medium enterprises.

These provisions should require multinational corporations to meet the highest standards to prevent the sale of products banned in that company's own country in countries with lower standards or lax enforcement. Only through broad and democratic processes of consultation and negotiation can consumer interests for high standards health and environmental protections be met and unilateral, illegal and covert protectionist measures avoided.

## Customs Procedures

1. Customs procedures should be harmonized while they are modernized to reduce bureaucracy and simplify procedures. Assistance should be given to the social sector and micro, small and medium producers and entrepreneurs who engage in foreign trade.

2. Customs valuation procedures should be linked to and integrated with those used for evaluating dumping and subsidy cases, the suppression of fraud, information gathering systems and dispute resolution mechanisms.

## Rules of Origin

Rules of origin are the criteria by which products come to be considered to be originating in a given place, which then affects their treatment in cross-border exchange under free trade agreements. The trend in such agreements is to establish regional rules of origin specifying a percentage of components or inputs to be included in order to qualify for designation of origin. While we do not exclude additional regional or sub-regional content requirements within the hemisphere, our view is that countries should be able to establish national content rules if the country feels that national economic development requires such designation. This demand or principle complements other proposals in Chapter 7 regarding the requirement for foreign companies to source a percentage of inputs in the country of production.

Countries may deem that, without national content rules, trade liberalization only benefits intra-firm integration and leads to the disintegration of national productive linkages. Lacking incentives to purchase production inputs within the country of production, large export companies revert to imports, which eliminates spin-off economic growth, despite increasing production. The neoliberal model assumes that the export sector is the engine of economic growth. In practice, this "engine" becomes disconnected from the rest of the train. Rules of origin that only require regional content transform the productive apparatus of many Southern countries into maquiladoras or export processing zones.

## XIII. ENFORCEMENT AND DISPUTE RESOLUTION

### Background

The rules and standards proposed in this document govern the conduct of nations, companies and individuals doing business in the hemisphere. They include specific regulations for investors and financial institutions; they ensure standards of environmental quality and the use of energy and natural resources; they specify the rights of workers, women, indigenous peoples, Black peoples and basic human rights of all peoples.

To make these rules and standards meaningful, it is critical that agreements include strong mechanisms for dispute resolution and rules enforcement. However, the development of such mechanisms raises complex issues. Hence, the formulation of such mechanisms must involve a process beyond the scope of the present document. To finalize such machinery will require continued multinational discussions. The present chapter is intended to be a starting point for such discussions. It includes some general principles discussed at the Peoples' Summit that serve as the foundation for future discussions leading to more specific rules and enforcement machinery.[1] These principles reflect the consensus that dispute resolution and enforcement mechanisms should be focused on reducing inequalities and based on fair and democratic processes. The chapter also raises the issue of whether agreements should include special safeguards for countries suffering as the result of surges in imports.

## Overarching Principle:

Labor and human rights and environmental quality controls cannot simply be tacked on to economic agreements through weak side agreements or simply through the addition of a social clause. They must be integral to the agreements themselves.

## INTERNATIONAL EQUITY ISSUES

### Guiding Principles:

The key objective of enforcement and the use of the rules discussed in this document should be to lessen development gaps among nations through a process in which all standards are harmonized upwards. Such a process must consider different levels of development in establishing the following:

- terms for the use of safeguards or other emergency measures;
- rules regarding the application of capital controls, performance standards and intellectual property rights limitations; and
- timelines for implementing rules and standards proposed in this document.

Less developed nations should not necessarily be held to the same standards as more developed nations, as long as their actions reduce asymmetries between nations.

## Specific Objectives:

- In terms of standards, there are some basic rights that can be universally defined and do not vary with levels of development. International Labour Organization (ILO) rules that give such status to freedom of association is an example. An initial task would be to identify all of the standards and rules we address in this document that can be considered to be universally defined human rights.

- Other standards such as minimum wages may vary with levels of development. A second task would be to identify such standards in general terms and define them in such a way that they can have region-wide applicability. For example it would be possible to define minimum wage standards in terms of what is required to avoid poverty—"a living wage." The specific amount will then vary from one nation to another.

- In some instances, the development process itself may cause hardships due to dislocations as resources are re-allocated and people lose jobs. In such cases, development through economic integration must be accompanied by compensation mechanisms for the losers. Thus part of the process of constructing an agreement for hemispheric development must include the establishment of mechanisms for adjustment assistance. In more developed nations, adjustment may come from general tax revenues, but for less developed nations a multinational adjustment institution will be required.

- Specific measures must be developed to prevent safeguard rules from being applied to the detriment of other nations. Safeguards or "escape clauses" are designed to allow countries to obtain relief when a surge of imports reduces output, employment or otherwise causes injury to a domestic industry. These rules allow countries to temporarily restrict imports to provide relief to domestic industries which are suffering as a result of import surges. However, it is important to deter the use of emergency measures by developed nations in ways that run counter to the objective of reducing development gaps in the hemisphere.

- Finally, nations without resources to enforce rules should be provided with funds for this purpose. Such funding can be implemented through the same mechanism developed for dislocation compensation.

# X. GENERAL PROPOSALS

## ENFORCEMENT AND PENALTIES

### Guiding Principles:

A critical aspect of the process of enforcement and the imposition of penalties for non-compliance is to institute a democratic and open process. Specific measures must be developed to ensure transparency and proper representation for civil society.

## SOME KEY ISSUES:

- One issue is the locale of adjudication. In general, this process should be the province of national governments and proceed to international arbitration only after recourse to national processes has been exhausted. Further dialogue is needed to determine the composition of the international forum.

- This raises the issue of representativeness which also presents some difficulties. Corporations and organized labor have well-established organizations through which representatives can be appointed or elected. But there are no comparable entities that can represent all environmental organizations or the spectrum of other NGOs with a stake in this process. Therefore some effort must be made to develop representative institutions for various interests.

### Specific Objectives:

- Compliance with the rules and standards agreed upon should be a pre-condition for participation on the part of both governments and corporations in any hemispheric agreement. There is thus a need to review the laws and practices of nations prior to membership. The review can be conducted by a multi-national panel of experts followed by open public hearings and discussions on recommendations. Governments that are not in compliance with the agreement should be put on a probationary status and a plan for compliance should be developed.

- There will also need to be ongoing audits of companies who operate within the hemisphere and thus enjoy the fruits of the agreement. Similarly, there must be a mechanism for responding to complaints about corporate conduct. Each government should have primary responsibility for the audits and response to complaints. But a hemispheric funding mechanism must be created for this purpose.

- All processes involving enforcement must be fully transparent. That includes a written public record of all proceedings and open hearings. There also needs to be a clear appeals process. Also this agreement must give standing to all stakeholders for participation in the process. Governments (including local governments), labor organizations, and NGOs should all have standing to bring complaints if they feel that they have an interest in the outcome of deliberations at both national and multi-national levels.

- Penalties for non-compliance should be imposed on both governments and companies. Prior to the imposition of such penalties, adequate notice should be given to provide opportunity for response and/or compliance. There should be stiff penalties available that can be directed at corporations and enforced by national governments.

## CONCLUSION

This document aims to lay the foundation for a social alliance that spans borders and unites us around the specific concerns of all of civil society. In contrast to the rules and standards embedded in NAFTA and the proposed FTAA, which benefit the few at the expense of most of us, our proposed rules and standards would enhance the every-day life of our citizens.

Of course, this is not a finished product. Much additional work is needed to disseminate, debate and educate around these points in order to reach consensus and create a solid basis for a hemispheric social alliance. We hope that this paper will serve as a basis for developing materials more oriented toward popular education work with various social sectors in our countries. Any interested organization should use it freely and creatively. Only through free and open debate can a true consensus be reached around serious, viable proposals for a sustainable continent and the well-being of our peoples.

## SUBMITTING COMMENTS

This is a living document that will be updated and distributed from time to time with everyone's additions.

*Comments can be addressed to:*

via email: ecoalt@web.net

via postal service: Common Frontiers, 15 Gervais Drive, Suite 305, Don Mills, Ontario, MDC-1Y8, Canada

via fax: 416/441-4073 (attention: Patty)

## SPONSORING ORGANIZATIONS:

ALLIANCE FOR RESPONSIBLE TRADE
c/o Development GAP
927 15th St. NW, 4th floor
Washington, DC 20005, USA
ph: 202/898-1566
fax: 202/898-1612
email: dgap@igc.org
Contact: Karen Hansen-Kuhn

COMMON FRONTIERS
15 Gervais Dr. Suite 305
Don Mills, Ontario, M3C 1Y8, Canada
ph: 416-443-9244
fax: 416-441-4073
email: comfront@web.net
Contact: Patty C. Barrera

RECHIP
Seminario 774, Nunoa
Santiago, 6841232, Chile
ph: 56-2-364-1738
fax: 56-2-364-1739
email: rechip@reuna.cl
Contact: Coral Pey

RMALC
Godard 20, Col. Guadalupe Victoria
CP. 07790, Mexico, D.F.
ph/fax: 52-5-355-1177
email: rmalc@laneta.apc.org
Contact: Sylvia Sandoval

RQIC
c/o Alternatives
3680 Rue Jeanne-Mance, 4e etage
Montreal P.Q, H2X-2K5, Canada
ph: 514-982-6606 ext:2243
fax: 514-982-6122
email: marcela@alternatives-action.org,
Contact: Marcela Escribano

# XI. Post-Santiago Evaluations

# XI. POST-SANTIAGO EVALUATIONS

*The Leadership Council for Inter-American Summitry, established in 1997, is an independent, non-partisan initiative composed of citizens from throughout the Americas working in private business, legislatures, academia, public policy institutes, the scientific community, and other civic organizations.*

*Project Directors are Richard E. Feinberg, Professor of International Political Economy and Director, APEC Study Center, University of California, San Diego, and Robin L. Rosenberg, Deputy Director, North-South Center, University of Miami.*

## Mastering Summitry:
### An Evaluation of the Santiago Summit of the Americas and Its Aftermath, Policy Report II

*March 1999*
*Leadership Council for Inter-American Summitry*

### PREFACE AND ACKNOWLEDGMENTS

This is the second Report of the Leadership Council for Inter-American Summitry. The Leadership Council issued its first Report, *From Talk to Action: How Summits Can Help Forge a Western Hemisphere Community of Prosperous Democracies,* just prior to the Second Summit of the Americas, held in Santiago, Chile, in April 1998. This second Report is intended to serve three purposes. First, it provides a critical account of what transpired at the Santiago Summit and compares and contrasts official actions with the recommendations made by the Leadership Council in its own pre-Summit Report. Second, it chronicles the actions taken — and not taken — in subsequent months to follow up on Summit initiatives. In this regard, the Report fills a void in public information. Third, the Leadership Council offers its appraisal of the current state of summitry in the Americas and offers recommendations for its improvement.

The work of the Leadership Council has been informed by two series of detailed working papers that surveyed implementation of the key initiatives of the Miami *Plan of Action* and by post-Santiago updates. We wish to thank those authors (acknowledged by name in section VIII) without whose efforts this Report would not have been possible. This project has been directed by Richard E. Feinberg and Robin L. Rosenberg, who attended both the Miami and Santiago Summits. The Ford Foundation has been generous in its support.

The members of the Leadership Council wholeheartedly endorse this report's overall content and tone and support its principal recommendations, even as each member may not agree fully with every phrase. Members subscribe as individuals; institutional affiliations are for purposes of identification only.

*Richard E. Feinberg*
*Professor of International Political Economy and Director,*
*APEC Study Center, University of California, San Diego*

*C. Fred Bergsten*
*Director, Institute for International Economics*

*Ambler H. Moss, Jr., Director*
*Dante B. Fascell North-South Center*
*University of Miami*

© *1999 University of Miami.*
*Published by the*
*University of Miami*
*North-South Center Press.*

## MISSION STATEMENT OF THE LEADERSHIP COUNCIL FOR INTER-AMERICAN SUMMITRY

The Leadership Council for Inter-American Summitry, established in 1997, is an independent, non-partisan initiative composed of citizens from throughout the Americas working in private business, legislatures, academia, public policy institutes, the scientific community, and other civic organizations. While many members have held high public office, none is currently employed in the executive branch of government. The Leadership Council is united in its aim to strengthen the forces fighting for effective democratic governance, market-oriented economic reforms, and social justice. These same goals are embedded in the declarations issued at the 1994 Summit of the Americas in Miami. The Leadership Council believes that periodic summits that gather the Western Hemisphere's heads of state and government can make a significant contribution toward achieving these goals but that significant reforms are required in the summitry process if its promise is to be fully realized.

The Leadership Council seeks to serve as a bridge between experts outside the executive branch of governments and the officials who organize the summits, between organized civil society and the public sector, and, in the spirit of inter-American summitry, between the northern industrialized nations and the southern developing nations of the region. The Council's membership includes individuals active in the civil society of their nations, as well as individuals with extensive experience at senior levels of government and in summit meetings in the Americas, the Asia Pacific region, and the industrialized world.

## EXECUTIVE SUMMARY

This second Report of the Leadership Council for Inter-American Summitry is intended to serve three purposes. First, it provides a critical account of what transpired at the Santiago Summit in April 1998 and compares and contrasts official actions with the recommendations made by the Leadership Council in its own pre-Summit Report. Second, it chronicles the actions taken — and not taken — since Santiago to follow up on Summit initiatives. Third, the Leadership Council offers recommendations for the improvement of summitry in the Americas.

## The Santiago Summit: An Evaluation

The first Leadership Council Report, *From Talk to Action,* offered a series of substantive and process recommendations for adoption at the Second Summit of the Americas. Of the eight substantive recommendations, the Santiago Summit followed two substantially (poverty and education); three partially (civil society, free trade, and institutional strengthening); and three weakly (corruption, environment, and finance). Of the process recommendations, the leaders at Santiago accepted two substantially (appointment of senior government coordinators and summit institutionalization); four partially (resources, functional networks, civil society participation, and monitoring responsibilities); and one weakly (targets and timetables). All in all, real progress was achieved in many respects; however, disappointments were also significant.

## Reverses and Advances Since Santiago

In the months since Santiago, there has been a notable, perhaps inevitable decline in senior-level focus on summitry in the Americas. Notwithstanding this generalized dip in energy, activity is proceeding. Among functional ministries, follow-up meetings are taking place throughout the hemisphere. In Washington, the outlines of a fortified implementation architecture are beginning to take shape. Some of the more noteworthy post-Santiago developments in summitry include:

**Trade:** Santiago officially launched negotiations toward the Free Trade Area of the Americas (FTAA). Nine negotiating groups held their first round of meetings in Miami in September 1998 to kick off what will be on-going meetings preparatory to the October 1999 ministerial in Canada.

**Finance:** The ministers of finance have not seen fit to accelerate the date for their next meeting, scheduled for Mexico in mid-1999. Vice ministers, however, have been meeting twice annually, and have built a "club" of officials whose personal ties facilitate the handling of crises as they arise.

**Corruption:** There is little evidence of implementation of the Inter-American Convention Against Corruption. However, the Organization of American States (OAS) and the Inter-American Development Bank (IDB) have begun to hold workshops to encourage ratification by more governments. Transparency International is planning to erect a monitoring system to track implementation of the Convention.

**Education:** Education was a centerpiece in Santiago; the World Bank, IDB, and U.S. Agency for International Development (USAID) pledged more than $8 billion over three years. Some of these projects are proceeding; however, so far the effort to transform the generalities of the Santiago *Plan of Action* into a concrete work plan have not prospered.

**Human Rights:** The Inter-American Human Rights Commission named its first Special Rapporteur on Freedom of Expression. USAID funded the new position.

**Women's Rights:** The IDB and U.S. government sponsored a well-attended "Vital Voices" conference in Montevideo, and the First Ladies of the Americas held a successful annual conference in Santiago.

**Health Technologies:** Health ministers advanced two Summit initiatives: the use of vaccines and the strengthening of epidemiological surveillance systems.

**Administrative Infrastructure:** The OAS created the Office of Summit Follow-Up to serve as the institutional memory for inter-American summitry and to provide technical support to the Summit Implementation Review Group (SIRG).

## Recommendations for More Effective Summitry

The Santiago Summit built on the lessons of the Miami process, but there is still a long way to go before summitry in the Americas fulfills its promise. In this spirit of continual summitry, the Leadership Council offers these recommendations:

1. The vision of the Free Trade Area of the Americas should be pursued even if the 1999 World Trade Organization (WTO) Ministerial charts an agenda that might accomplish some of the FTAA's economic objectives. In preparing the third Summit, Canada should take the lead in building a hemispheric consensus for a "democracy clause" that would circumscribe participation in the FTAA to democratically elected governments.

2. A ministerial-level Inter-American Financial Council should be formed to improve regional economic cooperation. The Financial Council would have more structure and influence than the current occasional meetings of regional finance ministers.

3. To spur ratification of the Inter-American Convention Against Corruption, the OAS should set target dates for ratification and entry into force. A new OAS mechanism should transform the Convention into a work plan, set priority goals, and issue an annual progress report.

4. The ministers of education should establish a series of issue-specific working groups that set concrete goals and that establish and publish useful monitoring guidelines with comparative data on each country's progress.

5. Canada should reassert the importance of the involvement of the private sector and civil society in summitry. Canada can set an example by involving its own civil society in preparations for the third Summit of the Americas.

6. The OAS's promising new Office of Summit Follow-Up should direct its network of staff experts to identify points of contact within national ministries, to complete standardized reports, and to publish them as a way to spur progress toward Summit goals.

7. The Troika (Canada, Chile, and the United States) and the OAS's Office of Summit Follow-Up should form a Summit Coordinating Committee (SCC) to coordinate overall Summit implementation. It might be appropriate for the World Bank and IDB to join the SCC, thereby bringing the key official actors together under a single umbrella.

8. Summit administrators should devise mechanisms to combat issue compartmentalization.

9. Canada should set a date for the Third Summit of the Americas without delay. A visible end-date prompts bureaucracies to fulfill mandates. The proposed SCC should develop a list of summit-approved items that can be completed by the third summit. Such an "early harvest" could include concrete progress toward the FTAA, agreement on a multilateral evaluation mechanism for counternarcotics efforts, entry into force of the Convention Against Corruption, agreement on the design and financial plan for a judicial studies center, and establishment of monitoring systems on key goals mandated on education and health.

## POLICY REPORT II
## I. INTRODUCTION:
## THE HEMISPHERE SINCE SANTIAGO

Since the Second Summit of the Americas in Santiago, Chile, on April 18-19, 1998, the Western Hemisphere has experienced serious shocks and has realized some worthy accomplishments. Peru and Ecuador delivered very good news when these traditionally rival states announced that their long-standing border dispute would be resolved peacefully through the mediation of other hemispheric nations. Recall that an outbreak of fighting between the two Andean nations in January 1995 had jarred the fresh "spirit of Miami," ignited at the First Summit of the Americas in December 1994.

In November 1998, the hemisphere confronted a very different threat: To prevent further infection of the Western Hemisphere by the Asian financial flu, Brazil sought the cooperation of the United States and the International Monetary Fund, who together mounted a massive $41.5 billion balance of payments package to try to stabilize Brazil's economy. Whereas on trade issues, Brazil and the United States were often on the opposite sides of the bargaining table, in this battle to protect the hemisphere from financial contagion, the region's two great democracies joined forces to defend their mutual interests.

Relations between the United States and Colombia improved markedly with the election in July 1998 of Andrés Pastrana, and the two nations announced agreement on a common approach to fighting narcotics traffickers. This entente removed a node of tension in hemispheric relations and renders progress on the Hemispheric Anti-Drug Strategy more feasible.

The most severe negative shock came in late October 1998, when Hurricane Mitch devastated Central America. The United States, Mexico, and other hemispheric countries rushed assistance to the storm-drenched region. Those same military bases that had funneled weapons into the civil wars of the 1980s now served to channel humanitarian aid. Paradoxically, the havoc wreaked by nature's destructive force created new conditions for hemispheric cooperation.

Obviously, none of these four events can be attributed primarily to the process of summitry in the Americas. Certainly neither the Central American calamity nor the Brazilian financial crisis were predicted in Santiago. Yet, the positive actions taken in response to these four problems were fully consistent with the spirit of summitry and its emergent hemispheric community of democracies. Summits and related ministerial meetings have contributed to an atmosphere of cooperation and have forged networks of working relationships that facilitated these affirmative responses to specific problems. Summit leaders noted that regional trade integration presupposed peaceful relations among nations and the resolution of outstanding controversies over boundaries. Summit leaders and related meetings of finance ministers have underscored the value of common action to stabilize capital flows. And Summit leaders have consistently sought common ground in the struggle against illegal narcotics.

At the next summit of the Americas in Canada in 2001, it will be perfectly appropriate for leaders to recall these four episodes of hemispheric cooperation and claim them as being fully in the spirit of hemispheric summitry and solidarity. In the face of unexpected shocks, the signals sent in Miami and Santiago helped guide decisionmakers and keep the hemisphere on the right track.

## II. THE SANTIAGO SUMMIT:
## AN EVALUATION

The first Report of The Leadership Council for Inter-American Summitry, *From Talk to Action: How Summits Can Help Forge a Western Hemisphere Community of Prosperous Democracies* — issued on the eve of the Santiago Summit — affirmed that summits can make a difference in the lives of the peoples of the Americas. As the Summit of the Americas in Miami in December 1994 demonstrated, summits can create a political process whereby the hemisphere can agree upon shared values and a common agenda, summits can codify norms and rules to guide the behavior of governments and civil society, and summits can place new issues on the international agenda and catalyze collective action behind consensus goals.

At the same time, The Leadership Council found that progress on key initiatives agreed upon in Miami was "on average modest" and that progress had fallen short of the promise of Miami. The Leadership Council pointed to a number of flaws in the Summit process. There were far too many initiatives and action items. Some initiatives lacked the essential elements of good public policy — measurable goals, timetables, priorities, and accountability. Leaders failed to allocate sufficient technical and financial resources for some initiatives. Many governments did not have the requisite institutional and financial capacities to carry out some of the action items. The regional organizations, notably the Organization of American States (OAS) and the Inter-American Development Bank (IDB), sought to implement some initiatives but allowed other mandates to slip. Monitoring mechanisms and compliance regimes were weak to nonexistent.

# XI. Post-Santiago Evaluations

## Chart I. Evaluation of Santiago Summit, Substantive Agenda

| Eight Challenges | Substantially | Partially | Weakly |
|---|---|---|---|
| *Centerpiece:* Creation of Inter-American Commission on Corruption | | | ✔ |
| Weakness of Civil Society | | ✔ | |
| Persistent Poverty and Worsening Inequality | ✔ | | |
| Failing Schools | ✔ | | |
| Environmental Degradation | | | ✔ |
| *Centerpiece:* Acceleration to 2002 for completion of FTAA process with participation open to democratic nations | | ✔ | |
| *Centerpiece:* Formation of an Inter-American Financial Council | | | ✔ |
| Insufficiency of Inter-American Institutions | | ✔ | |

*Policy Report Recommendations Followed*

## Chart II: Evaluation of Santiago Summit, Process Agenda

| Process Items | Substantially | Partially | Weakly |
|---|---|---|---|
| Initiatives should be responsibly crafted to contain practical goals, quantifiable targets, and realistic timetables. | | | ✔ |
| Initiatives should be assigned to mechanisms with adequate technical and financial resources with authority to mobilize them. | | ✔ | |
| Governments should appoint a senior official to coordinate Summit planning and implementation. | ✔ | | |
| Networks of functional ministries should be solidified. | | ✔ | |
| Participation of the private sector and other non-governmental organizations should be regularized. | | ✔ | |
| Monitoring responsibilities should be assigned for each initiative to an official regional mechanism with adequate capacity. | | ✔ | |
| *Centerpiece:* Institutionalization of the Summit Process. Summits should be institutionalized (every 2 years). | ✔ | | |

*Policy Report Recommendations Followed*

The Leadership Council Report, *From Talk to Action,* offered a series of substantive and process recommendations for adoption at the Second Summit of the Americas, convened in April 1998. Chart I evaluates the Santiago Summit's *Plan of Action* in light of the Leadership Council's Report. The chart is not meant to imply causality, although members of the Leadership Council personally presented their Report to heads of state and other senior officials and circulated the Report widely around the region. Of the eight substantive recommendations, the Santiago Summit followed two substantially (poverty and education); three partially (civil society, free trade, and institutional strengthening); and three weakly (corruption, environment, and finance). Of the process recommendations, the leaders at Santiago accepted two substantially (appointment of senior government coordinators and Summit institutionalization); four partially (resources, functional networks, civil society participation, and monitoring responsibilities); and one weakly (targets and timetables). All in all, while the Leadership Council went further in some areas than governments felt comfortable with in Santiago, real progress was achieved in many respects. Disappointments were also significant, however.

Specifically, the March 1998 Leadership Council Report proposed four centerpiece initiatives for Santiago:

1. The Leadership Council urged the heads of state to accelerate to 2002 the completion of negotiations for the Free Trade Area of the Americas. This proposal was intended to nudge leaders to bolder action, and the Council was not surprised when domestic opposition to trade liberalization in the United States and Brazil prevailed to force a slower pace. Nevertheless, Santiago did formally launch negotiations toward the FTAA, and trade ministers (in the San José Ministerial Declaration of March 1998) established an elaborate architecture for talks, replete with nine negotiating groups, a calendar for vice ministerial and ministerial meetings, and a sequence of venues and chairs, all to culminate in a final round of negotiations co-chaired by the two hemispheric heavyweights, the United States and Brazil.

In the spirit of the Leadership Council emphasis on institution-building, the Santiago Summit instructed the IDB to allocate resources to the Tripartite Committee (consisting of the IDB, the OAS, and the UN Commission for Latin America and the Caribbean [ECLAC]). Robert Devlin at the IDB, José Manuel Salazar at the OAS, and Inés Bustillo (who replaced the dedicated Isaac Cohen) at ECLAC bring strong leadership to the Tripartite Committee, which will serve as a technical secretariat for the FTAA negotiations.

Santiago did not announce that only democratic nations will be welcome to participate in the FTAA, as the Leadership Council had urged. Some governments argued this linkage was already implicit in the democratic spirit of the summits and in the exclusion of authoritarian Cuba. Several governments said they would favor such a formal democracy clause if it were proposed and suggested that the third Summit of the Americas in Canada may offer a propitious moment to make this linkage explicit.

2. As a response to the Asian financial crisis, the Leadership Council urged the formation of a ministerial-level Inter-American Financial Council to improve regional economic cooperation and enhance market confidence. Instead, the Santiago Summit largely ignored the global financial turbulence, although it did note ongoing work to strengthen domestic banking supervision, within the Miami-created Committee on Hemispheric Financial Issues (CHFI). Following the collapse of the Russian ruble, in early September 1998, the IMF convened a meeting with ministers of finance and central bank governors from 11 Latin American countries that have the greatest interaction with international financial markets and released a communiqué drawing attention to the region's generally sound macroeconomic policies. Several Latin American financial ministries and central banks are participating in the so-called Willard Group of 22 countries studying the architecture of the international financial system. But an opportunity was lost in Santiago for the hemisphere to get ahead of the curve: to advocate domestic reform measures to reassure investors, to distinguish the region and individual countries from unreliable financial markets elsewhere, and jointly to advocate reforms to inject more stability into international markets.

One explanation for Santiago's lack of focus on financial market turbulence was the preference among ministries of finance to remain apart from the centrality of the Summit process. Treasuries typically view the summits as overly dominated by foreign ministries and presidencies and seek to maintain their relative autonomy. Few finance ministers made an appearance at Santiago.

3. To spur implementation of the historic Convention Against Corruption — a major outcome of Miami — the Leadership Council proposed formation of an Inter-American Commission on Corruption. This Commission could monitor implementation of prior goals, issue periodic reports on country compliance, circulate model legislation, and help to coordinate technical assistance. However, in Santiago the corruption issue was given less salience than in Miami. Modestly, Santiago asked the

# XI. POST-SANTIAGO EVALUATIONS

OAS to hold workshops to disseminate the Convention's key provisions. Summit leaders did ask Chile to sponsor a symposium later in 1998 "to consider the scope of the Inter-American Convention against Corruption, and [its] implementation"; disappointingly, the symposium turned out to be more an information exchange among technicians than an agenda-setting event.

4. The pre-summit Leadership Council Report urged the institutionalization of summitry through biannual summits and a summit secretariat. Significantly, at Santiago the heads of state determined to meet "periodically," and it was announced that Canada would host the third hemispheric summit. The summiteers did not set an exact date, but it was widely expected to be in two to three years, in 2000 or 2001.

The Summit stopped short of establishing a full-fledged summit secretariat. The functions of the administrative bodies it did create were left somewhat vague, and the relations among them ambiguous. Nevertheless, significant steps were taken toward giving summitry in the Americas the administrative infrastructure it will need if the words of Summit texts are to be converted into on-the-ground realities. Two mechanisms that grew up spontaneously after Miami were given formal blessing. First, Santiago formalized the Summit Implementation Review Group (SIRG). Meetings are to be held two to three times a year, including mostly mid-level foreign ministry officials who will receive reports from countries (Responsible Coordinators) that have the lead in implementing Summit initiatives. To chair the SIRG, Santiago created a SIRG troika, composed of the two most recent hosts (the United States and Chile) and the future host (Canada) of summits. Significantly, representatives of the IDB and the World Bank, as well as of ECLAC and the Pan-American Health Organization (PAHO), will be invited to attend SIRG meetings to rope them into providing resources for Summit initiatives. Second, the Santiago text gives official recognition to the National Summit Coordinators, who provide points of contact for communications among governments. The Leadership Council had recommended naming such coordinators, albeit more explicitly at a senior level capable of pulling government agencies behind Summit accords.

In addition, Santiago assigned the OAS responsibility for providing technical support to the SIRG and for building an institutional memory for hemispheric summitry. Only experience will reveal just how relations will evolve among the OAS, the SIRG, and the functional national ministries involved in summit-mandated operations.

In sum, of the four centerpieces proposed by the Leadership Council, the Santiago Summit made significant advances on one (Summit administration) and chose caution on a second (trade), even as momentum from the Miami Summit process impelled trade talks forward. The Santiago Summit fumbled on two others (corruption and finance): It has fallen to the U.S. Treasury, the IMF, and individual country governments to tackle financial turbulence. While Western Hemisphere summitry elevated anticorruption as a legitimate issue for international diplomacy, it may cede leadership to other forums, such as the World Bank and the OECD, to carry the campaign forward.

## Other Substantive Issues

Both the Leadership Council Report and the Santiago *Plan of Action* addressed many other matters regarding democracy and civil society, economic integration and free trade, environmental protection, and poverty eradication. On this panoply of issues, the two documents enjoyed areas of significant overlap, no doubt reflecting the broad consensus around the hemisphere on basic interests and values. There were other areas where the Leadership Council recommended initiatives beyond those adopted in Santiago. And there were still other areas where the Summit delved more extensively or deeply than did the Leadership Council. In general, the Leadership Council underscored the limited capacity of the hemisphere to digest Summit initiatives and so imposed a self-discipline on its wish list. In contrast, the Summit organizers followed the Miami precedent and sought to satisfy the breadth of hemispheric concerns, approving, by one count, 171 action items.

### *Evaluating Santiago: Democracy, Human Rights, and Civil Society*

In the political realm, the Leadership Council focused on counternarcotics and civil society (and corruption, as noted above). The Council urged creation of a multilateral mechanism, probably within the OAS, to assess progress against illicit drugs as a replacement for unilateral judgments. Likewise, the Santiago leaders called for "an objective process of multilateral governmental evaluation" and directed the OAS to design such a monitoring mechanism. Both texts cited the consensus Anti-Drug Strategy approved prior to Santiago, but whereas the Leadership Council suggested that governments select a few priority, quantifiable goals from the 40-plus-point agreement, the Santiago text reiterated a comprehensive list of desirable — but not quantified — goals and objectives.

Believing that a vibrant civil society is a central pillar of a strong democracy, the Leadership Council expressed concern that many governments remain reluctant to provide opportunities for meaningful public participation. The Council urged that the Santiago Summit regularize the participation of non-governmental expertise and the private sector throughout the summitry process and that the proposed summit secretariat issue an annual report on civil society participation in Summit implementation. The Council also applauded the initiative of the IDB to establish a Foundation of the Americas to stimulate civil society within member countries.

Those officials who prepared the Santiago *Plan of Action* did not heed this call for deepening democracy through wider participation and enhanced transparency and accountability. Instead, the Santiago text seemed to shout down civil society by affirming, "The Governments will bear primary responsibility for implementation of the mandates of the Summit." In what appears as an oddly corporatist concept, the Santiago text remarked, "In accordance with Summit decisions . . . support will be provided by private sector organizations and civil society." This stands in sharp contrast with the Miami text, which had followed the assignment of primary responsibility to governments with the phrase, "with participation by all elements of our civil societies." As host, the United States had invited representatives of civil society to attend the public portion of the Miami Summit; there were few such opportunities in Santiago. Santiago convened no private sector gatherings, and some disgruntled NGOs chose to stage a separate, small "People's Summit." With regard to public access and influence over the summitry process, despite occasional references to civil society participation in the *Plan of Action*, Santiago stands as a setback against the gains of Miami, as foreign ministries reasserted their traditional prerogatives over foreign policy. It may be that a summitry secretariat, as advocated by the Leadership Council, might have constrained the officials negotiating the Santiago texts from such backsliding.

Just prior to the Santiago Summit, the IDB Executive Board turned aside a proposal to create the Foundation of the Americas. However, the Santiago text kept the issue alive by requesting the IDB to develop financial mechanisms to strengthen civil society and public participation.

In response to pressures to take into account environment and labor issues and to assure transparency during the trade negotiations, the San José trade ministerial in March 1998 established a special committee to hear the views of representatives of civil society. This new committee is to report to the deputy-level coordinating committee but would only transmit views on "trade related" matters presented in a "constructive" manner.

In the political realm, Santiago covered numerous areas that the Leadership Council did not directly address. The Summit commended the appointment of a Special Rapporteur for Freedom of Expression within the OAS Inter-American Commission on Human Rights, added a section on migrant workers not present in the Miami text, and called for the establishment of a justice studies center of the Americas to train law enforcement personnel.

## Evaluating Santiago: Economic Integration and Free Trade

In the realm of economics, the Leadership Council constrained itself to recommendations on the central matters of the FTAA and financial markets, as discussed above. The Santiago Summit's *Plan of Action* reaffirmed support for the Hemispheric Energy Initiative inaugurated at Miami and elaborated on several other topics not addressed by the Leadership Council, including infrastructure, transportation, and telecommunications.

## Evaluating Santiago: Eradication of Poverty

The Leadership Council and the Summit leaders agreed that poverty was an overriding concern and that the region's gains in the areas of macroeconomic reform and democratization were endangered by glaring inequality and deprivation. The Council noted that while private-sector-led growth with price stability provided the best context for poverty alleviation, more specific interventions were urgently needed to yield a more equitable distribution of the fruits of growth. The Summit underscored the importance of "second generation" reforms to improve the quality of life of all the peoples of the hemisphere.

Both the Leadership Council and the Santiago Summit gave prominence to education. The Summit *Plan of Action* gave education top billing and labeled it "the key to progress." Moreover, the substantive thrusts of both texts were strikingly similar. Both texts concurred in reaffirming Miami's call for completion of primary education by 100 percent of children and access for at least 75 percent of young people to secondary education by the year 2010. Both texts called for establishing standards and quantifiable indicators for basic skills and the use of new technologies, including distance learning. The Santiago text added calls for improved teacher training, increased availability of teaching materials, and more scholarship and exchange programs, all of which were complementary to the Council's briefer proposals.

The Leadership Council and the Summit leaders concurred on two other anti-poverty initiatives: microenterprises and health. Both texts recognized that the promotion of microenterprises required a comprehensive approach, including tax incentives, credit, management training, and partnerships with established private-sector firms. Both texts proposed building on the successful campaign against measles promoted at Miami, to use vaccines to reduce the incidence of such diseases as pneumonia, rubella, and mumps. Both texts underscored the importance of networks of health information and surveillance systems, in order to monitor and evaluate the impact of health reforms.

With regard to workers' rights, both texts urged the promotion of core labor standards, including the rights of free association. The Leadership Council text contained somewhat stronger language calling for ministers of labor to establish means to report on and assess national labor code reviews. The Summit text warned against "the use of labor standards for protectionist purposes."

The Santiago Summit added separate initiatives on women and indigenous populations.

Under poverty alleviation, the broad concurrence between the Leadership Council and the Santiago Summit reflects hemispheric agreement — at a general level — on measures that should be taken to attack poverty. Neither text, however, addressed the tough trade-offs and budgetary choices that governments confront in their strategic choices and daily skirmishes, as they battle over the distribution of income and wealth.

*Evaluating Santiago: Environmental Degradation*

The Miami Summit created three Inter-American Partnerships for Sustainable Development (Biodiversity, Pollution Prevention, and Sustainable Energy Use). The Summit on Sustainable Development in Santa Cruz in December 1996 approved another ambitious action plan addressing a wide range of social, economic, and environmental issues related to sustainable development. The first Leadership Council Report criticized the de facto establishment of two separate tracks for implementing sustainable development initiatives. The Summit Implementation Review Group (SIRG) oversees implementation of the Miami track, while the OAS monitors follow-up of the 65 initiatives of the Santa Cruz action plan. The Leadership Council recommended that in Santiago leaders put an end to this inefficient and divisive segregation of issues by consolidating oversight of implementation of sustainable development initiatives within a single institutional framework. The Leadership Council also proposed that Santiago select from Miami and Santa Cruz a limited number of initiatives for priority action.

Disappointingly, the Santiago Summit largely bypassed sustainable development. Action was reduced to the receipt of an OAS Report on Santa Cruz follow-up, a reiteration of commitments on climate change made at Kyoto, and an exhortation for the OAS and other inter-American institutions to "strengthen cooperation relating to implementation of the Santa Cruz Plan of Action." In fact, to help with Santa Cruz follow-up, the OAS, with support from USAID, the United Nations Environment Program (UNEP), and the World Bank's Global Environment Facility, has created the Inter-American Strategy for Public Participation in Sustainable Development Decisionmaking (ISP). The ISP seeks to bring together civil society representatives and government officials to develop, through research and demonstration projects, the elements of a strategy to strengthen public-private sector partnerships for sustainable development.

### III. REVERSES AND ADVANCES SINCE SANTIAGO

In the months since the Santiago Summit, there has been a notable decline in senior-level focus on summitry in the Americas. In part, this is inevitable, as the attention of senior officials shifts to the next international conference, more immediate crises, or the press of domestic politics. Yet, there were additional reasons for the rapid diversion of attention:

1. The delegates' mood in Santiago was positive and by the closing sessions even congratulatory. Still, the enthusiasm was tempered by the many problems plaguing summitry as well as the domestic constraints facing key leaders. The failure of President Clinton to secure "fast track" negotiating authority from the U.S. Congress in 1997 was fresh in delegates' minds and was reinforced when the U.S. House of Representatives voted down "fast track" legislation in September 1998.

2. The process of summitry was becoming the business of a narrowing circle of public officials. The private sector continued to follow FTAA developments, but the pace of negotiations was too slow to warrant their full engagement. Many NGOs lost touch with summitry, perhaps for lack of information and access or out of their

deepening cynicism regarding the likely fruits of the Summit process. Rather than growing its constituency, summitry was in danger of becoming the creature of an elite cadre of officials scattered within foreign ministries and particular functional agencies.

3. Summitry was institutionalized, but no date was set for the third summit. Bureaucrats lacked the certainty of near-term accountability before their leaders. Further, most initiatives still lacked strong monitoring, reporting, and evaluation mechanisms that could keep officials on their toes.

Notwithstanding this generalized dip in energy, activity is proceeding on two main fronts. Among functional ministries, follow-up meetings are taking place throughout the hemisphere. In Washington, the outlines of a fortified implementation architecture are beginning to take shape. Few of these activities capture the attention of the media or, for that matter, of most senior policymakers. The activities are the routine work of day-to-day multilateral diplomacy. A sample of some of the more noteworthy post-Santiago developments in summitry follow:

**Trade:** The Santiago Summit officially launched negotiations toward the FTAA. The vice ministerial-level Trade Negotiation Committee met in June and early December of 1998, and the nine negotiating groups held their first round of meetings in Miami in September 1998 to kick off what will be ongoing meetings preparatory to the October 1999 ministerial in Canada. The more than 800 officials who participate in these talks are becoming an inter-American community of trade negotiators.

In reality, the working groups are engaged in what might more precisely be termed "pre-negotiations," as they continue to gather data and define their work programs and agendas. Fundamental questions remain open: whether the FTAA will go substantially beyond WTO rules, what tariff rates (whether bound or applied rates) should be taken as the baseline for negotiations, and to what degree countries will be represented by their regional trading blocs. Santiago reaffirmed the Miami requirement for "concrete progress" in the negotiations by the year 2000 and instructed trade ministers to agree on specific business facilitation measures to be adopted before the end of the century. As yet, it is unclear what this "concrete progress" beyond business facilitation measures might consist of and whether such an early harvest is consistent with the ministerial agreement that the FTAA be a "single undertaking."

During 1998, subregional trade agreements — the building blocs of an FTAA — continued to make progress. Trade within NAFTA has been robust. The re-election of Fernando Henrique Cardoso was good news for MERCOSUR, although the collapse of the Brazilian currency in early 1999 was a shock to Argentine export competitiveness and monetary stability and confronted MERCOSUR with its gravest crisis. Caribbean and Central American governments have continued to draw closer together in their integration attempts (at least until Hurricane Mitch turned attention to reconstruction efforts), as have the Andean and MERCOSUR countries. Several additional bilateral agreements have been signed among countries or groups of countries, and others are still under negotiation.[1]

Among the major question marks looming over the FTAA are possible progress or lack thereof in other forums. The European Union is opening talks with Mexico and MERCOSUR on possible free trade pacts, and a summit of European Union and Latin American leaders is planned for June 1999. Such talks could serve as a spur to Washington to take more interest in the FTAA or could push trade liberalization efforts toward global forums. In another direction, the failure of the APEC Summit in Kuala Lumpur, in November 1998, to reach agreement on its sectoral liberalization agenda called into question the realism of its free trade vision and, therefore, the future of its regional free trade cousin, the FTAA. If the World Trade Organization launches negotiations at its December 1999 ministerial in Seattle on many of the issues being discussed within the FTAA, it could subtract from the incentive for liberalization at the regional level.[2]

For the moment, however, the FTAA remains very much at the center of the hemispheric trade agenda. The success of MERCOSUR and NAFTA confirms the contributions that trade and regional integration can make to economic progress. In his January 1999 State of the Union Address, President Clinton reasserted this vision of free trade in the Americas when, despite strong domestic opposition and financial instability in Brazil, he called once again for Congress to grant him trade authority to advance shared prosperity in the Western Hemisphere.

**Finance:** The ministers of finance have not seen fit to accelerate the date for their next meeting, scheduled for Mexico in mid-1999. Vice ministers, however, have been meeting twice annually, typically on the margins of the

---

1. Colleen S. Morton, 1999, "Update on Progress Toward Hemispheric Free Trade – October 1998," *this volume*.

# XI. POST-SANTIAGO EVALUATIONS

annual meetings of the IDB and the Bretton Woods institutions. These meetings allow the senior officials to keep track of the Miami-mandated IDB-led efforts to record country capital market practices, with an eye to enhancing regulatory regimes and market liberalization. The vice ministers also receive relevant briefings; for example, at the October 1998 meetings on the margins of the IMF/World Bank meetings, IMF Director of Research Michael Mussa briefed the vice ministers on the world economic outlook; Ricardo Hausmann, chief economist at the IDB, discussed policy options for confronting global financial market turbulence; and Daniel Zelikow, deputy assistant secretary for Latin America and Asia at the U.S. Treasury, elaborated upon U.S. proposals for IMF precautionary finance and for multilateral development bank enhancement of private credits. In addition, Brazil briefed the vice ministers on its stabilization program. These vice ministerials have built a "club" of officials whose personal ties facilitate the handling of financial crises as they arise. In a separate but reinforcing series of twice-yearly meetings, the IDB convenes the "Latin American Network of Central Banks and Finance Ministries"; these senior economists engage in informal discussions that seek to bridge the worlds of academia and public policy.

The IDB completed the Miami-mandated survey of financial markets, but the CHFI has not acted upon it to require periodic updating or to select priorities for regionwide action. The survey did, however, help to reveal weaknesses at the country level. The Bank's post-Miami plans to assist regionwide harmonization and integration of financial markets have also stalled. The IDB and the World Bank are following up on the Santiago request for assistance in establishing modern clearance and payments systems, along with diagnostic studies and technical assistance.

**Corruption:** As of February 1999, only 14 countries have ratified the Inter-American Convention Against Corruption, and there is little evidence of implementation in the sense of countries bringing their national laws into conformity with the Convention's articles and then enforcing them. However, the OAS and IDB have begun to hold workshops to encourage ratification by more governments and to provide technical assistance to those governments that have ratified the Convention and are looking to implement its provisions. The OAS is also building a database of institutions within member countries with a role in combating corruption.

Transparency International is planning to erect a monitoring system to track ratification and implementation of the anticorruption Convention. With 15 chapters in Latin America, this NGO may contribute to increasing public awareness of governments' actions — and inaction — in living up to summit-related commitments and thereby promote compliance.

**Narcotics:** Probably the most important post-Santiago development in the fight against the illicit drug trade was the coming to power of Colombian President Andrés Pastrana and his agreement with the United States to forge a bilateral Alliance Against Drugs. The United States doubled its annual assistance to Colombia to over $280 million. In the joint communiqué issued during President Pastrana's October 1998 state visit to Washington, Presidents Clinton and Pastrana "welcomed the work underway through the OAS to forge a hemispheric alliance, and to establish a multilateral process to monitor and evaluate national as well as collective performance toward agreed goals."

If this new bilateral cooperation between two major players in the drug wars holds, it will provide impetus for the OAS, through its Inter-American Drug Abuse Control Commission (CICAD), to construct a credible process for multilateral evaluation of implementation of the Summit-blessed Anti-Drug Strategy. Such a process could eventually persuade the U.S. Congress to drop its annual unilateral "certification" exercise. A CICAD working group, chaired by Canada and Chile, hopes to ready a blueprint for a Multilateral Evaluation Mechanism (MEM) for acceptance by the June 1999 OAS General Assembly.

**Education:** Education was a centerpiece in Santiago. The World Bank, the IDB, and USAID pledged more than $8 billion over three years. Some of the education projects are proceeding; for example, USAID is promoting reforms to strengthen the teaching profession, provide local communities with more control over schools, and establish and monitor standards for educational performance.[3] However, the same problems that stymied progress on education post-Miami have resurfaced, including rivalry among some governments for leadership, the difficulty of coordinating long-standing multilateral and bilateral programs, and the inherent complexity of educational reform itself. The post-Asian crisis slowdown in hemispheric growth and the attendant pressure on fiscal spending make it that much harder to improve educational systems.

---

2. José Manuel Salazar-Xirinachs, Chief Trade Advisor, OAS, "Free Trade in the Americas: Prospects and Obstacles," Address before the Andean Development Corporation Conference on Trade and Investment in the Americas, September 11, 1998.

Subsequent to the Santiago Summit, educational officials met in Mexico and in Washington; they also met in Brazil for an August 1998 ministerial. However, so far the effort to transform the generalities of the Santiago *Plan of Action* into a concrete work plan have not been successful. A series of governmental working groups have been established to promote work on Santiago's recommendations; group members hope to develop proposals for funding by early 1999.

Progress in other substantive areas:

**Human Rights:** The Inter-American Human Rights Commission named Argentine lawyer Santiago Canton as its first Special Rapporteur on Freedom of Expression. USAID announced a $150,000 contribution to fund the new position. The Special Rapporteur is to prepare an annual report on the right of freedom of expression in the Americas, as well as alert the Inter-American Human Rights Commission to any violations or threats involving freedom of expression.

**Women's Rights:** The IDB and the U.S. government sponsored a "Vital Voices" conference in Montevideo, Uruguay, in October 1998 that was attended by 400 women from around the hemisphere who are likely to assume positions of national leadership. This conference was a follow-up to Santiago's mandate to governments to "promote legal equality and equality of opportunities between women and men." Also, the First Ladies of the Americas held their annual conference in Santiago in late September and considered coordination of their ongoing agenda (women's rights, education, and health) with the Summit agenda.

**Labor Rights:** Labor ministers met in Viña Del Mar, Chile, in October to discuss the modernization of labor ministries and the effects of globalization on labor markets. Labor ministers, who have met 11 times since 1963, will now strive to execute relevant mandates from the summits of the Americas.

**Health Technologies:** During their September meeting at the Pan-American Health Organization (PAHO), health ministers advanced two Summit initiatives: the wide use of vaccines and the strengthening of regional epidemiological surveillance systems.

**Defense Ministerial:** The Santiago Summit brought the meetings of ministers of defense, which were an outgrowth of the Miami Summit, formally under the rubric of summitry. At the third ministerial in December 1998 in Cartagena, Colombia, ministers considered the roles and missions of militaries in democratic societies as well as ways to strengthen the inter-American security system.

**Administrative Infrastructure:** In the area of administrative infrastructure, the Summit Implementation Review Group (SIRG) held its fifteenth meeting in late October 1998. It heard reports of varying quality from several Responsible Coordinators (countries taking the lead in coordinating implementation of Summit initiatives). More promising, the SIRG was addressed by representatives from the World Bank, IDB, ECLAC, OAS, and PAHO, in a symbolic display of the greater integration of these international organizations in the summitry process. The Santiago Summit mandated that these organizations be invited to SIRG meetings.

Charged with chairing the SIRG, the Troika has begun to build working relations. This task is greatly facilitated by the fact that all three representatives reside in Washington as ambassadors to the OAS. The United States initially appointed a senior diplomat, Ambassador William Walker, to head the State Department's summit implementation office, but shortly after his appointment, he was reassigned to peacekeeping in the former Yugoslavia; thence the title of U.S. Summit Coordinator was bestowed upon the U.S. Ambassador to the OAS, Victor Marrero.

An important institutional development has been the creation in the OAS of the Office of Summit Follow-Up (OSF), headed by the able Bolivian diplomat, Jaime Aparicio. The OSF is tasked with being the institutional memory for inter-American summitry, as well as providing technical support to the SIRG. It also plans to coordinate civil society initiatives and disseminate information on the Summit process.[4] While the OSF's core staff has only three professionals, it draws on the expertise of the other OAS staff who specialize in Summit mandate issues. The OSF hopes to coordinate the OAS's Summit-related activities, and to assist Secretary General César Gaviria in his efforts to bring a rising proportion of OAS activities into line with Summit mandates. Certainly among the international organizations, summitry has had its greatest impact in the OAS, and some in the OAS see summitry as breathing new life into the institution and giving it a new raison d'être in the post-Cold War world.

---

3. Mark Schneider, Assistant Administrator of USAID, Remarks before the Latin American Studies Association, Chicago, September 26, 1998.

4. The OSF's valuable new web page address: < www.summit-americas.org >.

## IV. RECOMMENDATIONS FOR MORE EFFECTIVE SUMMITRY

Summitry is a continual process. When it functions well, at periodic summits the leaders set the agenda and a plan of action that their nations — the functional bureaucratic agencies, the private sectors, and the rest of organized civil society — fashion into more detailed work plans. In turn, this implementation process, with its successes and failures, informs the next summit, which modifies their mandates accordingly, and the process advances. While the Santiago Summit built on the lessons of the Miami process, there is still a long way to go before summitry in the Americas fulfills its promise.

In this spirit of continual summitry, the Leadership Council now offers the recommendations that follow. Some are addressed to the functional ministries that will be meeting during 1999-2000, and others are aimed at the next summit in Canada. Still other recommendations are intended for the private sector and non-governmental groups that must be the underpinning of any successful summitry process. Some of the following recommendations repeat those made in the first Leadership Council Report, while others respond to new circumstances. Together, these recommendations affirm key objectives in the areas of trade integration, financial stability, countercorruption, and educational reform; urge broadening the base of popular participation in summitry; and propose institutional reforms for more effective execution of Summit mandates.

**Recommendation 1:** *The vision of the Free Trade Area of the Americas remains the centerpiece of summitry in the Americas.* For this reason alone, it should be pursued with vigor even if the 1999 WTO ministerial charts an agenda that might accomplish some of the FTAA's economic objectives. Furthermore, progress in subregional trade integration underscores the contribution that open markets can make to hemispheric growth and prosperity.

In Santiago, some delegations expressed interest in a "democracy clause" that would circumscribe participation in the FTAA to democratically elected governments. *An explicit linkage between democracy and free markets would emblazon regional integration in the Americas with a special Bolivarian character. In preparing the third summit, Canada should take the lead in building a hemispheric consensus on this strategic political-economic linkage.*

The first Leadership Council Report urged leaders, particularly in the big markets of the United States and Brazil, to engage in concerted efforts to build the public case for the FTAA. We repeat this call. Specifically, the U.S. administration must mobilize sufficient political support to gain fast-track authority that encompasses regional trade agreements. A democracy clause would facilitate the construction of broad bipartisan support in the United States. For its part, the government of Brazil should explain to its citizens that the FTAA is in Brazil's national interest and is compatible with MERCOSUR's basic objectives; moreover, Brazil and other member countries could cite with pride the presence of a precedent-setting democracy clause in MERCOSUR.

The FTAA Government Committee on Civil Society should develop meaningful mechanisms for the participation of the private sector (corporate and financial), labor unions, and other non-governmental organizations (NGOs) in the construction of hemispheric free trade. It should hold public hearings as well as accept written submissions and make effective use of the FTAA website. The Committee should allow for a liberal interpretation of "trade related" and "constructive" in its transmission of public views to senior officials. The Leadership Council believes that a strong commitment to public participation in the FTAA process is an important means for broadening public support for free trade in the Americas.

**Recommendation 2:** *The Leadership Council believes that recent events have demonstrated the wisdom of its recommendation urging the formation of a ministerial-level Inter-American Financial Council to improve regional economic cooperation.* The proposed Financial Council would exercise self-surveillance of national macroeconomic policies as they affect the region and also review measures taken by the Bretton Woods institutions to cope with new market realities. Through the hemispheric participants in the Willard Group, the Financial Council could feed its views into the process, whereby the international financial architecture may be reformed. The Financial Council would meet more frequently and have more structure and influence than the current occasional meetings of regional finance ministers.

**Recommendation 3:** *To spur ratification of the Inter-American Convention against Corruption, the OAS should set target dates for ratification and entry into force.* At its June 1999 General Assembly, the OAS should create a mechanism, similar to the OECD Working Group on Bribery, to bring all signatories to the table, to provide technical assistance, and to carry out periodic peer evaluation of implementation efforts. This mechanism should transform the Convention into a work plan, set priority goals, and issue an annual progress report. In these efforts, the OAS should cooperate closely with Transparency International and its 15 country chapters in the Western Hemisphere.

**Recommendation 4:** The Santiago Summit labeled education "the key to progress," but it did not establish mechanisms for catalyzing a sustained process of change that has measurable goals and timetables. *Like the pursuit of free trade, the ministers of education should establish a series of issue-specific working groups that set concrete goals and that establish and publish useful monitoring guidelines with comparative data on each country's progress toward meeting those goals.*[5]

**Recommendation 5:** *Canada should reassert the importance of the involvement of the private sector and the other components of civil society in summitry.* Canada can set an example by involving its own civil society in preparations for the third Summit of the Americas. It can work with the OAS's Office of Summit Follow-Up to involve civil society in the many initiatives where the OAS is a convener or technical assistant. The healthy engagement of civil society inside the summitry process may negate interest in staging a counter "people's summit" at the Canadian Summit.

**Recommendation 6:** *The OAS's new Office of Summit Follow-Up holds the potential to fill the monitoring void left unfilled in Miami and Santiago. It should direct its network of staff experts to identify points of contact within national ministries to complete standardized reports.* The OAS could compile, evaluate, and publish this information as a way to spur progress toward Summit goals. These reports should replace existing reports by Responsible Coordinators and by national governments, which have too often lacked objectivity, standardization, quantification, and prioritization. The Office of Summit Follow-Up should become a major source of information for the SIRG, and consideration should be given to making it the SIRG's technical secretariat. Substantive direction, however, should remain with the functional ministries and their multilateral coordinating bodies (where the expertise lies) to best implement Summit mandates.

**Recommendation 7:** *The Troika (Canada, Chile, and the United States) and the OAS's Office of Summit Follow-Up should form a Summit Coordinating Committee (SCC) to coordinate overall Summit implementation.* Because the multilateral development banks are the primary source of funds for Summit implementation, it might be appropriate for them to join the SCC, thereby bringing the key official actors together under a single umbrella. The World Bank should follow the lead of the IDB and empower its senior coordinator to track its follow-through on Summit mandates and to serve as its representative to the SIRG and other Summit forums.

**Recommendation 8:** *Summit administrators should devise mechanisms to combat issue compartmentalization.* For instance, the Tripartite Committee should make trade negotiators aware of the Summit-related activities underway in forums dealing with environmental protection and labor rights. Trade negotiators also need to be aware of the agenda being pursued by the Committee on Hemispheric Financial Issues. As the Summit agenda amplifies, such coordination functions will grow in importance.

**Recommendation 9:** *Canada should set a date for the Third Summit of the Americas without further delay.* A visible end-date prompts bureaucracies to fulfill mandates and prepare "deliverables" and keys up important decisions for leaders. The Troika and the OAS Office of Summit Follow-Up (or a new SCC) should develop a list of summit-approved action items that can be completed by the third Summit. Such an "early harvest" could include, among others, concrete progress toward the FTAA, agreement on a multilateral evaluation mechanism for counternarcotics efforts, entry into force of the Convention Against Corruption, agreement on the design and financing of a judicial studies center, and establishment of monitoring systems on key goals mandated on education and health (including the eradication of measles by the year 2000).

In looking toward the Canadian Summit, the Troika should declare its intention to inject more discipline into the process of summit preparation and to seek to limit the scope of the negotiated Plan of Action. In response to problems and opportunities that have arisen since Santiago, the summiteers might add a few — but only a few — new initiatives to the already heroic hemispheric agenda.

The Leadership Council recommends that the Third Summit of the Americas be the "implementation Summit." Its preparatory phase should serve primarily to press for progress on the more promising of the Miami and Santiago initiatives. Its Plan of Action should set forth a realistic work plan that builds upon the previous Summits' comprehensive agendas. In that way, inter-Ameri-

---

5. Jeffrey M. Puryear, 1999, "Postscript: Education and the Summit," *this volume*.

can summitry can become a powerful instrument for the construction of the vision of Miami and Santiago: a hemispheric community of prosperous democracies.

## V. SUPPLEMENTAL COMMENTS

### Comments by Winston Dookeran

With respect to Recommendation 7, I would like to add that prior to the Summit to be held in Canada, consideration should be given to creating a platform that allows for the free and full discussion of the *historical promise* that this Summit holds for the hemisphere. Such a platform could solicit participation from a wide range of interested persons in academia and in public policy circles and civil societies. It should be structured to provide a better intellectual understanding as to the Summitry Process and a clearer articulation of the immediate and historical setting in which it is taking place. Perhaps the Leadership Council may reflect on the structure, content, and format for such a pre-summit action.

The recommendation to refer to the Third Summit of the Americas as an *implementation summit* may be premature, as there is a clear need to refocus on some of the realities that had emerged since the First Summit; and perhaps a different thinking on the strategy for implementation may now be required. If the summitry process is not given a new intellectual energy, the implementation process may not be sustainable. The peculiar problem of small economies in the FTAA process is still to be acknowledged at the policy and, indeed, the implementation stages.

*Dr. Winston Dookeran*

### Comments by Sonia Picado Sotela

1. The document is an excellent summary of the achievements and shortcomings of the Summit of the Americas in Santiago in April 1998. The document captures the most salient activities accomplished in relation to the Summit of the Americas process and furtherance of its institutionalization. It fulfills its objective completely and allows the reader (assuming he or she has some basic knowledge of the Summit process) to quickly grasp the new steps taken in this evolution.

2. The document's critical and clear focus is appropriate and valuable, even though it seems more critical of the Santiago Summit than necessary in light of the fact that it consistently fails to make no critical references to the Miami Summit. This creates a disparity in the presentation: notwithstanding delays or bottlenecks, the process has undoubtedly resolved the shortcomings and flaws that emerged from Miami. The very fact that we can now speak with authority of "a process" – beyond institutionalization of the Summits – is due in large part to the Santiago Summit of the Americas II.

3. The key point and the most important objection to the document is the reference – paragraph one, page six – and the strong recommendation – Recommendation 1, page 15 – concerning the incorporation of a "democratic clause" for the participation of countries in the FTAA. Repeatedly, the U.S. position throughout the Summit process, at Ministerial-level meetings and throughout the advance of the FTAA process, has been to link non-trade issues with the continent's progressive opening (environmental matters or labor conditions) that many south of the Rio Grande feel would be the basis for future nontariff barriers to the detriment of progress in the area of liberalization. These proposals have repeatedly been rejected by Latin American countries in different ways and at the various forums where they have surfaced. It seems convenient to keep progress in trade separate from such interference, which merely adds obstacles to a path that is already difficult in itself. There is ample room in the Summit process to insist on the importance of democratic unanimity in proceeding on the path proposed. There is no doubt in anyone's mind that Cuba is still a problem in the continent and its obstinacy in impeding democratic reforms alienates it from hemispheric integration processes, although taking this discussion to the level of trade perverts the nature of the proposal. On the other hand, it seems improbable that Cuba could, or would want to, even in the event of a democratic transition, become part of a trade liberalization process toward which many countries better prepared in this area continue to display their reticence. In summary, much risks being lost and the rewards will be almost nil with a proposal of this nature.

*Ambassador Sonia Picado Sotela*

## VI. LEADERSHIP COUNCIL FOR INTER-AMERICAN SUMMITRY

**Sergio Aguayo**
El Colegio de México
(Mexico)

**Bernard W. Aronson**
Acon Investments LLC
(United States)

**C. Fred Bergsten**
Institute for International Economics
(United States)

**Charles E. Cobb, Jr.**
Cobb Partners, Inc.
(United States)

**Charles H. Dallara**
Institute of International Finance
(United States)

**Winston Dookeran**
Central Bank of Trinidad and Tobago
(Trinidad and Tobago)

**Richard E. Feinberg**
APEC Study Center
University of California, San Diego
(United States)

**Alejandro Foxley**
Senator
(Chile)

**Kathryn Fuller**
World Wildlife Fund, Inc.
(United States)

**Irwin Jacobs**
Qualcomm
(United States)

**C. Kent Jespersen**
La Jolla Resources International
(Canada)

**Luis Moreno Ocampo**
Transparency International
(Argentina)

**Sylvia Ostry**
University of Toronto
(Canada)

**Sonia Picado Sotela**
Congresswoman
(Costa Rica)

**Beatrice E. Rangel**
Cisneros Group of Companies
(Venezuela)

**Gonzalo Sánchez de Lozada**
Former President
(Bolivia)

**José Serra***
(Brazil)
*on leave for government service

## CO-DIRECTORS
**Richard E. Feinberg** and **Robin Rosenberg**

## VII. BIOGRAPHICAL DATA

**Sergio Aguayo**, Ph.D., has been a Professor at the Colegio de México's Center for International Relations since 1977. He received a doctorate from the Johns Hopkins School of Advanced International Studies. In 1990, the John D. and Catherine T. MacArthur Foundation awarded him a Research and Writing Grant to examine national security issues of Mexico and the United States. He has been a visiting fellow or professor in several institutions, among others, the Center for U.S.-Mexican Studies at the University of California, San Diego; the Ortega and Gasset Foundation in Madrid; the New School for Social Research in New York; and the University of Chicago. He has also been active in the promotion of democracy and human rights through organizations such as Civic Alliance and the Mexican Academy of Human Rights. For those activities he was awarded the "Democracy Award" by the National Endowment for Democracies. He publishes a weekly column that appears in *La Reforma* and 14 other Mexican newspapers.

# XI. POST-SANTIAGO EVALUATIONS

**Bernard W. Aronson** is Chairman of Acon Investments and Chairman of Newbridge Andean Partners, L.P. Prior to assuming this position, Mr. Aronson was International Advisor to Goldman Sachs and Co. Mr. Aronson served as Assistant Secretary of State for Inter-American Affairs from 1989-1993, the longest tenure of any holder of that office. In 1993, then-Secretary Aronson was presented with the State Department's highest honor, the Distinguished Service Award. Prior government positions include Deputy Assistant to President Jimmy Carter in the Office of the White House Chief of Staff and Special Assistant to Vice President Walter Mondale. He serves as a Director of Royal Caribbean Cruise Lines, Inc. and Liz Claiborne Inc., is on the Board of Directors of the National Democratic Institute for International Affairs, and is a member of the Inter-American Dialogue and the Council on Foreign Relations.

**C. Fred Bergsten**, Ph.D., is Director of the Institute for International Economics, the only major research institution in the United States devoted to international economic issues. Dr. Bergsten has been Chairman of the Eminent Persons Group (EPG) of the Asia-Pacific Economic Cooperation (APEC) Forum and of the Competitiveness Policy Council, created by the U.S. Congress. He has served as Assistant Secretary of the Treasury for International Affairs and as Senior Fellow at The Brookings Institution and the Carnegie Endowment for International Peace. He has authored or co-authored 26 books on international economic issues, including *Global Economic Leadership and the Group of Seven* (1996). Dr. Bergsten frequently testifies before congressional committees.

**Charles E. Cobb, Jr.,** is Chairman of the Board of Directors and the Senior Partner of the investment firm, Cobb Partners, Inc. He served as U.S. Ambassador to Iceland during the Bush Administration. During the Reagan Administration, he was Under Secretary and Assistant Secretary at the U.S. Department of Commerce with responsibilities for the nation's trade development, export promotion, and international travel and tourism. Ambassador Cobb is a former Chairman and CEO of Arvida/Disney Corporation and a member of the Board and Executive Committee of The Walt Disney Company. Prior to that, he was the Chief Operating Officer and a Board member of Penn Central Corporation. He is also a former President and General Manager of several subsidiaries of Kaiser Aluminum. Ambassador Cobb earned undergraduate and graduate degrees at Stanford University. He was an officer in the U.S. Navy. He is active in many civic affairs and corporate organizations and currently serves on the Florida Governor's Commission on Education as Chairman of the Florida Business/Higher Education Partnership, and past Chairman of the Board of Trustees of the University of Miami, among others.

**Charles H. Dallara**, Ph.D., has been Managing Director and Chief Executive Officer of the Institute of International Finance in Washington, D.C., since 1993. The Institute represents more than 275 global financial institutions, including many of the world's largest banks. Before joining the Institute, Dallara was a Managing Director at J.P. Morgan and Co. (June 1991 to July 1993), where he chaired Morgan's Emerging Markets Risk Committee. He has held a number of senior positions in government, including Assistant Secretary of the Treasury for International Affairs in the Bush Administration, Assistant Secretary of the Treasury for Policy Development, and United States Executive Director of the International Monetary Fund. Dr. Dallara is a member of the Board of Directors or Trustees of the German Marshall Fund and The American Council on Germany, and has served as a member of the U.S.-Japan Business Council. He holds master's and doctoral degrees from Tufts University and an Honorary Doctor of Laws degree from the University of South Carolina.

**Winston Dookeran**, who holds an honorary Doctor of Laws degree from the University of Manitoba, is Governor of the Central Bank of Trinidad and Tobago. He served as Senior Economist at the Economic Commission for Latin America and the Caribbean. He earned a master's degree from the London School of Economics and Political Science and was a Lecturer in Economics at the University of the West Indies. Mr. Dookeran was also a Fellow at the Centre for International Affairs at Harvard University, where he edited *Choices and Change: Reflections on the Caribbean* (1996), published by the Inter-American Development Bank. He was Planning Minister in the government of Trinidad and Tobago and on several occasions served as Prime Minister.

**Richard E. Feinberg**, Ph.D., is Director of the Asia Pacific Economic Cooperation Study Center based at the Graduate School of International Relations and Pacific Studies (IRPS) at the University of California, San Diego. He also serves as Special Advisor to the Chancellor for Pacific Rim Affairs. Dr. Feinberg served as Special Assistant to President Clinton for National Security Affairs and Senior Director of the National Security Council's Office of Inter-American Affairs. He was one of the principal architects of the 1994 Summit of the Americas in Miami. Dr. Feinberg has served as President of the Inter-American Dialogue and Executive Vice President of the Overseas Development Council. He has held positions on the policy planning staff of the U.S. Department of State and in the Office of International Affairs in the U.S. Treasury Department. He has written more than 100 articles and books, most recently, *Summitry in the Americas,* published by the Institute of International Economics, where he is a visiting fellow.

**Alejandro Foxley**, Ph.D., is a Senator in the Chilean Senate and Chairman of the Senate Finance Committee. He has served as Minister of Finance to the Republic of Chile, Governor of the Inter-American Development Bank, and Chairman of the Development Committee at the World Bank. Dr. Foxley earned a doctorate in economics at the University of Wisconsin. He has authored or edited 11 books on economics, economic development, and problems of democracy, including *Economía Política de la Transición* (Ediciones Dolmen, 1993).

**Kathryn Fuller**, J.D., is President and CEO of the World Wildlife Fund based in Washington, D.C. She served previously as Executive Vice President, General Counsel, and Director of WWF's public policy and wildlife trade monitoring programs. Before joining WWF in 1982, Fuller worked at the U.S. Department of Justice as head of the Wildlife and Marine Resources Section. She was a special advisor to the United Nations at the Earth Summit in 1992 and serves on numerous boards, including the Board of Trustees of Brown University and the Board of Trustees of the Ford Foundation. Fuller has received the U.N. Environment Programme's Global 500 Award and is a member of the Council on Foreign Relations, the U.S. Advisory Committee for Trade Policy and Negotiations, the Overseas Development Council, and the World Bank's Advisory Group on Environmentally Sustainable Development.

**Irwin Jacobs**, Sc.D., is Founder, Chairman, and Chief Executive Officer of Qualcomm Incorporated. He has led the company, which has international activities in digital wireless telephony, mobile satellite communications, and internet software, through a period of rapid growth to over 7500 employees. He is a former President, CEO, and Chairman of Linkabit, which he also co-founded. From 1959-1966, Dr. Jacobs served as Assistant/Associate Professor of Electrical Engineering at Massachusetts Institute of Technology and from 1966-1972 was Professor of Computer Science and Engineering at the University of California, San Diego (UCSD). He is co-author of *Principles of Communication Engineering.* Dr. Jacobs is the recipient of many awards, including the National Medal of Technology Award bestowed by the President of the United States, the Alexander Graham Bell Medal, the Inventing America's Future Award, and the Albert Einstein Award. He is a member of the California Council on Science and Technology. Dr. Jacobs currently serves or has served on the boards of the National Academy of Engineering Industry Advisory Board, the University of California President's Engineering Advisory Council, UCSD Foundation Board of Trustees, UCSD Green Foundation for Earth Sciences, UCSD Cancer Center, San Diego Symphony, and San Diego Repertory Theater.

**C. Kent Jespersen** is Chairman of La Jolla Resources International Ltd. and Chairman of the Americas Business Forum for the Free Trade Area of the Americas in Toronto, 1999. His distinguished career in business and government service includes positions as Special Assistant to the Prime Minister of Canada, Special Assistant to the Canadian Federal Minister of Agriculture, President of NOVA Gas Services Ltd. and Gas International Ltd., and Senior Vice President of NOVA Corporation in Alberta, Canada. Mr. Jespersen is active in many business and public policy institutions as Chairman of the Institute of the Americas in La Jolla, California, Chairman of the C.D. Howe Institute in Toronto, and member of the board of directors of the Lester D. Pearson College of the Pacific in Victoria, British Columbia; Gasoducto GasAndes S.A., Santiago, Chile; Gainvest S.A., Buenos Aires, Argentina; and Bow Valley Energy, Calgary, Canada.

**Luis Moreno Ocampo** is Associate Professor of Criminal Law at the University of Buenos Aires Law School, where he received his law degree. In private law practice, Mr. Moreno Ocampo specializes in corruption control programs for large organizations. Through the auspices of the United Nations and the Inter-American Development Bank, he has aided governments in developing corruption control systems, specifically in the Dominican Republic, Bolivia, and Venezuela. Mr. Moreno Ocampo is co-founder of Poder Ciudadano, a non-governmental organization that promotes citizen responsibility and participation. He is also a member of the Advisory Committee of Transparency International, a worldwide organization that reduces corruption in international business transactions, and is President of its division for Latin America and the Caribbean. His books include *Self Defense: How to Avoid Corruption* (1993) and *When Power Lost the Trial: How to Explain the Dictatorship to our Children* (1996), which explains the functioning of the systems that were the causes of crimes during the Argentine military dictatorship. Mr. Moreno Ocampo also played a crucial role as prosecutor in trials related to Argentina's democratic transition.

# XI. POST-SANTIAGO EVALUATIONS

**Sylvia Ostry**, Ph.D., is Distinguished Research Fellow, Centre for International Studies, University of Toronto. She has a doctorate in economics from McGill University and Cambridge University. Dr. Ostry has held a number of positions in the Canadian Federal Government, among them, Chief Statistician, Deputy Minister of Consumer and Corporate Affairs, Chairman of the Economic Council of Canada, Deputy Minister of International Trade, Ambassador for Multilateral Trade Negotiations, and the Prime Minister's Personal Representative for the Economic Summit. Dr. Ostry has written numerous books and papers, most recently, *Who's on First? The Post-Cold War Trading System* (University of Chicago Press, 1997) and *Reinforcing the WTO* (Group of Thirty, Washington, 1998). She has received 18 honorary degrees from universities in Canada and abroad and the Outstanding Achievement Award of the Government of Canada. She is a Companion of the Order of Canada and a Fellow of the Royal Society of Canada. She is a director of Power Financial Corporation and a member of many distinguished councils and advisory boards. In 1992, the Sylvia Ostry Foundation annual lecture series was launched by Madam Sadako Ogata, U.N. High Commissioner for Refugees.

**Sonia Picado Sotela** is a Congresswoman for San José, Costa Rica, and Vice President of the Interamerican Institute of Human Rights. She served as Costa Rica's Ambassador to the United States from 1994 to 1998 and Justice and Vice President of the Interamerican Court of Human Rights from 1990 to 1994. From 1984 to 1994, she was Director of the International Institute of Human Rights. She was the first Latin American woman to be elected dean of a law school when she served as Dean of the University of Costa Rica School of Law (1980-1984). She has received many awards in recognition of her efforts to promote human rights and women's rights, including the United Nations Human Rights Award in 1993, an Inter-American Commission on Women award, and the Max Planc/Humboldt Award. She was an Edward Larocque Tinker Professor at Columbia University (New York) in 1991.

**Beatrice E. Rangel** is currently the Senior Vice President, Corporate Strategy, of the Cisneros Group of Companies in New York. Ms. Rangel's responsibilities include identifying, defining, and implementing business policies and investment projects. She is a personal advisor to the Office of the Chairman and the liaison between the Cisneros Group of Companies and governments and private enterprises for the development stage of projects. Ms. Rangel has served in a number of advisory positions in the private and public sectors of Venezuela. She was Advisor to former President of Venezuela, Carlos Andrés Pérez, and was elected Alternate Deputy of Congress for Miranda State. She served as General Secretary of the Ministry of Education in 1985 and the following year became Executive Secretary of the Presidential Commission in charge of drafting the National Education Reform Project. She later served as Minister of the Secretariat of the President. Ms. Rangel has served as a board member for several large companies and organizations, including Venezuelan Airways, The Vienna Institute for Development, and the Robert Kennedy Foundation for Human Rights. Ms. Rangel holds an M.A. in Public Administration from Harvard University and an M.S. in Development Economics from Boston University. Among her awards are The Order of Merit of May, conferred by the Republic of Argentina; Condor of the Andes Order, by the Republic of Bolivia; the Bernardo O'Higgins Order, by the Republic of Chile; the Order of Boyacá, by the Republic of Colombia; and the National Order of José Matías Delgado, by the Republic of El Salvador.

**President Gonzalo Sánchez de Lozada**, as a Senator and Minister of Planning in Bolivia, gained popular recognition as the author of the 1985 economic "shock therapy" program, which brought Bolivia's 25,000 percent hyper-inflation rate under control and created the foundation for future economic stability and growth. A graduate of the University of Chicago, he was inaugurated as President of Bolivia in August 1993 and served until August 1997. During his administration, President Sánchez de Lozada implemented his "Plan de Todos," based on profound economic, social, and political reforms. The Plan's main elements were administrative decentralization, which strengthened Bolivia's democratic process by transferring decision-making authority and revenue sharing to local regions and communities; popular participation, which allowed all citizens to be included in the process of administering and controlling revenue sharing in their communities; education reform, which incorporated multilingual and multicultural education into the educational system; capitalization, involving equity contributions in state-owned monopolies by strategic foreign partners and the transfer of government-owned shares to privately administered pension funds, which now distribute a yearly lifetime bonus to people over 65 years of age; and judicial reform.

## VIII. RESEARCH AUTHORS

The Leadership Council for Inter-American Summitry acknowledges the research contributions of the following authors in the indicated areas. Their original research provided an overview and analysis of the implementation of some of the major summit initiatives and helped to inform many of the Council's recommendations.

**Felipe Agüero,** Guaranteeing Democracy and Human Rights

**Richard L. Bernal,** Developing and Liberalizing Capital Markets

**Cristina B. Cunico,** Providing Equitable Access to Basic Health Services

**Ana María De Andraca,** Reforming Educational Systems

**Kimberly Ann Elliott,** Combating Corruption

**Marcela Gajardo,** Reforming Educational Systems

**Eduardo Gamarra,** Combating Illegal Drugs and Related Crimes

**Arturo García-Costas,** Building Sustainable Development Partnerships

**Inter-American Dialogue,** Strengthening the Role of Women in Society

**International Center for Research on Women,** Strengthening the Role of Women in Society

**Manuel Lasaga,** Developing, Liberalizing, and Integrating Financial Markets

**Luigi Manzetti,** Combating Corruption

**Colleen S. Morton,** Progress Toward Free Trade in the Western Hemisphere Since 1994

**Sean Neill,** Guaranteeing Democracy and Human Rights

**Jeffrey Puryear,** Reforming Educational Systems

**Robin Rosenberg,** Invigorating Civil Society Participation

**José Salazar-Xirinachs,** Promoting Free Trade in the Americas

**S. Jacob Scherr,** Partnerships for Sustainable Development

**Michael Shifter,** Guaranteeing Democracy and Human Rights

**Justin Ward,** Building Sustainable Development Partnerships

**Robert Watson,** Partnerships for Sustainable Development

To review the full content of research papers, visit the North-South Center's web page at http://www.miami.edu/nsc/

# XI. POST-SANTIAGO EVALUATIONS

*Transparency International (TI), a non-profit, non-partisan NGO headquartered in Germany, is the leading advocate of action to curb corruption. TI national chapters in over seventy countries, including seventeen in the Americas, are coalitions of leaders from major business enterprises, the legal and development communities, academia, and civic organizations. Some have held high public offices.*

*TI chapters are building public understanding of the adverse impact of corruption on open markets, democracy, and sustainable and equitable development. They are forging partnerships in support of constructive action by the public and private sector in both industrialized and developing countries around the world. To promote best practices by the private sector in foreign markets, TI chapters supported the recently signed OECD Convention on Combating Bribery of Foreign Public Officials, which criminalizes bribery of foreign public officials. Several countries in the hemisphere are signatories, including Argentina, Brazil, Canada, Chile, Mexico, and the United States. TI also contributed to the 1996 adoption of the International Chamber of Commerce Rules of Conduct on Extortion and Bribery, voluntary rules which would prohibit bribery for any purpose.*

*In the Americas, TI chapters encouraged the adoption of important anticorruption commitments by the leaders of the hemisphere at the 1994 Summit of the Americas in Miami. They have worked since that time for the implementation of those commitments through systemic reform at the national level. TI commends the OAS and the leaders for concluding the Inter-American Anticorruption Convention, an important milestone.*

# Report on Progress and Recommendations Toward Implementing the 1994 Summit Anticorruption Commitments

## I. COMMITMENT TO TRANSPARENT SYSTEMS TO PROMOTE INVESTMENT AND TRADE:

At the Summit of the Americas in December 1994, the leaders of the hemisphere recognized that prosperity depends on economic integration and free trade and, therefore, agreed to create a Free Trade Area of the Americas (FTAA) by 2005. They recognized that corrupt practices are impediments to growth in investment and trade and that their objectives would be undermined if corruption were not reduced. They committed to creating open and transparent markets and to a "comprehensive attack on corruption."

Corruption is an issue for all the FTAA working groups, threatening to undermine progress on investment, government procurement, intellectual property rights, services, customs, and market access. While this interconnection is widely recognized, few steps have been taken by the working groups in the four years since the Miami Summit to create the environment of integrity, transparency and predictability in which free trade will flourish.

There is still time before the Santiago Summit to demonstrate progress, and, at a minimum, the leaders should commit to concrete actions in the following areas.

• **Procurement:** At the 1994 Summit, leaders agreed to give priority to strengthening government procurement systems. Negotiations on a regional agreement on transparency in procurement have been underway for some time without tangible progress.

**Recommendation:** Leaders should commit to conclude the negotiation of a regional procurement agreement that ensures transparency, openness, and due process. The procurement agreement should go into effect expeditiously to enhance prospects for regional growth.

• **IDB Procurement Guidelines:** The InterAmerican Development Bank (IDB) can play a leadership role by establishing clear criteria for transparent procurement. The World Bank has adopted more stringent procurement guidelines, including requirements for disclosure of commissions paid to agents as well as procedures for investigating bribery allegations and for debarment of corrupt contractors. The IDB has been considering similar changes to its procurement rules, but there is reportedly resistance in the board which will have to be overcome.

**Recommendation:** Leaders should direct their IDB directors to adopt rules that closely track those of the World Bank so as to provide borrowers and bidders with a single set of consistent rules to ensure adequate anticorruption controls. The IDB should require antibribery pledges on bank-financed projects with commitments by bidders not to pay bribes, to adopt compliance programs, and to report commission payments.

• **Customs:** Corruption and bribery in customs matters have been long-standing problems in the region. Customs corruption is a serious non-tariff barrier that can deprive parties of the benefits of trade liberalization negotiated under an FTAA.

**Recommendations:** Efforts to eradicate customs corruption should be a priority. Progress should be made before entering into the FTAA agreement. Improvement in customs administration provides a good opportunity for early harvest actions that would show tangible results and a dedicated commitment to the negotiation of an effective FTAA agreement. Countries should, by a certain date, implement regionally compatible customs automation systems which would allow regional integration and facilitate the realization of benefits negotiated under the FTAA.

## II. COMMITMENT TO DEVELOP A HEMISPHERIC ANTICORRUPTION APPROACH:

• **InterAmerican Convention:** The OAS members moved quickly to fulfill the Summit commitment to negotiate a new hemispheric agreement against corruption by concluding and signing the InterAmerican Convention Against Corruption in March 1996. If implemented and enforced, this important agreement would strengthen existing regimes and add new tools, including criminalization of transnational bribery. Implementation of the convention would fulfill the Summit commitments to establish effective measures against illicit enrichment and to establish conflict of interest standards for public employees and penalties for abuse of public office for private gain.

However, to date, only seven countries have ratified, including Bolivia, Costa Rica, Ecuador, Mexico, Paraguay, Peru, and Venezuela.

**Recommendations:** Leaders should commit to conclude the ratification process prior to the Santiago Summit next April, 1998. Such action would demonstrate a dedicated commitment to the principles enumerated in the convention and permit the leaders to focus at the Santiago Summit on implementation of key provisions. This should include a commitment to provide adequate funding to the OAS to promote this process.

## III. COMMITMENT TO DOMESTIC REFORM:

In addition to calling for a regional convention, the leaders committed to take a broad range of steps to combat corruption. The following reflects a summary of reports received recently from some of the Transparency International chapters in the hemisphere on a few of the anticorruption initiatives by the public and private sectors. They indicate that progress to date has been uneven and more limited than hoped. Yet, as a member of TI-Bolivia cautions, credit should be given for the steady progress that has been made in many countries in the region on a range of institutional reforms to solidify the transition to democracy, strengthen the rule of law, and create more open markets.

### Argentina

President Menem has made public statements recognizing the need to reduce the perception of corruption in Argentina, and an Office of Government Ethics was established in 1997. Nonetheless, there are widespread allegations of corruption and bribery in the judiciary which have undermined public confidence.

Local actions include agreement by the governor of the province of Mendoza to create "islands of integrity," as proposed by the Argentina chapter of Transparency International, and to enhance transparency in the procurement process, by holding public hearings and requiring anti-bribery pledges to be signed by both the government and bidders. The Attorney General will have enforcement authority.

### Bolivia

Corruption is still perceived to be at a high level but privatization of six major state-owned enterprises in the last few years has had a positive effect on reducing it. Reforms are also proceeding to modernize the tax, financial, and accounting systems, and the comptrollers office was reportedly cited by the World Bank as among the best in Latin America. Moreover, at its first cabinet meeting, the new government, which took office on August 6, discussed a ten-point code of conduct for all public officials.

### Brazil

Despite some slight improvement in 1997, Brazil's performance is also limited. Recent allegations of corruption in the tendering of bids in the energy and health areas have been in the news, and Brazil is rated among the "top ten" money laundering countries.

# XI. POST-SANTIAGO EVALUATIONS

Several anticorruption measures have been initiated but are facing resistance:

- In the area of money laundering, the Central Bank will soon require banks to report all transactions over US$50,000, a high threshold. Historically, Brazil has allowed almost unfettered capital transfers in and out of Brazil, without interference from the Central Bank. The new Central Bank president may take firmer action in this area.

- In 1994, President Itamar Franco signed a "provisional measure" establishing a Federal Internal Control Secretariat with Inspectors General in each ministry. However, due to intense political pressure, authority has been renewed on a temporary basis monthly for the past forty-one months, and the Secretariat lacks adequate staffing or budget.

- Congress passed the first stage of the 1998 budget with an innovation which required the Executive Branch to be more "transparent" in reporting expenditures to the public. However, the President vetoed this provision, and the Congress is not expected to override.

- Requirements for reporting campaign finance sources were passed in 1993 for the 1994 elections. However, there is high level pressure to water down the requirements, leaving them only superficial.

## Canada

As a member of the OAS and the OECD, Canada is subject to both organization's antibribery commitments, particularly criminalizing transnational bribery. To date, however, it has not taken action to implement the commitments.

Since the Summit, the government has created an Office of the Ethics Counsellor. It has implemented codes of conduct for public sector employees in the ministries of Transport, Communications, Citizenship and Immigration, Foreign Service, and in 1997, for lobbyists. The Auditor General of Canada has issued a report on "Ethics and Fraud Awareness in Government", and a task force on public service values and ethics recently issued the Tait Report.

## Dominican Republic

Soon after taking office, President Fernandez announced an anticorruption program and established a Department for the Prevention of Corruption. The offices of Customs, Internal Revenue, Health and Human Services, and the Attorney General, who has responsibility for the program, are working with the assistance of representatives of the Latin American and Caribbean chapters of Transparency International to develop a work plan for public administration, procurement, and privatization. This is a "pilot" program for the IDB, which is providing the funding.

## Nicaragua

Shortly after taking office, the new Nicaraguan president Arnoldo Aleman became the first president to disclose his assets to the comptroller general. Most other incoming officials also made asset disclosures. The new government is seeking to enhance the public perception of the comptroller general's office and established a "Transparency Office." Nonetheless, in view of ongoing political tension, there is concern that transparency reform may be marginalized.

## Panama

The Government of Panama seems to be taking its commitments seriously with several concrete initiatives. An Intergovernmental Commission against Corruption, with representatives from the Public Ministry and the Controller General, was created to develop an anticorruption program. The program calls for improvement in community participation, and to this end, the government has undertaken a one-year anticorruption project, "National Dialogue for Civic Education and Control of Corruption" and created a hotline in the office of the Controller General to receive reports of corruption 24 hours a day.

The program also calls for analysis and modification of anticorruption legislation. A 1995 law simplifies public procurement and other administrative processes. The government has investigated numerous corruption cases and initiated judicial proceedings against one legislator, a judge of the Supreme Court, a governor, an ambassador, and various mayors for criminal acts. However, no decisions have been rendered for the period 1994-1997.

## United States

Despite its active participation in the negotiation process, the U.S. has not yet ratified the InterAmerican Convention against Corruption.

Although the U.S. has in place many anticorruption systems, including disclosure of assets and conflict of interest requirements for public officials, oversight of government functions, guarantees of a free press, an independent judiciary, freedom of information legislation and stringent procurement rules, one area where progress is still needed is campaign finance reform.

## Venezuela

President Caldera played a leadership role in the convention, and Venezuela ratified it this year. Nonetheless, despite the appointment of a special anticorruption commissioner, domestic measures to make the government operations more transparent and accountable are weak and corrupt acts by government officials go largely unpunished. A Code of Ethics for Public Employees has been established, but it has no stiff penalties. An exception is the work of the Ministry for State Reform which is trying to promote modernization.

**Recommendation:** A report from each national government on progress made since 1994 is expected to be delivered to the Santiago Summit. Monitoring on a more frequent basis and providing public access to such reports should be instituted. The OAS should provide technical assistance and promote progress.

## IV. COMMITMENT TO INCREASE CIVIL SOCIETY PARTICIPATION:

The Summit *Plan of Action* states that "[A]ll aspects of public administration in a democracy must be transparent and open to public scrutiny." It calls for more open discussion, "facilitating public access to information necessary for meaningful outside review," and reviewing regulations to facilitate the operation of non-governmental actors.

To date, there is little evidence that most governments have made meaningful progress on these critical aspects of civil society participation and more needs to be done.

An exception seems to be in Panama, where the government has found important ways to cooperate with the Transparency International chapter. Actions include collaboration on the design of the Intergovernmental Commission's anticorruption program and monitoring by the chapter of selected public procurement proceedings and privatizations, e.g., privatization in telecommunications. The Public Ministry opened an Office of Freedom of Information, permitting free access to government information to any citizen, and, at the suggestion of the chapter, agreed to establish anti-bribery pacts for its purchases.

Even without widespread government cooperation, there is a steady growth of civil society groups concerned with accountability of all branches of government and efficient delivery of public services. Transparency International chapters are now operating or in formation in 14 countries, including Argentina, Bolivia, Brazil, Canada, Colombia, Costa Rica, Ecuador, Jamaica, Panama, Paraguay, Peru, United States, Uruguay, and Venezuela.

They are coalitions bringing together the business sector, public officials, academics, professionals, and other members of civil society. For example, the Peruvian chapter's members include the Public Defender, an official of the Supreme Court, the President of the Diplomatic Academy, the ex-Dean of the Law School of Lima and other academics and professionals.

TI chapters determine their own agendas and objectives. In Venezuela, Pro Calidad de Vida has trained 1500 volunteers to fight corruption in Venezuela, Mexico, Bolivia, Ecuador, Nicaragua, and Panama. In Panama, activities include publishing monthly full page public bulletins about corruption in the country's major newspaper, holding seminars with trade unions and in the provinces, and sponsoring scholastic writing contests, studies of perceptions of corruption, and citizen debates.

In Guatemala, in the aftermath of the peace accords, many of the government's systems and powers are under review. Acción Ciudadana, the local NGO which has indicated interest in forming a Transparency International chapter, is monitoring the legislature's activities, keeping the public informed, and encouraging citizen participation in the implementation of the peace accords.

Civil society played an important role in formulating the commitments undertaken by the leaders in Miami. In the U.S., the government continues to solicit regularly the input of the Civil Society Task Force, comprised of numerous NGOs. During preparations for the Bolivia Summit on Sustainable Development, the OAS provided an opportunity for dozens of civil society organizations from around the hemisphere to make presentations.

**Recommendations:** It is crucial to the outcome of the Santiago Summit that there be a channel for citizens to provide input and to be present at the proceedings. Further, the leaders recognized that a vigorous democracy requires broad participation in public issues. This requires an informed citizenry that may freely participate. All governments should fulfill their commitment to "facilitate public access to information necessary for meaningful outside review" by passage of freedom of information legislation guaranteeing this right. Legislation should also be enacted to protect the right of citizens to criticize public officials.

#  XI. POST-SANTIAGO EVALUATIONS

*Transparency International (TI) USA*

# The Importance of the Organization of American States (OAS) Convention Against Corruption

Less than two years after the 1994 Miami Summit of the Americas called for the negotiation of a regional anticorruption initiative, the Inter-American Convention was signed by twenty-three nations. The Convention's rapid conclusion reflects the hemispheric consensus among government leaders, the private sector and citizens that addressing bribery and corruption is a priority. To date, fourteen countries have ratified the treaty, and several others including the United States have submitted it to their legislatures.

RATIONALE:

1. **Promotes Fair Competition:** Effective and prompt implementation will promote fair competition, reducing the opportunity for competitors to play by different rules, helping to reduce the risk to honest business, and maximizing returns for all.

2. **Creates Hospitable Investment Environment:** Anticorruption measures help economies create a hospitable environment for trade and investment and contribute to keeping private capital from shifting elsewhere.

3. **Establishes Transparency and Accountability:** Political stability and emerging democratic systems are strengthened with the elimination of bribery and corruption and the resultant enhanced public confidence.

4. **Maximizes Resource Allocation**: An anticorruption regime supports development by conserving resources for health, education and other basic needs.

5. **Contributes to Comprehensive Regime:** Implementation of the OECD Anti-bribery Convention will help reduce transnational bribery; complementary national-level efforts are necessary to achieve a comprehensive anticorruption regime.

PROPOSAL: AN AGREEMENT BY ALL HEMISPHERIC GOVERNMENT LEADERS TO RATIFY THE CONVENTION BY DECEMBER 31, 1999, AND:

6. **Active Monitoring:** The OAS should establish a monitoring and follow-up mechanism to promote ratification and to assist countries with implementation of the Convention, modeled on the OECD Working Group on Bribery and the Financial Action Task Force.

7. **Prompt Implementation:** Hemispheric leaders should demonstrate commitment to accountability to the public by promptly concluding an agreement on transparency in procurement.

## BACKGROUND:

The Convention obligates signatories to enforce anti-bribery laws and strengthen cooperation between countries on criminal investigations, judicial assistance and extradition. Parties are to criminalize transnational bribery and illicit enrichment, which requires only an unexplained increase in assets, rather than proof of receipt of a bribe. The Convention also encourages "preventive measures," including strengthening procurement, books and record practices, codes of conduct, and disclosure of assets.

## CONCLUSION:

Prompt ratification and implementation of the OAS Anticorruption Convention will promote fair competition and stimulate trade, investment and economic growth. Its transparency and anticorruption measures protect scarce resources and enhance public confidence. Ratification by the end of 1999, effective implementation, especially in highly visible areas such as transparency in procurement, and the creation of an OAS follow-up mechanism are needed for maximum benefit to governments, citizens and the private sector.

Co-authored by NAM and Transparency International-USA with input from members: 10/98

# XI. POST-SANTIAGO EVALUATIONS

*Transparency International (TI) USA*

# Recommendations of Transparency International on Combating Corruption to the Organization of American States (OAS) Symposium on Strengthening Probability and Civic Ethics
## November 16, 1998

Considering the pledges made to combat corruption in the Plans of Action of the 1994 and 1998 Summits of the Americas and the provisions of the Inter-American Convention against Corruption ("Convention"), governments should commit to:

### 1) TAKE THE FOLLOWING ACTIONS REGARDING THE CONVENTION:

- Complete ratification of the Inter-American Convention against Corruption by December 31, 1999;
- Establish an organ at the OAS to promote its implementation and to monitor progress;
- Report progress to the OAS General Assembly in June 1999 and annually thereafter.

### 2) TAKE THE FOLLOWING CONCRETE STEPS ON IMPLEMENTATION:

- Enact standards of conduct and rules regarding conflict of interest and the incompatibility of public office and private interests;
- Require public disclosure of assets of high level public officials (and their families) in the executive, legislative and judicial branches;
- Create or strengthen enforcement capacity of oversight bodies;
- Require the timely publication of information regarding government activities, including budgets and expenditures, public access to information, and public hearings for expression of the opinion of citizens.

## 3) PROMOTE INDEPENDENCE, INTEGRITY AND TRANSPARENCY IN THE ADMINISTRATION OF JUSTICE:

- Publish criteria for selection of judges and provide public review of candidates;
- Institute merit-based selection of judges;
  - Train in the highest ethical standards;
  - Create oversight mechanisms;
  - Strengthen the role of public prosecutors.

## 4) PROMOTE TRANSPARENCY AND INTEGRITY IN GOVERNMENT PROCUREMENT AND CUSTOMS:

- Implement a regional agreement on transparency in procurement by December 31, 1999;
- Experiment with Integrity Pact arrangements to learn from experience and replicate on a wider scale based on experience gained;
- Encourage the use of "no bribe commitments" and corporate codes of conduct that prohibit bribes in public bidding as well as in projects financed by the World Bank and Inter-American Development Bank (IDB);
- Encourage the Interamerican Development Bank to adopt uniform rules, documents, and policies of the highest standard for public bidding;
- Take immediate measures to simplify procedures and eradicate corruption in customs offices.

# XI. POST-SANTIAGO EVALUATIONS

*Transparency International (TI) USA*

# Transparency International-Americas Informe de Avances Anticorrupción/Anticorruption Progress Report

TI-AMÉRICAS PROGRAMA DE MONITOREO - CONVENCIÓN INTERAMERICANA CONTRA LA CORRUPCIÓN

TI-AMERICAS OAS ANTICORRUPTION CONVENTION MONITORING PROGRAM

This Progress Report on the Organization of American States' Anticorruption Convention was compiled on November 2, 1998, in the form of a table, which follows the Explanatory Notes.

## Explanatory Notes for the Table, Convención Interamericana contra la Corrupción/OAS Anticorruption Convention, 11/2/98.

1. **Signatarios/Signatories:** Sólo 25 de los 34 miembros de la OEA han firmado la Convención; paises que no la han ratificado son//Only 25 of the 34 OAS members have signed the Convention; countries that have not are: Antigua y Barbuda, Barbados, Belice, Canada, Dominica, Grenada, Santa Lucia, San Vicente y las Granadinas, St. Kitts y Nevis.

2. **Otros paises que han ratificado/Other countries that have ratified:** Honduras (5/25/98); México (5/27/97); Trinidad and Tobago (4/15/98).

3. **Soborno transnacional/Transnational bribery:** Seis miembros de la OEA (Argentina, Brasil, Canadá, Chile, México, y USA) firmaron la Convención de la OCDE contra el Soborno de Funcionarios Públicos Extranjeros, que prohibe el soborno transnacional.

Six OAS members (Argentina, Brazil, Canada, Chile, Mexico, and USA) signed the OECD Convention on Combating Bribery of Foreign Officials, which prohibits transnational bribery.

4. **Enriquecimiento ilícito/Illicit enrichment:** En algunos paises sin el tipo penal específico del enriquecimiento ilícito, existen o se ha propuesto delitos relacionados con un resultado similar.

In some countries without the specific offense of illicit enrichment, related offenses with a similar effect exist or have been proposed.

5. **Divulgación del patrimonio/Disclosure of assets:** Algunos paises exigen la declaración del patrimonio de los funcionarios públicos solamente a una agencia gubernamental, sin que haya un derecho ciudadano de acceso a los resultados, y en general hay pocos indicios que la información ha sido utilizada para comenzar acciones penales. También, en algunos paises, la cobertura se limita a ciertos funcionarios y/o cierto patrimonio. La Convención prevé la divulgación *pública,* que permite una mayor rendición de cuentas y el control ciudadano.

Some countries require the declaration of assets of public officials only to a government agency, without any right of citizen access to the information, and in gerneral there is little evidence that the information has been used to initiate prosecution. Also, in some countries, coverage is limited to certain officials and some types of assets. The Convention foresees *public* declaration, which permits greater accountability and citizen oversight.

6. **Transparencia en las licitaciones públicas/ Transparency in government procurement:** La Convención insta la licitación pública transparente, equitativa y eficiente. Actualmente, aún en paises con leyes sobre las licitaciones con algunos elementos de transparencia, muchas no son uniformes, comprensivas y facilmente disponibles. Los paises pueden lograr esta meta con la celebración e implementación para el año 2000 de un Acuerdo del ALCA sobre la Transparencia en las Licitaciones Públicas.

The Convention calls for transparent, equitable and efficient procurement. Currently, even in countries with procurement laws specifying some elements of transparency, many are not uniform, comprehensive or readily available. Countries can achieve this goal by concluding and implementing an FTAA Agreement on Transparency in Government Procurement by the year 2000.

7. **Acceso a la información/Access to information:** Algunos paises tienen derechos constitucionales a peticionar o sobre la libertad de expresión que en la práctica no brindan el acceso a la información. Para facilitar la transparencia y participación ciudadana, los paises deben establecer un derecho al acceso a la información, la difusión regular de la información, y audiencias públicas abiertas.

Some countries have constitutional rights to petition or of free expression that do not in practice afford access to information. In order to facilitate accountability, transparency and citizen participation, countries should establish a right to access information, a requirement for regular publication of information, and open public hearings.

8. Propuestas de reforma no enviadas a la legislatura. Reform proposals not yet sent to legislature.

Transparency International-Americas Informe de Avances Anticorrupción/Anticorruption Progress Report

# XI. POST-SANTIAGO EVALUATIONS

Convención Interamericana contra la Corrupción/OAS Anticorruption Convention, 11/2/98

| País/ Country (1) | Ratificación/ Ratification (2) | Soborno Transnacional/ Transnational Bribery (3) | Enriquecimiento to Ilícito/ Illicit Enrichment (4) | Códigos de Conducta/ Codes of Conduct | Divulgación de patrimonio/ Asset Disclosure (5) | Transparencia en las licitaciones/ Procurement (6) | Acceso a la información/ Access to Information (7) |
|---|---|---|---|---|---|---|---|
| Argentina | Sí/Yes (8/4/97) | No | Sí/Yes | Sí/Yes | No | No | No |
| Bolivia | Sí/Yes | No | Sí/Yes | No (8) | Sí/Yes (5) | Sí/Yes | Sí/Yes – (Derecho constitucional/ constitutional right) |
| Brasil | No – (Enviada al Congreso/ Submitted to Congress) | No | Sí/Yes – (No cumple con la Conv./Not in compliance with Conv.) | No (8) | Sí/Yes (5) | Sí/Yes | Sí/Yes – (Derecho constitucional/ constitutional right) |
| Canada | No | No | No (4) | Sí/Yes | No | Sí/Yes | Sí/Yes |
| Chile | Sí/Yes (9/22/98) | No | No (8) | No – (Pendiente en legislatura/ Pending in legislature) | No – (Pendiente en legislatura/ Pending in legislature) | No (8) | No – (Pendiente en legislatura/ Pending in legislature) |
| Colombia | Sí/Yes | No | Sí/Yes | Sí/Yes | Sí/Yes (5) | Sí/Yes | Sí/Yes |
| Costa Rica | Sí/Yes (5/9/97) | No (8) | Sí/Yes | No – (Pendiente en legislatura/ Pending in legislature) | No – (Pendiente en legislatura/ Pending in legislature) | No (8) | No – (Pendiente en legislatura/ Pending in legislature) |
| Ecuador | Sí/Yes (5/26/97) | No | Sí/Yes | No – (Pendiente en legislatura/ Pending in legislature) | Sí/Yes | No – (Pendiente en legislatura/ Pending in legislature) | Sí/Yes – (Derecho constitucional/ constitutional right) |
| Jamaica | No | No | No | Sí/Yes | No – (Pendiente en legislatura/ Pending in legislature) | No | No – (Pendiente en legislatura/ Pending in legislature) |

*Continued next page*

*Continued from previous page*

| País/ Country (1) | Ratificación/ Ratification (2) | Soborno Transnacional/ Transnational Bribery (3) | Enriquecimiento to Ilícito/ Illicit Enrichment (4) | Códigos de Conducta/ Codes of Conduct | Divulgación de patrimonio/ Asset Disclosure (5) | Transparencia en las licitaciones/ Procurement (6) | Acceso a la información/ Access to Information (7) |
|---|---|---|---|---|---|---|---|
| Panamá | Sí/Yes (7/20/98) | No – (Pendiente en legislatura/ Pending in legislature) | No – (Pendiente en legislatura/ Pending in legislature) | No | No – (Pendiente en legislatura/ Pending in legislature) (5) | Sí/Yes | Sí/Yes – (Derecho de petición/right to petition) (7) |
| Paraguay | Sí/Yes (11/29/96) | No | Sí/Yes (bajo reforma/ under reform) (4) | NO (5) | Sí/Yes | Sí/Yes | Sí/Yes (Derecho constitucional/ Const. right) (7) |
| Perú | Sí/Yes (4/4/97) | NO | Sí/Yes (No cumple con la Conv./Not in compliance with Conv.) | No | Sí/Yes | Sí/Yes | Sí/Yes |
| Uruguay | Sí/Yes (9/15/98) | No | No – (Pendiente en legislatura/pending in legislature) (4) | No | Sí/Yes (bajo reforma/ under reform) | No | Enviado al Congreso/ Transmitted to Congress 11/96 |
| USA | No (Enviada al Congreso/Submitted to Congress – 4/1/98) | Sí/Yes | No (4) | Sí/Yes | Sí/Yes | Sí/Yes | Sí/Yes |
| Venezuela | Sí/Yes (5/22/97) | No | No – (Pendiente en legislatura/Pending in legislature) | Sí/Yes | No | No | No |

# XI. POST-SANTIAGO EVALUATIONS

*Transparency International (TI) USA*

# TI-Americas Anticorruption Progress Report 2/8/99

At the 1994 Miami Summit, leaders called for a fight against corruption, starting with a hemispheric anticorruption agreement. In 1996, the Inter-American Convention against Corruption was concluded. The Convention is an important political commitment and requires signatories to take action, by enforcing existing anticorruption laws, providing mutual legal and judicial assistance, criminalizing transnational bribery and illicit enrichment, and enacting measures to enhance the accountability and integrity of public officials.

To encourage national implementation of this important agreement, TI chapters across the Americas have taken an initial tally of their governments' actions to date and today publish their findings in the TI Americas Anticorruption Progress Report. The TI Americas Anticorruption Progress Report is a snapshot, reflecting both progress achieved and areas where action is needed. The report covers the 15 countries in the hemisphere where there are TI chapters. Future reports will cover more countries and also evaluate the effectiveness of legislation and regulations and the extent of their enforcement. This effort supplements other TI anticorruption activities as TI chapters recognize that legal reform is only one important element of a comprehensive program to build integrity systems.

In brief, to date, only 25 of the 34 Organization of American States (OAS) members have signed and only 14 of 34 have ratified. The report also indicates whether there are laws related to key provisions, including criminalization of transnational bribery and illicit enrichment, codes of conduct and disclosure of assets, transparency in procurement, and access to information. These important commitments of the signatories are crucial elements of a national integrity system. Progress has been mixed. Of the countries surveyed:

• Only the US criminalizes transnational bribery and only 6 criminalize illicit enrichment in compliance with the Convention;

• Only 6 have codes of conduct, and, of those, not all have conflict of interest standards;

• Fewer than half require public disclosure of assets and even some of those apply only to certain officials or types of assets, and there is little evidence that the information is being used to initiate prosecution;

• Nine have laws on procurement with some transparency provisions, but the provisions are not uniform, comprehensive or readily available to the public;

• Many have established a right to access to information but few have effective procedures to permit citizens to pursue that right. Nor is there a government obligation to provide regular, timely government publication of information or public hearings.

TI chapters in the Americas urge their governments to move quickly to carry out their commitments and urge the National Ethics Authorities, representatives of international institutions, and civil society meeting at the OAS Symposium on Strengthening Probity and Civic Ethics in Santiago, Chile to include the attached recommendations in their final communiqué.

All OAS members should ratify by December 31, 1999 and should agree to create an OAS Monitoring Mechanism to conduct mutual evaluations, provide technical assistance, and report progress to ministers annually.

Transparency International, the global non-governmental coalition to curb corruption, and its fifteen chapters in the Americas stand ready to support the efforts of governments, business and other civil society groups to move forward on fighting corruption.

# XI. POST-SANTIAGO EVALUATIONS

*The Esquel Group Foundation (EGF), a non-profit private foundation created in 1984, provides a variety of services to non-governmental organizations, foundations, private corporations and international development agencies working in Latin America and the Caribbean. Its membership in the Grupo Esquel network of entities in Argentina, Bolivia, Brazil, Chile, Ecuador, Peru and Uruguay enhances the expertise it draws upon to provide quality services. It promotes alternative policies and programs that incorporate social equity and environmental concerns and strengthen the role of civil society. In addition, EGF works in collaboration with private sector entities to improve public policy for sustainable development, paying attention to political, economic, social, as well as natural resource considerations. Services include research, advocacy, technical cooperation and extensive advice regarding development in Latin America.*

## The Civil Society Task Force Dialogue with the Responsible Coordinators of the Civil Society Initiative of the Summit of the Americas

SEPTEMBER 18, 1998 — 8:30 A.M. TO 12:00
THE WASHINGTON CLUB, 15 DUPONT CIRCLE, NW
WASHINGTON, D.C.

**Ramón Daubón** welcomed the participants, noting that it was a privilege to be holding this special session with the Co-Coordinators of the Civil Society Initiative of the Summit of the Americas on the fourth anniversary of the Task Force and the second since being coordinated by the Esquel Group Foundation (EGF). He introduced Ambassador Juan Felipe Yriart, member of the Board and former Chairman of EGF.

**Amb. Yriart** expressed his gratitude for everyone's presence on behalf of EGF's President, Kenneth Cole. He noted that Grupo Esquel has been intimately involved in advocating the importance of civil society in Latin America and the Caribbean (LAC). **Amb. Yriart** explained that the great changes taking place in the region—market reforms, globalization, redefined states—have caused much confusion and misunderstanding as the traditional roles of different societal actors are necessarily questioned and realigned. In the midst of such change and confusion, he said, Esquel has come to the conclusion that the participation of civil society—by providing an umbrella under which such issues can be digested in their cultural, social, political and economic dimensions—has become even more critical for the sustainability of the processes of democratization and development. In that context, he welcomed the decision of **Ambassadors Espinal** and **Thompson** to seek this dialogue and offered the Task Force as a venue for continued exchange.

**Ambassador Flavio Darío Espinal** of the Dominican Republic expressed his country's commitment to their new role as co-coordinators of the Initiative and their sense of pride in sharing this responsibility with Jamaica. He highlighted that having civil society included in Summit language is an important accomplishment that responds to a new reality in which political opening and participation are increasingly important. In this sense, he noted, the strengthening of civil society is part of a general process of democratic consolidation which also requires institutional reform, tolerance, renewed judicial systems, a free press, the rule of law and pluralism. A variety of issues need to guide our efforts to move forward this Initiative, **Amb. Espinal** stated:

- This does not imply the search for a uniform model or a generalized prescription, as each society has its own specific characteristics. Therefore, we need to promote substantive discussion that will allow us to understand those different realities and define alternatives that take them into account.
- The issue of civil society has caused a political division along the lines of "good" (promoting its development) and "bad" (resisting its promotion). We need to seek a positive environment that promotes advancements in this area, acknowledging that no country is totally open or closed.
- We need to ensure the participation of a broad range of groups and prevent the development of an "elite" group of organizations with access to these processes.
- We need to create new possibilities and open new doors for keeping the momentum of the initiative.

**Amb. Espinal** concluded by inviting all participants to voice their suggestions on how to move forward the Civil Society Initiative.

**Amb. Arthur Thompson** of Jamaica thanked the organizers and participants, noting that he would try to complement the introduction of **Amb. Espinal.** He agreed on the need for pragmatism regarding uniform models and solutions, while emphasizing that there are common problems and key issues we should be addressing. He warned about resurfacing skepticism by some governments in Santiago to recognize civil society. Finally, **Amb. Thompson** called upon the participants to work for the integration of civil society vis à vis the governments of the region, explaining that the pressures of reduced budgets threaten the ability of bureaucracies to deal with a growing number of civil society groups.

**Daubón** introduced **Amb. William Walker** as the first speaker of the next session, "Negotiating the Civil Society Initiative: Miami to the Present." **Amb. Walker** introduced himself to the group, as he has recently replaced Amb. Richard Brown as US Senior Summit Coordinator. He explained that he has spent two-thirds of his 37-year foreign service career in LAC-related issues, including assignments in Argentina, Brazil, Bolivia, El Salvador and Honduras. Most recently, **Amb. Walker** was directing a U.S. Agency for International Development (USAID)-funded project on Administration of Justice throughout the region. He noted that as Summit Coordinator he plans to continue his predecessor's commitment to the promotion of civil society in the hemisphere.

**Daubón** explained that reaching a consensus on the Civil Society Initiative at the Miami Summit in 1994 was very hard, as a result of the reluctance of many governments to accept the importance of the topic. He highlighted the role of the Government of Jamaica along with other supporters that insisted on including civil society language in Summit documents. Miami has undoubtedly provided a good foundation, but it was in the Summit on Sustainable Development held in Santa Cruz, Bolivia, that the Initiative really "raised the floor" of minimally accepted participatory practices, **Daubon** mentioned. A key step in that process was the officially sanctioned conference of civil society held in Montevideo before the Summit. He explained that the meeting produced recommended language on civil society which had been drafted by 45 NGOs and 28 official representations. This language was ultimately approved by the Heads of State and included *in toto* in the Santa Cruz Declaration and Plan of Action.

**Mr. Sergio Jáuregui**, who came in representation of Minister Eric Reyes of Bolivia, explained that his country has approached participation in a serious and systematic way through its Popular Participation Law and its practical implementation.

**Robin Rosenberg** of the North-South Center of the University of Miami was a member of the US Delegation to the Santiago Summit. He noted that the Civil Society Initiative was advanced only marginally by the language at Santiago, and this after very difficult negotiations. Such advances included the following:

- Program to fill the gaps of Miami in terms of promoting an enabling environment for CSOs, including the issue of financing.
- Commitment to the promotion of Civil Society-Government partnerships.
- Positioning of the OAS as a focal point in these discussions and eventual programs.
- Endorsement of ongoing projects such as the Inter-American Strategy for Public Participation.
- Promoting the adoption of work plans for the establishment of legal and institutional frameworks for civil society that can be implemented at the national level.

**Rosenberg** believes that the challenge is now to ensure that the initiative moves forward by preventing the lowest common denominator from becoming the norm. This will be critical for the success of the Inter-American system, he noted, and will require the continued institutionalization of the Summit Process in Canada and beyond.

# XI. POST-SANTIAGO EVALUATIONS

The Civil Society Task Force Dialogue with the Responsible Coordinators of the Civil Society Initiative of the Summit of the Americas

Chilean Summit Coordinator **Ambassador Carlos Portales** highlighted the fact that in the Santiago Summit, civil society participation was seen as a cross-cutting theme running through the four baskets—education, democracy, poverty and economic integration. He also noted that the challenge of building civil society in the region goes beyond raising demands, but should necessarily include an active participation in seeking solutions to our pressing problems.

**Jaime Aparicio**, the new Coordinator for Summit Follow-up at the OAS, introduced the next section on concrete activities affecting civil society development in the region. He stressed that the Miami Summit marked the realization by governments that the incorporation of civil society is critical if the region is to accomplish the mandates of the new Inter-American Agenda. **Aparicio** explained that the OAS has had a positive evolution in the last couple of years with regards to civil society:

- the celebrations for the organizations' 50th Anniversary included, for the first time in its history, many civil society representatives on its panels;
- during the Bolivia Summit Process, over 60 civil society organizations addressed the Permanent Council of the OAS;
- emerging out of Santa Cruz, the Inter-American Strategy for Public Participation (ISP) was conceived at the OAS and is now developing the pilot projects which will allow it to assist governments in becoming more participatory on issues related to sustainable development;
- during the last General Assembly, the Ministers of Foreign Affairs directed the Permanent Council to design ways by which the OAS could involve civil society in its operations as well as assist member governments in becoming more participatory; and
- it has recently created the Office of Summit Follow-up, which will work closely with civil society in assisting and monitoring.

**Eric Dannenmaier** of USAID's Environmental Law Program explained that the ISP is a 1.5-year project designed to identify key elements of a strategy for participation that will be presented to governments in July 1999. The strategy has seven key components—six consist of information gathering and the seventh is the technical report containing strategic recommendations. One of the components of the project, entitled the "Legal and Institutional," is an empirical review of the regulations that govern public participation and how they work in practice. This component consists of a study, which is already under way, of legislation in 12 countries based on 21 indicators of participation. **Dannenmaier** shared some preliminary findings with participants:

- Aggregated figures indicate that less than 50% of the laws **do not** allow participation.
- The three types of "access" studied include access to process (most important in Latin America), access to justice and access to information.
- They noted a regional difference between Central and South America in terms of a distinct bias towards participation being an **obligation of government (CA) vs. a right of the citizen (SA)**. This conceptual difference has implications for policy choices affecting participation.
- Less than 25% of the laws provide the necessary financing for activities related to participation (i.e., staff time, resources for meetings and information dissemination, etc.).
- In terms of trends over time, there has been a consistent increase in the level of sensitivity of environmental laws to participation. In contrast, general legislation **excluding participation** increased until 1990 and has evened out since then.

He noted that in the last organizational meeting of the ISP held in Jamaica, three major conclusions were reached regarding the strategy to be formulated:

- that it be geographically balanced (taking into account the particular needs of small island states);
- that it focus on sustainable development as defined by the Santa Cruz Declaration and Plan of Action
- that it ensure sectoral diversity.

**Anne Marie Blackman** of the Unit for the Promotion of Democracy (UPD) at the OAS informed the group of efforts that Unit is undertaking to promote citizen participation. She noted that as the Unit mandated to provide support to Member States in consolidating their democratic systems and institutions, participation permeates all activities of the UPD. Particularly relevant is the "Program of Cooperation in Decentralization, Local Government and Citizen Participation," currently being undertaken and which focuses simultaneously on strengthening decentralization efforts and the functioning of local government as well as on opening space for citizen participation at the municipal/local/community levels. The program has four general objectives to be implemented across six program areas:

661

**Objectives**

- Contributing to policy debate and serving as a forum for creation, dissemination and exchange of information;
- Supporting institution-building in central, local government and civil society, principally through "horizontal cooperation" approaches among countries of the region;
- Enhancing the democratic legitimacy of local governance through increased citizen access and participation;
- collaboration with other agencies and institutions.

**Program Areas**

- Legal and regulatory frameworks
- Institutional development
- Relations between central and local government authorities
- Relations between legislatures and local authorities
- Aspects of economic and social development relating to local governance
- Information systems to support decentralization, local government and citizen participation.

**Blackman** also mentioned that the UPD is planning to hold a "Democratic Forum" specifically on the topic of civil society before the end of the year.

**Stahis Panagides** of Fundação Grupo Esquel Brasil (FGEB) and Esquel Group Foundation gave an overview of new proposed legislation to modernize the regulation of civil society organizations in Brazil. He emphasized that this is one of the most participatory legislative efforts, resulting from extensive analysis and dialogue conducted by senior public officials together with leaders of civil society. Accordingly, the proposed legislation is expected to produce a legal framework conducive to the expansion and strengthening of the third sector. **Luis Danin Lobo**, also of FGEB, stressed the importance of the new legislation in the context of the process of decentralization.

**Nelson Stratta** of Grupo Esquel Uruguay informed the group of recent events in Uruguay. He explained that one of the objectives of the process of modernization of the state in Uruguay was to "bring the state closer to the people" in response to a heightened awareness regarding the importance of civil society. This is conceived as increased openness and cooperation in the definition and implementation of social policy, including subcontracting of civil society organizations. In the reform of the state loan from the Inter-American Development Bank, he noted, are funds to be used in the setup of an Institution that would assist in the modernization of civil society so that it can effectively take on this enhanced role. **Stratta** mentioned that the Institution is currently bringing together interested parties in Government and both the private for-profit and non-profit sectors to explore cooperation in social investment—a win-win situation from a practical standpoint for all three actors: (a) for the state, it could mean increased impact for its social expenditures; (b) for the business sector, increased impact and recognition of their social investments; and (c) for CSOs, increased participation in social policy design, implementation and monitoring, including financial transfers. **Stratta** concluded by emphasizing that civil society needs to focus on modern approaches based on concepts of social capital and to seek cooperation with the for-profit sector in thinking and addressing social problems.

**Martha Cecilia Villada** of Partners of the Americas introduced participants to the Inter-American Democracy Network, a coalition of civil society organizations working together to promote citizen participation and strengthen democracies in the hemisphere. The network currently consists of 80 non-governmental organizations (NGOs) in sixteen countries and works across six program areas: (a) deliberation for citizen participation; (b) mobilizing citizens for community action; (c) civic and voter education; (d) social responsbility; (e) organizational capacity building; and (f) advocacy. **Villada** explained that most members are very experienced in transitions from authoritarian rule and are now exploring how to move into democracy-building and deepening. She said that the network has been successful at allowing for information exchange among members. The network also provides support that enhances the local advocacy efforts of members, she concluded.

**Aparicio** closed the section and invited participants to enjoy a short coffee break. Upon return from break, **Daubón** introduced **Amb. Peter Boehm** of Canada to kick off the next section on the future of the Civil Society Initiative.

**Amb. Boehm**, who has been Summit Coordinator for Canada for the last three years, confirmed his country's commitment to enhancing a broader role for civil society in the hemisphere. He explained that the first step in expressing that commitment is ensuring a broad and open consultative mechanism for the Summit in Canada in 2001. This openness should be ecumenical, avoiding domination by certain groups and ensuring space for all.

# XI. POST-SANTIAGO EVALUATIONS

## The Civil Society Task Force Dialogue with the Responsible Coordinators of the Civil Society Initiative of the Summit of the Americas

In terms of Canada 2001, **Amb. Boehm** called upon the participants to focus on a few tangible and realistic issues. He cited the Parliamentary Network of the Americas as a positive example of efforts that create opportunities for learning, modernizing and strengthening through the Inter-American Summit Process. He emphasized the need for the OAS to put a structure in place that allows it to play a major role in the Summit Process and the promotion of civil society within it. He concluded reiterating his interest in receiving feedback from participants.

**Daubón** opened up the floor for feedback from participants. **Bruce Jay** of the AFL-CIO Solidarity Center thanked and congratulated the organizers of the meeting, noting that it stimulated an open debate while allowing for useful information exchanges. He agreed with **Amb. Boehm**'s comment on the need for broader access—which he and many others feel is not the case. Many groups feel their views are not well represented and are calling for greater receptiveness from governments, he commented.

**Amb. Yriart** highlighted the need to distinguish between citizens participating and organizations of civil society engaging in advocacy. He stressed the need for a transformation of passive citizenship to participatory citizenship in Latin America, noting that a key aspect of that transformation is education because it is the means by which citizens will (or will not) be prepared to live in a globalized world.

**Atziri Ibañez** of the National Wildlife Federation urged the Co-Coordinators to link their efforts with other Summit initiatives in which citizen participation is critical. She mentioned specifically the recently created Committee of Government Representatives within the process of the Free Trade Area of the Americas (FTAA), noting that it would be useful for the Co-Coordinators to offer their assistance in ensuring that it fulfill its role of allowing for participation. There is much they can do for this and other initiatives to enhance citizen participation in those specific contexts, she stressed. **Rosenberg** agreed, adding that it will be very hard to establish a mechanism for involvement of civil society in negotiations at the Summit Level but that perhaps the sector should focus on monitoring and implementation. **Michael Franklin** of the Organization of Africans in the Americas brought to light the point of accountability by governments of the commitments made at Summits. Citing a case in Argentina, he asked for advice on actions that could be taken to increase the implementation of these participatory practices at the national level. **Carlo Dade** of the Enterprise Research Foundation commented on the need to incorporate the business sector into this process, a sector that is already involved extensively in social issues at the local and regional level.

**Amb. Boehm** emphasized the need to accept that when 34 countries are working together, it will be hard to reach agreement on certain topics. He clarified that currently the Summit Process has two separate tracks—the FTAA negotiations and the Summit Implementation Review Group (SIRG) which deals with all other initiatives—that will ultimately have to come together. He noted that Canada was very interested in seeing the CGR move ahead.

**Amb. Thompson** reminded the group that, ultimately, it is governments that will decide on implementation within their own countries, as the SIRG does not have enforcement capabilities. In light of this, civil societies must work with their governments and make sure that they group themselves so that the consultative mechanism is both manageable and accountable. He and **Amb. Espinal** thanked the participants for their attendance and comments, stating that they look forward to continued exchanges.

**Amb. Yriart** thanked the participants and the members of the Diplomatic Corps on behalf of Esquel. **Daubón** invited all to join us for the next session of the Civil Society Task Force, to be held Friday, October 23rd from 8:30 to 10:00 a.m.

# XII. Appendix: Summit Correspondence

# XII. APPENDIX: SUMMIT CORRESPONDENCE

- *Centro de Derecho Ambiental y de los Recursos Naturales* • *Centro Mexicano de Derecho Ambiental* • *Comité Nacional Pro Defensa de la Fauna y Flora* • *Centro de Derecho Ambiental de Honduras* • *Fundación AMBIO* • *Fundación Ambiente y Recursos Naturales* • *FLACSO* • *Instituto de Derecho Ambiental y Desarrollo Sustenable* • *National Audubon Society* • *Natural Resources Defense Council* • *National Wildlife Federation* • *Universidad Autónoma Metropolitana* • *Sociedad Conservacionista Audubon de Venezuela*

October 27, 1997

Mr. Carlos Murillo
President of the Preparatory Committee
Pro-Tempore Presidency
FTAA Office
Ministry of Foreign Trade
P.O. Box 96-2050
San Jose, Costa Rica

To the Honorable President of the Preparatory Committee of the Free Trade of the Americas office:

As you prepare to discuss the appropriate role in the Free Trade Agreement of the Americas negotiations (FTAA) for private parties, we urge you to legitimize and institutionalize participation and input from a broad spectrum of civil society sectors.

Under the Joint Declaration from the Third Ministerial Meeting at Belo Horizonte, Brasil, May 16, 1997 all signatory countries stated that they "... consider[ed] the inputs from stakeholders of ... civil societies to be important to ... deliberations ... and ... encourage[d] all countries to take them into account through mechanisms of dialogue and consultation". We understand that a private-sector business forum has been institutionalized and held in conjunction with each FTAA ministerial. We also understand that business sector's recommendations have been reviewed and analyzed by the Working Groups. We believe that recommendations by the business sector are an important contribution to trade deliberations; however, they represent only one view from stakeholders of civil society.

Public participation in trade policy deliberations needs to be balanced to achieve the stated goals of the Joint Declaration. First, the inclusion of representatives from a diverse cross-section of civil society sectors, such as the environmental sector, will help ensure that negotiators take into consideration the broader views of civil society. Broader public participation in the trade policy dialogue will ensure involvement from those directly affected by economic integration. Second, formal dialogue and consultation with a broad selection from civil society will help to ensure that "[f]ree trade and economic integration ... [raise] ... standards of living, improving the working conditions of people in the Americas and better protecting the environment."[1] Third, public participation in trade deliberations is also crucial to advancing the signatory countries' "... commitment to transparency in the FTAA process."[2] Finally, public participation is a fundamental element of democratic practice and the cornerstone of an effective decision-making process. "[A] vigorous democracy requires broad public participation in public issues."[3]

As you work toward the completion of the March 1998 Declaration of San Jose, we urge you to incorporate the language of the Declaration of Principles, Summit of the Americas of 1994[4] to include "...the right of all citizens to participate..." in the decision-making processes surrounding FTAA negotiations by creating an effective avenue for public dialogue and input. Integration should guarantee adequate mechanisms for participation and interaction with negotiators, including the resources necessary to provide all members of civil society routine access to working group meetings and negotiating sessions. Participation by the environmental sector should not depend solely on further developments at the WTO.

Economic development and environmental protection are two sides of the same coin and cannot be separated. We stand ready to work with you to develop and advance a coherent Western Hemispheric agenda for sustainable development.

Thank you for your attention to this important matter.

Respectfully submitted,

*Gustavo Alanis Ortega*
Centro Mexicano de Derecho Ambiental
(Mexico)

*Luis Castelli*
Fundacion Ambiente y Recursos Naturales (Argentina)

*John J. Audley*
National Wildlife Federation (U.S.A.)

On behalf of the following:

FLACSO (Argentina)

Comite Nacional Pro Defensa de la Fauna y Flora (Chile)

Centro de Derecho Ambiental y de los Desarrollo Sustenable (Guatemala)

Instituto de Derecho Ambiental y Recursos Naturales (Costa Rica)

Centro de Derecho Ambiental de Honduras (Honduras)

Universidad Autonoma Metropolitana (Mexico)

National Audubon Society (U.S.A.)

Sociedad Conservacionista Audubon de Venezuela (Venezuela)

Natural Resources Defense Council (U.S.A.)

Fundacion AMBIO (Costa Rica)

# Notes

1. *Summit of the Americas, Declaration of Principles*, subtitle "To Promote Prosperity through Economic Integration and Free Trade," (1994, page 2).

2. *Joint Declaration from the Third Ministerial Meeting at Belo Horizonte, Brasil*, (May 16, 1997, paragraph 14).

3. *Plan of Action, Declaration of the Summit of the Americas*, subtitle "Invigorating Society/Community Participation," (1994, page 4).

4. *Declaration of Principles, Summit of the Americas*, (Santa Cruz de la Sierra, Bolivia, 1996, paragraph 8).

# XII. Appendix: Summit Correspondence

*Organization of Africans in the Americas (OAA)*

*The OAA seeks to empower communities of African descent in the Americas by assisting these populations in the exercise of their social, political and economic privileges and responsibilities, in the expressions and acknowledgment of their cultural heritage and contributions, and of their past and current conditions.*

*The mission of the OAA is established for charitable and educational purposes to improve the life chances and conditions of communities of African descent with special regard for those populations who speak Spanish and Portuguese. Through involvement and promotion of cooperative efforts among diverse Black communities, OAA functions as a resource and referral center of data, service, support, and empowerment of Africans in the Americas.*

December 1, 1997

Ms. Madeleine Albright
Secretary of State
U.S. Department of State
2201 C Street N.W.
Washington. DC 20520

Dear Madam Secretary:

The Inter-American Development Bank (IDB) recently completed a study of Black communities in Latin America. The Study revealed that Black Latin Americans make up a minimum 40 percent of the Latin American poor. Neither U.S. government agencies nor multilateral institutions such as the IDB have ever invested in Black Latin American communities. Please find enclosed a copy of the IDB document.

We seek your good offices to include the issue of Black Latin Americans in the Summit of the Americas. We contacted the Summit Implementation and Review Group (SIRG) at the state department. The SIRG informed us that the next meeting between governments will occur in Washington, DC, between the 9th through 11th of December. This meeting represents the last realistic occasion for civil society organizations like OAA to influence the agenda. We are deeply concerned that, without your direct intervention, this cause will be marginalized.

Many Black Latin Americans have organized themselves under the AFROAMERICA XXI framework. This represents their vision for the next century. Please help us to strengthen democratic rule and participation in Latin America by including Black Latin American minorities and AFROAMERICA XXI on the summit agenda.

Best wishes for a productive and peaceful holiday season.

Sincerely,

*Michael J. Franklin*
President

# XII. APPENDIX:
## SUMMIT CORRESPONDENCE

*Organization of Africans in the Americas (OAA)*

*Organización Proavance de los Pueblos de Ascendencia Africana*

December 18, 1997
Mr. Richard C. Brown, Ambassador
Senior Summit Coordinator
United States Department of State
Washington, D.C. 20520

Dear Ambassador Brown:

We appreciate the acknowledgment and due consideration of our views by your deputy, Christian Kennedy. We also are pleased to hear that our work was praised in the Summit Implementation and Review Group's (SIRG) plenary, December 9 - 11, 1997. It is gratifying to hear that several delegations spoke about the conditions of people of African descent in the Americas. Our initiative to include Afro-Latin-Americans represents the aspiration of millions of humans in critical poverty throughout the region.

We understand that a principal objective of the SIRG is to develop policy to alleviate poverty and discrimination in all societies. This is precisely why Afro-Latin-Americans should be included on the agenda of the Summit. Afro-Latin-Americans, the largest minority in Latin America, are among the most discriminated and chronically poor. To date, U.S. cooperative assistance programs have failed to reach them.

The Andean and Central American parliaments support AFROAMERICA XXI, a process which includes most Black politicians, and a plurality of Black organizations in Spanish-speaking countries. AFROAMERICA XXI supports the initiative. Several Latin nations and several Caribbean nations have also indicated support. One country supporting inclusion, Costa Rica, has just now proposed that the term Afro-Latin-American be changed to "Afro-American." In their view, "Afro-Latin-American" is too restrictive a term. This infers the incorporation of all Blacks in the Americas into the summit agenda. OAA believes this to be an acceptable compromise in accord with the president's wish to have dialogue on race.

In addition, to meet the needs of the predominantly Black countries of the Caribbean who are not seeking to benefit by this initiative, the United States could introduce an "optionality" clause. This provision would place Caribbean countries as observers in the process rather than participants. We would like to communicate this position to foreign governments, and request your guidance and support.

We know that the U.S. position on race directly affects the lives of 150 million Afro-Latin-Americans. The accruing benefits to our foreign policy are many:

- Black Latin Americans may turn out to be the strongest of U.S. allies in the region, particularly because of their respect for the Black population in the United States.

- Bringing visibility to Blacks means bringing visibility to poverty since Blacks make up a minimum 40 percent of all the poor in Latin America. They represent an untapped market and a key to creating stability in the region.

- Participation of Blacks in political, social and economic processes will strengthen democratic rule, and over time hinder the need for migration to the United States or U.S. funding to relieve political crises.

Afro-Latin-Americans are invisible to national and international remedies because Latin governments do not include them in specific language that would identify them as a target group for support. Censuses and household surveys do not collect data by race. Supporting Afro-Latin-Americans without identifying them has proved historically impossible, and history will repeat itself at this Summit without that identification.

The IDB report sent to your office confirms the abhorrent treatment of Afro-Latin-Americans in the region. Failure to include Afro-Latin-Americans now on the Summit agenda provides fodder for those in Latin America who would continue unfair racial legacies into the next century, and it nullifies years of hard work by many people.

However, the single most important loss of all would be the example of openness, dialogue, and even honesty offered by the United States as it confronts the universal problems of discrimination and poverty. For, despite all our problems, no other American country in its internal affairs shows the depth of courage and resolve to address these issues.

For these reasons, we request to speak directly to you about this matter, and will make ourselves available at your disposal for such a meeting.

Sincerely,

*Michael Franklin*
President

cc:

The White House
Madame Secretary of State
Congressional Black Caucus

# XII. APPENDIX: SUMMIT CORRESPONDENCE

*• Centro de Derecho Ambiental y de los Recursos Naturales • Centro Latino Americano de Ecología Social • Centro Mexicano de Derecho Ambiental • Comité Nacional Pro Defensa de la Fauna y Flora • Centro de Derecho Ambiental de Honduras • Fundación Ambiente y Recursos Naturales • Fundación AMBIO • Fundación Salvadorena para el Desarrollo Económico y Social • National Audubon Society • National Wildlife Federation • PRONATURA, Mexico • PRONATURA, Republica Dominicana • Rainforest Alliance • Red Mexicana de Acción Frente al Libre Comercio • Patricia Gay, Environmental Consultant • Marie-Claire Segger, Trade Rules and Sustainability in the Americas Project • Mindahi Crescencio, Plural Group of Indigenous Peoples • Paulo Guilherme Ribiero, Universidade de Brasilia*

February 8, 1998

Mr. Carlos Murillo
President of the Preparatory Committee
Pro-Tempore Presidency
FTAA Office
Ministry of Foreign Trade
P.O. Box 96-2050
San Jose, Costa Rica

To the Honorable President of the Preparatory Committee of the Free Trade Area of the Americas office:

When government officials meet this February in San Jose, Costa Rica for the Third Free Trade Area for the Americas (FTAA) Vice-Ministerial meeting, we again urge you to take concrete steps to legitimize input and participation in trade negotiations from a broad spectrum of civil society. Public participation in trade and investment negotiations holds the key to successful completion of the proposed FTAA negotiations.

Since the First FTAA Trade Ministerial in 1995, negotiators have used the Business Forum proceedings to work directly with business community members on issues directly related to the scope and nature of trade negotiations. Some of the individual "working groups" have even developed more formal consultancy processes with the business sector, such as the meeting between the Services Working Group and the business community held on October 7, 1997 in Santiago, Chile. Unfortunately, similar opportunities to meet with negotiators do not exist for other sectors of civil society.

We believe that public participation should be integral to any trade or investment negotiations. Such a linkage confirms the relationship between open markets and democratic principles and provides citizens with the information they need to make sound and informed choices about policies that affect their future. But despite the fact that clear mandates which strongly support the full integration of civil society in the decision-making process, including policies and programs design, implementation and evaluation, exist in the Miami and Bolivia Summit Plans of Action, and in the Belo Horizonte Trade Ministerial Declaration, no such steps have yet been taken. The time has come to follow up on those commitments and make public participation a cornerstone of the FTAA process. We therefore urge the negotiators to adopt and implement the following recommendations as part of the Declaration of San Jose:

## PLACE PUBLIC PARTICIPATION ON A PAR WITH OVERALL TRADE NEGOTIATION OBJECTIVES

A general objective on public participation sends a strong signal to participating countries and to business interests that democratic decisionmaking is integral to good trade and investment policy.

## PROVIDE A SPECIFIC WORK PLAN DESIGNED TO OVERCOME THE OBSTACLES THAT RESTRICT CITIZEN PARTICIPATION

While members of the business community enjoy the financial resources, technical skills, and personal and professional relationships required to engage government officials in useful policy dialogue, citizen groups — especially those working in emerging economy nations — do not possess such resources. To overcome these obstacles to effective participation, we suggest the following specific work plan:

### 1. Establish an Information Clearing House

One of the biggest obstacles to participation is the lack of information; interested citizens around the hemisphere simply lack access to information detailing negotiating timetable, objectives, and participants. Because most citizen groups now have access to information available through the Internet, posting documents on a website or maintaining a communications "list-serve" are an inexpensive means of overcoming most information obstacles. A list-serve would also keep citizens abreast of upcoming meetings, workshops, and conferences and encourage dialogue among stakeholders.

The current official FTAA website provides useful information such as a chronology of the FTAA process; the official documents from the Ministerial meetings; information on the twelve Hemispheric Working Groups and access to some of the official documents prepared for the Working Groups. But, for citizens to be fully informed, information that states the different countries positions towards specific concerns on the trade agenda; the minutes of the past Vice Ministerial meetings; the agenda and issues of discussion for the future Vice Ministerial meetings, the future Ministerial meeting, and the Hemispheric Working Group meetings; as well as points of contact; links to related home pages; and access to position papers presented during negotiations will better help understand the process itself, the challenges and promote public access. Because of the diversity of languages spoken in the Hemisphere, we applaud and continue to encourage the current effort in providing this information in English, Spanish, French, and Portuguese.

We recommend you review both the websites and list-serves maintained by the North American Commission on Environmental Cooperation (CEC), and the North American Development Bank and Border Environmental Cooperation Commission (NADBank/BECC), for two examples of how to establish and maintain two important vehicles for citizen outreach and communication. We also recommend that you establish a single official FTAA website and avoid rotating responsibility for maintaining it between ministerial meeting hosts. The United Nations Economic Commission for Latin America and the Caribbean (ECLAC) or the Organization of American States (OAS) would be good candidates for such an important and permanent role in trade and investment negotiations.

### 2. Establish National Advisory Committees

Another obstacle blocking citizen participation in negotiations is the lack of formal access. National Advisory Committees, consisting of members of government and civil society, would be responsible for developing concrete negotiating recommendations and responses to the recommendations offered by other countries. Committee appointments should be made in a transparent manner, with the objective of ensuring broad representation of citizen groups and community perspectives.

### 3. Promote Research, Training, and Capacity Building

A third obstacle to effective citizen participation is the lack of popular understanding of the implications of expanded trade. The OAS recently allocated approximately $2.8 million for all trade-related projects in 1998, a portion of which is dedicated to government training programs. Equivalent budgetary efforts must be included into the Inter-American Strategy for Participation (ISP) of the OAS, regarding technical assistance and training addressed to civil society. Better understanding of the issues affecting citizens lives caused by economic integration will ultimately produce better policies that advance a sustainable development strategy for the Hemisphere.

Workshops and forums should also combine participation of environmental agency representatives to discuss trade issues as a way to establish communication between government agencies.

### 4. Fund Civil Society Participation in Trade and Investment Negotiations

The final major obstacle blocking citizen's participation in trade and investment negotiations is money; attending negotiating sessions, meeting with other stakeholders, and preparing useful position papers and analy-

# XII. APPENDIX: SUMMIT CORRESPONDENCE

Joint Letter to Vice-Ministers of Trade Attending the Third FTAA Vice Ministerial Meeting on Civil Society Participation

ses require resources most emerging economy NGOs do not have. By providing participation funds to NGOs, multinational institutions such as the Inter-American Development Bank (IDB) and the Organization for the American States (OAS), could play an important role ensuring that trade liberalization benefits the largest number of people possible.

Important steps need to be taken under the FTAA negotiations to expand the level of information dissemination and guarantee transparency. The objective recommendations would help to establish a minimum mechanism necessary to make public participation a reality under the FTAA process. We urge you to act now and help citizens prepare to take part fully in potentially the most significant political events affecting their lives today.

Respectfully submitted,

*Lic. Franklin Paniagua & Lic. Lizbeth Espinoza*
Centro de Derecho Ambiental y de los Recursos Naturales (Costa Rica)

*Eduardo Gudynas*
Centro Latino Americano de Ecología Social (Uruguay)

*Gustavo Alanis*
President
Centro Mexicano de Derecho Ambiental (Mexico)

*Miguel Stutzin*
Comite Nacional Pro Defensa de la Fauna y Flora (Chile)

*Lic. Mario Gerardo Galindo*
President
Centro de Derecho Ambiental de Honduras (Honduras)

*Roxana Salazar*
Executive Director
Fundación AMBIO (Costa Rica)

*Daniel Sabsay*
Executive Director
Fundación Ambiente y Recursos Naturales (Argentina)

*Eduardo Nunez*
Executive Director
Fundación Salvadorena para el Desarrollo Económico y Social (El Salvador)

*Kathleen Rodgers*
National Audubon Society (USA)

*John Audley*
Trade and Environment Program Coordinator
National Wildlife Federation (USA)

*Hans Herrmann*
General Director
PRONATURA Nacional, Mexico (Mexico)

*Rene Ledezma*
PRONATURA, Rep. Dominicana
Executive Director
(Republica Dominicana)

*Chris Willie*
Co-Director, Latin American Office
Rainforest Alliance (Costa Rica)

*Alejandro Villamar*
Red Mexicana de Acción Frente al Libre Comercio (Mexico)

*Patricia Gay*
Environmental and Development Policy Consultant
Latin America & the Caribbean

*Marie-Claire Segger*
Project Coordinator
Trade Rules and Sustainability in the Americas Project

*Mindahi Crescencio Bastida*
Plural Group of Indigenous People and Project Researcher
Trade Rules and Sustainability in the Americas Project

*Paulo Guilherme Ribiero Meireles*
Universidade de Brasilia and Project Researcher
Trade Rules and Sustainability in the Americas Project

# XII. APPENDIX: SUMMIT CORRESPONDENCE

*National Wildlife Federation (NWF), United States*

March 10, 1998

Mr. Peter F. Allgeier
Associate U.S. Trade Representative for the Western Hemisphere
U.S. Trade Representative
Washington, D.C. 20508
Fax #: 202 3954579

Dear Mr. Allgeier:

As you prepare to discuss with your counterparts next week the structure for the Free Trade Area of the Americas negotiations, and particularly the establishment of a Study Group on Trade and the Environment, you have asked for our reactions to a couple of recent conceptual proposals for inching toward a discussion on trade and the environment.

## I. NATIONAL MECHANISMS FOR PUBLIC PARTICIPATION

A proposal to have the U.S. and MERCOSUR jointly to develop a set of national consultative fora, which would probably rely on the MERCOSUR model for discussion processes, could have some useful potential. Nevertheless, recognizing that we do not have enough information to make concrete recommendations, we want to flag some potential pitfalls in such an approach. We have consulted with our counterparts in MERCOSUR countries and they have indicated several important limitations of the existing Consultative Fora for Economic and Social Issues that should be remedied if you pursue this model:

They do not feed into the MERCOSUR process. We believe it is important that if similar fora are created between the U.S. and MERCOSUR they should develop clear mechanisms that enable them to feed their recommendations throughout the FTAA framework. Developing national consultative mechanisms are just one of a series of steps that need to be taken to encourage citizen participation. We recommend that you look at the letter we sent you on February 10, 1998 for other concrete recommendations.

The MERCOSUR fora do not involve environmental NGOs, only business and labor. Of course we assume that your proposal would ensure environmental NGO participation.

The MERCOSUR groups are for consultation only and do not have an advisory role. There are presently many different fora that hold dialogues on trade and the environment, so we would not want this to be just another one. It would be very important to ensure that participating environmental NGOs can play an appropriate role in trade negotiations. You probably are aware that many NGOs need financial support to access documents and attend meetings. Such fora will need to mechanism to address this.

The proposal you are considering, to have a similar fora for the U.S. and MERCOSUR, could be a step in the right direction to start a dialogue. But, as you know, we will continue to encourage you to make sure similar steps are taken within the FTAA framework itself.

Others have suggested the OAS as a potential forum. But, we as well as other NGOs in Latin America are concerned that this would be an inadequate solution. At this time the OAS has a limited capacity to encourage citizen participation in trade negotiations, and even less to strengthen the trade and environment nexus. Nevertheless, encouraging this institution to develop a training and capacity-building project on trade and environment issues around the hemisphere could help produce a more positive atmosphere to advance a trade and environment agenda within the framework of the FTAA.

Encouraging regular meetings between the trade and environment ministers from the region would help build national and regional strategies to advance a sustainable development agenda for the Western Hemisphere. As we have found in our discussions with government officials in Latin America, most of the fear of the trade and the environment agenda is based on misunderstanding, which such meetings could begin to alleviate. But as we must continue to reiterate, making sure that a clear mechanism is devised which allows this process to feed into the FTAA negotiations would be of utmost importance.

The Central American countries, motivated by the Central American Commission for Environment & Development (CCAD) and the Permanent Secretary for the Central American Economic Integration Agreement (SIECA), have already taken this step, and have crafted a Declaration signed by both the Trade and Environment Ministers of each country geared towards incorporating the environmental dimension into trade liberalization and economic development in Central America. A copy of the first draft is attached to this document, but we understand there is a more recent version. A person to contact on this issue is Mr. Marco Gonzalez and Jorge Cabrera from the CCAD, tel. 502 3605426; fax: 502 3343876.

As we have said, any of these alternative fora for a trade and environment dialogue should be encouraged, but should not preclude the establishment of the Study Group or a formal working group within the context of the FTAA.

## II. STUDY GROUP ON TRADE AND THE ENVIRONMENT

Please remember that we applaud and continue to encourage your effort to keep environment in the trade dialogue. Nonetheless, it is probably obvious to you that a Study Group, at least the little we so far understand about it, would not meet our definition of fully integrating environmental priorities in trade negotiations. Nor does it reflect the agenda for trade negotiations articulated by President Clinton in his November 1997 "Statement of Executive Initiatives".

Therefore, although we fully understand the difficulties you have encountered in promoting a more straightforward negotiation on trade and the environment, we hope you will understand, in turn, that we would not be in a position to publicly support this concept, since we cannot see at this time how it would advance our goals.

On that basis, we offer the following observations:

a) There is a need to articulate stronger terms of reference. As you know, we believe this Study Group could play a key role in defining the relationship between the Western Hemisphere trading system and the environment, but only if it feeds into the negotiating framework of the FTAA, including all the relevant negotiating groups. A balance needs to be struck between "centralizing" the trade and environment discussion in a Study Group on Trade and the Environment and promoting the integration of environmental concerns into all aspects of the negotiating groups. While a dialogue on trade and the environment issues requires a focal point to ensure that they are advanced continuously, this will only work if trade and environment becomes an integral part of the agenda of all parts of the FTAA negotiating framework. We appreciate your efforts to secure a foothold for this dialogue, but we must continue to push for full integration.

The terms of reference should include the concrete steps for citizen participation and information dissemination that we listed in the letter we sent you dated February 10, 1998.

We are prepared to accept the need for the Study Group to begin in an oblique manner, with an evaluation of the linkages between trade and the environment contained in existing regional agreements (i.e., MERCOSUR, Andean Pact). This would certainly be an improvement over the Belo Horizonte agreement, which maintained that the issue of the environment and its relation to trade would only be kept under consideration "...in light of further developments in the work of the WTO Committee on Trade and the Environment" (Declaration of Belo Horizonte, paragraph 15.). That formulation would severely limit the possibilities of developing national and regional strategies to deal with the topic, and it would also reduce any possibility of dealing with each country's specific environmental peculiarities. Of course, the Belo Horizonte formulation would also limit citizen participation, contrary to what is encouraged under Agenda 21, the Summit of the Americas Declaration and the Declaration of Santa Cruz de la Sierra.

The terms of reference should include developing a real agenda for trade and the environment. For example, one topic could be developing a set of environmental indicators that would be comparable to economic indicators for the hemisphere.

The Study Group on Trade and the Environment should aim to develop concrete steps to enhance the capacity of national governments to have a constructive domestic dialogue and to create their own programs on trade and environment. It should also foster a working relationship between trade and environment ministers, as well as among their own relevant national agencies.

Nevertheless, please keep in mind that we await a Study Group that grapples with real trade and environment issues of this hemisphere, and that is linked to the negotiations. We urge you to work toward this in future steps.

b) As you know, we have the long term goal of linking the development of appropriate parallel institutions, dedicated to balancing trade and environment priorities, to the trade negotiations themselves. We are unclear how the Study Group might advance this goal; but perhaps this can be built into the formulation of that entity.

c) A clear commitment to make the Study Group on Trade and the Environment a reality should also include a budget proposal to realize its stated objectives.

## III. WE CONTINUE TO ENCOURAGE YOU TO ENSURE THAT THE FOLLOWING OBJECTIVE AND PRINCIPLE ARE PART OF THE FRAMEWORK OF THE DECLARATION OF SAN JOSE:

A general objective which places Trade Liberalization and Environmental Policies on a par as mutually supportive. This will reinforce the commitments made at the United Nations Conference on Environment and Development (Agenda 21) held in Rio de Janeiro in 1992; at the Summit of the Americas held in Miami in 1994; and those made at the Summit of the Americas in Santa Cruz de la Sierra, Bolivia in 1996. Trade agreements our nation enters from now on should be engines for sustainable development.

Procedural transparency in trade institutions and participation in the negotiations constitute fundamental principles for the way the negotiations will be led. Increased transparency and scope for participation play a key role in the attainment of basic goals of trade policy, such as ensuring that trade contributes to sustainability. The "right to know" and the "right of all citizens to participate" are fundamental elements of democratic practice and the cornerstone of effective decision-making process.

We again strongly encourage you to promote a stronger trade and environment agenda for the Western Hemisphere and to ensure effective steps will be taken so that a Free Trade Area of the Americas Agreement not be reached at the cost of environmental harm.

Thank you for your attention to this important matter.

Respectfully yours,

*Barbara Bramble*
Senior Director International Affairs
National Wildlife Federation

# XII. Appendix: Summit Correspondence

• AFL–CIO - USA • Centro Latino Americano de Ecología Social - Uruguay • Centro de Derecho Ambiental y de los Recursos Naturales - Costa Rica • Centro Mexicano de Derecho Ambiental - Mexico • Center for International Environmental Law - USA • Centro Ecuatoriano de Derecho Ambiental - Ecuador • Environmental Law Institute - USA • Fundación Ambiente y Recursos Naturales - Argentina • Fundación AMBIO - Costa Rica • Fundación Salvadorena para el Desarrollo Económico y Social • National Wildlife Federation - USA • PRONATURA - Dominican Republic • Programa Chile Sustentable - Chile • RENACE - Chile • Marie-Claire Segger, Trade Rules and Sustainability in the Americas Project - Canada

June 19, 1998

Ms. Kathryn McCallion
Chair of the Trade Negotiations Committee
Free Trade Area of the Americas

Dear Ms. McCallion:

Thank you for your willingness to work with non-governmental organizations to create a legitimate avenue for civil society to comment on the Free Trade Area of the Americas (FTAA) negotiations. As you prepare to discuss with your counterparts the structure and operating procedures of the Committee of Government Representatives for Civil Society (CGR), we offer these recommendations for your consideration.

## I. THE COMMITTEE OF GOVERNMENT REPRESENTATIVES MUST PRO-ACTIVELY SEEK PUBLIC INPUT

The CGR is faced with an important challenge: to provide the public with a legitimate and effective avenue for input and comment on hemispheric trade negotiations. To meet this challenge, FTAA negotiators must overcome many substantive and political obstacles that may weaken the success of the CGR if they are not addressed appropriately. The critical objective in the FTAA negotiations is to promote consultation and participation at the highest levels for other civil society groups. We are concerned that labor, environmental organizations and other representatives of civil society be able to advise negotiators with an access thus far afforded formally and informally to business representatives.

As we have mentioned in earlier letters sent to you and the former Presidency of the FTAA (see letters attached), most citizens groups throughout the hemisphere currently lack the financial and technical resources to engage fully in consultations. Moreover, many citizens do not trust governments to place their interests on a par with those of multi-national companies when negotiating trade and investment agreements. For these reasons, many citizens simply do not believe that the CGR will ever have either the capacity or the willingness to use public input to influence the negotiations themselves. Put simply, there is a great deal of fear, mistrust, lack of information and misinformation surrounding the CGR, factors that challenge its effectiveness and the legitimacy of the FTAA process itself.

We believe that the CGR's success depends on its ability to be an effective emissary for civil society concerns and on its ability to obtain hemispheric support for the FTAA negotiations. To achieve these goals, the CGR must provide citizens with evidence of its willingness to listen to their concerns and of its ability to overcome obstacles to citizen participation outlined above. Most importantly, the CGR should not act as a filter of views. Instead the CGR should clearly express these views and then articulate an agenda for trade and the environment in the FTAA negotiations. We believe these goals can best be achieved by adopting the proactive process for citizen participation outlined below.

## A) Establish a Timetable for Regional Meetings between Trade Ministers and Civil Society

We believe that the most effective way to overcome the level of misunderstanding and mistrust that currently exists between citizens and negotiators is to meet directly to discuss these concerns publicly. We encourage the CGR to arrange public meetings in accordance with the timetable of the negotiating groups. These public meetings could be modeled on an effective example of a similar proceeding, in which MERCOSUR meetings of the Social and Economic Council precede meetings of MERCOSUR's negotiating groups.

## B) Ensure Timely Citizen Access to Relevant Documents

Effective citizen input to trade negotiations requires timely access to the relevant documents and information that shapes day to day negotiations. We encourage the CGR to coordinate its work with the FTAA Administrative Secretariat to ensure citizens throughout the hemisphere have access to all relevant documents from the negotiations. Funding for computers, phone lines, and Internet services, as well as to purchase paper documents, must be made available to help citizen groups with limited resources.

One way to overcome information access problems is to create Public Information and Resource Centers (PIRCs). Located strategically throughout the Americas, PIRCs could provide citizens with timely access to important documents, and their staff could respond to questions and requests from the public and governments. We recommend that you consider MERCOSUR's Information System (SIM); the World Bank's Public Information Center and the North American Commission for Environmental Cooperation's (CEC) Resource and Public Information Center as examples of how these types of centers can operate.

While financial and technical resource constraints pose problems for some, increasingly the Internet is the most effective channel for information distribution. We recommend that you make extensive use of the Internet by maintaining a CGR Website, an electronic chat room and communications bulletin board, an FTAA news center and a calendar of meetings and events. There is a precedent in the United States for maintaining such a website; until just recently the United States Department of Commerce maintained the Transatlantic Business Dialogue website to encourage multinationals to maintain a dialogue with United States and European Union government officials. These electronic mechanisms have also been tested and proven to be successful means of communication for the Border Environmental Cooperation Commission (BECC). The website could provide the following information: general information about the CGR and its operations (contact information); formal reports of the CGR to the Trade Negotiations Committee (TNC); rules of procedure; public consultation guidelines; records of discussion; public meeting reports; documentation concerning countries' positions on topics addressed by the negotiating groups or factual summary of main elements of evolving discussions; technical documents and information disclosure policies (see attached copies of UNDP and the World Bank policies for an example).

The Internet should not be the CGR's only way of communicating with civil society in the Western Hemisphere. Faxing and old fashioned mail should also be used as alternate methods of communication, especially to ensure locating interested organizations before the CGR is well known.

## C) The CGR Should Be THE Legitimate Avenue for Citizen Input into FTAA Negotiations

One of the defining characteristics of the FTAA preliminary negotiations was the formal relationship between business representatives and government officials through the Business Forum. Trade ministers listened respectfully as business representatives presented their recommendations prior to each FTAA trade ministerial meeting. The Fourth Trade Ministerial, March 19, 1998, was no exception to this type of proceeding.

We appreciate the fact that the Forum itself was not an invention of government officials, and that the business community's effort to establish consensus positions prior to the ministerial meetings can provide useful information to government officials. At the same time, because government officials did not express a willingness to also meet formally with the other representatives of civil society who convened for each ministerial meeting, these groups felt naturally disadvantaged by the extraordinary access enjoyed by the business community.

Joint Letter to Ms. Kathryn McCallion in Preparation for the
Trade Negotiations Committee's (TNC) Meeting in Argentina

# XII. APPENDIX: SUMMIT CORRESPONDENCE

The CGR was mandated by the heads of state at the Second Summit of the Americas to receive input from labor, environment, business and the academic sectors. To facilitate other formal avenues for business input into these negotiations, beyond those required by national law, transgresses this mandate and would seriously damage the credibility of the CGR and FTAA negotiations with the rest of civil society. Recommendations from all sectors of civil society, not only the business sector, should be channeled into the CGR, and not directly to the Trade Ministers. We urge you to formally designate the CGR as THE legitimate avenue for citizen input.

The process established by the CGR should not preclude citizen groups to pursue other avenues for input into the negotiations, including direct access to the negotiating groups themselves, and routine consultation with national government officials and elected representatives. On the point of access to the negotiating groups there is an important precedent in Mercosur. Thus, given this and other experiences on trade agreements in the Western Hemisphere, the consultation process that will be established by the CGR with civil society should not be weaker or less than any of the already existing mechanisms these trade agreements have created.

## D) Work with Government Agencies, Intergovernmental Organizations, Philanthropic Foundations, and Multilateral Lending Institutions to Provide the Resources to Overcome the Financial Obstacles Blocking Citizen Involvement in Negotiations

If trade ministers engage civil society directly and more actively through the CGR, it will help overcome the mistrust that now exists between citizen groups and government officials in trade negotiations. Such engagement will reduce the level of misinformation that clouds the negotiations and clarify the key issues for public discussion. It will help provide each civil society sector with equal and fair access to the negotiations. Direct and transparent interaction with citizens will promote community understanding of the negotiations and lay the foundation for public support for the final negotiated agreement.

## II. OPERATIONAL PROCEDURES OF THE CGR

### A) Procedural transparency; access to information; notice and comment

Procedural transparency and access to information should be the rule — not the exception — for the CGR's agenda, meetings, and reports. As part of the transparency procedure, we recommend that the CGR post meeting timetables, deadlines for citizens submissions, and meeting agendas on the Internet. The CGR should provide at least thirty days notice of the dates, times, and deadlines for each meeting.

As mentioned in section I of this letter, priority should be given to developing Public Information and Resource Centers (PIRC). These will be an invaluable resource to foster informed participation in the CGR.

### B) Reports on Civil Society Input

We believe that the CGR should regularly produce **reports** that synthesize the concerns raised and proposed policies by civil society. These reports must accurately and impartially reflect the views of civil society groups, not the committee's own views in the form of commentary or edited version of civil society input.

The CGR should also produce **recommendations for the negotiating groups** on steps that could be taken to address issues raised by civil society.

The CGR should provide the public with a **full opportunity to comment** on the report and the recommendations. It should then issue a final report and final recommendations which will be passed to the TNC and **should be made public**. The CGR report and recommendations should incorporate all views of the CGR members and an appendix with all civil society submissions.

The CGR should consult or seek information or input from experts, specific groups and individuals on any relevant issues. **The CGR's Chair may invite experts to submit information to the Committee and may form subcommittees or task forces to review and report to the TNC.** The subcommittees may include individuals other than members of the Committee and should be balanced in terms of the interests represented.

In addition to this, the CGR should **provide relevant technical, scientific or other information to the TNC as it may deem necessary** to allow the TNC to be better informed to make a decision. If the TNC considers it requires more information on an issue raised by civil society it could ask the CGR to create a task force or subcommittee to address the issue at hand.

We appreciate the challenge you face to set up the CGR. Nevertheless, we again urge you to ensure that the structure and operating procedures defined for the CGR allow it to feed into the actual negotiating framework of the FTAA, including all the relevant negotiating groups. If it is established in this way, the CGR will be able to play a key role in defining a constructive relationship between the Western Hemisphere trading system and other aspects of regional integration.

We realize that many refinements will arise as the CGR receives wider public consideration. We will be pleased to work with you from this starting point and we thank you for the opportunity to share these suggestions with you.

Respectfully submitted by,

*Bruce Jay*
AFL-CIO, USA

*Eduardo Gudynas*
Centro Latino Americano de Ecología Social, Uruguay

*Leonel Umana*
Centro de Derecho Ambiental y de los Recursos Naturales, Costa Rica

*Gustavo Alanis*
Centro Mexicano de Derecho Ambiental, Mexico

*Brennan Van Dycke*
Center for International Environmental Law, USA

*Maria Amparo Alban*
Centro Ecuatoriano de Derecho Ambiental, Ecuador

*Susan Bass*
Environmental Law Institute, USA

*Patricia Vasquez*
Fundación Ambiente y Recursos Naturales, Argentina

*Roxana Salazar*
Fundación AMBIO, Costa Rica

*Jaime Acosta*
Fundación Salvadorena para el Desarrollo Económico y Social, El Salvador

*John Audley*
National Wildlife Federation, USA

*Rene Ledezma*
PRONATURA, Dominican Republic

*Sara Larrain*
Programa Chile Sustentable, Chile

RENACE
Chile

*Marie-Claire Segger*
Trade Rules and Sustainability in the Americas Project, Canada

cc:

Antigua and Barbuda, Hilroy Humphreys, Minister of International Trade

Argentina, Jorge Guillermo Campbell, Secretary of International Trade Relations

Bahamas, Mr. Wilfrid Horton, Permanent Secretary

Barbados, Courtney Blackman, Ambassador

Belize, Rodney H. Neal, Permanent Secretary

Bolivia, Ana María Solares Gaite, Vice Minister

Brazil, José Alfredo Graca Lima, Ambassador

Chile, Juan Gabriel Valdes, Director General

Colombia, Magdalena Pardo de Serrano, Vice Minister

Costa Rica, Anabel Gonzales, Vice Minister

Dominica, Irwin LaRocque, Permanent Secretary

Dominican Republic, Marcello Puello Abalo, Subsecretario de Industria y Comercio

Ecuador, Dumanny Sanchez Neira, Undersecretary of Foreign Trade and Integration

El Salvador, Eduardo Ayala Grimaldi, Vice Minister

Grenada, Gregory Renwick, Permanent Secretary

Guatemala, José Guillermo Castillo Villacorta, Viceministro de Economia

Guyana, Ramesh Sharma, Permanent Secretary

Joint Letter to Ms. Kathryn McCallion in Preparation for the Trade Negotiations Committee's (TNC) Meeting in Argentina

# XII. APPENDIX: SUMMIT CORRESPONDENCE

Haiti, Jean Daniel Elie, Directeur General du Ministere du Commerce et de l'Industrie

Honduras, José Hernan Erazo, Vice Minister of Economic Integration and Foreign Trade

Jamaica, George Anthony Hylton, Minister of State

Mexico, Eduardo Solis, Chief of Negotiations with America and Market Access Unit

Nicaragua, Azucena Castillo, Vice Minister

Panama, Laura Elena Flores, Vice Minister of Trade and Industry Paraguay, Dario Froillan Peralta Sosa, Vice Minister for Trade

Peru, Diego Calmet Mujica, Vice Minister of Tourism, Integration and International Trade Negotiations

St. Kitts and Nevis, Horatio Versailles, Permanent Secretary

Saint Lucia, Earl Huntley, Permanent Secretary

St. Vincent and the Grenadines, Bernard Willye, Minister of State

Suriname, Henridk A. Alimahomed, Permanent Secretary of Foreign Affairs

Trinidad and Tobago, Annette Gonzales, Director of International Economic Relations Division

United States, Peter Allgeier, Assistant US Trade Representative for the Western Hemisphere

Uruguay, Roberto Rodriguez Pioli, Viceministro

Venezuela, José Antonio Martinez Mena, Director General Sectorial de Comercio Exterior

# XII. APPENDIX: SUMMIT CORRESPONDENCE

*• Asociación Cívica Transparencia Internacional, Costa Rica • Asociación Nacional para la Conservación de la Naturaleza, Panamá • Centro Ecuatoriano de Derecho Ambiental, Ecuador • Defenders of Wildlife, USA • Environmental Law Institute, USA • Friends of the Earth, USA • Fundación Ambio, Costa Rica • Institute of Agriculture and Trade Policy, USA • National Wildlife Federation • PRONATURA, República Dominicana • Rainforest Alliance, Costa Rica • The Development Gap, USA*

October 16, 1998

Ms. Kathryn McCallion
Chair of the Trade Negotiations Committee and Temporary Chair of the Committee of Government Representatives for the Participation of Civil Society Free Trade Area of the Americas

Dear Ms. McCallion:

On the occasion of the first meeting of the Committee of Government Representatives (CGR) for the Participation of Civil Society in Miami, October 19-20, 1998, we would like to provide our recommendations and main concerns regarding the future work program and functioning of this committee.

We appreciate your efforts in advancing the formation of the CGR, and your commitment to civil society participation in the Free Trade Area of the Americas' (FTAA) negotiations. We realize that the large number of participating nations, and the diversity of opinions which are bound to arise, contribute substantially to this committee's formidable task. Yet in the seven months since its inception, the CGR has made no progress in defining its operating mechanisms or work agenda. This lack of progress leads us to question the current and future value of the CGR as a legitimate and effective avenue for public input, and to doubt the 34 countries' commitment to transparency and meaningful participation in the FTAA process. For example, statements made by you and Associate U.S. Trade Representative for the Western Hemisphere, Peter Allgeier, at the September 11, 1998 Andean Development Corporation Conference, imply that the role of the CGR is primarily to generate support for the FTAA through public education. While we agree that an informed public debate on the ramifications of the FTAA is critical, we contend that the goal of the CGR should be to enable all sectors of civil society to have a voice in the FTAA negotiations in order to ensure that the final FTAA agreement reflects the concerns of civil society. To enable non-discriminatory treatment of civil society participation in the FTAA negotiations, the CGR should allow for all sectors of civil society, and not just the business sector, to not only have prompt access information pertaining to the negotiations, but also to have regular and formal opportunities to discuss negotiating objectives, process, terms of reference and provisions.

Committee of Government Representatives

The October 19-20 meeting in Miami presents a critical opportunity to show your commitment to enabling civil society participation in the FTAA and provide an equal and non-discriminatory process to all sectors of civil society. We offer you some concrete recommendations which could, in our view, make measurable progress in advancing these objectives.

## DEFINE CLEAR MECHANISMS FOR ADDRESSING CIVIL SOCIETY CONCERNS WITHIN THE NEGOTIATING PROCESS.

During the People's Summit in Santiago, Chile, and during the Multilateral Agreement for Investment (MAI) negotiations, citizens indicated that they will not continue to support trade or investment policies which do not result from an open, transparent and participatory process. Full civil society participation requires not only that the CGR and its constituent governments solicit comments from the public, but that the CGR also establish a mechanism that allows these comments to influence the outcome of the negotiations, and be given the same possibility for adoption by the negotiators as the recommendations forwarded by the business sector. We urge you to create a CGR that achieves the following objectives:

- Establishes clearly defined and non-discriminatory mechanisms within the FTAA, to communicate citizens' recommendations to the individual negotiating groups;
- Sets reasonable time-frames for the functioning of these mechanisms; and
- Establishes methods of accountability.

Without these important components, the CGR will function only as a "mailbox" with no significant influence or impact on the negotiating process. We cannot support a citizen dialogue that serves only to provide negotiators a platform to promote policies that do not accurately reflect the concerns of civil society.

Another important aspect of an open and participatory process is that requests for comments should not be narrowly defined to restrict input from civil society to only trade-related issues. Trade rules have far reaching impacts, and though the relationship between trade rules and their effects might not be evident, civil society should be given the opportunity to demonstrate such relationships. As you are well aware, most trade ministers in the Western Hemisphere do not want to see environment linked to trade; in fact, the inclusion of representatives from environmental and other civil society organizations in the FTAA negotiations still faces serious opposition. This reluctance is, in some cases, not only an effort to elevate trade above other concerns, but also a lack of understanding of the existing linkages. It is important that the CGR ensure opportunities for civil society and government representatives to share their expertise and technical knowledge in an effort to overcome these barriers to understanding. This cannot be done by limiting the type of input from civil society.

Committee of Government Representatives

We note that the San José Trade Ministerial Declaration (March 1998) authorizes the other two committees (The Consultative Group on Smaller Economies and the Joint Government-Private Sector Committee of experts on Electronic Commerce) established in the FTAA to "make recommendations" on issues of importance to these committees. In contrast, the CGR is to "present the range of views for consideration" by Trade Ministers. At a minimum, we expect that these views be presented in a way that will facilitate action within the negotiating groups on areas of concern to civil society. Thus, it is imperative for the CGR to begin formulating mechanisms of civil society participation within the negotiating groups.

## Recommendation

1. This first meeting of the CGR (October 19-20), should focus on developing clearly defined and non-discriminatory mechanisms to receive and communicate citizens' recommendations to negotiating groups, reasonable time-frames for the functioning of these mechanisms, and established methods of accountability. A request for comments on negotiating objectives that does not provide these mechanisms does not provide a legitimate and effective avenue for participation in the FTAA negotiations. (See attached letter for further recommendations on operational procedures for the CGR.)

## ENSURE AN OPEN, TRANSPARENT AND PARTICIPATORY PROCESS IN THE FTAA FRAMEWORK.

As stated in an earlier letter sent to you (June 19), "effective citizen input to trade negotiations requires timely access to the relevant documents and information that shapes the day to day negotiations." Timely, convenient and inexpensive access to relevant, up-to-date information is the first step in empowering civil society in this process for formulating recommendations for the negotiations. The FTAA Administrators are *not* providing such information on the web site or in any other publicly accessible format. For example, neither a summary nor minutes of the negotiating groups' meetings in September 1998 are posted on the website or are available to the public in some other format. Transparency and participation in the CGR is of little value without transparency and participation throughout the negotiations process, including all negotiating groups.

## Recommendations

1. We request that the CGR provide for the timely release of relevant FTAA documents including the following:

   a) A schedule of the next meetings of the CGR and each of the FTAA negotiating groups;

   b) An outline of preliminary and official CGR and the negotiating group agendas for each of the meetings;

   c) Names and contact information of the national representatives to the CGR and the lead negotiators from each country in each of the negotiating groups.

Committee of Government Representatives

2. This first meeting of the CGR presents a critical opportunity to develop guidelines for transparency and participation which can be utilized by the FTAA negotiating groups. The procedures established by the CGR should help promote greater public participation and access to the negotiation process itself.

3. The CGR should also establish guidelines for NGO accreditation to observe and participate in the Negotiating Groups of the FTAA. A civil society representative should be invited to form part of the national delegation on each of the negotiating groups.

4. As part of the procedural issues of discussion, at the October 19-20 meeting the CGR should define information disclosure policies. Among rules of procedure which could be used to ensure transparency in the FTAA negotiating process the committee should define document de-restriction policies; public consultation guidelines; records of discussion; access to documentation concerning countries' positions on topics addressed by the negotiating groups or factual summary of main elements of evolving discussions. (See attached June 19 letter for further suggestions.)

## ACTIVELY ENGAGE CITIZENS IN PUBLIC DIALOGUE.

While we appreciate the opportunity to provide comments on the FTAA process, the effectiveness of the CGR depends primarily on its ability to promote dialogue between governments and all sectors of civil society. We therefore urge you to develop fora, such as public hearings or other platforms for oral presentations, where an exchange of ideas is possible. We suggest the use of existing regional dialogues on trade agreements to promote discussion on the FTAA.

As part of the preparatory process for this CGR meeting, the Second Meeting of the Trade Negotiations Committee (TNC) and future FTAA Negotiating Groups Meetings in Miami next year, governments in the hemisphere have the responsibility to develop national positions in close consultation with their citizens. We recognize that the CGR is not the forum where these national consultations should be determined or implemented; however, we feel it is important that the CGR offer formal, regular and timely opportunities for discussing the results of such national consultations as they pertain both to the work of the Trade Negotiations Committee (TNC) and the individual negotiating groups. Governments Representatives to the CGR and the CGR Chair should promote the participation of civil society organizations, through open dialogue, in the national decision-making process of the FTAA. Governments in this hemisphere have committed to encouraging all countries to take into account civil society input through mechanisms of dialogue and consultation (Belo Horizonte Ministerial Declaration, May 16, 1997) and it has not happened. This needs to take place at the outset of the negotiations.

Committee of Government Representatives

## Recommendation

1. We request that the CGR convene a public hearing after its first meeting in Miami and provide a timetable of meetings where citizens in this hemisphere have an opportunity to discuss issues of concern pertaining to the FTAA.

Successful fulfillment of the commitment to promote a dialogue among government officials and all sectors of civil society made by the heads of state at both the Santiago and Miami Summits of the America are particularly vital at this early stage in the FTAA negotiations. We pledge our support for your efforts to establish the CGR as an effective participatory mechanism before the rest of the negotiations proceed.

Sincerely,

*Ana Lucia Hernandez*
Asociación Cívica Transparencia Internacional
(Costa Rica)

*Angel Ureña Vargas*
Asociación Nacional para la Conservación de la
Naturaleza (Panama)

*Ma. Amparo Alban*
Centro Ecuatoriano de Derecho Ambiental (Ecuador)

*Bill Snape*
Defenders of Wildlife (USA)

*Susan Bass*
Environmental Law Institute (USA)

*Mark Vallianatos*
Friends of the Earth (USA)

*Roxana Salazar*
Fundación Ambio (Costa Rica)

*Steve Suppan*
Institute of Agriculture and Trade Policy (USA)

*John Audley*
National Wildlife Federation (USA)

*Rene Ledezma*
PRONATURA (Republica Dominicana)

*Chris Wille*
Rainforest Alliance (Costa Rica)

*Karen Hansen-Kuhn*
The Development Gap (USA)

# XII. APPENDIX: SUMMIT CORRESPONDENCE

*National Wildlife Federation (NWF), United States*

November 30, 1998

Mr. Peter F. Allgeier
Associate U.S. Trade Representative for the Western Hemisphere
Office of the United States Trade Representative
600 17th Street, N.W.
Washington, D.C. 20508

Dear Mr. Allgeier:

As you prepare for the December 2-3, 1998 Free Trade Area of the Americas (FTAA) Trade Negotiations Committee (TNC) meeting in Suriname, we are writing to briefly reiterate our earlier requests that the United States take significant and concrete steps towards strengthening public participation opportunities in the FTAA negotiations.

As we have noted on prior occasions, we urge you to work diligently to increase transparency in the individual sectoral negotiating groups and to ensure that the Committee of Government Representatives (CGR) does not simply become a "mailbox" repository of non-governmental organization (NGO) concerns with no significant corresponding influence, nor impact, on the negotiating process. In particular, the TNC meeting in Suriname provides a critical opportunity to make progress in the following three areas:

## DEFINE CLEAR MECHANISMS FOR ADDRESSING CIVIL SOCIETY CONCERNS WITHIN THE NEGOTIATING PROCESS

We commend the United States for its preliminary efforts in support of increasing public dialogue, producing a report of civil society comments and improving access to information. Despite these welcome initiatives, we remain concerned that the results of the first round of negotiations in Miami did not achieve concrete commitments to these important goals. In particular, we note that the current general request for comments on the FTAA with no clear steps or details as to the formal mechanisms through which civil society's comments will be addressed by the CGR, negotiating groups and/or Trade Ministers appears to be inadequate. While we are supportive of the modest proposal to post civil society comments on the official FTAA website as a means of promoting transparency, a new effort must be made at the upcoming TNC meeting in Suriname to ensure meaningful discussion of procedural mechanisms to address civil society concerns within the FTAA negotiations.

In this regard and as we have stated in the past, the establishment of the CGR as a forum to provide civil society with an opportunity to comment on the FTAA process is a step in the right direction. Nevertheless, in order for the CGR to successfully function as one of several potentially appropriate vehicles for ensuring that public participation and environmental protection are integrated into the context of trade negotiations, the CGR must adopt several important components into the core of its work program. These components include 1) an opportunity for public dialogue including proactive efforts on behalf of the

CGR to actively encourage public involvement in its activities; 2) the development of a comprehensive information disclosure policy and related communications policy; 3) providing creative funding mechanisms for citizen groups throughout the hemisphere which currently lack the financial and technical resources to engage fully in consultations; and 4) clear and measurable operational procedures which indicate how civil society concerns will be addressed within the context of the negotiations. (Please see attached letters.)

## DEFINE INFORMATION DISCLOSURE POLICIES AND FACILITATE THE DERESTRICTION OF RELEVANT DOCUMENTS

The results of the first round of negotiations in Miami made little concrete progress in promoting transparency in the FTAA negotiations. As part of the TNC's procedural issues of discussion at the December meeting, we again urge you to define information disclosure policies as a means to ensure public participation in the negotiations. Specifically, we believe the following "classes" or types of documents might be candidates for derestriction as an important *first* step in empowering civil society in a process to encourage "constructive" comments during FTAA negotiations:

1. Work plans and meeting schedules of the negotiating groups;

2. An outline of preliminary and official agendas of the CGR and the negotiating group meetings;

3. Working papers and draft texts of the negotiating groups, CGR and other committees;

4. Minutes, records of discussions or factual summary of the main elements stemming from the negotiating groups, TNC and Trade Ministers' meetings;

5. Countries' position papers on topics addressed by the negotiating groups;

6. The annotated outline produced by the negotiating groups;

7. Formal reports of the negotiating groups, CGR and other committees to the trade discussion;

8. A time schedule of the next meetings of each of the FTAA negotiating groups, CGR and other committees;

9. Names and contact information of the national representatives involved with the CGR, committees and negotiating groups and contact information for the lead negotiators from each country in each of the negotiating groups.

As you make progress on document derestriction in the FTAA negotiations, we strongly urge you to release a document describing the information disclosure policies to be utilized under the FTAA and to consider developing it into a comprehensive public document which would also integrate public consultation guidelines. We look forward to working with you and providing our assistance on both of these issues.

## INCORPORATE ENVIRONMENTAL ASSESSMENTS INTO FTAA NEGOTIATIONS

We call on you to introduce into the TNC's meeting agenda in Suriname a discussion with your counterparts on the need to develop environmental assessments early in the current stage of the FTAA negotiations and to take the lead in developing the framework for a social and environmental assessment of the FTAA negotiations. We believe that the application of environmental assessments can help identify relevant impacts, establish preventive and mitigative measures, and proffer reasonable alternative actions. The promotion of meaningful environmental assessments will strengthen public participation in FTAA negotiations by providing important data and by incorporating in a formal manner NGO and other civil society inputs and experiences of trade liberalization impacts in the Western Hemisphere.

As you know, the National Wildlife Federation is committed to engaging the United States and its important trading partners in the pursuit of an open and transparent trade policy that advances environmental protection as we move forward in integrating our diverse markets. We appreciate the opportunity to provide these comments and we look forward to working with you to address these important issues.

Sincerely,

*John J. Audley*
Director of International Affairs
National Wildlife Federation

# XII. APPENDIX: SUMMIT CORRESPONDENCE

cc:
Ms. Karen Lezny, US Trade Representative
Mr. Bryan Samuel, US Department of State
Ms. Rachel Schub, US Trade Representative
Mr. Matt Rhode, US Trade Representative
Mr. Claude Burcky, US Trade Representative
Mr. Bennet Harman, US Trade Representative
Ms. Susan Early, US Trade Representative
Ms. Lisa Kubiske, US Trade Representative
Mr. Steve Powell, Department of Commerce
Ms. Audrey Winter, US Trade Representative
Ms. Sandy Dembsky, US Trade Representative
Ms. Regina Vargo, Department of Commerce
Mr. Peter Collins, US Trade Representative
Ms. Jennifer Haverkamp, US Trade Representative
Ms. Serena Wilson, Environmental Protection Agency
Mr. Steve Wolfson, Environmental Protection Agency

# XII. Appendix

# Participating Organizations

Association of American Chambers of Commerce in
Latin America (AACLA)
1615 H Street, NW
Washington, D.C. 20062-2000
Tel: 202-463-5485
Fax: 202-463-3126

Canadian Foundation for the Americas (FOCAL)
55 Murray Street, Suite 230
Ottawa, Canada
K1N5M3
Tel: 613-562-0005
Fax: 613-562-2525

Caribbean/Latin American Action (C/LAA)
1818 N Street, NW; Suite 500
Washington, D.C. 20036
Tel: 202-466-7464
Fax: 202-822-0075
email: info@claa.org
http://www.claa.org

Corporación PARTICIPA
Almirante Simpson 014
Providencia
Santiago, Chile
Tel: 562-222-5384
Fax: 562-222-1374
email: participa@netup.cl

Corporation for Development Research (CINDE)
Santa Magdalena 75, Of. 1002
Providence, Santiago, Chile
Tel: 56-2 334-4302
Fax: 56-2 334-4303
email: preal@reuna.cl

Council of the Americas
690 Park Ave.
New York, NY 10021
Tel: 212-628-3200
Fax: 212-517-6247

ESQUEL Group Foundation (EGF)
1003 K St. NW, Suite 800
Washington, D.C. 20001-4425
Tel: 202-347-1796
Fax: 202-347-1797
email: info@esquel.org
http://www.esquel.org

Facultad Latinoamericana
de Ciencias Sociales (FLACSO)-Chile
Leopoldo Urrutia 1950
Santiago, Chile
Casilla 3213 Central de Casillas
Tel: 562-225-9938
Fax: 562-274-1004

Inter-American Development Bank (IDB)
1300 New York Ave., NW
Washington, D.C. 20577
Tel: 202-822-9002
Fax: 202-623-3615

Inter-American Dialogue
1211 Connecticut Ave., NW, Suite 510
Washington, D.C. 20036
Tel: 202-822-9002
Fax: 202-822-9553

International Center for Research on Women (ICRW)
1717 Massachusetts Ave., NW, Suite 302
Washington, D.C. 20036
Tel: 202-797-0007
Fax: 202-797-0020
email: icrw@igc.apc.org

International Institute for Sustainable Development
(IISD)
Head Office
161 Portage Avenue East, 6th Floor
Winnipeg, Manitoba, Canada
R3B 0Y4
Tel.: 1-204-958-7700
Fax: 1-204-958-7710
email: info@iisd.ca
IISDnet: http://iisd.ca/

National Association of Manufacturers (NAM)
1331 Pennsylvania Ave., NW
Washington, D.C. 20004-1790
Tel: 202-637-3000
Fax: 202-637-3182
email: manufacturing@nam.org

National Wildlife Federation (NWF)
1400 Sixteenth St., NW
Washington, D.C. 20036
Tel: 202-797-6898
Fax: 202-797-5486

North-South Center
1500 Monza Ave.
Coral Gables, FL 33146-3027
Tel: 305-284-6868
Fax: 305-284-6370
www.miami.edu/nsc/

Organization of Africans in the Americas
1234 Massachusetts Ave., NW; Suite C-1007
Washington, D.C. 20005
Tel: 202-638-1662
Fax: 202-638-1667

Organization of American States (OAS)
Office of Summit Follow-Up
17th and Constitution Ave., NW
Washington, D.C. 20006
Tel: 202-458-3609
Fax: 202-458-3967

Pan American Health Organization (PAHO)
Office of Information and Public Affairs
525 23rd Street, NW
Washington, D.C. 20037
Tel: 202-975-3459
Fax: 202-974-3143
www.paho.org

Partnership for Educational Revitalization in the Americas (PREAL)
c/o Inter-American Dialogue
1211 Connecticut Ave., NW, Suite 510
Washington, D.C. 20036
Tel: 202-822-9002
Fax: 202-822-9553
email: iad@thedialogue.org
www.preal.cl

Red Nacional de Acción Ecológica (RENACE)
Center for Environmental Law
Seminario 774, Nunoa
Santiago de Chile
Chile

The World Bank
1818 H Street, NW
Washington, D.C. 20433 U.S.A.
Tel: 202-477-1234

Transparency International (TI) USA
1615 L Street, NW, Suite 700
Washington, D.C. 20036
Tel: 202-682-7048
Fax: 202-682-7086

The U.S. Chamber of Commerce
1615 H Street, NW
Washington, D.C. 20062
Tel: 202-659-6000
Fax: 202-463-3190

# INDEX

## A

AACCLA (Association of American Chambers of Commerce in Latin America) 483, 485
ABF (Americas Business Forum) 139, 145, 232, 250, 393, 452, 455, 458-460, 467-472, 475, 483-484, 489, 491, 497, 498, 500, 502, 504, 509-510, 514-515, 667, 673, 682
Aboriginal peoples 589
abortion 181, 541, 544
Acción Ciudadana 648
accrediting professionals 469
ACS (Association of Caribbean States) 147, 251, 258
Action Plan 50
Ad-Hoc Committee of the World Health Organization 176
AD/CVD (antidumping/countervailing duty) 261, 264, 270
  decisions 261
Additional Protocol on Human Rights in the Area of Economic, Social, and Cultural Rights 161, 163
adjustment assistance 250, 253
administrative
  infrastructure 627, 636
  reform 278
Administrative Secretariat 72, 259, 306, 455, 463
adolescent
  prevention of pregnancies 91
  teen pregnancy 161
Advance New Opportunities for Natural Gas 237
AeroMexico 321
AFL-CIO Solidarity Center 274, 388, 663
African Growth and Opportunity Act 460, 461
Afro
  -Latin-Americans 579, 671
  Americans 576-577
Afroamerica XXI 572, 578-580, 669, 671
Agenda 21 97-98, 242
agrarian reform 561
Agreement on Copyright and Related Rights 260

Agreement on Trade-Related Aspects of Intellectual Property Rights. *See TRIPS*
agreements 298
  trade and investment liberalization 606
agricultural 97, 463
  subsidies 473
  subsistence 592
AIDIS (Inter-American Association of Sanitary Engineering) 101
AIDS. *See HIV/AIDS*
air
  pollution reduction of 133, 142
  quality 102
  safety 278
ALACBS (Association of Latin American and Caribbean Bank Supervisors) 196, 209, 211, 216
ALADI 198, 255, 310-311
Alianza coalition 320
ALIDES (Central American Alliance for Sustainable Development) 114
alien smuggling 11
Allende, Salvador 202
Alliance Against Drugs 635
Alliance for Sustainable Development 85
Amazon Cooperation Treaty. *See TCA*
American Bankers Association 200
American Chambers of Commerce 483
American Declaration of the Rights and Duties of Man 4
Americas Business Forum. *See ABF*
  private sector recommendations 483
Americas Financial Board 197
amnesty
  law 161, 164
  to military and civilian personnel 164
Amnesty International 158, 172
ANCOM (Andean Common Market) 266
Andean Community 251, 254-255, 263, 265, 271
Andean Pact 254, 258, 678
Andean Common Market. *See ANCOM*

Andean Council of Ministers of Foreign Relations. *See CAMARE*
Andean Development Corporation 72
Andean Tribunal of Justice 255
Andres Bello Pact 225, 227
anti
  -bribery 479, 490, 646, 648-650
  -corruption 33, 316, 318-319, 321, 322, 324, 327, 635, 645, 653, 657
    commissioner 648
    convention 139, 389, 653, 655
    legislation 147, 647
    measures 649
    procurement guidelines 513
    program 647-648
  -drug strategy 26, 628, 631, 635
    in the Hemisphere 58
  -money laundering measures 503
  -poverty policies 522
antidumping 264, 270, 277, 473-474, 503
  duties 293, 303, 463
  laws 264
  problem 263-264
antidumping/countervailing duty. *See AD/CVD*
Antigua and Barbuda 257
APEC (Asia-Pacific Economic Cooperation) 143-146, 249, 272, 274, 275, 407, 453, 468, 486-487, 490, 515, 556, 559, 634
  SCCP (Sub-Committee on Customs Procedures) 488
Areas of Democracy and Human Rights 156
Argentina 77-79, 81, 83, 87-88, 157, 160, 163, 184, 193, 202-203, 219-221, 223-224, 237-239, 243, 258-260, 262-263, 265-266, 275, 315, 317, 319, 320, 322, 388, 390-391, 395, 397, 401, 653, 660, 663, 675, 684
"Argentine miracle" 319
armed forces 157, 160-161, 163, 165
arms control 14, 49
ARPEL (Reciprocal Assistance of Latin American Oil Companies) 243
Aruba 77
Asia 134, 218, 252, 261, 275, 309, 349-350, 373-374, 453, 485, 486, 489, 635

697

*Asia, continued*
   East 133-134, 137, 144, 351-352, 354, 374
   financial crisis 453, 485
   monetary crisis 460, 461
   Pacific 131
   South 374
   Southeast 350, 351
Asia-Pacific Economic Cooperation. *See APEC*
Asian flu 278, 463, 478, 498
   financial flu 628
Association of American Chambers of Commerce in Latin America. *See AACCLA*
Association of Caribbean States. *See ACS*
Association of Latin American and Caribbean Bank Supervisors. *See ALACBS*
ATA Carnet Convention 480
auditing standards 201
Australia 263, 272
automotive industry products 255

# B

Bahamas 83, 257
balance of payments
   issues 252
   manual 201
   problems 309
Banco Nación 315
banking
   and securities markets 193, 196, 204, 209, 505
   associations, regional 200
   commercial
      privatization of 205
   development
      capital markets and pension funds 205
      closure and downsizing of 205
   direct ownership of 205
   dual-currency regimes 205
   law of 1993 205
   long-term financing options 211
   market supervision and examination 211
   multipurpose 204
   pension system 205
   privatize 203
   removal of subsidized lending 205
   securities law 205
   superintendent 203

   supervision 4, 216, 217
   system 193, 217, 453
      commercial crisis in 1982 202
      crises 198
      financial crisis of 1995 204
      reform of regulatory environment 205
bankruptcy 212
   regimes 196, 201, 212
Barbados 80, 97, 114, 257, 379, 466, 524, 653
Barshefsky, Charlene 273
Basic Health Care Plan 181
Basic Obstetric Emergency Care. *See BEOC*
basic rights of workers 20
   child labor 21
   forced labor 21
   non-discrimination in employment 21
basic sanitation services 561
BASICS 79
Basle Core Principles of Effective Banking Supervision 16, 216
   Agreement 205
   Committee 44, 195
BECC (Border Environmental Cooperation Commission) 674, 682
Belém do Pará Convention 156
Belize 83-84, 87-88, 114, 116, 119, 238-239, 257, 280, 334
Bellcore International 380
Belo Horizonte Trade Ministerial 58, 405, 452, 454-455, 464, 468, 472-473, 481, 484-485, 487, 506, 514
Belo Horizonte Ministerial Declaration 295, 673
BEOC (Basic Obstetric Emergency Care) 177
Bi-National Drug Threat Assessment 337
BID. *See IDB*
Big Bang 194, 197
bilateral
   agreements 250, 251, 255, 259, 260, 265, 272, 309
   arrangements 265
   investment treaties 266
   negotiations 249, 252
biodiversity 97, 101, 105, 235-236, 239, 240-241, 245, 595, 601-603, 614, 615, 633

   conservation 105, 241, 602
   preservation 603
   protection 240
   sustainable use 110
Biodiversity Partnership 246
biotechnology 108, 124, 617
black peoples
   discrimination 599
   neoliberal policy 598
   rights of 593, 619
BNHI (Business Network for Hemispheric Integration) 460, 468, 475, 477, 481
Bolivia 78-80, 84, 87-88, 90-91, 97-102, 104-107, 109, 111-116, 119-120, 122, 124-126, 133, 136, 138, 140, 142, 177, 184, 203, 235, 237-244, 250-251, 255, 260, 265, 268, 271, 317, 330-332, 334-336, 338, 340-341, 385-387, 392, 397-398, 403, 405-406, 453, 493, 511, 536-537, 541, 543, 546, 563, 573-574, 636, 643, 646, 648, 660, 679
Bolivia Summit of the Americas 221, 235-237, 239-240, 243-246, 386, 390, 394-395, 398, 661
Bolivia Summit Declaration 407
border control 11
Border Environmental Cooperation Commission. *See BECC*
Brady Bonds 199
Braga, Carlos Primo 265
Brazil 78-83, 85, 87, 91, 93-94, 102-104, 107, 109-110, 112-116, 119-120, 133, 143, 145, 148, 156-159, 173, 176-177, 179, 182-184, 193, 203, 223, 226, 232, 237-239, 242, 244, 249-250, 253, 258-260, 262-263, 265--267, 271-278, 297, 309-310, 320, 323, 327, 330, 336, 354, 373-374, 395, 397, 399, 405, 411, 453-455, 458-459, 461, 463-464, 466-468, 472, 479, 482, 485, 490, 497, 511, 536-538, 541-548, 557-559, 592, 628, 630, 634-637, 646, 647-648, 653, 660, 662
Brazil Amazon 241
Brazilian financial crisis 628
Bretton Woods 195
   institutions 635, 637
bribery 12, 138, 645

698

# INDEX

*bribery, continued*
  outlawing 141
  transnational
    criminalization of 657
"Budgetgate" 320
Buenos Aires Ministerial
  Communiqué 212
building mutual confidence 59
Bureau of Oceans and International
  Environmental and Scientific
  Affairs 387
Business Commission for International Trade Negotiations. *See
  CENCIT*
business facilitation 307
Business Network for Hemispheric
  Integration. *See BNHI*
business-education partnerships
  372, 376-378

## C

C/LAA (Caribbean/Latin American
  Action) 372, 380, 497-498, 500-506
  Agribusiness Team 503
  Business Teams 501
  Energy Business Team 503
  Transportation Business Team 506
CACM (Central American Common
  Market) 206, 251, 256-258, 265,
  269, 276
CAMARE (Andean Council of
  Ministers of Foreign Relations—
  Consejo Andino de Ministerios
  de Relaciones Exteriores) 255
campaign reform 328
Canada 33, 44, 58, 77-78, 83-84,
  106-108, 115, 118, 120, 135-139,
  156-158, 175, 182, 184, 190, 237-242, 249-251, 261-265, 268-269,
  273, 275, 281-282, 284, 288, 298-299, 300, 304, 317, 361, 385,
  387, 389-390, 393, 395, 398, 400-401, 403-408, 416, 453, 471, 473,
  482, 487, 495, 511, 525, 536,
  544-545, 555-559, 561-563, 568,
  571, 591-593, 606-607, 616, 626-628, 630-631, 634-639, 647-648,
  653, 655, 660, 662-663
Canada-U.S. Free Trade Agreement
  261
Canadian Centre for Foreign Policy
  Development 404

Canadian International Development Agency. *See CIDA*
Canadian Labour Congress. *See
  CLC*
capital
  flows
    liberalization of 191, 195-196
  markets
    full-scale integration of 193
    initiative 196
    integration of 191, 195, 209, 216,
      294, 301
    regulations 196, 216
    transactions, liberalization of 196
  movements 192, 195-196, 207, 209,
    216-218
  speculative 560
*carabineros* 162
Cardoso, Fernando Henrique 30,
  35, 153, 158-160, 275-276, 309,
  320, 321, 634
Care of the Sick Child Strategy 102
Caribbean Basin Initiative. *See CBI*
Caribbean Common Market and
  Community. *See CARICOM*
Caribbean Disaster Emergency
  Response Agency 103
Caribbean Economic Diversification
  Program 112
Caribbean Islands 78, 119
Caribbean Project for Planning for
  Adaptation to Climate Change
  116
Caribbean Water and Wastewater
  Association. *See CWWA*
Caribbean/Latin American
  Action. *See C/LAA*
CARICOM (Caribbean Common
  Market and Community) 33, 80,
  103, 112, 198, 251, 255, 257-258,
  265, 268-269, 271, 276, 337,
  390, 453, 466
Cartagena Accord 331, 332
Carvalho, Clóvis 320
CATIE (Tropical Agronomic
  Research and Teaching Center)
  106
Cayman Islands 77
CBI (Caribbean Basin Initiative)
  276, 459, 462
CBSA (Chilean Banking Supervisory Agency) 203
CCAD (Central American Commission on Environment and
  Development) 108, 678
CEAL (Latin American Business
  Council) 200, 227
CEC (North American Commission
  for Environmental Cooperation)
  674, 682
CENCIT (Business Commission for
  International Trade Negotiations)
  499
Center for Foreign Policy Development 409
Central America 193, 204, 239,
  243, 251-252, 256, 309-310, 329,
  390, 392, 454, 467, 501, 547,
  592, 606, 628, 634
Central American Alliance for
  Sustainable Development 108,
  115
Central American Commission on
  Environment and Development.
  *See CCAD*
Central American Common
  Market. *See CACM*
Central American Council on
  Forests and Protected Areas 107
Central American Institute for
  Administration and Supervision
  of Education. *See ICASE*
Central American Integration
  System. *See SICA*
Centre for Foreign Policy Development 408
CEPAL (Comisión Económica para
  América Latina y el Caribe—
  Economic Commission for Latin
  America and the Caribbean,
  ECLAC) 38, 49, 256, 269
CER (Closer Economic Relations)
  263
CET (four-tiered Common External
  Tariff) 255-260
CGIAR (Consultative Group for
  International Agricultural
  Research) 615
CGR (Committee of Government
  Representatives on Civil Society)
  388, 637, 681-689
Chairman's International Advisory
  Council of the Americas Society
  227

Chamber of Commerce of the U.S.A., 483, 485
CHFI (Committee on Hemispheric Financial Issues) 58, 143-144, 192, 195, 196, 198-204, 209-211, 216, 218, 630, 635, 638
   Deputies 212
child mortality 181-183
childcare for teen mothers 526
children
   health care 79
   mortality 77
      rates 139, 187
      reduction of 78
   rights 102
Chile 69, 77-78, 80-81, 83-85, 88, 105-108, 112, 119, 120, 124, 132, 137, 157-158, 160-163, 171, 173, 177, 179-80, 188, 192-193, 199, 202-203, 206, 219-224, 226, 231, 237-240, 243, 250-265, 267-268, 271, 275, 310, 322, 327, 329, 333-335, 341, 347-348, 356-357, 363-364, 372, 385, 387-388, 390, 395-396, 403-404, 406, 419, 453-454, 458, 462, 466, 479, 482-483, 485, 490, 493, 495, 498, 511, 521-522, 533, 536-539, 542, 544, 546, 547, 571-573, 592-593, 625, 627- 628, 631, 635-636, 638, 653, 658, 673, 688
Chilean Banking Supervisory Agency. *See CBSA*
China 106, 116, 184, 351
Church World Services/Lutheran World Relief 388
CICAD (Inter-American Drug Abuse Control Commission) 5, 12, 50, 333-337, 340, 421, 578, 635
   Model Regulations on the Control of Arms and Explosives Connected with Drug Trafficking 13
CIDA (Canadian International Development Agency) 80, 82-83, 101, 116, 122, 176, 278, 388, 404, 408, 557, 558-559, 561, 563
CIDI (Inter-American Council for Integral Development) 9, 58, 99-100, 123, 126, 242
   Executive Secretariat 72
   Strategic Plan for Partnership for Development 9

CIDS (Inter-American Commission on Sustainable Development) 111, 126
CIESS (Inter-American Center for Social Security Studies) 81, 177
CIM (Inter-American Commission of Women) 70, 523
CINDE (Corporation for Development Research) 347-348, 363-364
CITEL (Inter-American Telecommunications Commission) 18, 58
   guidelines on value-added services 18
CITES (International Convention on Trade in Endangered Species) 108
Citibank 321
citizen participation 385-386, 389, 392, 416, 571, 576, 648, 654, 661-662
citizens' rights 589
citizenship 41
civic ethics 658
civil
   society vii, viii, 4, 9-11, 13, 20, 22-23, 30, 34, 41-43, 45, 47-48, 50, 63, 66, 131-132, 134-136, 138, 141, 146-148, 155, 157, 178, 183, 185, 220, 223-227, 244-245, 279, 307, 310, 328, 352, 359, 363, 385-389, 391-394, 396-398, 400, 403-404, 406, 409, 411-412, 416, 421, 452-453, 458-459, 494, 511, 537, 540-541, 549, 555-557, 559, 562, 571-576, 589, 590, 599, 603, 621, 626-628, 630-633, 637-638, 648, 658-663, 667-668, 673-674, 681-684, 687-689, 691
   -government partnerships 660
   accreditation to groups 388
   participation vii, 385, 387, 390, 396, 398, 403, 406, 408, 411, 421, 500, 556, 559, 562, 574-575, 578, 632, 648, 687
   role of combating corruption 328
   responsibility 375
Civil Society Initiative 385-387, 390, 392, 394, 397-398, 400, 636, 659, 660, 662
Civil Society Task Force 386-387, 389, 394, 397, 401, 648, 663
civil-military relations 159, 162, 165

civilian
   -political supervision 163
   supremacy 158
CLC (Canadian Labour Congress) 405, 591
Clean Development Mechanism 17, 44
Clean Energy Database 237
Clean Energy Technologies 237
Clean Water Information System 114
Clearance and Settlements Systems 45
climate and energy
   El Niño 44
   human health 44
   pollution 44
Climate Change and Biodiversity Conventions 98
Clinton, William Jefferson 26, 29, 33, 35, 61, 66, 151, 236, 252, 253, 257, 272-275, 310, 314-316, 318, 332-336, 339, 396, 405, 456-457, 459, 460-463, 466, 484, 485, 593, 633-635, 641, 678
Closer Economic Relations. *See CER*
CMC (Common Market Council) 259-260
CNBV (National Banking and Securities Commission) 204
code of conduct 646
   international business 563
code of ethics 561
Code of Ethics for Public Employees 648
coercive instruments 157
collective bargaining 559
Collor de Mello, Fernando 160, 320, 323, 327-328
Colombia 78, 80, 83, 107, 109-114, 116, 119-120, 123, 173, 176, 178-182, 184, 219, 226, 238-239, 241-242, 255, 257, 262, 265, 271, 310, 317, 330-338, 341, 349, 357-358, 379, 388, 394-395, 453-455, 495, 497, 540-541, 544-545, 547-548, 628, 635-636, 648
Colosio, Luis Donaldo 321
commercial
   dispute resolution 196, 201, 212
   illicit practices 138

# INDEX

Committee of Government Representatives on Civil Society. *See CGR*
Committee on Administrative and Budgetary Affairs 73
Committee on Cooperation 243
Committee on Electronic Commerce 458
Committee on Hemispheric Financial Issues. *See CHFI*
Committee on Hemispheric Security 14
Committee on Inter-American Summits Management 58
Committee on Trade and Environment 306
Common Frontiers 405, 407, 591, 592
common law 473
Common Market Council. *See CMC*
Common Market Group 259
Community of Portuguese-speaking Countries. *See CPLP*
competition 649
    policy 196, 201, 212, 260-264, 270-272, 286, 301, 305, 310, 463, 473
computer-based trading systems 212
Comunidade de Países de Lingua Portuguesa. *See CPLP*
CONCAUSA alliance 239
concrete progress 452, 457-458, 465-468, 478, 483, 485, 502, 505, 509, 514, 627, 634, 638
Confederation des Syndicats Nationaux. *See CSN*
Conference on Women 24, 84
congressional investigative committee. *See CPI*
Consejo Andino de Ministerios de Relaciones Exteriores. *See CAMARE*
conservation 494, 602, 615
    biodiversity and raising of species 602
    of soil and natural resources 601
consolidated supervision 192, 195-196, 198-200, 203
Consultative Fora for Economic and Social Issues 677
Consultative Group for International Agricultural Research. *See CGIAR*

Consultative Group on Smaller Economies 306, 463
contributions to electoral campaigns 12
Convention of Belém do Pará 158, 161, 163
Convention on Biological Diversity 105, 109, 111, 603
Convention on Biological Diversity's Protocol on Biosafety 615
Convention on Combating Bribery of Foreign Public Officials 511
Convention on the Law of the Seas 108
Convention on the Prevention and Penalization of Torture 156
Convention on the Protection of the World's Cultural and Natural Heritage 108
Convention on Wetlands of International Importance. *See RAMSAR*
COPANT 269
Core Principles for Effective Banking Supervision 44-45
Corporación Participa. *See PARTICIPA*
corporate
    assets, expropriation of 613
    governance 201
Corporation for Development Research. *See CINDE*
corrupt business practices 490
corruption 5, 12, 49, 59, 147, 313-314, 316-318, 327-328, 331-332, 339, 375, 391, 393, 411, 419, 421, 453, 474, 476, 490, 504, 509, 511, 572, 578, 595, 597, 608, 626, 630, 631, 635, 642, 646, 647-649, 651, 657-658
    and narcotics trafficking 132, 140
    attack on 645
    bribery 12
    combating 210, 316, 328, 331, 393, 421, 578, 635, 651
    confronting 23
    counter 637
    related unlawful practices in commercial transactions 12
COSRA (Council of Securities Regulators of the Americas) 196, 198, 200, 209, 211

Costa Rica 77-78, 80, 83-85, 87-89, 103, 105-106, 108, 119-120, 124, 176, 238-239, 241, 256, 262-263, 265-266, 268, 271-273, 295-297, 317, 380, 395, 455, 464, 468, 473, 475, 483, 485, 493, 495, 497-498, 509, 522, 525, 536-538, 540-541, 543, 546, 640, 646, 648, 667, 671, 673
Council for the Rights of Children 159
Council of Judicial Coordination 164
Council of Ministers Responsible for Central American Economic Integration and Regional Development 256
Council of Securities Regulators of the Americas. *See COSRA*
Council of the Americas 483, 485
Council on the Condition of Women 538
counter-insurgency efforts 593
counterdrug
    accords, international 330
    initiatives 332
counternarcotics 59
    agenda 339
    alternative development 331, 337-339
    efforts 638
    policies 329, 335-336
counternarcotics agreements 333
Counternarcotics Alliance 335-336
counternarcotics apparatus 331
Counternarcotics Consensus 331
countervailing duties 264, 270, 293, 303, 463, 473, 475, 503
Court of Constitutional Guarantees 163
courts, independence of 157
CPI (congressional investigative committee) 320
CPLP (Community of Portuguese-speaking Countries—Comunidade de Países de Lingua Portuguesa) 184
credit limits 201, 205
crime
    organized 33
    transnational 331-332
Cristiani, Alfredo 203

cross-border transactions 216, 217
CSN (Confederation des Syndicats Nationaux) 405
CSOs (civil society organizations) 387-388, 390, 394, 396, 398-400, 403-408, 493, 511, 556, 559, 571-576, 648, 660-662
Cuba 77-78, 83, 120, 184, 258, 334, 453, 456, 539, 541, 548, 559, 597, 630, 639
  blockade of 590
cultural
  heritage 413
  values 59
currency
  management policies 217
  stability 192, 207
  volatility 249
customs 422, 488, 646
  code 499
  documentation 506
  facilitation 484
  procedures 261, 302, 456, 458-459, 469, 472, 475-476, 479-480, 488, 502, 506, 619
  rules 469, 480
  union 251, 267
Customs Cooperation Council 467
CWWA (Caribbean Water and Wastewater Association) 101

# D

Daubón, Ramón 386, 389, 391-393, 394, 396-398, 400-401, 659, 660, 662-663
DDM (Data for Decision Making) 177
de Prevoisin, Gerardo 321
debt
  crisis 193, 199-200, 217, 415, 417, 614
  external 257
  payments 613
  repayments 561
  reschedulings 200
  service 252
decentralization 231, 661-662
Declaration of Principles 155, 157-158, 161, 164, 486
Declaration of Principles on Fundamental Rights of Workers 21
Declaration of Santa Cruz 97

Declaration of Santa Cruz de la Sierra 64-65, 97
Declaration of Santiago vii, viii, 155
Declaration on Forests 98
Declaration on the Environment and Development 98
Declarations of the Regional Conferences on Confidence and Security Building Measures 5
Defense Ministerial of the Americas 157, 636
  Williamsburg and Bariloche 14
defense policy 14
deforestation, curbing 110
DeLors Commission on Education 222
demilitarization 160
democracy vii, 9, 29, 33, 59, 133, 557, 563, 572, 631
  and free elections 135
  consolidating 4, 57
  consolidation of 171
  corruption 70
  deepening 47
  education for 4, 10
  judicial cooperation 70
  participatory 39, 589, 590
  preservation and strengthening of 9, 23, 26, 59, 70, 555, 575, 578
    corruption, terrorism, and illegal narcotics 9
  public safety 70
  restoration of in Haiti 33
  security 70
  strengthening 3, 7
democracy and human rights 10, 158
  human rights education 10
  inhumane conditions in prisons 10
democratic
  equality 376
  governance 156-158, 411-412, 626
  institutions 132-133, 136, 140, 147
  norms 138
  principles 413
  rule 672
  values 134-135, 327
democratization 26, 65, 134, 155, 160, 165, 324, 332, 372, 397, 415-416, 493, 561, 596-597, 632, 659
Denmark 107
Department for the Prevention of Corruption 647

Department of Energy. See U.S. DOE
deregulation 474, 476, 486, 488-489, 592, 601
desertification 110
  management 105
DFAIT 404
direct investment 453, 456, 475, 479, 481
Director General of Carabineros 162
disappearance, forced 158, 164
disarmament and arms control 14
discrimination 5, 11, 38, 50, 57, 414. See also poverty
  against women 19, 590
  and poverty 672
  combat racial 27
  eradication of vii, 59, 555, 558, 575
    by public participation 70
  health, hunger, women, indigenous people 59
  racial 11
  women
    against 590
    eradication of 70
disease. See also health
  communicable 101
  dengue, eradication of 188
  eliminating Chagas 64
  infectious 181, 416
  prevention 79
  spread of infectious 26
  transmissible 174, 179-180, 183-184
dispute resolution 454, 463, 470, 488, 494, 594-595, 612, 619-620
Dispute Resolution Foundation 388
dispute settlement 264, 285, 286
  mechanisms 261, 264, 266
  procedures 470, 474
  process 261
diversity, cultural and ethnic 589, 590
DOE (U.S. Department of Energy) 44, 140, 242
dollarization 193, 205, 207
domestic
  financial markets, liquidity in 211
  reform 646
  savings 193, 211, 252, 472
  violence 84, 87, 89, 521, 523, 526, 543
    combating 10
    prevent 84

# INDEX

Domestic Violence Law 88
Dominica 257-258, 653
Dominican Republic 78-80, 83, 87, 91, 106-107, 116, 177, 219, 243, 257, 317, 330, 385, 387-390, 392, 397, 499, 501, 532, 537, 647, 659, 681
double taxation 471
Draft Ministerial Declaration 301
drug
  -related corruption 331-332
  abuse 33, 58, 72
  activity 417
  addicts, social reintegration of 13
  alliance against 33
  cartels 340
  combating production of 597
  consumption 336-337, 417, 597
    control budget 337
  counter-collaboration in 341
  dangers of abuse 13
  diversion of chemical precursors 13
  eradication and interdiction 13
  illicit
    consumption 12, 337
      prevention of 13
    crops 13
    production 58
  interdiction 278
  international narcotics agreements 13
  problem 5
  producing countries 336
  reducing demand 336
  rehabilitation 13
  reintegration programs 13
  trade 563
  traffic in narcotics 13
  traffickers, extradition of 340
  trafficking 12, 26, 49, 58, 72, 329-334, 336, 339, 340, 597
    illegal 453
    illicit 453
    related crimes 12
  use, rate of 336
drugs. *See also narcotics*
  coca 330, 332, 338-340
    crop substitution in 339
  cocaine 330, 336-337
  combating 329, 339-340
    illegal 329-330
  crop reduction programs 337-339
  demand-reduction efforts 337
  eradicate crops 329
  forced eradication 338
  illegal narcotics 628
  illicit 631

poppy 338-339
  war against 593
DSM (dispute settlement mechanism) 264
dumping 270
duty rates 458, 471
DVP (delivery versus payment) 212

## E

early harvest 627, 634, 638
Earth Summit 97, 99
Eastern Caribbean Central Bank 257
EC (European Community) 191, 195-196, 205, 225, 257, 321, 372, 461, 560
ECLAC (United Nations Economic Commission on Latin America and the Caribbean, CEPAL) 4, 9, 18-20, 22, 45, 64, 72, 82, 103, 116, 122-123, 138, 146, 176, 221-222, 232, 256, 258, 262, 266, 291, 310, 390, 395, 453-454, 464, 499, 545, 548, 630-631, 636, 674
ecological conservation 612
economic
  cooperation 453, 486, 627, 630, 637
  development vii, 4, 25, 64, 105, 111, 182, 197, 209, 231, 241, 266, 309, 337, 376, 380, 392, 414, 453, 478, 490, 497, 503-506, 544, 561, 579, 610, 612, 614-615, 618-619, 642, 668, 678
  growth 412, 486
    self-sustaining 500
  integration 4, 15-16, 38, 47, 70, 215, 257, 294, 296, 301, 306-307, 309-310, 398, 414, 417, 452-453, 455-456, 486, 493-494, 509, 555-557, 559, 560-561, 563-572, 574-576, 595-598, 605-607, 620, 631-632, 645, 661
    and free trade 7
    energy cooperation 16
    increased 3
    modernization of financial markets 16
    transportation and telecommunications 16
  liberalization 310
  modernization 411
  policies, market-based 3
Economic Commission on Latin America and the Caribbean. *See ECLAC. See also CEPAL.*
Economic Consultative Forum 259
Economic Cooperation Agreement 265
Economic Development Institute. *See EDI*
economic integration and free trade 59, 452
ecotourism 106
ECU (European Currency Unit) 195
Ecuador 78-81, 83-84, 87, 91, 93, 102-103, 105, 107, 112, 119, 120, 177, 238-240, 243, 245, 251, 255, 316-317, 330, 341, 391, 393, 495, 537, 541-542, 628, 646-648
EDE (Electronic Data Exchange System) 476-477, 480
EDI (Economic Development Institute) 81, 177
education 4, 7, 23, 26, 41, 47, 59, 70-72, 97, 133, 141, 171, 231, 347, 374, 412, 417, 479, 555, 557-558, 572, 575, 577, 589, 609, 627, 630. *See also women*
  access to 4, 231
  achievement in mathematics and science 352
  achievement tests 352
  adult 220
    programs 222
  advancement 221
  and communications policy 103
  and health 638
  assessment 226
  attainment, poor 350
  availability of textbooks 353
  basic skills 221
  bilingual
    intercultural, 223
    preschool 222
    primary programs 222
  business-, partnerships 227
  campaign for individual investors 200
  centralized administration 354
  certification of job skills 222, 223
  childhood 227
  civic and voter 662
  content and performance standards 233
  continuing adult 222

*education, continued*
- crisis 349-350, 353
- cross-national tests 353
- decentralization 220, 226-227, 232
  - programs 353
- delegating greater authority to schools 357
- democratic principles 223
- disadvantaged groups 222
- distance 42, 221, 223, 558
  - learning 222
- economic growth 352
- efficiency 222
- entrepreneurial skills 8
- equity 366
  - of basic 349
- evaluations of performance 233
- exchange programs 370
- expenditure 9
- failing schools 132, 137
- finance 226, 370
- for democracy 4, 10, 222
- formal 224, 226, 368, 579
- formation of ethical values 223
- gap in attainment 351
- gender
  - equality 352
  - equity 223
- health workers 177, 187
- higher 8, 220
- human resources training 220
- human rights 223
- illiteracy 41, 220-221
  - rate 577
- in Latin America 41
- inadequate evaluation of
  - school performance 353
  - student learning 353
- incapacitated students 221
- incentives for performance 354
- increased financing 360
- indigenous
  - children 222
  - peoples 221
- inequity 351
- information and communication technologies 223
- information networks 223
- initial and preschool programs 221
- institutional change 368
- institutions 376
- international
  - indicators 228
  - tests 356
- investments in 371
- job-related competencies 8

- lack authority and accountability 353
- limited school authority and accountability 353
- literacy programs 222
- little investment in primary schools and secondary schools 353
- low test scores 349
- management 223
- measurement and evaluation 232
- micro, small, and medium-sized enterprises training and technical assistance 19
- migrants 221
- ministries 233
  - national or state-level 357
- money
  - invested in public schools 358
  - investment per student 358
  - per-pupil spending 365
- multiculturalism 369
- multilateral cooperation 9
- national
  - and regional tests 232
  - assessment systems 227
  - assessments 356
  - standards 226
    - primary and secondary 222
  - testing 349, 356
    - regimes 227
  - system 356
- non-governmental actors 231
- parental choice 227
- per student investment 233
- performance 233
  - evaluations 353
  - standard 353
  - standards 356
- policy 347, 363
  - and practice 356
- poor
  - teaching 353
  - women 221
- post-secondary 558
- preparation for the world of work 368
- preschool 228
- primary 34, 41, 220
  - and secondary 222, 228, 349, 354-355, 358, 378
  - quality 133, 142
  - school, overcome nutritional deficiencies 220
- private
  - -public partnerships 228
  - and public schools 351
- professional training 220
- professionalism among teachers 8
- professionalize teaching and

- administration 223
- public
  - -private partnerships 221
  - expenditure on 355
  - spending per primary student 354
- quality 8, 30, 41, 220-222, 224-225, 231-232, 348, 352, 359, 365, 377, 526, 577, 609
  - primary 7, 222
  - secondary 7
  - teaching 358
- reform 38, 133, 139, 141-142, 219, 221, 224-228, 233, 347-348, 354, 359, 363, 365, 376, 379, 381, 413-414, 558, 573, 635, 637
  - Latin America and the Caribbean 221
- policy 139
- reforms
  - structural 221
- regional
  - program of internships 42
  - testing system 233
- relevance 222
- respect for the environment 223
- responsible coordinator
  - Mexico 220
- school
  - autonomy 227, 231
  - management 231-232, 349, 353, 356-357
  - performance 353
  - readiness activities 40
- sector
  - productivity of 360
- self-learning 221
- services 377
- spending 355
- standardized tests 42
- standards 349, 356, 378
  - and evaluations 366
- statistics 42, 233
  - and indicators 356
- strategies
  - cultural diversity of peoples 8
  - democratic principles 8
  - exchange programs 8
  - gender-related issues 8
  - human rights 8
  - indigenous populations and migrants 8
  - peace 8
  - respect for natural resources 8
  - teaching materials 8
  - tolerance 8
- strengthen ethical values 421
- student learning 353
- system 50

# INDEX

*education, continued*
    centralized 349, 356
    standards for 349, 356
    strong 359, 372
    women's access to 547
    internal efficiency of 221
    teacher (s) (ing)
        -training programs 353
        and student evaluations 360
        materials 353, 370
        preparation 232
        profession 349, 353, 357-358, 367, 635
        professionalism among 8
        training 220, 222, 231, 353, 358, 378
        unions 227, 353, 354, 359
        quality 353
    technology and distance 369
    testing, cross-national 350
    tolerance 223
    tracking 522
    truancy 220
    universal access to 220, 221
    university students 354, 359
    values 369
    virtual school 42
    vocational 41
        training 223
    women 526, 535, 547
        levels of attainment 547
        primary school 548
    workplace skills 221
education, democracy and sustainable development 573
Education for Democracy 573
Education for Hemispheric Integration 573
Education for Sustainable Development 573
Education, Preserving and Strengthening Democracy 452
Educational Excellence. *See IE*
EEC (European Economic Community) 217
EGF (Esquel Group Foundation) 385-388, 391-392, 394, 397, 399, 659, 662
EIA (Environmental Impact Assessment) 240
Eizenstat, Stuart 273
El Salvador 78-79, 84, 87-88, 91, 93, 102, 104, 119-120, 184, 192, 202-204, 238-239, 241, 243, 252, 256, 262, 265-266, 350, 353, 397, 538, 540, 544, 606, 660
    forestry statute in 241
elections
    transparent 49
electoral
    campaigns 12
        transparency in the origin of all contributions 12
    process
        support the integrity of 33
electronic commerce 18, 372, 459, 466, 469, 479, 489, 503, 688
Electronic Data Exchange System. *See EDE*
emergency preparedness 103
energy 97, 236
    Americas Business Forum 504
    and minerals 118
    and telecommunications 453
    biosphere reserves 240
    clean conventional 238
    conservation 240
        funding 240-241
    cooperation 118
    efficiency 237-239
        financing 237
        and renewable energy 118-119
        production 238
    environmental democracy 240
    geothermal 238
    indigenous
        rights groups' 240
        communities 240
        peoples
            rights 240
    initiatives 237
    innovative financing 241
    international cooperation 238
    land and resource management 240
    market-based pricing 238
    market-oriented pricing 238
    national parks 240
    natural gas 237
    non-conventional renewable 238
    per capita consumption 238
    plans, integrated least-cost national 238
    policy 616
    projects
        clean 118-119, 237
        renewable 239
        wind 119
    public participation 240
    regional cooperation 17
        development of renewable energy and energy efficiency 17
        integration of energy markets 17
    regulated market pricing 238
    renewable 239
        energy resources 239
    resources conventional 238
    rural electrification programs 237-239
    sector 5, 504
    security long-term 121
    small hydro and biomass 238
    solar 238
    strategies integrated least-cost 238
    sustainable 237-239, 602
        development 240
        forestry incentives 240
        projects 239
            financing mechanisms 237
            for priority financing 238
            priority financing for 238
        sources 239
        use of natural environments 240
    wind 238

Energy Efficiency in the Hemisphere 237
Energy Efficient and Renewable Technologies Consortium 616
Energy Ministers Meeting 237
Energy Mix Baseline and Projections 237
Energy Partnership 245
Entidades Promotoras de Salud. *See EPS*
entrepreneurial skills 8
entrepreneurship 141
environment 72, 133, 594, 596
    preservation of 57
    protection of 598
environmental
    assessments 692
    clean-up 612
    concerns 678
    degradation 121, 132-133, 137, 142, 453, 596, 601, 633
    deterioration 188
    groups 252
    hazards 101
    health
        improvement of sanitation 101
        Inter-American Water Day 101
        safe drinking water 101
    issues vii
    law network 122, 127
    policies 414, 479, 502
    pollution 104

*environmental, continued*
   protection 104, 106, 111-112, 114, 249, 273-274, 277, 493, 560, 668
   quality 493, 619-620
   standards 563
   sustainability 560, 601
   technologies 272
Environmental Forum 406
Environmental Impact Assessment. *See EIA*
Environmental Law Institute 388
Environmental Law Program 661
EPA (U.S. Environmental Protection Agency) 101, 114, 123, 140, 242-243
epidemiological surveillance 189
Episcopal Church 388
EPS (Health Care Promoting Entities—Entidades Promotoras de Salud) 181
equal
   rights 5
      child custody 10
      in the workplace 10
      inheritance 10
      property 10
   work
      among men and women 577
equality 590
   improving gender 41
   legal 172
   of opportunity 27
   women 521
equity 7
   cultural 7
   disability and ethnic 7
   gender discrimination 7
   markets 205
Eradication of Poverty and Discrimination 188-190, 403, 452, 571
   initiatives
      Health Technology 188
      Hunger and Malnutrition 188
      Women and Indigenous Populations 188
Esquel Group Foundation. *See EGF*
ethnic minorities 50
ethno-cultural identification 579
EU (European Union) 44, 143, 180, 239, 242-243, 260, 267, 272-274, 309, 317-318, 323-325, 338, 453, 456, 465, 468-469, 605, 606, 614
European Community. *See EC*

European Convention on Access to Information 385
European Currency Unit. *See ECU*
European Monetary System 195, 217
European Union. *See EU*
European Economic Community. *See EEC*
EX-IM Bank 316
exchange
   rate 472
      liberalization 194
   reserves 252
executions, extrajudicial 164
Executive Group for the Repression of Forced Labor 159
Executive Secretariat 72
export 257
   non-oil 255
   subsidies 270
external
   auditors 200
   debt 257, 613

# F

family planning services 90
FAO (UN Food and Agriculture Organization) 106-107, 110-111, 116
   Forestry Commission 100
fast track 252-253, 273-275, 277-279, 456, 458-466, 498, 633
   authority 249, 274, 309, 405, 456, 461
      negotiating 253, 272-273
   authorization 273, 275
   legislation 30, 310, 454, 456, 460, 462, 466, 485, 490, 498, 500
FCPA (Foreign Corrupt Practices Act) 313-315, 323-324
Federal Reserve 198, 217
Feinberg, Richard E. 197-199, 220, 625, 640
FELABAN (Latin American Federation of Banks) 198, 200
FGEB (Fundação Grupo Esquel Brasil) 662
finance 626, 634
financial
   conglomerates 201
   council 637
   crimes 196, 207, 211-212
      combating 197, 199

   technical assistance program for 202
   disclosure 201, 204, 212, 317
   flows 215-216
   global, crisis 309
   institutions 204
   integration 38, 191-192, 194, 197, 199
   management 194, 325
   markets 191, 196, 202, 210-211, 630
      banking and securities market clearance 16
      Basle Core Principles for Effective Banking Supervision 16
      deregulation of 196
      globalization of 192, 193, 206, 215
      integration 194, 200
      integration of 191, 196, 198, 211, 216, 635
      internal and cross-border transactions 16
      regional integration of 191, 195
      regulators 211
   sector 215-217
      agreements 192
      banking, securities, and insurance 191
      development 194, 196, 200, 202, 207
      integration 192-193, 195, 199, 201, 206-207
      legislation 192, 206
      reforms 191-192, 194, 205-206
      regulations 192, 197, 201
         analysis of 192
      restructuring and modernization of 192
   services 459, 468, 470, 481, 484, 488-489, 500, 505
      for micro, small, and medium-sized enterprises 19
   stability 637
      and trade integration 133
financial and organizational aspects of health sector reform 176
Financial Markets Development Initiative 44
Financial Sector Working Group on Small Economies 199
Financial Services Business Team 505
Financial System Superintendency 203
firearms and ammunition, illicit transnational traffic in 13
First Ladies of the Americas 177, 627
First Nations 561
   Forum 557

# INDEX

Fiscal Accounts Manual 201
Fiscalía Especial de Derechos Humanos 163
flat-tariff rate structure 255
Florida International Bankers Association 200
FOCAL (Canadian Foundation for the Americas) 404, 555, 562
FONASA (National Health Care Fund—Fondo Nacional de Salud) 179-180
Fondo Nacional de Salud. *See* FONASA
food bank networks 22
foreclosure 201
Foreign Corrupt Practices Act. *See* FCPA
foreign
   direct investment 256
   exchange
      markets 195
      regulations 204
      transactions 595, 614
   investment 29, 147, 192, 199, 255-256, 319, 371, 472, 489, 500, 595, 601, 610-613
      barriers 260
      greater 193
      laws 199
      adequacy of 192, 199
Foreign Investment Funds 203
forest 97
   sustainable management 108, 133, 142
Forest Stewardship Council. *See* FSC
forestry
   coastal zone management 241
   conservation 241
   indigenous peoples' rights 241
   law reforms in Jamaica 241
   legislation 241
   management 241
   Mexico's "PRODEFOR" program 241
   statute in El Salvador 241
   sustainable incentives 241
Formas y Reformas de la Educación 227
Forum of First Nations 561
Forum of the Americas on Sustainable Development 99-101, 111, 125-126
   agriculture and biodiversity 99
   cities and energy 99
   health and water 99

Forum on Social and Economic Alternatives 406
Foundation of the Americas 632
four-tiered Common External Tariff. *See* CET
Fourth International Conference on Women 103
Fourth Trade Ministerial 682
Fourth World Conference on Women 20, 220
France 116, 180, 184, 317, 328, 591
Franco, Itamar 160, 320
free
   elections, and democracy 135
   markets 30
   press 171, 648, 659
   trade 15, 38, 70, 171, 215, 255, 294, 555, 557, 563, 575-576, 596, 630, 632, 645
      agenda 406
      and economic integration 7
      area 27
      business facilitation measures to 16
      energy cooperation 16
      hemisphere
         -wide 250
         infrastructure 16
      internal 258-259, 260
      modernization of financial markets 16
      negotiations 277, 309, 599
      smaller economies 16
      transportation and telecommunications 16
free trade zones 563
free-floating exchange rates 217
freedom
   of information legislation 648
   of the press 563
Frei Ruiz-Tagle, Eduardo 25, 29-30, 33, 35-37, 49, 322
freight services 256
FSC (Forest Stewardship Council) 241
FTAA (Free Trade Area of the Americas) vii, 3-4, 15-17, 23, 27, 45, 49, 70, 133-134, 139, 142-143, 145-148, 172, 232, 249-250, 252-253, 256-258, 262-278, 309-310, 329, 332-333, 388-389, 392, 395-396, 400-401, 404-408, 415, 452-468, 470, 472-475, 478-479, 482-491, 493-494, 497-505, 509-511, 513-514, 556-557, 559-560, 562-563, 576, 590, 592, 594-595, 611, 626-627, 630, 632-634, 637-639, 645-646, 654, 663, 667, 673-675, 677-679, 681-684, 688-689, 691, 692.
   Administrative Secretariat 682
   negotiations 500-501
Fujimori, Alberto 155, 163-165, 205, 321-322
Fund for Biodiversity 109
Fundação Grupo Esquel Brasil. *See* FGEB
Fundación Carvajal 388

## G

GAAP (generally accepted accounting principles) 459, 470
GADIS 388
gas pipeline projects 374
GATS (General Agreement on Trade in Services) 262
GATT (General Agreement on Tariffs and Trade) 194, 262, 270-272, 289, 295, 302, 315, 317, 323, 456, 466, 472, 476, 480-481, 503
Gaviria, César 243
GEF (Global Environmental Facility) 109-111, 116, 127, 387, 404-405
gender
   equality 577
   equity 596, 598
      awareness training 600
   improving equality 41
   violence 89
General Agreement on Tariffs and Trade. *See* GATT
geothermal power development 119
Germany 106, 180, 182, 184, 317, 545
GII (Global Information Infrastructure) 381
GIIC (Global Information Infrastructure Commission) 380-381
Gingrich, Newt 274
GIS (Global Information Society) 18, 381
global
   economy 33, 608, 617
   financial crisis 309
   marketplace 3

Global Conference on Sustainable Development of Small Island Developing States 97
Global Environmental Facility. *See* GEF
Global Forum of Peoples Native to the Forests and Other Peoples Dependent on the Forests Regarding Preservation and Sustainable Management of Forests 107
Global Information Infrastructure. *See* GII
Global Information Infrastructure Commission. *See* GIIC
Global Information Society. *See* GIS
Global Program of Action for Land-Based Sources of Marine Pollution 117
Global Workshop on Indigenous Peoples and Forests 110
globalization 3, 45, 174, 249-250, 253, 273, 279, 309, 314, 317, 360, 397, 415, 417, 485-486, 557, 572, 590, 595-596, 599-600, 609, 659
globalized markets 210
Gore, Albert 274
governance 38
government
  accountability 412
  local 661-662
  procurement 258, 260-261, 265, 271, 277, 287, 304, 315-317, 319, 454, 456, 459, 463, 467, 470, 474, 479, 480, 484, 489-490, 509,-510, 513, 515, 610, 645, 654
  and customs 652
  disciplines 263
  discrimination suffered by U.S. companies 315
  purchasing 610
GPA (Government Procurement Agreement) 265
gradual approach 194, 197
Grassroots Development Model 412
Greece 614
Grenada 83, 257, 653
ground-water controls 120
Group of Experts on Demand Reduction 337
Group of Three 255
groups, technical working 250
Grupo Esquel Uruguay 662
Guasch, Luis 264, 270
Guatemala 78, 80, 83-84, 87-88, 91, 102, 109, 111, 113, 119, 120, 155, 238-239, 242, 256, 350, 391, 463, 495, 499, 501, 540-542, 546, 548, 593, 648
guns, illegal trade in 30
Guyana 77, 83, 109, 120, 257

# H

Haiti 77-79, 83, 91, 102, 116, 155, 238-239, 257, 453
Hazardous Merchandise Transportation Agreement 259
health 97, 141, 609, 633
  and education 638
  basic services 41
    better access 181
  campaign against measles 59
  care 34, 374, 414, 417
    preventive 80
    quality 609
  Chagas' disease, eliminating 64
  child 175, 183
    standards on 102
  cholera 64, 101, 416
    epidemic 179
  communicable diseases 101
  dengue, combating 103
  diarrhea 181
  diphtheria 187
  Ebola epidemic 65
  education 189
  emergency obstetric care 188
  environmentally safe drinking water 101
  epidemiological surveillance systems 636
  eradication of measles 638
  HIV/AIDS 65, 101, 102
  infants, nutrition 189
  influenza 141
  laboratories, public 184
  lead in gasoline 139
  maternal 175, 183, 188
    care facilities 184
  mumps 141, 189
  of indigenous populations 184
  pneumonia 141
  pregnant mothers 181
  reform 189
  rubella 141
  sector reform 80-82, 173-179, 181-182, 185, 187-188
  services 64
    basic 188
      equitable access to 173-178, 185, 187-188
    quality of 184
    rehabilitation of the infrastructure 184
    universal access to 182
  technologies 20, 64, 65, 627, 636
    basic sanitation 20
    epidemiological surveillance 20
    initiative 189
    needs-based health information systems 20
    new 188
    pneumonia, meningitis, measles, rubella and mumps 20
    quality of drinking water 20
    safety and efficacy of pharmaceutical products 20
    utilization of vaccines 20
  tetanus 187
  tuberculosis 179, 181, 187
  typhoid 179
  vaccines 636
  women 535, 543, 636
    reproductive and sexual 543
  workers, education 177, 187
Health Care Promoting Entities. *See* EPS
Health Service Provider Institutions. *See* IPS
Health Technology Linking the Americas 64-66
Health-Promoting Schools 102
Helms-Burton legislation 277
Hemisphere Working Groups 491
hemispheric
  community 639
  cooperation 628
  dialogue 73
  financial sector agreements 192, 197
  information systems 50
  infrastructure 17, 59
    transnational projects 17
  integration vii, 3, 476, 483, 493, 498, 500, 571, 573, 603, 616, 639
  political dialogue 50
  summit process 71
  trade agenda 634
  trade liberalization 483
Hemispheric Action Plan for Education 41
Hemispheric Anti-Drug Strategy 5, 12, 333-334, 628

# INDEX

Hemispheric Committee of Ministers of Finance 44
Hemispheric Energy Initiative 17
Hemispheric Energy Steering Committee. *See HESC*
Hemispheric Energy Symposium. *See HES*
hemispheric security 14
Hemispheric Working Group. *See HWG*
hemotherapy network 184
HES (Hemispheric Energy Symposium) 146, 236-237, 245
HESC (Hemispheric Energy Steering Committee) 44, 236-237
HIV/AIDS 65, 79,-80, 82-83, 101-102, 174, 179-180, 182, 184, 187-188, 543, 599
　prevention 79
Holland 180
Honduras 78-79, 81, 83-84, 87-88, 91, 102, 111-112, 119-120, 238-240, 256, 265, 269, 317, 350, 398, 411, 578-579, 653, 660
Hong Kong 275, 350, 374
Honorary Inter-American Council 58
hospitals 179, 181
　rehabilitation of 180
HTI (Western Hemisphere Transportation Initiative) 24
Hufbauer/Schott readiness indicators 253
human
　capital development 372, 376
　resources 379
　　development 561
human rights vii, 7, 9-11, 23, 26, 29, 49-50, 58-59, 62, 70, 89, 139, 155-159, 161, 165-166, 171-172, 221, 278, 405, 407, 413-414, 416, 523, 526-527, 540, 543, 547, 555-559, 561, 563, 573, 576, 580, 589, 593-594, 596-600, 607, 619-620, 631, 636
　agenda 594
　awareness training 600
　basic 161, 374
　black population 159
　children 156
　children and adolescents 159
　corruption 70

　crimes 165
　defense of 26
　democracy, and 164
　disabled persons 156, 161
　education 10
　eradicate violations of 11
　implementation of 599
　indigenous peoples 156, 161
　indigenous societies 159
　issues 162
　judicial cooperation 70
　migrant workers 156
　migrants 11
　minorities 156
　organizations 158
　plans and programs 9
　preservation and strengthening of 9, 23, 59, 70, 575, 578
　promotion of 4
　protection of 23
　public safety 70
　reforms to the judicial and prison systems 161
　respect for 7
　security 70
　seniors 159
　system 10
　violations 158-164
　women 156, 159, 161
Human Rights National Plan 158-159
Human Rights Ombudsman 163
Human Rights Secretariat 158
Human Rights Watch 158, 162
humanitarian aid 628
hunger and malnutrition 189
　fight against 22
　food bank networks 22
HWG (Hemispheric Working Group) 465, 472-477, 479, 482, 674

# I

IABIN (Inter-American Biodiversity Information Network) 110-111, 240
IACAC (Inter-American Convention Against Corruption) 12, 58, 133, 140, 146, 148, 314, 316, 323, 327, 421, 510, 512-513, 578, 626-627, 630-631, 635, 637-638, 646-647, 651
IAWG (Inter-Agency Working Group) 387

Ibero-American Summit 224
IBM (International Business Machines) 315
ICAO (International Civil Aviation Organization) 17
ICASE (Central American Institute for Administration and Supervision of Education) 104
ICRW (International Center for Research on Women) 521, 527, 535-536, 577
ICW (Inter-American Commission on Women) 20, 522-523
IDB (Inter-American Development Bank) 4, 9, 11-12, 15-22, 34, 38-40, 42, 44-45, 48-49, 58, 63-64, 72, 78, 80, 82, 84-85, 87-88, 100-101, 103, 107, 109, 111-113, 116, 118-119, 121-123, 126, 132-133, 137,-143, 145-146, 173, 175-176, 184, 188-190, 196-197, 199-202, 210-213, 216, 221-226, 232, 237, 242, 244, 246, 251-253, 256, 258, 261-262, 265-266, 268, 271, 279, 291, 310, 317, 319, 335-336, 338, 348, 363, 370-371, 373, 379, 388, 380, 390, 394-395, 400, 403, 406-407, 419, 421-422, 453-454, 464, 476, 499, 511, 513, 522-523, 526, 535, 541, 571-575, 578, 626-627, 628, 630-632, 635-636, 638, 645, 652, 662, 669, 672, 675
　national capital regulations 196
IDRC (International Development Research Centre) 175-176, 177, 226, 386, 408
IFS (International Financial Statistics) 201
Iglesias, Enrique 48
IICA (Inter-American Institute for Cooperation on Agriculture) 100-101, 106, 111, 122
illegal immigration 278
ILO (International Labour Organisation) 5, 15, 20-21, 546, 557, 559, 580, 599, 603-605, 611, 620
　Convention 169, 603
IMCI (Management of Childhood Illness) 79-80, 177, 187

709

IMF (International Monetary Fund) 44, 123, 143, 200-201, 210, 314, 318-319, 328, 335, 361-460, 466, 523, 608, 613-614, 628, 630-631, 635
   disclosure 210
immigration 486, 594, 606-607
   policies 594, 606-607
   status 607
immunization
   programs 189
   rates 102
IMO (International Maritime Organization) 17
import 278
   surcharges 257
   tariffs 256
import-substitution 256
impunity 159, 164
IMR (Infant Mortality Rate) 77-80, 86, 91. *See also infant*
IN (Intelligent Networks) 18
INAMPS (National Institute of Health Assistance and Social Security — Instituto Nacional de Assistência Médica da Previdência Social) 182-183
income
   -support programs 606
   disparity 30
   distribution 253
   inequality 40, 278
indemnification 158
Independent Group of Experts on Smaller Economies 501
India 184
indigenous
   communities 19, 561, 597, 599, 602-603, 609, 612, 615
   groups 77, 80
   peoples 27, 109, 110, 413-414, 558, 576, 590, 592, 594-595, 598, 601, 612, 615, 619
      education 221
      neoliberal policy 598
      rights of 593, 599
      traditional rights of 617
   populations 5, 19, 21, 24, 172, 188, 633
      access to education 21
      basic and secondary education services with training 21
      education strategies 8
      health care 21
      occupational training 21
      poverty and development 21
      women 40
Indigenous Peoples Fund 40
Indonesia 350
inequalities 597-598
inequality 132, 136, 141
   income 40
inequity
   social 41
infant. *See also children*
   malnutrition 21
      reduction of 189
   mortality 174, 177, 179, 561. *See also IMR (Infant Mortality Rate)*
      rates 63
      reducing 177
   nutrition of 189
information
   age 34
   disclosure policies 692
   exchange 237, 662
   systems security 503
   technology 43, 373, 378, 459, 468-469, 470, 488, 500
      case management in the judicial system 43
      health and education systems 43
      land title registration 43
      social security 43
      tax and customs administrations 43
Information Clearing House 674
Information System. *See SIM*
Information Technology Agreement. *See ITP*
infrastructure 38, 43, 468, 479
   and urban development 113
   energy supply systems 43
   investment 505
   projects 43
   public services 43
   roads, ports, airports 43
   telecommunications 43
   water and sewerage 43
INL (International Narcotics and Law Enforcement Affairs, U.S. Department of State) 335, 337
innovative financing 237
Instituciones de Salud Previsional. *See ISAPRE*
Instituciones Prestadoras de Servicios de Salud. *See IPS*
Institute for International Bankers 200
Institute for International Economics 220
Institute of the Americas 262, 264-265, 267, 269, 278
institution-building 38, 662
institutional reform 659
Institutional Revolutionary Party *See PRI*
institutional strengthening 630
Instituto Nacional de Assistência Médica da Previdencia Social. *See INAMPS*
insurance
   companies 205
   industry 193
Integrated Management of Childhood Illness. *See IMCI*
Integrated Resource Planning. *See IRP*
Integrated Water Resources Management 116
integration
   capital markets 216
   economic 4
      increased 3
   hemispheric 3
   markets 216
   regional 57
intellectual property 250, 256, 258, 260-261, 265, 271, 277, 288, 454, 463, 474, 506, 514, 516, 595, 602-603, 614-615
   implementation 272
   legislation 503
   negotiations 263
   protection 266
intellectual property rights. *See IPR*
intelligence adviser 322
Inter-Agency Task Force for Bolivia Summit Follow-up 101, 114, 122, 126
Inter-Agency Working Group. *See IAWG*
Inter-American Association of Sanitary Engineering. *See AIDIS*
Inter-American Biodiversity Information Network. *See IABIN*
Inter-American Center for Social Security Studies. *See CIESS*
Inter-American Commission on Corruption 133-134, 141, 146, 630

# INDEX

Inter-American Commission on Human Rights 10-11, 21, 158, 163-165, 632
Inter-American Commission on Sustainable Development 22, 58
Inter-American Commission on Women. *See ICW*
Inter-American Committee on Sustainable Development. *See CIDS*
Inter-American Conference on Hunger 22, 189
Inter-American Convention Against Corruption. *See IACAC*
Inter-American Convention Against the Illicit Production and Trafficking of Firearms 13, 33
Inter-American Convention on Forced Disappearance 156, 158, 161
Inter-American Convention on Human Rights 557
Inter-American Convention on the Prevention, Punishment and Eradication of Violence Against Women 522
Inter-American Council for Commerce and Production 200
Inter-American Counternarcotics Consensus 331-332
Inter-American Declaration of Protection for Human Rights Defenders 600
Inter-American Democracy Network 388, 662
Inter-American Development Bank. *See IDB*
Inter-American Dialogue 388, 521, 525
Inter-American Dialogue on Water Management 101
Inter-American Drug Abuse Control Commission. *See CICAD; OAS/CICAD*
Inter-American Financial Council 133-134, 144, 146, 627, 630, 637
Inter-American Human Rights Commission 159, 172, 627, 636
Inter-American Human Rights Institute 10, 165

Inter-American Human Rights System 600
Inter-American Hunger Conference 58
Inter-American Institute for Cooperation on Agriculture. *See IICA*
inter-American institutions 132
inter-American law 49
Inter-American Network 174, 176, 578
  Health Sector Reform 177
Inter-American Network on Health Economics and Financing. *See REDEFS*
Inter-American Program to Combat Corruption 12
Inter-American Regional Workers' Organization. *See ORIT*
Inter-American Strategy for Public Participation. *See ISP*
Inter-American Summit Process 663
inter-American summitry 626
Inter-American Telecommunications Commission. *See CITEL*
Inter-American Water Day 85, 101
Inter-American Water Resources Network. *See IWRN*
interdependence 29
interest rates, liberalization of 203
Intergovernmental Commission Against Corruption 647
Intergovernmental Panel on Forests. *See IPF*
Interministerial Working Group for the Valorization of the Black Population 159
international
  accounting standards 476, 481, 502
  alliances 331
  arbitration 265
  conferences 207
  counterdrug accords 330
  economic trends 143
  equity 620
  financial
    institutions 210
    system 613
    transactions 605, 609
  labor standards 604
  markets 630

  migration 606
  narcotics agreements 13
  securities exchange 203
  standards 480
  trade agreements 601
International Association of Securities Commissions. *See IOSCO*
International Bankers Advisory Council 200
International Bankers Association of California 200
International Business Machines. *See IBM*
International Center for Research on Women. *See ICRW*
International Chamber of Commerce, Rules of Conduct to Combat Extortion 319
International Civil Aviation Organization. *See ICAO*
International Committee of Experts in Hospital Mitigation 103
International Conference on Population and Development 20, 103, 174
International Convention on the Protection of the Rights of All Migrant Workers and Members of Their Families 607
International Convention on Trade in Endangered Species. *See CITES*
International Development Research Center. *See IDRC*
International Federation of Red Cross and Red Crescent Societies 103
International Financial Statistics. *See IFS*
International Initiative on Genetic Plant Resources 109
International Institute for Educational Excellence 380-381
International Instrument for Dangerous Substances 105
International Labour Organisation. *See ILO*
International Maritime Organization. *See IMO*
International Monetary Fund. *See IMF*

711

International Narcotics and Law Enforcement Affairs. *See INL*
International Organization for Migration 606
International Treaty on Trade in Tropical Woods. *See ITTA*
International Transit Guide 257
intraregional
 investment 260
 trade 200, 251, 257, 260, 278
investment 266, 285, 288, 303, 453, 463, 470, 645
 certificates 204
 liberalization 601
  agreements 606
 policy 594
 reform 310
 regulation 611
IOSCO (International Association of Securities Commissions) 45
IPF (Intergovernmental Panel on Forests) 107, 111
IPR (intellectual property rights) 255-256, 260, 262-263, 265-266, 285, 304, 310, 456, 474, 479-480, 484, 486, 490, 499, 502, 509, 563, 594, 601, 614, 620, 645.
IPS (The Health Service Provider Institutions—Instituciones Prestadoras de Servicios de Salud) 181
Ireland 614
IRP (Integrated Resource Planning) 615-616
ISAPRE (Instituciones de Salud Previsional) 179-180
ISP (Inter-American Strategy for Public Participation) 111, 125, 385, 389-391, 398-399, 403-406, 408, 572, 574, 633, 661, 674
 Project Advisory Committee 387
Italy 180, 184, 321, 324-325, 328, 411
ITC (International Trade Commission) 261
ITP (Information Technology Agreement) 272, 487
ITTA (International Treaty on Trade in Tropical Woods) 108
ITU (International Telecommunications Union) 18

IWRN (Inter-American Water Resources Network) 115, 117-118

## J

Jamaica 80, 114-115, 117, 238-239, 243, 257, 262, 269, 334, 385-392, 394, 396-399, 403, 463, 572, 574, 648, 659, 660-661
 forestry law reforms in 241
Japan 107, 116, 175, 180, 184, 314, 317, 323-325, 351, 456
job-related competencies 8
Joint Declaration from the Third Ministerial Meeting at Belo Horizonte 667
Joint Ministerial Declaration of the Second Hemispheric Summit on Transportation 17
Joint Parliamentary Commission 259
Joint United Nations Program on AIDS. *See UNAIDS*
journalists
 prevent violence against 33
judicial
 and legal cooperation 5
 cooperation 50
 reform 161-162, 164, 278
 studies center 638
 systems
  highest ethical standard 422
  renewed 659
  strengthening 23, 422, 453
judiciary 155, 157, 160-162, 164-166
 independence of 157
 independent 648
 reprofessionalization of 164
justice vii
 administration of 5, 171
 combating
  organized crime 15
  transnational crime 15
 courts
  transparency, efficiency and effectiveness 15
 preserving and strengthening 9
 studies center 15
 system 15, 33
 training of sector personnel 15

## K

Kennedy Round 461
Kettering Foundation 388
Korea 351, 354, 374

## L

La Cantuta crimes 164
labor 72, 594
 environmental
  groups 310
  standards 490
 forced 159
 incorporation of new technologies 15
 markets effects of globalization 636
 matters 15, 172
 norms 59
 organizations 45
 right 249, 273, 277
 rights 141, 636
 safety and health conditions 15
 standards 133, 142, 633
  basic 603-605
labour 556
 prohibition of child 559
 rights 561
 standards 559
Labour and Social Forum 560
LAC 270, 272, 277-278
LAIA 259
Land and Water Resource Management Project 116
land tenure issues 561
land-reform programs 107, 110
Latin America 250, 252, 260, 263, 272, 275, 280, 309, 313-314, 316-317, 319, 322-323, 328, 332, 336, 347-355, 358-359, 363, 371, 373-374, 376-378, 380, 386, 388-389, 393-395, 397, 399-400, 405-408, 413-417, 451, 453-454, 456-457, 462, 464, 478, 483, 485, 497, 499, 501, 506, 521-522, 525, 535, 537, 539, 540-545, 547-549, 557-559, 561-562, 579, 613, 617, 630, 635, 646, 659, 663
Latin American integration 25
Latin American Association of Banking Regulators 200
Latin American Business Council. *See CEAL*
Latin American Central Banks 196

# INDEX

Latin American Congress on National Parks and Protected Areas 240
Latin American Economic System. *See SELA*
Latin American Energy Organization. *See OLADE*
Latin American Federation of Banks. *See FELABAN*
Latin American Network of Central Banks and Finance Ministries 635
Latinobarometro 323
Law Against Domestic Violence 88
LDCs (Least Developed Countries) 257
Lead Risk Reduction 242
leaded gasoline phase-out
   initiative 236
   project 236
Leadership Council for Inter-American Summitry 131, 172, 452, 625-628, 630-633, 637-639
Least Developed Countries. *See LDCs*
legal
   and civil protection 523
   and judicial cooperation 5
   equality 172
   systems, adequate 26
León, Rene 266
Letelier, Orlando 161
liberalization 253, 256-257, 260, 268, 272, 275, 278-279, 634
   of capital transactions 196
   programs 202
life expectancy 63
literacy 377
long-term debt and equity instruments 212

## M

macroeconomic
   policies 485, 630, 637
   reforms 197
   stability 200, 255
MAI (Multilateral Agreement on Investment) 405, 470, 476, 502, 590, 595, 611-614, 688
Malaysia 351
malnutrition, reduction of infant 189

market access 252, 263-264, 266, 268, 272-274, 276, 285, 289, 294, 302, 310, 456, 463, 465, 472, 486, 503-505, 509, 594, 618, 645
marketplace, global 3
maternal mortality 77-78, 89-92, 174, 177, 179, 181-182, 188-190, 541. *See also women*
   rates 139, 187-188, 543-544
   reduction 78, 89-92
      programs 91-92
McCaffrey, Barry 333, 335, 337
MDCs (More Developed Countries) 257
Mead, Margaret 236
MEAs (Multilateral Environmental Agreements) 494
measles 64, 104, 177, 179, 187, 189. *See also health*
   campaign against 59
   eradication 34, 93-95, 139, 187-188
      plan of action 93
      regional surveillance system for 93
   surveillance needs 95
   vaccination 94, 141
      coverage 94
Measles Elimination Plan 82
Measles Eradication Plan of Action 188
Mejide, Graciela Fernández 320
MEM (Multilateral Evaluation Mechanism) 635
Menem, Carlos Saúl 30, 319-320, 646
meningitis 189
MERCOCYT (Common Market of Scientific and Technological Knowledge) 124
MERCOSUL. *See MERCOSUR*
MERCOSUR (Southern Cone Common Market) 25, 27, 105, 115, 133, 135, 143, 148, 184, 198, 206, 250-251, 255, 258-260, 262-264, 265-266, 268, 271, 273-278, 280, 309-310, 390, 415, 453-454, 456, 465-466, 487, 603, 634, 637, 677-678, 682
   Ministries of Health 185
      mechanisms of sanitary control 185
      medical devices 185
      standards of quality of services 185
   SIM (Information System) 682

Mexican Ministry of Environment, Natural Resources, and Fisheries 242
Mexico 78-79, 81, 83, 85, 87, 93, 103, 105, 107-109, 112-116, 119-120, 192-194, 202, 204-206, 219-223, 225, 232, 238-240, 243, 251-252, 255, 257-258, 261-262, 264-265, 268, 273, 275, 281, 317, 321, 323, 329, 332, 334-335, 337-338, 349, 354, 390, 395, 405, 416-417, 453, 458, 462, 466, 485, 495, 511, 536, 537-547, 558, 591-593, 603, 606, 616, 626, 628, 634, 636, 646, 648, 653
   peso crisis 194, 252, 261, 452, 454, 457-458, 485
   "PRODEFOR" program 241
Mexico City 112, 455, 540, 542, 543
MFN (most-favored nation status) 266, 268, 469, 473-474, 481-482
Miami Summit of the Americas 39, 62, 66, 327, 483, 486, 521
Miami
   Declaration;
   Plan of Action 57, 59, 71, 294, 521-522
microenterprise 40, 112, 142, 577, 633
   training 557. *See also SMEs*
MIF (Multilateral Investment Fund) 40-41, 45
   regulating and monitoring public services 43
migrants
   education 221
   strategies 8
   human rights 11
   peoples 50
   workers 5, 9, 11, 59, 171-172, 452, 594, 632
      rights of 590
      working conditions 11
migration 590
   policies 11
military
   authoritarian
      regime 155, 158, 160
      rule 157-158, 163
   authoritarianism 157
   prerogatives 160, 162-163

713

mines
- -free zone, antipersonnel 14
- effective awareness 14
- land, removal of 49

minimum wage 605
- standards 620

mining 97, 118, 120-121, 124
- small-scale 121

Mining and Education Ministerials 404

Ministerial Resolutions 307

ministerials 144
- trade 145

Ministerio de Salud. *See MINSAL*

ministers
- of education 232
- of trade 4, 232, 305
- of finance 216
- of labor 70

Ministry for Women and Human Development 163

Ministry of Health. *See MINSAL*

MINSAL (Ministry of Health—Ministerio de Salud) 179, 181, 183-184

Monetary Board 203

Monetary Council of the Americas 197

Monetary Stabilization Certificates 204

money market instruments 204

money-laundering 5, 50, 139, 329-333, 340, 470, 503, 614, 646, 647
- combat 210

Montesinos, Vladimiro 322

Montevideo Hemispheric Conference on Citizen Participation in Decision-making for Sustainable Development 386

Montserrat 257

More Developed Countries. *See MDCs*

mortality
- rates
  - child 139, 187, 190
  - maternal 139, 187, 188, 190
  - reduction, child 187

most-favored nation status. *See MFN*

Mother Care Project 177

MRA (Mutual Recognition Agreements) 18, 469, 473, 480, 488

Multi-modal Transportation Agreement 259

multilateral
- agencies 45, 193, 197-202, 207, 246, 322, 328-330
- approach 330, 339-340
- banks 70
  - development 210
- negotiations 462, 464, 494
- organizations 220, 222, 232, 296, 313
- political forum 72
- trade negotiations 461, 465

Multilateral Agreement on Investment. *See MAI*

Multilateral Counternarcotics Center 341

Multilateral Environmental Agreements. *See MEAs*

Multilateral Investment Fund. *See MIF*

multilateralism 556

multinational corporations 253

mutual
- funds, regulations affecting 200
- recognition agreements. *See MRAs*

Multilateral Evaluation Mechanism. *See MEM*

# N

NAALC (North American Agreement on Labor Cooperation) 603

NADBANK (North American Development Bank) 253, 674

NAFTA (North American Free Trade Agreement) 198, 205-206, 250-252, 255, 257-258, 261-268, 271, 273-277, 333-334, 405, 415, 452-454, 456-457, 461-462, 465, 474, 479, 557, 560, 592, 595, 600, 603, 611-616, 621, 634
- negotiations 194

NAM (National Association of Manufacturers) 460, 478-482, 650

narco-trafficking 33, 460
- confronting 23

narcotics 635. *See also drugs*
- traffic in 13
- trafficking 330, 332-334, 628
  - and corruption 132, 140
  - combating 329

"Nariño" Agreement of 1994   174

national
- education
  - standards 378
  - strategy 378
- testing 231

National Action Committee on the Status of Women 557

National Association of Manufacturers. *See NAM*

National Association of Securities Dealers 200

National Banking and Securities Commission. *See CNBV*

National Committee for Environmental Education 104

National Corporation for Reparation and Reconciliation 161

National Council on Women's Rights 159

National Councils for Sustainable Development 11, 407

national defense policy 160

National Environmental Funds. *See NEFs*

national financial market regulations 211

National Health Care Fund. *See FONASA*

National Health Care System. *See SNSS*

National Information Service 160

National Institute of Health Assistance and Social Security. *See INAMPS*

National Leaded Gasoline Phase-out Plans 242

National Officials' Seminar on the Elimination of Lead in Latin America and the Caribbean 243

National Plan for Equal Opportunities for Women 88

National Plan for Equality of Opportunities 161

National Plan to Combat Violence 88

National Register of Detainees 164

National Sanitation Foundation 101

National Security Council. *See NSC*

National Social Security System 181, 183

national tax regimes 192, 199

# INDEX

National Wildlife Federation. *See NWF*
National Women's Service. *See SERNAM*
Natural Disaster Reduction 103
Natural Resources Defense Council. *See NRDC*
Nature Conservancy (International) 388
NEFs (National Environmental Funds) 241
negotiating groups (FTAA) 16, 172, 263, 271, 276, 292, 296, 306, 310, 390, 454-455, 463-466, 468, 471, 485, 493-494, 626, 630, 634, 678, 682-684, 691-692
neoliberal 563, 590, 592-593, 595-596, 598, 619
neoliberalism 557, 592-594
Network of International Cooperation on Arid and Semiarid Zones 105
New Orleans Communiqué 191, 196-197, 200-201, 216
New Orleans Ministerial 196, 199-200
New Zealand 263, 272, 275
NGOs (non-governmental organizations) 41, 80, 82, 84, 88-90, 95, 102, 104-105, 107, 110, 115, 127, 134, 136-137, 142, 145, 148, 159, 166, 190, 200, 207, 219, 220, 222-226, 232, 235, 237, 240-241, 243, 245, 313, 319, 324-325, 328, 358, 385-386, 388, 390, 396, 398, 400, 404-406, 452, 493, 495, 499, 510, 537, 542, 544, 556, 559, 561-562, 575, 579, 604, 615, 621, 632-633, 637, 648, 660, 662, 674, 677, 678, 691-692
  environmental 452
  participation 677
Nicaragua 78-79, 83-85, 87-88, 91, 93, 102, 104, 111-112, 119-120, 156, 226, 238-240, 251-252, 256, 350, 353, 391, 538, 541, 647-648
  non-governmental health clinic 544
NII (national information infrastructure) 378
"no bribe commitments" 419, 422
non-governmental

actors 386, 389, 455, 511, 648
  groups 637
  international organizations 158
nontariff. *See also tariff*
  barriers 148, 250, 273, 484, 487, 595
  restrictions 486
NORDESTE Project 184
North American Agreement on Labor Cooperation. *See NAALC*
North American Commission for Environmental Cooperation. *See CEC*
North American Development Bank. *See NADBANK*
North American Free Trade Agreement. *See NAFTA*
North-South Center of the University of Miami 220, 224, 387, 398, 660
NRDC (Natural Resources Defense Council) 139-140, 145, 235-236, 238-242
  non-leaded gasoline 145
NSC (National Security Council) 160, 162
nuisance duties 499
NWF (National Wildlife Federation) 390, 663, 692

## O

OAS (Organization of American States) 3-5, 9-12, 14, 15, 21-22, 24, 31, 33, 38, 45, 48-50, 58, 69-73, 82, 85, 97, 100-101, 103-104, 109-112, 114, 116-117, 121-127, 132-133, 136-142, 145-148, 156, 158, 166, 171, 176, 202, 210, 212, 222-225, 232, 239-246, 252, 262, 264, 266, 268-269, 278, 291, 293, 296, 310, 313, 316-317, 319, 321-323, 327-328, 330, 333-337, 340, 342, 370-371, 385-395, 398-400, 403-408, 419, 421, 454, 464, 475-476, 479, 484, 490, 499, 510, 512, 522-523, 526, 540, 571-578, 600, 626-628, 630-633, 635-638, 649-651, 653, 657-658, 660-661, 663-675, 678
  Administrative Secretariat for Summits 72
  Anti-Corruption Convention 385, 655

  Monitoring Program 653
  General Secretariat 70-72
  Illegal Firearms Convention 33
  Inter-American Commission for Drug Abuse 58
  Inter-American Commission on Human Rights 141
  Inter-American Council on Integral Development 58
  Inter-American Strategy for Public Participation vii, 388
  observation mission 163
  Office of Summit Follow-Up. *See OSF*
  Permanent Council of 661
  Public Participation Initiative 388
  Special Committee on Inter-American Summits Management 58, 71, 73
  Sustainable Development and Environment Unit 101
  Technical Secretariat 72
  Trade Unit 139, 143, 146
  Unit for the Promotion of Democracy. *See UPD*
OAS/CICAD (Inter-American Drug Abuse Control Commission) 141
ODA (Overseas Development Administration) 175, 177, 558, 561
OECD (Organization for Economic Cooperation and Development) 228, 233, 249, 262, 272, 290, 316-317, 319, 324, 328, 354, 356, 470, 476, 479, 484, 490, 511, 611, 631, 647, 649, 653
  Guidelines Governing the Protection of Privacy 489
  Working Group on Bribery 637, 649
OECS (Organization of Eastern Caribbean States) 105, 257
off-shore financial center 203
Office of National Drug Control Policy. *See ONDCP*
OLADE (Latin American Energy Organization) 100, 119-121, 243
ONDCP (Office of National Drug Control Policy) 333, 335-336
open
  economies 134
  markets 135-136, 646
  regionalism 142
Organization for Economic Cooperation and Development. *See OECD*

Organization of Africans in the Americas 388, 663
Organization of American States. *See OAS*
Organization of Eastern Caribbean States. *See OECS*
ORIT (Inter-American Regional Workers' Organization) 593, 604
Orthodox Structural Adjustment 614
OSF (Office of Summit Follow-Up) 627, 636, 638, 661
Ouro Preto Protocol 259
Overseas Development Administration. *See ODA*

## P

PAC (Project Advisory Group) 404-405, 408
PAHO (Pan American Health Organization) 20, 22, 24, 38, 48, 58-59, 65-66, 77-85, 87-88, 91-94, 96, 100-104, 122, 140-141, 173-177, 180, 184, 187-190, 242, 390, 395, 526, 631, 636
  sustainable development 5
PAISM (Program for Integral Assistance to Women's Health) 543
Pan American Health Organization. *See PAHO*
Panama 77-78, 82-84, 87-88, 93, 115, 119, 137, 141, 238-240, 243, 256, 322, 330, 332, 336, 391, 453, 455, 457, 473, 537, 541, 546, 548, 647-648, 656
Paraguay 78-81, 83, 87-88, 90-91, 93, 106-107, 120, 139, 143, 155, 184, 238-239, 243, 258-259, 260, 275, 317, 332, 334-335, 453, 495, 538, 541, 646, 648
Paris Club 199
parliamentarism 159
Parliamentary Network of the Americas 663
PARTICIPA 387-388, 396, 403-405, 495, 571-572
Participants in the Biodiversity and Pollution Prevention Partnership 246
Partners of the Americas 662

Partnership for Biodiversity 235-236, 239, 245
Partnership for Educational Revitalization in the Americas. *See PREAL*
Partnership for Pollution Prevention 59, 187-188, 235-236, 242
Partnership for Sustainable Energy Use 235-236, 238-239
Partnerships for Health Reform. *See PHR*
Partnerships for Sustainable Development 235, 244, 633, 644
Pastrana, Andrés 338, 628, 635
Paulista Convention on the Elimination of All Forms of Discrimination Against Women 538
PCDEN Project 184
PCMAM Project 184
PECC (Pacific Economic Consultation Council) 477, 481
pension
  funds 196, 203, 205, 210, 612
  system 204
People's Summit of the Americas 405, 632, 638
Pérez, Carlos Andres 327
Permanent Council. *See OAS*
Permanent Forum of Regional Parliaments 576
Perot, Ross 274
pertussis 187
Peru 78-81, 83-4, 87-88, 91, 101-103, 105,-107, 111-113, 115-116, 119-120, 155, 158, 163, 176-177, 179, 192-193, 202-203, 205-206, 238-240, 243, 245, 251, 255, 271, 300, 317, 321-322, 330-332, 334-336, 338-339, 341, 393, 416, 453, 464, 536-538, 540-541, 544-545, 548, 628, 648
peso crisis 194, 252, 261, 452, 454, 457-458, 485
pesticides 105, 110
petroleum-based products 257
PHR (Partnerships for Health Reform) 177
phytosanitary specifications 619
PIAS 85
Pinochet, Augusto 161, 162, 396, 593

PIRCs (Public Information and Resource Centers) 682-683
Plan of Action for Measles Eradication 95
Plan of Action to Achieve Universal Access to Education 58
pneumonia 181, 189. *See also health*
Poder Ciudadano 328
Point of Lights Foundation 388
police 157-160, 162, 165
  bravery 159
polio 187. *See also health*
political
  democratization 415
  jurisdictions 611
  stability 330, 596, 616, 649
pollution
  Bolivia-Brazil natural gas pipeline 244
  clean water 244
  leaded gasoline phase-out 241-243, 246
  motor fuel production 243
  Partnership for Prevention of Pollution 59, 187-188, 235-236, 242-243, 246
  pesticides 242
  prevention 85, 111, 113, 235-236, 245, 633
  sustainable tourism 242
  water resources 242
Popular Participation Law 660
port infrastructure 506
Port of Spain 115-116
Portugal 614
poverty 8, 18-19, 25, 28-30, 34, 38, 40-41, 43, 64,-66, 84, 105-107, 110, 118, 124, 132-133, 136-137, 141, 174, 184, 188, 190, 225, 348, 393, 398, 405, 414, 416-417, 453, 493, 527, 548, 555-558, 561, 572, 577, 579, 592-593, 597, 601, 606, 611, 616, 618, 620, 626, 630-631, 633, 661, 671-672
  alleviation 188, 374, 633
  discrimination 38
    adequate health services 19
    basic rights of workers 18
    clean water and proper nutrition 19
    disadvantaged racial and ethnic minorities 19

# INDEX

discrimination against women 19
  eliminating 47
  eradication of 18, 24
  health technologies 19
  indigenous communities 19
effects of 147
eradication of vii, 7, 59, 395, 411-412, 414, 416, 421, 555, 558, 561, 572, 575-577, 632
  by public participation 70
  role of women 572
extreme 598
female and child 590
health, hunger, women, indigenous people 59
income disparity 30
international war on 597
Latin American 669
nutrition, social services, healthy environment 5
overcoming 5
reduction 39, 57
  policies 40
war on 598
women, eradication of 70
PREAL (Partnership for Educational Revitalization in the Americas) 226-227, 233, 347-348, 357, 363, 365
precursor traffic 329
prenatal care 83, 90
presidentialism 159
PRI (Institutional Revolutionary Party) 321
price liberalization 197
Principles for International Contracts 476, 481
prison
  conditions. 159
    subhuman 163
private sector 190, 210, 212, 232, 235-236, 239, 245, 271-272, 274-275, 278, 287, 294, 297, 307, 310, 318-319, 321, 368, 370, 372, 376-377, 379-381, 385-386, 388, 392, 394, 403-405, 407-408, 451-452, 454-455, 458-461, 466-472, 474-477, 479, 481-482, 484, 485-486, 489-491, 497-506, 510-511, 514-515, 522, 525, 527, 558, 561, 595, 627, 629, 632-633, 637-638, 646, 649, 650

financial institutions 205
  groups 455, 468, 470
  investment 378
  involvement 380
  recommendations 483
  labor, role of 271
  savings 196, 210
privatization 85, 147-148, 203, 210, 260, 275, 314, 319, 321, 323, 360, 469, 473-474, 486, 488-489, 510, 592, 608, 610, 646-648
  of the energy sector 121
procurement 645
  sound systems 515
product marking 481
Program for Integral Assistance to Women's Health. *See PAISM*
Program for Regional Seas of UNEP 108
Program for the Improvement of the Quality of Education 161
Program for the Support of Women's Leadership and Representation 526
Program of Community Health Agents 184
Project Advisory Group. *See PAC*
Project of Reduction of Child Mortality 184
Promoting Women in Development. *See PROWID*
property registration 19
  computer-generated 19
  georeferencing 19
  indigenous populations 19
  procedures 19
  records storage 19
property rights 196, 201, 212, 256
  intellectual 310
  protection of 212
Proposal for Implementation of the Plan of Action 156
Proposed American Declaration on the Rights of Indigenous Peoples 21
Protection of All Persons under Any Form of Detention or Imprisonment 162
Protocol of San Salvador 158, 163
Protocol on Biosecurity 108
Protocol on the Abolition of the Death Penalty 156

Protocol on the Harmonization of Rules 260
Protocol on Trade Marks, Indications of Source and Appellations 260
Protocol to Abolish the Death Penalty 158
Protocol to the Inter-American Convention on Human Rights 161
PROWID (Promoting Women in Development) 536
public
  access to information 648
  awareness 104
  bidding 419
  disclosure of assets 421
  information 625
  infrastructure 486
  notice 515
  participation 122, 124, 125, 127, 240, 667
  sector
    corporations 610
    procurement 475, 479, 513
  works contract 610
Public Information and Resource Centers. *See PIRCs*
Puerto Rico 241-242, 246, 392
Punishment and Eradication of Violence Against Women 522

## Q

quotas 525

## R

racial discrimination 11
Racketeer Influenced and Corrupt Organizations Act. *See RICO*
Rajapatirana, Sarath 264, 270
RAMSAR (Convention on Wetlands of International Importance) 108
Rapporteur for Freedom of Expression 171-172, 636
rebel insurgencies 278
Reciprocal Assistance of Latin American Oil Companies. *See ARPEL*
Red Cross 179
REDEFS (Inter-American Network on Health Economics) 81, 177, 188

717

REDESOL 388
REFORSUS Project 184
regional banking and securities associations 201
Regional Facility for Trade Development 45
Regional Fund for Agriculture 123
regional
   integration 136, 143, 147, 192, 194-195, 197-198, 200-201, 203-207, 210, 216-217, 256, 269, 392, 415-416, 573, 634, 637
      strategy 193-194, 199, 217
      markets liberalization and integration of 200
   securities exchange 204
Regional Integration Fund 197-198
Regional Oil Integration 237
Regional Surveillance System for Measles Eradication 93
regional value content 267
Regulatory Cooperation in the Hemisphere 237
regulatory
   reform 278
   transparency 515
rehabilitation 13
reintegration programs 13
Réseau Québécois sur l'Intégration Continentale. *See RQIC*
resources
   allocation 649
   coastal and marine 114, 116-117
   mineral 118
Responsible Coordinators 75, 156, 158, 219-224, 227, 246, 387, 393-394, 397, 390, 631, 636, 638, 659
RICO (Racketeer Influenced and Corrupt Organizations Act) 315
rights. *See also human, children, women*
   equal 5
   of children 172
   of families 172
   of youths 172
Robles, Rodolfo 164
Roman law (civil law) 473
Romo, Osvaldo 161
RQIC (Réseau Québécois sur l'Intégration Continentale) 405
rubella 189

Rubin, Robert 273
rule of law 157, 165, 646, 659
Rules of Origin 285, 290, 302, 456, 465, 472, 505, 618-619
Rules of Origin and Customs Procedures 267
rural electrification 120
Rural Home Program 107
Russia 184, 218, 309, 332, 411, 630

## S

safe motherhood 79-80, 91-92
   initiative 78
SAFTA (South American Free Trade Area) 453
SAIC (Science Applications International Corporation) 380
Salinas de Gortari, Carlos 321
Salinas, Raúl 321
Samper, Ernesto 332-333
San Antonio Declaration 331-332
San José Ministerial Declaration 630
San José Trade Ministerial 452, 454-455, 465, 475, 478, 483, 632
San Salvador Protocol 156
San Salvador Summit 256
Sánchez de Lozada, Gonzalo 335, 340, 643
sanitary and phytosanitary. *See SPS*
sanitation 188
   basic 184
Santa Cruz de la Sierra Declaration 97, 155
Santa Cruz de la Sierra Plan of Action 24, 58
Santiago Declaration vii-viii, 155
Santiago Summit of the Americas II vii, 43, 59, 64-66, 71, 483
   Plan of Action 231
Sarney, José 159, 320
savings rates 132, 137
   low 137, 142
SCC (Summit Coordinating Committee) 627, 638
Schiefelbein, Ernesto 225
schools. *See education*
Schwanen, Daniel 264
science and technology 16, 72
   communications and information industries 16

   earthquakes 16
   ecosystems 16
   floods 16
   hurricanes 16
   natural hazards 16-17
   volcanic eruptions 16
Science Applications International Corporation. *See SAIC*
Scientific and Cultural Organization. *See UNESCO*
Secretariat for Strategic Affairs 160
Secretariat of the Treaty on Central American Economic Integration. *See SIECA*
secretariat support facilities 485
securities
   and insurance markets 194
   exchange 204
      Bolsa 204
   markets 194, 202, 206, 209
      supervision and examination 211
security
   building measures 14
   international concepts 14
   personal security and law enforcement 136
SELA (Latin American Economic System —Sistema Económico Latinoamericano) 268, 310
Sendero Luminoso 163
Senior Telecommunications Officials Meeting 18, 58
SERNAM (National Women's Service) 47, 161
   equal opportunities for women 161
   pregnancy subsidies 161
   sexual harassment 161
   teen pregnancy 161
Serrano, Jorge 155
Services Working Group 673
Sherwood, Robert 265
SIECA (Secretariat of the Treaty on Central American Economic Integration) 245-256, 678
SIIFT (Society for Inter-American Interbank Financial Telecommunications) 217
Silber, Simão Davi 267
SIM (Information System) MERCOSUR 682
SIMBIOSIS (Specialized Information System on Biotechnology) 124

# INDEX

Simpson, John 267
Singapore 272, 275, 350, 374
Single Customs Form 257
SIRG (Summit Implementation Review Group) 22, 38, 57, 59, 63, 70, 72, 142, 144-146, 156, 161, 163, 172, 220, 235, 387, 390-393, 395-396, 401, 404, 408, 419, 571-572, 575, 627, 631, 633, 636, 638, 663, 669, 671
   VIII Meeting 58
Sistema Económico Latinoamericano. *See SELA*
Sistema Nacional de Servicios de Salud. *See SNSS*
Sistema Único de Saúde. *See SUS*
Sistema Unificado e Descentralizado de Saúde. *See SUDS*
small business financing 40
small economies 268, 291
Small Economies Group 197
Small Economies Working Committee 501
SMEs (small and medium-sized enterprises) 18
SMSE (Sustainable Markets for Sustainable Energy) 44, 119
smuggling aliens 11
SNSS (National Health Care System—Sistema Nacional de Servicios de Salud) 179
social
   development vii, 70, 72
   equity 39, 601
   expenditures 136
   inequities 41, 188
   investment funds 72
   justice 590, 607
   programs 147, 182, 556, 561, 598, 604-605, 614
   safety nets 250
   security 589
     benefits 11
     systems 609
     universal access to 182
   services, inadequate 136
Society for Inter-American Interbank Financial Telecommunications. *See SIIFT*
Society for World Interbank Financial Telecommunications. *See SWIFT*

South American Free Trade Area. *See SAFTA*
Southern Cone 64
Southern Cone Common Market. *See MERCOSUR*
sovereignty 561
Spain 182, 184, 239, 614
Special Committee on Inter-American Summits Management 58, 71, 73
Special Meeting on Health Sector Reform 176
Special Rapporteur for Freedom of Expression 171-172, 636
Specialized Information System on Biotechnology. *See SIMBIOSIS*
Spirit of Miami 628
SPS (Sanitary and Phytosanitary Standards) 258, 290, 471-472, 479, 488, 499, 502, 503, 617
   certifications 256
   measures 259
   restrictions 148
St. Kitts and Nevis 257
St. Lucia 238, 239, 257-258
St. Vincent and the Grenadines 257-258
Standards and Technical Barriers to Trade 292, 303
Standstill Agreement 478, 481
Stephenson, Sherry 269
stock exchange integration 505
Stroessner, Alberto 155
Study Group on Trade and the Environment 677, 679
Suárez, Hugo Banzer 330
subregional
   agreements 254, 265, 274, 278
   arrangements 249, 253
subsidies 270
   duties 293, 303, 463
SUDS (Unified and Decentralized Health System—Sistema Unificado e Decentralizado de Saúde) 183
Summit Conference on Sustainable Development. *See Bolivia Summit of the Americas*
Summit Coordinating Committee. *See SCC*
Summit Coordinating Office 387

Summit Implementation Review Group. *See SIRG*
Summit of the Americas vii, 20, 26, 47, 57, 64, 131, 146, 174, 176, 329, 411-412, 419, 493, 521, 573, 627. *See Miami Summit of the Americas, Bolivia Summit of the Americas, Santiago Summit of the Americas II*
summit planning 133, 145
Summit Process 69
   institutionalization of 660
summit secretariat 133-134, 141, 145-147, 631
summitry
   effective 144
   popular participation in 637
superintendency of banks 205
supervisory practices 192, 197
   discussion of 192
Supreme Decree Law on Protection from Family Violence 163
Suriname 257, 258
surveillance systems 633
survey of financial systems 58
SUS (Unified Health System—Sistema Único de Saúde) 183
sustainability 100, 598, 607
sustainable
   agriculture 105
   cities 38, 98, 111-112, 114
   development 5, 24, 40, 97, 99-101, 103-104, 108-111, 121-127, 134-136, 138-139, 142, 147, 236, 240-241, 244-246, 274, 294, 306, 399, 404, 407, 411-412, 414, 451, 453, 486, 493, 494, 556-557, 561-562, 571-572, 574, 576, 589, 594-597, 601-602, 607-609, 613, 616-617, 633, 661
   financial resources for 126
   economic growth 513
   energy 236-239, 602
     development 615
     project financing mechanisms 237
     projects 238-239
     sources 239
     use 633
   forestry
     incentives 241
     management of 108
   human development 85, 90
   transport 111, 113
   urbanization 112

Sustainable Development Councils viii
Sustainable Development Partnerships 142
Sustainable Energy Development 595
Sustainable Markets for Sustainable Energy Program. *See SMSE*
Sweden 84, 180
SWIFT (Society for World Interbank Financial Telecommunications) 217
Symposium on Enhancing Probity in the Hemisphere 12
Symposium on Health of the Children of the Americas 77
System of Active Epidemiological Surveillance 179

# T

TA (technical assistance) 501
Taiwan 374
tariff 255-256, 260, 277, 618. *See also nontariff*
  and non-tariff
    barriers 487, 500
    measures 487
  and services negotiations 466
  barriers 250, 273, 484
  capital goods 259
  code, common 258
  common external 267, 271
  elimination 484
    agreements 251
  enforcement 267
  harmonized 488
  import 256
  in the automotive sector 259
  informatics and telecommunications products 259
  level, two-tier national 255
  liberalization 472
  non-
    barriers 256, 258, 277, 471, 475, 479, 487, 500, 502, 619
    restrictions 259
  rates 634
  reductions 250, 259, 266, 267, 310, 618
  reforms 194
Task Force on Education, Equity, and Economic Competitiveness 227, 347, 365

TBT (Transportation Business Team) 506
TCA (Amazon Cooperation Treaty—Tratado do Cooperação Amazônica) 108, 184
TDA 316
teachers. *See education*
technical
  assistance. *See TA*
  barriers to trade 503, 618
Technical Action Service Unit 258
Technical Advisory Committee 405
Technical Assistance Program 212
Technical Working Group on National Financial Markets 210, 262
technologies
  access to new 133
    distance learning 142
  environmental 272
technology
  training 379
  transfer 213
Tegucigalpa Protocol 256
Tele-Escola 42
telecommunications 18, 72, 380, 453, 459, 467-470, 480, 488-489, 505-506, 592, 632, 648
  basic telephone service 18
  broadcast television and radio 18
  computers 18
  e-mail 145
  equipment certification 58
  GBT Agreement 18
  guidelines on value-added services 18
  independent regulatory bodies 18
  infrastructure 58, 378
  Internet 18
    and multimedia services 18
  networks 376
  regional infrastructure plan 18
  services 500, 505
  teleconferences 145
  universal access/service 18
  value-added services 58
telecommunications and information technology 505
Telecurso 2000 42
telemedicine 189
Telesecundaria 42
tequila effect 252
territorial integrity 5

terrorism 5, 13, 30, 49
  confronting 23
  elimination 13
Thailand 222, 351
Third Summit of the Americas
  Canada 627
TI (Transparency International) 319, 324-325, 328, 388, 509-512, 635, 638, 646-648, 651, 653, 657-658
  Anticorruption Progress Report 657
TIF (Trade and Investment Forum) 467
TMN (Telecommunications Management Network) 18
TNC (Trade Negotiations Committee) 16, 305, 455, 459, 463, 465-469, 471, 477, 514, 634, 682-684, 689, 691-692
Tokyo Round 456, 461
torture 159-162, 164
tourism 59
tourism development 580
trade 453
  agreements 556, 606
    regional 133, 143
  and investment liberalization 497
  barriers 488
  deficit 148
  development vii
  in services 268
  integration 137, 637
    and financial stability 133
  intraregional 135, 142
  liberalization vii, 148, 249-250, 253-254, 275, 277-279, 498, 601, 618-619
    process 639
    and economic cooperation 486
    hemispheric 253
  negotiations 677
  policy 310, 594
  subregional agreements 250, 252
Trade and Investment Forum. *See TIF*
trade and labor rights 307
trade barriers 257
Trade Liberalization and Environmental Policies 679
Trade Ministerials. *See Bela Horizonte, San José Trade Ministerials*
Trade Ministers 45
  annual meetings 250

# Index

Trade Negotiations Committee. *See TNC*
Trade Related Intellectual Property Rights. *See TRIPS*
Trade-Related Investment Measures. *See TRIMs*
traditional know-how and biological diversity 110
trafficking nations 336, 340
Transatlantic Business Dialogue 682
transmissible diseases 187
transnational
   corporations 406, 592-593, 599, 614
   law enforcement 331
   organized crime 331
transparency in procurement 419
Transparency International. *See TI*
transparent business practices 502
transportation 17, 255, 453
   improving infrastructure 17
   reliable passenger and cargo services 17
   safety in air 17
   sea and land transportation systems 17
Transportation Business Team. *See TBT*
transportation infrastructure 506
Tratado do Cooperação Amazônica. *See TCA*
Treaty of Asunción 259
Treaty of Rome 195
TRIMs (Trade-Related Investment Measures) 611
Trinidad and Tobago 81, 83, 114-115, 243, 251, 257, 276, 317, 464, 640, 653
Tripartite Committee 16, 45, 70, 146, 262, 266, 271, 306, 454-455, 464, 470, 630, 638
TRIPS (Trade Related Intellectual Property Rights) 260, 265, 474, 480, 484, 490, 506, 615
Troika 627, 631, 636, 638
Tropical Agronomic Research and Teaching Center. *See CATIE*

## U

UN Committee Against Torture 162
UN Convention to Combat Desertification 389
UNAIDS (Joint United Nations Program on AIDS) 83, 188
UNDCP (United Nations Drug Control Program) 336-338
UNDP (United Nations Development Program) 103, 122-124, 253, 392
UNECLAC. *See ECLAC*
unemployment 111, 136, 141, 252-253, 275-276, 375, 453, 545, 590, 592, 606, 609
   insurance 250, 606, 612
UNEP (United Nations Environmental Program) 108-109, 116-117, 122-123, 633
UNESCO (United Nations Scientific and Cultural Organization) 9, 104, 108, 125, 127, 221-222, 225, 227, 404, 548, 573
   Latin American Regional Office 222
unfair trade practices 270
UNFPA (United Nations Population Fund) 176
UNICEF (United Nations Children's Fund) 79, 82, 101, 173, 176-177, 187, 222, 225
Unified and Decentralized Health System. *See SUDS*
Unified Health System. *See SUS*
unilateral certification process 330
unions 252-253, 272, 559
Unit for the Promotion of Democracy 156, 165. *See UPD*
United Kingdom 175, 177, 184
United Nations Charter of Economic Rights and Duties of States 618
United Nations Children's Fund). *See UNICEF*
United Nations Conference on Environment and Development 679. *See also Earth Summit*
United Nations Conference on Population and Development 543
United Nations Conference on Trade and Development 614
United Nations Convention on the Rights of the Child 15
United Nations Development Program. *See UNDP*
United Nations Drug Control Program. *See UNDCP*
United Nations Economic Commission on Latin America and the Caribbean. *See ECLAC*
United Nations Food and Agriculture Organization. *See FAO*
United Nations Fourth World Conference on Women 522, 538, 577
United Nations Framework Convention on Climate Change 5, 17
   Clean Development Mechanism 17
   exchange of technology 17
United Nations Guidelines for Consumer Protection 574
United Nations Environmental Program. *See UNEP*
United Nations Population Fund. *See UNFPA*
United Nations Register of Conventional Arms 14
United Nations Working Group on Forced or Involuntary Disappearances 164
United Nations World Conference on Women 84
United States 77-78, 84, 94, 106, 108, 110, 115-116, 119-120, 132-136, 143, 146, 148, 171-173, 175, 180, 184, 193, 196, 199-200, 217, 237-240, 242-243, 245, 249-250, 252-253, 258, 260-267, 269-270, 272-280, 309-310, 314-317, 321, 324-325, 328-334, 336-337, 339, 351, 385-386, 388, 390, 392-393, 395, 411-412, 416, 451, 454-458, 460-462, 465-469, 471, 473, 482, 485, 487, 491, 495, 498, 500, 511, 522, 524-525, 536, 540, 545, 591, 593, 606-607, 627-628, 630-632, 635-638, 647-649, 671-672, 677, 682, 691-692
United States Environmental Training Institute. *See USETI*
Universal Access to Education 220
Universal and Regional Human Rights Protection System 600
Universal Declaration of Human Rights 4, 559, 599, 611

721

Universal Declaration of the Rights of Indigenous Peoples 561
UPD (Unit for the Promotion of Democracy) 10, 661-662
urban development 112, 113
Uruguay 77-78, 80-81, 83, 105, 107-108, 113, 116, 176, 184, 238-239, 240, 258-260, 264, 275, 386-388, 390, 392, 400, 403, 453, 456, 495, 541, 546, 548, 572, 574, 636, 648, 662
Uruguay Round 249-250, 252, 267, 272, 295, 301, 309-310, 459, 461-462, 464-466, 469-472, 498, 503
Uruguay Round Agreement Act 315
U.S. Agency for International Development. *See USAID*
U.S. business community 275
U.S. Congress 310
U.S. Department of Energy. *See DOE*
U.S. Environmental Protection Agency. *See EPA*
U.S. Foreign Bank Supervision Enhancement Act of 1991 198
U.S. Information Agency. *See USIA*
U.S. International Trade Commission. *See ITC*
U.S. Summit Coordinator 636
U.S. trade policy 310
U.S. Trade Representative. *See USTR*
U.S. Treasury Department 267, 631, 635
USAID (United States Agency for International Development) 44, 63, 78-83, 85, 101, 104, 111-112, 122-127, 173, 175-176, 177, 187-188, 190, 226, 242, 278, 386-387, 390-391, 395, 398, 404, 536, 627, 633, 635-636, 660
Environmental Law Program 661
USETI (United States Environmental Training Institute) 243
USIA (United States Information Agency) 278
USTR (United States Trade Representative) 256, 261-262, 265-266, 272-273, 461, 464, 466

## V

vaccination 94-95, 187. *See also health*
measles 94
coverage 94
preventable diseases 187, 189
Venezuela 77-78, 83, 87, 93, 102, 105-106, 112, 116, 118-120, 142, 184, 193-194, 237-239, 243, 245, 251, 255, 265, 271, 309, 316, 322-323, 327-328, 330, 341, 350, 393, 395, 454, 504, 537-539, 541, 545-546, 548, 572, 646, 648
Vienna Convention on Consular Relations 11, 332
violence 33
against women 84, 87-89, 523
domestic 87
urban 590
Virtual University 42
visa issuing procedures 481
Vital Voices 636

## W

water
-edge amendments 463
development projects 115
drinking systems 118
ground-
controls 120-121
management
sustainable 133, 142
potable 99, 101, 114
quality 102, 117
resources 114-117
and coastal areas 97-98
management 117
safe drinking 136
Water Management and Coastal Pollution Control Project 116
Water Resources Management System 115
weapons. *See also arms*
trafficking 5
Website of the Summit Process 72
Western Hemisphere Transportation Initiative. *See HTI*
WHO (World Health Organization) 176, 180, 187, 374
Winnipeg Principles for Trade and Sustainable Development 406
WIPO (World Intellectual Property Organization) 265, 490, 614
WLCA (Women's Leadership Conference of the Americas) 521-522, 525-527, 535-537, 549
Task Force on Monitoring 535
WMO (World Meteorological Organization) 44
women 20, 72, 601, 633. *See also education, maternal*
abortion 541
therapeutic 541
legal 541
adolescent pregnancies 548
affirmative action policies 537, 546
breast-feeding, nutritional needs 21
cervical cancer 545
SOS Corpo 545
Colombia's Intra-family Violence Law of 1996 540
congressional commissions 538
corporate and multilateral bank responsibility 527
day care services 546
discrimination 546
women of childbearing age 547
domestic violence 527, 535. *See also violence*
as criminal behavior 543
earnings 545
economic opportunities 535
education 521, 526-527, 535, 547, 636. *See also education*
drop out rates 548
enrolled in universities 548
family 548
levels of attainment 547
primary school 548
school textbooks 548
system, access to 547
emergency obstetric care 188
employment 521
equal opportunities for 161
equality 521
executive level 546
family planning 544
nationwide 544
gender
differences 547
equity 20
roles 546
stereotypes 548
studies 548, 549
government-run family planning programs 544
groups 89
health 535, 543, 636
care 90
inadequate coverage 545

# INDEX

*women, continued*
    conditions 20, 188
    Nicaraguan non-governmental clinic 544
    reproductive and sexual 543
  human rights commission 540
  illiteracy rates 547
  in private and political leadership 521
  in society, strengthening the role of 187
  income differentials 545
  indigenous 40
  informal sector, work in 546
  issues 40
  judicial reform 527
  labor markets 527
    mobility in the 546
  leadership 527, 537
  legal rights 535
  *maquiladoras* 547
  maternity 546
    mandatory leave 546
  microenterprise credit 545
  multilateral development 526
  multinational companies 546
  neoliberal policy 598
  occupational segregation 546
  occupations 545
  Outreach Strategy 527
  part-time employment 546
  Peruvian Defensoría del Pueblo 540
  police stations 542
  political leadership 535
    access to 525
  political participation 537
  politicians 537, 549
  poor, education 221
  pregnancy 546
    administration of tests 546
    mothers 181
    nutritional needs 21
    subsidies 161
  prenatal care 40
  private sector 526
  promotion of breast-feeding 189
  quotas 538
    in elections 538
    laws 539
    rules 537
  rape 540, 543
  representation 537
  rights 50, 156, 161, 277, 522, 593, 619, 636
    to land 577
    role of 576
  salaries consistently lower than men's 545
  sexual harassment 161
  sterilization 544
  sub-contracting 546
  unemployed 545
  violence against 541
    domestic or intra-family 541
    frequency of 542
  work 545
Women's Health Program 184
Women's Leadership Conference of the Americas. *See WLCA*
Women's World Banking. *See WWB*
workers. *See also basic rights of workers*
  basic rights 603
  migrant 11
    conditions 11
  rights 274, 593, 619
    provision 604
  training 376
Workers Rights Clause 604
Working Group on Democracy and Human Rights 58, 165
Working Group on Small Economies 58, 194, 198, 296, 501
Workshop on Market Access 468
World Bank 9, 12, 19-20, 22, 34, 58, 78, 79-82, 85, 91, 101, 123, 139, 142, 145, 173, 175-177, 180, 184, 186, 188-190, 194, 200, 210, 221-225, 232, 242-243, 245-246, 264, 268, 310, 314, 318-319, 324, 326, 328, 335, 338, 354, 370-371, 373, 388, 390-391, 395, 511, 513, 541, 571, 608, 613-614, 627, 631, 635-636, 638, 645, 652
  Global Environment Facility 633
World Bank's Public Information Center 682
World Conference of Vienna 10
World Conference on Education 222
World Conference on Human Rights 20
World for Non-Violence Against Women Day 88
World Health Organization. *See WHO*
World Intellectual Property Organization. *See WIPO*
World Meteorological Organization. *See WMO*
World Summit for Children 93, 77, 103, 174, 177
World Summit for Social Development 20, 103, 220
World Trade Organization. *See WTO*
WTO (World Trade Organization) 4, 21, 77, 142-143, 249-250, 252-253, 256, 259-260, 262-270, 272-277, 282, 286-293, 295, 297, 301-304, 306-307, 310, 317-318, 323-324, 328, 454, 456-457, 459-460, 462, 464-471, 473-474, 476, 479-482, 484, 487-490, 498-499, 503, 505, 511, 556, 559, 605, 611, 613-615, 627, 634, 637, 678
  GBT Agreement 18
  Government Procurement Agreement 490
  Services Agreement on Basic Telecommunications 505
WWB (Women's World Banking) 545

# X

xenophobia 11, 590

# Y

Yanomami Indians 160

# Z

Zamora, Jaime Paz 332
Zedillo, Ernesto 30, 321